THE OXFORD HANDBOOK OF

WHITE-COLLAR CRIME

THE OXFORD HANDBOOKS IN CRIMINOLOGY AND CRIMINAL JUSTICE

GENERAL EDITOR: MICHAEL TONRY

The *Oxford Handbooks in Criminology and Criminal Justice* offer authoritative, comprehensive, and critical overviews of the state of the art of criminology and criminal justice. Each volume focuses on a major area of each discipline, is edited by a distinguished group of specialists, and contains specially commissioned, original essays from leading international scholars in their respective fields. Guided by the general editorship of Michael Tonry, the series will provide an invaluable reference for scholars, students, and policymakers seeking to understand a wide range of research and policies in criminology and criminal justice.

OTHER TITLES IN THIS SERIES:

ORGANIZED CRIME
Letizia Paoli

CRIMINOLOGICAL THEORY
Francis T. Cullen & Pamela Wilcox

CRIME PREVENTION
Brandon C. Welsh & David P. Farrington

SENTENCING AND CORRECTIONS
Joan Petersilia & Kevin R. Reitz

JUVENILE CRIME AND JUVENILE JUSTICE
Barry C. Feld & Donna M. Bishop

THE OXFORD HANDBOOK OF

WHITE-COLLAR CRIME

Edited by

SHANNA R. VAN SLYKE, MICHAEL L. BENSON,

and

FRANCIS T. CULLEN

OXFORD

UNIVERSITY PRESS

OXFORD
UNIVERSITY PRESS

Oxford University Press is a department of the University of Oxford. It furthers
the University's objective of excellence in research, scholarship, and education
by publishing worldwide. Oxford is a registered trade mark of Oxford University
Press in the UK and in certain other countries

Published in the United States of America by Oxford University Press
198 Madison Avenue, New York, NY 10016, United States of America.

Library of Congress Cataloging-in-Publication Data
The Oxford handbook of white-collar crime / edited by Shanna R. Van Slyke,
Michael L. Benson, and Francis T. Cullen.
pages cm. — (The Oxford handbooks in criminology and criminal justice)
Includes bibliographical references and index.
ISBN 978–0–19–992551–3 (hardcover : alk. paper) — ISBN 978–0–19–094734–7 (paperback : alk. paper)
ISBN 978–0–19–998499–2 (online file)
1. White collar crimes.   I. Van Slyke, Shanna, editor.   II. Benson, Michael L., editor.
III. Cullen, Francis T., editor.
HV6768.O94 2016
364.16'8—dc23
2015023121

Contents

PART IV WHITE-COLLAR CRIME ACROSS THE LIFE COURSE

PART V CULTURAL AND INSTITUTIONAL CONTEXTS

PART VI ORGANIZATIONAL CONTEXT

PART VII REGULATORY OVERSIGHT

PART VIII CRIMINAL SANCTIONS

PART IX PUBLIC POLICY

PREFACE

LIKE it or not, we are emotional creatures, and one reason why crime is a perennially attention-grabbing subject of political discourse and scientific research is because it speaks to our emotions. It scares us. That is, most of us are scared of traditional forms of street crime. Who hasn't woken up in the middle of the night worried that the front door isn't locked? Who hasn't felt on edge entering a deserted parking garage late at night? The possibility of being the victim of a predatory attack in these situations provokes a viscerally primed alertness and a readiness to fight or flee. But such emotional reactions are rarely evoked by the types of crime that are the subject of this Handbook: that is, white-collar crime. The prospect of falling victim to a fraudulently marketed collateralized debt obligation is more likely to provoke bafflement than gut-wrenching fear. Not surprisingly, therefore, white-collar crime typically does not rank high as a matter of public concern even though the threat that it poses to the economy and to civil society exceeds that of street crime by several orders of magnitude. White-collar crime has also long occupied a marginal position in criminology, and the lack of attention that criminologists devote to it can be traced in part to its complexity.

Just because a problem is complex, however, does not mean that it is wise to ignore it. Indeed, complex problems are the ones we should worry about the most, because they pose harms that are hard to see and that cannot be solved with simple solutions. This volume was motivated by a desire to shed light on a problem that is all too often passed over by both researchers and policymakers. We hoped that by bringing together a collection of clearly written and approachable articles on the many facets of white-collar crime and white-collar crime control, we could advance both scholarly and public interest in this important global problem. The essays cover not only the traditional domains of white-collar crime scholarship but also new theoretical developments related to our understanding of the causal factors that underlie white-collar crime and new developments in public policy regarding its control.

This Handbook is divided into eight parts and begins with the debate over the definition of white-collar crime. This debate has gone on since the concept was introduced over three-quarters of a century ago. For many scholars, the white-collar criminal is envisioned as an older, wealthy, white male who orchestrates the theft of millions or who exploits others for personal or business advantage. Even though this stereotype is probably what the general public has in mind when it pictures the white-collar offender, scholars have proposed alternative definitions. These alternative definitions focus on the nature of the crime (clandestine and based on deception) rather than the social and demographic characteristics of the perpetrators. At present, both definitional approaches are used in the field, and as the two chapters in part I as well as chapters in other parts make clear, the choice of definition has theoretical, empirical, and policy implications.

Regardless how it is defined, though, the impact of white-collar crime cannot be denied. Two essays in part II explicate the monetary, physical, and social costs that are imposed by white-collar crime on those directly victimized by it as well as the costs it imposes indirectly on the economy and society in general.

"Why do they do it?" This question has intrigued criminologists, as well as just about everybody else, for a long time, but it seems especially puzzling in the case of white-collar crime. Perhaps this is because white-collar crime seems counterintuitive. It is easy to understand why a person who is homeless or addicted to illegal drugs might resort to criminal activity to stay alive or to avoid the pains of withdrawal. But this need-based reasoning does not seem to apply as well to the people who commit white-collar crimes. Some answers to the "why" question can be found in the chapters in part III. These chapters focus on the demographic and psychological characteristics of the people who commit white-collar crimes and on their reasons for doing so. Because of changes in the nature of work and the enlarging of economic opportunities for women and racial and ethnic minorities, there are reasons to believe that the pool of potential white-collar offenders is growing and changing in its demographic composition, suggesting that the prevalence of white-collar type crimes may also be increasing.

Throughout most of its history, the study of white-collar offenders has been based on the assumption that they are psychologically normal and socially well integrated into mainstream society. White-collar offenders are thought not to suffer from the developmental and social disadvantages that plague street offenders. Accordingly, investigations of white-collar offenders have been restricted to only one stage in the life course: adulthood. The exclusive focus on white-collar offenders as adults is now out of step with the rest of criminology, where life-course and developmental perspectives now dominate. However, as the chapters in part IV demonstrate, there are signs that this situation is changing. Researchers have begun to investigate whether there are adolescent precursors to white-collar crime, and they have started to apply the principles, concepts, and statistical techniques of developmental theory to white-collar offenders. It is too early to say where this new theoretical approach will lead, but, at a minimum, it represents a step toward bringing the study of white-collar crime closer to the theoretical mainstream of criminology.

One of the distinguishing features of white-collar crime is that it is almost always integrated into or parasitic upon legitimate economic activities. As the structure and organization of legitimate economic activities change so, too, does white-collar crime. Thus, the nature of the white-collar crime problem that is found in a particular society or a particular historical period depends on the larger cultural and institutional context. The essays in part V delve into the complex interconnections that exist among economic fluctuations, cultural variations, and trends in the nature and prevalence of white-collar crime.

Part VI deals with another contextual feature of white-collar crime. It is often situated in an organizational context. This context influences both opportunities and motivations for white-collar offending. While organizations provide a setting in which white-collar offenses by individuals can occur, organizations themselves can also be conceived as offenders. The chapters in this section explore the criminogenic properties and dynamics of organizations and also address the factors that may lead to organizational self-restraint.

The final three parts of the volume—VII, VIII, and IX—focus on the tough problem of controlling white-collar crime. The control of white-collar crime is complicated for two main reasons. First and more important, since white-collar crimes are almost always integrated into legitimate economic activities, it follows that steps taken to control white-collar criminals inevitably affect legitimate businesspeople. Although regulatory restrictions are necessary to protect the common good, they also impose costs on legitimate businesses and reduce their efficiency. Trade-offs have to be made, and this stubborn reality is a source of continual political conflict and debate. The chapters in part VII explore how regulatory policy is made, how it is enforced, and its overall effectiveness.

Second, the clandestine nature of white-collar offenses makes them difficult to detect and investigate using the traditional legal tools available to law-enforcement agencies. Nevertheless, even though regulation is the most important means of controlling white-collar crime, the criminal justice system also has a role to play. Unfortunately, it is a role that is fraught with logistical difficulties and confounded by policy conundrums. As the essays in parts VIII and IX show, white-collar crimes pose challenges for investigators and prosecutors because the crimes often involve organizations as well as individuals and raise ethical questions about who or what should be held accountable. Finally, when white-collar offenders are convicted in criminal court, what should be done with them? Should they be sentenced harshly to satisfy the principle of just deserts, or should the penalties they suffer as a result of their "fall from grace" mitigate the severity of their sanctioning?

Such questions animate the study of white-collar crime and make it an exciting and ever-changing area of criminological investigation and public policy. We believe the essays presented in this volume will help readers explore these questions and help them to see that even though white-collar crime may not speak to the emotions like violent crime does, it poses far more important and far-reaching challenges to all of us.

Michael L. Benson, Shanna R. Van Slyke, and Francis T. Cullen
April 23, 2015

Contributors

Michael L. Benson is Professor of Criminal Justice at the University of Cincinnati.

Lennon Y. C. Chang is a Lecturer in the School of Social Sciences at Monash University.

Hongming Cheng is Associate Professor of Sociology (Law, Crime, and Justice) at the University of Saskatchewan in Canada.

Mark A. Cohen is Justin Potter Professor of American Competitive Enterprise and Professor of Law at Vanderbilt University.

Hazel Croall is Professor Emeritus of Criminology at Glasgow Caledonian University.

Francis T. Cullen is Distinguished Research Professor Emeritus of Criminal Justice and Senior Research Associate at the University of Cincinnati

Dean A. Dabney is Associate Professor in the Department of Criminal Justice and Criminology at Georgia State University.

Lucian E. Dervan is Associate Professor of Law and Director of Faculty Development at the Southern Illinois University School of Law.

Mary Dodge is Professor in Criminology and Criminal Justice at the University of Colorado Denver.

Kimberly D. Dodson is Associate Professor of Law Enforcement and Justice Administration at Western Illinois University.

Peter Fleming is Professor of Business and Society at the Cass Business School, City University, London.

Gilbert Geis was Professor Emeritus, Department of Criminology, Law and Society University of California, Irvine.

Neil Gunningham is Professor in the Regulatory Institutions Network, Research School of Sciences, and in the School of Resources Environment and Society at the Australian National University.

John L. Hagan is John D. MacArthur Professor of Sociology and Law at Northwestern University and a Senior Research Fellow at the American Bar Foundation.

Spencer Headworth is a PhD Candidate in the Department of Sociology at Northwestern University and a Research Assistant at the American Bar Foundation.

Bill Hebenton is a Member of the Centre for Criminology and Criminal Justice, School of Law, University of Manchester, UK, and Research Associate of the University's Centre for Chinese Studies at the University of Manchester, School of Law.

Andy Hochstetler is Professor of Sociology at Iowa State University.

Wim Huisman is Professor of Criminology and Chair of the School of Criminology at VU University Amsterdam.

Susyan Jou is Professor of Criminology in the Graduate School of Criminology at National Taipei University.

Susanne Karstedt is Professor in the School of Criminology and Criminal Justice, Griffith University, Australia.

Jay P. Kennedy is Assistant Professor of Criminal Justice at Michigan State University.

Paul M. Klenowski is Assistant Professor and Director of Criminal Justice at the Clarion University of Pennsylvania.

Michael Levi is Professor of Criminology at Cardiff University.

William Mackey is a doctoral student at the University of Cincinnati.

Tamara D. Madensen is Associate Professor and Graduate Coordinate of Criminal Justice at the University of Nevada, Las Vegas.

Peter Mascini is Associate Professor of Sociology at Erasmus University of Rotterdam, The Netherlands.

Ray Paternoster is Professor of Criminology and Criminal Justice at the University of Maryland.

Brian K. Payne is Vice Provost for graduate and undergraduate academic programs at Old Dominion University.

Alex R. Piquero is Ashbel Smith Professor in the Program in Criminology in the School of Economic, Political, and Policy Sciences at the University of Texas at Dallas.

Nicole Leeper Piquero is Associate Dean of Graduate Programs and Professor of Criminology at the University of Texas at Dallas.

Ellen S. Podgor, J.D., LLM, is Gary R. Trombley Family White-Collar Crime Research Professor and Professor of Law at Stetson University College of Law.

Henry N. Pontell is Distinguished Professor of Sociology at John Jay College of Criminal Justice of The City of New York, and Professor Emeritus of Criminology in the School of Social Ecology at University of California, Irvine.

Amanda Pozzuto is a PhD Candidate in the College of Business and Economics at West Virginia University.

Harland Prechel is Professor of Sociology and College of Liberal Arts Cornerstone Fellow at Texas A&M University.

Mary Kreiner Ramirez is Professor of Law at Washburn University School of Law.

Donald J. Rebovich is Professor of Criminal Justice in Utica College's School of Business and Justice Studies.

Melissa Rorie is Professor of Criminal Justice and Faculty Advisor for the Criminal Justice Club at the University of Nevada, Las Vegas.

Sally S. Simpson is Professor of Criminology and Criminal Justice and Director of the Center for the Study of Business Ethics, Regulation, & Crime at the University of Maryland.

Simon I. Singer is Professor of Criminology and Criminal Justice at Northeastern University.

Stephen G. Tibbetts is Professor of Criminal Justice at the California State University, San Bernardino.

Edward C. Tomlinson is Associate Professor of Management at West Virginia University.

Shanna R. Van Slyke is Associate Professor of Criminal Justice in Utica College's School of Business and Justice Studies.

Wei Wang is Assistant Professor at China Police College.

Peter Cleary Yeager is Associate Professor of Law and Criminology at Boston University.

Stelios C. Zyglidopoulos is Reader in Management at the Adam Smith Business School, University of Glasgow.

THE OXFORD HANDBOOK OF

WHITE-COLLAR CRIME

CHAPTER 1

···

CORE THEMES
IN THE STUDY OF
WHITE-COLLAR CRIME

···

MICHAEL L. BENSON, SHANNA R. VAN SLYKE, AND FRANCIS T. CULLEN

THIS anthology was designed to present a wide-ranging collection of cutting-edge research and theory on white-collar crime and its control. The process of assembling and organizing the various strands of research was guided by eight interconnected themes: (1) concept, (2) offender, (3) organization, (4) choice, (5) opportunity, (6) context, (7) costs, and (8) control. Although all of the essays present important insights and findings related to their specific topics, a number of general conclusions that link to our eight themes and that apply across the articles stand out. They include the following:

- The definition of white-collar crime remains controversial and substantially influences who and what is studied as well as general conclusions about the nature of white-collar crime;
- Regardless of how white-collar crime is defined, white-collar offenders differ from street offenders in regard to their social backgrounds, demographic attributes, and psychological characteristics;
- Especially when compared to those who commit violent crimes, those who commit white-collar crimes appear to be more strongly influenced by rational choice considerations;
- Like other types of crime, white-collar crime is not gender neutral in either motivations or mechanics;
- Individuals who hold executive or managerial positions in organizations have abundant opportunities to engage in white-collar crime with a low likelihood of being caught;

- Certain organizational features can create a criminogenic context that facilitates the concealment of white-collar criminal activity and limits the likelihood of its punishment;
- Although difficult to measure with any degree of accuracy, the economic costs of white-collar crime outweigh the costs of other forms of crime; and
- Different control mechanisms are used against white-collar criminals as opposed to street criminals, with white-collar crime control oriented toward regulation and the fostering of compliance while street crime control focuses on punishment and deterrence.

Below we explicate the eight themes that guided the anthology.

I. CONCEPT

Although the term "white-collar crime" was not coined until near the middle of the 20th century, scholarly interest in what can only be called "white-collar criminals" goes back much farther in the history of criminology (Geis, Chapter 2 in this volume). For example, Lombroso (1887) compared "born criminals" to "criminaloids," some of whom were people "high in power, who society venerates as its chiefs ... their high position generally prevents their criminal character from being recognized" (p. 47). And at the turn of the 20th century, Ross also drew attention to the criminaloid or as he sometimes called such persons, the quasi-criminal: "He is a buyer rather than a practitioner of sin, and his middlemen spare him unpleasant details. Secure in his quilted armor of lawyer-spun sophistries.... The wholesale fleecer of trusting, workaday people is a 'Napoleon,' a 'superman'" (1907, p. 53). But neither Lombroso's criminaloid nor Ross's quasi-criminal captured the criminological imagination like Edwin H. Sutherland's white-collar criminal.

Even though Sutherland's catchy term—white-collar crime—is relatively new historically speaking, the behavior that it references is ancient. Fraud has a history that can be traced back millennia, long before Lombroso and Ross put pen to paper (Geis 1988; Johnstone 1998; Holtfreter, Van Slyke, and Blomberg 2005; Geis, Chapter 2 in this volume). In an analysis of Cicero's (44 B.C.) *On Duties* and Dante's (1314) *Inferno*, Chevigny (2001) showed that fraud and deception have been viewed as the most reprehensible of all crimes throughout much of human history. Indeed, it is only recently, as life has come to be seen as precious and as fear of death has heightened, that violence has come to be seen as the more reprehensible form of crime (Pinker, 2012). Still, despite the historical recognition and condemnation of fraud, Lombroso, Ross, and Sutherland highlighted a special feature of its waywardness: it is committed by *powerful offenders*—those who hold privileged positions and who use the trust of others to break the law in order to maximize their personal power and wealth. All three noted that the misdeeds of the powerful often go unpunished for long periods of time and that they can adversely affect the fortunes of entire nations.

Geis's (Chapter 2) essay in this volume illustrates how strands of thought from diverse scholarly and professional fields—all connected by the image of a powerful and power-abusing victimizer—merged in the conceptualization of white-collar crime that Sutherland presented in his Presidential Address to the American Sociological Society in 1939. Sutherland later defined it as "crime committed by a person of respectability and high social status in the course of his occupation" (1949, p. 9). From this definition and his other writings, five key features stand out in regard to Sutherland's view of white-collar crime. First, the offenders were, by definition, individuals of high social status and respectability. Second, the offenses were committed within an occupational context. Third, the offenses were committed in a particular way—that is, through the "violation of delegated or implied trust" (1940, p. 3). Fourth, the offenses involved massive financial and other costs (e. g., to "social relations" [1949, p. 13]). Fifth and finally, civil and administrative violations could be counted as white-collar crimes because civil laws often deal with practices that are fundamentally similar to those proscribed by criminal laws and because many illegal practices can be sanctioned under either criminal or civil law and often both.

Sutherland's approach to defining white-collar crime has been defended and followed by many distinguished white-collar crime scholars, such as, for example, Pontell (Chapter 3 in this volume) and Braithwaite (1985). This approach to defining white-collar crime has been labeled the "offender-based approach" because of its focus on the social characteristics of the offenders (Benson and Simpson 2014). Despite the fundamental importance of Sutherland's insight into lawbreaking among those of high social status, the meaning of the concept of white-collar crime has mutated radically since the term was introduced.

Although Sutherland's approach to defining white-collar crime is the one that resonates best with popular stereotypes of white-collar offenders, a competing conceptual approach emerged only a few decades after his address. This approach focuses on the nature of the offense rather than the offender. The most influential offense-based definition was promulgated by Edelhertz (1970, p. 3), who defined white-collar crime as "an illegal act or series of illegal acts committed by nonphysical means and by concealment or guile, to obtain money or property, to avoid the loss of money or property, or to obtain business or personal advantage." Edelhertz's definition differs from Sutherland's in important ways. It makes no reference to the social status of the actor or to the occupational location of the act. Rather, it focuses entirely on the means by which the illegal act is committed. Thus, for Edelhertz, *any* illegal act that is committed by "nonphysical means and by concealment or guile" for economic or personal advantage is a white-collar crime.

As both Geis (Chapter 2 in this volume) and Pontell (Chapter 3 in this volume) argue, offense-based definitions enlarge the conceptual boundaries of white-collar crime far beyond the high-powered corporate executives that so concerned Sutherland. In Pontell's view, this expansion has the effect of producing the "a priori operational trivialization of white-collar crime" as researchers end up studying a heterogeneous collection of small-time fraudsters and trust violators. He blames offense-based definitions for inadequate regulatory policies and largely inadequate if not entirely absent criminal laws against the harmful behaviors of society's elites. Whereas the objective of Sutherland was to call attention to the misdeeds of the powerful, the objective of Edelhertz was to provide a definition more consistent with legal norms—that is, offense-based definitions are designed to reflect justice system policy and practice. This conceptual bowdlerization not only perpetuates and reinforces existing disparities in the operation of the justice system between white-collar and street crimes, but it also diverts attention from those deceptive acts that cause the most harm and that are committed by economic and political elites.

The defenders of Sutherland's approach make a valid point regarding the potential dangers of defining white-collar crime in the manner suggested by Edelhertz. If using an offense-based approach means that high-status offenders end up being ignored, then criminology is not much better off than it would have been had the concept of white-collar crime never been invented. Sutherland was correct that crimes by powerful people in his day were ignored. If contemporary criminologists end up studying only small-time fraudsters and welfare mothers, then the theoretical value of the concept of white-collar crime is seriously diminished. Yet, it cannot be denied that people who do not have exalted social status commit crimes that for all intents and purposes are the same as the white-collar crimes committed by Sutherland's corporate executives (Weisburd et al. 1991). Corporate executives engage in accounting fraud and tax evasion, and so do small business owners. Bank presidents can misappropriate millions of dollars (Calavita and Pontell 1990) while bank tellers embezzle a few hundred bucks. Researchers using the offense-based approach have brought this reality sharply into focus, and they have also demonstrated that both elite and non-elite white-collar offenders differ substantially on a number of dimensions from ordinary street offenders (Wheeler et al. 1988; Weisburd et al. 1991; Benson and Kerley 2000; Benson and Simpson 2014).

At present, the term "white-collar crime" is used in both senses by researchers. For some researchers, it refers to the corrupt, exploitative, and socially harmful acts of respectable and powerful individuals and organizations; for others, it refers more broadly to economic crimes that involve deception. As this volume demonstrates, both definitional approaches have been used by researchers to produce important findings and insights on contemporary crime problems. Since both conceptual approaches are found in the literature, it is important to pay attention to how individual researchers operationalize the term in order to accurately assess the significance of their work for the field of white-collar crime. Different definitions lead to different questions and yield different results. Not surprisingly, almost every contributor to this anthology devotes at least a few words of explanation regarding the definition that guided his or her analyses.

II. Offenders

The answer to the question "Who is the white-collar offender?" depends on how one defines white-collar crime (Klenowski and Dodson, Chapter 6 in this volume; Hochstetler and Mackey, Chapter 8 in this volume). For those who follow Sutherland's approach, however, the question is hardly worth asking. The offenders who should concern us are, by definition, elite members of the corporate and political power structures of modern society. They are the ones who make decisions that affect the financial well-being of millions of people as well as the social and economic health of nations. What matters about them is their economic and political power, not their social or demographic characteristics. Nevertheless, it is implied in writings of Sutherland and his followers that white-collar offenders are predominantly white, male, psychologically normal, and unsullied by contact with the criminal justice system.

Sutherland undoubtedly was correct that the leaders of America's major corporations frequently engage in behavior that is prohibited by law and that warrants sanctioning in criminal courts, even though the perpetrators rarely see the inside of a courtroom. Wealthy, high-ranking, and highly respected offenders certainly do exist, and they even occasionally appear on the nightly news or nowadays on the webpages of both major and minor news outlets. But the spotlight that is shined on the perpetrators of these national scandals reveals only a small segment of the white-collar offending population.

Researchers using offense-based definitions of white-collar crime have found that those who commit white-collar crimes are much more heterogeneous in their social, demographic, and criminal-background characteristics than the stereotypical image of the white-collar offender would suggest. Consider, for example, gender, race, and social class. Although it is true that most white-collar offenders are white and male, the female share of some low-level forms of white-collar crime, such as embezzlement and identity theft, is substantial (Klenowski and Dodson, Chapter 6 in this volume; Dodge, Chapter 10 in this volume). But the involvement of women in elite frauds, especially in leadership roles, is still exceedingly rare (Steffensmeier et al. 2013; Benson and Gottschalk 2014). Likewise, non-whites also commit low-level white-collar offenses in significant numbers, and trend data suggest that for the past three decades both women and non-whites have been commanding an ever larger share of white-collar crime, especially in regard to low-level offenses (Shover and Hochstetler 2006; Benson and Simpson 2014). Perhaps the most surprising findings to emerge in the past three decades, however, concern the class standing of those who commit white-collar offenses. As several of the chapters presented here note (Klenowski and Dodson, Chapter 6; Hochstetler and Mackey, Chapter 8), most of the people who end up in the federal judicial system for white-collar offenses are not wealthy and are not high-ranking corporate executives. Rather, they occupy the middle levels of the class hierarchy (Karstedt, Chapter 9 in this volume).

The expansion of the population of white-collar offenders along gender, race, and class lines has led to a new body of theory and research on their social origins and backgrounds (Piquero and Benson 2004; Piquero and Piquero, Chapter 12 in this volume; Benson, Chapter 13 in this volume). Rather than simply assuming that early childhood and family experiences have little to do with white-collar offending in adulthood, researchers have begun to investigate whether involvement in white-collar crime may arise out of the childrearing practices of the middle and upper classes. Indeed, some have gone so far as to speculate that a middle-class upbringing has features that are the functional equivalents of the poverty, abuse, conflict, and neglect that play such prominent causal roles in street offending. These features include the inculcation of a sense of entitlement, an emphasis on competitive success, and a worldview in which the application of ethical norms and standards of behavior is always considered to be negotiable (Shover and Hochstetler 2006). In short, like ordinary offending, white-collar offending is beginning to be explored as a behavioral pattern that is part of the life course and that arises out of a developmental process (Singer, Chapter 11 in this volume; Piquero and Piquero, Chapter 12 in this volume; Benson, Chapter 13 in this volume). In one sense, this theoretical development represents a departure from Sutherland's perspective on white-collar offending, as he was opposed to class-based explanations of crime in general. On the other hand, it is consistent with his broader aim of reforming criminological theory, because white-collar offending is now being brought under the theoretical umbrella of life-course criminology, one of the dominant theoretical perspectives in criminology (Cullen 2011).

III. CHOICE

The life-course perspective calls upon us to view criminal offending as part of a broader process of human development that involves biological, psychological, and social domains. But, despite the all-inclusive nature of life-course theorizing about crime, in the end, specific acts of white-collar law violation occur because specific choices are made by specific individuals or groups of individuals working in concert. A corporate executive decides to ignore the expensive regulations for storing hazardous chemicals that end up polluting a river. Midlevel sales managers in competing companies get together and decide to share customers to ensure market stability and organizational survival for all. An accountant accedes to a demand from the company CEO to figure out a way, illegal if necessary, to improve the bottom line before the next quarterly report is due on Wall Street.

In regard to white-collar crime, choices are theorized to be a function of the actor's subjective assessment of the net rewards of crime compared to the net rewards of not engaging in crime—that is, of complying with the law (Paternoster and Simpson 1993; Simpson 2013). The net rewards of crime are defined as the benefits of crime minus its costs; the same definition applies to non-crime as well (Wilson and Herrnstein 1985). When the former exceed the latter, crime is expected to result. Although white-collar crimes are almost always economically oriented in one sense or another, the decision making of white-collar offenders involves much more than a simple assessment of how much money some particular offense might garner. In other words, decision making by business managers and executives involves more than just a cold-blooded calculation of the economic utility of different courses of action. In particular, decision makers are sensitive to the potential that they or their companies may suffer reputational costs as a result of the exposure of lawbreaking (Paternoster and Simpson 1996; Shover and Hochstetler 2006). Indeed, these informal costs appear to figure more prominently in the decision-making calculus of offenders than formal legal sanctions (Simpson 2013). Research also suggests that decision making in business is guided by moral and ethical considerations (Simpson 2002; Simpson, Gardner, and Gibbs 2007). Those who would engage in white-collar crime may refrain from doing so if they regard the act in question as immoral or socially harmful.

On the other hand, if potential offenders believe that their actions can be framed in morally acceptable terms, then the restraining effect of morality is greatly weakened. White-collar offenders are especially adept at framing their activities to themselves in such a way that the moral and reputational costs of crime are neutralized, at least in the offender's eyes (Benson 1985; Willott, Griffen, and Torrence 2001; Shover and Hochstetler 2006; Klenowski et al. 2011). The ability of white-collar offenders to deny the criminality of their actions is enhanced by the complex nature of business activity and the normative ambiguity that surrounds it (Green 2004, 2006). At what point does a conversation between competitors become a price-fixing conspiracy? When does boastful advertising shade into outright consumer fraud? White-collar offenders are also insulated from the moral costs of white-collar crime by the public's ambiguous view of government efforts to control and regulate business and economic activity (Cullen, Chouhy, and Jonson, forthcoming).

Like other people, white-collar offenders are not robots devoid of feelings and emotions. Indeed, emotional factors can influence choices in regard to white-collar crime (Benson and Sams 2013). For example, if business owners or managers feel that they have been unfairly stigmatized or sanctioned by legal authorities, they may respond with anger and defiance rather than compliance (Simpson 2013). Thus, even though the world of business is often portrayed as one in which rationality and cool calculation rule, research suggests otherwise. White-collar crime choice has an emotional component.

Finally, white-collar crime is often carried out in an organizational setting, and this setting influences criminal decision making (Tomlinson and Pozzuto, Chapter 18 in this volume). No discussion of choice in regard to white-collar crime would be complete if it did not acknowledge the organizational dimension of decision making. The idea of an isolated individual decision maker is not applicable to those who work in organizations, because people who work in organizations inevitably interact with coworkers, superiors, and subordinates as well as people who work in other organizations. In these interactions, the preferences and subjective assessments of the interacting parties are shared and become part of each individual's decision-making gestalt.

IV. Organization

As noted above, organizations can be conceptualized as providing a setting that influences decision making. Indeed, from the perspective of choice theory, the organization is simply another source of benefits and costs that individuals take into account when deciding on various courses of action. For example, variation in the degree to which organizations monitor employee performance in regard to ethical standards will make deviant behavior potentially more costly in some organizations than in others. And there are other organizational characteristics that influence how people behave (Huisman, Chapter 21 in this volume). Tomlinson and Pozzuto (Chapter 18 in this volume) argue that three particularly important characteristics are (1) the reward system, (2) the organizational culture, and (3) the organizational structure.

Consider how an internal reward system could be designed to provoke white-collar crime. Organizations are inherently goal-seeking entities (Gross 1978, 1980). To achieve their goals, they must organize and motivate individuals to behave in ways that promote organizational goals. One way to do this is to align the achievement of organizational goals with individual benefits—that is, to reward people for doing things that lead to organizational success. For example, raises or promotions can be granted to people who meet certain sales targets or other types of productivity standards, while those who fail to meet the standards are fired, demoted, or otherwise punished. Organizations vary in how quantifiable organizational goals are and how tightly personal rewards are tied to the achievement of these goals. Enron is a classic example of an organization that had very clear financial goals and a very tightly coupled system for aligning corporate goals and individual rewards. Its infamous review and reward system required supervisors to rate a specified percentage of their subordinates as unsatisfactory and sanction them accordingly (McLean and Elkind 2003). This brutal system pressured Enron's employees to try to enhance their performance by any means available, including illegal ones.

Although it makes intuitive sense to consider organizations as settings that influence how people make decisions, act, and interact, organizations have also been conceptualized as agents in and of themselves (Braithwaite and Fisse 1990; Huisman, Chapter 21 in this volume). Indeed, it has been asserted that the organizational form is inherently criminogenic (Gross 1978, 1980). A long line of research has focused on the organizational correlates of white-collar crime (Simpson 1987; Zey 1993; Simpson 2002; Clinard and Yeager 2006; Simpson, Garner, and Gibbs 2007; for a general overview, see Simpson 2013). Many different factors have been investigated, including size, culture, profitability, hierarchical structure, strategy, type, and competitive environment. But empirical findings are inconclusive and no concise set of factors has yet been identified that predicts organizational offending with any degree of accuracy (Simpson 2013).

The choice perspective assumes that criminal behavior is essentially goal-seeking behavior. The offender is viewed as an agent who wants something and chooses to use illegal means to get it. In regard to organizational offending, however, this agent-centered view is at times inappropriate, because in some cases organizations violate the law not because they choose to do so but rather because they are simply incompetent to comply with their legal obligations (Huisman, Chapter 21 in this volume). Small and medium-sized organizations in particular may not have the personnel resources or technical expertise to keep up with the voluminous regulations that govern almost all industries and economic enterprises. Their law-breaking behavior is perhaps more akin to the individual who forgets to file her taxes on time than it is to the amoral pursuit of illegal gains. Some instances of organizational deviance are best viewed as the inevitable byproduct or unintended consequences of organizational structures and routines (Vaughan 2005). Organizational incompetence is not a factor that criminologists have devoted much attention to, but if organizations are to be conceptualized as actors, then we must recognize that, like people, they do not always know what they are doing and their actions are not always intentional.

V. Opportunity

Opportunities are now recognized as an important cause of all crime (Felson and Eckert 2015), and in the past few decades, criminologists have focused increasingly on the situational and ecological factors that facilitate opportunities for street crime (Cohen and Felson 1979; Clarke 1983). As causal factors, opportunities are considered to be even more important for white-collar crime. One would be hard pressed to find any study of any form of white-collar crime that does not in one way or another blame the occurrence of the crime on the offender's having an opportunity to do it. For white-collar crime, the answer to the question "Why did they do it?" is almost always "Because they could." The list of case studies of particular white-collar crimes that blame them on the opportunities afforded by lax regulatory oversight is, to put it mildly, large.

The nature of white-collar crime opportunities, however, differs from that of street crime (Benson and Simpson 2014). Opportunities for street crime arise when a motivated offender encounters a suitable target that is not capably guarded (Cohen and Felson 1979). For most street crimes, guardianship involves either somehow inhibiting the offender's access to the target or somehow making the offender feel that undertaking the crime would be accompanied by a risk of detection that is unacceptably high. Typically, the risk of detection is raised by putting the target under surveillance.

But white-collar crime opportunities are different. The most important difference between white-collar and street crime opportunities is that white-collar offenders have legitimate access to the targets of their offenses (Benson and Simpson 2014; Felson and Eckert 2015; Madensen, Chapter 19 in this volume). This access almost always arises out of the offender's occupational role or position within an organization. Unlike the burglar who must break into a house to steal something, an embezzler can merely take money out of the cash register. Likewise, the doctor who submits a fraudulent claim to the Medicaid program has legitimate access to both patients and the Medicaid reimbursement system. As Marcus Felson has argued for a long time, the distinguishing feature of white-collar crimes is that the offender has specialized access to the target. Because white-collar offenders have legitimate access to the targets of their offenses, the standard crime-prevention technique of reducing crime by blocking the offender's access to the target is difficult if not impossible to use in the case of most white-collar crimes.

In addition to having specialized access to their targets, white-collar offenders have another advantage over their street-level counterparts. That advantage resides in the superficial appearance of legitimacy of white-collar offenses. In other words, the offenses are not obvious (Braithwaite and Geis 1982). For example, the doctor who submits a fraudulent claim to a healthcare insurer tries to make the claim appear like an ordinary legitimate claim. The manufacturer who illegally disposes of hazardous waste may take steps to make the waste appear nonhazardous, such as by mislabeling the barrel that contains it (Rebovich 1992). The fraudulent and misleading financial reports published by Enron were good enough to fool many sophisticated investors (McLean and Elkind 2003). The victims of Bernard Madoff's massive Ponzi scheme were blissfully unaware that the financial statements they received from him were wildly inflated (Henriques 2011). Indeed, a distinguishing feature of many white-collar crimes is that even the victim often is unaware of the offense until it is too late to respond, and in some cases victims may never learn of the offense. The superficial appearance of legitimacy means that the types of surveillance used to prevent street crime—such as reports from victims, observation by security guards, or closed-circuit cameras—are virtually useless in regard to white-collar crimes. Other forms of surveillance or oversight are needed to prevent white-collar crimes, and when they are lacking or insufficient opportunities for white-collar crime expand.

For white-collar crimes, surveillance must be specialized and usually is carried out by regulatory agencies. In theory, these agencies are supposed to provide oversight by inspecting places of business and reviewing business records and activities to make sure that they comply with the law. But, as scholars from Sutherland forward have repeatedly pointed out, regulatory oversight is almost always inadequate, and even when violations are discovered the penalties associated with them are usually bearable for offenders (Shover and Hochstetler 2006). As with ordinary street offenders, white-collar offenders feel much more comfortable executing their schemes if they are confident that no one is watching or that the costs of being caught are not too high. Under these conditions, opportunities to engage in white-collar crimes surely seem plentiful and attractive to potential offenders. Thus, the inadequacy of regulatory oversight is a major element in the opportunity structure of white-collar crime.

Regulatory oversight so often lacks credibility because both regulation and oversight are parts of a political process that is riddled with conflicting and competing interests (Ramirez, Chapter 23 in this volume). Every industry and profession in the United

States hires lobbyists to advocate for the special interests of their employers in the halls of Congress and in the offices and meeting rooms of regulatory agencies. These special interests work tirelessly to diminish regulatory restrictions, especially those that might lead to criminal accountability for anyone in the industry or profession (Ramirez, Chapter 23 in this volume). Occasionally, a scandal is so large and outrageous that the public demands action and as a result new rules and regulations are enacted. For example, after the accounting scandals of the early 2000s, the U.S. Congress passed the law popularly known as Sarbanes-Oxley that in theory is supposed to prevent future accounting frauds by strengthening regulatory oversight of the internal accounting practices of large companies and raising penalties for transgressions. As soon as the public's attention wanes and turns elsewhere, however, special interests begin whittling away at the strength of the enforcement process until eventually real enforcement gives way to the appearance but not reality of oversight and accountability.

Finally, opportunities for white-collar crime continually evolve as financial and technological innovations create new products and new forms of business activity. For example, the massive amount of fraud that occurred in the mortgage and investment banking industries between 2000 and 2008 was made possible in part by such financial innovations as the invention of the collateralized debt obligation (CDO) as an investment vehicle (Barnett 2013). CDOs were so complicated and so little understood by investors and regulators that it was not hard for the major investment banks to market them in a fraudulent manner (Barnett 2013). The evolution of the Internet and online banking coupled with the expansion of consumer credit has made identity theft both more feasible and more lucrative (Copes and Vieraitis 2012). As recent scandals involving such major corporations as Target and Home Depot show, it is now possible to steal the financial identities of millions of people at a time and get access to their lines of credit. For identity thieves, opportunity started knocking in the 1990s. As the economy and technology evolve over time, opportunities for white-collar crimes follow in their wake, leading some scholars to proclaim white-collar crime as the crime of the future (Weisburd et al. 1991; Shover and Hochstetler 2006; Benson and Simpson 2014).

VI. CONTEXT

As the preceding section discussed, opportunities for white-collar crime are shaped in part by political processes. These processes in turn are part of a larger institutional and cultural context that influences both opportunities and motivations for white-collar crime (Bonger and Horton 1916; Coleman 1987). Nearly a century ago, Bonger and Horton (1916) argued that capitalism itself created a moral climate of egoism that inflamed the desire for material success, thus providing a potent source of motivation for crime in all social classes (Simpson and Rorie, Chapter 16 in this volume). More recently, as Headworth and Hagan (Chapter 14 in this volume) show in their analysis of white-collar crime in the financial crisis of 2008, the cultural landscape of the

United States has for some time been dominated by an "orientation toward financial markets that privileges the notions of self-regulation and self-correction over government intervention." As a result of this orientation, individuals working in the financial markets prior to 2008 felt both entitled and empowered to develop complex and little-understood financial instruments, such as CDOs based on pools of subprime loans. Then, in the name of economic growth and with the unwitting backing of the U.S. government, these financial instruments were marketed using fraud and deceit to unsuspecting investors. And when the underlying assets—that is, subprime loans on which the instruments were based—began to fail, the economy followed suit.

Although it is tempting and to a certain degree correct to blame the economic collapse of 2008 on the financial malfeasance of greedy and self-serving investment bankers as well as the fraudulent activities of others who worked in the mortgage industry, this individualized view tells only a small part of the story. Before it can be activated, greed needs an outlet, an opportunity to manifest itself—and the opportunity to engage in the financial malfeasance with little risk of sanction throughout most of the first decade of the 21st century was created by the U.S. government. As Headworth and Hagan (Chapter 14 in this volume) and Prechel (Chapter 15 in this volume) show, the government played a key role in shaping and deregulating financial markets. It pushed the investment banking industry to develop the complex structured debt instruments that were marketed to investors (Barnett 2013). Through deregulation, it "altered the boundaries of legitimacy, legality, and criminality in finance, expanding the realm of explicitly or implicitly sanctioned behaviors" (Headworth and Hagan, Chapter 14 in this volume). The cultural milieu that infused capital markets provided actors with justifications for their risky financial innovations and transactions, while the structure of banking organizations as well as the market itself ensured that responsibility would be diffused to such a degree that finding responsible parties in the aftermath of the collapse became virtually impossible. Hence, almost none of the "big players" in the investment banking world have been criminally charged, let alone convicted, despite widespread agreement among commentators that fraud was rampant leading up to the collapse of 2008 (Benson 2012; Levi 2012; Barnett 2013).

The onslaught of fraud in the mortgage and investment banking industries prior to 2008 is only one example of how cultural and institutional contexts can create conditions in which white-collar and corporate crime can flourish. But it is certainly not the only example. Indeed, there is a strong theoretical and research tradition in the white-collar crime literature that focuses on interconnections between economic fluctuations, cultural contexts, and rates of white-collar and corporate crime (Simpson and Rorie, Chapter 16 in this volume). This research tends to show that the effects of economic fluctuations are crime specific—that is, some forms of white-collar crime are more sensitive to economic fluctuations than others. The research also shows that both economic booms and economic recessions can influence different forms of corporate and white-collar crime in different ways, because both booms and recessions can affect motivations and opportunities (Benson 2012; Levi 2012). For example, economic recessions can put struggling businesses under enormous pressure and threaten them with total failure. Under these conditions, it is almost axiomatic that some owners and executives will respond by breaking the law in an attempt to keep their failing enterprises from going under. On the other hand, an expanding economy can lead to a mad scramble to get in on the action and make money by any means necessary as quickly as one can. The thrift scandal of the 1980s is an excellent example of this dynamic (Calavita and Pontell 1990).

Thus, if anything has been learned since Sutherland introduced the world to white-collar crime, it is that (1) white-collar crime feeds off of and is inextricably linked to legitimate economic activity and (2) opportunities for white-collar crime expand or contract depending on the evolution of political-legal arrangements and the pendulum-like swings in cultural orientations that oscillate between belief in the efficacy of government regulation versus faith in the invisible hand of the free market (Prechel, Chapter 15 in this volume).

VII. Costs

Measuring social phenomena is often difficult, and this is especially true in regard to phenomena such as criminal activity, which is by its very nature meant to be clandestine. Nevertheless, those who study ordinary street crime have made some strides in measuring its extent, trends, and costs. The extent can be estimated by mathematically combining information about the number of offenses known to the authorities with information about reporting rates for those offenses to get a rough number for the overall annual crime rate. The number can then be tracked over time to determine whether crime is increasing or decreasing. And by employing a little more mathematical wizardry, researchers have even been able to get better-than-ballpark estimates of how many offenses active offenders commit in a given time period. Once the number of offenses is known, trends in the overall costs of street crime can be estimated by multiplying the average cost per offense by the number of estimated offenses.

It seems reasonable to expect that the costs of white-collar crime also vary over time, and that they also trend up or down depending on how active white-collar offenders are. If we could count the number of white-collar crimes, we would be on our way toward estimating its costs. Counting, however, turns out to be a problem, and very little is known about the dark figure of white-collar crime. As numerous scholars have noted, for various reasons estimating the amount of white-collar crime to any reasonable degree of accuracy seems to be a very difficult task, if not one that is outright unachievable (Sparrow 1996; Shover and Hochstetler 2006). Thus, estimating the costs of white-collar and corporate crime is a project accompanied by large margins of error.

Estimating the amount of white-collar crime is complicated for both conceptual and substantive reasons. Conceptually, estimation of the amount of white-collar crime depends crucially on how the term is defined (Croall, Chapter 4 in this volume).

Offense-based definitions, which typically include any property offense involving deceit or deception, result in dramatically higher white-collar offense counts than do offender-based definitions, which include only occupationally related offenses committed by high-status individuals. Dramatically higher counts are also achieved if regulatory violations are included along with criminal violations. Substantively, white-collar crime is difficult to count because the offenses are not obvious and do not leave easily observed traces of their occurrence (Braithwaite and Geis 1982; Benson, Kennedy, and Logan, forthcoming). Instead, the crime itself is typically hidden behind or integrated into legitimate occupational or financial activities (Benson and Simpson 2014). Often, even the victim may not realize that an offense has occurred. For example, healthcare professionals who submit fraudulent claims to the health insurers or government programs try to make them look like legitimate claims and hope, often correctly, that they will go unnoticed (Jesilow, Geis, and Pontell 1991; Sparrow 1996). Even when a white-collar offense has been discovered, it can still be difficult to put a dollar value on it (Cohen, Chapter 5 in this volume).

Nevertheless, despite these conceptual and substantive difficulties, there are a number of points of agreement about the amount and costs of white-collar crime. First, white-collar crime is widespread and its costs outweigh those of ordinary street crime by several orders of magnitude (Croall, Chapter 4 in this volume; Cohen, Chapter 5 in this volume). Second, either directly or indirectly white-collar crime affects almost everyone (Croall, Chapter 4 in this volume; Cohen, Chapter 5 in this volume). For example, fraud in the mortgage and investment banking industries recently has been implicated in the economic collapse of 2008 (Barnett 2013; Simpson and Rorie, Chapter 16 in this volume), and in the 1980s fraud in the savings and loan industry cost taxpayers literally billions of dollars (Calavita and Pontell 1990). And there are more subtle costs that cannot be so easily calculated in dollars and cents. Consider how the presence of harmful chemicals in the environment, food, or consumer products may lead to illness and reduced quality of life (Croall, Chapter 4 in this volume). In addition to the physical and financial costs of white-collar crime, it may also have severe psychological effects. For example, many of the victims of Bernard Madoff's Ponzi scheme described themselves as emotionally devastated by the loss of their life savings (Henriques 2011), as were the employees of Enron who lost their retirement accounts when it went bankrupt (McLean and Elkind 2003).

Finally, as Cohen (Chapter 5 in this volume) perceptively notes, the costs of white-collar crime also include what he calls "avoidance behaviors." Avoidance behavior refers to actions taken by individuals and businesses to avoid becoming a victim of a white-collar crime, or in the case of businesses to avoid being mistakenly charged with a crime. For example, purchasing a credit monitoring service to protect oneself against identity theft is a form of avoidance behavior and also can be considered a cost of white-collar crime. Avoidance behaviors also include actions taken by governments to help prevent crime. Consumer education campaigns and consumer protection agencies help prevent white-collar crimes, but they also cost tax dollars and add to the money lost to white-collar crime.

VIII. CONTROL

That white-collar crime and corporate crime pose a grave threat to individuals and society should, by now, be obvious. "Crime in relation to business," as Sutherland (1940) called it, has given us financial scoundrels who steal billions, environmental disasters that destroy habitats and require billions to clean up, and workplace tragedies whose emotional and physical costs are so appalling that it is tasteless to put a price on them. In light of the size and severity of the problem, one might think that white-collar crime control would be a top priority at all levels of government, but that would be a mistake. With as close to a universal consensus as one can get among scholars, those who study white-collar crime agree that the governmental responses to white-collar crime control are inadequate at best and laughable at worst. Nevertheless, even though official responses to white-collar crime can be fairly described as "limp" (Shover and Hochstetler 2006), they are not entirely absent, nor are they entirely ineffective. In the final section of this chapter, we describe the different approaches that are used to control white-collar crime, focusing primarily on regulatory oversight and criminal sanctions.

For a variety of reasons, white-collar crime poses special problems for criminal justice agencies. First, the crimes themselves are difficult to detect because they are often camouflaged as legitimate business activities (Braithwaite and Geis 1982; Benson and Simpson 2014). Second, even when a white-collar crime does come to light, if it is committed in an organizational setting, it can be difficult for investigators and prosecutors to pinpoint a responsible party—that is, an individual or group of individuals who can be convicted and sent to jail (Benson and Cullen 1998). Indeed, prosecutors often face a difficult decision over whether to charge the corporation itself or some individual involved in the offense (Dervan and Podgor, Chapter 27 in this volume). Third, the investigation of crimes committed in organizational settings can be extremely complex, time-consuming, and resource-intensive (Dervan and Podgor, Chapter 27 in this volume). Furthermore, the defendants in white-collar cases have abundant legal and financial resources with which to fight criminal charges by taking full advantage of the procedural safeguards that are built into modern legal systems to protect against the coercive use of authority by criminal justice officials (Mann 1985). For all of these considerations, prosecutors have reason to be chary of trying to use criminal sanctions to control white-collar crime.

On the rare occasions when prosecutors do move forward and secure convictions against "respectable offenders," it is not exactly clear how they should be sentenced or what the most appropriate sanction is (Levi, Chapter 28 in this volume). On the one hand, it seems important to send a message that the law applies to rich and poor alike, and therefore it is appropriate to send white-collar offenders to prison. On the other hand, however, one can ask if it makes sense to spend money incarcerating individuals who pose little risk of future dangerousness purely for the sake of punishment. Thus, in sentencing white-collar offenders, judges face a paradox of how to blend the severity that public opinion demands with the leniency that correctional theory would suggest is appropriate (Wheeler, Mann, and Sarat 1988; Levi, Chapter 28 in this volume). The evidence is mixed as to how they resolve this paradox, with some studies finding that upper-world offenders are sentenced more harshly than comparable lower-status counterparts (Tillman and Pontell 1992; Van Slyke and Bales 2012), while other studies find little in the way of class-based differences in sentence severity (Hagan and Nagel 1982; Wheeler, Weisburd, and Bode 1982; Hagan and Palloni 1986; Benson and Walker 1988). Even though there is some evidence that incarceration rates and sentence lengths for white-collar offenders have increased in the past two decades (Stadler, Benson, and Cullen 2013), the likelihood that we will ever witness a mass incarceration movement directed at business executives is vanishingly small.

Although the criminal justice system has an important role to play in controlling crime in relation to business, especially in egregious cases, responsibility for the day-to-day oversight and control of harmful activities in business falls mainly on regulatory agencies. And it is within the framework of regulation that the major policy initiatives regarding the control of business activities are put forth. Both the day-to-day administration and enforcement of regulatory rules and the overall form and structure of regulatory policy are perennially controversial topics.

Indeed, one would be hard pressed to find a more controversial and longstanding subject than the proper role of government in the marketplace. When is government intervention necessary and when should matters should be left to the invisible hand of the market (Gunningham, Chapter 24 in this volume)? Should regulatory inspectors act like law-enforcement agents seeking to find and punish all rule violations, or should they take a more conciliatory, responsive approach to their work with regulated entities and try to help them comply with the law (Fisse and Braithwaite 1993; Gunningham, Chapter 24 in this volume)? Do regulations work, or is their effectiveness inevitably eviscerated by special interests working behind closed doors (Ramirez, Chapter 23 in this volume)? What should be done with transnational organizations that seem to operate outside the jurisdiction of any single governmental authority (Braithwaite 1993)? These are but a few of the many ongoing debates over the need for and effectiveness of regulation.

Regarding the effectiveness of regulation, the idea that lax regulation or lack of credible oversight is a fundamental cause of white-collar crime has the status of something approaching a biblical truth among white-collar and corporate crime scholars. A particularly compelling analysis of the role of inadequate regulatory oversight in corporate crime can be found in Ramirez's study (Chapter 23 in this volume) of the financial scandals of the preceding decade. Ramirez recounts a familiar story in which the response to public outrage over some corporate scandal leads to the passage of new "tough" regulations. But after the public's attention turns elsewhere, special interests work to "diminish regulatory restrictions and to subvert criminal accountability" (Ramirez, Chapter 23 in this volume). Throughout the history of regulation, scandal and outrage have often led to new regulations that are passed with great fanfare only to be quietly eroded later by the lobbying and backroom deals of special interests.

But even regulations that have been eroded can still have some level of effectiveness, and there are differing opinions on how best to judge effectiveness (Mascini, Chapter 25 in this volume). If effectiveness is judged by the application of tough regulatory sanctions to rule violations, then there is little evidence of that. However, as Mascini (Chapter 25 in this volume) notes, the movements toward responsive regulation and regulatory governance take a more polycentric as opposed to state-centric view of regulation. Under a responsive regulation system, the effectiveness of regulation is judged not so much by how many rule violations are sanctioned but instead by the degree to which harm is reduced and the interests of civil society are protected. According to proponents of responsive regulation, this is most likely to be achieved when regulators work cooperatively with regulated entities (Ayres and Braithwaite 1992). Likewise, the regulatory governance model views the state, the market (i.e., corporations and other business entities), and civil society as part of a comprehensive and interlocking system through which socially responsible behavior by businesses is promoted.

Whether the happy and cooperative state of affairs envisioned by the regulatory governance and responsive regulation models is ever actually achieved in the market place is debated and depends on where you look (Mascini, Chapter 25 in this volume). There have been some success stories. For example, the airline industry has made important contributions to the safety of air travel. But there are also many industrial sectors where market participants have done little to improve the safety of workers or consumers and have vigorously resisted efforts by governments to do so ((Cullen et al. 2006). The effectiveness of different regulatory models is, therefore, difficult to evaluate as counterexamples can always be found. In the end, the "holy grail" of regulation may never be found, because "policy ideas on regulatory inspection are founded on conflicting conceptions of the good society" (Mascini, Chapter 25 in this volume).

IX. Conclusion

This Handbook was designed to bring together contemporary cutting-edge thinking on the problem of white-collar crime and its control. In regard to that goal, we believe we have succeeded, but we are also aware that a field as broad and deep as white-collar crime can never be captured in a single handbook, at least not in one that could be lifted by a normal person. Thus, in selecting what areas to cover and how many chapters to devote to them, we have necessarily had to be selective. This book could easily have had twice as many chapters and been twice as long. Nevertheless, we believe readers will find something of value here on each of the eight themes that guided our work—concept, offender, organization, choice, opportunity, context, costs, and control.

REFERENCES

Ayres, Ian, and John Braithwaite. 1992. *Responsive Regulation*. Oxford: Oxford University Press.

Barnett, Harold S. 2013. "And Some with a Fountain Pen: Mortgage Fraud, Securitization, and the Sub-Prime Bubble." In *How They Got Away with It: White-Collar Criminals and the Financial Meltdown*, pp. 104–29, edited by Susan Will, Stephen Handelman, and David C. Brotherton. New York: Columbia University Press.

Benson, Michael L. 1985. "Denying the Guilty Mind: Accounting for Involvement in a White-Collar Crime." *Criminology* 23: 583–608.

Benson, Michael L. 2012. "Evolutionary Ecology, Fraud, and the Global Financial Crisis." In *Contemporary Issues in Criminological Theory and Research: The Role of Social Institutions*, pp. 299–306, edited by Richard Rosenfeld, Karen Quinet, and Crystal Garcia. Belmont: Wadsworth.

Benson, Michael L., and Francis T. Cullen. 1998. *Combating Corporate Crime: Local Prosecutors at Work*. Boston, MA: Northeastern University Press.

Benson, Michael L., and Petter Gottschalk. 2014. "Gender and White-Collar Crime in Norway: An Empirical Study of Media Reports." *International Journal of Law, Crime, and Justice*. Available online January 28, 2015. http://www.sciencedirect.com.proxy.libraries.uc.edu/science/article/pii/S1756061615000026

Benson, Michael L., Jay P. Kennedy, and Matthew Logan. Forthcoming. "Issues, Challenges, and Opportunities in the Measurement of White-Collar and Corporate Crime." In *Handbook on Measurement in Criminology and Criminal Justice*, edited by Timothy S. Bynum and Beth M. Huebner. New York: John Wiley.

Benson, Michael L., and Kent R. Kerley. 2000. "Life Course Theory and White-Collar Crime." In *Contemporary Issues in Crime and Criminal Justice: Essays in Honor of Gilbert Geis*, pp. 121–36, edited by Henry N. Pontell and David Shichor. Upper Saddle River, NJ: Prentice Hall.

Benson, Michael L., and Tara L. Sams. 2013. "Emotions, Choice, and Crime." In *The Oxford Handbook of Criminological Theory*, pp. 494–510, edited by Francis T. Cullen and Pamela Wilcox. Oxford: Oxford University Press

Benson, Michael L., and Sally S. Simpson. 2014. *Understanding White-Collar Crime: An Opportunity Perspective*. 2nd ed. New York: Routledge.

Benson, Michael L., and Esteban Walker. 1988. "Sentencing the White-Collar Offender." *American Sociological Review* 33: 301–9.

Bonger, Willem A., and Henry P. Horton. 1916. *Criminality and Economic Conditions*. Boston: Little, Brown, and Company.

Braithwaite, John. 1985. "White-Collar Crime." *Annual Review of Sociology* 11: 1–25.

Braithwaite, John. 1993. "Transnational Regulation of the Pharmaceutical Industry." *The Annals* 525: 12–30.

Braithwaite, John, and Brent Fisse. 1990. "On the Plausibility of Corporate Crime Control." *Advances in Criminological Theory* 2: 15–37.

Braithwaite, John, and Gilbert Geis. 1982. "On Theory and Action for Corporate Crime Control." *Crime and Delinquency* 28: 292–314.

Calavita, Kitty, and Henry N. Pontell. 1990. "'Heads I Win, Tails You Lose:' Deregulation, Crime, and Crisis in the Savings and Loan Industry." *Crime and Delinquency* 36: 309–41.

Chevigny, Paul G. 2001. "From Betrayal to Violence: Dante's *Inferno* and the Social Construction of Crime." *Law and Social Inquiry* 26: 787–818.

Clarke, Ronald. V. 1983. "Situational Crime Prevention: Its Theoretical Basis and Practical Scope." In *Crime and Justice: An Annual Review*, pp. 225–56, edited by Michael Tonry and Norval Morris. Chicago: University of Chicago Press.

Clinard, Marshall B., and Peter C. Yeager. 2006. *Corporate Crime.* New Brunswick, NJ: Transaction.

Cohen, Lawrence E., and Marcus Felson. 1979. "Social Change and Crime Rate Trends: A Routine Activity Approach." *American Sociological Review* 44: 588–608.

Coleman, John W. 1987. "Toward an Integrated Theory of White-Collar Crime." *American Journal of Sociology* 93: 406–39.

Copes, Heith, and Lynne M. Vieraitis. 2012. *Identity Thieves: Motives and Methods.* Boston: Northeastern University Press.

Cullen, Francis T. 2011. "Beyond Adolescence-Limited Criminology: Choosing Our Future? The American Society of Criminology 2010 Sutherland Address." *Criminology* 49: 287–330.

Cullen, Francis T., Gray Cavender, William J. Maakestad, and Michael L. Benson. 2006. *Corporate Crime under Attack: The Fight to Criminalize Business Violence.* Newark, NJ: LexisNexis Matthew Bender.

Cullen, Francis T., Cecilia Chouhy, and Cheryl Lero Jonson. Forthcoming. "Public Opinion about White-Collar and Corporate Crime." In *The Handbook of White-Collar Crime*, edited by Nicole Leeper Piquero. New York: John Wiley and Sons.

Edelhertz, Herbert. 1970. *The Nature, Impact and Prosecution of White-Collar Crime.* Washington, D.C.: U.S. Department of Justice.

Felson, Marcus, and Mary Eckert. 2015. *Crime and Everyday Life.* 5th ed. Thousand Oaks, CA: Sage.

Fisse, Brent, and John Braithwaite. 1993. *Corporations, Crime, and Accountability.* Cambridge: Cambridge University Press.

Geis, Gilbert. 1988. "From Deuteronomy to Deniability: A Historical Perlustration on White-Collar Crime." *Justice Quarterly* 5: 7–32.

Green, Stuart P. 2004. "Moral Ambiguity in White-Collar Criminal Law." *Notre Dame Journal of Law, Ethics, and Public Policy* 18: 501–19.

Green, Stuart P. 2006. *Lying, Cheating, and Stealing: A Moral Theory of White-Collar Crime.* New York: Oxford University Press.

Gross, Edward. 1978. "Organizational Crime: A Theoretical Perspective." In *Studies in Symbolic Interaction*, pp. 55–85, edited by Norman Denzin. Greenwood, CT: JAI Press.

Gross, Edward. 1980. "Organization Structure and Organizational Crime." In *White-Collar Crime: Theory and Research*, pp. 52–76, edited by Gilbert Geis and Ezra Stotland. Beverly Hills: Sage.

Hagan John L., and Alberto Palloni. 1986. "Club Fed and the Sentencing of White-Collar Offenders before and after Watergate." *Criminology* 24: 603–21.

Hagan, John L., and Ilene H. Nagel. 1982. "White-Collar Crime, White-Collar Time: The Sentencing of White-Collar Offenders in the Southern District of New York." *American Criminal Law Review* 20: 259–89.

Henriques, Diane B. 2011. *The Wizard of Lies: Bernie Madoff and the Death of Trust.* New York: Times Books/Henry Holt.

Holtfreter, Kristy, Shanna Van Slyke, and Thomas G. Blomberg. 2005. "Sociolegal Change in Consumer Fraud: From Victim–Offender Interactions to Global Networks." *Crime, Law, and Social Change* 44: 251–75.

Jesilow, Paul, Gilbert Geis, and Henry N. Pontell. 1991. "Fraud by Physicians against Medicaid." *Journal of the American Medical Association* 266: 3318–22.

Johnstone, Peter. 1998. "Serious White Collar Fraud: Historical and Contemporary Perspectives." *Crime, Law and Social Change* 30: 107–30.

Klenowski, Paul, Heith Copes, and Christopher W. Mullins. 2011. "Gender, Identity, and Accounts: How White-Collar Offenders Do Gender When Making Sense of Their Crimes." *Justice Quarterly* 28: 46–69.

Levi, Michael. 2012. "Fraud Vulnerabilities, the Financial Crisis, and the Business Cycle." In *Contemporary Issues in Criminological Theory and Research: The Role of Social Institutions*, pp. 269–92, edited by Richard Rosenfeld, Karen Quinet, and Crystal Garcia. Belmont: Wadsworth.

Lombroso, Cesare. 1887. *L'homme Criminel*. Paris: F. Alcan.

McLean, Bethany, and Peter Elkind. 2003. *The Smartest Guys in the Room: The Amazing Rise and Scandalous Fall of Enron*. New York: Portfolio.

Paternoster, Raymond, and Sally S. Simpson. 1993. "A Rational Choice Theory of Corporate Crime." In *Advances in Criminological Theory*, pp. 37–58, edited by Ronald. V. Clarke and Marcus Felson. New Brunswick, NJ: Transaction.

Paternoster, Raymond, and Sally S. Simpson. 1996. "Sanction Threats and Appeals to Morality: Testing a Rational Choice Model of Corporate Crime." *Law and Society Review* 30: 549–83.

Pinker, Steven. 2012. *The Better Angels of Our Nature: Why Violence Has Declined*. New York: Penguin Books

Piquero, Nicole Leeper, and Michael L. Benson. 2004. "White-Collar Crime and Criminal Careers: Specifying a Trajectory of Punctuated Situational Offending." *Journal of Contemporary Criminal Justice* 20: 148–65.

Rebovich, Donald J. 1992. *Dangerous Ground: The World of Hazardous Waste Crime*. New Brunswick, NJ: Transaction.

Ross, Edward A. 1907. *Sin and Society: An Analysis of Latter-Day Iniquity*. Boston and New York: Houghton, Mifflin, and Company.

Shover, Neal, and Andrew Hochstetler. 2006. *Choosing White-Collar Crime*. New York: Cambridge University Press.

Simpson, Sally S. 1987. "Cycles of Illegality: Antitrust Violations in Corporate America." *Social Forces* 65: 943–63.

Simpson, Sally S. 2002. *Corporate Crime, Law, and Social Control*. New York: Cambridge University Press.

Simpson, Sally S. 2013. "White-Collar Crime." *Annual Review of Sociology* 39: 309–31.

Simpson, Sally S., Joel Garner, and Carole Gibbs. 2007. *Why Do Corporations Obey Environmental Law? Final Report*. Washington, D.C.: National Institute of Justice, U.S. Department of Justice.

Sparrow, Malcolm K. 1996. *License to Steal: Why Fraud Plagues America's Health Care System*. Boulder, CO: Westview Press.

Stadler, William, Michael L. Benson, and Francis T. Cullen. 2013. "Revisiting the Special Sensitivity Hypothesis: The Prison Experience of White-Collar Offenders." *Justice Quarterly* 30: 1090–114.

Steffensmeier, Darrell, Jennifer Schwartz, and Michael Roche. 2013. "Gender and 21st-Century Corporate Crime: Female Involvement and the Gender Gap in Enron-Era Frauds." *American Sociological Review* 78: 448–76.

Sutherland, Edwin H. 1940. "White-Collar Criminality." *American Sociological Review* 5: 1–12.

Sutherland, Edwin H. 1949. *White Collar Crime*. New York: Holt, Rinehart, and Winston.

Tillman, Robert, and Henry N. Pontell. 1992. "Is Justice 'Collar-Blind'? Punishing Medicaid Provider Fraud." *Criminology* 30: 547–74.

Van Slyke, Shanna, and William D. Bales. 2012. "A Contemporary Study of the Decision to Incarcerate White-Collar and Street Property Offenders." *Punishment and Society* 14: 217–46.

Vaughan, Diane. 2005. "The Normalization of Deviance: Signals of Danger, Situated Action, and Risk." In *How Professionals Make Decisions*, pp. 255–75, edited by Henry Montgomery, Raanan Lipshitz, and Brehmer Brehmer. Mahwah, NJ: Lawrence Erlbaum.

Weisburd, David, Stanton Wheeler, Elin Waring, and Nancy Bode. 1991. *Crimes of the Middle Classes: White-Collar Offenders in the Federal Courts*. New Haven, CT: Yale University Press.

Wheeler, Stanton, Kenneth Mann, and Austin Sarat. 1988. *Sitting in Judgment: The Sentencing of White-Collar Criminals*. New Haven, CT: Yale University Press.

Wheeler, Stanton, David Weisburd, and Nancy Bode. 1982. "Sentencing the White-Collar Offender: Rhetoric and Reality." *American Sociological Review* 47: 641–59.

Wheeler, Stanton, David Weisburd, Elin Waring, and Nancy Bode. 1988. "White-Collar Crime and Criminals." *American Criminal Law Review* 25: 331–57.

Willott, Sara, Christine Griffin, and Mark Torrance. 2001. "Snakes and Ladders: Upper-Middle-Class Male Offenders Talk about Economic Crime." *Criminology* 39: 441–66.

Wilson, James Q., and Richard J. Herrnstein. 1985. *Crime and Human Nature*. New York: Simon and Schuster.

Zey, Mary. 1993. *Banking on Fraud: Drexel, Junk Bonds, and Buyouts*. New York: Aldine De Gruyter.

PART I

DEFINITIONAL DEBATES

CHAPTER 2

THE ROOTS AND VARIANT DEFINITIONS OF THE CONCEPT OF "WHITE-COLLAR CRIME"

GILBERT GEIS

WHITE-COLLAR crime has become a prominent social and political issue since the global economic meltdown that began in the first decade of the present century. This essay discusses the history of concern with such behavior while focusing on the various definitions of what should be regarded by the criminal justice and regulatory systems as white-collar crime.

The core conclusions are as follows:

- Throughout history there has been social and political concern regarding the abuse of power by elites in business, politics, and the professions, and persons who exploit the citizenry by violations of customs, rules, and laws.
- Disapproval of these malevolent practices began to coalesce in the United States at the turn of the 20th century in the movement against persons labeled "robber barons" and in the work of a group of writers who were called muckrakers.
- This movement was specified as a crusade against "criminaloids" and "white-collar bandits" before the sociologist Edwin Sutherland in 1939 pinned the tag of "white-collar crime" on the illegal acts of the powerful in the course of their occupational work.
- Sutherland's definition has been challenged by people who insist that it should not be the status of the perpetrator but conviction for criminal acts with specific characteristics, such as securities fraud, that should define white-collar crime.
- Dissensus over the relative merits of offender-based and offense-based definitions of white-collar crime can be transcended in part by use of a hybrid approach that avoids some of the theoretical and empirical shortcomings of the latter.

Section I of this essay offers an inventory of behaviors in early times that would today come under the heading of white-collar crime. Section II reviews writings in the United States prior to the formal introduction of the term "white-collar crime." Section III reviews the emergence of the designation "white-collar crime" and the erratic nature of the definitions offered by its originator. Section IV discusses the appearance of an emphasis on the legal nature of the offense rather than the status of the offender, and notes the significance of the two major approaches to white-collar crime for research, theory, and policy. Finally, section V offers the writer's appraisal of the variant definitions of "white-collar crime."

I. The Pre-Sutherland Landscape

The belief that all humans are born equal is dear to the heart of many citizens of democracies, but throughout time it has been refuted by the fact that some persons, through birth, effort, good luck, or other arrangements, are a great deal more equal than others. The power that goes with being better situated in the social and economic hierarchy may be used to engage in actions that violate tradition and, as social systems evolve, formal legal rules. Early substantive information on elite wrongdoing can be gleaned from codes promulgated almost two thousand years before the beginning of the Christian calendar. Notable is the Code of Hammurabi, issued about 1780 B.C.E. by the ruler of Babylonia (Prince 1904; Bryant 2005). Among its 282 provisions are decrees proclaiming that "a judge who has given a verdict, rendered a decision, granted a written judgment, and afterward had altered his judgment" was to be fined twelve times the amount of the judgment and expelled from his position (Johns 1999). Presumably, the rules were intended to discourage payment of bribes to judges to induce them to change their verdict.

The ancient records also include other examples. Edicts, parables, imprecations, and curses directed at practices that later became known as white-collar crimes appear in the history of the offense of bribery in ancient Egypt (Taylor 2001) and political tyranny in early Greece (McGlew 1993). Corruption in the Roman Empire was classically portrayed by Shakespeare in *Julius Caesar* when Brutus levels the accusation: "Let me tell you, Cassius, you yourself/Are much condemned to have an itching palm/To sell and mart your offices for gold." (An itching palm, folklore claimed, could best be cured by scratching it with a metallic coin.) In Exodus 23:8 in the King James translation of the Old Testament, we again are met with a warning against bribery: "And you shall take no bribes, for the bribe blinds the wise, and perverts the words of the righteous." In Matthew 21:12, there is the story of Jesus overturning the tables of the unscrupulous money changers in the temple.

In the common law of England, as well as in colonial American statutes, there were provisions against what were called forestalling, engrossing, and regrating—offenses involving the creation of shortages of comestibles in order to reap greater profits for food deliberately withheld from the market (Geis 1988, pp. 9–13).

Harsh indictments of the kinds of behavior that would be labeled "white-collar crime" likewise appear in the more contemporary historical record. Perhaps (but perhaps not) the most influential prompt to interest in white-collar crime came from the work of Charles Richmond Henderson, Sutherland's Ph.D. advisor at the University of Chicago. Henderson had written in a textbook:

> The social classes of the highest culture furnish few convicts, yet there are educated criminals. Advanced culture modifies the form of crime, tends to make it less coarse and violent, but more cunning; restricts it to quasi-legal forms. But education also opens up the way to new and colossal kinds of crime. . . . Many of the "Napoleons" of trade . . . are cold-blooded robbers and murderers, utterly indifferent to the inevitable misery which . . . will follow their contrivances and deals. (Henderson 1901, p. 250)

In 1907, E. A. Ross, a preeminent sociologist, devoted a chapter in his *Sin and Society* to persons he labeled *criminaloids*. His roster included

> the director who speculates in securities, the banker who lends the depositors' money to himself . . . the railroad official who grants a secret rebate for his private graft, the builder who hires delegates to harass his rivals with ceaseless strikes, the labor leader who instigates a strike in order to be paid for calling it off, the publisher who bribes his text-books into the schools. (p. 50)

The criminaloid, Ross went on, "counterfeits the good citizen. Full well he knows that the giving of a fountain or a park, the establishing of a college chair on Neolithic drama or the elegiac poetry of the Chaldeans will more than outweigh the dodging of taxes, the grabbing of streets, and the corrupting of city councils" (p. 62).

The investigative work of the muckrakers—Ida Tarbell, Frank Norris, and Upton Sinclair, among others—documented harmful practices in the oil industry, the Chicago meatpacking plants, as well as corruption in the country's largest cities (Filler 1990). The term "robber barons" was fixed by Matthew Josephson (1933) on magnates who had engaged in self-serving financial craftiness, sucking funds from investors and the government, money that, for example, only marginally went into the building of the transcontinental railroads but largely ended up in the pockets of moguls such as Leland Stanford and Mark Hopkins (Lewis 1938; see generally Geis 2011, pp. 15–82).

Other writers also noted elite wrongdoing and likened the perpetrators to "white-collar bandits" (Schoepfer and Tibbetts 2011). In 1926, Hurnard J. Kenner, the manager of the Better Business Bureau, berated "the white-collar bandit, the gentleman thief who steals the savings of the uniformed or gullible by stock-swindling and fraudulent brokerage practices" (Kenner 1926, p. 54). Three years later, the same term was employed by George E. Q. Johnson, Jr. (1929), a federal district attorney in Illinois.

Finally, a law professor, writing about planned bankruptcies, attributed them to "white-collar bandits" (Wolfe 1938).

II. Edwin H. Sutherland

The term "white-collar crime" was introduced to the public arena by Edwin H. Sutherland in his 1939 presidential address to a joint meeting of the American Sociological Society and the American Economics Association. Sutherland had graduated in 1904 from Grand Island College in Nebraska, where his father, a Baptist minister, was president. He enrolled in the sociology department at the University of Chicago, staffed by what many people consider the most eminent group of sociology scholars ever assembled in one academic setting (Bulmer 1984).

There are no obvious clues that might explain Sutherland's emergent focus on white-collar crime in the latter part of his career. Notably, however, he was raised in Nebraska and absorbed the populist ideology that saw corporate leaders, particularly those running the railroads, mercilessly sucking the lifeblood out of farm communities by levying exorbitant and discriminatory rates (Cherry 1981). In the preface to his 1949 monograph on the subject he noted that he (in fact, primarily his students) had been assembling the material for the book during the previous twenty-five years. Eventually, he would publish this monograph and four papers on the subject of white-collar crime. In addition, the text of a talk on white-collar crime that Sutherland delivered at DePauw University was included in a collection of his journal writings.

A. "White-Collar Criminality" (1939)

A major theme of Sutherland's presidential address was that, in their research and theories, both sociologists and economists had failed to take account of what he labeled "white-collar crime." Had they attended to such crimes, inevitably they would have realized that notions that crime was caused by conditions such as poverty, broken homes, psychopathic ailments, immigrant status, and mental deficiency were inadequate. The reason, Sutherland argued, is that they failed to account for illegal acts by the powerful in their role in business, politics, and the professions.

Sutherland provided the first two of his various definitions of white-collar crime in his address. His aim, he proclaimed, was "a comparison of crime in the upper or white-collar class, composed of respectable or at least respected business and professional men, and crime in the lower class, composed of persons of low socio-economic status" (Sutherland 1940, p. 1). In a later footnote he elaborated on his definition:

> Perhaps it should be repeated that "white-collar" (upper) and "lower" classes merely designate persons of high and low socioeconomic status. Income and amount of

money involved in the crime are not the sole criteria. Many persons of "low" socio-economic status are "white-collar" criminals in the sense that they are well-dressed, well-educated, and have high incomes, but "white-collar" as used in this paper means "respected," "socially accepted and approved," "looked up to." Some people in this class may not be well-dressed or well-educated, nor have high incomes, although the "upper" usually exceed the "lower" classes in these respects as well as in social status. (p. 4)

This piece of obscurantism indicates the inconclusive wrestling bout that Sutherland had with himself trying to pin down the parameters of his subject.

Sutherland clearly was following the path of the muckrakers, as a newspaper reporter had no trouble recognizing. The story in the *Philadelphia Public-Ledger* (1939, p. 17) indicated that his speech offered a "withering denunciation" of acts of white-collar crime to "an astonished audience." In his talk, Sutherland harked back to the robber barons—Cornelius Vanderbilt, J. P. Morgan, and others—to make his case. He also added to that roster more current upper-crust crooks—Ivar Kreuger and Serge Alexandre Stavisky—and maintained that "in many periods more important crime news may be found on the financial pages of newspapers than on the front pages" (p. 2).

Sutherland insisted that the behaviors he was concerned with could have been handled as criminal offenses. He offered a roster of agencies that might move against white-collar offenders (e.g., the Interstate Commerce Commission) and acts that might be committed by white-collar offenders (e.g., false advertising). "White-collar crime is real crime," he claimed. "It is not ordinarily called crime, and calling it by this name does not make it worse, just as not calling it crime does not make it better" (p. 5). He was concerned not with criminal convictions but with "convict-ability" (p. 6). Sutherland argued that whether an act is defined as a crime or a violation often is determined by the power of likely offenders. An example others would offer is lobbying, which is self-evidently a form of bribery, except that the politicians who are lobbied are the ones who determine the legal dimensions of bribery.

Sutherland believed there was need for a theory that explained every kind of crime. For him, the etiological grail was "differential association," a set of postulates maintaining that criminal behavior is learned and that the essence of the learning involves an acquired understanding of outlawed behavior as acceptable or unacceptable and acting in accord with that belief. Sutherland, who often was his own most astute critic, would hedge that position in the textbook that he wrote and that Donald Cressey, a former Sutherland Ph.D. student, updated after Sutherland's death:

Just as the germ theory of disease does not explain all diseases, so it is possible that no one theory of criminal behavior will explain all criminal behavior. In that case, it will be desirable to define the areas in which any theory applies, so that the several theories can coordinate and, when taken together, can explain all criminal behavior. (Sutherland and Cressey 1960, p. 71; Sutherland 1948)

B. Published Papers, Lectures, and Controversy (1941–1949)

Less than a year after his presidential address Sutherland published an article that repeated many of his earlier points but also sought to clarify the foggy impression he had left regarding the behaviors with which he was concerned. He granted that his definition of white-collar crime was "arbitrary and not very precise" (Sutherland 1941, p. 11) and then offered a pair of examples of what he deemed white-collar crime to be: "[A] fraud committed by a realtor in the sale of a house," Sutherland wrote, "or a murder committed by a manufacturer in strike-breaking activity" (p. 11). He subsequently offered a laundry list of misrepresentations that he believed fell under his definition of white-collar crime:

> [M]isrepresentations occur in the financial statements of corporations, in advertising and other sales methods, in manipulation of the stock exchange, in short weights and measures and in the misgrading of commodities, in embezzlement and misapplication of funds, in commercial bribery, in the bribery of public officials, in tax frauds, and in the misapplication of funds in receiverships and bankruptcies. (p. 11)

Six years following his presidential address, Sutherland published a stalwart defense of the fact that he classified as crimes episodes that had not been dealt with by a criminal court (Sutherland 1945). Importantly, he had moved his attention from delicts of individuals to organizational offenses. He had examined 547 adverse decisions for violations of one of four federal statutes: antitrust, false advertising, offenses against the National Labor Relations Act, and infringement of copyrights, patents, and trademarks. Only 9 percent of these events had been tried as crimes; the large majority had been dealt with in equity or civil courts or by quasi-judicial commissions. Sutherland argued that 473 of the cases *were* crimes and *could* have been proceeded against as such if the authorities had chosen to do so. That they had not done so, he believed, was often the result of social homogeneity between the offenders and the enforcers, the political contributions that businesses make to officeholders and office-seekers, and a relatively indifferent public opinion. He also maintained that the cases showed that "the criminality of [the corporate] behavior was not made obvious by the conventional procedures of the criminal law but was blurred and concealed by special procedures . . . that eliminate or at least minimize the stigma of crime" (p. 136).

Sutherland granted that those penalized by fines, injunctions, and cease-and-desist orders had not enjoyed the presumption of innocence nor had the state had to prove criminal intent. But he argued (rather unpersuasively) that these guarantees were disappearing in the criminal law as strict liability principles gained a foothold in regard to crimes such as statutory rape and defrauding an innkeeper.

Sutherland's (1948) talk to the Toynbee Club, a group of sociology students and faculty at DePauw University, was a prelude to his monograph on white-collar crime that was published the following year. In this informal setting, he apparently felt freer to express his vitriolic distaste for law-breaking corporations, a category that his research indicated included virtually every large business in the United States. His depiction of the response of strikebreakers hired by the Ford Motor Company is tough prose for a "neutral" social scientist:

> The [strike] organizers . . . went with their literature up onto an overhead pass. They were informed that they were trespassing on private property. According to many witnesses, they turned quietly and started away. As they were leaving, they were attacked. They were beaten, knocked down, and kicked. Witnesses described this as a "terrific beating" and "unbelievably brutal." One man's back was broken and another's skull fractured. . . . While these assaults were being committed, city policemen were present and did not interfere. [Ford's] Director of the Service Department was also present. (pp. 87–88)

Sutherland maintained that "if the word 'subversive' refers to efforts to make changes in the social system; the business leaders are the most subversive influence in the United States" (p. 92). He summed up his presentation by noting: "I have attempted to demonstrate that businessmen violate the law with great frequency, using what may be called the methods of organized crime" (p. 96).

Sutherland stated in the 1939 talk (and later in his book) that he was employing the term "white-collar criminal" "to refer to a person in the upper socioeconomic class who violates the laws designed to regulate his business." He added that the term "white-collar" more generally referred to "the wage-earning class which wears good clothes at work, such as clerks in stores" (p. 79). He would omit this last observation in his book.

In an encyclopedia entry (Sutherland 1949b), Sutherland's first sentence offered a straightforward definition of his subject: "The white collar criminal is defined as a person of high socioeconomic status who violates the laws designed to regulate his occupational activities" (Sutherland 1949b, p. 511). He then proceeded, as usual, to muddy the semantic waters by ruminating about what was and what was not white-collar crime.

He eliminated matters such as adultery by persons of high socioeconomic standing from the white-collar crime category, but he specifically differentiated the person of lower socioeconomic status "who violates the . . . special trade regulations which apply to him" from the ranks of white-collar criminals (p. 511). Sutherland had no strong interest in pinning down the parameters of white-collar crime, and his neglect left the class emphasis that obviously was of special importance to him vulnerable to later attack.

C. *White Collar Crime* (1949)

Sutherland's classic monograph on white-collar crime contributed very little beyond what he already had indicated in his previous articles and talk. The 272-page book is almost exclusively a compilation of violations of laws, primarily regulatory rules, by seventy of the largest corporate entities in America (Sutherland 1949a). Sutherland presented information on violations by businesses under six different headings: (1) restraint of trade; (2) rebates; (3) patents, trademarks, and copyrights; (4) misrepresentation in advertising; (5) unfair labor practices; (6) war crimes; and (7) miscellaneous crimes. In regard to advertising, for instance, Sutherland noted a considerable roster of blatant deceptions—that footwear advertised as alligator shoes had no trace of alligator in them and that coffins claimed to be rustproof were not.

His findings led Sutherland to the hyperbolic observation that in terms of their records businesses were no different than organized criminals, an argument that takes up an entire chapter. He quotes with approval economist Thorstein Veblen's observation that the "ideal pecuniary man is like the ideal delinquent in his unscrupulous conversion of goods and persons to his own ends and in a callous disregard of the feelings and wishes of others and of the remoter effects of his actions" (Veblen 1912, p. 237). In Sutherland's view this made the "ideal" (perhaps but not assuredly meaning the typical) businessperson little different than a professional criminal (p. 217).

At the end of *White Collar Crime* Sutherland inserted a section called "Personal Documents," which was made up of submissions by students of their experiences working in enterprises such as selling typewriters, sewing machines, and shoes by employing crooked tactics (1949a, p. 234ff). Sutherland might have been including these vignettes to add a bit of further color to his monograph or perhaps merely to extend it to a more usual length, but the tactic only serves to confound further an understanding of what Sutherland truly regarded as white-collar crime.

Finally, under pressure from his publisher, who feared that it might end up in legal difficulty if companies labeled as criminal in the book but not so designated by a criminal court sued for defamation, Sutherland cut several chapters and removed identifying corporate names from the text. It would be thirty-four years before the unabridged version found its way into print (Sutherland 1983).

D. Nota Bene

My review of Sutherland's publications and his speech on white-collar crime lead to a conclusion that white-collar crime scholars, myself included, have largely ignored. It is that Sutherland never really studied white-collar crime by individuals but almost exclusively focused on business, usually corporate, wrongdoing. He buttressed his introduction of the term "white-collar crime" in 1939 with scattered references to particular notorious offenders and offered a smattering of observations (e.g., white-collar criminals are responsible for more financial losses than the entire traditional street offenders combined). But he must have come to realize that he did not possess the resources, nor could he locate the sources, to carry out the very demanding task of providing substantive information and theoretical conclusions about the cohort of persons he regarded as white-collar criminals. What could he say that would advance our understanding of people like John D. Rockefeller and Daniel Drew that would rise very far above the anecdotal?

III. Critiques and Alternatives

Sutherland, and probably all who prefer offender-based definitions of white-collar crime over definitions grounded in crime characteristics, refused to forfeit social scientific definitional autonomy to the lawmakers and enforcers. Social scientists might make "better" decisions than legislators in delineating what should be regarded as white-collar crimes, since they presumably (hopefully?) have no personal nor financial interest in their decisions and could be held to a standard of logical consistency. Attacks on Sutherland's definition were launched by legal scholars as well as by some prominent social scientists who participated in a Yale Law School study of white-collar crime.

A. Conviction by a Criminal Court

Sutherland's heresy in defining white-collar crime, according to some lawyers, was in categorizing as white-collar crime acts that the authorities had not treated as crimes. Thus, Tappan claimed that Sutherland's concept of white-collar crime had created a "widespread and seductive ... fashionable dogma" (1947, p. 98). Tappan faulted the study of white-collar crime for being marked by "blustering broadsides" against the "existing system" (p. 99). He noted that "[a]ll of these practices are within the framework of ordinary business practices" (p. 99), as if this means that they should be acceptable. Presumably, Sutherland would have found the National Labor Relations Board (NLRB) guilty judgment as validating the behavior as a white-collar crime.

In contrast to Sutherland's definitional approach, Tappan (1947) repeatedly argued that the only reasonable subject for criminological concern was the person who had been convicted in a criminal court. "Only those are criminals who have been adjudicated as such by the courts," he insisted (p. 100), and added: "In studying the offender there can be no presumption that arrested, arraigned, indicated, or prosecuted persons are criminals unless they also be held guilty beyond a reasonable doubt of a particular offense" (p. 100).

But this critique of Sutherland is flawed. How do we classify Kenneth Lay, the one-time president of Enron, who was convicted of multiple white-collar offenses but the record was wiped clean when he died before he could be sentenced (Eichenwald 2008)? Or Ivar Kreuger and other obvious white-collar criminals who killed themselves before they could be tried (Partnoy 2009)? While Tappan identified Sutherland's work by name, he failed to address its core point: white-collar crimes are acts that are dealt with by government agencies and that they could have been prosecuted in a criminal court had the authorities chosen to do so. Tappan's definition of the white-collar criminal is little more than a historical footnote today, and there are no contemporary advocates for it.

B. Crimes with Distinctive Characteristics

Unlike the earlier law-trained critics of Sutherland's delineation of white-collar crime, Herbert Edelhertz had led fraud investigations as chief of the fraud division of the U.S. Department of Justice. Edelhertz believed that Sutherland's definition was much too limited. White-collar crime was "democratic," he maintained, "and can be committed by a bank clerk or the head of his institution" (Edelhertz 1970, pp. 3–4). This position trivialized Sutherland's concern with the abuse of power by the powerful. Edelhertz saw white-collar crime as "an illegal act or a series of illegal acts committed by nonphysical means and by concealment or guile, to obtain money or property, to avoid the payment or loss of money or property, or to obtain business or personal advantage" (p. 4).

Edelhertz's core point was that the definition of white-collar crime ought to be tied directly to legal provisions, which reflect the characteristics of these crimes. The definition that he offered, however, has a number of questionable criteria. It is odd to specify one act or a series of acts since a single offense will do to meet the requirements of the definition. In addition, it could be argued that a reasonable categorization of white-collar offenses should include violent acts, such as when a doctor does cataract operations on patients who do not require the procedure and inflicts eyesight loss (Jesilow, Pontell, and Geis 1993). The focus on motive, which need not be proven in a criminal case, seems unnecessary. Nor is it clear if Edelhertz agreed with Sutherland or with Tappan regarding whether a criminal conviction was necessary for an act to be considered a white-collar crime.

Another legal definition of their subject based on crime characteristics marked the work of a group of scholars at Yale University. The Yale group decided to focus on eight federal statutes to provide a sample of white-collar criminals: (1) securities fraud; (2) antitrust violations; (3) bribery; (4) tax offenses; (5) bank embezzlement; (6) postal and wire fraud; (7) false claims and statements; and (8) credit- and lending-institution fraud. Their study sites were seven federal district courts. They examined a random sample of thirty persons convicted in each of the courts during the fiscal years 1976 through 1978 for offenses. Researchers were provided access to the presentence investigation reports prepared by probation officers, which typically contained detailed information about both the offender and the offense.

For white-collar crime scholars the flagship of the work at Yale was *Crimes of the Middle Classes* (Weisburd et al. 1991). While elites and the unemployed appeared in their sample of 1094 offenders, they concluded that in the main white-collar crime, as they defined it, was essentially the conduct of middle-class persons. Kathleen Daly, a member of the research team, would later state that the women in the study were characterized by "occupational marginality." As many as one third of the women in some of the offense categories were unemployed. Daly wondered if "white-collar criminal" was an appropriate designation for the women, given their "socioeconomic profile, coupled with the nature of their crimes" (Daly 1989, p. 790).

In ignoring corporate and civil offenses, the Yale investigators failed to attend to executives who were culpable but who escaped criminal prosecution because the government preferred to fine them or to act against the deeper-pocketed organizations for which they worked. Similarly and arguably the Yale Study was off-target by ignoring regulatory actions. The criminal law was only rarely invoked after the recent economic meltdown, although many prominent businessmen, such as Angelo Mozilo of Countrywide, were heavily fined by the Securities and Exchange Commission: his fine was $67.5 million (Madrick 2011). The offense roster used by Yale would also overlook persons such as Martha Stewart, who had seemingly violated the law against insider trading but was convicted on a charge of perjury (Heminway 2007).

In defense of defining white-collar crime on the basis of offense characteristics, Susan Shapiro, a participant in the Yale Study, maintained that there was a need to "liberate" the term from its Sutherland shackles, especially its focus on the wardrobe of the perpetrator. The designation "white-collar criminal," she argued, should be confined to violators of trust, such as persons who manipulate norms of disclosure, disinterest, and role competence, categories, Shapiro granted, that would not embrace antitrust violations. Shapiro defended her revisionist position with rousing rhetoric, claiming that Sutherland's approach to white-collar crime had "created an imprisoning framework for contemporary scholarship, impoverishing theory, distorting empirical inquiry, oversimplifying policy analysis, inflating our muckraking instincts, and obscuring fascinating questions about the relationship between social organization and crime" (Shapiro 1990, p. 346).

IV. Envoi

I have neither need nor predilection to be neutral on the matters discussed above, to cheer on with equal enthusiasm both my spouse and the bear. For my part, however ineptly Sutherland formulated his definition and however poorly he defended it, its essential focus on the abuse of power by elites in the course of their occupation stands out as an exceedingly important public policy issue that demands the keen attention of the public, policymakers, and research scholars.

A good starting point is the post-Sutherland definition of white-collar crime as "violations of the law to which penalties are attached that involve the use of the violator's position of significant power, influence or trust in the legitimate economic or political institutional order for the purpose of illegal gain, or to commit an illegal act for personal or organizational gain" (Reiss and Biderman 1980, p. 4). There are two major virtues of this definition. First, it sets out in a straightforward manner the essence of Sutherland's basic focus on the use of significant power, influence, and trust in violation of the law by persons holding legitimate positions. Recent high-profile white-collar crimes include the savings and loan bank debacles (Calavita, Pontell, and Tillman 1997). Then there were Enron and Arthur Andersen, WorldCom, Adelphia Communications, and other big-time perpetrators of financial crookedness (see, e.g., Swartz and Watkins 2003; Cooper 2008). Finally, and most dramatically, the world suffered from the subprime mortgage and hedge fund manipulations that brought about the great economic melt-down. Companies involved included Bear Stearns, the American International Group, Merrill Lynch, Countrywide Financial, and the Bank of America (Morris 2008; Geis 2012). The meltdown pinpointed behavior that is criminologically distinctive and of great public concern and should not be diluted by being associated with matters such as insufficient-funds checks that unemployed persons seek to pass.

Second, the Reiss–Biderman definition embraces serious law violations that are not necessarily dealt with in criminal courts. In the wake of the meltdown the failure of the government to seek criminal indictments was notorious. The U.S. Department of Justice allegedly brokered an agreement with state attorneys general not to file cases in criminal courts because the resultant dramatic public exposure of what had gone on would only further undermine a fragile financial world (Morgenson and Story 2012).

V. Conclusions

Disagreement over the variant definitions of white-collar crime has been identified as a conflict of Populist (in terms of the elite standing of the perpetrator) and Patrician per-spectives (focusing on violators of specified laws). In a pair of articles, Neal Shover and Francis Cullen contrasted the ingredients of the Sutherland definition of white-collar crime and definitions that are based on crime characteristics rather than the status of the offender (Shover and Cullen 2008, 2011).

Sutherland's position was labeled a "Populist" approach and said to be based on a call for equal justice, while the Yale definition, labeled Patrician, was held to be "more nar-row, technical and less reform-oriented" (2008, p. 156). The Patrician view was said to "lump together . . . frauds committed by itinerant door-to-door vinyl siding installers and the crimes of international bankers" (2011, p. 50). The result is that "unusually priv-ileged offenders thereby blend with and become less conspicuous among their more numerous middle-class cousins" (2011, p. 50). Neither did partisans of the Patrician approach "generally include inequality as a causal factor" (2008, p. 157). Adherence to the Patrician definition, Shover and Cullen pointed out, allowed the U.S. Department of Justice to arrest thieves and telemarketing fraudsters and broadcast to the public that it was focusing its energies on capturing white-collar criminals.

References

Bryant, Tamera. 2005. *The Life and Times of Hammurabi: Biography from Ancient Civilizations: Legends, Folklore, and Stories of Ancient Worlds*. Hockessin, DE: Mitchell Lane.

Bulmer, Martin. 1984. *The Chicago School of Sociology: Institutional Diversity and the Rise of Sociological Research*. Chicago: University of Chicago Press.

Calavita, Kitty, Henry N. Pontell, and Robert H. Tillman. 1997. *Big Money Crime: Fraud and Politics in the Savings and Loan Crisis*. Berkeley: University of California Press.

Cherry, Robert W. 1981. *Populism, Progressivism, and the Transformation of Nebraska Politics, 1895–1915*. Lincoln: University of Nebraska Press.

Cooper, Cynthia. 2008. *Extraordinary Circumstances: The Journal of a Corporate Whistle-Blower*. Hoboken, NJ: John Wiley.

Daly, Kathleen. 1989. "Gender and Varieties of White-Collar Crime." *Criminology* 27: 769–95.

Edelhertz, Herbert. 1970. *The Nature, Impact, and Prosecution of White-Collar Crime*. Washington, D.C.: U.S. Government Printing Office.

Eichenwald, Kurt. 2008. *Conspiracy of Fools: A True Story*. New York: Broadway Books.

Filler, Louis. 1990. *The Muckrakers*, rev. and enlarged ed. State College: Penn State University Press.

Geis, Gilbert. 1988. "From Deuteronomy to Deniability: A Historical Perlustration on White-Collar Crime." *Justice Quarterly* 5: 7–32.

Geis, Gilbert. 2011. *White-Collar and Corporate Crime: A Documentary and Reference Guide*. Santa Barbara, CA: ABC-Clio.

Geis, Gilbert. 2012. "The Great American Meltdown from 2007 and Onward." In *Reflections on White-Collar Crime: Discerning Readings*, edited by David Shichor, Larry Gaines, and Andrea Schoepfer. Long Grove, IL: Waveland Press.

Heminway, Joan MacLeod. 2007. *Martha Stewart's Legal Troubles*. Durham, NC: Carolina Academic Press.

Henderson, Charles R. 1901. *Introduction to the Study of Dependent, Defective, and Delinquent Children*, 2nd ed. Boston: Heath.

Jesilow, Paul, Henry N. Pontell, and Gilbert Geis. 1993. *Prescription for Profit: How Doctors Defraud Medicaid*. Berkeley: University of California Press.

Johns, Claude H. W. 1999. *Babylonian and Assyrian Law, Customs, and Letters*. Union, NJ: Lawbook Exchange.

Johnson, George E. Q., Jr. 1929. "Enforcement and Administration of the Criminal Law." *Commercial Law Legal Journal* 39: 432–41.

Josephson, Matthew. 1933. *The Robber Barons: Saints or Sinners?* New York: Holt, Rinehart, and Winston.

Kenner, Hunard J. 1926. "The Fight on Stock Swindlers." *Annals of the American Academy of Political and Social Science* 125: 54–58.

Lewis, Oscar. 1938. *The Big Four: The Story of Huntington, Stanford, Hopkins, and Crocker, and the Building of the Central Pacific*. New York: Knopf.

Madrick, Jeffrey G. 2011. *Age of Greed: The Triumph of Finance and the Decline of America, 1970 to the Present*. New York: Knopf.

McGlew, James F. 1993. *Tyranny and Political Culture in Ancient Greece*. Ithaca, NY: Cornell University Press.

Morgenson, Gretchen, and Louise Story. 2012. "In Financial Crisis, No Prosecutions of Top Figures." *New York Times* (April 14).

Morris, Charles R. 2008. *The Two Trillion Dollar Meltdown: Easy Money, High Rollers, and the Great Credit Crunch*, rev. ed. New York: Public Affairs Press.

Partnoy, Frank. 2009. *Match King: Ivar Kreuger, the Financial Genius behind a Century of Wall Street Scandal*. New York: Public Affairs Press.

Philadelphia Public Ledger. 1939. "Poverty Belittled as Crime Factor." (December 28).

Prince, J. Dynley. 1904. "Code of Hammurabi." *American Journal of Theology* 8: 601–09.

Reiss, Albert J., Jr., and Albert D. Biderman. 1980. *Data Sources on White-Collar Lawbreaking*. Washington, D.C.: U.S. Government Printing Office.

Ross, Edward Alsworth. 1907. *Sin and Society: An Analysis of Latter-Day Iniquity.* Boston: Houghton Mifflin.

Schoepfer, Andrea, and Stephen G. Tibbets. 2011. "From Early White-Collar Bandits and Robber Barons to Modern-Day White-Collar Criminals: A Review of the Conceptual and Theoretical Research." In *Reflecting on White-Collar and Corporate Crime: Discerning Reading,* edited by David Shichor, Larry Gaines, and Andrea Schoepfer. Long Grove, IL: Waveland Press.

Shapiro, Susan P. 1990. "Collaring the Crime, Not the Criminal: Liberating the Concept of White-Collar Crime." *American Sociological Review* 55: 346–68.

Shover, Neal, and Francis T. Cullen. 2008. "Studying and Teaching White-Collar Crime: Populist and Patrician Perspectives." *Journal of Criminal Justice Education* 19: 155–74.

Shover, Neal, and Francis T. Cullen. 2011. "White-Collar Crime: Interpretative Disagreement and Prospects for Change." In *Reflecting on White-Collar and Corporate Crime: Discerning Readings,* edited by David Shichor, Larry Gaines, and Andrea Schoepfer. Long Grove, IL: Waveland Press.

Sutherland, Edwin H. 1940. "White-Collar Criminality." *American Sociological Review* 5: 1–12.

Sutherland, Edwin H. 1941. "Crime and Business." *Annals of the American Academy of Political and Social Science* 217: 112–18.

Sutherland, Edwin H. 1945. "Is 'White-Collar Crime' Crime?" *American Sociological Review* 10: 32–39.

Sutherland, Edwin H. 1948. "Crime of Corporations." In *Edwin H. Sutherland on Analyzing Crime,* edited by Karl Schuessler. Chicago: University of Chicago Press.

Sutherland, Edwin H. 1949a. *White Collar Crime.* New York: Dryden.

Sutherland, Edwin H. 1949b. "The White Collar Criminal." In *Encyclopedia of Criminology,* edited by Vernon C. Branham and Samuel B. Kutash. New York: Philosophical Library.

Sutherland, Edwin H. 1983. *White Collar Crime: The Uncut Version.* New Haven, CT: Yale University Press.

Sutherland, Edwin H., and Donald R. Cressey. 1960. *Principles of Criminology,* 4th ed. Philadelphia, PA: Lippincott.

Swartz, Mimi, and Sherron Watkins. 2003. *Power Failure: The Insider Story of the Collapse of Enron.* New York: Doubleday.

Tappan, Paul W. 1947. "Who Is the Criminal?" *American Sociological Review* 12: 96–102.

Taylor, Claire. 2001. "Bribery in Athenian Politics: Part II: Ancient Reactions and Perceptions." *Greece and Rome* 48: 154–272.

Veblen, Thorstein. 1912. *Theory of the Leisure Class: An Economic Study of Institutions.* New York: Macmillan.

Weisburd, David, Stanton Wheeler, Elin Waring, and Nancy Bode. 1991. *Crimes of the Middle Classes: White-Collar Offenders in the Federal Courts.* New Haven, CT: Yale University Press.

Wolfe, Bertram K. 1938. "Detection of Fraud under the New Bankruptcy Law." *Temple University Law Quarterly* 13: 1–28.

CHAPTER 3

THEORETICAL, EMPIRICAL,
AND POLICY IMPLICATIONS
OF ALTERNATIVE
DEFINITIONS OF
"WHITE-COLLAR CRIME"
"Trivializing the Lunatic Crime Rate"

HENRY N. PONTELL

THIS essay considers the theoretical, empirical, and policy implications that emanate from different conceptualizations of white-collar crime. Building upon a theme introduced by the Harvard sociologist Daniel Patrick Moynihan that U.S. society has come to tolerate extreme amounts of common crime, thus "trivializing" serious lawbreaking, it has three main thrusts. First, it extends the reach of Moynihan's observation by focusing on white-collar and corporate crime. Second, it considers criminological definitions and theorizing that trivializes the term "white-collar crime" itself. Third, it provides a case study of how definitional trivialization affected policy and enforcement practices in the 2008 financial meltdown.

The main conclusions are these:

- Efforts by some in the scholarly community to revise Sutherland's original definition of white-collar crime have had the unintended effect of creating a downward view of white-collar and corporate crimes that neglects serious elite offenses.
- Definitional trivialization occurs because elite white-collar crimes are more hidden, less understood, less dramatic, and rarely criminally adjudicated, and because information about them is more difficult to obtain.

- The most consequential forms of white-collar crime and corporate crime are rarely considered or accounted for because of definitional trivialization, leading to inadequate social policies designed to prevent them.
- Schools of thought regarding the preferable definition of white-collar crime represent a conflict of positions with ideological underpinnings.
- The claim that the status of the offender needs to be separated from the act in order to avoid biased social analysis allows the most consequential forms of white-collar and corporate lawbreaking to fly well below the political, academic, and policy radar screens.
- As noted by Sutherland and others, the use of significant status, power, and privilege needs to be centrally considered—not removed—both in understanding the nature of white-collar and corporate offending and in designing policies to prevent them.

The essay is organized as follows. Section I considers a conceptual context introduced by Moynihan, who argued that American society tends to "define deviancy down," or, put another way, "trivialize the lunatic crime rate." Section II critiques and extends Moynihan's approach to include the lunatic white-collar crime rate. Section III analyzes efforts by some academics to revise Sutherland's original definition, which have created a downward view of white-collar and corporate crimes that neglects serious elite lawbreaking. Section IV examines the role of the Yale White-Collar Crime Project in trivializing the definition of white-collar crime and considers an earlier review of their research. Section V discusses how the traditional status-based meaning of white-collar crime raises important empirical and interpretative questions that avoid the definitional trivialization that the revisionist approach encourages. Section VI considers what researchers have labeled as the Patrician and Populist approaches to defining white-collar crime. Section VII notes how some researchers have used a trivialized definition of white-collar crime in theorizing about crime more generally. Section VIII uses a case study from the 2008 financial meltdown to illustrate policy and enforcement implications of alternative definitions of white-collar crime. Finally, section IX posits that there are formidable challenges to preventing white-collar crimes in today's global economy and that definitions directly influence policies aimed at such efforts.

I. Conceptual Context

The title of this essay derives in part from an observation by Edwin Torres, a judge on the New York Supreme Court, which was highlighted in an article, "Defining Deviancy Down," by Daniel Patrick Moynihan (1993). Trained as a sociologist, Moynihan would come to serve as a senator from the state of New York, a post held by, among others, Robert Kennedy and Hillary Rodham Clinton. Torres and Moynihan were expressing their indignation at the way that Americans had come to show a "so what," passive, and shoulder-shrugging indifference about what the two men saw as an intolerable level of criminal behavior. The judge had said that "the slaughter of innocents remains unabated; subway riders, bodega owners, cab drivers, babies; in laundromats, at cash machines, on elevators, in hallways" the victims and these crime sites were being treated with a "near narcoleptic state that could diminish the human condition to the level of combat infantrymen, who, in protracted campaigns, can eat their battlefield rations seated on the bodies of the fallen, friend and foe alike" (Moynihan 1993, p. 19). The grim lesson was that "a country that loses its sense of outrage is doomed to extinction" (Moynihan 1993, p. 20).

Moynihan lamented that Americans had gotten "used to a lot of behavior that is not good for us" (1993, p. 21). True to his disciplinary roots, he harkened back to Emile Durkheim to buttress his thesis that crime was being normalized (Durkheim 1982 [1895]). Durkheim had maintained that every society generates a certain level of waywardness and that this aberrancy serves to notify conformists regarding what constitutes acceptable behavior. In one of his best-known canards, Durkheim insisted that even a society of saints would nonetheless label as deviants those somewhat less saintly whose actions provided an object lesson in how not to behave. Moynihan had criticized Durkheim's idea of a "normal" crime rate, declaring that it failed to attend properly to the fact that at some point the "normal" becomes "abnormal" and unacceptable. For Moynihan, the United States had reached that over-the-top level.

Moynihan granted that distinctions must be made between various kinds of acts that are categorized as crime and deviance. Some behaviors, once regarded as wayward, may come to be seen as conventional, no longer objects of social disapproval. He failed to point out, however, that there also was at work a tendency to "define deviancy up," a pattern illustrated by new offenses, such as hate crime, child abuse, and marital rape. Moynihan maintained that huge amounts of crime result in only the most dramatic acts getting the public's attention, while the remainder elicit no fanfare, much less any real concern. He argued that Americans were "defining deviancy down." Judge Torres tagged the phenomenon as *"trivializing the lunatic crime rate"* (Moynihan 1993, p. 20; emphasis added).

Moynihan's position has not gone without critical reactions since it was enunciated. Some said that it was no more than political rhetoric directed against "permissiveness" in society and "leniency" in the criminal justice system, views dear to "law-and-order" conservatives. Moynihan was charged with implying that "the problem is public tolerance of intolerable behavior and that the solution is resuming traditional standards by stepping up repression of underclass conduct" (Karmen 1994, p. 105). In an ironic way, that position can be said to reflect poorly on the critics. After all, there are other possible approaches to reducing crime, including most notably altering elements of the social system that correlate with and might be causative of lawbreaking. Moynihan was saying that something ought to be done, not what that something might be.

II. Trivializing Lunatic White-Collar Crime

One gap in Moynihan's position—or perhaps the need to extend its reach—has not heretofore been noted. Moynihan's focus on traditional street crimes constitutes a myopic view of the problem, an astigmatism that characterizes many analysts who pretend that white-collar lawbreaking somehow belongs to a realm other than that of crime. His analysis totally ignored white-collar and corporate offenses, behaviors for which "defining deviancy down" and "trivializing the lunatic crime rate" are the norm. A considerable element in the trivialization of white-collar and corporate crime lies in the fact that politicians who set the tone and to a large extent dictate the decibel level of the response to such illegalities depend very heavily on campaign contributions from people and organizations that supply the roster of white-collar criminals. There is a folk saying about not biting the hand that feeds you or, in white-collar crime terms, "Don't defeat the elite."

Whether called "white-collar crime," "economic crime," or "abuse of power" or given some other label, higher forms of political, professional, and business delicts typically are complex, obscure, and somewhat esoteric. Unlike street offenses, there never has been, or likely will be, an annual tabulation of the extent of such behavior. As two writers recently noted, "No one can determine or estimate . . . costs with confidence; this would require systematically collected data on the prevalence of white-collar crime, the numbers of victims and their losses. These data do not exist and would be extremely difficult to collect in any case" (Shover and Cullen 2008, pp. 162–63).

Three major problems contribute to the trivializing of white-collar crime. First, white-collar crime is rarely dramatic. The Federal Bureau of Investigation, an organization famous for its public relations techniques, understands what "sells." In 2009, its "Famous Cases" page on its website listed scores of crimes—and Enron was the only white-collar case. Although some white-collar crimes inflict serious physical harm on individuals, much of it is what has been characterized as "diffuse" because it affects large numbers of people only indirectly. In addition to the major scandals that reach the headlines, the vast hidden bulk of white-collar crimes result in financial injuries that are "paper crimes." There is no chalk outline on the sidewalk, no yellow tape sequestering the crime scene, no blood-spattered walls. Of late, in what are referred to as "perp walks," law-enforcement personnel have taken to handcuffing persons arrested for white-collar offenses and hustling them between figures with "POLICE" prominently displayed on their jackets while television cameras record it all. The tactic appears to be an effort to raise the trivialization threshold level a bit.

Second, numerous important but complex cases by sophisticated white-collar offenders and organizations never come before a court. This is unlike the lunatic crime rate that concerned Moynihan. The power, wealth, sophisticated legal talent available to the well-heeled, the political atmosphere, and the sometimes arcane actions that are specifically designed to hide intent—especially at the heart of many of the largest and most costly crimes—come into play in determining whether or not criminal charges will prevail. The social reality of defining such acts as "criminal" is much more difficult and involved than for common crime. Studies of the savings and loan debacle in the United States empirically demonstrate that law enforcement and criminal justice agencies were not able to investigate and assuredly not prosecute offenses that they were aware of because of a shortage of personnel and resource capacity (Pontell, Calavita, and Tillman 1994; Calavita, Pontell, and Tillman 1997; Tillman, Calavita, and Pontell 1997). More recently, offenses associated with the current subprime lending frauds were featured obliquely in political debates, but the focus was almost exclusively on the economy as a whole and on consequent problems for the banking industry and for homeowners undergoing or contemplating foreclosure. The word "speculation" sometimes surfaced in discussions of high-pressure and misleading sales pitches that induced persons to buy a house they could not truly afford. But the word "crime" was not prominent, although later studies and reports found that it had permeated the behaviors (Nguyen and Pontell 2010; Financial Crisis Inquiry Commission [FCIC] 2011; Nguyen and Pontell 2011).

Moreover, white-collar crimes are very difficult to prove, as illustrated by the following hypothetical example of the elusiveness of demonstrating intent. "I always intended to sell my options on September first," says the corporate president accused of insider trading. "It just so happened that just before then, I found out that the company anticipated a considerable downturn. That information, however, had nothing to do with the sale of my stock," he says, with the subtext: "And I dare you to prove otherwise beyond a reasonable doubt."

Third, there is a reluctance to define captains of industry as "criminals," perhaps best illustrated by the odd response of Ernest Burgess, one of the most prominent stars in the sociological firmament, to an article on white-collar crime in which he found it out of order to label people as criminals who did not see themselves as such (Burgess 1950). It also is regarded by some as unpatriotic to consider those prominent in their community as lawbreakers. And, besides, the media often find it difficult to set out the details of a white-collar conspiracy in a way that will engage readers and, especially, television viewers who respond to visual imagery: the holdup, the auto chase, the murdered corpse (Rosoff et al. 2010). Filmmaker Michael Moore highlighted this in his Oscar-winning documentary, "Bowling for Columbine," by lampooning the popular U.S. television show *COPS* with another version called *CORPORATE COPS*, which depicted the police catching an executive on a busy New York City street, tackling him and tearing off his suit jacket and shirt before handcuffing him face down against a parked car.

Moreover, as Tombs and Whyte (2003) observed, entrepreneurship and market forces provide inherent hurdles that those seeking information must overcome to learn the details of white-collar crime. Perpetrators often are protected by a battery of powerful lawyers and public relations specialists. The organization often serves as both a weapon and a shield, and it is likely to cover the exorbitant legal expenses of its senior officers who may run afoul of the law (Wheeler and Rothman 1982). The *New York*

Post, for instance, learned that Angelo Mozilo and his co-defendants from the defunct lending company, Countrywide Financial, had hired a brigade of 19 lawyers to mount their defense against criminal charges—and that American taxpayers would foot the estimated $50 million in attorneys' fees. The Bank of America, which received $45 billion in bailout money, agreed when taking over Countrywide that for six years it would be responsible for the legal expenses incurred by the company and its officers (Tharp and Scanlan 2009).

III. Definitional Trivialization

Efforts by some in the scholarly community to revise Sutherland's original definition have had the unintended effect of creating a downward view of white-collar and corporate crimes that neglects serious elite lawbreaking. The redefinition campaign was inaugurated by Susan Shapiro, who argued that the term should be "de-collared" (Shapiro 1990). Shapiro cited Merton's claim that the role of conceptual analysis lies in "exposing specious empirical relationships latent in unexamined concepts and in debunking theories based on these relationships" (Shapiro 1990, p. 346). Merton observed that "conceptual language tends to fix our perceptions and, derivatively, our thought and behavior" and that sociologists often become "imprisoned in the framework of the (often inherited) concepts they use" (Merton 1949, pp. 88–89). Ironically, it was Merton himself who used Sutherland's introduction of the term "white-collar crime" to illustrate the defining process, and who was laudatory of the contribution, noting that it undercut mainstream theories viewing crime as a result of broken homes, Freudian complexes, and other forms of personal and social malaise.

Shapiro granted the revolutionary impact of the emergence of the term, pointing out that "the concept of white-collar crime was thus born of Sutherland's efforts to liberate traditional criminology from the 'cognitive misbehavior' reflected in the spurious correlation between poverty and crime" (Shapiro 1990, p. 346). But she maintained that the concept now had become an "imprisoning framework" that "causes sociologists to misunderstand the structural impetus for these offenses" (Shapiro 1990, p. 346). The problem she perceived was that the term "white-collar crime" focuses on some combination of characteristics of lawbreakers, specifying that they be upper-class, or upper-status individuals, organizations, or corporations, or incumbents of occupational roles, a position that inherently confuses "acts with actors, norms with norm breakers, and the modus operandi with the operator" (Shapiro 1990, p. 347).

Neither the reference to Merton's view as adopted by Shapiro nor her own critique survives close examination. That Merton called for revision of entrenched but outmoded concepts is not the same as a demonstration that his call is relevant to white-collar crime, a concept he heralded. For her part, Shapiro's concern that acts and actors and other elements of the traditional white-collar crime approach are "confused" is confusing. What is "inherently wrong" with studying and theorizing about acts carried out by specified actors, be they juveniles, professional athletes, or police personnel?

Separating the crime from the criminal is more problematic than Shapiro and those who have followed her lead have suggested. The element of power is centrally relevant in analyses of white-collar crime. Among other things, it permits only some perpetrators to engage in certain crimes while denying similar opportunities to others. Removing the notion of status from the definition of white-collar crime effectively skews examination of offenses downward, since power allows perpetrators to hide more effectively their illegalities; they will be more likely to escape detection or prosecution or reach civil settlements, and their offenses will not appear in government databases. Official statistics will therefore necessarily reflect the weakest and/or most careless offenders. Separating status from the offense thus results in the a priori *operational trivialization* of white-collar crime and more easily allows researchers—and others—to focus downward in assessing the nature of white-collar criminality. As Braithwaite (1985, p. 131) has argued, this lowers the conceptual bar to the point where the original term becomes almost meaningless in that it produces a portrait of white-collar crime that includes a sizeable percentage of unemployed persons who have passed insufficient-funds checks at the local supermarket.

IV. THE YALE WHITE-COLLAR CRIME PROJECT

Shapiro's contribution grew out of her connection with a large research grant awarded to a Yale Law School team headed by Stanton Wheeler to study white-collar crime, a particularly unusual funding development tied to concerns in the administration of President Carter. Driven to a considerable extent by the need to gather information on a readily discernible cohort of offenders, some of the Yale group elected to specify selected penal code offenses as constituting the true realm of white-collar crime. Anyone who committed these offenses became by definition a white-collar criminal. The approach ignored regulatory and administrative agency episodes that Sutherland regarded as essentially equivalent to acts proscribed by the criminal code. Nor did it attend to accusations of traditional white-collar crime that rarely show up in court statistics because astute and expensive lawyers negotiate compromise settlements for their wealthy and powerful clients (Mann 1985). The result is that those tried are the "fish that jumped into the boat."

Most notably, some of the Yale researchers concluded that Sutherland was wrong, that white-collar crime was the work of the middle class, although their sample inevitably included both upper-class and lower-class representatives. No longer would it be necessary to locate a nexus between status, power, and lawbreaking (Weisburd et al. 1994).

In a detailed critique of the Yale project, David Johnson and Richard Leo noted that the four major books produced from it did not attend to the definitional problems or ambiguities inherent in the concept of white-collar crime. Instead, each work offered different definitions that fit with varying approaches to the subject matter (1993, p. 65). But as the authors correctly point out, "How we define 'white-collar crime' strongly influences how we perceive it as a subject matter and thus what and how we research" (1993, p. 65). For example, in one of the Yale products that examined presentence investigations of criminals convicted of a collection of federal crimes, Weisburd and his colleagues (1993) found that many offenders do not comport with some definitions of white-collar crime; they are, by and large, middle class. While the researchers claimed not to take their data at face value, the problem is with the a priori decision to characterize and contrast Sutherland's definition through examination of conviction data. They avoided conceptual ambiguity and the definitional issue by in effect taking the side of Paul Tappan (1947), who had debated Sutherland early on, dubbed the term "white-collar crime" as "loose, derogatory, and doctrinaire," and argued that criminologists should confine themselves to the study of those adjudicated as guilty of certain crimes.

The definitional issue here is paramount (yet dodged, as Johnson and Leo pointed out), and the allure of the book (and its title, *Crimes of the Middle Classes: White-Collar Offenders in the Federal Courts*) is that it seemingly challenges common notions that white-collar offenders are necessarily of high status. This is a "challenge" only if one considers official data the true realm of white-collar crime, which many scholars do not. The work is thus not a treatise on white-collar crime per se, but on occupational or economic crimes that are most easily handled by the criminal justice system, or as Johnson and Leo noted, "*convictions of the middle classes*" (1993, p. 86, emphasis added). Viewed in this light, the book is not a direct challenge to Sutherland's original formulation, yet it effectively directed attention to the lowest levels of economic criminality (adjudicated cases) and the fact that most of them did not involve persons of particularly high status.

It could reasonably be claimed that the current critique "blames the messengers," as it was not the researchers who selected the cases that were studied, but rather the enforcement agents who decided to take on non-elite offenders and their less serious crimes. This defense, however, again avoids the central issue of the choices researchers make regarding which definitional approaches they use (in this case Tappan's, not Sutherland's), which data they analyze and why, and what conclusions they apply to their findings. The issue here is not one of internal validity, but one of external validity due to the subsample of violators. That the offenders in the study did not comport with the traditional definition of white-collar crime comes as no surprise at all, as "operational trivialization" had already occurred through the selection of convicted offenders. So the point here is not "blaming the messengers" for the news they discovered and shared but in identifying and understanding the misleading nature of the message *they chose* to deliver.

As Johnson and Leo argued, Weisburd and colleagues were engaged in a classic sociological debunking exercise aimed at showing how criminologists and others had incorrectly defined white-collar crime as an elite offense (1993, p. 88). But in stating that the authors "successfully expose and reorient much wrongheaded thinking" (1993, p. 88), they too fall prey to the same conceptual trivialization. While conceding that there could be particularly harmful elite offenders who were not represented in the sample studied, they had no hesitation (or any empirical evidence, for that matter) in claiming that "While it is true that most [convicted] white-collar criminals are not the elite deviants who so concerned Sutherland and his followers, it is equally true and no less important that a tiny handful of white-collar crimes may be especially harmful and thus deserving of our attention and concern" (1993, p. 89). The "tiny handful" estimate appears out of thin air, but they invoke the savings and loan crisis (which resulted in a "tiny handful" of more than a thousand major prosecutions of elite offenders and organizations in a single financial scandal) and its poster child, Charles Keating, to remind us that middle-class offenses differ greatly. While Johnson and Leo appear to agree with the trivialized portrait of white-collar crime, they also observed that it was a lack of a conceptual definition of white-collar crime up front that more easily allowed for the conclusion of Weisburd and colleagues that it was essentially a middle-class offense. The ad hoc selection of eight specific statutory offenses that the authors believed would fit most conceptions of white-collar crime avoids the definitional issue but nonetheless puts them squarely in the Tappan camp of focusing on adjudicated offenses as the way to characterize white-collar crime.

Finally, and perhaps most importantly, Johnson and Leo noted that after Weisburd and his colleagues acknowledge in the first chapter that "that they are only sampling convicted white-collar offenders . . . they seem to lose sight of this limitation [in subsequent chapters] when they generalize from this sample of convicted offenders to the universe of all white-collar criminals" (Johnson and Leo 1993, p. 89). This external validity issue is overlooked at the expense of trivializing white-collar crime. It also detracts from the significant, yet more modest, contribution of the study, which was to describe and further specify known forms of middle-class property offending—a topic overlooked by criminologists studying both common and more elite white-collar lawbreaking. Considering these acts as the true realm of white-collar crime is at best misleading; at worst, it trivializes the concept of white-collar crime by omitting serious elite and organizational offenses that are of much greater fiscal and physical consequence. How and why such crimes are omitted in practice is no mystery. The importance of status and power in influencing the trivialization of white-collar crime is clearly demonstrated in a study of arson cases in Boston. Barry Goetz (1997) illustrated how resource constraints and class bias provide a "structural cloak" that covers white-collar criminality. The fires were intentionally arranged by landlords in order to collect insurance, but for years, officials blamed them on lower-class occupants of the buildings. By keeping arson-for-profit a "non-issue" (and arson-for-profit was not one of the Yale categories), a significant form of white-collar crime was trivialized.

One need only consider the endemic wave of "collective embezzlement" (Calavita et al. 1997) and "control fraud" (Black 2005) in the savings and loan crisis; the corporate and accounting scandals of 2002 that included Enron, Arthur Andersen, Worldcom, and numerous other companies; or the recent subprime mortgage crisis that led to the largest global economic meltdown in history to see the unprecedented financial damage caused by white-collar and corporate crimes of the "non-middle-class." The gargantuan losses from fraud in these scandals do not include those occurring on a regular basis from corporate and elite offending that never reach the criminal justice system or the final stages of adjudication. Whether or not they truly constitute a "tiny handful" of white-collar lawbreaking remains to be seen (Rosoff et al. 2010).

V. Re-Collaring White-Collar Crime

The traditional status-based meaning of white-collar crime raises important empirical and interpretative questions that avoid the definitional trivialization that the revisionist approach encourages. We are led to determine why persons who live otherwise conventional and law-abiding lives and who often have great wealth commit white-collar crimes, and to consider the role of organizational settings. Removing those concerns denies the significance of privileged contexts and organizational structures in producing illegality. The ethos and curricula of business schools, corporate governance structures, bureaucratic considerations, and political power all become matters of interest when traditional definitions of white-collar crime are in play. Separating the crime from the criminal thrusts these matters into the etiological background or, at worst, eliminates them entirely. The "structural impetus" for these crimes emanates from the very institutions of power and privilege that Sutherland made part of his original definition. Denying the tie between "respectability" and "social status" with the commission of these offenses essentially denies the meaning of the term "white-collar crime" itself.

In a major review of the topic, Braithwaite (1985) concluded that using Sutherland's definition offers the best path to comprehension of an important form of criminal behavior. "This at least excludes welfare cheats and credit card fraud from the domain," Braithwaite observed (1985, p. 131). Explaining *how* and *why* these acts come about is quite different from identifying *who* engages in them. Sutherland's approach does not preclude focusing on the relationship between social class and crime and, indeed, might facilitate it. Failure to appreciate that only some persons can commit certain forms of criminality because of their social position reduces the likelihood of recognizing class considerations in lawbreaking. This was one of Sutherland's seminal points. Most persons can engage in crimes that are predominantly perpetrated by those in the lower echelons of society. The pattern, however, is not bidirectional.

Finally, Sutherland never conceived of the term "white-collar crime" as a "legal term," unlike some scholars who have challenged the idea (Shapiro 1990; Zimring and

Johnson 2007). Rather, he saw it as a social science construct that would guide research. Sutherland had cooperated with Sellin on his classic *Culture Conflict and Crime* (1938), in which Sellin argued forcefully that social scientists should not adhere to legal definitions appearing in penal codes. The law, he pointed out, is the product of power, lobbying, whim, and a host of idiosyncratic inputs that often lack logical coherence. Many harmful acts never are outlawed because those who commit them or contemplate doing so see to it that they are not. Sellin noted:

> The unqualified acceptance of legal definitions as the basic elements of criminological inquiry violates a fundamental criterion of science. The scientist must have freedom to define his own terms based on the intrinsic character of his material and designating properties in that material which are assumed to be universal. (1938, p. 31)

Sellin's goals were to identify personal and social injury and to examine those who inflict it and, in the course of that enterprise, to determine whether and, if not, why such acts were not forbidden. As Colin Goff and Gilbert Geis (2008, p. 253) noted, "Sellin's revisionist perspective pervades studies of what is called 'social deviance.'" For Sutherland, the goal was to shed light on a group of largely overlooked illegal acts that are committed by powerful persons and that generally fall well below the radar of conventional criminological and public attention.

VI. IDEOLOGICAL DIFFERENCES: POPULISTS VERSUS PATRICIANS

Many scholars, particularly those who might be regarded as "old-timers" in the field, use Sutherland's definition of white-collar crimes as an illegal act "committed by a person of respectability and high social status in the course of his occupation" (Sutherland 1949, p. 9). The definition contains an element that might reasonably be labeled as propaganda, as it focuses attention on wrongdoing by those in prestigious positions. In its way, it is a corollary of street crime that almost exclusively focuses on wrongdoing by underclass persons. As Anatole France (1894, p. 117) said, "The law in its majestic equality forbids both the poor man and the rich man from sleeping under the bridge." He had no need to mention that rich men are not very likely to be sleeping under bridges.

Sutherland's definition puts white-collar crime into an interpretative context. Removing it from that context—"de-collaring" it—leads to trivializing the structural elements that are basic to such crimes and to overlooking policies that best prevent them in the specific context in which they arise. This results in a failure to consider complex social, political, cultural, and economic settings and the emergence of a focus on heterodox congeries of offenders apprehended for breaking an array of rather amorphous laws that are tagged as "white-collar crime."

In a recent essay, Shover and Cullen (2008) argued that the two schools of thought regarding the preferable definition of white-collar crime can be seen as a conflict between positions with ideological underpinnings. The first is the "Populist" perspective, which locates the offenses within the framework of social inequality. The second is what they labeled the "Patrician" view, which offers a less politicized and more legal–technical perspective. They noted that adherents of the Patrician bloc tend to be characterized by elitist backgrounds and affiliations. Greatly broadening the embrace of white-collar crime has the effect of deflecting attention from the wrongdoing of elites onto others, those beneath them in the social hierarchy, whose misdeeds are of much greater concern to the general public than should be the case.

A lunatic rate of white-collar crime is apparent regardless of which prism is used, but the extent of such neglect is a function of definition. The Patrician view minimizes the impact of white-collar crime by considering only those cases found in official statistics. The Populist perspective highlights issues of power, respectability, and privilege as concepts for understanding the phenomenon and is thus more expansive.

This theoretical element is not unlike the debate between Sutherland and Tappan, the latter trained in both law and sociology, that took place shortly after Sutherland introduced his concept. Representing Patricians, Tappan dubbed the term "white-collar crime" as loose, derogatory, and doctrinaire, and he argued that criminologists should confine themselves to the study of those adjudicated as guilty of certain crimes (Tappan 1947). Sutherland, the Populist, argued that if criminology confined itself to the well-documented biases that feed into the content of the criminal law, researchers would forfeit claims to pursuing a social scientific enterprise (Sutherland 1945).

VII. More Theoretical Maneuvering

White-collar crime has persistently been the graveyard in which theories seeking to explain the entire gambit of criminal behavior have been buried. Edwin Sutherland began the interment process when he inveighed against some of the usual and largely unchallenged explanatory shibboleths of his time:

> We have no reason to think that General Motors has an inferiority complex or that the Alcoa Aluminum Company of America has a frustration-aggression complex or that U.S. Steel has an Oedipus complex, or that the Armour Company has a death wish or that the Duponts desire to return to the womb. (1973, p. 96)

Putting aside the anthropomorphic ingredient in this observation, a matter that had persistently bedeviled attempts to theorize about corporate crime (Cressey 1988; Braithwaite and Fisse 1990), and Sutherland's point is equally applicable to the persons who are responsible for committing crimes in the name of their corporations. He said as much as he concluded the paragraph, "The assumption that an offender must have some such pathological distortion of the intellect or the emotions seems to be absurd," he continued, "and if it is absurd regarding the crimes of businessmen, it is equally absurd regarding the crimes of persons in the lower economic class" (Sutherland 1973, p. 96). Sutherland also decried other interpretations of crime that were unable to explain the lawbreaking of persons in the upper classes, such as feeblemindedness, poverty, immigrant status, and backgrounds in families marked by divorce (Sutherland 1949).

In their self-control theory, Gottfredson and Hirschi (1990) sought to avoid the pit dug by Sutherland. They did so by accepting the trivialized definition of white-collar crime adopted by some of the Yale researchers that focused on all persons who broke specified laws, including grocery shoppers who passed insufficient-funds checks and a considerable corps of unemployed women arrested for petty offenses (Daly 1989; Hirschi and Gottfredson 1989; Weisburd et al. 1994). This allowed them to portray individuals they labeled as white-collar offenders as recidivists and perpetrators of variegated offenses. Critics wrote that they found it difficult to conceive of corporate CEOs as burglars or robbers, and they noted that it was not the absence of self-control but its abundance that typically had gotten executives, professionals, and politicians to the positions of power that they occupied (Steffensmeier 1989; Benson and Moore 1992; Reed and Yeager 1996).

White-collar crime to a considerable degree suffers not only from trivialization but also to a great extent from a failure of recognition, from invisibility, from its status, in Goetz's (1997) term, as a "non-issue."

VIII. POLICY AND ENFORCEMENT IMPLICATIONS OF ALTERNATIVE DEFINITIONS OF WHITE-COLLAR CRIME

Policy and enforcement implications of alternative definitions of white-collar crime are clearly seen in the aftermath of the 2008 financial meltdown, which was initiated by activities of the subprime mortgage industry, major banks, and related Wall Street firms. Prototypical corporate frauds resulted in no criminal indictments, such as those perpetrated by the behemoths American International Group, Countrywide, Lehman Brothers, and Bear Sterns (Bamber and Spencer 2009; Kelly 2009; McDonald and Robinson 2009; Michaelson 2009).

These companies—whose balance sheets were saturated with securities containing subprime mortgages—collapsed, were bought by competitors, or were bailed out by the federal government with huge infusions of taxpayer money. For most criminologists and the public in general, their actions represented intricate and arcane business practices that were difficult to understand fully and to portray in the mass media. Moreover, the government, for a number of reasons having to do with resources and enforcement capacity, political will, and flawed policies, did not initiate criminal proceedings against major companies and their executives (FCIC 2011; Morgenson and Story 2011; Friedrichs 2013; Pontell, Black, and Geis 2014). As of this writing, there has not been a single major criminal prosecution resulting from the largest financial meltdown in world history.

One telling illustration of the manner in which white-collar crime was trivialized in the 2008 crisis unfolded in the wake of the acquisition of the financially beleaguered Merrill Lynch Corporation by the Bank of America in 2008 for $50 billion. The Bank of America had been given some $40 billion by the federal government to keep it from going belly up. When the agreement to take over Merrill Lynch was reached, officials in the Bank of America knew that their acquisition had specified year-end bonus payouts to top-level Merrill Lynch employees totaling some $5.8 billion. Bank of America needed the approval of its shareholders to complete the merger deal. But the proxy statement lied by saying that the bonuses would not be paid so that when they voted, stockholders were unaware that they would be giving up a considerable sum that was going into the pockets of Merrill Lynch executives.

The Securities and Exchange Commission (SEC) negotiated a $33 million settlement with the Bank of America as a penalty for that negligent act. But the agreement had to be endorsed by a federal court. Judge Jed S. Rakoff's ruling cut to the quick. He refused to approve the settlement, saying that it did not "comport with the most elementary notions of justice and morality" (*Securities and Exchange Commission v. Bank of America* 2009, p. 3). He wanted to know why the SEC was allowing the Bank of America to pass off the fine onto its shareholders rather than pinpointing the persons who had violated the law by omitting crucial information from the proxy statement. The Bank of America claimed this was not its doing; it was lawyers who had put together the misleading statement. Then "why not go after the lawyers?" the judge asked. And what about the Bank of America executives, who were presumably being paid very well to see that the company's affairs were conducted legally (*Securities and Exchange Commission v. Bank of America* 2009, p. 3)?

The bank officials also said that they had arranged the settlement because to go to court would cost them more than $33 million. The judge thought that absurd and implied that perhaps they were reluctant to have their own behavior revealed in a public forum. He pointed out, "It is quite something for the very management that is accused of having lied to its shareholders to determine how much of those victims' money should be used to make the case against the management go away" (*Securities and Exchange Commission v. Bank of America* 2009, p. 3). The SEC's action, had it not been challenged, as it very rarely is, would have swept under the carpet what on its face was a very serious violation of the law; in that respect, the regulatory agency became complicit in the trivializing cover-up.

IX. Conclusion

The claim that white-collar crime is primarily a middle-class offense and that the status of the offender needs to be separated from the act in order to avoid biased social analysis implicitly allows the most consequential forms of white-collar and corporate lawbreaking to fly well below the political, academic, and policy radar screens. Put another way, such treatment trivializes the nature and extent of white-collar crime. This trivialization ensures that major white-collar crimes remain largely absent in the development of effective regulatory policies and the law more generally. Nor are they included in what Moynihan described as "a lot of behavior that's not good for us."

Preventing white-collar and corporate crime in the global economy presents formidable challenges. The proliferation of international business has led to efforts to put in place overarching regulatory bodies to attempt to control cross-border crimes. Neal Shover and Andy Hochstetler summarized the nature and difficulties that have accompanied these developments: "Global oversight develops in dozens of forms and a complex array of institutions. It relies on criminal prosecution primarily in the nations where crimes originate. Nations, however, are reluctant to grant other nations and international bodies the right to define and pursue global oversight on their soil" (2006, p. 108). They noted that most international cooperation has occurred in the areas of war crimes and international organized crime, but, regarding white-collar and corporate crime, they cited Michael Gilbert and Steve Russell (2002, p. 233): "All the while avoidable harms (often of equivalent or greater magnitude) by transnational corporations are ignored."

Trivializing the lunatic white-collar crime rate entails much greater social costs than those related to the crime and deviance considered by Moynihan. As noted by Sutherland and others, the use of significant status, power, and privilege needs to be centrally considered—not removed—both in understanding the nature of white-collar and corporate offending, and in policies designed to prevent them. This stands in direct contrast to more conservative approaches that use an adjudicative approach to defining white-collar and corporate crime and that end up aiming downward rather than considering the highest levels of lawbreaking. The most recent financial meltdown provides an excellent case in point.

References

Bamber, Bill A., and Andrew Spencer. 2009. *Bear Trap: The Fall of Bear Stearns and the Panic of 2008*. New York: Black Tower Press.
Benson, Michael L., and Elizabeth Moore. 1992. "Are White-Collar and Common Criminals the Same? An Empirical and Theoretical Critique of a Recently Proposed General Theory of Crime." *Journal of Research in Crime and Delinquency* 29: 25–72.

Black, William K. 2005. *The Best Way to Rob a Bank Is to Own One: How Corporate Executives and Politicians Looted the Savings and Loan Industry.* Austin: University of Texas Press.

Braithwaite, John. 1985. "White-Collar Crime." *Annual Review of Sociology* 11: 1–25.

Braithwaite, John, and Brent Fisse. 1990. "On the Plausibility of Corporate Crime Theory." *Advances in Criminological Theory* 2: 15–37.

Burgess, Ernest W. 1950. "Comment and Concluding Comment." *American Journal of Sociology* 56: 31–34.

Calavita, Kitty, Henry N. Pontell, and Robert Tillman. 1997. *Big Money Crime: Fraud and Politics in the Savings and Loan Crisis.* Berkeley: University of California Press.

Cressey, Donald R. 1988. "The Poverty of Theory in Corporate Crime Research." *Advances in Criminological Theory* 1: 31–56.

Daly, Kathleen. 1989. "Gender and Varieties of White-Collar Crime." *Criminology* 27: 769–94.

Durkheim, Emile. 1982 [1895]. *The Rules of Sociological Method.* Translated by W. D. Halls. New York: The Free Press.

Financial Crisis Inquiry Commission (FCIC). 2011. *The Financial Crisis Inquiry Report: Final Report of the National Commission on the Causes of the Financial and Economic Crisis in the United States.* Washington, D.C.: U.S. Government Printing Office.

France, Anatole 1894. *Le Lys Rouge* [The Red Ruby]. Paris: Calmann-Levy.

Friedrichs, David O. 2013. "Wall Street: Crime Never Sleeps." In *How They Got Away With It: White Collar Criminals and the Financial Meltdown,* edited by Susan Will, Stephen Handelman, and David C. Brotherton. New York: Columbia University Press.

Gilbert, Michael J., and Steven Russell. 2002. "Globalization of Criminal Justice in the Corporate Context." *Crime, Law, and Social Change* 38: 211–38.

Goetz, Barry. 1997. "Organization as Class Bias in Local Law Enforcement: Arson-for-Profit as a 'Nonissue.'" *Law and Society Review* 31: 557–88.

Goff, Colin, and Gilbert Geis. 2008. "The Michael-Adler Report (1933): Criminology under the Microscope." *Journal of the History of the Behavioral Sciences* 44: 350–63.

Gottfredson, Michael R., and Travis Hirschi. 1990. *A General Theory of Crime.* Stanford: Stanford University Press.

Hirschi, Travis, and Michael R. Gottfredson. 1989. "The Significance of White-Collar Crime for a General Theory of Crime." *Criminology* 27: 359–71.

Johnson, David T., and Richard Leo. 1993. "The Yale White-Collar Crime Project: A Review and Critique." *Law and Social Inquiry* 18: 63–99.

Karmen, Andrew. 1994. "'Defining Deviancy Down': How Senator Moynihan's Misleading Phrase about Criminal Justice Is Rapidly Being Incorporated into Popular Culture." *Journal of Criminal Justice and Popular Culture* 2: 99–112.

Kelly, Kitty. 2009. *Street Fighters: The Last 72 Hours of Bear Stearns, the Toughest Firm on Wall Street.* New York: Portfolio.

Mann, Kenneth. 1985. *Defending White-Collar Crime: A Portrait of Attorneys at Work.* New Haven, CT: Yale University Press.

McDonald, Larry G., and Patrick Robinson. 2009. *A Colossal Failure of Common Sense: The Insider Story of the Collapse of Lehman Brothers.* New York: Crown.

Merton, Robert K. 1949. *Social Theory and Social Structure: Toward the Codification of Theory and Research.* Glencoe, IL: Free Press.

Michaelson, Adam. 2009. *The Foreclosure of America: The Inside Story of the Rise and Fall of Countrywide Home Loans, the Mortgage Crisis, and the Default of the American Dream.* New York: Berkley Publishing Group.

Morgenson, Gretchen, and Louise Story. 2011. "In Financial Crisis, No Prosecutions of Top Figures." *The New York Times* (April 14): p. 1.

Moynihan, Daniel Patrick. 1993. "Defining Deviancy Down: How We've Become Accustomed to Alarming Levels of Crime and Destructive Behavior." *The American Scholar* 62: 17–30.

Nguyen, Tomson H., and Henry N. Pontell. 2010. "Mortgage Origination Fraud and the Global Economic Crisis: A Criminological Analysis." *Criminology and Public Policy* 9: 591–612.

Nguyen, Tomson H., and Henry N. Pontell. 2011. "Fraud and Inequality in the Subprime Mortgage Crisis." In *Economic Crisis and Crime*, edited by Mathieu Deflem. Bingley, UK: Jai Press/Emerald Publishing Group.

Pontell, Henry N., Kitty Calavita, and Robert Tillman. 1994. "Corporate Crime and Criminal Justice System Capacity: Government Response to Financial Institution Fraud." *Justice Quarterly* 11: 383–410.

Pontell, Henry N., William K. Black, and Gilbert Geis. 2014. "Too Big to Fail, Too Powerful to Jail? On the Absence of Criminal Prosecutions Following the 2008 Financial Meltdown." *Crime, Law, and Social Change* 61: 1–13.

Reed, Gary E., and Peter C. Yeager. 1996. "Organizational Offending and Neo-Classical Criminology: Challenging the Reach of a General Theory of Crime." *Criminology* 34: 357–82.

Rosoff, Stephen M., Henry N. Pontell, and Robert Tillman. 2010. *Profit without Honor: White-Collar Crime and the Looting of America*, 5th ed. Upper Saddle River, NJ: Pearson.

Securities and Exchange Commission v. Bank of America. 09-CIV.6829 (September 14, 2009).

Sellin, Thorsten. 1938. *Culture Conflict and Crime*. New York: Social Science Research Council.

Shapiro, Susan S. 1990. "Collaring the Crime, not the Criminal: Liberating the Concept of White-Collar Crime." *American Sociological Review* 55: 346–65.

Shover, Neal, and Francis T. Cullen. 2008. "Studying and Teaching White-Collar Crime: Populist and Patrician Perspectives." *Journal of Criminal Justice Education* 19: 155–74.

Shover, Neal, and Andrew Hochstetler. 2006. *Choosing White-Collar Crime*. New York: Cambridge University Press.

Steffensmeier, Darrell J. 1989. "On the Causes of White-Collar Crime: An Assessment of Hirschi and Gottfredson's Claims." *Criminology* 27: 345–58.

Sutherland, Edwin H. 1945. "Is 'White-Collar Crime' Crime?" *American Sociological Review* 10: 132–39.

Sutherland, Edwin H. 1949. *White Collar Crime*. New York: Dryden Press.

Sutherland, Edwin H. 1973. "Crimes of Corporations." In *Edwin H. Sutherland: On Analyzing Crime*, edited by Karl Schuessler. Chicago: University of Chicago Press.

Tappan, Paul W. 1947. "Who Is the Criminal?" *American Sociological Review* 12: 96–102.

Tharp, Paul, and Matthew Scanlan. 2009. "BofA $50m Toxic Avenger: Bailed-Out Bank Footing Mozilo's Legal Bills." *New York Post* (June 10): p. 34.

Tillman, Robert, Kitty Calavita, and Henry N. Pontell. 1997. "Criminalizing White-Collar Misconduct: Determinants of Prosecution in Savings and Loan Fraud Cases." *Crime, Law, and Social Change* 26: 53–76.

Tombs, Steve, and David Whyte. 2003. *Unmasking the Crimes of the Powerful: Scrutinizing States and Corporations*. New York: Peter Lang.

Weisburd, David, Elin Waring, and Ellen Chayet. 1993. "Specific Deterrence in a Sample of Offenders Convicted of White-Collar Crimes." *Criminology* 33: 583–607.

Weisburd, David, Stanton Wheeler, Elin Waring, and Nancy Bode. 1994. *Crimes of the Middle Classes: White-Collar Offenders in the Federal Courts*. New Haven, CT: Yale University Press.

Wheeler, Stanton, and Michael L. Rothman. 1982. "The Organization as Weapon in White-Collar Crime." *Michigan Law Review* 80: 1403–26.

Zimring, Franklin, and David Johnson. 2007. "On the Comparative Study of Corruption." In *International Handbook of White-Collar and Corporate Crime*, edited by Henry N. Pontell and Gilbert Geis. New York: Springer.

PART II

IMPACT OF WHITE-COLLAR CRIME

CHAPTER 4

WHAT IS KNOWN AND WHAT SHOULD BE KNOWN ABOUT WHITE-COLLAR CRIME VICTIMIZATION?

HAZEL CROALL

It is accepted widely that victimology has largely neglected victimization from white-collar crime and that, while the white-collar crime literature has done much to expose the harm and human misery caused by offenses, it has not explored systematically many aspects of victimization (Croall 2007; Whyte 2007; McGurrin and Friedrichs 2010). Section I of this essay will discuss briefly the characteristics of white-collar crime victimization, and section II will outline how it is researched. Section III will explore what we know about its overall cost and extent and its direct and indirect impact on victims. Section IV will look at how this affects different groups in the population. Section V will conclude by summarizing what we know and what we do not know and consider what we should know and why. It will be argued that white-collar crime victimization

- is widespread, involves multiple and repeat victimization, and exceeds that from conventional crime;
- directly and indirectly affects all of us and can have an extremely severe impact on individual victims as well as affecting citizens, communities, and business in general;
- affects most severely those least able to protect themselves, particularly the poorest within Western nations and across the globe; and
- is often invisible and should be researched more widely in order to render it visible and thereby help to avoid it.

I. What Is White-Collar Crime Victimization?

The many issues surrounding the definition of white-collar crime and its ambiguous criminal status are discussed in Part I of this Handbook and need little reiteration. Sutherland's (1949) definition, referring to white-collar crime as being crime committed in the course of a *legitimate* occupation or business, generally taken to encompass white-collar and corporate crime, raises many issues of inclusion. Critical scholars have queried for example whether the scope of white-collar crime should be restricted to activities specifically against the *criminal* law or should also include other illegal and harmful activities, particularly on the grounds that what is legally criminal changes over time, and business and corporate interests, from whom offenders are drawn, play a part in determining the "criminal" status of their activities. Some have gone so far as to suggest an approach referring to harm rather than crime (Tombs 2010), whereas others argue that this is overly subjective and suggest the use of some kind of benchmark. In respect of state and environmental crime for example, Green and Ward suggest that a way forward is to look at acts widely regarded as "deviant" by a "respected" audience, and subject to some form of formal or informal sanction, including widespread censure by a wide range of reputable organizations (Green and Ward 2000; Green, Ward, and McConnachie 2007). Following many other writers (Friedrichs 2006; Tombs 2010), this essay will take a broadly inclusive approach by encompassing activities subject to criminal law (criminal), regulatory law (often dubbed quasi-criminal), and administrative and other laws (broadly described as illegal but not criminal) and those widely recognized as immoral and subject to calls for regulation from respected individuals and organizations (broadly described by Passas [2005] as "lawful but awful") (Croall 2012). Also, there is a very narrow and contested line among legal, illegal, and criminal activities and between legitimate and illegitimate businesses (Shichor, Sechrest, and Doocy 2000; Levi 2008), and any one category of white-collar crime may involve "classic" white-collar offenders along with a range of what are essentially criminal "entrepreneurs" or "scampreneurs" (Levi 2008; Button, Tapley, and Lewis 2009). The success of many frauds depends on skilled perpetrators being able to present themselves as "respectable," and illegal businesses often use or set up legitimate ones as a "front" (Shover et al. 2003). In line with an inclusive approach, and because they are covered in relevant research, these offenses also will be included.

These considerations have several implications for victimization. As offenders are carrying out their legitimate occupation, and are trusted on the basis of their actual or assumed occupational role and expertise, victims often are unaware of any harm. In large legitimate organizations, the division of labor and its associated diffusion of responsibility mean that it is difficult to pinpoint a guilty individual intending to harm a specific victim or victims. In contrast to the immediate face-to-face situation in cases of interpersonal violence, offenders and victims are separated in time and space and there may be no identifiable criminal "event" (Tombs and Whyte 2010a).

Victimization is also relatively invisible and often denied or not defined as such by the putative victims themselves (Croall 2007). Thus, victims cannot detect some offenses such as an excess of harmful chemicals in the air, in household products, or in food. Sutherland (1949) pointed to the "rippling effect" of offenses such as underweight goods or price fixing, in which individual losses are negligible but illegal profits are enormous. Other activities, irrespective of their legal status, are tolerated widely and victims, even when aware of harm, do not define themselves as "victims" of "crime." In yet other cases, for example, victims willingly have purchased suspiciously cheap goods or attractive investments and may blame themselves, particularly in the context of the doctrine of *caveat emptor*.

II. How Do We "Know" About White-Collar Crime Victimization?

These characteristics limit the applicability of research tools such as victim surveys, most of which omit white-collar crime due to the technical difficulties posed by victims' unawareness along with a general failure to regard these offenses as the kind of serious crimes that governments—often the main funders of victim surveys—want to know about. Nonetheless, some surveys are carried out such as, in the United States, the National Public Survey on White-Collar Crime by the National White-Collar Crime Center (NWCCC). The British Office of Fair Trading (OFT) and the Australian government also have surveyed aspects of fraud victimization (Smith and Budd 2009). These inevitably are limited to offenses detected by victims; often do not distinguish among white collar, frauds, and other "scams"; and do not include corporate crimes such as those involving safety, health, or environmental regulations.

The statistics reported by law-enforcement agencies, often cited by researchers, also are limited as so few offenses are reported to law enforcement. Even when victims are aware of some harm, they may not know whom to complain to; in other circumstances, the embarrassment that so often accompanies victimization from fraud also inhibits reporting (Button et al. 2009). NWCCC (2010) found that just over half of victimization incidents were reported to any agency, with a mere 11.7 percent being reported to a law-enforcement or crime-control agency. The many regulatory agencies involved are known to detect only a very small proportion of offenses, and records do not distinguish consistently between "offenses," "complaints," "incidents," or even deaths and injuries (Croall 2009a). Only a small proportion of offenses is prosecuted, making conviction figures unreliable. There is no one major source of information, and collating the records of many agencies, accounting for variations in recording, deducing how many "complaints" or "incidents" might be seen as "crime" versus those due to managerial neglect or incompetence, carelessness, misuse, or ignoring instructions on the part of consumers or workers, or simply, an "accident," is, in itself, a major task. Nonetheless the records of agencies, used critically and creatively, can be a valuable source of information (Tombs 2000, 2010).

Despite all these difficulties, there *is* a considerable volume of information available, though this body of literature is small compared with studies of conventional crime victims. Research has examined victims of, for example, various kinds of investment and personal frauds (Levi and Pithouse 1992; Shover, Fox, and Mills 1994; Spalek 1999; Shichor et al. 2000; Titus 2001), and case studies of "scandals" such as the thrift debacle (Calavita, Pontell, and Tillman 1997) and the collapse of companies such as BCCI (Spalek 2001) and Enron (Friedrichs 2004) provide additional information. This literature also contains many studies of corporate crimes, including "disasters" subsequently found to be attributable to managerial responsibility (Tombs and Whyte 2007; Tombs 2010).

Looking outside the criminological box also reveals a wide range of information (Croall 2009a, 2009b). While not necessarily seen as "crime," many activities are recognized as public issues and subject to investigation. A variety of organizations, including government departments and interest groups such as consumer or employee associations, carry out the equivalent of victim surveys, asking consumers about such things as experiences with faulty products or food poisoning and workers about injuries and illnesses originating in the workplace (Tombs 2010). Investigative journalism also can provide invaluable details on the impact of offenses and major case studies.

III. Dimensions of White-Collar Crime Victimization

Taken together, these sources of information reveal many dimensions of white-collar crime victimization. Its scope has been explored in relation to its overall costs and the extent of victimization from different offenses. Other research has explored the impact of offenses on individual victims and experiences of primary and secondary victimization.

A. The Costs of White-Collar Crime

A typical way of exposing the vast amount of victimization has been to list the costs of specific offenses and cases and numbers of deaths, injuries, or illnesses. While these figures vary enormously in terms of reliability and accuracy, they provide a starting point to illustrate the broad scope of white-collar crime victimization. Some selected examples follow, dealing primarily with financial frauds and forms of corporate crime.

Often cited in relation to financial frauds are total losses associated with significant cases, such as the estimated losses of $473 billion by 2021 of the savings and loan debacle (Calavita et al. 1997) or, in the United Kingdom, the £11 billion losses attributed to the "mis-selling" of pensions in 1998 and the £130 billion lost to five million mortgage frauds (Tombs and Whyte 2010b). Behind these figures lie many personal tragedies such as unemployment, lost retirement funds, or ill health, as happened following the collapse of Enron (Friedrichs 2004). The impact of the financial crisis of 2008, associated with many different kinds of frauds and illegitimate activities, was felt worldwide. In the United States alone, families lost their homes, investors and savers suffered from stock market losses of $7 trillion, and citizens suffered devastating declines in retirement, college, and other savings (McGurrin and Friedrichs 2010).

While it is notoriously difficult to "count" the cost of fraud (Levi and Burrows 2008), it has been estimated to cost the Australian community $8.5 billion each year (Smith and Budd 2009), and one attempt to collate reliable research internationally estimates that losses to any organization. including government departments, in areas of expenditure such as payroll, procurement, health, social security, insurance, and pensions, will amount to at least 3 percent and possibly as much as 9 percent (Gee, Button, and Brooks 2009). Consumer frauds and scams have been associated by the Australian Bureau of Statistics with a total loss of $1 billion (Smith and Budd 2009), and the British Office of Fair Trading (OFT 2008), in a survey of consumer "detriment" involving organizations treating consumers unfairly, estimated a total annual cost of around £6.6 billion.

White-collar and corporate crime also involves a high toll of death, disease, and injury. The literature contains many well-known cases of "mass deaths" such as the Ford Pinto car (Cullen, Maakestead, and Cavendar 1987), the Bhopal poisoning (Pearce and Tombs 1998), and the Minamata disease (Yokoyama 2006). While no one source aggregates this toll, it far exceeds that of violent crime. In the United Kingdom, for example, Tombs (2000, 2010) has calculated that the total number of workplace deaths attributable to managerial responsibility far exceeds those from homicide—to which can be added the toll of industrially caused diseases. In Britain alone, asbestos, widely used after its dangers were known, has caused around 4,000 deaths per annum (Tombs 2010). In the United States, the Occupational Safety and Health Administration reports that 5,200 workers are killed by occupational injuries each year, while the Department of Labor estimates that over four million workers are injured at work annually and around 50,000 deaths are attributable to occupational diseases (McGurrin and Friedrichs 2010). While it is, as outlined above, very difficult to ascertain how many of these are due to crime or negligence, Tombs and Whyte (2007) cite research estimating that as many as 70 percent of the workplace fatalities in the United Kingdom could be attributed to managerial responsibility and violation of regulations.

Food and consumer products also cause death and illness (Croall 2009a, 2013). Mass deaths associated with food include those of six Chinese babies in 2008 when melamine was used in baby formula, with a further 300,000 suffering illness (Liu 2009). Food poisoning has been associated with the so-called killer bug *Escherichia coli* 0157E—the impact of which has been linked to poor regulation and negligence and which led to the deaths of 49 consumers in France and Germany in 2011 (Croall 2013). Consumer products, particularly toys, electrical goods, and cosmetic and pharmaceutical products, many now produced in countries with less stringent safety standards, also carry considerable dangers, although reliable figures of their effects, including deaths and injuries, are very hard to find, as is attributing these specifically to breaches or neglect of regulations. The U.S. Consumer Product Safety Commission estimates that consumer products are responsible for 27,100 deaths and 33.1 million injuries each year (McGurrin and Friedrichs 2011). While data are sparse, the U.K. consumer association Which? (2004) claimed that seven people each year are killed by the specific group of products that were deemed unsafe and that were recalled. The Department for Business, Innovation and Skills (2009) estimates that unsafe goods, particularly toys and fireworks, coming through one U.K. port alone cause or contribute to 95,000 injuries, 100 fires, and 3 deaths per annum. Also well documented are the deaths and illnesses associated with pharmaceutical products such as thalidomide, contraceptive devices such as the Dalkon Shield (Finlay 1996), and cosmetic products and surgery (Croall 2009a). Environmental crime is associated with further death and illness, often by exacerbating existing conditions—pollution, for example, has been said to cause as many as 800,000 premature deaths globally (Tombs and Whyte 2010b), and this also draws attention to the massive impact on animals and nonhuman species (White 2008). At a broader level, global industrial and production processes have been associated with new forms of slavery, exploitation, and environmental degradation, and the continued production of unhealthy junk food, aggressively marketed despite its dangers being known, has been associated with growing rates of heart disease and obesity (Croall 2013).

These examples, however unsystematic, serve to underline the point made by many scholars since Sutherland (1949) that the "human misery" and impact of white-collar crime far outstrip that of conventional crimes (Shover et al. 1994; Whyte 2007; Friedrichs and McGurrin 2011). These examples also suggest that we are all victims of white-collar crime—and likely to be victims of many of its forms, from financial frauds, mis-selling, and misrepresentation of products, to less common kinds of physical victimization (Croall 2010).

B. The Extent of Victimization from White-Collar Crime

The widespread nature of victimization is further underlined by exploring what can be learned from victim surveys, even though they inevitably are limited to those forms of crime about which victims are aware and funders of surveys wish to know. This latter consideration means that surveys generally are restricted to unambiguously "criminal" activities associated with illegitimate rather than legitimate enterprises (Button et al. 2013). Surveys of fraud victimization tend to variously include credit card fraud, identity theft, advance fee and other investment frauds, prize lottery frauds, and the sale of fake products and services such as weight-loss and diet scams. Much of this is not strictly white-collar crime and involves a range of offenders whose characteristics are not fully known or who could be described as "scampreneurs" (Button, Lewis, and Tapley 2009). These surveys do, however, highlight the frequency with which people are exposed to different forms of fraud, particularly with the growth of telemarketing and Internet sales. Few generalizations about rates are possible—nor are cross-national comparisons feasible—as surveys have very different methodologies and different samples and include different ranges of offenses, often differently defined (Smith and Budd 2009).

In the United States, the NWCCC (2010) found that nearly 40 percent of surveyed households reported victimization from credit card fraud; 16 percent from losing money through the Internet; 12 percent from identity theft; nearly 10 percent from a fraudulent business venture; around 7 percent from false stockbroker information; and 4 percent from mortgage fraud. It also found that, after credit card fraud, price misrepresentation and unnecessary home or auto repairs were the most commonly experienced white-collar crimes, each being reported by around 22 percent. A 2005 survey by the Federal Trade Commission found that 13.5 percent of adults had been victims of one or more consumer frauds, with the biggest category being fraudulent weight-loss products (2.1 percent), followed by fraudulent foreign lotteries and buyers' club memberships (1.5 percent), fraudulent prize promotions (1.2 percent), and fraudulent work-at-home schemes (1.1 percent) (Anderson 2007).

The British OFT (2008) survey cited above found that around one third of respondents reported at least one problem in 12 months. The majority involved losses below £5, but 4 percent involved over £1,000, typically involving telecommunications, domestic fuel, personal banking, insurance, and home maintenance. An OFT (2006) survey of mass marketing scams found that 48 percent of the population reported being targeted and around 8 percent admitted to being a victim. Drawing together a number of British surveys, Button and colleagues (2009) reported that the highest individual losses involved African advance-fee frauds, accounting for median losses of £2,858 for 70,000 victims, followed by median losses of £2,751 for high-risk investment frauds, involving 90,000 victims. Other median losses were smaller, involving less than £100; these scams include prize draw and foreign lottery scams, work-at-home and business opportunity scams, and miracle health and weight-loss scams.

In Australia, the 2007 personal fraud survey (which included identity fraud and consumer scams) found that 5 percent of the population over age 15 reported being the victim of a fraud, with 3 percent reporting identity fraud. A total of 35.8 percent of the population had been exposed to a scam, with 2 percent having fallen victim to the scam. Lotteries were more often responded to, as only 0.1 percent of respondents reported responding to advance-fee frauds. Average losses were in the region of $2,156, with only 3 percent of victims losing more than $10,000 (Smith and Budd 2009).

The European Crime and Safety Survey (EUICS) included "nonconventional" crimes such as consumer fraud, although many of the included deviant acts amount to cheating rather than serious fraud. On average, 12 percent of those interviewed in a range of European countries reported some kind of consumer fraud, with over one third of incidents involving shops and one tenth building or construction. Rates varied, with few clear trends being identified, although the authors point to global analyses that suggest a relationship between the size of the informal sector of the economy and cheating, thus accounting for higher levels in countries of transition (van Dijk et al. 2007).

While there is less information about the prevalence of victimization from other forms of white-collar crimes (particularly those not widely regarded as "crime"), U.K. labor force surveys, similar to victim surveys, suggest that injuries in 2006–7 affected 1,000 per 100,000 workers—a figure that, argues Tombs (2010), exceeds injuries received in "real crime" assaults recorded by criminal statistics, although it should be reiterated that not all of these are due to violations of regulations. The survey also reveals that over two million respondents suffered from an illness they believe to have been caused or made worse by work.

C. The Impact of Victimization

While studies of victimization from white-collar crime have been largely absent from criminological discussions of and policies supporting the victims of crime, a considerable amount of research has now indicated that many offenses have a severe and long-lasting impact and that victims are much in need of support and are less different from victims of violence than often assumed (Ganzini, McFarland, and Bloom 1990).

Inevitably, the impact of victimization varies from being almost negligible to being life-changing and life-threatening (Shover et al. 1994). Button and associates (2009) suggested that fraud victimization can be conceptualized as an iceberg (or pyramid), at the top of which are found the minority, "chronic" victims who have lost large proportions of their savings and are often repeat victims. In the middle are found "one-off" victims who have lost large amounts of money, and at the base lie the much larger number who are unaware of their victimization or have lost only a very little. The impact of an offense, however, may not always be related to the net sum lost but to, for example, victims' abilities to recoup their losses (Shover et al. 1994). Victims' reactions also vary—however small the loss, some nonetheless feel angry or let down. Shichor and colleagues (2000) found that 39 percent of victims cited anger and dismay, with a further 23 percent citing milder sentiments, and around 10 percent being "philosophical." Others, like victims of street crime, complain about loss of personal time to sort things out (OFT 2008).

Fraud victims, especially those experiencing greater losses, suffer many secondary effects. Many cite the actual or threatened loss of a home, an inability to plan for retirement, a need to work longer hours, or an inability to support children and grandchildren (Spalek 2001, 2007). Psychological effects such as stress, anxiety, and depression are reported widely (Button et al. 2009) along with major depressive disorders (Ganzini et al. 1990) and actual and threatened suicide (Shichor et al. 2000; Spalek 2001). In some cases, particularly where spouses have been unaware of the investment leading to a loss, divorce and family disintegration have followed (Shover et al. 1994; Shichor et al. 2000; Spalek 2001). The impact is said to be extremely severe for the elderly, who have less chance of recouping their losses; as Levi (1999) argues, fraud can lead to broken dreams and destroy happiness permanently. Many of these problems last many years after the initial losses (Shover et al. 1994; Shichor et al. 2000).

Victimization also may involve a sense of betrayed trust (Levi and Pithouse 1992), and a recurrent theme in the literature is a sense of self-blame and embarrassment— which inhibits reporting and seeking help (Shover et al. 1994; Shichor et al. 2000; Titus 2001). Much of this stems from the nature of many frauds in which victims feel that they have, particularly given the primacy of *caveat emptor*, cooperated with the offender by purchasing a product or investment, providing information, or having been greedy and careless. This aspect has led to many (Levi 1992; Shover et al. 1994; Shichor et al. 2000; Button et al. 2009) likening fraud to rape or domestic violence in that victims can be seen as "willing" or "undeserving." The negative impact of this on a victim's self-esteem may be more devastating than the material loss (Shichor et al. 2000) and may amount to a sense of stigma (Spalek 2001; Titus 2001).

Other forms of corporate crime involve severe secondary impacts. As seen above, many involve death, exploitation, life-changing injuries, and long-term illnesses with spillover effects on victims and their families. Some may not be able to work again. The British support group Families Against Corporate Killers noted that the repercussions of work-related death go on for many years, with spouses unable to work again, children traumatized and failing at school, and families thrown into poverty and insecurity (Snell and Tombs 2011). Victim support groups also suggest that families may struggle knowing who to "blame" and ascertaining "what happened." Incidents involving mass deaths affect relatives, friends, survivors who have suffered no immediate injuries but suffer from "survivor guilt," rescuers, and witnesses. In some cases, bodies take a long time to be found and parents may lose children—all of which can exacerbate grief and hamper recovery (Wells 1995). The victims of corporate crime, particularly where an employer is involved, also can experience a sense of betrayed trust.

A further form of secondary victimization has been found in relation to victims' encounters with criminal justice and other organizations (Shover and Hochstetler 2002), and victim support organizations generally do not deal with white-collar crime victims (Moore and Mills 1990). Studies refer to victims being passed from one organization to another in a kind of "merry-go-round" fashion (Button et al. 2013), and many cases take years or even decades to be settled, after which, for many, little or no relief is forthcoming (Shover et al. 1994). Indeed, victims often express more dissatisfaction with the system than with the perpetrators (Shover et al. 1994; Shichor et al. 2000). Workplace deaths, particularly "disasters," may involve years of inquiries, inquests, and dealing with regulatory bodies—a process that Snell and Tombs (2011) describe as a form of double victimization amounting to an official denial of victim status.

IV. The Social Distribution
of Victimization

There is less systematic information about how different groups in the population are affected; indeed, white-collar crime often is perceived to have a relatively indiscriminate impact on *all* consumers, workers, and citizens (Croall 2009a, 2010). We do know, however, that age, gender, socioeconomic status, and race are important for some offenses, although relationships are far from clear-cut. A combination of biological, cultural, and socioeconomic factors underlies the unequal impact of some offenses, as illustrated in the following subsections.

A. Age

It often is assumed that the very old and young are particularly vulnerable, with both physical factors and the social construction of age being important. For example, the Chinese milk case affected babies' as opposed to adults' kidneys (Liu 2009). Babies ingest chemicals in the environment and household products more rapidly, and *E. coli* generally has had a more severe effect on children and older people (Croall 2009a). Moreover, children in institutions may be subject to physical and sexual abuse, and the elderly in institutions are also at risk from physical abuse and financial exploitation (Croall 2007) as a result of employees abusing their occupational roles or management failures in respect of regulations or supervision.

The production and the marketing of products and services reflect the social construction of age, which in turn affects victimization. Children are vulnerable to unsafe, cheap, imitation toys, and teenagers' concerns with fashion, technology, risk, and excitement—so often associated with committing crime—can make them the victims of counterfeit and substandard fashion items, misleading mobile phone contracts, and safety offenses in nightclubs or outdoor pursuits (Croall 2009a). The importance of financial security in old age is reflected in the many frauds involving pensions and investments directed at maximizing retirement income and, as outlined above, the elderly, being unable to recoup their losses, suffer more severely from financial frauds (Levi 1999; Shichor et al. 2000). "Fear of ageing" can be exploited by the promotion of "assistive products" and security devices that may not work (Croall 2009a).

Nonetheless, it is important to avoid stereotypes. Younger people, being more prepared to take a risk, also are affected by investment frauds and scams (MacKenzie 2010), and those in middle years can be affected by mortgage frauds and sales from the Internet. A number of studies have reported that younger people are more at risk from some kinds of frauds (Van Wyk and Mason 2001), and an Australian study linked lifestyle factors such as an active social life and working with greater risks faced by those under 65 (Muscat, James, and Graycar 2002). Titus (2001) found the affluent elderly to be less at risk from fraud, commenting that they may have become older and wiser while it is possible that their lower rate of internet use also decreases their exposure to fraud (Smith and Budd 2009). However, consumer fraud remains a major form of victimization for the elderly (Button et al. 2009; Smith and Budd 2009).

B. Gender

While much white-collar crime literature has been "gender blind" (Snider 1996), women have been perceived as targets on the grounds of their assumed financial or technological incompetence, with "little old ladies" being archetypal fraud victims. Women have been found to suffer more from car sales and servicing and appliance repair frauds (Croall 2009a). Again, a combination of cultural and socioeconomic factors is significant.

Women have been affected most adversely by products and services affecting their bodies through conforming to dominant images of femininity (Simpson and Elis 1996), such as silicone breast implants and other dangers of cosmetic surgery, which often are regulated inadequately (Croall 2009a), as well as for miracle health and weight-loss scams (Button et al. 2009). Women, being more in the home, are more at risk from work-at-home and career-opportunity scams (Button et al. 2009).

Women are not necessarily more at risk as victimization reflects wider gender roles. So-called man's work carries risks of fatal injuries, and a "macho" culture may act against compliance with safety requirements (Whyte 2007). Men are more likely to be victimized by African advanced-fee frauds and high-risk investment frauds (Button et al. 2009). In general, victimization in the workplace reflects the gendered division of labor. Women are exploited in low-paid jobs, such as care work, where conditions and wages can fall below legal minima; a similar fate may be suffered by men in casual labor, particularly on building and construction sites, and this form of exploitation also adversely affects immigrant laborers (Croall 2010).

C. Socioeconomic Status

Age and gender are linked strongly to socioeconomic status, and the relationship between status and white-collar victimization is also complex. While it might be assumed popularly that "rich" or "powerful" offenders prey on the poor and powerless, white-collar crime has been said to have a more "democratic" effect, affecting the "well-heeled" and affluent (Moore and Mills 1990) as well as governments and organizations. All taxpayers suffer from tax evasion, and all citizens' health is endangered by pollution. Investors need money to invest, and retirement savings, mortgages, and luxury goods are not an option for the poorest. Indeed, victims' presumed affluence is said to underlie the lack of public sympathy for victims of fraud—although they are often less affluent than is assumed (Shichor et al. 2000). Titus (2001) found that greater education was not necessarily a protective factor and explained that better-educated people have wider interests and are more active consumers, which increases their exposure to fraudulent advances.

Nonetheless, there is strong evidence to suggest that the impact of some, if not most, white-collar crime falls most severely on the poorest. It is those most likely to need welfare and health support who suffer most from tax avoidance and evasion and the high costs associated with the 2008 financial crisis. Britain's National Consumer Council (2003) has identified low-income groups, residents of deprived areas, and those with "skills difficulties" as vulnerable consumers. Nonunion and casual workers are more likely to be seriously and fatally injured at work (Whyte 2007), while the lowest-paid, often migrant workers are most likely to be exploited.

Socioeconomic status also is associated with race, particularly in relation to environmental crime. U.S. research suggests that more hazardous chemical plants and waste sites are closer to lower-class communities and communities of color than to higher-class, white communities (Lynch, Stretesky, and McGurrin 2001). Lynch and Stretesky (2001), for example, established that chemical accidents are more likely to occur near African-American and low-income census tracts. In the United Kingdom, some of the worst cases of chemical pollution have had a disproportionate effect on lower-class communities (Tombs and Whyte 2010b).

A combination of socioeconomic and cultural factors underlies these inequalities. The more affluent, for example, have less need to purchase inexpensive imitations, second-hand cars, or cheap processed foods, and they can afford to move away from polluted neighborhoods. They are more likely to know how to avoid the most blatant investment frauds and consumer scams, to seek financial advice, and to be aware of the need to eat a healthy diet. The poorest people, on the other hand, have little choice but to work in unsafe workplaces, to accept exploitative conditions, and to live in polluted neighborhoods or what have been described as "food deserts," where little fresh, healthy produce is available at an affordable price. In short, the more affluent are protected by their economic, political, and cultural capital (Croall 2009a, 2010), and, in common with other forms of crime victimization, victimization from white-collar crime, and the ability to avoid it, reflects wider structures of inequality and stratification.

C. Global Inequalities

Many global white-collar crimes are related to the "race to the bottom" on the part of major corporations who exploit the spaces between laws and the less stringent financial, taxation, employment, safety, health, and environmental regulations of countries that need inward investment (Croall 2005). This is illustrated in cases such as Bhopal, where many safety aspects of the plant were inferior to those of a similar plant in the United States and would not have complied with U.S. regulations (Pearce and Tombs 1998). This pattern can be seen in the more recent examples of e-waste and toxic waste dumping, which effectively involve the transfer of dangers from richer to poorer countries (White 2008) and to the poorest within those countries. Workers from Third World countries are most likely to be exploited, whether at home or when they migrate.

V. Discussion: What Is Known and What Should Be Known About White-Collar Crime Victimization

A. What We Know

Despite the limited nature of available information, we know enough to argue that white-collar crime has serious economic, physical, and emotional effects on individuals as well as enormous economic and social costs—exceeding those of conventional crime. The losses from individual housebreaking or theft, for example, pale into insignificance compared with the loss of investments, retirement savings, and employment. As McGurrin and Friedrichs (2010, p. 152) argue, "robbery by banks" has higher costs than conventionally described bank robbery, and corporate "violence" exceeds that of conventionally described violent crime (Tombs and Whyte 2010). We also know that, as for conventional crime—whether as consumers, employees, investors, savers, or taxpayers—individuals are repeat and multiple victims. Victimization also is known to reflect wider social inequalities, with the poor and least powerful being more severely affected.

Much of the focus above has been on individual victims, but it also is important to recognize (however briefly) the spillover effect of white-collar and corporate crime on communities, neighborhoods, trade, commerce, and government. The devastating impact of serious frauds, company collapses, and chemical and environmental "disasters" on communities include loss of employment, local amenities, revenue from trade and commerce, as well as ill health (Croall 2009b). Crimes often described as "victimless," such as tax evasion, drain resources from local and national governments. Levi and Burrows (2008) cite estimates that tax fraud, for instance, cost the U.K. National Health Service around £6,434 billion in 2005 alone.

Many have also noted the delegitimation effect of white-collar crime (Shover et al. 1994). Friedrichs (2006) suggests that white-collar crime's most pernicious cost is the level of cynicism, distrust, and loss of confidence in major institutions that it engenders, which can have "real" effects on the economy. Victims of fraud may change their investment behavior (Button et al. 2009), for example, and the prevalence of mass marketing scams may reduce the extent to which consumers are prepared to buy from legitimate organizations (Spalek 2006). A report by Ernst and Young (2008) noted that corruption makes markets unfair, erodes public trust, and places a drag on long-term economic development.

As with forms of conventional crime, victimization can be denied and victims blamed (Croall 2007)—be they investors seeking high returns, workers "choosing" to work in unsafe workplaces, consumers buying suspiciously cheap items, women risking illness and injury to improve their appearance, or parents buying junk food for children. It also can be difficult to establish who the victims are. As McGurrin and Friedrichs (2010) pointed out, prior to the 2008 financial crisis, applicants had lied about their financial circumstances to obtain mortgages. Nonetheless, the financial institutions that had turned a blind eye and the banks that had accepted the loans ultimately were to blame.

B. What Should We Know?

Nonetheless, there remains much that we do not know. Indeed, given the enormous costs outlined above, it is surprising that there have been so few attempts to measure accurately the overall costs of, for example, financial frauds, tax avoidance and evasion, injuries and illnesses in the workplace, unsafe consumer goods, adulterated food, and chemical pollution. We know even less about the extent to which victimization mirrors wider social inequalities or about the complex interrelationships among age, class, gender, and race and the economic and cultural factors underlying offending and victimization. Despite the many difficulties outlined above, much more research is possible and desirable.

It is possible, for example, to survey more intensively victims' experiences of those crimes and harms that they know about (Croall 2009b), such as Internet frauds, defective or underweight consumer goods, food poisoning, some aspects of unsafe work environments and polluted local areas, along with misleading, aggressive, and intrusive marketing strategies. Detailed surveys could include estimates of the extent to which retailers, sellers, employers, and companies are to blame. Like other victim surveys, these could be analyzed by social class, gender, age, and race, and they could be combined with and compared to conventional crime surveys.

While inevitably victim surveys cannot tap offenses with unaware victims, even these victims can be investigated. Of considerable potential are the "mystery shopping" exercises carried out by enforcers and interest groups—in which researchers, posing as consumers, purchase goods or ask for estimates of work that has to be done in relation to car servicing (Croall 2009a). Moreover, notwithstanding technical difficulties, far more accurate estimates could be made of the total costs of serious frauds, tax avoidance, and evasion by government-sponsored research were there a stronger will to so do. There is also a need for research that "joins up" different aspects of white-collar crime to illustrate its effects. Local surveys looking at the impact of a range of crimes can highlight the higher risks of white-collar and corporate victimization than the "real" crimes or "antisocial" behavior that local crime surveys count (Whyte 2004; Croall 2009b). Better estimates of the total costs of many kinds of offending, when collated, can be used at a national level, while the enormous harms associated with corporate activities across the globe—revealed by investigative journalism and interest groups—could be much more systematically mapped.

C. Why Should We Know More?

Why we should fund this extensive research agenda? Since Sutherland (1949), the exposé tendency of white-collar and corporate crime research has attracted criticisms of subjectivity and political bias. Underlying this tendency, however, is a concern to raise awareness of the massive costs associated with white-collar crime in order to combat it and thereby reduce victimization.

"Crime as choice" and rational choice theories (see, e.g., Cornish and Clarke 1986) focus on offenders' choices; where white-collar offenders are concerned, it has been argued that business choices are based on profit maximization at the expense of, for example, health, safety, and environmental considerations (Croall 2004). As seen above, goods and services are targeted at particular groups for whom they are seen to be attractive. Were their dangers more widely known, consumers perhaps would no longer purchase these goods and services, thus removing their profitability. This kind of thinking underlies government policies toward such groups as consumers, with recent decades having seen a focus on the need to better inform consumers in preference to tougher regulation (Croall 2009b).

While these kinds of strategies may have some effect, a deeper understanding of the context of these choices and the structural basis of victimization indicates the limitations of this approach. Many victims' choices, such as those of workers, are far from freely made. Economic pressures affect other so-called choices, such as where to live or which goods and foods to consume. Cultural factors also are crucial, with many dangerous or harmful products being marketed as "must have" desirable products. As seen above, images of femininity underlie women's choices of beauty products and services, and the insecurities associated with old age are associated with offenses targeted at the middle-aged and elderly. Furthermore, many of these forms of victimization—along with the exploitation of children, migrant workers, Third World countries, and the environment—ultimately are rooted in "asymmetries of power" (Passas 2000).

Exposing and, as McGurrin and Friedrichs (2010) argue, expanding the conceptualization of crime victims by constructing harmful activities as "criminal" can play a part in combating them. Despite the widely acknowledged issues, outlined in Part VIII of this Handbook, surrounding the use of *criminal* sanctions, there is evidence to suggest that companies do fear adverse publicity and criminalization (Croall 2004). Otherwise, why do many global corporations shroud their operations and tax avoidance schemes in such secrecy? Exposure can produce change. During widespread adverse publicity surrounding the "aggressive" tax strategies of major corporations, Starbucks volunteered to pay back around £10 million in U.K. taxes in the face of proposed consumer boycotts (Neville and Treanor 2012). The importance of these kinds of exposures is outlined by McGurrin and Friedrichs (2010), who argue that a fundamental change in our understanding of crime victimization is necessary to avoid the potential catastrophe of another major financial meltdown. Moreover, the impact of these harmful activities on the most vulnerable across the globe illustrates that they involve considerations of social and environmental as well as criminal justice.

REFERENCES

Anderson, Keith B. 2007. *Consumer Fraud in the United States: The Second FTC Survey*. Staff Report of the Bureaus of Economics and Consumer Protection. Washington, D.C.: Federal Trade Commission.

Button, Mark, Chris Lewis, and Jacki Tapley. 2009. *Fraud Typologies and the Victims of Fraud: Literature Review*. Portsmouth, UK: University of Portsmouth.

Button, Mark, Jacki Tapley, and Chris Lewis. 2013. "The 'Fraud Justice Network' and the Infrastructure of Support for Individual Fraud Victims in England and Wales." *Criminology and Criminal Justice* 13: 37–61.

Calavita, Kitty, Henry N. Pontell, and Robert Tillman. 1997. *Big Money Crime: Fraud and Politics in the Savings and Loan Crisis*. Berkeley: University of California Press.

Cornish, Derek B., and Ronald V. Clarke, eds. 1986. *The Reasoning Criminal: Rational Choice Perspectives and Offending*. New York: Springer Verlag.

Croall, Hazel. 2004. "Combatting Financial Crime: Regulatory versus Crime Control Approaches." *Journal of Financial Crime* 11: 45–55.

Croall, Hazel. 2005. "Transnational White-Collar Crime." In *Transnational and Comparative Criminology*, pp. 227–45, edited by James Sheptycki and Ali Wardak. London: Glasshouse Press.

Croall, Hazel. 2007. "Victims of White-Collar and Corporate Crime." In *Victims, Crime, and Society*, pp. 78–108, edited by Pamela Davies, Peter Francis, and Chris Greer. London: Sage.

Croall, Hazel. 2009a. "White-Collar Crime, Consumers, and Victimization." *Crime, Law, and Social Change* 51: 127–46.

Croall, Hazel. 2009b. "Community Safety and Economic Crime." *Criminology and Criminal Justice* 9: 965–85.

Croall, Hazel. 2010. "Economic Crime and Victimology: A Critical Appraisal." *International Journal of Victimology* 8: 169–83.

Croall, Hazel. 2013. "Food Crime: A Green Criminology Perspective." In *International Handbook of Green Criminology*, pp. 167–83, edited by Nigel South and Avi Brisman. London: Routledge.

Cullen, Francis T., William J. Maakestad, and Gray Cavender. 1987. *Corporate Crime Under Attack: The Ford Pinto Case and Beyond*. Cincinnati, OH: Anderson.

Department for Business, Innovation and Skills. 2009. *A Better Deal for Consumers: Delivering Real Help Now and Change for the Future*. Presented to Parliament by the Secretary of State for Business, Innovation and Skills, July 2009. London: Department for Business Innovation and Skills. https://www.gov.uk/government/publications/a-better-deal-for-consumers-delivering-real-help-now-and-change-for-the-future

Dijk, Jan van, Robert Manchin, John van Kesteren, Sami Nevala, and Gergely Hideg. 2007. *The Burden of Crime in the EU: A Comparative Analysis of the European Crime and Safety Survey (EU ICS) 2005*. Brussels: Gallup Europe.

Ernst and Young. 2008. *Corruption or Compliance—Weighing the Costs, 10th Global Fraud Survey*. http://www.ncc.co.uk/article/?articleid=15621

Finlay, Lucinda, M. 1996. "The Pharmaceutical Industry and Women's Reproductive Health." In *Corporate Victimization of Women*, pp. 59–110, edited by Elizabeth Szockyj and James G. Fox. Boston: Northeastern University Press.

Friedrichs, David O. 2004. "Enron et al.: Paradigmatic White-collar Crime Cases for the New Century." *Critical Criminology* 12: 113–32.

Friedrichs, David O. 2006. *Trusted Criminals: White-Collar Crime in Contemporary Society*, 3rd ed. Belmont: Thomson Wadsworth.

Ganzini, Linda, Bentson McFarland, and Joseph Bloom. 1990. "Victims of Fraud: Comparing Victims of White-Collar and Violent Crime." *Bulletin of the American Academy of Psychiatry and Law* 18: 55–63.

Gee, Jim, Mark Button, and Graham Brooks. 2009. *The Financial Cost of Fraud*. London: MacIntyre Hudson/CCFS.

Green, Penny, and Tony Ward. 2000. "State Crime, Human Rights, and the Limits of Criminology." *Social Justice* 27: 101.

Green, Penny, Tony Ward, and Kirsten McConnachie. 2007. "Logging and Legality: Environmental Crime, Civil Society, and the State." *Social Justice* 34: 94–110.

Levi, Michael. 1992. "White-Collar Crime Victimization." In *White-Collar Crime Reconsidered*, pp. 169–94, edited by Kip Schlegel and David Weisburd. Boston: Northeastern University Press

Levi, Michael. 1999. "The Impact of Fraud." *Criminal Justice Matters* 36: 5–7.

Levi, Michael. 2008. "Organized Fraud and Organizing Frauds: Unpacking Research on Networks and Organization." *Criminology and Criminal Justice* 8: 389–419.

Levi, Michael, and John Burrows. 2008. "Measuring the Impact of Fraud in the U.K.: A Conceptual and Empirical Journey." *British Journal of Criminology* 48: 293–318.

Levi, Michael, and Andrew Pithouse. 1992. "The Victims of Fraud." In *Unraveling Criminal Justice*, edited by David Downes. London: Macmillan.

Liu, Chenglin. 2009. "Profits above the Law: China's Melamine Tainted Milk Incident." *Mississippi Law Journal* 79: 371–417.

Lynch, Michael J., and Paul Stretesky. 2001. "Toxic Crimes: Examining Corporate Victimization of the General Public Employing Medical and Epidemiological Evidence." *Critical Criminology* 10: 153–72.

Lynch, Michael J., Paul Stretesky, and Danielle McGurrin. 2001. "Toxic Crimes and Environmental Justice." In *Controversies in White-collar Crime*, pp. 109–36, edited by Gary Potter. Cincinnati, OH: Anderson.

Mackenzie, Simon. 2010. "Scams." In *Handbook on Crime*, pp. 137–52, edited by Fiona Brookman, Mike Maguire, Harriet Pierpoint, and Trevor Bennett. Cullompton, UK: Willan

McGurrin, Danielle, and David O. Friedrichs. 2010. "Victims of Economic Crime on a Grand Scale." *International Journal of Victimology* 8: 147–57.

Moore, Elizabeth, and Michael Mills. 1990. "The Neglected Victims and Unexamined Costs of White-Collar Crime." *Crime and Delinquency* 36: 408–18.

Muscat, Glenn, Marianne James, and Adam Graycar. 2002. *Older People and Consumer Fraud*. Trends and Issues in Crime and Criminal Justice (no. 220). Canberra: Australian Institute of Criminology.

National Consumer Council. 2003. *Everyday Essentials: Meeting Basic Needs—Research into Accessing Essential Goods and Services*. London: National Consumer Council.

National White-Collar Crime Center. 2010. *National Public Survey on White-Collar Crime.* Available at http://www.nw3c.org/docs/publications/2010-national-public-survey-on-white-collar-crime.pdf?sfvrsn=8

Neville, Simon, and Jill Treanor. 2012. "Starbucks to Pay £20m in Tax over Next Two Years after Customer Revolt." *The Guardian* (December 6). Available at http://www.guardian.co.uk/business/2012/dec/06/starbucks-to-pay-10m-corporation-tax?intcmp=239

Office of Fair Trading. 2006. *Research on Impact of Mass Marketed Scams.* London: Office of Fair Trading.

Office of Fair Trading. 2008. *Consumer Detriment: Assessing the Frequency and Impact of Consumer Problems with Goods and Services.* Available at http://www.oft.gov.uk?news?press?2008?49-08

Passas, Nikkos. 2000. "Global Anomie, Dysnomie, and Economic Crime: Hidden Consequences of Neo-liberalism and Globalization in Russia and around the World." *Social Justice* 27: 16–35.

Passas, Nikkos. 2005. "Lawful but awful: 'legal corporate crimes.'" *Journal of Socioeconomics* 34: 771–86.

Pearce, Frank, and Steve Tombs. 1998. *Toxic Capitalism: Corporate Crime and the Chemical Industry.* Aldershot, UK: Ashgate.

Shichor, David, Dale K. Sechrest, and Jeffrey Doocy. 2000. "Victims of Investment Fraud." In *Contemporary Issues in Crime and Criminal Justice: Essays in Honor of Gilbert Geis*, pp. 81–96, edited by Henry N. Pontell and David Shichor. Upper Saddle River, NJ: Prentice Hall

Shover, Neal, Glenn S. Coffey, and Dick Hobbs. 2003. "Crime on the Line: Telemarketing and the Changing Nature of Professional Crime." *British Journal of Criminology* 43: 489–505.

Shover, Neal, Greer Litton Fox, and Michael Mills. 1994. "Consequences of Victimization by White-Collar Crime." *Justice Quarterly* 11: 75–98.

Shover, Neal, and Andy Hochstetler. 2002. *Choosing White-Collar Crime.* Cambridge, UK: Cambridge University Press.

Simpson, Sally S., and Lori Elis. 1996. "Theoretical Perspectives on the Corporate Victimization of Women." In *Corporate Victimization of Women*, pp. 33–58, edited by Elizabeth Szockyj and James G. Fox. Boston: Northeastern University Press.

Smith, Russell G., and Carolyn Budd. 2009. *Consumer Fraud in Australia: Costs, Rates, and Awareness of the Risks in 2008.* Trends and Issues in Crime and Criminal Justice (no. 382). Canberra: Australian Institute of Criminology. Available at http://www.aic.gov.au/publications/current series/tandi/381-400/tandi382.aspx

Snell, Katy, and Steve Tombs. 2011. "How Do You Get Your Voice Heard When No One Will Let You? Victimization at Work." *Criminology and Criminal Justice* 11: 207–23.

Snider, Laureen. 1996. "Directions for Social Change and Political Action." In *Corporate Victimization of Women*, pp. 235–66, edited by Elizabeth Szockyj and James G. Fox. Boston: Northeastern University Press.

Spalek, Basia. 1999. "Exploring the Impact of Financial Crime: A Study Looking into the Effects of the Maxwell Scandal upon the Maxwell Pensioners." *International Review of Victimology* 6: 213–30.

Spalek, Basia. 2001. "White-Collar Crime and Secondary Victimization: An Analysis of the Effects of the Closure of BCCI." *Howard Journal of Criminal Justice* 40: 166–79.

Spalek, Basia. 2007. *Knowledgeable Consumers? Corporate Fraud and Its Devastating Impacts.* Briefing 4 London: Centre for Crime and Justice Studies.

Sutherland, Edwin. 1949. *White Collar Crime.* New York: Holt, Rinehart, and Winston.

Titus, Richard M. 2001. "Personal Fraud and Its Victims." In *Crimes of Privilege: Readings in White-Collar Crime*, pp. 57–66, edited by Neal Shover and John Paul Wright. New York: Oxford University Press.

Tombs, Steve. 2000. "Official Statistics and Hidden Crimes: Researching Health and Safety Crimes." In *Doing Criminological Research*, pp. 64–81, edited by Victor Jupp, Pamela Davies, and Peter Francis. London: Sage.

Tombs, Steve. 2010. "Corporate Violence and Harm." In *Handbook on Crime*, pp. 884–903, edited by Fiona Brookman, Mike Maguire, Harriet Pierpoint, and Trevor Bennett. Cullompton, UK: Willan.

Tombs, Steve, and Dave Whyte. 2007. *Safety Crime*. Cullompton, UK: Willan.

Tombs, Steve, and Dave Whyte. 2010a. "Reflections upon the Limits of a Concept: 'Victims' and Corporate Crime." *International Journal of Victimology* 8: 184–99.

Tombs, Steve, and Dave Whyte. 2010b. "Crime, Harm, and Corporate Power." In *Crime: Local and Global*, pp. 137–72, edited by John Muncie, Deborah Talbot, and Reece Walters. Cullompton, UK: Willan

Van Wyk, Judy, and Karen A. Mason. 2001. "Investigating Vulnerability and Reporting Behavior for Consumer Fraud Victimization: Opportunity as a Social Aspect of Age." *Journal of Contemporary Criminal Justice* 17: 328–45.

Wells, Celia. 1995. *Negotiating Tragedy: Law and Disasters*. London: Sweet and Maxwell.

Which? 2004. Products Recalls: A Burning Issue. *Which?* Online (March).

White, Rob. 2008. *Crimes against Nature: Environmental Criminology and Ecological Justice*. Cullompton, UK: Willan.

Whyte, Dave. 2004. "All that Glitters Isn't Gold: Environmental Crimes and the Production of Local Criminological Knowledge." *Crime Prevention and Community Safety* 6: 53–63.

Whyte, Dave. 2007. "Victims of Corporate Crime." In *Handbook of Victims and Victimology*, pp. 446–63, edited by Sandra Walklate. Cullompton, UK: Willan.

Yokoyama, Minoru. 2006. "Environmental Pollution by Corporations." In *International Handbook of White-Collar Crime*, pp. 327–46, edited by Henry N. Pontell and Gilbert Geis. New York: Springer.

CHAPTER 5

....

THE COSTS OF
WHITE-COLLAR CRIME

....

MARK A. COHEN

WHILE criminologists rarely think of quantifying crime in monetary terms, to most economists, there is no question that crime costs should be estimated. The study of economics is all about the allocation of scarce resources in society. Since criminal justice policy decisions inevitably involve choices between two or more alternatives, the enumeration of costs and benefits places these alternatives on a level playing field and can help policymakers make more informed decisions that enhance society's well-being.

Section I of this chapter provides background on the scope of white-collar crime and how it is defined here, along with a discussion of the purpose behind estimating the cost of white-collar crime. Section II defines the term "costs" as it is used in this literature and presents a comprehensive taxonomy of crime cost categories. Section III discusses the methodologies used to estimate white-collar crime costs and highlights some of the difficulties of defining and estimating costs. Section IV summarizes what is known and unknown about the costs of white-collar crime, providing national estimates of the costs of white-collar crime in the United States when they are available. A brief final section discusses the major research needed in order to further understand the magnitude of white-collar crime costs and to use these estimates to better inform policy decisions.

To summarize the main points of this essay:

- There are numerous reasons for studying the costs of white-collar crime. Most importantly, it allows policymakers to put harms on an equal footing for purposes of conducting cost–benefit analysis as well as to compare the severity of crimes across types and over time.
- The costs of white-collar crime go well beyond victimization costs. Business, government, and individuals all take costly actions to avoid and prevent becoming victims of white-collar crime. In addition, because many white-collar crimes occur

in the context of legitimate business activities and often no *mens rea* requirement is included in corporate criminal offenses, businesses may take costly actions to avoid becoming charged with a crime. However, little is known about the magnitude of many of these avoidance behaviors.

- In some cases, nonfinancial victimization costs may be a significant consequence of white-collar crime. Costs may include physical or psychological harm to people and the environment in addition to serious harm to public confidence in political and/or economic institutions. However, the evidence on these costs is scant and there are no comprehensive victimization surveys establishing the magnitude of these types of harms.

- Victimization costs that have been quantified total hundreds of billions of dollars annually in the United States. Once the nonquantified crimes are included, the total victimization costs of white-collar crime easily exceed the estimated cost of street crime in the United States. However, because avoidance behavior, precautionary expenditures, and other costs are not fully accounted for, we do not yet know how the total costs of white-collar versus street crime compare.

I. Background on White-Collar Crime: Why Estimate Costs?

There are three main reasons to estimate the costs of white-collar crime. First, policymakers are often interested in comparing the harm caused by different types of crime. For example, almost all theories of punishment rely to some extent on victim harm as one component of the appropriate criminal sanction. Is a financial fraud that costs a victim $10,000 worse than the theft of $5,000 in a home burglary? How do we compare identity theft in which the victim loses $500 to a home-repair scam where the victim loses $1,000? Although one can identify the various harms associated with each type of crime, without a common metric such as dollars, it is difficult to objectively compare these harms.

A second reason for estimating the costs of crime is to compare them to other social ills. For example, D. A. Anderson (2012) estimated that the costs of crime (including street crime) were $3.2 trillion in the United States in 2010—an amount similar to but slightly higher than the $2.7 trillion we spent on healthcare that year. While these comparisons provide few insights into appropriate policies to deal with either crime or health issues, they do provide some context in which to view the magnitude of the crime problem. Over time, it might even be possible to quantify the magnitude of any change in crime. In fact, D. A. Anderson (2012) estimated that the cost per capita of crime in the United States has fallen by about 10 percent from the mid-1990s, even controlling for inflation.

Perhaps the most important use of monetary estimates of the cost of crime is to compare the benefits and costs of alternative crime-control policies. There is no shortage of crime-prevention and crime-reduction programs and proposals that would benefit from government funding. However, the government can only fund so many of these programs. Should we spend more on preventing identity theft or financial fraud? Would spending more government money on white-collar crime enforcement be more or less effective than prevention programs by the private sector? Only by monetizing the cost of crime can one begin to answer these questions. Estimating the costs and benefits of proposed policies is not just an academic exercise: in the United States, federal regulatory agencies are required to conduct cost–benefit analyses as part of their regulatory development process (Office of Management and Budget 2012).

II. Definitions and Categories of Crime Costs

This chapter takes a broad view of white-collar crime, which has been defined as "an illegal act or series of illegal acts committed by nonphysical means and by concealment or guile, to obtain money or property, to avoid the payment or loss of money or property, or to obtain business or personal advantage" (Edelhertz 1970, p. 3). This broad definition would include more than Sutherland's (1949) original focus on crime "committed by a person of respectability and high social status in the course of his occupation" (p. 9). Thus, this definition includes crimes such as fraudulent home repairs and identity theft—crimes committed by individuals who would not normally be associated with a high-status individual. As with both Edelhertz and Sutherland, this definition would include crimes committed by corporations.

At first glance, it would appear that the costs of white-collar crime fall most squarely on its direct victims and can be calculated easily from the amount of money that is taken from them. For example, one might start with the presumption that the cost associated with mortgage fraud is the amount of money that the victim loses through higher interest or fees. But this might be just the tip of the iceberg. If the victim loses a considerable amount of money, it is possible that collateral consequences could accrue, such as a reduced credit rating or higher cost of borrowing. In the worst cases, the victim might lose her home and incur moving costs, higher rent payments, longer commute times, or other serious inconveniences. The victim might also suffer intangible losses such as increased anxiety or fear. Law-enforcement officials might become involved, and if there are criminal-law violations, the criminal justice system might incur costs. Finally, and perhaps as important as any other cost, the fact that all consumers are exposed to the risk of fraudulent mortgage brokers prompts us all to take expensive precautions to avoid becoming victimized. We might be less inclined to do business with smaller, newer, yet legitimate companies or individuals who we fear might be defrauding us and thus pay a "risk premium" for doing business with more established institutions. Worse yet, some consumers might simply refuse to purchase a home and continue to rent due to their fear of being victims of fraudulent mortgage lenders. Put differently, the threat of being a white-collar crime victim might cause many members of the public to lose faith in governmental and/or economic institutions (see, e.g., Shover, Fox, and Mills 1994; Meier and Short 1995). The bottom line is that the costs of white-collar crime are far-reaching—to offenders, victims, and society at large. This section provides definitions to help the non-economist wade through this somewhat unfamiliar territory as well as taxonomy of crime costs.

A. Definitions

As the discussion above begins to suggest, the concept of "cost" is itself difficult to define. Costs do not just appear when a crime is committed—they are the result of decisions by many different parties, including offenders, victims, the government, and society at large. When one party increases the costs associated with crime (or preventing crime), this action will likely have an impact on other parties. Increased government expenditures on reducing insider trading, for example, might not only reduce the costs associated with insider trading victimization, but also reduce investor anxiety and thus induce more consumers to invest their money in the stock market. Moreover, when the government spends tax dollars on police or courts to investigate and/or punish criminal activity, these costs might also deter others from committing crimes—thus reducing victimization costs in the future. Thus, while measuring the costs of crime is largely a static exercise that informs us about the current state of costs and who bears them, the distribution of costs will vary over time depending upon private and public crime-prevention policies and the behavior of potential victims and offenders.

An important issue in estimating the costs of crime is to understand the goals of the decision makers. For example, consider the costs of Internet fraud against a consumer. To make the example more concrete, suppose the average fraud cost the consumer $1,000 out of pocket, resulted in 10 hours of time spent by the victim in dealing with the aftermath of the fraud, and caused mental anguish. As a result of the fraud, assume that the state government loses $200 in tax revenue. A government budget analyst might be interested only in the tax implications of increased fraud enforcement; that is, the cost of increased enforcement and criminal justice costs versus the $200 increased tax revenue from reducing fraudulent behavior. A more informed government policy analyst might go beyond the tax revenue benefits to include the full $1,000 in reduced monetary victimization costs. However, from a social cost–benefit perspective, the full costs of victimization—including the value of the victim's time and mental anguish—should be accounted for. This chapter attempts to be as broad as possible in estimating costs and thus includes all costs of crime while taking care to try to identify who bears those costs. However, as will be shown below, while it is possible to be comprehensive in listing the potential costs of white-collar crime, it is much more difficult to estimate some of the components of crime costs.

One conceptual difficulty in estimating the cost of crime against business is how to value the items taken. If money is taken, the value is straightforward—the face value of the bills. However, if the loss is merchandise, whether the loss should be valued at retail or wholesale depends on the opportunity cost to the victim. If the victim can easily replenish the product and does not lose retail sales, the loss is the cost to the owner—not its retail price. However, if the item is scarce and cannot be readily replaced, the loss is now the full value the owner could have expected to receive. Some crimes against business involve theft of services (e.g., cable television or wireless Internet services) that involve essentially zero marginal costs to the victim and might not have been purchased at all in the absence of the theft. This is only a loss to the company, however, if the user would have actually purchased the service in the absence of the theft. If these services would not have been purchased, it is hard to label this a "cost." This is particularly true with "bootlegged" music and counterfeit luxury goods when the purchaser is aware that the product is a counterfeit—except to the extent the offender would otherwise purchase some of the legitimate product. Of course, in all cases, there may be other more subtle costs associated with the loss, such as diminishing the value of the legitimate product to all law-abiding purchasers or reducing the perceived moral implications of violating the law by the public at large—resulting in even more violations.

One of the most confusing and misunderstood concepts in the cost of crime literature is the difference between "social costs" and "external costs." This distinction is particularly important when assessing white-collar crimes. The traditional economic definition of "social cost" is something that reduces the aggregate well-being of society. However, when an offender swindles $10,000 from an investor, that money changes hands and makes the criminal better off at the expense of the victim. Some economists argue that these "transfers" are not social costs and thus would not include them in an analysis of the costs of crime. Others argue that offenders are not part of the social welfare calculus (and thus we should ignore their welfare gains from stealing). Cohen (2005) argued for the use of another concept for purposes of estimating the costs of crime: "external costs." The "external costs" of crime are imposed on victims who do not voluntarily accept these negative consequences—much like the "externality" of pollution imposes costs on the nearby community. The victim neither asked for nor voluntarily accepted compensation for enduring these losses. Moreover, society has deemed that imposing these external costs is morally wrong and against the law. Ultimately, it is important to identify which concept is being used because they may result in dramatically different cost estimates. In this chapter, the concept of "external costs" is used and transfers are considered to be real costs.

B. Taxonomy of Crime Costs

The costs of crime can be grouped into three major categories (Brand and Price 2000):

1. Costs incurred in anticipation of crime (e.g., prevention),
2. Costs incurred as a consequence of crime (e.g., victimization), and
3. Costs in response to crime (e.g., criminal justice expenditures).

Cohen (2005) provided a detailed taxonomy of individual crime costs based on these more general categories. Table 5.1 summarizes these costs and provides an initial characterization of "who bears the cost" of crime. Regardless of how these costs are grouped, it is useful to start with a comprehensive listing, which allows researchers and policymakers to understand which costs are included and which are not. Few cost–benefit analyses are able to fully monetize all costs and benefits. However, best practice in cost–benefit analysis calls for identifying all costs that have not been monetized so that policymakers can judge the importance of these remaining categories relative to the monetized costs and benefits.[1]

1. *Anticipation of Crime*

The first category, "anticipation of crime," affects virtually all members of society who might be engaged in the activity that is subject to the criminal offense. For example, the existence of identity theft might cause potential victims to both incur "precautionary expenditures," such as purchasing credit monitoring services, and "avoidance behaviors," such as frequently changing their passwords or avoiding Internet purchases. Despite all of these actions, however, potential victims might still suffer residual "fear" of victimization. To operationalize this concept, economists would ask how much potential victims might be willing to pay to reduce the fear of crime after already making precautionary expenditures and taking avoidance behaviors (section III). Some of the costs incurred in anticipation of crime are borne by governmental agencies, businesses, or nongovernmental institutions to help prevent crime. Examples of these activities include consumer protection agencies, consumer education campaigns, and regulatory disclosure requirements.

2. *Consequences of Crime*

Next, we turn to the consequences of crime—initially borne by victims. It is important to note that businesses and governments might also be victims of white-collar crime (although ultimately this cost might be borne by consumers, shareholders, and/or tax-payers). In addition, it is not always the case that the monetary "gain" to the offender from a fraud is equal to the "harm" to the victim. For example, a military contractor who gains a few hundred dollars by using cheaper screws than called for in a contract might cause millions of dollars in harm if an airplane crashes as a result of inferior

Table 5.1 Taxonomy of Crime Costs: Anticipation and Consequences of Crime

Crime Cost Category	Who Bears the Cost
Anticipation of Crime	
Precautionary expenditures	Potential victims
Avoidance behaviors	Potential victims
Fear of crime	Potential victims
Crime-prevention programs	Society/business/government
Consequences of Crime	
Monetary or physical property losses	Victims/insurers/society
Productivity losses	Victims/society/employers
Household service losses/Lost school days	Victims/family/society
Medical and mental health costs	Victim/family/insurers/society
Pain, suffering, and lost quality of life	
• Pain, suffering & lost quality of life	Victim
• Loss of affection/enjoyment, trauma	Victim family
Victim support services	Victim/government/society
Legal costs associated with tort claims	Victim/shareholders/society
Long-term consequences of victimization	Victim/family
Reduced confidence in public & economic institutions	Victim/society
Offender costs	Offender/society
Response to Crime	
Police	Society/government
Prosecution	Society/government
Courts	Society/government
Legal fees	
• Public defenders	Society/government
• Private lawyers	Offenders/shareholders
Criminal sanctions	Society/government/offenders/ shareholders
Victim and witness costs	Victim/witnesses
Jury service	Jurors
Victim compensation	Society/government
Offender costs	
• Productivity	Offender/society
• Injury/death to offender while incarcerated	Offender/society
• Loss of freedom to offender	Offender
• Offender's family	Offender's family/society
Over-deterrence costs	
• Innocent individuals accused of offenses	Innocent "offenders"
• Restrictions on legitimate activities	Society/shareholders
• Costs of additional detection avoidance by offenders	Offenders/shareholders
Justice costs	Society

Source: Adapted from Cohen (2005).

products. In some cases, white-collar crime might not directly harm people at all—but instead harm the environment, endangered species, and so on.

While white-collar crime victims often incur direct monetary losses, other indirect expenses might be incurred, such as lost wages while away from work dealing with the criminal justice system or even medical and/or mental health costs to the extent victims suffer psychological harm from victimization. Although psychological harm might be thought of as typically associated with crimes against the person that result in physical injury, some white-collar victims of fraud, for example, suffer psychological injury (Ganzini, McFarland, and Bloom 1990). In extreme cases, victims who require mental health care might also be unable to perform their normal household services or attend school. Even if mental health or medical costs are reimbursed through insurance or employee benefit programs, society bears the cost through higher insurance premiums. Since the provision of insurance requires administrative (overhead) costs, the loss is even higher than the medical cost itself. In addition to tangible costs incurred by victims (or paid by third parties), "intangible" consequences of crime such as pain, suffering, and reduced quality of life may be quantified in monetary terms (Cohen 2005).

In addition to the victim, the victim's family may incur costs in extreme cases. For example, family members might end up performing household chores that the victim can no longer undertake. Perhaps more likely, family members of victims might also suffer psychologically—whether because of any monetary losses incurred by the victim or mental health damages that cause the family member to lose enjoyment/affection from the victim.

In some cases, support services are available to victims of white collar crime through government as well as private foundations. These services might provide counseling as well as emergency financial assistance. Victims of white-collar crime may bring a private tort action against the offender. These suits involve various legal and court costs—often to third parties and insurance companies. Sometimes class-action lawsuits will be filed on behalf of victims or shareholders of companies engaging in corporate crimes. These legal costs can often represent a significant percentage of victim losses—and in many cases the combined costs incurred by plaintiffs and defendants could even exceed victim losses.

For completeness, and to compare white-collar crime to street crime, table 5.1 includes a category titled "long-term consequences of victimization." For example, there is some evidence that victims of child abuse are more likely to become child abusers themselves. Whether or not any of these types of intergenerational costs exist in the context of white-collar victimization is unknown.

A potentially significant cost of white-collar crime is the fact that the public's confidence in economic and/or political institutions might be significantly harmed in certain cases. Further, these harms might vary depending upon the perpetrator. For example, a $10 million fraud committed by an individual might have different social harm implications compared to a similarly sized fraud committed by a financial institution. Similarly, while both incidents might result in loss of life, a pharmaceutical manufacturer that falsifies test results and markets a drug that carries unreported risks might be viewed differently from an individual healthcare provider who substitutes inferior drugs. Thus, an important unresolved issue is whether or not there is additional harm when a white-collar crime is committed by a large organization as opposed to an individual.

Finally, one of the consequences of crime is the cost incurred by the offender. For example, in perpetrating a fraudulent mortgage operation, the offender might need to rent an office and purchase computer equipment. Some might think that these offender costs are not social costs and that they benefit society because people are employed and businesses earn profits from the sale of the computer equipment; instead, these resources should be considered wasteful as they do not serve any socially beneficial purpose. In addition to such socially wasteful spending, the time the offender spends on illegal behavior could be devoted instead to socially productive activity benefitting society.

3. *Response to Crime*

The most visible response to crime is the criminal justice system—including government expenditures for police, prosecutors, public defenders, courts, prisons, and other non-incarcerative sanctions. In addition to government costs, private costs include expenditures on criminal defense lawyers and time spent by victims, juries, and witnesses dealing with the criminal justice system. Victim compensation programs have also been established in many states to provide monetary assistance to victims of crimes.

Not only does white-collar crime impose costs on the victim, but some costs fall directly on the offender who is apprehended and subject to the criminal justice system. Other costs are borne by the offender's family. For example, if the offender was working in a legitimate occupation prior to incarceration, he or she will suffer from lost wages while in prison. Regardless of whether or not one wants to include the offender's well-being as part of society's interests, those lost wages are a measure of the productivity loss to society. There is also evidence that incarceration will reduce the future earning capacity of many offenders (particularly white-collar offenders) as they have a more difficult time finding quality employment with a felony record. Potentially more costly is the intangible loss to the family—especially children—of the incarcerated offender.

Another potential offender cost is the value of lost freedom to an incarcerated offender. Beyond the productivity loss, some would argue that society should consider the impact that prison has on the offender. For example, it is possible that alternatives to prison would still meet the goals of punishment at a lower cost. A related and potentially more troubling cost associated with incarceration of offenders is the risk that the prison experience will increase the propensity of the offender to recidivate. To the extent this is true, if one were to compare the cost of imprisonment to the cost of probation (for example), any marginal increase in future crimes might be attributed to the cost of imprisonment.

Finally, two often-overlooked categories of costs are "over-deterrence" and "justice" costs. Over-deterrence costs are collateral consequences of imposing penalties for illegal behavior. First, innocent parties who might be accused of committing a crime will take costly actions to avoid such allegations. This is particularly a problem with many types of white-collar and corporate crime where the underlying activity is often legitimate and provides benefits to society. In fact, many corporate crimes are strict liability offenses not requiring the *mens rea* that is typically associated with street crimes. For example, corporations in the United States can be held strictly (vicariously) liable for the actions of their employees even if they are against company policy. Thus, particularly high penalties for financial fraud, for example, might deter some firms from engaging in socially desirable financing activities that carry with them the risk of an errant employee who subjects the company to criminal prosecution. Even if the company decides to continue this line of business, it might take socially costly actions to avoid the risk of a violation. Thus, the risk of over-deterrence is a real and important consideration in virtually all policies that are designed to reduce white-collar crime.

Finally, "justice" costs are the government's analog to over-deterrence costs—they are primarily determined by society's willingness to take costly precautions to ensure that innocent individuals are not accused of crimes. For example, constitutional protections against self-incrimination or searches and seizures without probable cause are the price we pay for justice and avoiding incrimination of the innocent.

III. Methods of Estimating the Costs of White-Collar Crime

The costs of white-collar crime are notoriously difficult to quantify because victims often do not know they have been subject to a criminal offense. While a victim of robbery or assault is generally aware of his or her victimization and may report it to police or respond to a victimization survey, the company whose product has been counterfeited and the consumer who buys the fake product might have no idea they were victimized. Victims of price-fixing or bid-rigging conspiracies might have no idea they are paying higher prices due to these criminal activities. In some cases, elderly victims of fraud might not realize (or deny) they have been victimized—especially if they suffer from dementia (Templeton and Kirkman 2007).

Researchers have developed numerous methods to estimate the costs of white-collar crime—none of which is perfect. Government surveys have begun to ask a representative sample of households if they were victimized by various types of fraud. Of course, these surveys only capture those who know they have been victimized. Another method often used by government or private trade associations is to rely upon random audits or industry surveys and then apply this figure to aggregate industry or trade data. This approach is commonly used in the area of tax revenues and counterfeit goods. It is also problematic for many reasons. First, except for truly random audits, many of these estimates are based on biased samples, anecdotal evidence, or simply "informed guesses." Often it is difficult to verify the methodology and to know if figures can be compared in any meaningful way. Second, even if accurate, this approach focuses only on the dollar loss to victims and ignores many of the crime costs identified in table 5.1.

To go beyond the pure monetary costs of victimization, economists have applied various survey techniques to estimate the costs of white-collar crimes. The most typical approach is a "bottom-up" estimate of the individual components of the costs of crime included in table 5.1. For example, the Federal Trade Commission (FTC 2003, 2007) commissioned several surveys of identity theft victims and asked them how much was stolen, how much they ultimately had to pay out of pocket, and how much time they spent dealing with the consequences of the theft. Victims of identity theft frequently reported other negative consequences such as being harassed by debt collectors, denied credit cards, utilities cut off, and so forth. Many identity theft victims reportedly suffer psychological harm, including feelings of anxiety, fear, mistrust, and paranoia (Sharp et al. 2004, pp. 132–133). In theory, each of these cost components can be individually estimated and added up to estimate the cost of identity theft. However, all of these "bottom-up" approaches ignore some very important components of the costs of crime—including the "fear of crime," expenditures or actions taken by the public to avoid the risk of crime, as well as any residual loss to the community such as business development.

An alternative approach is to estimate costs from the "top down." One method is to elicit information on the public's willingness to pay (WTP) for reduced crime through carefully designed surveys (Cohen et al. 2004). This WTP method is controversial because it is based on "stated preferences" and not actual market transactions. However, the methodology has become well developed and used by economists to value such diverse amenities and disamenities as pollution, risk of cancer, national security, and protection of endangered species.

In theory, the "top-down" and "bottom-up" approaches should lead to the same estimate if the latter is all-inclusive. Cohen (2010) compared these two approaches in the case of street crimes and concluded that the "bottom-up" approaches thus far have not fully captured the costs of crime.

Piquero, Cohen, and Piquero (2010) used a "top-down" approach to estimate that the public is willing to pay $73 to $87 annually to reduce identity theft by 25 to 75 percent. This translates into a WTP of between $1,526 and $3,842 per identity theft. Table 5.2 reports on the "bottom-up" estimate of the cost of identity theft. According to the FTC (2007, pp. 9–10), while the average identity theft netted the offender $1,882, the out-of-pocket loss to victims averaged $371. Thus, the difference, $1,511 ($1,882–$371), was borne by business. Piquero et al. (2010, pp. 15–16) added $744 as "lost productivity" to this amount based on the average 30 hours spent by consumers in responding to identity theft. Adding these three costs together yields an estimate of $2,626. However, this total does not include intangible costs to victims, costs of avoidance, government-related criminal justice costs, and so on.

One important limitation of the WTP studies conducted to date is they have not assessed the cost categories included in the respondent's WTP. For example, we do not know whether respondents considered the fact that lowering identity theft might also

Table 5.2 Cost of the Average Identity Theft (in 2007 USD)

Component	Cost
Victim	
Out-of-pocket costs	$371
Lost productivity	$744
Intangible costs (including collateral consequences such as denial of credit, mental anguish, etc.)	?
Private Business	
Out-of-pocket costs	$1,511
Public	
Criminal justice costs	?
Avoidance Costs	
Insurance, monitoring services, actions taken to avoid victimization	?
Fear to General Public	?
Community Costs	
Lost productivity, resources devoted to criminal activity	?
Justice Costs	
Criminal-justice–related costs to protect the innocent	?
Over-Deterrence	
Lost business opportunities, inconvenience to legitimate credit card customers, etc.	?
Total	$2,626

Source: Piquero, Cohen, and Piquero (2011).

lower the cost of insurance, lower the need for law-enforcement expenditure (which might lower their taxes), and so forth. Thus, it is not entirely clear whether the estimated $1,526 to $3,842 WTP should be added to estimates of the business and government costs of identity theft. Piquero et al. (2010) assumed that respondents only considered the cost to victims and thus subtracted this amount from the WTP estimate before adding it to the cost to business. Thus, they estimated the total cost of identity theft to range from $2,760 to $5,076. Even this estimate, however, might ignore many of the cost categories shown in table 5.2 such as offender costs and over-deterrence. Thus, further research in this area is clearly needed.

One of the difficulties in assessing the costs of white-collar crime is identifying the appropriate unit of measure. With street crime, costs are typically measured based on the impact associated with the criminal offense—an "incidence-based" approach. Thus, if an assault occurred in 2013 but results in a lifetime of medical costs to the victim, costs are added up over the entire lifetime of the victim (discounted to present value) and counted as a cost incurred as a result of crime in 2013. This approach would normally be followed in the case of white-collar crime. However, many crimes themselves occur over a long time period. For example, a Ponzi scheme or antitrust violation might continue for many years and losses grow over time. Once exposed, it might be impossible to identify one year in which the crime occurred and to apportion costs to any particular year.

Another complication in measuring the costs of white-collar crime is that often the costs and benefits of the offense are dispersed over many victims as well as unintended beneficiaries. The recent LIBOR scandal is a good example of this problem. Numerous banks have admitted they falsified reports, causing the LIBOR interest rate to be lower than it should have been.[2] While the offenders presumably benefited from this crime, it hurt mortgage lenders and others who received less interest on loans than they otherwise would. Yet, many people benefited from lower LIBOR rates—including homeowners who were unintended beneficiaries. A similar argument has been made in the case of lost tourism following the BP Deepwater Horizon spill—much of the lost revenue was offset by revenue to other tourist destinations. While economists argue that the net losses are relevant for purposes of estimating "social costs" of these type of events, the "external-cost" approach taken in this chapter would consider only the cost to victims as being relevant and would not offset them for purposes of estimating the costs of white-collar crime.

IV. What Is Known (and Unknown) About the Costs of White-Collar Crime?

As discussed earlier, white-collar crimes such as fraud and antitrust violations are notoriously difficult to quantify because victims often do not know they have been subject to a criminal offense. Even for those crimes where victims know their losses, there is no central government survey or reporting mechanism to tally these crimes or their costs. Many of the estimates that have been made are of questionable methodological rigor; in fact, some appear to be more folklore than empirically based. This section recaps what is known and attempts to identify the largest gaps in our knowledge about the costs of white-collar crime.

Table 5.3 summarizes the best available and most recent estimates of the costs of white-collar crime in the United States, as well as significant areas where no national cost estimates are available. It *only* includes the cost of victimization—not society's response or attempts to prevent victimization. Table 5.3 also identifies when other significant "non-monetary" costs of victimization might need to be added to these estimates; for example, when victimization might involve reduced quality of life.

Table 5.3 Victim Costs of White-Collar Crime in the United States

Crime Type	Monetary Costs (billions of $)	Year	Source	Additional Nonmonetary Costs Likely
Occupational theft and employee fraud	$800	2012	(1)	no
Tax gap	$385	2006	(2)	no
Counterfeit products and piracy	$200–$250	2005	(3)	yes
Health insurance fraud	$80	2011	(4)	no
Computer security and viruses	$53	2005	(5)	no
Identity theft	$45–64	2010	(6)	yes
(identity theft w/o cost to business)	($1–$32)			
Retail fraud	$40.6	2010	(7)	no
Insurance fraud (non-healthcare)	$40	2011	(4)	no
Consumer fraud	$4–$12	2011	(8)	yes
Financial, securities, mortgage fraud	?	?		yes
Antitrust	?	?		no
Gvt. contract fraud, kickbacks, etc.	?	?		yes
Environmental crimes	?	?		yes
Worker safety crimes	?	?		yes
Food and drug crimes	?	?		yes
Import/export violations	?	?		yes

Notes: Costs associated with anticipation of and response to crime are not included. See table 5.1 for a full list of crime cost categories.

Sources: (1) Association of Certified Fraud Examiners (2012); (2) Internal Revenue Service (2012); (3) U.S. Special Trade Representative (2005); (4) FBI (2011); (5) Anderson (2012); (6) Lexis-Nexis (2011); Piquero, Cohen, and Piquero (2011); (7) Lexis-Nexis (2011); (8) K. B. Anderson (2013).

A. Occupational Theft and Employee Fraud

Perhaps one of the largest white-collar crimes is occupational theft and employee fraud. The Association of Certified Fraud Examiners (ACFE 2012) estimated that the average business loses about 5 percent of total revenue to employee frauds such as theft of cash receipts or inventory, false invoices, and other forms of skimming. This translates into about $3.5 trillion worldwide or $800 billion in the United States in 2012. It is important to note, however, that the ACFE study is not a representative sample of companies; it is based on the subjective assessment of the fraud problem as reported by certified auditors.

B. Tax Evasion

The Internal Revenue Service (2012) estimates the "tax gap" to be $450 billion in under-paid taxes in 2006—with $385 billion expected to be uncollected after $65 billion in late payments and penalties are paid. Some of this amount no doubt overlaps with the reported crime costs elsewhere in this chapter, although it is impossible to know how much overlap exists. For example, if an employee embezzles money by setting up a fraudulent invoicing scheme, that income is unlikely to be reported. However, the company that incurs the loss might reduce its taxes by deducting these expenses on its income statements. Thus, this type of fraud might increase the tax gap. On the other hand, a company that fraudulently bills Medicare for medical procedures not incurred might report that income on its taxes. In that case, to the extent the income never should have been received by the company, taxes might have been overpaid. Thus, it is impossible to know how much overlap occurs between the tax gap and other crime cost estimates.

C. Counterfeit Products and Piracy

According to an Organization for Cooperation and Development (OECD 2007) study, up to $200 billion in counterfeit goods entered international trade in 2005. This figure does not include items produced and sold domestically and digital products distributed over the Internet (such as downloaded music and movies). A report by the U.S. Special Trade Representative (2005) estimated that the "losses to U.S. industries" from counterfeit products range from $200 to $250 billion. While this number is reported in table 5.3, its estimation methodology is unclear.

As the OECD (2007 p. 11) study noted,

> Counterfeiting and piracy are not victimless crimes. The scope of products has broadened from luxury watches and designer clothing to include items which impact directly on personal health and safety—including food, pharmaceutical products, and automotive replacement parts.

The report goes on to identify additional costs imposed by counterfeiting, including anticipation costs (e.g., modification of products and/or packaging of legitimate products to make them difficult to copy or fake, awareness campaigns to reduce consumer demand), consequences (e.g., defective automotive replacement parts, ineffective pharmaceutical products), and response (e.g., government and private investigation and litigation).

Although one cannot claim that terrorism is a cost of white-collar crime, an important and interesting link has been made between organized crime and terrorist organizations and white-collar crimes such as counterfeiting and piracy. According to Interpol, terrorist organizations have used counterfeit goods to help finance their operations; for example, the sale of fake Nike t-shirts in New York City helped to finance the 1993 World Trade Center bombing (National Chamber Foundation 2005). A recent Rand Corporation study (Treverton et al. 2009) further documents the extent to which organized crime and terrorist organizations use counterfeit products to support their activities.

D. Insurance Fraud

Health insurance fraud has often been cited as accounting for 10 percent of all healthcare expenditures in the United States. Yet, Hyman (2002, p. 159) found that there is virtually no statistical evidence for this figure. Indeed, its origins appear to have been little more than a guess by unidentified individuals surveyed for a Government Accountability Office report. Further, as Hyman (2002) pointed out, the few studies that are based on randomized audits often include "unnecessary" or "undocumented" services—which are not followed up for verification or any fraud determination. The Federal Bureau of Investigation (FBI) found that health insurance fraud accounts for 3 to 10 percent of all healthcare expenditures, and ultimately reported an estimate of $80 billion (3 percent of expenditures) but they did not reference a source. D. A. Anderson (2012, p. 239) cited a higher figure based on the midpoint of this range: 6.5 percent. In addition to health insurance fraud, the FBI estimates about $40 billion annually is stolen through insurance frauds such as false or exaggerated claims, phony insurance companies, and other schemes (D. A. Anderson 2012, p. 240). There is little information on the source of this estimate from the FBI. Thus, while these figures are shown in table 5.3, their reliability is uncertain.

E. Retail Fraud

Lexis-Nexis (2011, p. 34) surveyed 1,000 retail establishments in the United States and estimated the magnitude of retail fraud—including stolen merchandise, bounced checks, and fraudulent transactions. The survey excludes employee or insider fraud. It estimated that retail fraud cost merchants approximately $40.6 billion in 2011—down significantly from $191.3 billion in 2009 and $70.04 billion in 2010.

F. Identity Theft

Piquero et al. (2010, p. 17) estimated the cost of identity theft to range between $22.9 and $42.1 billion in 2007. As discussed above, this includes out-of-pocket losses to business and consumers, the value of lost time to consumers, as well as the public's WTP to reduce identity theft. Thus, it is the only estimate in table 5.3 that goes beyond direct monetary losses. More recently, Lexis-Nexis (2011, p. 9) reported on a 2010 survey of identity theft in which they estimated a total of 8.1 million victims and an average total cost of $4,607 ($3,976 cost to companies and $631 to consumers). The cost to companies included their cost of dealing with the fraud—not just any monetary loss. They also found the average identity theft victim spent 33 hours dealing with the fraud (at a cost of $874 based on hourly wage rates in the United States).[3] Based on their WTP survey, Piquero et al. (2010, p. 15) estimated the average intangible costs associated with identity theft to range from $134 to $2,450. Adding intangible costs to the Lexis-Nexis survey results in an estimated cost per identity theft ranging between $5,615 and $7,931. Multiplied by 8.1 million victims, the annual cost in 2010 was approximately $45 to $64 billion. However, about $32 billion of this amount represents the cost to private business, which overlaps with the loss from retail fraud.

G. Consumer Fraud

The FTC commissioned a survey of over 3,600 consumers in 2011 that asked respondents to state whether they had been victimized by fraud—including products paid for that were not delivered, unauthorized charges, credit repair services that were not delivered, product claims that were not as described (e.g., fraudulent weight loss or health benefit claims), foreign lottery prizes, and so forth. K. B. Anderson (2013) summarized the findings of the FTC study, where an estimated 37.8 million cases of fraud were reported with a *median* monetary loss to victims of $100. Multiplying these two figures results in total losses of $3.8 billion. However, since some victims lose considerably more than this and losses are bounded by zero, the mean loss is likely to be higher than the median. While we do not know the "average" loss to fraud victims in the United States, the 75th percentile in the FTC study was reported to be $300. Thus, even if the average loss were $300, total monetary losses are under $12 billion. Accordingly, table 5.3 estimates these losses at $4 to $12 billion. However, whatever the out-of-pocket monetary losses to victims of consumer fraud, total losses are likely to be higher if one were to include the value of time dealing with complaints, trying to obtain refunds, replacing the product with a legitimate product, and so on.[4] More recently, Cohen (2015) estimated the WTP to reduce a consumer fraud to be $1,200. Based on this WTP estimate, total costs to society from consumer fraud would be approximately $45 billion—about four to 10 times victim losses.

H. Computer Security and Viruses

D. A. Anderson (2012, pp. 227–28) reported on a 2005 FBI survey of computer security breaches and estimated annual costs to business to be $53 billion after adjusting costs downward to account for thefts and fraud accounted for elsewhere. This only includes the costs associated with repairing the breaches, not prevention activities.

I. Financial, Securities, and Mortgage Fraud

There are no comprehensive estimates of the costs of financial frauds such as insider trading, Ponzi schemes, securities frauds, and mortgage fraud. Depending upon the fraud, victims vary from everyday consumers who are cheated out of small (or large) amounts of money to sophisticated investors, corporations, shareholders, or governments. Some of these frauds involve a few hundred or thousand dollars; others involve billions. While the number of victimizations is unknown, Cohen (2015) estimated the WTP to reduce one financial fraud victimization to be $12,000.

J. Other Regulatory Offenses

Numerous regulatory offenses may result in criminal sanctions. The major categories without national cost estimates include (1) antitrust, (2) environmental crimes, (3) worker safety offenses, (4) food and drug violations, (5) import or export violations, and (6) government contract fraud (aside from healthcare fraud included in table 5.3). Although national estimates are not available, individual cases can be quantified, and costs in some cases are enormous (Cohen 1989). For example, government military contractors might fraudulently bill for services not performed or substitute inferior products that could result in significant loss of life or property. While the offenses are not included in the monetary estimates in table 5.3, their total costs could easily dwarf those that are included. For example, the 2010 Deepwater Horizon oil spill in the Gulf of Mexico (which ultimately resulted in criminal pleas by both BP and Transocean) resulted in billions of dollars in costs—including loss of life, lost oil, cleanup costs, natural resource damages, and lost income to local businesses. As another example, the recent LIBOR scandal has likely resulted in hundreds of billions of dollars of losses to governments and businesses that paid higher interest rates than they otherwise would have.

Note that many regulatory offenses may be prosecuted either criminally or under civil/administrative authority. This highlights an important definitional issue when it comes to economic and regulatory crimes. Unlike street crime, often fraud and regulatory violations can be classified as civil, regulatory, or criminal—and the decision about how to label the incident is largely up to the prosecutor. Among the factors that might be considered by prosecutors are the weight of evidence, the burden/cost of proving criminal intent, and the willingness of corporate officials to "settle" the case if criminal charges are not pursued. In addition, the standards of corporate criminal liability in the United States are such that "intent" does not necessarily have to be shown as it does in most criminal charges filed against an individual. Thus, there is likely to be considerably more discretion in whether or not to prosecute a corporation as opposed to an individual (see Benson and Cullen 1998). One simple way to estimate the costs of white-collar crime such as this would be to only include offenses where criminal sanctions are imposed. But that would result in an underestimate of the true cost of corporate and white-collar crime. Further, it is not how we estimate the cost of street crime—where all criminal victimizations are included even if no offender is ever charged with a crime.

Some crimes with very large intangible costs, like betrayal of the public trust, may never be monetized. Nevertheless, we can conceptualize the social or external costs of these crimes. For example, the cost of exporting illegal military equipment to hostile nations might be thought of as the risk of harm to our national security. However, quantifying that risk and the possible harm is another matter.

V. Conclusion

D. A. Anderson (2012, pp. 245–49) estimated the cost of street crime victimization in the United States to be approximately $833.8 billion—including $40.2 billion in stolen or damaged property, $37.4 billion in medical costs and lost wages, and $756.2 billion in the value of injuries and death. As shown in table 5.3, the monetary cost of occupational theft and employee fraud alone has been estimated to be $800 billion. While there might be some overlap in table 5.3, total victimization costs exceed $1.6 trillion and many costly crimes are not included in these estimates. More importantly, aside from identity theft, none of the costs included in table 5.3 include intangible losses such as the psychological impact of victimization. Thus, it is clear that the costs of victimization from white-collar crime far exceed that of street crime in the United States. Far less is known, however, about the relative costs associated with society's anticipation of and response to white-collar crime.

This chapter has attempted to bring together a vast literature and data sources to paint a broad picture of the costs of white-collar crime. It should be clear to the reader that, while a comprehensive framework and approach can be sketched out, there is much to be done to fully understand the costs and consequences of white-collar crime. Future research needs to focus on three important areas: (1) the collateral consequences of victimization (including psychological impact), (2) the costs of avoidance and precautionary expenditures taken to prevent victimization, and (3) the costs incurred by individuals and businesses in preventing a false accusation or accidental commission of a white-collar crime (i.e., potential costs of over-deterrence). Without such information, criminal-justice policymakers will be at a huge disadvantage in prioritizing their expenditures and designing socially desirable policies to combat this costly social ill.

Notes

1 For more details on the use of cost–benefit analysis in the study of street crime, see Roman, Dunworth, and Marsh (2010) and Farrington, Welsh, and Sherman (2001). Boardman et al. (2011) is a standard economics textbook on cost–benefit methodology.

2 See for example, "The LIBOR Scandal: The Rotten Heart of Finance." *Economist*, July 7, 2012.

3 The average earnings for a full-time, year-round worker in 2010 were $55,093, or $26.49 per hour. Consumer Population Survey, U.S. Census Bureau, 2010. http://www.census.gov/hhes/www/cpstables/032011/perinc/new04_001.htm

4 Anderson (2012, p. 241) estimates the loss to victims to be $55 billion by combining the FTC with the "average losses" reported by the National Consumers League. However,

consumers who proactively contact the NCL fraud alert website are likely to be those most injured and motivated to complain—a less representative sample than the randomly selected set of consumers from the FTC survey. Note that Anderson (2013) is not the same author as Anderson (2012).

REFERENCES

Anderson, David A. 2012. "The Cost of Crime." *Foundations and Trends in Microeconomics* 7: 209–65.

Anderson, Keith B. 2013. *Consumer Fraud in the United States, 2011: The Third FTC Survey.* Staff Report. Washington, D.C.: Bureau of Economics, Federal Trade Commission.

Association of Certified Fraud Examiners. 2012. *2012 Report to the Nations on Occupational Fraud and Abuse.* Austin, TX: Author.

Benson, Michael T., and Francis T. Cullen. 1998. *Combating Corporate Crime: Local Prosecutors at Work.* Boston: Northeastern University Press.

Boardman, Anthony, David Greenberg, Aidan Vining, and David Weimer. 2011. *Cost–Benefit Analysis.* Upper Saddle River, NJ: Prentice Hall.

Brand, Samuel, and Richard Price. 2000. *The Economic and Social Costs of Crime.* London: Home Office.

Cohen, Mark A. 1989. "Corporate Crime and Punishment: A Study of Social Harm and Sentencing Practice in the Federal Courts, 1984–1987." *American Criminal Law Review* 26: 605–60.

Cohen, Mark A. 2005. *The Costs of Crime and Justice.* New York: Routledge.

Cohen, Mark A. 2010. "Valuing Crime Control Benefits Using Stated Preference Approaches." In *Cost–Benefit Analysis and Crime Control,* pp. 73–118, edited by John K. Roman, Terence Dunworth, and Kevin Marsh. Washington, D.C.: Urban Institute.

Cohen, Mark A. 2015. "Willingness to Pay to Reduce White Collar and Corporate Crime," *Journal of Benefit-Cost Analysis* 6: 305–24.

Cohen, Mark A., Roland T. Rust, Sara Steen, and Simon Tidd. 2004. "Willingness-to-Pay for Crime Control Programs." *Criminology* 42: 86–106.

Edelhertz, Herbert. 1970. *The Nature, Impact, and Prosecution of White-collar Crime.* Washington, D.C.: U.S. Government Printing Office.

Farrington, David P., Brandon C. Welsh, and Lawrence W. Sherman, eds. 2001. *Costs and Benefits of Preventing Crime.* Boulder, CO: Westview Press.

Federal Bureau of Investigation. 2011. *Financial Crimes Report to the Public, Fiscal Years* 2010–2011. Available at http://www.fbi.gov/stats-services/publications/financial-crimes-report-2010-2011/financial-crimes-report-2010-2011

Federal Trade Commission. 2003. *Identity Theft Survey Report, prepared by Synovate.* Available at http://www.ftc.gov/os/2003/09/synovatereport.pdf

Federal Trade Commission. 2007. *2006 Identity Theft Survey Report,* prepared by Synovate. Available at http://www.ftc.gov/os/2007/11/SynovateFinalReportIDTheft2006.pdf

Ganzini, Linda, Bentson McFarland, and Joseph Bloom. 1990. "Victims of Fraud: Comparing Victims of White Collar and Violent Crime." *Bulletin of the American Academy of Psychiatry and Law* 18: 55–63.

Hyman, David A. 2002. "HIPAA and Health Care Fraud: An Empirical Perspective." *Cato Journal* 22: 151–78.

Internal Revenue Service. 2012. "The Tax Gap." Available at http://www.irs.gov/uac/The-Tax-Gap

Lexis-Nexis. 2011. *2011 True Cost of Fraud Study*. Dayton, OH: Author.

Meier, Robert F., and James F. Short, Jr. 1995. "The Consequences of White-Collar Crime." In *White-Collar Crime: Classic and Contemporary Views*, 3rd ed., pp. 80–104, edited by Gilbert Geis, Robert F. Meier, and Lawrence M. Salinger. New York: Free Press.

National Chamber Foundation. 2005. *Why Are Counterfeiting and Piracy Costing the American Economy?* Washington, D.C.: Author.

Office of Management and Budget. 2012. *2012 Report to Congress on the Benefits and Costs of Federal Regulations and Unfunded Mandates on State, Local, and Tribal Entities*. Washington, D.C.: Author.

Organization for Economic Cooperation and Development. 2007. *The Economic Impact of Counterfeiting and Piracy*. Paris: Author.

Piquero, Nicole Leeper, Mark A. Cohen, and Alex R. Piquero. 2010. "How Much Is the Public Willing to Pay to be Protected from Identity Theft?" *Justice Quarterly* 28: 437–58.

Roman, John K., Terence Dunworth, and Kevin Marsh, eds. 2010. *Cost–Benefit Analysis and Crime Control*. Washington, DC: Urban Institute.

Sharp, Tracy, Andrea Shreve-Neiger, William Fremouw, John Kane, and Shawn Hutton. 2004. "Exploring the Psychological and Somatic Impact of Identity Theft." *Journal of Forensic Science* 49: 131–36.

Shover, Neal, Greer Litton Fox, and Michael Mills. 1994. "Long-Term Consequences of Victimization of White-Collar Crime." *Justice Quarterly* 11: 75–98.

Sutherland, Edwin H. 1949. *White Collar Crime*. New York: Holt, Rinehart and Winston.

Templeton, Virginia H., and David N. Kirkman. 2007. "Fraud, Vulnerability and Aging." *Alzheimer's Care Today* 8: 265–77.

"The LIBOR Scandal: The Rotten Heart of Finance." 2012. *Economist* (July 7). Available at http://www.economist.com/node/21558281

Treverton, Gregory F., Carl Matthies, Karla J. Cunningham, Jeremiah Goulka, Greg Ridgeway, and Anny Wong. 2009. *Film Piracy, Organized Crime, and Terrorism*. Santa Monica, CA: Rand Corporation.

U.S. Census Bureau. 2010. *Consumer Population Survey*. Available at http://www.census.gov/hhes/www/cpstables/032011/perinc/new04_001.htm

U.S. Trade Representative. 2005. *2005 Special 301 Report*. Washington, D.C.: Author. Available at http://www.ustr.gov/archive/assets/Document_Library/Reports_Publications/2005/2005_Special_301/asset_upload_file195_7636.pdf

PART III

UNDERSTANDING WHITE-COLLAR CRIMINALS

CHAPTER 6

WHO COMMITS WHITE-COLLAR CRIME, AND WHAT DO WE KNOW ABOUT THEM?

PAUL M. KLENOWSKI AND KIMBERLY D. DODSON

ALTHOUGH it has been determined that overall crime rates have continued to decrease for traditional street crimes during the past decade, the opposite is true regarding many acts of white-collar crime. Recent figures indicate that from 2007 to 2011 certain white-collar crimes were on the rise, including healthcare fraud (7 percent), corporate fraud (27 percent), securities and commodities fraud (34 percent), and mortgage and lending fraud (50 percent) (Federal Bureau of Investigation 2011). Additional statistics suggest that certain types of occupational frauds and abuse, including such offenses as asset misappropriation, falsifying or submitting fraudulent statements, and bribery and corruption, now cost U.S. businesses more than $600 billion annually (Association of Certified Fraud Examiners 2012). Furthermore, recent victimization surveys conducted primarily in Western nations show that white-collar offenses are occurring with greater frequency than conventional street crimes, and more alarmingly, the rates of these white-collar offenses are substantially higher than traditional street crimes of acquisition including burglary, robbery, and theft/larceny (Flatley 2007; Gordon et al. 2007; Levi et al. 2007; Nicholas et al. 2007; van Dijk et al. 2007; Shover and Hunter 2010). One recent U.S.-based victimization survey conducted by the National White-Collar Crime Center found that approximately two thirds (63 percent) of respondents reported being the victim of a white-collar crime (Kane and Wall 2006). Thus, it appears that these specific crimes are a pervasive problem affecting millions of lives globally.

In addition to official statistics, individual cases involving white-collar crime have appeared in daily news coverage with increasing regularity beginning with the significant financial scandals of the early 2000s (Friedrichs 2010). Names such as Ken Lay, Bernie Ebbers, and Bernie Madoff have become synonymous with white-collar crime, and their cases highlight the deleterious impact these types of offenses have had on the world economy. Lay, for example, served as the chief executive officer of the Enron

Corporation, an American energy, commodities, and service company, from 1985 to 2002. After years of manipulating Enron's accounting books to artificially inflate stock prices, Lay, along with a cadre of his chief officers, was arrested and charged with multiple counts of fraud and securities violations. As a result of these illegal acts, Enron was forced to file for bankruptcy protection to the tune of $64 billion, one of the largest bankruptcies in U.S. history. The Enron scandal not only jolted the nation's economy but also destroyed countless lives, costing thousands of people their jobs, pensions, and future economic stability (Friedrichs 2010).

It is important to note that such celebrity cases as these do not accurately reflect the population of those who commit these white-collar offenses. To be more precise, white-collar crime does not always take place on a national stage, nor are these crimes restricted to male corporate executives. For instance, authorities in Dixon, Illinois, recently charged the city comptroller, Rita Crundwell, with misappropriation of funds, embezzlement, and wire fraud. In November 2012, she admitted to stealing $53 million from the city over a twenty-year period. As part of a plea agreement, she pleaded guilty to one count of wire fraud and received a twenty-year sentence (Jenco 2013). The Crundwell case illustrates a valuable point that will be addressed later in this essay: any person—regardless of age, race, gender, class, educational level, or occupational status—can choose to commit a white-collar crime.

In the subsequent pages, we summarize the research that has been conducted about white-collar offenders. Based on our analysis, we offer the following conclusions:

- White-collar crime is a generic, yet relative, term that encompasses a wide array of illicit acts. A more definitive typological scheme, similar to those created for traditional street offenses, must be established and subsequently applied before substantial empirical conclusions can be rendered regarding what know about the large spectrum of offenders whose crimes range from basic identify thefts committed by conmen to highly complex financial frauds committed by corporate elites.
- To date, a significant proportion of the studies conducted have yielded a somewhat consistent demographic profile (i.e., age, race, gender, class, employment status, education level, marital status, community, religion, and familial ties) of the typical white-collar offender. Based on what is known, a considerable percentage of white-collar offenders are gainfully employed middle-aged Caucasian men who usually commit their first white-collar offense sometime between their late thirties through their mid-forties. However, recent research has noted an increase in commission by both females and minority offenders for certain types of white-collar crime. Finally, most offenders appear to hail from middle-class backgrounds, have some level of higher education, are married, and have moderate to strong ties to community, family, and religious organizations.
- Research on the criminal careers of white-collar offenders has determined that they usually have a criminal history, including infractions that span the spectrum

of illegality—ranging from traffic citations to both high-level street and white-collar offenses. The limited body of research on white-collar offenders' lifestyles shows that a majority of them do not engage in an over-indulgence of vice (i.e., drugs, alcohol, prostitution); in fact, it appears that only low-level white-collar offenders make these lifestyle choices.

- Although limited, the research regarding the personality traits of white-collar offenders has provided some promising areas for future analysis. Recent research that examined the five-factor personality trait model determined that white-collar offenders tend to be more neurotic and less agreeable and conscientious than their non-criminal white-collar counterparts. The type A personality research could hold promise for gaining added insights about white-collar offenders, but it has yet to be thoroughly examined.

We begin in section I by offering a brief historical overview of what is meant by white-collar crime, highlighting the problems that continue to plague its application in research. This section concludes by recognizing the importance of studying these offenses by specific type, not merely under the generic term of white-collar crime. In section II, we introduce the importance of assessing what we know about white-collar offenders and the approach we take to address this issue. Sections III, IV, and V then examine what is known, respectively, about white-collar offenders' demographic characteristics, criminal careers and lifestyles, and personality traits. Finally, section VI provides suggestions for future research.

I. WHAT IS WHITE-COLLAR CRIME?

A. Pioneering Efforts to Define the Problem

In 1939, during his presidential address to the American Sociological Society, Edwin H. Sutherland presented his conceptualization of the term "white-collar crime." Sutherland's decision to articulate his ideas about white-collar criminality was the product of his dissatisfaction with the academy's obsession with crimes committed by those of lower socioeconomic status, especially those committed by male juvenile delinquents. He argued that crime was not merely a lower-class phenomenon, and that more attention must be given to those crimes committed by members of the upper class. Sutherland (1949, p. 7) defined white-collar crime as "crimes committed by a person of respectability and high social status in the course of his occupation." He based this definition on his own groundbreaking study of the illegal and unethical conduct of the seventy largest corporations in America, a study that forever altered the landscape of the criminological world by expanding our categories of crime into this new realm of "elite" criminality.

Although it is important to pay homage to Sutherland's pioneering efforts on the topic, his efforts are not without shortcomings. The most notable failures of his work include the following: delineating clearly between the various forms of white-collar crime he examined; considering the influence of corporations over regulatory and legislative processes; and distinguishing between organizational and individual white-collar acts (Meier 2001; Geis 2007; Friedrichs 2010).

There were several immediate post-Sutherland efforts to refine the definition of white-collar crime. For example, Frank Hartung (1950) investigated violators of war-time regulations in the meat industry. He concluded that the actions of these workers, not just executives, could be construed as white-collar crimes, which extended Sutherland's definition beyond those of high social status to include blue-collar workers. In 1953, Donald Cressey also attempted to expand Sutherland's definition by focusing on "trust violating behavior" that occurred in the workplace. He claimed that occupational crimes (i.e., embezzlement) involved three elements: (1) presence of a non-shareable financial problem, (2) an occupational position that provided access to other people's money, and (3) verbalizations to pacify guilt prior to commission (Cressey 1953). Cressey's empirical contribution expanded the conceptualization of white-collar crime by highlighting the difference between corporate crime and what we now refer to as occupational crime. His research provides clear evidence that not all people who commit occupational crimes are affluent business executives; in fact, most people who hold a position of trust and fiduciary responsibility within any given occupation have the potential to commit an occupational crime, regardless of socioeconomic status. Cressey's work irrevocably changed how the criminological world viewed offenses committed in the workplace and provided the notion that anyone, including minimum-wage employees, can commit an occupation-related white-collar offense.

To provide a more concise picture of what is known about white-collar offenders, the research reviewed for this essay centers upon a definition of white-collar crime that is similar to the work of Cressey, a definition that is occupationally focused. Thus, white-collar crime, as discussed in the subsequent pages, is defined as criminal acts committed by an individual who takes advantage of his or her position of fiduciary trust and responsibility for either a personal or corporate gain.

B. Making the Case for Typologies

Aside from Hartung and Cressey, only two other noteworthy attempts to redefine white-collar crime occurred between 1950 and 1970. The first was by Geis in 1962, who suggested that the term "white-collar crime" should only be applied to violations committed by corporations, not by an individual (Geis, 1992). Edelhertz (1970) disagreed with Geis and suggested that the term be broken down into categories to allow for empirical investigation of the different forms of white-collar crime, especially those committed by individual offenders (Geis 1992). Building upon the suggestion of Edelhertz, Clinard and Quinney (1973) formally proposed separating white-collar offenses into two distinct categories for the purpose of gaining a better understanding of those who engaged in these types of crimes. Their categories are (1) occupational crimes, which are crimes carried out by any person at any level within an organization for his or her own purposes or gain (i.e., employee and against employer) and (2) corporate crimes, which are crimes committed by corporate officials for the benefit of or in the interest of the corporation. To date, many scholars contend that Clinard and Quinney's distinction has been the single most influential typological scheme of white-collar crime ever presented, a true turning point in regard to how these offenses should be examined (Geis 1992; Friedrichs 2010).

Since Clinard and Quinney's novel proposal, others have attempted to formulate their own typologies for studying white-collar crime (see Green 1990; Coleman 2006; Shover and Hochstetler 2006; Hagan 2008). It should be noted that the purpose of a criminological typology is to organize patterns of crime and criminal behavior into homogenous categories to assist with both the explanation of the illicit behavior and the appropriate response to it (Gibbons 2002; Dabney 2005). Most recently, Friedrichs (2007, 2010), building upon the work of his predecessors, suggested that white-collar crime is merely a generic term that encompasses a vast array of illegal activity; thus, to understand those who commit such acts, a crime typology is needed to permit proper empirical examination. Friedrichs provided basic criteria for differentiating between the types of white-collar crime that occur. His specific criteria consisted of the following: (1) the context in which the illegal activity occurred, including the setting (e.g., corporation, government office) and the level within the setting or the status or position of offender (e.g., wealthy or middle class, executive or employee); (2) the primary victims (e.g., general public or individual clients); (3) the principal form of harm (e.g., economic or physical injury/death); and (4) the legal classification of the act (e.g., fraud, embezzlement, and insider trading). Based on these criteria, Friedrichs has created a practical typology comprising five distinctive categories of white-collar crime that permits a more concise empirical assessment of these various offenses. His typology consists of the following: (1) corporate crime, (2) occupational crime, (3) governmental crime, (4) state or corporate crime/crimes of globalization/high-finance crimes, and (5) enterprise/contrepreneurial/avocational crime (see Friedrichs 2010, pp. 7–8, for a complete overview).

Although some scholars may disagree with his typological categories, at the least it appears that Friedrichs has created a logical framework that encourages a more thorough analysis of the various types of offenses that have been traditionally classified as "white-collar" crime. By systematically separating white-collar offenses into distinct typologies, more deliberate research can be conducted to understand further the specific kinds of crimes committed within the various occupational sectors (i.e., private, governmental, and nonprofit). Because past research has failed to disaggregate white-collar offenders by specific typologies, the empirical lines have been blurred with regard to what we actually know about these offenders. Research studies have examined a vast array of white-collar offenders that range from telemarketing conmen (see, e.g., Shover, Coffey, and Sanders 2004; Copes and Vieraitis 2009) to individuals who are engaged in legitimate professions but who use their position of trust to commit their crimes (Cressey 1953; Benson 1985; Jesilow, Pontell, and Geis 1993; Dabney 1995; Mason 1999; Gauthier 2001; Willott, Griffin, and Torrance 2001; Evans and Porche 2005; Klenowski 2008). Thus, until more deliberate efforts like Friedrichs' are made to categorize these offenses into discernible types based on agreed-upon empirical criteria, research regarding white-collar crime will only continue to yield limited information regarding those who choose to commit such offenses.

II. WHO ARE WHITE-COLLAR OFFENDERS?

The early literature on white-collar crime contains assumptions about the profile of the typical white-collar offender. Such assumptions were grounded in Sutherland's (1949) original description centering upon the idea that these offenders are highly educated men who belong to the upper ranks of their organizations and who only commit offenses involving their occupations within their respective businesses. Since Sutherland's classic work, scholars have made limited yet empirically productive strides to understand who chooses to commit these types of offenses. Based on our extensive review of the literature, a variety of research methodologies (i.e., both qualitative and quantitative) have been used to draw conclusions about these offenders that range from the professional conman to the corporate executive. More specifically, it appears that certain research methods have yielded a large percentage of what is known about white-collar offenders. Key examples include (1) case studies (Geis 1967; Simpson and Piquero 2001; Faulkner et al. 2003; Cullen et al. 2006); (2) historical ethnographies (Vaughan 1996; Lee and Ermann 1999; Vaughan 2007); (3) reviews of autobiographical accounts (Shover and Hunter 2010); (4) secondary data analyses (Pogrebin, Poole, and Regole 1986; Wheeler, Weisburd, and Bode 1988; Daly 1989; Scott 1989; Weisburd, Chayet, and Waring 1990; Weisburd, Wheeler, Waring, and Bode 1991; Benson and Moore 1992; Benson and Kerley 2001; Weisburd, Waring, and Chayet 2001; Lewis 2002; Holtfreter 2005; Shover and Hochstetler 2006; Alalehto and Larsson 2011); (5) comprehensive literature reviews (Elliott 2010; Ragatz and Fremouw 2010); (6) surveys (Collins and Schmidt 1993; Walters and Geyer 2004; Wells 2004; Blickle et al. 2006; Kane and Wall 2006; Poortinga, Lemmen, and Jibson 2006; Listwan, Piquero, and Van Voorhis 2010); and (7) in-depth qualitative interviews (Zietz 1981; Benson 1985; Jesilow et al. 1993; Dabney 1995; Mason 1999; Willott et al. 2001; Gauthier 2001; Shover et al. 2004; Evans and Porche 2005; Bucy, Formby, Raspanti, and Rooney 2008; Klenowski 2008; Copes and Vieraitis 2009; Klenowski, Copes, and Mullins 2011).

In this chapter, a comprehensive review of the post-Sutherland research regarding what we actually know about white-collar offenders will be discussed. In particular, three broad categories of known offender characteristics that have been examined since the late 1970s will be presented in sections III, IV, and V. These categories are white-collar offenders' demographic characteristics, criminal careers and lifestyles, and personality traits.

III. Demographic Characteristics of White-Collar Offenders

The social background and demographic characteristics of white-collar offenders are notably different from what is considered typical for traditional street-level thieves and common criminals (Shover and Hunter 2010). Both crime categories truly represent a broad spectrum of offenses and offender types, and this poses significant problems when attempting to draw legitimate comparisons between the two groups (Friedrichs 2010). Moreover, demographic differences are also quite profound when comparing types of white-collar offenders. For example, white-collar conmen who commit such acts as telemarketing fraud and identity theft vary greatly demographically compared with those who have legitimate occupations and use their positions of trust to embezzle from their company (Shover et al. 2004; Copes and Vieraitis 2009; Shover and Hunter 2010). In addition, other problems exist when comparing white-collar crimes by type, since each offense category encompasses diverse illegalities and is strongly correlated with one's position within one's respective company (Daly 1989; Weisburd et al. 1990, 1991, 2001). Based on prior criminological research, it appears that with some exceptions (i.e., identity thieves and telemarketing fraudsters), most conventional street criminals tend to commit more of the traditional street crimes (e.g., theft, burglary, and robbery), whereas white-collar offenders tend to engage in various forms of corporate and occupational-related offenses (e.g., embezzlement, fraud, asset misappropriation, and trade violations) (Leap 2007). However, some scholars have determined, based on how one chooses to define both street crime and white-collar crime, that it is not uncommon for street offenders to commit white-collar offenses and for white-collar offenders to engage in more traditional street crimes (Daly 1989; Weisburd et al. 1990, 1991; Benson and Moore 1992; Weisburd et al. 2001; Lewis 2002; Shover and Hochstetler 2006; Copes and Vieraitis 2009; Shover and Hunter 2010).

That stated, the following demographic information regarding white-collar offenders has been extracted from a narrow body of research consisting of a small group of studies with limited samples of participants. Thus, the information presented here should be interpreted cautiously as a mere foundation for future white-collar crime research.

A. Age

Historically speaking, the age of onset remains one of the strongest predictors of criminal activity. Decades of research on conventional street crime have consistently revealed that a large percentage of persons who commit these offenses begin doing so in their adolescent years (Shover and Hochstetler 2006). However, this is not the case for white-collar offenders. Research consistently demonstrates that these offenders tend to be considerably older, on average, and tend to commence their criminal activity later in life than the common street offender. In fact, most studies show that the majority of white-collar offenders are arrested, prosecuted, and convicted for their first offense anywhere between their late thirties to their mid- to late forties (Wheeler et al. 1988; Weisburd et al. 1990, 1991; Benson and Moore 1992; Benson and Kerley 2001; Weisburd et al. 2001; Lewis 2002; Walters and Geyer 2004; Holtfreter 2005; Shover and Hochstetler 2006; Ragatz and Fremouw 2010; Alalehto and Larson 2011). This finding should come as no surprise, since legitimate employment opportunities are often restricted by age, education, and prior work experience (Green 1990; Wells 1992; Holtfreter 2005; Friedrichs 2010). Thus, it might be that the opportunity that attracts these offenders generally does not become accessible until after they obtain a legitimate profession and amass years of service, which results in a later age of onset (Shover and Hochstetler 2006).

However, when white-collar crime types were compared, lower-level offenses such as embezzlement consistently appear to have a lower age of onset (Pogrebin et al. 1986; Wheeler et al. 1988; Weisburd et al. 1991, 2001; Lewis 2002; Poortinga et al. 2006). Most scholars contend that typical embezzlers tend to occupy lower-level positions within an organization; thus, embezzlers would be younger, since most people begin their professional careers as entry-level employees. Furthermore, prior research suggests that a moderately significant correlation exists between the offender's age and the level of sophistication of white-collar offenses committed, a point that would benefit from further examination (Weisburd et al. 1991; Benson and Moore 1992; Benson and Kerley 2001; Weisburd et al. 2001; Shover and Hochstetler 2006).

B. Race

With respect to race, most research indicates that conventional street crimes tend to be concentrated in lower-class settings and are committed by minority offenders from lower-class backgrounds (Braithwaite 1985; Benson and Kerley 2001; Friedrichs 2010; Parker 2013). However, the research regarding race and white-collar crime commission seems to be ambiguous. Some prior research suggests that white-collar offenders tend to be predominately white, especially when examining higher-level corporate federal offenses (e.g., antitrust, Securities and Exchange Commission [SEC] violations) (Pogrebin et al. 1986; Wheeler et al. 1988; Weisburd et al. 1991; Weisburd et al. 2001; Benson and Kerley 2001; Walters and Geyer 2004; Poortinga et al. 2006; Ragatz and Fremouw 2010). One notable exception focused on the accounts of forty-two sanctioned physicians from California and New York (Jesilow et al. 1993). Jesilow et al.'s results show that a significant percentage of non-white physicians (both foreign and American born) were responsible for a considerable portion of medical-related frauds. One hypothesis regarding this unique finding is that these particular doctors focused their practices in urban, low-income areas where oversight was closely regulated, and a majority of the funds were derived from federal and state social assistance programs (Jesilow et al. 1993). In addition, in their comparison of the characteristics of federal offenders convicted in U.S. district courts for both street and white-collar crimes between 1995 and 2002, Shover and Hochstetler (2006) discovered that roughly 48 percent of convicted street offenders and 32 percent of white-collar offenders were non-white (i.e., Hispanic or African-American), indicating that a larger-than-expected portion of federal white-collar offenses are committed by non-whites.

Aside from the aforementioned exceptions, it appears that the remaining research has determined that when lower-level white-collar crimes were examined (e.g., identity theft, embezzlement, and check fraud), African-Americans represented a more significant percentage of the offender population (Daly 1989; Lewis 2002; Shover and Hochstetler 2006; Copes and Vieraitis 2009). According to Uniform Crime Report (UCR) data, it appears that African-Americans are proportionately overrepresented for white-collar crime arrests (i.e., over 25 percent) (Federal Bureau of Investigation 2011). Some scholars contend that the reason for this overrepresentation lies in the fact that African-Americans tend to commit lower-level offenses unrelated to a legitimate occupation—offenses that are more likely to be reported, investigated, and officially processed by the authorities (Steffensmeier 1989; Lewis 2002; Friedrich 2010). In addition, some researchers argue that if the limited amount of data that we do have suggest that minorities are overrepresented for lower-level white-collar offenses, then whites may also be overrepresented for mid- to high-level occupational offenses (Weisburd et al. 1991, 2001; Shover and Hochstetler 2006). Regardless of these prior findings, a more concerted effort to investigate the relationship between race/ethnicity and white-collar offense type should be conducted before firm empirical conclusions regarding race and white-collar crime can be offered.

C. Gender

As is the case with street crime, females make up only a fraction of the arrests and convictions for white-collar offenses (Dodge 2009). However, a significant amount of evidence suggests that women are becoming increasingly involved as perpetrators of white-collar crimes (Albanese 1993; Lybarger and Klenowski 2001; Haantz 2002; Lewis 2002). The results of one particular 20-year longitudinal study of white-collar data from California determined that although men committed the majority of the 12,238 white-collar offenses analyzed, a considerable proportion of white-collar offenses (e.g. embezzlement, forgery, fraud) were committed by women both in and out of the workplace (Lewis 2002). To date, the bulk of the research has shown that women tend to commit higher percentages of lower-level white-collar crimes, especially such crimes as embezzlement, asset misappropriation, and embezzlement compared to other forms of white-collar crime (Pogrebin et al. 1986; Wheeler et al. 1988; Daly 1989; Weisburd et al. 1991; Benson and Kerley 2001; Weisburd et al. 2001; Holtfreter 2005; Simon and Ahn-Redding 2005; Poortinga et al. 2006; Copes and Veraitis 2009). Although no single reason can be pinpointed for the greater percentage of involvement in lower-level offenses, some scholars believe that this trend is a result of the continued male dominance of corporate America (Daly 1989; Steffensmeier 1993; Forsyth and Marckese 1995; Dodge 2009).

Other scholars contend that crime commission might be based purely on occupational opportunity (Green 1990; Holtfreter 2005; Shover and Hochstetler 2006). However, as the women of females into corporate America continues, one should anticipate that their patterns of involvement in occupational-related forms of white-collar crime will continue to increase and could one day rival their male counterparts for certain types of offenses (Dodge 2009; Klenowski, Copes, and Mullins 2011). For example, in regard to lower-level types of occupational white-collar crimes committed in the workplace (e.g., embezzlement), it has been determined that women are now responsible for a significant percentage of these types of offenses (Benson and Simpson, 2009). One analysis of UCR data for the specific crimes of fraud, embezzlement, and forgery/counterfeiting from 1943 to 1991 supports the claim that women's involvement in these specific types of white-collar offenses has been gradually increasing over time due in large part to their increased participation in the workforce (Forsyth and Marckese 1995). Lybarger and Klenowski (2001) found similar trends regarding the significant increase of female involvement in the same UCR offense categories from 1980 to 2000 and concluded that opportunity in the workplace opens the door for increased involvement in certain white-collar offenses. Thus, based on these analyses, if trends continue in this direction, female rates of criminality for these three offense categories will eventually equal that of their male counterparts. However, until more gender-specific research is conducted on the various aspects of female white-collar criminality, especially their involvement in higher-level crimes committed in the workplace (e.g., SEC violations, tax fraud) along with their specific motivations for commission, data regarding their involvement will continue to yield limited and ambiguous conclusions.

D. Class

As decades of criminological research have revealed, conventional street offenders tend to hail disproportionately from poor and working-class backgrounds and, according to official statistics, a significant percentage of street crimes are committed by minority offenders (Benson and Moore 1992; Benson and Kerley 2001; Shover and Hochstetler 2006). However, in regard to the relationship between white-collar crime and the social class of the offender, the research findings tend to be mixed. As previously noted, considerable debate has ensued since the time of Sutherland regarding whether only those from the upper strata of society are capable of committing white-collar offenses. In recent years, the work of numerous cohorts of white-collar scholars has provided a more decisive position on this topic. Most scholars now agree that in the broadest application of the term "white-collar crime," a large percentage of these offenders are gainfully employed and are members of the middle class—a finding that has been consistently supported in the research (Cressey 1953; Daly 1989; Weisburd et al. 1991; Mason 1999; Benson and Kerley 2001; Weisburd et al. 2001; Benson 2002; Holtfreter 2005; Shover and Hochstetler 2006; Shover and Hunter 2010). For example, researchers who analyzed the data from original Yale Study have collectively arrived at the same conclusion that most white-collar crimes are committed by members of the middle class. In fact, most analyses of this dataset confirm that managers and their subordinates, and not owners of the elite social classes, are often more directly implicated in the most serious white-collar acts (Wheeler et al. 1988; Daly 1989; Weisburd et al. 1991; Benson and Kerley 2001; Weisburd et al. 2001). This discovery seems logical since managers control key aspects of the organizational structure along with resource allocation and distribution for the day-to-day operations of their companies. Other scholars' efforts have supported the findings of the Yale analyses regarding the social class of white-collar offenders (see Pogrebin et al. 1986; Mason 1999; Lewis 2002; Piquero and Benson 2004; Poortinga et al. 2006; Shover and Hochstetler 2006; Shover and Hunter 2010; Ragatz and Fremouw 2010).

Most recently, researchers have attempted to appropriately categorize the social class of the wide spectrum of occupational offenders as "privileged" (Shover and Hochstetler 2006; Shover and Hunter 2010). The so-called privileged class includes gainfully employed individuals whose occupations range from low-level clerical staff to those who work in certain professions (e.g., doctors, lawyer, and accountants) to corporate executive officers. This categorization attempts to validate the prior research by solidifying the notion that white-collar offenders tend to be products of the middle and upper classes and are usually employed in what are referred to as "respectable" occupations within corporate America, many of which require certain standards for employment. The remaining members of society are employed in what is labeled as "dirty work" or the working-class occupations, which refers to jobs that most people understand must be carried out but are undesirable (e.g., construction worker, nursing home attendant, trash collector) (Shover and Hochstetler 2006; Shover and Hunter 2010). This recent attempt to categorize those who commit these occupational offenses as "privileged" provides a practical conceptual framework regarding the social class of "most" (i.e., middle and upper classes) occupational offenders. However, this categorization fails to adequately account for the countless acts of white-collar crime that are committed by both ordinary lower-class street offenders (who may or may not be employed) and those who are employed in the "dirty" working-class professions, two groups that commit a significant portion of white-collar offenders (see Lewis 2002; Shover et al. 2004; Copes and Vieraitis 2009). Thus, to eliminate future confusion resulting from comparisons of unemployed fraudsters with those who commit their crimes while legitimately employed, future research efforts should attempt to delineate between white-collar crime offense types, especially those committed by occupational offenders of all social class backgrounds, not just those of the privileged classes. Moreover, white-collar offenses committed by conmen and street offenders should be examined separately from the latter so that a more decisive understanding can be gathered regarding the variations (e.g., demographic variables and personality traits) between offender types, including information about their social class.

Overall, based on decades of more current and empirically focused efforts, it appears that Sutherland's claim that white-collar crimes are only committed by the elite in corporate America has been challenged and reopened for further scholarly debate. In fact, recent research (i.e., the past thirty years) has indicated that the bulk of those who choose to commit occupational white-collar crimes do in fact hail from the middle and upper-middle classes. However, the aforementioned results must be interpreted cautiously since these findings may be a function of the paucity of data available on white-collar crimes and the lack of accessibility to white-collar offender populations. In addition, it would be realistic to assume that most white-collar crime scholars would contend that the relationship between social class and white-collar criminality is relative and depends almost exclusively on how one chooses to define white-collar crime. Thus, until further research is conducted with more specific and mutually acceptable definitional and typological parameters, no definitive conclusions can be provided regarding the correlation between social class and white-collar criminality.

E. Other Demographic Variables

With respect to employment status, white-collar offenders are more likely to be employed, especially since employment is a necessary condition for many of these types of offenses (Green 1990; Wells 1992; Kerley and Benson 2001; Benson 2002; Weisburd et al. 2001; Shover and Hochstetler 2006). Those convicted of white-collar offenses who were unemployed would not meet most definitional schemes of an "occupational" white-collar offender; consequently, these offenders should be categorized as non-occupational offenders and assessed separately from the former. As previously mentioned, limited empirical value can be attained by comparing characteristics of legitimately employed professionals (e.g., doctors who commit Medicaid fraud) with conmen (e.g., telemarketers). Unfortunately, one of the pitfalls of the prior research in white-collar crime is that it fails to make this distinction (Jesilow et al. 1993; Shover et al. 2004).

In regard to education, the research shows that white-collar offenders, including some considered conmen (i.e., telemarketers), are more likely to be educated, with the completion of at least some college coursework (Weisburd et al. 1991; Benson and Moore 1992; Benson and Kerley 2001; Weisburd et al. 2001; Willott et al. 2001; Benson 2002; Shover et al. 2004; Holtfreter 2005; Poortinga et al. 2006; Shover and Hochstetler 2006; Ragatz and Fremouw, 2010). Those offenders found to be the least educated are those who occupy entry-level and clerical positions and commit such crimes as embezzlement and low-level frauds (Pogrebin et al. 1986; Daly 1989; Weisburd et al. 1991; Weisburd et al. 2001; Benson 2002).

White-collar offenders are also more likely to be married (some more than once), have children, and have what's considered relatively "stable" family situations (Pogrebin et al. 1986; Daly 1989; Benson and Kerley 2001; Weisburd et al. 2001; Benson 2002; Walters and Geyer 2004; Shover and Hochstetler 2006; Copes and Vieraitis 2009). This should be no surprise, especially since most of these offenders tend to commit their offenses later in life (Benson 2002). As for the role of religion, a few studies have found that white-collar offenders, compared to street offenders, have stronger community and church affiliations (Weisburd et al. 1991; Benson and Kerley 2001; Weisburd et al. 2001).

Last, there is limited empirical evidence regarding the differences in family backgrounds of street and white-collar criminals. For example, studies show that street criminals are more likely to come from single-parent households (Schroeder, Osgood, and Oghia 2010) while most white-collar criminals tend come from two-parent households (Shover et al. 2004; Shover and Hochstetler 2006). In addition, white-collar offenders have reported that their fathers were the principal source of income and that their financial circumstances growing up were secure and, in many cases, comfortable (Benson and Kerley 2001; Shover et al. 2004; Shover and Hochstetler 2006). Street criminals have reported that their mothers were the primary source of income and that their fathers were absent from the home, which meant their financial circumstances growing up were largely insecure and tenuous (National Institute of Justice 2013; Parker 2013). Finally, there appears to be significantly less abuse and criminality in the background of white-collar offenders compared to street offenders. According to one analysis, street offenders were nearly three times more likely to have a convicted offender in their immediate family while growing up, and 18 percent were abused or neglected as children compared to 6 percent of white-collar offenders (Benson 2002). Again, these findings should only be viewed as a foundation for future research; limited conclusions regarding these demographic variables should be made until further examination can be provided.

IV. Criminal Careers and Lifestyles of White-Collar Offenders

The examination of demographic characteristics undoubtedly puts us closer to formulating a more accurate understanding of white-collar offenders, but these factors only provide part of the picture. As the realm of criminological inquiry continues to evolve, more purposeful efforts to examine additional factors beyond demographic characteristics have provided new insights regarding the typical white-collar offender. Two such key areas of inquiry are information regarding the criminal career and lifestyle choices of these offenders. Although both areas require further empirical scrutiny, some practical information regarding white-collar offenders' criminal careers has yielded some promising suggestions, and this information has been summarized below.

A. Criminal Career

White-collar offenders have traditionally been stereotyped as one-time offenders who, when apprehended, never commit another offense (Green 1990). Recidivism rates for white-collar offenders usually are significantly lower than the comparable rates for conventional offenders largely because known risk factors for recidivism are less common among these white-collar criminals (Shover and Hochstetler 2006). However, research shows that these offenders have more in common with street offenders than originally imagined. In multiple analyses of federal court data from the original Yale Study, researchers determined that a significant percentage of convicted white-collar offenders are repeat offenders having multiple prior contacts with the law (i.e., for both white-collar and street-level offenses), with the highest rates found among those convicted of the least sophisticated white-collar offenses (Weisburd et al. 1990, 1991, 2001). The assertion that white-collar offenders are often repeat offenders is also supported by Benson and Moore (1992) and Benson and Kerley (2001) in their reexaminations of Forst and Rhodes' (1990) study of sentencing patterns in eight federal district courts from 1973 through 1978. Both of these secondary analyses determined that white-collar offenders did have prior contacts with the law, especially arrests for minor offenses and previous white-collar criminal activity. Most recently, the Association of Certified Fraud Examiners' (2004) survey of 363 perpetrators convicted of occupational crimes found that 12 percent of respondents had previous criminal histories. However, the results of these few studies, many which examine the same federal sample of offenders, only provide a limited picture of the white-collar offender as a career criminal; thus, further research examining the careers of such offenders is warranted.

B. Lifestyles

Decades of criminological research have revealed that a large percentage of convicted street offenders lead a self-indulgent lifestyle plagued with alcohol, drugs, and other vices (Shover 1996). The underlying issues leading street offenders to a lifestyle of addiction are varied, contradictory, and beyond the scope of this essay. However, although research has revealed a strong correlation between a lifestyle of addiction and the commission of conventional crimes, there is less than moderate support for this claim when examining white-collar offenders. In his groundbreaking work on occupational crime, Cressey (1953, p. 36) determined that "riotous living" was in fact a catalyst for a small proportion of people in his sample. Since Cressey, other scholars have reexamined the role of lifestyle—or what Mason (1999) refers to "life as a party"—and its connection to white-collar criminality (Zietz 1981; Shover et al. 2004; Klenowski 2008; Copes and Vieraitis 2009). The research suggests that the role of a self-indulgent lifestyle of vice (i.e., drugs, alcohol, and gambling) can be found predominately in the words of lower-level occupational offenders and professional conmen, not among mid- to upper-level employees and managers (Shover et al. 2004; Copes and Vieraitis 2009). In fact, one study of forty convicted occupational offenders found that approximately one third admitted they used alcohol and drugs, but they overwhelmingly proclaimed that these indulgences were not the cause of their particular acts (Klenowski 2008). Many of these same offenders reported that their drug and alcohol use was most prominent after the commission of their offense, with almost all referencing their use as a means to deal with the guilt and anxiety they felt after commission. Regardless of these findings, no significant answers can be offered regarding the role of offenders' lifestyles in their white-collar criminality. Future research should look to delineate between offender types (i.e., conman vs. legitimate worker) so more valid and reliable conclusions can be drawn. Moreover, questions regarding other addictive behaviors (i.e., frivolous spending, sexual liaisons) should be included so that a more concise picture of these offenders can be obtained.

V. Personality Traits of White-Collar Offenders

Although there are some notable studies on the demographic characteristics of white-collar offenders, there are fewer studies that have examined the personalities of such offenders. Most of these studies have focused on the five-factor trait model, which is the most widely used and accepted model in the personality literature. The "big five" factors are broad categories of personality traits that consist of openness, conscientiousness, extraversion, agreeableness, and neuroticism (OCEAN) (see McCrae and Costa 1987; Costa and McCrae 1992). Some of the studies on personality and white-collar criminals have examined self-control, which Hirschi (2004) explains was largely developed using the five-factor model. Identifying personality traits related to white-collar offending is important because it could help develop criminal profiles of such offenders and might provide insight into deterring white-collar offenders.

A. Five-Factor Trait Model

To date, three studies have used the five-factor personality model in an effort to identify the personality traits related to white-collar offending (Collins and Schmidt 1993; Kolz 2000; Blickle et al. 2006). One study conducted by Kolz (2000) examined employee theft among 218 individuals working at a women's clothing chain. The participants completed the conscientiousness, agreeableness, and neuroticism scale of the NEO Five-Factor Inventory (Costa and McCrae 1992). Results showed that low levels of conscientiousness and agreeableness were related to higher levels of employee theft.

Collins and Schmidt (1993) compared 365 prisoners convicted of white-collar offenses with 344 individuals employed in upper-level positions of authority. They administered the California Personality Inventory (CPI), which includes items designed to measure responsibility, socialization (e.g., adherence to social norms within an organization), and self-control. Low scores are indicative of a lack of responsibility, inadequate socialization, and low self-control. In addition, Collins and Schmidt (1993) included an Employment Inventory (EI), a personality-based measure designed to measure job stability, conscientious work attitudes and behaviors, and honesty. Both the CPI and EI survey items include measures of the five-factor trait model.

Collins and Schmidt (1993) found that white-collar offenders displayed a greater tendency toward irresponsibility; an inability to adhere to social norms set within the agency; and lower levels of self-control, especially-risk taking behaviors, than individuals working in upper-level management positions. They found that white-collar criminals were more likely than their managerial counterparts to have unstable or spotty job histories; had poor work habits, including a lack of conscientiousness and dependability regarding assigned tasks; and failed to conform to company rules and policies.

Blickle et al. (2006) extended the work of Collins and Schmidt (1993) by comparing 76 incarcerated white-collar offenders and 150 white-collar managers working from various agencies in Germany. They administered a survey including items intended to measure several personality traits such as hedonism, narcissism, and conscientiousness. People who are hedonistic place a high value on material success and individual wealth. Narcissistic individuals demonstrate a pervasive pattern of grandiosity (i.e., inflated self-esteem), a need for admiration, and a general lack of empathy. Those who are conscientious strive for competence, order, fulfillment of duties, achievement, and self-discipline.

Blickle et al.'s (2006) findings showed that white-collar offenders were more hedonistic than the non-criminal managers. Because white-collar offenders placed a higher value on material success, it seems they were willing to pursue it through criminal means if necessary. Narcissistic tendencies were stronger in white-collar criminals than in non-criminal managers. In other words, white-collar offenders' inflated sense of self-worth, coupled with their need to be respected or admired by others, appeared to increase the odds that they would commit white-collar offenses. In addition, their inability to empathize with others freed them from feelings of guilt and shame while allowing them to pursue criminal opportunities. However, contrary to theoretical expectations, the conscientiousness of the white-collar criminals was higher than that of the white-collar managers. Blickle et al. (2006) argued that this finding might not be wholly inconsistent with white-collar offending because white-collar criminals must be conscientious in order to ascend the managerial ranks and gain a position of trust to further their criminal behavior. Therefore, it seems plausible that conscientiousness would be high among white-collar offenders.

Blickle et al. (2006) also hypothesized that white-collar offenders would exhibit lower self-control than white-collar managers. Their operationalization of self-control included behavioral indicators of self-control because Hirschi and Gottfredson (1993) suggested that such indicators were preferable. Specifically, Blickle et al. (2006) created four scenarios that involved a description of a situation in which the actor has the opportunity to cheat a target. Participants were given the choice to cheat (low self-control) or not cheat (high self-control). The lower the score, the less self-control a person showed. As predicted, white-collar criminals demonstrated less behavioral self-control than white-collar managers.

The studies conducted by Kolz (2000), Collins and Schmidt (1993), and Blickle et al. (2006) attempted to identify personality traits that were associated with white-collar offending. In a related study, Listwan, Piquero, and Van Voorhis (2010) examined whether personality traits explained recidivism among a sample of white-collar offenders. They administered a survey to sixty-four inmates convicted of a white-collar crime. They examined four personality subtypes: (1) aggressive (manipulative, hostile, or possess antisocial values); (2) neurotic (highly anxious or insecure, self-conscious, and envious or jealous); (3) dependent (followers); and (4) situational (pro-social and conforming). These subtypes overlap conceptually with the five-factor personality traits.

The results showed that personality traits were significantly related to recidivism among white-collar offenders. More precisely, Listwan et al. (2010) found that the neurotic type had the highest rates of recidivism. Because neurotic individuals are more likely to experience anxiety, envy, and jealousy, they might resort to criminal behavior to offset these feelings. Research also shows that neurotic individuals tend to have trouble controlling their urges and delaying gratification (Thompson 2008).

B. Type A Traits

Taken together, the preceding studies lend support to the hypothesis that the five-factor personality traits help explain white-collar crime. However, Elliott (2010) argued that type A/B personality theory might hold additional promise for understanding the connection between personality and white-collar offending. According to Friedman and Rosenman (1974) in their groundbreaking work on the topic, type A individuals tend to be extremely competitive, to seek out financial gain, to exhibit impatience with others, and to display a chronic sense of urgency and an inability to relax, and often feel the need to challenge other type A people. Put differently, type A individuals tend to be extroverted, aggressive, and competitive and to seek out ways to increase their own financial well-being regardless of the consequences for others.

Although Elliott (2010) did not test her theory directly, she did use empirical research to bolster her claim that type A individuals may be prone to white-collar offending. For example, research shows that the competitive nature of type A individuals, coupled with their drive to succeed, might lead to maladaptive strategies, some of which are criminal (Houston and Snyder 1988; Carducci and Wong 1998). Type A individuals also have an increased propensity for taking financial risks to achieve success and the recognition that such success brings (Carducci and Wong 1998).

Bucy et al. (2008) interviewed forty-five white-collar crime experts in the United States, including federal prosecutors, *qui tam* (whistleblower) real estate agents' attorneys, and private defense attorneys who specialize in defending white-collar criminals. The experts divided white-collar criminals into two groups: leaders and followers. The participants consistently described leaders as having type A personalities; that is, they described leaders as intelligent, arrogant, cunning, successful, greedy, prone to take risks, aggressive, narcissistic, determined, and charismatic. Participants described the followers as less confident, less aggressive, less ambitious, passive, subservient, dominated, gullible, prone to blindly follow others, and less likely to take responsibility for their own actions.

While the research on personality and white-collar offending is sparse, it is clear that personality traits offer important insights for understanding who white-collar offenders are. The research reviewed here demonstrates that white-collar offenders are more likely to score high on the five-factor trait model; that is, they tend to be neurotic and less agreeable and conscientious than their non-criminal white-collar counterparts. The type A personality research could hold promise for gaining added insights about white-collar offenders, although this remains to be empirically tested with white-collar offenders.

VI. Conclusion: Implications for Future Research

Based on the reviewed research, it is apparent that our knowledge about white-collar offenders has increased substantially since Sutherland's groundbreaking efforts. Generations of scholars following in his footsteps have established a foundation of information that others should look to build upon. Thus, we will close our essay by first summarizing what we actually know about these offenders, including their demographic characteristics, patterns of offending, lifestyle choices, and personality traits. Next, we will offer a brief discussion of some of the more profound limitations regarding past and current research in the hopes of inspiring future scholars to address these shortcomings so that we may continue to build a more comprehensive understanding of who these offenders are, and more importantly, why they choose to commit these types of offenses.

A. What Do We Really Know?

With regard to the sociodemographic characteristics of white-collar offenders, the bulk of the research conducted to date has determined that a majority of them are gainfully employed middle-aged Caucasian men who usually commit their first white-collar offense sometime between their late thirties and their mid-forties. However, recent research has also discovered an increase in crime commission by both women and minority offenders for certain types of white-collar crime, especially lower-level frauds and embezzlements. A majority of offenders hail from middle-class backgrounds and have some level of higher education, are married, and have stronger ties to community, family, and religious organizations than traditional street offenders.

With respect to offending patterns, scholars have discovered that most white-collar offenders usually have a history of prior contact with the law, including infractions ranging from misdemeanors to both high-level street and white-collar felony offenses. As for their lifestyle behaviors, research shows that many do not engage in an over-indulgence of vice (i.e., drugs, alcohol, prostitution). In fact, it appears that only low-level white-collar offenders opt to participate in these hedonistic behaviors.

The research regarding the personality traits of white-collar offenders has provided some promising areas for future analysis. Although limited in variety and scope, recent research that examined the five-factor personality trait model determined that white-collar offenders tend to be more neurotic and less agreeable and conscientious than their non-criminal white-collar counterparts, especially in regard to controlling urges and delaying gratification. When compared to non-criminal colleagues, it has been discovered that white-collar offenders have lower levels of self-control, a greater tendency toward irresponsibility, and higher levels of narcissism. In addition, although not fully examined, the type A personality research could hold promise for gaining added insight about white-collar offenders, especially their proclivity toward the acquisition of power and control; however, it must be thoroughly assessed before its empirical worth can be applauded.

Considerable and valuable strides have been made by modern white-collar crime scholars, especially in establishing a baseline of understanding about these offenders. However, considerable work remains to be done before more decisive conclusions can be drawn regarding the various types of offenders who choose to commit these acts. Thus, to add to what is known about white-collar offenders, future scholars must attempt to address the empirical shortcomings of their predecessors—similar to the work that has been conducted on traditional street crime since the early 20th century.

B. Where Do We Go from Here?

With the intent of assisting future white-collar crime scholars, we conclude our essay by listing some of the major issues with the prior research so that continued efforts can be made to build upon what we know about these offenders.

First, a number of previous studies have relied heavily upon the exact same dataset of official records that were compiled as part of an original study undertaken by Yale University (Holtfreter 2005; Leap 2007; Friedrichs 2010). This one dataset has been analyzed numerous times over a thirty-year period (see e.g., Wheeler et al. 1982, 1988; Daly 1989; Weisburd et al. 1990, 1991, 2001). Thus, it should come as no surprise that the authors of these studies drew similar empirical conclusions regarding their demographic findings of white-collar offenders, especially when compared to common street criminals. Although these particular studies have provided new insights about the demographics of white-collar offenders, their results are dated, notably similar, and not applicable to the modern white-collar offender.

Aside from the issue of archaic data, other major limitations were exposed during our review. First, prior research fails to provide information regarding state-level white-collar offenders. Much of the data that exists focuses primarily on federal offenders, with the exception of minimal state-level research. This must be addressed to determine if any notable differences exist between state- and federal-level offenders. Understanding the differences between these different levels of offenders may help us to identify the factors that lead to such offending and to create policies to deter such behavior. Second, there is a noticeable shortage of longitudinal data regarding white-collar offenders from both federal and state jurisdictions (see for exception Lewis 2002). Longitudinal studies may reveal criminal behavior patterns (i.e., traits, sociodemographic variables) that may help to determine whether some white-collar offenders have a history of offending throughout the life course and subsequently could be classified as career criminals (Benson 2002). Based on the diminutive body of research on this topic, it appears that some white-collar offenders have repeated contact with the criminal justice system, with the highest rate found among those who could be classified as "blue-collar" and were convicted of the least sophisticated white-collar crimes (Weisburd et al. 1991; Benson and Kerley 2001; Holtfreter 2005; Shover and Hochstetler 2006; Shover and Hunter 2010). However, these results should be interpreted with caution since there is a lack of sufficient reliable data that would permit truly valid comparisons Third, little is known about white-collar offenders who live outside of major urban centers. Aside from the longitudinal study conducted by Lewis (2002), most of what is known is based primarily upon federal convictions in urban areas; thus, additional data regarding offenders living outside of major metropolitan areas would be beneficial when attempting to assess the importance of class and white-collar criminality. Fourth, previous information on white-collar offenders has been derived solely from a population of convicted offenders—a problem that has consistently plagued the field of criminology (Weisburd et al. 1991). This limitation may be more inherently troublesome when discussing white-collar offenders, since many victims are unaware that a crime has even taken place. Therefore, future research should attempt to include self-report studies of both corporate officers and employees at remaining organizational levels who have avoided arrest and prosecution for occupational offenses, including administrative and regulatory violations. Fifth, no one agency, state or federal, collects consistent information regarding the various forms of white-collar crime, including administrative and civil violations (Friedrichs 2010). In fact, none of the studies examined for this essay included violations of administrative and regulatory laws, both of which comprise various types of serious white-collar offenses. Although formally acknowledged as problematic by many early white-collar crime scholars, little has been done to address the offenses. Until a more concerted effort is made by state and federal officials to gather more detailed and reliable data about these crimes, criminologists will continue to be limited in their abilities to provide more substantial conclusions.

Again, regardless of the various empirical shortcomings of the early studies on white-collar crime analyzed for this essay, the efforts of these early scholars provide an important baseline of understanding regarding what we know about certain types of white-collar crime. However, much controversy remains regarding how white-collar crime should be defined and studied, especially the offense- versus offender-based criteria debate (Edelhertz 1970; Steffensmeier 1989; Shapiro 1990; Geis 1992; Friedrichs 2007, 2010). To date, much of the existing research has favored the former, so it makes up the majority of information compiled about what is known about white-collar offenders. Based on this fact, it appears that Merton (1949, pp. 8–9) might be correct in his statement that academics might have become "imprisoned in the framework of the (often inherited) concepts they use." Thus, we agree with those scholars who assert that the time has come to partition the domain of white-collar offenses into criterion-based typologies so that new data (i.e., demographic and personality-related information) can be amassed and examined regarding these crimes, and more importantly, the offenders who choose to commit them (Braithwaite 1985; Shapiro 1990; Geis 1992; Friedrichs 2010).

ACKNOWLEDGMENTS

We thank Mrs. Linda Cheresnowski, Clarion University-Venango College Librarian, along with Andrey Mojica, undergraduate student at Western Illinois University-Quad Cities, who assisted us on gathering the research for this essay.

REFERENCES

Alalehto, Tage, and Daniel Larsson. 2011. "Who Was the White-Collar Criminal? White-Collar Criminals in Sweden, 1865-1912." In *Capitalism in Business, Politics and Society*, edited by Eugene H. Shelton. Hauppauge, NY: Nova Science.

Albanese, Jay. 1993. "Women and the Newest Profession: Females as White-Collar Criminals." In *Female Criminality: The State of the Art*, edited by Concetta C. Culliver. New York: Garland.

Association of Certified Fraud Examiners. 2004. *Report to the Nations on Occupational Fraud and Abuse*. Austin, TX: Author.

Association of Certified Fraud Examiners. 2012. *Report to the Nations on Occupational Fraud and Abuse*. Austin, TX: Author.

Benson, Michael L. 1985. "Denying the Guilty Mind: Accounting for Involvement in a White-Collar Crime." *Criminology* 23: 66–73.

Benson, Michael L. 2002. *Crime and the Life-Course: An Introduction*. Los Angeles: Roxbury.

Benson, Michael L., and Kent Kerley. 2001. "Life Course Theory and White-Collar Crime." In *Contemporary Issues in Crime and Criminal Justice: Essays in Honor of Gilbert Geis*, edited by Henry Pontell and David Shichor. Upper Saddle River, NJ: Pearson.

Benson, Michael L., and Elizabeth Moore. 1992. "Are White-Collar and Common Offenders the Same? An Empirical and Theoretical Critique of a Recently Proposed General Theory of Crime." *Journal of Research in Crime and Delinquency* 29: 251–72.

Benson, Michael L., and Sally S. Simpson. 2009. *White-Collar Crime: An Opportunity Perspective*. New York: Routledge.

Blickle, Gerhard, Alexander Schlegel, Pantaleon Fassbender, and Uwe Klein. 2006. "Some Personality Correlates of Business White-Collar Crime." *Applied Psychology: An International Review* 55: 220–33.

Braithwaite, John. 1985. "White Collar Crime." *Annual Review Sociology* 11: 1–25.

Bucy, Pamela H., Elizabeth P. Formby, Marc S. Raspanti, and Kathryn E. Rooney. 2008. "Why Do They Do It? The Motives, Mores, and Character of White-Collar Criminals." *Saint John's Law Review* 82: 401–37.

Carducci, Bernardo J., and Alan S. Wong. 1998. "Type A and Risk Taking in Everyday Money Matters." *Journal of Business and Psychology* 12: 355–59.

Clinard, Marshall, and Richard Quinney. 1973. *Criminal Behavior Systems: A Typology*. New York: Holt, Rinehart and Winston.

Coleman, James. 2006. *The Criminal Elite*, 6th ed. New York: St. Martin's Press.

Collins, Judith M., and Frank L. Schmidt. 1993. "Personality, Integrity, and White-Collar Crime: A Construct Validity Study." *Personnel Psychology* 46: 295–311.

Copes, Heith, and Lynne Vieratis. 2009. "Bounded Rationality of Identity Thieves: Using Offender-Based Research to Inform Policy." *Criminology and Public Policy* 8: 237–62.

Costa, Paul T., and Robert R. McCrae. 1992. *Revised NEO Personality Inventory (NEO-PI-R) and NEO Five-Factor Inventory (NEO-FFI) Professional Manual*. Odessa, FL: Psychological Assessment Resources.

Cressey, Donald R. 1953. *Other People's Money: A Study in the Social Psychology of Embezzlement*. Glencoe, IL: Free Press.

Cullen, Frank, Gray Cavender, William Maaskestad, and Michael L. Benson. 2006. *Corporate Crime under Attack: The Ford Pinto and Beyond*. Cincinnati, OH: Anderson.

Dabney, Dean A. 1995. "Neutralization and Deviance in the Workplace: Theft of Supplies and Medicines by Hospital Nurses." *Deviant Behavior* 16: 313–31.

Dabney, Dean A. 2005. "Typologies of Crime and Criminal Behavior." In *Encyclopedia of Criminology*, edited by Richard Wright and J. Mitchell Miller. New York: Routledge.

Daly, Kathleen. 1989. "Gender and Varieties of White-Collar Crime." *Criminology* 27: 769–94.

Dodge, Mary. 2009. *Woman and White Collar Crime*. Upper Saddle River, NJ: Pearson.

Edelhertz, Herbert. 1970. *The Nature, Impact, and Prosecution of White-Collar Crime*. Washington, D.C.: Law Enforcement Assistance Administration, U.S. Department of Justice.

Elliott, Rebecca T. 2010. "Examining the Relationship between Personality Characteristics and Unethical Behaviors Resulting in Economic Crime." *Ethical Human Psychology and Psychiatry* 12: 269–76.

Evans, Rhonda D., and Dianne A. Porshe. 2005. "The Nature and Frequency of Medicare/Medicaid Fraud and Neutralization Techniques among Speech, Occupational, and Physical Therapists." *Deviant Behavior* 26: 253–70.

Faulkner, Robert R., Eric R. Cheney, Gene A. Fisher, and Wayne E. Baker. 2003. "Crime by Committee: Conspirators and Company Men in the Illegal Electrical Industry Cartel, 1954–1959." *Criminology* 41: 511–54.

Federal Bureau of Investigation. 2011. *Financial Crimes Report 2010–2011*. Washington, D.C.: Financial Crime Reports to the Public.

Flatley, John. 2007. "Mobile Phone Theft, Plastic Card and Identity Fraud: Findings from the 2005/06 British Crime Survey." Available at http://www.homeoffice.gov.uk/rds/pdfs07/hosb1007/pdf

Forst, Brian, and William Rhodes. 1990. "Sentencing in Eight United States District Courts, 1973–1978." Ann Arbor, MI: Inter-University Consortium for Political and Social Research.

Forsyth, Craig J., and Thomas A. Marckese. 1995. "Female Participation in Three Minor Crimes: A Note on the Relationship between Opportunity and Crime." *International Journal of Sociology of the Family* 25: 127–32.

Friedman, Meyer, and Ray Rosenman. 1974. *Type A Behavior and Your Heart*. New York: Alfred A. Knopf.

Friedrichs, David O. 2007. *Trusted Criminals: White Collar Crime in Contemporary Society*, 3rd ed. Belmont: Wadsworth.

Friedrichs, David O. 2010. *Trusted Criminals: White Collar Crime in Contemporary Society*, 4th ed. Belmont: Wadsworth.

Gauthier, Deann K. 2001. "Professional Lapses: Occupational Deviance and Neutralization Techniques in Veterinary Medical Practice." *Deviant Behavior* 22: 467–90.

Geis, Gilbert. 1967. "White-Collar Crime: The Heavy Electrical Equipment Antitrust Cases of 1961." In *Criminal Behavior Systems: A Typology*, edited by Marshall Clinard and Richard Quinney. New York: Holt, Rinehart, and Winston.

Geis, Gilbert. 1992. "White-Collar Crime, What Is It?" In *White-Collar Crime Reconsidered*, edited by Kip Schlegel and David Weisburd. Boston: Northeastern University Press.

Geis, Gilbert. 2007. *White-Collar and Corporate Crime*. Upper Saddle River, NJ: Pearson.

Gibbons, Don. 2002. "Typologies of Criminal Behavior." In *Encyclopedia of Crime and Justice*, edited by Joshua Dressler, Vol. 4. New York: Gale Group.

Gordon, Gary, Donald J. Rebovich, Kyung-Seok Choo, and Judith B. Gordon. 2007. *Identity Fraud Trends and Patterns: Building a Data-Based Foundation for Proactive Enforcement*. Utica, NY: Utica College, Center for Identity Management and Information Protection.

Green, Gary. 1990. *Occupational Crime*. Chicago, IL: Nelson-Hall.

Haantz, Sandy. 2002. *Women and White Collar Crime*. National White Collar Crime Center. Available at http://www.nw3c.org/downloads/women_wcc1.pdf

Hagan, Frank. 2008. *Introduction to Criminology*, 6th ed. Los Angeles, CA: Sage.

Hartung, Frank. 1950. "White-Collar Offenses in the Wholesale Meat Industry in Detroit." *American Journal of Sociology* 56: 25–34.

Hirschi, Travis. 2004. "Self-Control and Crime." In *Handbook of Self-Regulation: Research, Theory and Applications*, edited by Roy F. Baumeister and Kathleen D. Vohs. New York: Guilford Press.

Hirschi, Travis, and Michael R. Gottfredson. 1993. "Commentary: Testing the General Theory of Crime." *Journal of Research in Crime and Delinquency* 30: 47–54.

Holtfreter, Kristy. 2005. "Is Occupational Fraud 'Typical' White-Collar Crime? A Comparison of Individual and Organizational Characteristics." *Journal of Criminal Justice* 33: 353–65.

Houston, B. Kent, and Charles R. Snyder. 1988. *Type A Behavior Pattern: Research, Theory, and Intervention*. New York: Wiley.

Jenco, Melissa. "Ex-Dixon Comptroller Gets 19½ Years for $54 Million Fraud." *Chicago Tribune News* (February 14). Available at http://articles.chicagotribune.com/2013-02-14/news/chi-rita-crundwell-sentencing-20130214_1_rita-crundwell-dixon-coffers-paul-gaziano

Jesilow, Paul, Henry Pontell, and Gilbert Geis. 1993. *Prescription for Profit: How Doctors Defraud Medicaid.* Berkeley: University of California Press.

Kane, John, and April Wall. 2006. *The 2005 National Survey on White-Collar Crime.* Fairmont, WV: National White Collar Crime Center.

Klenowski, Paul M. 2008. *Other People's Money: An Empirical Examination of the Motivational Differences between Male and Female White-Collar Offenders.* Ph.D. dissertation, Indiana University of Pennsylvania, Department of Criminology.

Klenowski, Paul M., Heith Copes, and Chris Mullins. 2011. "Gender, Identity, and Accounts: How White-Collar Offenders Do Gender When Making Sense of Their Crimes." *Justice Quarterly* 28: 46–69.

Kolz, Arno R. 2000. "Personality Predictors of Retail Employee Theft and Counterproductive Behavior." *Journal of Professional Services Marketing* 19: 107–14.

Leap, Terry L. 2007. *Dishonest Dollars: The Dynamics of White-Collar Crime.* Ithaca, NY: Cornell University Press.

Lee, Matthew T., and M. David Ermann. 1999. "Pinto 'Madness' as a Flawed Landmark Narrative: An Organizational and Network Analysis." *Social Problems* 46: 30–47.

Levi, Michael, John Burrows, Mathew Fleming, and Matt Hopkins, with the assistance of Kent Mathews. 2007. *The Nature, Extent and Economic Impact of Fraud in the UK.* London, UK: Association of Chief Police Officers. Available at http://www.acpo.police.uk/asp/policies/Data/Fraud%20in%20the%20UK.pdf

Lewis, Roy. 2002. *White-Collar Crime and Offenders: A 20-Year Longitudinal Cohort Study.* San Jose, CA: Writers Club Press.

Listwan, Shelley J., Nicole L. Piquero, and Patricia Van Voorhis. 2010. "Recidivism among a White-Collar Sample: Does Personality Matter?" *Australian and New Zealand Journal of Criminology* 43: 156–74.

Lybarger, Jeff, and Paul M. Klenowski. 2001. "Identifying Trends in White-Collar Crime: A 20-Year Analysis of UCR Data." Fairmont, WV: National White Collar Crime Center.

Mason, Karen. 1999. *Middle-Class, White Collar Offenders: Needy Women, Greedy Men?* Ph.D. dissertation, University of Tennessee at Knoxville, Department of Sociology.

McCrae, Robert R., and Paul T. Costa. 1987. "Validation of the Five-Factor Model of Personality across Instruments and Observers." *Journal of Personality and Social Psychology* 52: 81–90.

Meier, Robert F. 2001. "Geis, Sutherland, and White-Collar Crime." In *Contemporary Issues in Crime and Criminal Justice*, edited by Henry Pontell and David Shichor. Upper Saddle River, NJ: Prentice Hall.

Merton, Thomas. 1949. *Social Theory and Social Structure: Toward the Codification of Theory and Research.* Glencoe, IL: Free Press.

National Institute of Justice. 2013. *Impact of Child Abuse and Maltreatment on Delinquency, Arrest and Victimization.* Available at http://www.nij.gov/topics/crime/child-abuse/impact-on-arrest-victimization.htm

Nicholas, Sian, Chris Kershaw, and Alison Walker. 2007. *Crime in England and Wales 2006/2007, Home Office Statistical Bulletin 11/07.* London: Home Office.

Parker, Wayne. 2013. *Statistics on Fatherless Children in America.* Available at http://fatherhood.about.com/od/fathersrights/a/fatherless_children.htm

Piquero, Nicole L., and Michael L. Benson. 2004. "White-Collar Crime and Criminal Careers: Specifying a Trajectory of Punctuated Situational Offending." *Journal of Contemporary Criminal Justice* 20: 148–65.

Pogrebin, Mark R., Eric D. Poole, and Robert M. Regoli. 1986. "Stealing Money: An Assessment of Bank Embezzlers." *Behavioral Sciences and the Law* 4: 481–90.

Poortinga, Ernest, Craig Lemmen, and Michael D. Jibson. 2006. "A Case Control Study: White-Collar Defendants Compared with Defendants Charged with Other Nonviolent Theft." *Journal of American Psychiatric Law* 34: 82–89.

Ragatz, Laurie, and William Fremouw. 2010. "A Critical Examination of Research of the Psychological Profiles of White-Collar Criminals." *Journal of Forensic Psychology Practice* 10: 373–402.

Schroeder, Ryan D., Aurea K. Osgood, and Michael J. Oghia. 2010. "Family Transitions and Juvenile Delinquency." *Sociological Inquiry* 80: 579–604.

Scott, Donald W. 1989. "Policing Corporate Collusion." *Criminology* 27: 559–87.

Shapiro, Susan. 1990. "Collaring the Crime, Not the Criminal: Reconsidering the Concept of White-Collar Crime." *American Sociological Review* 55: 346–65.

Shover, Neal. 1996. *Great Pretenders: Pursuits and Careers of Persistent Thieves.* Boulder, CO: Westview.

Shover, Neal, Glen S. Coffey, and Clinton R. Sanders. 2004. "Dialing for Dollars: Opportunities, Justifications, and Telemarketing Fraud." *Qualitative Sociology* 27: 59–75.

Shover, Neal, and Andy Hochstetler. 2006. *Choosing White-Collar Crime.* New York: Cambridge University Press.

Shover, Neal, and Ben Hunter. 2010. "Blue-Collar, White-Collar: Crimes and Mistakes." In *Offenders on Offending: Learning About Crime from Criminals,* edited by Wim Bernasco. Devon, UK: Willan Publishing.

Simon, Rita J., and Heather Ahn-Redding. 2005. *The Crimes Women Commit, the Punishment They Receive.* Lanham, MD: Lexington Books.

Simpson, Sally S., and Nicole L. Piquero. 2001. "The Archer Daniels Midland Antitrust Case of 1996." In *Contemporary Issues in Crime and Criminal Justice,* edited by Henry Pontell and David Shichor. Upper Saddle River, NJ: Prentice Hall.

Steffensmeier, Darrell. 1989. "On the Causes of 'White-Collar' Crime." *Criminology* 27: 345–58.

Steffensmeier, Darrell. 1993. "National Trends in Female Arrests, 1960–1990." *Journal of Quantitative Criminology* 9: 411–41.

Sutherland, Edwin H. 1949. *White Collar Crime.* New York: Holt, Reinhart, and Winston.

Thompson, Edmund R. 2008. "Development and Validation of an International Big-Five Mini-Makers." *Personality and Individual Differences* 45: 542–48.

Vaughan, Diane. 1996. *The Challenger Launch Decision: Risky Technology, Culture, and Deviance at NASA.* Chicago: University of Chicago Press.

Vaughan, Diane. 2007. "Beyond Macro- and Micro-Levels of Analysis, Organizations, and the Cultural Fix." In *International Handbook of White-Collar and Corporate Crime,* edited by Henry Pontell and Gilbert Geis. New York: Springer.

Van Dijk, Jan., Robert Manchin, John van Kesteren, Sami Nevala, and Gergely Hideg. 2007. *The Burden of Crime in the EU Research Report: A Comparative Analysis of the European Crime and Safety Survey.* Available at http://www.gallupeurope.be/euics/Xz38/downloads/ EUICS %20%20The%20Burden%20of%20Crime%20in%20the%20EU.pdf

Walters, Glenn D., and Matthew D. Geyer. 2004. "Criminal Thinking and Identity in Male White-Collar Offenders." *Criminal Justice and Behavior* 31: 263–81.

Weisburd, David, Ellen Chayet, and Elin Waring. 1990. "White-Collar Crime and Criminal Careers: Some Preliminary Findings." *Crime and Delinquency* 36: 342–55.

Weisburd, David, Elin Waring, with Ellen Chayet. 2001. *White-Collar Crime and Criminal Careers.* Cambridge, UK: Cambridge University Press.

Weisburd, David, Stanton Wheeler, Elin Waring, and Nancy Bode. 1991. *Crimes of the Middle Class: White-Collar Offenders in the Federal Courts.* New Haven, CT: Yale University Press.

Wells, Joseph T. 1992. Fraud Examination: Investigative and Audit Procedures. Westport, CT: Quorum.

Wells, Joseph T. 2004. *Corporate Fraud Handbook: Prevention and Detection.* New York: John Wiley & Sons.

Wheeler, Stanton, David Weisburd, and Nancy Bode. 1982. "Sentencing the White-Collar Offender: Rhetoric and Reality." *American Sociological Review* 47: 641–59.

Wheeler, Stanton, David Weisburd, Elin Waring, and Nancy Bode. 1988. "White-Collar Crime and Criminals." *The American Criminal Law Review* 25: 331–57.

Willott, Sara, Christine Griffin, and Mark Torrance. 2001. "Snakes and Ladders: Upper-Middle Class Male Offenders Talk About Economic Crime." *Criminology* 39: 441–65.

Zietz, Dorothy. 1981. *Women Who Embezzle or Defraud: A Study of Convicted Felons.* New York: Praeger.

CHAPTER 7

···

WHITE-COLLAR CRIMINALS

*Ethnographic Portraits of Their Identities
and Decision Making*

···

DEAN A. DABNEY

CRIMINOLOGY long has struggled to establish a sense of legitimacy within the scholarly community (Pontell and Geis 2007). Similar to other fields of study, criminology has partitioned itself into subareas in hopes of generating concentrated, statistically rigorous, and cumulative understandings of complex social phenomena. For example, in his 1939 presidential address to the American Sociological Society, Edwin Sutherland coined the term "white-collar crime" and used it as an exemplar of an understudied and underappreciated type of crime in need of added scholarly inquiry (Sutherland, 1940). While Sutherland's impassioned plea carved out a new conceptual space for the field and stimulated much substantive debate, a review of the literature reveals that white-collar offending remains a relatively understudied and underappreciated subarea of criminology.

Analyses seeking to identify the most influential books in criminology or criminal justice, either in terms of citations generated (Gabbidon and Martin 2010) or as ranked by modern-day scholars (Vito and Tewksbury 2008), yield sparse representation for white-collar crime monographs; only Sutherland's 1949 text *White Collar Crime* is represented on the list. Cohn, Farrington, and Wright's (1998) longitudinal analysis of top criminology and criminal justice journals revealed that the hybrid category "white-collar crime/organized crime/corporate crime" yielded the lowest percentage of published articles of the seven substantive areas that they operationalized. Similarly, their parallel analysis of the scholars most frequently cited in top journals identified very few people who have earned a solid reputation as white-collar crime researchers.

Comprehensive reviews of the white-collar crime literature by Braithwaite (1985) and Geis (1985, 1988) reveal a paucity of data-driven research on the topic. Geis (1985, 1988) broke the history of white-collar crime inquiry down into three eras: 1939–1963, 1964–1975, and 1976–1988. While he noted an uptick in the research effort during the liberal era that spanned the mid-1960s to the mid-1970s, the overall levels during this era or any other era do not even approach what one observes for other crime types such as murder, assault, sexual violence, robbery, burglary, common property crime, or public order crime (Dabney 2013).

This essay seeks to provide a historical review of the individual and organizational ethnographic work on white-collar criminal offending. As the subtitle indicates, it reviews individual-level inquiries derived from interviews, observations, and archival data on known white-collar offenders. This tradition of research can be traced back to Cressey's (1953) interviews with embezzlers and extends through modern qualitative investigations such as Klenowski's (2012) work on incarcerated white-collar criminals. This brand of ethnographic research should be quite familiar to the readers of this Handbook, as it grows directly from the sociological and anthropological disciplines and is a tried-and-true facet of the white-collar crime research landscape.

The reader may find a bit more awkward the inclusion of other empirical works under the heading of "organizational ethnographies." Given the organizational context in which much white-collar crime occurs, a number of empirical works on the topic of white-collar offending have adopted a corporate- or collective-level unit of analysis, seeking to theorize the culture of criminality. This latter category, which I am calling organizational ethnography, can be traced to Sutherland's (1949) archival review of misconduct among a sample of the largest U.S. corporations in the 1940s and includes recent case studies on the criminogenic culture within NASA (Vaughan 2006) and scandalous conduct within the fertility clinics of California (Dodge and Geis 2003). Some of these empirical and theoretically informed endeavors, such as the work of Dodge and Geis or Vaughan, fit within the anthropological or sociological tradition of organizational ethnography as championed by Geertz (1988) and van Maanen (1979), in that the theorizing is inductive in nature, devoid of quantitative analysis, and rich with unmistakably ground-level reflexivity.

Conversely, it may strike readers as odd to see some of the works included in this essay, especially since the work of scholars such as Sutherland (1949) and Clinard and Yeager (1980) appears to bear little resemblance to what social science scholars include under the heading of ethnographic work, given that their research endeavors include the conversion of evidence into numerical form, the use of correlational and other computational methods, and findings presented as statistical coefficients. However, as a close reading of these works clearly shows, their data were uniformly derived from fieldwork within organizations (including such techniques as face-to-face interviews, direct observation, and document review) followed by the rigorous recording and coding of this source material. The methodologies they employed were in many ways inductive and interpretivist in nature, even though other parts of their analytical approach are more typical of the positivist tradition. The contention here is that these works spring from interpretive practices, informed by thick description efforts and grounded theorizing; thus it is reasonable to include them under the umbrella of organizational ethnographies. This broadened application of the term "organizational ethnography" is in line with the mission statement of the newly formed *Journal of Organizational Ethnography*, inasmuch as the inaugural editor's introduction states

> We recognize that ethnography is a contested term, and we acknowledge the growth in recent times in the new and somewhat diverse ways in which ethnographic research is now conducted. Our use of the terms ethnography is therefore broad based, and loosely defined. We do not seek to use the journal to demarcate or draw fine distinctions between what is, and what is not, ethnography. The journal is primarily interested in receiving high-quality organizational ethnographies, so-called "thick" descriptive studies, informed by robust empirical and theoretical underpinnings that examine, critique or challenge the "received wisdom" of current "knowledge claims" within the field. (Brannan, Rowe, and Worthington 2013, pp. 7–8)

This new tradition reflects an ongoing effort to blend the ethnographic traditions of anthropology and sociology with those of the organizational and managerial sciences (Cefkin 2009; Yanow 2009; Ybema 2009). In an effort to provide a broad treatment of the topic, these organizational ethnographies constructed in the tradition of the organization sciences commonly associated with the business discipline, as opposed to the more familiar social science disciplines, are included in the current discussion.

That said, this essay excludes loosely structured case studies that seek to provide largely descriptive accounts of single instances of corporate wrongdoing. Anthologies such as the ones produced by Punch (1996), Mokhiber (1988), or Gerber and Jensen (2007) are excluded. Also excluded are the insightful but heuristic case studies often found in white-collar crime textbooks or monographs, such as Geis's (2007) analysis of the Moeves Plumbing Company as an example of the occupationally related dangers to which workers can be exposed. Case studies such as this do not contain the level of systematic inquiry or theory development commonly associated with ethnographic studies. Also omitted from this review are journalistic accounts such as Broad and Wade's (1982) work on scientific misconduct and Stewart's (1991) exposé on the savings and loan scandal of the 1980s. Trade books written by industry insiders—such as Sarna's (2010) account of the Bernie Madoff case or Stern's (1976) account of the Buffalo Creek flood disaster—also are omitted from the analysis. While informative, these journalistic accounts and trade books tend to lack empirical rigor and theoretical bases. Conversely, this essay does cover rigorously designed and implemented individual and organizational ethnographies and case studies published as selections within anthologies, such as Ermann and Lundman's (2002) six editions of *Corporate Crime and Governmental Deviance* and similar research-driven readers, including Pearce and Snider (1995), Pontell and Shichor (2001), and Shover and Wright (2001). Finally, the text excludes purely deductively conceived and quantitatively delivered studies such as the work of Hollinger and Clark (1983), Weisburd, Waring, and Chayet (2001), or Piquero and Benson (2004).

Scholars have noted that for a variety of reasons qualitative studies tend to make up a majority of the data-driven inquiries into individual or organizational white-collar offending (for examples of this observation, see Clinard and Yeager 1978; Friedrichs 2010; Levi 1995; Pontell and Geis 2007; Shapiro 1980; Shichor 2009). Meager levels of federal funding, a paucity of large and representative datasets, and the practical difficulties involved in entering corporate bureaucracies to access proprietary data have been proposed to account for the traditional and ongoing reliance on qualitative research designs among scholars seeking to advance our understanding of the nature and dynamics of white-collar offending. As Presser (2010) reminds us, the published accounts of known offenders, while few in number, provide rich detail on how and why complex criminal acts are perpetrated. Given the complex and hidden nature of white-collar offending, the necessity of qualitative work is all the more obvious. That said, we are only beginning to grasp the behavioral dynamics and underlying cognitive mechanisms associated with white-collar offending. As such, we only have scratched the surface in identifying the relevant recurring relationships and theorizing about their antecedents and connections. Ethnographic inquiry thus remains a valuable means through which we can advance our understanding of white-collar crime. Describing ethnographic inquiry, Shover noted that "it offers the opportunity to understand the abstract in human terms. When the theoretical focus shifts to individuals, foundational assumptions usually are explicit or readily apparent to all" (Shover 2012, p. 141).

In this regard, the goal of this essay is to provide a historical account of published individual- and organizational-level ethnographies that privilege white-collar offenders. With many potential theoretical and empirical horizons ripe for future exploration, it draws upon a rational choice framework in hopes of illuminating what Diane Vaughan astutely calls "the situated individual action in a structure/culture/agency nexus that influences interpretation, meaning, and action at the local level" (Vaughan 1998, p. 23). For heuristic purposes, the essay partitions the history of ethnographic work on white-collar offending into four eras, as shown in table 7.1.

Section I discusses ethnographic work done during the Formative Era, a period beginning in the late 1940s and running into the early 1960s. During these early years, luminaries such as Edwin Sutherland, Donald Cressey, Marshall Clinard, and Richard Quinney used systematic reviews of corporate documents or interviews with known offenders to both describe and theorize the behavioral and motivational underpinnings of specific forms of corporate-based criminality. Not privy to official datasets or ready access to information, in many respects these early scholars were crafting the first "playbook" on how to access information about white-collar offending and make sense of its etiology. Section II fleshes out work done during the Cautious Era of the mid-1960s and 1970s. Facing a backlash against critical thinking during the time of McCarthyism, scholars of this era tended to play it safe, focusing less attention on the wrongdoing of large corporations and more on forms of misconduct deemed less threatening to the establishment. Section III speaks to the Expansion Era of the 1970s and 1980s, a time when ethnographers embarked upon wide-ranging and creative qualitative work on a host of industries and professions. Finally, Section IV details work done during the

Table 7.1 Four Eras of White-Collar Crime Research

Noteworthy Ethnographies	Major Contributions
Formative Era (1940s–Early 1960s)	
Sutherland (1949)	Documented a record of pervasive forms and levels of criminal wrongdoing in a sample of seventy of America's largest nonfinancial institutions and provided empirical support for the concept of white-collar crime
Hartung (1950)	Documented unsafe working conditions and unfair business practices in the U.S. wholesale meat industry
Clinard (1952)	Documented and conceptually organized corporate participation in black market operations during World War II
Cressey (1953)	Study of known embezzlers provided the first detailed theoretical insights into the individual-level behavioral and cognitive intricacies of white-collar offenders
Quinney (1953)	Study of sanctioned retail pharmacists theorized connections between individual violators and occupational culture
Cautious Era (Mid-1960s–Mid-1970s)	
Geis (1967)	Study of bid-rigging practices among heavy electrical equipment corporations was the first to theorize industry-level corporate wrongdoing
Horning (1970)	Extended study of crimes in complex organizations to lower-level employees, showing individual and workgroup norms guiding wrongdoing among shop floor-level electrical plant workers
Ditton (1977)	Broadened the lens of business crime to include salesmen, theorizing individual and collective dimensions within the sales force of a bread company
Vandiver (1972)	Case study of events surrounding unsafe product development at B. F. Goodrich Co. set the stage for future theoretically driven reviews of a scandal
Denzin (1977)	Thick description of the criminogenic environment within the American liquor industry
Expansion Era (Late 1970s–1980s)	
Clinard & Yeager (1978)	Comprehensive study of regulatory action against all Fortune 500 companies offered taxonomy of major forms of violations and their pervasiveness
Zietz (1981)	Study of female embezzlers that theorized a gendered dimension to embezzlement and stimulated subsequent gender-based inquiries of white-collar crime
Vaughan (1983)	Study of the investigation into Medicaid fraud by a retail pharmacy chain provided insight into the dynamics of white-collar crime investigation and organizational structure and process underlying systematic fraud
Braithwaite (1984)	Study of corporate collusion and financial misconduct in the worldwide pharmaceutical industry added further articulated structural factors shaping individual- or corporate-level wrongdoing

(Continued)

Table 7.1 Continued

Noteworthy Ethnographies	Major Contributions
Benson (1985)	Study of sanctioned white-collar offenders theorized the behavioral patterns and accounts of persons apprehended and formally processed for white-collar crimes
Modern Era (1990s–Present)	
Passas (1992)	Study of fraud within the Third World banking industry theorized class- and race-based dimensions of predatory corporate misconduct
Szockyj (1993)	Study of insider-trading practices shed light on a complex form of white-collar crime
Calavita, Pontell, & Tillman (1997)	Study of the savings and loan industry linking deregulation to wide-ranging individual and collective forms of fraud
Vaughan (1996)	Case study of the Challenger space shuttle catastrophe was among the first studies of state–corporate crime
Dodge & Geis (2003)	Case study of the individual- and profession-level factors surrounding fertility clinic scandal

Modern Era—a time since the 1990s when researchers have been largely opportunistic in their approach—further illuminating and theorizing new and emerging forms of white-collar offending.

Based upon this historical review, this essay reaches several conclusions:

- Qualitative research on white-collar crime long has served as the foundational form of inquiry shaping the discovery of and theorizing about the behavioral and motivational aspects of corporate misconduct.
- Ethnographic work has spanned a broad array of topics and empirical approaches, ranging from individual-level work that targets the people who commit the crimes to organizational-level ethnographies that seek to articulate the cultural underpinnings of corporate- or industry-wide wrongdoing.
- The current state of our understanding of white-collar offending is built largely upon ethnographic field work done by a relatively small number of scholars. Their inductively framed works informed the conceptual and methodological facets of more deductive research efforts that have followed at the same time they stimulated additional creative research and policy initiatives.
- There is much to be gained from applying a historical lens to the ethnographic work done on white-collar offending over the past three quarters of a century, as one gains an appreciation of how societal developments as well as the trends of the sociological and criminological fields shaped the theoretical and methodological approaches pursued by scholars over time.
- It is useful to organize the evolution of white-collar crime research into four historical eras: Formative, Cautious, Expansion, and Modern.

- The Formative Era, which spanned a decade and a half beginning in the late 1940s, introduced the scientific method and grounded theorizing to the topic of criminal offending occurring in an organizational context.
- The Cautious Era, which is associated with the tumultuous late 1960s and early 1970s, produced two strains of research on misconduct perpetrated in an organizational context. First, some scholars focused on crime and misconduct among low- and mid-level managers as opposed to upper echelons of the corporate machine, but second, other researchers focused on conspiratorial crimes perpetrated by large corporate entities.
- The Expansion Era, which spanned the 1970s and 1980s, involved a growing number of inductively centered inquiries of corporate wrongdoing, usually coming in the form of single-site case studies or multiple-site amalgams. Collectively this work drove home the point that localized organizational behavior (be it at different levels of a single organization or across multiple organizations in the same industry) is best understood when it is situated within an industry context, as this broader context shapes pervasive criminogenic pressures and opportunities. Factors such as gender and social status were prominently featured in this regard.
- Finally, white-collar crime research during the Modern Era, which started in the early 1990s and continues to the present, has been largely opportunistic in nature. Scholars have waited for technology or industry change to produce new manifestations of white-collar crime and then centered their inquiries on large scandals that bring these phenomena to light. Work has been mostly descriptive in nature.

I. THE FORMATIVE ERA

Not surprisingly, inductive research designs dominated the earliest empirical inquiries into the nature and dynamics of white-collar offending. Left without official data sources such as the Uniform Crime Reports or anything like self-report data, scholars pursued the only functional data collection alternative: they rolled up their sleeves and started from scratch by reviewing media reports or bringing together in piecemeal fashion available documents and testimonials of known or suspected offenders (Reiss and Biderman 1980). Sutherland (1949) got the ball rolling with his comprehensive analysis of sanctioned acts attributed to large American corporations. The most detailed account of the project's methodology can be found in Gilbert Geis and Colin Goff's introduction to the reprinting of Sutherland's original treatise (Sutherland 1983). According to Geis and Goff, Sutherland began amassing his archival database of court and regulatory decisions taken against large U.S. corporations in 1928. His final sample included 70 corporate entities, each of which was identified among the 200 largest nonfinancial corporations in America.[1] Over the course of twenty years, he assembled copious official and unofficial documents detailing the full historical record of wrongdoing attributable to each corporation in the sample. This archival analysis takes on characteristics of a multiple-site organizational ethnography of sorts in that Sutherland and his student assistants meticulously gathered and reviewed untold numbers of documents, assembling them into descriptive and theoretically informed categories. While the results were reported as descriptive statistics along with textual examples, the project was a massive exercise in inductive analysis.

In the end, Sutherland (1949) found widespread evidence of officially sanctioned corporate wrongdoing, in that these 70 firms accumulated 980 adverse court or administrative decisions. Descriptive accounts were offered with the names of the violators redacted from the 1949 edition of the book. Incident data also were provided, with the data-collection effort revealing double-digit criminal or administrative decisions being levied against more than half the sample. Moreover, a clear majority of the firms (60 percent) were subject to at least one criminal conviction, with the average firm racking up four convictions. Sutherland went on to organize the various acts of wrongdoing according to general offense categories, including restraint of trade; rebates, patents, trademarks, and copyrights; misrepresentation in advertising; unfair labor practices; financial manipulations; war crimes; and miscellaneous violations of laws.

Sutherland's (1949) work was not purely descriptive in nature; it also contained several theoretically oriented chapters. Not surprisingly, his theoretical approach was informed by the tenets of differential association theory. Through the official and unofficial records he had at his disposal, Sutherland sought to articulate common behavioral techniques and cognitive motives associated with acts of corporate wrongdoing. With a keen emphasis on the roles of individual power and privileged social status, he meticulously situated these antecedents in culturally based learning processes. As Geis (1988) noted:

> He believed that corporate crime was caused by the transmission of an ethos of crookedness within the business milieu. Sutherland maintained that this ethos involved an arrogant apathy to government as well as the corruption of the political process and politicians by businessmen. (p. 23)

Sutherland situated his explanations in culturally based learning processes and the opportunities that were afforded high-status employees due to a lack of ethical standards or direct oversight. Given this focus, Sutherland's groundbreaking work is best described as the first multiple-site organizational ethnography of white-collar crime.

Other organizational studies would follow in the coming years; for noteworthy examples, see Clinard's (1952) study of black-market operations that thrived during World War II, Hartung's (1950) study of wrongdoing in the wholesale meat industry, and Lane's (1953) work on New England shoe-manufacturing companies. Most of these works were carried out by young scholars who were directly or indirectly mentored by Sutherland. It should not be surprising, then, that the methods and theoretical orientations that they pursued placed a heavy emphasis on culturally derived patterns and processes cutting across diverse forms of corporate wrongdoing. An emphasis on personal status, culturally based learning patterns, and opportunity structures afforded by weak oversight were common elements in this regard.

The early era of white-collar crime research also is marked by a series of individual-level ethnographic inquiries. Here again, the work tended to be conducted by students of Edwin Sutherland, with the most widely cited example being Donald Cressey's (1953) research monograph *Other People's Money*, which systematically chronicled the behavioral and motivational characteristics of people convicted for some form of criminal violation of financial trust occurring within an organizational context (i.e., embezzlement). Cressey assembled a sample of 133 inmates who were confined in one of three prisons located in Indiana and California. Each inmate was interviewed on at least two occasions. Preliminary interviews (ranging from 30 to 90 minutes) sought to confirm that the inmates fit the study's inclusion criteria and then to build rapport between the researcher and subject. Follow-up interviews of varied lengths and frequencies were conducted with each member of the sample. In the end, several hours of summary and verbatim field notes were amassed on each participant.

Key concepts emanating from Cressey's work include "trust violation," "non-sharable problem," and "vocabularies of adjustment." He focused his efforts squarely on persons occupying a position of financial trust, seeking to differentiate their motives and social circumstances from those who occupy a position of financial trust but do not violate it. To wit, he stated

> The central problem is that of determining whether a definable sequence of conjuncture of events is always present when criminal trust violation is present and never present when trust violation is absent, and the correlated problem is that of explaining genetically the presence or absence of those events. (Cressey 1953, p. 12)

Clearly, Cressey aspired to lofty goals of identifying generalizable causal factors and situating them within a theory of trust violation.

Cressey saw trust violations as the result of a cumulative series of antecedents, explaining that "the origin of the trust violation could not be attributed to a single event, but that its explanation could be made only in terms of a series or conjuncture of events, a process" (1953, p. 29). A key component of this antecedent process was the "non-sharable problem"—debt that accrued from inappropriate behaviors (e.g., gambling, substance abuse, extramarital affairs) that could not be met through legitimate sources of income. Cressey surmised that embezzlement emerges as a reasonable means to resolve the financial discord while preserving the secrecy of the problem and thus perpetuating its existence. However, the choice to violate financial trust would only follow in those cases where the perpetrator was able to conceive of "vocabularies of adjustment," or situational verbalizations that preserved his or her moral and ethical standing in light of the unauthorized use of entrusted funds. In short, Cressey theorized that the person must occupy a position of trust, be pressured by a non-sharable problem, recognize embezzlement as a viable relief source, and be capable of articulating a viable explanation to account for theft as legitimate.

One can see tenets of both learning and choice theories within Cressey's theoretical frame. By emphasizing the culturally bound aspects of the non-sharable problem and vocabulary of adjustment concepts, he was able to tap nicely into Sutherland's ideas regarding definitions and differential association. It is noteworthy that Cressey's focus on the importance of a position of financial trust parallels the notion of "generative worlds" that Shover and Hochstetler (2006) detail in their choice-based discussion of white-collar crime. Furthermore, the recognition of embezzlement as a workable solution to a non-sharable problem approximates what Shover and Hochstetler would deem "lure," or the presence of criminal opportunities without effective oversight. Cressey's inclination to blend choice and learning perspectives in his model is driven by the solitary context that he affixes to the embezzlement process. For while learning theorists often have struggled to operationalize concepts such as differential association, differential reinforcement, definitions, and imitation in instances of solitary offending—choosing mostly to enlist the concept of discriminative stimuli as a catchall remedy (Akers 1998)—choice theorists are more keen to the idea of an inner dialogue that occurs in the head of the offender that is not so bound to the social context.

Written under the direction of Marshall Clinard, Quinney's (1962) dissertation on the topic of prescription violations by retail pharmacists stands as another exemplar of the sort of ethnographic work conducted during the early era of white-collar crime scholarship. As one of Sutherland's students, Clinard (1952, 1990) wrote widely on the topic of corporate crime, usually adopting a learning-based framework to account for the factors that correlate with individual or collective wrongdoing. Not surprising, then, is the fact that Quinney sought to "offer an explanation of criminal behavior which occurs in retail pharmacy in terms of an analysis of the occupation" (1963, p. 180). Specifically, Quinney compared interview data from twenty New York pharmacists who had been formally sanctioned for drug-dispensing violations to conversations carried out with a comparison group of sixty pharmacists who had been investigated for similar violations but were subsequently absolved of wrongdoing, exploring how their orientations to their work roles affected their occupational behaviors. He identified a tension between professional work roles couched in the compounding and dispensing of prescription drugs and business-oriented roles driven by the retail demands of the drugstore. He demonstrated that pharmacists who adopted professional occupational role identities exhibited no prescription violations, while those gravitating toward the business-oriented identity were much more likely to be violators.

In Quinney's (1963) interview-centered work, we again see an effort to pursue Sutherland's notion of offender typologies and culturally derived definitions, motives, and routines to a specific form of white-collar crime. These learning-based frameworks, coupled with a focus on specific types of offending, were hallmarks of the early era of white-collar crime research. Clearly, the Sutherland tradition shaped most systematic inquiries conducted during these years. Moreover, working without large datasets or much at all in the way of official data, researchers gravitated toward the inductive development of what Merton (1957) would deem white-collar theories of the middle range, in that they aimed at identifying a set of sensitizing concepts that could be organized using a clear and concise theoretical framework to account for a specific type of criminal conduct.

There was much in the way of scholarly contributions that are readily attributable to the Formative Era of work on white-collar offenders. First and foremost, given the lack of datasets based upon survey research efforts or geographically broad official records, these inquiries represent the sum total of empirical research on the topic.[2] Early white-collar crime researchers were advocates of the scientific method and theory development, and thus each of the early inquiries was systematic in nature, built around creative research designs, and directed toward generalizable observations drawn directly from ethnographic data and other types of data and used to formulate clear and concise theoretical statements about the behavior in question. Many of these inquiries—such as the work of Quinney (1962) and Hartung (1950)—were dissertation projects, and thus there is a clear structure to the work and a discernible connection to their mentors or the home sociology departments from which they sprung. Finally, while oriented more toward discovery of trends than definitive policy implications, it is worth noting that there was a forward reaching dimension to the conclusions and implications presented in these early works. Namely, white-collar crime research during the Formative Era spoke to gaps in the literature and presented future research directions that undoubtedly stimulated much debate, creative thinking, future research projects, and published commentaries.

II. The Cautious Era

Despite the excitement generated by the Formative Era, Geis (1988) notes a decade-long dormancy in white-collar crime research from the mid-1960s through the mid-1970s, attributing it to fear among other things generated by the McCarthy hearings, the Cold War, and a preoccupation with the various controversial wars of the time. During this period, sociologists and criminologists did not generate much in the way of original research on white-collar crime. Most of the work that was done focused on offending by low-level employees who, while occupying positions of trust, generally were not of high social status. Ditton's (1977) work on salesmen in a bread company and Horning's (1970) study of theft on the shop floor of an electrical plant represent solid examples of the sort of ethnographic work done in this era. While somewhat different in their theoretical leanings, both Ditton (1977) and Horning's (1970) work combined face-to-face interviews with fieldwork within a single occupational environment to reveal the techniques that employees used and the corresponding meanings assigned to various forms of trust violation. This sort of strategy closely aligns with the sociological or anthropological tradition of an organizational ethnography, vis-à-vis van Maanen (1979).

In many ways, this era of offender-based research is aptly described as taking a "low-hanging fruit" approach in that it targeted wrongdoing among relatively powerless employees within isolated work settings. Insights into the cultural development of the behaviors and corresponding cognitive neutralizations clearly follow the Sutherland (1949) and Sykes and Matza (1957) learning-based tradition. The work represents incremental (not significant) developments in the way of research design, theory construction, and policy implications. It is not that this was a lost decade as much as it was a slowdown in the momentum that had been so arduously built by the earlier pioneers of white-collar crime scholarship.

Geis's (1967) report on the antitrust cases spawned by an elaborate bid-rigging scheme among large heavy electrical equipment companies stands as one of the few broad-based, multiple-site organizational-level ethnographies published during the Cautious Era of the mid-1960s and 1970s.[3] Referring to the work of Sutherland and others before him, Geis (1967) noted, "the antitrust cases provide the researcher with a mass of raw data against which to test and to refine the earlier hunches and hypotheses regarding white-collar crime" (p. 141). While recognizing the limitations associated with a case-study design built solely on secondary sources (e.g., court transcripts, investigative files, media reports), the absence of access to pertinent files and individuals led Geis to rely on data "drawn together from diverse secondhand sources" (Geis 1967, p. 142). The overall methodological and theoretical contribution of Geis's work represents more of an incremental extension of previous efforts rather than path-forging work. Substantively, he provided another well-written case study that traces widespread and diverse acts of misconduct to a series of individual- and corporate-level calculations and decisions. He pieced together the intricate techniques of the broad-based bid-rigging conspiracy that was orchestrated by the corporate executives. He drew upon the testimony of the accused offenders to ferret out common explanations or accounts for the bid-rigging; invariably these accounts downplayed the significance and maliciousness of the wrongdoing. These cognitive and behavioral processes are presented in a learning-based framework that stresses cultural norms and power relationships. On the methodological front, Geis took advantage of the limited secondhand data readily available as a result of formal and media accounts of the wrongdoing.

While not alone, Geis's case study of a specific kind of wrongdoing perpetrated by a single corporate entity is one of the few organizational studies published during the Cautious Era. Another example of an organizational-based ethnography is Vandiver's (1972) study of the events surrounding B. F. Goodrich's manufacturing of faulty brake pads that ended up causing fatalities for Air Force pilots flying the LTV Aerospace Corporation's A7D aircraft. Leonard and Weber's (1970) case study showing how market forces within the American auto industry link to criminal misconduct among automakers and dealers, as well as Denzin's (1977) insightful analysis of the criminogenic structure of the American liquor industry, should also be noted. All of these examples focus scholarly attention on structural forces that exist within and across a specific market of the American economy. In doing so, the authors added a new and insightful theoretical layer to the discussion of how patterns of wrongdoing emerge, spread, and proliferate within a specific market milieu.

III. The Expansion Era

Perhaps reflecting upon his own work, Geis (1988) posited that the early ideas along with the repressive political climate of the preceding time period may have served as an incubator for scholars seeking to shed light on and account for the abuses of power that were hallmarks of the decade that spanned the mid-1960s through the mid-1970s. This premise is given credence by Peter Yeager's (2008) recollections on how the societal context of the 1970s motivated him to embark upon several corporate crime inquiries during the 1980s. The late 1970s and the 1980s saw an impressive spate of scholarship in criminology in general, including the sub-area of white-collar crime. Organizational- and individual-level ethnographies of offenders remained prominent features of white-collar crime scholarship during this period.

Regarding organizational-level studies, Clinard and Yeager (1978) jumpstarted the conversation with their seminal work on criminal wrongdoing among Fortune 500 corporations, their purpose being to

> Establish systematically the largest database ever constructed on major American corporations' violations of federal law . . . to determine patterns of offending, to identify the structural and economic correlates of these patterns, and to discover patterns in government sanctioning of these offenses. (Yeager 2008, p. 10)

The authorship team received a large Department of Justice grant to study corporate wrongdoing using the official files of twenty-five federal agencies during a two-year period (1975–1976). They also analyzed newspaper reports, reports to the Securities Exchange Commission, and Law Services Reports. While the findings of this report come in the way of descriptive statistics and rudimentary correlational analyses, the quantitative analyses were derived from the meticulous interpretation and coding of copious amounts of formal and informal documents, thus giving it an interpretivist bent. The inquiry uncovered widespread evidence of criminal and regulatory wrongdoing, including 1,533 federal cases pursued against the 582 corporations in their sample. The researchers categorized wrongdoing into a series of types, including administrative violations (e.g., creative accounting and noncompliance with reporting requirements), financial violations (e.g., illegal payments to vendors and politicians), labor violations (e.g., union busting and unsafe work conditions), and violations that compromised the competitive market (e.g., price fixing and bid rigging). They attributed corporate offending types and levels to the loose culture of control developed and maintained by members of top management and regulatory entities. In effect, the authors described incubators of diverse forms of wrongdoing within many of the top U.S. corporations (Clinard et al. 1979). While the data detailing the incidence and prevalence figures were eye-catching, it was the rich qualitative data that they uncovered on the complex schemes, cover-ups, and networks of corroboration that provided the inductive core for the theoretical observations that were detailed in their research monograph (Clinard and Yeager 1980).

This inquiry was followed closely by John Braithwaite's (1984) work on collusion and wrongdoing within the pharmaceutical industry and Diane Vaughan's (1983) seminal work on Medicaid fraud within the Revco drugstore chain. Both studies are ethnographic in nature, with the first being an industry-level case study of broad-based wrongdoing across an entire business sector and the latter representing a case study of misconduct perpetrated in a single corporate environment. These two works demonstrate a new methodological direction and a corresponding heightened level of empirical rigor compared to the early works.

In the introduction to his book, Braithwaite (1984) detailed four stages of social science inquiry: theorizing, qualitative inquiry, statistical studies, and experimental work. He observed that white-collar crime scholarship in the 1980s had matured beyond stage one but that stage three was premature. That said, it is clear that Braithwaite deemed a design based upon an industry-wide case study approach to be more timely and rich than a repeat performance of localized case studies: "I am more convinced than ever that a superior understanding of a particular crime in a particular firm is gained when the researcher has a grasp of how the industry works as a whole" (1984, p. 8).

At the same time that Braithwaite's approach was deductive in its vantage point on the problem, it was more inductive in its sampling strategy than earlier studies had been. Namely, Braithwaite relied on interpersonal interviews as his primary source of information. He used a snowball sampling strategy to identify and speak directly to 131 senior-level executives employed within 32 different prominent pharmaceutical corporations worldwide. He also conducted supplemental interviews with regulators, trade association officials, and informants who had left the industry that were "much more valuable . . . [and] almost equal in number to the formal industry interviews" (Braithwaite 1984, p. 9). This large collective of loosely structured conversations was bolstered by a comprehensive review of hundreds of thousands of pages in company documents and official transcripts emanating from trial proceedings and various government investigations. The resulting monograph details patterns of bribery, scientific misconduct, unsafe manufacturing practices, antitrust, fiddling, and unseemly marketing practices that cut across the industry as a whole. Braithwaite used these patterns to map out a regulatory approach for controlling corporate crime within the pharmaceutical industry and beyond.

Diane Vaughan's (1983) case study represents another important development in our understanding of white-collar offending. In her discussion of the study's development, she explains that her original plan sought to flesh out the link between the social structure of the Revco corporation and its involvement in a wide-ranging and costly Medicaid overbilling scheme, for which the company and two managers were held criminally responsible. When confronted with problems gaining access to corporate employees, she was forced to redesign the study as one that operationalized the nature and dynamics of the misconduct through the eyes of seven different government bureaucracies involved in the investigative and adjudication process. Unlike previous localized ethnographies that relied almost exclusively on official documents, court transcripts, and news reports, Vaughan introduced a new dimension to her research design by spending time immersed in the regulatory agencies and also interviewing staff members who were involved in the fact-finding effort. This approach afforded her a more comprehensive dataset fashioned largely from previously untapped information sources.

Vaughan set the stage for her research monograph by acknowledging that the study of organizational structure and process traditionally had been the purview of organizational sociologists, while the study of crime within organizations long had been done by criminologists. She adopted the perspective of a "social control network . . . merging conceptual tools and knowledge of interorganizational relations with what is known about organizational misconduct" (1983, p. xiii). She not only detailed the structure and processes within Revco that brought about more than a half million dollars in fraudulent Medicare claims within Franklin County, Ohio, but also she mapped the development of the interagency regulatory environment that first missed the misconduct but then later vigorously sought to uncover it and hold both individuals and the corporation criminally responsible. Vaughan's (1983) juxtaposing of the offenders and social control agents within a single study represents an important development in the ethnography of white-collar offending. In some way, it parallels the approach used by Shapiro (1984) to frame up the relationship between insider traders and investigative entities within the Securities and Exchange Commission; and by Cullen, Maakestad, and Cavender (1987) when accounting for the events surrounding the Ford Pinto case.

The 1980s also saw an expansion of individual-level qualitative work using creative sampling and interview approaches to gain firsthand insights from known white-collar offenders. These inquiries cover a broad array of white-collar offenders and offense types. For space purposes, the current discussion centers on a series of studies targeting convicted white-collar offenders accessed with the assistance of state correctional authorities. The first example is Benson's (1985) interview-based study of thirty men convicted (in prison or on parole at the time of the study) in federal courts for misdeeds ranging from antitrust violations to embezzlement to tax evasion. In focusing on how these men account for their misconduct, Benson identified common forms of denial that correspond to different offense types; for example, tax violators tended to point to complexities in the tax code, while embezzlers pointed to non-sharable problems, as was the case in Cressey's (1953) classic study.

Zietz's (1981) interview-based study of 100 convicted female embezzlers stands as another example of an individual-level inquiry designed to provide rich description and theoretical insight on the behaviors and cognitions of white-collar criminals. What is most significant about Zietz's work are her choices to place center stage the issue of gender and to demonstrate via comparison to Cressey's (1953) work how the pre-event circumstances and post-commission accounts offered by female offenders differ substantially from those of their male counterparts. In particular, Zietz used an inductive frame to uncover gender-specific motivations for embezzlement. Unlike their male counterparts detailed in earlier work by Cressey and others who oriented to non-sharable problems seated in vices or greed, the women were driven to bilk their employers out of a sense of loyalty to their families. This study set the stage for future gender-based studies of white-collar offending.

There is much to like about the qualitative research on white-collar offending that emerged during the 1970s and 1980s. It provides vivid descriptions and theoretically diverse explanations for the behaviors and cognitions of a broad array of white-collar offenders. Expansion was a hallmark of this period of research, a time in which researchers fanned out into different industries to isolate and illuminate all sorts of harmful behaviors perpetrated by individuals and corporate entities around the world. Important theoretical observations were made with respect to gender and social status factors that shape white-collar offending. Methodologically, there were not many new wrinkles introduced. Most of the organizational-level ethnographies continued to rely heavily on existing documentation. It was encouraging, however, to see researchers move toward research designs that yielded first-hand accounts from victims, perpetrators, and social control agents that allowed for a depth of insight that was not possible from secondhand sources. Theoretically, researchers continued to rely heavily on learning and choice perspectives to produce both micro- and macro-level explanations of white-collar offending.

IV. THE MODERN ERA

Since the 1990s, ethnographic work on white-collar offending has become largely opportunistic in nature, generally waiting for new forms of offending to emerge or for high-profile scandals to erupt and then diving in with an inductive frame to both describe and explain the phenomenon. When new methods of fraud and abuse emerged on the scene, scholars were quick to enlist ethnographic strategies to shed light on the emergent phenomenon. Examples include telemarketing fraud (Stevenson 1998; Shover, Coffey, and Hobbs 2003), creative insider-trading schemes (Reichman 1993; Szockyj 1993), fertility clinic fraud (Dodge and Geis 2003), and the manipulation of emerging Third World banking systems (Passas 1992; Tillman and Indergaard 2005). As one example, Dodge and Geis provided a wide-ranging ethnographic account of how doctors and staff from the Center for Reproductive Health at the University of California, Irvine engaged in acts of fraud and research misconduct. In addition to defrauding federal agencies, donors, and the state out of millions of dollars due to illegal and unethical medical procedures, doctors were shown to be harvesting eggs from unsuspecting female patients and implanting them in others for profit. Studies such as this one provide important descriptive accounts that organize our understanding of emerging forms of white-collar crime.

During this period, scholars have continued to enlist qualitative research designs to detail and account for understudied forms of white-collar misconduct. For example, ethnographic work emerged revealing such problems as drug abuse among nurses

(Dabney 1995) and pharmacists (Dabney and Hollinger 2002), harmful medical procedures by veterinarians (Gauthier 2001) and doctors (Rosenthal 1995), professional misconduct among academics (LaFollette 1992), and various abuses within the health insurance industry (Jesilow, Pontell, and Geis 1993; Tillman 1998). While there is nothing particularly new about the misconduct under consideration in these studies, this work does serve to provide descriptive and theoretical insights on understudied topics. For example, Dabney (1995) used interviews with a sample of nurses involved in drug use and/or drug or supply theft to extend the tenets of neutralization theory. The work shows how nurses downplay the significance of supply theft or treat it as a fringe benefit of the job. With respect to drug theft and use, nurses were accepting of the practice when it involved non-narcotics being used for the treatment of ailments that were seen as inhibiting patient care but opposed it when it involved narcotics or the impairment of skills.

Finally, as was the case in previous eras, scholars continue to employ ethnographic methods within the capacity of high-profile case studies of corporate wrongdoing, as can be seen in Barnett's (1994) study of Superfund abuses and Calavita, Pontell, and Tillman's (1997) research into the savings and loan scandal of the 1980s. Diane Vaughan's (1996) case study of the 1986 explosion of the Challenger space shuttle stands as a prime example in this regard. Weaving together interviews with the key organizational actors within government agencies such as NASA and private corporations such as the engineering firm Morton Thiokol, Vaughan provided both a historical ethnography of the short- and long-term events leading up to the failed launch and a rich theoretical frame through which one might account for state–corporate crime in general. Further, on the theoretical front, Vaughan (1998) drew upon tenets of the rational-choice perspective to frame the Challenger explosion as a "situated action" or "normal accident" resulting from the nexus of an organizational culture built around a high tolerance for risk and a passive posture on the part of managers who grew accustomed to letting political and economic factors shape their daily directives.

Both individually and collectively, the ethnographic work of the past several decades has served to advance our empirical and theoretical insight on white-collar offending patterns incrementally. A host of topics has been explored, adding various methodological and theoretical contributions along the way. The use of ethnography as a means of investigating individual- and organizational-level misconduct remains a vibrant and well-used lens through which scholars study white-collar crime. The resulting descriptive and conceptual insights have laid the way for a generation of survey researchers or persons conducting secondary analyses of official data seeking to confirm, extend, or generalize these ideas to different venues and/or broader samples. For example, the definitional and methodological issues that emerged from a generation of qualitative research with white-collar offenders undoubtedly played a part in the Yale studies of the late 1990s (Weisburd et al. 2001), wherein court data shed light on the criminal careers and socioeconomic background of persons convicted of economic crimes. Similarly, Michael Benson, Nicole Leeper Piquero, Sally Simpson, and a host of other talented quantitatively oriented scholars have drawn upon existing cross-sectional and longitudinal datasets to test the theoretical tenets of early white-collar crime researchers who spent five decades applying an interpretivist frame to the subject matter.

V. CONCLUSION

This chapter sought to provide a historical overview of the ethnographic work on the topic of white-collar offending since Edwin Sutherland's 1939 speech. In doing so, the discussion has placed in the foreground methodological and theoretical trends and sought to showcase prominent pieces of work that illustrate the various sorts of research being done. Clearly, white-collar crime scholarship has morphed from a fringe endeavor within criminology into a legitimate and well-respected area of study that adds substantially to our nuanced understanding of criminal wrongdoing. What began as a series of critical essays and patchwork studies of misconduct within organizations has evolved into different strains of research addressing everything from offending patterns, to victimization patterns, to research on formal and informal social control efforts, and proposed policy directions. The current state of our understanding is fundamentally built upon and thus informed by the painstaking ethnographic fieldwork done by the scholars identified in this chapter (as well as those not included due to space constraints). We have come to appreciate a host of new variations of white-collar crime, ranging from bank fraud, to medical fraud, to retail fraud, as a result of these inquiries. On the cognitive front, we have come to appreciate the normative tightrope that these otherwise law-abiding citizens often walk as they embark upon and continue with their complex wrongdoing. Finally, ethnographers have done well to flesh out the interplay between individual-level agency and cultural norms within the organizations that house these sorts of offenders. Not only have these inductively framed works informed the conceptual and methodological facets of more deductive research efforts that have followed, but they also have stimulated everything from additional ethnographic research to crudely fashioned policy initiatives. In short, one cannot begin to appreciate the advances we have made in the area of white-collar crime scholarship and policymaking without acknowledging the ethnographic work available on small groups of white-collar offenders.

NOTES

1. Sutherland chose to exempt firms operating primarily in the public utilities, transportation, communications, and petroleum industries.
2. Relatedly, early white-collar crime research mostly focused on the behavior and decision making of perpetrators, as opposed to of victims or social control agents.
3. It is worth noting that the federal inquiry into alleged antitrust violations was launched in 1959, with the resulting federal court cases playing out in 1961 and 1962. As such, one could argue that this study is more aptly situated in the Formative Era detailed above.

Such a conclusion would explain how and why he was able to gain a sponsor and audience for a study so critical of powerful corporations.

REFERENCES

Akers, Ronald L. 1998. *Social Learning and Social Structure: A General Theory of Crime and Deviance*. Boston: Northeastern University Press.

Barnett, Harold C. 1994. *Toxic Debts and the Superfund Dilemma*. Chapel Hill: University of North Carolina Press.

Benson, Michael. L. 1985. "Denying the Guilty Mind: Accounting for Involvement in a White-collar Crime." *Criminology* 23: 589–99.

Braithwaite, John. 1984. *Corporate Crime in the Pharmaceutical Industry*. London, UK: Routledge and Kegan Paul.

Braithwaite, John. 1985. "White-Collar Crime." *Annual Review of Sociology* 11: 1–25.

Brannan, Matthew, Mike Rowe, and Frank Worthington. 2013. Editorial for the *Journal of Organizational Ethnography*: Time for a New Journal, a Journal for New Times. *Journal of Organizational Ethnography* 1: 5–14.

Broad, William, and Nicholas Wade. 1982. *Betrayers of the Truth: Fraud and Deceit in the Halls of Science*. New York: Simon and Schuster.

Calavita, Kitty, Henry N. Pontell, and Robert Tillman. 1997. *Big Money Crime: Fraud and Politics in the Savings and Loan Crisis*. Berkeley: University of California Press.

Cefkin, Melissa. 2009. *Ethnography and the Corporate Encounter: Reflections on Research in and of Corporations*. New York: Berghahn Books.

Clinard, Marshall B. 1952. *The Black Market: A Study of White-Collar Crime*. New York: Holt, Rinehart, and Winston.

Clinard, Marshall B. 1990. *Corporate Corruption: The Abuse of Power*. New York: Praeger.

Clinard, Marshall B., and Peter C. Yeager. 1978. "Corporate Crime: Issues in Research." *Criminology* 16: 255–72.

Clinard, Marshall B., and Peter C. Yeager. 1980. *Corporate Crime*. New York: Free Press.

Clinard, Marshall B., Peter C. Yeager, Jeanne Brissette, David Petrashek, and Elizabeth Harries. 1979. *Illegal Corporate Behavior*. Washington, D.C.: U.S. Department of Justice.

Cohn, Ellen G., David P. Farrington, and Richard A. Wright. 1998. *Evaluating Criminology and Criminal Justice*. Westport, CT: Greenwood.

Cressey, Donald. 1953. *Other People's Money*. Glencoe, IL: Free Press.

Cullen, Francis, William J. Maakestad, and Gray Cavender. 1987. *Corporate Crime under Attack: The Ford Pinto Case and Beyond*. Cincinnati, OH: Anderson.

Dabney, Dean A. 1995. "Neutralization and Deviance in the Workplace: Theft of Supplies and Medicines by Hospital Nurses." *Deviant Behavior* 16: 313–31.

Dabney, Dean A. 2013. *Crime Types: A Text-Reader*, 2nd ed. Boulder, CO: Aspen.

Dabney, Dean A., and Richard C. Hollinger. 2002. "Drugged Druggists: The Convergence of Two Criminal Career Trajectories." *Justice Quarterly* 19: 201–33.

Denzin, Norman. 1977. "Notes on the Criminogenic Hypothesis: A Case Study of the American Liquor Industry." *American Sociological Review* 42: 905–20.

Ditton, Jason. 1977. *Part-Time Crime: An Ethnography of Fiddling Pilferage*. New York: MacMillan.

Dodge, Mary, and Gilbert Geis. 2003. *Stealing Dreams: A Fertility Clinic Scandal.* Boston: Northeastern University Press.

Ermann, M. David, and Richard J. Lundman. 2002. *Corporate Crime and Governmental Deviance,* 6th ed. New York: Oxford University Press.

Friedrichs, David O. 2010. *Trusted Criminals: White Collar Crime in Contemporary Society,* 4th ed. Belmont: Wadsworth.

Gabbidon, Shaun L., and Favian Martin. 2010. "An Era-Based Exploration of the Most Significant Books in Criminology/Criminal Justice: A Research Note." *Journal of Criminal Justice Education* 21: 348–69.

Gauthier, DeAnn K. 2001. "Professional Lapses: Occupational Deviance and Neutralization Techniques in Veterinary Medical Practice." *Deviant Behavior* 22: 467–90.

Geertz, Clifford J. 1988. *Works and Lives: The Anthropologists as Author.* Stanford: Stanford University Press.

Geis, Gilbert. 1967. "The Heavy Electrical Equipment Antitrust Cases of 1961." In *Criminal Behavior Systems,* pp. 103–18, edited by Marshall Clinard and Richard Quinney. New York: Holt, Rinehart, and Winston.

Geis, Gilbert. 1985. "Criminological Perspectives on Corporate Regulation: A Review of Recent Research." In *Corrigible Corporations and Unruly Law,* pp. 101–36, edited by Brent Fisse and Peter A. French. San Antonio, TX: Trinity University Press.

Geis, Gilbert. 1988. "From Deuteronomy to Deniability: A Historical Perlustration on White-Collar Crime." *Justice Quarterly* 5: 7–32.

Geis, Gilbert. 2007. *White-collar and Corporate Crime.* Upper Saddle River, NJ: Prentice Hall.

Gerber, Jurg, and Eric L. Jensen. 2007. *Encyclopedia of White-Collar Crime.* Westport, CT: Greenwood.

Hartung, Frank E. 1950. "White-Collar Offenses in the Wholesale Meat Industry in Detroit." *American Journal of Sociology* 56: 25–34.

Hollinger, Richard C., and John P. Clark. 1983. *Theft by Employees.* Lexington, MA: Lexington Books.

Horning, Donald M. 1970. "Blue-Collar Theft: Conceptions of Property, Attitudes toward Pilfering, and Work Group Norms in a Modern Industrial Plant." In *Crimes against Bureaucracy,* pp. 49–64, edited by Erwin O. Smigel. New York: Van Nostrand Reinhold.

Jesilow, Paul, Henry N. Pontell, and Gilbert Geis. 1993. *Prescription for Profit: How Doctors Defraud Medicaid.* Berkeley: University of California Press.

Klenowski, Paul M. 2012. "Learning the Good with the Bad: Are Occupational White-Collar Offenders Taught How to Neutralize Their Crimes?" *Criminal Justice Review* 37: 461–77.

LaFollette, Marcel C. 1992. *Stealing into Print: Fraud, Plagiarism, and Misconduct in Scientific Publishing.* Berkeley: University of California Press.

Lane, Robert E. 1953. "Why Businessmen Violate the Law." *Journal of Criminal Law, Criminology, and Police Science* 44: 151–65.

Leonard, William N., and Marvin Glen Weber. 1970. "Automakers and Dealers: A Study of Criminogenic Market Forces." *Law and Society Review* 20: 407–20.

Levi, Michael. 1995. "The Use and Misuse of Citations as a Measure of Influence in Criminology." *British Journal of Criminology* 35: 138–42.

Merton, Robert K. 1957. *Social Theory and Social Structure.* Glencoe, IL: Free Press.

Mokhiber, Russell. 1988. *Corporate Crime and Violence: Big Business Power and the Abuse of the Public Trust.* San Francisco, CA: Sierra Book Club.

Passas, Nikos. 1992. "I Cheat, Therefore I Exist? The BCCI Scandal in Context." In *Emerging Global Business Ethics*, pp. 69–78, edited by W. Michael Hoffman, Judith B. Kamm, Robert E. Frederick, and Edward S. Petry, Jr. Westport, CT: Quorum Books.

Pearce, Frank, and Laureen Snider. 1995. *Corporate Crime: Contemporary Debates*. Toronto: University of Toronto Press.

Piquero, Nicole Leeper, and Michael L. Benson. 2004. "White-Collar Crime and Criminal Careers: Specifying a Trajectory of Punctuated Situational-Dependent Offending." *Journal of Contemporary Criminal Justice* 20: 148–65.

Pontell, Henry N., and Gilbert Geis. 2007. *International Handbook of White-Collar and Corporate Crime*. New York: Springer.

Pontell, Henry N., and David Shichor. 2001. *Contemporary Issues in Crime and Criminal Justice: Essays in Honor of Gilbert Geis*. Upper Saddle River, NJ: Prentice-Hall.

Presser, Lois. 2010. "Collecting and Analyzing the Stories of Offenders." *Journal of Criminal Justice Education* 21: 431–46.

Punch, Maurice. 1996. *Dirty Business: Exploring Corporate Misconduct: Analysis and Cases*. London, UK: Sage.

Quinney, Earl R. 1962. *Retail Pharmacists as a Marginalized Occupation: A Study of Prescription Violation*. Madison: University of Wisconsin.

Quinney, Earl R. 1963. "Occupational Structure and Criminal Behavior: Prescription Violation by Retail Pharmacists." *Social Problems* 11: 179–85.

Reichman, Nancy. 1993. "Insider Trading." In *Beyond the Law: Crime in Complex Organizations*, pp. 55–96, edited by Michael Tonry and Albert J. Reiss, Jr. Chicago: University of Chicago Press.

Reiss, Albert J. Jr., and Albert D. Biderman. 1980. *Data Sources on White-Collar Law-Breaking*. Washington, D.C.: U.S. Department of Justice, National Institute of Justice.

Rosenthal, Marilynn M. 1995. *The Incompetent Doctor: Behind Closed Doors*. Philadelphia, PA: Open University Press.

Sarna, David. 2010. *History of Greed: Financial Fraud from Tulip Mania to Bernie Madoff*. New York: Wiley.

Shapiro, Susan P. 1980. *Thinking about White-Collar Crime: Matters of Conceptualization and Research*. Washington, D.C.: U.S. Department of Justice, National Institute of Justice.

Shapiro, Susan P. 1984. *Wayward Capitalists: Target of the Securities and Exchange Commission*. New Haven, CT: Yale University Press.

Shichor, David. 2009. "Scholarly Influence and White-Collar Crime Scholarship." *Crime, Law, and Social Change* 51: 175–87.

Shover, Neal. 2012. "Ethnographic Methods in Criminological Research: Rationale, Reprise, and Warning." *American Journal of Criminal Justice* 37: 139–45.

Shover, Neal, Glenn S. Coffey, and Dick Hobbs. 2003. "Crime on the Line: Telemarketing and the Changing Nature of Professional Crime." *British Journal of Criminology* 43: 489–505.

Shover, Neal, and Andrew Hochstetler. 2006. *Choosing White-Collar Crime*. New York: Cambridge University Press.

Shover, Neal, and John P. Wright. 2001. *Crimes of Privilege: Readings in White-Collar Crime*. New York: Oxford University Press.

Stern, Gerald M. 1976. *The Buffalo Creek Disaster: How the Survivors of One of the Worst Disasters in Coal-Mining History Brought Suit against the Coal Company—and Won*. New York: Vintage.

Stevenson, Robert J. 1998. *The Boiler Room and Other Telephone Sales Scandals.* Chicago: University of Illinois Press.

Stewart, James B. 1991. *Den of Thieves.* New York: Simon and Schuster.

Sutherland, Edwin H. 1940. "White-Collar Criminality." *American Sociological Review* 5: 1–11.

Sutherland, Edwin H. 1949. *White Collar Crime.* New York: Dryden.

Sutherland, Edwin H. 1983. *White Collar Crime: The Uncut Version,* with an introduction by Gil Geis and Colin Goff. New Haven, CT: Yale University Press.

Sykes, Gresham, and David Matza. 1957. "A Theory of Delinquency." *American Sociological Review* 22: 664–70.

Szockyj, Elizabeth. 1993. "Insider Trading: The SEC Meets Carl Karcher." *Annals of the American Academy of Political and Social Science* 525: 46–58.

Tillman, Robert. 1998. *Broken Promises: Fraud by Small Business Health Insurers.* Boston: Northeastern University Press.

Tillman, Robert H., and Michael L. Indergaard. 2005. *Pump and Dump: The Rancid Rules of the New Economy.* New Brunswick, NJ: Rutgers University Press.

Vandiver, Kermit. 1972. "Why Should My Conscience Bother Me?" In *In the Name of Profit,* pp. 3–31, edited by Robert L. Heilbroner. Garden City, NY: Doubleday.

Van Maanen, John. 1979. "The Fact of Fiction in Organizational Ethnography." *Administrative Science Quarterly* 24: 539–50.

Vaughan, Diane. 1983. *Controlling Unlawful Organizational Behavior: Social Structure and Corporate Misconduct.* Chicago: University of Chicago Press.

Vaughan, Diane. 1996. *The Challenger Launch Decision: Risky Technology, Culture, and Deviance at NASA.* Chicago: University of Chicago Press.

Vaughan, Diane. 1998. "Rational Choice, Situated Action, and the Social Control of Organizations." *Law and Society Review* 32: 23–61.

Vaughan, Diane. 2006. "NASA Revisited: Theory, Analogy, and Public Sociology. *American Journal of Sociology* 112: 353–93.

Vito, Gennaro F., and Richard Tewksbury. 2008. "The Great Books in Criminal Justice: As Ranked by Elite Members of the Academy of Criminal Justice Sciences." *Journal of Criminal Justice Education* 19: 366–82.

Weisburd, David, Elin Waring, and Ellen F. Chayet. 2001. *White-Collar Crime and Criminal Careers.* Boston: Cambridge University Press.

Yanow, Dvora. 2009. "Organizational Ethnography and Methodological Angst: Myths and Challenges in the Field." *Qualitative Research in Organizations and Management: an International Journal* 4: 186–99.

Ybema, Sierk. 2009. *Organizational Ethnography: Studying the Complexities of Everyday Life.* Los Angeles, CA: Sage.

Yeager, Peter C. 2008. "Science, Values and Politics: An Insider's Reflections on Corporate Crime." *Crime, Law and Social Change* 51: 5–30.

Zietz, Barbara. 1981. *Women Who Embezzle or Defraud: A Study of Convicted Felons.* New York: Praeger.

CHAPTER 8

THE POOL OF POTENTIAL WHITE-COLLAR CRIMINALS
Whence?

ANDY HOCHSTETLER AND WILLIAM MACKEY

AMID declining rates of street crime, white-collar crime abounds. Between 2007 and 2012, federal district court convictions for white-collar offenses increased 5.7 percent (TracFed 2012), and nearly one in four U.S. households currently reports victimization for white-collar crime annually (Huff, Desilets, and Kane 2011). This chapter locates the source of white-collar crimes in an obvious place: the pool of persons with the motivation and the opportunity to commit them.

Nevertheless, to engage in crime is to make a choice. Before pursuing a discrete offense, individuals, who may spring from different pools of likely offenders, apply moral and maximizing calculation to evaluate whether the opportunity for crime is sufficiently rewarding and acceptable to offset its accompanying risks. Those who make that choice share certain psychological and social characteristics. While hardship and other familiar sources of street criminals' motivations increase some forms of white-collar offending, affluence also might play a role in generating predisposed offenders. This view of the sources of crime undergirds most of the conclusions of the essay. The conclusions are these:

- Characteristics of white-collar offenders are contingent on the definition of white-collar crime investigators use.
- Long-term changes in the workplace have increased the size of the offender pool.
- Assessments of costs and benefits of crime are important in shaping individual offenders' discrete choices to offend and the size of the pool of potential offenders. Chief among costs are the chances of being detected and penalized.
- Economic conditions influence the pool of offenders and the rate of offending. Both peaks and troughs in economic conditions lead to increases. Competition and inequality in an economy and the relations they produce also increase rates.

- White-collar offenders' psychological characteristics differ from those of the general population. They share characteristics with street offenders, but unlike most street offenders, white-collar offenders often enjoyed comfortable upbringings and hold occupational positions in affluent working conditions.

Section I of this essay discusses definitions of white-collar crime and provides the one that will be used in this chapter. Section II explores social and economic conditions that shape the size or behavior of offender pools, including changing payoff, workforce and economic variation, and cultural variation. Section III elaborates by examining the characteristics of those in offender pools, with emphasis on the offenders' backgrounds and predispositions and how these contribute to offenses.

I. Defining White-Collar Crime

In studying white-collar crime, much is contingent on how investigators define it. A key distinction is whether to rely on offender-based or offense-based definitions. Those who prefer offense-based definitions select general characteristics of white-collar offenses and then identify acts in the criminal code that fit these criteria. For example, investigators might note that white-collar crimes are "crimes of deception" or "abuses of trust" and then locate crimes that fit the criteria for analysis.

In contrast, offender-based definitions focus on the traditional, upward-looking emphasis in white-collar crime analysis. By concentrating on crimes of the privileged, investigators avoid the mistake of assuming that the pathologies of poverty cause crime. Offender-based definitions typically include crimes by both the corporate elite, as well as middle-class fraudsters, but exclude grandmothers who commit welfare fraud and street-level check forgers. Because large numbers of con artists, deceptive tradesmen, small embezzlers, and credit thieves threaten to obscure the distinctiveness of white-collar crime and its causes, there is value in offender-based definitions. For similar reasons, classification of white-collar crime into crimes committed by privileged *upper-world* white-collar offenders or by *ordinary* white-collar offenders also is practical.

Ordinary white-collar offenders are more financially stable and privileged than street thieves but generally less well off than the general population; almost half have a prior arrest (Weisburd et al. 1994). Many hail from the middle classes, and 15 percent of white-collar offenders come from families that had trouble providing necessities (compared to 25 percent of street offenders) (Benson 2002). Table 8.1 compares characteristics of white-collar and street offenders sentenced in federal courts between 2005 and 2011. It illustrates that even offense-based definitions yield offenders who are on average older and more educated than street offenders are. More white-collar compared to ordinary street offenders are female, in part reflecting the now-predominant presence of females in the white-collar workforce, particularly in the lower ranks.

Table 8.1 Characteristics of Individuals Sentenced for Federal Street Crimes and White-Collar Crimes, United States, 2005–2011

Characteristic	Street Offenders[a]	White-Collar Offenders[b]
Race (percent African-American and Hispanic)	41.7	44.1
Gender		
Male	89.7	69.7
Female	10.3	30.3
Education		
Less than high school	35.5	18.2
High school graduate	42.2	29.3
Some college	19.2	31.0
College graduate	3.1	21.5
Age		
Under 21	6.9	1.8
21–30	36.6	21.0
31–40	28.1	28.7
41–50	19.8	25.3
50+	9.6	23.2
Average age (weighted)	34.5	41.0
Average number of cases annually	1,891	8,993

[a] Includes defendants convicted of murder, manslaughter, assault, robbery, burglary, and auto theft.

[b] Includes defendants convicted of fraud, embezzlement, bribery, tax offenses, antitrust offenses, and food and drug violations.

Occupational crimes are offenses committed for direct personal enrichment in the course of an occupation and are composed largely of embezzlement or misappropriation of asset schemes. They serve as an example of the analytical significance of attention to privilege in the definition of crime. While one third of those who commit white-collar crime have a prior criminal conviction (Weisburd et al. 1994), 87 percent of those committing occupational crime have no prior conviction (Association of Certified Fraud Examiners 2012). In 2012, occupational crimes in the United States committed by employees resulted in average losses of $50,000. The figure for managers and owners, however, was $150,000 and $373,000 respectively. Those with tenure of more than ten years had crimes with ten times the losses of those with tenure of less than a year. Losses increase at every level of education (Association of Certified Fraud Examiners 2012). These findings suggest that investigators might get a different picture of white-collar crime and the privilege of offenders if they weighted offenses by harmfulness. They also make clear that the definition researchers use significantly influences descriptive findings.

In this essay, we define white-collar crimes as criminal offenses committed for direct or indirect financial gain by way of account manipulation, fraud, misrepresentation or deception in documents, or through the misuse of position as an employee or enterprise owner to such ends. We include "crimes by pen," or acts that involve manipulation of records to commit or obscure illegal practices including embezzlement. This includes misrepresentations on bills of sale, statements of collateral, services rendered, in transactions, and in communications with regulators, investors, or customers. Such acts sometimes occur when offenders circumvent legal restrictions on business practices for achievement of organizational objectives to secure career advancement, job security, or financial reward. Due to the abuse of public trust in the rules of trade they entail, the definition includes illegal manipulation of markets and deceptive financial accounting. While broad, our use excludes many forms of cheating, ordinary and physical crimes that occur at work, simple street cons, and crimes outside business.

II. Shaping Offender Pools

There are standing pools of offenders who are predisposed, tempted, and motivated to commit crime. This is true even if they flow toward crime only when events open channels of opportunity. The pools vary in size by location and time, and this is contingent partially on the numbers of persons prepared by circumstance to accomplish the tasks that particular offenses demand. On average, the preferences and outlooks of those who are structurally positioned to take advantage of or respond to a particular white-collar crime opportunity are shaped by a number of different factors.

A. Payoff

Survey research shows that the perceived benefits of white-collar crime and the perceived costs affect willingness to offend (Piquero, Exum, and Simpson 2007). Evidence from research into responses to increased regulatory efforts and penalties also demonstrates that corporate malefactors are responsive to penalties. Investigators employing a wide range of methodologies and data find significant and inverse relationships between resources devoted to regulating behavior and misconduct (Gray and Shimshack 2011). Dubin, Graetz, and Wilde (1990) found that $25 million expended on investigating, prosecuting, and punishing tax violators yielded $1.7 billion in increased revenues, for example. The vast majority of this money represented the effect of general deterrence of violators and not collections and penalties of those targeted.

Most opportunities for crime result when malefactors see a valued outcome as accessible by crime. Such valued outcomes include influence, power, a competitive advantage, material goods, or in the most usual instance money. Therefore, the presence and the rate of occurrence of valued ends or objects are important in criminal calculations. For example, lax oversight has played an integral role in the increasing scale of state largesse in the past half-century by creating lucrative and diverse opportunities such as welfare fraud, misappropriation of money from military contracting, and Medicare and Medicaid fraud. Understandably, lack of oversight makes crime seem a much more worthwhile risk.

Abundant opportunities in a particular sphere of commerce often occur when regulations and enforcement efforts or resources lag behind emergent criminal opportunities in those markets. Such ineffective control may occur when authorities do not recognize the potential for crime, perhaps because a market or transaction changes abruptly or evolves in unnoticed ways. Change in business and trade practices can also happen in ways that are so complex that they escape the understanding and attention of regulators. Notably, financial institutions often sweep in and recruit potential candidates with the credentials to understand, foresee, or investigate these intricate possibilities by offering salaries and benefits unmatchable by regulatory or investigative agencies who seek high-finance experts as employees (Lewis 2010).

Unforeseen crises or imperatives sometimes demand that allocators expend resources without regard for increased safeguards with predictable results. Disaster funds and charitable relief monies, used in situations such as Hurricane Katrina, inspire fraudsters large and small. Governmental estimates indicate that between approximately $600 million and $1.4 billion was paid out in improper or fraudulent assistance payments for the hurricane (Government Accountability Office 2006). Likewise, common sense suggests that when governments or international agencies pour large amounts of cash into failed and corrupt states in hopes of stabilizing them, much of the money disappears (Carroll 2012).

It is important to recognize the theoretical distinction between "pulls" toward white-collar crime created by opportunities and "pushes" that form pools of motivated or predisposed offenders. Investigators usually portray increased benefits of crime and lowered costs as pulls: when a crime is attractive, offenders respond. Attractive opportunities also push toward crime, however, by altering aggregate perceptions of the wrongfulness of offending. Lucrative and abundant criminal opportunities in a place or time shape the pool of offenders by altering collective moral assessments of citizens so that the number of predisposed persons increases.

Legal scholars' recognition of these pushes and pulls extends contemporary models of criminal choice beyond simple and individualistic portrayals of morally neutral individuals to examine the inculcation by law and law enforcement of moral standards in a population or group. Penalties form and reinforce public conceptions of right and wrong, and an "educative" or "declarative" effect results from eventual cultural calibration and support of the wrongness and contemptibility of an act by predictable punishment. Over time, the public learns to see acts that result in certain and severe penalty as not only wrongheaded but also morally wrong. When people think that offenders get away with crime routinely, however, they are unlikely to judge harshly and are more likely to follow suit (Welch et al. 2005). As the likelihood of penalties increases, individual willingness to commit discrete crimes declines due to fear of being caught, but an enduring effect is found in the depletion of pools of persons who would even consider the material costs and benefits because it has become morally deplorable to the public. It is worrisome, therefore, that the public believes authorities treat white-collar crime leniently and are unlikely to catch offenders (Schoepfer, Carmichael, and Piquero 2007).

B. Workforce Conditions

An often-overlooked source of increasing numbers of predisposed organizations and tempted individuals may be changes in the workplace. Reiss and Tonry (1993, p. 1) pointed out that "[p]erhaps the most striking revolution of the 20th century was the rapid expansion of the population of organizations." The continuation of this trend is reflected in the increasing number of employer firms, which has expanded from 5 million to 6 million in the past twenty years (Small Business Administration 2010). It has now been true for decades that "the population of profit, not-for-profit, and governmental organizations in the United States rivals in number the population of individuals" (Reiss and Tonry 1993, p. 1). As the numbers of organizations expand, the geographic span and the hierarchical complexity of many organizations also grow. This is relevant because infractions are likely to occur in large firms and may be more common in firms where top management intercedes from afar or manages mainly based on financial criteria rather than through up-close monitoring of operations (Hill et al. 1992). Infractions also occur more commonly in decentralized organizations (McKendall and Wagner 1997).

In keeping with a worldwide trend, changes in the nature and location of work have prepared more U.S. residents to take advantage of white-collar criminal opportunities (Weisburd et al. 1994). The proportion of the U.S. workforce reporting white-collar employment increased from 18 percent in 1900 to more than 61 percent in 2010. Today, there are more than 86 million white-collar workers (U.S. Department of Commerce 1975; U.S. Census Bureau 2011).

C. Economic Conditions

Crime is more tempting in some economic conditions than in others. The relationship between economic conditions and the supply of potential white-collar criminals likely reflects a curvilinear distribution: slow and steady growth is unlikely to drive crime, but economic busts and booms increase the proportion of individuals and organizations weighing criminal options (Staw and Szwajkowski 1975; Clinard and Yeager 1980; Simpson 1987; Baucus 1994; Alalehto 2010). During boom times, when there is the widespread belief that "everyone is getting rich," risk-taking increases. When everyone seems to be doing well by playing fast and loose, the belief that it is foolish to hold back becomes appealing. The belief that a rising economic tide obscures questionable activities and decreases the vigilance of law enforcement also emboldens many. Authorities are less likely to ferret out and detect schemes as long as money flows and culprits avert apparent catastrophes. For example, if pyramid-scheme proprietors invest some principal and return a solid yield, and checks to investors clear, this surely obscures their activity and postpones the reckoning that a weak economy would bring.

The relationship of measures of aggregate economic well-being to crime is complex, and there is mixed evidence for hypotheses asserting that economic indicators correlate with crime. The number of countervailing and moderating variables that affect crime rates at the same time as economic variables practically ensures that this is so. Nevertheless, there is some evidence that certain economic variables measuring hardship or economic sentiment correlate with some forms of offending (Rosenfeld and Fornango 2007). Difficult economic times lead many to think that they must cut corners in order to maintain their position. Commentators assert often that this is due to the salience of "fears of falling" when the economy makes apparent the grim consequences of losses (Wheeler 1992; Piquero 2012). Because it can depress both income and prospects for the future, an economic downturn increases general economic insecurity, anxiety about failing, competition, and psychological desperation; the term "fear of falling" encapsulates all of these conditions.

This is not to imply that fear of falling is a psychological trait that extends into many aspects of life. Evidence suggests that those who worry most about slippages in status also worry about the costs of crime, so their stable insecurities tend to reduce offending, all else held equal (Piquero 2012). As it pertains to white-collar offending, investigators should cast fear of falling as situational (Benson 1984). Potential offenders faced with perceived situational risks to income or status offend, while those who are secure in their current positions are less likely to experience fear and seek criminal opportunity. The insulating effect of job security may be why banked resources, often called slack, reduce infractions in challenging times (Baucus and Near 1991). It is likely that the prevalence of fear of falling in a populations waxes and wanes with economic conditions. In challenging economic environments or unsettled markets, personal and career hardships are common and make bending and breaking rules more tempting. Such circumstances cause individuals of many careers, stations, and temperaments to experience fear of falling and to consider behavioral options that they normally find unacceptable.

Inequality is another economic source of criminal inclination and crime. It predicts rates of street crime at various geographic aggregates (Hsieh and Pugh 1993). The typical theoretical interpretation is that, in areas and times with high degrees of inequality, the concentration of resources frustrates the disadvantaged. They respond by attempting to acquire money and property illegitimately, lashing out, or giving up on conventional means of achievement. To the casual observer, it is not difficult to understand that the pressures to commit crime are higher for those in Miami, Florida, where inequality is very high and easily seen than they are in Sheboygan, Wisconsin, where it is very low.

Inequality affects the pool of both ordinary and upperworld white-collar offenders. In addition to the motivation it provides the relatively disadvantaged, inequality diminishes the ability of a population to control the behavior of the privileged. When inequality makes it appear that relatively powerless members of society cannot control upper echelons, those in higher ranks come to feel that some forms of white-collar crime are ordinary business. Supporting this notion is that cross-national variation in inequality affects corruption (You and Khagram 2004). Estimates from a panel study of 102 countries from 1995 to 2005 show that a high level of development, human capital, and political rights reduces corruption, but economic inequality increases it (Badinger and Nindl 2012). In U.S. states, there is a bidirectional relationship or cycle between inequality and corruption over time (Apergis, Dincer, and Payne 2010). There also is evidence that there is less temptation to commit white-collar crime in civilly engaged places (Schoepfer and Piquero 2006). Upperworld malefactors can be expected where inequality and resultant civic disengagement leave the decisions of the powerful unchecked.

D. Crime-Facilitative Culture

In its various aspects, culture plays an essential role in the formation of potential pools of offenders. It affects the rate of occurrence and helps guide prevalent forms of crime. Culture can harbor a predominant ethos of competitiveness, provide ready justification for crime, or sustain a shared stance that some forms of white-collar offending are acceptable.

Locales and times vary in how powerfully and pervasively an ethos of competitiveness dominates interpersonal relationships and individual actions. In some environments, whether they are places, occupations, or organizations, competition is endemic and ruthless. Cultures of competition drive individuals to strive for success in an environment that allows few victors. Whether they seek fortune, fame, power, or respect, many worry ceaselessly about conditions that might stand in their way. For example, children of elites in China face immense pressure to gain entry or scholarships to prestigious and selective universities. Parents often hire agents to assist with applications, contributing to the growth of illicit cottage industries offering help with fabricating academic records, résumés, and writing samples (Jacobs 2010). Competitive environments might operate on criminal decisions indirectly by shifting decision-making approaches toward manipulative strategies (Verbeke, Ouwerkerk, and Peelen 1996). These worlds transform normative restraints and rules into challenges that some circumvent to disadvantage legitimate competitors.

A crime-facilitative culture—whether in an organization, industry, geographic locale, or historical era—makes available beliefs that others permit or normatively mandate noncompliance, or that circumstances justify it (Needleman and Needleman 1979). Salient rhetorical devices construe as acceptable choices that conflict with legal norms and perspectives that call them into question. These techniques of neutralization or accounts excuse infraction by blunting the moral force of law and neutralizing the guilt of criminal participation (Sykes and Matza 1957; Maruna and Copes 2004).

The stance toward misconduct permeates culture, and members perpetuate it in everyday understandings and the interactions that form them. A study on reporting illegal or irregular behavior among officers in the Israeli defense forces revealed that the effects of subjective understandings of reporting norms were much stronger predictors of personal intentions to report than were personal attitudes toward reporting (Ellis and Arieli 1999). Surveying 300 persons in two large certified public accounting firms revealed that assessments of corporate ethical culture and a strong rule-following orientation in the firm predicted individual ethical judgment, primarily by shaping respondents' ethical idealism (Douglas, Davidson, and Schwartz 2001).

Crime-facilitative cultures often accompany and sustain entrenched criminal practices in organizations and serve to educate the uninitiated into local conduct norms. For example, a salesperson might work with ostensive competitors in a territory to rig bids and joke that such practices are not part of the job—they *are* the job. If old hands conversationally mark those who are fastidious with rules and laws as being bothersome rubes, then new hires catch on quickly. A focus on the ridiculous burdens of regulatory red tape and the ineffectiveness and ineptitude of internal compliance departments also sends a message that few miss.

Conversely, cultures of compliance exist. There are highly ethical organizations where superiors endorse, support, and reward ethical conduct. Evidence suggests that where this is the case, subordinates in the organization respond to the model and to incentives for compliance (Simpson 2002). In corporations where respondents report strong ethical cultures, pressure for unethical behavior declines threefold, rates of misconduct decline by half, failure to report misconduct declines markedly, and retaliation for reporting diminishes from 1 in 4 incidents to 1 in 20 (Ethics Resource Center 2011).

Cultural forces may influence how entire geographies or nations respond to shifting opportunities. For example, a national survey reveals that at times of perceived increases in scrutiny from the outside, respondents are more likely to report strong ethical climates in their workplace (Ethics Resource Center 2011). A small study by the economist Steven Levitt (2006) demonstrates ethical variation by firm and time. His associate, also trained in economics, delivered bagels and donuts on an honor payment system to more than 100 New York office buildings; take a bagel and leave the money. Analysis of losses to theft revealed that there was a great deal of stability in which firms had high and low rates, and that large firms had more. However, the overall rate of theft dropped significantly (thefts declined by 15 percent) in the aftermath of the attacks on September 11, 2001. In the wake of the terrorist attack, stealing a bagel seemingly was 85 percent as attractive as it had been prior to the tragedy. Surely, it is more difficult to justify stealing from neighbors in such times. While generalizing this result to white-collar crime takes imagination, this curious natural experiment reinforces the notion that public moral stances ebb and flow with events. Wherever a crime-conducive culture takes hold, it increases the supply of the tempted and predisposed. Where cultures of restraint are in place, the pool of offenders dwindles.

III. Backgrounds and Mental Predisposition

The pool of white-collar offenders shares psychological characteristics and traits that distinguish it from the general population. Some of these characteristics, such as low levels of self-control among some (Benson and Moore 1992), high rates of mental illness, and certain psychopathologic traits (Poortinga, Lemmen, and Jibson 2006; Ragatz, Fremouw, and Baker 2012), distinguish both street and white-collar lawbreakers from the population of non-offenders. In fact, one study found higher rates of unipolar and bipolar disorders among evaluated white-collar offenders than among street offenders (Poortinga et al. 2006). Obviously, where these characteristics generally are disadvantageous to social status and upward mobility, a higher percentage of street offenders exhibit them (Ragatz et al. 2012). The fact that many white-collar crimes require occupational achievement suggests that severe disabilities and the most apparent personality problems are rarer in their ranks, and this should be especially so among upperworld offenders. Less apparent mental problems and positions on the mental health disorder spectrum often appear in white-collar worlds, however. For example, psychopathy may suit a person for certain corporate positions and be more common there (Babiak, Newmann, and Hare 2010). Indeed, many mental illnesses, including substance abuse, occur across ranks and probably contribute to explaining the occurrence of white-collar offending across individuals in all strata.

There is little reason to think that "serious and chronic mental illnesses" or psychoses like schizophrenia vary significantly by time or place. Therefore, they have little influence on variation in the pool of predisposed offenders or changing rates of crime. Yet, other mental illnesses and bad habits vary significantly and likely shape the size of the pool by time and place. For example, drug- and alcohol-related disorders have prevalence and incidence proportions that vary significantly over time and by place (Haffner 1985).

A high rate of addiction characterizes the white-collar offender pool. Like street offenders, those with deliberative capacity clouded by substance abuse fill pools of the tempted and predisposed. The financial costs and workplace failures associated with addiction also lead to crime, and this effect may span social classes. Because rates of substance abuse and addiction vary significantly by class background, it is probably an especially prominent problem for ordinary white-collar offenders; their motives are not likely very different from those that drive others to burglary. A comparison of white-collar offenders referred by courts for psychiatric evaluation with nonviolent thieves found that rates of substance abuse were 65 percent and 90 percent, respectively (Poortinga et al. 2006). Substance abuse occurs in all ranks, however. Indeed, there is some evidence that both poverty and affluence contribute (Luthar and Latendresse 2007). Space precludes reviewing what drives drug and alcohol addiction in populations, but it is likely that when use of addictive drugs increases, and particularly if it increases among the privileged segments of society, we should expect more white-collar crime.

In addition to psychological problems and bad habits, attitudinal characteristics distinguish white-collar offenders from non-offenders. For example, it is clear that the ethical stance of people confronted with prohibited opportunities predicts their choices. Belief about whether a practice is acceptable ethically may influence an individual's intention and likelihood of pursuing it (Simkin and McLeod 2010). Crime can be unthinkable for a person who adheres to a general code that forbids acting in his or her self-interest and against the interest of others and who values obeying the law. When investigators present quasi-experimental vignettes containing organizational incentives for and against offending (including formal and informal punishments), results reveal that opportunities provide significant incentives, but that those who are highly ethical are unresponsive to changes in the risks and rewards of offending (Paternoster and Simpson 1996; Simpson 2002).

Ethical stances vary not only between individuals but also by place and time. For example, there has been a recent turn for the worse in tolerance for unethical behavior in the U.S. workforce, perhaps in response to reduced job security (Ethics Resource Center 2011). By nation, structural conditions vary and shape ethics. Trust in government, trust in the legal system, and national pride predict attitudes related to tax compliance, for example. This pattern suggests that variation in the legitimacy granted government and institutions shapes the numbers of persons attitudinally predisposed to offend and subsequently affects rates of some forms of white-collar crime (McGhee 1998).

White-collar (particularly upperworld) offenders come from more comfortable backgrounds and circumstances than others do, and social-psychological characteristics rooted in relatively affluent backgrounds may forebode their crimes. For example, lower-class individuals turn to family and community as means of coping when dealing with chaotic situations, while upper-class individuals place increased emphasis on making money and seek financial gain when their environments become chaotic (Piff et al. 2012). It requires a small leap, therefore, to link chaotic and troublesome work environments, perhaps rooted in larger economic troubles, theoretically to increased chances of seeking criminal payoff among the well-heeled.

Such differences might have roots in distinctive family relationships among the privileged. Family life in the middle and upper classes centers on cultivating certain skills in children. Parents and educators devote time, attention, and money to instilling verbosity, creativity, and the educational background that will prepare their children to fit in among similar company, manage abstract concepts, and negotiate social worlds of middle- or upper-class work and life (Shover and Hochstetler 2005).

Parents of privileged children teach that life is a competition, and that social manipulations and long-term investments in advantageous relationships provide a competitive edge. There is a great deal of emphasis on performance, particularly in academics and career development.

Lareau (2002) and her students spent hours participating in and observing the daily lives of a sample of working- and middle-class families. They noted that parents of poor and working-class children employ practices of childrearing (Lareau 2002, p.747) described as "natural growth." Lareau (2002) explained that "parents viewed children's development as spontaneously unfolding, as long as they were provided with comfort, food, shelter and other basic support" (p. 773). Poor and working-class parents try to provide basic conditions for children to grow but do not structure leisure.

Blue-collar parents use directives rather than reason to control children (Lareau 2002). In blue-collar households, communication is implicit; much is understood but goes unsaid, and children do not engage in conversation with adults so much as receive edicts. When there is rule breaking or mistakes, parents point them out and correct without question or delay. In households that are familiar with simple authority, contesting or discussing the implications or reasons for the error or negotiating is out of the question. Parental discipline in poor and working-class families often is gruff and runs to the immediate, painful, and quick. Corporal punishment is used more often by working-class parents than those at higher levels of the class structure (Strauss and Donnely 1994). Many working-class children develop a generalized conformism, and they generally see legal threats as legitimate and binding (Kohn 1977). They might be less likely to develop self-assurance in dealing with superiors and impersonal organizations.

Middle-class parents encourage children verbally and include them in conversation with adults. Conversations in these homes center on interpreting and puzzling over events far removed from daily life. Children learn to search for complex motives and learn that others value their opinions and perspectives. Parents not only defer to children in conversation, but also children witness parents' juggling family schedules around their activities. Lareau (2002) suggested that parents' deference and attentiveness and other aspects of middle-class childrearing produce a sense of entitlement in middle-class children, one that may find expression throughout life.

Backgrounds and experiences have a significant influence on the formation of mental traits. Some of these traits serve as conduits for translating predispositions formed early in life into adult decisions. The traits of entitlement and arrogance are conceptually similar and equally likely to be risk factors in white-collar criminal decision making. Arrogance is an unrealistic appraisal of one's personal abilities and importance that undermines one's realistic prediction of the consequences of one's behavior. The arrogant are confident that if they commit a criminal action, authorities will never treat it as such. They might be accustomed to a malleable world that they can manipulate with ease. Arrogant white-collar offenders generally see themselves as respectable and reasonable people whose responses to problems should be understandable (Shover and Hunter 2010). To white-collar offenders, the spirit of the law does not intend criminal penalties for people like them; when laws interfere, then, they might deem them as overly cumbersome intrusions or as misguided.

Entitlement lends itself to the belief that benefits of some kind are due, and that any disruption of delivery is illegitimate. This sense affects a range of crimes and unethical behaviors and is consistent with larger personality patterns reflected in scales designed to measure narcissism, criminal thinking, and psychopathy (Campbell et al. 2004; Hare 2006). The entitled expect their abilities and credentials to be viewed as special, their ends to be achieved, and their efforts to be rewarded richly.

As with their overall style of childrearing, middle-class parents believe competition is a positive experience and one they try to provide for their children (Lareau 2002). Children reared in middle-class circumstances or with even greater privilege expect to compete and win and for things to go well in their lives. Later in life, they strive for improved position and constantly compare their efforts and remunerations to work-mates and neighbors (Langston 1993).

Competitiveness might manifest in crime only in the face of impending failure. In experimental tasks, persons who cannot complete the tasks or who fall behind within the provided rules are more likely to cheat in competitive circumstances (Schwieren and Weichselbaumer 2010). This finding suggests that all else held equal, the ability to compete fairly has an inverse relationship to offending. Shover, Coffey, and Hobbs (2003) found that the telemarketing fraudsters they interviewed had high aspirations but, prior to discovering their penchant for fraud, had not achieved the lifestyle or success they had expected. Many desired the toys and property of the middle and upper classes—but they also wanted to party lavishly, get money quickly, and work only in conditions they enjoyed. Predictable loss motivates the highly competitive and enti-tled to crime. Those who emphasize competitive outlooks and the necessity of success in their children perhaps should not be surprised when their children have problems accepting failure or are dissatisfied persistently with their achievements and position (Luthar 2003).

Desire for control is another trait linked to white-collar crime. Those individuals with high levels of desire for control are assertive and decisive and seek to influence oth-ers for personal advantage. White-collar employees and executives desire and exhibit these traits (Kaiser, Hogan, and Craig 2008). Piquero et al. (2007) applied a standard measure of desire for control to 131 M.B.A. students and managers. The respondents interpreted a corporate-crime scenario where situational factors varied randomly. In addition, the investigators asked questions about the payoff and costs of offending. Situational, individual, and personality characteristics were significant predictors of intentions to offend. Desire for control was a significant aspect of personality that pre-dicted it. The origins of desire for control might begin in lives where things tend to turn out well; in this way, it is extremely unlike the learned helplessness that often plagues those befallen by lifetimes of difficulty. Moreover, being accustomed to greater control and self-determination leads to sensitivity to situations where there is inability to exert control and to greater expectations of autonomy (Schwartz 2000).

What we know about why some people embezzle from their employers while oth-ers do not highlights the importance of self-conversations in framing prospective acts. Embezzlers are able to steal in part because they define the act of stealing in a way that enables them to maintain a favorable sense of self (Cressey 1953). Some define it as bor-rowing or as compensation due them for work beyond their official duty and hours.

Others see it as something done to provide for their families that cannot be provided for legitimately. Studies spanning more than five decades consistently have shown that people who have offended and been caught tell stories that minimize their guilt; it remains uncertain whether they do this in advance of crime and whether some are adept at crafting and using such neutralizations (Maruna and Copes 2004).

Working-class citizens have available a narrow range of acceptable explanations for their crimes. Ordinary thieves generally refer to their activities as "doing dirt," "stealing," or "doing wrong." Upper-class and middle-class children gain acuity with a more diverse array of neutralizing justifications (Hazani 1991). Fraudsters often point to the similarities of what they did and what others in business do. They highlight that salesmanship involves deception and that *caveat emptor* is the rule. They contend either that their crimes are part of ordinary business or that the line between licit and illicit transactions is so thin that one inadvertently slips across. Upperworld offenders refer to cumbersome regulation and see their illicit actions as mere circumventions of arbitrary and capricious intrusions. In this way, "social controls that serve to check or inhibit deviant motivational patterns are rendered inoperative, and the individual is freed to engage in [crime] without serious damage to his self-image" (Sykes and Matza 1957, p. 667).

Perspectives and skills acquired in generative worlds and reinforced in affluent occupational lives facilitate this process. They make it possible for respectable citizens to weigh criminal options without adopting a criminal identity (Ragatz et al. 2012). Their verbal intelligence, flexibility, and tendency to see many moral choices as gray areas allow them to construe acts as understandable and allowable rather than criminal. Decision makers are more likely to offend when they inhabit a culture of excuse making that provides ready evasions, but backgrounds also prepare some to craft explanations that explain moral departures.

Social and cultural conditions of middle-class life appear to generate ample and increasing numbers of individuals prepared to commit white-collar crime. Hagan (1992) noted that both social power and risk taking, which are characteristic of affluent classes, might contribute to crime and delinquency in privileged children. Others point out that social class "alters a variety of life contexts and chances" from differences in economic opportunities to culture, and this can increase delinquency by privileged youth (Wright et al. 1999, p. 178).

It is possible, perhaps even likely given what we know of the high levels of dissatisfaction and pathologies of the affluent (Luthar 2003), that prospering eras yield greater numbers of persons predisposed to commit some forms of crime, and that not all of these motivated offenders come from disadvantaged backgrounds. Affluent societies might yield increasing numbers of persons whose backgrounds and experiences lead them to believe that they are entitled to resources, positions, and control, and this entitlement might lead some to crime.

If affluence shapes the criminal psychology of a time or place, its effect probably is especially significant for upperworld offenders. The outlooks it engenders might result in increasing rates of crime among the privileged when temporary economic setbacks make it appear that their rightful position is slipping and their goals are receding. Increasing numbers of affluent persons, many of whom are reared in privileged circumstances, might contribute to increases in numbers of persons prepared to rationalize and justify the offenses they commit in pursuit of sustained success.

IV. CONCLUSION

When it comes to seizing opportunities for crime, some will and some will not. Ultimately, persons morally and circumstantially situated so as to perceive crime as lucrative compose the pool of offenders. Just as is the case for street offenders, the pool of white-collar offenders has no single line of demarcation separating it from the general population. In large part, historical and cultural forces that affect entire populations form the shape and depth of the pool's basin. However, opportunity draws individuals to discrete, detectable crimes.

One cannot deny the structural sources of crime, but prevailing sentiments to authority and the law shape the pool as well. Valerie Braithwaite (2001) found that citizens approach the requirement to comply with tax law from a variety of "motivational postures." Many citizens and business owners comply due to obligations of citizenship. Among the noncompliant, some are openly resistive and question the legitimacy of taxation policy (Andreoni, Errard, and Feinstein 1998). Such sentiments to regulatory and legal interferences might wax and wane in large populations, communities, or nations. Moreover, when government intervention in corporate behavior is sporadic and legal threats are uncertain, increased numbers consider intrusions into questionable activities as both unlikely and illegitimate.

Fortunately, many white-collar workers live and work in contexts that promote prudent decision making. Therefore, the proximity of law enforcement and its response to citizen concerns of white-collar malfeasance are likely to thwart potential offenders. Improved chances of detection dissuade potential individual offenders as they contemplate discrete crimes. The more important effects of deterrence, however, occur when the state demonstrates through certain and shameful punishment the immorality, criminality, and dishonor of committing crimes of deception.

REFERENCES

Alalehto, Tage. 2010. "Wealthy White-Collar Criminals: Corporations as Offenders." *Journal of Financial Crime* 17: 308–20.

Andreoni, James, Brian Errard, and Jonathan Feinstein. 1998. "Tax Compliance." *Journal of Economic Literature* 36: 818–35.

Apergis, Nicholaus, Oghuzan C. Dincer, and James E. Payne. 2010. "The Relationship between Corruption and Inequality in U.S. States." *Public Choice* 135: 125–35.

Association of Certified Fraud Examiners. 2012. *Report to the Nations on Occupational Fraud and Abuse: 2012 Global Fraud Study*. Austin, TX: Author.

Babiak, Paul, Craig Newmann, and Robert Hare. 2010. "Corporate Psychopathy: Talking the Walk." *Behavioral Sciences and the Law* 28: 174–93.

Badinger, Harald, and Elisabeth Nindl. 2012. *Globalization, Inequality, and Corruption*. Vienna University of Economics and Business, Department of Economics Working Paper Series, 139.

Baucus, Melissa S. 1994. "Pressure, Opportunity and Predisposition: A Multivariate Model of Corporate Illegality." *Journal of Management* 20: 699–721.

Baucus, Melissa S., and Janet P. Near. 1991. "Can Illegal Corporate Behavior Be Predicted? An Event History Analysis." *Academy of Management Journal* 34: 9–36.

Benson, Michael L. 1984. "The Fall from Grace: Loss of Occupational Status as a Consequence of Conviction from White-Collar Crime." *Criminology* 22: 573–94.

Benson, Michael L. 2002. *Crime and the Lifecourse: An Introduction*. Los Angeles: Roxbury.

Benson, Michael L., and Elizabeth Moore. 1992. "Are White-Collar and Common Offenders the Same? An Empirical and Theoretical Critique of a Recently Proposed General Theory of Crime." *Journal of Research in Crime and Delinquency* 29: 251–72.

Braithwaite, Valerie. 2001. "A New Approach to Tax Compliance." In *Taxing Democracy*, edited by Valerie Braithwaite. Aldershot, UK: Ashgate.

Campbell, W. Keith, Angelica M. Bonachi, Jeremy Shelton, Julie J. Exline, and Brad J. Bushman. 2004. "Psychological Entitlement: Interpersonal Consequences and Validation of a Self-Report Measure." *Journal of Personality Assessment* 83: 29–45.

Carroll, Kevin T. 2012. "Afghan Corruption—The Greatest Obstacle to Victory in Operation Enduring Freedom." *Georgetown Journal of International Law* 43: 873–96.

Clinard, Marshall B., and Peter C. Yeager. 1980. *Corporate Crime*. New York: Free Press.

Cressey, Donald R. 1953. *Other People's Money: A Study in the Psychology of Embezzlement*: Glencoe, IL: Free Press.

Douglas, Patricia Casey, Ronald A. Davidson, and Bill N. Schwartz. 2001. "The Effect of Organizational Culture and Ethical Orientation on Accountants' Ethical Judgments." *Journal of Business Ethics* 34: 101–21.

Dubin, Jeffrey, Michael J. Greatz, and Louis L. Wilde. 1990. "The Effect of Audit Rates on the Federal Individual Income Tax, 1977–1986." *National Tax Journal* 43: 395–409.

Ellis, Shmuel, and Shaul Arieli. 1999. "Predicting Intentions to Report Administrative and Disciplinary Infractions: Applying the Reasoned Action Model." *Human Relations* 52: 947–67.

Ethics Resource Center. 2011. *National Business Ethics Survey*. Arlington, VA: National Business Ethics Survey.

Government Accountability Office. 2006. *Hurricane Katrina and Rita Disaster Relief, GAO-06 844T*. Washington, D.C.: Author.

Gray, Wayne B., and Jay P. Shimshack. 2011. "The Effectiveness of Environmental Monitoring and Enforcement: A Review of the Empirical Evidence." *Review of Environmental and Economic Policy* 5: 3–24.

Haffner, Heinz. 1985. "Are Mental Disorders Increasing over Time." *Psychopathology* 18: 66–81.

Hagan, John. 1992. "The Poverty of a Classless Criminology." *Criminology* 30: 1–20.

Hare, Robert D. 2006. *Snakes in Suits: When Psychopaths Go to Work*. New York: Harper Business.

Hazani, Moshe. 1991. "Aligning Vocabulary, Symbol Banks, and Sociocultural Structure." *Journal of Contemporary Ethnography* 20: 179–205.

Hill, Charles W., Patricia C. Kelley, Bradley R. Agle, Michael A. Hitt, and Robert E. Hoskisson. 1992. "An Empirical Examination of the Causes of Corporate Wrongdoing in the United States." *Human Relations* 45: 1055–76.

Hsieh, Ching-Chi, and M. D. Pugh. 1993. "Poverty, Income Inequality, and Violent Crime: A Meta-Analysis of Recent Aggregate Data Studies." *Criminal Justice Review* 18: 182–202.

Huff, Rodney, Christian Desilets, and John Kane. 2011. *The National Public Survey on White Collar Crime*. Fairmont, WV: National White Collar Crime Center.

Jacobs, Andrew. 2010. "Rampant Fraud Threat to China's Brisk Ascent." *New York Times* (October 7): A1.

Kaiser, Robert B., Robert Hogan, and Craig S. Bartholomew. 2008. "Leadership and the Fate of Organizations." *American Psychologist* 63: 96–100.

Kohn, Melvin T. 1977. *Class and Conformity*, 2nd ed. Chicago: University of Chicago Press.

Langston, Doris. 1993. "Who Am I Now? The Politics of Class Identity." In *Working Class Women in the Academy*, edited by Michelle M. Tokarcysk and Elizabeth A. Fay. Amherst: University of Massachusetts.

Lareau, Annete. 2002. "Invisible Inequality: Social Class and Childrearing in Black and White Families." *American Sociological Review* 67: 747–76.

Levitt, Steven D. 2006. "White-Collar Crime Writ Small: A Case Study of Bagels, Donuts, and the Honor System." *American Economic Review* 96: 290–4.

Lewis, Michael. 2010. *Liars Poker: Rising Through the Wreckage on Wall Street*. New York: Norton and Company.

Luthar, Suniya S. 2003. "The Culture of Affluence: Psychological Costs of Material Wealth." *Child Development* 74: 1581–93.

Luthar, Suniya S., and Shawn Latendresse. 2007. "Children of the Affluent: Challenges to Well-Being." *Current Directions in Psychological Science* 14: 49–53.

Maruna, Shadd, and Heith Copes. 2004. "Excuses, Excuses: What Have We Learned from Five Decades of Neutralization Research?" In *Crime and Justice: A Review of Research*, Vol. 32, edited by Michael Tonry. Chicago: University of Chicago Press.

McGhee, Robert W. 1998. *The Ethics of Tax Evasion: Perspectives in Theory and Practice*. Dumont, NJ: Dumont Institute for Public Policy.

McKendall, Marie A., and John A. Wagner, III. 1997. "Motive, Opportunity, Choice, and Corporate Illegality." *Organization Science* 8: 624–47.

Needleman, Martin L., and Carolyn Needleman. 1979. "Organizational Crime: Two Models of Criminogenesis." *Sociological Quarterly* 20: 517–28.

Paternoster, Raymond, and Sally S. Simpson. 1996. "Sanction Threats and Appeals to Morality: Testing a Rational Choice Model of Corporate Crime." *Law and Society Review* 30: 549–83.

Piff, Paul K., Daniel M. Sancato, Andres G. Martinez, Michael W. Kraus, and Dachner Keltner. 2012. "Class, Chaos, and the Construction of Community." *Journal of Personality and Social Psychology*. Advance online publication. doi:10.1037/a0029673

Piquero, Nicole Leeper. 2012. "The Only Thing We Have to Fear Is Fear Itself: Investigating the Relationship between Fear of Falling and White-Collar Crime." *Crime and Delinquency* 58: 362–79.

Piquero, Nicole Leeper, M. Lyn Exum, and Sally S. Simpson. 2007. "Integrating the Desire-for-Control and Rational Choice in a Corporate Crime Context." *Justice Quarterly* 22: 252–80.

Poortinga, Ermest, Craig Lemmon, and Michael D. Jibson. 2006. "A Case-Control Study: White-Collar Defendants Compared with Defendants Charged with Other Nonviolent Theft." *Journal of the American Academy of Psychiatry and Law* 34: 82–89.

Ragatz, Laurie L., William Fremouw, and Edward Baker. 2012. "The Psychological Profile of White-Collar Offenders: Demographics, Criminal Thinking, Psychopathic Traits, and Psychopathology." *Criminal Justice and Behavior* 20: 1–20.

Reiss, Albert J., Jr., and Michael Tonry. 1993. "Organizational Crime." In *Beyond the Law: Crime in Complex Organizations*. In *Crime and Justice: A Review of Research*, Vol. 18, edited by Michael Tonry and Albert J. Reiss, Jr. Chicago: University of Chicago Press.

Rosenfeld, Richard, and Robert Fornango. 2007. "The Impact of Economic Conditions on Robbery and Property Crime: The Role of Consumer Sentiment." *Criminology* 5: 735–69.

Schoepfer, Andrea, Stephanie Carmichael, and Nicole Leeper Piquero. 2007. "Do Perceptions of Punishment Vary between White-Collar and Street Criminals?" *Journal of Criminal Justice* 35: 151–63.

Schoepfer, Andrea, and Nicole Leeper Piquero. 2006. "Exploring White-Collar Crime and the American Dream: A Partial Test of Institutional Anomie Theory." *Journal of Criminal Justice* 34: 227–35.

Schwartz, Barry. 2000. "Self-Determination: The Tyranny of Freedom." *American Psychologist* 55: 79–88.

Schwieren, Christianne, and Doris Weichselbaumer. 2010. "Does Competition Enhance Performance or Cheating: A Laboratory Experiment." *Journal of Economic Psychology* 31: 241–53.

Shover, Neal, Glen S. Coffey, and Dick Hobbs. 2003. "Crime on the Line: Telemarketing and the Changing Nature of Professional Crime." *British Journal of Criminology* 43: 489–505.

Shover, Neal, and Andy Hochstetler. 2005. *Choosing White-Collar Crime*. Cambridge, UK: Cambridge University Press.

Shover, Neal, and Ben W. Hunter. 2010. "Blue-Collar, White-Collar: Crimes and Mistakes." In *Offenders on Offending: Learning about Crime from Criminals*, edited by Wim Bernasco. Collompton, UK: Wilan.

Simkin, Mark, and Alexander McLeod. 2010. "Why Do College Students Cheat?" *Journal of Business Ethics* 94: 441–53.

Simpson, Sally S. 1987. "Cycles of Illegality: Antitrust Violations in Corporate America." *Social Forces* 65: 943–63.

Simpson, Sally S. 2002. *Corporate Crime, Law and Social Control*. New York: Cambridge University Press.

Small Business Administration. 2010. *Private Firms, Establishments, Employment, Annual Payroll and Receipts by Firm Size, 1988–2007*. Available at http://archive.sba.gov/advo/research/us88 07.pdf

Staw, Barry M., and Eugene Szwajkowski. 1975. "The Scarcity Munificence Component of Organizational Environments and the Commission of Illegal Acts." *Administrative Science Quarterly* 20: 345–54.

Strauss, Murray, and Denise A. Donnelly. 1994. *Beating the Devil out of Them: Corporal Punishment in American Families*. New York: Lexington.

Sykes, Gresham M., and David Matza. 1957. "Techniques of Neutralization: A Theory of Delinquency." *American Sociological Review* 22: 664–70.

TracFed. 2012. *Tracreports: White Collar Crime Convictions for May 2012*. Syracuse, NY: Author. Available at http://trac.syr.edu/tracreports/bulletins/white_collar_crime/month-lymay12/gui/

U.S. Census Bureau. 2011. *Current Population Survey: Annual Social and Economic Supplements*. Washington, D.C.: U.S. Government Printing Office.

U.S. Department of Commerce. 1975. *Historical Statistics of the U.S.: Colonial Times to 1970*. Washington, D.C.: Author.

Verbeke, Willem, Cok Ouwerkerk, and Ed Peelen. 1996. "Exploring Contextual and Individual Factors on Ethical Decision Making of Salespeople." *Journal of Business Ethics* 15: 1175–84.

Weisburd, David, Stanton Wheeler, Elizabeth Waring, and Nancy Bode. 1994. *Crimes of the Middle Classes: White-Collar Offenders in the Federal Courts*. New Haven, CT: Yale University Press.

Welch, Michael R., Xu Yili, Thoroddur Bjarnason, Tom Petee, Patricia O'Donnell, and Paul Magro. 2005. "'But Everybody Does It . . .': The Effects of Perceptions, Moral Pressures, and Informal Sanctions on Tax Cheating." *Sociological Spectrum* 25: 21–52.

Wheeler, Stanton. 1992. "The Problem of White-Collar Motivation." In *White-Collar Crime Reconsidered*, edited by Kip Schlegel and David Weisburd. Boston: Northeastern University Press.

Wright, Bradley R., Aushalom Caspi, Terrie E. Moffit, Richard A. Miech, and Phil A. Silva. 1999. "Reconsidering the Relationship between SES and Delinquency: Causation but not Correlation." *Criminology* 37: 175–94.

You, Jong-Sung, and Sanjeev Khagram. 2004. "A Comparative Study of Inequality and Corruption." *American Sociological Review* 70: 135–57.

CHAPTER 9

MIDDLE-CLASS CRIME

*Moral Economies between Crime in the Streets
and Crime in the Suites*

SUSANNE KARSTEDT

MIDDLE-CLASS crime is as difficult a concept as white-collar crime, and it critically shares a number of the inbuilt problems of the latter. This chapter follows Sutherland's original and path-breaking concept; it links a group of offenders to particular types of crime by way of the access to opportunities that this group shares. "Ordinary people" are believed to commit white-collar crimes in increasing numbers, due to changes in consumption, finances, and banking, and foremost the revolution in technology that came with the Internet. However, they are equally often the targets and victims of crime, resulting in a considerable overlap between offending and victimization among them (Karstedt and Farrall 2006a, 2007; Karstedt 2015). Their crimes are located between the crimes in the suites and crimes in the streets, and they are representative of the broad middle of society. Contemporary developments of middle-class crime and victimization are analyzed against the backdrop of a globally growing middle class and the profound changes in which its members work, consume, and own property in different parts of the world.

Section I provides a brief history of the concept within the context of white-collar crime research and conceptualization. In section II, I will define middle-class crime, give an overview of its most important characteristics, and outline a theoretical approach to middle-class crime. This section also introduces the framework of the "moral economy" (Thompson 1971). Section III charts the scope of middle-class crime, including types of offenses, offenders and victims, as well the costs of these types of crime. Sections IV and V analyze the moral economies of the middle classes in their capacity both as consumers and citizens from a comparative perspective. Greed and need have been both made responsible for white-collar crime in general and middle-class crime in particular. Section VI explores the dominance of greed or need in the reservoir of motives of middle-class offenders. Section VII concludes with a perspective on the future of middle-class crime. Conclusions reached in this chapter include the following:

- White-collar crime is essentially middle-class crime. Like any white-collar crimes, these crimes mostly include cheating and lying: making false insurance claims; claiming for refunds one is not entitled to; all types of tax evasion, with the most common forms of requesting and paying "cash in hand" in order to avoid taxes or contributions to social security; cheating on benefits; deceiving fellow citizens in secondhand sales; and small-scale and street-level corruption in terms of favors asked. This is "white-collar crime writ small," and most of these illegal practices and moral transgressions are just the everyday crimes of ordinary people.
- Middle classes share essential features that are decisive for their engagement in crime and shady practices. They are consumers and citizens alike. The rise of the middle classes and the welfare state occurred concomitantly in the global North and intricately linked the middle classes to the state bureaucracy. This opens up a range of opportunities for typical middle-class crimes of small-scale tax evasion, and false benefit or subsidies claims.
- White-collar crime writ small—and offenders from the "respectable middle classes" at the center of contemporary societies—share a number of defining characteristics with white-collar crime and criminals generally as originally defined by Sutherland. These acts are often moral transgressions and situated in a gray zone between illegality and immorality; offenders evade detection and prosecution, even if for different reasons; and denial is widespread among the respectable, whether in the middle or at the top of the social pyramid.
- Two conceptual frameworks advance our understanding of middle-class crime. First, choice theories are based on causal factors that juxtapose the supply of "lure" with control and oversight over the alluring goods, and both external and internal oversight or self-restraint of those who are tempted. These factors create the supply of criminal opportunities on the one hand, and a pool of motivated offenders on the other hand. Second, middle-class crime is part of contemporary moral economies; these represent the structural and moral constraints in which individual choices are embedded, but also the incentives and justifications for crimes and shady practices.
- In contrast to street crime and common notions of fraud and white-collar crime, victims of the crimes of everyday life are neither from different social backgrounds nor life circumstances than offenders; rather, they share the same social space. The result is a comparably high victim–offender overlap in European countries in general, in particular for countries with larger and more affluent middle classes. This corroborates the typical relationship between this specific social group and its access to opportunities of crime.
- Middle-class crimes, like other white-collar crimes, result in a multiple of monetary losses in comparison to more common crimes; even if they are individually small, they cause considerable damage and losses. Fraud and similar crimes

have surpassed ordinary property crimes in terms of costs. The state and government are particularly affected, as are financial services, small businesses, and even charities.

- In contemporary European moral economies, fairness and the balance of power relations emerge as a decisive correlate of middle-class victimization and offending. Unfair procedures in consumer markets include little concern for consumers and preoccupation with profits as well as price fixing, both leading to unfair deals for consumers. Perceptions of and actually unfair business practices shape the moral economy and the "generalized morality" in markets, as well as the readiness of consumers to engage in transgressions and crimes of everyday life.

- As distrust of business and perceptions of their unfair dealings lead to moral disengagement, so too does corruption of government officials. Where corruption reaches high levels in European countries, tax compliance decreases significantly. As main contributors of taxes and recipients of healthcare, education, and pensions, the allegiance of citizens from the broad middle classes is decisive but might be easily lost.

- Middle-class crimes, both as transgressions and victimizations, are highest in European societies with comparably larger and also more affluent middle classes. This indicates that greed rather than need motivates these types of illegal and morally dubious practices, and simultaneously makes consumers vulnerable to being victims. Given the range of the middle classes in contemporary societies and huge differences in their financial situation, both need and greed play a role in the reservoir of motives for engaging in morally dubious or illegal practices.

- The crimes of everyday life are constitutive of the criminality of the middle classes and simultaneously illuminate their "inner moral life" and moral commitments, both as consumers and as citizens. Collective perceptions of procedural fairness in markets of goods and services are the lynchpin of contemporary moral economies as they were in 18th-century Britain. Regulating and prosecuting unfair and semi-legal practices of businesses, tightly monitoring abuse of their power, and empowering consumers to protect their interests seem to be reasonable strategies for business and governments to reduce losses from the crimes of everyday life committed by the middle classes.

I. A Short History
of Middle-Class Crime

With the term "white-collar crime," Edwin Sutherland coined one of the most successful and popular concepts of criminology, and simultaneously one of the most difficult for criminologists. Today, the term is vernacular in most languages whether translated or not and appeals to the public as well as the criminological imagination. Its appeal stems from the fact that it evokes images of the rich and powerful who commit serious crimes with impunity and escape from prosecution and punishment due to their social status and the power they can wield. The recent global financial crisis and involvement of banks and bankers indeed gave rise to globally shared sentiments and resentment against the global financial powers who had not only engaged and were involved in seemingly criminal activity, but who obviously enjoyed their—if not illegal then at least immoral—gains with impunity. Donald Newman (1958, p. 753) noted that "no longer is the criminologist a middle-class observer studying lower-class behavior. He now looks upward at the most powerful and prestigious strata." From early on, the concept of white-collar crime has been shifted toward the "higher end" of these types of crimes, where crimes are complex, damage is normally huge, and victims are numerous. White-collar crime has been increasingly superposed and identified with "crimes of the powerful" (Tombs and Whyte 2003; Karstedt 2007), "elite deviance" (Simon 2011), or "corporate crimes," and white-collar criminals have been seen as a "criminal elite" (Coleman [1988] 2002). Heeding Newman's directions, criminologists started to address "crimes in the suites" as synonymous with white-collar crimes and to neglect the same type of crimes committed by the general public and ordinary citizens comfortably situated in the middle strata of contemporary societies.

This is the result of Sutherland's difficult legacy and its inbuilt ambiguities. On the one hand, Sutherland defined a group of offenders in contrast to lower-class and blue-collar offenders; on the other hand he—if only vaguely—delineated a range of crimes, to which positions in organizations and agencies gave access. As such, white-collar crime is as much a specific type of crime that is linked to specific activities, as it signifies a specific type of offender, however merely identified by his or her social status. Both ways to define white-collar crime are difficult to reconcile, and this has contributed to numerous problems of conceptualizing and researching it. However, Sutherland developed the concept within a historical context, where both were indeed linked through the rapid and inexorable rise of the middle classes in the course of industrialization and modernization. The sociologist Siegfried Kracauer had written the most insightful observations on the rise of the "Salaried Masses" (1930 [1998]) in Germany after World War I. As their numbers exponentially increased in all types of organizations, in companies and the state bureaucracy, their particular lifestyle and political orientations shaped the landscape of the industrialized countries during the first half of the 20th century. Their emerging consumerism, which set them apart from working-class culture, became a signature feature of the major cities in Europe and the Americas. Even if the United States was still a predominantly agricultural country, corporations and their administrations started to grow rapidly. White-collar workers defined the urban landscape, and a bulge of middle-class people emerged. The changes in financial and retail markets, in corporate structure and the composition of economic sectors, as well as the flows of goods and new transport facilities opened up numerous opportunities for white-collar employment as well as for new types of crime, such as fraud and embezzlement, starting in the 19th century (Locker and Godfrey 2006). The new class of white-collar workers saw themselves confronted with these opportunities and "lure" (Shover and Grabosky 2010, p. 432), both at the workplace and as consumers.

Sutherland himself shifted his own analytical focus to the upper strata of this social group and to educated professionals and business leaders. At the time of his writing, U.S. society was still stratified into a powerful and small upper class and a large (immigrant) working class, with a comparably smaller white-collar class in its middle. He thus blazed the trail toward the higher end of white-collar crimes and criminals, which is dominating contemporary theory and debate with very few exceptions (e.g., Weisburd et al. 1991; Shover, Coffey, and Hobbs 2003). By shifting white-collar crimes to the higher end of complexity, damage, and seriousness, and white-collar criminals to the upper social strata, Sutherland could draw attention to the bias with which criminal justice agencies targeted the lower classes and crimes of the poor and needy. He argued that white-collar crimes and criminals easily slipped through the net of criminal justice, partially because of the social status of the offenders and partially because of the very complex nature of the crimes—and thus enhanced opportunities for covering them up. In addition, the focus on the top allowed for a neat distinction between powerful white-collar offenders and the large numbers of their powerless victims at the lower end of the social pyramid.

Weisburd et al. (1991) were among the first to realign white-collar crime with its historical roots in the middle classes. Based on empirical research on sentenced white-collar offenders in the United States, they developed a far "broader portrait of white-collar crime" (p. 171). Their results showed that white-collar crimes in their sample of convicted offenders were of a "mundane, common, everyday character" (p. 171) rather than highly sophisticated schemes such as tax evasion (Braithwaite 2005), fraudulent accounting (McBarnet and Whelan 1999), and complex Ponzi schemes. The basic ingredients were "lying, cheating and stealing" (p. 171; see also Green 2006), and the truly complicated offenses were drowned out by the bulk of simple ones, which could be (and actually were) carried out by almost everyone. However, the type of offenses clearly differed from those committed by the underclass, and they varied widely, including securities fraud, antitrust violations, bribery and bank embezzlement, false claims and statements, and credit- and lending-institution fraud (Weisburd et al. 1991, p. 11). Offenses thus ranged from sophisticated schemes open to high-ranking offenders to the simplest ones. The offenders were neither drawn from the highest ranks of status and class in American society, nor did they have an underclass background. With few exceptions they represented "the broad middle of the society, much above the poverty line, but for most part far from elite social position and status" (p. 171). Daly (1989), in her analysis of the same dataset of convicted white-collar offenders used by Weisburd et al., took this a step further. She found that many of these offenders were located at the lower end of what can be termed middle classes, and a large proportion of them, in particular women, were unemployed. "Marginality" rather than a social status at the center or upper strata of society might explain this type of white-collar crime.

Weisburd et al. (1991, p. 172) found "virtually every possible combination of offense and offender," from professionals committing the simplest forms of crime to individuals at the lower ranks of organizations committing the most sophisticated schemes. Even the most prominent of recent cases of white-collar crime that produced huge losses for banks and even led to their demise were committed by young middle-class men, who stood out—if in anything—by their normal behavior and inconspicuous ways. White-collar offenders like accountants, physicians (Jesilow, Pontell, and Geis 1993), and lawyers are of solid middle-class background rather than of high status. Simple tax evasion schemes are shared by the many and the elites. The British expenses scandal of 2009 that implicated numerous members of Parliament did not involve more complex schemes than those that small businesses might use, and a telling comment from a member of the public was, "I would have done the same" (Winnett and Rayner 2009).

Weisburd et al. thus (re)confirmed that white-collar crimes are essentially "crimes of the middle classes," and white-collar offenders are mostly from the center of society. They restored a class of crime in between the well-established notions of "crimes in the suites" and "crimes in the streets," and with it the middle ground of society as a source of potential offenders. Karstedt and Farrall (2006a) identify this as an "under-explored terrain" at the core of contemporary societies, where we find not only varying degrees of "white collarness" of offenders, but also a range of crimes and fraudulent and unfair practices. These are committed at the kitchen table, on the settee, from home computers and laptops, from office desks and call centers, at cash points in restaurants and supermarkets, and in face-to-face interaction with builders and other tradespeople, as well as with fellow citizens. Karstedt and Farrall (2006a, p. 1011) term these the "crimes of everyday life," often falling into a gray zone of legality and morality, and committed by "ordinary people." They are neither committed at powerful nor at professional positions, and very often not even in any workplace-related capacity. Most of them are committed by people in their capacity as consumers, citizens, taxpayers, or beneficiaries of state subsidies. This is the group that politicians like to address as the "law-abiding majority" (Karstedt and Farrall 2007), in a comfortable contrast to the criminality of the rich and the crimes of the poor (Weisburd et al. 1991, p. 3).

II. Middle Classes and Their Crimes: Definition, Delineation, and Context

A. The Global Rise of the Middle Classes

In 2008, Goldman Sachs issued a report stating that "we are in the middle of an unprecedented explosion in the 'world middle class' and witness a globally "expanding middle" with "a shift in income towards middle-income countries and people." The report predicted that "by 2030, two billion new people may join the world middle class" (p. 7), leading to less global inequality and sweeping changes in consumption and spending patterns. The report was not ignorant of the fact that this would mainly apply to developing or the so-called BRIC countries (Brazil, Russia, India, China), and that in the developed world middle classes were increasingly embattled. The growing middle class of China epitomizes this global process (Kharas 2010; Kharas and Gertz 2010).

This development mirrors the rise of the middle classes in Europe and the United States in the 19th and most of the 20th century, with increasing consumption, increasing numbers of white-collar workers, declining inequality, and the emergence of a welfare state. Then, their income and share of income grew substantively during the second half of the past century (Offer 2006). The rise of the middle classes in the global North contributed to higher levels of equality in income distribution that we still observe today. This process has tended to level off during the last decades of the past century and the first decade of the 21st century (Wilkinson and Pickett 2009), which contributed to the present distress of the middle classes. Until today, they represent the "middle" or center of contemporary societies, both in the sense of income and lifestyle and as the normative center of gravity, where they stand for the core of shared beliefs and norms. Globally, the middle classes diverge, with a decline in income, lifestyle, and economic prospects in the global North and a burgeoning economy and increasing purchasing and political power in the global South. Even as the development in the global South partially mirrors the earlier rise of the middle classes in the global North, we find more divergence than convergence among the global middle classes, a fact that defines the prevalence of different types of middle-class crimes and victimization in different parts of the globe, and across global regions.

However, the "old" and "new" middle classes share essential features that are decisive for their engagement in crime and shady practices. They are consumers and citizens alike. As consumers they navigate markets and interact with retailers, banks, insurers and other financial services, or their fellow citizens when they participate in auctions on the Internet. As citizens, they provide the bulk of government income as taxpayers, but they are also the recipients of welfare payments from the government; the beneficiaries of healthcare, education, and pension programs, of government student loans and support, and of subsidies for families and businesses; and claimants of benefits when unemployed. The rise of the middle classes and the welfare state occurred concomitantly in the global North and intricately linked the middle classes to the state bureaucracy. This opened up a range of opportunities for typical middle-class crimes of small-scale tax evasion and false benefit or subsidies claims.

B. Contemporary Middle Classes: Offenders and Victims

Sutherland mainly based his concept of white-collar crime on the salaried workforce, the rise of employment in the administration of business and government, and the increase of professionals in all realms of administration. Today, new occupations and workplaces give the middle classes privileged access to a range of opportunities for crime and shady practices, including small-scale and street-level corruption in offices, in sales departments (Price Waterhouse Cooper 2007), or within the police forces (Klockars, Kutnjak, and Haberfeld 2003). As the sector of higher education and research expanded, academic fraud has increased to worrying levels (Transparency International 2013; Cokol, Ozbay, and Rodriguez-Esteban 2008; Fang, Steen, and Casadevall 2012). In particular, retail markets on the Internet open up opportunities where middle-class people are simultaneously offenders and victims (for offenders, see Shover, Coffey, and Hobbs 2003; for victims, see Holtfreter, Reisig, and Pratt 2008).

Contemporary middle-class crime is decisively shaped by changes in consumption, finances and banking, and foremost the revolution in technology that came with the Internet. As these technologies thoroughly change the ways in which people work, consume, and own property across the globe (Albanese 2005), offending and victimization among the middle classes should converge across the globe in the decades to come, with the emerging middle classes in many ways taking the lead and paving the way, notwithstanding the considerable differences in their overall economic and social position. This might affect their victimization rather than offending, as contemporary middle classes across the globe seem to be vulnerable to victimization in equal measure. However, they are mainly victimized by their fellow white-collared citizens. They find themselves victimized by unfair and illegal practices by banks and insurers, or other large companies, at the hands of small retailers and tradespeople, by fellow citizens in car boot sales and on the Internet, and by fraudulent telemarketing offers (Shover, Coffey, and Hobbs 2003), and exploited by corrupt officials at borders or when in need of government certificates or permissions. In particular, the emerging middle classes in China seem to suffer from government officials as well as from fraudulent retailers on the Internet (Chang 2012). With victimization and offending considerably overlapping among the middle classes, victimization might act as an important motivational factor for offending.

The middle classes comprise a range of income, levels of financial security, and living standards; they include those who live comfortably as well as those who struggle financially (Karstedt and Farrall 2007). Given these different circumstances of this group, some crimes, like benefit fraud, might still be predominantly caused by need, while others, like tax evasion, are mainly caused by greed (for need: Daly 1989; Katungi, Neale, and Barbour 2007; Tunley 2011; for tax: Braithwaite 2005, 2009; on cultural differences: Lundström 2013). However, newly emerging middle-class crimes like academic fraud are incentivized by gains in reputation rather than by material ones (Fang, Steen, and Casedavall 2012). The majority of middle-class victims of fraud do not seem to be the powerless and helpless victims, as in a bankruptcy case in the United Kingdom (Spalek and King 2007).

C. Middle-Class Crime Defined

"Everybody does it" is the title of Thomas Gabor's (1994) probe into "crime by the (general) public." Accordingly, his definition is based on the group of offenders, who are mainly seen as the law-abiding majority, and not on specific types of crime. There cannot be any doubt that members of the middle classes commit all types of crimes, ranging from the most heinous acts of mass violence and atrocities to domestic violence, and from large-scale corporate crimes to shoplifting. Weisburd et al. (1991), and likewise Karstedt and Farrall (2006a), define middle-class crime in a different way and according to the access that ordinary people and the middle classes have to criminal opportunities. The rise of the middle classes—now and then—gives its members access to goods and services, and to government agencies and their support, far beyond the opportunities of the lower strata of society; their crimes are related to these opportunities, which are at present changing due to new technologies, and their often-privileged access to these. It is from this vantage point that middle-class crimes are defined and their realm is delineated. What does this position between the upper echelons of society, and their crimes in the suites, and the lower strata of society, and their crimes on the street, imply?

According to this approach, middle-class crimes are essentially white-collar crimes, as they mostly include cheating and lying: making false insurance claims; claiming for refunds one is not entitled to; all types of tax evasion, with the most common forms of requesting and paying "cash in hand" in order to avoid taxes or contributions to social security; cheating on benefits; deceiving their fellow citizens in secondhand sales; and small-scale and street-level corruption in terms of favors asked. This is "white-collar crime writ small" (Levitt 2006), and at the lowest end of the scale of white-collar crime that makes it into the public sphere (Levi 2006); Karstedt and Farrall (2006a, b) use the term "crimes of everyday life."

Importantly, Sutherland defined white-collar crime as serious moral transgressions independent of the illegal nature of the act itself, and in a way he designed a "moral theory" of white-collar crime (Green 2006). Obviously it is as difficult to draw a line between outright illegal and criminal acts in the realm of the "crimes of everyday life" as it is to nail down crimes and criminals "in the suites." There is a "wide array of peripheral cases in which the line between criminal and noncriminal conduct is unfathomable" (Henning 2008, p. 325), and there are numerous actions that teeter on the boundaries of normative and moral acceptability. Legal and moral boundaries are equally blurred: there is a fine line between bribes and gifts, between "aggressive tax planning," still legal, and illegal tax evasion (Braithwaite 2005; Tetlock and McGraw 2005, p. 35; Braithwaite 2009), or between not declaring a fault when not asked and lying about it in a secondhand sale to a fellow citizen. Karstedt and Farrall (2006a, p. 1011) point out that these types of behaviors "fall into a gray zone of legality and morality." The range of illegal, immoral, and illegitimate practices, mostly at the lower end of damage, sophistication, and complexity, and the type of offenders make these crimes just the everyday crimes of normal people, who would be filled with indignation if the label of "criminal" were ever applied to them. As the middle classes indeed see themselves as representing the "respectable" and "law and order" in society, they nearly always deny the criminality of their own acts (Karstedt and Farrall 2007; Tunley 2011; Stadler and Benson 2012).

Widespread denial of the immorality and/or illegality of these behaviors is facilitated by three factors. First, any kind of reaction—be it from criminal justice authorities or other citizens—is rare. Ordinary people are not shielded from prosecution by their status but simply by the sheer amount of often-negligible transgressions that would, if prosecuted, bring the criminal justice system to a creaking halt, and make punishment seemingly senseless. Second, middle-class crimes differ from white-collar crimes proper, as they rarely cause moral outrage among the population (Levi 2009). While the legal and moral ambiguities of white-collar crimes result from the contrast between often widely shared "moral intuitions" (Mikhail 2007; Henning 2008) and lacunae in the law itself, a lack of prosecution, or application of existing laws, middle-class crimes are firmly embedded in shared moral intuitions of the general public. These give rise to a reservoir of justifications of shady practices and illegal and immoral actions, and to an array of techniques of neutralization. They in particular give space to frank and uninhibited discussions of such actions among relatives and friends, at the workplace and the dinner table, amounting to requests for collusion in these practices and outright illegal acts (Karstedt and Farrall 2006b, 2007; for white-collar criminals, Stadler and Benson 2012). In particular, the belief is widespread that "everybody does it," whether it is insurance (Karstedt and Farrall 2006a) or benefit fraud (Dean and Melrose 1997). Finally, as victimization and offending are closely related in this group, the former might give justification and reason to the latter, and notions of unfair treatment at the hands of large corporations seem to be a driving force of offending in the marketplace (Karstedt 2015).

In sum, white-collar crime writ small and offenders from the "respectable middle classes" at the center of contemporary societies share a number of defining characteristics with white-collar crime and criminals generally as originally defined by Sutherland. These acts are often moral transgressions and situated in a gray zone between illegality and immorality; offenders evade detection and prosecution, even if for different reasons; and denial is widespread among the respectable, whether in the middle or at the top of the social pyramid.

D. The Moral Economy of Middle-Class Crime: Choice, Opportunity, and Moral Constraints

The basic ingredients of middle-class crime are "lying, cheating and stealing" (Weisburd et al. 1991, p. 171; Green 2006), though stealing in this context stands for all types of fraudulent activities. Middle-class crime is essentially fraud. In 2005, Albanese noted that fraud, which had overtaken theft as the most common property crime in the crime statistics of most rich societies in the global North, had become the defining crime of the 21st century. Albanese named three processes that accounted for the exponential growth of fraud over the past decades. Ownership and storage of goods and money have decisively changed, with credit cards, online transactions, and online retailing. Rather than goods being stored in small shops and warehouses, they are now concentrated within a few locations; banks are no longer "where the money is." Finally, and concomitantly, movements of goods, moneys, and services has changed. It is a characteristic of Internet and cybercrime that huge numbers of potential victims can be simultaneously addressed at large distances and in foreign countries. These processes generate the "cornucopia of new criminal opportunities" that Shover, Coffey, and Hobbs (2003, p. 490) identify, which give rise to both widespread victimization and offending, in particular among the middle classes.

The "ordinary people" in the center of society, who transgress legal and moral norms, do not suffer from the many problems that have been associated with those committing street crimes. It therefore makes sense to see them as actors who make informed, even if not always well-informed, decisions. "Opportunities become crimes only because of decisions made by volitional actors," and "crime-as-choice theory" provides a valuable framework for middle-class crime (Shover and Grabosky 2010, p. 430; Simpson 2011). Choice theories are based on causal factors, which apply to both the most complex white-collar crimes that are committed by a few and the least complex ones committed by the many. Shover and Grabosky's (2010, p. 430) model aims at explaining variations in the prevalence of white-collar crime. It essentially juxtaposes the supply of "lure" (i.e., something "attractive and covetable" [p. 431]), and the temptation this arouses in individuals and organizations with control and oversight over the alluring goods, and both external and internal oversight or self-restraint of those who are tempted. These factors create the supply of criminal opportunities on the one hand, and a pool of motivated offenders on the other hand.

The model is particularly pertinent for the analysis of middle-class crime. External oversight over economic actors has been weakened across the past decades, and this has turned out to be a major cause for the increase in white-collar crime (Shover and Grabosky, 2010, p. 432). Government policies and programs target middle-class and middle-income households with complex tax and benefit programs alike, thus creating incentives for tax evasion and "lure" for acquiring benefits. Insurers create "moral hazards" that tempt citizens into not only reckless but also illegal behavior (Ericson, Barry, and Doyle 1999). Karstedt and Farrall (2006a) argue that moral commitment has widely changed and given way to "legal cynicism" (Sampson and Bartusch 1998) among consumers and citizens, making them more inclined to exploit illegal opportunities when they present themselves. Thus, to understand middle-class crime, it is the behavior of consumers that needs to be understood rather than the behavior of seasoned fraudsters (Holtfreter, Reisig, and Pratt 2008, p. 207). In the same vein, we need to understand the behavior of ordinary citizens and taxpayers

(Braithwaite 2009) rather than of persistent benefit fraudsters or international law firms (Braithwaite 2005).

External oversight and internal constraints are embedded in what Granovetter (1985) has termed the "generalized morality" of markets and the economy. Generalized morality provides the "communal norms that guide everyday life as a means of evaluating the propriety of conduct" (Henning 2008, p. 328). Their observance by others provides vital information for actors as to their actual "generalizability": if others do not comply with legal or moral norms, this has an impact on both external oversight and internal constraints (Dean and Melrose 1997; Kotzian 2011). Regard for others, acknowledgment of the moral values that guide economic behavior, and principles of fairness thus act as constraining forces against temptation and lure. In contrast, perceptions of unfair treatment at the hands of business and government (Tyler [1990] 2006; Sondak and Tyler 2007) and information about high-level and elite white-collar crimes (Levi 2006, 2009), or about what colleagues at work and neighbors at home do, loosen such constraints and act as incentives for criminal choices. Like any economic action, criminal choices in markets are embedded in the fabric of moral values. Middle-class crime thus potentially illuminates the relationship between markets and moral order, and the patterns of the "moral economy" of contemporary societies.

The concept of a "moral economy" was pioneered by the historian E. P. Thompson (1971), who originally developed it as an explanation for the riotous transition from premodern to liberal corn markets in 17th- and 18th-century Britain (and more encompassing of class relations). More recently, the concept has been used in a wider sense to describe the particular set of justice perceptions and the moral order of the economy (Booth 1994; Arnold 2001; Sayer 2007) and the welfare state (Mau 2003). With the inclusion of the welfare state into the moral economy of contemporary societies, the relationship between citizens and the state bureaucracy becomes as important as the one between consumers and business. Thompson posited two basic "laws" of markets: first, that they are grounded in a morality of fairness, justice, roles, and rules, and shared notions of acceptable behaviors, profits, and entitlements, and second, that economic changes inevitably have an impact on the moral economy, by shifting relations of power and the moral constraints imposed on actors, in particular on the powerful.

Contemporary moral economies can be defined as an ensemble of institutional patterns, generalized morality, and moral commitment; as such, they represent the structural and moral constraints in which individual choices are embedded, but also the incentives and justifications for crimes and shady practices. According to Karstedt and Farrall (2006a), changes in the moral economy have in particular disadvantaged consumers; they are exercised by "value for money," mis-selling, hidden charges, and inaccurate product descriptions. However, they resist and hit back by inflating insurance claims as a reaction to small-print rules or overpriced premiums; they retreat into a shadow economy in which they pay cash-in-hand to circumvent tax and social security laws, and try to circumvent red tape by offering favors to officials (Schneider and Enste 2000; Schneider, Torgler, and Schaltegger 2008; Buehn and Schneider 2012). Three dimensions of the moral economy are particularly relevant for middle-class crime, and they complement the original model by Shover and Grabosky (2010) as shown in figure 9.1. These include, first, the general level of commitment to moral and legal norms by other actors ("generalized morality," per Granovetter 1985) and, second, the perceived fairness and legitimacy of market rules and actors (Sandok and Tyler 2007). Finally, individual norm commitment functions as additional enhancement of internal oversight and constraint. Thus, the moral economy works like a lock on the pool of tempted offenders by either increasing or decreasing the level.

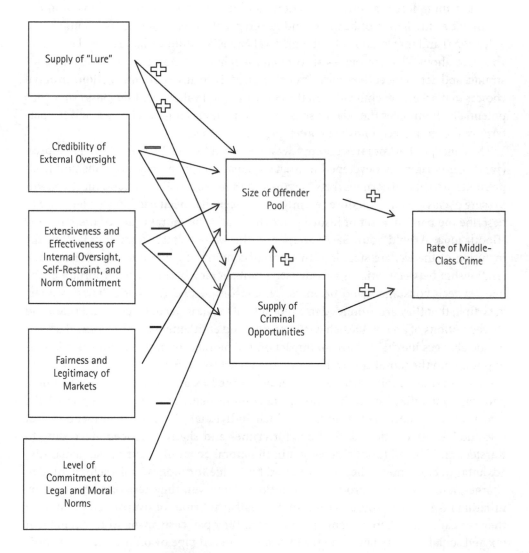

FIGURE 9.1 A Model of Variation in Middle-Class Crime

Source: Karstedt 2015; adapted from Shover and Grabosky (2010).

III. The Scope of Contemporary Middle-Class Crime

A. Victimization and Transgression

The development of the Internet changed established interpersonal relationships in banking, consumption, and retailing. These changes coincided with policies of deregulation of markets that took up momentum at the same time. The movement of neoliberalism started in the United States and the United Kingdom in the 1980s and has swept through all global regions since then. Both developments affected the established middle classes in the global North and the emerging ones in the global South, with the latter taking the lead in adopting the new technologies in all realms of life (for China and the greater China region: Chang 2012; Anti-Phishing Alliance of China 2013; McKinsey Global Institute 2014). In the global North, transitional and postcommunist societies were in particular affected by neoliberal policies of decreasing welfare and the transition from a state economy to free markets. Across the globe, new technologies and new opportunities and rewards transformed economic citizenship in the direction of active self-advancement and "entrepreneurial comportment" of the individual (Rose 1996, p. 340). Consumers had to take responsibility and risks. As markets were deregulated, a new "risk environment" with little oversight or regulation was created, with ample opportunities for fraudulent transactions and sharp practices on both sides of the counter (Ericson, Barry, and Doyle 1999). In many countries, citizens were urged to become "consumers" of government services, and they were forced into markets of welfare or security. Middle classes found themselves in a new environment where the relation between risk and blame, responsibility and conformity, for consumers and business alike had thoroughly changed, and with it the relationships between buyers and vendors (Karstedt and Farrall 2006a). These developments did not amount to a total demise of the "moral" in the economy, but on the contrary instigated a renewal of "market-embedded morality," driven by increasing demands of corporate and consumer responsibility and accountability (Shamir 2008).

In this environment, consumers feel victimized by the practices of insurance companies and financial services. They are sold allegedly useless insurance and financial packages, they are not properly informed about the products, and they feel that they are being defrauded by small-print clauses (Karstedt and Farrall 2004, 2006a, 2006b, 2007). They find themselves charged for undelivered services, bogus repairs, and used parts sold as new. "Consumer revolts" against overcharging banks gained momentum in 2007, and since then, British banks have been forced on numerous occasions to compensate consumers for high-risk products, overcharging for bouncing checks, and other forms of malpractice, mirroring in our time the corn riots that the historian Thompson had observed. With increased use of the Internet, cyberfraud is equally on the rise, and consumers are increasingly victimized by being lured into a range of scams, such as inheritance scams, phishing scams, work-from-home scams, and auction and Internet sales scams (Jorna and Hutchings 2013). Telemarketers and Internet retailers victimize consumers in Europe and the United States (Shover, Coffey, and Hobbs 2003; Holtfreter, Reisig, and Pratt 2008; Federal Trade Commission 2013). In many countries, citizens are asked to supply favors and bribes in encounters with officials, be it the police or civil servants in the state bureaucracy with responsibility for issuing licenses and benefits (Karstedt 2014); in these cases both offenders and victims mostly come from a middle-class background.

Table 9.1 gives an overview of the prevalence of different types of victimization in European countries, based on data from the 2004 European Social Survey, which included questions about the moral economies of 25 European societies, including Turkey.[1] One third (34.6 percent) of Europeans report having been overcharged by tradespeople, a quarter (27.3 percent) felt that they did not get the best deal from banks and insurers, and one fifth (21 percent) had been cheated in a secondhand sale by their fellow citizens. In contrast, victimization by corrupt officials is rare, although countries differ widely. Consumers are more vulnerable in the postcommunist and newly emerging market economies of central and southeast Europe rather than in the advanced economies of its western parts, while the citizens of the latter suffer more often at the hands of banks and insurers.

Mirroring the mounting complaints by consumers and citizens are complaints from insurers and representatives from health services about the increase in fraud committed by their customers and clients in the United Kingdom, as well as in other European countries (Insurance Europe 2013). Retailers find themselves as victims of customers who take unfair and often illegal advantage of generous terms and offers. Small tradesmen report that their customers try fraudulently to make them responsible for damages. Citizens do not hesitate to take illegal and unfair advantages, often as a reaction to feeling victimized by the practices of insurance companies and financial services, as well as by government policies.

Data from the United Kingdom and Germany confirm that small and large businesses are indeed victims of middle-class offending; however, the national government, the state, and its agencies turn out to be the most common target when citizens avoid taxation, do not pay their TV license, or deliberately misclaim benefits. Table 9.2 shows that 26.7 percent of European citizens engage in such behavior, with the western and northern European countries taking a lead. This dwarfs the respective rates for all other types of shady practices and crimes, like fraudulent insurance claims or cheating on fellow citizens. The study by Broadhurst et al. (2011) gives an impression of the involvement of the emerging middle classes in China in fraudulent practices as well as of their victimization. If we take business victimization as a proxy, 13.4 percent report having been a victim of fraud, which includes fraud by outsiders and employees and Internet-related fraud. Six percent report having been asked for a bribe by officials and other businesspersons. If fraud by outsiders and employees, as well as victimization by corrupt officials, is seen as indicative of middle-class crime, emerging middle classes

Table 9.1 Europe: Victimization in the Last 5 Years (Percent at Least Once)

Country	Overcharged by Tradespeople (%)	Bank/Insurer Did Not Offer Best Deal (%)	Cheated upon in Second-Hand Sale (%)	Official Asked for Favor/Bribe (%)
20% highest	– Luxembourg (47.1)	– Norway (41.8)	– Slovakia (52.3)	– Ukraine (32.5)
	– Czech Republic (45.8)	– Iceland (40.0)	– Estonia (43.3)	– Slovakia (14.8)
	– Austria (41.3)	– Austria (37.5)	– Ukraine (36.4)	– Czech Republic (12.6)
	– Estonia (41.0)	– United Kingdom (37.0)	– Czech Republic (34.9)	– Greece (12.5)
	– Slovakia (40.3)	– Germany (35.8)	– Slovenia (34.2)	– Poland (12.1)
20% lowest	– Portugal (18.2)	– Turkey (7.6)	– Greece (9.8)	– Finland (0.9)
	– Finland (22.3)	– Greece (10.7)	– Spain (11.9)	– United Kingdom (1.2)
	– Turkey (24.2)	– Portugal (14.9)	– Portugal (12.3)	– Netherland (1.3)
	– Iceland (27.3)	– Ukraine (19.3)	– Switzerland (14.3)	– France (1.5)
	– Ireland (27.9)	– Poland (20.4)	– France (16.6)	– Switzerland (1.5)
Europe	34.6	27.3	21.7	5.8

Notes: Percentage who responded that this happened to them at least once or more often: How often, if ever, have each of these things happened to you in the last five years? a) A plumber, builder, car mechanic or other repair person overcharged you or did unnecessary work. b) You were sold food that was packed to conceal the worse bits. c) A bank or insurance company failed to offer you the best deal you were entitled to. d) You were sold something second-hand that quickly proved to be faulty. e) A public official asked you for a favor or a bribe in return for a service.

Source: European Social Survey (2004).

Table 9.2 Europe: Immoral and Illegal Behavior in the Last 5 Years (% at Least Once)

Country	Avoid VAT/Tax	Cheated in Second-Hand Sale	Fraudulent Insurance Claim	Fraudulent Benefit Claim	Offered Bribe
20% highest	– Iceland (45.5)	– Ukraine (7.7)	– Austria (6.7)	– Ukraine (5.4)	– Ukraine (16.7)
	– Denmark (38.4)	– Estonia (5.6)	– Denmark (5.2)	– Iceland (4.5)	– Slovakia (8.1)
	– Belgium (33.7)	– Finland (5.6)	– Iceland (4.8)	– Czech Republic (3.6)	– Czech Republic (7.5)
	– Germany (32.8)	– Czech Republic (4.9)	– Germany (4.4)	– Austria (3.5)	– Poland (5.0)
	– Turkey (32.6)	– Poland (4.6)	– Czech Republic (4.3)	– Slovakia (3.2)	– Greece (3.0)
20% lowest	– Switzerland (12.8)	– Greece (0.6)	– Greece (0.2)	– Netherland (0.1)	– Finland (0.2)
	– Ukraine (13.7)	– Hungary (1.0)	– Turkey (0.4)	– Hungary (0.3)	– Ireland (0.3)
	– Portugal (15.1)	– Switzerland (1.2)	– Ireland (0.7)	– Greece (0.5)	– Switzerland (0.3)
	– Ireland (15.6)	– France (1.5)	– Slovenia (1.2)	– Belgium (0.7)	– United Kingdom (0.4)
	– United Kingdom (19.1)	– Turkey (1.7)	– Norway (1.4)	– Switzerland (0.7)	– Netherlands (0.5)
Europe	26.7	3.5	2.7	1.7	2.7

Notes: Percentage who responded that they had done this once or more often: How often, if ever, have you done each of these things in the last five years? a) Kept the change from a shop assistant or waiter knowing they had given you too much? b) Paid cash with no receipt so as to avoid paying VAT or other taxes? c) Sold something second-hand and concealed some or all of its faults? d) Misused or altered a card or document to pretend you were eligible for something you were not? e) Made an exaggerated or false insurance claim? f) Offered a favor or a bribe to a public official in return for a service? g) Over-claimed or falsely claimed government benefits such as social security or other benefits?

Source: European Social Survey (2004).

Table 9.3 Crimes of Everyday Life: Victims and Offenders in Europe

Country	Victimization (%)	Offending (%)	Victim and Offender (%)
20% highest	– Hungary (76.6) – Slovakia (76.5) – Norway (75.1) – Luxembourg (75.0) – Austria (73.2)	– United Kingdom (37.6) – Belgium (34.2) – Luxembourg (33.3) – Ukraine (30.9) – Austria (30.2)	– Luxembourg (28.6) – Ukraine (28.2) – United Kingdom (28.0) – Belgium (25.4) – Austria (25.0)
20% lowest	– Portugal (36.3) – Turkey (42.7) – Greece (44.1) – Ireland (56.1) – Finland (57.8)	– Turkey (5.8) – Greece (8.1) – Portugal (8.9) – Hungary (13.2) – Poland (18.9)	– Turkey (4.6) – Greece (5.8) – Portugal (6.7) – Hungary (12.2) – Ireland (13.9)
Europe	63.2	24.1	19.2

Notes: See notes for Table 9.1 and 9.2. Percentage of victims (at least once), percentage of offenders (at least once), and percentage of those who were both victims and offenders (at least once); computations based on individual data.

Source: European Social Survey (2004).

seem to be only slightly less involved in such practices than those in western European societies.

In contrast to common notions of fraud and white-collar crime, victims of the crimes of everyday life are not from different social backgrounds or life circumstances than offenders; rather, they share the same social space (Karstedt and Farrall 2006a, 2007). The factors that drive victimization might be the same as those for offending: little restraint and self-control, and a high temptation by "lure." Such individuals are easy prey if targeted, and they are also more inclined to offend (Holtfreter, Reisig, and Pratt 2008). Offending might also constitute a kind of self-help justice for those who feel victimized or treated unfairly in the marketplace (Karstedt and Farrall 2006a), or might be an act of defiance in the face of government authorities (Braithwaite 2009). The result is a rather high victim–offender overlap that is well documented, especially for violent crimes in the more deprived strata of society, but rather uncommon for this social group (Germany and the United Kingdom, Karstedt and Farrall 2006a; European countries, Karstedt 2015). Table 9.3 shows that one fifth (19.2 percent) of European consumers and citizens are victims *and* offenders, nearly two thirds (63.2 percent) were victimized over the past five years, and one quarter (24.1 percent) engaged in offending. The victim–offender overlap is more pronounced in western European countries and advanced market societies that underwent the changes in their moral economies as outlined above. Moreover, as Karstedt (2015, pp. 81–82) demonstrates, European countries with larger and more affluent middle classes have higher levels of offender–victim overlap, thus corroborating the typical relationship between this specific social group and its access to opportunities of crime. In the United Kingdom those who are frequent offenders *and* victims are typically from the higher social strata, are better educated, and have higher incomes, and thus have a distinct middle-class background (Karstedt and Farrall 2006a, 2007).

B. The Costs of Middle-Class Crime

Sutherland's observation (1940, 1949; see Weisburd et al. 1991, pp. 5–8) that these crimes result in a multiple of monetary losses in comparison to more common crimes equally applies to the crimes of the middle classes; even if they are individually small, they cause considerable damage and losses (Karstedt and Farrall 2006a, p. 1013). Fraud and similar crimes are surpassing ordinary property crimes in terms of costs. In the early 2000s, the costs of fraud outstripped the costs of burglary. The 2001 British Crime Survey estimated that there were slightly over 1 million burglaries in the year 2000 and that the costs of burglaries were £2.7 billion (using 1999 prices, Brand and Price 2000, pp. 32–33). The Brand and Price report, however, puts the costs of fraud and forgery at £13.8 billion, roughly four times as much as the costs of this type of common crime.

The following estimations are from the United Kingdom, but other European countries with similar economies and welfare systems should not substantively differ. Karstedt and Farrall (2006a) report that the Department of Work and Pensions estimated that 5 percent of their claims were fraudulent in 2003, resulting in losses of £573 million, or 4 percent of social security payments. The Association of British Insurers (ABI) claims that 4 percent of household insurance claims made in 2000 were fraudulent (ABI 2000). The Association for Payments and Clearing Services (APACS) set the cost of losses due to counterfeit credit card fraud at £108 million in 2000, with a steep increase in the previous years (APACS, n.d.). Levi et al. (2007; Levi and Burrows 2008) estimated losses separately for the private and public sector in 2005. Financial services suffered losses from fraud of about £1 billion, while for other businesses this figure was estimated at about £2.75 billion, the same as for private households. However, these figures are dwarfed by losses in the public sector, both on the national and local level. Tax evasion and fraud, in particular Value Added Tax (VAT; sales tax or goods and services tax), amount to £5.5 billion, a figure that does not include income-tax fraud, which, presumably, is the most common type (Levi et al. 2007, p. 4); benefit fraud creates losses of up to £0.5 billion. These figures are mirrored by cross-national estimates of the shadow or informal economy in a number of European countries, and a global sample (Schneider, Buehn, and Montenegro 2010); these estimates include lost VAT and undeclared income tax (Schneider, Torgler, and Schaltegger 2008). Schneider (2003) estimated the losses incurred by the informal economy in Germany, Austria, and Switzerland at 10 to 16 percent of the official GDP in 2002; for Germany this amounted to €350 billion. Levi et al. (2007, p. 87) report a range for benefit fraud between 1 and 4 percent of payments for different types of benefits and allowances. According to the Committee of Public Accounts, in 2008 the largest losses were accrued from undeclared earnings, fraudulent claims of household size, and clients living abroad (in sum at about £70 million [Tunley 2011]). Charities are vulnerable to fraud by their own members and outsiders; a survey revealed that £147 million was lost, about one third to internal fraud (National Fraud Authority 2013). In 2013, the National Fraud Authority claimed that the British economy had lost £52 billion from fraud. Data on businesses in China estimate a total loss of US$15 million for a sample of 5,000 businesses, with half of the losses being incurred due to fraud by employees (Broadhurst et al. 2011, p. 117).

Even less is known about the losses that consumers incur when being overcharged by tradespeople or banks or being left out-of-pocket by insurers. An indication might be given by the amounts that banks are forced to pay to their customers for different forms of malpractice, as recently in the United Kingdom. Jorna and Hutchings (2013, p. 11) calculated reported losses from a survey on cyberscam victims in Australia. Notably, the middle- and higher-income groups were slightly overrepresented among the victims of such scams. The mean loss was calculated at AUS$8,000, with a median of AUS$500, indicating a wide range of losses and considerable amounts at the top end.

IV. The Moral Economy of Middle Classes: Consumers and Business

Thompson's (1971) original conceptualization of the moral economy focuses on the acceptance and legitimacy of power relations in market exchanges, and foremost on the perceptions of fairness of prices and profits. Besides being judged on distributive fairness or just outcomes by consumers, markets and moral economies are also defined by "procedural justice" (i.e., that vendors and buyers act according to rules and regulations that can guarantee "fair deals" for all). In particular, the powerful big businesses have to play by the rules of markets, and this involves transparency, avoidance of bias, and honest communication (Sondak and Tyler 2007). The ways in which power, fairness, and moral commitment shape contemporary moral economies and middle-class crime can be gauged from data on 25 European societies (including Turkey). Given the collective nature of the moral economy, all data are aggregated on country level, and analyses are based on country-level data.[2]

In contemporary European moral economies, fairness and the balance of power relations emerge as decisive correlates of middle-class victimization and offending. Unfair procedures in consumer markets include little concern for consumers and preoccupation with profits as well as price fixing, both leading to unfair deals for consumers. They also imply that businesses are powerful enough to engage in such practices, and as such they indicate an imbalance of power in markets, where consumers have little chance of being properly informed and receiving fair deals. Karstedt and Farrall (2006a, 2007) report a number of incidents where people felt in particular powerless in dealing with banks, insurers, and retailers, and recent regulation of banks has focused on the provision of full information for consumers as a necessary counterbalance against their powerful positions.

As Karstedt (2015) shows, the majority of European citizens deem unfair practices to be widespread in contemporary consumer markets: the majority agree that businesses ignore the interests of consumers, and nearly three quarter assume that they fix prices, mostly in the established market economies of western and southern Europe. However, a majority also see consumers in a better position to protect their interests. Such perceptions of power (or powerlessness) in markets are related to actual and structural power differentials in society: the higher the level of income inequality, the more businesses are perceived as unfair actors in markets. Perceptions of unfair dealings by businesses have decisive repercussions on the pattern of moral economies. They increase distrust, with the financial services particularly affected; they reduce moral commitment; and they generally cause disallegiance from moral and legal norms and a cynical attitude toward these. The more citizens perceive businesses as unfair in their country, the more they agree that one cannot make money without acting dishonestly. If, however, consumers feel empowered to protect their interests, commitment to legal norms increases substantially. In addition, consumers are more fearful of being treated dishonestly and victimized by shady practices if they generally perceive that businesses are engaging in unfair practices.

Nonetheless, on the aggregate level, norm commitment does not seamlessly translate into changes in aggregate rates of actual offending in the marketplace. It seems that such commitment hardly acts as a restraint on the pool of potentially motivated offenders in a society, when opportunities and lure are abundant; consequently, on the aggregate level, opportunities seem to be the dominant causal factor shaping the level of middle-class crime.[3] However, individual-level analyses of these European data show that widely held beliefs about the validity of norms and the commitment of others are major factors in determining individual compliance (Kotzian 2011). In sum, perceptions of and actually unfair business practices shape the moral economy and the "generalized morality" in markets, as well as the readiness of consumers to engage in transgressions and crimes of everyday life. Such perceptions can be realized as part of a reservoir of motives should the opportunity for transgression arise, independent of whether these perceptions are based on actual and personal experience or just on hearsay.

V. The Moral Economy of Democracy: Citizens and Governments

The moral economy of markets and their distinct patterns of fairness, trust, and moral commitment are mirrored in the economic transactions of citizens as taxpayers, or as recipients of welfare payments with their governments. The perceived legitimacy of tax burdens and welfare payments, the fairness and equity of distributing these among citizens, the transparency of regulations and decision making, and procedural justice in these transactions largely determine the compliance of citizens with rules and regulations (for tax: Murphy 2003, 2004, 2005; Braithwaite 2009; Buehn and Schneider 2012; for welfare states: Mau 2003). Fair treatment at the hands of authorities and their trustworthiness have been identified as important factors in securing compliance with rules and regulations (Tyler [1990] 2006) and enhancing "tax integrity" (Braithwaite 2009). The quality of public-sector services, the credibility of governments to deliver, and equal and fair treatment of citizens are defining characteristics of the moral economy of contemporary relationships between citizens and their governments. These are important factors in enhancing their moral commitment, in particular in securing tax compliance as well as preventing fraudulent claims of government subsidies and welfare payments (Buehn and Schneider 2012). Where the quality of public-sector services is low and corruption is pervasive, and where citizens cannot expect fair and equal treatment and thus withdraw trust from government, their reactions as taxpayers

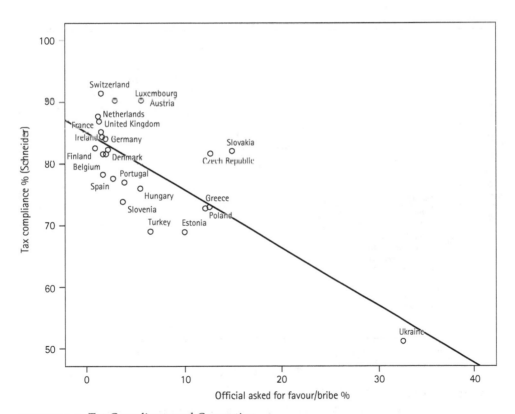

FIGURE 9.2 Tax Compliance and Corruption

Source: Schneider, Buehne, and Montenegro (2010); European Social Survey (2004). Percentage of those who responded that this had happened to them at least once: How often, if ever, have each of these things happened to you in the last five years? A public official asked you for a favor or a bribe in return for a service.

Notes: R-square: .57; $F_{(1, 22)} = 29.28^{***}$; $p < .001$.

and welfare recipients range from dismissiveness and subversion to outright defiance. Dissent and resentment can amount to silent or overt tax revolts, or to playing games on tax authorities (Braithwaite 2009) and welfare agencies. Buehn and Schneider (2012) have shown a positive and recursive relationship between corruption and the size of the "shadow economy," where business and citizens avoid tax and other social security payments, for 51 countries across the globe.

Using Schneider's Index of Tax Compliance, which is based on a range of indicators (Schneider, Buehn, and Montenegro 2010),[4] the relationship between corruption and tax compliance can be confirmed for the moral economies of government–citizen relationships in 25 European countries. As seen in figure 9.2, victimization by corrupt officials reduces the overall tax compliance of citizens significantly. It also increases fraudulent claims of government benefits (figure 9.3). Likewise distrust of markets and business and perceptions of their unfair dealings lead to moral disengagement corruption of government officials has the same effect on citizens in interactions with their

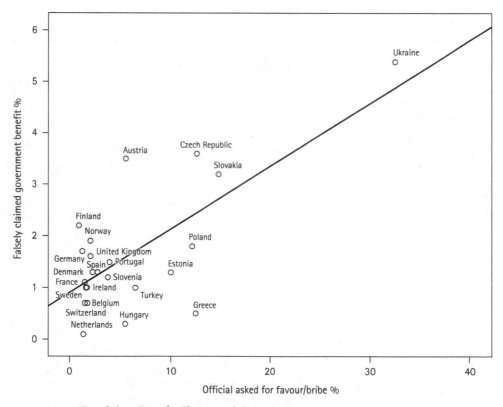

FIGURE 9.3 Fraudulent Benefit Claims and Corruption

Source: European Social Survey (2004). Percentage who responded that they had done this once or more often: How often, if ever, have you done each of these things in the last five years? Over-claimed or falsely claimed government benefits such as social security or other benefits? Percentage of those who responded that this had happened to them at least once: How often, if ever, have each of these things happened to you in the last five years? A public official asked you for a favor or a bribe in return for a service.

Notes: R-square: .52; F(1, 21) = 22.29***; $p < .001$.

governments. In European countries, distrust in government officials increases where citizens are asked for bribes and favors ($r = .54$; $p < .001$); consequently, where distrust reaches high levels, tax compliance decreases significantly ($p < .05$), with the latter indicating general discontent with the quality and fairness of public-sector services. As citizens from the broad middle classes are the main contributors of taxes and recipients of healthcare, education, and pensions, their allegiance is decisive but might be easily lost. The moral economy of contemporary democracies is grounded in an intricate pattern of fairness, trust, and mutuality between governments and their middle classes.

VI. Middle-Class Morality: Need, Greed, and Lure

Average-income earners in the very center of society have access to a range of illegitimate means that are not available to the less well-to-do strata in society and not alluring to the well-off upper classes. These include products like insurance (Ericson, Barry, and Doyle 1999), services in the banking sector, use of shops and services with generous policies for replacements and refunds (Karstedt and Farrall 2004), and further access to specific tax refunds and entitlements (Braithwaite 2005, 2009), to government benefits and services and finally opportunities that arise in their capacity as professionals. These constitute opportunities for offending and engaging in illegal and morally dubious practices, but they also make the average-income earner susceptible to fraud victimization. Such opportunities tend to increase for the better-off among the average-income earners. The middle classes comprise a range of income, and different levels of financial security and living standards; they include those who live comfortably as well as those who struggle financially. Average-income earners are particularly hit by economic and financial crises, which are exacerbated by the "fear of falling" (Wheeler 1992, p. 118) engrained in the "inner life of the middle classes" (Ehrenreich 1989). An individual or household crisis might tempt them to take to illegal practices, like fraudulently claiming benefits (Tunley 2011) or retreating into the shadow economy.

How much of the motivation of potential middle-class offenders (and victims) can be accounted for by greed, and how much by need? Greed loosens the internal constraints that play a decisive role in our choice model of middle-class crime, and thus makes this group not only more motivated to engage in illegal practices but also easy targets for lure, for investment schemes with incredibly high returns, or for the not-to-be-missed deal on the Internet and in secondhand sales. Greed makes them both predators and prey. Karstedt and Farrall (2006a, 2007) report for the United Kingdom that the crimes of everyday life are more often committed by offenders with average to high income, and frequent victim-and-offenders are significantly more often found in this group. Holtfreter, Reisig, and Pratt (2008) found for a U.S. sample of consumers engaging in remote purchasing activities via the Internet that low self-control (i.e., risk taking) significantly increased the likelihood of fraud victimization among a group of people with typical middle-class incomes; they were even more prone to such practices if they expected an increase in income rather than a decline of their purchasing power. The Federal Trade Commission (2013) found "risky purchasing practices" in particular on the Internet to be a decisive factor in fraud victimization. Australian consumers who had been victims of Internet scams mainly came from the full social spectrum, although there was a slight overrepresentation of middle-income earners (Jorna and Hutchings 2013). These results indicate that greed rather than need motivates these types of illegal and morally dubious practices, and simultaneously makes consumers vulnerable to being victims. However, the large proportion of unemployed and marginalized individuals that Daly (1989) found among sentenced white-collar offenders indicates at least a personal financial crisis and struggle behind their offending. Karstedt and Farrall (2006a, 2006b) found that those who are struggling, independent of the level of their income, are more inclined to engage in such transgressions and crime. According to a study from the United Kingdom (Katungi, Neale, and Barbour 2006), need is the driving force for working in the informal and shadow economy among low-paid earners, who are mostly in a financially troubling situation. The respondents in this study were well aware that they were both avoiding taxes and often fraudulently claiming benefits. Given the range of the middle classes in contemporary societies and huge differences in their financial situation, both need and greed play a role in the reservoir of motives for engaging in morally dubious or illegal practices.

Karstedt (2015, pp. 80–83) shows for the moral economies of Europe that middle-class crime, both transgressions and victimization, is highest in societies with comparably larger and also more affluent middle classes. Egalitarian countries like the Nordic countries, Germany, Austria, and the Netherlands have high rates of offenders—and also of victim–offenders. When comparing European moral economies according to their median level of household income (i.e., the income that half of the population achieve),[5] the overall rates of crimes of everyday life are significantly higher in countries where average consumers and earners are decisively better off (e.g., in Norway and Luxembourg). This indicates that greed slightly crowds out need as motivation for the middle classes, which is corroborated by the fact that the relationship is strong both for offenders only and victim–offenders. The average-income earners in these countries are coveted consumers who are offered and have access to the higher range of consumer goods and services, with an array of criminal opportunities attached. In Europe, the more egalitarian countries with large middle classes are countries with well-developed welfare states and consequently higher tax burdens and social security contributions. Both set incentives and provide opportunities for small businesses and consumers to retreat into the shadow economy. Markets and the state both offer more "lure" to average earners than societies with less equal distributions of income, less developed welfare systems, and lower tax burdens. At least in European societies, more equality thus does not encourage higher levels of commitment to moral and legal norms that might restrain middle-class consumers from engaging in morally dubious and illegal behavior, but to the contrary (see also Offer 2006).

VII. Crimes and Everyday Life: Into the "Inner Life of the Middle Classes"

The crimes of the middle classes are "crimes of everyday life," small in monetary value but large in number and directly related to the ways in which they consume, pay, save and invest, and store goods. The middle class is a social group with a considerable overlap of victimization and transgression. The crimes of everyday life are constitutive of the criminality of the middle classes and simultaneously illuminate their "inner moral life" and moral commitments, both as consumers and as citizens. These white-collar crimes "writ small" are signature crimes of contemporary moral economies, the generalized morality and communal norms that guide them, and the power relations that shape them.

In line with the original concept by Thompson (1971), power relations, and linked to these collective perceptions of procedural fairness in markets of goods and services, are the lynchpin of contemporary moral economies as they were in 18th-century Britain. If businesses are seen to be involved in unfair practices that disadvantage consumers, this coincides with disallegiance to legal norms, distrust of businesses, and fear of being treated dishonestly. Collectively shared perceptions of fair treatment and fair exchanges are cornerstones of "generalized morality" in the moral economies of the mostly affluent countries of Europe. Regulating and prosecuting unfair and semilegal practices of businesses, tightly monitoring abuse of their power, and empowering consumers to protect their interests seem to be reasonable strategies to reduce losses from the crimes of everyday life committed by the middle classes. Rather than deploring ever-increasing fraud by consumers and citizens, businesses need to realize that their practices are equally important in shaping the moral economy in which they themselves operate, and can have repercussions on consumer behavior. In a similar vein, this applies to the moral economy of citizens and governments. Fairness and clarity of rules and regulations, and just treatment of taxpaying and benefit-claiming citizens are cornerstones on which citizens' tax integrity is built (Braithwaite 2009), and government practices of setting incentives and applying controls are decisive in achieving this.

As can be seen from a comparison of European countries, the crimes of everyday life are more common in more equal societies, with higher levels of median incomes. Thus, their increase cannot be counted among the social dysfunctions of income inequality (Wilkinson and Pickett 2009) but might rather be part of the "challenge of affluence" (Offer 2006). On the one hand, as self-control is loosened when societies become more affluent, members of the middle classes might shed moral restraints and engage in morally dubious and outright illegal behaviors, both as consumers and citizens. On the other hand, with lower self-control they are prone to engaging more often in risky purchasing practices and thus become victimized.

The concepts of middle-class crime or crimes of everyday life share the fuzziness of the concept of white-collar crime and a number of its characteristics. They are useful in directing attention to a category of crimes and transgressions in between crimes in the suites and crimes in the streets. As middle classes are on the rise globally, and the ways in which they consume, pay, and invest are changing rapidly, it seems that this category will become more important over the next decades.

ACKNOWLEDGMENTS

This essay uses material published in Karstedt (2015). I am grateful to Stephen Farrall, University of Sheffield, and Kai Bussmann, Martin-Luther University Halle, with whom I conducted the original research between 2001 and 2003, and designed the module for Round Two of the European Social Survey in 2004. Most of all, I thank Lucy Strang, Cambridge, and Michael Koch, University of Bielefeld, for research, data collection and analysis, and graphics.

NOTES

1. European Social Survey 2004 is available at www.europeansocialsurvey.org
   The module "Economic morality" on which this research is based is one of the rotating modules and only available for 2004 (see http://www.europeansocialsurvey.org/data/module-index.html). However, there is no reason to assume that opportunities for middle-class crime have changed dramatically since then. In addition, there is no reason to assume that the theorized relationships have changed following, for example, the economic crisis in 2008, which hit European countries quite differently. It can be firmly posited that even if some of the data might change, the ranks of countries will be mainly unchanged and correlations will be robust and stand the test of time. Weighted data were used to account for differences in sampling design and population size. The Design Weight corrects for slightly different probabilities of selection, thereby making the sample more representative of a "true" sample of individuals aged 15+ in each country. The Population Size weight is used when examining data for two or more countries combined. This weight corrects for the fact that most countries taking part in the European Social Survey have very similar sample sizes, no matter how large or small their population. The Population Size weight makes an adjustment to ensure that each country is represented in proportion to its population size. For more information, see the ESS Documentation Report at www.europeansocialsurvey.org
2. See note 1 for details of the survey. For in-depth analyses of countries see Karstedt (2015); for individual-level analyses see Hirtenlehner, Farrall, and Bacher (2013) and Kotzian (2011).
3. If instead of actual offending rates intentions to offend are used, moral commitment has an impact in a comparative individual-level analysis of Germany (West and East) and England and Wales (Karstedt and Farrall 2006a). This result indicates that actual offending to a large extent depends on the availability of opportunities rather than the moral constraints on the pool of potential offenders.

4. This index measures the shadow economy, which includes all legal products and services that are concealed from public authorities in order to avoid payment of taxes, social security contributions, or any contributions based on other business and labor laws. The index is calculated as the difference between a country's estimated tax income, based on a number of economic and government indicators, and the actual tax revenues; it ranges from 0 to 100, with higher ranks indicating higher levels of compliance and vice versa a smaller size of the shadow economy (Schneider, Buehn, and Montenegro 2010).

5. The median household income is a particularly suitable measure for the income of average consumers and the "middle classes." It is based on data for annual household income, in euros, from the European Survey 2004; the value is the middle of the category of income that 50% of the population achieve (e.g., for the category of €12,000 to under €18,000, the value of €15,000 was used). Data for Estonia and Ukraine were not included.

REFERENCES

Albanese, Jay S. 2005. "Fraud: The Characteristic Crime of the Twenty-First Century." *Trends in Organized Crime* 8: 6–14.

Anti-Phishing Alliance of China. 2012. *Annual Report of Anti-Phishing Alliance of China.* Beijing: Author.

Arnold, T. Clay. 2001. "Rethinking Moral Economy." *American Political Science Review* 95: 85–95.

Association for Payment and Clearance Services (APACS). n.d. *Fraud in Focus 2001.* London: APACS.

Association of British Insurers (ABI). 2000. *Update 2000.* London: ABI.

Booth, William. 1994. "On the Idea of the Moral Economy." *American Political Science Review* 88: 653–67.

Braithwaite, John. 2005. *Markets in Vice, Markets in Virtue.* Sydney: Federation Press.

Braithwaite, Valerie. 2009. *Defiance in Taxation and Governance: Resisting and Dismissing Authority in a Democracy.* Cheltenham: Edward Elgar.

Brand, Stephen, and Richard Price. 2000. *The Economic and Social Costs of Crime.* Home Office Research Study 217. London: Home Office.

Broadhurst, Roderic, John Bacon-Shone, Brigitte Bouhours, and Thierry Bourhours. 2011. *Business and the Risk of Crime in China.* Canberra: ANU E-Press.

Buehn, Andreas, and Friedrich Schneider. 2012. "Corruption and the Shadow Economy: Like Oil and Vinegar, Like Water and Fire?" *International Tax and Public Finance* 19: 172–94.

Chang, Lennon. 2012. *Cybercrime in the Greater China Region.* Cheltenham: Edward Elgar.

Cokol, Murat, Fatih Ozbay, and Paul Rodriguez-Estaban. 2008. "Retraction Rates on the Rise." *European Molecular Biology Organization Reports* 9: 2.

Coleman, James W. [1988] 2002. *Criminal Elite: Understanding White-Collar Crime.* New York: Worth Publishers.

Daly, Kathleen. 1989. "Gender and Varieties of White-Collar Crime." *Criminology* 27: 769–94.

Dean, Hartley, and Margaret Melrose. 1997. "Manageable Discord: Fraud and Resistance in the Social Security System." *Social Policy and Administration* 31: 103–18.

Ehrenreich, Barbara. 1989. *Fear of Falling: The Inner Life of the Middle Classes.* New York: Pantheon Books

Ericson, Richard V., Dean Barry, and Aaron Doyle. 1999. "The Moral Hazards of Neo-Liberalism: Lessons from the Private Insurance Industry." *Economy and Society* 29: 532–58.

Fang, Ferric, Grant Steen, and Arturo Casadevall. 2012. "Misconduct Accounts for the Majority of Retracted Scientific Publications." *Proceedings of the National Academy of Science* 109: 17028–33.

Federal Trade Commission (FTC). 2013. *Consumer Fraud in the United States, 2011: The Third FTC Survey*. Washington, D.C.: Author.

Gabor, Thomas. 1994. *Everybody Does It! Crime by the Public*. Toronto: University of Toronto Press.

Goldman Sachs. 2008. *The Expanding Middle: The Exploding World Middle Class and Falling Global Inequality*. Global Economics Paper 170. New York: Goldman Sachs.

Granovetter, Mark. 1985. "Economic Action and Social Structure: The Problem of Embeddedness." *American Journal of Sociology* 91: 481–510.

Green, Stuart P. 2006. *Lying, Cheating, and Stealing: A Moral Theory of White-Collar Crime*. Oxford: Oxford University Press.

Henning, Peter J. 2008. "The DNA of White-Collar Crime." *New Criminal Law Review* 11: 323–54.

Hirtenlehner, Helmut, Stephen Farrall, and Johann Bacher. 2013. "Culture, Institutions, and Morally Dubious Behaviors: Testing Some Core Propositions of the Institutional Anomie Theory." *Deviant Behavior* 34: 291–320.

Holtfreter, Kristy, Michael D. Reisig, and Travis C. Pratt. 2008. "Low Self-Control, Routine Activities, and Fraud Victimization." *Criminology* 46: 189–220.

Insurance Europe. 2013. *The Impact of Insurance Fraud*. Brussels: Author.

Jesilow, Paul, Henry N. Pontell, and Gilbert Geis. 1993. *Prescription for Profit: How Doctors Defraud Medicaid*. Berkeley: University of California Press.

Jorna, Penny, and Alice Hutchings. 2013. *Australasian Consumer Fraud Task Force: Results of the 2012 Online Consumer Fraud Survey*. Canberra: Australian Institute of Criminology.

Karstedt, Susanne. 2007. "From the Crimes of the Powerful to the Crimes of Power: An Uncomfortable Situation." *Monatsschrift für Kriminologie und Strafrechtsreform* 90: 78–90.

Karstedt, Susanne. 2014. "State Crime: The European Experience." In *The Routledge Handbook of European Criminology*, pp. 125–53, edited by Sophie Body-Gendrot, Mike Hough, Klara Kerezsi, Renee Lévy, and Sonja Snacken. Oxford: Routledge.

Karstedt, Susanne. 2015. "Charting Europe's Moral Economies: Citizens, Consumers, and the Crimes of Everyday Life." In *The Routledge Handbook of White-Collar and Corporate Crime*, pp. 57–88, edited by Judith van Erp, Wim Huisman, and Gudrun Vande Walle. London: Routledge.

Karstedt, Susanne, and Stephen Farrall. 2004. "The Moral Maze of the Middle Class: The Predatory Society and Its Emerging Regulatory Order." In *Images of Crime II: Representations of Crime and the Criminal in Politics, Society, the Media, and the Arts*, pp. 65–94, edited by Hand-Joerg Albrecht, Telemach Serassis, and Harald Kania. Freiburg: Edition Iuscrim.

Karstedt, Susanne, and Stephen Farrall. 2006a. "The Moral Economy of Everyday Crime: Markets, Consumers, and Citizens." *British Journal of Criminology* 46: 1011–36.

Karstedt, Susanne, and Stephen Farrall. 2006b. "Crimes of Everyday Life: Business Practices and Consumer Compliance." *Compliance and Regulatory Journal* 1: 49–59.

Karstedt, Susanne, and Stephen Farrall. 2007. *Law-Abiding Majority? The Everyday Crimes of the Middle Classes*. Briefing 3 (July). London: Centre for Crime and Justice Studies. Available at http://www.crimeandjustice.org.uk/

Katungi, Dennis, Emma Neale, and Aaron Barbour. 2006. *People in Low-Paid Work: Need not Greed*. London: Joseph Rowntree Foundation.

Kharas, Homi. 2010. *The Emerging Middle Class in Developing Countries*. OECD Development Centre. Working Paper No. 285. Paris: OECD.

Kharas, Homi, and Geoffrey Gertz. 2010. *The New Global Middle Class: A Cross-Over from West to East*. Wolfensohn Center for Development at Brookings. Washington, D.C.: Brookings Institution.

Klockars, Carl B., Sanja Kutnjak Ivkovic, and Maria Haberfeld. 2003. *The Contours of Police Integrity*. London: Sage.

Kotzian, Peter. 2011. "Cosi Fan Tutte: Information, Beliefs, and Compliance with Norms." *Zeitschrift für Soziologie* 40: 158–73.

Kracauer, Siegfried. [1998] 1930. *The Salaried Masses: Duty and Distraction in Weimar Germany*. New York: Verso Books.

Levi, Michael. 2006. "The Media Construction of Financial White-Collar Crimes." *British Journal of Criminology* 46: 1037–57.

Levi, Michael. 2009. "Suite Revenge? The Shaping of Folk Devils and Moral Panics about White-Collar Crimes." *British Journal of Criminology* 49: 48–67.

Levi, Michael, and John Burrows. 2008. "Measuring the Impact of Fraud in the UK." *British Journal of Criminology* 48: 293–318.

Levi, Michael, John Burrows, Matthew H. Fleming, and Matthew M. Hopkins. 2007. *The Nature, Extent and Economic Impact of Fraud in the UK*. London: Association of Chief Police Officers (ACPO).

Levitt, Stephen D. 2006. "White-Collar Crime Writ Small: A Case Study of Bagels, Donuts, and the Honor System." *American Economic Association Papers and Proceedings* May 2006: 290–4.

Locker, John, and Barry Godfrey. 2006. "Ontological Boundaries and Temporal Watersheds in the Development of White-Collar Crime." *British Journal of Criminology* 46: 976–92.

Lundström, Ragnar. 2013. "Framing Fraud: Discourse on Benefit Cheating in Sweden and the UK." *European Journal of Communication* 28: 630–45.

Mau, Steffen. 2003. *The Moral Economy of Welfare States: Britain and Germany Compared*. London: Routledge.

McBarnet, Doreen J., and Chris Whelan. 1999. *Creative Accounting and the Cross-Eyed Javelin Thrower*. Chichester, UK: Wiley.

McKinsey Global Institute. 2014. *China's Digital Transformation: The Internet's Growing Impact on Productivity and Growth*. London: Author.

Mikhail, John. 2007. "Universal Moral Grammar: Theory, Evidence, and Future." *Trends in Cognitive Science* 11: 143–52.

Murphy, Kristina. 2003. "Procedural Justice and Tax Compliance." *Australian Journal of Social Issues* 38: 379–408.

Murphy, Kristina. 2004. "The Role of Trust in Nurturing Compliance: A Study of Accused Tax Avoiders." *Law and Human Behavior* 28(2): 187–209.

Murphy, Kristina. 2005. "Regulating More Effectively: The Relationship between Procedural Justice, Legitimacy, and Tax Non-Compliance." *Journal of Law and Society* 32: 562–98.

National Fraud Authority. 2013. *Annual Fraud Indicator*. London: Author.

Newman, Donald J. 1958. "White-Collar Crime." *Law and Contemporary Problems* 23: 735–53.

Offer, Avner. 2006. *The Challenge of Affluence: Self-Control and Well-Being in the United States and Britain since 1950*. Oxford: Oxford University Press

PricewaterhouseCoopers. 2007. *Economic Crime: People, Culture, and Controls.* London: PricewaterhouseCoopers.

Rose, Nikolas. 1996. "The Death of the Social? Re-Figuring the Territory." *Economy and Society* 25: 327–56.

Sampson, Robert J., and Dawn J. Bartusch. 1998. "Legal Cynicism and (Subcultural?) Tolerance of Deviance: The Neighborhood Context of Racial Differences." *Law and Society Review* 32: 777–804.

Sayer, Andrew. 2007. "Moral Economy as Critique." *New Political Economy* 12: 261–70.

Schneider, Friedrich. 2003. "The Size and Development of the Shadow Economies and Shadow Economy Labor Force of 22 Transition and 21 OECD Countries: What Do We Really Know?" In *The Informal Economy in the EU Accession Countries*, pp. 23–62, edited by Boyan Belev. Sofia: Center for the Study of Democracy.

Schneider, Friedrich, Andreas Buehn, and Claudio Montenegro. 2010. "New Estimates for the Shadow Economies All over the World." *International Economic Journal* 24: 443–61.

Schneider, Friedrich, and Dominik Enste. 2000. *Schattenwirtschaft und Schwarzarbeit.* Munich: Oldenbourg.

Schneider, Friedrich, Benno Torgler, and Christoph Schaltegger. 2008. *Schattenwirschaft und Steuermoral.* Zürich: Rüegger.

Shamir, Ronen. 2008. "The Age of Responsibilization: On Market-Embedded Morality." *Economy and Society* 27: 1–19.

Shover, Neal, and Peter Grabosky. 2010. "White-Collar Crime and the Great Recession." *Criminology and Public Policy* 9: 429–33.

Shover, Neal, Glenn S. Coffey, and Dick Hobbs. 2003. "Crime on the Line: Telemarketing and the Changing Nature of Professional Crime." *British Journal of Criminology* 43: 489–505.

Simon, David R. 2011. *Elite Deviance.* 10th ed. London: Pearson.

Simpson, Sally S. 2011. "Making Sense of White-Collar Crime: Theory and Research." *Ohio State Journal of Criminal Law* 8: 481–502.

Sondak, Harris, and Tom R. Tyler. 2007. "How Does Procedural Justice Shape the Desirability of Markets?" *Journal of Economic Psychology* 28: 79–92.

Spalek, Basia, and Sam King. 2007. *Farepak Victims Speak Out: An Exploration of the Harms Caused by the Collapse of Farepak.* London: Centre for Crime and Justice Studies. Available at http://www.crimeandjustice.org.uk/

Stadler, William A., and Michael L. Benson. 2012. "Revisiting the Guilty Mind: The Neutralization of White-Collar Crime." *Criminal Justice Review* 37: 494–511.

Sutherland, Edwin H. 1940. "White-Collar Criminality: Presidential Address to the American Society of Sociology." *American Sociological Review* 5: 1–12.

Sutherland, Edwin H. 1949. *White Collar Crime.* New York: Holt, Rinehart, and Winston.

Tetlock, Philip E., and A. Peter McGraw. 2005. "Theoretically Framing Relational Framing." *Journal of Consumer Psychology* 15: 35–37.

Thompson, Edward P. 1971. "The Moral Economy of the English Crowd in the Eighteenth Century." *Past and Present* 50: 76–136.

Tombs, Steve, and David Whyte, eds. 2003. *Unmasking the Crimes of the Powerful: Scrutinizing States and Corporations.* Berne and London: Peter Lang.

Transparency International. 2013. *Global Corruption Report: Education.* Abingdon: Routledge.

Tunley, Martin. 2011. "Need, Greed, or Opportunity? An Examination of Who Commits Benefit Fraud and Why They Do It." *Security Journal* 24: 302–19.

Tyler, Tom R. [1990] 2006. *Why People Obey the Law,* 2nd ed. New Haven, CT: Yale University Press.

Weisburd, David, Stanton Wheeler, Elin Waring, and Nancy Bode. 1991. *Crimes of the Middle Classes. White-Collar Offenders in the Federal Courts.* New Haven, CT, and London: Yale University Press.

Wheeler, Stanton. 1992. "The Problem of White-Collar Crime Motivation." In *White-Collar Crime Reconsidered,* pp. 108–23, edited by Kip Schlegel and David Weisburd. Boston: Northeastern University Press.

Wilkinson, Richard G., and Kate E. Pickett. 2009. "Income Inequality and Social Dysfunction." *Annual Review of Sociology* 35: 493–511.

Winnett, Robert, and Gordon Rayner. 2009. *No Expenses Spared.* London: Transworld Publishers.

CHAPTER 10

GENDER CONSTRUCTIONS

MARY DODGE

HISTORICALLY, criminologists have studied the population responsible for committing the highest number of crimes—men. Research clearly shows that males commit more crime than females; consequently, theoretical perspectives and applied studies focus on the former, especially in the area of white-collar crime. The reasons for the higher number of male criminals are complex and may include, for example, social, environmental, biological, or psychological factors (see Cullen, Agnew, and Wilcox 2014). Also, criminological theories suggest that opportunity, variability in self-control, risk-taking tendencies, and/or strain may influence behavior—legal and illegal (Gottfredson and Hirschi 1990; Broidy and Agnew 1997; Agnew 2006; Benson and Simpson 2009; Holtfreter et al. 2010). Whether or not existing theoretical perspectives offer insight into female criminality is a subject of some controversy. Explanations for the gender gap are evolving as scholars continue to explore the causes, pathways, and participation of women in crime, particularly in the field of white-collar crime (Daly and Chesney-Lind 1988; Simpson 1989; Chesney-Lind and Shelden 1992; Steffensmeier and Allan 1996; Belknap 2001).

Early gender studies redefined the manner in which female criminality was viewed and brought attention to a neglected area of research. In 1975, Freda Adler and Rita James Simon introduced a discussion of how and why the involvement of women in white-collar crimes was likely increasing. Forty years later, studies of women and white-collar crime are rare and the full extent of women's participation in corporate and occupational crime remains unknown, although substantial variation in gender and crime still exists (Dodge 2009).

This essay summarizes what we know about women and white-collar crime, and it explores possible explanations for how and why women may or may not participate in this type of offending. This review includes historical and current perspectives and research related to gender and white-collar crime. Section I offers an overview of white-collar crime and explores how definitional issues hinder efforts to more fully understand the gender gap in the commission of corporate and occupational crime. This section also briefly describes the historical development of white-collar crime and the controversies surrounding the labeling of offense types and offenders. Section II examines the gendered stereotypes associated with women, work, and white-collar crime. This section also explores how gendered practices and opportunity structures influence behavior. Section III provides an overview of past and current research on women and white-collar crime. Section IV offers an analysis of the differences and similarities between men and women engaging in different forms of white-collar crime, despite low participation by the latter. Gendered patterns of behavior in how offenses are committed and justifications also are explored. In summary, section V addresses future directions for reflection and research on gendered forms of white-collar crime. The primary conclusions addressed in this essay include the following:

- Women's involvement in white-collar crime remains limited, except in crimes of embezzlement.
- Ongoing definitional disputes of what constitutes white-collar crime marginalize efforts to gain an in-depth understanding of women involved in occupational and corporate crime.
- Further research is needed to understand fully the gender dynamics of white-collar crime and the roles women assume in the workplace.
- Women continue to face glass ceilings that limit occupational advancement and criminal activities.

The following section provides a brief history of occupational and corporate crime and the controversy over defining offenders and offenses as white-collar and pink-collar. The discussion establishes a historical context for current examinations of gender and white-collar crime.

I. An Overview of Historical Perspectives of White-Collar Crime and Gendered Offending

In 1939, when Edwin Sutherland introduced the widespread and serious nature of white-collar crime at a meeting of the American Sociological Society and the American Economics Association, he paid little attention to detailed definitional issues. His description of white-collar crime at the time, though it became somewhat more refined during his career, is described as "unacceptably vague" (Geis, Meier, and Salinger 1995, p. 25). He emphasized that these crimes depended on the offender's occupational status. According to Sutherland (1945), white-collar crime involves respectable, upper-class business and professional men whose occupations facilitate the commission of the crime. In many definitions, the social status of the individual, the financial aspects of the crime, and the occupational means of committing the illegal—and in some cases unethical—act are key components. The debate over the definition of white-collar crime varies because of the wide range of possible acts and whether or not the focus is on the offense, the offender, or both.

The status of the offender, more often than not, is central to many proposed white-collar crime definitions. Narrow definitions address elite criminals and corporations engaging in nonviolent, complex financial frauds. Arguably, however, holding a high-status work position is not a necessary condition for committing some types of occupational and financial crime, and many scholars believe the definition of white-collar crime should include middle- and working-class people (see, e.g., Hagan, Nagel, and Albonetti 1980; Shapiro 1981; Vaughan 1992). Bank tellers, bookkeepers, and low-level managers, for example, lack status but often commit financial fraud. Research on white-collar crime also includes Internet schemes, juveniles, and police officers (Pontell and Rosoff 2009; Rosoff, Pontell, and Tillman 2014). Some researchers, however, argue that lower-level crimes such as embezzlement fail to rise to the level of white-collar crime because the offender lacks status. Steffensmeier, Schwartz, and Roche (2013) noted that including "low-profit, less complex financial schemes" is "stretching definitions of white-collar crime and failing to capture the breadth and diversity of serious economic and corporate financial crimes" (p. 450). The latter perspective limits white-collar research to crimes such as insider trading, antitrust violations, complex Ponzi schemes, and accounting frauds by large corporations and high-placed business executives. In some cases, the "color of the collar" has established categories of offenses and offender, further complicating definitional issues.

White-collar offenders typically are educated men in positions of power engaging in nonviolent financial schemes. Pink collar, a term coined by Kathleen Daly (1989), describes female involvement in fiduciary fraud and commonly refers to low-level schemes such as embezzlement. Men who commit financial fraud are seldom, or never, labeled pink-collar criminals. In 2007, Perri and Litchenwald introduced the term red-collar crime as a label for white-collar criminals who employ violent means to conceal fraudulent acts (Perri and Litchenwald 2007, 2008; Brody and Kiehl 2010). Overall, the list of white-collar crimes is extensive, and categorizing them as nonviolent or committed exclusively by men seems foolhardy and exclusionary; this approach also ignores the intersection of gender and race (Simpson 1991; Simpson and Elis 1995). Moreover, white-collar crime scholars have long acknowledged the possible violent nature of some offenses, which diminishes the need for conceptualizing acts as red collar (Friedrichs 2010).

White-collar crime encompasses many types of offenses and offenders, and males are engaged in the majority of cases of corporate and professional malfeasance. White-collar crime is distinguished from street crime because offenders hold positions of trust and financial gain serves as the primary motive. The level of female participation varies according to the breadth and width of the definition. The inclusion of embezzlement as a white-collar crime, for example, substantially raises the number of women offenders. Women embezzlers account for approximately 50 percent of all such offenses in arrest data (FBI Uniform Crime Report 2012).

II. Women, Work,
and White-Collar Crime

The discourse on how and why women commit crime has evolved along with structural and attitudinal societal changes. Numerous early explorations on the misdeeds of female offenders emphasized biological differences focusing on promiscuity as a reason, motivation, and/or explanation of delinquency and crime (see, e.g., Thomas 1923; Glueck and Glueck 1950; Pollak 1950; Cohen 1955). Also, the mores associated with the proper treatment and behavior of women influenced and perpetuated stereotypical beliefs that marginalized women and established gendered boundaries for them in the private and public spheres. Aggregate-level crime patterns, for example, show that men offend at higher rates for all crimes except prostitution (Steffensmeier and Broidy 2001). According to Steffensmeier and Broidy, "gender differences in norms, moral development and affiliate concerns, social control, physical strength and aggression, and sexuality dictate patterns of female crime by shaping both criminal opportunities and criminal motivations among women" (2001, p. 128).

Scholars who questioned the historically traditional normative standards associated with women who commit crime ultimately challenged many of the stereotypes. Initially, the idea that women can, do, and will commit crime in a manner similar to men was viewed as unorthodox. Academic and public reactions to the work of Freda Alder (1975) and Rita James Simon (1975), for example, were mixed. Critics of the emerging scholarship on female criminality argued that the idea of a liberation hypothesis, as many people referred to the work of Adler and Simon, created a backlash that interfered with efforts to establish equal rights for women. The idea that women, suddenly unfettered from domestic responsibilities, would behave in a masculine and criminal manner in the workforce was deemed offensive by some commentators. The reality of the controversy was intertwined with historical events, such as efforts to pass the Equal Rights Amendment, and was immersed in stereotypes associated with persistent dichotomies of the characteristics associated with being feminine or masculine. Ultimately, their provocative ideas predicting an increased involvement of women and crime were embraced and lauded as a crucial area of study otherwise ignored. Simon and Adler both postulated that the low rate of female participation in crime was related to the lack of opportunity. Simon, who reflected on her initial work thirty years later, noted: "Women are no more honest, no more decent, and no more moral than men. The only reason they had lower crime rates, particularly white-collar crime, was because they had fewer opportunities to commit crime" (Dodge 2009, p. 12). Similarly, Adler commented: "The kinds of crimes one commits are related to the illegal opportunities to commit them. While a shopper might pilfer from commercial establishments, it is not possible to be involved in insider trading, unless one is 'inside' the corporate community" (Dodge, 2009, p. 180). The workplace offers the opportunity to engage in legitimate and illegitimate acts; in other words, the milieu further delineates white-collar crime from street crime (Benson and Simpson 2009).

Many people believed women would continue their domestic role in the workplace as caregivers by introducing empathy and nurturance to the business world. Extant studies show how male and female behavior differs in positive and negative ways in the workplace. On the one hand, women in high-ranking positions, according to some reports, show less aggression, competitiveness, and violence than their male counterparts (Fukuyama 1998). Women in the workplace, on the other hand, face the same strain, lures, and demands that push men into committing acts of white-collar crime (Shover and Hochstetler 2006; Dodge 2007; Benson and Simpson 2009; Dodge 2009). Women may engage in high-risk activities to protect and sustain relationships, whereas men are more likely to commit financial fraud for profit (Cressey 1953; Zeitz 1981; Steffensmeier and Broidy 2001).

The one consistent pattern in examinations of the role of women in the workplace is related to the stereotypes that define how women handle legitimate and illegitimate behavior. Men in positions of power likely have risen to the top by adopting an aggressive, risk-taking style of management. Vande Walle (2002) described the production of gender as being embedded in perceived characteristics associated with masculinity such as "aggression, competition, rationality, machismo, power." In contrast, femininity entails "sweetness, sensitivity, irrationality, and obedience" (p. 282). Many feminist scholars agree that the hegemonic masculine structure of the corporate workplace continues to subjugate and marginalize women (Murrell and James 2001; Bravo 2007).

West and Zimmerman (1987) are credited with expanding both the concept of doing gender and the idea that behavior occurs based on situational societal contexts, which defines how one acts as a man or woman. Martin (2003) persuasively argued that social constructions at work continue to be "gendering practices and practicing gender" (p. 343). Gendering practices, according to Martin, create inequalities in the workplace and diminish the identity and confidence of many women. Organizational emphasis on characteristics such as "competence, leadership, effectiveness, excellence, rationality, strength, and authority" is conceptualized as masculine (Martin 2003, p. 345; see also Ely and Meyerson 2000; Martin 2001; Quinn 2002). Martin's research identified several differential impacts of gender in corporate entities. First, women are held accountable for pleasing men. Second, women are placed in a no-win situation, even at the highest levels of management. A woman who challenges gendered practices may be viewed as "overly sensitive" and as acting like a girl more than an executive (p. 348). Women who abide by the masculine norms and fail to practice femininity remain outside the formal and informal networks, lose peer approval, and hold lower status (West and Zimmerman 1987; McGuire 2000; Martin 2001). Men label women as "not one of the boys."

Workplace gendered stereotypes connected to white-collar criminality may limit a female's opportunity to commit such crimes because "men do not like having women as crime partners; they neither trust women nor think them capable in a jam" (Daly 1989, p. 280). Higher-level white-collar crimes often involve multiple executives, incorporating a team concept. Recent research on gender and corporate crime shows that women are rarely part of these conspiracies (Steffensmeier, Schwartz, and Roche 2013). The exclusion of women in such high-level crimes may be nothing more than men's sexism translated to the upper corporate echelons (Daly 1989). Men typically establish close personal bonds at the office. This social bonding comes about by dedicating long hours and spending more time with colleagues, rather than family. As women enter the workplace, they are subjected to enhanced supervision and slower promotion rates than men—partially because they lack the collectivist "corporate" mentality (Daly 1989).

Overfelt (2012) reported that entrepreneurial women must relinquish luxuries many females consider essential to being a mother in order to be successful in the business world. Women in executive positions face extensive social pressure to balance work and effective childrearing (Overfelt 2012). The collective bond required for corporate conspiracies may be interrupted by women's parental and familial obligations.

Females often are placed in no-win situations in the workplace. To be successful in corporate America, they must attempt to fit into a masculine role while still preserving a ladylike self-image (Dodge 2009; Klenowski, Copes, and Mullins 2011). Stabile (2004) discovered that female white-collar offenders are much more likely to be portrayed harshly in the media and tabloids. When female white-collar criminality is reported in the news, the stories are derogatory, transforming the typical profile of a corporate leader from a "tough, aggressive, competitive" person to a "bitchy, pushy, manipulative, and unfeminine" individual (Dodge 2009, p. 73).

The difference in public treatment of female offenders in the media compared to male offenders is dramatic. From June 1, 2002, to June 30, 2003, *The New York Times*, for example, published 271 stories about Martha Stewart and two about Kenneth Lay (Stabile 2004). The trend is fairly consistent—further analysis found a total of 1,507 stories about Martha Stewart and 12 about Kenneth Lay in all New York newspapers from November 2003 to May 2004 (Stabile 2004). Gender stereotypes also are salient in accounts of women who have committed white-collar crime. As Vande Walle (2002) noted, media reports of known white-collar crimes tend to be gender neutral unless a woman is involved.

Crime statistics may reveal that women are advancing through the corporate ranks to executive positions and adopting a more traditional corporate mindset that can result in illegal activities. Simon and Ahn-Redding's (2005) exploration of arrest statistics through 2001 showed a relationship between the increased number of women in high-status positions with access to financial assets and higher rates of arrests for white-collar crime among females. Their research found that almost 37 percent of the employed women held managerial, professional, and technical positions in 2000, and 17 percent held jobs categorized as administrative and executive. In 2001, women accounted for more than one third of all arrests for larceny and almost half of all arrests for embezzlement and fraud. Simon and Ahn-Redding concluded that women were committing more white-collar crimes because of greater participation in the labor force, which creates opportunity.

III. RESEARCH ON WOMEN
AND WHITE-COLLAR CRIME

Women do commit white-collar crimes, although the number of incidents remains low. Croall (2003) argued that the maleness of white-collar crime continues to dominate academic studies, though a more substantial base of literature is developing. Much of the current work on women and white-collar crime follows the tradition of the case study methodology (Geis, Meier, and Salinger 1995). Quantitative studies are rare because of the difficulties of gathering sufficient data. Gottschalk (2013), for instance, noted the importance of developing real data in a recent research publication: "Rather than presenting some cases and anecdotal evidence, the paper [described below] presents substantial statistical evidence to conclude on [sic] gender differences in white-collar crime" (p. 362). The small sample size of Gottschalk's studies, however, fails to offer substantial statistical evidence.

In 1986, the Bureau of Justice Statistics (BJS) reported that females represent a higher proportion of arrests for white-collar crimes than for any other types of crime (Manson 1986). According to Manson's BJS report, arrests in 1983 for "nonviolent crime for financial gain committed by means of deception" show females were involved in 34 percent of the white-collar felony offenses. Albanese (1993) discovered, in the United States and Canada, an increase in the number of women who were employed in white-collar occupations and a similar pattern in arrests for fraud, forgery, counterfeiting, and embezzlement during the 1970s and 1980s. Data from the BJS indicate a "55 percent increase in the number of women convicted of fraud felonies in state courts between 1990 to 1996" (cited in Haantz 2002, p. 1). Haantz's (2002) research showed that, of the 1,016 federal prisoners incarcerated for white-collar crime in 2000, nearly one in four was a woman.

Daly's (1989) research offered many new insights on women and white-collar crime. She discovered that women who committed financial fraud or embezzlement were younger and less educated, held lower-status positions, and earned less compared to men. Daly found that female arrests for pink-collar offenses had increased, perhaps further closing the gap between male and female offending. Her findings suggest that marginality, rather than liberation or occupational mobility, is a more appropriate manner in which to frame female white-collar crime.

An analysis of media reports from 2009 to 2011 in Norway discovered that of the 161 convicted white-collar offenders identified in major newspaper articles, 153 were males and eight were females (Gottschalk 2012). The research compared female and male offenders on a variety of variables but, because of the low sample size, found no statistically significant differences. The females in the sample, overall, appeared to have earned lower incomes and garnered less profit from their crimes. In a subsequent study employing much of the same data, Gottschalk (2013) identified additional newspaper articles of high-profile, large-yield offenses from 2009 to 2012. He found that of the 255 convicted white-collar criminals in Norway, 20 were female. This comparison of females and males also suggests the latter stole higher dollar amounts, earned more money, paid higher taxes, and reported larger personal wealth.

Perhaps the most sophisticated study on women and white-collar crime is represented in the work of Steffensmeier, Schwartz, and Roche (2013). These researchers offered the first in-depth examination of female participation in recent high-level corporate crimes. The database included 83 corporate frauds and 436 defendants. The findings show that women were rarely involved in conspiracy groups and, when they did participate, they were minor players and made less profit compared to the males in the group. The results, according to the authors, "do not comport with images of highly placed or powerful white-collar female criminals" (p. 448). The findings suggest that women have encountered a new glass ceiling in the upper echelons of the corporate world. In lower-level crimes, however, female participation continues to increase. A global study of lower-level and midlevel corporate fraud showed that females in 2012 accounted for 41 percent of the perpetrators (Association of Certified Fraud Examiners 2012).

IV. Gender Similarities and Differences in the Commission of White-Collar Crime

Specific gender differences in white-collar offending are somewhat unexplored, and the limited research that exists is contradictory. A common notion is that women are typically more remorseful than men for their illegal actions and almost always commit white-collar offenses for someone other than themselves (Goldstraw-White 2012). Men and women often view white-collar crimes differently from a gendered standpoint. Traditionally, women have been more likely to commit a white-collar offense "for their families or for others with whom they have a close personal relationship" (Goldstraw-White 2012, p. 163; see also Zeitz 1981). Men, who are more likely to own businesses than women, justify their offenses in terms of protecting the profits during slow times (Goldstraw-White 2012).

Goldstraw-White (2012) examined roles that may contribute to white-collar offending and discovered several important gender differences. Men were far more likely than women to engage in a detailed and sophisticated planning process before committing a white-collar crime. Both male and female employees who committed white-collar offenses cited poor oversight within the organization or the ability to take advantage of a position of power or authority. In the Goldstraw-White study, one of the main differences found between males and females is the ability of women to manipulate the resources of an organization. Women typically find themselves in middle-management positions and are "more able to exploit opportunities or weaknesses in systems and procedures, because they know and understand them in detail" (p. 179).

In past research, men and women have cited financial need as a reason for committing white-collar crime, although the extent of true need has varied. Many white-collar criminals reveal financial concern as a motive, regardless of the "severity" of monetary need (Langton and Piquero 2007; Goldstraw-White 2012). Men also seem to commit offenses based on their own prerogative, and evidence exists that men turn to crime because of pressures to maintain an upper-class lifestyle. Women more commonly cite a hardship as a reason for their criminal behavior rather than maintenance of an established lifestyle. Some reasons cited by women for their involvement in criminal acts include personal debt, familial medical hardships, and intervention in a family member's problem such as drug addiction. Klenowski, Copes, and Mullins (2011) found that women used the excuse of "necessity" as a justification more often than men.

People engage in crime for a variety of reasons and often adopt techniques of neutralization or rationalization to hasten or justify their illegal behavior. Recent research has explored gendered differences among white-collar offenders and justifications for their actions. The use of techniques of neutralization, first proposed by Sykes and Matza (1957), is common among all types of offenders. The list of possible neutralizations has been extended from the original five set forth by Sykes and Matza—that is, denial of responsibility, denial of injury, denial of victim, condemnation of the condemners, and appeal to higher loyalties. Other researchers have found that offenders also claim metaphor of the ledgers, entitlement, normality, necessity, and justification by comparison (see, e.g., Klockars 1974; Benson 1985; Cromwell and Thurman 2003; Coleman 2006).

Vieraitis et al. (2012) explored the process of gendered neutralizations among master of business administration students. The research employed a corporate-crime scenario to help determine how gender influences the types of neutralizations used in corporate-offending decisions. They found that male students were more likely than females to agree to market or sell a banned drug, while men were more likely to deny injury compared to women who condemned the condemners (e.g., blamed prosecutors or regulatory agencies).

The financial motive behind white-collar crime appears to be gender neutral. Both men and women engage in many criminal behaviors for money (Copes and Vieraitis 2012). The justifications between males and females, according to Copes and Vieraitis, differ. Men are more likely to defend their behavior based on their roles as breadwinners. In contrast, women justify their crimes as concerned caregivers, as previously mentioned. Similarly, Klenowski, Copes, and Mullins (2011) discovered through semistructured interviews that male offenders frequently focus on providing for their families as excuses, whereas women claim they are caring for their families.

V. Conclusions

Only recently has the role of women who commit corporate and occupational crime garnered substantial scholarly attention. The existing literature and research lend support to four major conclusions regarding women and white-collar crime. First, women in the workplace are just beginning to obtain positions that are more conducive to white-collar crime, but they still face many occupational barriers. Second, financial crime by women is more likely to be labeled as pink collar, particularly embezzlement, because of disagreements over what constitutes white-collar crime. Third, perceived gender roles of appropriate female and male behavior and "in-groups" leave little room for women's participation in major corporate frauds. Finally, existing research is limited and the role of women in white-collar crime is evolving.

Before women entered the upper echelons of the occupational and corporate worlds, few were afforded the opportunity to engage in traditional white-collar crimes such as price-fixing, insider trading, bribery, and medical fraud. Women are still blocked from many workplace opportunities, which restricts their access to white-collar crime. In 2012, about 20 women (just over 4 percent) were employed as chief executive officers in Fortune 500 companies (Lennon 2013). Women are no longer just in retail, beauty, and consumer-related positions as they take the helm of companies such as Lockheed Martin, General Dynamics, Yahoo!, General Motors, and Hewlett-Packard. Although a low number of women are working as CEOs, "female chiefs are leading multibillion [dollar] businesses in oil, energy, and steel—fields that are obviously not just for the boys anymore" (Sellers 2012). Despite these advances, women still more commonly work as midlevel managers than corporate leaders.

Considerable academic debate has developed as the involvement of women in white-collar crime has become fodder for speculation and empirical testing. Often the problems in identifying who is involved and what is entailed in white-collar crime are frustrating and mired in polemics, because definitions of white-collar crime continue to be imprecise. Ideas about the participation of women in elite crime may depend on basic assumptions about who commits what crime. Vande Walle (2002) argued that the concept of white-collar crime refers to white middle-class men and is studied with a clear understanding of the absence of gender. She noted: "And even if they [women] can commit a crime that has the characteristics of a white-collar offence, they cannot commit 'white-collar crime,' because their blouses may not be white" (p. 283). Consequently, the discourse often excludes women and stereotypes their behavior as "pink" or, in other words, less important.

Current research shows several differences between males and females associated with criminal behavior and white-collar crime. First, women steal less money in fraudulent acts than men do. Prostitution and embezzlement are the only areas where female offending is higher than or equal to that of men (Becker and McCorkel 2011). Second, women tend to justify or rationalize their illegal behavior as more "altruistic" than men do. Third, the glass ceiling continues to block opportunities in the workforce and for white-collar crime offenses. Fourth, one of the key differences between male and female offending is that women typically act alone rather than as part of a group; this is especially true when considering embezzlement.

Clearly, additional data are needed to determine the actual involvement of women in white-collar crime using a broad definition. However, it would be remiss to assume that women are strictly relegated to the realm of pink-collar crime, because their opportunities to commit white-collar crime continue to increase as females assume professional and leadership positions in the workforce. The commission of white-collar crime depends on positioning in male-dominated corporate and professional work environments. In other words, one key component to female participation is opportunity. Women represent 50 percent of all arrests for embezzlement, according to the FBI's Uniform Crime Report (2012)—a longstanding trend reflecting the importance of opportunity.

In summary, occupational, professional, and political crimes by women are on the increase, although the gender gap in the overall number of women arrested for or convicted of white-collar crimes remains low. Institutional norms and expectations create an environment where legal and illegal behaviors are defined through socialization. Success in many professions is characterized by risk-taking behavior and the competitive edge to win at all costs. The pushes toward white-collar crime as a means of achieving financial rewards, power, and respectability continue to be connected to gender. Understanding gender and white-collar crime is a work in progress, and women's participation in the workplace is changing the landscape. Currently, there is little empirical evidence to suggest that women's involvement in high-level corporate crime is increasing, and whether or not this trend will change remains to be seen.

REFERENCES

Adler, Freda. 1975. *Sisters in Crime: The Rise of the New Female Criminal*. New York: McGraw-Hill.

Agnew, Robert. 2006. *Pressured into Crime: An Overview of General Strain*. Los Angeles: Roxbury.

Albanese, Jay. 1993. "Women and the Newest Profession: Females as White-Collar Criminals." In *Female Criminality: The State of the Art*, pp. 119–31, edited by C. C. Culliver. New York: Garland.

Association of Certified Fraud Examiners. 2012. *Report to the Nations on Occupational Fraud and Abuse: 2012 Global Fraud Study*. Available at http://www.acfe.com/uploadedFiles/ACFE_Website/Content/rttn/2012-report-to-nations.pdf

Becker, Sarah, and Jill A. McCorkel. 2011. "The Gender of Criminal Opportunity: The Impact of Male Co-Offenders on Women's Crime." *Feminist Criminology* 6: 79–110.

Belknap, Joanne. 2001. *The Invisible Woman: Gender, Crime, and Justice*. Belmont: Wadsworth.

Benson, Michael. L. 1985. "Denying the Guilty Mind: Accounting for Involvement in a White-Collar Crime." *Criminology* 23: 583–607.

Benson, Michael L., and Sally S. Simpson 2009. *White-Collar Crime: An Opportunity Perspective*. New York: Routledge.

Bravo, Ellen. 2007. *Taking on the Big Boys: Or Why Feminism Is Good for Families, Business, and the Nation*. New York: The Feminist Press at the City University of New York.

Brody, Richard G., and Kent A. Kiehl. 2010. "From White-Collar Crime to Red-Collar Crime." *Journal of Financial Crime* 17: 351–64.

Broidy, Lisa, and Robert Agnew. 1997. "Gender and Crime: A General Strain Theory Perspective." *Journal of Research in Crime and Delinquency* 34: 275–306.

Chesney-Lind, Meda, and Randall G. Shelden 1992. *Girls, Delinquency, and Juvenile Justice.* Pacific Grove, CA: Brooks/Cole.

Cohen, Albert Kircidel. 1955. *Delinquent Boys: The Culture of the Gang.* New York: Free Press.

Coleman, James W. 2006. *The Criminal Elite,* 6th ed. New York: St. Martin's Press.

Copes, Heith, and Lynne M. Vieraitis. 2012. *Identity Thieves: Motives and Methods.* Boston: Northeastern University Press.

Cressey, Donald R. 1953. *Other People's Money: A Study of the Social Psychology of Embezzlement.* New York: Free Press.

Croall, Hazel. 2003. "Men's Business? Some Gender Questions about White-Collar Crime." *Criminal Justice Matters* 53: 26–27.

Cromwell, Paul, and Quint Thurman. 2003. "The Devil Made Me Do It: Use of Neutralizations by Shoplifters." *Deviant Behavior* 24: 535–50.

Cullen, Francis T., Robert Agnew, and Pamela Wilcox. 2014. *Criminological Theory: Past to Present.* New York: Oxford University Press.

Daly, Kathleen. 1989. "Gender and Varieties of White-Collar Crime." *Criminology* 27: 769–93.

Daly, Kathleen, and Meda Chesney-Lind. 1988. "Feminism and Criminology." *Justice Quarterly* 5: 497–538.

Dodge, Mary. 2007. "From Pink to White with Various Shades of Embezzlement: Women Who Commit White-Collar Crimes." In *International Handbook of White-Collar and Corporate Crime,* pp. 379–404, edited by Henry N. Pontell and Gilbert Geis. New York: Springer.

Dodge, Mary. 2009. *Women and White-Collar Crime.* Upper Saddle River, NJ: Prentice Hall.

Ely, Robin J., and Debra E. Meyerson. 2000. "Theories of Gender in Organizations: A New Approach to Organizational Analysis and Change." *Research in Organizational Behavior* 27: 105–53.

Federal Bureau of Investigation (2012). *Crime in the United States: Uniform Crime Reports.* Available at http://www.fbi.gov/about-us/cjis/ucr/crime-in-the-u.s/2012/crime-in-the-u.s.-2012/tables/33tabledatadecovervarviewpdf

Friedrichs, David O. 2010. *Trusted Criminals: White Collar Crime in Contemporary Society,* 4th ed. Belmont: Wadsworth Cengage Learning.

Fukuyama, Francis. 1998. "Women and the Evolution of World Politics." *Foreign Affairs* (October): 24–40. Available at http://fullaccess.foreignaffairs.org

Geis, Gilbert, Robert F. Meier, and Lawrence M. Salinger. 1995. *White-Collar Crime: Classic and Contemporary Views.* New York: Free Press.

Glueck, Sheldon, and Eleanor Glueck. 1950. *Unraveling Juvenile Delinquency.* New York: The Commonwealth Fund.

Goldstraw-White, Janice. 2012. *White-Collar Crime: Accounts of Offending Behavior.* England: Palgrave Macmillan.

Gottfredson, Michael R., and Travis Hirschi. 1990. *A General Theory of Crime.* Stanford: Stanford University Press.

Gottschalk, Petter. 2012. "Gender and White-Collar Crime: Only Four Percent Female Criminals." *Journal of Money Laundering Control* 15: 362–73.

Gottschalk, Petter. 2013. "Women's Justifications of White-Collar Crime." *International Journal of Contemporary Business Studies* 4: 24–32.

Haantz, Sally. 2002. *Women and White-Collar Crime.* National White Collar Crime Center. Available at http://www.nw3c.org/downloads/women_wcc1.pdf

Hagan, John, Ilene H. Nagel, and Celesta Albonetti. 1980. "The Differential Sentencing of White-Collar Offenders in Ten Federal District Courts." *American Sociological Review* 45: 802–20.

Holtfreter, Kristy, Kevin M. Beaver, Michael D. Reisig, and Travis C. Pratt. 2010. "Low Self-Control and Fraud Offending." *Journal of Financial Crime* 17: 295–307.

Klenowksi, Paul M., Heith Copes, and Christopher W. Mullins. 2011. "Gender, Identity, and Accounts: How White-Collar Offenders Do Gender When Making Sense of Their Crimes." *Justice Quarterly* 24: 46–69.

Klockars, Carl B. 1974. *The Professional Fence*. New York: Free Press.

Langton, Lynn, and Nicole Leeper Piquero. 2007. "Can General Strain Theory Explain White-Collar Crime? A Preliminary Investigation of the Relationship between Strain and Select White-Collar Offenses." *Journal of Criminal Justice* 35: 1–15.

Lennon, Tiffani. 2013. *Benchmarking Women's Leadership in the United States*. University of Denver, Colorado Women's College. Available at http://www.womenscollege.du.edu/media/documents/BenchmarkingWomensLeadershipintheUS.pdf

Manson, Donald A. 1986. *Tracking Offenders: White-Collar Crime*. U.S. Department of Justice Bureau of Justice Statistics. Available at http://www.bjs.gov/index.cfm?ty=pbdetail&iid=3630

Martin, Patricia Y. 2001. "Mobilizing Masculinities: Women's Experiences of Men at Work." *Organization* 8: 587–618.

Martin, Patricia Y. 2003. "Said and Done Versus Saying and Doing: Gendering Practices, Practicing Gender at Work." *Gender and Society* 17: 342–66.

McGuire, Gail. 2000. "Gender, Race, Ethnicity, and Networks: The Factors Affecting the Status of Employees' Network Members." *Work and Occupations* 27: 500–23.

Overfelt, Maggie. 2012. "What Maternity Leave? For Entrepreneurial Women, Long Breaks from Work Aren't Always an Option." *Crain's New York Business* (August 26): 12. Available at http://www.crainsnewyork.com/article/20120826/SMALLBIZ/308269982/what-maternity-leave#

Perri, Frank S., and Terrance G. Lichtenwald. 2007. "A Proposed Addition to the FBI Criminal Classification Manual: Fraud-Detection Homicide." *The Forensic Examiner* 16: 18–30.

Perri, Frank S., and Terrance G. Lichtenwald. 2008. "The Arrogant Chameleons: Exposing Fraud-Detection Homicide." *The Forensic Examiner* 17: 26–33.

Pollak, Otto. 1950. *The Criminality of Women*. New York: A. S. Barnes.

Pontell, Henry N., and Steven M. Rosoff. 2009. "White-Collar Delinquency." *Crime, Law, and Social Change* 51: 147–62.

Quinn, Beth. 2002. "Sexual Harassment and Masculinity: The Power and Meaning of 'Girl Watching.'" *Gender and Society* 16: 386–402.

Rosoff, Stephen M., Henry N. Pontell., and Robert Tillman. 2014. *Profit without Honor: White-Collar Crime and the Looting of America*, 6th ed. Upper Saddle River, NJ: Pearson/Prentice Hall.

Sellers, Patricia. 2012. "Fortune 500 Women CEOs Hit a Milestone." *CNNMoney* (November 12). Available at http://postcards.blogs.fortune.cnn.com/2012/11/12/fortune-500-women-ceos-3/

Shapiro, Susan P. 1981. *Thinking about White Collar Crime: Matters of Conceptualization and Research*. Washington, D.C.: U.S. Department of Justice.

Shover, Neal, and Andrew Hochstetler. 2006. *Choosing White-Collar Crime*. Cambridge: Cambridge University Press.

Simon, Rita James. 1975. *Women and Crime*. Lexington, MA: Lexington Books.

Simon, Rita James, and Heather Ahn-Redding. 2005. *The Crimes Women Commit: The Punishments They Receive*, 3rd ed. Lexington, MA: Lexington Books.

Simpson, Sally S. 1989. "Feminist Theory, Crime, and Justice." *Criminology* 40: 605–31.

Simpson, Sally S. 1991. "Caste, Class, and Violent Crime: Explaining Differences in Female Offending." *Criminology* 29: 115–35.

Simpson, Sally S., and Lori Elis. 1995. "Doing Gender: Sorting Out the Case and Crime Conundrum." *Criminology* 33: 47–81.

Stabile, Carol A. 2004. "Getting What She Deserved: The News Media, Martha Stewart, and Masculine Domination." *Feminist Media Studies* 4: 315–32.

Steffensmeier, Darrell J., and Emile Allan. 1996. "Gender and Crime: Toward a Gendered Theory of Female Offending." *Annual Review of Sociology* 22: 459–87.

Steffensmeier, Darrell J., and Lisa Broidy. 2001. "Explaining Female Offending." In *Women, Crime, and Criminal Justice: Original Feminist Readings*, pp. 111–31, edited by Claire Renzetti and Lynne Goodsteing. Los Angeles: Roxbury.

Steffensmeier, Darrel J., Jennifer Schwartz, and Michael Roche. 2013. "Gender and Twenty-First-Century Corporate Crime: Female Involvement and the Gender Gap in Enron-Era Corporate Frauds." *American Sociological Review* 78: 448–76.

Sutherland, Edwin H. 1945. "Is 'White Collar Crime' Crime?" *American Sociological Review* 10: 132–9.

Sykes, Gresham M., and David Matza. 1957. "Techniques of Neutralization: A Theory of Delinquency." *American Sociological Review* 22: 664–70.

Thomas, William I. 1923. *The Unadjusted Girl: With Cases and Standpoint for Behavior Analysis*. Boston: Little, Brown.

Vande Walle, Gudrun. 2002. "'The Collar Makes the Difference'—Masculine Criminology and Its Refusal to Recognize Markets as Criminogenic." *Crime, Law, and Social Change* 37: 277–91.

Vaughan, Diane. 1992. "The Macro–Micro Connection in White-Collar Crime Theory." In *White Collar Crime Reconsidered*, pp. 124–45, edited by Kip Schlegel and David Weisburd. Boston: Northeastern University Press.

Vieraitis, Lynne M., Nicole Leeper Piquero, Alex R. Piquero, Stephen G. Tibbetts, and Michael Blankenship. 2012. "Do Women and Men Differ in Their Neutralizations of Corporate Crime?" *Criminal Justice Review* 37: 478–93.

West, Candace, and Don Zimmerman. 1987. "Doing Gender." *Gender and Society* 1: 3–37.

Zeitz, Dorothy. 1981. *Women Who Embezzle or Defraud: A Study of Convicted Felons*. New York: Praeger.

PART IV

WHITE-COLLAR CRIME ACROSS THE LIFE COURSE

CHAPTER 11

··

ADOLESCENT PRECURSORS
OF WHITE-COLLAR CRIME

··

SIMON I. SINGER

ADULT white-collar criminals developed their techniques of deception early in their lives. They may have learned as adolescents how to achieve their objectives by ignoring the stated rules. As students in school, they may have been rewarded with excellent grades, despite having cheated on an exam or plagiarized a school paper. In their familial settings, they may have experienced the sneaky thrill of conning their parents into believing they were studying at a friend's house when they were actually partying. When hanging out at the local mall, they may have figured out how to slip that attractive wallet or bracelet into their pocket without having to pay for it. Whether as students, family members, or consumers of all that a good middle-class life has to provide, adolescence is that period of time when the techniques, rationalizations, and definitions in favor of violating legal and administrative rules are most likely to be learned.

There is a structure to adolescence that is both transitional and formative (Steinberg 2002). The transitional reflects the fact that adolescents are on their way to adulthood; they are not yet fully responsible adults. An adolescent's childlike modern-day dependency is often coupled with desires for status in one social setting after another. Expectations to succeed in each of these settings can be formative, particularly if success is generated through the clever concealment of the truth. The habits of youth can transcend adolescence. Most adolescents know this about their delinquencies. They often are warned or just realize that their offenses in adolescence are no longer worth pursuing.

Although the vast majority of adolescents desist from their offending, we know that a small segment of adolescents become life-course or chronic offenders. A familiar conclusion from the criminological literature is that the best predictor of persistent criminal behavior is the frequency and seriousness of offending in adolescence (Moffitt 1993). As repeatedly documented, chronic adult offenders usually began their criminal careers as adolescent delinquents (Farrington 1994; Farrington et al. 2006). Although the frequent and serious delinquents are the subject of contemporary criminological research (Loeber and Farrington 2012), they are strangely absent from the literature on white-collar crime.

So why has the criminological literature been relatively slow to recognize the importance of adolescence in its explanations of white-collar crime? One reason is that definitions of white-collar crime preclude adolescence. Several definitions draw on Edwin Sutherland's (1949) conception of white-collar crime as an act committed by adults who are in high-status occupational positions. Adolescents as students or dependent family members are generally of low status. They are assumed to be relatively powerless in avoiding the kinds of punishment that white-collar criminals could potentially face (Sutherland 1949, p. 247). Last but not least are the consequences of adolescent cheating, conning, or lying. In contrast to adult white-collar criminals, the cost of an adolescent lying to his or her parents or cheating on a school exam is directed to the family or the school. This sort of conning is seen as not hurting society. Instead, it is seen as administrative—an infraction that is far removed from the problem of crime.

Yet acts of deception and the abuse of trust also characterize adult white-collar criminality. Although adolescents are not in positions of high occupational status, they may be in the fortunate position of residing in upper-middle-class families. Their parents may have the money, authority, and connections to insulate them from punishment. The harm perpetuated by their offending could be even more significant in producing the justifications for repeated acts of fraud in adulthood.

This essay illustrates how adolescence can be considered a precursor to adult white-collar crime. Edwin Sutherland's (1949) focus on adult occupational status and adult group associations in the commission of white-collar crime should not be viewed as entirely negating the importance of adolescence (Geis 2010). His theory of learned offending by means of association with others explained adolescent as well as adult crime. A theory of differential association is typically referenced to explain the group context of adolescent delinquency (Warr 2002). But group definitions of a situation relate to social class (Singer 2010). The expectations for success among middle- and upper-class parents produce a set of social definitions that can be quite different from those of less affluent parents. For instance, upper-middle-class parents expect their children to attend a highly ranked college so that the offspring can reproduce their own high-paying careers (Nelson 2010). But there is a leap between the pressure to succeed legitimately and the pressure to succeed by any means necessary. Why some infamous white-collar criminals like Bernard Madoff felt pressure to succeed by any means necessary can only be speculated upon based on anecdotal evidence (Arvedlund 2009).

In section I, the type of offending that is the most comparable to adult white-collar criminality is defined as *white-collar delinquency*. This term stems from the writings of its proponents (Hagan and Kay 1990; Friedrichs 2007; Pontell and Rosoff 2009). The term has been drawn upon to refer to general and specific types of fraudulent behaviors, such as the illegal copying of copyrighted materials. It has also been drawn upon to refer to sensational kinds of cybercrime by adolescents. Both the more general and specific uses of the term *white-collar delinquency* have emphasized the affluence of middle-class youths and their capacities to cheat or deceive.

Section II identifies conditions of *adolescence* that might be conducive to white-collar delinquencies. Adolescence is a time of extended dependency and emerging independence. The route toward status during this transitional period of time is quite difficult for a segment of youth, who generally account for the small proportion of high-offending delinquents. They lack the law-conforming social bonds that would minimize their rate of delinquency. Moreover, the self in adolescence is increasingly emphasized in modern-day society. Today, adolescents have considerable opportunity to be on their own in their suburban developments and on their own computers.

Section III explores how the *social class* of an adolescent's parents might influence white-collar delinquency. The middle and upper classes have the luxury of more time and resources to be expended on longer stays in school. There appears to be more of a negotiated order among today's middle- and upper-class parents. Success is measured by performance and is celebrated through honor-student status or acceptance into a good college.

Section IV considers how white-collar delinquency relates to *social status*. Good grades might not be good enough. For a segment of youths, the competitive search for status can be a never-ending pursuit. The pressure to succeed for a segment of adolescents might be so great that an A-minus may not satisfy their self-serving desires. In contrast to boys, girls have been observed to be more relational, more nurturing in their pursuits, and less competitive (Hagan and Kay 1990; Steffensmeier, Schwartz, and Roche 2013).

The essay concludes in section V with stories and survey data on white-collar delinquency. The survey data reveal that gender, age, and social class are significant predictors of white-collar delinquencies. The main conclusions are as follows:

- Acts of copying software and other copyrighted materials, cheating in school, and other acts of fraud by affluent youth are acts of white-collar delinquency.
- Class matters in adolescence as well as adulthood. Aspects of middle- and upper-class lifestyles are identified as emphasizing autonomy, self-efficacy, and self-actualization. An emphasis on the self to the exclusion of others places middle-class adolescents at risk of chronic white-collar offending.
- White-collar acts of delinquency are related to gender, age, and social class.
- When adolescents are identified for their white-collar delinquencies, the penalties are generally not severe.
- Minimizing the adolescent precursors to adult white-collar crime requires recognizing the reasons for white-collar delinquency.
- The complex transitional and formative qualities of adolescence should be examined as they relate to white-collar delinquencies.

I. WHITE-COLLAR DELINQUENCY

Criminological discussion of white-collar acts of delinquency is surprisingly sparse. The term *white-collar delinquency* is not nearly as popular as the term *white-collar crime*. Sutherland (1949) was focused on adult white-collar crime, and for that reason he incorporated an age-dependent definition of white-collar criminals. Of course, adolescents are not in a position of high occupational status. Yet the major theories of crime are also the theories of delinquency. The learning of definitions, values, and norms that are conducive to delinquency are the same as those that are conducive to criminality. For this reason, except for factors that are age graded (e.g., marriage), the predictors of offending in adolescence are usually no different than those of crime in adulthood, as numerous cohort studies continue to illustrate (e.g., Loeber and Farrington 2012).

The term *white-collar delinquency* is both a legal and social construction. It derives from the legal concept of delinquency, which emerged in the early part of the 19th century with the creation of reformatories. The juvenile court at the end of the 19th century completed the process of recognizing that the offenses of the young should be legally distinguished from those of adults. The founders of the juvenile court were less concerned with offense categories. They tended to negate the criminal law's classification of offenses, preferring to focus on the reasons for an adolescent's troubling behaviors. But this early tendency to lump all types of adolescent offending together made little practical sense. Offense categories are indicative of the reasons for adolescent offending, and for considering the most appropriate type of response. Generally, the response to an adolescent's addiction to illicit substances should be different than from occasional acts of petty theft. These offense distinctions are not new; they are part of public knowledge about offenders and have become critical to the delinquency literature. Most recently they have incorporated the notion of white-collar delinquency.

A Google search of *white-collar delinquency* reveals less than a hundred references, including duplicate entries of the articles produced by Hagan and Kay (1990) and Pontell and Rosoff (2009). The 1990 article by Hagan and Kay appears to be the first use of the words *white-collar delinquency*. They use it to refer to offenses that involve the illicit copying of software and other copyrighted materials. Friedrichs's (2007, pp. 203–4) textbook on white-collar crime refers to the Hagan and Kay's article and notes its significance in relating to delinquency. In the context of delinquency, Friedrichs refers to Gottfredson and Hirschi's (1990) general theory of criminality and delinquency, which suggests that the determinants of delinquency are no different than that of white-collar crime.

But there would seem to be little need for a separate category of delinquency if the dimensions of offending by adolescents are invariant across offense categories. Although Gottfredson and Hirschi's (1990) general theory of crime acknowledges offense variation, the perspective tends to see such differences as situational rather than motivational. The reasons for a particular type of offense remain the same; that is, all acts of delinquency and crime are a function of an individual's capacities to control short-term desires and to avoid offending for a quick and easy gain. Neglected in the case of adult as well as adolescent offending is the fact that white-collar criminality can require considerable forethought, planning, and sophistication in the choice of deceptive practices (Geis 2008). The point here is that not everyone can cheat and get away with it. Those who are able to get away with their offenses as adolescents can be expected to try to get away with their offending as adults.

By referring to a segment of delinquents as white-collar delinquents, all adolescent delinquencies are not to be considered equally. Matza (1964) distinguished between the chronic, committed delinquent and the occasional delinquent based on a theory of adolescence and delinquency. He argued that an adolescent subculture of delinquency exists alongside a delinquent subculture, indicating varying degrees of commitment to law-violating behaviors. Hagan (1991) examined the self-reported delinquency of adolescents and was able to identify a segment of affluent youths who were embedded in a subculture of delinquency that he further identified as a party subculture. These affluent youths were largely from the middle and upper class and were socially bonded with one another through their acts of drinking. Their partying did not impede their adult occupational and educational status. In contrast, the adolescents who became embedded in a delinquent subculture were less able to obtain the kind of adult educational and occupational status of their more affluent peers.

The more specialized vision of delinquency is contained in Pontell and Rosoff's (2009) use of the term *white-collar delinquency*. They relate sensational acts of cybercrime leading to costly acts of fraud perpetrated against corporations and individual victims. The capacity to create computer viruses and perform acts of online fraud requires computer skills and forethought as to how best to perpetrate a particular kind of con. The ability to con another requires ingenuity and the capacity to deceive in a way that exhibits a high degree of self-control (Goffman 1990; Friedrichs and Schwartz 2008). White-collar acts of delinquency, like white-collar acts of adult crime, can require technical skills if they are to be committed successfully over a lengthy period of time.

Hagan and Kay's (1990) definition and discussion of white-collar delinquency refers to a wide array of offenses, including offense types that could be considered as bordering on the trivial, such as an act of copying copyrighted materials. Pontell and Rosoff's (2009) definition of white-collar delinquency is more restrictive: they confine their analysis to sensational and egregious acts of crime. But they locate these serious acts of crime within the middle class—a class that has the intelligence, computers, and technical skills to produce considerable amounts of financial loss. White-collar delinquency reflects the class of the youth and the seriousness of the offending. This more restrictive use of the term would deny less sensational offenses that affluent youths commit, such as their acts of cheating in school.

The appropriateness of using an inclusive or exclusive definition of white-collar delinquency depends on the research question to be addressed. The more general use of the term is specific to adolescents. According to state law, the offenses of adolescents are acts of delinquency, not acts of crime. The status of delinquent as opposed to criminal varies by age, usually somewhere between sixteen and eighteen. The term is specific not only to adolescence but also to a range of possible infractions, including status-offense behaviors such as truancy and disobeying a parent. For serious acts of crime, there is the criminal court, particularly for older adolescents. Indeed, the acts that Pontell and Rosoff (2009) refer to as serious acts of white-collar crime are committed by older adolescents who may not be eligible for juvenile justice. In contrast, the more inclusionary use of the term *white-collar delinquency*, as initially conceived by Hagan and Kay (1990), would fit a range of deceitful as well as manipulative behaviors. Moreover, the inclusion of offenses that are more typically committed by middle-class and upper-class youths would fit Sutherland's classic definition, whereby "the white-collar criminal is defined as a person with high socioeconomic status who violates the laws designed to regulate its occupational activities" (Benson and Simpson 2009, p. 5). Sutherland's examples would fit the delinquency category more generally because they are violations of regulatory or civil law rather than criminal law. Similarly, the white-collar delinquent facing juvenile court is technically subject to a civil or administrative court rather than a criminal court.

II. ADOLESCENCE

The term *white-collar delinquency* is grounded in adolescence, as a transitional and formative period of time (Scott and Steinberg 2008). Adolescents are neither dependent children nor independent adults. Their main or only occupation is that of a student. In middle-class households, adolescents are expected to attend college. But upper-middle-class parents are not interested in just any college for their adolescents; they desire a good college that can enable their children to compete for the most desirable occupational pursuits (Nelson 2010).

The transitional period is critical to loosening whatever parental social bonds and social control might have existed in childhood. The teenage years are a critical turning point of tremendous physical, social, and biological change (Steinberg 2002; Coleman 2010). Essentially, many adolescents are lost between their earlier childhood and future adulthood. This is not the case for all adolescents, but it is the case for a significant proportion, who become involved in drugs and other illegal behaviors.

More generally, the adolescent literature refers to a significant amount of risk taking. These are negative risks, such as unprotected sex or experimenting with drugs. The consequences of this sort of risky behavior are often felt early in life. Frequent drug use and risky sexual activity often produce negative consequences, such as poor school performance or unwanted pregnancy. Many adolescents learn by their mistakes. But suppose the risky behavior pays off? Suppose an adolescent who is really good at cheating in school has learned that his ability to con others is enjoyable—a sneaky thrill worth repeating in future endeavors?

Another factor to consider is peer support for delinquency (Warr 2002). Peer-group affiliations act to provide status to adolescents through status-generating groups (Danesi 1994; Milner 2004). They are intended to provide adolescents with the strength in numbers that they lack in their powerless position as adolescents. They revolve not just around one delinquent or non-delinquent group, but through a web of group-identifying affiliations, such as particular styles of dress, music preferences, athletic abilities, or school status. Today there is more of a choice of group affiliations, thanks to the Internet. Along with this choice, peer-group associations should be more individualized.

Contemporary middle-class adolescents have more to choose from among their Facebook friends, Internet sites, and places to hang out. Individual identities as opposed to group identities can facilitate a focus on the self, as in self-esteem, self-actualization, or self-efficacy (Maslow 1970; Taylor 1989; Bandura 1997; Dweck 1999; Jang and Thornberry 1999). Each of these terms has its own meaning and has been advocated by sophisticated theorists of human development. Becoming an adolescent today means recognition of self. According to survey data compiled by Duane Alwin (2004), middle-class parents today are more inclined to encourage their adolescents' sense of self. In earlier generations, parents were more likely to value obedience over autonomy. For good reason parents expect their children to think for themselves as they compete in their educational and occupational pursuits.

So expectations of individual achievement begin early in adolescence. The shift that Alwin identifies emphasizes an individual self. Undoubtedly, it includes inculcating middle-class values of honesty and the need to achieve by the stated rules. In an educational setting such as a high school, this means honesty in doing homework assignments and taking exams. But there can be a gap between how well adolescents can meet their objectives when playing by the stated rules. Adolescents know that their grade-point average and test scores are important; their parents expect them to perform well so they can attend the right colleges and subsequently attain high occupational status.

III. Social Class

The pressure to succeed by any means necessary may be facilitated by the efforts of middle-class and upper-class parents. They believe that their children are too good to fail on their own. As previously mentioned, Margaret Nelson's (2010) study of parenting insightfully shows how upper-middle-class parents are especially protective of their children. She relates how the more affluent and more educated parents will go to greater personal lengths to secure their children's future. She compared parents with graduate degrees with those who had a bachelor's degree or less and found that graduate-degree parents expressed more protective beliefs about their adolescent and young adult children. Graduate-degree parents expressed greater concern about their children growing up too quickly. They tried to extend the period of time their child would remain in school, often insisting that they attend graduate school. The more professionally oriented parents were not only more involved in their children's activities; they were also assisting and guiding them in their competitive educational and occupational pursuits.

Middle- and upper-class adolescents are also in a more desirable position to compete for educational and occupational status. They have more of the resources that would enable them to pursue college and secure good jobs. These resources include not only material assets but also the kind of social capital that is known to increase the likelihood of being in a position of authority. The assumption here is that parental authority and power provide the sense of personal entitlement that enables white-collar delinquency. Others have drawn on the term *social capital* to indicate not only the economics of class but also the cultural capital of class that produces subtle distinctions that can advantage the affluent. For instance, Hagan's (1989) power-control theory suggests that the authority parents derive from their positions of work is reproduced among their adolescents. Critical to Hagan's power-control theory is the interplay between class and gender. More specifically, boys raised by parents in employer or management positions should be the most free to be delinquent.

Indeed, Hagan found support for his thesis in a series of articles beginning in 1985. Hagan et al. showed that delinquency rates peaked for adolescents in the employer class, which would be comparable to those in the middle and upper classes (Hagan, Gillis, and Simpson 1985). There is other support for the delinquency of affluent adolescents and their ability to avoid arrest, prosecution, and labeling as delinquents (Cicourel 1968; Chambliss 1973). Observational and ethnographic studies show that class enables middle- and upper-class youths to avoid punishment. Cicourel (1968) observed the formal and informal proceedings of juvenile court decision making in two communities. Officials in the more affluent suburban community felt more compelled to give adolescents another chance. He observed, moreover, that affluent parents would confront officials more about their adolescent's behavior, and as a consequence they would save their children from being adjudicated as delinquent.

Another example of how affluent youths avoid official delinquent labels is Chambliss's (1973) study of two groups of adolescents: one middle-class group named the Saints and the lower-class group of youths named the Roughnecks. Chambliss made the point that class matters in predicting an arrest. Although the Saints were engaged in just as much offending as the Roughnecks, they could repeatedly avoid arrest, unlike the Roughnecks. The difference Chambliss attributed to the kind of neighborhood in which the Saints lived and to their types of offenses. In contrast to the Saints, whose offenses were deemed less serious, the Roughnecks' offenses were viewed by the police as more serious because they more often involved acts of fighting. The police were more inclined to arrest the Roughnecks to prevent further acts of violence. Chambliss further attributed the ability of the Saints to avoid any official arrest to their ability to convince the police that they were remorseful and good kids. The middle- and upper-class Saints knew the art of impression management.

There are other criminological distinctions to note. Serious and frequent delinquency is a phenomenon of disadvantage. The more chronic delinquents are more troubled adolescents (Moffitt 1993). One major disadvantage is familial and neighbor-hood impoverishment. Sampson (2011) most convincingly stated that neighborhoods and the social capital that endures in advantaged neighborhoods make a difference in controlling crime. The critical elements to social capital are the trust and empathetic identification that neighbors have with one another so they can assist with all sorts of troubles, including reporting on each other's kids when they are misbehaving. Social capital assumes community and a network of neighbors who know one another and are willing to trust others to come to their assistance unselfishly.

But there are signs that there is less community or a sense that "we are in this world together" among middle- and upper-class families. Shover and Hochstetler (2006) sug-gested in their analysis of why adults choose to commit white-collar crime that middle-class youths acquire a manner of thinking and acting that reflects their privileged status. They explained that middle- and upper-class youths can become "ready recruits to white-collar crime [and] the ease with which the products of privilege turn to crime suggests there may be qualities and pathologies in their generative worlds" (Shover and Hochstetler 2006, p. 55). But what is it about these worlds? Shover and Hochstetler speculated about the possible influence of living in larger homes where children have their own room. In other words, the affluent have more time to be on their own; they are less likely to have to negotiate densely populated spaces. In contrast, lower-class youths reside in more densely populated settings, often in inner cities where they must take into account the constant presence of others.

Another dimension to Shover and Hochstetler's analysis is middle- and upper-class competitiveness. Most recently, the competitive stance of affluent parents was noted by Margaret Nelson (2010). As discussed above, parents with graduate degrees not only were highly protective of their children but also instilled a strong competitive orienta-tion, insisting that their children extend their education as long as possible and attend the best possible schools (Nelson 2010). She observed less pressure among the less edu-cated parents in her sample.

Middle- and upper-class parents are also likely to employ the "best" kind of parent-ing style, as advocated in the parenting literature. The importance of self-esteem is repeatedly advocated, and as it has been popularized so too have the more sophisti-cated versions been reduced to an ethos that repeatedly emphasizes a sense of self, as in self-efficacy and self-actualization. The authoritative parenting study is the preferred style—the one most recommended by experts in adolescent development (Baumrind 1991). This kind of parenting style places "a high value on the development of auton-omy and self-direction" (Steinberg 2002, p. 141). Unlike authoritarian parents, who are dogmatic about the rules, "authoritative parents deal with their child in a rational, issue-oriented manner, frequently engaging in discussion and explanation with their children over matters of discipline" (p. 141). Children raised by parents who practice an authoritative style of parenting tend to perform better than those raised by authoritar-ian parents (Steinberg et al. 1992; Hay 2001).

There has been little critical analysis of an authoritative style of parenting. An unin-tended consequence of this type of modern-day parenting is to increase ambiguity about the stated rules (Smelser 1998; Haines and Beaton-Wells 2012), which is located more in middle- and upper-class households. Duane Alwin (2004) found this to be the case and has drawn on the term *parental modernity* to indicate how autonomy trumps obedience. Based on several generations of survey data, he found that parents increasingly value their adolescents' ability to think for themselves. This kind of autonomy of self is emphasized over obedience to a group and is located more among the middle and upper class (Popenoe 1988; Alwin 2005).

So a competitive and autonomous self appears more likely to emerge in middle- and upper-class households. Distinguished early 20th-century sociologists like Simmel (1995) identified this sort of competitive streak in a blasé attitude that would develop among what Veblen (1899) referred to as the leisure class. For instance, Baumgartner (1988) found a preference among white-collar/professional-class suburbanites for what she terms moral minimalism. In contrast to blue-collar/working-class families, she found that the more affluent tended to have "an aversion to confrontation and conflict and a preference for spare, even weak strategies of social control." They tended "to tolerate or do nothing at all about behavior they find disturbing." Moreover, the more affluent suburbanite neighborhood approached disputes in a "conciliatory fashion" (pp. 10–11). Baumgartner further concluded her analysis by stating that the suburban life of the more affluent revolves around a culture of avoidance. A tolerance for deviance among the middle and upper class when it comes to their own youths makes sense, given that most adolescents mature out of their delinquent behaviors. Yet for a segment of adolescents, there is a risk in ignoring their white-collar acts of delinquency. These acts are rationalized based on the notion that they are trivial and of little consequence.

IV. Status-Generating Desires

Not everyone is equally capable of obtaining recognition in a status-oriented society by following the stated rules. Bending the rules in pursuit of status may be more common today than in premodern times (Thomas 1923). In earlier times, a person's status was often dictated by birth; it was ascribed based on familial or tribal affiliations. Modern-day societies are meritocracies. They look to promote and assign status based on achievement scores, money earned, or occupational prestige. Adolescents are not in a position to earn vast amounts of money or to take prestigious jobs. Instead, they only have their achievement scores through their school pursuits and money that they might be able to earn through their allowances and part-time work. Today's teenagers cannot depend on their place of birth alone as an indication of their status; familial connections matter less. Instead, middle-class and upper-class adolescents are expected to perform well in one achievement test after another. Status must be earned and displayed through achieved grades, clothes, fame, and admiration by others.

In a modern-day society, the school is the most important source for legitimating status. Based on their performance on various standardized tests, the school is a place where students are placed in honor tracks and non-honor tracks. One way to confront this need for status is for adolescents to generate their own alternative status-generating groups. Milner (2004) related how status-generating groups provide alternative venues in which adolescents can perceive themselves as *cool*. Earlier, Cohen (1955) highlighted, in his theory of lower-class delinquent boys, the importance of lower-class status frustration with middle-class values as first confronted in school. While Cohen's classic analysis dealt primarily with a single lower-class delinquent culture, Milner's 2004 analysis looked at a variety of adolescent groups across the class culture. Yet Cohen also mentioned middle-class boys who suffer from status frustration by not being able to identify and understand the professional pursuits of their parents. The important point is that adolescents in a modern or postmodern society can draw on more than one culture in pursuit of status.

Although the group context of delinquency is indisputable, the reasons for it are less than clear. Based on research that has distinguished various kinds of delinquent groups, the associations leading to status are different for impoverished and affluent youths. Impoverished inner-city youths tend to associate more in organized gangs; status is derived through their neighborhood turf and ethnic and racial identities. For middle and upper-class youths, who live largely in affluent suburbs, peer-group associations are loose. They are less attached to their suburban subdivisions, particularly since they are all too willing to relocate as their parents have for educational and occupational pursuits.

Over a half-century ago, David Riesman (1950) described the American middle class as increasingly outer directed. They were less likely to be inner directed in their values and beliefs than those of an earlier era. He argued that middle-class Americans were more conscious of what others think of them—for example, by buying the most popular consumer items. This need for status based on what others think did not disappear in the 21st century. Adolescents have their designer jeans, smartphones, and other must-have consumer items. Whether this is more so the case for youth who are raised in affluent versus impoverished circumstances is an empirical question. What certainly remains the same are the transitional aspects of adolescence and the search for status.

V. Stories and Data on White-Collar Delinquency

A. Adolescence and Bernie Madoff

Implicit in the sensational story of this century's largest Ponzi scheme is the untold story of white-collar delinquency. In December 2008, 70-year-old Bernard Madoff pleaded guilty in federal criminal court to operating an investment firm that persuaded hundreds of highly intelligent investors to believe that he could be trusted with millions of their dollars (Lewis 2012). That part of Madoff's story is already well known and confirmed. Madoff had produced fraudulent monthly financial statements over several decades. If not for the financial downturn of 2008, he might have been able to continue his con even longer. His life could have ended without him ever having faced the legal consequences of his acts of fraud.

Less known is Madoff's biography and when his habit of defrauding people actually began. He was raised in a solidly upwardly mobile middle-class family. He was reported to have lied early on in his adulthood, pretending to have graduated from law school when he actually did not. Clearly, he was a master at deception. Few have the innate skill to fool so many successful and well-educated individuals. Madoff mastered the fine art of impression management (Goffman 1990; Lewis 2012).

It is not possible to know when exactly Madoff started to develop his con-artist skills. In her book *Too Good to Be True: The Rise and Fall of Bernie Madoff*, Erin Arvedlund (2009) speculated that Madoff might have started his habit of deceiving others in high school. Arvedlund interviewed several of Madoff's high-school friends and acquaintances. She quoted one of them as stating that he "showed pride of appearance, willingness to deceive, [and] no fear of the eventual consequences when there was a good chance of success." The same high-school friend stated that Madoff faked a book-report presentation. Madoff might have learned to get away with his misdeeds because "nobody could really get mad at Bernie. He had a put-upon Charlie Brown persona that carried him through" (p. 18). But plenty of adolescents cheat, so Madoff could not be considered unique for his ability to fake a book report. Moreover, there is little that is unique about an adolescent who shows pride in his appearance.

Just as revealing is when Madoff, on the day of his sentencing, gave a reason to the judge and those present for his grand act of fraud. He stated that he could never accept the loss of status that would come from having failed to succeed. He stated:

> Although I may not have intended any harm, I did a great deal of harm. I believed when I started this problem, this crime, that it would be something I would be able to work my way out of, but that became impossible. As hard as I tried, the deeper I dug myself into a hole. I made a terrible mistake, but it wasn't the kind of mistake that I had made time and time again, which is a trading mistake. In my business, when you make a trading error, you're expected to make a trading error, it's accepted. My error was much more serious. I made an error of judgment. *I refused to accept the fact, could not accept the fact, that for once in my life I failed. I couldn't admit that failure and that was a tragic mistake.* (*New York Times* 2009, p. B4, emphasis added)

Many white-collar criminals were sheltered from failure. Otherwise, they could not be in their positions of trust, if they had a record of having been caught and punished for their offenses. Madoff was able to escape detection early. It is not possible to know exactly when he could have been sanctioned to the point that it would have prevented his serious acts of crime. The fact that he had defrauded investors for at least several decades suggests that his fraudulent behavior did not just suddenly happen in adulthood.

B. Adolescent Cheating in New Hampshire

Hanover, New Hampshire, is the home of Dartmouth College, and the town where the sons of upper-middle-class parents were caught stealing and cheating on their final exams. Many of them were graduating honor students on their way to prestigious Ivy League schools. On a weekend night, the students broke into their high-school office, copied the answers, and distributed them to a large cadre of students. The end-of-the-semester exams for this group of juniors and seniors might have determined their ultimate acceptance into many of the same prestigious colleges that their parents had attended. The local town prosecutor wanted to prosecute the older adolescents in criminal court for breaking and entering, but their parents objected, thereby creating a major uproar that received national media attention (Schweitzer 2007).

The parents of the charged youths included professors at Dartmouth College, a journalist, and a hospital president. They claimed that a criminal court charge—even if it did not involve incarceration—was too harsh a penalty. In media reports, the parents of the youths argued that a criminal court conviction might prevent their children from attending the school of their choice. They argued that any penalty should be administered by the school, and there should be confidentiality of the youth's conviction. This is an example of where persons of high occupational status can avoid prosecution when committing their white-collar crimes. According to one student quoted in a National Public Radio story, "kids know they won't get in trouble for things like sharing homework or finding out what's on a test from kids who've already taken it . . . Some teachers don't classify that as cheating." One parent commented that "Hanover [High School] is a place where the college you go to is more of a status symbol than the car you drive, and parents put big-time pressure on kids" (Seabrook 2007, transcript).

Hanover is not alone. This past year, the front page of *The New York Times* was filled with stories of adolescents cheating in elite schools. At Harvard, 125 students were caught cheating on a take-home exam. At an elite public high school in New York City (Stuyvesant High), cheating became systematic, involving a network of youths who would photograph the exams using their phones and then text them to their fellow students who were about to take the same test (Kolker 2012). *The New York Times* also reported systematic cheating on college aptitude exams among students in an affluent Long Island, New York, school district (Anderson 2011).

C. Survey Data on White-Collar Delinquency

Estimates of cheating in school are the most thoroughly studied indicators of white-collar delinquency. National estimates of cheating vary considerably. Based on their survey data, Davis, Drinan, and Gallant (2009, p. 45) reported that 85 percent of high-school students cheat. This figure includes exam cheating, plagiarism, and copying homework. The percentage of youths cheating on exams is 62 percent, they report. Even more striking, Singer's (2014) analysis of white-collar delinquency in an afflu-ent suburb of Buffalo, New York, found that 81 percent of youths admitted to having cheated in school or copied copyrighted materials without permission at least once in their lives. However, when the survey questions were limited to within the past year, the incidence of white-collar delinquency decreased to 26 percent. Boys report more white-collar delinquency than do girls. Boys are particularly higher in reporting that they copied copyrighted materials: 43 percent versus 37 percent. The incidence of white-collar delinquency appears to peak between 16 and 17, which would also be the peak period for delinquency in general.

In Singer's (2014) Buffalo suburb study, the vast majority of adolescents who stated they cheated said they did so only a few times. Only 12 percent of adolescents said they cheated five or more times. A further analysis of the frequency of white-collar delin-quency suggests that the students who report higher grades cheated more. This is con-trary to what we would expect if low grades were taken as an indication of the need to cheat. The best predictor of white-collar delinquency is school attachment: adolescents who are most dedicated to the stated goals of the school are the least likely to cheat.

The relationship between the incidence of having ever committed white-collar acts of delinquency and several personal background characteristics is illustrated in the fig-ures. They refer to self-reported mean rates, standardized on a 15-point scale to mini-mize the impact of outliers.

First, age and gender are significant, as indicated in figures 11.1 and 11.2. The effect of gender supports a recent study by Steffensmeier, Schwartz, and Roche (2013), which shows the overrepresentation of males in adult white-collar corporate crime. They hypoth-esized that male rates of white-collar criminality should be higher because males are more "individualistic" in their orientations (p. 451). They further argue that males are more status conscious, and they are more likely to be autonomous in their business pursuits. In Singer's Buffalo suburb study, the peak age of white-collar delinquency generally and of the subcategory of cheating is 16. Notably, at that age, a significant dif-ference exists between male and female rates of white-collar delinquencies, 5.6 points for boys and 3.7 points for girls. For the subcategory of cheating (figure 11.2), the differ-ence at age 16 is equally significant in the expected direction, 3.5 points and 2.2 points.

In Singer's study, the gender difference in white-collar delinquency can be further examined by indicators of social class. An archived measure based on the officially recorded assessed housing value of parents would avoid the response bias that is associ-ated with adolescents exaggerating their social class. When this largely suburban com-munity is divided into quartiles, boys who live in the most expensive housing have the highest level of white-collar delinquency and cheating. Figure 11.3 shows that boys have a rate of 5.0 points in the upper-class dimension, nearly twice the rate for girls in the lowest class. The gender–class difference persists for cheating (figure 11.4). These data support Hagan's assertion that upper-class (employer-class) youth are the most

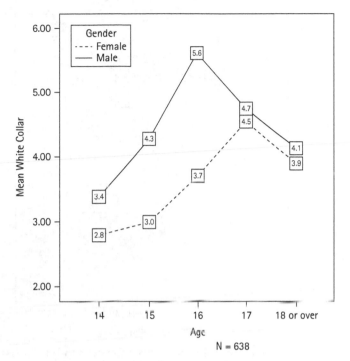

FIGURE 11.1 White-Collar Delinquency by Gender and Age

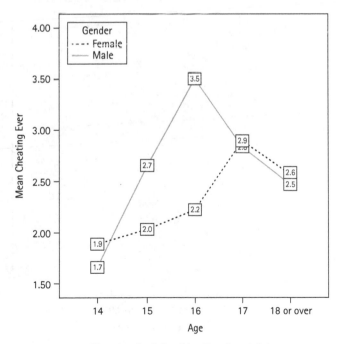

FIGURE 11.2 Cheating in School by Gender and Age

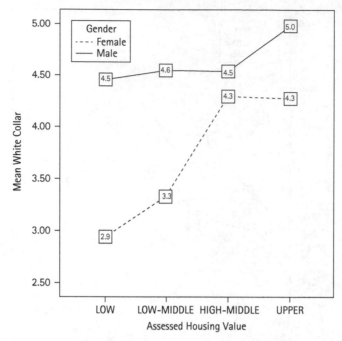

FIGURE 11.3 White-Collar Delinquency by Gender and Social Class

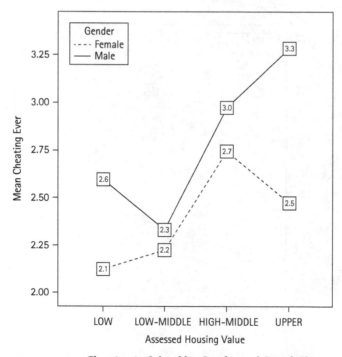

FIGURE 11.4 Cheating in School by Gender and Social Class

delinquent; that is, adolescents in the higher class categories have higher rates of white-collar delinquency, controlling for gender.

Other data from Anderman and Murdock (2007) suggest that social-organizational goals predict white-collar delinquency. They specifically looked at cheating in school. They found that students who were less concerned with their grades are more dedicated to mastering their subjects (the love of learning) and less inclined to cheat. They stated:

> The basic argument is that when students are mastery oriented, they are unlikely to engage in academic cheating behaviors because cheating will not serve a useful purpose. If the goal of an academic task is to truly master the material, and to truly improve one's own learning, then an academic shortcut such as cheating will not lead to the attainment of one's goal. (Anderman and Murdock 2007, p. 93)

Still, an emphasis on mastery must be assessed eventually. The assessment has consequences. A competitive, status-conscious society is not likely to be kind to its adolescents who do not test well. Even if they score well, it might not be good enough for those adolescents who, like Madoff, cannot confront the possibility that they might fail to be the very best.

V. Conclusion

The life-course literature has long recognized that the precursors for adult criminality reside in adolescence. Yet theories of delinquency tend to focus on the crimes of those who are disadvantaged. The main precursor to being an adult is adolescence. It is surprising that more of the characteristics of middle-class and upper-class adolescence are not taken into account in explanations of adult white-collar criminals. Still, the limited literature on white-collar delinquency (Hagan and Kay 1990; Pontell and Rosoff 2009) and the recent scholarship of Shover and Hochstetler (2006) indicate the importance of relating adolescence to adult white-collar criminality. The delinquency of the affluent tends to be ignored because their offenses are not considered serious. The seriousness of adolescent offending is frequently linked to acts of violence. Too often, white-collar delinquencies are considered trivial and of no consequence, since the victims are the school or family members.

Just as the criminological literature has been obsessed with identifying the risk factors related to serious violence (e.g., Farrington et al. 2006), so too should white-collar crime scholars look deeply at the risk factors that produce middle-class and upper-class delinquents. This means moving beyond mere opportunities for white-collar crime; it means considering how social class enables value orientations that lead to high rates of white-collar delinquency.

The story of Bernard Madoff is a sensational one about how past minor acts of offending might relate to serious acts of fraud, but the story is an unofficial one. Before his Ponzi scheme, Madoff had never been arrested for any kind of offense. This is the case for the vast majority of middle- and upper-class adolescents who have committed an act that could have landed them in juvenile court. Affluent youths in affluent communities are less likely to be identified as delinquent and to face official sanctions, as indicated by several studies cited in this chapter. If middle- and upper-class white-collar delinquents had received the status degradation that lower-class youths receive in their routine confrontations with the police, then they might be less inclined to repeat their offending.

The impact of formal and informal reactions by officials, parents, and teachers to white-collar acts of delinquency should be examined in considerably more detail. Teenagers' lives are organized differently today than in earlier times. Middle- and upper-class youths are on their own in many of their daily pursuits. From the privacy of their basement recreational rooms to the cyberspace of their websites, adolescents are increasingly on their own. As a consequence, there is more of an emphasis on the self, as in self-efficacy and self-actualization. How that sense of self needs to be tempered with a sense of others should be examined in more detail than this chapter has been able to identify in terms of adolescent precursors to adult white-collar crime.

Data should be collected on white-collar delinquency as a subcategory of delinquency. Analyses of adolescent cheating are framed largely in terms of educational objectives, with little discussion of criminological theory. The data presented on white-collar delinquency not only are sparse but were collected for the purpose of understanding general acts of delinquency. More needs to be examined in terms of how white-collar delinquency in adolescence and involvement in white-collar crime in adulthood may be connected. Are adult white-collar criminals merely on a continuum of deceitful behaviors that were initially committed in their adolescence?

The biography of white-collar criminals, like Madoff, should be explored for their adolescence. It is too easy to gloss over the commonality of adolescent or young-adult cheating based on the successful careers of the famous (Dionne 1987). Further trivializing the significance of white-collar delinquency is to suggest that everyone at some point in their lives is a delinquent (Gabor 1994). A mix of case study, personal interview, and survey data would ideally find distinctions in the adolescence of white-collar offenders. Just as any analysis of an adult's criminal career would certainly incorporate his or her youthful offending, so too should adolescence be considered first as a general precursor and then a more specific reason for the white-collar crimes of adulthood.

REFERENCES

Alwin, Duane F. 2004. "Parenting Practices." In *The Blackwell Companion to the Sociology of Families*, pp. 142–58, edited by Jacqueline Scott, Judith Treas, and Martin Richards. Hoboken, NJ: Wiley-Blackwell.

Alwin, Duane F. 2005. "Attitudes, Beliefs, and Childbearing." In *The New Population Problem: Why Families in Developed Countries Are Shrinking and What It Means*, pp. 115–26, edited by Alan Booth. Mahwah, NJ: Lawrence Erlbaum Associates.

Anderman, Eric M., and Tamera Burton Murdock. 2007. *Psychology of Academic Cheating*. Amsterdam and Boston: Elsevier Academic Press.

Anderson, Jenny. 2011. "After Arrest, a Wider Inquiry on Sat Cheating." *New York Times* (September 29). Available at http://www.nytimes.com/2011/09/30/nyregion/after-arrest-a-wider-inquiry-on-sat-cheating.html?_r=0

Arvedlund, Erin. 2009. *Too Good to Be True: The Rise and Fall of Bernie Madoff*. New York: Portfolio.

Bandura, Albert. 1997. *Self-Efficacy: The Exercise of Control*. New York: Worth.

Baumgartner, M. P. 1988. *The Moral Order of a Suburb*. New York: Oxford University Press.

Baumrind, Diana. 1991. "The Influence of Parenting Style on Adolescent Competence and Substance Use." *Journal of Early Adolescence* 11: 56–95.

Benson, Michael L., and Sally S. Simpson. 2009. *White-Collar Crime: An Opportunity Perspective*. New York: Routledge.

Chambliss, William J. 1973. "The Roughnecks and the Saints." *Society* (November/December): 24–31.

Cicourel, Aaron. 1968. *The Social Organization of Juvenile Justice*. New York: John Wiley.

Cohen, Albert K. 1955. *Delinquent Boys: The Culture of the Gang*. New York: The Free Press.

Coleman, John C. 2010. *The Nature of Adolescence*. New York: Routledge.

Danesi, Marcel. 1994. *Cool: The Signs and Meanings of Adolescence*, 2nd revised ed. Toronto: University of Toronto Press.

Davis, Stephen F., Patrick F. Drinan, and Tricia Bertram Gallant. 2009. *Cheating in School: What We Know and What We Can Do*. Hoboken, NJ: Wiley-Blackwell.

Dionne, E. J., Jr. 1987. "Biden Admits Plagiarism in School but Says It Was Not 'Malevolent.'" *New York Times* (September 18). Available at http://www.nytimes.com/1987/09/18/us/biden-admits-plagiarism-in-school-but-says-it-was-not-malevolent.html?pagewanted=all&src=pm

Dweck, Carol S. 1999. *Self-Theories: Their Role in Motivation, Personality, and Development*. Philadelphia: Psychology Press.

Farrington, David P. 1994. "The Development of Offending and Antisocial Behavior from Childhood: Key Findings from the Cambridge Study in Delinquent Development." *Journal of Child Psychology and Psychiarty and Allied Disciplines* 36: 929–64.

Farrington, David P., Jeremy W. Coid, Louise M. Harnett, Darrick Jolliffe, Nadine Soteriou, Richard E. Turner, and Donald J. West. 2006. *Criminal Careers Up to Age 50 and Life Success Up to Age 48: New Findings from the Cambridge Study in Delinquent Development*. Home Office Research, Development and Statistics Directorate.

Friedrichs, David O. 2007. *Trusted Criminals: White Collar Crime in Contemporary Society*, 3rd ed. Belmont, CA: Thomson Higher Education.

Friedrichs, David O., and Martin D. Schwartz. 2008. "Low Self-Control and High Organizational Control: The Paradoxes of White-Collar Crime." In *Out of Control: Assessing the General Theory of Crime*, pp. 145–59, edited by Erich Goode. Stanford: Stanford University Press.

Gabor, Thomas. 1994. *"Everybody Does It!" Crime by the Public*. Toronto: University of Toronto Press.

Geis, Gilbert. 2008. "Self-Control: A Hypercritical Assessment." In *Out of Control: Assessing the General Theory of Crime*, pp. 203–16, edited by Erich Goode. Stanford: Stanford University Press.

Geis, Gilbert. 2010. "Sutherland, Edwin H.: White-Collar Crime." In *Encyclopedia of Criminological Theory*, pp. 910–15, edited by Francis T. Cullen and Pamela Wilcox. Thousand Oaks, CA: Sage.

Goffman, Erving. 1990. *The Presentation of Self in Everyday Life*. New York: Doubleday.

Gottfredson, Michael R., and Travis Hirschi. 1990. *A General Theory of Crime*. Stanford: Stanford University Press.

Hagan, John. 1989. *Structural Criminology*. New Brunswick, NJ: Rutgers University Press.

Hagan, John. 1991. "Destiny and Drift: Subcultural Preferences, Status Attainment, and the Risks and Rewards of Youth." *American Sociological Review* 56: 567–86.

Hagan, John, and Fiona Kay. 1990. "Gender and Delinquency in White-Collar Families: A Power–Control Perspective." *Crime and Delinquency* 36: 391–407.

Hagan, John, A. R. Gillis, and John Simpson. 1985 "The Class Structure of Gender and Delinquency: Toward a Power–Control Theory of Common Delinquent Behavior." *American Journal of Sociology* 90: 1151–78.

Haines, Fiona, and Caron Beaton-Wells. 2012. "Ambiguities in Criminalizing Cartels." *British Journal of Criminology* 52: 953–73.

Hay, Carter. 2001. "Parenting, Self-Control, and Delinquency: A Test of Self-Control Theory." *Criminology* 39: 707–36.

Jang, Sung Joon, and Terence Thornberry.1999. "Self-Esteem, Delinquent Peers, and Delinquency: A Test of the Self-Enhancement Thesis." *American Sociological Review* 63: 586–98.

Kolker, Robert. 2012. "Cheating Upwards: Stuyvesant Kids Do It. Harvard Kids Do It. Smart Kids May Especially Do It. But Why?" *New York Magazine* (September 24). Available at http://nymag.com/news/features/cheating-2012-9/

Lewis, Lionel S. 2012. *Con Game: Bernard Madoff and His Victims*. New Brunswick, NJ: Transaction.

Loeber, Rolf, and David P. Farrington. 2012. *From Juvenile Delinquency to Adult Crime: Criminal Careers, Justice Policy, and Prevention*. New York: Oxford University Press.

Maslow, Abraham. 1970. *Motivation and Personality*. New York: Harper and Row.

Matza, David. 1964. *Delinquency and Drift*. New York: John Wiley.

Milner, Murray. 2004. *Freaks, Geeks, and Cool Kids: American Teenagers, Schools, and the Culture of Consumption*. New York: Routledge.

Moffitt, Terrie E. 1993. "Adolescence-Limited and Life-Course-Persistent Antisocial Behavior: A Developmental Taxonomy." *Psychological Review* 100: 674–701.

Nelson, Margaret K. 2010. *Parenting Out of Control: Anxious Parents in Uncertain Times*. New York: New York University Press.

New York Times. 2009. "Bernard L. Madoff's Statement to the Court." (June 29). Available at http://www.nytimes.com/2009/06/30/business/30bernietext.html

Pontell, Henry N., and Stephen M. Rosoff. 2009. "White-Collar Delinquency." *Crime, Law and Social Change* 51: 147–62.

Popenoe, David. 1988. *Disturbing the Nest: Family Change and Decline in Modern Societies*. New York: Aldine de Gruyter.

Riesman, David. 1950. *The Lonely Crowd: A Study of the Changing American Character*. New Haven, CT: Yale University Press.

Sampson, Robert J. 2011. *Great American City: Chicago and the Enduring Neighborhood Effect.* Chicago: University of Chicago Press.

Schweitzer, Sarah. 2007. "School Cheating Scandal Divides N.H. Town: Criminal Charges too Harsh, Some Say." *Boston Globe* (September 19). Available at http://www.boston.com/news/education/higher/articles/2007/09/19/school_cheating_scandal_divides_nh_town/?page=full

Scott, Elizabeth S., and Laurence Steinberg. 2008. *Rethinking Juvenile Justice.* Cambridge, MA: Harvard University Press.

Seabrook, Andrea. 2007. "New Hampshire Split over High School Cheating." National Public Radio, Transcript of Broadcast. Available at http://www.npr.org/templates/transcript/transcript.php?storyId=14811147

Shover, Neal, and Andy Hochstetler. 2006. *Choosing White-Collar Crime.* New York: Cambridge University Press.

Simmel, Georg. 1995. "The Metropolis and Mental Life." In *Metropolis: Center and Symbol of Our Times*, pp. 30–45, edited by Phillip Kasinitz. New York: New York University Press.

Singer, Simon I. 2010. "Thomas, W. I.: The Unadjusted Girl." In *Encyclopedia of Criminological Theory*, pp. 942–48, edited by Francis T. Cullen and Pamela Wilcox. Thousand Oaks, CA: Sage.

Singer, Simon I. 2014. *America's Safest City: Delinquency and Modernity in Suburbia.* New York: New York University Press.

Smelser, Neil J. 1998. "The Rational and the Ambivalent in the Social Sciences: 1997 Presidential Address." *American Sociological Review* 63: 1–16.

Steffensmeier, Darrell J., Jennifer Schwartz, and Michael Roche. 2013. "Gender and Twenty-First-Century Corporate Crime: Female Involvement and the Gender Gap in Enron-Era Corporate Frauds." *American Sociological Review* 78. 448–76.

Steinberg, Laurence D. 2002. *Adolescence.* Boston: McGraw-Hill Higher Education.

Steinberg, Laurence, Susie D. Lamborn, Sanford M. Dornbusch, and Nancy Darling. 1992. "Impact of Parenting Practices on Adolescent Achievement: Authoritative Parenting, School Involvement, and Encouragement to Succeed." *Child Development* 63: 1266–81.

Sutherland, Edwin H. 1949. *White Collar Crime.* New York: Dryden Press.

Taylor, Charles. 1989. *Sources of the Self: The Making of the Modern Identity.* Cambridge, MA: Harvard University Press.

Thomas, William Isaac. 1923. *The Unadjusted Girl: With Cases and Standpoint for Behavior Analysis.* Boston: Harper Torchbooks.

Veblen, Thorstein. 1899. *The Theory of the Leisure Class.* Boston: Houghton Mifflin.

Warr, Mark. 2002. *Companions in Crime: The Social Aspects of Criminal Conduct.* New York: Cambridge University Press.

CHAPTER 12

WHITE-COLLAR CRIMINAL PARTICIPATION AND THE LIFE COURSE

NICOLE LEEPER PIQUERO AND ALEX R. PIQUERO

DESCRIBING the longitudinal course of criminal offending among criminal offenders has been a key feature of criminological work. The focus here has been on providing a portrait of the main relationship between age and crime, to include both aggregate (i.e., at what age is the prevalence of crime the highest) and individual (i.e., what is the modal age of first offense) depictions. Beginning with the 1945 Philadelphia Birth Cohort Study, the seminal criminal careers analysis of 9,945 males followed to age 18 (Wolfgang, Figlio, and Sellin 1972) and its companion study, the 1958 Philadelphia Birth Cohort Study, which traced the offending careers of 27,160 persons through age 26 (Tracy and Kempf-Leonard 1996), a wealth of evidence has accumulated on such patterns of criminal careers, especially at the individual level, from numerous longitudinal data sources around the world. Examples include studies conducted in the United Kingdom (Piquero, Farrington, and Blumstein 2007; Farrington, Piquero, and Jennings 2013), Sweden (Wikström 1990), Dunedin, New Zealand (Moffitt et al. 2001), Christchurch, New Zealand (Fergusson, Horwood, and Nagin 2000), and Montreal (Tremblay et al. 2003). Longitudinal studies have also been undertaken in the United States, including one at the national level (Elliott 1994) and several city-specific investigations from Pittsburgh, Rochester, and Denver (Loeber et al. 1999).

The sum of this work has been the development and subsequent modification of what has come to be known as the criminal career paradigm/framework, which depicts individual offending patterns over the life course in relation to the onset, persistence, and desistance of offending, as well as several aspects of specific offending features such as specialization, seriousness, career length, and co-offending. A key observation about the various empirically based criminal career studies is their largely singular focus on "street" offenders, offenders whose crimes are generally limited to the common violent and property index offenses. Although this is certainly very important for theory and policy matters, it is unfortunate that this focus—which may have something to do with the field's interest in street offending but also may have something to do with available data—has led to a gap in the knowledge about the criminal careers of non-street offenders, including for example sex offenders and the focus of this essay, white-collar offenders.

Accordingly, this essay provides a broad overview of criminal careers and white-collar offenders. Our main conclusions are as follows:

- The criminal career paradigm has much to offer to the study of longitudinal patterns of white-collar offending.
- Researchers are slowly beginning to apply the lessons learned from criminal career research among street offenders to the study of white-collar crimes and criminals.
- Research shows that white-collar offenders, who are older, already educated, often employed, and married, offer a unique challenge to existing developmental/life-course explanations of offending behavior.
- Lessons learned from both sets of researchers (white-collar crime and developmental/life course) can and should continue to build bridges to help more fully describe the patterning of white-collar offending over the life course.
- Directions for future theoretical and empirical research are outlined.

We begin in section I by discussing the criminal career paradigm, including the main elements of the framework as well as a summary of the main findings from the extant empirical literature. After identifying the lack of criminal career research on white-collar offenders, and highlighting its relevance, section II provides a review of what is known about patterns of white-collar criminal careers, which have been generated from two primary databases. From there, section III reviews the main criminologically based theoretical frameworks that have been applied to understanding white-collar criminal careers as well as a few theories that have been specifically developed to understand this understudied offense and offender type. Section IV concludes the essay with some suggestions for future research on white-collar criminal careers.

I. The Criminal Career Paradigm

The criminal career paradigm is concerned with the longitudinal patterning and progression of an individual's criminal career, beginning with the onset of offending, the persistence of offending among those with two or more offenses, and the eventual cessation or desistance from criminal offending (Blumstein et al. 1986). Within these main features are various aspects of a criminal career, including the extent to which offenders concentrate or specialize in specific crime types, the extent to which offenders co-offend with other offenders, and the extent to which offenders increase in the severity or seriousness of their offending as they progress throughout their careers. As can be seen, this framework offers some potentially useful insights into the various aspects of criminal offending, permitting interesting theoretical and empirical investigations of the reasons for why people offend, why some may continue and why some may stop, as well as why some may concentrate in specific crime types or domains of crime.

At least four reviews of the vast criminal career literature are available (Blumstein et al. 1986; Farrington 2003; Piquero, Farrington, and Blumstein 2003; Soothill, Fitzpatrick, and Francis 2009), so a detailed review of the various findings is beyond the scope of this chapter. Nevertheless, it is worth highlighting some key findings. For example, the age of first offense (i.e., onset) is typically in early adolescence (though it emerges earlier in self-reported data as compared to official records), participation in offending tends to peak in late adolescence (with participation in violence in early adulthood), there is very little specialization in offending, and desistance is common by the late twenties or early thirties. It is also important to note that this line of research helped to spur the development of advanced methodological techniques that were designed to identify unique patterns of offending, referred to as trajectories, that follow different shapes and patterns over age (Nagin and Land 1993). The results from that line of research show that the commonly depicted aggregate age–crime curve, with its rise in adolescence, peak in late adolescence, and precipitous decline in early adulthood, is not characteristic of all criminal offenders. In fact, although some offenders do in fact follow this aggregate curve, others begin early and offend at continuously high rates into adulthood, others follow a low-level chronic trajectory of moderate involvement over a sustained period, while a smaller group of persons begin offending in late adolescence and continue thereafter (see Piquero 2008; Jennings and Reingle 2012).

One of the gaps in the extant criminal careers research has been its concerted focus on the more common street offenses and offenders. This may not be too surprising, for most criminological theories are focused on this type of crime and offender, but also because most self-report and official sources of criminal records contain mainly violent, property, drug, and status offenses. Noticeably absent from most longitudinal criminal career studies has been the attention paid to specific types of offenders and offense types, such as sex offenders (Piquero et al. 2008; Zimring, Jennings, and Piquero 2008; Piquero et al. 2012) and, in particular, white-collar offenders (Benson and Moore 1992; Weisburd and Waring 2001; Piquero and Weisburd 2009). However, there is considerable value in understanding the criminal careers of white-collar offenders, primarily because the relationship between age and crime among such offenders and of such crime types may not resemble that of street offenses, largely because the opportunity to commit white-collar crimes may not emerge until well after adolescence and certainly into adulthood. Next, we review empirical research regarding the criminal careers of white-collar offenders, with a focus on what is known about individual-level patterns of offending.[1]

II. What Do We Know About Patterns of White-Collar Criminal Careers?

The first observation to be made about the criminal careers of white-collar offenders is that there is very little empirical research available, due in large part to the lack of longitudinal data on these types of offenders. For the most part, what is known about white-collar criminal careers comes from three main data sources, which are described below along with their main findings.

The first data source—referred to as the Yale study—was conducted between 1976 and 1978 in U.S. federal courts and was collected under the guidance of Stanton Wheeler (Wheeler, Weisburd, Waring, and Bode 1988). This study was based on a sample of 1,342 offenders convicted of eight white-collar–oriented offenses (bank embezzlement, tax fraud, credit card fraud, mail fraud, securities fraud, false claims, bribery, and antitrust offenses). Importantly, the researchers also collected data from a sample of persons convicted of non–white-collar offenses (postal fraud and postal forgery) for use as a comparison group. The white-collar offenders were primarily male and white, and on average were about ten years older than the non–white-collar offenders. This data source has been analyzed extensively to study criminal career issues and in particular the dimensions of criminal careers.

For example, Weisburd et al. (1990, 1991) reported that the age of onset among white-collar offenders in the Yale study was thirty-five. Although it must be remembered that this information is based on a sample of convicted offenders, it was still much later than for the comparison group of offenders. In a subsequent investigation, these authors also reported that 34 percent of the white-collar offenders with prior arrests also had at least one other arrest for a white-collar crime. Weisburd and Waring (2001) obtained ten years of follow-up data from the original sample to further investigate the sample's criminal careers after the date of the offenders' original criterion offense. Aside from the minor evidence in favor of specialization (limited mainly to those whose criterion offense was securities fraud), a number of key findings emerged from their study. First, they observed that almost half of the sample was at some point arrested for at least one offense other than the criterion white-collar crime, and that 31 percent of the sample was arrested at least once after the criterion offense (with the greatest proportion found among credit fraud and mail fraud offenses). An important related finding was that for almost half of the sample, the criterion white-collar crime was the only event reported on their criminal rap sheet (Weisburd and Waring 2001, p. 49). The second key finding concerned the age at desistance. Although it is difficult to study the desistance issue while persons are still alive (and potentially still actively offending), Weisburd and Waring (2001, pp. 37–38) reported that some white-collar offenders were still offending into their forties, fifties, and beyond. In fact, among those repeat offenders who reached age fifty, 47.4 percent had an arrest after that age. Third, with respect to career length, a not-so-commonly studied criminal career dimension, the average duration of a criminal career, comparing the first and last arrest recorded on the rap sheets, was about fourteen years—almost double the average career length among street offenders (see Piquero et al. 2003). Fourth, when Weisburd and Waring (2001) examined patterns of recidivism, their findings showed that for almost half of the sample who were arrested in the follow-up period, "three years or more passed before they had another arrest event reported on their rap sheets" (p. 95), a finding that contradicts the research among common street offenders, which tends to find very high recidivism patterns at the first couple of years. Related to the issue of recidivism, Weisburd and Waring (2001, pp. 134–5) also examined the effect of prison sentences on subsequent offending but failed to find evidence of a deterrent effect or even an aggravating effect of sanctions. What they did find with respect to the correlates of recidivism mimicked what has been found among street offenders; that is, persons who were unmarried, have a history of drug use, have a lengthier prior criminal record, and are male are more likely to be re-arrested. Weisburd and Waring (2001) concluded their work by interpreting the criminal careers of their white-collar sample not through the lens of individual characteristics but instead by considering the situations in which their crimes occur. We expand upon their theoretical distinctions regarding the white-collar offenders in a later section.

More recently, Piquero and Weisburd (2009) used the ten-year follow-up data and performed a group-based trajectory analysis on the criminal histories of the convicted offenders to assess the extent to which the offenders' careers were marked by distinct offending patterns. The authors identified three offender trajectories (low-rate, intermittent, and persistent offenders), each of whom followed distinct crime trajectories. The low-rate group of offenders made up about 71 percent of the total sample, and their offending was characterized by low episodic involvement in crime. A second group of offenders followed a medium rate of offending, more sustained over time than a high-level offending. That is, persons in the medium-rate trajectory offended at a slightly higher rate than the low-rate group, but their offending was more stable than unstable over time. Of the overall sample, medium-rate offenders accounted for about 25 percent of the sample. The final group of offenders was termed "high-rate" offenders. The offending pattern of this group was fairly high and stable over the ten-year follow-up period. On the one hand, the volume and stability of "high-rate" offenders are not common among general criminal career studies—especially those that track offenders into middle adulthood; on the other hand, this "high-rate" group made up about 5 percent of the overall sample, roughly the same percentage that criminal career researchers (Wolfgang et al. 1972) and developmentalists (Moffitt 1993) argue are responsible for the higher overall volume of crime. Piquero and Weisburd's (2009) findings underscore the importance of recognizing the variability of offending among white-collar offenders and confirm observations made by Weisburd et al. (1991) that persons in the white-collar crime category are more diverse than similar.

In sum, the pattern of findings from the Yale study suggests that while there are some similarities between the white-collar and the comparison group of non–white-collar offenders, white-collar offenders do not necessarily follow the typical criminal career patterns detected among common offenders with respect to onset age, prior criminal record, and age of desistance.

The second data source, compiled by Brian Forst and William Rhodes, included over 5,000 persons convicted in U.S. federal courts between 1973 and 1978 for six white-collar crimes (n = 2,643 persons: bank embezzlement, bribery, false claims and statements, income-tax violations, mail fraud, postal embezzlement) and for four common crimes (n = 2,512 persons: bank robbery, homicide, narcotics offenses, postal forgery). As was the case in the Wheeler data source, the white-collar offenders in the Forst and Rhodes data were primarily male, white, and older than the common offenders. These data have been used to assess several important criminal career issues (see Benson and Kerley 2000).

With respect to basic criminal career dimensions, the white-collar offenders in the Forst and Rhodes data have much in common with those in the Yale Study. For example, the average age of onset for the white-collar offenders in the Forst and Rhodes data was forty-one, compared to thirty for common offenders. The Forst and Rhodes data have also been analyzed with respect to the specialization dimension. Benson and Moore (1992) provided one of the few empirical investigations of the extent to which there is specialization between white-collar and non–white-collar offenders and reported evidence that white-collar offenders were more specialized in their offending than non–white-collar offenders. For example, among the white-collar convictees, 28 percent of the repeat offenders had at least one prior arrest for a white-collar crime (Benson 2013, pp. 206–7). In a subsequent analysis, Benson (2013, pp. 206–7) defined white collar specialists as those who have prior arrests in addition to the criterion offense, with at least half of their total number of arrests being for white-collar offenses, and identified a relatively small degree of specialization, with white-collar specialists representing 7 percent of the sample (with one-time offenders [61 percent] and generalists [32.3 percent] making up the remainder of the sample).[2]

The final data source comes from a twenty-year retrospective analysis of the criminal careers of a cohort of 17,053 adult (age eighteen or older) offenders from California whose first adult arrest occurred in 1973, with subsequent offenses updated through the end of 1992 (Lewis 2002). Specific felony and misdemeanor white-collar (embezzlement, bribery, fraud, forgery, tax law violations) and street (violent, property, drugs, other) offenses were used for the 1973 criterion offense (p. 97). Lewis then compared the criminal careers of white-collar offenders to street crime offenders (as well as to mixed-offense-type offenders)[3] to examine central criminal careers issues such as chronicity and specialization. Among the many findings from his investigation, the following are most relevant.

First, of the original 17,053 offenders, 1,424 were initially arrested for a white-collar offense in 1973 and were only arrested for white-collar offenses during the twenty-year follow-up. This white-collar-only group contrasts with a street-crime-only group comprising 10,150 offenders, whose first offense in 1973 was for a street crime and whose subsequent arrests were also only for street crimes. Lewis identified two additional groups: (1) those arrested in 1973 for a white-collar offense but who were subsequently arrested for one or more street crimes ($n = 1,272$) and (2) those arrested in 1973 for a street crime but who were subsequently arrested for one or more white-collar offenses ($n = 4,207$). Second, among the white-collar-only group (8.3 percent of the sample), and unlike the Yale Study and the Forst and Rhodes data, the majority were female, while among the street-crime-only group the majority were male. Moreover, the white-collar-only offenders were primarily white, and with respect to age, the white-collar-only group was older, on average, than any of the other group comparisons.

Third, with respect to criminal history characteristics, Lewis reported that while some white-collar offenders were chronically recidivistic, the majority were generally one-time-only offenders, and their crimes were mainly limited to fraud and forgery (as embezzlement, bribery, and tax law violations were extremely rare among this white-collar-only group). On the other hand, street-crime-only offenders had a higher overall average and volume of crimes compared to the white-collar-only group. But perhaps most interesting, the two mixed-offense groups were very chronic with respect to their offending, averaging between five and ten arrests over the twenty-year period. Thus, diversity and chronicity closely paralleled each other in the mixed-offense groups, a finding consistent with some of the more common criminal careers research (see Piquero et al. 2003).

In sum, although there are virtually no longitudinal data sources that track the criminal careers of white-collar offenders—especially data sources collected since the original studies of the 1970s—the research shows that most white-collar offenders (at least as measured and defined in these data sources) are typically male, white, and about ten years older than non–white-collar offenders, and are from the middle class of society (i.e., average citizens with moderate incomes); are experienced with previous arrests and convictions (though not at the same rate as non–white-collar offenders); and have prior experience with both white-collar and non–white-collar types of crimes. We return to these data-related issues in the concluding section of the chapter.

III. Theoretical Applications

Research emerging from work conducted within the criminal career framework gave rise to new theoretical approaches, primarily those concerned with the development of offending over the life course. Also referred to as Developmental/Life-Course Criminology (DLC) (Farrington 2003), theories within this perspective attempt to explain not only the aggregate age–crime curve, but also the variation that exists within this curve (e.g., Why do some offenders start early and persist longer? What sorts of life events may alter age-crime curves?) As can be seen, then, DLC and the study of crime over the life course more generally may offer a unique theoretical lens with which to view white-collar criminal careers—primarily because such careers do not appear to follow the common age–crime curve, nor do they evince similar offending trajectories—for example, exhibiting a much later age at onset of offending. In this section, we discuss the life-course perspective and the extent to which it (or parts of it) may help understand or explain variation in white-collar criminal careers.

The life course has been defined by Elder (1985, p. 17) as "pathways through the age differentiated life span," and according to Sampson and Laub (1993, p. 8), two central concepts tend to underlie the analysis of life-course dynamics: trajectory and transitions. Trajectories refer to a pathway of development in a particular domain, including employment, crime, and so forth, while transitions refer to specific life events that are embedded within a trajectory, such as first job versus second job, or first crime versus fourth crime. In this regard, "life-course analyses are often characterized by a focus on the duration, timing, and ordering of major life events and their consequences for later social development" (Sampson and Laub 1993, p. 8).

In their early 1990s, Sampson and Laub, working in the field of criminology, and Moffitt, working in the field of psychology, sought to use the life-course framework as a backdrop from which to study antisocial and criminal behavior. Sampson and Laub focused on pathways and turning points throughout the life course, arguing for the importance of studying processes of continuity and change over the life course as well as how life events altered (upward or downward) offending patterns. Moffitt's developmental taxonomy hypothesized the existence of two distinct groups of offenders who offended at different rates and for different reasons, and whose longitudinal offense patterning was unique. These theoretical developments spurred an immense amount of empirical research that helped bring forth additional theoretical frameworks that incorporated the life-course framework. These theories became unified, more or less, under the rubric of DLC.

At the core, DLC allows for the possibility that different risk and protective factors relate to different effects on distinct groups of offenders in different ways over the life course. In this regard, the predictors of the onset, persistence, and desistance of offending may vary among, for example, low-rate versus high-rate offenders, and at different periods of the life course, such as childhood, adolescence, and adulthood. According to Farrington (2003), research investigating various developmental/life-course frameworks has generated several widely accepted conclusions, some of which include (1) the prevalence of offending peaks between the middle to late teenage years; (2) the onset of offending peaks between ages eight and fourteen, while desistance peaks between twenty and twenty-nine; (3) an early onset of offending predicts a longer career duration and a greater frequency of offending; (4) a small proportion of the population commits a greatly disproportionate amount of crime; (5) most offender careers are marked by versatility—not specialization—in offending; (6) during the teenage years, most crimes are committed with others, while during the adult years most crimes are committed alone; (7) there is a stepping stone from less to more serious among those offenders who offend regularly and progress into a criminal career; and (8) active criminal involvement is typically part of a larger syndrome of antisocial behavior that includes substance abuse, limited education success, and failed employment opportunities.

Although these conclusions are important and based on an extensive amount of empirical research using a variety of longitudinal studies conducted around the world, a limiting feature is that these studies rely almost exclusively on samples of common/ street offenders and thus do not consider white-collar crime or white-collar offenders in any great detail—largely because of the lack of longitudinal data on such offenders. Nevertheless, some exceptions exist, reported upon earlier in this chapter, and they have started to come together to form the application of DLC to white-collar crime and white-collar offenders.

Weisburd and Waring (2001) observed important variation in the frequency of offending among their white-collar sample, as well as some key differences in the factors that were able to distinguish across them. While also observing patterns of offending that resembled those in the non–white-collar crime research more generally, Weisburd and Waring developed a typology that characterized the offending of the white-collar offenders in the Yale Study. The first group of individuals included low-frequency offenders who had one or two arrests. For the most part, these offenders were conventional persons, with some very limited criminal experience. Two variants within the "crime as aberration" group did stand out, with one set of offenders appearing as "crisis responders" and a second set appearing as "opportunity takers." The first group, which largely conforms to normative expectations and exhibits prosocial behavior, offends in response to a specific situation that threatens them, their families, or their companies (Weisburd and Waring 2001, p. 146). These offenders feel they have no choice but to offend. Also believed to be generally conforming, the second group offends because they encounter a specific opportunity. Thus, for the first two white-collar offender typologies, "the crimes they commit appear as aberrations on otherwise law-abiding records" (p. 147). Another group, characterized by intermittent offending patterns, was referred to by Weisburd and Waring as "opportunity seekers." Offenders following this pathway were low-frequency chronic offenders whose lives were characterized by achievement and social stability. Yet, their pattern of offending appears to be characterized by an active "seeking out" of criminal opportunities, one that stretches from the earliest point in their lives (p. 90). Much like the chronic offenders of the more common criminal careers research, the third typology was persistent in their offending. Termed "stereotypical criminals," persons in this trajectory had extensive prior criminal histories and lives characterized by difficult circumstances with employment, relationships, and substance abuse. Thus, Weisburd and Waring (2001) are amenable to the notion that white-collar offenders do not follow the same age–crime relationship, that there are important variations in the shape and level of their respective trajectories' offending styles, and that different factors may be able to distinguish membership across the three groups. In short, Weisburd and Waring's theoretical outline of three distinct white-collar offender trajectories is in line with recent developmental/life course-related theoretical work.

Piquero and Benson (2004) reviewed the theoretical development of life-course criminology and noted that this area of research has fallen prey to the same mistake pointed out by Sutherland, which is acting as though common street crime is the only crime type that exists. They (2004, p. 149) argued that failing to recognize the uniqueness of white-collar criminals and crimes will "inevitably lead to a biased and incomplete understanding of trajectories in crime." In trying to fill the theoretical gap in understanding criminal trajectories, the researchers suggest another pattern of offending, which they call "punctuated situationally dependent offending" (Piquero and Benson 2004, p. 158), which assumes white-collar offenders follow the same trajectories as described by Moffitt's (1993) adolescence-limited offender. That is, they engage in crime and delinquency during their adolescent years but age out of such behaviors in young adulthood. However, after a brief period of conformity this group of offenders begins to offend again—only this time because of their position in the workplace (i.e., their deviance manifests in the form of white-collar crime). They note this is a distinct period of offending because these offenses differ from the previous indiscretions of youth, and it is situational because it is triggered by factors external to the offender. The situational dependence can come about in one of two ways: (1) the opportunity to offend does not present itself until the individual has secured a certain occupational position, or (2) it is motivated by a crisis that demands immediate attention (Piquero and Benson 2004, p. 158).

Benson (2013, pp. 211–4) recently considered how the life-course perspective may be applied to understand the offending of the (largely middle-class) white-collar offender and in doing so outlined some of the key findings from the burgeoning scholarship on longitudinal research on white-collar crime. First, he noted that white-collar offenders did not seem to follow conventional trajectories of crime anticipated and empirically identified by life-course theory. For example, Moffitt's focus on antisocial behavior anticipates two distinct groups of offenders, adolescence-limited and life-course-persistent, both of which evince unique age–crime curves and both of whom offend for different reasons. Importantly, neither group is anticipated to have any involvement in white-collar offending. Absent from Moffitt's taxonomy (as well as most other developmental/life-course theories) is a recognition of the importance of occupational position. For many white-collar offenses to occur, persons must find themselves occupied in a suitable position that provides the opportunity to engage in certain crimes—situations that more common offenders typically do not find themselves in. Importantly, white-collar offenders do not find positions that afford such offending opportunities until early to middle adulthood—thereby painting a contradictory picture of the age–crime curve that is characteristic of more common street offenses.

A second observation made by Benson (2013) is that, for the most part, white-collar offending does not appear to be a function of antisocial personality—at least not as currently observed in the literature. On the other hand, different individual differences or personality characteristics appear to be uniquely related to white-collar styles of offending, such as the desire for control (Piquero, Exum, and Simpson 2005) and other situationally based factors (Piquero and Benson 2004) such as the fear of falling, or the prospect of losing status and prestige (Piquero 2012), that relate to white-collar offending. It remains to be seen how well these factors may predict white-collar criminal careers.

Third, when studying patterns and correlates associated with the distinction between persistence and desistance from crime, DLC tends to focus on traditional forms of informal social control, including primarily marriage, education, and employment, which may represent important turning points away from crime. Sampson and Laub's (1993; Laub and Sampson 2003) age-graded informal social control pays particular attention to marriage—especially good marriages—in the movement away from crime among their sample of offenders followed into late adulthood. Thus, for previous offenders, getting married and investing in a marriage offers one pathway out of a life of crime. Yet, many white-collar offenders are already married; as such, that particular turning point would not operate as something that may help them move away from crime. Instead, there may be other turning points that trigger desistance, and perhaps more importantly there may be context-specific turning points that lead to offending (i.e., some sort of situational stressor in the family or workplace).

Thus, it appears from Benson's (2013) perspective that white-collar offenders do not necessarily follow the prototypical pattern of offending found within developmental/life-course theory and research. However, the life-course perspective might still be a useful perspective from which to theorize and empirically study the motives of white-collar offenders and the patterning of white-collar offenses. For example, several themes emerging from DLC may be especially relevant for white-collar offending and white-collar offenders. These themes include things such as continuity and change as well as the influence of adult stressors, but the point is that these are materially different aspects for white-collar as opposed to common street crimes. Consider, for example, the notions of continuity and discontinuity. A significant amount of developmental/life-course theory and research is focused on the continuity of antisocial behavior over the life course. Yet, although with an exception to the "high-rate" chronic offenders observed in the Yale Study (Weisburd and Waring 2001; Piquero and Weisburd 2009), many white-collar offenders do not exhibit a continuity of antisocial and criminal behavior over the life course. Thus, for these persons discontinuity (changing from a state of non-offending to a state of offending) occupies a central place. Also, for these persons offending does not generally seem to resemble some sort of antisocial personality but instead a different set of personality characteristics coupled with situational circumstances that create the impetus to offend.

In short, although there is some evidence to suggest that many white-collar offenders appear to be more middle than upper class (at least as judged from conviction records), they do not appear to easily fit into Sutherland's (1949) view of the powerful, elite offender nor do they necessarily fit into Moffitt's (1993) dual trajectory classification of adolescence-limited and life-course-persistent offender. As Benson (2013, p. 211) recognizes, white-collar offenders exhibit differences in some of the basic criminal career dimensions (i.e., later onset age, later age at desistance, more specialization than common offenders) as well as some differences with respect to the portrait of demographic differences (i.e., mainly male, white, educated, employed) compared to non–white-collar/common offenders. All of this is to suggest that criminological theories must seriously consider the nuanced differences between white-collar and non–white-collar offenders and consider focusing efforts on identifying the different triggers or risk factors that increase the likelihood of offending—such as occupational opportunity, adult stressors, company culture, and business-related pressures—that are unique to white-collar offenders.

IV. Future Research Directions

This chapter set out to review what has been learned about the criminal careers of white-collar offenders and white-collar offending over the life course. Key findings from the empirical research suggest that the longitudinal patterning of white-collar offending shares some of the same features that characterize street offending, but there are also some important differences. In particular, white-collar offenders tend to begin their offending later in the life course and tend to offend for somewhat different reasons than do street offenders. And while much of the empirical research has relied on a limited number of studies, some of that work can be considered within the emerging paradigm of DLC. In the remainder of the chapter, we chart out several directions for subsequent theoretical and empirical research on the criminal careers of white-collar offenders and white-collar offending.

First, there is a pressing need for longitudinal data on white-collar offenders. The main data sources that have provided the empirical research discussed earlier in the chapter were collected in the 1970s, were of convicted offenders, included a very narrow range of white-collar crime types, and contained very little by the way of predictors. What is needed are longer-term follow-ups, with an extensive set of offense types considered, as well as consideration of criminological variables believed to be related to white-collar offending. We also need to consider the context of white-collar offending in much greater detail to see if this has any effect above and beyond individual-level predictors (see Simpson, Paternoster, and Piquero 1998).

Second, it would be especially useful to consider the collection of qualitative data, especially since key insights about street offenders have emerged from adoption of this methodology (see Shover 1996; Laub and Sampson 2003). In particular, data collected in this fashion not only may provide unique insight that may not be detectable in large-scale data collections but also may help to identify themes, processes, and variables that should be considered in subsequent research.

Third, theorists need to think carefully about the nature of white-collar crime and how those criminal careers may be different from the criminal careers of corporations more generally. Although the focus of this essay was on white-collar offenders, it is still important to recognize that corporations have criminal careers and trajectories as well.

Finally, the developmental/life-course framework offers a useful way to think about the risk and protective factors associated with offending generally and can be easily applied to white-collar crimes and white-collar offenders. Of course, there may be differences with respect to the types of variables, types of offenders, and types of circumstances that may be specific to the white-collar crime context that varies from the traditional street context, but this kind of analysis should not be difficult to undertake.

In closing, much has been learned regarding the criminal careers and life-course trajectories of common street offenders, and researchers are slowly beginning to apply these lessons to the study of white-collar crimes and criminals. What is also true is that much has been learned that distinguishes white-collar criminals from their street counterparts. As such, white-collar offenders—who are older, already educated, often employed, and married—offer a unique challenge to existing developmental/life-course explanations of offending behavior. Lessons learned from both sets of researchers, white-collar crime and developmental/life course, can and should continue to build bridges to help more fully describe the patterning of white-collar offending over the life course.

NOTES

1. The criminal careers of organizational offenders are also an important question, but theory and especially empirical research are very rare (see Simpson and Koper 1992).
2. To be sure, there are multiple ways of measuring specialization and multiple methods of empirically investigating the extent to which offenders specialize in their offending, and alternative approaches may yield different conclusions regarding white-collar specialization.
3. Mixed-type offenders correspond to the sizable number of persons in the data who were arrested for both white-collar and street offenses.

REFERENCES

Benson, Michael L. 2013. *Crime and the Life Course: An Introduction.* 2nd ed. New York: Routledge.

Benson, Michael L., and Kent R. Kerley. 2000. "Life Course Theory and White-Collar Crime." In *Contemporary Issues in Crime and Criminal Justice: Essays in Honor of Gilbert Geis*, edited by Henry N. Pontell and David Shichor. Upper Saddle River, NJ: Prentice Hall.

Benson, Michael L., and Elizabeth Moore. 1992. "Are White-Collar and Common Offenders the Same: An Empirical and Theoretical Critique of a Recently Proposed General Theory of Crime." *Journal of Research in Crime and Delinquency* 29: 251–72.

Blumstein, Alfred, Jacqueline Cohen, Jeffrey A. Roth, and Christy A. Visher, eds. 1986. *Criminal Careers and Career Criminals.* Washington, D.C.: National Academy Press.

Elder, Glenn H., Jr. 1985. "Perspectives on the Life Course." In *Life Course Dynamics: Trajectories and Transitions, 1968–1980*, edited by Glenn H. Elder, Jr. Ithaca, NY: Cornell University Press.

Elliott, Delbert S. 1994. "1993 Presidential Address—Serious Violent Offenders: Onset, Developmental Course, and Termination." *Criminology* 32: 1–22.

Farrington, David P. 2003. "Developmental and Life-Course Criminology: Key Theoretical and Empirical Issues—The 2002 Sutherland Award Address." *Criminology* 41: 221–55.

Farrington, David P., Alex R. Piquero, and Wesley G. Jennings. 2013. *Offending from Childhood to Late Middle Age: Recent Results from the Cambridge Study in Delinquent Development.* New York: Springer.

Fergusson, David M., L. John Horwood, and Daniel S. Nagin. 2000. "Offending Trajectories in a New Zealand Birth Cohort." *Criminology* 38: 525–52.

Jennings, Wesley G., and Jennifer M. Reingle. 2012. "On the Number and Shape of Developmental/Life-Course Violence, Aggression, and Delinquency Trajectories: A State-of-the-Art Review." *Journal of Criminal Justice* 40: 472–89.

Laub, John H., and Robert J. Sampson. 2003. *Shared Beginnings, Divergent Lives: Delinquent Boys to Age 70*. Cambridge, MA: Harvard University Press.

Lewis, Roy V. 2002. *White Collar Crime and Offenders: A 20-Year Longitudinal Cohort Study*. San Jose, CA: Writers Club Press.

Loeber, Rolf, Evelyn Wei, Magda Stouthamer-Loeber, David Huizinga, and Terence P. Thornberry. 1999. "Behavioral Antecedents to Serious and Violent Juvenile Offending: Joint Analyses from the Denver Youth Survey, Pittsburgh Youth Study, and the Rochester Youth Development Study." *Studies in Crime and Crime Prevention* 8: 245–63.

Moffitt, Terrie E. 1993. "Adolescence-Limited and Life-Course-Persistent Antisocial Behavior: A Developmental Taxonomy." *Psychological Review* 100: 674–701.

Moffitt, Terrie E., Avshalom Caspi, Michael Rutter, and Phil A. Silva. 2001. *Sex Differences in Antisocial Behaviour: Conduct Disorder, Delinquency, and Violence in the Dunedin Longitudinal Study*. Cambridge, UK: Cambridge University Press.

Nagin, Daniel S., and Kenneth C. Land. 1993. "Age, Criminal Careers, and Population Heterogeneity: Specification and Estimation of a Nonparametric, Mixed Poisson Model." *Criminology* 31: 327–62.

Piquero, Alex R. 2008. "Taking Stock of Developmental Trajectories of Criminal Activity over the Life Course." In *The Long View of Crime: A Synthesis of Longitudinal Research*, edited by Akiva M. Liberman. New York: Springer.

Piquero, Alex R., David P. Farrington, and Alfred Blumstein. 2003. "The Criminal Career Paradigm: Background and Recent Developments." In *Crime and Justice: A Review of Research*, Vol. 30, edited by Michael Tonry. Chicago: University of Chicago Press.

Piquero, Alex R., David P. Farrington, and Alfred Blumstein. 2007. *Key Issues in Criminal Career Research: New Analyses of the Cambridge Study in Delinquent Development*. Cambridge, UK: Cambridge University Press.

Piquero, Alex R., David P. Farrington, Wesley G. Jennings, Brie Diamond, and Jessica Craig. 2012. "Sex Offenders and Sex Offending in the Cambridge Study in Delinquent Development: Prevalence, Frequency, Specialization, Recidivism, and (Dis)Continuity over the Life-Course." *Journal of Crime and Justice* 35: 412–26.

Piquero, Alex R., Nicole Leeper Piquero, Karen J. Terry, Tasha Youstin, and Matt Nobles. 2008. "Uncollaring the Criminal: Understanding Criminal Careers of Criminal Clerics." *Criminal Justice and Behavior* 35: 583–99.

Piquero, Nicole Leeper. 2012. "The Only Thing We Have to Fear Is Fear Itself? Investigating the Relationship between Fear of Falling and White-Collar Crime." *Crime and Delinquency* 58: 362–79.

Piquero, Nicole Leeper, and Michael L. Benson. 2004. "White-Collar Crime and Criminal Careers: Specifying a Trajectory of Punctuated Situational Offending." *Journal of Contemporary Criminal Justice* 20: 148–65.

Piquero, Nicole Leeper, M. Lyn Exum, and Sally S. Simpson. 2005. "Integrating the Desire-for-Control and Rational Choice in a Corporate Crime Context." *Justice Quarterly* 22: 252–80.

Piquero, Nicole L., and David Weisburd. 2009. "Developmental Trajectories of White-Collar Crime." In *The Criminology of White-Collar Crime*, edited by Sally S. Simpson and David Weisburd. New York: Springer.

Sampson, Robert J., and John H. Laub. 1993. *Crime in the Making*. Cambridge, MA: Harvard University Press.

Shover, Neal. 1996. *Great Pretenders: Pursuits and Careers of Persistent Thieves*. Boulder, CO: Westview.

Simpson, Sally S., and Christopher Koper. 1992. "Deterring Corporate Crime." *Criminology* 30: 347–76.

Simpson, Sally S., Raymond Paternoster, and Nicole L. Piquero. 1998. "Exploring the Micro-Macro Link in Corporate Crime Research." In *Research in the Sociology of Organizations: Special Volume on Deviance in and of Organizations*, edited by Peter Bamberger and William J. Sonnenstuhl. Greenwich, CT: JAI Press.

Soothill, Keith, Claire Fitzpatrick, and Brian Francis. 2009. *Understanding Criminal Careers*. Cullompton, UK: Willan.

Sutherland, Edwin H. 1949. *White Collar Crime*. New York: Holt, Rinehart, & Winston.

Tracy, Paul E., and Kimberly Kempf-Leonard. 1996. *Continuity and Discontinuity in Criminal Careers*. New York: Plenum.

Tremblay, Richard E., Frank Vitaro, Daniel S. Nagin, Linda Pagani, and Jean R. Seguin. 2003. "The Montreal Longitudinal and Experimental Study: Rediscovering the Power of Descriptions." In *Taking Stock of Delinquency: An Overview of Findings from Contemporary Longitudinal Studies*, edited by Terrance Thornberry and Marvin D. Krohn. New York: Kluwer/Plenum.

Weisburd, David, Ellen F. Chayet, and Elin J. Waring. 1990. "White-Collar Crime and Criminal Careers: Some Preliminary Findings." *Crime and Delinquency* 36: 342–55.

Weisburd, David, and Elin Waring (with Ellen F. Chayet). 2001. *White-Collar Crime and Criminal Careers*. New York: Cambridge University Press.

Weisburd, David, Stanton Wheeler, Elin Waring, and Nancy Bode. 1991. *Crimes of the Middle Classes: White-Collar Offenders in the Federal Courts*. New Haven, CT: Yale University Press.

Wheeler, Stanton, David Weisburd, Elin Waring, and Nancy Bode. 1988. "White-Collar Crime and Criminals." *American Criminal Law Review* 25: 331–57.

Wikström, Per-Olof H. 1990. "Age and Crime in a Stockholm Cohort." *Journal of Quantitative Criminology* 6: 61–83.

Wolfgang, Marvin E., Robert M. Figlio, and Thortsen Sellin. 1972. *Delinquency in a Birth Cohort*. Chicago: University of Chicago Press.

Zimring, Franklin, Wesley Jennings, and Alex R. Piquero. 2008. "Juvenile and Adult Sexual Offending in Racine, Wisconsin: Does Early Sex Offending Predict Later Sex Offending in Youth and Young Adulthood?" *Criminology and Public Policy* 6: 507–34.

....

CHAPTER 13

DEVELOPMENTAL PERSPECTIVES ON WHITE-COLLAR CRIMINALITY

....

MICHAEL L. BENSON

WHITE COLLAR crime and white-collar offenders have always posed a problem for criminology. White-collar offenses do not resemble the offenses that most people, including criminologists, think of when the subject of crime comes up, and white-collar offenders do not look like the offenders whom politicians and the news media endlessly castigate for our crime problem. Neither white-collar offenses nor white-collar offenders fit the common stereotypes of crime and criminals. Although some valiant efforts have been made to bring the etiology of white-collar crime into the conceptual domain of standard criminological theory (Sutherland 1949; Coleman 1987; Hirschi and Gottfredson 1987; Lasley 1988; Passas 1990), these efforts have failed to generate sustained lines of research, and, with the possible exception of choice theory (Paternoster and Simpson 1993; Shover and Hochstetler 2006), there is at present no consensus on which one has the most promise. This essay represents yet another attempt to integrate white-collar crime into mainstream criminology by exploring how the life-course perspective might be applied to the lives and criminal careers of white-collar offenders.

In the past two decades, the life-course perspective has become such an influential force in criminology that an eminent criminologist has declared it one and the same as the discipline itself (Cullen 2011). As Francis Cullen (2011) put it: "Life-course criminology now is criminology" (p. 310). Despite its dominant role in contemporary criminology, most of the theorizing about crime and the life course simply ignores white-collar crime. With only a few exceptions, little effort has been made to apply the life-course perspective to white-collar crime (Benson and Kerley 2000; Piquero and Benson 2004), and the accounts that have been put forth to date to explain offending patterns over the life course simply do not fit what is known about white-collar offenders (see, e.g., Sampson and Laub 1993; Moffitt 1997). Thus, to describe or account for white-collar criminal participation over the life course requires one to set aside many of the taken-for-granted assumptions and commonly accepted findings that guide contemporary theorizing in the life-course perspective. Yet, for both white-collar crime research and for life-course theory, there may be some value to exploring patterns in white-collar offending using the life-course perspective as an orienting or heuristic framework.

Section I of this essay will briefly review the life-course perspective and the contemporary developmental and life-course accounts that have been promulgated to explain offending over the life course. Section II addresses the definition of white-collar crime and briefly reviews what is currently known about white-collar offenders. Section III focuses on white-collar criminal careers and the degree to which their careers resemble the careers of other types of offenders. Section IV treats propensities, controls, and motivational paths as they apply to white-collar offending. Section V discusses how social, historical, and legal changes influence motivations and opportunities for white-collar crime. Finally, section VI presents suggestions regarding (1) what white-collar crime researchers might take from the life-course perspective to advance our understanding of white-collar offenders and (2) what the life-course perspective might take from the study of white-collar crime.

The main conclusions of this essay are as follows:

- Contemporary developmental and life-course theories of the etiology of crime are inconsistent with white-collar crime offending patterns and are therefore incomplete as general theories of crime.
- As with other forms of crime, individual involvement in and rates of white-collar crime are influenced by evolving social, economic, and legal conditions.
- Although current evidence suggests that participation in white-collar crime is driven primarily by situational considerations, the potential role of ontogenetic factors deserves further investigation and should not be entirely discounted.

I. THE LIFE-COURSE PERSPECTIVE AND CRIMINOLOGY

The life-course perspective is an interdisciplinary intellectual movement that focuses on human development and behavior over time. The term "life course" refers to a sequence of age-graded stages and social roles that are socially constructed within particular societies at particular points in time. Because societies and historical periods differ in regard to the opportunities for and constraints on development and success that they provide to people, the shape of any particular individual's life course is determined in part by the time and place in which he or she lives (Elder 1998). As discussed later in this chapter, the influence of historical and social change may be particularly important in regard to understanding white-collar criminal participation and the life course. Within the parameters set by historical time and place, the life course is shaped by individual endowments and characteristics, relationships with other people, the nature and timing of life events, human agency, and the vagaries of chance (Benson 2013).

As applied to criminal behavior, the life-course perspective pictures offending as arising out of a developmental process that extends from birth through adulthood, in which people follow different trajectories in crime. Researchers have investigated a number of important questions in regard to these trajectories, including when and why offending starts, how long it lasts, and when and why people stop offending. One theory posits that there are basically only three patterns in offending: (1) those who are not involved in antisocial or criminal behavior at all or only minimally ("non-offenders"); (2) those who show no signs of antisocial behavior early in life but who undergo a brief period of criminality during adolescence ("adolescence-limited offenders); and (3) those who show signs of antisocial behavior early and who persist in criminal and antisocial behavior throughout adulthood ("life-course-persistent offenders") (Moffitt 1997). In regards to life-course-persistent offending, Moffitt (1997) argued that this pattern develops when a child with certain neuropsychological deficits has the misfortune to be raised in an adverse home environment. Because of dysfunctional interactions with parents, the child develops an antisocial behavioral style that persists throughout adulthood. Other theorists disagree about the number of offending patterns and their causes (Laub and Sampson 2003; Sampson and Laub 2003). Laub and Sampson (2003), for example, contended that there are many more than just three offending patterns, and even serious long-term offenders can and do desist in adulthood if they experience a prosocial turning point. Further, in their view, early childhood predictors cannot explain offending patterns in adulthood. Although disagreement persists over these and other issues in regard to offending patterns over the life course, all of the major contemporary theoretical approaches assume that offending begins relatively early in life—that is, sometime in the first or second decade—and that patterns in criminal offending are determined by a combination of ontogenic and sociogenic factors (Thornberry 1987; Gottfredson and Hirschi 1990; Sampson and Laub 1993; Moffitt 1997; Farrington 2005). However, as shown below, the emphasis on the early ontogenic and sociogenic determination of criminal trajectories that characterizes much of life-course theorizing appears not to correspond with what is known about white-collar offenders or their criminal careers.

The lack of congruence between life-course theory and white-collar crime arises in part from methodological reasons involving the nature of the samples and measures used by life-course researchers. Life-course and developmental studies tend to use longitudinal datasets that focus on high-risk youth and not on people who become successful in adulthood. Until quite recently, longitudinal studies also tended to end when the subjects reached their thirties, and the samples typically did not contain or attempt to measure people committing white-collar crime. As a result, except for Laub and Sampson (2003), life-course theories typically do not focus on adult change, and even

Laub and Sampson (2003) look primarily at the factors that lead people *out of* crime in adulthood and ignore the factors that might lead them *into* crime.

II. White-Collar Crime and White-Collar Offenders

Sutherland (1983) defined white-collar crime as "a crime committed by a person of respectability and high social status in the course of his occupation" (p. 7). Because of its emphasis on the social characteristics of the offender and the occupational location of the offense, this definition has been criticized as being overly restrictive and for confusing definition with explanation (Edelhertz 1970; Shapiro 1990). In opposition to Sutherland's offender-based definition, others have argued that white-collar crime should be defined by the nature of the illegal act (Edelhertz 1970; Shapiro 1990). What distinguishes white-collar crime from other types of crime is that offenders use some combination of deception, guile, or abuse of trust to commit the offense as opposed to overt physical action. While the offense-based approach to defining white-collar crime is not without its critics (Braithwaite 1985; Geis 1988), it has the advantage of permitting researchers to investigate how variations in the social status of offenders influence motivations and opportunities for white-collar crime as well as the nature and seriousness of offenses (Benson and Simpson 2014). In addition, defining white-collar crime from an offense-based perspective makes it more compatible with the life-course perspective and permits one to take advantage of recent research on white-collar offenders that has adopted this approach. Hence, for the purposes of this article, white-collar crime is defined along the lines suggested by Edelhertz (1970) as an illegal act committed by concealment, guile, or deception to obtain business or personal advantage or to avoid the loss of the same.

Sutherland's imagery of the white-collar offender as a respectable and high-social-status person still resonates today in the popular news media, which seems never to tire of promoting the stereotype of the high-profile corporate executive as the *sine qua non* of white-collar crime. Although there is certainly no shortage of crooked executives, research has found that the perpetrators of white-collar types of crimes often come from less elevated positions in the social structure (Croall 1989; Weisburd et al. 1991; Benson and Moore 1992; Weisburd and Waring 2001; Benson and Simpson 2014). Statistical analyses of the social backgrounds of persons convicted for white-collar crimes (i.e., nonphysical, financially oriented crimes involving deceit or concealment) in the federal judicial system indicate that the typical white-collar offender is neither highly educated nor wealthy and would be most accurately described as a member of the middle class (Wheeler et al. 1988; Benson and Kerley 2000). Yet, even though most white-collar offenders do not conform to Sutherland's image, they are nevertheless clearly drawn from a different sector of the American social structure than are common criminals. They typically do not suffer from the developmental deficits, personal pathologies, or social disadvantages that are so prevalent among common criminals and that are assumed to be a source of their criminal propensities (Wheeler et al. 1988; Benson and Kerley 2000; Weisburd and Waring 2001; Benson and Simpson 2014). Obviously, the developmental and social differences between white-collar offenders and street offenders are even more pronounced if only people of high social status and respectability are considered to be true white-collar offenders. Nevertheless, regardless of how white-collar offenders are identified, the relative absence of the personal and social characteristics that life-course theories identify as factors that lead people to crime has implications for our understanding of participation in white-collar crime through the life course.

In developmental and life-course theories of crime, offending is theorized to arise out of an underlying criminal propensity. Some theorists view propensities as being fixed relatively early in life and then not subject to much change (Gottfredson and Hirschi 1990; Moffitt 1997), while others view propensities as more malleable and changeable, depending on the individual's response to life-course events and experiences (Laub and Sampson 2003; Sampson and Laub 2005). White-collar offenders, however, tend not to have the personal and social characteristics that life-course theories identify as factors that lead people to crime. Indeed, they tend to have the "social bonds" such as good jobs and marriages that are thought to lead to desistance from crime rather than onset. These characteristics of white-collar offenders suggest that white-collar criminal participation through the life course is perhaps driven more by situational factors than by underlying propensities (Weisburd and Waring 2001; Piquero and Benson 2004). Nevertheless, the role of propensities should not be discarded entirely in regard to white-collar crime. Shover (2007), for example, argued that three cultural conditions found in middle- and upper-class homes generate a propensity for white-collar crime: "normatively unbridled competition, a pervasive sense of arrogance and an ethic of entitlement" (p. 88).

Just as developmental and life-course theories have been based on particular types of samples that have limited their generalizability, the same is true of most studies of white-collar offenders. They tend to be based on samples of adults and thus are not good at tracking how earlier events, conditions, and experiences may have contributed to adult offending. There is an implicit assumption that nothing in the lives of white-collar offenders matters until they get their first job or until they rise to a certain level of occupational success. This assumption is debatable. It is also often assumed that white-collar offenders have little to no experience with the criminal justice system. As discussed in the next section, this assumption needs qualification.

III. White-Collar Criminal Careers

Describing the criminal careers of white-collar offenders is difficult because of the paucity of longitudinal data on these offenders. Indeed, the whole notion of a criminal career may seem inappropriate in regard to white-collar offenders, because they are typically assumed to be "one-shot" offenders, whose first encounter with the criminal justice system is their last (Weisburd, Chayet, and Waring 1990). However, the stereotypical image of the white-collar offender as a "one-shot" offender is not entirely accurate. Two studies of individuals convicted of white-collar crimes in the federal judicial system found that approximately 40 percent of them had at least one prior arrest, and between 12 and 15 percent had four or more prior arrests (Weisburd et al. 1991; Benson and Kerley 2000; Benson 2002). Thus, a notable proportion of white-collar criminals have committed multiple offenses, and the term "white-collar criminal career" is not an oxymoron as applied to them.

Some important dimensions of career offending are age of onset, age of desistance, and rate of offending (Blumstein et al. 1986). With respect to age of onset, white-collar offenders do not follow the standard pattern. For offenders with multiple arrests, the mean age of onset for white-collar criminals is five to ten years older than it is for common criminals, and for one-time offenders the average age of first arrest for a white-collar offender is close to forty compared to an average of thirty for common offenders (Benson and Kerley 2000; Benson 2002). As measured by arrests, then, most white-collar offenders are "late starters."

White-collar offenders also diverge from the standard criminal trajectories in regard to desistance. What little is known about desistance in white-collar crime comes from a study that followed a sample of white-collar offenders who had been convicted in federal court for ten years after their convictions (Weisburd and Waring 2001). The results suggest that white-collar offenders do not follow the patterns typically found among street criminals. Even among relatively serious street criminals, a majority "age out" of offending by the time they reach their thirties (Laub and Sampson 2003). In the Weisburd study, however, the average age of desistance for white-collar offenders who had any arrests after the criterion offense is forty-three. Close to half (47 percent) of the white-collar offenders who reached the age of fifty by the end of the study had been arrested after age fifty. With a longer follow-up period, the percentage of new arrests would go up (Weisburd and Waring 2001, p. 37). Ten percent of the offenders who made it to age seventy had arrests in their eighth decade of life. Overall, compared to common crime samples, a larger proportion of white-collar offenders appear to continue offending late in the life course (Weisburd and Waring 2001, p. 38).

The causes of desistance from white-collar crime probably are not the same as those for desistance from street crime. Street offenders may quit some types of crimes simply because the ability to commit certain offenses, such as robbery and burglary, may decline with age. This explanation does not seem to fit in the case of white-collar crime because the offenses are not physically demanding and because opportunities for white-collar crime may actually increase with age. As offenders grow older, they may move into more trusted occupational positions and hence have more opportunities to take advantage of their employers or others.

Another explanation often given for desistance from crime involves changes in informal social control. Street offenders appear to be most likely to desist when they establish strong informal social bonds to family or work as a result of experiencing a turning point (Laub and Sampson 2003). But white-collar offenders are much more likely to already have these bonds when they commit their offenses (Benson and Moore 1992; Benson and Kerley 2000). Therefore, increases in informal social control perhaps do not play a significant role in desistance from white-collar crime.

Weisburd and Waring (2001, p. 41) speculated that the most likely cause of desistance from white-collar crime may be the cognitive changes associated with aging. As they reach middle age, white-collar offenders may come to the realization that time is passing them by and that they do not want to risk wasting any more of their remaining time in trouble with the law. The hard-driving executives who are willing to do anything for company and career when they are young may have a change of heart as they enter their fifties. Even the relatively small risk of incarceration that goes with white-collar crime may strike older offenders as an unacceptably high risk to take.

Overall, the picture of white-collar criminal participation through the life course that one gets from official records suggests that white-collar offenders start their involvement in crime later in life than other types of offenders. Although they offend at a lower rate, they appear to offend longer and desist later in the life course than ordinary street offenders.

As measures of the timing, duration, and intensity of criminal careers, however, arrest records suffer from obvious flaws. Many offenses never lead to an official arrest, and therefore, arrests provide only an estimate of when criminal careers start and end. Arrest records may also underestimate the frequency of offending that occurs during a criminal career (Blumstein et al. 1986). In the case of white-collar offenders, the degree of correspondence between arrests and actual involvement in criminal activities may be particularly tenuous because of the inherent nature of white-collar crimes. Unlike most ordinary street crimes such as burglary, robbery, or auto theft, white-collar offenses are not obvious. White-collar offenders, particularly those who are successful, take special pains to hide their offenses both from their victims and from law enforcers (Geis 1977; Sparrow 1996; McLean and Elkind 2003; Henriques 2011). Indeed, detecting the offense has long been recognized as one of the major problems that law enforcers face in their efforts to control white-collar crime (Braithwaite 1981; Benson and Simpson 2014).

Thus, official records provide a picture of white-collar criminal participation that does not accurately portray many forms of white-collar offending, because the offenses may go undetected for long periods of time. For example, Bernie Madoff was arrested in 2008, when he was seventy years old, but his Ponzi scheme began as much as twenty years earlier (Henriques 2011). Likewise, the infamous accounting frauds at Enron and WorldCom went on for several years before they came to light (McLean and Elkind 2003). In the 1960s, the famous heavy electrical antitrust conspiracy existed on and off for a decade or more (Geis 1977), and employees of the W. R. Grace illegally dumped hazardous waste in Woburn, Massachusetts, for decades before being discovered (Benson and Simpson 2014). Even relatively small-time offenders who are not involved in major multimillion-dollar scams may, nevertheless, engage in a single type of criminal endeavor, such as embezzlement, for years (Rosoff, Pontell, and Tillman 2006, pp.

508–09). The group-oriented nature and the extended duration of some white-collar offenses complicate the task of assigning beginning and ending points to white-collar criminal careers.

IV. PROPENSITIES, CONTROLS, TURNING POINTS, AND MOTIVATIONAL PATHS

As applied to non-white-collar offenders, the life-course perspective typically pictures offending propensities as arising out of the interaction of ontogenic and sociogenic factors. For example, in their age-graded theory of informal social control, Sampson and Laub (1993) contended that individuals are least likely to offend when they are strongly bonded to others via the institutions of marriage, employment, and education. Sampson and Laub recognized that for ontogenic reasons people may vary in how they react to the social controls imposed by these social institutions, with some being more amenable to control and conformity than others, but, nevertheless, in their view the institutions of marriage and employment usually have crime-inhibiting effects on those who participate in them. Indeed, in standard life-course theory, the institutions of family and work offer turning points to offenders, which facilitate desistance. But the relationships among marriage, employment, and crime may be different in regard to white-collar crime.

The lack of full-time, stable employment has long been recognized as an important cause of involvement in crime. Indeed, for ordinary street offenders, finding a good job is typically thought of as a prosocial turning point that can lead to desistance. In theory, work creates a sense of interdependency between the offender and conventional others, thus amplifying informal social controls on the offender. With its expectations regarding regular attendance and performance of duties, work alters the offender's pattern of routine activities and provides an opportunity to develop a prosocial identity, leading to reduced recidivism (Laub and Sampson 2003; Sampson and Laub 2003). Although the evidence on the effects of work on recidivism is mixed (Uggen 2000; Bushway and Apel 2012; Latessa 2012), the idea that work might actually promote involvement in offending would certainly be regarded by most criminologists as unorthodox. Yet, in regard to white-collar crime, such is the case.

Work facilitates white-collar offending by providing potential offenders with both opportunities and motivations that encourage rather than inhibit offending. Obviously, one way in which work facilitates white-collar offending is by granting the offender access to a particular target or the opportunity to commit a particular type of offense. Bank embezzlement, for example, requires employment in a bank. The position provides the opportunity, and this applies to many other types of white-collar crime, such as healthcare and securities fraud (Shapiro 1984; Sparrow 1996; Weisburd and Waring 2001).

Besides providing individuals with opportunities to offend, work organizations may also create an environment in which white-collar offending for the benefit of the organization is either facilitated or coerced (Gross 1978; Needleman and Needleman 1979; Hochstetler and Copes 2002). As Sutherland (1983) noted long ago, illegal practices are found in many, if not all, businesses and industries, and as new employees assume their occupational positions they may be encouraged, socialized, and sometimes coerced to participate in these business-related crimes. Sutherland (1983, pp. 243–45) provided numerous examples of young people in occupations ranging from accountants to shoe salesmen being socialized into disreputable and exploitative practices. In these cases, the offender's motivation is not necessarily predatory or acquisitive; rather, it may be defensive: the individual engages in white-collar crime to keep his or her job. Organizations also can create an ethical climate or culture in which certain types of white-collar offending are framed in ways that make them acceptable to otherwise law-abiding individuals (Needleman and Needleman 1979; Clinard 1983; Hochstetler and Copes 2002).

The life-course perspective holds that the individual life course is structured by the cultural and social structural conditions that prevail during an individual's life. Societies and cultures vary in regard to the opportunities that they provide to men and women to pursue certain activities and lines of action. This is true in regard to involvement in white-collar crime, where gender differences are pronounced because of differences in opportunities and in gender roles and relationships.

As with almost all other forms of crime, men dominate in white-collar crime. Official records indicate that their levels of participation are considerably higher than women's, and that is not the only difference (Weisburd et al. 1991; Benson and Simpson 2014). When women do become involved in white-collar crime, they do so for different reasons and in different ways than men (Zietz 1981; Daly 1989). For example, women are much more likely than men to participate in relatively low-level and uncomplicated offenses (Weisburd et al. 1991; Holtfreter 2005), and their reasons for offending are more likely to involve family and personal troubles rather than pecuniary gain or self-indulgence (Zietz 1981; Daly 1989; Klenowski, Copes, and Mullins 2011). The gender gap in the level and character of white-collar offending is particularly pronounced in conspiratorial offenses committed in large organizations. In a recent study of persons indicted by the Corporate Fraud Task Force of the U.S. Department of Justice, Steffensmeier, Schwartz, and Roche (2013) found the usual gender gap between men and women, but they also found that women were much less likely than men to play leading roles in corporate conspiracies—even women who occupied high-level positions within corporate hierarchies. When women are involved in corporate crime groups, it is usually because they are personally affiliated in some way with one of the male conspirators or because they occupy some position in the organization that is essential for carrying out the offense—but they are almost never the organizers or leading figures in corporate conspiracies. Opportunities for corporate crime are structured, then, not only by occupational position but also by larger historical and cultural traditions regarding gender roles and relationships.

Gender is not the only demographic characteristic that influences the rate and nature of involvement in white-collar crime. Race and social class, both independently and in combination, are strongly related to participation in white-collar crime. Race is highly correlated with involvement in traditional street crimes, with blacks being overrepresented. But the relationship between race and crime changes dramatically when the lens is shifted to white-collar crimes. Like the gender gap in corporate crime, there is also a race gap in corporate crime. Blacks tend to be overrepresented in both low-level white-collar crimes and serious street crimes, while whites tend to be overrepresented in high-level white-collar crimes (Harris and Shaw 2000). Because race and social class are so strongly correlated, it is difficult to determine with certainty whether the underrepresentation of blacks in high-level corporate offenses is simply because there are so few blacks who hold high-level corporate positions or because blacks experience the same lack of opportunity to get involved in workplace crime groups that women do. In short, for several reasons blacks may lack access to the occupational and organizational networks that provide the freedom and power that one needs to commit large-scale white-collar crimes (Hagan 1994).

With their middle- and upper-class positions, white-collar offenders are different from ordinary street offenders in that they often have something to lose, such as social status, a job, or, in many cases, a small business. The fear or threat of loss of these tangible and valued resources may provide a unique motivation for white-collar offending that is not seen among street offenders (Benson and Moore 1992; Wheeler 1992). Small-business owners, for example, may engage in a host of fraudulent practices simply to stay in business or to earn a living wage (Benson 1985; Barlow 1993; Croall 2001). The idea of engaging in crime to prevent a loss suggests a unique motivational path for white-collar offenders and contrasts sharply with the idea of an impulsive undercontrolled offender who simply pursues his or her own hedonistic self-interest.

V. Social Change, the Life Course, and White-Collar Crime

Forms of crime and the availability of opportunities to commit them evolve over time. For example, stealing another person's identity for illicit purposes is not a recent invention of the criminal mind. Identity theft has been around for centuries, but opportunities for engaging in this form of theft have expanded dramatically in the past decade or so (Copes and Vieraitis 2012). Consumer fraud has been recognized for centuries, too, but opportunities to commit this type of fraud have expanded dramatically over the past two hundred years, in part because consumer products have become so much more plentiful and technically complex and because of the geographical separation between buyers and manufacturers that characterizes modern global trade networks

(Holtfreter, Van Slyke, and Bloomberg 2005). More generally, opportunities to engage in various forms of white-collar crime have been expanding for over a century, as America has evolved from a rural agricultural-based society to one in which most people work in offices that are increasingly based on advanced technologies. Because of these changes in the nature of work, more people have access to the "white-collar world of paper fraud" (Weisburd et al. 1991, p. 183). Faxes, computers, scanners, and mobile phones are the tools of the trade of white-collar crime, and more people have access to these tools in the modern world. In addition to changes in work, the expansion of government programs creates new opportunities and incentives for people to take illegal advantage of the government's largesse (Shover and Hochstetler 2006), and as Shapiro (1990) noted, the rise of agency relationships makes crimes based on abuse of trust increasingly available. Thus, from the perspective of life-course theory, these historical changes have expanded opportunities for individuals to follow certain types of white-collar criminal trajectories that were simply not available to most people throughout most of human history.

The past few decades have witnessed several examples of social and legal change that have created new opportunities for white-collar crime and attracted scores of white-collar "opportunity takers" (Weisburd et al. 1991). In the early 1980s, in response to economic conditions that had undermined the financial solvency of many savings and loan institutions ("thrifts"), the rules and regulations governing this industry were reformed. Most notably, rules regarding ownership and loans were relaxed to give thrifts more flexibility (Calavita and Pontell 1990). Although deregulation was intended to shore up an important segment of the banking industry, it had the perverse effect of creating conditions in which fraud became easier and more lucrative for the owners and operators of thrift institutions (Pontell and Calavita 1993). Not surprisingly, word that money was there for the taking spread quickly, and hundreds of new applications for savings and loan institution charters were filed with state and federal regulatory bodies (Pontell and Calavita 1993; Black 2005). Many of the new owners of thrifts were clearly opportunity takers who recognized that as a result of deregulation thrifts had become vulnerable and poorly guarded targets ripe for financial exploitation (Pontell and Calavita 1993). As a result of fraud and other willful criminal activity, many thrifts became insolvent and had to be bailed out by taxpayers (Pontell and Calavita 1993; Black 2005). According to government reports, criminal activity was involved in 70 to 80 percent of insolvencies in the thrift industry (Calavita and Pontell 1990; Pontell and Calavita 1993). For white-collar offenders, the law sometimes becomes a source of opportunities rather than a source of risks.

Another example of the connection between social and legal change and white-collar criminal participation can be found in the mortgage industry. When thrift institutions began to falter in the 1980s, regular banks and the largely unregulated mortgage lenders stepped in to fill the breach and developed new mortgage instruments, such as the adjustable-rate mortgage and the subprime mortgage. Pushed by a Republican Congress and signed by then president Bill Clinton, the Financial Services Modernization Act of 1999 allowed commercial banks, investment banks, securities firms, and insurance companies to merge. What followed is now well known—a boom of epic proportions in the housing industry accompanied and spurred by massive fraud in the mortgage industry (Benson 2010). According to a report from the Treasury Department's Financial Crimes Enforcement Network (FCEN), suspicious activity reports related to mortgage fraud increased by over 1,400 percent between 1997 and 2005 (U.S. FCEN 2006). From that point on, the annual rate of increase in suspected mortgage fraud cases slowed and in some years even declined. However, after the housing bubble burst, new forms of fraud, such as foreclosure fraud, began to rise.

Two developments appear especially significant in regard to the explosion of mortgage fraud that occurred in the first decade of the 21st century. First was the rise of the secondary mortgage market, in which mortgages were bundled together and turned into commodities that could be traded among investors. Because banks and other lenders no longer had to hold on to mortgages to make a profit, they had less incentive to make loans only to well-qualified borrowers. Lenders now had a vested interest in making as many loans as possible, regardless of their quality, and then selling them to other parties. The second change was the expansion in the number of mortgage brokers. Like the savings and loan industry, once the legal and social landscape for the mortgage industry changed, new operators in the form of mortgage brokers were drawn to the field. Mortgage brokers act as intermediaries between individual home buyers and banks or mortgage lending companies. Both banks and other nonfinancial lenders came to rely increasingly on these third-party brokers, which created opportunities for organized fraud groups to operate (U.S. Federal Bureau of Investigation 2005). These groups often involved real estate agents, appraisers, straw buyers, bank loan officers, and mortgage brokers, and they engaged in a variety of different types of mortgage fraud, including predatory lending, equity skimming, property flipping, and mortgage-related identity theft.

A report from the U.S. Bureau of Labor Statistics documents that, as the housing bubble expanded in the early 2000s and then burst around 2007, employment trends in the mortgage and housing industries mirrored that pattern. Between 2001 and 2006, employment in the field of mortgage brokers increased by 119 percent, and in the following two years after the housing bubble burst, it declined by close to 60 percent (Byun 2010). It is not possible now to know what the prevalence rate for fraud among mortgage brokers was in the mid-2000s. Nor is it possible to know whether the new entrants to the field were lured there because they saw opportunities for fraud or simply discovered that opportunities existed after they were employed. However, regardless of whether the mortgage industry was populated by predatory white-collar crime opportunity seekers or by normal people who simply took advantage of opportunities as they saw them, there is little reason to doubt that the combination of mortgage deregulation and a classic boom in the housing market created conditions that greatly facilitated white-collar offending and hence either enticed or permitted previously law-abiding individuals to become white-collar criminals.

VI. White-Collar Crime and Life-Course Theory

As noted in the opening sections of this chapter, the life-course perspective views involvement in criminal and antisocial behavior as arising out of a developmental process that begins in early childhood. Depending on their early childhood and adolescent experiences, people enter conforming or nonconforming trajectories that then influence their subsequent opportunities and life chances in adulthood. White-collar crime researchers, however, for the most part have ignored childhood and adolescence as potential starting points for white-collar criminal careers (but see Shover and Hochstetler 2006; see also Singer, Chapter 11 in this volume). For most white-collar crime researchers, individual involvement in white-collar crime is envisioned as arising during adulthood out of the pressures and opportunities that accompany engagement in different occupations and industries. Obviously, most white-collar offenders do not suffer from low self-control of the sort envisioned by Gottfredson and Hirschi (1990). Nor are they likely to be plagued by Moffitt's (1993) neuropsychological deficits. However, even though most white-collar offenders are unlikely to suffer from these sorts of behavioral and cognitive disorders, this does not rule out the possibility that some white-collar offenders have distinctive psychological characteristics that contribute to their offending, and these characteristics may have ontogenetic origins.

Indeed, the idea that white-collar offenders may somehow be "different" from ordinary people has a long historical pedigree in white-collar crime. Over a century ago, Ross (1907) argued that the distinguishing characteristic of the robber barons of his day, the "criminaloids" whom today we would call white-collar criminals, was *moral insensitivity*—that is, the psychological capacity not to be troubled by the harms that they imposed on others in pursuit of their own goals and objectives. Since then, a multitude of case studies and qualitative research efforts have developed similar themes to portray the personalities of white-collar criminals. They are variously described as being arrogant and having a sense of entitlement (Shover and Hochstetler 2006; Shover 2007); as possessing a sense of superiority over their victims (Stotland 1977); as being narcissistic (Perri 2011), aggressive, and self-seeking (Spencer 1965); and as displaying an impenetrable unwillingness to admit the criminality of their actions (Benson 1985).

In recent years, these largely anecdotal reports have been supplemented by a small but growing body of quantitative research efforts. Collins and Schmidt (1993) compared persons convicted of white-collar crimes to a matched control sample of noncriminal white-collar employees on several personality scales. The white-collar offenders scored significantly lower than the white-collar controls on social conscientiousness but significantly higher on social extraversion. Conscientious individuals are responsible, dependable, rule-abiding, and committed to social and civic values. The white-collar offenders in this study were less likely to display these traits than noncriminal white-collar employees. Extraverted people have outgoing personalities, make friends easily, and can be effective in social situations. White-collar offenders appear in general to be more socially extraverted than their noncriminal counterparts (Alalehto 2003).

Other studies have compared incarcerated white-collar offenders to other types of offenders on psychological assessment instruments designed to measure criminal thinking patterns, criminal lifestyles, the centrality of a criminal identity, and psychopathology (Walters and Geyer 2004; Ragatz, Fremouw, and Baker 2012). The findings must be interpreted cautiously because they come from relatively small samples of incarcerated offenders, who may differ in systematic ways from offenders who avoid detection and conviction. These studies also suggest that we must be careful in whom we call the white-collar offender. There are distinctive psychological differences between people who commit only white-collar crimes versus people who commit a mixed bag of offenses, some of which happen to be white-collar offenses. For example, Walters and Geyer (2004) reported two relevant results. First, they found that persons with convictions for a mix of white-collar and non-white-collar offenses register higher on scales measuring criminal thinking, criminal identification, and deviance than do persons whose prior history includes only white-collar offenses. Second, persons who specialize in white-collar crime score higher on the "social potency" subscale of the Psychopathic Personality Inventory-Revised (PPI-R) than more versatile or mixed-bag offenders (see also Ragatz et al. 2012).

It is too early yet to tell how much and in what ways the psychological profiles of white-collar offenders differ from normal parameters, but the growing body of research suggests that Sutherland's dismissal of psychological factors in regard to white-collar offending was premature. Not only does research indicate that white-collar offenders often do have psychological profiles that vary from the norm, but recent research also suggests that psychopathology and other types of personality disorders are not uncommon among individuals who are successful in the corporate world (Board and Fritzon 2005; Babiak, Neumann, and Hare 2010). Indeed, some have suggested that in certain industries and environments, psychopathic traits may actually facilitate business success (Babiak and Hare 2006). Sutherland undoubtedly was correct that values favorable to law violations permeate many industries and corporate organizations and that socialization into these values is common and promotes white-collar crime. Nevertheless, his sociological background and training may have kept him from considering individual-level factors in white-collar offending. In particular, he gave no weight to the possibility that certain personality types may be more likely than others to internalize values favorable to law violations, succeed in the world of business, and engage in white-collar crime (Gross 1978, 1980). Involvement in white-collar offending, then, is a function not only of culture and opportunity but also of individual-level factors.

If, as hypothesized above, individual-level factors, such as particular personality profiles, are implicated in involvement in white-collar crime, then extrapolating from life-course theory and behavioral genetic research, it follows that ontogenetic factors may play a role in the etiology of white-collar offending through the life course. According to life-course theory, behavioral trajectories are established early in life through the interaction of individual endowments and social environments. Decades of behavioral genetics research have demonstrated that all individual-level traits, including psychological characteristics, are to some degree influenced by heredity (Moffitt 2005; Rutter 2007). Theoretical understanding, then, of individual involvement in white-collar crime will remain forever inadequate if efforts are not made to recognize that, like other forms of offending, white-collar offending involves to some degree developmental processes and interactions that begin in early life.

Saying that white-collar offending can be viewed from the perspective of developmental processes, however, does not mean that white-collar offenders are born and not made. Indeed, in regard to white-collar crime, it would be a mistake to succumb to the "tyranny of infant determinism" (Kagan 1998). If anything, research on individual involvement in white-collar crime finds that the vast majority of white-collar offenders do not follow the standard trajectories in crime and antisocial behavior that prevail among non–white-collar offenders. Accordingly, the factors that shape the parameters of these standard trajectories—such as neuropsychological deficits, inadequate parenting, cumulative disadvantages, turning points, informal social controls, and the structuring effects of routine activities—either are not relevant to white-collar crime or work in different ways. Participation in white-collar crime through the life course is more likely determined by a mix of personal characteristics; occupationally based opportunities and motivations; and evolving conditions in the social, economic, and legal environments. Thus, despite its undeniable promise, contemporary life-course theory will remain incomplete if it continues to act as if common street crime is the only type of crime there is (Piquero and Benson 2004). This was a criticism leveled by Sutherland against the contemporary theories of his day, and it is still valid today.

To sum up, most white-collar crime researchers have unwisely ignored the important finding from the life-course perspective that individual differences that arise early in the life course can have a substantial influence on subsequent trajectories in crime. At the same time, life-course researchers have been shortsighted in ignoring the white-collar crimes of the middle and upper classes that occur in adulthood and that may have unique age-graded causes. Indeed, to the extent that the life-course and developmental perspectives continue to ignore adult white-collar offending, their generalizability as theories of crime and antisocial behavior will inevitably be as limited as the criminological theories of Sutherland's day.

REFERENCES

Alalehto, Tage. 2003. "Economic Crime: Does Personality Matter?" *International Journal of Offender Therapy and Comparative Criminology* 47: 335–55.

Babiak, Paul, and Robert D. Hare. 2006. *Snakes in Suits: When Psychopaths Go to Work.* New York: Regan Books.

Babiak, Paul, Craig S. Neumann, and Robert D. Hare. 2010. "Corporate Psychopathy: Talking the Walk." *Behavioral Sciences and the Law* 28: 174–93.

Barlow, Hugh D. 1993. "From Fiddle Factors to Networks of Collusion: Charting the Waters of Small Business Crime." *Crime, Law, and Social Change* 20: 319–37.

Benson, Michael L. 1985. "Denying the Guilty Mind: Accounting for Involvement in a White-Collar Crime." *Criminology* 23: 583–608.

Benson, Michael L. 2002. *Crime and the Life-Course: An Introduction*. Los Angeles: Roxbury.

Benson, Michael L. 2010. "Evolutionary Ecology, Fraud, and the Global Financial Crisis." In *Contemporary Issues in Criminological Theory and Research: The Role of Social Institutions*, pp. 299–306, edited by Richard Rosenfeld, Kenna Quinet, and Crystal Garcia. Belmont: Wadsworth.

Benson, Michael L., and Kent R. Kerley. 2000. "Life Course Theory and White-Collar Crime." In *Contemporary Issues in Crime and Criminal Justice: Essays in Honor of Gilber Geis*, pp. 121–36, edited by Henry N. Pontell and David Shichor. Upper Saddle River, NJ: Prentice Hall.

Benson, Michael L., and Elizabeth Moore. 1992. "Are White-Collar and Common Offenders the Same: An Empirical and Theoretical Critique of a Recently Proposed General Theory of Crime." *Journal of Research in Crime and Delinquency* 29: 251–72.

Benson, Michael L., and Sally S. Simpson. 2014. *Understanding White-Collar Crime: An Opportunity Perspective*, 2nd ed. New York: Routledge.

Black, William K. 2005. *The Best Way to Rob a Bank Is to Own One: How Corporate Executives and Politicians Looted the S&L Industry*. Austin: University of Texas Press.

Blumstein, Alfred, Jacqueline Cohen, Jeffrey A. Roth, and Christy A. Visher. 1986. *Criminal Careers and "Career Criminals."* Washington, D.C.: National Academy Press.

Board, Belinda J., and Katarina Fritzon. 2005. "Disordered Personalities at Work." *Psychology, Crime, and Law* 11: 17–32.

Braithwaite, John. 1981. "The Limits of Economism in Controlling Harmful Corporate Conduct." *Law and Society Review* 16: 481–504.

Braithwaite, John. 1985. "White-Collar Crime." *Annual Review of Sociology* 11: 1–25.

Bushway, Shawn D., and Robert Apel. 2012. "A Signaling Perspective on Employment-Based Reentry Programming." *Criminology and Public Policy* 11: 21–50.

Byun, Kathryn J. 2010. "The U.S. Housing Bubble and Bust: Impacts on Employment." *Monthly Labor Review* December: 3–17.

Calavita, Kitty, and Henry N. Pontell. 1990. "'Heads I Win, Tails You Lose': Deregulation, Crime, and Crisis in the Savings and Loan Industry." *Crime and Delinquency* 36: 309–41.

Clinard, Marshall B. 1983. *Corporate Ethics and Crime*. Beverly Hills: Sage.

Coleman, James W. 1987. "Toward an Integrated Theory of White-Collar Crime." *American Journal of Sociology* 93: 406–39.

Collins, Judith M., and Frank L. Schmidt. 1993. "Personality, Integrity, and White-Collar Crime: A Construct Validity Study." *Personnel Psychology* 46: 295–311.

Copes, Heith, and Lynne M. Vieraitis. 2012. *Identity Thieves: Motives and Methods*. Boston: Northeastern University Press.

Croall, Hazel. 1989. "Who Is the White-Collar Criminal?" *British Journal of Criminology* 29: 157–74.

Croall, Hazel. 2001. *Understanding White-Collar Crime*. Buckingham, UK: Open University Press.

Cullen, Francis T. 2011. "Beyond Adolescence-Limited Criminology: Choosing Our Future, The American Society of Criminology 2010 Sutherland Address." *Criminology* 49: 287–330.

Daly, Kathleen. 1989. "Gender and Varieties of White-Collar Crime." *Criminology* 27: 769–94.

Edelhertz, Herbert. 1970. *The Nature, Impact, and Prosecution of White-Collar Crime.* Washington, D.C.: U.S. Department of Justice.

Elder, Glen H. 1998. "The Life Course as Developmental Theory." *Child Development* 69: 1–12.

Farrington, David P., ed. 2005. *Integrated Developmental and Life-Course Theories of Offending.* New Brunswick, NJ: Transaction.

Geis, Gilbert. 1977. "The Heavy Electrical Equipment Antitrust Cases of 1961." In *White-Collar Crime: Offenses in Business, Politics, and the Professions*, pp. 117–132, edited by Gilbert Geis and Robert F. Meier. New York: The Free Press.

Geis, Gilbert. 1988. "From Deuteronomy to Deniability: A Historical Perlustration on White-Collar Crime." *Justice Quarterly* 5: 7–32.

Gottfredson, Michael R., and Travis Hirschi. 1990. *A General Theory of Crime.* Stanford: Stanford University Press.

Gross, Edward. 1978. "Organizational Crime: A Theoretical Perspective." In *Studies in Symbolic Interaction*, pp. 55–85, edited by Norman Denzin. Greenwood, CT: JAI Press.

Gross, Edward. 1980. "Organization Structure and Organizational Crime." In *White-Collar Crime: Theory and Research*, pp. 52–76, edited by Gilbert Geis and Ezra Stotland. Beverly Hills: Sage.

Hagan, John. 1994. *Crime and Disrepute.* Thousand Oaks, CA: Pine Forge Press.

Harris, Anthony R., and James A. W. Shaw. 2000. "Looking for Patterns: Race, Class, and Crime." In *Criminology: A Contemporary Handbook*, pp. 129–64, edited by Joseph F. Sheley. Belmont: Wadsworth/Thompson Learning.

Henriques, Diana B. 2011. *The Wizard of Lies: Bernie Madoff and the Death of Trust.* New York: Times Books/Henry Holt.

Hirschi, Travis, and Michael Gottfredson. 1987. "Causes of White-Collar Crime." *Criminology* 25: 949–74.

Hochstetler, Andrew, and Heith Copes. 2002. "Organizational Culture and Organizational Crime." In *Crimes of Privilege: Readings in White-Collar Crime*, pp. 210–21, edited by Neal Shover and John Paul Wright. New York: Oxford University Press.

Holtfreter, Kristy. 2005. "Is Occupational Fraud 'Typical' White-Collar Crime? A Comparison of Individual and Organizational Characteristics." *Journal of Criminal Justice* 33: 353–65.

Holtfreter, Kristy, Shanna Van Slyke, and Thomas G. Blomberg. 2005. "Sociolegal Change in Consumer Fraud: From Victim–Offender Interactions to Global Networks." *Crime, Law and Social Change* 44: 251–75.

Kagan, Jerome. 1998. *Three Seductive Ideas.* Cambridge, MA: Harvard University Press.

Klenowski, Paul M., Heith Copes, and Christopher W. Mullins. 2011. "Gender, Identity, and Accounts: How White-Collar Offenders Do Gender when Making Sense of Their Crimes." *Justice Quarterly* 28: 46–69.

Lasley, James R. 1988. "Toward a Control Theory of White-Collar Offending." *Journal of Quantitative Criminology* 4: 347–62.

Latessa, Edward. 2012. "Why Work Is Important, and How to Improve the Effectiveness of Correctional Reentry Programs that Target Employment." *Criminology and Public Policy* 11: 87–91.

Laub, John H., and Robert J. Sampson. 2003. *Shared Beginnings, Divergent Lives: Delinquent Boys to Age 70.* Cambridge, MA: Harvard University Press.

McLean, Bethany, and Peter Elkind. 2003. *The Smartest Guys in the Room: The Amazing Rise and Scandalous Fall of Enron.* New York: Penguin Books.

Moffitt, Terrie E. 1997. "Adolescence-Limited and Life-Course-Persistent Offending: A Complementary Pair of Developmental Theories." In *Developmental Theories of Crime and Delinquency*, pp. 11–54, edited by Terence P. Thornberry. New Brunswick, NJ: Transaction.

Moffitt, Terrie E. 2005. "Genetic and Environmental Influences on Antisocial Behavior: Evidence from Behavioral-Genetic Research." *Advances in Genetics* 55: 41–104.

Needleman, Martin L., and Carolyn Needleman. 1979. "Organizational Crime: Two Models of Criminogenesis." *Sociological Quarterly* 20: 517–28.

Passas, Nikos. 1990. "Anomie and Corporate Deviance." *Contemporary Crises* 14: 157–78.

Paternoster, Raymond, and Sally Simpson. 1993. "A Rational Choice Theory of Corporate Crime." In *Routine Activity and Rational Choice*, pp. 37–58, edited by Ronald V. Clarke and Marcus Felson. New Brunswick, NJ: Transaction.

Perri, Frank S. 2011. "White-Collar Criminals: The 'Kinder, Gentler' Offender?" *Journal of Investigative Psychology and Offender Profiling* 8: 217–41.

Piquero, Nicole Leeper, and Michael L. Benson. 2004. "White-Collar Crime and Criminal Careers: Specifying a Trajectory of Punctuated Situational Offending." *Journal of Contemporary Criminal Justice* 20: 148–65.

Pontell, Henry N., and Kitty Calavita. 1993. "The Savings and Loan Industry." *Crime and Justice* 18: 203–46.

Ragatz, Laurie L., William Fremouw, and Edward Baker. 2012. "The Psychological Profile of White-Collar Offenders." *Criminal Justice and Behavior* 39: 978–97.

Rosoff, Stephen, Henry N. Pontell, and Robert Tillman. 2006. *Profit without Honor: White-Collar Crime and the Looting of America*. Upper Saddle River, NJ: Prentice Hall.

Ross, Edward A. 1907. *Sin and Society: An Analysis of Latter-Day Iniquity*. Boston: Houghton Mifflin.

Rutter, Michael. 2007. "Gene–Environment Interdependence." *Developmental Science* 10: 12–18.

Sampson, Robert J., and John H. Laub. 1993. *Crime in the Making: Pathways and Turning Points through Life*. Cambridge, MA: Harvard University Press.

Sampson, Robert J., and John H. Laub. 2003. "Life-Course Desisters? Trajectories of Crime among Delinquent Boys Followed to Age 70." *Criminology* 41: 555–92.

Sampson, Robert J., and John H. Laub. 2005. "A Life-Course View of the Development of Crime." *Annals of the American Academy of Political and Social Science* 602: 12–45.

Shapiro, Susan P. 1984. *Wayward Capitalists: Target of the Securities and Exchange Commission*. New Haven, CT: Yale University Press.

Shapiro, Susan P. 1990. "Collaring the Crime, Not the Criminal: Reconsidering the Concept of White-Collar Crime." *American Sociological Review* 55: 346–65.

Shover, Neal. 2007. "Generative Worlds of White-Collar Crime." In *International Handbook of White-Collar and Corporate Crime*, pp. 81–97, edited by Henry N. Pontell and Gilbert Geis. New York: Springer.

Shover, Neal, and Andrew Hochstetler. 2006. *Choosing White-Collar Crime*. New York: Cambridge University Press.

Sparrow, Malcolm K. 1996. *License to Steal: Why Fraud Plagues America's Health Care System*. Boulder, CO: Westview.

Spencer, John C. 1965. "White-Collar Crime." In *Criminology in Transition*, pp. 233–66, edited by Tadeusz Grygier, Howard Jones, and John C. Spencer. London: Tavistock.

Steffensmeier, Darrell J., Julian Schwartz, and Michelle Roche. 2013. "Gender and 21st-Century Corporate Crime: Female Involvement and the Gender Gap in Enron-Era Corporate Frauds." *American Sociological Review* 78: 448–76.

Stotland, Ezra. 1977. "White-Collar Criminals." *Journal of Social Issues* 33: 179–96.

Sutherland, Edwin H. 1949. *White Collar Crime.* New York: Holt, Rinehart and Winston.

Sutherland, Edwin H. 1983. *White Collar Crime: The Uncut Version.* New Haven, CT: Yale University Press.

Thornberry, Terence P. 1987. "Toward an Interactional Theory of Delinquency." *Criminology* 25: 863–92.

Uggen, Christopher. 2000. "Work as a Turning Point in the Life Course of Criminals: A Duration Model of Age, Employment, and Recidivism." *American Sociological Review* 65: 529–46.

U. S. Federal Bureau of Investigation. 2005. *Financial Crimes Report to the Public, May 2005.* Washington, D.C.: U.S. Department of Justice, Federal Bureau of Investigation.

U. S. Financial Crimes Enforcement Network. 2006. *Mortgage Loan Fraud: An Industry Assessment Based on Suspicious Activity Report Analysis.* November. Washington, D.C.: Office of Regulatory Analysis.

Walters, Glenn D., and Matthew D. Geyer. 2004. "Criminal Thinking and Identity in Male White-Collar Offenders." *Criminal Justice and Behavior* 31: 263–81.

Weisburd, David, Ellen F. Chayet, and Elin J. Waring. 1990. "White-Collar Crime and Criminal Careers: Some Preliminary Findings." *Crime and Delinquency* 36: 342–55.

Weisburd, David, and Elin J. Waring. 2001. *White-Collar Crime and Criminal Careers.* New York: Cambridge University Press.

Weisburd, David, Stanton Wheeler, Elin Waring, and Nancy Bode. 1991. *Crimes of the Middle Classes: White-Collar Offenders in the Federal Courts.* New Haven, CT: Yale University Press.

Wheeler, Stanton. 1992. "The Problem of White-Collar Crime Motivation." In *White-Collar Crime Reconsidered*, pp. 108–23, edited by Kip Schlegel and David Weisburd. Boston: Northeastern University Press.

Wheeler, Stanton, David Weisburd, Elin Waring, and Nancy Bode. 1988. "White-Collar Crime and Criminals." *American Criminal Law Review* 25: 331–57.

Zietz, Dorothy. 1981. *Women Who Embezzle Or Defraud: A Study of Convicted Felons.* New York: Praeger.

PART V

CULTURAL AND INSTITUTIONAL CONTEXTS

CHAPTER 14

WHITE-COLLAR CRIMES
OF THE FINANCIAL CRISIS

SPENCER HEADWORTH AND JOHN L. HAGAN

THIS essay explores U.S. society's relationship to wrongdoing in financial markets, using the 2008 financial crisis as a case study. Our analysis reveals a social situation in which "wrong" actions caused clear and serious social harm. The behaviors in question meet standards for substantiating criminalization from a philosophical point of view and provide multiple opportunities for pursuit of criminal fraud charges. Despite a general trend toward criminalization in U.S. social control and pressure for criminal charges against those whose illegal actions contributed to the 2008 collapse, formal state response has largely been limited to civil proceedings; those criminal charges that have resulted have been concentrated against relatively minor players in the financial world, with only one Wall Street executive receiving prison time. As the five-year statute of limitations on the actions that led to the crisis has taken effect, it is now evident that the top Wall Street executives and firms responsible for creating the financial crisis will avoid criminal prosecution.

We contend that the lack of elite criminalization in connection to the 2008 crisis demonstrates a social situation in which wrongs that benefit some at the expense of many others for the most part constitute a "cost of doing business" that is imposed on society in general. While this "cost" is far from universally accepted as legitimate, it is widely seen as inevitable or beyond the scope of formal social control through the criminal justice system. On the other hand, the civil penalties assessed as a consequence of lawbreaking are also essentially a "business cost," but one that is imposed on elite financial actors who routinely operate on the margins of legality. Below we analyze the causal structures underlying this construction of elite fraud, using the 2008 crisis as an example. Our perspective reflects the multiple and reciprocal causal forces at work in the construction of financial crime as a social fact, showing the intersection of agentic, structural, and cultural influences, rather than relying on an "either/or" style of analysis (Calavita, Pontell, and Tillman 1997, p. 19). Section I explores the role of the state, which plays a key role in shaping markets and which through (de)regulatory action altered the boundaries of legitimacy, legality, and criminality in finance, expanding the realm of explicitly or implicitly sanctioned behaviors. Section II addresses the commission of key categories of action, including pertinent aspects of the finance industry—such as the rise of exotic debt instruments and vertical integration—and the role of both structural and agentic forces in explaining behavior. Section III shifts attention to the aftermath of the crisis and formal and informal attributions of blame, focusing on justifications of key actors' behaviors, framings of wrongdoing and punishment, and how the structure of organizations and markets contributed to the diffusion of responsibility and complicated the process of investigation.

The main conclusions reached in this essay are the following:

- Elite actors provide an exception to the general trend toward criminalization in the United States.
- Combinations of opportunity, rationalization, and "collective delusion" help generate misdeeds in financial markets.
- Framings of the behaviors in question played key roles in both their ex-ante rationalizations and ex-post justifications.
- Organizational, market, and legal structures; state–market interconnections; and the characteristics of financial offenses impede formal social control efforts, particularly criminalization.

I. Role of the State

There is evidence of a cyclical relationship between legal restrictions and ethics in the business world; the two are currently relatively decoupled, with a dominant "law and economics" framework that lauds the invisible hand (Hirsch and Morris 2010). Associated with this decoupling is an orientation toward financial markets that privileges the notions of self-regulation and self-correction over government intervention. "The market," however, is by no means an entity that exists independent of the state (see Harcourt 2011); rather, the state has played a central role in the formation of financial markets and their development over time. The U.S. government's role in developing the financial instruments at the heart of the 2008 financial crisis provides a good example.

Mortgage-backed securities (MBS) are asset-backed investment vehicles that are intended to yield a predictable and continuous cash flow. The assets underlying such securities sometimes extend beyond mortgages to include other forms of debt—for example, car loans and credit card payments. In the case of MBS, the underlying assets are mortgage payments. Banks pool mortgages to create the securities and the resulting stream of future cash payouts—assuming, of course, that reliable payments are made on the mortgages in the pool.

The federal government developed the idea of MBS in the 1960s. Looking to facilitate the growth of mortgage lending without contributing to the national debt (which had expanded notably in the wake of the Vietnam War and the social programs of the Great Society initiative), they transformed the Federal National Mortgage Association from a government organization into a publicly traded company, technically a "government-sponsored enterprise." The Johnson administration also created a competitor for Fannie Mae—the Federal Home Loan Mortgage Corporation, or Freddie Mac—and the Governmental National Mortgage Association, or Ginnie Mae, a government-owned corporation designed to protect against mortgage defaults (Fligstein and Goldstein 2010). Using MBS allowed the state to avoid holding the mortgages and thereby avoid expanding the national debt, while at the same time stimulating the housing market through offering additional home loans. With MBS, investors own the mortgages as bonds, keeping the mortgages off the government's books. Ginnie Mae issued the first MBS in April 1970 (Fligstein and Goldstein 2010).

After the Keynesian orientation of earlier decades, the 1980s marked the beginning of a renaissance for laissez-faire, free-market thinking in Western developed economies. At the core of this ideology is a belief in the efficiency of markets. Over the past three decades, popular and political discourse has shifted toward the conviction that minimally regulated market mechanisms are the best-functioning tools for socioeconomic development. This "neoliberal turn" represented a transition away from the liberal democratic model of the state that dominated the post-World War II political economy. The liberal democratic approach advocated a substantial role for government intervention in the economy to ensure economic stability and growth and to reduce unemployment and promote public welfare. The neoliberal approach, in contrast, prioritized the entrepreneurial activity of economic actors and firms and the free movement of capital (Harvey 2005). Although states remain thoroughly intermeshed in markets, this opinion has proven popular among the general public and among mainstream politicians of varying party identifications.

Ronald Reagan's adamant assertion that "government is not the solution to our problem, government is the problem" offers a succinct summation of the neoliberal vision of the state's role in the economy. The promised benefits of neoliberal economic policies for middle- and lower-class individuals were suggested with aphorisms such as "a rising tide lifts all boats" and with supply-side "trickle-down" tax-cutting policies. The actual results were the accumulation of vastly unequal concentrations of wealth and income among the rich in the United States and other nations since the neoliberal policies gained prominence in the 1980s (Harvey 2005, pp. 16–17; Dobbin and Jung 2010, p. 37).

This is the background context of financial malfeasance in the 2008 crisis. Shifts in political orientations and popular opinion regarding the appropriate role of the state in the economy have provided new opportunities for both licit and illicit practices by powerful actors in the marketplace. In some cases, legal definitions have changed, turning "crime" into "not-crime," officially legitimating once-prohibited forms of profiteering, and reframing white-collar crime scenes as sites of lawful, if unfortunate, market occurrences.

Thus, regulation (and deregulation) of MBS needs to be understood as a dynamic interplay between representatives of the government—which created, developed, and protected the market—and the private-sector actors to whom the government transferred partial ownership and hence ceded additional power, in the context of the neoliberal turn toward "liberated" markets. Lax regulations were crucial in attracting banks to become involved in MBS trading, and banks were successful in deterring expanded regulatory involvement as the market grew and derivative instruments multiplied in complexity in the 1990s and 2000s, resulting in a "passive form of regulatory capture" (Fligstein and Goldstein 2010, p. 63). Firms invested substantial resources in their efforts to shape regulatory policy. The CEO of one subprime company—Ronald Arnall of Ameriquest—and his associates spent more than $20 million on lobbying efforts between 2002 and 2006 (Pozner, Stimmler, and Hirsch 2010, p. 194).

Significant deregulatory activity in this period also reduced state control of the market in important ways. Rollbacks in the regulation and oversight of financial practices received widespread leadership and support from representatives of both major U.S. political parties. In 1999, the banking industry won a major victory with the passage of the Gramm-Leach-Bliley Act, which was sponsored by Republicans but garnered Democratic congressional support and was signed into law by Democrat Bill Clinton.

This legislation repealed major portions of the 1933 Glass-Steagall Act. Passed in response to the Great Depression, Glass-Steagall had prohibited the leveraging of financial speculation based on mergers of investment and commercial banks. Gramm-Leach-Bliley removed these limitations, allowing holding firms to engage simultaneously in investment banking, commercial banking, and insurance. New opportunities opened for financial speculation, leveraging, and riskier forms of profitmaking. Where Glass-Steagall had aimed to reduce the speculative activity linked to the onset of the Great Depression, Gramm-Leach-Bliley permitted banks to devise and deal in debt instruments that had long been off limits to them, including MBS.

The Commodity Futures Modernization Act of 2000—also passed with bipartisan congressional support and signed by President Clinton—helped to fuel a growing Wild West atmosphere surrounding Wall Street trading of derivative instruments, which were in turn based on securitized mortgages. This act removed derivatives from the supervision of the Commodity Futures Trading Commission and the Securities Exchange Commission (SEC).[1] These derivative instruments were based on MBS and credit-default swaps associated with the securitized mortgages.

Removing regulators from the equation greatly increased opportunities for leveraged trading. The Commodity Futures Modernization Act also functioned to displace responsibility for assessing the quality of increasingly complex kinds of derivative instruments from public regulatory agencies to the individuals and firms entering the market as investors. These individual and institutional investors, in turn, relied heavily on the evaluations of an emerging functional oligopoly of major credit-rating agencies.

Credit-rating agencies are private companies that analyze firms and the financial instruments that they produce and provide assessments of their quality as investment vehicles. They occupy a unique position in the world of finance. Because of the complexity of the U.S. financial system, simple categorical ratings and rankings hold great evaluative appeal (see Espeland and Sauder 2007).[2] The agencies' assessments provide essential pieces of information that often drive financial markets. They produce a specialized form of judgmental knowledge that can increase the liquidity of these markets. A credit agency's "seal of approval" can remove for potential investors much of the mystery of debt instruments and thereby lubricate their exchange (Carruthers 2010).

According to standards of best practice, investors and traders should engage in their own due diligence before acquiring an asset-backed security: they should examine the quality of the underlying asset and reach an independent assessment of the investment's riskiness. In practice, however, carrying out such reviews is a difficult and time-intensive process, while speed and efficiency are regarded as essential for successful financial dealings. In lower Manhattan's Wild West atmosphere, as in its 19th-century predecessor, swiftness on the trigger can make the difference in financial terms between the quick and the dead.

So, there is considerable pressure to rely on the assessments of credit-rating agencies. Even among those market actors who do conduct their own evaluations, it is unusual to remove the specialized assessments of credit-rating agencies from the equation (Rona-Tas and Hiss 2011). In theory, these expert assessments should carry a considerable degree of validity; in practice, however, both banks and credit-rating agencies failed to identify accurately the risks of housing mortgages and other kinds of loans and did not fulfill their supposed protective functions.

In a global economic system increasingly driven by finance and credit (Davis 2009; Krippner 2011), the agencies' rankings and analyses of performance and credit worthiness can have massive implications. This notable influence lies almost entirely in the hands of three U.S. firms, which essentially function as a "trio-poly" (Rona-Tas and Hiss 2011, p. 230): Fitch Ratings, Moody's Investors Service, and Standard & Poor's. These "Big Three" credit-rating agencies collectively hold about 95 percent of market share (Alessi and Wolverson 2012, p. 2) in the rating of financial instruments and assets, with about 40 percent each for Moody's and Standard & Poor's and 15 percent for Fitch Ratings. Together, they are responsible for 99 percent of ratings of outstanding asset-backed securities (Rona-Tas and Hiss 2011, p. 230).

The U.S. government has shown considerable reluctance to regulate credit-rating agencies. Despite their great influence, these organizations are primarily self-regulated and operate largely outside the purview of government oversight and control. Further, the SEC allows banks to pay fees to the rating agencies that evaluate the quality of the financial instruments they produce and sell. A partner in the former investment bank Bear Stearns equated this situation to "cattle ranchers paying the Department of Agriculture to rate the quality and safety of their beef" and went on to say that "subprime credit has become the mad cow disease of structured finance" (quoted in Cohan 2009, p. 332).

The high level of complexity of many contemporary structured debt instruments that rating agencies are tasked with assessing further exacerbates this manifest conflict of interest. Innovation in construction of investment vehicles has proceeded so rapidly that even highly trained experts who specialize in evaluating the quality of debt instruments encounter major difficulties fully comprehending them. Of particular note in this regard are collateralized debt obligations. These multifaceted instruments consist of collections of mortgage-backed and other forms of asset-backed securities. These instruments are dynamic in that they can change over time, with byzantine sets of rules expected to maintain consistency in their risk profiles despite changes in their makeup. With these sorts of financial products growing in importance in the market, raters increasingly have found themselves relying on input from the issuers of the instruments, with whom they work in carrying out assessments (Rona-Tas and Hiss 2011). Indeed, some amount of "co-learning" has become an indispensable element of regulatory efforts to deal with the tight coupling and uncertainties inherent in current financial market arrangements; regulation needs to be dynamic, accounting for fast-moving and ongoing changes in the makeup of financial products and their relationships to each other. Regulators are in an "arms race" of financial knowledge with private-sector actors but often must rely substantially on the latter for information (Schneiberg and Bartley 2010).

II. KEY CATEGORIES OF ACTION

Investor demand for MBS grew quickly and was bolstered by deregulation. An expanding collection of mortgage-granting institutions found themselves at the bottom of a vertical chain populated by elite financial organizations. This hierarchical, vertically integrated structure created pressure to increase the number of mortgages that could be pooled into securities for resale through banks to both individual and institutional investors.

A. The Tactic of Subprime Lending

The mortgage lending industry adopted the term "subprime" to refer to loans made to high-risk borrowers. Despite reduced likelihoods of repayment, lenders were able to extend loans to these low-credit-score individuals—often through the use of disguised and escalating interest-rate payment schedules. While the saleable real estate at the core of mortgage-backed instruments hypothetically offered some presumed security in the event of nonpayment, loan defaults at a minimum meant interruptions to the cash flow underlying the securities. One rationale for expanding lending to disadvantaged borrowers was that pooling the mortgages would disperse the risks and thereby help to ensure a profitable return. The assumption was that spreading the pooled risks across different geographical markets, for example, would cushion the effects of possible localized repayment problems.

As was widely reported in the crisis' aftermath, less reputable as well as more reputable mortgage lenders increasingly made home loans available to individuals without requiring evidence of employment or assets consistent with the capacity to make regular payments reliably. In many cases, predatory lending practices were aimed directly and disproportionately at the poor and people of color. This was an ironic reversal of the redlining practices that prevented home loans to the disadvantaged in earlier decades, with the consequence, if not purpose, of exacerbating racial and socioeconomic segregation and inequality (Massey and Denton 1998; Satter 2009). A Wells Fargo loan officer working in Baltimore reported that "the company put 'bounties' on minority borrowers . . . loan officers received cash incentives to aggressively market subprime loans in minority communities" (Powell 2009b, p. 2). Loan officers also received bonuses for issuing high-interest subprime loans to borrowers who qualified for prime rates (Davis 2010).

When pooled and resold as securities, these loans in the aggregate became tantalizing products. In securitizing mortgages, banks organized loans into tranches, ranking them by the ostensible risk of default for the mortgages in the pool. This creation of risk hierarchies through securitization catered to the preferences of different investor categories. The highest tranches were ranked lowest in risk and accordingly paid the lowest interest rates to investors. Lower-ranked tranches boosted interest payments but also brought greater risks. In the event of homeowner defaults, investors in the lowest tranches were the first to stop receiving payments.

One example of the pressure to issue high-risk loans is found in the business of Lehman Brothers, the busiest loan originator on Wall Street before the financial collapse. Lehman used a Colorado-based firm called Aurora Services as its lower-level mortgage-origination arm. Aurora was pressured to make "no-doc loans" to borrowers without documented incomes. A Lehman senior vice president recalled the pressure to make these highly dubious loans: "Anyone at our level who had a different view from senior management would find themselves going somewhere else quick . . . You are not paid to rock the boat" (Story and Thomas 2009, p. 4).

In many cases, adjustable-rate subprime mortgages started with relatively low interest rates for the first year, followed by a dramatic spike in interest charges. This arrangement contributed to the housing market bubble by temporarily propping up unsustainable lending practices. However, as more and more borrowers were unable to make mortgage payments, foreclosures rapidly began to pile up, precipitating the 2008 collapse.

B. The Fallacies and Frauds of Risk Rating

Authoritative assessments of the riskiness of various tranches in pools of securitized mortgages were provided by credit-rating agencies, which in turn were supported through fees paid to them for their rankings by the banks, placing the credit-rating agencies in a classic conflict of interest. Banks also created shell "shadow banks" to sell the highest-risk tranches, avoiding regulation and oversight from federal agencies with authority over the banks but not the shadow institutions they created partly to evade state control; this activity was rendered possible by deregulation under the Gramm-Leach-Bliley Act of 1999 (Campbell 2010; Angelides et al. 2011).

The credit-rating agencies' compromised fee arrangements effectively made raters structurally subordinate to the bankers who employed them. When rating financial instruments involved in trades, agencies did not receive full fee payment until the deal was closed. The high ratings obtained by the asset-backed securities created from subprime mortgages prior to the 2008 crisis suggest the capacity of this conflict of interest to influence and alter assessments of the creditworthiness of such investment vehicles. Banks also demonstrated willingness to patronize other credit-rating agencies if one agency was unwilling to give the superb ratings they desired for their products (Fligstein and Goldstein 2010).

Subprime loans were in high demand by investment banks as the assets to be pooled in forming MBS. In a reversal of conventional practice, investment banks "bundled" the subprime high-interest-paying loans with more ordinary and presumably less risky mortgages. Investors could choose among instruments of varying durations and presumed risks. Subprime-based MBS grew from around 10 percent of the total MBS market in 2003 to nearly 70 percent in 2007 (Fligstein and Goldstein 2010, p. 32).

The appeal of the banks' risk-spreading strategy produced a strong and growing demand for increasing numbers of loans of various types. The large banks at the top of this mortgage-securitization chain pressured the lower-level lenders to increase the supply of high-interest subprime mortgages to mix into the securitization pools. As the pressure for subprime mortgages increased, the quality control over the mortgages decreased, and when mortgage holders started to default not just in one region but all across the country, a foreclosure crisis began.

The Countrywide Financial firm provides an instructive example. This subprime pioneer and national leader in mortgage lending received consistently high evaluations from leading rating agencies, despite its deteriorating lending standards and risky behavior. CEO Angelo Mozilo acknowledged within his company major doubts about the quality of the company's loan portfolio. In one instance, after arranging a nearly $140 million stock selloff, he wrote an e-mail that seemingly acknowledged fraudulent behavior, saying to two other high-ranking Countrywide executives that "We are flying blind on how these loans will perform in a stressed environment of higher unemployment, reduced values and slowing home sales . . . We have no way, with any reasonable certainty, to assess the real risk of holding these loans on our balance sheet" (Scheer, Gullo, and Levy 2009, p. 1). It was not in the interest of Countrywide or the ratings agencies to acknowledge this view publicly, however, since they were being encouraged by higher-level financial institutions such as Bank of America (which ultimately acquired Countrywide) to keep increasing their provision of mortgages.

The three major ratings agencies exaggerated the safety of MBS in the years leading up to the financial crisis, and they did not begin to downgrade their assessments of financial instruments backed by subprime mortgage debt until after the mortgage crisis was under way. After the bubble in the housing market burst, though, downgrades came hot and heavy: in the several months immediately following the collapse, the ratings agencies in total reduced their assessments of MBS by $1.9 trillion. Overnight, instruments regarded as "prime"—the lowest-risk, most secure rating category—were transformed to junk status. Not only were these downgrades too late to ameliorate the impact of the bursting bubble, but they actually exacerbated the damage, as regulations forced banks holding downgraded securities to sell them while simultaneously prohibiting other financial institutions from purchasing them (Surowiecki 2009, p. 25).

While it is clear in retrospect that agencies gave falsely inflated ratings to MBS in the run-up to the 2008 meltdown, there is also evidence to suggest that at least some of those employed by credit-rating agencies were well aware of the problem in advance of the crash. One e-mail exchange between analysts at Standard & Poor's began, "By the way, that deal was ridiculous." A colleague replied, "I know, right—[the] model def[initely] does not capture half the risk," and then, in response to a comment questioning whether the firm should be rating the deal at all, "We rate every deal. It could be structured by cows and we would rate it" (Cohan 2009, pp. 331–32).

Historically, mortgage issuers retained ownership of the asset collateral until the loan matured and was paid off. Securitization, though, can curtail lenders' incentive to see a mortgage paid off. Pooling and selling off mortgages as parts of asset-backed securities diminishes the significance of the risk of default to the original lender. However, as Fligstein and Goldstein (2010) demonstrated, all the major mortgage and MBS issuers retained significant volumes of the securities—except Goldman Sachs and to some extent JPMorgan—all the way up to the crisis. Indeed, banks and MBS bundlers increased their holdings by hundreds of billions of dollars in the years leading up to the crisis, at the same time as these instruments were growing more and more high risk (Fligstein and Goldstein 2010).[3]

The best explanation for these actions is that the banks substantially believed assessments of the risks as controllable—or they believed they ultimately were protected by their "too big to fail" status. For their part, authoritative state figures did not dispute the elite rankings that credit-rating agencies gave to subprime MBS; the Federal Reserve's open-market committee agreed with the agencies' view that risks within the housing market were manageable (Sorkin and Walsh 2013). This suggests the importance of a "collective, field-wide delusion" (Fligstein and Goldstein 2010, p. 59) or diffused "irrational exuberance" (Shiller [2000] 2006, pp. 1–2) in inflating the housing bubble and precipitating the crisis. Powerful actors shared the belief that the market was characterized primarily by risk—unknown but knowable—rather than uncertainty and that that risk could be managed effectively (Levi 2009; Schneiberg and Bartley 2010).

Thus, the evidence suggests an important systematic causal role for a shared set of understandings about the nature of the market. Although the fact that firms retained their own MBS holdings creates a problem for any purely rational choice perspective that depicts profit-oriented firms acting rationally to fleece investors, damning statements like Mozilo's "flying blind" remarks show that individuals representing these firms acted deceptively. Deregulation and market structures undoubtedly created environments of "lure," with opportunities and temptations for this type of deception-based lawbreaking (Shover and Hochstetler 2006), and the role of agency within this context should not be abandoned. Elite actors acted deliberately and deceptively, aware of the potential for social harm, even if they genuinely underestimated the riskiness of the situation. Intentionality intersected with structural characteristics, with complexity and tight coupling exacerbating the consequences (Perrow 2010).

Actors used techniques of neutralization such as appeals to higher loyalties to rationalize their wrongdoing (Sykes and Matza 1957; Cressey [1953] 1973; Maruna and Copes 2005). These rationalizations or techniques of neutralization were deployed as motivations that "permit" illegal behaviors, not just justifications of them after the fact. In the case of mortgage lending and securitization, the dominant expressed logic was "expanding opportunities for home ownership."

C. Subprime Mortgages and the Ownership Society

Those involved in the process suggested that the existence of subprime mortgages provided the chance to obtain a home loan and build equity for people who otherwise might not have had such options available to them: the poor and people with either bad credit or no credit. This framing of the push for high-interest loans to finance the purchase of a home was indicative of a wider move toward an "ownership society," championed by the George W. Bush administration in the middle to late 2000s. This program sought to make individual Americans into "agents of their own destiny" (in the president's words) and to tie outcomes for households to the market performance of owned (or borrowed) assets such as homes and securities (Davis 2009, pp. 3–4). The ownership society meant finding novel finance-based tools to replace the disintegrating welfare state and decline of corporate welfarism and to take on issues of retirement and healthcare.

The existence of securitization and mortgage-backed financial instruments, this line of reasoning argued, made it possible for lenders to hedge the risks of delinquency and default and to continue offering the loans that propelled a broad-based shift toward an ownership society. In the abstract, this sounded like an attractive goal, with possibilities of ameliorating some of the past injustices in U.S. housing practices and expanding the socioeconomic opportunities engendered by home ownership and equity building.

But the realities of subprime lending in the run-up to the 2008 crisis tell a different story. In one particularly telling example, an e-mail from the Goldman Sachs mortgage department referred to the "shitty deal" the bank was giving its investor clients by recommending investments based on a pool of questionable subprime mortgages (Adams 2010), which clearly illustrates the disconnect between the language of empowerment and equality and the banks' deliberate profiteering practices. Conflicting value sets operated simultaneously in such situations: banks were striving to maximize profits while also expressing an interest in broadening economic opportunities. Observable outcomes, however, suggest that one of these value sets (i.e., profits) characteristically took precedence over the other.

Many banks disproportionately sought borrowers of color using predatory lending practices, subprime loans, and their accompanying exorbitant interest rates. More than 50 percent of home loans held by African-American and Latino borrowers were subprime loans with elevated interest rates, and these borrowers were three times more likely than their white counterparts to hold such loans. In the years leading up to the 2008 crash, middle-income African-American households were nearly five times more likely than their white counterparts to hold subprime mortgages.

The NAACP led a class-action suit that named more than a dozen banks in allegations of racially discriminatory lending practices (Powell 2009a, 2009b, 2009c, 2010). Even before the widespread delinquencies and defaults of the mortgage crisis, predatory lending in communities of color had cost homeowners tens of billions in lost equity (Rivera et al. 2008). More broadly, expanding home mortgage lending to higher-risk homebuyers ended up raising interest rates for all mortgage borrowers, while investors lost countless millions on high-risk securities that investment banks marketed to their own advantage with fees, insurance, and short sales (Morgenson and Rosner 2011). By late 2009, 25 percent of U.S. mortgages were underwater (Davis 2010, p. 341).

III. AFTERMATH OF THE CRISIS

The philosophical question at the heart of considerations of criminalization is that of *wrongdoing*. Whereas noncriminal sanctions are designed to prevent harm and compensate, criminal sanctions serve another purpose. Criminalization functions to express social condemnation for actions that constitute "public wrongs" (Duff and Green 2005). According to the Harm Principle (Feinberg 1984), to substantiate a crime, it must be shown that harm resulted from the action in question, and that the seriousness of the crime trumps competing considerations, such as the autonomy of the actor. "Pure" property crimes such as theft constitute clear harms against victims that outweigh claims to independent action. Offenses that are based on obtaining property by means of deception are doubly harmful, in that they do harm both directly to victims and indirectly to the broader community by harming social trust and transactional confidence (Simester and Sullivan 2005; see also Sutherland [1949] 1983; Shapiro 1984, 1987).

Some of the actions that precipitated the 2008 collapse, while of dubious ethicality, were not illegal (Hirsch and Morris 2010). Others, however, clearly were. The SEC actively pursued civil and administrative actions in connection with this lawbreaking against many of the country's largest financial firms and their representatives, including Bank of America, Bear Stearns, Charles Schwab, Citigroup, Countrywide, Fannie Mae and Freddie Mac, Goldman Sachs, JPMorgan Chase, and Wells Fargo. In total, it has brought noncriminal charges against more than 150 organizations and individuals, including 65 senior corporate officials. These actions have resulted in more than $2.5 billion in penalties, disgorgement, and other monetary relief (SEC 2013). The settlements also come with statements that no wrongdoing is acknowledged by the penalized parties, however, and thereby they explicitly avoid the condemnatory element that distinguishes criminalization.

In the bulk of these cases, criminal charges could have been pursued in conjunction with, or in place of, noncriminal legal action, under state or federal statutes. Certainly, actions under consideration meet the two-pronged standard of a public wrong posed by property crimes of deception, with enormous direct losses and serious damage to trust and confidence both domestically and abroad. Yet, there have been no criminal prosecutions of top Wall Street firms in response to deceptive actions in financial markets in the run-up to the crisis. And only one Wall Street executive was sent to prison for his actions—Kareem Serageldin, a former Credit Suisse investment banker, who received a two-and-a-half year federal prison sentence for misrepresenting the value of securities in the heat of the crisis. The mortgage executives and bank CEOs directly responsible for the creation of the climate in which he acted all avoided similar punishment (Eisinger 2014).[4]

A handful of smaller players have been criminally charged for their roles in the crisis. A notable conviction came against Lee B. Farkas, who in June 2011 was sentenced to thirty years in federal prison for a long-running scheme at a relatively small Florida mortgage firm that defrauded investors and the government of billions (Protess 2011). Criminal justice authorities significantly expanded attention to mortgage fraud in response to the housing market collapse, with a particular focus on subprime loans. In 2008, the FBI carried out "Operation Malicious Mortgage," charging more than 400 defendants across the country in connection with mortgage fraud and netting scores of convictions. This action was carried out with an explicit commitment to general deterrence, with a concordant emphasis on Beccarian swiftness, certainty, and severity. FBI Director Robert Mueller stated: "To persons who are involved in such schemes, we will find you, you will be investigated, and you will be prosecuted . . . to those who would contemplate misleading, engaging in such schemes, you will spend time in jail" (FBI 2008, p. 1).

As noted, Bear Stearns was among the major Wall Street firms targeted for civil action by the SEC. Earlier, two disgraced Bear Stearns fund managers brought up on federal criminal fraud charges were found not guilty in November 2009. Jurors in the case concluded that the two men may have been foolhardy and greedy, but that prosecutors failed to prove beyond a reasonable doubt the intent necessary to substantiate criminal fraud (Kouwe and Slater 2009). Since the failure to obtain a conviction in this case, authorities have demonstrated reluctance to pursue criminal cases. After a high-profile investigation of former Countrywide chief Mozilo, prosecutors abandoned their effort to bring criminal charges in the case in favor of a civil settlement. American

International Group's (AIG) Joseph Cassano saw his criminal charges dropped (Kerem 2012). It is now apparent that no major criminal charges will be pressed against those most responsible for the subprime debacle.

With the clear public wrongs represented by actions precipitating the crisis, the ability to bring civil and administrative actions successfully against elite actors and criminal charges against others, widespread popular support for condemnation through criminalization, and a new administration carried into office in 2008 in substantial part on a wave of populist anti-Wall Street rhetoric, one might ask why criminal charges against elite parties did not eventuate. Individual decisions to prosecute or not prosecute lie with prosecutorial authorities; in these cases, the rationales between prosecuting agents' decisions not to pursue charges obviously vary between different potential defendants. However, it is possible to identify some common threads uniting the body of noncriminalized elite actors.

A. Difficulties of Criminal Convictions

Two aspects of U.S. criminal proceedings are particularly noteworthy in complicating their application to financial offenses: the necessity of proving intent and the "beyond a reasonable doubt" standard for conviction (Benson and Cullen 1998). Both of these characteristics of criminal trials came up in the acquittal of the two Bear Stearns representatives. In general, substantiating criminal intent and proving charges beyond a reasonable doubt can be very difficult in large and complex cases of the sort that are brought against high-level Wall Street firms or their leaders. Civil proceedings, on the other hand, do not require demonstration of criminal intent, and instead require a more lenient "preponderance of the evidence" standard.

In instances of street crime, investigators usually begin with the "what" of the case: a specific offense, reported or observed, for which they attempt to identify and apprehend the responsible party. In financial crime cases, however, it is common for investigations to begin with the "who": a suspected wrongdoer (individual or organization), whose actions must be traced carefully in an effort to identify clearly illegal or criminal offenses (Calavita et al. 1997; see also Benson 2001). This process is time-consuming, laborious, expensive, and often extremely daunting, in terms of obtaining the necessary evidence, processing it, and presenting it in a way that is deemed likely to lead to a guilty plea or conviction. While research has demonstrated the greater likelihood of criminal charges eventuating in cases with larger numbers of victims and greater visible costs, it is also the case that individuals are more likely than organizations to face criminal prosecution (Shapiro 1984). The difficulty of substantiating *mens rea* for actions committed over an extended timeframe in a large organizational setting goes a substantial way toward explaining the tendency for criminal charges to eventuate in high-profile cases with a clearly blameworthy individual architect, such as the Madoff and Stanford Ponzi schemes, but not in cases where misrepresentation and deception are submerged in a corporate context, such as Countrywide's Mozilo and AIG's Cassano.

B. Defendants' Status, Resources, and Connections

In general, research has suggested that criminal justice systems in Western democracies tend to favor higher-status offenders over their lower-status counterparts in cases of potential white-collar crime at the stages of legislation (Savelsberg and Brühl 1994), prosecution (Hagan and Parker 1985; Benson and Cullen 1998), and defense (Mann 1985). Criminal laws directed at white-collar offending may be proposed with an eye toward elite offenders but can end up being applied to lower-status actors (Savelsberg and Brühl 1994). Their financial resources and social capital provide high-status individuals with many opportunities to influence social response to potentially criminal behavior (Levi 2009).

Large financial firms also employ the finest defense lawyers that money can buy. In recent years, a "new normal" has developed for high-level finance-crime defendants: not only do defense lawyers of the highest caliber represent them, but their lawyers are of a particular type—from elite corporate law firms, and mostly former federal prosecutors (Weisselberg and Li 2011). White-collar defense includes a phase of discussion and negotiation between defense and prosecution that is almost entirely unheard of in other types of criminal proceedings (Mann 1985); one author calls the process "conference room litigation" (Buell 2013, p. 50). The result is that negotiated settlements in the form of deferred prosecution agreements, nonprosecution agreements, and other deals often replace plea bargains involving admission of wrongdoing or the advancement of a conventional adversarial process. As in regulatory initiatives, state efforts to sanction wrongdoers demonstrate the interconnection of market actors and state authorities, with officials regularly moving through the "revolving door" between financial firms, law firms, and the public sector.

C. Negative Socioeconomic Consequences

The idea of "too big to fail" encouraged bank bailouts after the housing collapse; "too big to jail" or "too big for trial" have become buzzwords in the discussion around the lack of criminal prosecution for elite actors in the aftermath of the crisis. Attorney General Eric Holder recently reiterated such sentiments in defending the Department of Justice's failure to bring charges against those most culpable in bringing about the crisis and subsequent recession. The collapse of Arthur Andersen in the wake of the Enron scandal is pointed to as evidence of a "corporate death penalty" that results from criminalization efforts; in that case, charges were later dropped, but not before the firm had collapsed and 28,000 jobs had been lost (Protess 2013). Many fear the consequences of pursuing criminalization of more economically central entities.

Authorities favor economic stability and a rationalist "risk management" approach over the retributive, emotive impulses given greater influence in cases of more immediate and visible street crimes. Offenders may be seen as generally within tolerable limits of deviance, or their actions as a part of capitalism that is difficult or impossible to prevent or is ultimately acceptable in light of perceived benefits of the system itself (Levi 2009). Although research suggests that U.S. residents generally perceive white-collar crime as serious and favor its punishment (Holtfreter et al. 2008), both before and after the 2008 crash, polls of public opinion showed high levels of support for a relatively unfettered market economy. In the years immediately following the collapse, Gallup found that only a quarter of U.S. respondents believed there was "too little government regulation of business and industry," while more than half "worried that there will be too much government regulation of business" (Harcourt 2011, p. 11).

IV. Conclusions

In a recent interview with *The New York Times*, Preet Bharara, the U.S. Attorney for the Southern District of New York (which includes Wall Street), spoke frankly about white-collar criminals and potential white-collar criminals working in the elite world of high finance. He noted that many people in the field "are highly skilled at cost-benefit analysis. They're highly intelligent. They've been to the best schools. They weigh the risk of getting caught against the potential reward, and they decide it's worth the risk. We're trying to tilt that equation" (quoted in Stewart 2012, p. 2).

Yet Bharara and others who seek to prevent and prosecute white-collar crime face an uphill battle. The quote suggests the influence of the rational actor model and deterrence strategies on white-collar criminal justice practice. Yet, an array of structural factors beyond rational agency are at work. In recent years, a neoliberal political context and accompanying public opinion have made financial crime easier and more profitable to commit with impunity. Deregulation and vertical integration have expanded opportunities for crime, and its criminalization has grown more difficult. The 2008 crisis starkly demonstrated the devastating socioeconomic consequences that can result from such financial abuses.

As suggested and encouraged by Bharara, the financial crisis has sparked a critical reevaluation of permissive attitudes toward questionable business practices in both the political and financial spheres. These efforts respond to the kinds of concerns raised by the perspective we have advocated. Yet the results of U.S. social control efforts have been uneven across areas of financial crime.

Bharara's U.S. Attorney's Office has been successful in obtaining criminal convictions against individuals for insider trading. The courts have allowed aggressive investigative tactics in pursuit of these crimes. In contrast, civil rather than criminal prosecutions have been the norm in the mortgage securitization market central to the financial crisis. There is a notable failure to hold high-ranking financial elites criminally accountable for practices associated with mortgage securitization. The Department of Justice, however, has shown signs of interest in pushing for guilty pleas in place of fines and reforms. Prosecutors obtained guilty pleas to criminal fraud charges from Japanese subsidiaries of UBS and the Royal Bank of Scotland (RBS) in connection with the Libor rate-fixing scandal. While these are remote subsidiaries of non-U.S. banks, the UBS and RBS guilty pleas represent U.S. authorities' first successful criminal action against a major financial institution in more than ten years (Scott and Protess 2012), and officials have asserted their intentions to use a similar approach more widely in financial fraud cases (Protess 2013). It remains to be seen how realistic or effective the tool of criminalization can be for preventing or ameliorating financial disasters like the 2008 crisis.

Notes

1. In general, derivatives are financial instruments based on speculation regarding future changes in the value of various assets and comprising contracts to buy or sell under particular conditions.
2. Instead of continuous quantitative scores, credit-rating agencies use categorical letter-based assessments. The specifics of these grading schemes vary slightly between organizations.
3. It is unclear exactly how higher-ups perceived the riskiness of the business in which their subordinates were increasingly miring them. It is not unlikely that they relied on a general belief in the fundamental safety of the housing market as an area of investment, assuming that if a collapse did ensue, the government would bail them out in fear of wider economic catastrophe (Fligstein and Goldstein 2010). Subsequent events, of course, demonstrated the error of the first belief but the soundness of the second.
4. There have in recent years been successful criminal charges against some other high-profile fraudsters whose crimes were not connected to the 2008 crisis, such as convicted Ponzi schemers Bernard Madoff and Allen Stanford. The relatively straight-forward nature of the fraud and clear individual culpability in these cases make them more conducive to criminal prosecution.

References

Adams, Richard. 2010. "Goldman Sachs Senate Hearing: As It Happened." *The Guardian* (April 27).

Alessi, Christopher, and Roya Wolverson. 2012. "The Credit Rating Controversy." Council on Foreign Relations. Available at http://www.cfr.org/united-states/credit-rating-controversy/ p223–28

Angelides, Phil, Brooksley Born, Byron Georgiou, Bob Graham, Heather H. Murren, and John W. Thompson. 2011. *The Financial Crisis Inquiry Report*. Washington, D.C.: The Financial Crisis Inquiry Commission.

Benson, Michael L. 2001. "Investigating Corporate Crime: Local Responses to Fraud and Environmental Crime." *Western University Law Review* 28: 87–116.

Benson, Michael L., and Francis T. Cullen. 1998. *Combating Corporate Crime: Local Prosecutors at Work*. Boston: Northeastern University Press.

Buell, Samuel W. 2013. "Is the White-Collar Offender Privileged?" *Duke Law Journal* 63: 823–90.

Calavita, Kitty, Henry N. Pontell, and Robert H. Tillman. 1997. *Big Money Crime: Fraud and Politics in the Savings and Loan Crisis*. Berkeley: University of California Press.

Campbell, John L. 2010. "Neoliberalism in Crisis: Regulatory Roots of the U.S. Financial Meltdown." In *Markets on Trial: The Economic Sociology of the U.S. Financial Crisis: Part B*, pp. 65–101, edited by Michael Lounsbury and Paul M. Hirsch. Bingley, UK: Emerald Group.

Carruthers, Bruce. 2010. "Knowledge and Liquidity: Institutional and Cognitive Foundations of the Subprime Crisis." In *Markets on Trial: The Economic Sociology of the U.S. Financial Crisis: Part A*, pp. 157–82, edited by Michael Lounsbury and Paul M. Hirsch. Bingley, UK: Emerald Group Publishing.

Cohan, William D. 2009. *House of Cards: A Tale of Hubris and Wretched Excess on Wall Street*. New York: Doubleday.

Cressey, Donald R. [1953] 1973. *Other People's Money: A Study of the Social Psychology of Embezzlement*. Montclair, NJ: Patterson Smith.

Davis, Gerald F. 2009. *Managed by the Markets: How Finance Re-Shaped America*. New York: Oxford University Press.

Davis, Gerald F. 2010. "After the Ownership Society: Another World Is Possible." In *Markets on Trial: The Economic Sociology of the U.S. Financial Crisis: Part B*, pp. 331–56, edited by Michael Lounsbury and Paul M. Hirsch. Bingley, UK: Emerald Group.

Dobbin, Frank, and Jiwook Jung. 2010. "The Misapplication of Mr. Michael Jensen: How Agency Theory Brought Down the Economy and Why It Might Again." In *Markets on Trial: The Economic Sociology of the U.S. Financial Crisis: Part B*, pp. 29–64, edited by Michael Lounsbury and Paul M. Hirsch. Bingley, UK: Emerald Group.

Duff, R. A., and Stuart P. Green. 2005. *Defining Crimes: Essays on the Special Part of the Criminal Law*. New York: Oxford University Press.

Eisinger, Jesse. 2014. "Why Only One Top Banker Went to Jail for the Financial Crisis." *New York Times Magazine*, May 4, 2014: MM34.

Espeland, Wendy Nelson, and Michael Sauder. 2007. "Rankings and Reactivity: How Public Measures Recreate Social Worlds." *American Journal of Sociology* 113: 1–40.

Federal Bureau of Investigation. 2008. "'Malicious' Mortgage Fraud: More than 400 Charged Nationwide." Washington, D.C.: Author.

Feinberg, Joel. 1984. *Harm to Others*. New York: Oxford University Press.

Fligstein, Neil, and Adam Goldstein. 2010. "The Anatomy of the Mortgage Securitization Crisis." In *Markets on Trial: The Economic Sociology of the U.S. Financial Crisis: Part A*, pp. 29–70, edited by Michael Lounsbury and Paul M. Hirsch. Bingley, UK: Emerald Group.

Hagan, John, and Patricia Parker. 1985. "White-Collar Crime and Punishment." *American Sociological Review* 45: 802–20.

Harcourt, Bernard E. 2011. *The Illusion of Free Markets: Punishment and the Myth of Natural Order*. Cambridge, MA: Harvard University Press.

Harvey, David. 2005. *A Brief History of Neoliberalism*. New York: Oxford University Press.

Hirsch, Paul M., and Mary-Hunter Morris. 2010. "Immoral but not Illegal: Monies vs. Mores Amidst the Mortgage Meltdown." *Strategic Organization* 8: 60–75.

Holtfreter, Kristy, Shanna Van Slyke, Jason Bratton, and Marc Gertz. 2008. "Public Perceptions of White-Collar Crime and Punishment." *Journal of Criminal Justice* 36: 50–60.

Kerem, David. 2012. "Change We Can Believe In: Comparative Perspectives on the Criminalization of Corporate Negligence." *Transactions: The Tennessee Journal of Business Law* 14: 95–115.

Kouwe, Zachery, and Dan Slater. 2009. "2 Bear Stearns Fund Leaders Are Acquitted." *New York Times* (November 10).

Krippner, Greta R. 2011. *Capitalizing on Crisis: The Political Origins of the Rise of Finance.* Cambridge, MA: Harvard University Press.

Levi, Michael. 2009. "Suite Revenge? The Shaping of Folk Devils and Moral Panics about White-collar Crimes." *British Journal of Criminology* 49: 48–67.

Mann, Kenneth. 1985. *Defending White-Collar Crime: A Portrait of Attorneys at Work.* New Haven, CT: Yale University Press.

Maruna, Shadd, and Heith Copes. 2005. "What Have We Learned from Five Decades of Neutralization Research?" *Crime and Justice* 32: 221–320.

Massey, Douglas, and Nancy Denton. 1998. *American Apartheid: Segregation and the Making of the Underclass.* Cambridge, MA: Harvard University Press.

Morgenson, Gretchen, and Joshua Rosner. 2011. *Reckless Endangerment: How Outsized Ambition, Greed, and Corruption Created the Worst Financial Crisis of Our Time.* New York: St. Martin's Griffin.

Perrow, Charles. 2007. *The Next Catastrophe: Reducing Our Vulnerabilities to Natural, Industrial, and Terrorist Disasters.* Princeton, NJ: Princeton University Press.

Powell, Michael. 2009a. "Blacks and Latinos Are Hit Hardest as New York Foreclosures Rise." *New York Times* (May 17).

Powell, Michael. 2009b. "Suit Accuses Wells Fargo of Steering Blacks to Sub-Prime Mortgages in Baltimore." *New York Times* (June 7).

Powell, Michael. 2009c. "Memphis Accuses Wells Fargo of Discriminating against Blacks." *New York Times* (December 30).

Powell, Michael. 2010. "Federal Judge Rejects Suit by Baltimore against Bank." *New York Times* (January 8).

Pozner, Jo-Ellen, Mary Kate Stimmler, and Paul M. Hirsch. 2010. "Terminal Isomorphism and the Self-Destructive Potential of Success: Lessons from Subprime Mortgage Origination and Securitization." In *Markets on Trial: The Economic Sociology of the U.S. Financial Crisis: Part A*, pp. 183–218, edited by Michael Lounsbury and Paul M. Hirsch. Bingley, UK: Emerald Group.

Protess, Ben. 2011. "Mortgage Executive Receives 30-Year Sentence." *New York Times* (June 30).

Protess, Ben. 2013. "Prosecutors, Shifting Strategy, Build New Wall Street Cases." *New York Times* (February 18).

Rivera, Amaad, Brenda Cotto-Escalera, Anisha Desai, Jeannette Huezo, and Dedrick Muhammad. 2008. *Foreclosed: State of the Dream 2008.* Boston: Institute for Policy Studies, United for a Fair Economy. Available at http://www.faireconomy.org/files/pdf/StateOfDream_01_16_08_Web.pdf

Rona-Tas, Akos, and Stefanie Hiss. 2011. "Forecasting as Valuation: The Role of Ratings and Predictions in the Subprime Mortgage Crisis in the United States." In *The Worth of Goods: Valuation and Pricing in the Economy*, pp. 223–46, edited by Jens Beckert and Patrick Aspers. New York: Oxford University Press.

Savelsberg, Joachim, and Peter Brühl. 1994. *Constructing White-Collar Crime: Rationalities, Communication, Power.* Philadelphia, PA: University of Pennsylvania Press.

Scheer, David, Karen Gullo, and Ari Levy. 2009. "Mozilo Saw Countrywide 'Flying Blind,' Dumped Stock, SEC Claims." *Bloomberg* (June 5).

Schneiberg, Mark, and Tim Bartley. 2010. "Regulating or Redesigning Finance? Market Architectures, Normal Accidents, and Dilemmas of Regulatory Reform." In *Markets on*

Trial: The Economic Sociology of the U.S. Financial Crisis: Part A, pp. 281–308, edited by Michael Lounsbury and Paul M. Hirsch. Bingley, UK: Emerald Group.

Scott, Mark, and Ben Protess. 2012. "As Unit Pleads Guilty, UBS Pays $1.5 Billion over Rate Rigging." *New York Times* (December 19).

Securities and Exchange Commission (SEC). 2013. *SEC Enforcement Actions Addressing Misconduct that Led to or Arose from the Financial Crisis.* Washington, D.C.: Author.

Shapiro, Susan P. 1984. *Wayward Capitalists: Target of the Securities and Exchange Commission.* New Haven, CT: Yale University Press.

Shapiro, Susan P. 1987. "The Social Control of Impersonal Trust." *American Journal of Sociology* 93: 623–58.

Shiller, Robert J. [2000] 2005. *Irrational Exuberance*, 2nd ed. Princeton, NJ: Princeton University Press.

Shover, Neal, and Andy Hochstetler. 2006. *Choosing White-Collar Crime.* New York: Cambridge University Press.

Simester, A. P., and G. R. Sullivan. 2005. "The Nature and Rationale of Property Offenses." In *Defining Crimes: Essays on the Special Part of the Criminal Law*, edited by R. A. Duff and Stuart P. Green. New York: Oxford University Press, pp. 168–95.

Sorkin, Andrew Ross, and Mary Williams Walsh. 2013. "U.S. Accuses S. & P. of Fraud in Suit on Loan Bundles." *New York Times* (February 4).

Stewart, James B. 2012. "In a New Era of Insider Trading, It's Risk vs. Reward Squared." *New York Times* (December 7).

Story, Louise, and Landon Thomas, Jr. 2009. "Tales from Lehman's Crypt." *New York Times* (September 13).

Surowiecki, James. 2009. "Ratings Downgrade." *New Yorker* (September 28).

Sutherland, Edwin H. [1949] 1983. *White Collar Crime: The Uncut Version.* New Haven, CT: Yale University Press.

Sykes, Gresham M., and David Matza. 1957. "Techniques of Neutralization: A Theory of Delinquency." *American Sociological Review* 22: 664–70.

Weisselberg, Charles D., and Su Li. 2011. "Big Law's Sixth Amendment: The Rise of Corporate White-Collar Practices in Large U.S. Law Firms." *Arizona Law Review* 53: 1221–99.

CHAPTER 15

ORGANIZATIONAL POLITICAL ECONOMY AND WHITE-COLLAR CRIME

HARLAND PRECHEL

THE financial failures of large corporations in the early 2000s (e.g., Adelphia, Enron, WorldCom), the 2008 financial crisis, and the Great Recession had widespread effects on individuals and societies. These effects include the loss of wealth through the precipitous decline in housing values, persistently high unemployment, decreased economic mobility, and record levels of income and wealth inequality.[1] While these issues received considerable attention by researchers, much less is known about the mechanisms that permitted the behaviors that contributed to corporate failures and the crisis. Even less attention has been given to the mechanisms that encouraged the middle and working classes to shift their assets from savings accounts, pensions, and other relatively secure investments to riskier corporate securities and mutual funds. To fill this gap in the literature, the analysis here examines how organizational and political–legal changes in the social structure (1) created incentives for the working classes to shift their savings into riskier investments and (2) permitted the managers of those investments to engage in risk-taking behaviors and corporate wrongdoing.

A key concept in this chapter is *financialization*. Financialization is a complex concept that has been defined in different ways. In general, financialization is the expansion of financial organizations and markets in national and international economies. In this essay, financialization is defined more precisely as the organizational and political–legal arrangements that facilitate making profits and increasing value for companies and their shareholders through financial transactions. Making profits and increasing the value of a company through financial transactions contrast with the production and sale of physical commodities such as automobiles and providing services such as healthcare.

To illustrate, in the United States, after a bank makes a mortgage loan to a home buyer, it can sell the mortgage on the secondary mortgage market to another company, such as an investment bank. The investment bank can in turn accumulate hundreds of mortgages and combine them into mortgage-backed securities that it can then sell to investors. In each of these transactions, the parties hope to make a profit even though the underlying asset has not changed. In the case of a home mortgage, the underlying asset is the house. The bank makes a profit by selling the home mortgage on the secondary market and the investment bank makes a profit by selling mortgage-backed securities. Investors in these securities, which may be individuals or mutual fund managers, hope to make a profit from the interest and principal paid by the homeowner. All of these transactions are facilitated by organizational and political–legal arrangements. And just as mortgages can be transformed into securities, virtually all other products and services can be transformed into financial instruments that can be bought and sold on financial markets. However, profits at all levels of this process are dependent on the value of the underlying asset (e.g., houses purchased by homeowners). If the value of houses declines and homeowners default on their mortgages, the value of the securities sold to investors also declines.

Researchers who focus on the organizational and political dimension of the 2007-2008 crisis maintain that the co-evolution of regulators and banks put the government in a position to create new financial markets (Fligstein and Goldstein 2010) or assume that an autonomous state created policies that facilitated financialization (Campbell 2010; Krippner 2010). Others suggest that the financial crisis was a normal accident that occurs in complex structures where events cannot be predicted (Palmer 2010). Still others maintain that the crisis was caused by cultural shifts inside organizations that created a norm of risk-taking behavior (Abolafia 2010).

Although these perspectives provide insight into the financial crisis, they ignore corporate–state relations or assume that the state acted autonomously in creating laws and rules that facilitated financialization. As a result, these perspectives fail to examine how the exercise of corporate and class power redefines corporate–state relations in ways that permit new markets to emerge in the first place (Prechel and Morris 2010). Therefore, it is necessary to examine how class power, which has its origins outside the state, is exercised in ways that permit new markets to emerge. The analysis here suggests that (1) prevailing theoretical perspectives are too narrowly focused to capture the complex mechanisms that permit new financial markets to emerge and wrongdoing to occur and (2) empirical studies do not operate within a sufficiently long timeframe and lack sufficient depth of analysis. What are needed, therefore, are a broader theoretical framework and a more in-depth historical analysis that investigates *how* changes in the social structure permitted new financial markets to emerge and malfeasance, chicanery, and crime in them to occur.

The conceptual framework focuses on how corporate and class powers were exercised to redefine the organizational and political–legal arrangements in ways that created the conditions for managers to engage in financialization and financial wrongdoing. The central theoretical tenets suggest that capitalists exercise power to redefine state policies and structures in ways that make behaviors, which were previously illegal or not viable, perfectly legal. This social structure, in turn, creates opportunities and incentives for corporate managers to pursue their self-interest with guile.

The analysis focuses on *financial wrongdoing*, which is defined here as (1) acts that violate a law or the intent of a law established by government or nongovernmental agencies responsible for corporate financial oversight and (2) acts that violate the public's understanding of the code of conduct that is supposed to define business behavior.[2] This focus on financial wrongdoing is consistent with the tradition in criminology that adopts Durkheim's (1933) conception of *morality*: activity that is oriented toward the benefit of the social whole and is characterized by feelings of obligation and desirability. The political and economic analysis also addresses Durkheim's underlying concern with the consequences for society when self-interests prevail.

Although financialization is frequently conceptualized as a market phenomenon and associated with investment banking activities such as underwriting of securities and creating financial products, the specific historical form of financialization is defined by the political–legal arrangement in which corporations and markets are embedded. Despite the increased attention to financialization by social scientists in recent years, there is nothing new about financialization as a means to accumulate capital. To illustrate, financialization in the form of derivatives existed for most of the 20th century. Derivatives represent future streams of income for investors from underlying assets that can include anything representing ownership, such as currency, agricultural commodities, home mortgages, and corporate securities (Levitt 2002; Partnoy 2004). To illustrate, derivatives were used in the early 20th century to coordinate the production of agricultural commodities such as corn, soybean, wheat, hogs, and cattle to ensure an adequate supply of food for the expanding urban population. Agricultural derivatives are simply contracts that ensure farmers a price for their products when they are delivered to buyers. These futures contracts are traded on regulated exchanges such as the Chicago Mercantile. Derivatives are also widely used in the banking sector, where contracts on foreign-exchange rates ensure an adequate supply of currency to carry out international transactions (*Oxford Dictionary of Business Management* 2006, p. 164).

What is different about the late 20th century is the rapid expansion of financial markets, nonfinancial corporations participating in financialization, and the increase in information asymmetries in financial markets. The analysis that follows identifies the underlying political, economic, and organizational mechanisms that permitted these characteristics to emerge, thereby creating opportunities for corporate managers to engage in wrongdoing. The primary conclusions include the following:

- Neoliberal ideology and market fundamentalism emerged as a guide to public policy.
- In response to capital accumulation constraints and capital shortages, capitalists and managers successfully lobbied government officials to redefine the political–legal arrangements in ways that encouraged the middle and working classes to invest in corporate securities.

- Although some of the first innovative financial instruments were created in the manufacturing sector, the energy and financial sectors formed a powerful political coalition that pressured government officials to extend the outside parameters of the law to permit new forms of financialization.
- The emergent organizational and political–legal arrangements created opportunities for managers to engage in activities that were previously not viable or were illegal.

Section I presents a political economy framework to explain the emergence of the institutional arrangements in the late 20th century that created opportunities for corporations to engage in financial wrongdoing. Section II examines how public policy changes created a "new social frontier" where new political–legal arrangements facilitated the shift of assets owned by the working and middle classes to financial markets and permitted corporations to create structures to access that capital. Section III focuses on how managers and capitalists engaged in political capitalism to create new forms of financialization and hide high-risk and, in some cases, illegal behavior from the investing public and government oversight. Section IV summarizes the four transformative changes that occurred during this historical period and juxtaposes the "ideal with the real," where the neoliberal ideology of market efficiency and transparency is in sharp contrast with the concrete organizational and political–legal arrangements that created asymmetric information and opportunities for financial wrongdoing.

I. Theoretical Framework

The focus on the relationship between social structure and white-collar crime was first articulated by Sutherland (1949) in his seminal observation of differential social organization, where some social structures provide different opportunities to commit crime than others. Subsequent research in this tradition has shown that variation in regulatory policy, enforcement structures, and economic conditions affect white-collar crime (Clinard and Yeager 1980; Simpson 1986; Yeager 1991; Prechel and Morris 2010). The conceptual framework here extends Sutherland's framework by elaborating three pillars (i.e., like legs of a stool) that explain how the historically specific social structure that emerged in the late 20th century created opportunities for executives to engage in financial wrongdoing.

First, this framework builds on the insight of modern political economy, which suggests that the parts of the social structure are intrinsically intertwined and can only be understood in relationship to one another (Marx 1867 [1977]; Weber 1921 [1978]; Durkheim 1933; Polanyi 1944 [2001]; Selznick 1949; Mills 1956).[3] The primary focus is on how corporations and markets are embedded in political–legal arrangements and how political embeddedness varies over time.

Second, it draws on recent conceptions of *political capitalism*: the use of political outlets by business interests to attain conditions of economic stability and predictability to facilitate capitalist growth and development (Kolko 1963). Political capitalism encompasses the exercise of power (1) outside the state, where capitalists attempt to control the political debate, (2) in the legislative process, where broad policy parameters are established, and (3) in state agencies that have authority over policy implementation and enforcement (Prechel 2000).

Third, it incorporates a central idea from organizational political economy: when capital accumulation opportunities decline, business interests become more politically active and mobilize to redefine corporate–state linkages in ways that create new opportunities for capital accumulation. The emergent political–legal arrangements are manifested as changes in the organizational structure of the state that, in turn, establish the parameters for future policy. After policies are enacted as state structures, they affect subsequent policy through the alignments they provide for competing interests both inside and outside the state (Prechel 1990, 2000). This path-dependent process affects the content and form of future policies and state structures.

The historically contingent feature of modern capitalism is articulated by social structure of accumulation theory, which draws on long-wave theories of capitalist growth and development. Research in this tradition has shown that variation in the rate of capital accumulation is a primary cause of historical shifts in economic, ideological, and political arrangements. Social structure of accumulation theorists maintain that capitalism goes through a cycle that is repeated over time (Gordon, Edwards, and Reich 1982; McDonough, Reich, and Kotz 2010). The cyclic characteristic of capitalism exists because corporate profits depend on institutional arrangements that are external to the firm: the ideological, political, and economic spheres. These institutional arrangements are designed to ensure conditions favorable to capital accumulation and the reproduction of class relations. However, periodic breakdowns in one dimension of the institutional arrangements undermine capital accumulation, which initiates a shift to a new phase of the cycle.

There are three distinct phases in each social structure of accumulation. The initial *exploration* phase follows periods of economic decline. During this stage, politicians and capitalists experiment with restructuring the institutional arrangements. After new institutional arrangements are enacted, *consolidation* occurs, where the ideological, political, and economic arrangements are reintegrated. This new social structure of accumulation provides the foundation for higher profits and contributes to stable capitalist growth and development. The last stage is *decay*, which is characterized by incompatibility within the institutional arrangements. Markets weaken during periods of economic decline, resulting in economic instability. Decay and the subsequent capital accumulation crisis result in a new exploration phase and the cycle is repeated.

Research that examines *decay–exploration* transitions focuses on how new institutional arrangements are politically constructed to create the conditions that facilitate stable capitalist growth and development (Prechel 2000). During the early stages of this transition, conflict becomes more pronounced among capitalist class factions because their distinct location in the economy creates economic requirements that are manifest as political interests that are incompatible with the interests of other capitalist class factions. As a result, capitalist class factions have different political agendas and frequently disagree on policy. However, as economic decline continues, capitalist recognize that realignment of the institutional arrangements is dependent on their collective political power and unify politically to form a "power bloc" to advance a coherent policy agenda (Poulantzas 1974 [1978]). The specific policy outcomes that are designed to reinvigorate capitalism are negotiated inside the state because it is the only organization in society with the capacity to mediate conflict between competing classes and class factions.

Using this conceptual framework, the following examines how corporate management engaged in political capitalism to redefine the organizational and political–legal arrangements in which corporations and markets are embedded. It also shows how extending the outside parameters of the prevailing institutional arrangement (1) legitimated behaviors that were previously illegal or not viable and (2) created opportunities for managers to engage in financial wrongdoing.

II. Creating a New Social Frontier

A. Prevailing Ideas: Neoliberalism and Market Fundamentalism

A fundamental premise of neoliberalism is that government interference with markets is the cause of poor economic performance and that free markets ensure economic growth and prosperity. In contrast to neoliberalism, economic sociologists maintain that markets are always embedded in cultural and political institutions. In precapitalist societies, markets are embedded in cultural arrangements and exchanges are based on normative considerations (Weber 1921 [1978]). One of the primary ways that culture affects markets in modern society is through the ideas about how markets should be organized and the transformation of those ideas into policies, laws, and state structures that establish and enforce the outside parameters of market behavior.

During the middle decades of the 20th century, embedded liberalism limited managers' capacity to engage in risky behavior (Ruggie 1982). In contrast, late-20th-century neoliberalism assumes that, through price changes, markets spread the relevant information to individuals who use this information to make decisions that advance their interests (Hayek 1991, pp. 12–13). This perspective maintains that the inefficiencies of markets are small; the inefficiencies of government are high; and social, economic, and political problems can be solved with information provided by markets. Market fundamentalism, which is the extreme version of neoliberal ideology, entails the religion-like certitude that all social problems can be resolved by market forces (Stiglitz 2002; Somers and Block 2005). In contrast to the prevailing belief that market deregulation occurred in the late 20th century, which implies that laws governing markets were eliminated, the analysis here shows that *reregulation* more accurately captures how existing markets were changed and new markets emerged. Specifically, existing political–legal arrangements were replaced with new arrangements that permitted a wider range of corporate and market behaviors. Most important, the emergent form of political embeddedness created greater risk to, especially, small investors and opportunities for managers to advance their profitmaking agenda and engage in financial wrongdoing.

B. Creating and Distributing Risk: Socializing Capital

By the late 20th century, scholars began to acknowledge the shift from fated risk in traditional societies to created risk in modern society, where the intersection of technical knowledge and economic decision making that creates risk is protected by the state (Beck 2009, p. 25). The following describes the mechanisms that exposed more segments of society to greater financial risk in the late 20th century. Although many parallels have been drawn between the Great Depression and the Great Recession, one important difference exists. By the end of the 20th century, a much larger portion of the middle and working classes had invested in corporate securities and other risky financial instruments. As a result, when financial crises occur, losses to the middle and working classes include a loss of value in their homes, pensions, and other retirement funds.

Historically, efforts to socialize capital are enacted when the amount of capital generated by corporations is insufficient to advance their capital accumulation agendas. The first major public policy that socialized capital occurred in the late 19th century, when corporations mobilized to create the legal framework for the stockholding company (Hilferding 1910 [1981]; Roy 1997). Socializing capital during this historical period took two forms: (1) individuals made direct stock purchases and (2) bankers invested deposits from individuals' saving accounts into corporate securities.[4] However, the rate of ownership of corporate securities by individuals was relatively low in the late 19th and early 20th centuries, in part because some of the largest corporations, such as Carnegie Steel Company, continued to be organized as private partnerships. However, the value of corporate securities in manufacturing increased from less than $1 billion in 1897 to more than $6.8 billion in 1904 (Roy 1997, p. 5). By 1927, estimates suggest that four to six million people, or only 3.4 to 5 percent of the population, owned corporate stock (Burk 1988, pp. 260–67).

Although the first mutual funds were created in 1924, they did not provide a substantial source of capital and could not fill the widespread capital shortages during the Great Depression. In response, Congress passed legislation in 1933 and 1934 to facilitate the development of mutual funds. Despite these changes, mutual funds were not used widely, and the percentage of the working and middle classes who invested in corporate securities was relatively low during the middle decades of the 20th century. However, the interest in mutual funds as a mechanism of accessing the public's capital gained more attention in the early 1970s, when the manufacturing sector experienced declining profits, global competition accelerated, and a sharp increase in energy costs undermined capitalist growth and development. The capacity of U.S. firms to generate reinvestment capital was hampered further by their strategy of maintaining high shareholder value (e.g., paying stock dividends). As a result, corporations in key industries (e.g., automobile, steel) did not have an adequate supply of capital to invest in more efficient production technology and restore profit to previous levels.

To increase the availability of capital to modernize production facilities, capitalists and managers lobbied Congress to redefine the political–legal arrangements in ways that encouraged a wide range of citizens to invest in corporate securities. Congress was receptive to this policy because it coincided with the state's agenda to ensure stable economic growth and development. In 1971, Congress enacted legislation to create money-market mutual funds, and in 1974 individual retirement accounts (IRAs) were created for workers who did not have employee-funded pension funds. In 1978, legislation was passed that permitted employees to create 401(k) retirement plans. Then, in 1982, company-sponsored retirement accounts were approved by the Internal Revenue Service (IRS) (Levitt 2002, p. 257). In the following decade, more investment options were made available to individuals, including the Roth IRA in 1997.

In a separate policy arena, in response to the recession in the early 1990s, the Federal Reserve reduced interest rates, which lowered returns on savings account deposits to historically low levels. Despite the economic recovery, the Federal Reserve kept interest rates low throughout the decade. These neoliberal policies, which were enacted under the leadership of Alan Greenspan, created incentives for more members of the middle and working classes to invest in corporate securities. Other incremental Federal Reserve policies permitted financial services firms to engage in activities that were previously limited to more tightly regulated commercial banks, savings and loans, and credit unions. The subsequent expansion of the financial services sector provided a range of banking and investing services that allowed customers to easily shift their savings into corporate securities.

These policies resulted in a massive shift of capital into financial markets. In 1980, 5.7 percent of households invested directly or indirectly through mutual funds in corporate securities, which was approximately the same as the estimate for 1927. However, by 1990, 23.4 percent of families owned shares in mutual funds, and mutual fund assets passed $1 trillion (Investment Company Institute 2013). Investments by the middle and working classes continued to increase in the 1990s. By 2001, 51.9 percent of American families directly or indirectly owned corporate securities (Kennickell, Starr-McCluer, and Surette 2003).

The expansion of mutual funds also created new sources of wealth and power in the financial sector. Whereas the fees charged to manage mutual funds increased the wealth of fund managers, control over the large sums of capital provided fund managers with power over corporate management. By the 1980s, institutional investors began to exercise this power by pressuring corporate managers to increase *shareholder value*: firms' worth as judged by stockholders that is measured by dividend payments and growth in company stock value (Useem 1996). During this same historical moment, to encourage managers to behave more like owners and increase shareholder value, corporate boards increased stock options as a form of executive compensation. Because stock options only have value if stock prices increase, this form of executive compensation created incentives for managers to pursue high-profit ventures, which are typically coupled with high risks.

C. Redefining Corporate Structures

Although the transfer of capital to mutual funds was well under way by the early 1980s when the back-to-back recessions occurred, the organizational mechanisms to readily access this capital did not exist. Moreover, the record-high interest rates in the 1980s made debt financing expensive during a historical period when many manufacturing companies were experiencing severe capital accumulation constraints. During the same period, financial analysts began to argue that the stock market undervalued large corporations. These analysts maintained that the sum of the parts was more valuable than the whole (Jensen 1984; LeBaron and Speidell 1987; Porter 1987). These claims were supported by the success of wealthy investors such as T. Boone Pickens and Carl Icahn who made fortunes taking over corporations, breaking them up into parts, and selling the parts as legally independent corporations.

The challenge for management was to set up a corporate structure that allowed them to unlock capital in the firms that they managed. One option was to use the holding-company structure that prevailed in the late 19th and early 20th centuries, where parent holding companies could issue stock in their legally independent subsidiary corporations. However, with two notable exceptions (banks and public utilities), this structure was deinstitutionalized by New Deal legislation that taxed capital transfers between subsidiaries and parent companies. This public policy was enacted because many politicians and scholars believe that this structure created opportunities for managers to engage in risk-taking behavior and financial wrongdoing, which contributed to the Great Depression. By the 1960s, most large corporations changed to the multidivisional form, where divisions and the central office are all part of a single legal entity (Chandler 1962; Fligstein 1985; Palmer, Jennings, and Zhou 1993).[5]

To re-institutionalize the parent company/subsidiary structure, corporate management lobbied Congress to eliminate the New Deal capital transfer tax. This political coalition, which included large nonfinancial corporations and several trade associations, succeeded when a little-known provision was included in the mid-1980s tax policy to eliminate this tax. After the legislation was enacted, corporations began to restructure their divisions as *subsidiaries*: legally independent companies in which the parent company is the majority shareholder. Because subsidiaries are legally independent corporations, the parent company can issue up to 50 percent of the stock in its subsidiary corporations while retaining ownership control over them.

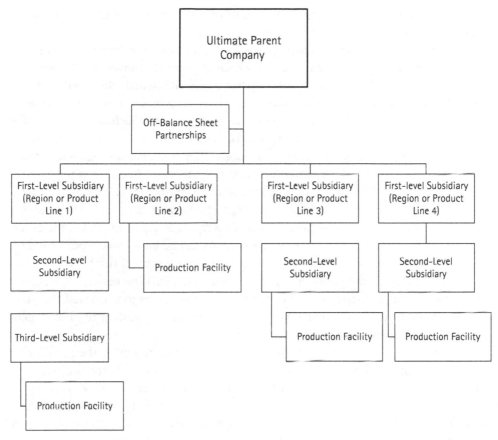

FIGURE 15.1 The Multilayer-Subsidiary Form

This public-policy change was followed by a transition from the multidivisional form to the *multilayer-subsidiary form*: at the top of this corporate structure, a legally independent parent company replaces the general office of the multidivisional form and divisions are replaced by legally independent subsidiary corporations (figure 15.1). The parent company operates like a financial management company and engages in financial transactions with its subsidiaries and third parties (e.g., banks, financial services firms), ensures that the operating subsidiaries have adequate cash flow to maintain their operations, and monitors the portfolio of corporate entities to ensure that they meet profit and stock value targets (Prechel and Boies 1998; Prechel 2000). Under certain conditions, this corporate structure creates a liability firewall between the subsidiary and the parent company, which protects the parent company from liabilities that occur in its subsidiaries.

By 1993, 42 percent of the largest 100 industrial corporations had one or no divisions, the mean number of divisions per corporation declined from 8.8 in 1981 to 4 in 1993, and the mean number of domestic subsidiary corporations increased from 23 to 51 (Prechel and Boies 1998). By 2004, this structure had spread throughout U.S. industry, when 84.7 percent of the 500 largest companies were structured under the multilayer-subsidiary form (Prechel and Morris 2010).

These organizational and political–legal arrangements have important implications. First, abolishing the capital transfer tax simultaneously eliminated the need for management to report internal capital transfers to the IRS, which abolished a crucial oversight mechanism. Second, corporations used this structure to lower their tax obligations. By the late 1980s, U.S. parent companies were devising mechanisms to transfer capital among their domestic and foreign subsidiaries in order to lower their U.S. tax obligation. Third, restructuring divisions as subsidiaries is often associated with an initial public stock offering of corporate securities (i.e., stocks and bonds) in their newly formed subsidiaries. This dimension of the corporate form change had two implications. On the one hand, corporations obtained a larger share of their capital from equity markets, which reduced their dependence on debt markets (e.g., banks). On the other, a large portion of these corporate securities (i.e., stocks and bonds) were purchased by institutional investors who managed retirement and other mutual funds, which drew a larger percentage of the public into the securities market. Whereas eliminating the capital transfer tax reduced oversight on how corporate managers invested the public's money, investing in subsidiary initial public offerings by mutual fund managers increased financial risk among the working classes.

Although subsidiaries are the most widely used corporate entity, the multilayer-subsidiary form accommodates other legally independent corporate entities. Corporate managers also used this structure to diversify their assets by investing in *affiliate* corporations, where the parent company owns less than 50 percent of their stock. The use of affiliate corporations became more widespread in the 1990s, when corporations revised their earlier strategy to focus on core product lines and diversified their financial portfolio (Prechel, Morris, Woods, and Walden 2008). Because the parent company owns less than 50 percent of an affiliate's stock, in contrast to subsidiaries, it is not required to report these corporate entities on its consolidated financial statement.

Management also made greater use of *partnerships*: a business association of two or more people who share risks and profits. Throughout the middle decades of the 20th century, partnerships were used primarily by small firms such as private investment banks and professional organizations (e.g., accounting and law firms). However, after the multilayer-subsidiary became viable, financial managers began to devise ways to use partnerships to manage firms' assets. One of the crucial features of partnerships is that they are not taxed and profits and taxes are passed on to the partners, which could be another corporation.[6] Partnerships often have several partners, no single partner has controlling interests, and the contracts creating partnerships specify the extent of each partner's liability. Unlike parent companies and subsidiaries, partnerships do not have the right to sell securities to the investing public. As a result, partnerships are lightly regulated and not required to adhere to corporate law (*Oxford Dictionary of Business Management* 2006), even when they are majority owned by a public corporation. For example, accounting rules do not require parent companies to include partnerships in their financial statements.[7]

III. Political Capitalism and New Forms of Financialization

A. The Industrial Sector

Although most explanations for the spread of financialization in the late 20th century focus on the financial sector, some of the first innovative financial instruments emerged in nonfinancial sectors of the economy. For most of the 20th century, manufacturing firms generated most of their reinvestment capital internally, focused on accounting to monitor costs, and employed few financial managers. However, by the 1970s, competition in domestic and global markets created internal capital shortages and greater dependence on external capital markets. In response, manufacturing firms employed more financial managers and placed them in key decision-making positions. Some of these financial managers were hired from the investment banking sector. In addition to negotiating external financing with banks (e.g., loans, bond offerings, and stock offerings), financial managers began to develop alternative forms of low-cost financing during this period when the Federal Reserve Bank attempted to control inflation with record high interest rates.

To advance their agenda, the manufacturing sector created the Business Roundtable to develop a unified political strategy and pressure Congress and the Reagan administration to pass legislation to reduce its tax obligations. This lobby effort succeeded when Congress passed the Economic Recovery Tax Act of 1981. The tax breaks from this legislation were so lucrative for low-profit firms that they could not use them all. To maximize the benefit from this tax policy, financial managers in low-profit firms proposed that they securitize their unused tax deductions by selling them to third parties (i.e., high-profit corporations) who could use them.[8] Securitization provides a clear benefit to corporations with immediate capital needs: instead of waiting for capital to trickle in over a long time, the owner of the asset can estimate its value and sell it at a discount to investors.

Partnerships provide a convenient mechanism to organize economic activities such as securitized assets because they are loosely regulated and easily created and dismantled (U.S. Congress 2003, p. 9). Most important, if the assets are not managed actively, partnerships have off-balance-sheet status and are given the designation of special-purpose entities (SPEs), a specialized type of partnership created to carry out a specific financial purpose or activity (Financial Accounting Standards Board 1959; Powers, Troubh, and Winokur 2002, p. 38).

In response to low profit levels, manufacturing corporations claimed that their survival depended on using off-balance-sheet entities to raise additional capital to modernize their production facilities. After convincing the Treasury Department that these assets were not actively managed, financial managers packaged physical assets (e.g., computers, blast furnaces) with unused tax deductions into leaseback agreements and placed them in off-balance-sheet partnerships.

These organizational and political–legal arrangements permitted the low-profit firms to (1) lease physical assets with the unused tax deductions to high-profit firms, who could use them to lower their tax bill, and (2) lease the physical asset back to the original owner, who would continue to use it (Prechel 2000, pp. 218–19). These agreements were purely financial transactions to benefit corporations and entailed no physical change or movement of the securitized asset. Financial managers argued that it was appropriate to use off-balance-sheet entities to hold leaseback arrangements because the contract represents a steady flow of income that is not actively managed.

There are several implications of these organizational and political–legal arrangements. First, these SPEs benefitted both firms by increasing their cash flow. Whereas high-profit companies acquired the tax deductions below their actual value, low-profit companies received payment for their unused tax credits. Second, these organizational and political–legal arrangements also reduced government oversight of corporate finances because parent companies are not required to report off-balance-sheet partnerships on their consolidated financial statement (U.S. Congress 2002, p. 38). Third, these arrangements lowered corporate tax obligations, which reduced government revenues.

While this change in political embeddedness substantially increased corporations' organizational and financial flexibility, it also increased opportunities for financial wrongdoing. First, because off-balance-sheet partnerships exist at the edge of the regulatory system, they are virtually impossible for oversight agencies to monitor. Second, securitization is complex, with hundreds of pages of rules on how to securitize assets, which makes them ripe for abuse. Although there is nothing new about corporations employing lawyers, accountants, and financiers to discover ways to circumvent the intent of a rule or law without formally breaking it, off-balance-sheet partnerships create new opportunities to circumvent the intent of the law because these corporate entities are not transparent to investors. As a result, these organizational and political–legal arrangements can be used in ways that give the appearance of fiscal strength when it does not exist. To illustrate, to qualify for off-balance-sheet status, only 3 percent of the capital in an SPE must come from an independent source. This rule assumes that 3 percent ownership is adequate to ensure oversight of the partnership by a third party. The rule also means that 97 percent of the capital in the off-balance-sheet partnership could be debt that is not reported on the balance sheet (Levitt 2002). Most important, the 3 percent rule is completely arbitrary, with no evidence to support that it will result in adequate financial oversight.

By extending the use of off-balance-sheet partnerships, the Treasury Department's ruling created new mechanisms and opportunities for managers to pursue financialization strategies. Soon, investment bankers began to view financialization as a profit-making opportunity and worked with corporate management to devise new financial products to cope with their capital needs. Partnerships were set up to conduct a wide range of business activities, and by 1990 approximately 600,000 partnerships existed. The number of partnerships continued to increase in the 1990s (Levitt 2002; Gladwell 2007), and, by the early 21st century, there were approximately two million partnerships in corporate America. In 2002, hundreds of billions of dollars were located in partnerships that reported almost $3 billion in income and $2.5 billion in tax deductions (Johnston 2003).

B. More Risks and Opportunities to Engage in Financialization: The Gramm-Leach-Bliley Financial Services Modernization Act

As knowledge spread of how organizational structures facilitated financialization in ways that improved corporate balance sheets and raised shareholder value, more corporations incorporated financial strategies into their capital accumulation agendas. The implementation of financial strategies was accelerated in nonfinancial firms after management discovered that selling its commodities was easier if it offered financial services to prospective customers. For example, in the 1980s, large retail firms such as Sears and manufacturing firms such as Ford, General Electric, and General Motors created subsidiaries to provide finance services to customers purchasing their products. Expanding the corporate structure to accommodate financialization was accomplished easily in the parent company/subsidiary structure, where management could create a financial services entity and organize it as a legally independent subsidiary. In the two decades between 1981 and 2001, when most firms restructured as the multilayer-subsidiary form, the percentage of profits reported from financing increased from 12 to 39 percent (Phillips 2002, Drenner 2004).

The rapid spread of financialization is also associated with the widespread acceptance of neoliberal ideology and market fundamentalism. These ideas were embraced by the leadership of the Federal Reserve Bank and the Treasury Department, where changes in the rules governing banks weakened the 1933 Glass-Steagall Act and the Bank Holding Company Act of 1956. These laws were initially enacted to prohibit the same corporation from engaging in commercial banking, investment banking, and insurance. In response to the reversal of the laws and regulations, financial conglomerates emerged that engaged in commercial banking, investment banking, and insurance activities.

By the late 1990s, neoliberal ideology became so entrenched in the Executive Branch, Congress, and the Federal Reserve Bank that giant corporations assumed that the federal government would acquiesce to their demands. To illustrate, in 1998 Citicorp merged with the insurance company Travelers Property and Casualty to create the giant financial conglomerate Citigroup, even though this form of corporate consolidation was still prohibited by law. Congress did not vote to dismantle the Glass-Steagall Act and the Banking Company Act of 1956, which prohibited mergers among financial firms that operated in different markets, until the following year, when it passed the 1999 Gramm-Leach-Bliley Financial Services Modernization Act. These organizational and political–legal arrangements created the potential for multiple conflicts of interests because they permitted a single bank to engage in a wide range of transactions with the same corporate client, including loans, stock analyses, underwriting corporate securities, advising on mergers and acquisitions, insurance, and investment advising. Corporate managers defended these new organizational and political–legal arrangements by maintaining that they would create effective "Chinese walls" between corporate entities where the potential for conflicts of interest exists.

The problem with these corporate–state relations is that they are based on trust; they assume that managers will not violate laws or the intent of laws and rules established by government or nongovernmental agencies or engage in acts that violate the public's understanding of the business code of conduct. While trust can contribute to the smooth operation of markets (Polanyi 1944), corporations are not markets, and many decisions are buried deep inside very large and complex organizations. Moreover, profitmaking agendas create incentives for firms and their managers to not establish or enforce Chinese walls among corporate entities that have conflicts of interest (figure 15.1).

C. The Convergence of Interests in Energy and Finance: The Commodity Futures Modernization Act of 2000

Although the Roosevelt Administration succeeded in convinced Congress to dismantle the holding company structure by imposing a tax on capital transfers between subsidiaries and their parent holding companies, exceptions were permitted in two economic sectors: banking and energy. These economic sectors were exempted from this policy because economic concentration in these sectors was considered essential to capitalist growth and development. However, these economic sectors were more tightly regulated than other sectors. A core component of the subsequent Utilities Holding Company Act of 1935 and later legislation established price-setting mechanisms in energy markets based on fuel type, age of the facility, and other cost-based variables. To stabilize the production of natural gas, prices were set by "take or pay" contracts where pipeline companies made long-term commitments to purchase natural gas from producers. Although these political–legal arrangements stabilized prices, natural gas firms maintained that prices and profits were so low that there was little incentive to invest in exploration for new natural gas reserves. As a result, the natural gas market grew at a modest pace during the middle decades of the 20th century.

One of the early advocates of market reform was an undersecretary of energy in the Department of Interior, Ken Lay, who was appointed in 1972 to assist in developing a national energy policy. Lay spent his short career in the government advocating for reregulation of the natural gas market and developing relationships with government officials. In 1973, Lay left the government to work for a small pipeline company that purchased natural gas from producers and transported and sold it to consumers.

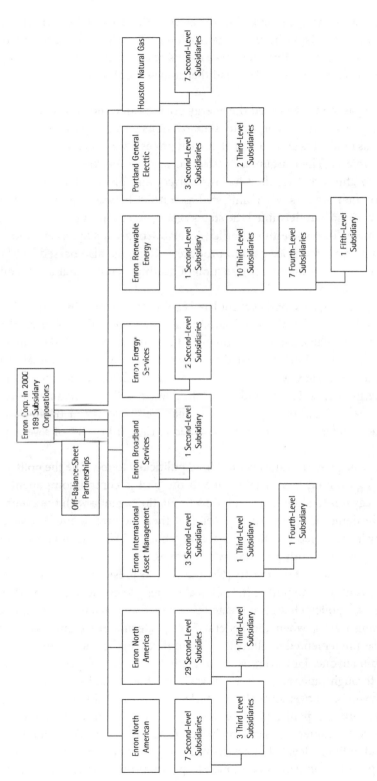

FIGURE 15.2 Enron Corporate Structure

In that same year, shortages emerged in the electrical and natural gas markets, which coincided with the decision by the Organization of Petroleum Exporting Countries (OPEC) to raise oil prices. Together these events resulted in a national energy crisis. Natural gas shortages were so widespread that some schools and factories were forced to close.

The natural gas industry viewed the energy crisis as an opportunity to pressure the federal government to revise corporate–state relations governing the natural gas market. Natural gas producers argued that at current prices it was too risky to invest in new exploration projects. Their argument rested, in part, on periodic and unpredictable warmer temperatures that resulted in lower prices and profits. The failure to invest in new exploration projects was manifested as conflict between the industry and the government because it undermined the state's agenda to ensure stable capitalist growth and development. To resolve this conflict, in 1978 Congress acquiesced and enacted legislation to increase the price paid to producers. Congress also passed legislation to restrict demand by limiting the construction of heating facilities that used natural gas (Eichenwald 2005, p. 9).

The rules governing this market stimulated exploration, which increased the supply of natural gas, boosted the profits of natural gas producers, and advanced the state's agenda to maintain stable capitalist growth and development. Moreover, the ongoing oil embargo and high oil prices created incentives for many large wholesale consumers to switch to natural gas, which contributed to higher demand and prices. However, when the energy crisis subsided and prices dropped, pipeline companies were locked into the long-term "take or pay" contracts that were negotiated during the crisis. These contracts undermined profits and resulted in the bankruptcy of several pipeline companies.

In response, the pipeline industry mobilized politically to redefine the political–legal arrangements governing this market. Like in the past, a central component of their political strategy was to align their capital accumulation agenda with the state's agenda to increase the domestic energy supply. Ken Lay, then the president of the small pipeline company Transco, led a political coalition whose primary agenda was to replace "take or pay" contracts with a market where prices were negotiated "on the spot." In 1984, Lay became president of Houston Natural Gas. As president of this larger pipeline company, Lay continued to pursue his political strategy to create a "spot market."

The first major policy change to create this market was enacted in 1984, under the Reagan administration, when the Federal Energy Regulatory Commission (FERC) Order 380 was implemented to allow local natural gas distribution companies to purchase gas from anyone. However, because much of the natural gas supply had to be transported through pipelines, producers and distributors had to negotiate with the pipeline companies. To overcome this obstacle, in 1985 the FERC passed Order 436 to encourage pipeline companies to make their lines accessible to utility companies and other wholesale consumers (Fusaro and Miller 2002; Fox 2003). Although these organizational and political–legal changes created mechanisms to buy, transport, and sell natural gas, pipeline companies continued to pressure the state to release them from their long-term obligation under the take-or-pay contracts. In 1987, the FERC acquiesced and permitted pipeline companies to renegotiate these contracts.

Together, these changes created the conditions to establish a spot market. In 1984, Houston Natural Gas formed a consortium with five other pipeline companies, a law firm, and the investment bank Morgan Stanley to create the Natural Gas Clearinghouse.[9] Natural gas trading became so successful that it was taken over by Morgan Stanley in the following year. Eventually, more than 75 percent of natural gas sales were conducted on the spot market (Fusaro and Miller 2002). However, the spot market could not overcome the problem of supply-and-demand fluctuations associated with changing weather patterns and other difficult-to-predict conditions. As a result, producers refused to make large capital investments to explore and develop natural gas reserves.

In the meantime, to take advantage of the capital accumulation opportunities in this emerging market, in 1985 Houston Natural Gas merged with its much larger competitor InterNorth to create Enron Corp. The underlying logic for the merger was simple. Anticipating reregulation of the industry, both pipeline companies were acquiring small companies and competing over these acquisitions. Instead of competing with each other, these companies combined to form one of the largest pipeline companies in the United States, with the capacity to purchase, transport, and sell natural gas to many customers dispersed over a large geographic region.[10]

Despite InterNorth's substantially larger size, Lay negotiated to relocate corporate headquarters to Houston and, after a few years, become the chief executive officer. Enron continued to employ the consulting firm McKinsey & Company, which was hired by InterNorth, to help develop the natural gas market. McKinsey assigned a consultant with a background in finance to develop the strategy, Jeffrey Skilling. During this transition period, Enron and other pipeline companies struggled with how to succeed in this market. For decades, wholesale customers were accustomed to purchasing natural gas at a fixed rate and were hesitant to participate in a spot market. Further, in response to the uncertainty of the spot market, many large consumers shifted to coal and oil.

After numerous failed proposals, Skilling came up with the idea of using the pipeline business to connect producers and consumers. However, this entailed a fundamental transformation of Enron's business model. Instead of selling its pipeline services to transport natural gas, Enron would broker contracts between producers and buyers. That is, Enron would operate like a bank for natural gas. Using the "Gas Bank" as a metaphor, Skilling proposed that producers would make deposits in the Gas Bank (i.e., sell natural gas at a guaranteed low price) and customers would withdraw from the Gas Bank (i.e., purchase natural gas at a guaranteed above-market price). Skilling's business model assumed that producers would sell at below-market prices and customers would buy at above-market prices to reduce their risk. In short, Enron proposed to create a natural gas *derivatives* market: contracts that are based on the value of an underlying commodity that specify an obligation to deliver a product at a set price at a future date.

Skilling presented the idea to Rich Kinder, who was one of Enron's rising managers and soon became president and chief operating officer. Kinder agreed to allow Skilling to present his proposal to a group of executives. However, the executives were unconvinced that producers would sell at below-market prices and consumers would buy at above-market prices. Although Kinder was cautious, he was also concerned that if this market did develop, Enron must be ready or it would miss out on tremendous capital accumulation opportunities. For the next few months, Kinder worked with Skilling on presenting this idea to potential customers. After two weeks, Kinder and Skilling had more than $1 billion of multiyear natural gas contracts (Eichenwald 2005, p. 43). In the meantime, traders outside Enron began to agree that a derivatives market for natural gas would be created and, in 1990, the New York Mercantile began to trade natural gas derivatives (McLean and Elkind 2003).

Concerned that the regulated exchanges would control this market, Skilling and Kinder quickly created the organizational arrangements to trade in this market. The Gas Bank also benefitted from bank policy that tightened the credit of exploration and drilling companies in this uncertain natural gas market. Enron's business model filled this capital void by agreeing to make loans to natural gas producers for exploration and production in return for a guaranteed supply of natural gas at a fixed price in the future. Producers accepted these terms because it guaranteed a profit. The Gas Bank also guaranteed customers a fixed price at a future date. In short, the Gas Bank shifted risk for both producers and consumers in this market to Enron. Despite Kinder and Skilling's success in obtaining futures contracts, key Enron executives remained skeptical and the strategy was only partially implemented. Kinder and Skilling continued to argue that if Enron did not implement this strategy, another company would benefit from these capital accumulation opportunities. However, implementing this strategy required a tremendous amount of capital, which Enron did not have.

D. An Early Warning: Too Much Risk and Complexity to Manage, Financial Wrongdoing, and Near Bankruptcy

When Enron was created, it was organized under the multilayer-subsidiary form. This structure accommodated its merger and acquisition strategy; acquired or merged companies could be incorporated as legally independent subsidiaries and continue to operate as they did prior to consolidation. Together with its aggressive merger and acquisition strategy, management used this corporate form to create a complex of subsidiary corporations operating in many markets in multiple geographic locations in the domestic and global economies.

The first major sign that Enron was too complex to manage emerged in the mid-1980s. One of Enron's subsidiary corporations that was located in Valhalla, New York, Enron Oil, employed a small group of forty traders who speculated on crude oil and refined products. In 1985, subsidiary management began to manipulate the books and set up offshore corporate entities in Panama to hide misleading and false transactions.

Using this organizational structure, subsidiary managers reported rapidly increasing revenues that resulted in bonuses of $3.1 million and $9.4 million for themselves in 1985 and 1986, respectively. This corporate wrongdoing was exposed in 1987 when the parent company discovered that subsidiary managers were engaging in the illegal behavior of shifting profits to future months. In their defense, managers claimed that they engaged in this behavior to cover unexpected future shortfalls.

The parent company's investigation of the wrongdoing concluded that subsidiary managers had suffered some trading losses but these were manageable. Although the traders had falsified bank statements, they were neither fired nor punished. Instead, they were permitted to continue trading, in part because the parent company was dependent on capital from this trading subsidiary to make its debt payments and finance the Gas Bank (Bryce 2002, p. 39).

In mid-1987, a much worse crisis emerged in the same trading subsidiary. As a result of market volatility caused in part by the war between Iran and Iraq and the subsequent unpredictability of oil shipments through the Strait of Hormuz, Enron Oil suffered huge trading losses. To offset these losses, traders made riskier bets, which resulted in additional losses. The parent company's investigation revealed that the subsidiary was responsible for the delivery of almost $1.5 billion of crude oil, which it did not have.

At that time, Enron's total debt had reached approximately $3.5 billion and its stock valuation was about $4.7 billion. When the $1.5 billion loss was included, Enron had a negative net worth of about $300 million (Bryce 2002, p. 41). If Enron could not solve the problem before it was exposed to the public, the company would be forced into bankruptcy. In a desperate attempt to avoid bankruptcy, Enron sent a team of its most experienced traders to the subsidiary, who renegotiated enough of these trades to save the company. The president and treasurer of Enron Oil received short sentences for their financial crimes. Although information asymmetries permitted this illegal behavior to go undetected until it became a crisis, these organizational arrangements were not modified.

The near bankruptcy of Enron had little effect on the spread of market fundamentalism among top management. One exception was Kinder, who continued to approach the natural gas market with caution. To limit the firm's risk while pursuing this capital accumulation opportunity, Kinder argued for a business model where profits from trading would be limited to 30 percent, and the remaining 70 percent would come from physical assets (e.g., pipelines and processing plants).

D. More Political Capitalism, Risk, and Opportunities for Financial Wrongdoing

To further increase their capital accumulation opportunities in this market, pipeline companies mobilized politically to change more rules governing how energy trades could be conducted. They maintained that the natural gas market would operate more efficiently if derivatives contracts could be sold on unregulated exchanges. However, with a few exceptions (e.g., short-term derivatives such as currency exchange rates), derivatives trading was limited to regulated exchanges such as the Chicago Mercantile that were monitored by the Commodities Futures Trading Commission (CFTC).

Enron, which had become one of the most politically active firms in corporate America, led a strategy to change this public policy. The natural gas coalition accelerated its political strategy when Bill Clinton defeated President George H. W. Bush in November 1992. Anticipating resistance to further reregulation of this market from a Democratic president, days after the election the energy lobby began pressuring the CFTC to further relax the rules governing natural gas trades. Like in the past, this political lobby aligned its capital accumulation agenda with the state's agenda to increase domestic energy supplies. The energy industry continued to argue that unregulated derivatives trading would increase predictability in the market and reduce the risk to producers, who, in turn, would make greater investments in natural gas exploration and production.

Wendy Gramm, chair of the CFTC and spouse of Senator Phil Gramm (R-TX), whose state was the home of numerous energy companies and the recipient of large financial contributions from energy companies, agreed with the industry that energy trades should not be under the CFTC's jurisdiction. The commission voted along party lines, and the Republican majority passed a provision by a 2-to-1 vote to exempt energy companies from oversight by the CFTC. The committee's dissenting vote was cast by Sheila Blair, who viewed the exemption as a "dangerous precedent."

This decision permitted energy companies to set up their own internal trading floors, which exempted them from complying with the rules governing regulated exchanges. In fact, energy companies engaged in derivatives trading were not required to report to any regulatory agency (e.g., CFTC, Securities and Exchange Commission [SEC], or the Federal Reserve Bank). Because energy trading firms were permitted to engage in high-risk transactions on unregulated exchanges, no one knew how much capital they had to back their derivatives trading business.

However, critics were not silenced by the CFTC decision, and energy trading companies became concerned that the decision might be overturned under a future Democratic administration. An opportunity to make this provision more permanent emerged in the late 1990s when Congress was due to reauthorize the Commodity Exchange Act. By the late 1990s, the global derivatives market had grown to $88.2 trillion, and advocates in the financial sector argued that the current regulatory structure prohibited U.S. firms from entering this rapidly expanding and profitable market. To advance their coinciding economic interests, investment banks, financial services firms, and energy companies formed a coalition and launched a well-financed strategy to pressure Congress to enact legislation allowing derivatives futures to be traded on unregulated markets.

This political coalition was augmented by the emergence of increased economic and political unity within the financial sector. In 1993, the Association of Reserve City Bankers and the Association of Registered Bank Holding Companies merged to create the Bankers Roundtable. This organization changed its name in 2000 when the insurance sector joined banks to form the Financial Services Roundtable. The goal of this organization was to advance policy benefitting the financial sector. During this same period, the American Securitization Forum was created to advocate for expansion of the securitization market.

Despite the expansion of this political coalition, oversight agencies and several members of Congress opposed further reregulation of financial markets. After several political defeats in Congress, Senator Gramm and the Republican leadership in the House attached the Commodity Futures Modernization Act of 2000 to the 11,000-page Consolidated Appropriations Act for FY2001. This omnibus budget bill passed with a 290-to-60 vote in the House and by unanimous consent in the Senate. With virtually no discussion of the attached derivatives trading legislation, President Clinton signed the bill into law on December 21, 2000. This provision, which became known as the Enron Loophole, exempted a wide range of derivatives trades from regulation and virtually guaranteed that corporations could create their own over-the-counter derivatives exchanges that were removed from public scrutiny and government oversight (U.S. Congress 2002).

Despite the risks, virtually no countervailing political–legal arrangements were enacted to monitor or oversee these trades. Although natural gas traders developed complex financial models to structure derivatives contracts, the core problem remained: it was difficult to predict the future value of the underlying commodity. To compete with Enron in this market, other Fortune 500 energy corporations, including Dynegy, El Paso, and Williams, also entered this market. However, Enron captured a large share of the energy derivatives market, which confirmed Skilling and Kinder's previous claim that early market entry was important. In fact, by the end of 2000, Enron's unregulated exchange was ranked third in energy trades behind the regulated London and New York exchanges.

E. The Expansion of Shadow Banking: Financing Enron's Gas Bank

Given its high debt load, Enron was not able to finance the Gas Bank with conventional financing. However, by the mid-1990s, securitization was no longer considered an exotic means to raise capital. As described above, manufacturing corporations pooled their tax breaks from assets and sold them to other firms in the 1980s. As early as 1987, Skilling's employer, McKinsey & Company, began to view securitization as a mechanism to remove "capital and balance sheets as constraints on growth" (McLean and Elkind 2003, pp. 66-67). Soon, financial services and consulting firms were advising managers on how to use these financial instruments to strengthen their balance sheets. By the late 1990s, securitization had spread to many types of business enterprises: banks securitized credit card loans, composers securitized song royalties, and states securitized proceeds from tobacco litigation (McLean and Elkind 2003, p. 157).

This new social frontier of securitization represents a historical turning point from the mid-20th century when the primary mechanisms to finance firms' ongoing operations were limited to adding debt, issuing securities, or drawing from cash flows.

Concerned that another company would take advantage of the capital accumulation opportunities in the emerging natural gas market, in June 1990 Kinder convinced Skilling to leave his consulting career at McKinsey & Company and join Enron as chairman and chief executive of the subsidiary Enron Finance (Eichenwald 2005). Although Skilling was not an expert in securitization, his experience at McKinsey provided him with enough information to know that securitization could provide a viable form of off-balance-sheet capital. To obtain the necessary human capital, Skilling hired a personnel firm to locate an investment banker who specialized in structured financing. His name was Andrew Fastow, and he was employed as an investment banker at Continental Bank Corp., where he advised corporations on how to reduce their debt and improve their financial statements.

Investment in human capital to advance Enron's financialization agenda was not limited to off-balance-sheet financing. Enron also hired recent graduates from top-ranked MBA programs and accountants who were employed by the major accounting firms. In addition to providing Enron with the human capital to develop cutting-edge financing and accounting instruments, these financial managers and accountants provide the social capital to create networks between Enron and investment banks and audit firms. Whereas the investment banks provided information on structuring financing and underwrote many of Enron's partnerships, the audit firms provided information on how to maneuver through accounting rules and financial reporting requirements.

To outmaneuver its competitors in the emerging natural gas trading market, management also needed an organizational structure that facilitated rapid decision making and a means to finance its natural gas trading business. To create this structure, in 1991 the parent company combined Enron Gas Marketing, where its natural gas trading business was located, and Enron Finance under second-level subsidiaries Enron Capital and Trade Resources (McLean and Elkind 2003). This organizational structure internalized the finance function that previously was done by banks. Now, Enron was operating much like an investment bank. Traders in Enron Gas Marketing could negotiate contracts with customers and send the contract to managers in Enron Finance for approval. Moreover, effective Chinese walls were not established between these legally independent subsidiary corporations.

The first SPEs created at Enron were perfectly legal. These off-balance-sheet entities, which were named the Cactus Funds, were created because Enron did not have the capital to loan to producers and wait years for repayment. To raise capital, the Cactus Funds borrowed money from banks, invested some of it into securities, and used the return on these securities to make their bank payments. Financial managers also securitized the natural gas futures contracts in Cactus and sold them to investors, which typically included other corporations such as General Electric, who were paid from profits on these futures contracts when they began generating revenues. Technically, these partnerships met the legal criteria of off-balance-sheet financing because the payments on both sides of the deal were negotiated in advance. By mid-1993, Enron had raised $900 million with the Cactus off-balance-sheet partnerships (Fox 2003).

However, these complex financial instruments and corporate structures did nothing to mitigate the risk associated with off-balance-sheet treatment of assets: the value of the underlying commodity at a future time is not known. That is, unlike securitization of physical assets such as the depreciation allowance guaranteed by the government that were used in the mid-1980s by the industrial sector, futures derivatives markets are less predictable. Despite this shortcoming, management pursued this market aggressively and provided financing for both natural gas producers and buyers, which gave Enron a tremendous advantage in this new market. Moreover, whereas Enron's arrangements with producers guaranteed a supply of natural gas at a predictable price, its strategy to finance these trades gave its traders an important advantage over traders in companies whose customers had to obtain external financing from banks. To compete in this market, other pipeline companies developed similar organizational arrangements. In short, these capital accumulation opportunities contributed to isomorphism in organizational strategies and structures in this market.

To capture a large share of this market, Enron rewarded traders who met their trading targets with large bonuses and routinely dismissed traders who did not meet their targets. Although these policies were intended to create incentives for traders to sell more derivatives contracts, they also created perverse incentives, such as encouraging traders to inflate the deal value. As a result, many contracts lacked financial integrity, which placed more responsibility on Enron's internal risk-assessment department. However, effective Chinese walls were not constructed between the risk-assessment unit and the trading unit, and traders routinely pressured risk-assessment managers to approve contracts that lacked financial integrity (Cruver 2002).

Although Enron began to lose money on these derivatives contracts, little corrective action was taken because the revenues were needed to shore up Enron's balance sheets. If revenues declined, a stock devaluation could trigger a debt payment that Enron could not meet. In short, the goal to capture a large market share morphed into maintaining shareholder value. To give the appearance of a strong balance sheet during this period, Enron began to use mark-to-market accounting; this accounting mechanism places revenues on the books when the contract is negotiated versus when the product is delivered and the transaction is completed.

These organizational arrangements and managerial strategies had two important consequences. First, they exposed Enron to additional risks. On the one hand, if a producer failed to deliver natural gas at the agreed-upon date, then to meet the terms of its contracts Enron would have to purchase natural gas that was often more expensive and sell it at a loss. On the other hand, if a customer failed to purchase the natural gas at the agreed-upon price, Enron would be stuck with natural gas that it often had to sell at below current market prices. Second, financing the producers and underwriting the contracts with customers increased Enron's capital dependence. Thus, as Enron expanded its share of this rapidly growing market, it became more dependent on off-balance-sheet capital.

E. A Catastrophic Failure in the New Social Frontier

By the mid-1990s, Enron had changed from a pipeline to a financial company. Because many of Enron's energy derivatives lacked financial integrity, its trading subsidiary continued to lose money. After Fastow was promoted to chief financial officer and top manager of the subsidiary Global Finance in 1998, he suggested that Enron use the equity market to raise capital to finance its ongoing operations. Although Skilling was concerned that a stock offering might saturate the market and push the stock price down, Fastow convinced Lay and Skilling that a stock offering in the parent company would succeed. In addition to the $800 million raised in the parent company's stock offering, Enron raised several hundred million dollars by issuing stock in its subsidiaries. However, Skilling resisted additional equity financing. Because Enron had reached the limits of its debt ceiling, Skilling's decision eliminated all forms of conventional financing. To fill Enron's capital needs, Fastow pursued more off-balance-sheet financing. In the years immediately preceding Enron's bankruptcy, Enron Finance raised approximately $20 billion annually through structured financing that was approved by top management and the board of directors (Fusaro and Miller 2002; McLean and Elkind 2003). Many of these off-balance-sheet partnerships violated one or more of the rules governing securitization. For example, in one case, the third-party partner was an employee. However, most Enron managers were unaware of these arrangements because they were off-balance-sheet and, thus, not transparent.

By keeping its financial obligations off-balance-sheet, Enron was able to report ever-increasing revenues, which gave the impression of increased shareholder value. Enron stock value increased from $19 a share on November 5, 1997, to $82 on January 25, 2001, when the firm was listed as the seventh largest U.S. corporation. Throughout this period, Enron appeared to be financially sound to the public and to many of its employees. These appearances aided top managers in their efforts to encourage Enron employees to invest all or most of their 401(k) retirement accounts into Enron stock, which provided Enron with an additional source of capital. It is estimated that of the $2.1 billion in Enron's employee pension fund, $1.3 billion was in Enron stock in late 2000 (Fox 2003).

Unknown to most employees, investors, and oversight agencies, management's use of off-balance-sheet financing dramatically increased Enron's risk. That is, if the partnerships failed, shareholders were responsible. As widely understood now, this is precisely what occurred. In October 2001, Enron had to report a $618 million loss in a partnership; three weeks later, management restated net income by $586 million; and two weeks later, it had to repay $690 million in partnership debt (Levitt 2002). These events triggered an SEC investigation of its off-balance-sheet partnerships (Fusaro and Miller 2002). By late October, the value of Enron's stock dropped to $11 per share and management filed for bankruptcy on December 2, 2001. In the aftermath of the Enron meltdown, Andrew Fastow (2006) stated that he had engaged in transactions with banks that had a material impact on Enron's financial statements. In other words, structured financing in Enron's off-balance-sheet partnership was not limited to passive assets that, by definition, were not to have a material impact. Enron's $60 billion bankruptcy, which was the largest in U.S. history, resulted in substantial costs to society. While many large investors could absorb their losses, the same was not true of small investors. In addition to losing their jobs, thousands of Enron employees lost most of their retirement savings. Some of these employees were close to retiring, with little opportunity to rebuild their retirement savings. The retirement funds of the working classes also lost value because institutional investors, who managed their retirement funds, invested in Enron stock. For example, the retirement funds of 50,000 California state employees were managed by the California Public Employees' Retirement System, which held a substantial amount of Enron stock. Other investor losses occurred in investment banks and other financial firms that invested in Enron's off-balance-sheet partnerships. Losses to their shareholders were twofold. On the one hand, these firms lost much of the capital that they invested in Enron's off-balance-sheet partnerships. On the other, the SEC used securities laws to bring charges against several of the world's largest financial firms for financial wrongdoing associated with the Enron bankruptcy. Most of these firms settled without admitting guilt. By 2007, settlements from these lawsuits reached $7.3 billion, which lowered shareholder value in these firms.

Lawsuits were also brought against thirty-two Enron employees for violating securities and related laws. In return for testifying against Ken Lay and Jeffrey Skilling, Chief financial officer Andrew Fastow was given a six-year prison sentence for pleading guilty to two conspiracy counts. Skilling was sentenced to a 24-year prison term for conspiracy, securities fraud, false statements, and insider trading. Skilling, who continues to claim that he is innocent of any wrongdoing, is appealing his case. Other Enron executives involved with wrongdoing were charged with a range of financial crimes, including securities fraud, wire fraud, insider trading, falsifying records, and conspiracy. Several of these executives successfully fought the charges brought against them. Others were given probation or received prison terms that ranged from less than a year to 5.5 years.

Despite the widespread damage to society, few substantive changes were made to contain financial risk. Free-market advocates attributed the Enron bankruptcy to a "few bad apples." As a result, corporations continued to engage in high-risk derivatives trading and securitization in energy and other financial markets.

Ironically, the Enron failure created capital accumulation opportunities for the same investment banks that were the underwriters of Enron's off-balance-sheet partnerships. After the Enron bankruptcy, Bear Stearns, Credit Suisse, Citigroup, Deutsche Bank, Lehman Brothers, and Merrill Lynch all set up energy trading operations in Houston. Moreover, these and other investment banks continued to engage in political capitalism to redefine corporate–state relations in ways that allowed them to expand financial markets.

IV. CONCLUSION

The above analysis supports the central tenet of the organizational political economy framework. In response to capital accumulation constraints in the mid-1970s and early

1980s, corporate management engaged in political capitalism to redefine the organizational and political–legal arrangements in which corporations and markets are embedded. They exercised corporate and class power to transform the ideological, economic, and political–legal arrangements in ways that facilitated capitalist growth and development through financialization. However, these organizational and political–legal arrangements also increased firms' financial risks and created opportunities for managers to engage in financial malfeasance, chicanery, and crime. The new power bloc that emerged consisted primarily of the energy and financial capitalist class factions. Although the initial expansion of financialization occurred in the manufacturing sector (Prechel 2000, pp. 218–19) the energy and banking sectors were the most politically active sectors to advance financialization as a means to accumulate capital. However, many manufacturing and retail corporations (e.g., Ford, General Electric, General Motors, Sears) engaged in financialization because they realized that raising capital by restructuring their divisions as subsidiaries, selling securities in them, and creating subsidiaries to provide financing for their customers were means to advance their capital accumulation agendas. As a result, the lines between economic sectors became blurred and most sectors supported changes to policies and laws that permitted firms to participate in financial markets.

Four transformative changes contributed to this new social frontier. The first occurred in response to capital shortages during a period when U.S. manufacturing corporations needed capital to modernize their facilities so they could compete in global markets. The emergent political–legal arrangements expanded mutual funds and corporate retirement plans. Together with low interest rates, these arrangements encouraged the working and middle classes to invest their pretax income in mutual funds. These organizational and political–legal arrangements expanded the power of institutional investors, who began to pressure corporate managers to increase shareholder value. In response, corporate management increased the use of stock options as a form of executive compensation. Because stock options only have value if stock prices increase, this form of executive compensation created perverse incentives for managers to pursue strategies that increased their own wealth and placed small investors at risk. To illustrate, while many small investors, which included Enron employees, lost a substantial portion of their savings after the bankruptcy, many Enron executives exercised (i.e., sold) their stock options before the bankruptcy.

The second transformative change entailed the spread of more complex and flexible corporate structures that contributed information asymmetry between management and small investors. Throughout the middle decades of the 20th century, most large corporations were organized as the multidivisional form, where all parts of the corporation were part of a single legal entity. The primary exceptions were commercial banks and utilities, which were more tightly regulated by government oversight agencies. To unlock capital in the corporation, capitalists pressured the Executive Branch and Congress to eliminate the tax on internal capital transfers. Passage of the Tax Reform Act of 1986, which eliminated the capital transfer tax between legally independent corporate entities, simultaneously made the holding company/subsidiary structure viable and eliminated an important means to monitor capital transfers. The emergent organizational and political–legal arrangements created opportunities for parent companies to transfer capital in ways that overvalued their assets. To illustrate, in 1996 Enron acquired Mariner Energy for $185 million. Because Mariner was privately owned when it was acquired and Enron incorporated it as a wholly owned subsidiary, it never issued stock and therefore its value was not determined by the market. Mariner's speculative deep-water exploration business further contributed to the uncertainty of its value. These conditions created an opportunity for Enron to mark up the value of Mariner Energy, which strengthened the parent company's financial position when the parent company did not meet its earnings target. When Enron was forced to file for bankruptcy in 2001, management had valued Mariner at $347.4 million. However, the postbankruptcy accountant valued the subsidiary at less than a third of the parent company's valuation (McLean and Elkind 2003).

The third transformative change redefined the rules governing off-balance-sheet financing. While this form of financialization was extended first from banking to the manufacturing sector in the early 1980s, it quickly spread. By the 1990s, these and other forms of securitization were used widely throughout corporate America. Off-balance-sheet financing created opportunities for managers to mislead the investing public by giving the impression that a corporate balance sheet was strong when it was not. Moreover, many assets that qualify for off-balance-sheet treatment are not truly passive, as investors discovered when the underlying commodity (e.g., houses) lost value in 2007–2008.

The fourth transformative change occurred in derivatives trading markets. After experimenting with policies designed to revitalize the manufacturing sector, corporate and political leaders directed their attention toward the energy and financial sectors. The convergence of economic interests of energy and financial corporations resulted in a powerful and well-financed political coalition that successfully pressured Congress and the Executive Branch to pass financialization legislation. Whereas incremental changes in corporate political embeddedness occurred during the two decades following the economic downturns in the early 1980s, two political–legal arrangements were particularly important in creating opportunities for management to engage in financial wrongdoing. Whereas the decision by the CFTC paved the way for corporations to engage in unregulated derivatives trading, the Commodity Futures Modernization Act of 2000 revised the Commodity Exchange Act in a way that gave these arrangements more permanency and further legitimated the use of securitization and other forms of financialization. These new organizational and political–legal arrangements allowed managers to create a wide range of over-the-counter derivatives markets that were removed from public scrutiny and government oversight.

The historical transition to financialization of markets has important consequences for class power in American society. Managerial power increased to unprecedented levels in the late 20th century. Managerial power was enhanced by the spread of neoliberal ideology that championed the efficiency of markets and the inefficiency of government oversight, the emergence of corporate structures that concealed capital transfers from oversight agencies and the investing public, and the asymmetry of information between management and working- and middle-class investors.

By juxtaposing the ideology of neoliberalism (i.e., ideal) with the concrete organizational and political structures (i.e., real), the analysis shows that the markets that were created in the late 20th century did not distribute the kind of information that permitted most individuals to use it in ways that advanced their interests. Instead, these markets provided information that misled investors, especially small investors. Moreover, the exercise of managerial power after the Enron implosion curtailed efforts to change the organizational and political–legal arrangements in ways that limited opportunism and financial wrongdoing.[11]

Although neoliberal ideology, the financialization of the economy, and a decline in state power and an increase in managerial power suggest that a new social structure of accumulation has emerged (McDonough et al. 2010), these institutional arrangements have not achieved the stable capitalist growth and development similar to previous consolidation stages. This suggests that the institutional arrangements are still in the exploration stage. Sources of continued instability include record levels of income and wealth inequality, underemployment and unemployment, and crises inside large and complex corporations where financial transactions are hidden from the public and oversight agencies. These crises include the $6 billion trading loss at JP Morgan in 2012 where financial transactions were hidden from third-party oversight. Thus, the current level of state power remains insufficient in relationship to managerial power to implement public policies that protect society from risk-taking behaviors, market failures, and financial malfeasance.

Notes

1. The worst consequences of the 2008 crisis occurred in less developed societies whose economies (e.g., foreign exchange rates) are dependent on stability in financial markets (Prechel 2012).
2. The previous definition of financial wrongdoing (Prechel and Morris 2010) was expanded because consumers make financial decisions based, in part, on their understanding of the business code of conduct.
3. The theoretical framework is in contrast to the general trend in the social sciences where increased specialization of each new field and subfield examines a narrower set of research questions. This trend is problematic because society is moving toward greater complexity. Therefore, theories to explain social behavior must be sufficiently complex to capture how the emergent social structure affects behavior.
4. These investments into corporate securities were typically made without informing depositors.
5. Although some industrial corporations organized their assets as subsidiaries, they were concentrated in the largest automobile, food products, oil and gas, and pharmaceutical corporations. These subsidiaries typically operated independent of the central office.
6. This arrangement is viable because under the law corporations are artificial persons.

7. Sometimes management will refer to partnerships in a footnote in their annual report to stockholders. However, this information typically does not make the financial arrangements held in partnerships transparent to investors.

8. Historically, securitization was limited to short-term agreements that banks had with other banks (e.g., contracts on currency exchange rates).

9. The firm later became Dynegy.

10. InterNorth had the added incentive to merge because the corporate raider Irwin Jacobs was acquiring a large share of its stock. A merger would dilute Jacobs' shares and prevent the takeover.

11. Even after the 2008 crisis and the Great Recession, the capitalist class organized politically to block the implementation of key provisions of the 2010 Frank-Dodd Wall Street Reform and Consumer Protection Act.

REFERENCES

Abolafia, Mitchel. 2010. "The Institutional Embeddedness of Market Failure: Why Speculative Bubbles Still Occur." *Research in the Sociology of Organizations* 30: 177–200.

Beck, Ulrich. 2009. *World at Risk*. Malden, MA: Polity.

Brenner, Robert. 2004. "New Boom or New Bubble?" *New Left Review* 25: 76–100.

Bryce, Robert. 2002. *Pipe Dreams: Greed, Ego, and the Death of Enron*. New York: Public Affairs.

Burk, James. 1988. *Values in the Marketplace*. New York: Walter de Gruyter.

Campbell, John. 2010. "Neoliberalism in Crisis: Regulatory Roots of the U.S. Financial Meltdown." *Research in the Sociology of Organizations* 30: 65–101.

Chandler, Alfred. 1962. *Strategy and Structure*. Cambridge, MA: The M.I.T. Press.

Clinard, Marshall B., and Peter C. Yeager. 1980. *Corporate Crime*. New York: The Free Press.

Cruver, Brian. 2002. *Anatomy of Greed: The Unshredded Truth from an Enron Insider*. New York: Carroll & Graf Publishers.

Durkheim, Emile. 1933. *The Division of Labor in Society*. New York: The Free Press.

Eichenwald, Kurt. 2005. *Conspiracy of Fools*. New York: Broadway Books.

Fastow, Andrew. 2006. "*United States of America v. Andrew S. Fastow*: Declaration of Andrew S. Fastow." United States District Court Southern District of Texas Houston Division, September 25.

Financial Accounting Standards Board. 1959. *Accounting Research Bulletin No. 51, Consolidated Financial Statements*. Norwalk, CT: Financial Accounting Standards Board.

Fligstein, Neil. 1985. "The Spread of the Multidivisional Form among Large Firms, 1919–1979." *American Sociological Review* 50: 377–91.

Fligstein, Neil, and Adam Goldstein. 2010. "The Anatomy of the Market Securitization Crisis." *Research in the Sociology of Organizations* 30: 29–70.

Fox, Loren. 2003. *Enron: The Rise and Fall*. Hoboken, NJ: John Wiley and Sons, Inc.

Fusaro, Peter, and Ross Miller. 2002. *What Went Wrong at Enron*. Hoboken, NJ: John Wiley and Sons.

Gladwell, Malcolm. 2007. "Open Secrets: Enron, Intelligence, and the Perils of Too Much Information." *The New Yorker* (January 8).

Gordon, David, Richard Edwards, and Michael Reich. 1982. *Segmented Work, Divided Workers: The Historical Transformation of Labor in the United States*. New York: Cambridge University Press.

Hayek, Friedrich. 1991. *The Road to Serfdom*. London, UK: Routledge.

Hilferding, Rudolf. 1910 [1981]. *Finance Capital: A Study of the Latest Phase of Capitalist Development*. London: Routledge and Kegan Paul.

Investment Company Institute. 2013. *2013 Investment Company Fact Book*. Available at http://www.icifactbook.org/fb_ch6.html

Jensen, Michael. 1984. "Takeovers: Folklore and Science." *Harvard Business Review*, November-December: 109–21.

Johnston, David Cay. 2003. *Perfectly Legal*. New York: Penguin Books.

Kennickell, Arthur, Martha Starr-McCluer, and Brian Surette. 2003. "Recent Changes in U.S. Family Finances: Results from the 1998 and 2001 Survey of Consumer Finances." *Federal Reserve Bulletin*, January.

Kolko, Gabriel. 1963. *The Triumph of Conservatisms*. Glencoe IL: The Free Press.

Krippner, Greta. 2010. *Capitalizing on Crisis: The Political Origins of the Rise of Finance*. Cambridge, MA: Harvard University Press.

LeBaron, Dean, and Lawrence Speidell. 1987. "Why Are the Parts Worth More than the Sum? 'Chop Shop,' a Corporate Valuation Model." In *The Merger Boom*, edited by Lynn E. Browne and Eric S. Rosengren. Boston: Federal Reserve Bank of Boston.

Levitt, Arthur. 2002. *Take on the Street: What Wall Street and Corporate America Don't Want You to Know*. New York: Pantheon Books.

Marx, Karl. 1867 [1977]. *Capital*. New York: Vintage Books.

McDonough, Terrence, Michael Reich, and David Kotz. 2010. *Contemporary Capitalism and Its Crisis: Social Structure of Accumulation Theory for the 21st Century*. Cambridge: Cambridge University Press.

McLean, Bethany, and Peter Elkind. 2003. *The Smartest Guys in the Room: The Amazing Rise and Scandalous Fall of Enron*. New York: Fortune.

Mills, C. Wright. 1956. *The Power Elite*. Oxford, UK: Oxford University Press.

Oxford Dictionary of Business Management. 2006. Oxford, UK: Oxford University Press.

Palmer, Donald, P. Devereaux Jennings, and Xueguang Zhou. 1993. "Late Adoption of the Multidivisional Form by Large U.S. Corporations." *Administrative Science Quarterly* 38: 100–31.

Palmer, Donald, and Michael Maher. 2010. "The Mortgage Meltdown as a Normal Accident." *Research in Organizational Behavior* 30: 219–56.

Partnoy, Frank. 2004. "Enron and the Derivatives World." In *Enron: Corporate Fiascos and Their Implications*, edited by Nancy B. Rapoport and Bala G. Dharan. New York: Foundation Press.

Phillips, Kevin. 2002. *Wealth and Democracy: A Political History of the American Rich*. New York: Broadway Books.

Polanyi, Karl. 1944 [2001]. *The Great Transformation: The Political and Economic Origins of Our Time*. Boston: Beacon Press.

Porter, Michael. 1987. "From Competitive Advantage to Corporate Strategy." *Harvard Business Review* 65: 43–59.

Poulantzas, Nicos. 1974 [1978]. *Classes in Contemporary Capitalism*. London: Verso.

Powers, William Jr., Raymond S. Troubh, and Herbert S. Winokur, Jr. 2002. *Report of Investigation by the Special Investigation Committee of the Board of Directors of Enron Corp.* February 1.

Prechel, Harland. 1990. "Steel and the State: Industry Politics and Business Policy Formation, 1940–1989." *American Sociological Review* 55: 648–68.

Prechel, Harland. 2000. *Big Business and the State: Historical Transitions and Corporate Transformation, 1880s–1990s*. Albany: State University of New York Press.

Prechel, Harland. 2012. "Political Capitalism, Markets, and the Global Financial Crises." In *The Wiley-Blackwell Encyclopedia of Globalization*, 1st ed., edited by George Ritzer. Oxford: Blackwell Publishing.

Prechel, Harland, and John Boies. 1998. "Capital Dependence, Financial Risk, and Change from the Multidivisional to the Multilayered Subsidiary Form." *Sociological Forum* 13: 321–62.

Prechel, Harland, Theresa Morris, Tim Woods, and Rachel Walden. 2008. "Corporate Diversification Revisited: The Political-Legal Environment, the Multilayer-Subsidiary Form, and Mergers and Acquisitions." *Sociological Quarterly* 49: 849–78.

Prechel, Harland, and Theresa Morris. 2010. "The Effects of Organizational and Political Embeddedness on Financial Malfeasance in the Largest U.S. Corporations: Dependence, Incentives, and Opportunities." *American Sociological Review* 75: 331–54.

Roy, William. 1997. *Socializing Capital: The Rise of the Large Industrial Corporation in America*. Princeton, NJ: Princeton University Press.

Ruggie, John. 1982. "International Regimes, Transactions, and Change: Embedded Liberalism in the Postwar Economic Order." *International Organization* 36: 379–415.

Selznick, Phillip. 1949. *TVA and the Grass Roots*. Berkeley: University of California Press.

Simpson, Sally. 1986. "The Decomposition of Antitrust: Testing a Multi-Level, Longitudinal Model of Profit-Squeeze." *American Sociological Review* 51: 859–75.

Somers, Margaret, and Fred Block. 2005. "From Poverty to Perversity: Ideas, Markets, and Institutions over 200 Years of Welfare Debate." *American Sociological Review* 70: 260–89.

Stiglitz, Joseph. 2002. *Globalization and Its Discontents*. New York: W.W. Norton.

Sutherland, Edwin. 1949. *White Collar Crime*. New York: Dryden.

U.S. Congress. 2002. "How Lax Regulation and Inadequate Oversight Contributed to the Enron Collapse." House of Representatives, Minority Staff, Committee on Government Reform, 107th Congress, February.

U.S. Congress. 2003. "Investment Banks: The Role of Firms and Their Analysts with Enron and Global Crossing." Report to the Senate Committee on Banking, Housing and Urban Affairs and the House Committee on Financial Services, GAO-03-511. Washington, D.C.: Government Printing Office.

Useem, Michael. 1996. *Investor Capitalism: How Money Managers Are Changing the Face of Corporate America*. New York: Basic Books.

Weber, Max. [1921] 1978. *Economy and Society*, edited by Guenther Roth and Claus Wittich. Berkeley: University of California Press.

Yeager, Peter C. 1991. *The Limits of Law: The Public Regulation of Private Pollution*. New York: Cambridge University Press.

CHAPTER 16

··

ECONOMIC FLUCTUATIONS
AND CRISES

··

SALLY S. SIMPSON AND MELISSA RORIE

SOON after the global financial crash of 2008, speculation began in earnest about the recession's likely impact on crime rates (Police Executive Research Forum 2009; United Nations Office of Drug Control [UNODC] 2010). Even though the economic decline was hastened by a wide array of financial shenanigans by business (Shover and Grabosky 2010; Friedrichs 2012) and most citizens believe that white-collar crime contributed to the economic crisis (National White Collar Crime Center 2010), prognostication has centered primarily on the relationship between economic deterioration and changes in traditional crime (for exceptions, see DeFlem 2011; Levi, 2011; Benson, 2012).

Much of the recent conjecture about the financial crisis and crime appears to be tied to a countertrend spike in homicide (especially) rates (ABC News 2012; Press TV 2012), but scholarly interest in the impact of economic conditions on crime is longstanding. Bonger (1916), for instance, held capitalism responsible for creating a moral climate of egoism that inflamed material desires across all social classes. Criminal behavior, in class-appropriate forms, was the inevitable result. Durkheim (1951) linked rapid changes in social conditions associated with industrialization and a "disembodied market economy" (Bernburg 2002) to a breakdown in social control and subsequent normlessness (anomie). Increasing crime rates were not tied to economic deterioration per se. Rather, any rapid change in the economy—booms or depressions—could cause anomie.

Contemporary criminologists have also associated crime rates with economic fluctuations, producing an extensive body of empirical research on "street" crime. Much less attention has been directed at the impact of economic conditions on "suite" crimes, yet it stands to reason that corporate crimes (which are, by definition, committed in pursuit of financial gain) should exhibit a stronger relationship with economic dynamics.[1] The intent of this essay is to explore, theoretically and empirically, this connection. Is corporate offending affected by economic cycles and, if so, in what way? To frame our discussion, in section I we describe what is known about the relationship between economic fluctuations and street crimes. This literature guides our discussion in section II, where we review theory and research on economic fluctuations and corporate crime.[2] Section III provides a critical look at the existing literature by examining the sensitivity of research results to methodological and measurement matters, sampling issues, and simultaneity considerations. Finally, section IV concludes with recommendations for further study. The main conclusions discussed in this essay include the following:

- Most research on economic fluctuations and crime concentrates on traditional offenses, not white-collar or corporate crime.
- The dominant theoretical perspectives that predict a relationship between economic conditions and corporate crime are anomie-strain, rational choice, and routine activity theory. There is more empirical support for rational choice and routine activity predictions than for anomie-strain as the former explain a rise in corporate crime associated with both economic crisis and boom periods.
- Some crime types are more sensitive to economic fluctuations than are others.
- Research in this area needs to give greater consideration to the measurement of indicators and outcomes, sampling, temporal considerations, simultaneity, and political influences (how corporate behavior is monitored and policed).

I. Economic Fluctuations
and Street Crimes

Criminologists have offered a variety of opinions regarding the anticipated relationship between economic fluctuations and traditional crime rates. Perhaps the most common view is that certain types of crime will increase as the economy restricts and moves into recession; more particularly, economically driven crimes—"parasitic crimes" (Rosenfeld and Fornango 2007)—as well as those tied to stress (drugs and violence) are expected to rise. This pattern should reverse itself during boom periods. A counterargument anticipates that property crime, especially burglary, will decrease during recessions as higher levels of unemployment leave more people at home with fewer economic resources to purchase the kind of material items that are attractive for criminals to steal (Cohen and Felson 1979). Finally, noting the "paradox of crime amid plenty" (Wilson 1975) and a literature showing weak, inconsistent, and/or nonexistent empirical relationships between crime rates and economic indicators (Peterson 2011), a sizeable number of criminologists dismiss the relationship altogether.

There are good reasons to believe, however, that economic conditions promote crime. Contractions and expansions in the economy are thought to have an impact on street crime in two main ways—through criminal motivations and/or through criminal opportunities. In the first case, recessions may *exacerbate* the crime problem because people will experience higher levels of material deprivation. Such hardship is thought to create or exacerbate feelings of frustration and inadequacy or, alternatively, the perceived benefits of crime will come to outweigh the perceived costs. Second, economic busts may *alleviate* the crime problem because contraction naturally limits criminal opportunities (Cantor and Land 1985; Cook and Zarkin 1985). Economic booms are generally assumed to have the opposite effect—people are less motivated to offend, but there are more opportunities to do so. Criminal motivation theorists typically draw on strain theory or rational choice theory while opportunity theorists tend to use routine activity explanations.[3]

The empirical research on economic fluctuations and street crime has been somewhat inconsistent, with some studies supporting the motivation thesis and others the opportunity–crime link. Many studies find that economic hardships lead to more crime (e.g., Chiricos 1987; Freeman 1994; UNODC 2010; Nunley, Seals, and Zietz 2011) and some find that recession indicators predict less crime (Cohen, Felson, and Land 1980; Wilson 2011), but in general it appears that economic fluctuations have a differential impact depending on the type of crime (Cantor and Land 1985; Cook and Zarkin 1985; Levitt 2001; Arvanites and Defina 2006; Bushway, Cook, and Phillips 2012). Specifically, most research finds that unemployment and other economic indicators affect property but not violent crime (Cook and Zarkin 1985; Levitt 2001; Levitt 2004; Rosenfeld and Fornango 2007; Yearwood and Koinis 2011).[4]

Not all scholars treat opportunity and motivation as distinct processes. For instance, Cantor and Land (1985) suggest that recessions likely have a short-term effect by reducing the opportunity for crimes to occur, but if a recession lasts for a long time, frustration and stress will build and eventually motivate offending. Using data on the FBI's Uniform Crime Report (UCR) index crimes, they found some support for this argument. Specifically, property crimes exhibited this mixed effect whereby a higher unemployment rate had a short-term negative relationship and a long-term positive effect. The same was not true, however, for violent crimes, which had an inconsistent relationship with unemployment. Arvanites and Defina (2006) retested Cantor and Land's (1985) theory using different data. They found a negative relationship between the gross state product and the UCR index crime rates, which supports motivation theories; property crimes and robbery increased as a result of poor economic conditions. However, they found no support for the relationship between opportunity and property crime, nor was there a relationship between economic trends and more expressive violent crimes.

More recently, Kruger (2011) examined the effect of the entire business cycle (e.g., recession and economic expansion) on crime rates. He confirmed that economic cycles affect specific types of crime differently. Property crimes, violent crimes, and sex crimes increased during recessions. Alcohol/drug-related crimes and economic (white-collar) crimes increased during economic expansions. He concluded by suggesting that property crimes increase because of motivation due to economic inequality while violent and sex crimes increase because of feelings of distress or inadequacy, or because more leisure time is available. During economic expansions, higher levels of alcohol use correspond with increases in substance-related crimes. White-collar crimes likely increase during expansions because offenders expect more returns on such crimes (i.e., they are profitable), because there are more opportunities for such crimes, or because greed and a desire for status among certain groups are more manifest during conditions of economic plenty.

The next section examines theories and studies more specifically focused on economic conditions and a particular type of white-collar offending—corporate crime. For our purposes, we define corporate crime as acts by corporations and their representatives that are proscribed by law (civil, regulatory, and criminal) and involve guile, deception, and concealment for illicit advantage while giving the appearance of legitimacy in the organizational setting (Braithwaite 1984; Shover and Hochstetler 2006; Benson and Simpson 2009). Although managerial self-interest may play an indirect role in the offense, corporate crimes occur in the pursuit of organizational goals. Thus, conceptualization about the effect of economic fluctuations on corporate offending should give consideration to individuals embedded within the organizational/corporate context. In the next section, we review relevant theoretical approaches and their predictions about economic conditions and corporate crime followed by an assessment of the empirical evidence as it relates to these predictions.

II. Economic Fluctuations and Corporate Crimes

A. Theoretical Approaches

Similar to street crime, explanations for variations in corporate crime rates as a function of economic conditions typically draw upon motivational and opportunity theories.[5] Of these theories, anomie-strain is by far the most commonly used, although rational choice, opportunity, and organizational (institutional) theories appear to have more empirical support than strain explanations. The specific applications of these approaches to corporate crime are described in more detail below.

1. *Anomie-Strain Theory*

Anomie theory as elaborated by Passas (1993) and Vaughan (1983) advances Merton's (1938) observation that the upper classes are not immune from strains associated with means–ends disjunctures. Cultural pressures for material success are reinforced by the capitalist mode of production. Pressures on firms to make a profit and remain competitive are inherent to the system. Indeed, the major (and some would claim only) goal of a business corporation is to make the maximum possible profit (Conklin 1977; Passas 1993). Failure to achieve and sustain profitability can threaten the survival of the firm. Others suggest that strains due to blocked access, competition for resources, and constant pressures to expand market share increase the likelihood of firm innovation (Wang and Holtfreter 2012). Generally, the intense and continuous pressure to compete and be successful creates the conditions and motivation for corporate crime.

There are a few important differences in how anomie-strain theory has been applied to corporations compared with how it is theorized to affect individuals. First, competition among firms is inherent and non-stop. The capitalist race is unending—some competitors fall by the wayside but are replaced with new firms. Competitive volatility and rapid structural differentiation contribute to anomic conditions. In this context, moral/ethical socialization within business is disrupted and definitions of deviant behavior often are in flux. Second, economic goal achievement for firms can be blocked in two ways (Vaughan 1983, p. 58): (1) the means to the goals are blocked because companies cannot compete for legitimate opportunities (e.g., they are barred from entry by controllers) and (2) the goals themselves are restricted. Here, companies may gain entrance to the competition (means), but the outcome (ends) is a zero–sum game with only one winner (e.g., when firms compete for a contract).

From this perspective, deteriorating economic conditions affect corporate crime rates by exacerbating competitive pressures to stay afloat. When firm profitability is threatened and other means to profits are limited, decision makers within firms are likely to innovate. Under normal economic conditions, threats to company profits can come from within the company (ineffective management, poor products or services, bad investment decisions), but declining economic conditions that are associated with recessions affect the corporation from the outside—from its external environment. Recessionary periods affect supply and demand and market stability. Contraction affects "corporate abilities to obtain, legally, the resources that are necessary for survival" (Simpson 1986, p. 859). Profits are uncertain at the same time that competition among firms for scarce resources increases. Scarcity, therefore, is expected to cause corporate crime rates to rise.

Messner and Rosenfeld (1994) also extended anomie theory by highlighting how the natural anomic tendencies of modern capitalist societies have been aggravated by institutional power imbalances that tend to privilege the economy over the other social institutions primarily responsible for control and regulation (e.g., family, polity, religion, and education). This structural dynamic, coupled with the materialist goal orientation among actors, encourages an outcome orientation that favors efficiency over legitimacy to achieve goals. Amid anemic controls, a weakened economy should trigger more offending as corporations and their managers will have fewer legitimate means to achieve wealth.

2. *Rational Choice Theory*

In contrast to anomie-strain perspectives, rational choice theory could explain a rise in corporate crime rates during both economic crisis and boom periods. As a micro-level theory, rational choice focuses on decision makers within the firm and presumes that offending is a choice—the product of a rational process that takes into account the costs and benefits of crime vis-à-vis legitimate alternatives. The decision process operates similarly for both street and white-collar offenders (Shover and Hochstetler 2006), but it is more nuanced for corporate offenders than it may appear on the surface because offending choices are framed by managerial roles. In other words, corporate managers take into account their own situations as well as that of the business.

As articulated by Paternoster and Simpson (1993, 1996), the rational calculus for corporate managers is sensitive to personal as well as organizational considerations and may include a variety of different normative and instrumental considerations. Decision makers may consider the perceived certainty/severity of formal legal and informal sanctions; the perceived certainty/severity of loss of self-respect; the perceived cost of rule compliance; the perceived benefits of noncompliance; their moral inhibitions; perceived sense of legitimacy/fairness of rules; the situational characteristics of the criminal event; and their prior offending record (1993, p. 47). Moreover, as Shover and Hochstetler suggest, the benefits of crime are tied to the lures or attractions in the corporate environment (2006); lure is the perception that one's interests may be advanced at the expense of others with relatively little risk to oneself. The opportunity for self-benefit is too attractive to be ignored even when the potential risks of crime are obvious if due diligence is practiced (Barnett, 2011, p. 67). Lure for corporations and their managers may be the billions that can be made from mortgage origination fees or the immediate profit margin from the stocks traded on insider information. It may be the easy fix to the corporate pollution problem when managers believe that purchasing and installing expensive pollution abatement equipment in an old factory simply cannot be justified based on a cost/benefit assessment. Lure does not need to be illegal per se, but the short-term opportunity to benefit can cascade quickly into criminal activity.

How corporate crime rates respond to financial crises depends on how costs and benefits are affected by the economic constraints or, as Shover and Hochstetler (2006, p. 109) put it, "the structural conditions and generative worlds that lie 'behind' readiness to choose crime . . . shape offenders' evaluation of potential costs and benefits." Institutional theorists understand that economics and the broader cultural-cognitive, normative, and regulatory aspects of institutions affect the construction of rationality within companies (Fligstein 1990; Scott 2004). Consequently, the link between economic conditions and the regulatory environment (political-economy) also is considered part of the decision process. How does crisis affect regulatory processes? Is there more or less risk of discovery and punishment during economic downturns than during periods or expansion? Certainly police and regulatory budgets are negatively affected by recessionary periods and positively by prosperous ones (Irwin 2011). However, justice responses to illegality are likely more complex than this simple model. Building on Warren Buffett's observation that it is obvious who is swimming naked when the tide goes out, Levi (2011, 286) notes that "corporate indebtedness is a major trigger for the revelation of fraud, as it becomes impossible to hide large-scale fraud." But theorizing about crime and the economy tends to focus more on the effect of downturns, with less emphasis on the effect of economic booms on opportunities, motivations, and the possibilities for learning the techniques of crime (Benson 2012).

Opportunity and rational choice theory can be joined to account for higher levels of corporate crime during periods of economic crises. If crime is the consequence of the confluence of motivated offenders, an attractive target, and a lack of capable guardians, the supply of motivated offenders will increase with economic deterioration.[6] The supply of capable guardians, however, is a function of whether the firm's environment is constrained or munificent. During periods of crisis, there are fewer capable guardians—both within and external to the firm. And regulators may be unwilling to "kick business when it's down." So corporate offending would be expected to rise. However, crimes may also rise during boom periods. When the economy is growing, lure attracts not just corporate decision makers and firms but potential gatekeepers, who become co-conspirators (e.g., auditors). Formal and informal oversight may be overtaxed by the supply of opportunities (Levi 2012). Thus, boom and bust periods may not affect crime rates in predictable ways as economic effects are varied at the macro and micro levels.

Drawing from Finney and Lesieur's contingency model of organizational crime (1982, p. 261), we can depict the anticipated relationships predicted by each theory as economic conditions fluctuate. In figure 16.1, anomie-strain is linked to offending via anomic societal conditions (A, societal and cultural conduciveness), culture of competition (B, performance emphasis), and means–ends disjunctions linked to economic downturns (C, external and internal constraints and pressures). Criminogenic mechanisms exist both at the macro level, where crime "rates" for corporations will rise as the market becomes more uncertain and competitive, and at the micro level, as managers confront these challenges and assess choice options.

The rational choice model of offending is depicted via paths between B, C, D, E, F, and H. As individual actors, managers are subject to evaluations and assessments of their performance and that of the company (B). Consequently, their decision processes are influenced by financial considerations, which are tied to economic conditions (C and D—both growth and decline), along with other factors (H—the risk of getting caught, effectiveness of internal compliance systems, moral beliefs). Not all of these elements are depicted in the schematic (e.g., morality); however, we expect that some of the represented illustrated relationships are reciprocal. For instance, economic conditions affect the decisions managers make, and vice versa. Finally, although the literature is unclear how "lure" fits into decision-making processes (and how to measure it), we show it as a societal/individual state created by sociocultural conduciveness and performance emphasis (B) whose influence on crime depends on context. In this case, economic conditions mediate its influence on managerial decisions.

Finally, opportunity theory is depicted in the links between C, D, and H. Both economic growth and decline may be linked to crime in that economic fluctuations affect the supply of motivated actors, capable guardians, and opportune targets. As noted, during periods of recession the supply of motivated offenders (profit pressures) may increase at the same time that control mechanisms weaken (within and outside of the firm). Growth, on the other hand, can increase crime as opportunities for success increase, as potential offenders learn the techniques of crime (through market mimicry

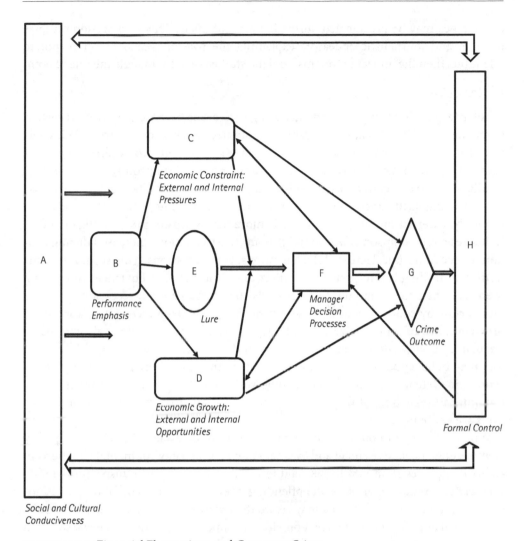

FIGURE 16.1 Financial Fluctuations and Corporate Crime

and diffusion), and motivations to take advantage of a growing and stable market accelerate (Benson 2012).

B. Empirical Findings

Research on white-collar and corporate crime demonstrates that such crime increases during economic contractions as well as during booms. Scholars interpret these contradictory results by drawing from both motivational and opportunity theories. Criminal motivations can be affected by both poor and good economic conditions, but different crime types may be precipitated during booms and busts. This next section outlines research and journalistic endeavors explaining the role of recessions on corporate offending, then the impact of "booms," and the studies that disentangle the role of both.

1. Recessions

Scholars argue that companies offend during recessions because they are less certain of making a profit or because they cannot obtain necessary resources from their environment. When a company is uncertain about how it is going to perform, the managers engage in certain behaviors to stabilize their assets (Simpson 1987; Keane 1993; Mulligan 2009) and extract resources from their environment (Staw and Szwajkowski 1975). During such times, there is a strong pressure to achieve financial goals and, generally, external monitoring of firms is more lax (Simpson 1987; Mulligan 2009). In her research, Simpson (1987) found that antitrust violations increased during economic recessions but decreased during more severe recessions. This seemingly contradictory finding is interpreted as a reflection of the structural balance confronting the state when the economic system is threatened. In general, recessions produce more crime by companies due to scarcity. But long and deep recessions/depressions provoke more of a protective stance by formal (and possibly informal) guardians. Regulatory policies de-emphasize sanctions and monitoring. In other words, regulators may believe that penalizing firms threatens the legitimacy and stability of the economic system as a whole. The Arthur Andersen "hangover" is a contemporary reminder to regulators of what can happen when regulatory enforcement and sanctions are exuberant.

When it comes to nonfinancial crimes and economic cycles, the relationship may be more equivocal. McKendall and Wagner (1997) studied environmental violations in eighty companies from 1983 to 1987 and found that while lower industry profitability was related to more environmental offending, there were many conditional relationships. Although industry factors may create the motivation to engage in crime, there are internal and external factors that provide the opportunity to do so. They also noted that the factors explaining serious environmental crimes are different from those explaining less serious offending.

2. Booms

Although many studies find a relationship between economic recessions and corporate crime, just as many studies find that these offenses increase during economic expansions. They generally explain these contradictory findings by examining investor expectations and monitoring: firms engage in misconduct to increase profits and keep their stakeholders happy, while stakeholders monitor company performance and conduct less closely. During booms, investors become irrationally exuberant and expect better earnings and are less likely to monitor firms who put out positive information (Rajgopal, Shivakumar, and Simpson 2007; Povel, Singh, and Winton 2007; Wang, Winton, and Yu 2010; Davidson 2011). Davidson (2011), for example, finds that accounting fraud is especially likely during the two years before an economic peak (measured using the GDP) because while expectations remain high, it becomes more difficult to maintain performance levels that meet those expectations. When corporations know that investors expect higher earnings, corporate leadership may choose to inflate earnings in order to avoid stock price declines (Rajgopal et al. 2007) or to inflate initial public offerings (Wang et al. 2010). Essentially, the corporation "caters" to investors' expectations for high returns (Rajgopal et al. 2007).

At the same time that investor expectations are high, investors' optimism means they are likely to only superficially monitor companies, thereby increasing opportunities for crime. For example, investors may only examine readily available public announcements if firms are performing well (Povel et al. 2007; Wang et al. 2010). Povel et al. (2007) go so far as to argue that regulations mandating public release of information may actually increase fraud because it reduces the cost of monitoring; in a booming economy, investors will rely on public information to tell them whom they should be scrutinizing (see also Wang et al. 2010).

In addition to investors' beliefs, managers' expectations about the economy as well as their companies' performances relative to others in their industry may drive offending behavior—again, due to an increased sense of pressure to perform strongly. Mishina et al. (2010) found a relationship between firm performance (relative to other corporations in the industry) and external expectations (deviance from expected returns based on past performance) and illegal corporate behavior among manufacturing firms listed in the S&P 500 from 1990 to 1999. They found that when a firm's performance exceeded that of their competitors and exceeded prior recorded returns (external expectations), corporate crime is more likely.

Fernandes and Guedes (2010) distinguished between managerial expectations about the economy and actual economic performance. Examining Securities and Exchange Commission enforcement actions from 1978 to 2004, they found that managers inflate company earnings when managers *expect* the economy to be good because they want to appear competitive with other companies, but few managers overstate earnings when the economy is *actually* strong. When the economy is strong, the company is likely performing well and therefore there is no need to misstate earnings.

3. *Both Recessions and Expansions*

Given the inconsistent results outlined above, it is not surprising that many studies find an effect of recessions *and* booms when including both in one study. Similar to the theories for street crime, scholars argue that both strain and opportunity matter; therefore, economic booms and busts both have the potential to affect crime rates. For example, Baucus and Near (1991) used event-history analysis to examine corporate crime in eighty-eight convicted and forty-two randomly selected companies over the time period from 1974 to 1983. They found that both economic recessions and economic expansion predicted more illegality but that corporate crimes were most likely during economic booms. During such expansions, firms were more likely to take advantage of opportunities to improve their position. Baucus (1994) elaborated on these results and argued that, similar to Durkheim, both booms and busts can be seen as times of uncertainty. Booms create more opportunities for crime, while busts are more likely to create pressure or motivations for crime. Similarly, Simpson (1986) found that anti-competitive behavior increased as *both* stock prices and unemployment increased. This implies that such behavior may be more likely during the transition of a business-cycle contraction to a business-cycle expansion (i.e., the time in which we pull out of a recession). Basically, some economic environments create unpredictability for companies, and managers will engage in illicit behaviors in their attempts to stabilize the company's earnings.

The effect of an uncertain economic environment can be seen at the industry level as well. Using Clinard and Yeager's (1980) data on manufacturing companies in the late 1970s, Wang and Holtfreter (2012) examined the role of strain and opportunity at both the corporate and the industry level. Although they found that poorly performing firms located in poorly performing industries were more likely to offend, growing firms in growing industries were more likely to offend as well. Industry growth may offer more opportunities whereby firms can grow via different methods (including crime). Furthermore, growing industries may be more competitive and necessitate criminal methods to maintain competitiveness at the firm level.

Other scholars argue that different types of crime respond to different economic environments. Simpson (1986) found that economic pressures can have opposing effects on trivial as opposed to serious offenses: trivial crimes seem to increase with increased industry profitability, while more serious collusion occurs when the industry is experiencing economic pressure. It appears that antitrust offending will occur under all economic conditions, but the form it takes differs according to what is happening in the larger economy. Interestingly, a recent report by National Public Radio, which detailed how the recession is affecting the occurrence of financial crimes, argues the exact opposite. Small-scale financial crimes such as mortgage fraud and identity theft appeared to be on the rise during the first part of the recession, but major financial crimes were few and far between. The author argued that the increase in small-scale financial crimes was due to increased motivation (i.e., economic hardship, anger with employers) as well as the fact that more people were getting caught with increased enforcement efforts. Conversely, he suggested that corporations were subject to more scrutiny in a bad economy, and therefore major financial crimes are less likely to occur (Whitelaw 2009).

Overall, the literature is mixed as to the impact of financial crises on corporate offending patterns. Theoretical arguments can be used to predict increasing crime rates during both retraction and boom periods, and the empirical literature finds support for both arguments. In the next section, we assess the sensitivity of the empirical data to measurement, sample, and other sources of bias and conclude with recommendations for future research.

III. Assessing the Literature: Contradictions and Consistencies

The review of the literature shows inconsistencies in the relationship between economic cycles and corporate crime. Some inconsistencies may be explained theoretically since motivational theories and opportunity theories typically predict different outcomes, but there are other reasons we may not have a clear consensus about the impact of economic recessions or booms on corporate crime. Measurement or recording issues affect the reported empirical relationships in different studies. This section will review potential explanations for the inconsistent findings in the research.

A. Economic Indicators

How economic conditions are measured affects empirical findings. Rosenfeld and Fornango (2007) discussed the use of various economic instruments—unemployment, the gross state product, consumer perceptions—on the street crime/economic cycle relationship and the limitations of each. Certain measures may too broad and fail to capture the specific economic issue at hand, other measures may be too narrow and miss relevant factors related to crime, or it may be more important to assess how *perceptions* of the economy influence crime (i.e., whether people are truly feeling strained during recessions) as opposed to using objective economic measures. Rosenfeld and Fornango (2007) showed that using alternative measures of economic status affected the observed relationship between economic conditions and crime. Similarly, Yearwood and Koinis (2011) found that different measures of the economy (supplemental social security income, average wage and salary disbursements, the consumer price index, and per capita personal income) had differential effects by crime type. Most relevant to the current discussion is their fraud and embezzlement outcomes: they found unemployment to be unrelated to these white-collar crimes, but *increases* in wage and salary disbursements and per capita personal income were associated with increases in these crimes. We could not find any studies comparing different economic indicators of financial crisis and their associations with corporate crime,[7] although it is clearly an important avenue for future research.

B. Outcomes Measured

It is also likely that economic conditions affect different types of corporate crimes in unique ways. Although all corporate crimes are (by definition) committed to benefit the company, the opportunity structures for various crimes are likely to be very different. For example, during booms, it may be easier to hide accounting fraud with profits but harder to hide environmental offending when regulatory resources are plentiful. Corporate crime scholars should emulate the research done that compares the economy–crime relationship of index property crimes to violent crimes (Cantor and Land 1985; Cook and Zarkin 1985; Levitt 2001; Aravintes and Defina 2006; Bushway et al. 2012) to gain a better understanding of when and how changing economic conditions may differentially affect corporate crime types. In addition, the corporate crime empirical research relies on different types of crime data—offender and victimization self-reports, inspection data, and prosecution or enforcement data. Unlike street crime, where there have been extensive comparisons of data sources over time, nothing of the sort has been done in the corporate crime area. It would be useful to learn more about how these different sources of crime data parallel or diverge from one another as economic conditions shift.

C. Sampling Issues

Inconsistent findings from both street and corporate crime research are also a likely consequence of the different population samples used across studies. One research question of interest is how the economy–corporate crime relationship occurs internationally. We know that certain countries and regions were affected more than others by the recent economic crisis and that the models predicting street crimes differ across countries (UNODC, 2010). It may be that certain areas or countries have more protective factors in place that promote resistance to offending in the face of economic uncertainty. For example, Cao, Zhao, and Ren (2010) found that national-level measures of social support reduce anomie among individuals. Does social support have a similar protective effect against corporate offending? Similarly, certain companies may exhibit resistance in the face of uncertainty. Some research indicates that the attitudes of top management or the presence of a corporate culture of compliance protects against offending (Gunningham, Kagan, and Thornton 2003; Gibbs 2006; Parker and Nielsen 2009); we should do more to assess how salient these factors are under different economic conditions.

D. Temporal Considerations

Another measurement issue of import is the temporal aspect. As the UNODC (2010) noted, results may be affected by whether economic and crime trends are measured over the long term as opposed to taking a more short-term snapshot:

> [C]rime series data demonstrate that crime levels are often subject to *long-running* trends that may be related to a complex interplay of gradually changing

socio-economic factors. Such factors have been proposed to determine an "equilib-rium" or underlying level of crime, with short-term changes tending to be "corrected back" in subsequent years. In addition to long-running trends, crime levels may also be affected on a medium-term *seasonal* basis. Seasonal crime level increases may typically be observed during summer, for instance. As such, any time series analysis of the act of (comparatively) short term economic crisis must be placed within the context of such long-run and medium term trends. (UNODC 2010, p. 9, emphasis in the original)

Given that individual offenses by corporations often occur over a long period of time, temporal factors should be considered especially relevant when examining the relationship between economic fluctuations and such crimes.

E. Simultaneity Issues

A corollary to temporal issues is the question of whether offending or economic instability comes first. Although most research assumes that recessions or booms drive offending, it is likely that corporate behavior has an impact on economic sta-bility (see Barnett 1981). An obvious example is the prevalence of unethical and ille-gal practices in the mortgage industry that purportedly led to the worst economic crisis in recent history (National White Collar Crime Center 2010; Shover and Grabosky 2010; Friedrichs 2012). Statistical models must take such concerns into account to more accurately represent the relationship, but Levi (2012) cautions that it is extremely difficult to disentangle cause and effect, especially because the social reaction to criminals (moral panics and "folk devils") differs not only between tradi-tional and white-collar offenders but also between high-status and low-level white-collar offenders.

F. Recording by Regulatory Agencies

In addition to methodological concerns, the association between corporate crime and the economy is likely tempered by the capacity of formal and informal parties to prevent such behavior. As discussed above, in times of recession regulators may be less punitive toward corporations and therefore the relationship between recession and crime would appear to be negative, as offending will not be recorded as often. During booms, regulators may have more resources to conduct investigations and inspections and therefore may discover more crime. For example, Simpson (1987) argued that the apparent discrepancy between the severity of the recession and anti-trust offending may be due more to regulatory recording behavior than to actual offending. Clearly, there is a need to move beyond regulatory and law enforcement data to avoid such biases.

IV. CONCLUSION

In this chapter, we have demonstrated that economic fluctuations have inconsistent effects on corporate offending. In contrast to the empirical research on street crimes, studies show that profit-oriented crimes by corporations occur during both recessions and times of economic euphoria. Limited research suggests that certain types of crimes may be more likely during different economic cycles, but results are somewhat contradictory and may vary across different categories of crimes (e.g., antitrust violations vs. financial frauds). Because research in this area is sparse and does not do enough to account for alternative explanations, future research needs to consider issues related to operationalization, modeling, sampling, and the recording of offending data. Without more rigorous research, it is difficult to make informed recommendations for policy based on our current state of knowledge.

NOTES

1. Note that although we may mention white-collar offending briefly, this essay is focused on explaining the role of economic cycles on *corporate* crime.
2. It is interesting to note that the empirical data on street crimes focus on the relationship between economic cycles and crime *rates*, while the studies on corporate crime focus on how economic cycles affect offending by individual corporations.
3. These theories will be developed in greater detail in section II.
4. For example, Rosenfeld and Fornango (2007) use the Index of Consumer Sentiment, while Levitt (2001) discusses alternative methods of measuring unemployment's effects (specifically panel data, instrumental variable analysis, natural experiments, comparative data, and individual-level data). Levitt (2004) mentions unpublished works that use measures such as wages of low-income workers (p. 170). Yearwood and Koinis (2011) contrast unemployment to indicators of supplemental social security income, average wage and salary disbursements, the consumer price index, and per capita personal income.
5. The terms *white-collar* and *corporate crime* are conceptual, not legal, expressions. Although certain crimes known to police may be classified as white collar or corporate, there are a myriad of challenges to creating a crime rate for these offense types (Simpson, Harris, and Mattson 1993; Gibbs and Simpson 2009). In the next sections, we link economic conditions to patterns of corporate offending and not to crime rates *per se*.
6. As Conklin (1977) reminds us, "Completely, the only goal of a business corporation is to make the maximum possible profit over a long period" (p. 41).
7. There is abundant research on how different measures of corporate financial performance affect corporate crime (see, e.g., Shaw and Szwajkowski 1975; Clinard and Yeager 1980; Simpson 1986; Jamieson 1994; Simpson, Garner, and Gibbs 2007). In her study of corporate antitrust violations, Simpson (1987) uses multiple indicators of business cycles to assess whether leading indicators of recession (stock price) have different effects than those that lag (unemployment) or if one type of recession (inventory) has a different effect on crime than other types.

REFERENCES

ABC News. 2012. "Will Recession Make Cities Dangerous Again?" *ABC News* (December 4). Available at http://abcnews.go.com/US/story?id=92121&page=1

Arvanites, Thomas M., and Robert H. Defina. 2006. "Business Cycles and Street Crime." *Criminology* 44: 139–64.

Barnett, Harold C. 1981. "Corporate Capitalism, Corporate Crime." *Crime and Delinquency* 27: 4–23.

Barnett, Harold C. 2011. "The Securitization of Mortgage Fraud." In *Economic Crisis and Crime*, pp. 65–84, edited by Mathieu DeFlem. Bingley, UK: Emerald Group Publishing.

Baucus, Melissa S. 1994. "Pressure, Opportunity, and Predisposition: A Multivariate Model of Corporate Illegality." *Journal of Management* 20: 699–721.

Baucus, Melissa S., and Janet P. Near. 1991. "Can Illegal Corporate Behavior Be Predicted? An Event History Analysis." *Academy of Management Journal* 34: 9–36.

Benson, Michael L. 2012. "Evolutionary Ecology, Fraud, and the Global Financial Crisis." In *Contemporary Issues in Criminological Theory and Research: The Role of Social Institutions*, pp. 299–305, edited by Richard Rosenfeld, Kenna Quinet, and Crystal Garcia. Belmont: Wadsworth (Cengage Learning).

Benson, Michael L., and Sally S. Simpson. 2009. *White-Collar Crime: An Opportunity Perspective*. New York: Routledge.

Bernburg, Jon G. 2002. "Anomie, Social Change, and Crime." *British Journal of Criminology* 42: 729–42.

Bonger, Willem A. 1916. "Criminality and Economic Conditions." Boston: Little Brown. (F. H. Norcross, Trans.)

Braithwaite, John. 1984. *Corporate Crime in the Pharmaceutical Industry*. London: Routledge and Kegan Paul.

Bushway, Shawn, Philip J. Cook, and Matthew Phillips. 2012. "The Overall Effect of the Business Cycle on Crime." *German Economic Review* 13: 436–46.

Cantor, David, and Kenneth C. Land. 1985. "Unemployment and Crime Rates in the Post–World War II United States: A Theoretical and Empirical Analysis." *American Sociological Review* 50: 317–32.

Cao, Liqun, Rouhui Zhao, and Ling Ren. 2010. "Social Support and Anomie: A Multilevel Analysis of Anomie in Europe and North America." *International Journal of Offender Therapy and Comparative Criminology* 54: 625–39.

Chiricos, Theodore G. 1987. "Rates of Crime and Unemployment: An Analysis of Aggregate Research Evidence." *Social Problems* 34: 187–212.

Clinard, Marshall B., and Yeager, Peter C. 1980. *Corporate Crime*. New York: Free Press.

Cohen, Lawrence E., and Marcus Felson. 1979. "Social Change and Crime Rate Trends: A Routine Activity Approach." *American Sociological Review* 44: 588–608.

Cohen, Lawrence E., Marcus Felson, and Kenneth C. Land. 1980. "Property Crime Rates in the United States: A Microdynamic Analysis, 1947–1977; with Ex Ante Forecasts for the Mid-1980s." *American Journal of Sociology* 86: 90–118.

Conklin, John E. 1977. *Illegal but not Criminal*. Englewood Cliffs, NJ: Prentice Hall

Cook, Phillip J., and Gary A. Zarkin. 1985. "Crime and the Business Cycle." *Journal of Legal Studies* 14: 115–28.

Davidson, Robert H. 2011. *Accounting Fraud: Booms, Busts, and Incentives to Perform*. Ph.D. dissertation, The University of Chicago, School of Business.

Deflem, Mathieu. 2011. *Economic Crisis and Crime*. Sociology of Crime Law and Deviance, Vol. 16. Bingley, UK: Emerald Group Publishing.

Durkheim, Emile. 1951. *Suicide: A Study in Sociology*. Glencoe, IL: The Free Press.

Fernandes, Nuno, and Jose Guedes. 2010. "Keeping Up with the Joneses: A Model and a Test of Collective Accounting Fraud." *European Financial Management* 16: 72–93.

Finney, Henry C., and Henry R. Lesieur. 1982. "A Contingency Theory of Organizational Crime." In *Research in the Sociology of Organizations*, pp. 255–59, edited by Samuel B. Bacharack. Greenwich, CT: JAI Press.

Fligstein, Neil 1990. *The Transformation of Corporate Control*. Cambridge, MA: Harvard University Press.

Freeman, Richard B. 1994. *Crime and the Job Market*. Working Paper #4910 for the National Bureau of Economic Research. Available at http://www.nber.org/papers/w4910

Friedrichs, David O. 2012. "Wall Street: Crime Never Sleeps." In *How They Got Away with It: White-Collar Criminals and the Financial Meltdown*, pp. 1–44, edited by Susan Will, Stephen Handalman, and David C. Brotherton. New York: Columbia University Press.

Gibbs, Carole. 2006. *Corporate Citizenship, Sanctions, and Environmental Crime*. Ph.D. dissertation, University of Maryland, Department of Criminology and Criminal Justice.

Gibbs, Carole, and Simpson, Sally S. 2009. "Measuring Corporate Environmental Crime Rates: Progress and Problems." *Crime, Law, and Social Change* 51: 87–107.

Gunningham, Neil, Robert A. Kagan, and Dorothy Thornton. 2003. *Shades of Green*. Palo Alto, CA: Stanford University Press.

Irwin, Darrell D. 2011. "The Showdown with Shrinking Budgets: Police Departments in Economic Downturns." In *Economic Crisis and Crime*, pp. 195–212, edited by Mathieu Deflem. Sociology of Crime Law and Deviance, Vol. 16. Bingley, UK: Emerald Group Publishing.

Jamieson, Katherine M. 1994. *The Organization of Corporate Crime: Dynamics of Antitrust Violation*. Thousand Oaks, CA: Sage.

Keane, Carl. 1993. "The Impact of Financial Performance on the Frequency of Corporate Crime: A Latent Variable Test of Strain Theory." *Canadian Journal of Criminology* 35: 293–308.

Kruger, Niclas A. 2011. "The Impact of Economic Fluctuations on Crime: A Multiscale Analysis." *Applied Economics Letters* 18: 179–82.

Levi, Michael. 2011. "Social Reactions to White-Collar Crimes and Their Relationship to Economic Crisis." In *Economic Crisis and Crime*, pp. 87–105, edited by Mathieu DeFlem. Bingley, UK: Emerald Group Publishing.

Levi, Michael. 2012. "Trends in Fraud." In *Contemporary Issues in Criminological Theory and Research: The Role of Social Institutions*, pp. 270–98, edited by Richard Rosenfeld, Kenna Quinet, and Crystal Garcia. Belmont: Wadsworth (Cengage Learning).

Levitt, Steven D. 2001. "Alternative Strategies for Identifying the Link between Unemployment and Crime." *Journal of Quantitative Criminology* 17: 377–90.

Levitt, Steven D. 2004. "Understanding Why Crime Fell in the 1990s: Four Factors That Explain the Decline and Six That Do Not." *Journal of Economic Perspectives* 18: 163–90.

McKendall, Marie A., and John A. Wagner. 1997. "Motive, Opportunity, Choice, and Corporate Illegality." *Organization Science* 8: 624–47.

Merton, Robert K. 1938. "Social Structure and Anomie." *American Sociological Review* 3: 672–82.

Messner, Steven F., and Richard Rosenfeld. 1994. *Crime and the American Dream.* Belmont: Wadsworth.

Mishina, Yuri, Bernadine J. Dykes, Emily S. Block, and Timothy G. Pollock. 2010. "Why 'Good' Firms Do Bad Things: The Effect of High Aspirations, High Expectations, and Prominence on the Incidence of Corporate Illegality." *Academy of Management Journal* 53: 701–22.

Mulligan, Michael. 2009. "The Devil on Recession's Shoulder." *Accountancy Magazine* 143: 44.

National White Collar Crime Center. 2010. *National Public Survey on White Collar Crime.* Fairmont, WV: Author.

Nunley, John M., Rihcard A. Seals, and Joachim Zietz. 2011. "Demographic Change, Macroeconomic Conditions, and the Murder Rate: The Case of the United States, 1934–2006." *Journal of Socio-Economics* 40: 942–8.

Parker, Christine, and Vibeke L. Nielsen. 2009. "Corporate Compliance Systems: Could They Make Any Difference?" *Administration and Society* 41: 3–37.

Passas, Nikos. 1993. "Anomie Theory and Corporate Deviance." *Contemporary Crisis* 14: 157–78.

Paternoster, Raymond, and Sally S. Simpson. 1993. "A Rational Choice Theory of Corporate Crime." In *Routine Activity and Rational Choice,* pp. 37–58, edited by Ronald V. Clarke and Marcus Felson. Vol. 5 of *Advances in Criminological Theory.* New Brunswick, NJ: Transaction Publishers.

Paternoster, Raymond, and Sally S. Simpson. 1996. "Sanction Threats and Appeals to Morality: Testing a Rational Choice Model of Corporate Crime." *Law and Society Review* 30: 549–84.

Peterson, Richard R. 2011. "Employment, Unemployment, and Rates of Intimate Partner Violence: Evidence from the National Crime Victim Surveys." *Sociology of Crime, Law, and Deviance* 16: 171–93.

Police Executive Research Forum. 2009. *Violent Crimes and the Economic Crisis: Police Chiefs Face a New Challenge.* Washington, D.C.: Author.

Povel, Paul, Rajdeep Singh, and Andrew Winton. 2007. "Booms, Busts, and Fraud." *Review of Financial Studies* 20: 1219–54.

Press TV. 2012. "Crime Rates Increased in Spain Due to Worsening Economic Crisis." (August 1). Available at http://www.presstv.ir/detail/2012/08/01/253812/economic-crisis-ups-crime-rates-in-spain/

Rajgopal, Shivaram, Lakshmanan Shivakumar, and Ana V. Simpson. 2007. *A Catering Theory of Earnings Management.* Working paper. Available at http://papers.ssrn.com/sol3/papers.cfm?abstract_id=991138

Rosenfeld, Richard, and Robert Fornango. 2007. "The Impact of Economic Conditions on Robbery and Property Crime: The Role of Consumer Sentiment." *Criminology* 45: 735–69.

Scott, W. Richard. 2004. "Institutional Theory: Contributing to a Theoretical Research Program." In *Great Minds in Management: The Process of Theory Development,* pp. 460–84, edited by Ken G. Smith and Michael A. Hitt. Oxford, UK: Oxford University Press.

Shover, Neal, and Peter Grabosky. 2010. "Editorial Introduction White-Collar Crime and the Great Recession." *Criminology and Public Policy* 9: 429–33.

Shover, Neal, and Andy Hochstetler. 2006. *Choosing White-Collar Crime.* New York: Cambridge University Press.

Simpson, Sally S. 1986. "The Decomposition of Antitrust: Testing a Multi-Level, Longitudinal Model of Profit-Squeeze." *American Sociological Review* 51: 859–75.

Simpson, Sally S. 1987. "Cycles of Illegality: Antitrust Violations in Corporate America." *Social Forces* 65: 943–63.

Simpson, Sally S., Joel Garner, and Carole Gibbs. 2007. *Why Do Corporations Obey Environmental Law?* U.S. Department of Justice, National Institute of Justice Final Report. Washington, D.C.: National Institute of Justice.

Simpson, Sally S., Anthony R. Harris, and Brian A. Mattson. 1993. "Measuring Corporate Crime." In *Understanding Corporate Criminality*, pp. 115–40, edited by Michael Blankenship. New York: Garland.

Staw, Barry M., and Eugene Szwajkowski. 1975. "The Scarcity-Munificence Component of Organizational Environments and the Commission of Illegal Acts." *Administrative Science Quarterly* 1975: 345–54.

United Nations Office on Drugs and Crime. 2010. *Monitoring the Impact of Economic Crisis on Crime.* GIVAS Final Report. Vienna, Austria: Author.

Vaughan, Diane. 1983. *Controlling Unlawful Organizational Behavior: Social Structure and Corporate Misconduct.* Chicago: University of Chicago Press.

Wang, Tracy Y., Andrew Winton, and Xiaoyun Yu. 2010. "Corporate Fraud and Business Conditions: Evidence from IPOs." *Journal of Finance* 65: 2255–92.

Wang, Xia, and Kristy Holtfreter. 2012. "The Effects of Corporation- and Industry-Level Strain and Opportunity on Corporate Crime." *Journal of Research in Crime and Delinquency* 49: 151–85.

Whitelaw, Kevin. 2009. "Is Recession Causing Rise in Financial Crimes?" *National Public Radio* (November 13). Available at http://www.npr.org/templates/story/story.php?storyId=120096862

Wilson, James Q. 1975. *Thinking about Crime.* New York: Basic Books.

Wilson, James Q. 2011. *If Unemployment Has Shot Up, Why Has the Crime Rate Gone Down?* Lecture given to the Manhattan Institute. Available at http://www.manhattan-institute.org/html/wilson.htm

Yearwood, Douglas L., and Gerry Koinis. 2011. "Revisiting Property Crime and Economic Conditions: An Exploratory Study to Identify Predictive Indicators beyond Unemployment Rates." *Social Science Journal* 48: 145–58.

CHAPTER 17

··

CULTURAL VARIATION

··

SUSYAN JOU, BILL HEBENTON, AND LENNON
Y. C. CHANG

ON the significance of "culture," one notable commentator rightly asserted, "the concept of culture has moved from the periphery to the very center of scientific investigation, and culture figures as a primary rather than dependent variable in global change" (Karstedt 2001, p. 286). Criminology has been no exception in this foregrounding of culture both as a theoretical concept and as an object of analysis (Parnell and Kane 2003; Garland 2011). Tylor (1920, p. 5) offered, perhaps, the most famous inclusive definition: "Culture is that complex whole which includes knowledge, belief, art, morals, law, customs, and any other capabilities and habits acquired by man as a member of society."

Culture, then, can be understood as a set of meanings, values, and interpretations that forms a specific social force independently and partially autonomous from social structure and institutional contexts. Thus, cultural patterns originate from and result in prototypical environmental constraints and patterns of social structure, producing and reproducing economic and institutional arrangements. Operating as "shared restraints" on behavior, culture, properly understood, has both cognitive and material outcomes (Karstedt 2001). Yet, of course, because of their all-embracing referents, cultural explanations run the serious risk of tautology. Inevitably, we need to be mindful of the potential for problems of conceptual confusion that may arise from the multivalent nature of the concept of culture and of the need and importance of teasing out how one's research question determines culture as an object of analysis (Garland 2011; Melossi, Sozzo, and Sparks 2011).

Cultural explanation has two senses broadly recognized in the literature (Brightman 1995; Sewell 1999): (1) culture opposed to not culture and (2) culture as totalizing term, which encompasses the impact of contrasting cultures. The first marks an analytical abstraction, artificially separated from other drivers and constraints that help determine social action; the second uses the notion of culture as shorthand for a bounded (normally taken as nation-state) cluster of beliefs, values, and customary "understandings."

For comparative criminology, the intriguing question concerns whether culture, in either sense, can be adduced as a meaningful independent variable affecting rates of white-collar crime (see Coleman 1987). As we will illustrate, few credible claims to any kind of generalization can be made regarding this question, largely because of the elusiveness of adequate data.

The nature of white-collar crime—its complexity, the power of its perpetrators—means that only an unrepresentative minority of offenses is detected and officially recorded. Not only is the problem of underreporting less severe with regard to common offenses, but also alternative measures such as self-reports and victim surveys are problematic when applied in the arena of white-collar crime. The latter are questionable because many victims of white-collar crime are unaware that they have been victimized, whereas the former are questionable because such offenders will not respond to surveys or do not consider their activities as criminal in the first place. The enormous difficulties of assessing the level of white-collar crime in one country at one point in time have been well rehearsed in the literature (Reiss and Biderman 1980).

On the other hand, questions on whether "cultural values" or certain "organizational cultures" generate greater white-collar criminality than others are somewhat more manageable and consequently have attracted significant empirical work. Furthermore, it is apparent that some societies suffer more than others from specific forms of governmental corruption and graft (Quah 2003, 2013). Given similarities and/or differences in social, political, and economic systems—at an aggregate and collective level—some commentators reach for explanations rooted in cultural patterns (Sandholtz and Taagepera 2005; Kirkman et al. 2006; Minkov 2011). In part, this preference may occur because, despite profound and rapid social change, basic cultural patterns seem to have a higher degree of inertia than is often assumed. As Inglehart and Hofstede have shown in their classic studies of modernization and value patterns, the relative position of cultural patterns remains stable through decades (Hofstede 1984; Inglehart 1997).

In section I of this essay, we consider the conceptual underpinnings of cultural variation and its uses and implications within particular forms of cultural values research on corruption (including bribery and intellectual property fraud). Section II considers the Chinese cultural practice of *guanxi*, defined as a network of personal relationships emerging from the fundamentals of Chinese culture, traditions, and social organization. In particular, it analyzes how *guanxi* in Chinese culture relates to forms of white-collar crime, including corruption, and is illustrative of how structure and agency can act as constraints on culture. Section III draws a number of pertinent conclusions, substantive and methodological, about cultural variation and white-collar criminality. The main conclusions reached in this essay are as follows:

- Cultural values function as factors or explanatory variables. Their impact can be direct, and culture can be conceptualized either as an independent or a meditating variable. Indirectly, culture can be construed as either a contextual or moderating variable.

- A growing body of research has sought to conceptualize societal values in different ways, and past research has identified correlations between various values and various forms of white-collar crime, such as, for instance, corruption.
- If they are to inform better our understanding of white-collar crime, explanations that invoke cultural variation require careful parsing of the roles of structure and agency, ideally detailing how processes and mechanisms translate culture into action. This undertaking can be best accomplished by drawing upon dialectical and historical sources.
- Culture is just one partial aspect of any adequate explanation for white-collar crime, part of the mix with other aspects of action that are more commonly understood as political or economic. Indeed, one of the problems with cultural theories of white-collar crime derives from this very variety of independent constructs.

I. Culture and Cultural Variation

When the idea of culture is invoked as an independent variable in an attempt to explain aggregate rates of white-collar crime, it is normally the intention to isolate specifically cultural forces and to distinguish them from other kinds of social/political/economic factors—that is, culture as opposed to not culture (Garland 2011). Such analyses are typically reductive in their conception of culture and often rely on "thin" description of what culture is (Geertz 1988). Further, there is a broader conceptual problem of isolating "the culture," for example, from "the economic"—a category error recognized by the classic writers on the subject. Culture (values) is embodied in both economic ends and means, with culture integral to economic life (Geertz 1988). Such distinctions rarely can withstand close scrutiny, because they operate largely as analytical "convenient fictions," artificially separating out aspects of human action and social practice that are intermeshed and integrated.

If we turn to culture as a "totalizing" concept—its second use—then the key analytical distinction is upon the social whole, and not between different aspects of the social world. Here, culture refers to a distinctive world, ethnic group, class, or nation-state. Culture used in this sense demarcates a distinctive social world that is created and recreated by individuals and is marked by tradition, frameworks of values, and implicit learned understandings. Deployed in this way, cultural variation linked to another variable (e.g., aggregate levels of white-collar crime) is thus a form of identifiable casual contrast—between this and that culture. Yet, this second use of culture carries its own problems and draws one onto well-rehearsed yet troublesome and contested literature.

The practice of treating nations as units of cultural variation (i.e., of cross-cultural comparison) has been subject to two key criticisms. First, studies of individuals show significant within-nation variance; second, nations have regional, ethnic, or other subcultures (Karstedt 2001; Peterson and Smith 2008). The first is grounded in correct empirical findings but is itself logically flawed. When national cultures are compared, it does not matter whether individual differences are large and whether they are longer or smaller than national differences. The existence of intranational subcultures is a more serious argument against using nations as a unit of cross-cultural analysis. One might wonder if the cultures of large countries, such as China, India, and Indonesia, or even those of far smaller but seemingly diverse nations, such as Belgium, Spain, and Switzerland, are homogeneous enough to be studied as single entities. A number of studies have compared in-country regions on cultural indicators. The totality of their evidence is inconclusive (Hofstede 1984; Schwartz 1994; Hofstede 2001). There is evidence to refute some of the arguments against the concept of national culture, but the weight of existing research points to the conclusion that when basic cultural values are compared, in-country regions tend to cluster along national lines rather than be scattered and intermixed with the regions of other countries in the same cultural or geographic area (Lenartowicz, Johnson, and White 2003; Hofstede et al. 2010; Minkov and Hofstede 2012).

More abstractly, on the matter of culture and nation, one is, in essence, dealing with the matter of the internal complexity of the modern world—a product of imperial/colonial ambitions, global trade, and electronic technological communication and where the confusion of forms of life is increasingly the common state of things (Brightman 1995). To this end, culture may be best seen as a toolbox, or conceptualized as elective affinities of motive (Garland 2011). Cultural variation, if invoked, needs careful explication, where one seeks to bring dialectical and historical knowledge to bear, contesting the grand narrative of any simple form of cultural variation as explanation. Yet, the state of this field of research is far removed from this, with imprecise and multiple definitions of culture coupled with assumptions of cultural uniformity, excessive reliance on methodologically weak research designs and post hoc interpretations of atypical and enigmatic findings, and failure to acknowledge and explore the effects of hierarchy and agency as constraints on culture (Shover and Hochstetler 2002; Trahan 2011). The resulting ambiguities have made it difficult for researchers in this field to operationalize key terms and incorporate them into research designs (Hochstetler and Copes 2001). We return to this theme as part of this essay's conclusions.

Cultural variation, whether at societal or organizational levels, has been explored either via cross-national studies of cultural values or with case studies often in societies of high-contrast value, such as Asia. Societal values can be conceptualized in several different ways. Past research has identified correlations between various societal values and corruption. In the later 1960s, Geert Hofstede became interested in cultural differences across nations and was presented with the opportunity to study the values of employees working in IBM in fifty countries around the world. He discovered that the nations differed along four dimensions: power distance, collectivism versus individualism, femininity versus masculinity, and uncertainty avoidance. Later, he added a fifth dimension (long-term vs. short-term orientation; Hofstede 2001). His work became a catalyst for cross-cultural research, including correlates of white-collar crime (Davis and Ruhe 2003; Park 2003; Moores 2007; Seleim and Bontis 2009).

In this context, Cateora and Graham (2004, p. 151) found that "Americans are mono-chromic time oriented, linguistically direct, foreground focused and they achieve efficiency through competition"; thus they asserted that bribery is less common. "Alternatively, Japanese culture is high-context, collectivistic, high power distance, lin-guistically indirect and background focused, and they achieve efficiency through reduc-tion in transactions costs" (p. 151); thus bribery is more common. Cateora and Graham summed up cultures along a continuum as relationship oriented versus information oriented: countries with a more relationship-oriented culture exhibit higher levels of corruption.

The basic argument is that government or business regulation in one nation is the reflection of attitudes and beliefs about justice, responsibility, and social relations, and these are significantly affected by cultural values (Jing and Graham 2008). More recently, 170 investigators in 62 cultures around the world have worked on the Global Leadership and Organizational Behavior Effectiveness Research Program (GLOBE) (House et al. 2002; Javidan et al. 2006). They measured culture at the levels of the industry, organization, and society and examined the ways in which culture affected societal, organizational, and leadership effectiveness. Nine cultural dimensions were identified from the results of the GLOBE project (see generally House et al. 2002; Javidan et al. 2006):

1. Performance orientation is the degree to which an organization or society encour-ages and rewards group members for performance improvement and excellence.
2. Future orientation is the degree to which individuals in organizations or societies engage in future-oriented behaviors such as planning, investing in the future, and delaying individual or collective gratification.
3. Humane orientation is the degree to which individuals in organizations or societ-ies encourage and reward individuals for being fair, altruistic, friendly, generous, caring and kind to others.
4. Institutional collectivism is the degree to which organizational and societal insti-tutional practices encourage and reward collective distribution of resources and collective action.
5. In-group collectivism is the degree to which individuals express pride, loyalty, and cohesiveness in their organizations or families.
6. Uncertainty avoidance is the extent to which members of an organization or soci-ety strive to avoid uncertainty by relying on established social norms, rituals, and bureaucratic practices.
7. Gender egalitarianism is the degree to which an organization or a society mini-mizes gender role differences while promoting gender equality.
8. Assertiveness is the extent to which societies are assertive, confrontational, and aggressive in social relationships.
9. Power distance is the extent to which a society expects and agrees that power should be stratified and concentrated.

Although some of these dimensions are similar to those proposed by Hofstede, new dimensions were unveiled (e.g., institutional collectivism, humane orientation). There are advantages to using the GLOBE dimensions over Hofstede's: (1) the GLOBE findings are particularly strong, as the researchers were able to benefit from methodologies developed over a period of five decades and used state-of-the-art methodologies to conduct their research and (2) they were able to discover new dimensions that had previously been unavailable for cross-cultural research. A significant fact about GLOBE's nine cultural dimensions is that each one was conceptualized in two ways: practices, or "as is," and values, or "should be" (Seleim and Bontis 2009). As yet, little research has been conducted examining the effects of these new dimensions on behaviors.

O'Connor and Fischer (2012) investigated the two values dimensions developed by Inglehart and Baker (2000). The first contrasts traditional values with rational values (which emphasize greater egalitarianism and tolerance). The second dimension contrasts survival values (which emphasize hard work, limited leisure, materialism, and authoritarian rule) with self-expression values (which emphasize quality of life and individuals' rights to express themselves freely and challenge the existing order). These dimensions not only are encompassing of alternative value frameworks (i.e., they are broad and conceptually very similar to and show convergent validity with other value domains) but also represent the only value set that is based on representative samples across nearly forty years of study. Both dimensions are likely to be important for understanding corruption. For example, self-expression values may decrease incentives for corruption as they emphasize interpersonal trust and civic-mindedness over personal gain (Welzel 2010; Welzel and Inglehart 2010).

In support of this prediction, Welzel, Inglehart, and Klingemann (2003) found that countries that initially had high self-expression value scores subsequently had lower corruption levels (a time-lagged correlation between values and corruption). Sandholtz and Taagepera (2005) observed a similar correlation between self-expression values and lower corruption cross-sectionally, noting that country self-expression value scores accounted for more than half of the variance in average corruption between countries.

Similarly, rational values may create fewer opportunities for corruption, because they favor more egalitarian society in which there are fewer entrenched hierarchies and power imbalances, meaning that individuals in societies with more rational values are less likely to have the opportunity to wield—and potentially misuse—high discretion and power. In line with this prediction, Sandholtz and Taagepera (2005) found that rational values were inversely correlated with corruption and accounted for approximately a quarter of the variance in average corruption between countries.

While previous studies on corruption have investigated the relationships between these variables and corruption at single time points (e.g., Welzel et al. 2003) or averaged across time points (e.g., Sandholtz and Taagepera 2005), only O'Connor and Fischer (2012) have investigated relationships across multiple time points, taking longitudinal data from fifty-nine countries in a two-level linear growth model (within countries over a twenty-eight-year period) as well as differences between countries. As predicted, results showed that self-expression values are related to lower corruption across but not within countries, corroborating evidence that this value dimension is linked to important differences between societies.

Societal values research has produced a rich literature in relation to intellectual property fraud and bribery; in what follows, we highlight some of the core tropes and findings.

1. Intellectual Property Fraud

Cultural values research on intellectual property fraud (e.g., software piracy) is evident from the literature. There is, undoubtedly, increasing concern about relationships between intellectual property fraud and other white-collar crimes (Beresford et al. 2007). Such crimes may include investment fraud (e.g., using a trademark of a legitimate company to deceive potential investors), money laundering (e.g., concealing funds acquired from "sales"), fraudulent sales (e.g., using an Internet site to deceive customers), identity theft, and tax evasion (e.g., failing to declare income acquired through fraudulent intellectual property activities). National economic wealth and Hofstede's national culture dimensions (Hofstede 2001; Hofstede and Hofstede 2005) are commonly used to explain differences in levels of software piracy across countries. The economic wealth of a nation influences some forms of intellectual property fraud because most software vendors use the same pricing strategy across the globe (Gopal and Sanders 2000), but what is affordable in the United States might be too expensive for people in the countries such as Vietnam, where per capita income is lower. Culture contributes because in societies that encourage close ties between members of the in-group over individuality and personal property, sharing is the norm and piracy rates tend to be higher (Moores 2003; Shin et al. 2004). While the global software piracy rate has fluctuated, the average national rate continues to decline. This decline may be partly explained by an increase in the economic wealth of almost all countries (World Development Indicators 2006). However, associated declines in software piracy have not always followed suit (Business Software Alliance 2003). This would suggest that wealth, or the lack of it, is not the sole driver of software piracy.

Hofstede's national culture dimensions indicate differences in work value perspectives between national cultures. In relating national culture to software piracy, individualism/collectivism (IDV) is often the only cultural factor shown to be significantly related, along with some measure of economic wealth (Husted 2000; Marron and Steel 2000; Moores 2003; Shin et al. 2004). A strong negative relationship between IDV and piracy is expected: the higher the individualism of a country, the lower the software piracy rate. When considering declines in piracy, it follows that if economic wealth is a strong predictor of the level of software piracy, then countries that experience the greatest increase in economic wealth will also experience the greatest decline in software piracy. Although habit may lead some people to continue pirating software, one expects a strong positive relationship among wealth and declines in the piracy rate. Using the same argument, and given the expected strong relationship between wealth and IDV, one also expects a strong positive relationship between IDV and declines in piracy.

The relationship between power distance, masculinity/femininity, uncertainty avoidance, and declining piracy rates is more difficult to determine. Few studies have found a significant relationship between these three culture variables and levels of piracy, although masculinity/femininity has occasionally been found to be significant (e.g., Ronkainen and Guerrero-Cusumano 2001). If we assume that software piracy is an example of corruption, then there is indeed literature that has found a significant relationship between Hofstede's national culture variables and national corruption levels (Husted 1999; Getz and Volkhema 2001; Davis and Ruhe 2003; Park 2003; Robertson and Watson 2004).

The key results from the above studies are that, in cultures with high power distance, there is an expectation and acceptance of unequal distributions of power. "Whistle-blowing" is not tolerated, and those in power will seek to prevent or punish any such attempts. In this context, corruption and other types of illegal behavior can be rife. In cultures with high masculinity, traditional masculine roles are encouraged, and individuals, especially males, are expected to be ambitious and competitive and to strive for material success. It is suggested that this "get ahead" mentality breeds corruption. In cultures with high uncertainty avoidance, there is a need to reduce uncertainty, and corruption, often in the form of bribes, is one means of securing a certain result. It seems reasonable to suggest, therefore, that when levels of national corruption are high, software piracy will flourish. For instance, corruption would lead to a "blind eye" being turned toward the existence of arcades and other outlets that sell pirated software, and for "tipoffs" to be given should a police raid be imminent. Using a larger sample than has previously been available (fifty-seven countries) and software piracy data from 1994 to 2002, Moores (2008) indeed found the expected negative relationship between economic wealth, culture (individualism and masculinity), and levels of software piracy. The rate of decline over time in software piracy, however, was found to be a cultural phenomenon, with two factors (power distance and uncertainty avoidance) working in opposition. Similar results were found for a subset of thirty-seven relatively poor countries (Moores 2008).

When we turn our attention to assessing declines in software piracy, the issue appears to be a function of culture, not economic wealth. The significant negative relationship between power distance and declines in piracy suggests that, in cultures where power distance is high, such as Russia, China, Indonesia, and Vietnam, any declines in software piracy are significantly attenuated. This result is consistent with studies that relate Hofstede's national culture dimensions of levels of corruption, where power distance tends to be the most significant cultural factor (Husted 1999; Getz and Voljema 2001; Davis and Ruhe 2003; Park 2003). Any expected decline in software piracy due to growing gross domestic product (GDP) is significantly attenuated by national corruption levels. Further studies have found Hofstede's individualism variable had an inverse relationship with piracy, often with more than 75 percent of variance explained by GDP and cultural variables (Ronkinen and Guerrero-Cusumano 2001; Shore et al. 2001; Yang and Somnez 2007).

2. Bribery

There is a growing body of work on bribery and cultural values (Sanyal and Samanta 2004; Sanyal and Guvenli 2009). Husted (1999) examined the role of economic and cultural variables and found a significant inverse relationship between perceived levels of bribery in a country and its per capita income (purchasing power parity). Cultural dimensions—using Hofstede's classification—of masculinity and power distance were significant factors (Hofstede 1984). Sanyal and Samanta (2003) confirmed Husted's findings and found that income distribution in a country was another significant economic factor. Similarly, Getz and Volkema (2001) found that bribery in a country was related to wealth, as were power distance and uncertainty avoidance. Uncertainty avoidance moderated the relationship between economic adversity and bribery. Thus, there is an empirical basis to suggest that certain economic and cultural factors determine perceived levels of bribery. Sanyala and Samanta (2003) also found that economic freedom and level of human development are associated with levels of perceived bribery in a country, with open economies and a high level of human development inversely related to bribery. All these studies found that per capita income is inversely related to bribery.

One of the few studies that looked at the supply side found a high correlation between countries with companies with a high propensity to receive bribes and those most likely to be giving bribes (Sanyal and Samanta 2004). Using Transparency International's Bribe Payers Index, the authors found that the propensity to give bribes is determined by economic factors such as per capita income (for details on the Index, see Transparency International 2006). Their sample was restricted to nineteen countries and did not look explicitly at cultural factors.

We now have a good understanding of the demand side of bribery, especially the characteristics of countries where bribe taking is widespread. Both economic and cultural factors have been found to explain the prevalence of bribe taking (Sanyal and Guvenli 2009). Much less work has been done on the supply side of bribery. Using Hofstede's cultural values framework and the Corruption Perceptions Index and Bribe Payers Index as principal measures of bribery, such studies would appear to provide strong endorsement of the thesis that economic determinism (rather than culture) explains the propensity to bribe (Sanyal and Guvenli 2009). Yet this is not the complete picture.

Studies also show that some national cultural factors do play a role, albeit perhaps a secondary one; countries that have lower power distance, long-term orientation scores, or higher individualism scores are significantly less likely to give bribes. Long-term orientation scores are consistently associated with high bribe giving. This suggests that a commitment to success over the long haul and being persistent in the pursuit of over-arching goals leads to corporate behavior in which bribe giving is a significant element. It could be that the firm sees bribe giving as a temporal and necessary aspect of doing business that would be beneficial over the long run.

Baughn et al. (2009) addressed the propensity of firms from thirty different countries to engage in international bribery. The study incorporates both domestic (economic development, culture, and domestic corruption in supplying country) and international factors (those countries' patterns of trade and involvement in international accords) in explaining the willingness to bribe abroad. The finding that firms from high-power-distance countries may be particularly prone to pro-vide bribes in less developed countries may be a function of the greater tolerance for corruption in high-power-distance countries (see Husted 1999; Getz and Volkema 2001; Hofstede 2001; Sanyal 2005). In this case, the culture of the bribe payer and the culture of the receiver would both be more tolerant of bribery. Sung (2005) noted that high tolerance for corruption in a society leads to the supply of foreign bribery from that society's multinational firms to recipients in other countries. Two hypotheses on the dynamics of transnational bribery were formulated and tested in this study. The demand-pull hypothesis views multinational corporations as victims of corruption in host countries and predicts a positive relationship between corrup-tion in host countries and bribery by guest businesses. The supply-push hypoth-esis treats multinationals as proactive parties and proposes a positive relationship between pro-bribery conditions in exporting countries and the inclination of their multinationals to engage in foreign bribery. Analysis of cross-national data yielded no support for the demand-pull hypothesis but strong backing for the supply-push hypothesis. Similarly, Sanyal and Samanta (2004) argued that country-level deter-minants of bribe taking would be also associated with bribe giving in international transactions.

Whereas regression has been the predominant method of analyzing variables related to the dynamics of supply and demand in bribery research (and indeed tax evasion and other "suspect" behaviors), recent innovative work by John Cullen and colleagues using multilevel hierarchical modeling has now begun to produce some rich and theoretically contextualized findings (Parboteeah, Bronson, and Cullen 2005; Martin et al. 2007; Bame-Aldred et al. 2013). Cullen and colleagues explicitly adopted a theoretically derived multilevel approach to investigate cultural, institu-tional, and organizational drivers of such behaviors. Using anomie theory (Merton 1968; see Messner and Rosenfeld [2001] for the wider application in criminology), with its basic premise that cultural and social drivers result in conditions in which pressures for goal achievement through any means displace normative control mechanisms, Cullen and colleagues provided a powerful foundation for investigat-ing these kinds of behaviors and are able to generate theoretically derived country-level and organization-level characteristics from anomie frameworks and articulate their relationships.

II. How Cultural Factors Work:
The Case of *Guanxi*

Earlier, we noted that cultural variation, if invoked, needs careful explication, and one particularly sharp example is how recent studies have sought to parse the mechanisms through which *guanxi* in Chinese culture relates to forms of white-collar crime, including corruption, and can be illustrative of how structure and agency act as constraints on culture (a point of critique raised previously by Shover and Hochstetler [2002]). *Guanxi* can be defined as a network of personal relationships emerging from the fundamentals of Chinese culture, traditions, and social organization (for an excellent general introduction to *guanxi*, see the collection of essays in Gold, Guthrie, and Wank 2002). It is essentially an expression of particularism—the felt personal obligation to help and give resources to closely related persons, such as family, friends, and membership groups. As a particular form of a culturally embedded social network, it shares considerable similarities with social networks prevalent in other cultures, such as *blat* in Russia (Ledeneva 1998; Wedel 2003), and has been implicated as a facilitator of corruption in Chinese societies (Sun 2004; Yu 2008; Li 2011; Zhan 2012).

However, available data from the Corruption Perception Index (CPI) published by Transparency International reveal significant differences in corruption across Chinese societies (Mainland China, Hong Kong, Taiwan), which is indicative of how constraints of political and regulatory context modulate the uses of *guanxi*. The international ranking and the average score of Hong Kong, Taiwan, and China for the CPI are categorized in table 17.1. The highest score is 10, which indicates the country is relatively free of corruption. Hong Kong scores best, Taiwan is placed in the middle rank, and China is at the other extreme.

Similar results can be found in the survey published by *Forbes* in 2011. In the "Best Countries for Business," *Forbes* ranked countries for business based on various

Table 17.1 Corruption Perception Index of Hong Kong, Taiwan, and China, 2010–2012

	2010		2011		2012	
	Standings	Score	Standings	Score	Standings	Score
Hong Kong	13	8.4	12	8.4	14	6.7
Taiwan	33	5.8	32	6.1	37	6.1
China	78	3.5	75	3.6	80	3.9

Source: Transparency International (2010–2012).

Table 17.2 *Forbes* "Best Countries for Business," 2011

Country	Business ranking	Corruption
Hong Kong	3	13
Taiwan	26	32
China	82	66

Source: Forbes (http://www.forbes.com/lists/2011/6/best-countries-11_rank.html).

indicators (including corruption). As table 17.2 shows, among the 134 countries surveyed, Hong Kong was ranked 13th in terms of corruption, Taiwan was ranked 32nd, and China was ranked 66th.

Confirmation of the modulating effects on *guanxi* also comes from surveys of business activities across Chinese societies (Anderson and Lee 2008). Yet, from the cultural perspective, *guanxi*'s direct corruptive outcomes are the least interesting; of greater significance is its facilitative function.

If we look at the case of Mainland China, it would appear that there has been an intensification of corruption in the postreform era: the most common types of white-collar crimes include corruption, bribery, misappropriation, collective embezzlement, abuse of public position, dereliction of duty, and fraud, with bribery one of the largest of these categories (Guo 2008; Zhan 2012). The *guanxi* practice is a trust-building process that uses affective interpersonal connections, but central to its establishment and maintenance is a stable reciprocal tie. The reciprocal tie normally builds upon a series of exchanges of gifts or favors and may take a long time to consolidate; each transaction is a step to deepen the relationship. These transactions are not instantly paid off but would keep the relationship of obligation ongoing. Because of this centrality of reciprocal ties, *guanxi* can be constructed for purely instrumental purposes, although the instrumentality is always camouflaged by interpersonal sentiments.

Thus, the facilitative role of *guanxi* is apparent from studies of bribery in China. In terms of bribe selection, delivery, and acceptance, the facilitative role provided by *guanxi* is evident. Bribe/gift selection is a fine art, and in general, gifts are preferred over pure money at the initial stage when the trust relationship is not yet strong. Later, existing cultural routines are chosen as ideal vehicles, such as Mahjong, a popular gambling game in China after dining banquets. It is a service provided by almost all dining and entertaining establishments. While playing the game, bribers can bribe, for instance, by deliberately losing and so on. The need to disguise the delivery of the bribe is also a key part of the transaction, and language plays its part. The Chinese language in its written forms can be radically and endemically ambiguous (Hodge and Louie 1998). As Li noted,

"There is no specific, unambiguous word for bribe" and "no common terms designating and denigrating the briber and the bribe." Bribers with some common sense would understand that a bribe should not be addressed as a 'bribe' or explained as an 'inducement' for an illicit service, since those words project dashing instrumentality of the briber and illegality to its recipient, who is the last person a briber wants to offend. (Li 2011, p. 11)

Linguistic terms are only used in relation to certain persons, with whom a trusting relationship has been established. Euphemisms dominate, and the trust context is built entirely upon intersubjective perceptions, which respond to the slightest observation of changes in behavior. This certainly is the case in Chinese culture, where reading between the lines is a regular communicative practice. *Guanxi* spawns its own self-referential agency-obscuring vocabulary that can be conveyed only in context and is only roughly translatable. Terms describing informal "arranging" serve to mask the nature of the particular transaction at hand and build an expedient ambiguity into the language and its "everyday" nature. The relationship between guilt-neutralizing linguistic devices and the commission of white-collar crimes, of course, is not new. After all, in his study of embezzlement some sixty years ago, Cressey (1953) discovered that white-collar offenders use "techniques of neutralization" (Sykes and Matza 1957).

To make the taking of the bribe more acceptable, such transactions often use other "traditions" as cultural stages in which to play out the transaction: gifts at traditional holidays or other ritual occasions, including weddings, baby showers, and funerals in the family, provide greater "legitimacy" to cash bribes, addressed as *lijin* (gift-money) wrapped in red envelopes (*hongbao*) for celebrations or white envelopes (*baibao*) for funerals. *Guanxi* only functions on the condition that a mutual understanding of the evolved meanings of the gift-giving process is shared by the gift givers and the gift receivers.

By ineluctably shaping norms in favor of closely related persons over the wider public, *guanxi* enhances the ends and the means for engagement in corruption, especially transactional corruption through particularistic ties. Obligation and reciprocity are at the normative center of the *guanxi* relationship but are modulated by structural barriers and, of course, perceived risk. Under China's increasingly stringent anticorruption measures, an envelope of cash may appear risky to accept; some studies reveal that bribes can be presented to some middlemen first and then transmitted onward (see work by Huang and Li [2006] quoted in Zhan [2012]). While the norm-inducing role is not specific to *guanxi* but exists within all networks, the norm-distorting effects of *guanxi* have particular resonance in the wider structure of both the communist economies of shortage and indeed postreform China (Ledeneva 1998; Rose-Ackerman 1999; Wedel 2003). Network peer pressure modulates individual moral judgment in a complex spiral of "dirty togetherness"; thus the bribe is legitimized by a changed context, a context transformed by the briber into one filled with sentiments of kindness, care, and understanding (Li 2011).

III. Conclusion

In the research reviewed for this essay, values have been seen as central to the concept of culture. The cultural values literature influenced by Hofstede and others has adopted a primarily dimensional-extensive strategy (Karstedt 2001), which is mostly quantitative and based on fairly large samples of different nations. The strategy implies that different cultures are mainly studied with parallel research designs that use the same variables, operational devices, and sampling techniques. It also has a starting assumption that cultures can be compared with regard to specific common dimensions. Typical dimensional concepts have been reviewed here alongside the empirical findings. As such, cultural values function as factors or explanatory variables. Their impact can be direct, and culture is conceptualized either as an independent or mediating variable. Indirectly, culture is either a contextual or a moderating variable.

Undoubtedly, the shadow of naïve empiricism has the potential to hover over such empirical efforts, and results must be interpreted cautiously because of certain methodological and conceptual problems. Cultural values research, like many cross-cultural studies, takes the following form. There is some variable on which a difference in score distributions is found between samples of subjects that have been drawn from at least two cultural populations. This difference is interpreted in terms of some cultural variable. However, such research often is characterized by ad hoc selection of cultural populations. Cultures differ from each other in many ways, and it is often unclear how interpretations other than the one preferred by a researcher can be ruled out. The interpretation of results in such cross-cultural research is affected by another problem, namely that measurement procedures are likely to lead to scores that are biased or inequivalent across cultures. Inequivalence means that a given score does not have the same meaning for a subject from one cultural population that it does for a subject from another population.

These methodological concerns aside, in the dimensional-extensive approach, culture defines the context in which other causes of white-collar crime operate, and it affects the way they do. White-collar crime becomes an expression and illumination, however refracted, of the wider culture, pointing to something more intrinsic. Yet, as argued earlier in the essay, if the analysis of cultural variation is to inform our understanding of white-collar crime, we need an account of the processes and mechanisms that translate culture into action. If cultural values are to be accorded causal efficacy in explaining matters, then we require an account of the mechanism that transmits this value both through time and in the contemporary period. Our analysis of Chinese *guanxi* is illustrative of both the richness and challenge inherent in such interpretive work (for more on the interpretive challenge, see Jou and Hebenton 2007; see also Jou, Hebenton, and Cao 2014).

Furthermore, as discussed earlier, culture is only a partial aspect of any adequate explanatory account of white-collar crime, only part of the mix with other aspects of action that are more commonly understood as political or economic. Indeed, one of the problems with cultural theories of white-collar crime derives from this very variety of independent constructs, with Ott's (1989) meta-analysis revealing that approximately seventy-three different constructs have been used to define the term "organizational culture" (Trahan 2011). In any concrete social analysis, we should see the cultural operating together with the interests and actions that obey different logics, whether economic, political, or legal. Arguably, a case-study approach can assist by analyzing specific forms of white-collar crime; funeral home fraud is a particularly interesting and pertinent example. Aside from differences in regulatory context and opportunity factors, bribery and fraud surrounding the funeral business in, for instance, the United States and Taiwan can be understood only by incorporating appropriate cultural understandings of beliefs regarding death and the afterlife (Jou 2005; Palombo 2007). As Jou found, this type of fraud in Taiwan involves a complex interplay of the symbolic necessity of large-scale funeral outlays related to the "face" culture, where the funeral ceremony symbolizes how influential, prestigious, powerful, and well connected the deceased and his or her family are; demands for *feng shui* graveyards and belief in "lucky" days and "proper" times to cremate or bury the deceased together create "economies of shortage" (i.e., not enough cremation facilities, mourning halls, and staff) and thus create motivations to bribe. Such case studies illustrate how both motivation and opportunity structures can be mediated by cultural forms. As researchers and scholars, we should, of course, seek to isolate and analyze cultural variation, but only as a start to more integrated analyses that fold cultural forms into multidimensional accounts of causes and consequences of white-collar crime.

REFERENCES

Anderson, Alistair R., and Yiu-Chung (Edward) Lee. 2008. "From Tradition to Modern: Attitudes and Applications of Guanxi in Chinese Entrepreneurship." *Journal of Small Business and Enterprise Development* 15: 775–87.

Bame-Aldred, Charles, W., John B. Cullen, Kelly D. Martin, and K. Praveen Parboteeah. 2013. "National Culture and Firm Level Tax Evasion." *Journal of Business Research* 66: 390–96.

Baughn, Chris, Nancy Bodie, Mark Buchanan, and Michael Bixby. 2009. "Bribery in International Business Transactions." *Journal of Business Ethics* 92: 15–32.

Brightman, Robert. 1995. "Forget Culture: Replacement, Transcendence, Reflexification." *Cultural Anthropology* 4: 509–46.

Business Software Alliance. 2003. *Eighth Annual BSA Global Software Piracy Study*. Business Software Alliance. Available at http://global.bsa.org/globalstudy/2003_GSPS.pdf

Cateora, Philip, and John L. Graham 2004. *International Marketing*, 12th ed. Burr Ridge, IL: McGraw-Hill.

Coleman, James W. 1987. "Toward an Integrated Theory of White-Collar Crime." *American Journal of Sociology* 93: 406–39.

Cressey, Donald R. 1953. *Other People's Money: A Study in the Social Psychology of Embezzlement*. Glencoe, IL: Free Press.

Davis, James H., and John A. Ruhe. 2003. "Perception of Country Corruption: Antecedents and Outcomes." *Journal of Business Ethics* 43: 275–328.

Garland, David. 2011. "Concepts of Culture in the Sociology of Punishment." In *Travels of the Criminal Question: Cultural Embeddedness and Diffusion*, edited by Dario Melossi, Maximo Sozzo, and Richard Sparks, pp. 17–43. Oxford, UK: Hart Publishing.

Geertz, Clifford. 1998. *Works and Lives: The Anthropologist as Author*. Stanford: Stanford University Press.

Getz, Kathleen, and Roger J. Volkema. 2001. "Culture, Perceived Corruption, and Economics." *Business and Society* 40: 7–30.

Gold, Thomas, Douglas Guthrie, and David Wank, eds. 2002. *Social Connections in China: Institutions, Culture, and the Changing Nature of Guanxi.* Cambridge, UK: Cambridge University Press.

Gopal, Ram D., and Lawrence Sanders. 2000. "Global Software Piracy: You Can't Get Blood Out of a Turnip." *Communication of the ACM* 43: 82–89.

Guo, Yong. 2008. "Corruption in Transitional China: An Empirical Analysis." *China Quarterly* 194: 357–87.

Hochstetler, Andy, and Heith B. Copes. 2001. "Organizational Culture and Organizational Crime." In *Crimes of Privilege: Readings in White-Collar Crime,* edited by Neal Shover and John Paul Wright, pp. 221–51. New York: Oxford University Press.

Hodge, Bob, and Kam Louie. 1998. *The Politics of Chinese Language and Culture: The Art of Reading Dragons.* London and New York: Routledge.

Hofstede, Gerstedt. 1984. *Culture's Consequences: International Differences in Work-Related Values,* 2nd abridged ed. Beverly Hills: Sage.

Hofstede, Gerstedt. 2001. *Culture's Consequences: Comparing Values, Behaviors, Institutions, and Organizations across Nations.* Beverly Hills: Sage.

Hofstede, Gerstedt, Adriana Garibaldi de Hilal, Sigmar Malvezzi, Betania Tanure, and Henk Vinken. 2010. "Comparing Regional Cultures within Country: Lessons from Brazil." *Journal of Cross-Cultural Psychology* 41: 336–52.

Hofstede, Gerstedt, and Gert Jan Hofstede. 2005. *Culture's Consequences: Software of the Mind* 2. New York: McGraw-Hill.

House, Robert J., Mansour Javidan, Paul J. Hanges, and Peter Dorfman. 2002. "Understanding Cultures and Implicit Leadership Theories across the Globe: An Introduction to Project GLOBE." *Journal of World Business* 37: 3–10.

Huang, Guo, and Ren Li (2006). *Haizhuqu Jianchayuan dui Xinghui Renyuan de Wenjuan Diaocha Baogao.* Survey Report of Bribe-Giving, Hazhu District Procuratorate [in Chinese].

Husted, Bryan W. 1999. "Wealth, Culture, and Corruption." *Journal of International Business Studies* 30: 339–59.

Husted, Bryan W. 2000. "The Impact of National Culture on Software Piracy." *Journal of Business Ethics* 26: 197–211.

Inglehart, Ronald. 1997. *Modernization and Postmodernization: Cultural, Economic, and Political Change in 43 Societies.* Princeton, NJ: Princeton University Press.

Inglehart, Ronald, and Wayne Baker. 2000. "Modernization, Cultural Change, and the Persistence of Traditional Values." *American Sociological Review* 65: 19–51.

Javidan, Mansour, Robert J. House, Peter Dorfman, Paul J. Hanges, and Mary S. de Luque. 2006. "Conceptualizing and Measuring Cultures and Their Consequences: A Comparative Review of GLOBE's and Hofstede's Approaches." *Journal of International Business Studies* 37: 897–914.

Jing, Runtian, and John L. Graham. 2008. "Values versus Regulations: How Culture Plays Its Role." *Journal of Business Ethics* 80: 791–806.

Jou, Susyan. 2005. "Illegal Conduct and the Funeral Business in Taiwan." *Journal of Criminology* 8: 1–24 [in Chinese].

Jou, Susyan, and Bill Hebenton.2007. "Insurance Fraud in Taiwan: Reflections on Regulatory Effort and Criminological Complexity." *International Journal of the Sociology of Law* 35: 127–42.

Jou, Susyan, Bill Hebenton, and Liqun Cao. 2014. "The Development of Criminology in Modern China: A State-Based Enterprise." In *The Routledge Handbook of Chinese Criminology*, edited by Liqun Cao, Ivan Sun, and Bill Hebenton, pp. 16–26. Abingdon, UK: Routledge.

Karstedt, Susanne. 2001. "Comparing Cultures, Comparing Crime: Challenges, Prospects, and Problems for a Global Criminology." *Crime, Law, and Social Change* 36: 285–308.

Kirkman, Bradley L., Kevin B. Lowe, and Cristina B. Gibson. 2006. "A Quarter Century of Culture's Consequences: A Review of Empirical Research Incorporating Hofstede's Cultural Values Framework." *Journal of International Business Studies* 37: 285–320.

Ledeneva, Alena V. 1998. *Russia's Economy of Favors: Blat, Networking, and Informal Exchange.* Cambridge, UK: Cambridge University Press.

Lenartowicz, Tomasz, James P. Johnson, and Carolyn T. White. 2003. "The Neglect of Intracountry Cultural Variation in International Management Research." *Journal of Business Research* 56: 999–1088.

Li, Ling. 2011 "Performing Bribery in China: Guanxi Practice, Corruption with a Human Face." *Journal of Contemporary China* 20: 1–20.

Marron, Donald B., and D. G. Steel. 2000. "Which Countries Protect Intellectual Property? The Case of Software Piracy." *Economic Enquiry* 38: 159–74.

Martin, Kelly D., John B. Cullen, Jean L. Johnson, and K. Praveen Parboteeah. 2007. "Deciding to Bribe: A Cross-Level Analysis of Firm and Home Country Influences on Bribery Activity." *Academy of Management Journal* 50: 1401–22.

Melossi, Dario, Maximo Sozzo, and Richard Sparks, eds. 2011. *Travels of the Criminal Question: Cultural Embeddedness and Diffusion.* Oxford, UK: Hart Publishing.

Merton, Robert. K. 1968. *Social Theory and Social Structure.* New York: Free Press.

Messner, Steven, and Richard Rosenfeld. 2001. *Crime and the American Dream.* Belmont: Wadsworth.

Minkov, Michael. 2011. *Cultural Differences in a Globalizing World.* Bradford, UK: Emerald Publishing.

Minkov, Michael, and Gerstedt Hoststede. 2012. "Is National Culture a Meaningful Concept? Cultural Values Delineate Homogeneous National Clusters of In-Country Regions." *Cross-Cultural Research* 46: 133–59.

Moores, Trevor T. 2003. "The Effect of National Culture and Economic Wealth on Global Software Piracy Rates." *Communications of the ACM* 46: 207–15.

Moores, Trevor T. 2008. "An Analysis of the Impact of Economic Wealth and National Culture on the Rise and Fall of Software Piracy Rates." *Journal of Business Ethics* 81: 39–51.

O'Connor, Seini, and Ronald Fischer. 2012. "Predicting Societal Corruption across Time: Values, Wealth, or Institutions?" *Journal of Cross-Cultural Psychology* 43: 644–59.

Ott, Steven J. 1989. *The Organizational Culture Perspective.* Chicago: The Dorsey Press.

Palombo, Bernadette J. 2007. "Fraud in the Funeral Industry." In *Encyclopedia of White-Collar Crime*, edited by Jurg Gerber and Eric L. Jensen, pp. 60–80. Westport, CT: Greenhaven Press.

Parboteeah, Praveen K., James W. Bronson., and John B. Cullen. 2005. "Does National Culture Affect Willingness to Justify Ethically Suspect Behaviors?" *International Journal of Cross Cultural Management* 5: 123–38.

Parnell, Philip C., and Stephanie C. Kane. 2003. *Crime's Power: Anthropologists and the Ethnography of Crime.* New York: Palgrave Macmillan.

Park, Hun. 2003. "Determinants of Corruption: A Cross-National Analysis." *Multinational Business Review* 11: 29–48.

Peterson, Mark F., and Peter B. Smith. 2008. "Social Structures and Processes in Cross-Cultural Management." In *The Handbook of Cross-Cultural Management Research*, edited by Peter B. Smith, Mark F. Peterson, and David C. Thomas, pp. 35–58. Thousand Oaks, CA: Sage.

Quah, Jon S. T. 2003. *Curbing Corruption in Asia: A Comparative Study of Six Countries*. Singapore: Eastern Universities Press.

Quah, Jon S. T. 2013. "Curbing Corruption and Enhancing Trust in Government: Some Lessons from Singapore and Hong Kong." In *Handbook of Asian Criminology*, edited by Jianhong Liu, Bill Hebenton, and Susyan Jou, pp. 25–48. New York: Springer.

Reiss, Albert J., and Albert Biderman. 1980. *Data Sources on White-Collar Law Breaking*. Washington, D.C.: United States General Printing Office (LXXXVI).

Robertson, Christopher J., and Andrew Watson. 2004. "Corruption and Change: The Impact of Direct Foreign Investment." *Strategic Management Journal* 25: 385–96.

Ronkinen, Ilkka A., and Jose-Luis Guerrero-Cusumano. 2001. "Correlates of Intellectual Property Violation." *Multinational Business Review* 9: 59–65.

Rose-Ackerman, Susan. 1999. *Corruption and Government: Causes, Consequences, and Reform*. New York: Cambridge University Press.

Sandholtz, Wayne, and Rein Taagepera. 2005. "Corruption, Culture, and Communism." *International Journal* 16: 287–300.

Sanyal, Rajib, and Turgut Guvenli. 2009. "The Propensity to Bribe in International Business: The Relevance of Cultural Variables." *Cross-Cultural Management: An International Journal* 16: 287–300.

Sanyal, Rajib, and Subama Samanta. 2004. "Correlates of Bribe Giving in International Business." *International Journal of Commerce and Management* 14: 1–14.

Schwartz, Shalom H. 1994. "Beyond Individualism/Collectivism: New Cultural Dimensions of Values." In *Individualism and Collectivism: Theory, Method, and Application*, edited by Uichol Kim, pp. 85–122. Thousand Oaks, CA: Sage.

Seleim, Ahmed, and Nick Bontis. 2009. "The Relationship between Culture and Corruption: A Cross-National Study." *Journal of Intellectual Capital* 10: 165–84.

Sewell, William H. Jr. 1999. "The Concept of Culture." In *Beyond the Cultural Turn*, edited by Victoria E. Bonnell and Lynn Hunt, pp. 35–61. Berkeley: University of California Press.

Shin, Seung Kyoon, Ram D. Gopal, G. Lawrence Sanders, and Andrew B. Winston. 2004. "Global Software Piracy Revisited." *Communications of the ACM* 47: 103–07.

Shore, Barry, A. R. Venkatachalam, Eleanne Solorzano, Janice M. Burn, Syed Zahoor Hassan, and Lech J. Janczewski. 2001. "Softlifting and Piracy: Behavior across Cultures." *Technology in Society* 23: 563–81.

Shover, Neal, and Andy Hochstetler. 2002. "Cultural Explanation and Organizational Crime." *Crime, Law, and Social Change* 37: 1–18.

Sun, Yan. 2004. *Corruption and Market in Contemporary China*. Ithaca, NY: Cornell University Press.

Sung, Hung En. 2005. "Between Demand and Supply: Bribery in International Trade." *Crime, Law, and Social Change* 44: 111–31.

Sykes, Gresham, and David Matza. 1957. "Techniques of Neutralization: A Theory of Delinquency." *American Sociological Review* 22: 664–70.

Trahan, Adam. 2011. "Filling in the Gaps in Culture-Based Theories of Organizational Crime." *Journal of Theoretical and Philosophical Criminology* 3: 89–109.

Transparency International. 2006. *Bribe Payers Index (BPI) 2006—Analysis Report*. Berlin: Transparency International Secretariat.

Tylor, Edward B. 1920. *Primitive Culture*, 6th ed. London, UK: J. Murray.

Wedel, Janine. 2003. "Mafia without Malfeasance, Clans without Crime: The Criminality Conundrum in Post-Communist Europe." In *Crime's Power: Anthropologists and the Ethnography of Crime*, edited by Philip C. Parnell and Stephanie C. Kane, pp. 221–44. New York: Palgrave Macmillan.

Welzel, Christian. 2010. "How Selfish Are Self-Expression Values? A Civicness Test." *Journal of Cross-Cultural Psychology* 41: 152–74.

Welzel, Christian, and Ronald Inglehart. 2010. "Value, Agency, and Well-Being: A Human Development Model." *Social Indicators Research* 97: 43–63.

Welzel, Christian, Ronald Inglehart, and Harold Klingemann. 2003. "The Theory of Human Development: A Cross-Cultural Analysis." *European Journal of Political Research* 42: 341–79.

World Development Indicators. 2006. *World Development Indicators Online*. Washington, D.C.: WorldBank.

Yang, Deli, and Mahmut Sonmez. 2007. "Economic and Cultural Impact on Intellectual Property Violations: A Study of Software Piracy." *Journal of World Trade* 41: 731–45.

Yu, Olivia. 2008. "Corruption in China's Economic Reform: A Review of Recent Observations and Explanations." *Crime, Law, and Social Change* 50: 174–87.

Zhan, Jing. 2012. "Filling the Gap of Formal Institutions: The Effects of Guanxi-Network on Corruption in Reform-Era China." *Crime, Law, and Social Change* 58: 93–109.

PART VI

ORGANIZATIONAL CONTEXT

CHAPTER 18

CRIMINAL DECISION MAKING IN ORGANIZATIONAL CONTEXTS

EDWARD C. TOMLINSON AND AMANDA POZZUTO

ORGANIZATIONS provide a context in which employed individuals carry out their work. This context is intentionally constructed such that it powerfully shapes individual behavior in particular ways (Trevino 1986; Tomlinson 2009). Moreover, contextual influences can affect behavior in both positive and negative ways. Unfortunately, evidence suggests that one of the outcomes resulting from the organizational context is the commission of white-collar crime. Our purpose here is to review research on contextual factors that appear to influence an individual's decision to engage in such criminal behavior.

Toward that end, our review is structured as follows. To delineate the scope of our review, section I presents our guiding definition of white-collar crime, describes the rationale for viewing this phenomenon within a decision-making paradigm, and explains how organizational factors may shape the decision-making calculus. Section II draws from extant research to describe prominent organizational factors implicated in decisions to engage in white-collar crime (i.e., the reward system, organizational culture, and organizational structure) and situates this literature into a decision-making framework. Section III discusses the policy implications stemming from our analysis. Finally, section IV summarizes the chapter's main themes and suggests that future research should continue to elaborate how the decision to engage in white-collar crime is shaped by the relationship between the individual and contextual factors.

The major conclusions of this chapter are as follows:

- Reward systems should be tied to legitimate goals that are challenging but attainable. The process of goal accomplishment should be monitored to ensure that unethical means are not chosen to obtain the goal. In short, valuable rewards should only be contingent on reaching ethical goals in ethical ways.

- Organizational leaders should create a formal, comprehensive ethics program. Beyond the mere presence of an ethics code, it is also necessary to have ethics training, enforcement mechanisms, and top management support.
- Top management teams must be careful when calibrating the degrees of centralization, departmentalization, and formalization in their organizational structures. Extant research suggests that when any of these elements are either too high or too low, white-collar crime may become more likely.

We now turn to developing the basis for these conclusions in the sections that follow.

I. WHITE-COLLAR CRIME AND CRIMINAL DECISION MAKING

We view white-collar crime as "an illegal act or series of illegal acts committed by non-physical means and by concealment or guile, to obtain money or property, to avoid the payment or loss of money or property, or to obtain business or personal advantage" (Edelhertz 1970, p. 3). We further situate our analysis in a paradigm that views such criminal behavior as a choice (as opposed to a more deterministic perspective) (Paternoster and Simpson 1993; Shover and Hochstetler 2006; Benson and Simpson 2009). That is, the act of committing a white-collar crime is regarded as stemming from a choice among alternative courses of action. Even if such choices are made based on biased perceptions that fail to satisfy key assumptions of perfectly "rational" decision making (e.g., perfect information, lack of time or cost constraints; March 1994), they still represent calculated decisions intended to obtain highly valued outcomes illicitly with minimal likelihood of detection and/or punishment (Paternoster and Simpson 1993; Shover and Hochstetler 2006). In other words, individuals choose to engage in white-collar crime when the perceived benefits of doing so are believed to outweigh the perceived costs, relative to other potential courses of action.

This cost–benefit analysis is a more recent development in criminological theory. In part, this has occurred because prior models focusing exclusively on costs (i.e., deterrence) have failed to obtain empirical support, likely because they ignore the powerful enticement of potential benefits or rewards (Paternoster and Simpson 1993). In this regard, a more complete decision-making model considers the potential costs (i.e., credibility of oversight and likelihood of punishment) in relation to the prospect of securing an attractive benefit (Shover and Hochstetler 2006; see also Paternoster and Simpson 1993).

Shover and Hochstetler (2006) use the concept of "lure" to describe the benefits that might accrue from crime. Lure refers to the prospect of a highly valued gain, "something that is attractive and covetable" (Shover, Hochstetler, and Alalehto 2012, p. 478). Such prospective benefits can take many forms, such as higher compensation, higher revenues and profits, and higher stock values (Paternoster and Simpson 1993). Once the desire for this benefit is aroused, it initiates a cognitive search for alternative ways of securing it. When one means toward this end is illicit, individuals might evaluate the potential costs involved (such as likelihood of detection) and how such costs might be minimized (Shover and Hochstetler 2006). Some evidence also suggests that potential rewards from criminal gains loom larger than potential risks of detection and/or punishment (Simpson and Koper 1992).

This theoretical framework is adopted here because similar models of decision making have been empirically shown to predict behavior in a wide range of human activity (e.g., Vroom 1964). Indeed, Shover and Hochstetler (2006) reviewed the applicability of the choice model to street crime and posited that this framework should be just as, if not more, useful in predicting white-collar crime. Relative to street crime, white-collar crime is committed in contexts that are more likely to stress and reward value-maximizing choices.

Indeed, the context that organizations provide is intended to shape individual decisions (although this context is not always intended to result in white-collar crime per se). For example, organizational executives establish and prioritize goals and regulate patterns of communication (March and Simon 1993). Such controls exert an influence on what goals employees pursue and how they will attempt to attain them. Therefore, we now turn to a discussion of prominent organizational factors posited to influence individual decisions to engage in white-collar crime.

II. Prominent Organizational Factors

Organizations are complex social structures with myriad components and features. Space limitations preclude an exhaustive review, so we will focus on three of the most prominent contextual factors that extant research has implicated in individual decisions to engage in white-collar crime: the reward system, organizational culture, and organizational structure. (For a more comprehensive review of organizational factors, see Tomlinson [2009].) Furthermore, we organize these factors in terms of how we believe they fit into the decision-making calculus reviewed earlier, where white-collar criminal choices are posited to be a function of perceived benefits in relation to perceived costs. We believe organizational factors influence these aspects, and we summarize our predictions in table 18.1.

Table 18.1 Perceived Benefits and Costs of White-Collar Crime

	Perceived Benefits	Perceived Costs	
	Lure	Credibility of Oversight	Likelihood of Punishment
Reward system	▓		
Organizational culture		▓	▓
Organizational structure		▓	▓

A. Perceived Benefits

Many commentators have noted that the coordination and accomplishment of goals is central to an organization's existence (e.g., Gross 1978; Clinard and Yeager 1983). In fact, organizations are under continual pressure to achieve goals and often attempt to motivate employees to accomplish such goals via the *reward system* (Eisenhardt 1989; Agnew, Piquero, and Cullen 2009; Milkovich, Newman, and Gerhart 2011). Accordingly, the reward system attempts to align the organization's interests with employees' self-interest: goals become worthwhile for employees to obtain insofar as they are instrumental in obtaining valued benefits (which could be intangible, such as feelings of accomplishment or affiliation with a successful organization, or tangible, such as promotions and monetary compensation; Milkovich, Newman, and Gerhart 2011). These potential benefits represent lure, insofar as they present situations that potential offenders can take advantage of for their own benefit (Eisenhardt 1989). Stated simply, "crime and corruption seem to be flourishing today in organizations because 'that's where the money is'" (Burke 2011, p. 69).

To the extent that employees find the reward system's benefit to be desirable, the reward system should invoke a search for ways to obtain it. Ideally (and, we contend, usually), the goal to which the benefit is tied is legitimate (e.g., to be profitable, to gain market share, to reduce expenses). Employees might choose from a variety of alternatives to achieve the goal and thereby obtain the benefit (reward). They might enact legitimate courses of action, or they might select more illicit means. A closer look at how reward systems are constructed and administered can shed light on this process.

An impressive body of research supports the conclusion that goals significantly enhance both employee and organizational performance (for one review, see Latham 2004). Yet we also acknowledge that there can be a "dark side" to such reward systems (Dunn and Schweitzer 2005; Ordonez et al. 2009). For example, in the early 1990s, Sears revised the reward system for its auto centers: the sales goal for each center was $147/hour, and meeting the goal became the basis for both incentive pay and retention on the payroll. This goal was regarded by the auto repair staff as so high that it could not be obtained unless unnecessary repairs were recommended to customers. This is precisely what happened, and authorities in California conducted an undercover sting operation that brought this practice to light (Dishneau 1992).

Similarly, executives at Enron fixated so heavily on increasing their company's stock price to ever-higher levels that they were willing to bend and outright break accounting rules to create the illusion that they were a profitable enterprise (McLean and Elkind 2003). Enron richly rewarded oil and gas traders who reaped windfall profits as well as those who developed financial structures that created the appearance of fiscal strength by masking major problems. In short, Enron was famous for minting millionaires. The lavish compensation system clearly oriented employees toward a focus on *appearing* to be a successful company, when the reality was that day-to-day management of the enterprise was incompetent at best (McLean and Elkind 2003). If the reward system is not managed correctly, it can actually induce more favorable employee attitudes toward unethical behavior (Anand, Ashforth, and Joshi 2004). More specifically, poorly specified reward systems tend to unwittingly reward undesirable behaviors and fail to generate truly desired behaviors (Kerr 1995).

B. Perceived Costs

Shover and Hochstetler (2006) articulated two perceived costs that individuals are believed to weigh in contemplating the commission of a white-collar crime: the credibility of oversight and the likelihood of punishment if detected. Clearly, these are linked in a sequential manner. If an individual believes that no one is monitoring his or her actions, then accountability appears to be low, and the likelihood of punishment is also deemed to be low. However, even if oversight is credible and sufficient to detect criminal behavior, the likelihood of punishment might still be low. Some organizations intentionally ignore criminal behavior that comes to their attention instead of enforcing their discipline policies (Tomlinson and Greenberg 2007). We consider how organizational culture and organizational structure influence these perceptions.

1. Organizational Culture

Organizational culture refers to "the shared social knowledge within an organization regarding the rules, norms, and values that shapes the attitudes and behaviors of its employees" (Colquitt, LePine, and Wesson 2011, p. 557). Norms (or shared standards of conduct) are often tacit and informal, and because they are essentially guidelines for social approval they are a powerful influence on individual behavior. In fact, researchers have demonstrated that informal social norms are a more powerful influence on individual behavior than either their own independent attitudes (Ellis and Arieli 1999) or formal managerial sanctions (e.g., Hollinger and Clark 1982). This is not surprising, since most adults determine what is right versus wrong in the workplace on the basis of internalized, shared moral norms of their work group (Kohlberg 1969). Most people desire to behave according to the expectations that respected others have for them.

Although the terminology employed was different, this notion of organizational culture affecting white-collar crime was evident in the seminal work by Sutherland (1949). Specifically, he attributed white-collar crime to "differential association," whereby individuals learn to engage in such behaviors in the workplace because they are surrounded by others who endorse those behaviors. In this manner, individuals are socialized into environments that provide them with cues on what behaviors are acceptable (and unacceptable) and even with rationalizations (Sykes and Matza 1957) for neutralizing any reservations about the ethicality or legality of certain questionable behaviors (Gross 1980; Hochstetler and Copes 2001; Anand, Ashforth, and Joshi 2004).

Such indoctrination into this type of organizational context can strongly affect an individual's perception regarding the credibility of oversight and the likelihood of punishment, as several examples from the extant literature readily attest. In a study of British dockworkers, a carefully orchestrated system was created whereby dockworkers could systematically steal freight they were employed to transport. Norms in this work group evolved to assign each member a vital role: receivers altered the invoices, while forklift operators moved crates to obstruct any potential monitoring, and lookouts were stationed to warn of any uninvited interruptions to cargo theft (Mars 1974). Similar dynamics were at play in other forms of organizational crime, such as the savings and loans "land flip" frauds (Calavita, Pontell, and Tillman 1997) and price-fixing conspiracies in the electrical equipment industry (Faulkner, Cheney, Fisher, and Baker 2003). Other studies have revealed that work groups sometimes conduct meetings to discuss how any potential monitoring systems might be overcome (Altheide et al. 1978; McLean and Elkin 2003).

Managers can also shape norms by the example they set with their own behavior. In fact, unethical behavior among employees is most likely when managers are seen as espousing high standards that they personally do not enact (Dineen, Lewicki, and Tomlinson 2006). Employees look to their managers for cues regarding acceptable behavior (Lewicki et al. 1997), and it is believed that when employees observe managers flouting the law with impunity, the credibility of oversight over their own behavior will be low (Shover et al. 2012). In a similar vein, researchers have uncovered instances where managers purposely turn a blind eye toward subordinates' criminal behaviors (Gouldner 1954; Sieh 1987). Norms of this nature clearly operate to signal that the chance of being caught while committing a white-collar crime is low. Moreover, some managers convey a "wink" whereby public statements that criminal behavior will be punished are accompanied by a nonverbal indication that this is truly not the case (Altheide et al. 1978). The Code of Ethics from Enron is often used as a contemporary example of this phenomenon (Sims and Brinkman 2003). In this manner, norms can also convey the perception that even if white-collar crime is detected, the chance of punishment is actually very low.

2. *Organizational Structure*

Organizational structure "defines how job tasks are formally divided, grouped, and coordinated" (Robbins and Judge 2011, p. 488). While there are several facets of an organization's structure, we focus on three for our analysis: centralization, departmentalization, and formalization. Centralization refers to where decision-making authority in the organization is formally situated; organizations can range from being highly centralized (where decision-making authority is concentrated at the top management level) to highly decentralized (where decision-making authority is pushed down to the lowest managerial levels). Departmentalization describes the way that jobs are grouped together to coordinate work flow. Formalization describes the degree to which work is standardized and enforced by rules, procedures, and other control mechanisms.

All three of these elements are predicted to influence employees' perceptions of the credibility of oversight and likelihood of punishment because they each create a context whereby employees would perceive less personal responsibility for their criminal decisions (although they do so in different ways). In the case of centralization, where formal decision-making authority is concentrated among top managers, considerable emphasis is placed on the hierarchy of authority. While authority is an invaluable tool that permits managers to discharge their responsibilities, too much emphasis on deference to authority can have dangerous consequences. In such an environment, there is considerable pressure for an employee to obey managerial directives even if such orders diverge from what the employee knows to be appropriate.

A legendary experiment by Milgram (1963) is instructive. Ostensibly to study the effects of punishment on learning, experimental participants were told to "teach" certain word pairings to a "learner" who appeared to be connected to an electric shock apparatus. When the learner made mistakes in reciting these word pairs, the teacher was to administer an iteratively higher electric shock via a console in front of the dividing wall that separated the two individuals. Whenever a participant would balk at the instructions to administer additional shock, Milgram would simply state, "You have no choice, you must go on! Your job is to punish the learner's mistakes." This directive was sufficient to prompt most participants to comply. Probing this alarming behavior, it was determined that participants complied (even though they were reluctant) because they felt a need to obey authority, and that in doing so they psychologically absolved themselves of any responsibility. Since they were just following orders, they reasoned that the ultimate responsibility for any harm should be attributed to the authority figure. Recent research has provided additional support for this effect in the context of financial reporting (Bishop 2013; Mayhew and Murphy 2014).

In hierarchical structures of authority, top management issues directives to specialists at lower levels. In turn, these lower-level employees feel compelled to carry out such orders, even if it entails illegality. In this case, both executives and employees might argue that they are not responsible: executives can claim that they were not aware of the criminal means employees used to follow their orders, while employees can claim that they were simply doing what they had to do to meet the requirements imposed on them (Clinard and Yeager 1983). Regardless, the perception that one is not responsible for one's actions aligns with the perception that any monitoring system (if it even exists) is not aimed at oneself; the lack of perceived culpability dismisses the notion of punishment. Many researchers have documented instances where white-collar criminals express amazement over their convictions because they did not see themselves as being personally responsible for a crime (e.g., Anand, Ashforth, and Joshi 2004).

Ironically, too much decentralization could produce the same effects. Rather than relying on directives from top management, employees themselves are granted significant decision-making authority, thus creating much diffused responsibility. Once again, it becomes increasingly difficult to isolate the individual(s) responsible for criminal activities (Dugan and Gibbs 2009).

With respect to departmentalization, organizations may choose to group jobs on the basis of functional departments (e.g., marketing, finance, manufacturing), the type of product or service that is offered (e.g., a household products company might have separate departments for shampoo, laundry detergent, and paper goods), the stage in the work process (e.g., those who receive insurance claims might work separately from those who ultimately send reimbursement), or geography (e.g., North America, Europe,

Asia). Departmentalization in any of these ways allows jobs with common tasks to be coordinated as it puts specialists in a particular area together. Ultimately, the organization seeks to choose a form of departmentalization that is optimal for the work flow. However, some forms of departmentalization might have the effect of creating a diffusion of responsibility among employees. This segmentation of jobs involved in different aspects of a complex process, in turn, might have the effect of (1) creating myopia that overlooks the potential impact that questionable behaviors undertaken in one department may have on other parts of the organization (Gross 1978, 1980) and (2) reducing any sense among employees that they might be participating in criminal behavior (e.g., a manufacturing manager determining that responsibility for any product liability issues resides with the legal department). It can also make it more difficult to pinpoint specific individuals responsible for a criminal act.

These dynamics are perfectly illustrated in the infamous case of the Ford Pinto. Company president Lee Iacocca directed the company to produce a new car "under 2,000 pounds and under $2,000" by 1970. Designing a new automobile is a complex process and involves highly specialized work in distinct areas, including chassis design, styling, and component testing. All of these processes must occur before factories can be tooled for production. While engineers conducted crash tests prior to production and uncovered initial evidence of gas tank explosions upon rear impact, the findings did not appear to be out of the ordinary, and results even appeared to be comparable to crash tests on competitors' vehicles. Moreover, the findings were not passed along to the recall coordinator prior to production. The normal segmentation process at work in this case meant that the engineers did not perceive a problem that exceeded their threshold for further action, and their findings were archived until much later, when the recall coordinator had to respond in the wake of numerous tragic accidents (Trevino and Nelson 2007; Benson and Simpson 2009).

Organizational structures also vary in terms of how formalized they are. As described earlier, formalization is the extent to which jobs are standardized by rules and procedures. High formalization employs structural tools to both guide and enforce employee conduct. This accountability is enabled by control mechanisms to disseminate standards, as well as to oversee compliance proactively (e.g., monitoring) or retrospectively (e.g., auditing). Organizations with little formalization might unwittingly send the message that no one is "minding the shop." Thus, employees might be more likely to perceive that there is no credible oversight and, hence, little chance of punishment. Conversely, high formalization might deter employees from criminal acts because they believe that they cannot escape detection (Dunn and Schweitzer 2005); the presence of such oversight suggests that if a crime is detected, it will be punished.

For example, Prudential Insurance employees were engaging in illegal "churning," whereby customers were persuaded to exchange the cash value for existing policies to purchase new and more expensive policies without being aware of the full costs and benefits of doing so (Scism 1996). Investigators attributed this to a lack of formal structure to ensure that proper procedures were employed in selling upgraded policies. Among the several reforms to correct this problem was the new procedure of having underwriters (who were not paid on commission) finalize policy upgrades directly with customers after reviewing a detailed checklist to ensure adequate understanding. The company was also reorganized to implement more direct oversight of this process. Such changes would make employees more likely to perceive that any subsequent efforts to "churn" would be detected and punished.

Moreover, these facets of organizational structure might combine in certain ways that further fuel the perception that credibility of oversight and likelihood of punishment are low. Shover et al. (2012) concluded, for example, that "growing specialization in industrial activities and organizational structures [departmentalization] requires and generates specialized pools of competence and skill that make effective oversight [via formalization] more difficult and costly" (p. 476).

III. Policy Implications

In this section, we draw out the implications of our foregoing analysis with an eye toward practical steps to reduce white-collar crime. Once again, we organize our points according to the benefit–cost framework. As we will see, in some cases clear solutions are elusive; many policies that might initially seem promising have drawbacks that lie beneath the surface.

A. Perceived Benefits

As we argued above, we believe that the organizational factor most likely to influence the perceived benefits of white-collar crime is the reward system. The examples we used earlier to establish this point actually serve to reiterate conclusions from major prescriptive writings on the use of goals in reward systems. Goals should be challenging but attainable (Latham 2004), as unrealistically high goals might stimulate white-collar crime because that is the only method perceived to be viable (Agnew, Piquero, and Cullen 2009). This stipulation also presupposes that employees charged with carrying out the goal have the necessary ability, tools, and training to achieve the goal in an appropriate manner. Goals should also be comprehensive enough to capture the true essence of what is desired and should be monitored to ensure that undesirable behavior is not the chosen means by which the goal is achieved. The reward system should also be tied to goals that are stable and easily measured, under conditions that employees can control (Agnew, Piquero, and Cullen 2009; Milkovich, Newman, and Gerhart 2011). For example, incentive pay programs are not appropriate when tied to electricity usage for utility company executives, as such metrics are determined by actual weather conditions (Pfeffer and Sutton 2006). Finally, goals should be ethically legitimate. Research suggests that individuals tend to make more unethical choices when the reward system rewards unethical behaviors and/or punishes ethical behaviors (Hegarty and Sims 1978; Trevino, Sutton, and Woodman 1985).

When organizations use their reward systems to offer employees an attractive benefit contingent upon goal accomplishment yet do not attend to legitimate design and administrative issues, they take one step forward only to take several backward (Ordonez et al. 2009). We contend that it is fully appropriate to set legitimate goals; it does indeed create "pressure" (Gross 1978) or motivation to achieve goals (Latham 2004). But the pressure to achieve them "at any cost" (Gross 1978) is more likely when illicit means are perceived to meet with greater likelihood of goal accomplishment (because the goal itself is otherwise deemed unobtainable) or have lower cost than more legitimate means. We proceed to consider organizational factors that relate to these perceived costs.

B. Perceived Costs

1. Organizational Culture

Managers can attempt to create a more ethical culture by developing a formal corporate ethics program. Such programs are characterized by several components: a formal *ethics code* that articulates standards for ethical behavior, *ethics training* to communicate these standards to employees, *enforcement mechanisms* to detect unethical practices (e.g., confidential hotlines) as well as to reward ethical behavior and punish unethical behavior, and *top management support* (including leading by example) (Weaver, Trevino, and Cochran 1999).

Because ethics codes are often the cornerstone of formal ethics programs, researchers have investigated the direct effects of these codes on employee behavior. This body of research has generated somewhat equivocal results (Kapstein and Schwartz 2008). However, Schwartz (2011) found that while ethics codes might not affect employee behavior directly, they do appear to have several indirect effects. Specifically, they can serve as (1) a "signpost" prompting employees to consult others to determine the appropriateness of certain behaviors, (2) a "shield" allowing employees to refuse unethical requests (whether they come from suppliers, customers, or even managers), (3) a "smoke detector" providing employees with a tool to deter others from unethical behavior, and (4) a "fire alarm" compelling employees to report ethical violations to the appropriate authority.

Ethics training is instrumental in disseminating the ethics code and providing organizational members on guidance pertaining to its application in their day-to-day duties. Delaney and Sockell (1992, p. 723) found that "the existence of an ethics training program lowers the extent to which respondents perceived that they had to do unethical things to get ahead in their firm." These training programs also led to the perception that the sponsoring organizations were more sensitive to moral issues, and as a result, these employees were "less likely to perceive that they have 'to do things that are not right' to get ahead than are employees in firms without such programs" (p. 725). Moreover, the presence of an ethics training program reinforces an ethical culture by explicitly recognizing that jobs occasionally present their incumbents with moral dilemmas, and the organization is committed to guiding employees to handle those dilemmas in ethically appropriate ways.

Enforcement mechanisms are another tool to shape the ethicality of an organization's culture. Confidential reporting hotlines provide one specific example whereby misconduct can be reported and handled by organizational officials (Dunn and Schweitzer 2005). The provision of enforcement mechanisms reiterates the value placed on ethical behavior and signals that infractions will be detected and punished. Prior research has shown that ethics code enforcement is effective to the extent that it is performed consistently and equitably, such that violations are dealt with regardless of who the perpetrator is, and in a manner proportionate to the severity of the violation (for a review, see Schwartz [2011]). Beyond punishment of unethical behavior, organizations might also shape an ethical culture by weaving rewards for ethical behavior into the performance review process (e.g., Dunn and Schweitzer 2005).

Management support refers to creating the perception among employees that those in positions of authority throughout the organization are committed to ethical behavior. Management support necessarily entails managers setting a good behavioral example for their employees to emulate, rather than merely promulgating ethical standards. Employees look to managers as salient sources of information regarding the norms, standards, and practices that are expected in organizations (Lewicki et al. 1997). Indeed, research has found that deviant workplace behavior among employees is lowest when managers both provide sound ethical guidance and actually practice that guidance themselves. On the other hand, deviant workplace behavior is highest when managers provide sound ethical guidance but do *not* enact the standards they promulgate to their subordinates (Dineen, Lewicki, and Tomlinson 2006).

2. *Organizational Structure*

As we reviewed above, it is difficult to prescribe an appropriate degree of centralization, as prior work suggests that unethical behaviors can result from either highly centralized or highly decentralized structures. Similarly, it is difficult to specify a priori an appropriate level of departmentalization: too much can lead to insular departments that tend to make ethical issues less salient, but too little can compromise organizational efficiency. Finally, formalization can be increased in ways that may contribute to reducing white-collar crime. We already discussed how formal ethics codes affect an organization's culture; we believe codifying formal ethical standards and policies is also related to the formalization component of an organization's structure. Formalizing a monitoring program has also been recommended as a promising management tool (e.g., Dunn and Schweitzer 2005). Of course, it is indeed more expensive to add monitoring, and in fact, the administrative burden may increase as the work supervised becomes more complex (Dunn and Schweitzer 2005). Moreover, there is some evidence that those formally charged with oversight duties might become less trusting of those they oversee (Strickland 1958). This mistrust might contribute to efforts to defeat the system by the employees who live under its scrutiny (Dunn and Schweitzer 2005), although research on this issue is still equivocal (Tomlinson 2011).

However, monitoring might be effective to the extent that affected individuals determine that the chances of committing criminal behaviors without detection and punishment are very low and avoid these behaviors as a result (Dunn and Schweitzer 2005). Frankly, even if a monitoring system does not deter white-collar crime, it might still be instrumental in detecting such behavior, which is a necessary precursor to organizational intervention. Extant research also suggests that random monitoring is more effective than routine and predictable monitoring (Ho and Schweitzer 2003).

IV. Conclusion

The purpose of this chapter has been to review research on contextual factors that appear to influence an individual's decision to engage in white-collar crime. Individuals choose to engage in white-collar crime when the perceived benefits of doing so are believed to outweigh the perceived costs, relative to other potential courses of action. Although there are numerous contextual factors that could influence the decision to engage in white-collar crime, in this chapter we chose to focus on the three most prominent ones: reward system, organizational culture, and organizational structure. We posited that the reward system primarily influences the perceived benefits of white-collar crime, whereas features of the organization's culture and structure primarily influence the perceived costs. In future research, there is a need for model testing of our predicted effects of organizational factors. We acknowledge the possibility that some factors might be empirically related to other elements in the decision-making calculus (e.g., organizational culture might convey social approval for committing white-collar crime, and thus might be a form of "reward"). Even so, we expect that the predominant effects are the ones we specify here.

Future research should also continue to elaborate on the relationship between the role of the individual and these contextual factors. For example, individuals react to ethical dilemmas as a function of their stage of cognitive moral development, and this likely interacts with contextual factors such as the ones we discuss here (Trevino 1986; Greenberg 2002; Tomlinson 2009). In other words, notwithstanding any arguments we make here regarding contextual factors, we cannot completely exonerate individuals from culpability for white-collar crime, as it is individuals who ultimately choose to engage in this harmful behavior. We simply hope that our analysis is useful in creating contexts that are more conducive to guiding the choices of organizational members more constructively.

REFERENCES

Agnew, Robert, Nicole Leeper Piquero, and Francis T. Cullen. 2009. "General Strain Theory and White-Collar Crime." In *The Criminology of White-Collar Crime*, pp. 35–60, edited by Sally S. Simpson and David Weisburd. New York: Springer.

Altheide, David L, Patricia A. Adler, and Duane A. Altheide. 1978. "The Social Meaning of Employee Theft." In *Crime at the Top*, pp. 90–124, edited by John M. Johnson and Jack D. Douglas. Philadelphia: J. B. Lippincott.

Anand, Vikas, Blake E. Ashforth, and Mahendra Joshi. 2004. "Business as Usual: The Acceptance and Perpetuation of Corruption in Organizations." *Academy of Management Executives* 18: 39–53.

Benson, Michael L., and Sally S. Simpson. 2009. *White-Collar Crime: An Opportunity Perspective*. New York: Routledge.

Bishop, Carol C. 2013. "The Impact of Social Influence Pressure on CFO Judgments." DBA dissertation, Kennesaw State University, Coles College of Business.

Burke, Ronald J. 2011. "Show Me the Money." In *Crime and Corruption in Organizations: Why It Occurs and What to Do About It*, pp. 69–95, edited by Ronald J. Burke, Edward C. Tomlinson, and Cary L. Cooper. Surrey, UK: Gower.

Calavita, Kitty, Robert Tillman, and Henry N. Pontell. 1997. "The Savings and Loan Debacle, Financial Crime, and the State." *Annual Review of Sociology* 23: 19–39.

Clinard, Marshall B., and Peter C. Yeager. 1983. *Corporate Crime*. New York: Free Press.

Colquitt, Jason A., Jeffery A. LePine, and Michael J. Wesson. 2011. *Organizational Behavior*, 2nd ed. New York: McGraw-Hill Irwin.

Delaney, John Thomas, and Donna Sockell. 1992. "Do Company Ethics Training Programs Make a Difference? An Empirical Analysis." *Journal of Business Ethics* 11: 719–27.

Dineen, Brian R., Roy J. Lewicki, and Edward C. Tomlinson. 2006. "Supervisory Guidance and Behavioral Integrity: Relationships with Employee Citizenship and Deviant Behavior." *Journal of Applied Psychology* 91: 622–35.

Dishneau, David. 1992. "Sears Admits Mistakes, Takes Workers Off Commission." The Associated Press (June 22). Available at http://news.google.com/newspapers?n id=1955&da t=199206237id=9IkxAAAAIBAJ&sjd=2aIFAAAAIBAJ&pg=1248, 4064341

Dugan, Laura, and Carole Gibbs. 2009. "The Role of Organizational Structure in the Control of Corporate Crime and Terrorism." In *The Criminology of White-Collar Crime*, pp. 111–28, edited by Sally S. Simpson and David Weisburd. New York: Springer.

Dunn, Jennifer, and Maurice E. Schweitzer. 2005. "Why Good Employees Make Unethical Decisions: The Role of Reward Systems, Organizational Culture, and Managerial Oversight." In *Managing Organizational Deviance*, pp. 39–60, edited by Roland E. Kidwell Jr. and Christopher L. Martin. Thousand Oaks, CA: Sage.

Edelhertz, Herbert. 1970. *The Nature, Impact, and Prosecution of White-Collar Crime*. Washington, D.C.: U. S. Department of Justice.

Eisenhardt, Kathleen M. 1989. "Agency Theory: An Assessment and Review." *Academy of Management Review* 14: 57–74.

Ellis, Shumel, and Shaul Ariel. 1999. "Predicting Intentions to Report Administrative and Disciplinary Infractions." *Human Relations* 52: 947–67.

Faulkner, Robert R., Eric R. Cheney, Gene A. Fisher, and Wayne E. Baker. 2003. "Crime by Committee: Conspirators and Company Men in the Illegal Electrical Industry Cartel, 1954–1959." *Criminology* 41: 511–54.

Gouldner, Alvin W. 1954. *Wildcat Strike: A Study in Worker-Management Relationships*. New York: Harper and Row.

Greenberg, Jerald. 2002. "Who Stole the Money, and When? Individual and Situational Determinants of Employee Theft." *Organizational Behavior and Human Decision Processes* 89: 985–1003.

Gross, Edward. 1978. "Organizational Crime: A Theoretical Perspective." In *Studies in Symbolic Interaction*, pp. 55–85, edited by Norman Denzin. Greenwich, CT: JAI Press.

Hegarty, W. Harvey, and Henry P. Sims. 1978. "Some Determinants of Unethical Decision Behavior: An Examination of Existing Studies and the Development of an Integrated Research Model." *Journal of Business Ethics* 77: 111–27.

Ho, T., and Maurice Schweitzer. 2003. "Transparency and Trust: What You See Is What You Get." Unpublished manuscript. Philadelphia: University of Pennsylvania.

Hochstetler, Andy, and Heith Copes. 2001. "Organizational Culture and Organizational Crime." In *Crimes of Privilege*, pp. 210–21, edited by Neal Shover and John Wright. Oxford, UK: Oxford University Press.

Hollinger, Richard C., and John P. Clark. 1982. "Formal and Informal Social Controls of Employee Deviance." *The Sociological Quarterly* 23: 333–43.

Kapstein, M., and Mark S. Schwartz. 2008. "The Effectiveness of Business Codes: A Critical Examination of Existing Studies and the Development of an Integrated Research Model." *Journal of Business Ethics* 77: 111–27.

Kerr, Steven. 1995. "On the Folly of Rewarding A While Hoping for B." *Academy of Management Executive* 9: 7–14.

Kohlberg, Lawrence. 1969. "Stage and Sequence: The Cognitive Development Approach to Socialization." In *Handbook of Socialization Theory and Research*, pp. 347–80, edited by David A. Goslin. Chicago: Rand McNally.

Latham, Gary P. 2004. "Motivate Employee Performance through Goal-Setting." In *Handbook of Principles of Organizational Behavior*, pp. 107–19, edited by Edwin A. Locke. Malden, MA: Blackwell.

Lewicki, Roy J., Timothy Poland, John Minton, and Blair Sheppard. 1997. "Dishonesty as Deviance: A Typology of Workplace Dishonesty and Contributing Factors." In *Research on Negotiation in Organizations*, pp. 53–86, edited by Roy J. Lewicki, Robert J. Bies, and Blair Sheppard. Greenwich, CT: JAI Press.

March, James G. 1994. *A Primer on Decision Making*. New York: Free Press.

March, James G., and Herbert Simon. 1993. *Organizations*, 2nd ed. Cambridge, MA: Blackwell.

Mars, Gerald. 1974. "Dock Pilferage: A Case Study in Occupational Theft." In *Deviance and Social Control*, pp. 209–28, edited by Paul Rock and Mary McIntosh. London, UK: Tavistock.

Mayhew, Brian W., and Pamela R. Murphy. 2014. "The Impact of Authority on Reporting Behavior, Rationalization, and Affect." *Contemporary Accounting Research* 31: 420–43.

McLean, Bethany, and Peter Elkind. 2003. *The Smartest Guys in the Room: The Amazing Rise and Scandalous Fall of Enron*. New York: Penguin.

Milgram, Stanley. 1963. "Behavioral Study of Obedience." *Journal of Abnormal and Social Psychology* 67: 371–8.

Milkovich, George T., Jerry M, Newman, and Barry Gerhart. 2011. *Compensation*. 10th ed. New York: McGraw-Hill Irwin.

Ordonez, Lisa D., Maurice E. Schweitzer, Adam D. Galinsky, and Max H. Bazerman. 2009. "Goals Gone Wild: The Systematic Side Effects of Overprescribing Goal Setting." *Academy of Management Perspectives* 23: 6–16.

Paternoster, Raymond, and Sally S. Simpson. 1993. "A Rational Choice Theory of Corporate Crime." In *Routine Activity and Rational Choice*, pp. 37–58, edited by Ronald V. Clarke and Marcus Felson. New Brunswick, NJ: Transaction.

Pfeffer, Jeffrey, and Robert I. Sutton. 2006. "What's Wrong with Pay-for-Performance?" *Industrial Management* 48: 12–17.

Robbins, Stephen P., and Timothy A. Judge. 2011. *Organizational Behavior*. Upper Saddle River: NJ: Pearson.

Schwartz, Mark S. 2011. "How to Minimize Corruption in Business Organizations: Developing and Sustaining an Ethical Corporate Culture." In *Crime and Corruption in Organizations: Why It Occurs and What to Do about It*, pp. 273–96, edited by Ronald J. Burke, Edward C. Tomlinson, and Cary Cooper. Surrey, England: Gower.

Scism, Leslie. 1996. "Prudential Insurance to Change Way It Sells Policies in Wake of Criticism." *The Wall Street Journal* (June 17): B5. Available at http://search.proquest.com/docview/1441124412?accountid=2837

Shover, Neal, and Andy Hochstetler. 2006. *Choosing White-Collar Crime*. New York: Cambridge University Press.

Shover, Neal, Andy Hochstetler, and Tage Alaehto. 2012. "Choosing White-Collar Crime." In *The Oxford Handbook of Criminological Theory*, 475–93, edited by Francis T. Cullen and Pamela Wilcox. New York: Oxford University Press.

Sieh, Edward W. 1987. "Garment Workers: Perceptions of Inequity and Worker Theft." *British Journal of Criminology* 27: 174–90.

Simpson, Sally S., and Christopher Koper. 1992. "Deterring Corporate Crime." *Criminology* 30: 47–75.

Sims, Ronald R., and Johannes Brinkman. 2003. "Enron Ethics: Culture Matters More Than Codes." *Journal of Business Ethics* 45: 243–56.

Strickland, Lloyd H. 1958. "Surveillance and Trust." *Journal of Personality* 26: 200–15.

Sutherland, Edward H. 1949. *White Collar Crime*. New York: The Dryden Press.

Sykes, Gresham M., and David Matza. 1957. "Techniques of Neutralization: A Theory of Delinquency." *American Journal of Sociology* 22: 664–70.

Tomlinson, Edward C. 2009. "Teaching the Interactionist Model of Ethics: Two Brief Case Studies." *Journal of Management Education* 35: 142–65.

Tomlinson, Edward C. 2011. "The Role of Trust in Employee Theft." In *Crime and Corruption in Organizations: Why It Occurs and What to Do about It*, pp. 121–41, edited by Ronald J. Burke, Edward C. Tomlinson, and Cary C. Cooper. Surrey, England: Gower.

Tomlinson, Edward C., and Jerald Greenberg. 2007. "Understanding and Deterring Employee Theft with Organizational Justice." In *Research Companion to the Dysfunctional Workplace*, pp. 285–301, edited by Janice Langan-Fox, Cary L. Cooper, and Richard J. Klimoski. Cheltenham, UK: Edward Elgar.

Trevino, Linda Klebe. 1986. "Ethical Decision Making in Organizations: A Person-Situation Interactionist Model." *Academy of Management Review* 11: 601–17.

Trevino, Linda Klebe, and Kate A. Nelson. 2007. *Managing Business Ethics: Straight Talk about How to Do It Right*. Hoboken, NJ: John Wiley and Sons.

Trevino, Linda Klebe, Charlotte D. Sutton, and Richard W. Woodman. 1985. "Effects of Reinforcement Contingencies and Cognitive Moral Development on Ethical Decision Making." Paper presented at the Annual Meeting of the Academy of Management, San Diego, CA.

Vroom, Victor H. 1964. *Work and Motivation*. New York: Wiley.

Weaver, Gary R., Linda Klebe Trevino, and Philip L. Cochran. 1999. "Corporate Ethics Programs as Control Systems: Influences of Executive Commitment and Environmental Factors." *Academy of Management Journal* 42: 41–57.

CHAPTER 19

OPPORTUNITIES FOR WHITE-COLLAR CRIME

TAMARA D. MADENSEN

THERE has been increasing recognition among criminologists that opportunity, as an independent construct, is worthy of in-depth examination. This recognition has been fostered by recent theoretical advancements. Several opportunity-based theories have been proposed over the past few decades. These theories explain how attractive crime opportunities form and how motivated offenders exploit them. Three of the most prominent opportunity theories—routine activity theory, crime pattern theory, and situational crime prevention—form the basis of a theoretical paradigm referred to as crime science (Clarke 2010).

Crime science theories already have been applied to white-collar crime prevention and research (Benson and Madensen 2007; Benson, Madensen, and Eck 2009). Yet, the crime science perspective appears to be grossly underused in studies of white-collar crime when compared to its use in the study and prevention of traditional street crimes. Researchers' lack of familiarity or training in this perspective might help explain the limited application of crime science to white-collar crime. As empirical evidence demonstrating the usefulness of crime science continues to grow, it might be time to revisit its potential to advance white-collar crime research.

The general purpose of this chapter is twofold. First, it explains how and why opportunities play an important role in white-collar crime. Second, it argues that the crime science perspective offers a useful framework for the study and prevention of white-collar crime opportunities. The main conclusions are as follows:

- Opportunities both permit and cause white-collar crime. While opportunity is a necessary condition for all crime, attractive crime opportunities also can provoke criminal behavior.
- The ten principles of opportunity and crime—frequently used to illustrate the importance and causal role of opportunity in street crimes—also can be used to explain white-collar crime patterns and events. The characteristics of white-collar

crimes are compatible with the underlying assumptions of opportunity-focused crime theories.

- Three opportunity-focused crime theories—routine activity theory, crime pattern theory, and situational crime prevention—form the basis of the crime science perspective. The crime science approach, also known as environmental criminology, is used to uncover highly specific crime opportunity structures, with the primary goal of finding ways to prevent crime.
- Crime opportunities have both structural and perceptual features that can be manipulated to discourage crime. Crime science theories draw attention to these features of white-collar crimes and suggest specific ways to disrupt crime opportunities.
- Characteristics unique to white-collar crimes do not hinder applications of the crime science perspective; rather, in some instances, these characteristics strengthen the explanatory power and applicability of crime science theories.
- Recent advances in crime science offer promising new directions for white-collar crime research. These advancements include typologies of crime-facilitating places, the influence of place management, crime script analysis, and studies of crime displacement and diffusion of benefits.

Section I begins with a discussion of the role of opportunity in white-collar crime. It demonstrates how white-collar crime events and patterns relate to the principles and underlying assumptions of opportunity theories. Section II provides an overview of the three opportunity-based theories that form the basis of the crime science perspective, and section III describes how the crime science perspective can be applied to the study and prevention of white-collar crime. Section IV explains how recent advancements in crime science provide new directions for white-collar crime research.

I. The Role of Opportunity in White-Collar Crime

Criminal actions are not possible in the absence of criminal opportunities. Yet, traditional criminologists largely ignored the relationship between crime and opportunity throughout the 20th century. Many early theorists focused their efforts toward understanding and explaining the origins of criminal motivation. Criminal behavior was most often attributed to individual or group differences rooted in biological determinants, psychological profiles, or social experiences.

Those who initially "discovered" and studied white-collar crime drew our attention to the social processes through which people become criminal. Sutherland's (1949) differential association theory explains how those who commit crime learn this behavior by interacting with others. People are more likely to engage in crime if they have close relationships with others who define crime as favorable and teach them techniques for committing crime. The role of opportunity is referenced here indirectly—individuals must be exposed to others who value criminal behavior and must learn how to commit crime. Criminal motivation and skills do not provide access to crime opportunities; they only prepare individuals to take advantage of opportunities, should such prospects arise. For many white-collar criminals, crime opportunities are encountered in the course of their occupation.

Several theories now recognize opportunity as a root cause of crime. These theories explain why crime rates vary over time and across places, how criminal activity patterns develop, and what should be done to prevent future events. Ten principles summarize the underlying assumptions of these theories and are collectively referred to as "crime opportunity theory" (Felson and Clarke 1998). These principles describe how opportunity influences crime and can be used to explain the central role of opportunity in all crime events, including white-collar crimes. The following examples demonstrate the principles' applicability to white-collar crime.

A. The Ten Principles of Opportunity and Crime

1. *Opportunities Play a Role in Causing All Crime*

Opportunities cause crime in two ways. First, opportunity is a necessary condition for crime. One must first encounter and recognize criminal opportunity in order to engage in crime. Second, opportunity also might provoke criminal behavior. Attractive crime opportunities might encourage normally law-abiding individuals to engage in behaviors they ordinarily would define as objectionable. Cressey (1953) acknowledged that opportunity must be present for someone to commit fraud, but he did not argue that opportunity alone provides the incentive for criminal behavior. However, interviews with white-collar offenders suggest that some offenders take advantage of opportunities simply because they offer substantial rewards. Offenders do not act uniformly in premeditated ways to solve pressing personal problems; rather, many offenders are opportunistic (see interview excerpts in Benson [1985]).

2. *Crime Opportunities Are Highly Specific*

Legal crime definitions can mask important differences between crime types. Consider embezzlement, for instance. Siphoning money from a cash register, forging checks from company bank accounts, inflating expense claims, falsifying overtime records, and adding family members to a company's payroll each require access to different opportunities. Positions of trust garnered through employment make each of these crimes possible, but the nature of one's specific employment position determines which type of crime can be committed. The person operating a cash register might not have access to payroll accounts, while those managing payroll departments might never have direct physical access to company cash. Since crime opportunities are highly specific, the methods used to commit various offenses also differ. These differences become important when attempting to devise prevention strategies.

3. Crime Opportunities Are Concentrated in Time and Space

Commonly observed fluctuations in police calls-for-service data illustrate the principle of concentrated opportunities for street crime, and research has found similar fluctuations in white-collar crime. Levels of specific white-collar crime types have varied across time. Major economic crises—such as the U.S. savings and loan scandal in the 1980s and 1990s and the housing bubble and subprime mortgage crisis in the 2000s—represent the culminating effects of periodic increases in illegal or unethical market dealings. White-collar crime levels also vary across organizations (Ashforth and Anand 2003; Shover and Scroggins 2009), industries (Apel and Paternoster 2009), and countries (see Gibbs, McGarrell, and Axelrod [2010] for a discussion of place concentrations within the transnational e-waste market). Time and place "signatures," or patterns of white-collar offenses, also are crime-specific and can vary from one crime type to the next. Crime signatures associated with bribing foreign governments to win contracts will likely differ from the crime signatures of stock manipulation involving fraudulent accounting. We can predict that foreign government bribery will be concentrated in countries where lucrative business opportunities are concentrated during periods of lax governmental oversight. Alternatively, fraudulent accounting may be more likely to occur in companies that offer managers larger stock and options holdings and during periods of high stock market valuations (Kedia and Philippon 2007).

4. Crime Opportunities Depend on Everyday Movements of Activity

Crime opportunities arise in the course of our everyday activities. White-collar criminals stumble across crime opportunities in the course of their business dealings much like residential burglars who locate attractive targets as they travel through familiar neighborhoods. White-collar offenders might encounter crime opportunities as a result of their employment positions or through their interactions with other people (e.g., investment schemes) or with financial entities (e.g., insurance fraud). Routine interactions between people and their environments create the conditions necessary for crime.

5. One Crime Produces Opportunities for Another

Those who are in the process of committing an offense might encounter opportunities for other crimes. Someone who breaks into a house with the intent to commit burglary might unexpectedly encounter the homeowner and subsequently commit an assault. Likewise, individuals might find additional crime opportunities while committing white-collar crimes. Someone who hacks into computer servers to disrupt an online business, for instance, also might find customers' personal and credit card information. The hacker might then commit identify theft and use the customers' information to open new credit cards or to make fraudulent purchases. The offender might then decide to sell the stolen credit card numbers to other cyber-criminals through illegal fencing websites. Because one opportunity often produces another, preventing one form of white-collar crime might also prevent future criminal offenses.

6. *Some Products Offer More Tempting Crime Opportunities*

Most white-collar crimes involve offenders using some form of deception to produce financial gain. Because the "product" desired by white-collar criminals is typically monetary in nature, the payoffs associated with some targets provide more tempting opportunities than others. Physicians who seek to increase their profits might be more tempted to bill Medicaid illegally than to bill individual patients for work not performed. Research has found the payoffs and risks associated with defrauding the Medicaid system to be exceptionally high and low, respectively (Jesilow, Pontell, and Geis 1993; Sparrow 2000). Alternatively, individual patients might be more likely to notice and refuse payment for services not rendered, particularly if they are paying out of pocket.

7. *Social and Technological Changes Produce New Crime Opportunities*

A substantial increase in white-collar crime occurred after World War II (Shover and Hochstetler 2006). Much of this increase has been attributed to new crime opportunities that developed as a result of both social changes (the growth of the insurance industry, increases in credit-based relationships and transactions, and increasing globalization) and technological changes (mass availability and use of personal computers, development of the Internet, and digitization of records). The major stock market crash of 1987, also known as Black Monday, has been blamed on changes in social exchanges that led to market overvaluation and technological innovations, including the computerized selling of stocks (Waldrop 1987; Bookstaber 2007). Social and technological changes commonly precede dramatic increases in crime levels or the emergence of new crime types (Felson and Clarke 1998).

8. *Crime Can Be Prevented by Reducing Opportunities*

If opportunities are a root cause of crime, then blocking opportunities should stop crime. But it is not always possible to eliminate crime opportunities, particularly if doing so hinders legitimate activities. We can stop physicians from performing unnecessary tests by restricting their access to patients or laboratories, but this would also prevent them from performing their legitimate duties. If an opportunity cannot be eliminated, it is often possible to make the opportunity less attractive. For years, people could claim tax deductions by simply listing numbers of dependent children on tax returns, but then the Tax Reform Act of 1986 and subsequent amendments to it required parents to list the Social Security numbers of dependent children. By increasing the risk that false claims would be detected, approximately 7.5 million fewer dependents were claimed in 1987 than 1986, which increased collections of federal government tax revenue by approximately $2.8 billion in a single year (House of Representatives Subcommittee on Social Security 2001).

9. *Reducing Opportunities Usually Does Not Displace Crime*

Displacement is not an inevitable outcome of prevention efforts. Opportunity theorists argue that offenders' commitment to crime is often exaggerated. Combating corporate crime by making it more difficult to deceive auditors is more likely to encourage non-criminal practices than it is to cause corporate executives to seek similar crime opportunities through employment in other industries (geographic displacement). Preventing employee theft of high-end products is not likely to cause a significant increase in the theft of far less desirable items (target displacement), nor is preventing cash-register theft likely to cause equal cash losses from highly secure safes (tactical displacement). Reducing opportunities for insider trading is not likely to encourage money laundering (crime type displacement). Displacement is not impossible in these circumstances—it can and does occur—but it is less likely than often assumed, because alternative crime opportunities are not always equally attractive. To assume that all offenders are driven to commit crime regardless of perceived costs ignores the causal role of tempting opportunities (see Benson and Simpson 2009).

10. *Focused Opportunity Reduction Can Produce Wider Declines in Crime*

The benefits of prevention efforts often extend beyond the crime opportunities initially targeted. This "diffusion of benefits" (Clarke and Weisburd 1994) occurs for at least two reasons. First, potential offenders might be unaware of the precise scope of a new prevention measure and thus overestimate the risk involved or the effort needed to continue their criminal behaviors. Use of the FBI's antipiracy warning seal on films might lead some to believe that the FBI has initiated a new detection system for all pirated copyrighted works and thereby decrease instances of both pirated film and music. Second, as previously described, we can block opportunities for additional crimes that unfold during the commission of criminal events. By reducing opportunities for falsification of financial information, for example, we might prevent insider trading based on falsely inflated earnings reports as well as obstruction-of-justice incidents during ensuing criminal investigations.

The ten principles of opportunity and crime frequently are used to illustrate the importance and causal role of opportunity in street crimes. This essay is the first attempt to apply each principle specifically to white-collar offenses. The examples above support Felson and Clarke's (1998) assertion that opportunity is a critical element in all crimes, and these examples suggest that opportunity frameworks might prove useful to those who study white-collar crime patterns and events.

As previously mentioned, the ten principles of opportunity and crime stem from the underlying assumptions of specific opportunity-focused theories. These theories explain how everyday activities create crime opportunities. Before discussing the potential application of specific opportunity theories to white-collar crime, it is useful to consider the ways in which crime opportunity theories differ from traditional criminological theories. These differences matter, especially to those concerned with preventing white-collar crime.

B. Alternative Assumptions of Crime Opportunity Theories

Several assumptions of crime opportunity theories distinguish them from traditional criminological theories. The most significant assumptions can be grouped into four general categories.

1. *Crime Is an Event Requiring the Study of Multiple Elements*

The criminal event perspective best summarizes the idea that crime is an event (Sacco and Kennedy 2002). A crime involves more than criminal action. To understand crime, we must consider multiple elements of the criminal event: offenders, victims, methods used to commit offenses, and social contexts in which crimes take place. Since the characteristics of these elements are likely to vary across offenses, it is important to examine very specific forms of crimes. A general focus on crime, or even on white-collar crime, will do little to promote productive inquiries into why specific criminal events occur.

To understand and prevent phishing e-mail scams designed to steal personal identification from computers, for instance, we would need to learn the following:

- Who commits phishing e-mail scams,
- Why certain people are more likely to become phishing victims than others,
- How offenders commit phishing e-mail scams, including the steps taken in preparation to commit these crimes, and
- Where, when, and under what conditions phishing e-mail scams are most likely to take place.

A focus limited to the characteristics of offenders or victims of these scams will produce an incomplete understanding of phishing crime opportunities and might thereby reduce the effectiveness of phishing prevention efforts. Designing effective responses requires the careful consideration of all criminal event elements. Crime opportunity theories suggest that highly tailored responses to specific opportunities are more likely to produce substantial decreases in crime than general prevention efforts aimed at all criminal offending.

2. *Proximal Factors Are More Influential in Criminal Events than Distal Factors*

Previous theorists have drawn distinctions between "criminality" and "crime" (Gottfredson and Hirschi 1990; Clarke 1997). Criminality is a behavioral disposition that manifests itself as a propensity or willingness to engage in criminal behavior, whereas crime, as the criminal event perspective argues, is an event that results from the intersection of multiple factors that create opportunities for specific types of behaviors. Crime opportunity theories focus on the latter; they are less concerned with the distal factors that produce criminal motivation (e.g., upbringing, neurological deficits) and are more concerned with immediate or proximal situational factors that provide the incentives or structures necessary for crime events to occur.

The opportunity perspective assumes that motivated offenders are always likely to be present (or will become present at some future point in time), and so the most effective responses to crime will involve using situational techniques to block existing crime opportunities. The opportunity approach absolves researchers from attempting to predict who will and who will not commit white-collar crime. Opportunity theorists would not try to identify those most likely to engage in predatory lending practices. Instead, they would focus on when, where, and how offenders target vulnerable people and then devise strategies to change the conditions that facilitate predatory lending activities.

3. Not All Opportunities Are Equal

As described within the ten principles of opportunity and crime, opportunity is considered a root cause of all crime. The opportunity perspective recognizes that criminal motivation alone does not result in crime; instead, motivation must be coupled with opportunity in order for crime to occur. When crime opportunities are encountered, people make deliberate choices either to abstain from or to engage in criminal behavior. This assumption is compatible with crime-as-choice theory (Shover and Hochstetler 2006), which posits that crime is the outcome of purposeful and calculated action. Given the same opportunities, some people will choose to offend and some will not (Shover, Hochstetler, and Alalehto 2013). While the opportunity perspective is not generally concerned with differences among offending and nonoffending groups, it draws attention to the characteristics of specific crime opportunities that generate more offending than others.

Crime opportunities are not ubiquitous (multiple elements must be in place for crime to occur), constant (crime is concentrated in time and space), or equal (some are more attractive than others). Different situational contexts produce different opportunities. The specific characteristics of crime opportunities define their opportunity structures. Crime opportunity structure characteristics, or choice-structuring properties, directly influence offender decision making (Cornish and Clarke 1987). In other words, the choice-structuring properties of various crime opportunity structures make some crimes more accessible and attractive to potential offenders than others. The attractiveness of a crime opportunity matters just as much as its availability. All U.S. citizens have the opportunity to refrain from paying taxes, but most pay anyway. A sizable number of people, however, are presumed to engage in some form of tax fraud to reduce their tax burden (Weisburd et al. 1991). For most people, underpayment of taxes provides a more attractive crime opportunity structure than does complete tax evasion.

4. *The Main Goal Is Prevention*

Theorists who study crime events assert that the main goal of the crime opportunity perspective is prevention. Interventions subsequent to the criminal offense, including incarceration and rehabilitation, are seen as less efficient and effective than efforts aimed at blocking crime opportunities. Prevention involves manipulating crime opportunity structures in ways that render them less attractive to offenders.

Crime opportunity theories can be used to develop targeted interventions for crime problems that meet the CHEERS criteria: (1) members of our communities are affected; (2) these individuals or organizations experience harm; (3) there is an expectation for police or other authorities to act; (4) the events can be described; (5) the events are recurring; and (6) the recurring events share similarities (Clarke and Eck 2003). White-collar crimes meet these criteria. The harms suffered by individuals, and by society in general, as a result of white-collar crime have been well documented (Cullen et al. 2006). Opinion surveys reveal that the public sees many forms of white-collar crime as serious events and therefore as worthy of police or government response (Cullen, Hartman, and Jonson 2009). Media reports and government data show recurring patterns of similar white-collar crime events (Rosoff, Pontell, and Tillman 2004).

This discussion demonstrates that (1) opportunities play an important role in all types of crimes, including white-collar crimes; (2) characteristics of white-collar crimes are congruent with the fundamental assumptions of opportunity theories; and (3) white-collar crimes meet criteria that suggest an opportunity-focused prevention approach can be used to reduce offending. Specific opportunity-focused theories are used to analyze crime opportunity structures. Together, these theories form the basis of the crime science perspective. The section that follows briefly describes how crime science theories are used to study crime problems and develop prevention strategies.

II. CRIME SCIENCE AND PREVENTION

Crime science, also known as environmental criminology, promotes the study of crime opportunity structures with the primary goal of finding ways to prevent crime. Crime science theories are grounded in the rational choice perspective (Cornish and Clarke 1986). A similar perspective, crime-as-choice theory, is often discussed in relation to white-collar crime. The central tenets of the rational choice perspective overlap with crime-as-choice theory, but the latter theory does not assume rationality in criminal choices (reasons for the rejection of the rationality assumption are discussed in Shover and Grabosky [2010]). Both perspectives, however, assert that offenders are volitional actors who choose a course of action based on perceptions of their circumstances and environments.

Three theories help form the basis of the crime science perspective: routine activity theory, crime pattern theory, and situational crime prevention. These theories explain how opportunities are created, how offenders find opportunities, and why offenders choose one crime opportunity over another. In doing so, they help us identify features of opportunity structures that can be manipulated to prevent crime.

A. Routine Activity Theory: How Opportunities Are Created

Crime opportunities are created when offenders are able to interact, unabated, with targets. Three elements create the necessary conditions for crime: a motivated offender, an attractive target, and a place where the offender can gain access to the target (Cohen and Felson 1979; Eck 1994). Crime will occur when all three elements converge at the same time, unless an effective controller is present. Controllers serve to disrupt crime opportunities by mitigating the role of each element. Each element has its own type of controller: handlers restrain offenders (Felson 1986), guardians protect targets (Cohen and Felson 1979), and place managers regulate places (Eck 1994). The presence of just one effective controller is sufficient to prevent crime, even if all three necessary elements are drawn together.

Routine activity theory can be used to investigate the opportunity structure of any particular crime. Once each "player" is identified, the structure can be assessed to find ways to disrupt the crime event. We can examine the three elements that provide the conditions necessary for crime and ask whether one of them can be removed from the situation. If removing the offender, target, or shared place is impossible or impractical, then we turn our attention to the controllers. If controllers are present, we can ask whether something can be done to increase their effectiveness. If controllers are not present, we can consider whether handlers, guardians, or place managers can be added to disrupt the crime opportunity. Figure 19.1 depicts the crime triangle commonly used to represent routine activity theory and shows the relationship between the elements and controllers. Figure 19.1 also references the systematic approach to considering crime prevention solutions promoted by this framework.

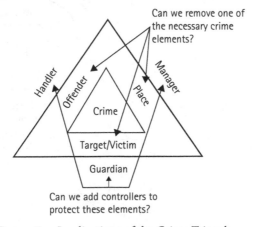

FIGURE 19.1 Crime-Prevention Implications of the Crime Triangle

B. Crime Pattern Theory: How Offenders
Find Opportunities

Crime pattern theory, also known as offender search theory, draws upon the principles of routine activity theory. This theory states that offenders encounter (or stumble across) crime opportunities as they conduct their everyday activities (Brantingham and Brantingham 1991, 1993). Many, if not all, of these everyday activities are legitimate rather than crime-related. Offenders encounter crime opportunities as they travel the *paths* that take them to and from their various activity nodes. *Nodes* represent places where the offender engages in both public and private activities, such as home, food establishments, work, school, and entertainment locations. Connected nodes and paths form crime opportunity structures. The nodes and paths frequented by offenders represent offenders' *action spaces*. Offenders are more likely to become aware of crime opportunities that fall on or near their action spaces. The primary assertion of the theory is this: If attractive targets fall within the action spaces of motivated offenders, then crime is likely to occur in the absence of intervention.

To disrupt crime opportunities, crime pattern theory suggests restricting offender access to crime-generating paths and nodes. Figure 19.2 depicts nodes within a hypothetical action/awareness space of an automotive repair shop owner. In the course of everyday business activities, the owner interacts with potential crime targets in a variety of places, including the repair shop, the shop's business insurance agency, parts suppliers, manufacturers or the parent corporation, the state's Department of Motor Vehicles office, and vehicle insurance companies. Each of these nodes provides different potential crime opportunities. Restricting access to these nodes can prevent crime.

FIGURE 19.2 Nodes and Crime Opportunities within an Awareness/Action Space

However, limiting access is not always a feasible or desirable option since it can also disrupt legitimate business activities. Under such conditions, it may be more useful to make available crime opportunities appear less attractive.

C. Situational Crime Prevention: How Offenders Perceive Opportunities

When offenders encounter potential targets during their everyday routine activities, they choose whether or not to offend based on five dimensions (or characteristics) of crime opportunities:

1. The *effort* needed to complete the offense,
2. The *risk* of being detected while committing the crime,
3. The *rewards* to be gained from committing the crime,
4. Situational conditions that *provoke* criminal action, and
5. Their ability to *excuse* or rationalize their behavior (Cornish and Clarke 2003).

All else being equal, offenders will be attracted to crime opportunities that require little effort, offer low risks and high rewards, encourage criminal behavior, and allow them to easily rationalize their behaviors.

Situational crime prevention offers twenty-five specific techniques for preventing crime—five for each dimension of opportunity. Table 19.1 lists these techniques and gives examples of how they have been used in practice. Use of situational prevention techniques alters offenders' perceptions of specific crime opportunities. In particular, these techniques make crime opportunities less attractive. Crime can be prevented if offenders perceive that the effort and risks are too high and the rewards are too low. Further, crime is less likely if offenders do not feel provoked or if they find it difficult to excuse their behavior.

Understanding crime opportunity structures requires well-organized inquiry into how opportunities are created, how they are discovered, and why some tempt criminals more than others. Crime science theories help guide such systematic inquiries. They draw attention to aspects of opportunities that enable crime and suggest specific ways to disrupt crime events. Crime science theories are used regularly to study and prevent common street crimes. They have also been applied in response to terrorism (Clarke and Newman 2006), crowd violence (Madensen and Eck 2008), illegal animal poaching (Lemieux and Clarke 2009; Pires and Clarke 2012), child sexual abuse (Wortley and Smallbone 2006a), and prison violence (Wortley 2002). Crime science also can be used to study and prevent white-collar crime, although some argue that features specific to white-collar crime opportunity structures might require the modification of crime science concepts and prevention strategies (Benson and Madensen 2007; Benson, Madensen, and Eck 2009).

Table 19.1 Techniques of Situational Prevention

Increase the Effort	Increase the Risks	Reduce the Rewards	Reduce Provocations	Remove Excuses
1. Target harden • Steering column locks and immobilizers • Anti-robbery screens • Tamper-proof packaging	**6. Extend guardianship** • Take routine precautions: go out in group at night, leave signs of occupancy, carry phone • "Cocoon" neighborhood watch	**11. Conceal targets** • Off-street parking • Gender-neutral phone directories • Unmarked bullion trucks	**16. Reduce frustrations and stress** • Efficient queues and polite service • Expanded seating • Soothing music/muted lights	**21. Set rules** • Rental agreements • Harassment codes • Hotel registration
2. Control access to facilities • Entry phones • Electronic card access • Baggage screening	**7. Assist natural surveillance** • Improved street lighting • Defensible space design • Support whistleblowers	**12. Remove targets** • Removable car radio • Women's refuges • Pre-paid cards for pay phones	**17. Avoid disputes** • Separate enclosures for rival soccer fans • Reduce crowding in pubs • Fixed cab fares	**22. Post instructions** • "No Parking" • "Private Property" • "Extinguish camp fires"
3. Screen exits • Ticket needed for exit • Export documents • Electronic merchandise tags	**8. Reduce anonymity** • Taxi driver IDs • "How's my driving?" decals • School uniforms	**13. Identify property** • Property marking • Vehicle licensing and parts marking • Cattle branding	**18. Reduce emotional arousal** • Controls on violent pornography • Enforce good behavior on soccer field • Prohibit racial slurs	**23. Alert conscience** • Roadside speed display boards • Signature for customs declarations • "Shoplifting is stealing"
4. Deflect offenders • Street closures • Separate bathrooms for women • Disperse pubs	**9. Utilize place managers** • CCTV for double-deck buses • Two clerks for convenience stores • Reward vigilance	**14. Disrupt markets** • Monitor pawn shops • Controls on classified ads • License street vendors	**19. Neutralize peer pressure** • "Idiots drink and drive" • "It's OK to say NO" • Disperse troublemakers at school	**24. Assist compliance** • Easy library checkout • Public lavatories • Litter bins
5. Control tools/weapons • "Smart" guns • Disable stolen cell phones • Restrict spray paint sales to juveniles	**10. Strengthen formal surveillance** • Red light cameras • Burglar alarms • Security guards	**15. Deny benefits** • Ink merchandise tags • Graffiti cleaning • Speed humps	**20. Discourage imitation** • Rapid repair of vandalism • V-chips in TVs • Censor details of modus operandi	**25. Control drugs and alcohol** • Breathalyzers in pubs • Server intervention • Alcohol-free events

Source: Center for Problem-Oriented Policing (2014).

III. Applying Crime Science
to White-Collar Crime

Benson and Simpson (2009) noted that white-collar crime opportunity structures differ from those of street crimes. There are at least four notable differences (see Benson and Madensen [2007] for an earlier discussion of white-collar differences). First, there are physical differences between white-collar and street crime opportunity structures. White-collar offenders sometimes find targets in places and along paths that do not exist in physical spaces. Second, white-collar offenders use different tactics, or modi operandi, to carry out their offenses. Unlike many street crime offenders, white-collar offenders use specialized access to victims to hide their intentions and criminal actions. Third, the nature of white-collar offenses differs from street offenses. The complexity, duration, and rewards associated with white-collar crimes produce different crime opportunity structures than those typically encountered by street offenders. Fourth, average white-collar criminals are different from average street criminals. These differences affect offenders' perceptions of and reactions to crime opportunity structures. The following subsections explore whether these seemingly unique white-collar crime characteristics affect applications of opportunity-based theories.

A. The Concept of Place

All criminal behavior occurs within a situational context. For traditional street crimes, this context usually is defined by the characteristics of a physical space: open-air drug dealing along a major thoroughfare, burglary of a single-family home in a residential neighborhood, robbery at a downtown convenience store, and assault at a neighborhood bar, for example. The social and physical characteristics of these places help form the crime opportunity structure. Crime scientists study place characteristics with the goal of eliminating or modifying features of the opportunity structure that make crime attractive in these locations. Effective crime-reduction strategies often require changes in place-management activities within well-defined crime locations. These locations, called proprietary places, usually are defined by a single address (Madensen and Eck 2012). Proprietary places represent a central concept in crime science theories.

The concept of *place* becomes muddled when dealing with white-collar crimes. White-collar offenders often are physically distant or separate from their victims at the time of the offense (Benson and Madensen 2007). White-collar crimes frequently occur during transactions that do not take place in a discrete physical space. Insider trading, for example, can occur over the telephone, while credit card fraud can take place over the Internet, and foreign lottery scams typically are conducted through e-mail. For these crime types, there is no single proprietary place that fully captures the situational context of any crime's opportunity structure.

If the concept of place is expanded to include *networks*, crime science theories can be applied to white-collar crimes, even in the absence of a well-defined physical location (Eck and Clarke 2003). Crime opportunities are dependent upon offenders' abilities to interact with targets in specific places (routine activity theory), and offenders become aware of crime opportunities as they move through familiar places (crime pattern theory). Networks provide the specific and familiar places that facilitate the necessary offender–victim interactions for many white-collar offenses.

Using the previous crime examples, networks include telephone communication services, Internet websites, and postal services. It is possible to disrupt crime opportunities involving networks, such as by shutting down those designed only to promote criminal behaviors. Peer-to-peer file-sharing service websites that allow the illegal distribution of music and videos, for instance, have been removed through court orders (Langenderfer and Lloyd 2001). It is impractical to shut down networks that serve legitimate functions, however, such as an insurance claims system, in order to prevent illegal activities. Yet this type of network can be modified to make crime opportunities less attractive. Claim submission standards and frequent random audits are examples of methods for increasing offenders' perceptions of the effort and risk associated with fraudulent insurance billing (Benson, Madensen, and Eck 2009).

B. Modus Operandi

The methods used by white-collar offenders appear to differ from the modi operandi of street offenders in at least two ways: (1) they use their occupational positions to gain access to victims and (2) they use deception to hide their offenses and resulting harms. Legitimate occupational positions provide many white-collar offenders with specialized access to targets and victims. They use this access and their employment privileges to carry out their offenses (Wheeler and Rothman 1981). A used car salesman who engages in odometer fraud naturally gains access to potential victims who willingly visit his business to purchase a motor vehicle, for example, while physicians motivated to commit healthcare fraud have legitimate access to patients, their records, and government reimbursement systems. Sometimes, offenders' specialized access to victims conflates the controller and offender roles outlined by routine activity theory. Consider the business of cybersecurity. The assigned role of cybersecurity company employees is that of guardian; they protect the private data of their clients. Yet, these guardians also act as offenders when they sell these data to unauthorized third parties.

Specialized access to victims and role conflation are not wholly unique to white-collar crime (see Eck and Madensen 2015), as many crimes committed against children involve similar opportunity structures. Parents and trusted others have specialized access to children. When trusted adults act to harm children, their guardianship roles are conflated with offending roles. Yet, we know that situational prevention measures can reduce opportunities for child sexual abuse by guardians (Wortley and Smallbone 2006b). Specialized victim access and role conflation common to many white-collar crimes complicate the dynamics of these events, but they do not negate the potential for effective opportunity-based prevention efforts.

White-collar offenders also use deception or concealment to hide their offenses and resulting effects from authorities. Cybersecurity company employees who access client information to sell it to others will attempt to do so without alerting authorities or supervisors to their criminal objectives. The offenders have legitimate access to the data, and they will structure their actions to appear as though they are simply performing their assigned security duties.

Deception and concealment behaviors are also common methods of operation among street criminals. Pickpockets use a variety of techniques to conceal their criminal actions. They may appear to be performing legitimate activities in a crowd (e.g., shopping, gambling, parade watching) as they commit their offense. Their goal is not to hide from others. Although in plain sight, they only work to conceal their criminal intentions and acts. Their methods leave some victims wondering whether they have been victimized or if they were simply careless with their belongings. Since deceit and concealment are important elements of pickpocketing opportunity structures (Maurer 2003), strategies to increase detection of these activities and block opportunities have proven highly effective (La Vigne 1997). White-collar crime opportunity structures involving deception and concealment also can be manipulated to prevent crime and overcome challenges commonly associated with using traditional policing approaches (see Friedrichs [2010] for a discussion on policing and regulating white-collar crime).

C. Nature of Offenses

The prevalence and precise nature of many white-collar crimes are unknown. Scholars recognize the limits of existing data for studying white-collar crimes and criminals; for example, official crime data provide a limited picture of white-collar criminal activity (Shover, Hochstetler, and Alalehto 2013). Much of what we know about white-collar crimes has been gathered from incomplete official data or detailed case studies of a few high-profile incidents. Still, available data suggest that white-collar crimes differ in many ways from traditional street crimes. In general, we know that white-collar crimes tend to be more complex, organized, profitable, and longer-lasting than street crimes (Weisburd et al. 1991).

While the profitability of white-collar crimes might make them highly attractive and more difficult to deter, their increased complexity, duration, and organization renders them highly suitable for opportunity-focused prevention activities. All crimes involve processes composed of multiple stages (or steps) that unfold over time. At each step, offenders make decisions and conduct preparations that allow them to commit the crime (see Cornish 1994). These steps occur before, during, and after a criminal event. Each step in the crime-commission sequence represents a possible intervention point. Therefore, complex white-collar crimes carried out over an extended period of time provide more intervention opportunities than hastily committed crimes. Highly organized crimes, such as many of those leading to the savings and loan crisis of the 1980s, involve predictable step sequencing. Anticipated sequencing can help focus intervention efforts.

Case studies of the savings and loan crisis revealed highly complex fraud schemes that lasted for years. There were countless steps involved in committing the various fraudulent activities that took place while establishing financial institutions (thrifts), attracting capital, and, eventually, attempting to avoid insolvency (Calavita and Pontell 1990). Many of the steps taken by thrift operators to commit criminal activities were facilitated by regulatory practices. Regulators increased the attractiveness of crime opportunity structures by the following:

- *Decreasing effort*—regulatory changes allowed thrifts to be started using noncash assets;
- *Decreasing risk*—lax reporting procedures reduced oversight and allowed frauds to continue unabated for extended periods of time;
- *Increasing rewards*—insurance protection was increased from $40,000 to $100,000, making fraud practices appear safer and more profitable;
- *Increasing provocations*—the most at-risk thrifts were forced to pay the highest interest rates, which encouraged unlawful risk-taking; and
- *Removing excuses*—regulatory agencies adopted the dual role of promotion and regulation, which sent mixed messages to thrift operators about acceptable banking practices.

Ineffective regulatory action at each stage of the crime-commission process promoted perceptions that unlawful behaviors were easy, safe, rewarding, necessary, and justified. In response to the crisis, the government reinstituted mechanisms for detecting and preventing criminal activity. These mechanisms involved introducing new controllers, including the Office of Thrift Supervision and the Federal Housing Finance Board, which acted to disrupt crime opportunities at various stages of crime-commission processes and to make criminal behaviors less attractive to banking operators.

D. "Street" Versus "Suite" Offenders

The demographics of white-collar offenders vary by offense. Check kiters, for example, are often different from those who engage in corporate price fixing. But studies generally show that even heterogeneous groups of white-collar offenders differ in many ways from street crime offenders. As a group, white-collar criminals tend to be older and more educated, socially integrated, and affluent than traditional street criminals (Weisburd et al. 1991; Benson and Kerley 2001).

Differences between street crime and white-collar crime offenders can affect their respective perceptions of crime opportunity structures. On one hand, these differences could make it easier to deter white-collar offenders: stronger educational backgrounds facilitate rational decision making, and white-collar criminals are less likely to suffer from problems that undermine rational thinking, like alcohol or drug abuse (Benson and Moore 1992). Greater rationality on the part of white-collar offenders might allow them to detect more quickly changes in crime opportunity structures. Slight increases in effort or risk can have large effects on white-collar offender decision making (Benson and Madensen 2007). Thus, prevention efforts might have a greater deterrent effect on white-collar criminals. This assumption has been at least partially supported by deterrence-focused studies (see Pratt et al. 2006).

Alternatively, white-collar offenders also display traits of entitlement and arrogance. These traits encourage unethical behaviors and the belief that interference or questioning by authorities is illegitimate (Shover, Hochstetler, and Alalehto 2013). Organizational cultures and peers can reinforce this perspective if language commonly used to discuss criminal activities minimizes associated harmful effects and helps offenders escape shame and justify their actions (Geis and Salinger 1998). Traits of entitlement and arrogance, coupled with the ability to offer excuses, might reduce the effectiveness of crime-prevention efforts.

Regardless of whether it is more or less difficult to deter white-collar offenders than street crime offenders, choices are products of offenders' assessments of their immediate situations. Evaluations show that efforts to reduce the attractiveness of situational opportunity structures have decreased criminal offending across diverse crime types (Clarke 1997; Wortley and Mazerolle 2008), including white-collar crimes. For crime to occur, offenders must have access to crime opportunities—regardless of their demographic, background, and personality characteristics. And, according to the crime science perspective, even the most motivated offenders can be blocked or deterred if changes to crime opportunity structures are substantial (Benson and Madensen 2007).

IV. Conclusion: Refocusing White-Collar Crime Research

Over the past several years, there has been greater recognition of the importance of opportunity as it relates to white-collar crime. Researchers have proposed situational crime-prevention tactics to address a wide variety of crimes, including employee computer crime (Willison and Siponen 2009) and cyberstalking (Reyns 2010). Empirical research has shown that specific routine activities can increase the likelihood of white-collar victimization; for example, particular consumer behaviors have been linked to increased risks of fraud victimization (Holtfreter, Reisig, and Pratt 2008). While many white-collar researchers have acknowledged the role of opportunity in white-collar crime (see Benson and Simpson 2009), the crime science perspective has not yet been adopted as the principal theoretical framework for most white-collar crime research.

The applications in this chapter suggest that crime science theories hold great promise for exploring and preventing white-collar crimes. With little or no modification, the principles and underlying assumptions of these theories can explain white-collar crime patterns and events. It is argued here that a reframing of white-collar crime investigations within the crime science paradigm offers at least three significant benefits. First, the crime-specific approach advocated by the crime science perspective would shift our focus away from longstanding, unresolved debates concerning appropriate crime classifications and definitions of white-collar crime. Second, crime science theories will provide a highly systematic and structured approach to white-collar crime research and prevention. Third, recent developments within the crime science perspective suggest new directions for future white-collar crime research.

A. Crime-Specific Approach

Two definitional approaches to white-collar crime have been the focus of a great deal of scholarly discourse. *Offender-based* definitions emphasize the occupational and social characteristics of an offender. To be labeled as a white-collar criminal using this approach, the people involved in such crimes must possess a prestigious or powerful occupational position and specific attributes, including high social status and respectability (Sutherland 1949). *Offense-based* definitions, in contrast, emphasize the characteristics of offenses rather than offenders. Those who prefer offense-based definitions apply the white-collar crime label to property crimes committed through the use of deception or concealment rather than by physical means (Edelhertz 1970).

Crime science theories suggest that the key aspects of both offender- and offense-based definitions are important. Offenders' social and occupational positions can offer access to specific types of crime opportunities. Further, the ways in which offenses are carried out have important implications for prevention measures. Both offender and offense characteristics are relevant from the crime science perspective. To ignore either would limit our understanding of how and why particular crime opportunities are exploited. It would also hinder attempts to devise effective crime-reduction strategies.

The crime-specific approach advocated by the crime science perspective requires researchers to abandon vague and heterogeneous crime categorizations. Crime scientists might study specific forms of insider trading or false advertising, but they would not mask differences between or draw sweeping conclusions about groups of crimes labeled as white-collar crimes. Since every crime has a distinctive opportunity structure that is not fully replicated by other crime types, a focus on highly specific forms of crime makes it easier to identify potentially effective interventions. Adopting the crime science perspective and its crime-specific approach would allow us to move beyond unresolved definitional debates by simultaneously acknowledging the influence of both offender and offense characteristics on particular crimes.

B. Structured Research and Prevention Focus

Theories are important. They guide research activities by suggesting what is, and what is not, worthy of attention and help us interpret specific findings. They can also suggest potential interventions. As previously discussed, crime science theories focus researchers' attention on how specific crime opportunities are created, how offenders find these opportunities, and why offenders choose one type of opportunity over another. Use of crime science theories could help advance white-collar crime research by offering a new approach to inquiry and response.

Unlike other theoretical perspectives, crime science theories promote a highly structured and systematic approach to the study of crime opportunity structures. Routine activity theory focuses attention on the characteristics of the three necessary crime elements and the presence or absence of associated controllers. Crime pattern theory requires researchers to map action spaces of offenders to identify sources of crime-generating paths and nodes. Situational crime prevention forces researchers to consider features of the situational context that make crime attractive based on five dimensions of opportunity: effort, risk, reward, provocation, and excuses. More comprehensive understanding of specific crime opportunity structures can be assembled using information gathered as a result of these focused inquires.

Crime science theories likewise offer a highly structured and systematic approach to crime prevention. They suggest specific ways to eliminate or reduce crime by systematically manipulating opportunity structures. Using routine activity theory, we can think about the removal of crime elements or the introduction of controllers into criminogenic environments. Using crime pattern theory, we can think about ways to eliminate or restrict access to paths and nodes that permit access to vulnerable targets. Situational crime prevention structures our thinking about crime-prevention responses by offering twenty-five techniques that reduce the attractiveness of existing crime opportunities. Researchers can use this framework to assess the influence of existing interventions. Categorizing interventions within the framework draws attention to dimensions of the opportunity structure that may be neglected by current strategies; for example, existing interventions may only focus on increasing risk while neglecting the other four dimensions of opportunity. This analysis brings attention to additional techniques that could be used to disrupt a specific crime opportunity.

Using the systematic approach advocated by the crime science perspective to uncover specific white-collar crime opportunity structures should produce two secondary benefits. First, it should ease cross-study comparisons of similar crimes. Detailed analyses of opportunity structures might reveal how different contexts influence the ways in which crimes are committed. Second, framing white-collar crime within the crime science perspective could facilitate dialogue between researchers and regulators because its concepts and language are simple and straightforward. The absence of technical and overly academic jargon within crime science theories provides a common simplified language for all who are interested in crime prevention.

C. New Directions

Extensions to crime science concepts also offer new directions for future white-collar crime research. There have been several advancements in crime science since the late 1970s and early 1980s. This chapter concludes with brief descriptions of four developments that may prove particularly useful for future white-collar crime research.

First, research has identified four different types of places involved in crime or crime-related activities (Felson 2003; Hammer 2011; Madensen and Eck 2013):

1. *Crime sites*—a location (e.g., address, building, or land parcel) at which crime repeatedly occurs;
2. *Convergent settings*—a place where potential offenders routinely meet with other potential offenders;
3. *Comfort spaces*—a place offenders use to hide or prepare for future offenses; and
4. *Corrupt spots*—a place that promotes crime at other places, such as a metal recycling business that encourages offenders to steal metal from other places.

These crime places are not always bound by physical space. Table 19.2 provides examples of crime places in virtual environments.

Future white-collar crime research might consider how offenders use different places to commit specific crimes. For example, while it is helpful to know where price fixing occurs (crime sites), it also might be useful to know where offenders routinely meet to discuss the coordination of pricing (convergent settings), where schedules and records of such meetings are kept (comfort spaces), and whether particular industry practices of specific companies are generating pressure for others to engage in price-fixing conspiracies (corrupt spots). Researchers can explore how each of these places might be addressed as part of a comprehensive prevention strategy.

Second, the role of place managers in preventing crime at places has been better explicated. Owners and their representatives engage in four processes to organize the physical and social environment of places (Madensen 2007): organizing space,

Table 19.2 Virtual Crime-Facilitating Places

Place	Virtual Example
Crime Sites	A website the routinely corrupts computers that link to it
Convergent Settings	A website where offenders can exchange information
Comfort Spaces	A protected private website only particular offenders can access
Corrupt Spots	A server that controls illicit activity at other websites

regulating conduct, controlling access, and acquiring resources. Since place owners have legal authority over their spaces, they are ultimately responsible for all behaviors that occur in a given place. This includes both criminal and crime-prevention behaviors. A renewed focus on place management has brought greater attention to the impact of specific place-management decisions on crime opportunities.

As previously discussed, not all white-collar crimes occur within the context of physical space. Some situational contexts involve networks that allow offenders to gain access to victims. Future white-collar crime research might focus on how network owners and operators carry out the four processes involved in place management and how decisions made related to each process serve to suppress or facilitate criminal behavior. For example, researchers can examine how the management of health insurance reimbursement systems influences crime opportunities. The personnel structure of insurance organizations (space organization), procedures established for claims submittal (conduct regulation), methods used to verify submitters' identification (access control), and approaches used to generate revenue (acquire resources) all directly influence the attractiveness of submitting fraudulent insurance claims. Reducing the frequency of such claims will require changes in these place-management practices.

Third, the steps involved in the commission of specific crimes have been analyzed using crime script analysis (Cornish 1994). A crime script analysis details the stages and activities involved in the crime-commission process. It has been applied to study various forms of crime, including stalking violence, drug dealing, human trafficking, child sexual abuse, and the illegal sales of endangered species (Leclerc and Wortley 2013). With regard to white-collar crime, crime script analysis has been used to study patterns in check forgery (Lacoste and Tremblay 2003).

Use of crime script analysis in future white-collar research can provide more detailed descriptions of crime events. Further, the systematic documentation of all stages of the crime-commission sequence will draw attention to a wider range of possible intervention points (Cornish and Clarke 2002). For example, many who illegally download movies or music online must (1) search for online file-sharing websites, (2) identify a file-sharing website with their desired content, (3) learn to navigate the site and avoid malicious files or malware, (4) download and store the media on a local device, and (5) play the media. Each of these steps provides a potential opportunity for intervention. It may be possible to make searching for illegal file-sharing sites more difficult by partnering with major search engines, shutting down or disrupting sites with desirable content, publicizing the risks associated with acquiring malware commonly found on these sites, and so forth.

Fourth, the impact of crime-prevention efforts often extends beyond the crime events initially targeted. Crime scientists focus on two outcomes of offender responses to crime interventions: crime displacement (Cornish and Clark 1987) and diffusion of benefits (Clarke and Weisburd 1994). Crime displacement occurs when offenders adapt in ways that allow them to continue offending after an intervention is implemented. Diffusion of benefits occurs when offenders overestimate the scope of prevention efforts and reduce offending against targets not specifically addressed by the intervention. Using crime science principles, researchers have shown that is it possible to predict how offenders are likely to react to specific prevention efforts (Brantingham and Brantingham 2003).

Future white-collar crime research can examine displacement and diffusion of benefits associated with specific crime-prevention techniques. For example, it is possible that stricter control and oversight of casino operations can reduce money laundering in this industry. If opportunities are blocked in the casino industry, it is important to consider how offenders might adapt to these circumstances. Researchers should carefully examine the impact of this intervention on other industries to which money-laundering activities might be displaced. Researchers should also be aware that reductions in other types of offenses (e.g., tax fraud) might occur in the casino industry as an indirect result of increased oversight aimed at reducing money laundering. It is impossible to estimate the true impact of an intervention without measuring both displacement and diffusion of benefits.

The impact of crime science theories on the study and prevention of traditional street crimes has been remarkable. The perspective continues to grow through the introduction of new concepts and potential applications, including the four advancements described in this concluding section. While it remains to be seen whether more white-collar crime researchers will embrace this opportunity-focused approach, current evidence suggests that the crime science perspective holds great promise for new directions in white-collar crime research.

REFERENCES

Apel, Robert, and Raymond Paternoster. 2009. "Understanding 'Criminogenic' Corporate Culture: What White-Collar Crime Researchers Can Learn from Studies of the Adolescent Employment–Crime Relationship." In *The Criminology of White-Collar Crime*, pp. 15–33, edited by Sally S. Simpson and David Weisburd. New York: Springer.

Ashforth, Blake E., and Vikas Anand. 2003. "The Normalization of Corruption in Organizations." *Research in Organizational Behavior* 25: 1–52.

Benson, Michael L. 1985. "Denying the Guilty Mind: Accounting for Involvement in a White-Collar Crime." *Criminology* 23: 583–607.

Benson, Michael L., and Kent R. Kerley. 2001. "Life Course Theory and White-Collar Crime." In *Contemporary Issues in Crime and Criminal Justice: Essays in Honor of Gilbert Geis*, pp. 121–36, edited by Henry N. Pontell and David Schichor. Upper Saddle River, NJ: Prentice Hall.

Benson, Michael L., and Tamara D. Madensen. 2007. "Situational Crime Prevention and White-Collar Crime." In *International Handbook of White-Collar and Corporate Crime*, pp. 609–26, edited by Henry N. Pontell and Gilbert Geis. Dordrecht, The Netherlands: Kluwer Academic/Plenum.

Benson, Michael L., Tamara D. Madensen, and John E. Eck. 2009. "The Criminology of White-Collar Crime." In *The Criminology of White-Collar Crime*, pp. 175–93, edited by Sally S. Simpson and David Weisburd. New York: Springer.

Benson, Michael L., and Elizabeth Moore. 1992. "Are White-Collar and Common Offenders the Same? An Empirical and Theoretical Critique of a Recently Proposed General Theory of Crime." *Journal of Research in Crime and Delinquency* 29: 251–72.

Benson, Michael L., and Sally S. Simpson. 2009. *White-Collar Crime: An Opportunity Perspective*. New York: Routledge.

Bookstaber, Richard. 2007. *A Demon of Our Own Design: Markets, Hedge Funds, and the Perils of Financial Innovation*. Hoboken, NJ: Wiley.

Brantingham, Patricia L., and Paul J. Brantingham. 1993. "Nodes, Paths and Edges: Considerations on the Complexity of Crime and the Physical Environment." *Journal of Environmental Psychology* 13: 3–28.

Brantingham, Paul J., and Patricia L. Brantingham. 1991. "Notes on the Geometry of Crime." In *Environmental Criminology*, pp. 27–54, edited by Paul J. Brantingham and Patricia L. Brantingham. Prospect Heights, IL: Waveland Press.

Brantingham, Paul J., and Patricia L. Brantingham. 2003. "Anticipating the Displacement of Crime Using the Principles of Environmental Criminology." In *Theory for Practice in Situational Crime Prevention*, pp. 119–48, edited by Martha J. Smith and Derek B. Cornish. Vol. 16 of *Crime Prevention Studies*, edited by Ronald V. Clarke. Monsey, NY: Criminal Justice Press.

Calavita, Kitty, and Henry N. Pontell. 1990. "Heads I Win, Tails You Lose: Deregulation, Crime, and Crisis in the Savings and Loan Industry." *Crime and Delinquency* 36: 309–41.

Center for Problem-Oriented Policing. 2014. "Twenty-Five Techniques of Situational Prevention." Available at www.popcenter.org/25techniques

Clarke, Ronald V., ed. 1997. *Situational Crime Prevention: Successful Case Studies*, 2nd ed. Guilderland, NY: Harrow and Heston.

Clarke, Ronald V. 2010. "Crime Science." In *The SAGE Handbook of Criminological Theory*, pp. 271–83, edited by Eugene McLaughlin and Tim Newburn. Thousand Oaks, CA: Sage.

Clarke, Ronald V., and John E. Eck. 2003. *Crime Analysis for Problem Solvers: In 60 Small Steps*. Washington, D.C.: Center for Problem-Oriented Policing.

Clarke, Ronald V., and Graeme R. Newman. 2006. *Outsmarting the Terrorists*. Westport, CT: Praeger Security International.

Clarke, Ronald V., and David Weisburd. 1994. "Diffusion of Crime Control Benefits: Observations on the Reverse of Displacement." In *Crime Prevention Studies*, vol. 2, pp. 165–84, edited by Ronald V. Clarke. Monsey, NY: Criminal Justice Press.

Cohen, Lawrence E., and Marcus Felson. 1979. "Social Change and Crime Rate Trends: A Routine Activity Approach." *American Sociological Review* 44: 588–608.

Cornish, Derek B. 1994. "The Procedural Analysis of Offending and Its Relevance for Situational Prevention." In *Crime Prevention Studies*, vol. 3, pp. 151–96, edited by Ronald V. Clarke. Monsey, NY: Criminal Justice Press.

Cornish, Derek B., and Ronald V. Clarke. 1986. *The Reasoning Criminal: Rational Choice Perspectives on Offending*. New York: Springer-Verlag.

Cornish, Derek B., and Ronald V. Clarke. 1987. "Understanding Crime Displacement: An Application of Rational Choice Theory." *Criminology* 25: 933–47.

Cornish, Derek B., and Ronald V. Clarke. 2002. "Analyzing Organized Crimes." In *Rational Choice and Criminal Behavior: Recent Research and Future Challenges*, pp. 41–64, edited by Alex R. Piquero and Stephen G. Tibbetts. New York: Routledge.

Cornish, Derek B., and Ronald V. Clarke. 2003. "Opportunities, Precipitators, and Criminal Decisions: A Reply to Wortley's Critique of Situational Crime Prevention." In *Theory for Practice in Situational Crime Prevention*, pp. 41–96, edited by Martha J. Smith and Derek B. Cornish. Vol. 16 of *Crime Prevention Studies*, edited by Ronald V. Clarke. Monsey, NY: Criminal Justice Press.

Cressey, Donald R. 1953. *Other People's Money: A Study of the Social Psychology of Embezzlement*. New York: Free Press.

Cullen, Francis T., Gray Cavender, William J. Maakestad, and Michael L. Benson. 2006. *Corporate Crime under Attack: The Fight to Criminalize Business Violence*. Cincinnati, OH: Anderson Publishing.

Cullen, Francis T., Jennifer L. Hartman, and Cheryl Lero Jonson. 2009. "Bad Guys: Why the Public Supports Punishing White-Collar Offenders." *Crime, Law and Social Change* 51: 31–44.

Eck, John E. 1994. "Drug Markets and Drug Places: A Case-Control Study of the Spatial Structure of Illicit Drug Dealing." Ph.D. dissertation, University of Maryland, Department of Criminology and Criminal Justice.

Eck, John E., and Ronald V. Clarke. 2003. "Classifying Common Police Problems: A Routine Activity Approach." In *Theory for Practice in Situational Crime Prevention*, edited by Martha J. Smith and Derek B. Cornish. Vol. 16 of *Crime Prevention Studies*, pp. 7–39, edited by Ronald V. Clarke. Monsey, NY: Criminal Justice Press.

Eck, John E., and Tamara D. Madensen. 2015. "Meaningfully and Artfully Reinterpreting Crime for Useful Science: An Essay on the Value of Building with Simple Theory." In *The Criminal Act*, pp. 5–18, edited by Martin Andresen and Graham Farrell. New York: Palgrave Macmillan.

Edelhertz, Herbert. 1970. *Nature, Impact, and Prosecution of White-Collar Crime*. Washington, D.C.: National Institute of Justice.

Felson, Marcus. 1986. "Linking Criminal Choices, Routine Activities, Informal Control, and Criminal Outcomes." In *The Reasoning Criminal: Rational Choice Perspectives on Offending*, pp. 119–28, edited by Derek B. Cornish and Ronald V. Clarke. New York: Springer-Verlag.

Felson, Marcus. 2003. "The Process of Co-Offending." In *Theory for Practice in Situational Crime Prevention*, edited by Martha J. Smith and Derek B. Cornish. Vol. 16 of *Crime Prevention Studies*, pp. 149–68, edited by Ronald V. Clarke. Monsey, NY: Criminal Justice Press.

Felson, Marcus, and Ronald V. Clarke. 1998. *Opportunity Makes the Thief: Practical Theory for Crime Prevention*. London: Home Office, Policing and Reducing Crime Unit.

Friedrichs, David O. 2010. *Trusted Criminals: White Collar Crime in Contemporary Society*, 4th ed. Boston: Cengage Learning.

Geis, Gilbert, and Lawrence S. Salinger. 1998. "Antitrust and Organizational Deviance." *Research in the Sociology of Organizations* 15: 71–110.

Gibbs, Carole, Edmund F. McGarrell, and Mark Axelrod. 2010. "Transnational White-Collar Crime and Risk: Lessons Learned from the Global Trade in Electronic Waste." *Criminology and Public Policy* 9: 543–60.

Gottfredson, Michael R., and Travis Hirschi. 1990. *A General Theory of Crime*. Stanford: Stanford University Press.

Hammer, Matthew. 2011. *Crime Places of Comfort*. M.S. Demonstration Project Paper, University of Cincinnati, Division of Criminal Justice.

Holtfreter, Kristy, Michael D. Reisig, and Travis C. Pratt. 2008. "Low Self-Control, Routine Activities, and Fraud Victimization." *Criminology* 46: 189–220.

House of Representatives Subcommittee on Social Security. 2001. *Use and Misuse of Social Security Numbers*. Washington, D.C.: U.S. Government Printing Office.

Jesilow, Paul, Henry N. Pontell, and Gilbert Geis. 1993. *Prescription for Profit: How Doctors Defraud Medicaid*. Berkeley: University of California Press.

Kedia, Simi, and Thomas Philippon. 2007. "The Economics of Fraudulent Accounting." *Review of Financial Studies* 22: 2169–99.

Lacoste, Julie, and Pierre Tremblay. 2003. "Crime and Innovation: A Script Analysis of Patterns in Check Forgery." In *Theory for Practice in Situational Crime Prevention*, edited by Martha J. Smith and Derek B. Cornish. Vol. 16 of *Crime Prevention Studies*, pp. 169–96, edited by Ronald V. Clarke. Monsey, NY: Criminal Justice Press.

Langenderfer, Jeff, and Don Lloyd Cook. 2001. "Copyright Policies and Issues Raised by A&M Records v. Napster: 'The Shot Heard Round the World' or 'Not with a Bang but a Whimper?'" *Journal of Public Policy and Marketing* 20: 280–88.

LaVigne, Nancy G. 1997. *Visibility and Vigilance: Metro's Situational Approach to Preventing Subway Crime*. Washington, D.C.: National Institute of Justice.

Leclerc, Benoit, and Richard Wortley, eds. 2013. *Cognition and Crime: Offender Decision Making and Script Analyses*. New York: Routledge.

Lemieux, Andrew M., and Ronald V. Clarke. 2009. "The International Ban on Ivory Sales and Its Effects on Elephant Poaching in Africa." *British Journal of Criminology* 49: 451–71.

Madensen, Tamara D. 2007. "Bar Management and Crime: Toward a Dynamic Theory of Place Management and Crime Hotspots." Ph.D. dissertation, University of Cincinnati, Division of Criminal Justice.

Madensen, Tamara D., and John E. Eck. 2008. *Spectator Violence in Stadiums*. Washington, D.C.: Office of Community Oriented Policing Services, U.S. Department of Justice.

Madensen, Tamara D., and John E. Eck. 2013. "Crime Places and Place Management." In *The Oxford Handbook of Criminological Theory*, pp. 554–78, edited by Francis T. Cullen and Pamela Wilcox. New York: Oxford University Press.

Maurer, David W. 2003. *Whiz Mob: A Correlation of the Technical Argot of Pickpockets with Their Behavior Pattern*. Lanham, MD: Rowman and Littlefield Publishers, Inc.

Pires, Stephen, and Ronald V. Clarke. 2012. "Are Parrots CRAVED? An Analysis of Parrot Poaching in Mexico." *Journal of Research in Crime and Delinquency* 49: 122–46.

Pratt, Travis C., Francis T. Cullen, Kristie R. Blevins, Leah E. Daigle, and Tamara D. Madensen. 2006. "The Empirical Status of Deterrence Theory: A Meta-Analysis." In *Taking Stock: The Status of Criminological Theory*, pp. 367–96, edited by Francis T. Cullen, John Paul Wright, and Kristie R. Blevins. Vol. 15 in *Advances in Criminological Theory*, edited by William S. Laufer and Freda Adler. New Brunswick, NJ: Transaction.

Reyns, Bradford W. 2010. "A Situational Crime Prevention Approach to Cyberstalking Victimization: Preventive Tactics for Internet Users and Online Place Managers." *Crime Prevention and Community Safety* 12: 99–118.

Rosoff, Stephen M., Henry N. Pontell, and Robert Tillman. 1998. *Profit without Honor: White-Collar Crime and the Looting of America*. Upper Saddle River, NJ: Prentice Hall.

Sacco, Vincent F., and Leslie W. Kennedy. 2002. *The Criminal Event: Perspectives in Space and Time*. 2nd ed. Belmont: Wadsworth.

Shover, Neal, and Peter Grabosky. 2010. "White-Collar Crime and the Great Recession." *Criminology & Public Policy* 9: 429–33.

Shover, Neal, and Andrew Hochstetler. 2006. *Choosing White-Collar Crime*. New York: Cambridge University Press.

Shover, Neal, Andy Hochstetler, and Tage Alalehto. 2013. "Choosing White-Collar Crime." In *The Oxford Handbook of Criminological Theory*, pp. 475–93, edited by Francis T. Cullen and Pamela Wilcox. New York: Oxford University Press.

Shover, Neal, and Jennifer Scroggins. 2009. "Organizational Crime." In *The Oxford Handbook of Crime and Public Policy*, pp. 273–303, edited by Michael Tonry. New York: Oxford University Press.

Sparrow, Malcolm K. 2000. *License To Steal: How Fraud Bleeds America's Health Care System*. Boulder, CO: Westview Press.

Sutherland, Edwin H. 1949. *White Collar Crime*. New York: Dryden Press.

Waldrop, M. Mitchell. 1987. "Computers Amplify Black Monday: The Sudden Stock Market Decline Raised Questions about the Role of Computers; They May Not Have Actually Caused the Crash, but May Well Have Amplified It." *Science* 238: 602–04.

Weisburd, David, Stanton Wheeler, Elin Waring, and Nancy Bode. 1991. *Crimes of the Middle Classes: White-Collar Offenders in the Federal Courts*. New Haven, CT: Yale University Press.

Wheeler, Stanton, and Mitchell Lewis Rothman. 1981. "The Organization as Weapon in White-Collar Crime." *Michigan Law Review* 80: 1403–26.

Willison, Robert, and Mikko Siponen. 2009. "Overcoming the Insider: Reducing Employee Computer Crime through Situational Crime Prevention." *Communications of the ACM* 52: 133–37.

Wortley, Richard. 2002. *Situational Prison Control: Crime Prevention in Correctional Institutions*. Boston: Cambridge University Press.

Wortley, Richard, and Lorraine Mazerolle, eds. 2013. *Environmental Criminology and Crime Analysis*. New York: Routledge.

Wortley, Richard, and Stephen Smallbone. 2006a. "Applying Situational Principles to Sexual Offending against Children." In *Situational Prevention of Child Sexual Abuse*, edited by Richard Wortley and Stephen Smallbone. Vol. 19 of *Crime Prevention Studies*, pp. 7–35, edited by Ronald V. Clarke. Monsey, NY: Criminal Justice Press.

Wortley, Richard, and Stephen Smallbone, eds. 2006b. *Situational Prevention of Child Sexual Abuse*. Vol. 19 of *Crime Prevention Studies*, edited by Ronald V. Clarke. Monsey, NY: Criminal Justice Press.

CHAPTER 20

··

EMPLOYEE THEFT

··

JAY P. KENNEDY

ACCORDING to the U.S. Census (2013), at the beginning of 2012, there were a total of 5,684,424 businesses in the United States, employing a total of 113,425,965 people. In 2012, these individuals, and the businesses for which they worked, helped produce over $16 trillion in gross domestic product. These businesses manufactured products such as cars, computers, and golf clubs; they also provided services from financial planning to specialized elder care and a host of other necessary functions within society. In light of the amount of money, goods, and services that are generated by or that pass through American businesses, it is perhaps not surprising that they are attractive targets for thieves. Sadly, for many businesses, the thieves are actually insiders—that is, their own employees. The magnitude of the problem of employee theft and the extent of its impact on the U.S. economy only can be estimated at this point in time, but a good deal of evidence indicates that employee theft is a significant social problem and an important form of white-collar crime.

Employee theft is an occupational crime that occurs within an organizational setting and fits offense-based definitions of white-collar crime. In particular, it fits Edelhertz's (1970) conceptualization of white-collar crime in that it is committed through non-physical means and necessitates the use of concealment or guile in order to obtain money or property. While employee theft clearly falls under this offense-based definition of white-collar crime, it is less consistent with the criteria used in offender-based definitions of the concept. For example, Sutherland (1983) defined white-collar crime as illegal acts committed by business people of high social status and respectability in the course of their occupation. This offender-based definition may apply to employee theft that is committed by business executives or managers but it would not include thefts by lower-level employees who do not occupy positions of high status and respectability.

Organizational theorists consider employee theft a type of counterproductive work behavior (Robinson and Bennett 1995; Bennett and Robinson 2000), meaning that it is behavior directed at the business and committed by business insiders, which creates serious economic harm for the business. It is also a very serious crime, one that creates large social and economic problems (McDaniel and Jones 1988; Kulas et al. 2007), yet it has received relatively little attention from crime scholars. These crimes typically are underreported, and because they are not violent in nature but rather are acquisitive acts where the victim is a faceless organization, they do not receive the scholarly or popular attention that traditional street crimes receive. Yet, while employee theft might not pose a physical threat to people, as do many forms of street crime, its impact is nevertheless significant. Indeed, its costs are estimated to be ten times the costs of traditional street crimes (Mustaine and Tewksbury 2002). Furthermore, business losses attributable to employee theft far exceed the value of losses attributable to nonemployee theft within the same businesses (Taylor and Prien 1998), and across the United States employee thefts cost businesses up to $10 million per day in the late 1970s (McNees et al. 1980).

These high financial costs are likely to be a major factor behind the failure of many restaurants (Ghiselli and Ismail 1998; Holmes 2011), as well as many other types of small businesses (Niehoff and Paul 2000). Employee theft likely increases the prices consumers pay for products (Bailey 2006; Hoffer 2010) and decreases tax revenue for communities (Lipman and McGraw 1988), while increasing operational expenses for the victimized business. For example, following an incident of employee theft, businesses might expend large amounts of money to increase prevention efforts within the business and guard against future occurrences of employee theft (Challinger 1998; Mishra and Prasad 2006). Increases in theft-prevention mechanisms represent an indirect cost of employee theft; it is a cost that a victimized business assumes as a result of theft but one that is also intended to reduce future opportunities for theft to occur within the business.

Beyond the financial costs of employee theft, businesses also might experience non-financial harms, such as higher rates of employee turnover and lower levels of interpersonal and organizational trust (Payne and Gainey 2004). Furthermore, the motivational, emotional, and psychological toll these acts can take on the owners and managers, and through them upon the employees of the business, could be far more significant than the financial losses associated with the theft (Dunlop and Lee 2004). The effects of employee theft, therefore, are wide-ranging and potentially very significant in nature. Understanding how these crimes occur, the motivations behind acts of theft, and how business should respond to employee theft are important steps that must be taken to develop mechanisms to reduce opportunities for thefts in the future. A deeper understanding of employee theft also has the potential to expand overall knowledge about white-collar offenders, public and private responses to white-collar crimes, and the ways in which organizations inadvertently create opportunities for this type of crime.

This chapter is divided into four sections. Section I focuses on the variety of behaviors considered employee theft, as well as what is known about the extent of employee theft. Section II discusses several sources of motivation for employee theft through a review of the literature related to the individual and organizational factors behind employee theft motivation, as well as the role opportunity plays in these crimes. Section III addresses the role the criminal justice system and businesses play in addressing employee theft through the use of prevention mechanisms and the reduction of opportunities for employee theft. Section IV discusses the potential for partnerships among criminal justice agencies and businesses to reduce the occurrence of theft, and the need to examine how business strategy affects, and is affected by, employee theft. Overall, this chapter draws several major conclusions regarding the problem of employee theft:

- It is a poorly defined concept, and there is no consensus regarding the specific types of behaviors that constitute employee theft.
- There is a significant amount of overlap between organizational theory and criminological theory when it comes to explaining individual-level motivations for employee theft.
- When compared to street thieves and burglars, employee thieves enjoy greater access to targets of theft and possess greater knowledge of the theft-prevention mechanisms present within the business.
- The most dedicated and trusted and the longest-tenured employees have the greatest opportunities to commit large-scale employee theft, yet this does not mean they are the most likely to engage in theft.
- Employee theft will continue to be an underreported crime until business owners recognize the potential value of working with the criminal justice system and criminal justice officials take steps to address the unique needs of victimized businesses.

I. An Overview of Employee Theft

Although there is no generally accepted definition of employee theft, these crimes always involve the unauthorized taking of business resources (e.g., cash, finished goods, raw materials) by an employee of the business. Employee theft results in a tangible loss for the business, meaning that the business can quantify the value of the loss in some way, typically in terms of a financial cost. This crime is committed against a business by offenders who possess specialized knowledge about the business, knowledge that comes from their role as employees. As employees, these individuals have legitimate access to sensitive parts of the business, legitimacy that is used to mask their criminal acts (Benson and Simpson 2009).

Furthermore, because of their employment within the business, employee thieves have the ability to become familiar with the business's use of surveillance and monitoring equipment, the work schedules of employees who might serve as guardians of the business's property, and other forms of guardianship present at the business. A motivated employee's intimate knowledge of guardianship mechanisms presents an interesting twist on the relationship between the target and the offender, because offenders—employees in the case of employee theft—typically have legitimate access to the targets of theft as a function of their job. The employees' position in the company gives them enhanced or even unobstructed access to the targets of theft because employees are typically not questioned about their access to business property, computer files, or the business's equipment and materials.

Laws that specifically target employee theft in the United States are virtually nonexistent because there are no state-level statutes that address theft committed by employees and because only a handful of federal statutes address these crimes. Those federal statutes that do address employee theft are limited to government employees, except for a few statutes (i.e., U.S. Code title 18, chap. 31, sections 656 and 664) that apply to theft by a bank employee or theft from employee benefit or pension plans. When prosecuting all other types of employee theft, states will typically use a combination of general theft, fraud, or embezzlement statutes. One potential reason for the lack of laws focused specifically upon employee theft might be the ambiguity that surrounds the term "theft" within this context. For example, one business owner may consider the taking of peripheral office supplies such as paper, pens, markers, and cleaning chemicals to be theft from the business, because employees are not authorized to take these products home for personal use. However, another owner may look at the taking of such items as simply a perk of employment, not as an offense against the company requiring legal action.

The taking of peripheral office supplies might seem like a trivial matter compared to the theft of large sums of money or the theft of expensive tools and equipment. Indeed, there is a lack of consensus among business owners as to whether the taking of small-value, or insignificant, items actually constitutes a theft from the business. Thus, the range of behaviors believed by business owners to be theft does not have clear boundaries, highlighting the ease with which employees are able to access resources of the business. Because employee thieves have access to the targets of theft, and because they are legitimate handlers of business resources, it can be difficult even to identify when employee theft is occurring.

Situations where an employee is the guardian of business resources, as well as a potentially motivated offender, give employee thieves opportunities to hide their acts for long periods of time (Benson and Simpson 2009). This is because the employee's position within the business allows him or her regular, legitimate access to the target, while also affording him or her knowledge of guardianship and theft-prevention mechanisms present within the business. In short, employees sit in the perfect position to assess the risks and rewards attendant to acts of theft within the workplace.

However, as noted above, not all employee thefts occur within the workplace, since employees might not necessarily complete all of their assigned tasks at the physical location of the business. When employees engage in business activities away from the physical location of the business, while also having access to business resources, they might have a greater ability to manipulate the level of guardianship exerted over their activities. As such, the opportunity for employee theft to occur could increase when employees work away from the business's physical location, given that employee offenders have the luxury of determining both when and where a theft will occur. On the other hand, those employees who are trusted as guardians of the business's resources while away from the physical location of the business might be the most trustworthy employees and, therefore, the least likely to steal from the business.

In addition to being able to determine, and potentially control, the optimal circumstances for a theft to occur, employee thieves have the ability to determine the value of any potential targets prior to engaging in the theft. Unlike other forms of theft, where offenders might have no clue about the likelihood of obtaining a particular item or the value associated with any items stolen prior to actually committing the crime, employee thieves know what they will obtain and likely know the value of the item they intend to steal before the actual theft. This knowledge aids the rational decision-making process behind the theft by influencing the employee's cost–benefit analysis. Their estimates of the respective costs and benefits of crime are likely to be more precise than those of street offenders.

Inherent to this calculation of costs and benefits is an assessment of the perceived utility that possession of an item will bring, or the utility received from what can be obtained by trading that item for something else. Employees who steal materials from their place of work yet have no interest in using the items themselves must have the means to exchange the stolen goods for cash or other items they desire. When there is no opportunity to dispose of these items, the attractiveness of the item is reduced, and the perceived benefit (or gain) from the theft decreases.

A. Varieties of Employee Theft

The term "employee theft" refers to a wide range of deviant and criminal behaviors that occur within the workplace, but there is no consensus on the proper definition and there are no generally accepted criteria for the types of behaviors that qualify as employee theft (Greenberg and Barling 1996). Because of this ambiguity, the term serves as a type of catch-all category for many different, yet seemingly related, kinds of behavior. These behaviors include acts of interpersonal deviance committed by an employee against coworkers, customers, or suppliers, as well as the theft of time through social loafing or timecard manipulation.

As an illustration of this conceptual vagueness, consider that some scholars have classified the theft of patients' property by healthcare workers as a type of employee theft (Harris 1999; Harris and Benson 2000; Weber, Kurke, and Pentico 2003; Lindbloom et al. 2007). This categorization is because the perpetrator gained access to the targets via his or her role as an employee of a healthcare organization and typically engaged in this criminal behavior during working hours. In committing these acts, the employee has violated the rules of the workplace, the trust of the organization, and the trust of the patients. The actions produced harm not only for the victimized patients and their families, but also for the business, which is likely to be liable for any remuneration paid to the victims. Even though the business itself was not the target of theft, many business owners consider the theft of another person's property by an employee, when the victim is connected in some way to the business (i.e., customer, employee, supplier), to be employee theft (Kennedy 2014). Because the perpetrator was an employee of the business, and because the theft occurred within the business or within the course of the employee completing his or her tasks away from the business, the business owner classified the act as employee theft.

As another example of the conceptual ambiguity surrounding the concept of employee theft, consider behaviors that do not produce an immediate tangible benefit for the employee, such as the theft of intellectual property or "stealing" customers when changing jobs (Hettinger 1989; Green 2002; Kennedy 2014), which some might also consider to be acts of employee theft. Intellectual property is not always thought of as a tangible business resource. While it could exist on paper or in a computer file some-where, it is the product of collective employee mental effort, effort originally intended to produce tangible business returns. When employees steal company secrets, pro-cesses and procedures, formulations, ideas, or plans, the theft might not be an actual taking of physical property. Rather, it is the unauthorized transfer of knowledge from one business to another, where such transference creates harm, typically financial, for the victimized business.

Because employees are trusted guardians of the knowledge they help to create for the business, it is difficult for businesses to monitor for this type of theft. While these employees might have signed an agreement stating that all creations and ideas devel-oped for the business belong to the business, it is easy to see how employees could argue that such property is owned by them personally, not by the company. In these cases, employees might take the property of the business not out of spite for the busi-ness or its management, but rather because they perceive that they have created and thus have a legitimate right to the property in question. An employees' perception that he or she is entitled to a business's resources—that he or she owns the property of the business and can transfer said property to personal uses—highlights the fact that many times employees and employers have very different ideas regarding the acts considered employee theft (Greenberg and Barling 1996).

Despite the ambiguity that might surround the term, the vast majority of people would consider an act to be employee theft whenever an employee takes advantage of opportunities to steal business resources from his or her employer. Using this defini-tion, the most documented occurrences of employee theft come from studies of fast-food establishments and convenience stores (Boye and Wasserman 1996; Wimbush and Dalton 1997; Snider 2001, 2002). According to these studies, typical employee theft involves taking cash (Hawkins 1984) or food intended for sale (Hollinger, Slora, and Terris 1992). Hollinger, Slora, and Terris (1992) pointed out that within fast-food and other retail establishments, the giving away of food and other items intended for sale is also considered theft. In these instances, employee theft might not provide a direct ben-efit to the employee but might rather be a means for the employee to show generosity to friends and family. However, the altruistic nature of these actions does not remove the inappropriate nature of the behavior, and these acts are still considered theft.

The theft of food and other products representing finished goods or work in process (Sieh 1987) serves to reduce the value of the business in two distinct ways. First, the business loses the opportunity to earn revenue from the stolen items; second, the businesses must pay to replace the stolen items (Rosenbaum 1976). When employee theft centers on the loss of tangible business property, it is not very difficult for a victimized business to assess the value of the loss. However, other times it is difficult for a business to ascertain the specific value of a loss attributable to employee theft.

While the theft of food, work in process, finished goods, and cash can create significant harms for victimized businesses, other types of theft are more difficult to quantify and therefore might be very difficult to identify. The theft of time is one such example. The theft of time is typically defined as the misuse or abuse of an employer's time by an employee (Snider 2001). This definition leaves the terms "misuse" and "abuse," as well as "employer's time," open to interpretation.

Some scholars have operationalized the theft of time in terms of the extent to which employees engage in social loafing, the taking of unearned breaks, and persistent tardiness (Kulas et al. 2007; Martin et al. 2010). Yet, while some business owners consider these acts to be "theft," they acknowledge that it is very difficult to catch employees engaging in these behaviors and even more difficult to stop the behavior from occurring (Kennedy 2014). Instead, managers often choose to focus upon more tangible forms of the theft of time, such as timecard manipulation and falsification of the number of hours worked.

While it might be difficult to find consensus regarding all of the specific behaviors that constitute employee theft, research has produced estimates of the extent of certain types of employee theft.

B. Extent of Employee Theft

Employee theft likely affects all businesses, albeit to varying extents. While it has been difficult to discern the specific impact of employee theft, scholars have estimated it to be one of the most frequently occurring crimes against business (McDaniel and Jones 1988). In the 1980s, for example, the estimated rate of victimization was 70 percent (Terris 1985). Although some evidence suggests that shoplifting, vandalism, and credit card fraud are more prevalent within certain types of businesses (Perrone 2000), employee theft, in general, appears to be a significantly underreported crime (Fisher and Looye 2000; Taylor 2002). The underreporting of employee theft makes it difficult to determine the full extent of this problem, as official data on these crimes present an inaccurate picture of their totality.

What information we do have indicates that, depending upon the industry examined, 6 to 70 percent of businesses have experienced some form of employee theft (Jones and Terris 1985; Sieh 1987; Ash 1991; Dalton and Metzger 1993; Fisher and Looye 2000). However, most scholars exploring the extent of this problem have found rates of employee theft victimization hovering around 60 percent (Wimbush and Dalton 1997; Krippel et al. 2008). Finding such high rates of business victimization is, perhaps, unsurprising given that several scholars have found that 35 to 70 percent of surveyed employees admit to employee theft (Slora 1989; Kamp and Brooks 1991; Hollinger, Slora, and Terris 1992; Boye and Slora 1993).

However, it must be remembered that different industries offer different opportunities for employee theft, and as a result, certain industries will experience more theft than others. For example, thefts are likely to be more common within "high-theft" industries such as fast-food establishments, convenience stores, and service stations. While businesses in other industries, such as manufacturing or financial services, may not see rates of employee theft as high as 60 percent, research has shown that even in these industries there is a considerable amount of employee theft. For example, Hollinger and Clark (1983) found that the total percentage of employees admitting to theft in non-high-theft industries varied slightly by industry, with 35.1 percent of employees admitting to theft within retail establishments, 33.3 percent within hospitals, and 28.4 percent within manufacturing firms.

While the prevalence of theft is likely to vary by industry, the type of employee theft that is most likely to occur across all industries is the theft of cash. This type of theft can occur in a number of different ways (Association of Certified Fraud Examiners [ACFE] 2012). The most prevalent type of cash theft identified by the ACFE involves billing schemes or schemes where employees cause their employers to issue payment for a fraudulent invoice. These acts cost businesses an average of $100,000 per incident and typically represent a series of ongoing thefts by a single individual rather than a one-time theft. According to the ACFE (2012), ongoing schemes create greater total losses for businesses, with payroll schemes (when an employee submits a fraudulent claim for compensation) having the longest average duration (3 years). Check tampering is the second-longest-lasting form of employee theft, lasting a median duration of 30 months. This form of theft also has the highest median loss per incident, with victimized businesses standing to lose about $143,000 per identified incident.

Specific estimates of the total costs of employee theft within the United States vary from between the tens of billions of dollars to $400 billion annually (Rosenbaum 1976; Murphy 1993; Myers 1999; Appelbaum et al. 2006). Not surprisingly, the vast majority of these costs are borne by the victimized business, with the owners of the business being those most affected by these acts (Gross-Schaefer et al. 2000; Chen and Sandino 2012). In fact, in 2010 the ACFE estimated that, on an annual basis, organizational losses due to employee theft reached as high as 5 percent of total business revenues. Other research on the financial harms of employee theft has shown that restaurants might lose between 7 and 10 percent of their gross sales to employee theft (Hawkins 1984).

III. Causes of Employee Theft

Criminologists and organizational theorists take two different, yet complementary, approaches to the study of the causes of employee theft. Organizational theorists conceptualize employee theft as a type of counterproductive work behavior (Robinson and

Bennett 1995) or a voluntary extra-role behavior that harms the organization. From this perspective, organizational theorists have sought to understand the workplace factors that facilitate the development of individual motivations to engage in theft. This approach includes a consideration of personality factors, other individual-level factors tied to the workplace, interactions in the workplace with peers and superiors, and the ethical climate of the organization. By contrast, crime scholars consider employee theft to be a crime and thus are more likely to attempt to explain these acts through theories of criminal behavior.

Criminologists have argued that a crime event occurs when a person motivated to offend is given the opportunity to engage in a crime, even if the victim and offender do not come into direct contact (Reyns 2013). Opportunities for crime exist when suitable targets are present at the same place and time as a lack of capable guardianship (Sherman, Gartin and Buerger 1989; Groff 2007). With regard to employee theft, addressing offender motivation and reducing opportunities for crime are viable routes to reducing or preventing crimes within a business. Addressing individual motivations to steal is an approach that may be well suited for dealing with employee theft given the relationships that exist among owners, managers, and employees. Working to reduce opportunities for offending by addressing the situations in which opportunity develops is also likely to be successful in combating employee theft as businesses exercise a large amount of control over their operations.

A. Individual and Organizational Motivations

The vast majority of research conducted on employee theft and the majority of the crime-prevention literature aimed at business owners focuses solely upon developing, or assessing, theories related to how employees become motivated to engage in theft. Much of this literature has found support for the role of strain in the development of offender motivation, despite the fact that strain theory (Merton 1938) has not been directly tested in this context. For example, stress that results from an employee's dissatisfaction with his or her job or employer, as well as stress that creates desires to retaliate against the business, is related to acts of employee theft (Greenberg and Barling 1996; Greenberg 2002). Employee theft, therefore, might represent a way for an employee to "even the score" against an employer whom the employee perceives to have wronged him or her in some way (Greenberg 1990).

Stress created by economic need has been found to influence an employee's intentions to steal from his or her employer (Machin and Meghir 2004; Rickman and Witt 2007; Chen and Sandino 2012). Likewise, the disjuncture between employment outcomes and expectations can lead to deviance-producing strain (Agnew 1992). These feelings of strain, particularly when they occur in the presence of antisocial peers or when the employee lacks prosocial coping mechanisms, can lead the employee to cope with these negative feelings through acts of employee theft. Under these circumstances, employee theft is most likely to result when the perceived mistreatment is thought to be severe, there are few internal or external controls to prevent the occurrence of theft, and the act of theft provides a way to bridge the divide between anticipated and actual workplace outcomes (Agnew 2001).

Because of the goal-directed nature of employment—people perform a job, in part, to receive wages—pay dissatisfaction is one type of strain within the workplace that is highly likely to lead to feelings of anger (Broidy 2001), which are then likely to lead to employee theft and other deviant workplace behaviors (Rebellon et al. 2009). While pay satisfaction is also closely associated with job satisfaction and perceptions of distributive justice (Organ and Konovsky 1989), it stands apart from these areas when considering the problem of employee theft. This is because employee theft is often associated with an employee's desire to extract gain from his or her employer in an attempt to close the gap between expected and actual remuneration (Agnew 2001; Rebellon et al. 2009).

When workers feel underpaid for their work, they might steal from the business in order to recoup their "losses," yet when these same workers begin to feel fairly compensated the theft is likely to subside (Greenberg 1990). This suggests that employees might steal only to create balance between the value they have placed on their services and the value of what they receive in compensation from the business (Ambrose, Seabright, and Schminke 2002; Tang and Chiu 2003). Yet, it is not likely that workers will only engage in theft as a reaction to pay dissatisfaction, because they are more likely to exhibit other less serious forms of counterproductive behavior, as well as to display a decrease in general workplace motivation, prior to engaging in theft (Rynes, Gerhart, and Minette 2004; Jones 2009).

The literature on employee theft is clear that the factors most likely to be associated with employee theft intentions, as well as the actual occurrence of employee theft, are job dissatisfaction, perceptions of inequality/injustice, pay dissatisfaction, and the presence of workplace or role-based stressors. The term "job satisfaction" refers to one's positive feelings about one's level of job performance and the rewards one receives as a result of that performance (Locke 1969). People can also experience job dissatisfaction, which relates to the negative feelings one experiences regarding one's job performance, or the rewards associated with that performance. High levels of job dissatisfaction can lead to the externalization of this dissatisfaction through counterproductive work behaviors (Lau, Au, and Ho 2003; De Cremer 2006; Mount, Ilies, and Johnson 2006; Roberts et al. 2007).

Similar to job satisfaction, issues of justice and fairness within the business relate to an employee's perception that he or she is treated appropriately by the business. While some workplace situations might clearly be unjust or unfair (e.g., abusive behavior on the part of supervisors that is aimed toward employees), other behavior is more ambiguous, and perceptions of justice/fairness rest in the individual employee's interpretation of the particular situation. The subjective interpretation of workplace events can lead some employees to engage in counterproductive behaviors, with employee theft being one such behavior (Greenberg 1993, 2002). Employee theft might be a likely outcome of feelings of injustice or unfairness when employees perceive that the outcomes they have received from the business are less than what they should have received.

Job dissatisfaction, pay dissatisfaction, and issues of justice in the workplace can all create stress for employees, and this stress can lead to acts of employee theft as well as other counterproductive work behavior (Bowling and Eschleman 2010). Surprisingly, the presence of role-based stressors is more likely to lead to acts of employee theft than are other conflicts, even when those conflicts involve one's superiors (Fox, Spector, and Miles 2001). Stress in the workplace can develop from a number of different sources, including a poor fit between employees and the jobs they are asked to perform, issues within the group with which an employee associates, or problems within the company (Kristof 1996). However, a poor fit between the employee and the business does not necessarily mean that employee theft will occur; it represents only one potential outcome.

The employee is also likely to feel large amounts of stress when there is a breach of an implicit relational or transactional contract, referred to as a psychological contract, between the employee and the employer (Graen and Uhl-Bien 1995). Stress can result from severing of the psychological contract because the negative feelings associated with this breach will likely have a significant influence on the range of on-the-job behaviors displayed by the employee (Zhao et al. 2007). Such a breach of the psychological contract can create stress because it could be a signal to the employee that his or her contributions to the business are not valued or respected (Coyle-Shapiro and Conway 2005). When employees feel that their contributions are not valued, they may experience negative affective responses to otherwise normal workplace conditions, and these responses might lead the employee to engage in a prolonged series of counterproductive behaviors.

The literature on employee theft has shown that there is no shortage of reasons as to why employees might choose to engage in acts of theft against their employer. Irrespective of the reason, these acts can create serious harm for the victimized business. However, even the most highly dissatisfied employee, who is likely to be the most highly motivated offender, will have a difficult time committing acts of theft against his or her employer if there are few opportunities within the business for theft to occur.

Other research on employee theft has found that factors such as age and tenure are significant to understanding an employee's motivation to engage in theft (Robin 1969; Hollinger 1986; Hollinger, Slora, and Terris 1992; Harris and Benson 2000; Huiras, Uggen, and McMorris 2000; Mustaine and Tewksbury 2002). These studies suggest that employee theft is concentrated among younger, short-tenured employees for several reasons. Compared to older, longer-tenured peers, these employees typically display lower levels of attachment to the business (Feldman 2003; Ng and Feldman 2009), have higher levels of impulsivity, perceive there to be lower opportunity costs associated with theft, and see the results of their actions as less harmful (Rickman and Witt 2007).

Another commonly studied set of antecedents to employee theft are factors associated with personality. Organizational theorists have used the five-factor model (McCrae and Costa 1987) of personality to study the relationships that exist among prominent features of personality and the propensity to engage in deviant behavior. The five-factor model of personality captures broad categorizations of characteristics that are used to explain individual variations in personality (Salgado 1997; Gosling,

Rentfrow, and Swann 2003); commonly called "The Big Five," these factors are neuroticism, extraversion, openness, agreeableness, and conscientiousness. Individuals who are high in conscientiousness are more likely than those with low conscientiousness to refrain from engaging in counterproductive work behaviors (Bowling 2010; Bowling and Eschelman 2010). Even when their level of job satisfaction is low, which typically indicates lower investment in the business, individuals who are high in conscientiousness are significantly less likely to engage in behaviors like employee theft than are individuals low in conscientiousness.

Another personality trait that has been found to be highly correlated with the occurrence of employee theft is agreeableness, or the propensity to work in cooperative rather than competitive ways. Penney and Spector (2002) found that individuals low in agreeableness were more likely to engage in counterproductive behaviors when they were faced with challenges on the job, while individuals high in agreeableness displayed low levels of intent to engage in such behaviors irrespective of the difficulties they encountered on the job. These authors also found that as difficulties and challenges on the job increased, so did the intention to engage in counterproductive behavior, suggesting that workplace factors help determine whether individuals will engage in deviant acts while on the job (Jackson et al. 2002; Spector and Fox 2002; Berry, Ones, and Sackett 2007).

Ironically, theft also might occur because employees feel a strong attachment to their position as well as to the business. Such feelings of attachment are typically accompanied by high levels of workplace commitment and the feeling that the employee has made significant contributions to the business. Under these circumstances, employees might feel that because of their hard work and dedication, they own a part of the business, or a part of its outputs (Pierce, Kostova, and Dirks 2001). Organizational theorists consider such behavior to be an indication of high levels of psychological ownership (Pierce, Van Dyne, and Cummings 1992). Psychological ownership is the perception among employees that they are responsible for, and have ownership rights over, the business, either in part or in whole. While psychological ownership has been found to influence positively the performance of extra-role behaviors and levels of organizational commitment (Vandewalle, Van Dyne, and Kostova 1995), a connection between psychological ownership and counterproductive work behaviors has also been theorized (Pierce, Kostova, and Dirks 2001).

When their feelings of psychological ownership take on a counterproductive tone, employees might steal from the business because they feel the property they are taking belongs to them by virtue of the effort they have exerted on behalf of the business—effort they believe has not been properly compensated. Employee theft might result when psychological ownership is high because employees come to identify their contributions to the business, as well as the tangible or intangible outputs of the business, as an extension of themselves (Van Dyne and Pierce 2004). As such, they view the taking of these items not as stealing from the business, but as merely gaining possession of, or in some way protecting, property they already consider to be their own (Avey et al. 2009).

B. The Role of Opportunity

As criminologists have stated, crimes like employee theft cannot occur without a motivated offender, as well as the presence of an opportunity for theft (Madensen and Eck 2008; Tillyer and Eck 2011). In other words, an employee identifies an opportunity to engage in employee theft and for some reason or another is motivated to victimize his or her employer. Crime scholars consider employee theft to be a crime that is committed against the business (Clark and Hollinger 1981; Hollinger and Clark 1983; Mars 1982; Payne and Gainey 2002) by offenders who possess specialized knowledge about the business. Employees gain this specialized knowledge by virtue of the fact that their position inside the business affords them legitimate access to sensitive parts of the business. This legitimacy is used by motivated employee thieves to complete, as well as to mask, their criminal acts (Benson and Simpson 2009).

As a result of their ability to access sensitive business resources, employees are in the best position to determine the optimal items to steal and the optimal time to steal from the business, which are factors that increase the chances of a successful theft (Clarke 1997). Furthermore, as employees engage in their normal and legitimate workplace tasks, they learn about the levels and types of guardianship present within the business. For example, employee thieves can become familiar with the business's use of surveillance and monitoring equipment, the work schedules of employees who might serve as guardians of the business's property, and other forms of guardianship present at the business. Motivated employee offenders can capitalize upon this knowledge and select the optimal circumstances to engage in theft, thereby taking full advantage of any opportunities for theft within the business.

This situation presents an interesting twist on the relationship between the target and the offender, as offenders—employees in this case—typically have legitimate access to the targets of theft as a function of their job. Legitimate access to business resources allows potential offenders enhanced or even unobstructed access to the targets of theft, as employees are not generally questioned about their access to business property, computer files, or the business's equipment and materials. The opportunity to steal from the business is also dependent upon the employee's perception of the target suitability of available business resources, which is influenced in part by the employee's ability to access desired items.

It is common for some employees to access sensitive material or information on a daily basis as they go about completing their assigned tasks, and it is also common for some employees to take the business's property away from the business location and away from guardianship measures present at the business. In some occupations, it is expected that employees will take materials, information, and equipment home with them, as needed, to complete their jobs. In these situations, employees are trusted as guardians of the business's property, and it is this trusted position that makes it easy for motivated employees to victimize their employer (see Sheppard and Sherman [1998] for a discussion of interdependence and trust within organizations, and see Shapiro [1990] for a review of the problem of abuse of trust).

With regard to employee theft, cash is the most preferred item for employees to steal (Kennedy 2014), as it allows them to obtain easily things they desire. However, the theft of finished goods could allow the employee to sell products produced by the business in order to obtain cash or some other desired item. When an item is not viewed as enjoyable yet is still considered to be a target suitable for theft, the employee likely perceives that he or she can sell or trade the item for something more desirable. In cases of employee theft, it is the owner or manager of the business who is likely in the best position to implement changes to the business that may reduce opportunities for employee theft.

Furthermore, within the context of employee theft, the ability to conceal the actual item might be just as important as having the ability to conceal the means by which the item has been obtained. Because employee thieves spend most their time at the location of the crime, concealing their acts is key to the continuance of their illegal behavior. After all, employees will only continue to benefit from their acts as long as they are hidden from owners and managers. Unlike traditional street crimes, where offenders typically flee the locations where they commit crimes so as to avoid detection, employee thieves may remain at the crime scene because their role in the offense is concealed. In fact, it is very likely that the longer the employee remains at the crime location, the more lucrative his or her theft schemes will become.

While the specific resources with which an employee is trusted vary by his or her position within the business, all employees are trusted to some extent with business resources that might be viewed as targets suitable for theft. As employees go about completing their legitimate job functions, they might have the opportunity to alter their performance in a negative way and use their knowledge of the business to engage in theft. Ironically, it is likely through the proper performance of one's job that an employee gains the trust and knowledge needed to engage in employee theft, which also allows the employee to create greater harms for the business than could a nonemployee thief.

IV. Combating Employee Theft

Despite the hidden nature of employee theft, and despite the fact that employee thieves enjoy significant advantages in the planning and execution of their crimes, resources exist to combat this problem. Specifically, two groups can have a significant influence on the occurrence of employee theft: business owners and managers and the criminal justice system. While the influence of each group is discussed separately, it is important to note that each group is less effective when pursuing a solution to the problem alone as opposed to working in a manner in which each complements the other. The owners and managers of businesses can combat the problem of employee theft by reducing opportunities for theft within the business through changes in guardianship, addressing offender motivation, and capitalizing upon appropriate place-management strategies. The criminal justice system can assist business owners and managers through the proper handling of identified instances of employee theft, dedicating resources to collaborating with businesses, and working with businesses to identify the best ways to address employee theft.

A. Owner/Manager Responses

Criminologists who study situational crime prevention have identified three roles through which the opportunity to offend can be curtailed: guardians, handlers, and place managers (Felson 1995; Graham et al. 2005; Hollis-Peel et al. 2011). Guardians are people who watch over targets of crime, serving as a protective buffer between the targets of crime and motivated offenders (Hollis-Peel et al. 2011). Handlers are directly related to motivated offenders and in some way act to reduce offender motivation through the relationship they share with a potential offender (Felson 1987). Place managers are individuals who may never have direct contact with offenders or targets, yet they control the activities at places where criminal opportunities exist (Sherman 1995). These concepts can successfully be applied to business owners and managers, as they have direct contact with offenders and targets and control the processes and procedures that influence theft opportunities within the business.

Specifically, business owners and managers may serve as (1) guardians of business resources, (2) handlers of potential offenders, and (3) place managers influencing the development of opportunities for employee theft. As guardians of the business and its resources, owners and managers are tasked with protecting business resources likely to be targeted for theft. In their role as handlers of potential offenders they must exercise control over employees, especially those at risk of theft. And their role as place managers is to ensure that the rules of the business are followed (Sampson, Eck, and Dunham 2010). While Felson (1995) argued that place managers are the most important of the three types of controllers, all three roles are interrelated (Hollis-Peel et al. 2011), and for business owners and managers all three roles are inextricably linked.

Business owners and managers are responsible for ensuring the business operates with optimal levels of efficiency. This requires them to become intimately involved with overseeing key business operations as well as monitoring the use of business resources to ensure that maximum output is gained from these operations. A focus upon output maximization, with its resultant emphasis upon surveillance of the business and its resources, will also reduce the likelihood of many types of crimes against the business (Burrows and Hopkins 2005). However, businesses will differ in regard to the types of resources available to address the development and occurrence of employee theft (Cardon and Stevens 2004).

The role that owners and managers play as guardians of the business affects their availability to monitor the business, which in turn influences their ability to deter theft (Hollis-Peel et al. 2011). The desire of owners and managers to succeed in the prevention of employee theft likely is tied to the level of personal responsibility they feel they have for the protection of the business (Felson 1995). Because the owner, or some other person with a strong investment in the owner, typically manages the business, the personal responsibility that owners and managers feel regarding the protection of the business should be high. However, when business owners and managers are unaware of theft, or they feel there is little they can do about it, they may be less likely to take proactive measures to curtail criminal opportunities (Eck 1994). In these cases, guardianship weakens not out of a lack of investment in the business, but rather out of a lack of awareness, or because of feelings of helplessness, on the part of business owners or managers.

As place managers, the owners and managers of businesses can influence the development of opportunities for crime within the business by exercising guardianship over the business and its resources (Eck 1994; Eck and Wartell 1998; Mazerolle, Kadleck, and Roehl 1998). In this role, owners and managers protect the business by monitoring resources, raw materials, and finished products and providing oversight of employees. An essential part of managerial oversight involves ensuring that employees follow the rules and regulations of the business and that rule violations are addressed (Graham et al. 2005). Rule enforcement, or the monitoring and maintenance of business processes and procedures, is one tangible output of the active guardianship of potential motivated offenders by business owners and managers.

The presence of items available for employee theft is determined by the activities of the business as well as the business's use of resources necessary for the completion of business tasks. As such, the opportunity for particular types of theft to occur will likely vary by industry; therefore, the types of theft that occur within a business are dependent, in part, upon the type of business. This creates a situation where businesses in different industries will come to define the actions that constitute employee theft in different, and sometimes conflicting, ways. Research into the problem of employee theft has acknowledged this trend, as scholars have studied many different behaviors that businesses have classified as employee theft.

Irrespective of the business type, when business owners and managers act as place managers, they help to make their workplaces less conducive to employee theft by showing clearly, through rule enforcement and active monitoring, that the business will not tolerate deviant activity (Eck and Weisburd 1995). Furthermore, owners and managers have the ability to affect the development of opportunities for employee theft through the relationships they have with others within the business who can also serve as guardians and protect the business against employee theft (Poyner and Webb 1997). In addition to the owners and managers, other employees, suppliers or business partners, and even customers can engage in guardianship activities that help to reduce opportunities for employee theft (Felson 1995). It also is relevant that employees potentially are not only guardians but also motivated offenders. Maintaining strong relationships with employees is important because it is through these ties that owners and managers can serve as better handlers of potential offenders.

Owners and managers occupy the role of handlers not only because of the close oversight they give to the employees, but also because of the investment they have in protecting the business against theft (Brown et al. 1987; O'Bannon, Goldfinger, and Appleby 1989; Sackett, Burris, and Callahan 1989; Rieke and Guastello 1995; Eck and Wartell 1998; Wanek 1999). For example, the investment of business owners and managers in the business, and in the relationships they maintain with employees, might allow them to leverage the emotional capital employees have in the business in such a way that employees become invested in protecting business resources (Willison 2000). The outcome of leveraging emotional capital is the ability of business owners and managers to influence the behavior of all employees on a routine basis, as well as the ability to focus upon specific employees when unique opportunities of theft or deviance are identified (Hollis-Peel et al. 2011). Leveraging emotional relationships within the business is similar to the idea of removing excuses from potential offenders, as the actions of business owners and managers can help employees to see how theft creates serious harms for the business (Clarke 1997; Clarke and Homel 1997). When emotional relationships are strong, owners and managers may be more cognizant of their employees' actions. Furthermore, they may be more closely connected to their employees, which may help identify workplace issues that provide opportunities for employee theft and other counterproductive work behaviors.

B. Criminal Justice System Responses

Businesses can do much to prevent employee theft by reducing opportunities for theft within the business, yet by themselves these efforts cannot prevent all thefts from occurring. Once thefts do occur within the business, the criminal justice system can play an important role in addressing these specific occurrences as well as preventing future opportunities for employee theft within the business. The most straightforward criminal justice system intervention comes in the form of police involvement in initiating the process of prosecuting employee thieves. However, business owners and managers may not always seek the help of the police when employee theft occurs, choosing not to seek assistance from the criminal justice system.

The results from a recent qualitative study of small business owners and managers suggest that many business owners are reluctant to contact the police when theft occurs, as they feel the police are an ineffective means of dealing with this problem (Kennedy 2014). In some cases, business owners perceive that contacting the police is inappropriate because the theft committed is trivial, or too small to warrant police intervention. Some business owners think that it is better to handle some thefts internally rather than involving the police because an arrest or conviction would be too harsh a punishment for the employee's deviant act. However, these same business owners often have difficulties identifying where to draw the line on the internal handling of theft, as they are ambiguous about the specific circumstances that would lead them to contact the police (Kennedy 2014).

Other business owners have stated they would not contact the police irrespective of the financial loss associated with the theft, as they have ideological stances against using the criminal justice system in such instances. These individuals are rare, and many business owners would contact the police in what they perceive to be severe cases of employee theft. However, even in cases where an act of employee theft is large and significant, certain business owners may still refuse to contact the police as they perceive the police cannot do anything about the theft. Furthermore, business owners may believe the police will not do anything about the theft. It is in these situations that the greatest gains can be made in finding partnerships between business owners and the criminal justice system.

Collaborations between the police and business owners can help reduce opportunities for employee theft in many ways, yet the key to the success of such partnerships lies in the quality of information shared between these two parties. For example, police officers might be able to share tips with businesses owners regarding what types of evidence and information are most valuable to a police investigation of employee theft. If business owners know the best practices to follow once they have identified an instance of employee theft, they might be better able to gather the most important information about the theft in a way that is easiest for the police to act upon. Furthermore, some police departments have specialized units that focus on financial or white-collar crimes, and these units might be better able to assist victimized business owners than street-level officers. While it is street-level officers who are more likely to interact with business owners on a regular basis, connecting victimized business owners with specialized financial crimes units will likely allow for more productive collaborations between business owners and the police.

As business owners become more familiar with the individuals who might serve as a resource to them in instances of employee theft (e.g., police detectives, street-level officers, prosecutors), they might become more likely to report employee theft within their business. Furthermore, business owners might be more open to sharing the challenges they face in dealing with theft as well as working with law enforcement to craft prevention mechanisms and procedures for dealing with theft. While the police are very knowledgeable about dealing with crimes generally, it is likely that the majority of officers do not fully understand the specific needs of businesses dealing with employee theft victimization. Through a strengthened partnership, business owners might be able to help police officers understand the specific issues they face. Such an understanding might lead to more effective investigations of employee theft as well as to a greater level of reporting of employee theft by businesses.

V. Conclusion

Beyond a handful of exceptions, employee theft has managed to fly under the criminological radar. Indeed, few scholars have paused to give attention to the scale of harm it creates for victimized businesses as well as for society as a whole. This lack of attention may be due in part to the fact that many businesses choose to deal with their victimization in silence and do not report thefts to the police. However, another reason for the lack of attention may be the ambiguity surrounding the true size of the problem. Employee thieves use their positions within businesses to mask their crimes, effectively shielding their acts from detection, while also suppressing suspicion of their existence.

Yet, what is known about employee theft suggests that the problem is widespread and that businesses of all shapes and sizes, operating in all manner of industry, are vulnerable to employee thieves. The threat of employee theft has led many businesses to implement controls designed to mitigate their exposure to these crimes, yet those within the organization often overcome these controls because, as employees, they have access to the most sensitive parts of the business. However, these crimes can be prevented, and if they do occur there are means to control the losses that result from an employee's deviant actions. It is likely that the most effective prevention mechanisms will be based on a mix of organizational theory, crime-prevention strategies, and law enforcement collaborations. Each of these elements contributes a different, yet important, piece to the puzzle.

Organizational theories define the focus of the prevention strategies and outline how best to implement these strategies to produce the desired change. Crime-prevention strategies can help define the elements of employee theft opportunity structures and identify which actors are responsible for controlling the development of these opportunity structures. As an integrated whole, these two approaches will be able to craft prevention strategies that lead to successful organizational changes that reduce the opportunity for employee theft without significantly altering the climate of the business. Such advancements will also aid law enforcement in assisting businesses dealing with employee theft. However, such a victory might be a silent victory because the effectiveness of such strategies will likely remain less apparent than similar crime-prevention strategies aimed at addressing more visible, conspicuous crimes.

REFERENCES

Agnew, Robert. 1992. "Foundation for a General Strain Theory of Crime and Delinquency." *Criminology* 30: 47–88.

Agnew, Robert. 2001. "Building on the Foundation of General Strain Theory: Specifying the Types of Strain Most Likely to Lead to Crime and Delinquency." *Journal of Research in Crime and Delinquency* 38: 319–61.

Ambrose, Maureen L., Mark A. Seabright, and Marshall Schminke. 2002. "Sabotage in the Workplace: The Role of Organizational Injustice." *Organizational Behavior and Human Decision Processes* 89: 947–65.

Appelbaum, Steven H., Jennifer Cottin, Remy Paré, and Barbara T. Shapiro. 2006. "Employee Theft: From Behavioral Causation and Prevention to Managerial Detection and Remedies." *Journal of American Academy of Business* 9: 175–82.

Ash, Philip. 1991. "A History of Honesty Testing." In *Preemployment Honesty Testing: Current Research and Future Directions*, pp. 3–20, edited by John W. Jones. Westport, CT: Quorum.

Association of Certified Fraud Examiners. 2012. *Report to the Nations on Occupational Fraud and Abuse*. Austin, TX: Author.

Avey, James B., Bruce J. Avolio, Craig D. Crossley, and Fred Luthans. 2009. "Psychological Ownership: Theoretical Extensions, Measurement and Relation to Work Outcomes." *Journal of Organizational Behavior* 30: 173–91.

Bailey, Ainsworth A. 2006. "Retail Employee Theft: A Theory of Planned Behavior Perspective." *International Journal of Retail and Distribution Management* 34: 802–16.

Bennett, Rebecca J., and Sandra L. Robinson. 2000. "Development of a Measure of Workplace Deviance." *Journal of Applied Psychology* 85: 349–60.

Benson, Michael L., and Sally S. Simpson. 2009. *White-Collar Crime: An Opportunity Perspective*. New York: Routledge.

Berry, Christopher M., Deniz S. Ones, and Paul R. Sackett. 2007. "Interpersonal Deviance, Organizational Deviance, and Their Common Correlates: A Review and Meta-Analysis." *Journal of Applied Psychology* 92: 410–24.

Bowling, Nathan A. 2010. "Effects of Job Satisfaction and Conscientiousness on Extra-Role Behaviors." *Journal of Business and Psychology* 25: 119–30.

Bowling, Nathan A., and Kevin J. Eschleman. 2010. "Employee Personality as a Moderator of the Relationships between Work Stressors and Counterproductive Work Behavior." *Journal of Occupational Health Psychology* 15: 91–103.

Boye, Michael W., and Karen B. Slora. 1993. "The Severity and Prevalence of Deviant Employee Activity within Supermarkets." *Journal of Business and Psychology* 8: 245–53.

Boye, Michael W., and Amy R. Wasserman. 1996. "Predicting Counterproductivity among Drug-Store Applicants." *Journal of Business and Psychology* 10: 337–49.

Broidy, Lisa M. 2001. "A Test of General Strain Theory." *Criminology* 39: 9–36.

Brown, Thomas S., John W. Jones, William Terris, and Brian D. Steffy. 1987. "The Impact of Pre-Employment Integrity Testing on Employee Turnover and Inventory Shrinkage Losses." *Journal of Business and Psychology* 2: 136–49.

Burrows, John, and Matt Hopkins. 2005. "Business and Crime." In *The Handbook of Crime Prevention*, pp. 468–515, edited by Nick Tilley. Cullompton, UK: Willan.

Cardon, Melissa S., and Christopher E. Stevens. 2004. "Managing Human Resources in Small Organizations: What Do We Know?" *Human Resource Management Review* 14: 295–323.

Challinger, Dennis. 1998. "The Realities of Crime against Business." Paper presented at the AIC Crime Against Business Conference, Melbourne, Australia, June 18–19, 1998.

Chen, Clara Xiaoling, and Tatiana Sandino. 2012. "Can Wages Buy Honesty? The Relationship between Relative Wages and Employee Theft." *Journal of Accounting Research* 50: 967–1000.

Clark, John P., and Richard C. Hollinger. 1981. *Theft by Employees in Work Organizations*. Minneapolis: University of Minnesota Press.

Clarke, Ronald V. 1997. *Situational Crime Prevention: Successful Case Studies*, 2nd ed. Albany, NY: Harrow and Heston.

Clarke, Ronald V., and Ross Homel. 1997. "A Revised Classification of Situational Crime Prevention Techniques." In *Crime Prevention at a Crossroads*, pp. 17–27, edited by Stephen Lab. Cincinnati, OH: Anderson.

Coyle-Shapiro, Jacqueline and Neil Conway. 2005. "Exchange Relationships: Examining Psychological Contracts and Perceived Organizational Support." *Journal of Applied Psychology* 90: 774–81.

Dalton, Dan R., and Michael B. Metzger. 1993. "'Integrity Testing' for Personnel Selection: An Unsparing Perspective." *Journal of Business Ethics* 12: 147–56.

De Cremer, David. 2006. "Unfair Treatment and Revenge Taking: The Roles of Collective Identification and Feelings of Disappointment." *Group Dynamics: Theory, Research, and Practice* 10: 220–32.

Dunlop, Patrick D., and Kibeom Lee. 2004. "Workplace Deviance, Organizational Citizenship Behavior, and Business Unit Performance: The Bad Apples Do Spoil the Whole Barrel." *Journal of Organizational Behavior* 25: 67–80.

Eck, John E. 1994. "Drug Markets and Drug Places: A Case-Control Study of the Spatial Structure of Illicit Drug Dealing." Unpublished Ph.D. dissertation, University of Maryland, College of Criminology and Criminal Justice.

Eck, John E., and Julie Wartell. 1998. "Improving the Management of Rental Properties with Drug Problems: A Randomized Experiment." *Civil Remedies and Crime Prevention* 9: 161–85.

Eck, John E., and David Weisburd. 1995. "Crime Places in Crime Theory." *Crime and Place: Crime Prevention Studies*, Vol. 4, edited by John E. Eck and David Weisburd. Monsey, NY: Criminal Justice Press.

Edelhertz, Herbert. 1970. *The Nature, Impact, and Prosecution of White-Collar Crime.* Washington, D.C.: National Institute of Law Enforcement and Criminal Justice.

Feldman, Daniel C. 2003. "The Antecedents and Consequences of Early Career Indecision among Young Adults." *Human Resource Management Review* 13: 499–531.

Felson, Marcus. 1987. "Routine Activities and Crime Prevention in the Developing Metropolis." *Criminology* 25: 911–32.

Felson, Marcus. 1995. "Those Who Discourage Crime." *Crime and Place: Crime Prevention Studies*, Vol. 4, edited by John E. Eck and David Weisburd. Monsey, NY: Criminal Justice Press.

Fisher, Bonnie, and Johanna W. Looye. 2000. "Crime and Small Businesses in the Midwest: An Examination of Overlooked Issues in the United States." *Security Journal* 13: 45–72.

Fox, Suzy, Paul E. Spector, and Don Miles. 2001. "Counterproductive Work Behavior (CWB) in Response to Job Stressors and Organizational Justice: Some Mediator and Moderator Tests for Autonomy and Emotions." *Journal of Vocational Behavior* 59: 291–309.

Ghiselli, Richard, and Joseph A. Ismail. 1998. "Employee Theft and Efficacy of Certain Control Procedures in Commercial Food Service Operations." *Journal of Hospitality and Tourism Research* 22: 174–87.

Gosling, Samuel D., Peter J. Rentfrow, and William B. Swann Jr. 2003. "A Very Brief Measure of the Big-Five Personality Domains." *Journal of Research in Personality* 37: 504–28.

Graen, George B., and Mary Uhl-Bien. 1995. "Relationship-Based Approach to Leadership: Development of Leader-Member Exchange (LMX) Theory of Leadership over 25 Years: Applying a Multi-Level Multi-Domain Perspective." *Leadership Quarterly* 6: 219–47.

Graham, Kathryn, Sharon Bernards, D. Wayne Osgood, Ross Homel, and John Purcell. 2005. "Guardians and Handlers: The Role of Bar Staff in Preventing and Managing Aggression." *Addiction* 100: 755–66.

Green, Stuart P. 2002. "Plagiarism, Norms, and the Limits of Theft Law: Some Observations on the Use of Criminal Sanctions in Enforcing Intellectual Property Rights." *Hastings Law Journal* 54: 167–205.

Greenberg, Jerald. 1990. "Employee Theft as a Reaction to Underpayment Inequity: The Hidden Cost of Pay Cuts." *Journal of Applied Psychology* 75: 561–68.

Greenberg, Jerald. 1993. "Stealing in the Name of Justice: Informational and Interpersonal Moderators of Theft Reactions to Underpayment Inequity." *Organizational Behavior and Human Decision Processes* 54: 81–103.

Greenberg, Jerald. 2002. "Who Stole the Money, and When? Individual and Situational Determinants of Employee Theft." *Organizational Behavior and Human Decision Processes* 89: 985–1003.

Greenberg, Liane, and Julian Barling. 1996. "Employee Theft." *Trends in Organizational Behavior* 3: 49–64.

Groff, Elizabeth R. 2007. "Simulation for Theory Testing and Experimentation: An Example Using Routine Activity Theory and Street Robbery." *Journal of Quantitative Criminology* 23: 75–103.

Gross-Schaefer, Arthur, Jeff Trigilio, Jamie Negus, and Ceng-Si Ro. 2000. "Ethics Education in the Workplace: An Effective Tool to Combat Employee Theft." *Journal of Business Ethics* 26: 89–100.

Harris, Diane K. 1999. "Elder Abuse in Nursing Homes: The Theft of Patients' Possessions." *Journal of Elder Abuse and Neglect* 10: 141–51.

Harris, Diana K., and Michael L. Benson. 2000. "Theft in Nursing Homes: An Overlooked Form of Elder Abuse." *Journal of Elder Abuse and Neglect* 11: 73–90.

Hawkins, Richard. 1984. "Employee Theft in the Restaurant Trade: Forms of Ripping off by Waiters at Work." *Deviant Behavior* 5: 47–69.

Hettinger, Edwin C. 1989. "Justifying Intellectual Property." *Philosophy and Public Affairs* 18: 31–52.

Hoffer, Erik. 2010. "The Mechanics of Supply Chain Theft." In *Supply Chain Security: International Practices and Innovations in Moving Goods Safely and Efficiently*, pp. 1–51, edited by Andrew R. Thomas. Santa Barbara, CA: ABC-CLIO.

Hollinger, Richard C. 1986. "Acts against the Workplace: Social Bonding and Employee Deviance." *Deviant Behavior* 7: 53–75.

Hollinger, Richard C., and John P. Clark. 1983. "Deterrence in the Workplace: Perceived Certainty, Perceived Severity, and Employee Theft." *Social Forces* 62: 398–418.

Hollinger, Richard C., Karen B. Slora, and William Terris. 1992. "Deviance in the Fast-food Restaurant: Correlates of Employee Theft, Altruism, and Counterproductivity." *Deviant Behavior* 13: 155–84.

Hollis-Peel, Meghan E., Danielle M. Reynald, Maud van Bavel, Henk Elffers, and Brandon C. Welsh. 2011. "Guardianship for Crime Prevention: A Critical Review of the Literature." *Crime, Law, and Social Change* 56: 53–70.

Holmes, Hayley. 2011. "Employee Theft in Restaurants: Perceptions about Theft-related Activities and Reporting Behaviors." Unpublished Ph.D. dissertation, Oklahoma State University, School of Restaurant and Hotel Administration.

Huiras, Jessica, Christopher Uggen, and Barbara McMorris. 2000. "Career Jobs, Survival Jobs, and Employee Deviance: A Social Investment Model of Workplace Misconduct." *Sociological Quarterly* 41: 245–63.

Jackson, Chris J., Stephen Z. Levine, Adrian Furnham, and Nicole Burr. 2002. "Predictors of Cheating Behavior at a University: A Lesson from the Psychology of Work." *Journal of Applied Social Psychology* 32: 1031–46.

Jones, David A. 2009. "Getting Even with One's Supervisor and One's Organization: Relationships among Types of Injustice, Desires for Revenge, and Counterproductive Work Behaviors." *Journal of Organizational Behavior* 30: 525–42.

Jones, John Walter, and Terris, William. 1985. "Screening Employment Applicants for Attitudes Towards Theft: Three Quasi-Experimental Studies." *International Journal of Management* 2: 62–75.

Kamp, John, and Paul Brooks. 1991. "Perceived Organizational Climate and Employee Counterproductivity." *Journal of Business and Psychology* 5: 447–58.

Kennedy, Jay P. 2014. "A View from the Top: Managers' Perspectives on the Problem of Employee Theft in Small Businesses." Unpublished Ph.D. dissertation, University of Cincinnati, School of Criminal Justice.

Krippel, Gregory L., Linda R. Henderson, Marvin A. Keene, Mariana Levi, and Kelly Converse. 2008. "Employee Theft and the Coastal South Carolina Hospitality Industry: Incidence, Detection, and Response (Survey Results 2000, 2005)." *Tourism and Hospitality Research* 8: 226–38.

Kristof, Amy L. 1996. "Person–Organization Fit: An Integrative Review of Its Conceptualizations, Measurement, and Implications." *Personnel Psychology* 49: 1–49.

Kulas, John T., Joanne E. McInnerney, Rachel Frautschy DeMuth, and Victoria Jadwinski. 2007. "Employee Satisfaction and Theft: Testing Climate Perceptions as a Mediator." *Journal of Psychology* 141: 389–402.

Lau, Vivian, Wing Tung Au, and Jane Ho. 2003. "A Qualitative and Quantitative Review of Antecedents of Counterproductive Behavior in Organizations." *Journal of Business and Psychology* 18: 73–99.

Lindbloom, Erik J., Julie Brandt, Landon D. Hough, and Susan E. Meadows. 2007. "Elder Mistreatment in the Nursing Home: A Systematic Review." *Journal of the American Medical Directors Association* 8: 610–16.

Lipman, Mark, and W. R. McGraw. 1988. "Employee Theft: A $40 Billion Industry." *Annals of the American Academy of Political and Social Science* 498: 51–59.

Locke, Edwin A. 1969. "What Is Job Satisfaction?" *Organizational Behavior and Human Performance* 4: 309–36.

Machin, Stephen, and Costas Meghir. 2004. "Crime and Economic Incentives." *Journal of Human Resources* 39: 958–79.

Madensen, Tamara D. and John E. Eck. 2008. "Violence in Bars: Exploring the Impact of Place Manager Decision-Making." *Crime Prevention and Community Safety* 10: 111–25.

Mars, Gerald. 1982. *Cheats at Work: An Anthropology of Workplace Crime*. London, UK: George Allen and Unwin.

Martin, Laura E., Meagan E. Brock, M. Ronald Buckley, and David J. Ketchen Jr. 2010. "Time Banditry: Examining the Purloining of Time in Organizations." *Human Resource Management Review* 20: 26–34.

Mazerolle, Lorraine Green, Colleen Kadleck, and Jan Roehl. 1998. "Controlling Drug and Disorder Problems: The Role of Place Managers." *Criminology* 36: 371–404.

McCrae, Robert R., and Paul T. Costa. 1987. "Validation of the Five-factor Model of Personality across Instruments and Observers." *Journal of Personality and Social Psychology* 52: 81–90.

McDaniel, Michael A., and John W. Jones. 1988. "Predicting Employee Theft: A Quantitative Review of the Validity of a Standardized Measure of Dishonesty." *Journal of Business and Psychology* 2: 327–45.

McNees, Patrick, Sharon W. Gilliam, John F. Schnelle, and Todd R. Risley. 1980. "Controlling Employee Theft through Time and Product Identification." *Journal of Organizational Behavior Management* 2: 113–19.

Merton, Robert K. 1938. "Social Structure and Anomie." *American Sociological Review* 3: 672–82.

Mishra, Birendra K., and Ashutosh Prasad. 2006. "Minimizing Retail Shrinkage Due to Employee Theft." *International Journal of Retail and Distribution Management* 34: 817–32.

Mount, Michael, Remus Ilies, and Erin Johnson. 2006. "Relationship of Personality Traits and Counterproductive Work Behaviors: The Mediating Effects of Job Satisfaction." *Personnel Psychology* 59: 591–622.

Murphy, Kevin R. 1993. *Honesty in the Workplace*. Belmont, CA: Thomson Brooks/Cole.

Mustaine, Elizabeth Ehrhardt, and Richard Tewksbury. 2002. "Workplace Theft: An Analysis of Student–Employee Offenders and Job Attributes." *American Journal of Criminal Justice* 27: 111–27.

Myers, Stacey. 1999. "Employee Theft Costs Billions." *Providence Business News* 14: 1–3.

Ng, Thomas W. H., and Daniel C. Feldman. 2009. "Re-examining the Relationship between Age and Voluntary Turnover." *Journal of Vocational Behavior* 74: 283–94.

Niehoff, Brian P., and Robert J. Paul. 2000. "Causes of Employee Theft and Strategies that HR Managers Can Use for Prevention." *Human Resource Management* 39: 51–64.

O'Bannon, R. Michael, Linda A. Goldfinger, and Gavin S. Appleby. 1989. *Honesty and Integrity Testing: A Practical Guide*. Atlanta, GA: Applied Information Resources.

Organ, Dennis W., and Mary Konovsky. 1989. "Cognitive versus Affective Determinants of Organizational Citizenship Behavior." *Journal of Applied Psychology* 74: 157–64.

Payne, Brian K., and Randy R. Gainey. 2004. "Ancillary Consequences of Employee Theft." *Journal of Criminal Justice* 32: 63–73.

Penney, Lisa M., and Paul E. Spector. 2002. "Narcissism and Counterproductive Work Behavior: Do Bigger Egos Mean Bigger Problems?" *International Journal of Selection and Assessment* 10: 126–34.

Perrone, Santina. 2000. "Crimes against Small Business in Australia: A Preliminary Analysis." *Trends and Issues in Criminal Justice*, No. 184. Canberra, AUS: Australian Institute of Criminology.

Pierce, Jon L., Tatiana Kostova, and Kurt T. Dirks. 2001. "Toward a Theory of Psychological Ownership in Organizations." *Academy of Management Review* 26: 298–310.

Pierce, Jon L., Linn Van Dyne, and Larry Cummings. 1992. "Psychological Ownership: A Conceptual and Operational Exploration." *Southern Management Association Proceedings* 203–11.

Poyner, Barry, and Barry Webb. 1992. "Reducing Theft from Shopping Bags in City Center Markets." In *Situational Crime Prevention: Successful Case Studies*, 2nd ed., pp. 99–107, edited by Ronald V. Clarke. Albany, NY: Harrow and Heston.

Rebellon, Cesar J., Nicole Leeper Piquero, Alex R. Piquero, and Sherod Thaxton. 2009. "Do Frustrated Economic Expectations and Objective Economic Inequality Promote Crime?" *European Journal of Criminology* 6: 47–71.

Reyns, Bradford W. 2013. "Online Routine and Identity Theft Victimization: Further Expanding Routine Activity Theory Beyond Direct-Contact Offenses." *Journal of Research in Crime and Delinquency* 50: 216–38.

Rickman, Neil, and Robert Witt. 2007. "The Determinants of Employee Crime in the UK." *Economica* 74: 161–75.

Rieke, Mark L., and Stephen J. Guastello. 1995. "Unresolved Issues in Honesty and Integrity Testing." *American Psychologist* 50: 458–59.

Roberts, Brent W., Peter D. Harms, Avshalom Caspi, and Terri E. Moffitt. 2007. "Predicting the Counterproductive Employee in a Child-to-Adult Prospective Study." *Journal of Applied Psychology* 92: 1427–36.

Robin, Gerald D. 1969. "Employees as Offenders." *Journal of Research in Crime and Delinquency* 6: 17–33.

Robinson, Sandra L., and Rebecca J. Bennett. 1995. "A Typology of Deviant Workplace Behaviors: A Multidimensional Scaling Study." *Academy of Management Journal* 38: 555–72.

Rosenbaum, Richard W. 1976. "Predictability of Employee Theft Using Weighted Application Blanks." *Journal of Applied Psychology* 61: 94–98.

Rynes, Sara L., Barry Gerhart, and Kathleen A. Minette. 2004. "The Importance of Pay in Employee Motivation: Discrepancies between What People Say and What They Do." *Human Resource Management* 43: 381–94.

Sackett, Paul R., Laura R. Burris, and Christine Callahan. 1989. "Integrity Testing for Personnel Selection: An Update." *Personnel Psychology* 42: 491–529.

Salgado, Jesus F. 1997. "The Five-Factor Model of Personality and Job Performance in the European Community." *Journal of Applied Psychology* 82: 30–43.

Sampson, Rana, John E. Eck, and Jessica Dunham. 2010. "Super Controllers and Crime Prevention: A Routine Activity Explanation of Crime Prevention Success and Failure." *Security Journal* 23: 37–51.

Shapiro, Susan P. 1990. "Collaring the Crime, not the Criminal: Reconsidering the Concept of White-Collar Crime." *American Sociological Review* 55: 346–65.

Sheppard, Blair H., and Dana M. Sherman. 1998. "The Grammars of Trust: A Model and General Implications." *Academy of Management Review* 23: 422–37.

Sherman, Lawrence W. 1995. "Hot Spots of Crime and Criminal Careers of Places." *Crime and Place* 4: 35–52.

Sherman, Lawrence W., Patrick R. Gartin, and Michael E. Buerger. 1989. "Hot Spots of Predatory Crime: Routine Activities and the Criminology of Place." *Criminology* 27: 27–56.

Sieh, Edward W. 1987. "Garment Workers: Perceptions of Inequity and Employee Theft." *British Journal of Criminology* 27: 174–90.

Slora, Karen B. 1989. "An Empirical Approach to Determining Employee Deviance Base Rates." *Journal of Business and Psychology* 4: 199–219.

Snider, Laureen. 2001. "Crimes against Capital: Discovering Theft of Time." *Social Justice* 28: 105–20.

Snider, Laureen. 2002. "Theft of Time: Disciplining through Science and Law." *Osgoode Hall Law Journal* 40: 89–110.

Spector, Paul E., and Suzy Fox. 2002. "An Emotion-centered Model of Voluntary Work Behavior: Some Parallels between Counterproductive Work Behavior and Organizational Citizenship Behavior." *Human Resource Management Review* 12: 269–92.

Sutherland, Edwin Hardin. 1983. *White Collar Crime: The Uncut Version*. Edited by Gilbert Geis and Colin Goff. New Haven, CT: Yale University Press.

Tang, Thomas Li-Ping, and Randy K. Chiu. 2003. "Income, Money Ethic, Pay Satisfaction, Commitment, and Unethical Behavior: Is the Love of Money the Root of Evil for Hong Kong Employees?" *Journal of Business Ethics* 46: 13–30.

Taylor, Natalie. 2002. "Under-Reporting of Crime against Small Businesses: Attitudes toward Police and Reporting Practices." *Policing and Society* 13: 79–89.

Taylor, Robert R., and Kristin O. Prien. 1998. "Preventing Employee Theft: A Behavioral Approach." *Business Perspectives* 10: 9–13.

Terris, William. 1985. *Employee Theft: Research, Theory, and Application*. Park Ridge, IL: London House Press.

Tillyer, Marie Skubak, and John E. Eck. 2011. "Getting a Handle on Crime: A Further Extension of Routine Activities Theory." *Security Journal* 24: 179–93.

U.S. Census. 2013. *Employer Firms, Employment, and Annual Payroll by Employment Size of Firm and Industry*. Economic Census. Washington, D.C.: U.S. Census Bureau.

Vandewalle, Don, Linn Van Dyne, and Tatiana Kostova. 1995. "Psychological Ownership: An Empirical Examination of Its Consequences." *Group and Organization Management* 20: 210–26.

Van Dyne, Linn, and Jon L. Pierce. 2004. "Psychological Ownership and Feelings of Possession: Three Field Studies Predicting Employee Attitudes and Organizational Citizenship Behavior." *Journal of Organizational Behavior* 25: 439–59.

Wanek, James E. 1999. "Integrity and Honesty Testing: What Do We Know? How Do We Use It?" *International Journal of Selection and Assessment* 7: 183–95.

Weber, James, Lance B. Kurke, and David W. Pentico. 2003. "Why Do Employees Steal? Assessing Differences in Ethical and Unethical Employee Behavior Using Ethical Work Climates." *Business and Society* 42: 359–80.

Willison, Robert. 2000. "Understanding and Addressing Criminal Opportunity: The Application of Situational Crime Prevention to IS Security." *Journal of Financial Crime* 7: 201–10.

Wimbush, James C., and Dan R. Dalton. 1997. "Base Rate for Employee Theft: Convergence of Multiple Methods." *Journal of Applied Psychology* 82: 756–63.

Zhao, H. A. O., Sandy J. Wayne, Brian C. Glibkowski, and Jesus Bravo. 2007. "The Impact of Psychological Contract Breach on Work-related Outcomes: A Meta-Analysis." *Personnel Psychology* 60: 647–80.

....

CHAPTER 21

CRIMINOGENIC ORGANIZATIONAL PROPERTIES AND DYNAMICS

....

WIM HUISMAN

POPULAR sentiment holds that criminals choose their actions, anticipating the benefits of crime. The concept of rational choice is also the foundation of several influential criminological theories, although the assumption that offenders rationally choose their actions is highly contested. Unlike perpetrators of street crime, white-collar offenders, acting in a business context, are generally seen as more purposive and rational. Although some white-collar crimes might be committed without clear criminal intent (Levi 2008), offenders are assumed to be sensitive to changes in their environment that influence costs and benefits, possibly more so than street criminals.

Yet, some of the most prominent or widely written-about endeavors in criminological theory have explained organizational offending with reference to organizational characteristics (Slapper and Tombs 1999, p. 111). Clinard and Quinney (1973) argued that white-collar crime can be divided into two types: (1) *corporate crime*: offenses committed by corporate officials for their corporation and the offenses of the corporation itself and (2) *occupational crime*: offenses committed by individuals in the course of their occupations and the offenses of employees against their employers. This distinction between the individual and the corporate offender paved the way for looking not only at individual but also at organizational dispositions for crime. In their landmark studies, Sutherland (1949) and Clinard and Yeager (1980) discovered that corporate offending was strongly concentrated in certain types of industries, and that a small percentage of violating corporations committed a highly disproportionate share of all offenses. These findings brought Clinard and Yeager to question whether "certain factors in the economic structure of corporations tend to produce violations" (Clinard and Yeager 1980, p. 127). Many white-collar crimes are committed in the context of an organization. Especially for the study of corporate crime, insights from organizational sciences were introduced in criminological frameworks. "Corporate crime is *organizational* crime, and its explanation calls for an *organizational* level of analysis. . . . The task for criminologists is to identify and examine the organizational factors that account for the illegal and/or socially harmful acts of individuals within corporations on behalf of the corporations themselves" (Kramer 1982, pp. 79–80).

This perspective became popular and has been applied to landmark cases of organizational deviance, such as the unsafe Ford Pinto and the explosion of the NASA Challenger space shuttle, which were initially officially framed as outcomes of rational choice, wherein managers weighed the costs and benefits of different decisions, such as changing product design in the case of the Pinto or delaying the shuttle's launch in the case of the Challenger (Lee and Ermann 2002; Vaughan 2002a). Organizational deviance was seen not as the outcome of individual choice, but as the result of organizational processes and characteristics. Organizational shortcomings were seen as a source of variation in the conduct of individual organizations. This perspective was used to analyze cases of corporate deviance and crime not only in the United States but also in Australia and Europe (Braithwaite 1989; van de Bunt and Huisman 2007).

Rational choice theory and organizational theory, however, need not be thought of as mutually exclusive approaches to explaining organizational offending. Contemporary scholars try to integrate organizational context and culture with a rational choice model of corporate offending (Paternoster and Simpson 1996; Simpson, Piquero, and Paternoster 2002; Simpson and Rorie 2011). Organizational characteristics and organizational processes influence individual decision making.

The aim of this chapter is to explore the organizational factors that have been identified to account for the illegal and/or socially harmful acts of individuals within corporations on behalf of the corporations themselves. Section I explores how organizational characteristics account for corporate crime. General organizational characteristics, as distinguished in the organizational sciences, include organizational strategy, organizational structure, and organizational culture. Sections II, III, and IV discuss theorizing and empirical research findings regarding each these organizational factors as explanatory variables for corporate crime. Section II discusses organizational strategy factors and shows how organizational goals and the means to achieve them can produce organizational offending. Section III discusses organizational structure as an explanation for organizational offending. Section IV discusses criminogenic organizational culture. In section V, the following conclusions will be reached:

- Organizational properties and dynamics are crucial in the process of understanding white-collar crime, as the defining characteristic of occupational crime is an organizational context.
- Organizational properties and dynamics are relevant to explain both corporate behavior and individual agency in the following ways: (1) corporate behavior is shaped by its organizational traits; (2) corporate noncompliance might be the result of organizational incompetence; (3) organizational factors influence individual choice of action of corporate officials.

- Criminological study has barely overcome the initial level of theorizing and case-study research. More and more rigorous empirical research is needed to test and refine theories of the relations between white-collar crime and organizational properties and dynamics.
- More needs to be learned about the interaction of organizational characteristics with environmental factors such as industry culture and regulation in producing white-collar crime.

I. Criminogenic Organizational Properties

This section explores how organizational characteristics account for corporate crime. It explores how organizational characteristics can explain organizational or individual behavior. Organizational characteristics can influence motivations and opportunities for corporate lawbreaking as well as for corporate regulatory compliance.

A. Organizational Actors

An important question in studying corporate crime is this: Whose crime is to be explained, that of individuals or that of the corporation as a whole? In organizational sciences, a corporation is seen as an independent actor manifesting behavior that can be scientifically studied. In this view, corporations have a "life" that is independent from the lives of the individuals who make up the organization (just like the life of the human body is independent from the lifespan of the individual cells that form the human body). Corporations can be described by their organizational characteristics: strategy, structure, and culture. Strategy refers to the goals of an organization and the means and processes by which it aims to achieve these goals. Structure refers to the way the corporation is organized and the division of tasks and responsibilities between the organizational members. Culture refers to the set of beliefs, values, and norms that represents the unique character of an organization and provides the context for action in it and by it (Morgan 2006). Thus, from the perspective of the field of organizational science, organizations can be viewed as capable of acting to achieve their goals and can therefore be held accountable for the consequences of their actions. This view is also in line with legal systems in which corporations are seen as legal entities that can be held (criminally) liable for their actions (Wells 2001).

In defining corporate crime, criminologists follow this approach: "Any act committed by corporations that is punished by the state, regardless of whether it is punished under administrative, civil, or criminal law" (Clinard and Yeager 1980, p. 16).

Sutherland, who coined the term "white-collar crime" with reference to the individual offender's wardrobe, wrote, "Corporations have committed crimes" and "the criminality of corporations" (Sutherland 1983, p. 217).

Following this view on organizations as actors, corporations could also have criminogenic dispositions (Gross 1978, 1980). These dispositions are related to specific features of the organizational strategy, structure, and culture. Just as individual behavior is a function of the interaction of individual dispositions and environmental conditions, it is the interaction between organizational traits and environmental factors that results in organizational behavior (Vaughan 2002b).

For criminologists, a central question is how these organizational characteristics can explain corporate behavior. The idea of organizations having criminogenic properties and dynamics seems to be widely accepted. "The sources and precise nature of what distinguishes the criminally predisposed is varied, and it differs for individuals and organizations. Organizations that are *predisposed* to exploit lure are distinguished by structural, cultural, or procedural characteristics that increase the odds that their personnel will recognize and exploit lure" (Shover and Hochstetler 2006, p. 51). Like the personality traits and disorders that predispose individual offenders to commit violent crimes or property crimes, organizations in this view also have characteristics that create a tendency to seek out or take advantage of criminal opportunities to advance organizational interests. Slapper and Tombs (1999) even speak of the "pathology of corporations."

B. Shaping Behavior of Agents

Critics of the organizational science view on organizations stress that in the end, the actions that are labeled as corporate crime are executed by people (Cressey, 1989). However, also in this view, organizational properties are relevant to explain the behavior of individual organizational agents. Agency theory helps to understand how the structural properties of agency relationships facilitate misconduct and confound systems of social control. In agency theory, organizations can be seen as principals and the employees as the agents carrying out the principals' actions. Principals have various mechanisms at their disposal to control agents pursuing the principals' interest: selection of agents, incentives such as rewards, limiting agents' discretion, and monitoring measures to oversee and evaluate the output of agent behavior. Therefore, it should not be surprising that incentives designed to align the interests of corporate executives and shareholders, such as giving the former stock options and equity ownership, might result in these executives contriving illicit schemes to inflate stock prices (Shapiro 2005). The particularities of organizations can greatly affect the distribution and availability of opportunities for illegality within an organization (Slapper and Tombs 1999, p. 127), since such corporations provide the motives, opportunity, and means for corporate crime by their own agents (Punch 2008, p. 119).

C. Organizational Incompetence to Comply

The previous two paragraphs discussed how organizational properties and dynamics influence the motivation of corporations and their members to violate the law. According to Coleman, an integrated theory on white-collar crime should contain two central explanatory variables: motivation and opportunity (Coleman 1995). Business regulations usually require corporations to take certain action to prevent harm and to protect the interests of consumers, employees, creditors, the environment, or the public at large (Clinard and Yeager 1980, pp. 113–6; Friedrichs 2010). But these corporations also have to be willing and able to comply. Besides illegal action (such as fraud), corporate crime can also be due to omission: corporations violate rules because they did not take the prescribed action, such as financial reporting, installing prescribed equipment, or avoiding environmental pollution (Huisman and Van Erp 2013). Therefore, motivation and opportunity are variables that can explain both corporate compliance and corporate noncompliance. Opportunities to comply might just as well be as relevant to understand corporate crime as opportunities to offend.

As such, motivation to comply is of secondary importance if a firm does not possess the capacity to comply (Parker and Nielsen 2011, pp. 14–15). Organizational factors not only provide the motive to violate, but organizational shortcomings can also limit the opportunity to comply. Although the importance of organizational factors in explaining corporate crime is widely acknowledged, organizational incompetence as a particular causative factor is often neglected. However, it is plausible that much corporate crime is the result of organizational shortcomings and incompetence. Researchers have failed to recognize the ubiquity and causal importance of incompetence in organizations, because a considerable amount of corporate crime research is based on serious but therefore also relatively exceptional cases, often occurring in large and well-known corporations (Shover and Hochstetler 2002). It is plausible that in these cases, lawbreaking is based on motivational decision making. The empirical reality, however, is that most—and less serious—offending takes place in the daily routines of small and medium-sized businesses (Vaughan 1999; van de Bunt and Huisman 2007). Routine nonconformity might not be the result of a decision. In fact, a company might not even be aware it is breaking the law.

Only a few scholars have discussed organizational incompetence as a cause of corporate crime. Stone (1975) studied a number of scandals of corporate lawbreaking from which he saw corporate mismanagement or what he called "dis-organization" as the main cause. Kagan and Scholz (1984) also presented organizational incompetence as an explanation for corporate noncompliance:

> Just as individuals can fail to learn and internalize social norms, business firms can fail to develop organizational units responsible for studying and implementing regulatory requirements, responsible for checking the purely profit-oriented impulses of other corporate units and the indifference of individual employees. Just as some individual criminals seem totally oblivious to the harm they inflict on others,

corporations with limited views of their social responsibility can fail to study or take seriously the human risks posed by their operations. Just as individuals may violate driving laws or miss tax-report deadlines through simple inattention or preoccupation with personal problems, corporations may allow established precautionary routines to slip gradually into disuse. (pp. 80–81)

Also, in his extensive case analysis, Punch (1996) attributed much of the corporate misconduct to "system failure": "Some companies set out to break the law; some end up breaking the law; and some cannot manage the messes they get into" (p. 216). Vaughan sees organizational deviance as an unanticipated suboptimal outcome and a routine byproduct of the system itself. She views the systematic production of organizational deviance as the inevitable outcome of all socially organized systems: "It follows that the same characteristics of a system that produce the bright side will regularly provoke the dark side from time to time." (Vaughan 1999, p. 274). Especially the use of technology—common in every contemporary corporation—and a certain level of uncertainty and imperfect knowledge that comes with technology produce unanticipated outcomes. This is even more likely when innovative, risky technology is involved (Vaughan 2002a). In a study on rule transgressions in the Dutch textile and waste-processing industries, Huisman (2001) found three varieties of incompetence: (1) the company is not aware of the rules and regulations; (2) the company knows the rules but does not know how to comply; and (3) the company knows both the rules and how to comply but lacks the means to do so. It is well established that regulated firms vary in relation to economic recourses, technical knowhow, knowledge about the law, managerial capacity and oversight, and other resources, and that these differences to a large degree explain differences in compliance behavior (Parker and Nielsen 2011, p. 15).

Again, it is not always clear whether corporate incompetence or inability to comply is the result of organizational dispositions or of individuals' shortcomings attributed to the organization: "Many violations of regulations are attributed to *organizational failure*—corporate managers fail to oversee subordinates adequately, to calculate risks intelligently, to establish organizational mechanisms that keep all operatives abreast of and attentive to the growing dictates of the law" (Kagan and Scholz 1984, p. 68). Also in the work of Punch organizational failures are—at least partly—deduced from factors at the managerial level, such as narcissism and cognitive dissonance (Punch 1996, 2008). Although in the organizational paradigm individual offenders are seen as psychologically normal (Braithwaite 1984), recent research reveals increasing evidence of particular personality traits and psychological disorders among white-collar offenders, just as research has documented among street offenders (Blickle et al. 2006; Bucy et al. 2008; Piquero, Schoepfer, and Langton 2010; Ragatz and Fremouw 2010). Biomedical research has even linked taking risks in the financial market to masculine hormones (Coates and Herbert 2010). One implication of this research is that it calls into question the rational choice perspective, because it implies that decisions are also influenced by personality factors and disorders rather than solely by the rational weighing of costs and benefits.

In the case of pure incompetence, the element of intent is missing. Although intent is not an element of common definitions of white-collar or corporate crime, unintentional offending might not *feel* like a crime, at least not to the larger audience. However, as many cases of incompetence to comply might be related to culpable negligence or managerial decisions not to invest in the competence to comply (in legal terms, dolus eventualis of conditional intent), the legal requirement of *mens rea* will usually still be met.

D. Conclusion

For several reasons, organizational properties and dynamics are important elements in the explanation of corporate crime. These reasons include the fact that corporate behavior is shaped by its organizational traits, corporate noncompliance might be the result of organizational incompetence, the individual behavior of employees is influenced by organizational factors, and organizational factors are influencing individual choice of action of corporate officials. In the next sections, we will look at the variables that explain variations in compliance and crime across organizations.

II. Organizational Strategy

In the traditional, functionalist approach in organizational sciences, organizations are viewed as "goal-seeking entities" (Kramer 1982, p. 81; Morgan 2006, p. 23). To achieve a goal, organizations—explicitly or implicitly—employ a strategy. An organizational strategy tells us what the goals of the organization are and by what means organizational members should attain them. A strategy is "the determination of the long term goals and objectives of an enterprise, and the adoption of courses of action and the allocation of resources necessary for carrying out these goals" (Chandler 1962, p. 13). Organizational strategy is relevant for understanding variations in compliance, because the corporate goal might contribute to the motivation to commit crime, and the allocation of the means influences the opportunity for corporate compliance and noncompliance.

A. Organizational Goals and Means

According to some scholars, the goal-seeking characteristic makes organizations inherently criminogenic (Gross 1980; Box 1983; Punch 1996). Goal seeking itself provides organizational members with a reason to violate the law in circumstances when this violation would be beneficial for achieving organizational goals. The motive is particularly powerful when corporate strategy puts a strong emphasis on attaining goals and little on using the appropriate means. In these circumstances, the risk exists that the ends will justify the means. "Some organizations seek profit, others seek survival, still others seek to fulfil government-imposed quotas, others seek to serve a body of professionals who run them, some seek to win wars, and some seek to serve a clientele. Whatever the goals might be, it is the emphasis on them that creates the trouble" (Gross 1978, p. 209). In this view, it is not so much the nature of the goals that is criminogenic, but rather the pressure to attain them.

Other scholars attribute risk to the goal of profit itself (Barnett 1981). Private for-profit firms, companies, and corporations differ from other types of organizations—such as governmental agencies—in that they have a profit motive. According to Kramer (1982), numerous studies have suggested that the "pressure for profits" is the single most compelling factor behind corporate crime (p. 81). Others have repeated this thesis (Slapper and Tombs 1999; Shover and Hochstetler 2006). Vold and Bernard (1986) stated that the question of "why white-collar offenders behave the way they do can be answered in a relatively straightforward way; they want to make a profit" (p. 338).

The assumption that the profit goal makes corporations inherently criminogenic—more than nonprofit organizations—might sound plausible, but it lacks a sound empirical basis. As will be discussed in the next section, many studies look at the *level of profit* to explain variations in compliance, but few compare profit and nonprofit organizations for this purpose. However, in support of the idea that profit motivates crime and noncompliance, a study of the nursing home industry in Australia by Jenkins and Braithwaite (1993) found substantially higher noncompliance with the law among for-profit nursing homes. A significant source of noncompliance is pressure on senior management from proprietors to reach financial goals that can only be attained by cutting corners on quality of care. This source of noncompliance is stronger among for-profit nursing homes than nonprofit nursing homes.

The idea of organizations having central and clear goals has been criticized. First, the corporation as a whole as well as its subsidiaries can try to achieve multiple goals, such as making a profit for shareholders *and* achieving a certain market position *and* achieving a reputation of corporate social responsibility. In the normative literature on business ethics and good corporate governance, the balance in corporate goals is often referred to as "PPP"—profit, people, planet. Second, a hierarchy of goals can be constructed. Some goals are conditional in relation to the others. The so-called systems approach assumes that organizations of any size are so complex that it is not possible to define a finite number of goals meaningfully. Instead, organizations develop the overall goal of survival (Jackson 2003). For business organizations, profit is a condition necessary to attaining that ultimate goal. There are, however, other—possibly competing—goals that are necessary for corporate survival. These goals can concern the health and safety of employees and the relationship with customers, local residents, and regulatory agencies.

Furthermore, a distinction can be made between short-term and long-term profit. A short-term focus can be due to limited cognitive competences and "greedy" personality of the leading managers, but it can also originate from deficits in decision-making procedures and certain features of corporate culture, as discussed in sections III and IV. To survive, corporations that try to maintain long-term profit will try to do so by being socially responsible and in compliance with governmental regulation.

The profit motive can also lead corporations to do more than is legally required—so-called over-compliance or beyond compliance (Pearce and Tombs 1997, p. 82). For example, Borck and Coglianese (2011) found that firms that join voluntary environmental self-regulation programs may increase sales to customers who value environmental protection, attract more productive employees, enhance the productivity of current employees who value working for an environmentally friendly firm, or win favorable treatment from the regulator in the enforcement of other mandatory environmental regulations. While regulatory scholars propose that affirmative motivations for compliance such as good intentions and a sense of obligation to comply can explain over-compliance (May 2004; Parker and Nielsen 2011), modern versions of rational choice theory incorporate individual moral views and cost–benefit calculations into managerial decision making regarding corporate crime (Paternoster and Simpson 1996; Gibbs 2012). Also, various studies find a positive correlation between profitability and corporate social responsibility (Orlitzky, Schmidt, and Rynes 2003). In this case, the corporate goals provide the motivation for compliance rather than for lawbreaking. So the goal-seeking character—if it even exists—might not be, in itself, motivation for noncompliance. It depends on the organizational strategy: the goals and the means and the balance between.

B. Strain

While detection rates and sanction severities regarding corporate violations are usually perceived as low, there is not much empirical evidence regarding the deterrent effect of law enforcement on corporate crime (Simpson et al. 2012) Therefore, if maximizing profits is the main motive behind corporate crime, we would expect many more violations than measurements of the prevalence of corporate crime are showing. Although such measurements suffer from many flaws (Friedrichs 2010, pp. 44–49), it seems fair to say that not all companies are violating the law when it seems profitable to do so. In many cases of corporate crime, the desire to minimize loss seems to be the dominant theme. Regulatory compliance and compliance management involve considerable sums of money. Thus, corporations need to have the financial resources to enable compliance; this might be difficult for companies facing bleak economic situations. Moreover, for such companies, saving costs of compliance or the opportunity for illegal earnings can prove to be very tempting. For these reasons, a corporation's economic situation is relevant for the degree of regulatory compliance.

The inability to achieve economic goals is one of the most frequent explanations given for white-collar crime, both theoretically (Box 1983; Vaughan 1983; Passas 1990; Braithwaite 1992; Agnew, Piquero, and Cullen 2009) and empirically (Clinard and Yeager 1980; Simpson 1986; Baucus and Near 1991; Jamieson 1994; Waring, Weisburd, and Chayet 1995; Simpson and Koper 1997; Simpson, Paternoster, and Piquero 1998; Wang and Holtfreter 2012; Ramdani and van Witteloostuijn 2013). In many texts, this causal factor is analyzed from the perspective of Merton's (1938) strain theory, which links crime to the strain generated from the blockage of success goals. Thus, assuming that the goals of corporations are profit maximization and market share expansion, the theory would predict that the motivation to engage in illegal behavior increases when these goals are more difficult to achieve by using legal means. Then, corporations opt for illegitimate means to achieve the goals set by the capitalist economy.

Most studies find a positive relation between economic strain and the occurrence of corporate crime. However, the available studies use a number of different ways to conceptualize and measure economic strain. First, studies look at different types and specificities of offenses. Simpson (1986), for example, found that economic strain was associated with higher levels of anticompetitive behavior. Yet when she distinguished anticompetitive acts by type, only some were linked to economic strain.

Second, the central elements of Merton's strain formula—goals and means—are operationalized in different ways. Benson and Simpson (2009, p. 60) assumed that the goal of profit produces more strain than other types of organizational goals. Results also vary by how profits are measured (e.g., stockholders' equity, return on sales, return on assets) (Simpson and Rorie 2011). According to Agnew, Piquero, and Cullen (2009, p. 39), financial stress is a rough surrogate for goal blockage. Agnew, Piquero, and Cullen say that studies have found that corporate crime is more common among companies with relatively low profits, companies with declining profits, companies in depressed industries, and companies suffering from other types of financial problems. Further, they argued that organizational crime may result not only from the inability to satisfy economic goals but also from the experience or threat of economic problems (p. 43). This shows that there are various types of strains, such as the fear of not being able to reach the goals and the fear of losing what has already been achieved. Also, there might be various variables producing different levels of strain: the magnitude of the gap between expected goals and actual achievement, the level of pressure put on organizational agents to achieve goals, and the availability of legitimate and illegitimate alternatives.

Building upon Merton's (1938) strain theory, Cloward and Ohlin (1960) argued that strained individuals are unlikely to engage in crime unless illegitimate opportunities are available. Also for corporations, studies have found that opportunities must be available for strained corporations to commit corporate crime (Simpson and Koper 1992; Vaughan 2002b). At the industry level, these opportunities are often conceptualized by industry-level prevalence of violations; at the organizational level, opportunities are conceptualized by size as a proxy for organizational complexity and by a criminogenic corporate culture in which offending to attain goals is accepted (Wang and Holtfreter 2012).

Third, strain as a cause of crime may be less about the factual impossibility of reaching goals than the *perception* of having to meet certain goals and the *perception* of legitimate means being insufficient—a psychological anomie (Cohen 1995). Besides being the result of external factors dictating goals and distributing means, strain could also be self-inflicted. Many case studies give examples of overly ambitious CEOs, such as in the case of large-scale accounting fraud at the grocery giant Ahold, dubbed by *The New York Times* and *The Economist* as "Europe's Enron" (Leng 2009, p. 31). Because Ahold's leaders assumed that globalization would leave room for only a few big players in the market, they set the ambiguous target of an annual increase of turnover of 15 percent, which evidently became attainable only by cooking the books (van de Bunt and Huisman 2007).

Fourth, studies locate strain as a factor contributing to crime at various levels (at the industry, the organizational, or the individual level). At the industry level, Clinard and Yeager (1980) found that the goal of financial success and profit maximization is more heavily emphasized in some industries, such as oil, automobile, and pharmaceutical industries, than in others. Industry-level strain can also be operationalized in different ways, producing different outcomes. Wang and Holtfreter (2012) assumed that operating in a munificent environment and a rapidly growing industry could potentially lessen performance pressure on a failing corporation, whereas operating in a scarce environment and a declining industry could increase the pressure. However, they found that corporations in rapidly growing industries have higher violation rates than corporations in financially depressed industries. Yet they also found that corporation- and industry-level financial strains will interact to produce greater effects on corporate crime: it appears that in industries that experience more strain, financially strained corporations have higher violation rates than their counterparts in industries that experience less strain. Baucus and Near (1991) also found that large firms operating in dynamic, munificent environments were the most likely of the firms studied to behave illegally. Wang and Holtfreter argued that fast-growing industries might be highly competitive. In these industries where markets are expanding and there is potential for corporations' growth, some violations might be considered as competitive strategies for corporations to survive and prosper. Following the same logic, Ramdani and van Witteloostuijn (2013) and Martin et al. (2007) found a positive relationship between competitive intensity and firm bribery.

At the organizational level, organizational strain can be a motive for corporate crime when legitimate means are insufficient to achieve corporate goals (Passas 1990), as various studies have found (Simpson and Koper 1997). However, strain can be experienced on the various hierarchical levels within the organization: by top management when it sets overly ambitious goals and by the shop floor when standard operating procedures are insufficient. The latter concept is best illustrated by the classic case of "the tap": a special tool illegally used for assembling aircraft as a last resort to meet production targets (Bensman and Gerver 1963). Several studies show that strain is often experienced at the middle-management level, when middle managers are responsible for executing the ambitious targets set by top management while not being provided with the appropriate means of so doing (Clinard 1983; Dean, Beggs, and Keane 2010). Besides vertical strain, horizontal strain might be due to the competition between subunits regarding scarce resources in the achievement of common corporate goals. Conceivably, this might even be a deliberate strategy of top management: By giving various subunits similar targets but limited resources, top management organizes subunit competition to achieve corporate goals (Breton and Wintrobe 1986).

In cases of organizational crime, the experience of organizational and individual strain may go hand in hand: when personal interests are linked to achieving corporate goals (e.g., substantial bonuses that are linked to reaching ambitious sales targets). Further, it is possible that some individuals identify so closely with the corporations in which they work that they vicariously experience the strains of the corporation (Agnew, Piquero, and Cullen 2009, p. 48). However, on the individual level, strain is usually operationalized as a fear of "falling" or losing what has already been gained. In their study on the criminal career patterns of 1,100 convicted white-collar criminals, Weisburd and Waring (2001) labeled a group of low-frequency offenders as "crisis responders," engaging in criminality in response to some type of perceived crisis in their professional or personal lives. Coleman (1987) suggested that the fear of failure is the inevitable correlate of the demand for success and that it is a strong motivator in committing crime to prevent anticipatory loss. Wheeler (1992) argued that "it should be among those in fear of falling rather than those holding steady or on the rise, where a higher proportion of the white-collar offenders may be found" (p. 117).

The fear-of-falling motivation should give us reason to reconsider the rational choice perspective. For white-collar offenders, the avoidance of a loss is a potential benefit from crime, thus making this choice more "rational." But the rational choice perspective as traditionally discussed often fails to account for this possibility. Rather, "benefits" are typically conceptualized as gains. There is considerable psychological research, however, demonstrating that avoiding loss is a more powerful motivator than reaping a gain (Kahnman and Tversky 1991, 2000). Beside individual case studies, in criminological research on corporate crime, the fear-of-falling hypothesis has hardly been empirically tested. In a first attempt to measure empirically the fear of falling, Piquero (2012) found that the effect of fear of falling is significant, but it exerts a negative—not the expected positive—effect on intentions to engage in white-collar crime.

III. Organizational Structure

According to *Businessdictionary.com*, organizational structure is "The framework, typically hierarchical, within which an organization arranges its lines of authority and communications, and allocates rights and duties. Organizational structure determines the manner and extent to which roles, power, and responsibilities are delegated, controlled, and coordinated, and how information flows between levels of management." Organizational structure can be a relevant variable in the causation of corporate crime: "There is no doubt that corporate crime needs to be partially understood with respect to the organizational characteristics of different corporations, and any full-blown theory of corporate crime needs to take account of various aspects of organizational form and structure" (Slapper and Tombs 1999, p. 126). Yet, not many criminological theories on corporate crime include organizational structure, at least not directly, since structure is related to common explanatory factors for corporate crime such as the size and complexity of corporations; the level of autonomy of subsidiaries and internal competition; the allocation of accountability; the structure of decision-making processes and the lines of internal control; and the organization of compliance management. These variables will be discussed below.

A. Size and Complexity

In many studies, the size of the organization, measured as the number of employees, is seen as a relevant variable to explain the level of organizational compliance. However, it is not clear how size is correlated to regulatory compliance and violation. Both theoretical assumptions and research findings are contradictory. On one hand, it is assumed that compliance is positively correlated to organizational size. Smaller firms might lack the expertise to comply with the great amount of business regulation. Large firms have the resources to invest in specialized compliance officers and departments and equipment to ensure compliance. On the other hand, it is assumed that compliance is negatively correlated to organizational size. The compliance issues of smaller firms might be less complex and easier to deal with. Nevertheless, the business processes of large firms might be more complex and more difficult to manage. Also, larger firms could attract more attention from various regulatory agencies, but there might also be a countervailing effect that would reduce their discovery in such activities or minimize their prosecution if discovered (Dalton and Kesner 1988).

In this sense, organizational complexity but not size is the relevant variable for understanding variation in compliance. Vaughan (2002b) distinguished formal organizations, which have a formalized division of labor and hierarchy, and complex organizations, which have more layers of hierarchy, more specialized division of labor, greater degrees of formalization, geographic dispersion, and so forth. Structural complexity is more specifically defined as the "degree of spread and segmentation in an organization's structure" (McKendall and Wagner 1997, p. 627). McKendall and Wagner saw at least three dimensions of complexity or differentiation: vertical, horizontal, and spatial. Vertical differentiation refers to layers of hierarchy and supervision. Horizontal complexity increases with the number of interdependent subunits working on pieces of a larger and more complex task. Finally, organizations that have many operating sites in geographically dispersed locations have a high degree of spatial differentiation (McKendall and Wagner 1997; Dugan and Gibbs 2009).

For a number of reasons, organizational complexity might be positively correlated to regulatory noncompliance. Complex organizations might be more difficult to control and might provide more opportunities for subsidiaries to use illegal means to achieve goals. Vertical differentiation might diffuse responsibility for regulatory compliance and therefore also for corporate crimes. Horizontal differentiation might increase subsidiaries' competition for scarce resources and create strain. Spatial differentiation might hinder internal control on regulatory compliance. These elements will be elaborated upon below.

Wang and Holtfreter (2012) remarked that previous studies used size and diversification as proxies for organizational complexity and assessed their direct effects on corporate crime. However, they claimed that the extant studies had not considered the conditioning effects of size and diversification. Given the argument that an organization's social status is positively associated with organizational size (Stinchcombe 1965), and that the central goal of people in capitalistic societies is to accumulate wealth and to achieve higher social status (Coleman 1987), Ramdani and van Witteloostuijn (2013) developed the hypothesis that large organizations are less motivated to engage in illegal activities than small ones because large organizations already enjoy a social status that is far above par. Accordingly, the marginal incentives of an organization to engage in crime diminish with organizational size.

As mentioned, empirical research findings cannot confirm or reject the various theoretical assumptions about the relation between organizational size and regulatory compliance. Already in 1982, Finney and Lesieur, having reviewed the limited evidence regarding organizational size and illegal activity, concluded that "although evidence is mixed, 'big' does not necessarily mean 'bad' when it comes to corporate crime" (p. 272). Later, Simpson and Rorie (2009) claimed that the most consistent finding across studies is a positive relationship between firm size and noncompliance. Simpson (1986) found such a relationship, and Dalton and Kesner (1988) found that larger firms are far more likely to engage in illegal behavior and more likely to be multiple violators than their smaller counterparts. Tillman and Pontell (1995) also found that corporate crime is more often found in larger organizations, organizations that are growing quickly, and organizations with complex ownership structures. In contrast, Borck and Coglianese (2011) found that larger firms are more likely to participate in voluntary compliance programs and more often go beyond compliance. Borck and Coglianese assumed that larger companies are more visible and connected to the public and might therefore face greater pressure from the public to be good environmental stewards. Another interpretation is that larger firms might simply have more resources to devote to compliance programs (p. 159). Parker and Nielsen (2009) found that larger companies are better able to implement compliance systems, which then increase compliance-promoting practices by business management. Wang and Holtfreter (2012) found no statistically significant interaction between any strain measure and size. Ramdani and van Witteloostuijn (2013) found that the effect of competitive intensity on firm bribery is smaller for larger organizational size, indicating that larger enterprises are better equipped to neutralize competitive pressures.

B. Autonomy and Responsibility

The founding fathers of organizational science—such as Taylor (1911), Fayol (1916), and Weber (1922)—saw the first bureaucratic type of structure as ideal for modern corporations. Until the mid-20th century, larger companies generally followed this functional form, which resembles a pyramid with integrated levels of management (Chandler 1962). In a centralized structure, decision-making power is concentrated in the top layer of management, and tight control is exercised over departments and divisions. Activities are divided into specialized departments with unique functions, but department heads report to a chief coordinator who continuously reconciles the subgoals of each department (Caves 1980). Efficiency is achieved by a fixed division of tasks and a limited autonomy of the execution of these tasks, while being guided by hierarchical supervisions and detailed rules and regulations.

This organizational structure has been linked to the causation of organizational crime. The rigidity of bureaucratic structures might create strains at the middle-management level, when top managers put high pressure on attaining set goals while limiting the resources to achieve these goals (Clinard 1983). Furthermore, the long lines between the shop floor ("What they don't know won't hurt them") and executive offices ("We don't want to know, as long they get it done") might provide the opportunity to diffuse responsibilities for rule breaking. Multiple hierarchical levels and divisionalized structures can create barriers to the discovery or reporting of illegal activity (Szwajkowski 1985; Dugan and Gibbs 2009). According to Kramer (1984), a potential result is "a de facto immunity . . . at least for highly placed officers who can stay a safe distance from criminal acts performed lower in the corporate hierarchy" (p. 70).

With growth and globalization in the second half of the 20th century, multinational corporations faced higher degrees of external and internal uncertainty. Therefore, many corporations shifted to a more decentralized, independent structure referred to as the corporate multidivisional form (Chandler 1962; Dugan and Gibbs 2009). In a decentralized structure, decision-making power is distributed, and the departments and divisions have varying degrees of autonomy. In these "loosely-coupled systems," the number of hierarchical levels is decreased and subunits are permitted more autonomy (Keane 1995).

Loose coupling might enable corporations to respond better to changes in the regulatory environment—and therefore might be positively related to corporate compliance (Vaughan 1999). Nevertheless, Keane (1995) and Tombs (1995) identified several dysfunctions of loose coupling that may be connected to illegal behavior. First, a parent company might not be attentive to disreputable practices of distant subsidiaries. According to Tombs, decentralization and autonomy create an institutionalized "willful blindness" and mobilize techniques of distancing and neutralization, making corporate crimes more possible and more likely (Tombs 1995, p. 141). Second, a very loosely coupled system might lack internal control, which can leave it vulnerable to illegal behavior. Freedom and distraction can provide an opportunity for abuse and the avoidance of detection. Third, this is especially so when compliance monitoring departments become separated from the decentralized subsidiaries. Autonomy minimizes their clout. Fourth, decoupling may be used to distance or even outsource business activities that have a high(er) risk of noncompliance. Thus, organizational structure can deny liability and evade responsibility when noncompliance is detected. Subcontracting partners might even be used to designate a scapegoat "when shit hits the fan" (Keane 1995).

C. Decision-Making Structures and Processes

Organizational structure also influences decision-making processes, of which law-breaking could be the outcome. The many hierarchical layers in a bureaucratic structure might lead to information loss as commands and data are communicated up and down the hierarchy. This can prevent crucial information from reaching the top—strategic decision-making—level. In a loosely coupled structure, top management might be isolated from critical information from autonomies subsidiaries. In the revisionist account of the Ford Pinto scandal, Lee and Ermann (2002) referred to the "loosely allied decision making units" (p. 280). In both cases, nonoptimal processes and outcomes are the result. Violation might be a deliberate choice based on invalid information about costs and benefits of compliance and noncompliance alternatives. However, noncompliance might also be the unanticipated outcome of flawed decision-making processes.

According to Simpson et al. (2002), firm size and complexity affect the rationality in strategic decision making. "As firms grow, they shift into a planning mode which requires a more detailed strategic process—more data, more analysis, and strategizing. Similarly, as firms stop growing, comprehensiveness decreases" (p. 31). Nonstrategic, day-to-day routine decisions are facilitated by the corporate structure. Along the lines of the division of tasks, these decision types are guided formally by so-called standard operation procedures (SOPs). These SOPs are rational for preventing time-consuming decision-making processes over routine activities, but they might be a poor fit for new problems, and economically irrational behavior may result. When environmental conditions change—such as regulatory requirements over business practices—adjustment of the SOPs might be constrained by organizational structure, a phenomenon termed by Simpson et al. (2002) as "creeping rationality" (p. 32). This creeping rationality might also contribute to the normalization of routine nonconformity (Vaughan 1999). It produces a decision framework in which "risky" decisions fall within the parameters of acceptable and normative behavior. Then, illegality and the thought that what one is doing is breaking the law are "not even on the radar screen" (Simpson et al. 2002, p. 29).

D. Internal Oversight

Organizational structure is also relevant for understanding the organization and functioning of internal control regarding regulatory compliance. In most modern corporations, compliance-management systems have been introduced to serve this purpose. These systems consist of structured measures aimed at ensuring more systematic compliance with regulations (Parker and Gilad 2011). Compliance officers—ranging from single individuals to whole departments—are appointed to monitor the execution of these systems. These officers translate social demands and regulatory obligations into internal instructions and monitor observance of these corporate regulations.

One might expect a positive effective of compliance-management systems on actual organizational compliance, as this is the reason they are put in place. Yet, compliance programs might be more cosmetic than real, thus serving a public relations function (Friedrichs 2010, p. 304). In some cases, they might actually increase the levels of or facilitate corporate offenses, by regulatory capture or keeping up appearances. Not much research has been done on the actual impact that compliance programs have on the level of compliance and on what determines the effectiveness of the programs. Below, the available studies are summarized.

Although "compliance" is seen as a fairly novel area for corporate attention, especially after the accounting fraud cases in the 1990s and the credit crunch in the first decade of the 21st century, it was already one of the most important variables in explaining differences in safety-regulation compliance in Braithwaite's (1985) study in the coal-mining industry. In a large survey of 999 large Australian businesses about their implementation of competition and consumer protection law compliance systems, Parker and Nielsen (2009) found that at least some elements of compliance systems can translate into good management of compliance in practice; however, management commitment to compliance values, managerial oversight and planning, and organizational resources are just as important.

Two studies on the waste-processing industry in the Netherlands found that the effectiveness of compliance officers very much depends on their formal and informal positions (Huisman 2001; van Wingerde 2012). Their effectiveness increases when they operate more independently from the business line and when they enjoy a certain level of organizational clout. Friedrichs (2010) commented that the effectiveness of corporate compliance officers is compromised to the extent that they report to the CEO, and not the corporate board, and that they are dependent upon the CEO for the conditions of their employment (p. 305).

IV. Organizational Culture

As mentioned in the introduction, the public framing of the corporate crime phenomenon in the financial industry by parliamentary and congressional committees and the media is that this is due to a criminogenic corporate culture of individual banks and the financial industry as a whole. It is this culture that makes bankers take excessive risks, rip off their clients, facilitate money laundering, and fix interest rates. Also in white-collar criminology, strong explanatory value is attributed to organizational culture. Organizational culture, however, is very difficult to define, operationalize, and measure. Finding a causal relationship with corporate crime is therefore even more difficult.

A. Organizational Culture

Since the 1980s, companies and other organizations are perceived as communities having their own, distinctive culture (Schein 1992). Schein (1992) defined corporate culture as "A pattern of shared basic assumptions that the group learned as it solves its problems of external adaptation and internal integration, that has worked well enough to be considered valid and, therefore, to be taught to new members as the correct way to perceive, think and feel in relation to those problems" (p. 12). Organizational culture has also been typified as the collective programming of the organizational members. Culture is the "software" that "programs" their behavior (Hofstede 1980). Behavior expresses values and norms, expectations, attitudes, beliefs, and ideas that are shared by the majority of the members of the organization. Together this is referred to as the organizational culture.

Organizational culture has two functions: standardization of problem solutions and reduction of uncertainty. Organizational culture can lead to standardization when employees and managers have programmed patterns of conduct and problem solving at their disposal. Organizational culture dictates how to perceive certain situations and how employees should (re)act. Organizational culture leads to the reduction of uncertainty through a referential framework by which organizational members can assess new situations and by which they can design their course of action (Schein 1992).

It is generally assumed that corporate leaders play a crucial role in the formation of the organizational culture. Through various mechanisms, they have a strong influence on the corporate culture: the issues that capture the attention of leaders (what is criticized, praised, or asked about), the way they respond to crisis (as crisis tests what the leader values and brings these values to the surface), their role modeling and signaling behavior (action speaks louder than words), the allocation of rewards (rewarding is a powerful instrument to communicate desired behavior), and the criteria they use for selection and dismissal (same idea: showing what is important and what is not) (Schein 1992). In management-speak, this collection of mechanisms is generally referred to as "the tone at the top."

Large, complex organizations might accommodate multiple and perhaps even contradictory cultures. Shover and Hochstetler (2002) pointed out the existence of inter- and intra-organizational cultures. Relatively autonomous—loosely coupled—subunits might have cultures that differ considerably from that of the parent company (Keane 1995).

Although a strong influence on organizational members' agency is attributed to culture and it is seen as an important variable in explaining organizational success or failure, organizational culture is not a very tangible concept. While many definitions have been formulated, most are difficult to operationalize and to measure. Nevertheless, several models have been developed to diagnose organizational culture, such as by Quinn (1988) and Schein (1992).

B. Organizational Ethical Culture

While a correlation between organizational culture in general and corporate crime is often assumed, the concept of the organizational ethical culture seems especially relevant to the study of lawbreaking, as most lawbreaking will be viewed as unethical. The concept of organizational ethical culture refers to the shared moral beliefs of organizational members. Organizational ethical culture is a specific dimension of organizational culture that describes organizational ethics and predicts organizational ethical behavior (Key 1999). This suggests a continuum, with on the one side corporations with highly ethical cultures and on the other side corporations with unethical cultures. Especially on the latter side, corporate crime could be expected.

Closely related to organizational ethical culture is the concept of ethical climate. Ethical climate is usually defined as those aspects that determine what constitutes ethical conduct (Victor and Cullen 1988). Ethical culture is usually defined as those aspects that stimulate ethical conduct (Kaptein 2008a). Nevertheless, the concepts are often used as synonyms. Several instruments have been developed to measure ethical climates and ethical cultures in organizations. Victor and Cullen (1988) developed the Ethical Climate Questionnaire for assessing the ethical climate, and Kaptein (2008a) developed the Corporate Ethical Virtues Model for measuring organizational ethical culture. Both models have been tested and validated. Less studied is the impact of ethical climate and ethical culture and their dimensions on different types of ethical and unethical conduct.

C. Organizational Culture and Corporate Crime

The instruments discussed above measure attitudes, not conduct. A general assumption in studies on ethical culture is that ethical culture has an effect on ethical conduct by the organization and its members. Especially in companies with an unethical culture, unethical conduct would be prevalent. This could result in rule breaking and criminality. Contrastingly, a strong ethical culture would create a moral threshold for managers and employees and prevent them from getting involved in law violation and other unethical conduct. This assumed relation between ethical culture and ethical conduct has been tested by using the Corporate Ethical Virtues Model (Kaptein 2008b, 2010, 2011). Most dimensions of this model are strongly related to self-reported unethical conduct.

The results of empirical studies in the field of business ethics confirm criminological theorizing on the relation between corporate culture and crime. It is possibly not a coincidence, therefore, that the founding father of white-collar crime, Edwin Sutherland, also developed the differential association theory on crime, which views criminal behavior as a result of social learning processes. Following up on this, Coleman (1995) described the processes of normalization of deviance within organizations that create a moral numbness of employees to the unethical aspects or harmful consequences of their actions when they become part of daily routines. According to subculture theory, in a social group a culture can evolve in which norms and values contradict societal norms and values that are laid down in the law. Due to their isolation, subcultures within corporations can define certain actions as acceptable or even desirable, while these actions are condemned by society as a whole. Moreover, following the theory of neutralization techniques, organizational cultures could transmit rule transgression by normalizing lawbreaking by neutralization and rationalization (Shover and Hochstetler 2002).

However, empirical research on the causal relationship between organizational culture and corporate crime in criminology is not particularly strong. Often, research is based on case studies that post hoc reconstruct a corporate culture and thereafter ascribe criminal conduct. Furthermore, the cases often involve high-profile or unusually harmful crimes and the organizations in which they occurred are singled out repeatedly, in the process becoming "landmark narratives" of scholarship on organizational crime (Shover and Hochstetler 2002, p. 9). A good example is the case of Enron, where various post hoc analyses show how Enron executives molded a corporate culture of individualism, competition, and aggressive underhand tactics that resulted in unethical behavior, fraud, and, finally, the collapse of the company (Sims and Brinkman 2003; Knottnerus et al. 2006). Another example is the largest fraud case in the Netherlands, which occurred in the real-estate industry (van de Bunt et al. 2011). The widespread corruption in this case was explained by the culture of the real-estate business in the Netherlands ("a culture of reciprocity"), the culture at the corporation where the suspects were employed ("a culture in which the goal of rapid growth justifies the means"), and the culture of the department of which the prime suspect was director ("a culture of non-transparency and fear"). In retrospect, culture seems to explain everything— and therefore it explains nothing.

So, although criminological theorizing attributes a strong explanatory value to the concept of organizational culture, the empirical proof for this alleged relationship is rather weak. More state-of-the-art research is currently being conducted by business ethics scholar Kaptein. In testing his Corporate Ethical Virtues Model Kaptein has found evidence for a strong correlation between organizational ethical culture and observed (2008b) and self-reported (2010) rule breaking.

V. CONCLUSION

Organizational properties and dynamics are crucial in understanding white-collar crime, given the central role of organizational context in occupational crimes. In all theoretical perspectives, organizational characteristics are important variables for explaining white-collar crime.

Considering the early recognition of the importance of organizational properties and characteristics in white-collar crime scholarship, it is striking that criminological study has barely overcome the initial level of theorizing and case-study research. More and more rigorous empirical research is needed to test and refine theories of the relations between white-collar crime and organizational properties and dynamics. For this advancement, new methodologies and better research designs have to be introduced. White-collar criminologists do not necessarily have to develop these themselves; novel theories and cutting-edge methodologies from mainstream criminology can be tested for their applicability in studying white-collar crime. For instance, as organizational dynamics produce routine nonconformity in SOPs (Vaughan 1999), criminological routine activities theory might be well suited for studying white-collar crime, as was already noted by Felson and Boba (2010) and Benson, Madensen, and Eck (2009).

Also, these methodologies will need better data. Qualitative research will always be needed to get a good understanding of organizational crime. Yet, because of the lack of quantitative data, most empirical research is based on the analysis of probably atypical cases (Shover and Hochstetler 2002). Obtaining longitudinal data on organizational characteristics and organizational lawbreaking might be challenging, but it is not impossible (Gibbs and Simpson 2009).

Furthermore, the relationship between white-collar crime and organizational characteristics is often portrayed as rather static: a company has a certain culture that contributed to the criminal conduct occurring at that company. However, longitudinal studies should give a more dynamic perspective on the development and processes of the interaction between organizational variables and criminal conduct. For this, random- and fixed-effects models should be combined. The random-effects model estimates the effect of both time-stable and time-varying variables. Although such studies should take into account a number of time-stable differences between organizations that are likely to be related to crime, the estimated effect of time-varying variables in these kinds of analyses should be interpreted cautiously, as bias resulting from unobserved variables could be at play. For that reason, a fixed-effects model should be used as well. A fixed-effects model examines only within-organizational change and controls for all stable organizational characteristics, measured or unmeasured, as long as those characteristics do not change over time. A disadvantage of the fixed-effects model is that the effect of stable background characteristics cannot be estimated, because the model controls for these characteristics (Verbruggen, Blokland, and van der Geest 2012).

Also, much more is to be learned from other scientific disciplines, such as economics, business administration, and organizational psychology. For instance, life-course criminology could be connected to organizational life-cycle models (Lester, Parnell, and Carraher 2003) to study how "organizational" life events influence organizational criminal careers and vice versa. In white-collar crime academia, there is the occasional use of theoretical models, methodologies, or results from such disciplines, as was also done in this paper. However, a systematic meta-analytic review of research in organizational sciences for its relevance for the study of white-collar crime would be better (Lipsey and Wilson 2001).

Finally, more is to be learned about the interaction of organizational characteristics with environmental factors such as industry culture and regulation in producing white-collar crime. Again, this is a topic of much theorizing, while rigorous empirical study surpassing the occasional case study is underdeveloped. Parker and Nielsen (2011) distinguished two methodological approaches. The first "objectivist" approach is straightforward testing of theories that identify organizational characteristics and external factors that are associated with (non)compliance as a dependent variable. The second "interpretive" approach aims at the social construction of the very notions of compliance and noncompliance. Looking at environmental factors is not only relevant for the objectivist study of regulatory noncompliance but is also important for understanding the interactive processes between regulator and regulated and the way organizational capacities are used to influence the meaning and definition of compliance, noncompliance, and crime (Vaughan 1999; Edelman and Talesh 2011).

REFERENCES

Agnew, Robert, Nicole Leeper Piquero, and Francis T. Cullen. 2009. "General Strain Theory and White-Collar Crime." In *The Criminology of White-Collar Crime*, pp. 35–60, edited by David Weisburd and Sally Simpson. New York: Springer.

Barnett, Harold C. 1981. "Corporate Capitalism, Corporate Crime." *Crime and Delinquency* 27: 4–23.

Baucus, Melissa S., and Janet P. Near. 1991. "Can Illegal Corporate Behavior Be Predicted? An Event History Analysis." *Academy of Management Journal* 34: 9–36.

Bensman, Joseph, and Israel Gerver. 1963. "Crime and Punishment in the Factory: The Function of Deviancy in Maintaining the Social System." *American Sociological Review* 28: 588–98.

Benson, Michael L., Tamara D. Madensen, and John E. Eck. 2009. "White-Collar Crime from an Opportunity Perspective." In *The Criminology of White-Collar Crime*, pp. 175–93, edited by Sally S. Simpson and David Weisburd. New York: Springer.

Benson, Michael L., and. Sally S. Simpson. 2009. *White-Collar Crime: An Opportunity Perspective*. New York: Routledge.

Blickle, Gerhard, Alexander Schlegel, Pantaleon Fassbender, and Uwe Klein. 2006. "Some Personality Correlates of Business White-Collar Crime." *Applied Psychology: An International Review* 55: 220–33.

Borck, Jonathan C., and Cary Coglianese. 2011. "Beyond Compliance: Explaining Business Participation in Voluntary Environmental Programs." In *Explaining Compliance: Business Response to Regulation*, pp. 139–69, edited by Christine Parker and Vibeke Lehmann Nielsen. Cheltenham, UK: Edward Elgar Publishers.

Box, Steven. 1983. *Power, Crime, and Mystification*. London, UK: Tavistock.

Braithwaite, John. 1984. *Corporate Crime in the Pharmaceutical Industry*. London: Routledge and Kegan Paul.

Braithwaite, John. 1985. *To Punish or to Persuade: Enforcement of Coal Mine Safety*. Albany: State University of New York Press.

Braithwaite, John. 1989. "Criminological Theory and Organizational Crime." *Justice Quarterly* 6: 333–58.

Braithwaite, John. 1992. "Poverty, Power, and White-Collar Crime." In *White-Collar Crime Reconsidered*, pp. 78–107, edited by Kip Schlegel and David Weisburd. Boston: Northeastern University Press.

Breton, Albert, and Ronald Wintrobe. 1986. "The Bureaucracy of Murder Revisited." *Journal of Political Economy* 94: 905–26.

Bucy, Pamela H., Elizabeth P. Formby, Marc S. Raspanti, and Kathryn E. Rooney. 2008. "Why Do They Do It? The Motives, Mores, and Character of White-Collar Criminals." *St. John's Law Review* 82: 401–571.

Bunt, Henk G. van de, and Wim Huisman. 2007. "Organizational Crime in the Netherlands." *Crime and Justice: A Review of Research* 35: 217–60.

Bunt, Henk G. van de, Nina L. Holvast, Huisman, K., Clarissa A. Meerts, Arnt G. Mein, and Dieneke Struik. 2011. *Bestuurlijke Rapportage Vastgoedfraudezaak 'Klimop' ['Administrative Report on Real Estate Fraude Case 'Klimop'].* Rotterdam/Utrecht: Erasmus School of Law and Verwey-Jonker Instituut.

Caves, Richard E. 1980. "Industrial Organization, Corporate Strategy, and Structure." *Journal of Economic Literature* 18: 64–92.

Chandler, Alfred D. 1962. *Strategy and Structure: Chapters in the History of the American Industrial Enterprise.* Cambridge, MA: MIT Press.

Clinard, Marshall B. 1983. *Corporate Ethics and Crime: The Role of Middle Management.* Beverly Hills: Sage.

Clinard, Marshall B., and Richard Quinney. 1973. *Criminal Behavior Systems: A Typology*, 2nd ed. New York: Holt, Rinehart and Winston.

Clinard, Marshall B., and Peter C. Yeager. 1980. *Corporate Crime.* New York: Free Press.

Cloward, Richard, and Lloyd Ohlin. 1960. *Delinquency and Opportunity: A Theory of Delinquent Gangs.* Glencoe, IL: Free Press.

Coates, John M., and Joe Herbert. 2010. "Endogenous Steroids and Financial Risk Taking on a London Trading Floor." *Proceedings of the National Academy of Sciences* 105: 6167–72.

Cohen, Deborah V. 1995. "Ethics and Crime in Business Firms: Organizational Culture and the Impact of Anomie." In *The Legacy of Anomie Theory*, pp. 183–206, edited by Freda Adler and William S. Laufer, Vol. 6 of *Advances in Criminological Theory*. New Brunswick, NJ: Transaction.

Coleman, James W. 1987. "Toward an Integrated Theory of White-Collar Crime." *American Journal of Sociology* 93: 406–39.

Coleman, James W. 1995. "Motivation and Opportunity: Understanding the Causes of White-Collar Crime." In *White-Collar Crime: Classic and Contemporary Views*, pp. 360–81, edited by Gilbert Geis, Robert F. Meier, and Lawrence M. Salinger. New York: Free Press.

Cressey, D. 1989. "The Poverty of Theory in Corporate Crime Research." In *Advances in Criminological Theory*, Vol. 1, pp. 31–56, edited by William S. Laufer and Freda Adler. New Brunswick, NJ: Transaction.

Dalton, Dan R., and Idalene F. Kesner. 1988. "On the Dynamics of Corporate Size and Illegal Activity: An Empirical Assessment." *Journal of Business Ethics* 7: 861–70.

Dean, Kathy Lund, Jeri Mullins Beggs, and Timothy P. Keane. 2010. "Mid-Level Managers, Organizational Context, and (Un)ethical Encounters." *Journal of Business Ethics* 97: 51–69.

Dugan, Laura, and Carole Gibbs. 2009. "The Role of Organizational Structure in the Control of Corporate Crime and Terrorism." In *The Criminology of White-Collar Crime*, pp. 111–28, edited by Sally S. Simpson and David Weisburd. New York: Springer.

Edelman, Lauren B., and Shauhin A. Talesh. 2011. "To Comply or Not to Comply—That Isn't the Question: How Organizations Construct the Meaning of Compliance." In *Explaining Compliance: Business Response to Regulation*, pp. 103–12, edited by Christine Parker and Vibeke Lehmann Nielsen. Cheltenham, UK: Edward Elgar Publishers.

Fayol, Henry, 1916. *Administration Industrielle et Générale [General and Industrial Administration]*. Paris: H. Dunod et E. Pinat.

Felson, Marcus, and Rachel L. Boba. 2010. *Crime and Everyday Life*, 4th ed. Beverly Hills: Sage.

Finney, Henry C., and Henry R. Lesieur. 1982. "A Contingency Theory of Organizational Crime." In *Research in the Sociology of Organizations*, pp. 255–99, edited by S. B. Bacharach, Vol. 1. Greenwich, CT: JAI Press.

Friedrichs, David O. 2010. *Trusted Criminals: White-Collar Crime in Contemporary Society*, 4th ed. Belmont: Wadsworth Cengage Learning.

Gibbs, Carole. 2012. "Corporate Citizenship and Corporate Environmental Performance." *Crime, Law, and Social Change* 57: 345–72.

Gibbs, Carole, and Sally S. Simpson. 2009. "Measuring Corporate Environmental Crime Rates: Progress and Problems." *Crime, Law, and Social Change* 51: 87–107.

Gross, Edward. 1978. "Organizations as Criminal Actors." In *Two Faces of Deviance: Crimes of the Powerless and Powerful*, pp. 198–213, edited by Paul R. Wilson and John Braithwaite. Brisbane: University of Queensland Press.

Gross, Edward. 1980. "Organization Structure and Organizational Crime." In *White-Collar Crime: Theory and Research*, pp. 52–70, edited by Gilbert Geis and Ezra Stotland. Beverly Hills: Sage.

Hofstede, Geert. 1980. *Culture's Consequences: International Differences in Work-Related Values*. Beverly Hills: Sage.

Huisman, Wim. 2001. *Tussen Winst en Moral. Achtergrond van Regelnaleving en Regelovertreding door Ondernemingen [Between Profit and Morality. Background Factors of Regulatory Compliance and Violation by Corporations]*. The Hague: Boom Legal Publishers.

Huisman, Wim, and Judith van Erp. 2013. "Opportunities for Environmental Crime: A Test of Situational Crime Prevention Theory." *British Journal of Criminology* 53: 1178–200.

Jackson, Michael C. 2003. *Systems Thinking: Creative Holism for Managers*. Chichester, UK: John Wiley and Sons.

Jamieson, Katherine M. 1994. *The Organization of Corporate Crime: Dynamics of Antitrust Violations*. Thousand Oaks, CA: Sage.

Jenkins, Anne, and John Braithwaite. 1993. "Profits, Pressure, and Corporate Lawbreaking." *Crime, Law, and Social Change* 20: 221–32.

Kagan, Robert A., and John T. Scholz. 1984. "The 'Criminology of the Corporation' and Regulatory Enforcement Strategies." In *Enforcing Regulation*, pp. 67–96, edited by Keith Hawkins and John M. Thomas. Boston: Kluwer Nijhoff Publishing.

Kaptein, Muel. 2008a. "Developing and Testing a Measure for the Ethical Culture of Organizations: The Corporate Ethical Virtues Model." *Journal of Organizational Behavior* 29: 923–47.

Kaptein, Muel. 2008b. "Developing a Measure of Unethical Behavior in the Workplace: A Stakeholder Perspective." *Journal of Management* 34: 978–1008.

Kaptein, Muel. 2010. "The Ethics of Organizations: A Longitudinal Study of the U.S. Working Population." *Journal of Business Ethics* 92: 601–18.

Kaptein, Muel. 2011. "Understanding Unethical Behavior by Unraveling Ethical Culture." *Human Relations* 64: 843–69.

Keane, Carl. 1995. "Loosely Coupled Systems and Unlawful Behavior: Organization Theory and Corporate Crime." In *Corporate Crime: Contemporary Debates*, pp. 168–81, edited by Frank Pearce and Laureen Snider. Toronto: University of Toronto Press.

Key, Susan. 1999. "Organizational Culture: Real or Imagined?" *Journal of Business Ethics* 20: 217–25.

Knottnerus, J. David, Jason S. Ulsperger, Summer Cummins, and Elaina Osteen. 2006. "Exposing Enron: Media Representations of Ritualized Deviance in Corporate Culture." *Crime Media Culture* 2: 177–95.

Kramer, Ronald C. 1982. "Corporate Crime: An Organizational Perspective." In *White-Collar and Economic Crime: Multidisciplinary and Cross-National Perspectives*, pp. 75–95, edited by Peter Wickman and Timothy Dailey. Lexington, VA: Lexington Books.

Kramer, Ronald C. 1984. "Corporate Criminality: The Development of an Idea." In *Corporations as Criminals*, pp. 13–37, edited by Eileen Hochstedler. Beverly Hills: Sage.

Lee, Matthew T., and M. David Ermann. 2002. "Pinto Madness: Flaws in the Generally Accepted Landmark Narrative." In *Corporate and Governmental Deviance: Problems of Organizational Behavior in Contemporary Society*, pp. 277–305, edited by M. David Ermann and Richard J. Lundman. New York: Oxford University Press.

Leng, J. 2009. *Corporate Governance and Financial Reform in China's Transition Economy*. Hong Kong: Hong Kong University Press.

Lester, Donald L., John A. Parnell, and Shawn Carraher. 2003. "Organizational Life Cycle: A Five-Stage Empirical Approach." *International Journal of Organizational Analysis* 11: 339–54.

Levi, Michael. 2008. "Combating Identity and Other Forms of Payment Fraud in the UK: An Analytical History." In *Perspectives on Identity Theft*, pp. 111–32, edited by Megan M. McNally and Graeme R. Newman. Monsey, NY: Criminal Justice Press.

Lipsey, Mark W., and David B. Wilson. 2001. *Practical Meta-Analysis*. Thousand Oaks, CA: Sage.

Martin, Kelly D., John B. Cullen, and Jean L. Johnson, and K. Praveen Parboteeah. 2007. "Deciding to Bribe: A Cross-Level Analysis of Firm and Home Country Influences on Bribery Activity." *Academy of Management Journal* 50: 1401–22.

May, Peter J. 2004. "Compliance Motivations: Affirmative and Negative Bases." *Law and Society Review* 38: 41–68.

McKendall, Marie A., and John A. Wagner, III. 1997. "Motive, Opportunity, Choice, and Corporate Illegality." *Organization Science: A Journal of the Institute of Management Sciences* 8: 624–48.

Merton, Robert K. 1938. "Social Structure and Anomie." *American Sociological Review* 3: 672–82.

Morgan, Gareth. 2006. *Images of Organization*. Beverly Hills: Sage.

Orlitzky, Marc, Frank L. Schmidt, and Sara L. Rynes. 2003. "Corporate Social and Financial Performance: A Meta-Analysis." *Organization Studies* 24: 403–41.

Parker, Christine, and Sharon Gilad. 2011. "Internal Corporate Compliance Management Systems: Structure, Culture, and Agency." In *Explaining Compliance: Business Responses to Regulation*, pp. 170–99, edited by Christine Parker and Vibeke Nielsen. Cheltenham, UK: Edward Elgar Publishers.

Parker, Christine, and Vibeke Lehmann Nielsen. 2009. "Corporate Compliance Systems: Could They Make Any Difference?" *Administration and Society* 41: 3–37.

Parker, Christine, and Vibeke Lehmann Nielsen, eds. 2011. *Explaining Compliance: Business Response to Regulation.* Cheltenham, UK: Edward Elgar Publishers.

Passas, Nikos. 1990. "Anomie and Corporate Deviance." *Contemporary Crises* 14: 157–78.

Paternoster, Raymond, and Sally S. Simpson. 1996. "Sanction Threats and Appeals to Morality: Testing a Rational Choice Model of Corporate Crime." *Law and Society Review* 30: 549–83.

Pearce, Frank, and Steve Tombs. 1997. "Hazards, Law, and Class: Contextualizing the Regulation of Corporate Crime." *Social and Legal Studies* 6: 79–107.

Piquero, Nicole Leeper. 2012. "The Only Thing We Have to Fear Is Fear Itself: Investigating the Relationship between Fear of Falling and White-Collar Crime." *Crime and Delinquency* 58: 362–79.

Piquero, Nicole Leeper, Andrea Schoepfer, and Lynn Langton. 2010. "Completely Out of Control or the Desire to Be in Complete Control? An Examination of How Low Self-Control and the Desire-for-Control Relate to Corporate Offending." *Crime and Delinquency* 56: 627–47.

Punch, Maurice. 1996. *Dirty Business: Exploring Corporate Misconduct: Analysis and Cases.* London: Sage.

Punch, Maurice. 2008. "The Organization Did It: Individuals, Corporations, and Crime." In *Corporate and White-Collar Crime*, pp. 102–21, edited by John Minkes and Leonard Minkes. London: Sage.

Quinn, Robert E. 1988. *Beyond Rational Management.* San Francisco: Jossey-Bass.

Ragatz, Laurie, and William Fremouw. 2010. "A Critical Examination of Research on the Psychological Profiles of White-Collar Criminals." *Journal of Forensic Psychology Practice* 10: 373–402.

Ramdani, Dendi, and Arjen van Witteloostuijn. 2013. "Bribery." In *Encyclopedia of Criminology and Criminal Justice*, pp. 1–5, edited by Jay S. Albanese and Jacqueline L. Schneider. Malden, MA: Wiley-Blackwell.

Schein, Edgar H. 1992. *Organizational Culture and Leadership: A Dynamic View*, 2nd ed. San Francisco: Jossey-Bass.

Shapiro, Susan P. 2005. "Agency Theory." *Annual Review of Sociology* 31: 263–84.

Shover, Neal, and Andy Hochstetler. 2002. "Cultural Explanation and Organizational Crime." *Crime, Law, and Social Change* 37: 1–18.

Shover, Neal, and Andy Hochstetler. 2006. *Choosing White-Collar Crime.* New York: Cambridge University Press.

Simpson, Sally S. 1986. "The Decomposition of Antitrust: Testing a Multi-Level, Longitudinal Model of Profit-Squeeze." *American Sociological Review* 51: 859–75.

Simpson, Sally S., and Christopher S. Koper. 1992. "Deterring Corporate Crime." *Criminology* 30: 347–75.

Simpson, Sally S., and Christopher S. Koper. 1997. "The Changing of the Guard: Top Management Characteristics, Organizational Strain, and Antitrust Offending." *Journal of Quantitative Criminology* 13: 373–404.

Simpson, Sally S., Raymond Paternoster, and Nicole Leeper Piquero. 1998. "Exploring the Micro-Macro Link in Corporate Crime Research." In *Research in the Sociology of Organizations: Deviance in and of Organizations*, pp. 35–68, edited by Peter A. Bamberger and William J. Sonnenstuhl, Vol. 15. Stamford, CT: JAI Press.

Simpson, Sally S., Nicole Leeper Piquero, and Raymond Paternoster. 2002. "Rationality and Corporate Offending Decisions." In *Rational Choice and Criminal Behavior*, pp. 25–39, edited by Alex R. Piquero and Steven G. Tibbetts. New York: Taylor and Francis.

Simpson, Sally S., and Melissa Rorie. 2011. "Motivating Compliance: Economic and Material Motives for Compliance." In *Explaining Compliance: Business Response to Regulation*, pp. 59–77, edited by Christine Parker and Vibeke Lehmann Nielsen. Cheltenham, UK: Edward Elgar Publishers.

Sims, Rondal R., and Johannes Brinkmann. 2003. "Enron Ethics: Culture Matters More Than Codes." *Journal of Business Ethics* 45: 243–56.

Slapper, Gary, and Steve Tombs. 1999. *Corporate Crime*. Harlow: Longman.

Stinchcombe, Arthur L. 1965. "Social Structure and Organizations." In *Handbook of Organizations*, Vol. 7, pp. 142–93, edited by James G. March. Chicago, IL: Rand McNally.

Stone, Christopher D. 1975. *Where the Law Ends: The Social Control of Corporate Behavior*. New York: Harper and Row.

Sutherland, Edwin H. 1949. *White Collar Crime*. New York: Dryden.

Sutherland, Edwin H. 1983. *White Collar Crime: The Uncut Version*. New Haven, CT: Yale University Press.

Szwajkowski, Eugene. 1985. "Organizational Illegality: Theoretical Integration and Illustrative Application." *Academy of Management Review* 10: 558–67.

Taylor, Frederick Winslow. 1911. *Principles of Scientific Management*. New York: Harper and Brothers.

Tillman, Robert, and Henry Pontell. 1995. "Organizations and Fraud in the Savings and Loan Industry." *Social Forces* 73: 1439–63.

Tombs, Steve. 1995. "Corporate Crime and New Organizational Forms." In *Corporate Crime: Contemporary Debates*, pp. 132–47, edited by Frank Pearce and Laureen Snider. Toronto: University of Toronto Press.

van Wingerde, Karin. 2012. *De afschrikking voorbij. Een empirische studie naar afschrikking, generale preventie en regelnaleving in de Nederlandse afvalbranche. [Beyond Deterrence: Punishment, Deterrence, and Compliance in the Dutch Waste Industry]*. Oisterwijk, NL: Wolf Legal Publishers.

Vaughan, Diane. 1983. *Controlling Unlawful Organizational Behavior: Social Structure and Organizational Misconduct*. Chicago: University of Chicago Press.

Vaughan, Diane. 1999. "The Dark Side of Organizations: Mistake, Misconduct, and Disaster." *Annual Review of Sociology* 25: 271–305.

Vaughan, Diane. 2002a. "The Challenger Space Shuttle Disaster: Conventional Wisdom and a Revisionist Account." In *Corporate and Governmental Deviance: Problems of Organizational Behavior in Contemporary Society*, 6th ed., pp. 306–34, edited by M. David Ermann and Richard J. Lundman. New York: Oxford University Press.

Vaughan, Diane. 2002b. "Criminology and the Sociology of Organizations: Analogy, Comparative Social Organization, and General Theory." *Crime, Law, and Social Change* 37: 117–36.

Verbruggen, Janna, Arjan Blokland, and Victor van der Geest. 2012. "Effects of Employment and Unemployment on Serious Offending in a High-Risk Sample of Men and Women from Ages 18 to 32." *British Journal of Criminology* 52: 845–69.

Victor, Bart, and John B. Cullen. 1988. "The Organizational Bases of Ethical Work Climates." *Administrative Science Quarterly* 33: 101–25.

Vold, George B., and Thomas J. Bernard. 1986. *Theoretical Criminology*, 3rd ed. New York: Oxford University Press.

Wang, Xia, and Kristy Holtfreter. 2012. "The Effects of Corporation- and Industry-Level Strain and Opportunity on Corporate Crime." *Journal of Research in Crime and Delinquency* 49: 151–85.

Waring, Elin, David Weisburd, and Ellen Chayet. 1995. "White-Collar Crime and Anomie." In *The Legacy of Anomie Theory*, pp. 207–25, edited by Freda Adler and William S. Laufer, Vol. 6 of Advances in Criminological Theory. New Brunswick, NJ: Transaction.

Weber, Max. 1922. *Wirtschaft und Gesellschaft*. Tübingen: Mohr.

Weisburd, David, and Elin Waring. 2001. *White-Collar Crime and Criminal Careers*. Cambridge: Cambridge University Press.

Wells, Celia. 2001. *Corporations and Criminal Responsibility*. New York: Oxford University Press.

Wheeler, Stanton. 1992. "The Problem of White-Collar Motivation." In *White-Collar Crime Reconsidered*, pp. 108–23, edited by Kip Schlegel and David Weisburd. Boston: Northeastern University Press.

CHAPTER 22

ORGANIZATIONAL SELF-RESTRAINT

STELIOS C. ZYGLIDOPOULOS AND PETER FLEMING

ACCORDING to Sutherland (1949), white-collar crime is "a crime committed by a person of respectability and high social status in the course of his occupation" (p. 9). Sutherland also pointed out that corporations commit crimes. This became abundantly clear with the recent Enron wave of scandals, in which white-collar criminals operated within and sometimes even on behalf of major corporations. In other words, corporations, which for many years were good upstanding corporate citizens, at some point in time could not restrain themselves, lost their moral compass, one might say, and descended into white-collar criminal behavior.

However, organizations are not human beings that personally possess self-restraint or a moral compass. Moreover, organizations do not commit white-collar crimes; it is the managers within them that do. In the case of organizations, then, we take organizational self-restraint to mean that organizations are able to avoid facilitating and able to prevent their managers from engaging in criminal activities. Following this rationale, two interrelated, important issues are: (1) why some corporations facilitate their managers engaging in white-collar crimes (while others do not) and (2) how organizations can manage to restrain their managers from engaging in white-collar criminal behavior.

In this chapter, building on the idea that there are two ways of viewing white-collar crime—a "bad-apples" approach and a "bad-barrels" one—we examine the above issues and identify the mechanisms through which corporations can prevent their managers from engaging in white-collar crime. The bad-apples approach views white-collar crime as the result of the personal characteristics of individuals (Bass, Butterfield, and Skaggs 1998; Fleming and Zyglidopoulos 2009). On the other hand, the bad-barrels approach views white-collar crime as resulting from the context within which individuals find themselves (Keane 1993). Drawing on social psychological research (Milgram 1974; Zimbardo 2007), this view holds that any individual under the right conditions could descend into white-collar crime. In this chapter, we use these two perspectives in a complementary way, as they allow us to identify different factors (drivers) that contribute to white-collar crime within corporations and thus allow us to identify how corporations can prevent their managers from getting involved in white-collar criminal behavior. Our main conclusions are as follows:

- There is no single measure through which organizations can prevent white-collar crime, but a combination of measures can significantly reduce the chances that white-collar crime will occur.
- Organizations should rationalize their managerial incentives to follow directly from the organization's goals, so that the possible motives behind white-collar crimes are reduced.
- Organizations should create adequate controls, so that the opportunities to engage in white-collar criminal behavior are reduced.
- Organizations should safeguard their whistleblowers, because whistleblowing can be a healthy antidote to social compliance and can often reveal or prevent a white-collar crime from continuing and/or escalating.
- Organizations should simplify and make visible their procedures to the greatest extent possible, thus reducing the risk that criminal activity will be hidden in complex structures and procedures.
- Organizations should provide ethical training to their employees so they can create an ethics-based culture.

The remainder of this chapter proceeds as follows. In section I, we expand on the two ways of viewing white-collar crime, the bad-apples and bad-barrels approaches. In section II, we discuss the four drivers of white-collar crime. In section III, we identify and discuss three corporate-specific factors that facilitate white-collar crime by influencing these drivers. Section IV draws on the previous two sections and discusses the organizational restraints that can prevent corporations from engaging in white-collar crime. In section V, we conclude with some comments on the importance of preventing corporations from engaging in white-collar criminal behavior.

I. Two Ways of Viewing White-Collar Crime Within Organizations

White-collar criminal behavior can be viewed in two ways: through a bad-apples perspective or a bad-barrels perspective. Both make simplifying assumptions about human behavior and so enable us to focus better on particular aspects of white-collar crime while necessarily ignoring others. Of course, neither of the two is complete without the other, and we use these two perspectives here to complement each other. In short, a bad-apples perspective assumes that white-collar crimes result from the few white-collar criminals (bad apples), who act in such a way because of who they are, with the majority of individuals being good. In the wake of the Enron wave of scandals, this approach toward white-collar crime was adopted by the U.S. government and the media to maintain that it was only a few individuals in a few corporations who were the problem, while the majority of corporations as well as the financial system as a whole were fundamentally sound (Zyglidopoulos and Fleming 2009). On the other hand, a bad-barrels perspective assumes there are no good or bad individuals, and it is the situation that makes the criminal. Most individuals finding themselves in particularly difficult situations will turn to criminal behavior, and it is not the individual but the situation that is at fault (Milgram 1974; Gioia 1992; Zimbardo 2007).

The first approach, the bad-apples one, has some affinity with the rational choice theory of crime, which sees criminal activity as "a purposive behavior which is designed to meet the offender's commonplace needs for such things as money, status, sex, and excitement" (Clarke and Felson 1993, p. 6) and allows moral responsibility to be attributed to the perpetrator. Of course, one could argue that criminal behavior is not necessarily a rational choice, as Shover and Hochstetler (2006) pointed out. But even if we do not see criminal behavior as rational in the sense that the offender might be misguided about the consequences of his or her actions (Trasler 1993), this way of viewing criminality still presumes that the offender performs some kind of cost–benefit analysis before the act (Clarke and Felson 1993). In other words, as Trasler (1993, p. 308) said, the perpetrator might still make "a logical inference from the data available to him," even though he (or she) might be misguided about his (or her) premises. This bad-apples approach allows us then to focus on the individual performing the act (Bass et al. 1998; Fleming and Zyglidopoulos 2009) and to identify two particular individual-level factors that play a role in white-collar crimes: agency and neutralization (Zyglidopoulos and Fleming 2009), which we discuss in section II. But first a few words about the bad-barrels perspective.

The bad-barrels approach absolves individual perpetrators from moral responsibility. The main idea behind this approach, in its strongest version, is that anyone finding himself or herself under the right conditions can perform a crime (Fleming and Zyglidopoulos 2009). As Plato said, "there are not many very good or very bad people, but the great majority are something between the two" (Plato's *Phaedo* 90a), and it is this great majority that is capable of criminal behavior under the right conditions. Particularly in the case of white-collar crime within organizations, Keane (1993) pointed out:

> Just over forty years ago, ground-breaking work by Sutherland (1949) focused attention on corporate crime. His research informed us that corporate offenses cannot be explained by individual pathology, and that any search for the causes of corporate crime should begin with an examination of the context wherein most corporate crimes occur—the organization. (p. 293)

A number of rather disturbing experiments in social psychology have shown that randomly selected individuals are capable, under the right conditions, of performing the cruelest acts and thus provide some legitimacy for the bad-barrels perspective. For example, in his famous obedience experiments, Milgram (1974) found that under the right conditions some randomly assigned college students were willing to inflict lethal electric shocks to others whom they considered to be experimental subjects. Milgram was so shocked by his findings that he performed his study again with a different population, blue-collar workers, and found that they responded in pretty much the same way as college students had. Similarly, in his Stanford experiments, Zimbardo (2007) found that randomly assigned university students turned into sadistic guards in less than a week, just because they were asked to play the guard in a hypothetical jail simulation game. Zimbardo had randomly assigned half of the students to be guards and half to be prisoners and wanted to observe how this week-long role-playing would affect the participants' behavior. However, the behavior of the guards became so cruel that he had to stop the experiment after a few days. Therefore, the organizational context within which one finds oneself appears to play an important role in criminal behavior. Following this rationale, the bad-barrels approach focuses on the organizational context within which an individual performs a crime, and thus we identify two particular organizational-level factors that play a role in white-collar crimes: social conformity and ethical distance (Zyglidopoulos and Fleming 2008). We discuss these factors in addition to agency and neutralization in more detail in section II.

II. Drivers of White-Collar Crime

Viewing white-collar crime from both bad-apples and bad-barrels perspectives, we identified four drivers of crime: agency, neutralization, social conformity, and ethical distance, which we expand on in the following paragraphs.

First, agency refers to the moral agency of individuals, which can be more formally defined as "an individual's ability to make moral judgments based on some commonly held notion of right and wrong and to be held accountable for these actions" (Taylor 2003, p. 20). In other words, agency refers to the ability individuals have to choose to act in a particular way. Focusing on the agency aspect of white-collar crime allows us to appreciate the importance of individual choice in criminal behavior.

Thus, in discussing the Holocaust and the implementation of the Final Solution by Nazi Germany in many European countries, Hannah Arendt (1963) described many situations where individuals found themselves in extreme situations and were forced to do criminal things if they wanted to save their lives or the lives of their loved ones. An important conclusion she reached from this is that "under conditions of terror most people will comply but some will not" (p. 233). She observed, in other words, that some individuals—even though they faced death or the death of their loved ones—did not choose to engage in what they considered criminal behavior. And she concluded that the role of individual choice cannot and should not be excluded from the reasons behind criminal behavior; even though environmental conditions play an important role in explaining criminal behavior, they can never justify it. But just as there are individuals who will never choose to commit a crime, there are others who choose criminal behavior as a way out of their particular situation, as the managers of Enron did (McLean and Elkind 2003). Does this mean, however, that those individuals who choose to commit a crime have no sense of morality or that they have a different code of morals than everybody else?

Second, from a number of studies in social psychology, it appears that many perpetrators have the ability to disengage themselves morally from their acts by using various neutralizations (Cressey 1953; Sykes and Matza 1957; Cressey and Moore 1983; Bandura 1990; Anand, Ashforth, and Joshi 2004). The term "neutralization" refers to the "excuses" said to oneself to make the beneficial-but-criminal act easier and to square with one's moral values. As many have noticed, individuals performing criminal activities tend not to see themselves as criminals (Cressey 1953; Sykes and Matza 1957; Cressey and Moore 1983; Benson 1985; Anand, Ashforth, and Joshi 2004). Instead, they find ways to disengage themselves morally from their own acts, using neutralizations such as "I was just obeying orders," "I was just borrowing the money, not stealing it," and "if I did not do it, someone else would" (Bandura 1990).

Cressey (1953), one of the earliest researchers to study the role of neutralizations in white-collar crimes, found that by using the excuse "that they are borrowing, trust violators [were] able to remain in full contact with the values and ideals of former and present associates who condemn crime" (p. 121). For instance, he reported that one trust violator "borrowed" many thousands of dollars from the bank he was working for but kept a very detailed account of the amount of money he owed on the back of the folder containing the titles of a property he owned and intended to sell to pay back the money he owed his bank. In his mind, we could say "he had somewhat 'mortgaged' his property for 'the loan' he took. So, when he was caught, he saw it not as fraud but just as having bad timing" (Zyglidopoulos and Fleming 2009, p. 112). Building on Sykes and Matza's work and applying it to business crime, Anand, Ashforth, and Joshi (2004) identified a number of neutralizations: denial of responsibility ("not my fault"), denial of injury ("nobody got hurt"), denial of victim ("they deserved it"), social weighting ("others did much worse"), appeal to higher loyalties ("I did it for the good of the company"), and balancing the ledger ("they owe me this much"). In the case of Enron, for example, Jeff Skilling said that, through his criminal actions, he was trying to save the firm from bankruptcy, and it seems that to a great extent he believed his own excuses. In short, then, neutralizations allow perpetrators to continue to performing crimes and benefit from them while at the same time not to see themselves as criminals (Anand, Ashforth, and Joshi 2004).

Third, social conformity, or group conformity, refers to the tendency of individuals within groups to conform to what they consider to be the norm (Ash 1951, 1956; Aronson 2004). This tendency to conform has been vividly shown to exist within groups through a famous experiment performed by Ash (1951, 1956). Ash found that a large proportion (35 percent) of his subjects conformed to group pressures and agreed with statements that clearly went against what their physical senses were telling them was not so. In other words, "the task was so easy, and physical reality was so clear-cut, that Ash himself firmly believed that there would be little, if any, yielding to group pressure" (Aronson 2004, p. 17). Furthermore, other researchers have supported Ash's findings by performing the same experiment in different cultural settings (Deutsch and Gerald 1955; Wolosin, Sherman, and Cann 1975). This social conformity of individuals contributes to white-collar criminal behavior as we have seen in many corporate scandals. For example, in the WorldCom saga, the company board approved a number of illegal requests due to peer pressure (Haddad 2002). And there are other examples of instances in which individuals within corporations were unwilling to go against the prevailing norm, even if this norm was clearly leading them into illegal behavior.

Fourth, ethical distance refers to the "distance between an act and its ethical consequences" (Zyglidopoulos and Fleming 2008, p. 266), the rationale being that the greater the ethical distance, the easier it will be for an individual to engage in a criminal activity. Bauman (1991) captured very well the role of proximity in matters of morality between act and ethical consequence when he said:

> Being inextricably tied to human proximity, morality seems to conform to the law of optical perspective. It looms large and thick close to the eye. With the growth of distance, responsibility for the other shrivels, moral dimensions of the object blur, till both reach the vanishing point and disappear from view. (p. 192)

In the Enron case, for example, the overly optimistic projections, tied into the criminal acts perpetrated by managers, were projections dealing with events supposed to take place twenty or more years into the future, thus being temporally very far from current acts and rewards (McLean and Elkind 2003). And beyond temporal considerations, individuals could be unable to see the consequences of their acts because their position in the business organization does not provide access to all the relevant information they need to appreciate fully the consequences of their actions (Zyglidopoulos and Fleming 2008).

III. Facilitating Factors

In addition to the above factors contributing to white-collar crimes, within business organizations in particular, two more factors facilitate white-collar criminal behavior. These factors are (1) increased and increasing pressure for economic performance and (2) organizational complexity.

As has become evident from the number of corporate scandals over the years, an increasing pressure for economic performance has motivated white-collar criminal behavior within corporations. On one hand, corporations seem to be faced with increased pressures to perform, whereas on the other, they are facing increased and increasing levels of competition that prevent them from achieving the desired results (Engardio and Roberts 2004). It is not surprising, then, that researchers (Asch and Seneca 1976; Baucus and Near 1991; Baucus 1994) have found that "lower industry profitability is associated with greater corporate illegality" (McKendall and Wagner 1997, p. 626). Similarly, strain theory suggests that when societies pressure individuals to achieve goals that they cannot achieve given the societal rules they have to adhere to, these individuals often "innovate" by breaking the rules to achieve their desired results (Merton 1968). Often, these extreme performance pressures are the result of the unrealistic choices a firm's leaders make. And we have seen many examples of such pressures—real or perceived—leading to criminal behavior by managers of corporations trying to achieve unachievable financial results. Take, for example, the Arthur Andersen case. As Ashforth et al. (2008) reported,

> Management's message to employees might have been implicit, but it was also clear: do anything necessary to ensure clients' return of consulting business and retain revenue flow, even if it means padding prices or creating problems for those clients. . . . The Andersen example is consistent with the widely and long-held notion that senior leaders are often responsible for corrupt actions by setting unrealistic financial goals. (p. 673)

Therefore, we can say that, under intense pressure for economic performance, the propensity of managers to choose to engage in criminal activity in order to achieve their economic goals is higher.

Organizational complexity is another factor that often facilitates white-collar crimes within corporations. Organizational complexity refers to the level of organizational differentiation and specialization of an organization (Thompson 1967; Khandwalla 1977; Dooley and Van de Ven 1999). Organizational complexity facilitates criminal activity within organizations for a number of reasons. First, it increases the ethical distance that any individual within the organization might encounter. The more complex an organization is, the less access the individuals working within it will have to the information necessary to be able to appreciate fully the ethical consequences of their actions and the more likely they will be to participate in criminal activities, because they cannot perceive the consequences of what they are engaged in (Bauman 1991; Zyglidopoulos and Fleming 2009). Elliot and Schroth (2002) referred to this phenomenon as the "fog of complexity." Second, the more complex an organization, the more credible some neutralizations sound. For example, in a complex structure where responsibilities and information are broken down, saying "it was not my fault" or "I was just doing my job" become understandable and acceptable characterizations of one's actions (Fleming and Zyglidopoulos 2008).

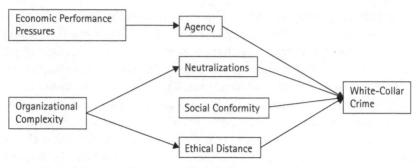

FIGURE 22.1 Drivers and Facilitators of White-Collar Crime Within Organizations

Concluding sections II and III, figure 22.1 illustrates our argument about the drivers and facilitating factors of white-collar criminal activities within organizations.

IV. ORGANIZATIONAL SELF-RESTRAINT

An organization can show self-restraint and minimize the possibility that its managers will engage in white-collar criminal behavior by intervening and severing the links identified in figure 22.1. In other words, an organization should try in different ways to influence the seven arrows depicting the influences of the various factors, which have a positive impact on white-collar crime. These influences are depicted in figure 22.2. We propose five ways through which organizations can achieve such

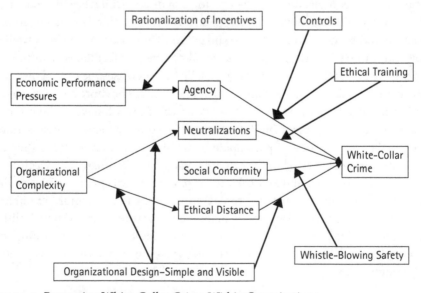

FIGURE 22.2 Preventing White-Collar Crime Within Organizations

self-restraint: (1) rationalizing incentives, (2) creating adequate controls, (3) creating a safe mechanism for whistleblowers, (4) focusing on simplicity and visibility in the organization, and (5) providing ethical training to employees.

First, rationalizing the incentives of managers that follow from the organization's goals plays an important role in decreasing the probability of white-collar crime. Quite often business organizations ask their managers and employees to achieve goals that are not possible given the nature of the business. In such cases, then, given that incentives are most often tied up with performance, some might find a way out by breaking the rules and even engaging in white-collar criminal activity. The Enron case is a good illustration of this. As McLean and Elkind (2003) put it:

> This was Enron's dirty little secret: a company built around trading and deal making cannot possibly count on steadily increasing earnings. . . . As one former Enron managing director says, "A business that had stable and predictable earnings that's primarily engaged in the trading of commodities is a contradiction in terms." (p. 126)

Therefore, if corporations want to prevent their managers from being tempted into "achieving" unrealistic results illegally, then they should first of all remove the incentives that unrealistic targets impose on them.

Second, creating adequate control systems can significantly reduce the probability of white-collar crime in organizations. Organizational control systems are supposed to align "the interests of the individuals with the interests of the organization" (Rosanas and Velilla 2005, p. 85). However, given the emphasis that the organizational control systems allocate to financial results, they tend not to control adequately for the morality or even legality of the various corporate actions (Fleming and Zyglidopoulos 2008). Therefore, in recent decades after each wave of corporate scandals, legislation (i.e., the sentencing reform act of 1984 and 1991 in the United States, the Sarbanes-Oxley Act of 2002 in the United States, and the Bribery Act of 2010 in the United Kingdom) has increased the pressure on business organizations to develop effective ethics and compliance programs. Siemens, for example, after its recent international bribery scandal, designed and implemented one of the most sophisticated compliance systems to prevent its managers from engaging in criminal activities in the future (Dietz and Gillespie, 2012). If designed and implemented well, compliance programs or systems can complement existing state laws and organizational controls. The combination of different types of internal and external controls is necessary for a couple of reasons. On one hand, state laws and regulations cannot—without turning societies into police states—effectively prevent white-collar crime within business organizations. On the other hand, the auditing and financial systems of corporations are not adequate for the task. However, when such controls are supplemented by internal compliance systems, the probability that those who chose to engage in white-collar crime will get away with it can be reduced (Fleming and Zyglidopoulos 2009).

Third, whistleblowing can be a healthy antidote to social compliance and often reveals or prevents a white-collar crime from continuing and/or escalating. According to Near and Miceli (1985), whistleblowing refers to "the disclosure by organization members (former or current) of illegal, immoral, or illegitimate practices under the control of their employers, to persons or organizations that may be able to effect action" (p. 4). Whistleblowers are very important for a number of reasons. According to Avakian and Roberts (2012), whistleblowers not only challenge "the established order of an organization as this is comprised of institutional structures, policies and procedures" but also take a moral stance and "display a concern for moral values" (p. 71). Thus, whistleblowers can be seen as an antidote to social compliance when some employees within an organization seem to be complying with criminal activities. However, their actions often result in their suffering significant social penalties (Mesmer-Magnus and Viswesvaran 2005). Thus, organizations in conjunction with governmental agencies must make a concerted effort to design custom-made whistleblowing policies (Loyens 2013) and legislative incentives that will encourage and protect those who disclose corporate wrongdoing.

Fourth, simplicity and visibility can help a great deal in preventing white-collar criminal activity. Given that organizational complexity can influence white-collar criminal behavior by making neutralizations more legitimate and by increasing the ethical distance that managers and employees experience, it follows that by simplifying procedures and making the outcomes visible to all organizational members, organizations can decrease the probability that their employees will fall into criminal activity. Of course, there are competitive secrets that no corporation wants to be made public. But these are few, and more often than not the matter is exaggerated in order to hide irregularities or illegalities—as was the case with Enron, whose managers hid their crimes behind a curtain of complexity disguised as an innovative business model (McLean and Elkind 2003).

Finally, organizations have to provide ethical training and support to their managers and employees so they can create an ethics-based culture. According to a number of studies (Paine 1994; Trevino et al. 1999; Tyler, Dienhart, and Thomas 2008), an ethical culture contributes a lot more toward the reduction of corporate illegality than simple regulatory compliance. Therefore, organizations should emphasize the ethical training of their employees in an attempt to make them not just comply with regulations but also espouse the values behind such regulations aimed at preventing criminal behavior.

V. CONCLUSION

Viewing white-collar crime within organizations from two complementary perspectives, bad-apples and bad-barrels perspectives, we identified four of its drivers (agency, neutralization, social conformity, and ethical distance), which along with two facilitating factors (economic performance pressures and organizational complexity) provide us with a more elaborate picture of white-collar crime in organizations (see figure 22.1). Of course, these factors are not exclusive, and different aspects of white-collar criminal activity within organizations could be important. But given the recent experiences of the various corporate scandals (e.g., Enron, Siemens, WordCom), these factors seem to emerge as important enough as driving and facilitating forces of white-collar crime.

The challenge for corporate leaders is then to recognize the potential for company wrongdoing and to engage actively in organizational self-restraint in the face of likely drivers and facilitating factors of white-collar criminal activities. Toward this end, to prevent or at least minimize the chances of white-collar crime, organizations should try to interrupt the influences identified in figure 22.1. We propose here that they can do this by implementing five measures: rationalizing incentives, creating adequate controls, creating a safe mechanism for whistleblowers, focusing on simplicity and visibility in the organization, and providing ethical training to employees. No one of these measures alone can address all of the drivers and facilitating forces behind white-collar crime, as each one addresses a different aspect of white-collar crime (see figure 22.2). Therefore, to the extent possible, organizations should try to engage in all of these measures, because when dealing with white-collar crime in large organizations, there is, unfortunately, no silver bullet.

REFERENCES

Anand, Vikas, Blake E. Ashforth, and Mahendra Joshi. 2004. "Business as Usual: The Acceptance and Perpetuation of Corruption in Organizations." *Academy of Management Executive* 18: 39–53.

Arendt, Hannah. 1963. *Eichmann in Jerusalem: A Report on the Banality of Evil.* London: Penguin.

Aronson, Elliott. 2004. *The Social Animal,* 9th ed. New York: Worth Publishers.

Asch, Peter, and J. J. Seneca. 1976. "Is Collusion Profitable?" *Review of Economics and Statistics* 58: 1–12.

Ash, Solomon. 1951. "Effects of Group Pressure upon the Modification and Distortion of Judgment." In *Groups, Leadership, and Men: Research in Human Relations,* edited by Harold S. Guetzkow. Pittsburgh, PA: Carnegie Press.

Ash, Solomon. 1956. "Studies of Independence and Conformity: A Minority of One against a Unanimous Majority." *Psychological Monographs* 70: 1–70.

Ashforth, Blake E., Dennis A. Gioia, S. L. Robinson, and Linda K. Trevino. 2008. "Reviewing Organizational Corruption." *Academy of Management Review* 33: 670–84.

Avakian, Stephanos, and Joanne Roberts. 2012. "Whistleblowers in Organizations: Prophets at Work?" *Journal of Business Ethics* 110: 71–84

Bandura, Albert. 1990. "Mechanisms of Moral Disengagement." In *Origins of Terrorism: Psychologies, Ideologies, Theologies, States of Mind,* edited by Walter Reich. Cambridge, UK: Cambridge University Press.

Bass, Daniel J., Kenneth D. Butterfield, and Bruce C. Skaggs. 1998. "Relationships and Unethical Behavior: A Social Network Perspective." *Academy of Management Review* 23: 14–31.

Baucus, Melissa S. 1994. "Pressure, Opportunity, and Predisposition: A Multivariate Model of Corporate Illegality." *Journal of Management* 20: 699–721.

Baucus, Melissa S., and Janet P. Near. 1991. "Can Illegal Corporate Behavior Be Predicted? An Event History Analysis." *Academy of Management Journal* 34: 9–36.

Bauman, Zygmunt. 1991. *Modernity and the Holocaust.* London: Polity.

Benson, Michael L. 1985. "Denying the Guilty Mind: Accounting for Involvement in a White-Collar Crime." *Criminology* 23: 583–607.

Clarke, Ronald V., and Marcus Felson. 1993. *Routine Activity and Rational Choice: Advances in Criminological Theory,* Vol. 5. New Brunswick, NJ: Transaction.

Cressey, Donald R. 1953. *Other People's Money: A Study in the Social Psychology of Embezzlement.* New York: Free Press.

Cressey, Donald R., and Charles A. Moore. 1983. "Managerial Values and Corporate Codes of Ethics." *California Management Review* 25: 53–77.

Deutsch, Morton, and Harold B. Gerard. 1955. "A Study of Normative and Informational Social Influence upon Individual Judgment." *Journal of Abnormal and Social Psychology* 51: 629–36.

Dietz, Graham, and Nicole Gillespie. 2012. "Rebuilding Trust: How Siemens Atoned for its Sins." *The Guardian* (26 March). Available at http://www.theguardian.com/sustainable-business/recovering-business-trust-siemens

Dooley, Kevin J., and Andrew H. Van de Ven. 1999. "Explaining Complex Organizational Dynamics." *Organization Science* 10: 358–72.

Elliot, A. Larry, and Richard J. Schroth. 2002. *How Companies Lie: Why Enron Is Just the Tip of the Iceberg.* London: Nicholas Brealey Publishing

Engardio, Pete, and Dexter Roberts, with Brian Bremner. 2004. "The China Price." *Business Week.* (December 6). Available at http://www.businessweek.com/stories/2004-12-05/the-china-price

Fleming, Peter, and Stelios C. Zyglidopoulos. 2009. *Charting Corporate Corruption: Agency, Structure, and Escalation.* Surrey, UK: Edward Elgar Publishing.

Gioia, Dennis A. 1992. "Pinto Fires and Personal Ethics: A Script Analysis of Missed Opportunities." *Journal of Business Ethics* 11: 379–89.

Haddad, Charles. 2002. "How Ebbers Kept the Board in His Pocket." *Business Week.* (October 14). Available at http://www.businessweek.com/stories/2002-10-13/how-ebbers-kept-the-board-in-his-pocket

Keane, Carl. 1993. "The Impact of Financial Performance on Frequency of Corporate Crime: A Latent Variable Test of Strain Theory." *Canadian Journal of Criminology* 35: 293–308.

Khandwalla, Pradip N. 1977. *The Design of Organizations.* New York: Harcourt Brace Jovanovich.

Loyens, Kim. 2013. "Towards a Custom-Made Whistleblowing Policy. Using Grid-Group Cultural Theory to Match Policy Measures to Different Styles of Peer Reporting." *Journal of Business Ethics* 114: 239–49.

McKendall, Marie A., and John A. Wagner III. 1997. "Motive, Opportunity, Choice, and Corporate Illegality." *Organization Science* 8: 624–47.

McLean, Bethany, and Peter Elkind. 2003. *The Smartest Guys in the Room: The Amazing Rise and Scandalous Fall of Enron.* New York: Penguin Books.

Merton, Robert K. 1968. *Social Theory and Social Structure.* Rev. Ed. Glencoe, IL: Free Press.

Mesmer-Magnus, Jessica R., and Chockalingam Viswesvaran. 2005. "Whistleblowing in Organizations: An Examination of Correlates of Whistleblowing Intentions, Actions, and Retaliation." *Journal of Business Ethics* 62: 277–97.

Milgram, Stanley. 1974. *Obedience to Authority: An Experimental View.* New York: Harper Perennial.

Near, Janet P., and Marcia P. Miceli. 1985. "Organizational Dissidence: The Case of Whistle-Blowing." *Journal of Business Ethics* 4: 1–16.

Paine, Lynn S. 1994. "Managing for Organizational Integrity." *Harvard Business Review* 72: 106–17.

Plato. 1989. "Phaedo" Translated by Hugh Tredennick, in *Plato: The Collected Dialogues*, edited by E. Hamilton and H. Cairns, Bollingen Series LXXI. Princeton, NJ: Princeton University Press.

Rosanas, Josep M., and Manuel Velilla. 2005. "The Ethics of Management Control Systems: Developing Technical and Moral Values." *Journal of Business Ethics* 57: 83–96.

Shover, Neal, and Andy Hochstetler. 2006. *Choosing White-Collar Crime*. New York: Cambridge University Press.

Sutherland, Edwin H. 1949. *White Collar Crime*. New York: Holt, Reinhart, and Winston.

Sykes, Gresham M., and David Matza. 1957. "Techniques of Neutralization: A Theory of Delinquency." *American Sociological Review* 22: 664–70.

Taylor, Angus. 2003. *Animals and Ethics: An Overview of the Philosophical Debate*. Peterborough, Ontario: Broadview Press.

Thompson, James D. 1967. *Organizations in Action: Social Science Bases of Administrative Theory*. New York: McGraw-Hill.

Trasler, Gordon. 1993. "Conscience, Opportunity, Rational Choice, and Crime." In *Routine Activity and Rational Choice: Advances in Criminological Theory*, Vol. 5, edited by Ronald V. Clarke and Marcus Felson. New Brunswick, NJ: Transaction.

Trevino, Linda Klebe, Gary R. Weaver, David G. Gibson, and Barbara Ley Toffler. 1999. "Managing Ethics and Legal Compliance: What Works and What Hurts." *California Management Review* 41: 131–51.

Tyler, Tom, John Dienhart, and Terry Thomas. 2008. "The Ethical Commitment to Compliance: Building Value-Based Cultures." *California Management Review* 50: 31–51.

Wolosin, Robert, Steven Sherman, and Arnie Cann. 1975. "Predictions of Own and Other's Conformity." *Journal of Personality* 43: 357–78.

Zimbardo, Phillip. 2007. *The Lucifer Effect: How Good People Turn Evil*. London: Random House.

Zyglidopoulos, Stelios C., and Peter Fleming. 2008. "Ethical Distance in Corrupt Firms: How Do Innocent Bystanders Become Guilty Perpetrators?" *Journal of Business Ethics* 78: 265–74.

Zyglidopoulos, Stelios C., and Peter Fleming. 2009. "The Escalation of Corruption." In *Research Companion to Corruption in Organizations*, edited by Ronald J. Burke and Cary L. Cooper. Surrey, UK: Edward Elgar Publishing Ltd.

PART VII

REGULATORY OVERSIGHT

CHAPTER 23

....

OVERSIGHT AND RULE MAKING AS POLITICAL CONFLICT

....

MARY KREINER RAMIREZ

THE 2008 financial crisis highlights once again the importance of sound financial regulation. In a period of deregulation and laissez-faire oversight, the financial sector engaged in high-risk investments and fraudulent activities that led to the crash of global financial markets and recession at home. Financial elites pocketed millions of dollars in earnings and bonuses while their companies lost billions, the government bailout of the industry cost trillions, and the accompanying global recession cost trillions more.

Governmental efforts to restore quickly confidence in the financial markets placed a costly bill on the American public without reforming the underlying regulation or oversight that permitted such recklessness and misconduct to flourish. The Securities and Exchange Commission (SEC), Commodities Futures Trading Commission (CFTC), Federal Reserve, and Federal Deposit Insurance Corporation (FDIC) have the power to enact regulations subject to criminal penalties through their rule-making authority.[1] In addition to being responsible for investigating misconduct, they may refer cases for criminal prosecution. The processing of these criminal referrals as well as the pursuit of other indicia of criminality within the financial sector reflects the administrative structure of the U.S. Department of Justice (M. Ramirez 2010). Although these agencies and other governmental authorities agreed to a number of civil settlements with the largest companies, the leaders at the apex of those organizations deemed "to big to fail" escaped criminal liability and many retained their positions within those organizations and the powerful financial influence they wield (Breslow 2013; M. Ramirez 2013; S. Ramirez 2013).

Early white-collar crime studies considered both civil liability cases and criminal liability cases, preferring to categorize by the type of offender or association of the act with one's occupation rather than relying upon the labels (e.g., criminal, civil, regulatory) placed on the offense (Clinard et al. 1979; Sutherland 1983). Within this context, this chapter explores the various inputs to oversight and rule making, the considerations that frustrate or favor effective oversight, and the political conflict that complicates long-term stability in rule making, oversight, and enforcement. In an age where reliance on self-regulation and ethical conduct has failed, this chapter concludes by identifying some avenues to redirect long-term confidence in the rule of law toward a public good.

To examine these issues more fully, this analysis focuses on the U.S. financial markets because they are attractive targets for white-collar crime; yet, the stability and success of such markets are critical to the economic well-being, national security, and stability of the U.S. government. The main conclusions are as follows:

- Financial markets are critical to a robust economy but also attract white-collar criminals. Regulations to prevent crime and oversight to detect crime are necessary to protect the fiscal health of the nation. Oversight is achieved through rule making.
- Once public attention has waned and markets have stabilized, special interests that benefit from a lack of oversight will exercise influence to diminish regulatory restrictions and subvert criminal accountability.
- Rules give the appearance of oversight and accountability, but those responsible for oversight fail to protect the public good because they are beholden to special interests, leadership is compromised by the mixed motives of revolving-door regulators, and special interests act persistently to frustrate the regulatory mission. Special interests operate across the political spectrum.
- Without structural reform that imposes controls and punishes their breach effectively, economic concentration will proceed unabated and the application of the rule of law to financial elites will continue to diminish as punishment is diluted even in clear cases of criminality, imposing a costly burden on the public and threatening stability.

Section I examines the need for oversight and rule making, reviewing the historical pattern of financial industry failures and legislative corrections. Section II identifies the limits of such rules and highlights the need for effective oversight once public attention wanes and special interests exploit the resulting political vacuum. Section III describes how self-interest by governing elites undermines effective implementation of regulations and prosecution of white-collar crime. Finally, section IV surveys proposals to reform the regulatory process and strengthen oversight and enforcement, to protect the public good (Santos 2006), and to reduce elite subversion of criminal accountability.

I. The Political Necessity of Regulation

Major advances in financial regulation have been born out of political and financial necessity, resetting the financial markets and banking industry during times of crisis. Regulations are not made in a vacuum. They require the expertise of the industry, even though driven by public interest in the outcome. Central to their success is the need to have the force of law behind them and to be sufficiently reasonable to enlist the governed in operating under them. Several key instances of significant legislation bearing on the financial markets have occurred over the past eighty years.

A. The 1929 Stock Market Crash and the Great Depression

New Deal legislation enacted in the 1930s after the stock market crash of 1929 and the ensuing Great Depression resulted from political pressure to fix the unregulated financial system. During 1933–1934, the U.S. Senate Committee on Banking and Currency investigated the securities and banking markets in response to the stock market crash and the Great Depression (Pecora 1968). In his 1939 book, Ferdinand Pecora described the testimony as revealing "a shocking corruption in our banking system [and] a widespread repudiation of old fashioned standards of honesty and fair dealing" (Pecora 1968, pp. 283–84).

The Roosevelt administration enacted the Banking Act of 1933, also known as Glass-Steagall (separating commercial banking and creating the FDIC), the Securities Act of 1933 (mandating full disclosure in the sales of securities), and the Securities Exchange Act of 1934 (regulating the securities markets) (Pecora 1968; S. Ramirez 2013). It also criminalized market manipulation, fraud, and violations of SEC rules (Securities and Exchange Act 1934; Pecora 1968; Kessler 1997). The New Deal slate of financial industry regulatory safeguards restored confidence in the banking system (Pecora 1968; Kessler 1997). The legislation even gained the support of business interests (Gordon 1994; s. Ramirez 2004).

B. The Savings and Loan Crisis

Deregulation in the savings and loans industry included repeal of controls on interest rates paid to depositors and elimination of restrictions on thrift activities (Black 2005). Hundreds of thrifts failed (Calavita and Pontell 1990). Total costs exceeded $1 trillion, bankrupted the Federal Savings and Loan Insurance Corporation, and led to the enactment of the Financial Institutions Reform, Recovery, and Enforcement Act (Friedrichs 2009). A new agency, the Resolution Trust Corporation, sold the assets of failed thrifts and pursued recovery from negligent officers and directors (Friedrichs 2009). Although the government's response "focused on containing the financial crisis, rather than on punishing wrongdoing . . . a high proportion of those formally charged in major thrift cases were convicted" (Rosoff, Pontell, and Tillman 2004, pp. 337–38).

The U.S. Department of Justice prosecuted Charles Keating and his cohorts on racketeering and bank fraud, among other charges (Rosoff et al. 2004; Black 2005).

C. Financial Accounting Fraud

Widespread fraud led to the stock market crash in 2002. Congressional efforts to deregulate the financial markets again played a key role (cummings 2007).[2] Rampant accounting fraud involving hundreds of corporations yielding bonuses and rewards for executives but huge losses for shareholders led to legislation prior to the fall mid-term elections creating stronger terms of enforcement and oversight than preferred by the administration (M. Ramirez 2007). The Sarbanes-Oxley Act of 2002 was enacted to address the accounting fraud and market manipulation that captured national attention beginning with the bankruptcy of Enron in the fall of 2001, but it did not reverse deregulatory efforts (Rosoff et al. 2004; cummings 2007). The act added key criminal provisions punishing securities and commodities fraud (18 U.S.C. §§ 1348, 1349) and providing criminal penalties prospectively for corporate officers who knowingly or willfully certify any financial statement pursuant to section 13(a) or 15(d) of the Securities Exchange Act of 1934 (15 U.S.C. §§ 78m[a] or 780[d]) that fails to comport with the requirements of those sections, and in particular with supplying information that "fairly presents, in all material respects, the financial condition and results of operation of the issuer" (18 U.S.C. § 1350).

The Department of Justice responded by forming the Enron Task Force, which led to the prosecution of thirty-three former employees of Enron, including successful prosecutions of former chief executives Ken Lay and Jeffrey Skilling, and Chief Financial Officer Andrew Fastow (M. Ramirez 2005, 2010; Emschwiller 2006). A Corporate Fraud Task Force, established in 2002 to address the broader corporate accounting fraud scandal, also reported "nearly 1,300 corporate fraud convictions . . . includ[ing] convictions of more than 200 chief executive officers and corporate presidents, more than 120 corporate vice presidents, and more than fifty chief financial officers" (M. Ramirez 2010, p. 978). Indeed, CEOs from some of the largest corporations embroiled in accounting scandals at the time were prosecuted, including Bernard Ebbers of WorldCom, Richard Scrushy from HealthSouth, John Rigas from Adelphia Communications, and Dennis Kozlowski from Tyco (M. Ramirez 2005; Rosoff et al. 2007; Friedrichs 2009).

D. The Financial Crisis of 2008

The tightening of credit markets in August 2007 and the bankruptcy of Lehman Brothers in September 2008 lent credence to Federal Reserve Chairman and the U.S. Treasury Secretary warnings to Congressional leaders that the United States was facing a financial market meltdown, and it could not wait for reforms to be attached to a bailout (S. Ramirez 2013). Congress passed the Emergency Economic Stabilization Act of 2008, agreeing to fund a $700 billion Troubled Asset Relief Program (TARP) to bail out the financial industry (Prins 2009; Financial Crisis Inquiry Committee [FCIC] 2011). Many of the bailouts of the 2008 financial crisis were initially hidden from public view, as the Federal Reserve used its powers to lend trillions of dollars to the largest banks and insurance companies with virtually no governmental oversight (FCIC 2011). Indeed, the Federal Reserve withheld the scope of the secret bailout from Congress as it debated the TARP bailout and regulatory oversight of the industry (Ivry, Keoun, and Kuntz 2011). By the summer of 2010, the U.S. bailout sat at over $16 trillion, which is more than the cost of all U.S. wars and conflicts combined at that time (Prins 2009; S. Ramirez 2013). The losses were not limited to the United States; rather, the global loss of wealth was estimated at $50 trillion in the summer of 2009 (Prins 2009).

In the United States, bailed-out firms gave massive bonuses to the top executives who had crashed the economy (Prins 2009; M. Ramirez 2013). With delinquent mortgages at record highs, a second wave of criminality emerged as banks submitted thousands of forged documents in courts across the country in support of foreclosure filings, and still no major banks or mortgage servicers were prosecuted (Paltrow 2012; U.S. Department of Justice, Office of Public Affairs 2012; M. Ramirez 2013). Described as "the biggest expansion of government power over banking and markets since the Depression," the Dodd-Frank Wall Street Reform and Consumer Protection Act aimed to promote financial stability by improving accountability and transparency, and to protect consumers from abusive financial services practices, among other purposes (Paletta and Lucchetti 2010).

Dodd-Frank offered no new criminal authority. Significantly, it did not affirmatively reverse many of the deregulatory measures that the FCIC concluded laid a foundation for manipulation (FCIC 2011). Instead, Dodd-Frank's chief Wall Street reforms were to be implemented over an eighteen-month period by regulatory agencies exercising rule-making authority (Funk 2010; Easton 2012; Taibbi 2012). Moreover, unlike prior financial crises, seven years after the crisis, top executives in the financial industry have not been prosecuted for any crimes, nor have the institutions been criminally charged (Breslow 2013; M. Ramirez 2013; S. Ramirez 2013; Cohen 2015). In many instances, the Department of Justice has announced it has no plans to prosecute the top executives despite evidence of wrongdoing and recommendations to investigate (Valukas 2010; FCIC 2011; Ferguson 2012; M. Ramirez 2013; PBS 2013).

II. Laissez-Faire Governance and Regulatory Retreat

Reform via regulation is "no panacea; nor are [these laws] self-regulating" (Pecora 1968, p. 303). As confidence is restored, financial and business interests often begin to oppose the need for additional regulation. Mancur Olsen long ago recognized the ability of small, cohesive, well-organized special-interest groups to prevail over diffused broad-based citizen concerns (Olsen 1971; Canova 2009; Coffee 2012). Extending this theory regarding special-interest groups, discrete but motivated groups may capture regulatory institutions, undermining their oversight and "assuring regulation will be uncoordinated and ineffective" (Canova 2009, p. 391). Corporate executives, as agents, often have interests that may diverge from those of the corporation and are able to use the financial power and wealth of the corporation to further their interests at the expense of the organization (S. Ramirez 2013). Corporate elites in the financial industry wield power and use corporate wealth to manipulate the legislative process through lobbying, through special access to government, and through government recruitment from corporate executives (Dye and Zeigler 2009; Baxter 2011). Left unchecked, corporate elites and the companies they run could become "financial super predators" able to "defeat all internal and external controls" because they are "ultimately in charge of the controls" (Black 2005, p. xiii).

A. Laissez-Faire Ideology: Markets Are Self-Correcting

Regulatory oversight is a first step in policing white-collar crime. When the leadership of the country or of the regulatory industry openly rejects regulatory oversight, it conveys the message to fraudsters that the agencies will not be scrutinizing the industry and that the time is ripe for special interests to harvest profits.

The Federal Reserve is a key regulator of the financial system. In 1987, Alan Greenspan, an "anti-regulator" who believed in the self-correcting nature of the financial markets, was appointed chairman (Stiglitz 2009). As a major proponent of deregulation, Greenspan encouraged alternative mortgage products that led to the subprime lending fiasco, supported the repeal of Glass-Steagall, and pressed to keep derivatives trading from falling under regulatory oversight (Prins 2009). In support of his ideology, Greenspan recognized that risk had to be managed but maintained that "private regulation generally has proved far better at constraining excessive risk-taking than has government regulation" (Federal Reserve Board 2005; Prins 2009).

Greenspan's belief that the market is self-correcting without need for oversight was roundly disproved in the financial crisis of 2008. Greenspan avoided numerous opportunities to use the Federal Reserve's oversight authority to clamp down on reckless mortgage lending and leverage ratios of $60 of debt to $1 of equity, relying instead on the "self-correcting nature of the markets and the ability of financial institutions to effectively police themselves" (FCIC 2011, p. xviii; S. Ramirez 2013). The commission (2011) found that a reliance on self-policing and an erosion of ethical conduct contributed to the crisis. Despite clear warnings from economists regarding the risks posed by the derivative markets, Greenspan claimed surprise when confronted by the enormity of the financial crisis, acknowledging a "flaw" in his ideology (Prins 2009; Stiglitz 2009). His ideology ignored a basic premise of market manipulation that some actors will place self-interest above the interest of their firms, rejecting optimal market behavior for self-interested profit maximization.

Throughout each of the crises in the financial markets, special interests have maintained that regulation restricts growth and burdens businesses (O'Brien 2003; Easton 2012). Despite the historical record of recurrent financial crises, the attacks on regulation waged by special interests nevertheless often received a sympathetic hearing in both the executive and legislative branches of government.

B. Deregulation

The leadership in both political parties has shifted to support deregulatory policies over the past forty years (O'Brien 2003; Canova 2009). Regulatory protections enacted from the 1930s to the 1950s that had provided for decades of financial stability were forsaken as legislation was enacted "abolishing selective credit controls and deregulating banking and finance" (Canova 2009, pp. 376–77). The severe financial losses during the thrift crisis in the early 1980s, spurred by deregulation and regulatory inaction, did not stem the prevailing march toward deregulation (Friedrichs 2009).

In 1998, Long Term Capital Management nearly collapsed due to the weight of its over-the-counter derivatives, serving as an early warning of a shadow banking system that was undercapitalized and overleveraged (cummings 2007). Nevertheless, efforts by the Commodity Futures Trading Commission to impose regulations on the derivatives market to limit its expansion and related losses were stifled by financial titans, including Henry Paulson, then chairperson of Goldman Sachs, who aligned against the effort thirteen major banks, Treasury Secretary Robert Rubin, Federal Reserve Chairman Alan Greenspan, and SEC Chairman Arthur Levitt (PBS 2009). In 2000, Congress effectively eliminated oversight of the over-the-counter derivatives market by both the Commodity Futures Trading Commission and the SEC (cummings 2007; FCIC 2011). Thus, when the financial crisis of 2008 came to the forefront of the American consciousness, many of the regulatory protections put in place in response to the 1929 market crash and the Great Depression had been gutted. Moreover, the regulatory responses to the widening trail of financial crises were unresponsive to the failed policy of deregulation of the financial industry. This period of deregulation, coupled with a move toward industry self-regulation, set the stage for the financial crisis of 2008 (Canova 2009; FCIC 2011). The Commission (2011) concluded in its report: "More than 30 years of deregulation and reliance on self-regulation by financial institutions, championed by former Federal Reserve chairman Alan Greenspan and others, supported by successive administrations and Congresses, and actively pushed by the powerful financial industry at every turn, had stripped away key safeguards, which could have helped avoid catastrophe" (p. xviii).

III. Undermining Oversight

The passage of legislation and the enactment of regulations to impose oversight and address market failures is only the first victory in an ongoing battle between the public's desire to protect markets and special interests' desire to subvert markets. It is far easier to make changes to oversight at the regulatory level because public attention wanes once legislation is passed. Special-interest groups remain committed to issues, whereas the public is dispersed and disorganized. Those responsible for enforcing laws fail to do so for a variety of reasons. Special interests may use politicians' need for financing elections to influence appointments to top posts in regulatory agencies or to receive favorable treatment (Canova 2009; Johnson and Kwak 2011). Oversight is undermined by revolving-door leadership that is at odds with the regulatory mission of government oversight and by the perpetual underfunding or understaffing of agencies as well as by the persistent failure to impose meaningful sanctions. Nowhere have the efforts to reduce oversight been more successful than they have been in short-circuiting criminal accountability.

A. Campaign Financing

Campaigning for political office is a costly affair in the United States. The 2012 federal elections, at over $5.8 billion, were the most expensive in history (Center for Responsive Politics 2012). The need to raise money to finance campaigns consumes politicians on all points of the political spectrum and encourages cozy relationships between those who seek public office and those seek legislative influence.

In his first presidential election in 2000, George W. Bush enjoyed financial support from Kenneth Lay, CEO of Enron Corporation, one of the fastest-growing and largest corporations in the United States at that time. Lay was part of a select group of fund-raisers for the presidential election, called "Pioneers," bringing in more than $602,000 from Enron and its employees in 2001, and donating with his wife $139,500 to George W. Bush's political campaigns over the years. From 1989 to 2001, he and his wife donated $882,580 to federal candidates, with over 90 percent of those funds going to Republican candidates (Associated Press 2009). With the collapse of Enron, the Department of Justice prosecuted Lay and Bush stepped back from the relationship.

In 2008, Barack Obama was in a tight primary campaign against Hillary Clinton when Wall Street committed its substantial financial support to Obama, contributing $9.5 million to him during the primary season, while also contributing $5.3 million to the Republican frontrunner, John McCain, in a pointed effort to have a friend in the White House just as the financial markets were failing (Saltonstall 2008; Yost 2008). Obama eventually clinched the Democratic nomination and went on to victory in the general presidential election. "Four out of Obama's top five contributors were employees of financial industry giants—Goldman Sachs ($571,330), USB AG ($364,806), JPMorgan Chase ($362,207) and Citigroup ($358,054)" (Saltonstall 2008). Despite the near meltdown of the financial markets, Obama retained the chairman of the Federal Reserve and appointed Timothy Geithner as treasury secretary, Larry Summers as director of the White House National Economic Council, and Eric Holder as attorney general (Canova 2009; Wachtel 2011). Eric Holder appointed Lanny Breuer as deputy attorney general of the Criminal Division (Paltrow 2012). Each of these appointees had strong links to the financial industry (Barofsky 2012; Barth, Caprio, and Levine 2012). Collectively, this group was unlikely to pursue criminal actions against those responsible for the crisis (Stiglitz 2010). Given the generous terms of the bailout and the lack of criminal prosecutions against leaders in the industry, one is forced to recall that Obama might not have been elected president but for early and generous support by the financial industry.

Reliance upon special interests to finance elections (Santos 2006) increased with the U.S. Supreme Court decision in *Citizens United v. Federal Election Commission* (558 U.S. 310 [2010]), which prohibited the government from restricting independent political expenditures by corporations and unions under the U.S. Constitution. Lower courts have used the decision to strike down limits on lobbying, including ethics rules that prohibit individuals from lobbying the government for a limited time period, such as twelve months, after they leave government employment (Hasen 2012). Spending on federal election campaigns in 2010, 2012, and 2014 subsequent to *Citizens United* broke records, with Congressional races far outpacing pre-2010 costs (Center for Responsive Politics 2010, 2012, 2015; Kurtzleben 2011). Funding political campaigns affects the executive and legislative branches (Santos 2006; Center for Responsive Politics 2012).

B. Revolving Door

Through its rule-making power, the government sets limits on cost externalization (Calavita and Pontell 1990). Business leaders complain such limits risk stifling capitalism by squelching innovation and adding compliance costs (Pecora 1968; Easton 2012). Sensitivity to the nature of limits and the risk of harm to business leads to a compromise. Oversight via administrative regulations is conducted by experts who have industry experience and are sensitive to the demands that such rules may place on business. Thus, the regulators are drawn from the industries they are asked to police (Prins 2009; Warren 2013).

The presence of industry beneficiaries in governmental positions highlights the influence of the financial industry in the years leading up to the 2008 crisis (S. Ramirez 2013). The passage of the Financial Services Modernization Act of 1999—significant for its deregulatory impact on the industry—legalized an earlier merger between Traveler's Insurance Company and Citicorp that would have been in violation of existing laws except for a grant by the Federal Reserve permitting the corporation a two-year grace period to divest the insurance company or convince legislators to change the law (PBS

2003; M. Ramirez 2013; S. Ramirez 2013). Then Treasury Secretary Robert Rubin championed the proposed legislation prior to leaving government after its passage to work for Citigroup (O'Brien 2003; Prins 2009; S. Ramirez 2013). Likewise, as chairman of Goldman Sachs, Henry Paulson had been a key supporter of the legislation and of efforts to ensure that derivatives would not be regulated by the Commodity Futures Trading Commission. Paulson left that post when he was appointed as U.S. treasury secretary in 2005, and he remained as secretary while the financial industry spiraled out of control beginning in 2006 and eventually crashed in 2008. This left Paulson at the helm proposing bailout legislation that would end up greatly benefiting his old firm (FCIC 2011; Johnson and Kwak 2011; S. Ramirez 2013).

In 2009, President Obama appointed Timothy Geithner as treasury secretary. Geithner had been the president of the Federal Reserve Bank of New York as the crisis unfolded and had worked closely with Paulson in the waning days of 2008 to develop a bailout (Sorkin 2009). One of his first acts as treasury secretary was to appoint Mark Patterson, a lobbyist for Goldman Sachs, as his chief of staff (Prins 2009). Although expertise in the industry would seem to be essential for both oversight and reform, it is also quite likely that individuals who have lobbied for a particular industry and who will inevitably return there after government service will advance perspectives that do not differ significantly from those of industry leaders (Stiglitz 2009).

Those who enter government service to promote the public good may be co-opted through subtle efforts. While at the Federal Reserve, Geithner was contacted by Sanford Weill, a former Citigroup CEO, regarding the possibility of Geithner becoming CEO of Citigroup after Charles Prince stepped down with a $38 million pay package in late 2007 due to the company's poor performance (Sorkin 2009). In contemplating the question, Geithner contacted one of his mentors, Robert Rubin, who informed Geithner that Rubin had placed his support behind Vikram Pandit to become CEO and advised Geithner to remain at the Federal Reserve, which Geithner did (Sorkin 2009). Pandit went on to earn about $56.5 million in compensation over the next five years (Enrich, Kapner, and Fitzpatrick 2012). Given the downturn in the financial markets, the excessive risk taking that was apparent in 2007, and the massive lending program that the Federal Reserve administered within the following year, Citigroup might hope Geithner would view the industry favorably, with a desire to please its leaders to perhaps increase lucrative employment opportunities in the future. Full-fledged efforts to break up the banks or impose new regulatory measures would be unlikely to enhance one's opportunities in the private sector. Moreover, Geithner gained the treasury secretary title and experience, earned pro-industry credentials aiding the financial industry with bailouts and sweetheart civil settlements, yet virtually ignored the home mortgage foreclosure crisis and the lackluster Affordable Home Modification Program (Suskind 2011; Barofsky 2012).

Harvey Pitt chaired the SEC from 2001 to 2003, after having previously represented corporate raider Ivan Boesky (Stewart 1992) and the "big five" accounting firms in their efforts to resist the SEC's campaign to separate the accounting industry's consulting business from its auditing business (Stephenson 2002). As SEC chairman, Pitt clashed with New York Attorney General Eliot Spitzer, who pursued conflicts of interest identified in Spitzer's investigation of Merrill Lynch and the rest of Wall Street in the early 2000s (O'Brien 2003). Asserting that the widespread nature of the activity suggested systemic breakdown, Pitt agreed to a global settlement between regulators and banks only because Spitzer refused to back down (O'Brien 2003). The banks were required to sever the links between research and investment banking (O'Brien 2003; Berenson and Sorkin 2012). Ultimately, the chairman of the New York Stock Exchange brokered an agreement between the feuding regulators and the banking sector, and Spitzer agreed to back off and to allow the SEC to lead any enforcement measures (Berenson and Sorkin 2002; O'Brien 2003). After leaving the SEC, Pitt founded a global business consulting firm associated with at least three hedge funds (Kalaroma Partners, LLC 2013).

The revolving-door temptation to please potential employers and the affinity with the industry one plans to join or rejoin emerges within the regulatory ranks as well (Hilzenrath 2011; Smallberg 2011; Taibbi 2012). A 2011 report by the Project on Government Oversight studying the SEC's revolving door identified 789 disclosure filings within a five-year period by former employees who planned to represent industry interests before the commission within two years of their departure from the agency (Smallberg 2011). More significantly, "the SEC Office of Inspector General has identified cases in which the revolving door appeared to be a factor in staving off SEC enforcement actions and other types of SEC oversight, including cases involving Bear Stearns and the Stanford Ponzi scheme" (Smallberg 2011, p. 2). The report further relied upon an empirical study that "found indirect evidence to support the contention that post-agency employment at higher salaries may operate as a quid pro quo in return for favorable regulatory treatment'" (Smallberg 2011, p. 26). The view that the revolving door distorts and undermines agency oversight and enforcement is broadly held and empirically supported.

Congressional policy expertise and access to members of Congress make former members valuable for private industry roles and as lobbyists (Santos 2006; Dye and Zeigler 2009; Center for Responsive Politics 2013). Adolfo Santos's (2006) study of former members of Congress who served between the early1970s and the early 2000s concluded that members of Congress who become lobbyists behave differently in their last term in Congress relative to those who do not become lobbyists, citing "numerous examples of lawmakers who used their position to enact legislation that benefited specific groups. These same lawmakers would then leave office only to become employed by the very group that they sponsored legislation for" (Santos 2006, p. 140).

The revolving door does not stop at the regulatory doorstep. The Department of Justice holds ultimate oversight authority through its ability to prosecute fraud and other federal financial crimes. As the 2008 financial crisis emerged, Attorney General Michael B. Mukasey refused to create a task force similar to that created in response to Enron's collapse and the corporate accounting frauds earlier in the decade (Lichtblau, Johnston, and Nixon 2008). In 2009, President Obama appointed Eric Holder as attorney general, and Holder selected Lanny Breuer as chief of his Criminal Division. Both Holder and Breuer came from private practice at Covington and Burling. Significantly,

Covington and Burling had represented the four largest U.S. banks and Freddie Mac prior to the financial crisis (Paltrow 2012; M. Ramirez 2013). When the foreclosure crisis hit, the banks involved drew up fraudulent mortgage assignments with forged signatures to foreclose on properties, an effort that came to be known as "robo-signing" (M. Ramirez 2013). Despite unquestionably fraudulent conduct, no criminal charges were brought against the banks. Instead, a global civil settlement involving forty-nine states and the Department of Justice was negotiated (U.S. Department of Justice, Office of Public Affairs 2012). Upon leaving the DOJ, both Holder and Breur returned to white collar defense work at Covinton & Burling (de la Merced 2015). Both have been criticized for failing to indict any of the top banks, mortgage companies, or top executives in the wake of the crisis (Breslow 2013; M. Ramirez 2013).

Thus, the revolving door between the private sector and the government undermines the effectiveness of both regulatory agencies and governmental departments, because self-interest interferes with effective oversight and enforcement, including criminal enforcement.

C. Withholding Resources

Underfunding or understaffing also undermines regulatory effectiveness. Congress holds the power of the purse and may use that power to withhold appropriations to fund statutory mandates and regulatory activities (U.S. Constitution, Article I, sections 8 and 9; Stith 1998). Using this power, legislators effectively have quashed oversight of the financial markets by withholding the funding necessary to effectuate the mission of various regulatory agencies. Because the federal budget involves so many different factors, reducing or limiting funding levels for a particular agency is less likely to gain widespread attention, while being pursued by special interests and those doing its bidding.

As early as 2004, the FBI requested additional funds to investigate the burgeoning number of mortgage-fraud complaints (Lichtblau et al. 2008). Personnel and other resources had been shifted from white-collar crime investigations to national security concerns after the 9/11 attacks (Lichtblau et al. 2008). From 2001 through 2007, the number of cases against financial institutions decreased 48 percent, from 2,435 cases to 1,257 cases, while the number of FBI agents working on white-collar crime cases during that period decreased 35 percent (Lichtblau et al. 2008). Despite clear evidence of increasing reports of fraud, neither additional personnel nor funds were provided.

The FBI acts as the criminal investigator for many white-collar crimes, although there are many other agencies that provide investigative support depending upon the nature of the crime (M. Ramirez 2010). The SEC lacks criminal prosecution authority, but it has authority to refer cases to the Department of Justice for criminal prosecution. From 2005 through 2012, the SEC faced flat or declining budgets (Carton 2011; Stewart 2011; U.S. SEC 2014). Its failure to investigate credible reports of fraud in the securities industry and its failure to provide effective oversight were cited as contributing factors to the financial market's collapse (FCIC 2011). The Dodd-Frank and Consumer

Protection Act, passed in 2010, imposed substantial new burdens on the agency to "create five new offices within its existing structure, conduct and publish 67 one-time reports or studies, conduct and publish another 22 reports on a periodic basis, and promulgate more that 240 new rules" (Carton 2011). The legislation also provided that the SEC's budget would double over the next five years, but Congress failed to appropriate additional funding in 2011 (Carton 2011). Critically, Dodd-Frank had included a plan to shift SEC to self-funding—a measure that has been attempted before and failed—but a last-minute legislative compromise removed the self-funding measure and replaced it with the promise to escalate funding and access to a $100 million reserve fund (Carton 2011). The failure to increase funding led to the SEC "curtail[ing] travel by its investigators and inspectors" and cutting back on expanding the facilities to meet the Dodd-Frank legislative mandates, including the delayed opening of an SEC Whistleblower Office (Carton 2011). Funding for the agency continues to lag well behind need, creating significant resource constraints. The SEC chair testified before Congress that "the number of examiners per trillion dollars in investment-adviser assets under management dropped from 19 in 2004 to 8 in 2014" (U.S. GAO Report 2014, p. 123).

In late 2010, unable to repeal Dodd-Frank, House Majority Leader Eric Cantor stated that Congress has the power to deny funding to the SEC and other executive agencies and that this is what the American people expect (Garofalo 2010; Carton 2011). Tight control over the SEC's budget had been used before. In 1995, U.S. senators reportedly "threatened to turn off the lights" at the SEC if it continued to oppose legislation curbing private securities litigation (Paltrow 1995; S. Ramirez 2000). Arthur Levitt, as chairman of the SEC, ended his efforts to reform auditor independence standards in 2000, fearing funding cuts by Congress in retribution (Levitt 2002; S. Ramirez 2002).

In the wake of Enron, the Department of Justice created a Corporate Fraud Task Force to address the massive accounting frauds, but the task force lacked its own prosecutorial staff or budget, and no additional staff or budgetary support was given to U.S. Attorneys' offices to pursue corporate crime (M. Ramirez 2010). With the increase in prosecutions that followed, the White House and Treasury Department expressed concerns that the pursuit of corporate criminality demonstrated "an antibusiness attitude that could chill corporate risk-taking"; major corporate fraud cases dropped significantly after 2005 (Lichtblau et al. 2008, p. A1; M. Ramirez 2010). The investigation and prosecution of white-collar crimes is costly due to the complex nature of the crimes (M. Ramirez 2010). Without resources devoted to pursuing such criminality, laws prohibiting criminal conduct are useless.

D. Additional Means of Undermining Regulatory Effectiveness

The Dodd-Frank Act of 2010 expands whistleblower protections, in part to expand upon the narrowly drawn and interpreted language of a whistleblower provision included in the Sarbanes-Oxley Act (M. Ramirez 2007). Recognizing the broad participation by many actors in concealing financial crimes, Congress sought to encourage employees to step forward with information of suspicious conduct to aid in early detection of fraud, while adopting measures to protect the employees from retaliation, a common occurrence when a whistleblower steps forward (M. Ramirez 2007; Levin and Coburn 2011; Westman and Modesitt 2012). Little opposition to including whistleblower provisions in Dodd-Frank reforms gave way to concerted opposition to the structure and rule-making process (U.S. Chamber of Commerce 2010; Securities Whistleblowers Incentives and Protections, 76 Fed. Reg. 34,300 [June 13, 2011]). Initially, a host of factors threatened its success, including inadequate funding and resources, proposed legislative amendments to undercut its provisions, threats of lawsuits from lobbyist groups and special interests, and the possibility that the scope of the legislation would be narrowed by conservative court interpretations (U.S. Securities and Exchange Commission 2011; Whistleblower Improvement Act of 2011 [H.R. 2483]).

E. Superficial Enforcement

Resolving matters civilly without requiring admission of wrongdoing or with fines substantially below reasonable amounts based upon the seriousness of the violations, failing to refer for criminal prosecution cases of known criminal conduct, and accepting plea deals that grossly understate criminal responsibility creates the appearance that the government is enforcing the rule of law, but the overall effect is superficial and instead may weaken the law.

The SEC and other government agencies frequently agree to civil settlements without requiring admission of wrongdoing (Lazo and Reckard 2011). Judge Jed Rakoff has criticized the SEC's practice of agreeing to consent judgments that do not require defendants to admit or deny the allegations of the complaint because such agreements hide the truth. He refused to approve a settlement where the SEC failed to provide sufficient information regarding the underlying facts establishing fraud in the case and the defendant bank was a recidivist, having violated prior agreements to follow the law (Wyatt 2011). Judge Rakoff's rejection of the settlement prompted several other federal district courts to withhold approval of agency settlements as well (Lattman 2013).[3] The SEC maintains that settlements are in the public's best interests because—due to limited resources—it cannot afford to bring the fraud cases to trial, and the Second Circuit that reviewed Judge Rakoff's decision held that the judge had not given sufficient deference to the agency's decision (Lattman 2013). The courts' willingness to step into the void left by regulator failure to protect the public interest reportedly has prompted some shift within the agency to require admissions of wrongdoing when the defendant acknowledges guilt in a related federal criminal case (Ax 2014).

Judge Rakoff also has criticized such settlements and initially rejected one between the SEC and Bank of America as unfair to the victims because the agency had grossly undervalued the claims (Kouwe 2009; Raymond 2011). Settlements by agencies and the Department of Justice arising from the 2008 crisis, although sometimes for substantial sums, are proportionately undervalued given the scope of the harm addressed in the settlements (Prins 2009; Warren 2013).

The U.S. Sentencing Guidelines, its Economic Crime Package, and the Sarbanes-Oxley Act strengthened punishment for white-collar crime (M. Ramirez 2003). With harsher terms of imprisonment recommended under the guidelines, the Department of Justice and financial elites have nurtured alternatives to prosecution, especially for large and public corporations, such as deferred prosecution agreements and nonprosecution agreements for those instances in which criminality cannot be ignored but meaningful punishment is sought to be avoided (M. Ramirez 2005, 2013; Garrett 2014).

Not only have the major investment banks become too big to fail, but also they have become too big to indict, as evidenced by a decision at the Department of Justice to enter into a global settlement with HSBC that included a nonprosecution agreement in lieu of indictment because of "concerns that criminal charges could jeopardize one of the world's largest banks and ultimately destabilize the global financial system" (Keshner 2012, p. 3; Protess and Silver-Greenberg 2012; U.S. Senate Committee on Homeland Security and Governmental Affairs 2012). Despite a wide-ranging money laundering operation and ties to terrorists and drug cartels, the decision not to indict can be contrasted with the 1991 guilty plea by the Bank of Commerce and Credit International (BCCI) to federal and state charges of racketeering, fraud, larceny, and falsification of business documents, as well as the largest forfeiture agreement in a criminal case at that time (Friedrichs 2009). At the time it was shut down due to the criminal investigation, BCCI had branches in seventy countries and assets between $20 and $30 billion (Friedrichs 2009). Moreover, BCCI's CEO pled guilty to federal charges stemming from the case (Friedrichs 2009).

The revolving door—and the support of powerful members of both political parties with financial favors—creates a sympathetic cartel of actors eager to distract the general public from the misconduct of the few by redirecting the focus of the American public to external risks. Thus, resources are shifted from investigating fraud to protecting our physical security from terrorists set to destroy us and to prosecuting and deporting illegal immigrants who allegedly threaten our jobs (Lichtblau et al. 2008; Eskrow 2011). Instead of being criminally investigated, banks are bailed out.

IV. ENLISTING EFFORTS TOWARD
A PUBLIC GOOD

Without reform from within, the rule of law continues to be eroded insofar as financial elites are concerned. The belief that markets are efficient and self-regulating benefits the special interests that want to remain free of restrictive government oversight (Stiglitz 2010). Now that the financial crisis of 2008 has demonstrated that the laissez-faire approach to financial markets is inefficient, the question remains as to what can be done to turn the economy back onto the path toward stability and growth. If regulations were in place and meaningful oversight by dedicated agencies were to occur, the need for criminal prosecutions would be lessened because high-risk fraudulent activity would be addressed before it reaches crisis proportions.

The underlying causes of the latest financial crisis point to systemic oversight and enforcement failures. Some proposed reforms relevant to enforcement are identified below.

A. Eliminating "Too Big To Fail"

Many have suggested that enacting an updated version of Glass-Steagall that would once again separate commercial banking and investment banking would remove the resources used by these institutions to gamble depositors' funds (Canova 2009; Prins 2009; Johnson and Kwak 2011; S. Ramirez 2013). As the major investment banks have diminished in number due to consolidations occurring prior to and in response to the financial crisis, an oligarchy of firms "too big to fail" has diminished options that current economic leaders consider viable (Baxter 2011; Johnson and Kwak 2011; Macey and Holdcroft 2011). During the savings and loan crisis regulators stepped in and closed thrifts that could not be saved (Black 2005). A number of experts have advocated breaking up the big banks, in part because they have become too big to manage (Johnson 2011; Macey and Holdcroft 2011). Calls by politicians asking regulators to break up the big banks have led to threats by the banks to withhold broader financial support of Democratic senate campaigns (Flitter 2015).

B. Enhanced Regulation of the Financial Industry

Unregulated derivatives remain "financial weapons of mass destruction" in our midst waiting to be detonated once more (Stiglitz 2009). For shadow banking and over-the-counter derivatives, disclosure offering full transparency regarding risk levels and financial soundness of the institutions would be appropriate. Dodd-Frank tapped the SEC and Commodity Futures Trading Commission to promulgate rules by July 2011 to mandate clearing of certain derivatives but, in the wake of significant lobbying, inserted a number of exemptions to derivatives oversight during the conference committee (Dodd-Frank Act, §§716, 721, 723; S. Ramirez 2010). The Trading Commission's rules were implemented on December 31, 2012, but the SEC's rules were delayed (Protess 2012; S. Ramirez 2013). The SEC has implemented a host of derivative-related rules with a view toward investor and market protection, although exemptions remain problematic (SEC 2015). Nevertheless, Wall Street traders and bankers have maintained tenacious efforts pursuing repeal of rules with legislators (Eavis 2015).

C. Enhancing Limits on the Revolving Door

"The revolving door out of government is more strictly regulated than the revolving door into government," and legal restrictions seem to consist primarily of limits on the postgovernment employment of former regulatory agents in the private sector as opposed to the hiring by the government of powerful corporate executives who are likely to still have connections with the industries they are called upon to regulate (Hill and Painter 2011, p. 1667). The Project on Government Oversight recommended measures to address these issues, including that Congress and the SEC strengthen pre-employment and postemployment restrictions, use ethics enforcement authority, make postemployment statements and recusals publicly available, and extend regulation to other financial regulatory agencies (Smallberg 2011). Such recommendations depend upon a Congress willing to impose tougher standards, agency leaders committed to enforcing such standards, and courts willing to uphold such standards—all of which remain uncertain and as structural obstacles to monitoring the revolving-door problem.

D. Meaningful Enforcement

Legislation that restricts the opportunity for private parties to police their investment through civil litigation or that heightens the burden of proof prior to discovery (e.g., Private Securities Litigation Reform Act of 1995, Securities Litigation Uniform Standards Act of 1998) should be eliminated because civil liability provides a means to target misconduct without relying upon a captured government agency to affirmatively act or fail to act (S. Ramirez 2002; M. Ramirez 2003).

In negotiated settlements, the government can require removal of the top management in the firm without prosecuting the organization (U.S. Department of Justice 2012). Removal of such actors at least offers an opportunity for different leadership within the organization. Leadership is central to the corporate culture and to effect real change it must be altered (M. Ramirez 2003, 2005).

The Department of Justice should establish a Corporate Crimes Division specializing in investigating and prosecuting corporate and financial fraud (M. Ramirez 2010). The department has prosecuted hundreds of low-level business individuals for financial fraud but not those involved at the large institutions who committed the same crimes in the 2008 crisis (Schweizer 2012). The Corporate Crimes Division would have civil and criminal authority and focus on multidistrict or multinational organizations with complex corporate structures or significant financial holdings capable of disrupting markets (M. Ramirez 2010). Faced with the potent risk of severe economic harm from another financial crisis and in the wake of the devastating impact of the financial crisis of 2008, the division would place priority on overseeing the lawful functioning of the financial markets and would develop significant expertise to advise the executive and legislative branches regarding security measures that could be taken, whether regulatory or enforcement based, to reinstate long-term confidence in U.S. financial markets (M. Ramirez 2010). The division would be available to assist in settlements with such major organizations to better evaluate the true costs to the country and recommend appropriate accountability. Moreover, through focused expertise and dedicated resources, it would better hold top agents within those organizations accountable as well as interrupt criminal enterprises before they could impose devastating costs on the economy (M. Ramirez 2010). Without a calculated effort to rein in the power of financial elites—who as control frauds use internal and external forces to impose costly criminality on the public (Black 2005)—the rule of law is undermined and financial lawlessness threatens national security (M. Ramirez 2013).

V. CONCLUSION

Regulatory oversight is the first pillar in maintaining a free and open market economy and stands with civil and criminal enforcement to guard against abuses in the marketplace. Well-financed special interests enlist political conflict to further goals that benefit only a few well-placed actors at the apex of the financial markets while imposing external costs on the public. History has demonstrated that relying on corporate self-regulation and ethical conduct is ineffective in protecting the economy from the unlawful manipulations of control frauds. Each new round of crises is costlier than the ones that preceded it. Reform that imposes oversight, limits self-interested conduct, and punishes those who violate the law will redirect long-term confidence in the rule of law toward a public good as well as promote economic well-being, national security, and the stability of the U.S. government.

NOTES

1. *Securities and Exchange Act of 1934*, 15 U.S.C. § 78ff; *Commodities Exchange Act of 1936*, 7 U.S.C. §13(a)(5); *Federal Deposit Insurance Act of 1950*, 31 U.S.C. § 5322; *Bank Holding Company Act of 1956*, 12 U.S.C.A. § 1847.
2. *Private Securities Litigation Reform Act of 1995*, Pub. L. No. 104-67, 109 Stat. 737 (1995); *Securities Litigation Uniform Standards Act of 1998*, Pub. L. No. 105-353, 112 Stat. 3227 (1998) (codified in scattered sections of 15 U.S.C.); *Commodity Futures Modernization Act of 2000*, Pub. L. No. 106-554, 114 Stat. 2763 (2000); cummings (2007).
3. *SEC v. Citigroup Global Markets, Inc.*, 752 F.3d 285 (2nd Cir. 2014).

REFERENCES

Associated Press. 2009. "Bush Edges Away from 'Kenny Boy.'" *CBS News.com* (February 11). Available at http://www.cbsnews.com/2100-250_162-628320.html

Ax, Joseph. 2014. "U.S. Judge Reluctantly Approves SEC–Citigroup $285 Million Deal." Reuters.com (August 5). Available at http://www.reuters.com/article/2014/08/05/us-citigroup-sec-idUSKBN0G51OC20140805

Barofsky, Neil. 2012. *Bailout: An Inside Account of How Washington Abandoned Main Street While Rescuing Wall Street*. New York: Free Press.

Barth, James, Gerard Caprio, and Ross Levine. 2012. *Guardians of Finance: Making Regulators Work for Us*. Cambridge, MA: MIT Press.

Baxter, Lawrence. 2011. "'Capture' in Financial Regulation: Can We Channel It toward the Common Good?" *Cornell Journal of Law and Public Policy* 21: 175–98.

Berenson, Alex, and Andrew Ross Sorkin. 2012. "How Wall Street Was Tamed." *New York Times* (December 22). Available at http://www.nytimes.com/2002/12/22/business/how-wall-street-was-tamed.html?pagewanted=all&src=pm

Black, William K. 2005. *The Best Way to Rob a Bank Is to Own One: How Corporate Executives and Politicians Looted the S&L Industry*. Austin: University of Texas Press.

Breslow, Jason M. 2013. "Too Big to Jail? The Top Ten Civil Cases against the Banks." *PBS Frontline* (January 22). Available at http://www.pbs.org/wgbh/pages/frontline/business-economy-financial-crisis/untouchables/too-big-to-jail-the-top-10-civil-cases-against-the-banks/

Calavita, Kitty, and Henry N. Pontell. 1990. "'Heads I Win, Tails You Lose': Deregulation, Crime and Crisis in the Savings and Loan Industry." *Crime and Delinquency* 36: 309–41.

Canova, Timothy A. 2009. "Financial Market Failure as a Crisis in the Rule of Law: From Market Fundamentalism to a New Keynesian Regulatory Model." *Harvard Law and Policy Review* 3: 369–96.

Carton, Bruce. 2011 "How Can Congress Kill Dodd-Frank? By Underfunding It." *Securities Docket* (January 20). Available at http://www.securitiesdocket.com/2011/01/20/how-can-congress-kill-dodd-frank-by-underfunding-it/

Center for Responsive Politics. 2010. "Bad News for Incumbents, Self-Financing Candidates in Most Expensive Midterm Election in U.S. History." *Open Secrets Blog* (November 4). Available at http://www.opensecrets.org/news/2010/11/bad-night-for-incumbents-self finan.html

Center for Responsive Politics. 2012. "2012 Election Spending Will Reach $6 Billion, Center for Responsive Politics Predicts." *Open Secrets Blog* (October 31). Available at http://www.opensecrets.org/news/2012/10/2012-election-spending-will-reach-6.html

Center for Responsive Politics. 2013. "Revolving Door." *Open Secrets Blog* (February 27). Available at http://www.opensecrets.org/revolving/

Center for Responsive Politics. 2015. "Final Tally: 2014's Mid-Term Was Most Expensive, with Fewer Donors." *Open Secrets Blog* (February 18). Available at http://www.opensecrets.org/news/2015/02/final-tally-2014s-midterm-was-most-expensive-with-fewer-donors

Clinard, Marshall B., Peter C. Yeager, Jeanne Brisette, David Petrashek, and Elizabeth Harries. 1979. *Illegal Corporate Behavior*. Washington, D.C.: U.S. Government Printing Office.

Coffee, John. 2012. "The Political Economy of Dodd-Frank: Why Financial Reform Tends to Be Frustrated and Systemic Risk Perpetuated." *Cornell Law Review* 97: 1019–78.

Cohen, William D. 2015. "Instead of Wall St. Prosecutions, Holder Delivers a Deadline." *New York Times* (February 28). Available at http://www.nytimes.com/2015/02/28/business/dealbook/instead-of-wall-st-prosecutions-holder-delivers-a-deadline.html

cummings, andré douglas pond. 2007. "Still 'Ain't No Glory in Pain': How the Telecommunications Act of 1996 and Other 1990s Deregulation Facilitated the Market Crash of 2002." *Fordham Journal of Corporate and Financial Law* 12: 467–548.

de la Merced, Michael J. 2015. "Eric Holder Returns to Covington & Burling." *New York Times* (July 6). Available at http://www.nytimes.com/2015/07/07/business/dealbook/eric-holder-returns-to-covington-burling.html

Dye, Thomas R., and Harmon Zeigler. 2009. *The Irony of Democracy*, 14th ed. Boston: Wadsworth Cengage Learning.

Easton, Tom. 2012. "The Dodd-Frank Act: Too Big Not to Fail." *The Economist* (February 18). Available at http://www.economist.com/node/21547784

Eavis, Peter. 2014. "Wall St. Wins a Round in a Dodd-Frank Fight." *Wall Street Journal* (December 13): B3.

Emschwiller, John, Gary McWilliams, and Ann Davis. 2006. "Lay, Skilling are Convicted of Fraud. *Wall Street Journal* (May 26). Available at http://www.wsj.com/articles/SB114789594247955693

Enrich, David, Suzanne Kapner, and Dan Fitzpatrick. 2012. "Pandit Ousted as CEO of Citi." *Wall Street Journal* (October 17): A1.

Eskrow, Richard J. 2011. "The Department of Justice: Indicting Immigrants, Ignoring Wall Street Crooks." *Huffington Post* (March 29). Available at http://www.huffingtonpost.com/rj-eskow/justice-by-the-numbers-ch_b_841802.html

Federal Reserve Board. 2005. *Remarks by Chairman Alan Greenspan—Risk Transfer and Financial Stability*. Speech. May 5, 2005. Available at http://www.federalreserve.gov/Boarddocs/Speeches/2005/20050505/default.htm

Ferguson, Charles H. 2012. *Predator Nation: Corporate Criminals, Political Corruption, and the Hijacking of America*. New York: Crown Business.

Financial Crisis Inquiry Commission (FCIC). 2011. *The Financial Crisis Inquiry Report: Final Report of the National Commission on the Causes of the Financial and Economic Crisis in the United States*. Washington, D.C.: U.S. Government Printing Office.

Flitter, Emily. 2015. "Exclusive: Upset by Warren, U.S. Banks Debate Halting Some Campaign Donations." *Reuters.com* (March 27). Available at http://www.reuters.com/article/2015/03/27/us-usa-election-banks-iduskbn0mnobv20150327

Friedrichs, David O. 2009. *Trusted Criminals: White-Collar Crime in Contemporary Society*, 4th ed. Belmont: Thomson Wadsworth.

Funk, T. Markus. 2010. "Getting What They Pay for: The Far-Reaching Impact of the Dodd-Frank Act's 'Whistleblower Bounty' Incentives on FCPA Enforcement." *BNA White-Collar Crime Report* 5: 640–42.

Garofalo, Pat. 2010. "Cantor Confirms GOP Wants to Defund Financial Reform: 'That's What the American People Are Expecting.'" *Think Progress Blog* (November 3). Available at http://thinkprogress.org/economy/2010/11/03/173613/cantor-confirm-defund/

Garrett, Brandon L. 2014. *Too Big to Jail: How Prosecutors Compromise with Corporations*. Cambridge, MA: Harvard University Press.

Gordon, Colin. 1994. *New Deals: Business, Labor, and Politics in America, 1920–1935*. New York: Cambridge University Press.

Hasen, Richard L. 2012. "Fixing Washington." *Harvard Law Review* 126: 550–85.

Hill, Claire, and Richard Painter. 2011. "Compromised Fiduciaries: Conflicts of Interests in Government and Business." *Minnesota Law Review* 95: 1638–91.

Hilzenrath, David S. 2011. "SEC Staff's 'Revolving Door' Prompts Concerns about Agency's Independence." *Washington Post* (May 13). Available at http://articles.washingtonpost.com/2011-05-13/business/35232119_1_sec-employees-sec-inspector-sec-enforcement-actions

Ivry, Bob, Bradley Keoun, and Phil Kuntz. 2011. "Secret Fed Loans Gave Banks $13 Billion Undisclosed to Congress." *Bloomberg* (November 27). Available at http://www.bloomberg.com/news/2011-11-28/secret-fed-loans-undisclosed-to-congress-gave-banks-13-billion-in-income.html

Johnson, Simon. 2011. "Tunnel Vision, or Worse, from Banking Regulators." *New York Times Economix Blog* (January 20). Available at http://economix.blogs.nytimes.com/2011/01/20/tunnel-vision-or-worse-from-banking-regulators/

Johnson, Simon, and James Kwak. 2011. *13 Bankers: The Wall Street Takeover and the Next Financial Meltdown*, 2nd ed. New York: Vintage Books.

Kalaroma Partners, LLC. 2013. "Biographies: Harvey Pitt, Chief Executive Officer." Available at http://www.kaloramapartners.com/people/harvey-l-pitt/

Keshner, Andrew. 2012. "HSBC Agrees to $1.9B Penalty in Money Laundering Probe." *New York Law Journal* (December 12). Available at http://www.law.com/corporatecounsel/PubArticleCC.jsp?id=1355068443857&HSBC_Agrees_to_19B_Penalty_in_Money_Laundering_Probe&slreturn=20130030174259

Kessler, Ronald. 1997. *The Sins of the Father: Joseph P. Kennedy and the Dynasty He Founded*, 2nd ed. New York: Grand Central Publishing.

Kouwe, Zachery. 2009. "Judge Rejects Settlement over Merrill Bonuses." *New York Times* (September 14). Available at http://www.nytimes.com/2009/09/15/business/15bank.html?hp

Kurtzleben, Danielle. 2011. "2010 Set Campaign Spending Records." *U.S. News and World Report* (January 7). Available at http://www.usnews.com/news/articles/2011/01/07/2010-set-campaign-spending-records

Lattman, Peter. 2013. "Judge's Rejection of Citigroup Deal Is Heard on Appeal." *The New York Times* (February 9): B2.

Lazo, Alejandro, and E. Scott Reckard. 2011. "Banks, Regulators to Act to Correct Foreclosure Flaws." *Los Angeles Times* (April 14). Available at http://waters.house.gov/news/documents-ingle.aspx?DocumentID=236765

Levin, Carl, and Tom Coburn. 2011. *Wall Street and the Financial Crisis: Anatomy of a Financial Collapse*. Report to the Congress by the U.S. Senate Permanent Subcommittee on Investigations, Committee on Homeland Security and Governmental Affairs. Washington, D.C.: Permanent Subcommittee on Investigations.

Levitt, Arthur. 2002. *Take on the Street: What Wall Street and Corporate America Don't Want You to Know*. New York: Pantheon Books.

Lichtblau, Eric, David Johnston, and Ron Nixon. 2008. "FBI Struggles to Handle Financial Fraud Cases." *New York Times* (October 19): A1.

Macey, Jonathan R., and James P. Holdcroft, Jr. 2011. "Failure Is an Option: An Ersatz-Antitrust Approach to Financial Regulation." *Yale Law Journal* 120: 1368–418.

O'Brien, Justin. 2003. *Wall Street on Trial: A Corrupted State*. Hoboken, NJ: John Wiley and Sons.

Olsen, Mancur, Jr. 1971. *The Logic of Collective Action: Public Goods and the Theory of Groups*, rev. ed. Cambridge, MA: Harvard University Press.

Paletta, Damian, and Aaron Lucchetti. 2010. "Law Remakes U.S. Financial Landscape: Senate Passes Overhaul that Will Touch Most Americans; Bankers Gird for Fight over Fine." *Wall Street Journal* (July 16). Available at http://online.wsj.com/article/SB10001424052748704682604575369030061839958.html

Paltrow, Scot J. 1995. "SEC Chief Shift on Investor Bill Is Linked to Senate Pressure." *Los Angeles Times* (November 22): D1.

Paltrow, Scot J. 2012. "Insight: Top Justice Officials Connected to Mortgage Banks." *Reuters* (January 20). Available at http://www.reuters.com/article/2012/01/20/us-usa-holder-mortgage-idUSTR E80J0PH20120120

PBS. 2003. "Frontline: Mr. Weill Goes to Washington: The Long Demise of Glass-Steagall." *PBS.org* (May 8). Available at http://www.pbs.org/wgbh/pages/frontline/shows/wallstreet/weill/demise.html

PBS. 2009. "Frontline: The Warning." *PBS.org* (October 20). Available at http://www.pbs.org / wgbh/pages/frontline/warning/interviews/born.html

PBS. 2013. "Frontline: The Untouchables." *PBS.org* (January 22). Available at http://www.pbs. org/wgbh/pages/frontline/untouchables/

Pecora, Ferdinand. 1968. *Wall Street under Oath: The Story of Our Modern Money Changers.* New York: Sentry Press. First published 1939 by Simon and Schuster.

Prins, Nomi. 2009. *It Takes a Pillage: Behind the Bailouts, Bonuses, and Backroom Deals from Washington to Wall Street.* Hoboken, NJ: John Wiley and Sons.

Protess, Ben. 2012. "Wall Street Is Bracing for the Dodd-Frank Rules to Kick In." *New York Times* (December 12): F10.

Protess, Ben, and Jessica Silver-Greenberg, 2012. "Bank Said to Avoid Charges over Laundering." *New York Times* (December 11): A1.

Ramirez, Mary K. 2003. "Just in Crime: Guiding Economic Crime Reform after the Sarbanes-Oxley Act of 2002." *Loyola University Chicago Law Journal* 34: 359–427.

Ramirez, Mary K. 2005. "The Science Fiction of Corporate Criminal Liability: Containing the Machine through the Corporate Death Penalty." *Arizona Law Review* 47: 933–1002.

Ramirez, Mary K. 2007. "Blowing the Whistle on Whistleblower Protection: A Tale of Reform versus Power." *University of Cincinnati Law Review* 76: 183–233.

Ramirez, Mary K. 2010. "Prioritizing Justice: Combating Corporate Crime from Task Force to Top Priority." *Marquette Law Review* 93: 971–1017.

Ramirez, Mary K. 2013. "Criminal Affirmance: Going Beyond the Deterrence Paradigm to Examine the Social Meaning of Declining Prosecution of Elite Crime." *Connecticut Law Review* 45: 865–931.

Ramirez, Steven A. 2000. "Depoliticizing Financial Regulation." *William and Mary Law Review* 41: 503–93.

Ramirez, Steven A. 2002. "Fear and Social Capitalism: The Law and Macroeconomics of Investor Confidence." *Washburn Law Journal* 42: 31–77.

Ramirez, Steven A. 2004. "Games CEOs Play and Interest Convergence Theory: Why Diversity Lags in America's Boardrooms and What to Do about It." *Washington and Lee Law Review* 61: 1583, 1604–06.

Ramirez, Steven A. 2010. "Dodd-Frank VII: Joseph Stiglitz Says It Will Happen Again." *Corporate Justice Blog* (July 30). Available at http://corporatejusticeblog.blogspot.com/2010/07/dodd-frank-vii-joesph-stiglitz-says-it.html

Ramirez, Steven A. 2013. *Lawless Capitalism: The Subprime Crisis and the Case for an Economic Rule of Law.* New York: New York University Press.

Raymond, Nate. 2011. "Rakoff Again Blasts SEC Settlements Where Defendants Admit No Wrong." *New York Law Journal* (March 24). Available at http://www.newyorklawjournal.com/PubArticleNY.jsp?id=1202487437732&Rakoff_Again_Blasts_SEC_Settlements_Where_Defendants_Admit_No_Wrong

Rosoff, Stephen M., Henry N. Pontell, and Robert H. Tillman. 2004. *Profit without Honor: White-Collar Crime and the Looting of America*, 3rd ed. Upper Saddle River, NJ: Pearson Prentice Hall.

Saltonstall, David. 2008. "Barack Obama Has Collected Nearly Twice as Much Money as John McCain." *New York Daily News* (July 1). Available at http://www.nydailynews.com/news/politics/barack-obama-collected-money-john-mccain-article-1.351304 - ixzz2IvP3U3nz

Santos, Adolfo. 2006. *Do Members of Congress Reward Their Future Employers? Evaluating the Revolving Door Syndrome*. Lanham, MD: University Press of America.

Schweizer, Peter. 2012. "Obama's DOJ and Wall Street: Too Big For Jail?" *Forbes* (May 7). Available at http://www.forbes.com/sites/realspin/2012/05/07/obamas-doj-and-wall-street-too-big-for-jail/

Smallberg, Michael. 2011. "Revolving Regulators: SEC Faces Ethics Challenges with Revolving Door." *Project on Government Oversight* (May 13). Available at http://www.pogo.org/pogo-files/reports/financial-oversight/revolving-regulators/fo-fra-20110513.html

Sorkin, Andrew Ross. 2009. *Too Big to Fail*. New York: Penguin Group.

Stephenson, Wen. 2002. "Frontline: A Tale of Two Chairmen." *PBS.org* (June 20). Available at http://www.pbs.org/wgbh/pages/frontline/shows/regulation/lessons/two.html

Stewart, James B. 1992. *Dens of Thieves*. New York: Touchstone.

Stewart, James. 2011. "As a Watchdog Starves, Wall Street Is Tossed a Bone." *New York Times* (July 16): A1.

Stiglitz, Joseph E. 2009. "Capitalist Fools." *Vanity Fair* (January 1). Available at http://www.vanityfair.com/magazine/2009/01/stiglitz200901

Stiglitz, Joseph E. 2010. *Freefall: America, Free Markets, and the Sinking of the World Economy*. Reprint Edition. New York and London: W.W. Norton and Company.

Stith, Kate, and Jose Cabranes. 1998. *Fear of Judging: Sentencing Guidelines in the Federal Courts*. Chicago, IL: University of Chicago.

Suskind, Ron. 2011. *Confidence Men: Wall Street, Washington, and the Education of a President*. New York: Harper Perennial.

Sutherland, Edwin. 1983. *White Collar Crime: The Uncut Version*. New Haven, CT: Yale University Press.

Taibbi, Matt. 2012. "How Wall Street Killed Financial Reform." *Rolling Stone* (May 24). Available at http://www.rollingstone.com/politics/news/how-wall-street-killed-financial-reform-20120510

U.S. Chamber of Commerce. 2010. "U.S. Chamber Urges SEC to Consider Potential Consequences of Whistleblower Bounty Program." (November 30). Available at http://www.uschamber.com/press/releases/2010/november/us-chamber-urges-sec-consider-potential-consequences-whistleblower-boun

U.S. Department of Justice. 2012. "Deferred Prosecution Agreement." *U.S. v. HSBC USA*, Cr. No. 12-763 (E.D. N.Y. December 12), Exhibit 10.1.

U.S. Department of Justice Office of Public Affairs. 2012. "Federal Government and State Attorneys General Reach $25 Billion Agreement with Five Largest Mortgage Servicers to Address Mortgage Loan Servicing and Foreclosure Abuses." U.S. Department of Justice. gov (February 9). Available at http://www.justice.gov/opa/pr/2012/February/12-ag-186.html

U.S. Government Accountability Office. 2014. *Financial Audit: Securities and Exchange Commission's Fiscal Years 2014 and 2015 Financial Statements*. GAO-15-166R. Washington, D.C.: Author. Available at http://www.gao.gov/products/GAO-15-166R

U.S. SEC. 2011. *Remarks at Georgetown University by Sean McKessey, Chairman, Office of the Whistleblower* (August 11).

U.S. SEC. 2012. "In Brief: FY 2013 Congressional Justification." SEC.gov (February). Available at http://www.sec.gov/about/secfy13congbudgjust.pdf

U.S. SEC 2014. *FY 2014 Congressional Budget Justification.* Washington, D.C.: Author. Available at http://www.sec.gov/about/reports/secfy14congbudgjust.pdf

U.S. Senate Committee on Homeland Security and Governmental Affairs, Permanent Subcommittee On Investigations. 2012. "HSBC Exposed U.S. Financial System to Money Laundering, Drug, Terrorist Financing Risks." (July 16). Available at http://www.hsgac .senate.gov/subcommittees/investigations/media/hsbc-exposed-us-finacial-system-to-money-laundering-drug-terrorist-financing-risks

Valukas, Anton R. 2010. "Report of Anton R. Valukas, Examiner." Report to the United States Bankruptcy Court, Southern District of New York *In re Lehman Bros. Holdings Inc.,* 439 B.R. 811 (Bankr. S.D.N.Y. 2010).

Wachtel, Katya. 2011. "The Revolving Door: 29 People Who Went from Wall Street to Washington to Wall Street." *Business Insider* (July 31). Available at http://www.businessinsider.com/wall-street-washington-revolving-door-2011-4?op=1

Warren, Elizabeth. 2013. "Avoiding Wall St. Shuffle's Perils." *Politico* (January 24). Available at http://www.politico.com/story/2013/01/elizabeth-warren-oped-key-indicators-for-filling-economic-posts-86690.html

Westman, Daniel P., and Nancy M. Modesitt. 2012. *Whistleblowing: The Law of Retaliatory Discharge,* 2nd ed. Arlington, VA: Bloomberg

Wyatt, Edward. 2011. "Judge Rejects an S.E.C. Deal with Citigroup." *The New York Times* (November 19): A1.

Yost, Pete. 2008 "Battered Wall Street Gives to Obama, McCain." *USA Today* (September 17). Available at http://usatoday30.usatoday.com/news/politics/2008-09-17-1694999833_x.htm

CHAPTER 24

REGULATION

From Traditional to Cooperative

NEIL GUNNINGHAM

REGULATION is one of the most important mechanisms used to curb white-collar and corporate crime. That is, attempts are made to limit wrongdoing not through the traditional mechanisms of the criminal law enforced by police, but through statutory schemes administered by specialist agencies. For example, insider trading of securities by individuals with access to material nonpublic information about a company is the quintessential financially motivated nonviolent crime committed for illegal monetary gain, and it—together with multiple means of manipulating markets—is banned by statute. But in contrast to "mainstream" criminal law, these statutes are enforced by the Securities and Exchange Commission, not by police.

In part, regulatory enforcement is used because such statutes involve technical and complex provisions that a specialist agency is best capable of administering. But behavior that is subject to economic or social regulation is also distinguishable from conventional crime in that it is only "qualifiedly disfavored." While we see no social virtue in such conventional crimes as robbery or assault, we do want financial markets to flourish not just for the benefit of those operating within them but also for the good of society. Similarly, we want corporations to manufacture goods and make profits. It is the *way* they go about pursuing these generally valued goals that we seek to regulate. For example, environmental regulation seeks to curb the manner in which corporations engage in production to prevent damage to the environment (but does not seek to ban production itself). In these circumstances, specialist regulatory agencies are seen as a more appropriate and effective means of balancing social benefits and costs than the police and mainstream criminal law.

Their role, moreover, is viewed primarily as one of oversight rather than of policing (as befits activity that is only qualifiedly disfavored). For example, in the wake of the global financial crisis, much regulatory attention has focused on how to mitigate potential systemic risks associated with financial markets in general and shadow banking in particular. Here, the aim is to develop a system of prudential regulation and other safeguards without unduly constraining the legitimate business of such markets. To this end, a set of overarching principles is being developed, the aim of which is "to ensure non-bank financial entities that are identified as posing shadow banking risk ... are subject to oversight by authorities" (Financial Stability Board 2012, p. 3). Monitoring in conjunction with an appropriate regulatory toolkit (more below on this) is a vehicle to achieve this objective. Notwithstanding the manifest failings of "light-handed regulation" and a cooperative (and very trusting) approach by regulators in the lead-up to the global financial crisis, a more directive and perhaps deterrence-oriented approach is apparently not on the agenda.

The behavior that is subject to regulation is most commonly committed in the context of a business, and some of it at least is committed by rational actors. Sometimes that behavior is intentional. Business decision makers might, for example, decide to externalize some of their costs (e.g., their pollution), passing them on to those downstream in terms of polluted water and dead fish, rather than investing the money in prescribed pollution-control devices or cleaner, less polluting (but more expensive) technology. Others might be reckless. Many breaches of occupational health and safety legislation can be seen as a consequence of a calculated choice made by business owners or managers who are tempted to maximize profits by cutting corners with health and safety precautions. Although these decision makers do not intend to inflict injury, disease, or death, they are well aware of the collateral damage likely to be caused by their actions. More commonly, however, business organizations and decision makers within them are simply negligent in their behavior. That is, even if they did not recognize the hazards or what they should have done to address them, the fact that a reasonable person would have done so will be sufficient to demonstrate a breach of regulation.

As such, *some* of the behavior that is governed by social or economic regulation might arguably be regarded as crime by choice. That is, decision makers have opportunities for crime (whether it is insider trading, risking workers' lives, or damaging the environment by their business activities), and some decision makers at least make a rational choice to engage in prohibited activities—balancing costs and benefits (e.g., profits from engaging in the illegal behavior vs. the likelihood of being detected, likely level of penalty in event of detection). But whereas breaching regulations is indeed an unambiguously purposeful and calculated action for some, this is not the case for others. For example, many businesspeople who breach work health and safety regulations, and in so doing endanger workers or others, simply fail to pay attention to the likely consequences of their actions in circumstances where a reasonable person would have done so.

These distinctions are important. Although deterrence might be a sensible response to those who embrace crime by choice, it is largely unhelpful as a response to those who are negligent or inadvertent. Indeed, the journey from traditional deterrence-based regulation to a much more cooperative style—which this chapter will describe—in part was prompted by recognition of the limits of rational choice theory and of deterrence as an across-the-board strategy for regulating qualifiedly disfavored behavior.

The distinction between choice and mere failure to pay attention raises the broader question of the relationship between regulation and white-collar crime. If we take a conventional definition of the latter (financially motivated nonviolent crime committed for illegal monetary gain), then clearly some regulated activities fall squarely within its ambit (e.g., insider trading, deliberate dumping of toxic substances, reckless activity causing serious injury or death on the job). But the farther we move on the continuum from intent through recklessness and criminal negligence to civil negligence and blameless inadvertence, the less likely is the activity to be regarded as crime, although it may still be the subject of regulatory oversight. Accordingly, white-collar crime and the regulation of social and economic activity overlap substantially but certainly are not synonymous.

Within the sphere of economic and social regulation, two of the longest-standing debates concern (1) the appropriate design of that legislation and (2) the appropriate nature of its enforcement. This debate can be characterized as one concerning the appropriate nature of that regulation. Should regulatory design itself and/or its enforcement be traditional in its approach, or should it, in contrast, function by means of cooperation? Couching the question in this way implies that a traditional approach is in some way coercive or at least non-cooperative. As will become apparent, this may be a helpful means of characterizing the debate concerning appropriate enforcement (at least in the United States), but it may do less than justice to the debate concerning regulatory design where the diversity of regulatory styles cannot be encapsulated in a simple coercion–cooperation dichotomy. But even here, traditional regulation and cooperation arguably do reflect two opposite ends of a policy continuum that helpfully can be contrasted.

Accordingly, with this important qualification, both debates will be examined through the lens of the traditional-versus-cooperative dichotomy. Given the considerable constraints of space, but also to ensure consistency, examples of how these debates have played out, and with what consequences, will be drawn from one particular field of social regulation: environmental protection. Nevertheless, although some of the examples given are specific to that field, the large majority of claims made as to the strengths and limitations of different approaches can be extrapolated readily to other areas of economic or social regulation.

Also for reasons of space, the analysis is confined to developments in "Anglo-Saxon" jurisdictions, primarily Australia, Canada, New Zealand, the United Kingdom (noting the constraints imposed by EU directives), and the United States. In any event, this focus may be appropriate given that it is in the Anglo-Saxon world that regulation has been most invoked and most relied upon as a mechanism to address white-collar crime.

In terms of its structure, following this introduction, section I will examine regulatory design, section II will examine compliance and enforcement, and section III will provide a conclusion. In each of the two substantive sections, the essay not only will describe the distinctive characteristics of traditional and cooperative approaches, but also will seek to explain why regulation has shifted from traditional to cooperative and to ask: Which approach works better, and why?

In broad terms, the essay argues the following:

- In terms of regulatory design, there has been a swing away from traditional command-and-control regulation to a range of less interventionist, more cooperative alternatives.
- Some of these alternatives, most notably management-based regulation and meta-regulation, have been largely successful, but others, not least voluntarism and negotiated agreements and regulatory flexibility initiatives, have not.
- Nevertheless, sweeping generalizations are dangerous. In determining the success of a particular instrument, much depends upon the nature and context of the policy issue to be addressed.
- There is value in designing complementary combinations of instruments, compensating for the weaknesses of each with the strengths of others, while avoiding combinations deemed to be counterproductive or at least duplicative. Much the same is true as regards compliance and enforcement.
- Similarly, in terms of compliance and enforcement, rather than seeking to identify a single intervention strategy that works best in all circumstances, what is needed is to consciously apply different intervention strategies according to their suitability for particular regulatory contexts.
- One of the many virtues of responsive regulation is its capacity to adjust the regulator's response according to the behavior and motivations of the regulatee and to build in the very flexibility that many other intervention strategies lack.
- It is important to be reminded that—not just with enforcement but also with the design of regulation—even cooperative strategies work best when they are underpinned by the threat of powerful sanctions if cooperation fails.

I. Designing Regulation

Regulation is a relatively recent phenomenon. In the financial sphere, it arguably dates back to 1933–34 when the U.S. Congress enacted the Glass-Steagall Act, the Securities Act, and the Securities and Exchange Act—the last of which created one of the most important of contemporary regulatory agencies: the Securities and Exchange Commission.[1] But social, as distinct from economic, regulation only really blossomed some decades later. For example, the U.S. Environmental Protection Agency (concerned primarily with curbing pollution and protecting the environment) was established in 1970, as was the Occupational Safety and Health Administration, which was charged with reducing work-related injury, disease, and death.

These forms of regulation are "traditional" in two senses. First, they involve *government-imposed* restrictions designed to discourage or prohibit harmful (commonly corporate) behavior (as distinct, for example, from self-regulation, co-regulation, or voluntarism). Second, they have a distinctive architecture central to which are command-and-control mechanisms of social control. Take, for example, environmental regulation. The dominant approach was to promulgate legislation designed to prohibit or restrict environmentally harmful activities (particularly pollution) by using direct or command-and-control (to use the unfairly but widely adopted pejorative label applied by free-market economists) mechanisms. Specifically, the preferred technique was to identify an environmental target, such as a limit on emissions of a pollutant to water or the air (the command), with penalties that would be imposed if this target is not met (the control).

This architecture, at least in the way it dealt with point-source pollution from large business enterprises, achieved some significant victories in halting, or at least slowing, some forms of environmental degradation. Indeed, traditional command and control, in imposing technology-based standards on large industries, sometimes has achieved quite dramatic improvements in environmental performance (Gunningham, Kagan, and Thornton 2003). Nevertheless, by the 1980s, traditional command-and-control regulation was criticized widely, both within the United States and elsewhere, for being inflexible and excessively costly for business. Centralized, bureaucratic standard setting—the centerpiece of traditional forms of direct regulation—was castigated routinely by its critics for being "inherently inefficient and cumbersome" (Elliott 1994, p. 1847). This critique of traditional regulation can be overstated, but the fundamental critique—that traditional command and control, whatever its effectiveness, scores poorly in terms of efficiency—has some substance.

In any event, traditional regulation was falling into disfavor as a consequence of broader shifts in the political and ideological landscape. By the 1980s, there had been, particularly in the United States and United Kingdom, a considerable turn toward neoliberalism—essentially the enterprise of embedding market values and structures within economic *and* social and political life. This project took a particularly strident form under Ronald Reagan and Margaret Thatcher. During their reign, assisted by the economic and political collapse of the former Soviet Union, the triumph of neoliberalism was almost unchallenged, and environmental policy received a sharp injection of free-market ideology. During the same period, governments also experienced considerable pressure from industry to reduce the economic burden of compliance. Thus, the confluence of economic pressures and political ideology sometimes constrained the introduction of further traditional regulation (though many earlier forms of traditional command and control remained on the statute book).

One important change was the shift toward economic instruments that, by "mimicking the market," were perceived to be far more efficient than command-and-control regulation and capable of providing industry with the flexibility and autonomy to make the lowest-cost decisions. Thus, there was an increasing focus on the use of price signals in the shape of taxes or charges, property rights in the form of tradable permits, and supply-side instruments in terms of subsidies. Also important was the shift away from regulation and toward a variety of voluntary, much more cooperative initiatives such as self-regulation, voluntary codes, co-regulation, and negotiated agreements. The reasons for this interest in voluntarism and cooperation are many but include the limits of command-and-control regulation and the interest of industry itself in seeking (at best) a flexible, cost-effective, and more autonomous alternative to direct regulation or (at worst) a means of avoiding the imposition of binding standards altogether (Moffet and Bregha 1999). Unfortunately, by the late 1990s, a number of systematic reviews of the various voluntary initiatives had concluded either that there were few demonstrated benefits, or that those benefits were confined to soft issues (e.g., information diffusion and consciousness raising). There could be a variety of reasons for the limited success of many voluntary, cooperative approaches more generally, including the central role of industry in the target-setting process, the scope for free riding, the uncertainty over regulatory threats, unenforceable commitments, poor monitoring, and lack of transparency.

By this time, in part because of the manifest failings of many of the alternatives to traditional regulation and in part because of a change in the political flavor of government, a further shift in the architecture of environmental regulation could be identified. Whereas in the Thatcher and Reagan years the emphasis had been on voluntarism and (where this was manifestly impracticable) on economic instruments, their successors placed greater emphasis on a return to government regulation. However, even under a Blair Labour government in the United Kingdom and a Clinton Democratic administration in the United States (and under state and federal Labour governments in Australia), neoliberalism still held sway (albeit in a gentler form). "New regulation" (rather like "New Labour") proved to be very different from "old regulation" and especially from the traditional command-and-control regulation that characterized the 1970s. In these and other Anglo-Saxon jurisdictions, concerted efforts were made to avoid measures that might intrude on business flexibility or competitiveness, and regulation—to the extent that it was back in fashion—was to be very light-handed and cooperative, both in its design and its application.

The Clinton-Gore administration played an influential role in rethinking what neoliberal regulation might look like. Its agenda to reinvent environmental regulation, unveiled in President Clinton's State of the Union Address in January 1995, outlined the future program as follows:

> It is time to draw upon the lessons we have learned over the last 25 years to reinvent environmental protection for the 21st century. We have learned that the American people are deeply committed to a healthy environment for their children and communities. We have learned that pollution is often a sign of economic inefficiency and business can improve profits by preventing it. *We have learned that better decisions result from a collaborative process with people working together, than from an adversarial one that pits them against each other. And we have learned that regulations that provide flexibility—but require accountability—can provide greater protection at a lower cost.* (Clinton 1995, emphasis added)

Under this agenda, the Clinton-Gore administration sought to nurture an explicitly cooperative relationship with business based on trust and reciprocity.

The Clinton-Gore administration, along with a number of other Anglo-Saxon governments (most notably in Canada and some Australian states), also began experimenting with an innovative approach to standard setting variously termed "process-based," "systems-based," or "management-based" regulation (Coglianese and Lazar 2003, p. 691). This approach involves firms developing their own process and management system standards and developing internal planning and management practices designed to achieve regulatory goals. Such standards have the considerable attractions of providing flexibility to enterprises to devise their own lowest-cost solutions to social challenges, as well as facilitating the likelihood that they would go beyond mere compliance with minimum legal standards. Finally, in contrast to direct regulation, they hold the promise of being applicable to a broad range of circumstances and to heterogeneous enterprises. For present purposes, such initiatives will be termed "management-based regulation."

Management-based regulation is now to be found in a variety of policy domains (Coglianese and Lazar 2003; Coglianese and Nash 2006). In broad terms, such regulation offers regulatory rewards and incentives in return for a commitment to adopt and implement an environmental management system, sometimes coupled with a process of dialogue with the local community or even with some more formal means of direct community participation in the decision-making process.[2] Again, this approach is a long way from the prescriptions of command and control and offers regulated organizations a cooperative approach that provides them with considerable autonomy in how they address environmental problems, often in dialogue with governmental regulators and others. Taken one step further, as it was in the early years of the new millennium, management-based regulation can become a form of meta-regulation or meta-risk management, in which government (or corporations seeking to regulate their multiple facilities)—rather than regulating directly—oversight the risk management of individual enterprises or facilities. Under such an approach, the role of regulation ceases to be primarily about inspectors or auditors checking compliance with rules and becomes more about encouraging the industry or facility to put in place processes and management systems, which then are scrutinized by regulators or corporate auditors.

The ultimate test of the success or otherwise of regulatory flexibility initiatives, management-based regulation, or meta-regulation as described above is an empirical one. Although the evidence on regulatory flexibility initiatives is at best mixed (Crow 2000; Holley and Gunningham 2006), it appears that management-based regulation can be an effective regulatory tool, at least in some circumstances. For example, plants subject to this form of regulation in the United States have experienced greater reductions in toxic chemical releases than they would have in the absence of these regulatory initiatives (Bennear 2005). In the case of meta-regulation, the evidence also is largely positive.[3]

To summarize, there have been major shifts in the architecture of social regulation in general and environmental regulation in particular during the past four decades.

These changes are in large part due to shifts in politics and ideology. In the 1970s, the sort of thinking that had led to the New Deal was still prevalent. The state was believed best placed to address major social challenges, and the tool most widely used for this purpose was the command-and-control type of regulation. But by the end of the decade, a business backlash—in conjunction with a reframing of the debate in terms of the tenets of neoliberalism—saw a shift to market-based instruments and less interventionist strategies such as self-regulation and voluntary agreements. By the time the Democrats (in the United States) and New Labour (in the United Kingdom) were returned to power, regulation was to be reinvented—not in terms of command and control, but with a focus on a light touch, greater flexibility, and an emphasis on rewarding high performers rather than punishing the recalcitrant. "Cleaner, cheaper, smarter" was Environmental Protection Agency Administrator Carol Browner's mantra in this period. And the tools that subsequently have been developed—not least, management-based and meta-regulation—also fitted comfortably within neoliberal discourse, being less intrusive, imposing a lower regulatory burden and less "red tape," and emphasizing management-technocratic rationality (Dryzek, 1997).

II. COMPLIANCE AND ENFORCEMENT

The area where it can be argued that there has been a shift from traditional to cooperative forms of regulation is that of compliance and enforcement. Here, as figure 24.1 illustrates, multiple regulatory models (adopted by different regulatory agencies) can be identified in the literature, and policymakers have far more choices than simply to punish or persuade.

Space precludes an analysis of all these models. Instead, the following account will focus on the first three models because these are the ones that might best illuminate the broad shift that is identifiable from traditional to cooperative regulation: rules and deterrence, advice and persuasion, and responsive regulation.

Turning first to *rules and deterrence* and *advice and persuasion*, it is clear that neither of these has proved to be an effective or efficient intervention strategy by itself. In principle, *rules and deterrence* can play a positive role, especially in reminding organizations to review their compliance efforts and in reassuring them that, if they comply, others will not be allowed to get away with noncompliance. Nevertheless, in practice, its impact is very uneven. Deterrence is, for example, better at influencing rational actors, who consciously balance costs and benefits, than the incompetent (Kagan and Scholz 1984; Braithwaite and Makkai 1991, p. 25). However, if not carefully targeted, deterrence actually can prove counterproductive, as when it prompts organizations and individuals to develop a culture of regulatory resistance, or to take a defensive stand, suppressing information and failing to explore the underlying cause of accidents for fear that this information will be used against them in a court of law (Bardach and Kagan 2002; Gunningham 2007). Finally, in terms of general deterrence, the evidence shows that

From a review of the regulatory literature, six distinctive (but often mutually compatible) regulatory enforcement and compliance strategies can be identified:

1. Advice and Persuasion: Emphasizes cooperation rather than confrontation and conciliation rather than coercion. The aim is to prevent harm, which is achieved by bargaining, persuasion, and negotiation rather than by sanctioning. Recourse to the legal process here is rare, the assumption being that the large majority of regulatees are willing to comply voluntarily.

2. Rules and Deterrence: Emphasizes a coercive, formal, and adversarial style of enforcement and the sanctioning of rule-breaking behavior. It assumes that regulatees are rational actors capable of responding to incentives and that, if offenders are detected with sufficient frequency and punished with sufficient severity, then they and others will be deterred from future violations.

3. Responsive Regulation: Suggests that best outcomes will be achieved if inspectors employ a blend of persuasion and coercion, the actual mix being adjusted to the particular circumstances and motivations of the regulatee. Regulators should begin by assuming virtue (to which they should respond by offering cooperation and information) but, when their expectations are disappointed, they should respond with progressively punitive and deterrence-oriented strategies until the regulated group conforms (a form of "tit for tat"; see, generally, Ayres and Braithwaite 1992; Braithwaite 2011).

4. Smart Regulation: Expands on some of the insights of responsive regulation and the enforcement pyramid by suggesting how markets, civil society, and other institutions can sometimes act as surrogate regulators and accomplish public policy goals more effectively, with greater social acceptance and at less cost to the state. It also argues that complementary mixes of enforcement strategies and tools will be more effective than "stand-alone" strategies.

5. Risk-Based Regulation: Argues that the kind of intervention in the event of non-compliance should depend upon an evaluation of degree of risk posed by the infraction and calculations regarding the impact that the noncompliance will have on the regulatory body's ability to achieve its objectives.

6. Meta-Regulation: Involves placing responsibility on the regulated organizations themselves (usually large organizations) to submit their plans to the regulator for approval, with the regulator's role being to "risk manage" the risk management of those individual organizations. The goal is to induce companies to acquire themselves the specialized skills and knowledge to self-regulate, subject to external scrutiny. Accordingly, the regulator's main intervention role is to oversee and audit the plans put in place by the regulated organization. Where it finds inadequacies, the regulator may invoke a responsive approach as described above.

Note. This figure and the wider arguments made in this section were published first in Neil Gunningham. 2011. "Enforcing Environmental Regulation." *Journal of Environmental Law* 23: 169–201, Box 1. This figure is reproduced by permission of Oxford University Press, USA.

FIGURE 24.1 Regulatory Strategies: Models Identified in the Regulatory Literature

regulated business organizations' perceptions of legal risk (primarily of prosecution) play a far more important role in shaping organizational behavior than the objective likelihood of legal sanctions (Simpson 2002). However, even when perceptions of legal risk are high, this is not necessarily an important motivator of behavior (Braithwaite and Makkai 1991, p. 35).

The evidence suggests that *advice and persuasion*, while valuable in encouraging and facilitating those willing to comply with the law to do so, may prove disastrous when used against those who are not disposed to voluntary compliance.[4] More broadly, advice and persuasion actually might discourage improved regulatory performance among better actors if agencies permit lawbreakers to go unpunished. This happens because even those who are predisposed to be "good apples" may feel at a competitive disadvantage if they invest money in compliance at a time when others are seen to be getting away with noncompliance (Shapiro and Rabinowitz 1997, p. 14). In short, a strategy of advice and persuasion will have different impacts on organizations according to their motivations. The strategy may be appropriate for corporate leaders but it will not be effective for engaging with reluctant compliers or the recalcitrant and may be effective only for the incompetent when coupled with education and advice.[5] A further problem with advice and persuasion is that regulators who are committed to this approach are particularly susceptible to being captured by the very industry they are overseeing and could end up being unduly sympathetic to its interests. For example, they might give advance notice of inspections; fail to take enforcement action even in the most egregious cases of social harm; and routinely adopt health, safety, and environmental policies proposed by the industry itself (Shapiro 2012).

Remarkably, both of these diametrically opposed regulatory strategies can stake a claim to being traditional. *Rules and deterrence*—or what Robert Kagan has characterized as "adversarial legalism"—has had, as he ably and comprehensively demonstrates, a profound influence on enforcement in the United States (Kagan 2003; see also Bardach and Kagan 2002). Yet in other Anglo-Saxon jurisdictions, the dominant regulatory style, at least until perhaps the past decade, has been that of compliance and persuasion.[6] Since the evidence suggests that neither of these traditional approaches is remotely optimal, is there a better alternative? This was the question addressed by Ian Ayres and John Braithwaite (1992) in their seminal work, *Responsive Regulation*.

Responsive regulation seeks to overcome the limitations of both rules-and-deterrence and advice-and-persuasion strategies by taking advantage of the strengths of both while compensating for their weaknesses. Ayres and Braithwaite argued that, because regulated enterprises have a variety of motivations and capabilities, regulators must invoke enforcement strategies that deter egregious offenders while at the same time encouraging virtuous employers to comply voluntarily and rewarding those who are going beyond compliance. Thus, good regulation means invoking different responsive enforcement strategies depending upon whether one is dealing with leaders, reluctant compliers, the recalcitrant, or the incompetent. However, the dilemma for regulators is that it is rarely possible to be confident in advance as to the motivation of a regulated firm.

If regulators assume that all firms will behave as good corporate citizens, they may devise a regulatory strategy that stimulates voluntary action but that is incapable of effectively deterring those who have no interest in responding to encouragement to voluntary initiatives. On the other hand, if regulators assume that all firms will need to be threatened with a big stick to bring them into compliance, then they will unnecessarily alienate (and impose unnecessary costs on) those who willingly would comply voluntarily, thereby generating a culture of resistance to regulation (Bardach and Kagan 2002).

The challenge is to develop enforcement strategies that punish the worst offenders while at the same time encouraging and helping employers who comply voluntarily. The mechanism proposed by Ayres and Braithwaite for resolving this challenge is for regulators to apply an enforcement pyramid (figure 24.2), which employs advisory and persuasive measures at the bottom, mild administrative sanctions in the middle, and punitive sanctions at the top. On their view, regulators should start at the bottom of the pyramid assuming virtue: that business is willing to comply voluntarily. However, when this assumption is shown to be ill founded, regulators should escalate up the enforcement pyramid to increasingly deterrence-oriented strategies (see Ayres and Braithwaite 1992; Gunningham and Johnstone 1999). In this manner, they find out, through repeated interactions, whether they are dealing with occupational health and safety leaders, reluctant compliers, the recalcitrant, or the incompetent, and they respond accordingly.

Central to this model are the needs for (1) gradual escalation up the face of the pyramid and (2) the existence of a credible peak or tip that, if activated, will be sufficiently powerful to deter even the most egregious offender. The former (rather than any abrupt

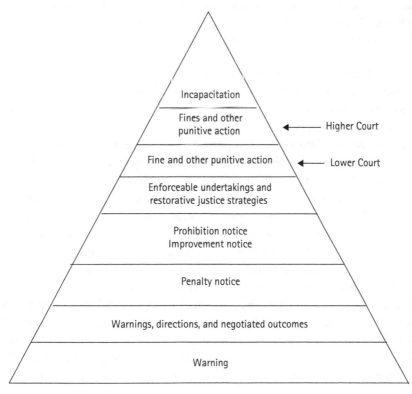

FIGURE 24.2 The Enforcement Pyramid

Note: This enforcement pyramid is illustrative of the sorts of carrots and sticks that an agency might want to invoke as part of an escalating strategy of enforcement, but it is not intended to be exclusionary. Many different mechanisms might be used under this general approach.

shift from low to high interventionism) is desirable because it facilitates the tit-for-tat response on the part of regulators, which forms the basis for responsive regulation (i.e., if the duty holder responds as a good citizen, he or she will continue to be treated by the inspectorate as a good citizen; Ayres and Braithwaite 1992). The latter is important not only because of its deterrent value, but also because it ensures a level playing field in that the virtuous are not disadvantaged.

While the pyramid concept and variations on it (see Gunningham, Grabosky, and Sinclair 1998; Gunningham and Johnstone 1999) offer a powerful heuristic, in practice a responsive approach (which in itself can take a number of different forms; see Nielsen 2006, p. 395) is best suited to the regulation of large organizations with which the regulator has frequent interactions (enabling a strategy of tit-for-tat to play out). As Johnstone (2003) pointed out:

> For the pyramid to work in the interactive, "tit-for-tat" sense envisaged by its proponents, the regulator needs to be able to identify the kind of firm it is dealing with, and the firm needs to know how to interpret the regulator's use of regulatory tools, and how to respond to them (Black 2001, p. 20). This requires regulators not only to know what is entailed in effective compliance programs and systematic [preventive] approaches, but also to have a sophisticated understanding of the contexts within which organizations operate, and the nature of an organization's responses to the various enforcement measures. (p. 11)

All this is a tall order. The result is likely to be that the less intense and less frequent the level of inspection—and the less knowledge the regulator is able to glean as to the circumstances and motivations of regulated organizations—the less practical it becomes to apply responsive regulation.

But even where regulators find it impractical to use the pyramid in its entirety (as where regulators make only infrequent inspections), it nevertheless could be useful in determining which regulatory tool to employ in a given instance (i.e., at what point in the pyramid it would be appropriate to intervene, given the characteristics of the regulated entity and the degree of risk or type of breach; Gunningham and Johnstone 1999, pp. 124–25). This involves a hybrid approach: gleaning as much information as possible from the previous history and track record of the duty holder using such indicators as are available and managers' attitudes, so as to inform an at least partially responsive approach as to where in the enforcement pyramid to intervene.

Finally, the pyramid approach "has the great merit that when shown the various pyramids, many regulators and policy-makers immediately seem to understand them descriptively and offer examples" (Scott 2004, p. 160). That is, connecting the theoretical construct of the pyramid to the concrete and practical experience of regulators is not a substantial problem, although their conception of it is usually more static than responsive.

Overall, it is fair to say that responsive regulators have found that they will gain better results by developing more sophisticated strategies that employ a judicious blend of persuasion and coercion, the actual mix being adjusted to the particular circumstances and motivations of the entity with whom they are dealing.[7] Having said this, empirical analysis suggests that responsive regulation in its tit-for-tat form has a greater effect on behavior than on attitudes (Mascini and Van Wijk 2009; Nielsen and Parker 2009; Braithwaite 2011). Indeed, Nielsen and Parker found no evidence that positive attitudes transformed low-performing enterprises into "good apples." Finally, there is some evidence that voluntary initiatives (e.g., voluntary environmental audits) by enterprises increase when authorities adopt responsive regulation (Maxwell and Decker 2006).

What implication does this cooperative turn have for regulation's fundamental oversight function? As will be apparent from the above, the most influential theory to endorse a cooperative approach is responsive regulation, which, in sharp contrast to pure advise-and-persuade approaches, does not assume that all businesses will respond positively and emphasizes the importance of escalating up the enforcement pyramid for those who do not. This unfortunately is a lesson that financial market regulators failed to heed in the years preceding the global financial crisis. Senior decision makers, including Alan Greenspan, assumed that regulation could be applied with the lightest of touches and without the need for escalating sanctions, because the financial industry could be trusted to monitor itself and to take the appropriate action voluntarily. In retrospect, as Greenspan himself now acknowledges, this was naïve and one of the primary causes of the crisis. But it was also the case that even this very limited oversight function itself was entirely lacking in some areas. For example, regulation as regards complex financial derivatives like collateralized debt obligations, credit-default swaps, and the hedge funds that invest in them was limited or nonexistent (see generally National Commission 2011). One lesson among others is that regulators need to be empowered with a broad oversight role. Another is that even where they purport to operate cooperatively, such cooperation must be underpinned by strong sanctions so that cooperation operates in the shadow of deterrence. In short, oversight remains of central importance, and even where cooperative approaches are preferred, their credibility depends on their being underpinned by the willingness to invoke sanctions, thereby "transcending the deregulation debate."

To return to the broader picture, while in the case of regulatory design it was overarching political economic dynamics that largely shaped change, in the case of compliance and enforcement, the writings of some scholars and accumulated academic research as to the empirical tenability of different approaches demonstrably played a much greater role. Nevertheless, they have not done so in isolation from broader social and political forces. The enforcement pyramid in particular (on which attention has focused far more than the broader model of responsive regulation), as Mascini (2013, p. 48) pointed out, "is congruent with the neoliberal reflex to depoliticize regulation of capitalist economies." It is also consistent with neoliberalism's privileging of the market over regulation. For example, Tombs and Whyte argued that with the enforcement pyramid, "enforcement of the law . . . is set against its notional opposite, 'partnership'" (Tombs and Whyte 2010, p. 51), with enforcement being something undertaken with regret, and only exceptionally. By implication they suggested that the pyramid characterizes the large majority of businesses as good citizens who, for reasons of enlightened self-interest or moral conviction, will comply voluntarily. Notwithstanding that a broader reading of responsive regulation reveals that its authors explicitly identify with a tradition of civic republicanism rather than neoliberalism, there indeed is evidence that, in practice, the enforcement pyramid—albeit not the broader theory— has been used for neoliberal ends.

III. Conclusion

This chapter has analyzed approximately four decades of environmental regulation in various Anglo-Saxon jurisdictions. It has shown how, after the heydays of command-and-control regulation and the swing to markets and voluntarism, a new, more cooperative phase evolved, with the most important manifestations of the new phase being regulatory flexibility, management-based regulation, and meta-regulation. Stepping back from the detail of these developments and the particular successes and failures of individual instruments, the broader question remains: What sorts of strategies are likely to work best in terms of effectiveness and efficiency? Unfortunately, the general answer to such questions is: It all depends.

Each of the frameworks described earlier has something valuable to offer (though some have more to offer than others), and none of them is "right" or "wrong" in the abstract. Rather, they make differing contributions depending upon the nature and context of the policy issue to be addressed. For example, voluntarism has value where self-interest and the public interest largely coincide.[8] Command-and-control regulation has worked well in dealing with large point-source polluters, particularly where one-size-fits-all technologies can be mandated. Such regulation has considerable power when it comes to changing the behavior of large reputation-sensitive companies, which are vulnerable not only to shaming but also to market forces and consumer pressure. Meta-regulation appears to be effective in dealing with complex and sophisticated environmental issues such as regulating major hazardous facilities, but it might be redundant when it comes to more traditional challenges. Regulatory flexibility has potential in engaging with "good apples"—large corporations who have reason to contemplate going beyond regulation in return for greater flexibility and less "green tape"—but it may do so at the cost of downplaying the resources necessary to drag "bad apples" into compliance with minimum legal standards.

The limitations of each of the major policy innovations, and of the architectures that underpin them, lead to a plea for pragmatism and pluralism. None of the policy instruments or perspectives examined above works well in relation to all sectors, contexts, or enterprise types. Each has weaknesses as well as strengths, and none can be applied as an effective standalone approach across the spectrum. Such a conclusion suggests the value of designing complementary combinations of instruments, compensating for the weaknesses of each with the strengths of others, while avoiding combinations deemed to be counterproductive or at least duplicative. This multimodal strategy indeed was the central message of "smart regulation" (Gunningham and Grabosky 2008). From this perspective, no particular instrument or approach is privileged. Rather, the goal is to accomplish substantive compliance with regulatory goals by any viable means using whatever regulatory or quasi-regulatory tools might be available.

Much the same is true regarding compliance and enforcement. Rather than seeking to identify a single intervention strategy that works best in all circumstances, what is needed is to apply consciously different intervention strategies according to their suitability to particular regulatory contexts. Different types of regulated enterprises confront different external pressures and have different skills, capabilities, and motivations. The environmental risks posed by different operations are also intrinsically different. Accordingly, best practice may mean applying different intervention strategies in different circumstances. Indeed, one of the many virtues of responsive regulation is its capacity to adjust the regulator's response according to the behavior and motivations of the regulated entity and to build in the very flexibility that many other intervention strategies lack.

Finally, and in the spirit of responsive regulation, it is important to be reminded that—not just with enforcement but also with the design of regulation—even cooperative strategies work best when they are underpinned by the threat of powerful sanctions should cooperation fail. That is, notwithstanding the enthusiasm of governments of a range of political persuasions for more cooperative approaches, the evidence suggests that many such strategies are far less likely to succeed if they are not underpinned by traditional regulation. For example, under regulatory flexibility, some enterprises may be tempted to develop "paper" management systems and tokenistic responses that independent third-party auditors might fail to detect (O'Rourke 2000). However, the threat of sanctions if they fail to deliver on performance targets set by the state would reduce substantially the risk of free riding. So too in the case of small business, the fear of regulation or its enforcement can be used to good effect to complement other more innovative approaches (Gunningham et al. 2005, p. 89). Even some market-based instruments, such as tradable emission rights, on closer examination involve a combination of markets and direct regulation (since although trading is a market mechanism, governments design the trading scheme, impose caps on emissions, and police compliance).

The more general conclusion is that "in some cases, nationwide laws and regulations will continue to be the best way to reduce risk. But in others, tailored strategies that involve market based-approaches, partnerships, or performance incentives may offer better results at lower costs'" (U.S. Environmental Protection Agency 2000, p. 4). However, even these less demanding and more conciliatory approaches, it must be emphasized, are likely to work best "in the shadow of regulation" (U.S. Environmental Protection Agency 2000, p. 4). So in this sense, while the trend from the 1980s to the present day has been one marked by the retreat of command-and-control regulation, these twin pillars of traditional regulation—commands and controls—often lurk in the background, providing an effective underpinning to cooperative approaches in their multiple manifestations.

NOTES

1. This section borrows from Gunningham (2009a).
2. See, for example, Gunningham (2009b, p. 145).
3. See, for example, Saksvik and Nytrø (1996).
4. See, for example, Gunningham (1987, p. 69).
5. Winter and May (2001).
6. See, for example, Hawkins (1984).
7. For reviews, see Baldwin and Black (2008).
8. Market solutions also may be credible when the environmental challenge involves a small number of players, all of whose self-interest could be harnessed by the provision of property rights. The tragedy of the commons is the classic example (see Hardin 1968). However, the larger the number of players, the greater the transaction costs, and the greater the potential for free riding, and the less credible a property-rights approach becomes.

REFERENCES

Ayres, Ian, and John Braithwaite. 1992. *Responsive Regulation: Transcending the Deregulation Debate*. New York: Oxford University Press.

Baldwin, Robert, and Julia Black. 2008. "Really Responsive Regulation." *Modern Law Review* 71: 59–94.

Bardach, Eugene, and Robert A. Kagan. 2002. *Going by the Book: The Problem of Regulatory Unreasonableness*. Philadelphia, PA: Temple University Press.

Bennear, Lori S. 2005. "Evaluating Management-Based Regulation: A Valuable Tool in the Regulatory Toolbox?" In *Leveraging the Private Sector: Management-based Strategies for Improving Environmental Performance*, edited by Cary Coglianese and Jennifer Nash. Washington, D.C.: Resources for the Future Press.

Black, Julia. 2001. "Managing Discretion." Paper presented at the Australian Law Reform Commission Conference on Penalties: Policy and Practice in Government Regulation, Sydney, Australia, June.

Braithwaite, John. 2011. "The Essence of Responsive Regulation." *University of British Columbia Law Review* 44: 475–520.

Braithwaite, John, and Toni Makkai. 1991. "Testing an Expected Utility Model of Corporate Deviance." *Law and Society Review* 25: 7–40.

Clinton, Bill. 1995. "Reinventing Environmental Regulation." Available at http://govinfo. library.unt.edu/npr/library/rsreport/251a.html#overview

Coglianese, Cary, and David Lazar. 2003. "Management-based Regulation: Prescribing Private Management to Achieve Public Goals." *Law and Society Review* 37: 691–730.

Coglianese, Cary, and Jennifer Nash, eds. 2006. *Leveraging the Private Sector: Management-based Strategies for Improving Environmental Performance*. Washington, D.C.: Resources for the Future.

Crow, Michael. 2000. "Beyond Experiments." *Environmental Forum* 17: 18–29.

Dryzek, John S. 1997. *The Politics of the Earth: Environmental Discourses.* New York: Oxford University Press.

Elliott, Donald E. 1994. "Environmental TQM: Anatomy of a Pollution Control Program that Works!" *Michigan Law Review* 1994: 1840–54.

Financial Crisis Inquiry Commission. 2011. Final Report of the National Commission on the Causes of the Financial and Economic Crisis in the United States. http://www.gpo.gov/fdsys/pkg/GPO-FCIC/pdf/GPO-FCIC.pdf

Financial Stability Board. 2012. *Strengthening Oversight and Regulation of Shadow Banking: Policy Framework for Strengthening Oversight and Regulation of Shadow Banking Entities.* Available at http://financialstabilityboard.org/publications/r_130829c.pdf

Gunningham, Neil. 1987. "Negotiated Non-compliance: A Case Study of Regulatory Failure." *Law and Policy* 9: 69–95.

Gunningham, Neil. 2007. "Prosecution for OHS Offences: Deterrent or Disincentive?" *Sydney Law Review* 29: 359–90.

Gunningham, Neil. 2009a. "Environmental Law, Regulation, and Governance: Shifting Architectures." *Journal of Environmental Law* 21: 179–212.

Gunningham, Neil. 2009b. "The New Collaborative Environmental Governance: The Localization of Regulation." *Journal of Law and Society* 36: 145–66.

Gunningham, Neil. 2011. "Enforcing Environmental Regulation." *Journal of Environmental Law* 23: 169–201.

Gunningham, Neil, and Peter Grabosky. 2008. *Smart Regulation: Designing Environmental Policy.* Oxford, UK: Oxford University Press.

Gunningham, Neil, Peter Grabosky, and Darren Sinclair. 1998. *Smart Regulation: Designing Environmental Policy.* Oxford, UK: Clarendon Press.

Gunningham, Neil, and Richard Johnstone. 1999. *Regulating Workplace Safety: System and Sanctions.* Oxford, UK: Oxford University Press.

Gunningham, Neil, Robert A. Kagan, and Dorothy Thornton. 2003. *Shades of Green: Business, Regulation, and Environment.* Stanford: Stanford University Press.

Hardin, Garrett. 1968. "The Tragedy of the Commons." *Science* 162: 1243–48.

Hawkins, Keith. 1984. *Environment and Enforcement: Regulation and the Social Definition of Pollution.* New York: Clarendon Press.

Holley, Cameron, and Neil Gunningham. 2006. "Environment Improvement Plans: Facilitative Regulation in Practice." *Environmental and Planning Law Journal* 23: 448–64.

Johnstone, Richard. 2003. "From Fiction to Fact: Rethinking OHS Enforcement." National Research Centre for Occupational Health and Safety Regulation Working Paper 11.

Kagan, Robert A. 2003. *Adversarial Legalism: The American Way of Law.* Cambridge, MA: Harvard University Press.

Kagan, Robert A., and John T. Scholz. 1984. "The Criminology of the Corporation and Regulatory Enforcement Styles." In *Enforcing Regulation*, edited by Keith Hawkins and John M. Thomas. Boston: Kluwer-Nijhoff.

Mascini, Peter. 2013. "Why Was the Enforcement Pyramid So Influential? And What Price Was Paid?" *Regulation and Governance*, 7: 48–60.

Mascini, Peter, and Eelco Van Wijk. 2009. "Responsive Regulation at the Dutch Food and Consumer Product Safety Authority: An Empirical Assessment of Assumptions Underlying the Theory." *Regulation and Governance* 3: 27–47.

Maxwell, John W., and Christopher S. Decker. 2006. "Voluntary Environmental Investment and Responsive Regulation." *Environmental and Resource Economics* 33: 425–39.

Moffet, John, and Francois Bregha. 1999. "An Overview of the Issues with Respect to Voluntary Environmental Agreements." CAVA (Concerted Action on Voluntary Approaches) Working Paper 98.

Nielsen, Vibeke Lehmann. 2006. "Are Regulators Responsive?" *Law and Policy* 28: 395–416.

Nielsen, Vibeke Lehmann, and Christine Parker. 2009. "Testing Responsive Regulation in Regulatory Enforcement." *Regulation and Governance* 3: 376–99.

O'Rourke, Dara. 2000. "Monitoring the Monitors: A Critique of PricewaterhouseCoopers (PWC) Labor Monitoring." Cambridge, MA: MIT Department of Urban Studies and Planning. Available at http://www.bollettinoadapt.it/old/files/document/18107 ROURKE_2000.pdf

Saksvik, Per Øystein, and Kjell Nytrø. 1996. "Implementation of Internal Control of Health, Environment, and Safety (HES) in Norwegian Enterprises." *Safety Science* 23: 53–61.

Scott, Colin. 2004. "Regulation in the Age of Governance: The Rise of the Post-regulatory State." In *The Politics of Regulation: Institutions and Regulatory Reforms for the Age of Governance*, edited by Jacint Jordana and David Levi-Faur. Cheltenham, UK: Edward Elgar.

Shapiro, Sidney A. 2012. "The Complexity of Regulatory Capture: Diagnosis, Causality, and Remediation." *Roger Williams University Law Review* 102: 221–58.

Shapiro, Sidney A., and Randy S. Rabinowitz. 1997. "Punishment versus Cooperation in Regulatory Enforcement: A Case Study of OSHA." *Administrative Law Review* 49: 713–62.

Simpson, Sally S. 2002. *Corporate Crime and Social Control*. Cambridge, UK: Cambridge University Press.

Tombs, Steve, and David Whyte. 2010. "A Deadly Consensus: Worker Safety and Regulatory Degradation under New Labour." *British Journal of Criminology* 50: 46–65.

Tombs, Steve, and David Whyte. 2013. "Transcending the Deregulation Debate? Regulation, Risk, and the Enforcement of Health and Safety Law in the UK." *Regulation and Governance* 7: 61–79.

U.S. Environmental Protection Agency. 2000. *A Decade of Progress: Innovation at the Environmental Protection Agency*. Washington, D.C.: U.S. Environmental Protection Agency, Office of the Administrator.

Winter, Søren C., and Peter J. May. 2001. "Motivation for Compliance with Environmental Regulations." *Journal of Policy Analysis and Management* 20: 675–98.

....

CHAPTER 25

COMPARING ASSUMPTIONS UNDERLYING REGULATORY INSPECTION STRATEGIES

Implications for Oversight Policy

....

PETER MASCINI

FOUR fundamentally different policy ideas about regulatory inspection can be found throughout the literature on regulation.[1] These policy ideas differ with respect to the role they ascribe to compliance motives as well as to the dominance of the state as a regulatory inspection agent. First, the criminalization of corporate non-compliance is based on the assumption that, in capitalist economies, entrepreneurs use their hegemonic power to evade regulation by rational calculation. Second, reintegrative shaming is based on the assumption that corporate actors comply with social norms out of a need to be socially accepted. Third, the enforcement pyramid assumes that compliance motives vary. Fourth, compliance motives are ignored in risk-based regulation because the aim of this policy idea is to objectify the hazards posed by products or processes.

While the role of compliance motives differs between these four policy ideas, they share a focus on the state as the dominant regulatory inspection agent. In this respect, these regulatory inspection strategies differ from the polycentric view characteristic of responsive regulation and regulatory governance. The polycentric view on regulatory inspection is based on the assumption that the capacity and willingness to regulate and inspect are dispersed over different social actors and that it is important to harness the assets of these actors optimally.

To some extent, the different policy ideas on regulatory inspection can be viewed as criticisms of each other's assumptions. Moreover, each of these ideas is most suitable for particular situations, yet at the same time, none of these policy ideas is without challenges or difficulties. This implies that the popularity of the different policy ideas on regulatory inspection is context bound and that political preferences contribute to their popularity. In this chapter, I develop the following points:

- First, four influential policy ideas about regulatory inspection—criminalizing corporate non-compliance, reintegrative shaming, the enforcement pyramid, and risk-based regulation—can be distinguished in terms of assumed compliance motives. The implementation of each of these ideas has its challenges.
- Subsequently, the state-centeredness of these four policy ideas can be contrasted with the polycentric point of view underlying responsive regulation and regulatory governance. The latter two polycentric regulatory inspection ideas grapple with implementation problems just like the four state-centered policy ideas do.
- Finally, it is concluded that general perspectives underlie each of the aforementioned policy ideas on regulatory inspection. Regulation is viewed in terms of conflict or harmony or as a social or scientific process, and regulatory power is conceived of as concentrated or dispersed. These perspectives are so abstract that it will always be possible to find situations where they do or do not apply. This means the popularity of the different policy ideas on regulatory inspection depends not only on their applicability but also on the political preferences of their beholders.

This chapter deals with the differences in assumed compliance motives underlying four different policy ideas on regulatory inspection as well as their limitations (sections I through IV). These policy ideas subsequently pertain to the criminalization of corporate non-compliance (section I), reintegrative shaming (section II), the enforcement pyramid (section III), and risk-based regulation (section IV). The state-centeredness of these first four policy ideas is contrasted with the polycentric perspective underlying responsive regulation and regulatory governance (section V). This review leads to the conclusion (section VI) that the holy grail of regulatory inspection has not yet been discovered and that it is unlikely that it will ever be found because the policy ideas on regulatory inspection are founded on conflicting conceptions of the good society.

I. Criminalizing Corporate Non-Compliance

The first policy idea about regulatory inspection problematizes the difference in evaluation and handling of street crime versus corporate non-compliance. Corporate non-compliance is considered at least as detrimental to society as is street crime. Supposedly, numerous disasters have shown that rules have been broken for which employers should be held responsible. That these kinds of accidents are recurrent indicates that employers intentionally break rules, thereby causing harm to employees, consumers, citizens, and the environment (Pearce and Tombs 1990; Tombs and Whyte 2010; Bittle 2015). Nonetheless, it appears as though the public shows significantly less concern about corporate crime than it does about street crime (although this seems to be changing [Simpson 2013, p. 320]). Moreover, supposedly, the handling of both types of crime differs significantly. While a punitive approach dominates responses to street crime, the handling of corporate crime is dominated by informing and persuading, administrative sanctions, and different forms of self-regulation (Tombs and Whyte 2012; see also Braithwaite 2003).

Proponents of the criminalization of corporate non-compliance try to understand why corporate crime is taken less seriously and is handled more leniently than is street crime even though its negative consequences are at least equivalent and its underlying intentions are at least as bad. Their answer is that employers abuse their privileged position of power in capitalist societies. Employers use their dominant position to depict regulation and enforcement as unwelcome impediments that inhibit economic growth (Bittle 2015). As a result, regulation and inspection are presented as problems instead of means to serve the common good. The dominance of this discourse is conceived of as the hegemonic power of business (Pearce and Tombs 1990).

Inspectors internalize the conviction that they have to restrain themselves in order to prevent obstructing economic growth. This explains, for instance, why inspectors predominantly use a trusting, persuasive enforcement style (Wilthagen 1993, Fineman and Sturdy 1999, pp. 641–42; Pautz and Rinfret 2012) and why inspectors gradually grow less inclined during their careers to prosecute companies for transgressions (Pearce and Tombs 1991, referring to a finding by Hawkins 1984). The internalization of the idea that market parties ought not to be disturbed unduly implies "the state's disciplin ary measures are constrained by an unwavering commitment to the capitalist endeavor. As such, state intervention to address corporate wrongdoing . . . supports rather than threatens the long-term viability of corporate capitalism" (Bittle 2015, p. 134). Allegedly, the hegemonic power of capital has increased since the rise of neoliberalism in the 1970s. In the neoliberal discourse, the state is depicted as the cause of societal problems, while the market is presented as their solution (Bittle 2015). The domination of this ideology has enticed governments during recent decades to shift their regulatory inspection policies to deregulation, persuasion, and forms of self-regulation (Tombs and Whyte 2010, 2012).

What spurs the proponents of the criminalization of corporate non-compliance most is the perceived gap between the self-image presented by businesses and their actual behavior. This perceived discrepancy makes criminalization proponents deeply suspicious of the intentions of corporations (Abel 1985, p. 788; Neale 1997; Shover 2008). They assume entrepreneurs are profit-driven, amoral, rational calculators who will violate the law when the benefits of crime outweigh the costs (Simpson 2013, p. 323):

> We believe that there is an inherent contradiction between, on the one hand, the profit-making goal of business enterprises within competitive capitalism, and, on the other hand, the taking of a socially responsible attitude to the consequences of these activities, that is, to their "externalities." (Pearce and Tombs 1990, p. 415)

Supposedly, even those entrepreneurs who sincerely support corporate social behavior cannot be trusted. After all, when they follow their good intentions, they will no longer be able to compete in a capitalist market. Because of this fundamental mistrust of business compliance motives, a punitive regulatory strategy is favored: "We attempt to demonstrate the desirability and feasibility of a punitive regulatory strategy for controlling corporate conduct" (Pearce and Tombs 1990, p. 423). This means, among other implications, that the scope of criminal law and the certainty and severity of (mostly) criminal sanctions have to be extended (Pearce and Tombs 1990; Bittle 2015). The criminalization of corporate non-compliance is thought to be in the interest of well-intended companies as well because, allegedly, such companies incur the costs of complying with the rules while their unscrupulous competitors profit from the indulgence of inspectors. The criminalization of corporate crime demands a strong state. Even though the state is thought to function nowadays as an extension of the market, potentially the state is also the only serious countervailing power of the market (Bittle 2015). This explains why Tombs and Whyte (2010) hope that events such as the financial crisis of 2008 will make the public aware that the trend of increasingly depending on the market as a regulatory inspection agent has had disastrous consequences and that the responsibility of regulatory inspection will be reverted to the state.

II. Reintegrative Shaming

The policy idea of reintegrative shaming has emanated from the empirical finding that, on average, a punitive approach like the criminalization of corporate non-compliance is counterproductive because of its stigmatizing character (Makkai and Braithwaite 1994a). Moreover, numerous studies have established that a punitive enforcement style may result in compliance—but at the cost of substantial perverse consequences such as decreasing involvement with regulation, inefficiency due to time-consuming lawsuits, deteriorating relationships between inspectors and regulatees, individual and collective opposition by regulatees, and withholding information from inspectors (see, e.g., Ayres and Braithwaite 1992, p. 83; Short 2012, p. 663). Reintegrative shaming promises a strategy that shares with the criminalization of corporate non-compliance the expression of disapproval for rule violations but that does not produce the negative consequences of the latter.

Reintegrative shaming aims to combine the expression of disapproval for noncompliance (shaming) with bringing the deviant actor back into the community (reintegration). More specifically, reintegrative shaming involves showing disapproval for deviance combined with showing respect for the perpetrator, inserting a specific moment wherein the episode is closed, judging the deed but not the rule violator, and not equating the deviant act with the culprit: "hate the sin, but love the sinner." It is expected that stigmatizing shaming decreases compliance while reintegrative shaming increases it: "re-integrative shaming is our best shot at inducing guilt and responsiveness in the wrongdoer; stigmatizing is most likely to induce anger and resistance" (Ayres and Braithwaite 1992, p. 92). Crucial for this policy idea is the assumption that feelings of shame and guilt are the main drivers of compliance. Regulatees are supposed to comply because they care about what others think of them. The assumed importance of the need for social acceptance as a compliance motive is underscored by other theoretical arguments as well. Makkai and Braithwaite (1994b) argued that reintegrative shaming is most likely to spur on feelings of guilt and shame when regulatees and inspectors are interdependent. Allegedly, the more interdependent a community is, the more regulatees care about other people's opinion of them. The assumed importance of the need for social acceptance as a compliance motive is also expressed by the expectation that gossiping—confirming social norms by expressing disapproval of deviance committed by others—has a positive impact on compliance. Supposedly, gossiping induces feelings of guilt and shame and, consequently, increases the inclination to comply. So, while the criminalization of corporate non-compliance assumes that cost–benefit calculations are the main compliance motive, reintegrative shaming is based on the assumption that compliance primarily depends on the need to be socially accepted.

Makkai and Braithwaite (1994b) found confirmation of the effectiveness of reintegrative shaming in a large-scale compliance study of Australian nursing home directors. Nursing home directors who had undergone stigmatizing shaming as well as those who had encountered toleration and understanding without disapproval for noncompliance worsened their compliance record, while those who had faced reintegrative shaming improved their compliance record. Moreover, reintegrative shaming proved to be effective only when a situation of interdependence existed between directors and inspectors (i.e., when directors already knew the inspectors from previous encounters). However, their findings have been contested. Botchkovar and Tittle (2005) extensively reviewed the tenability of the theoretical assumptions underlying reintegrative shaming and tested these assumptions themselves. Their test was an improvement for several reasons.

First, Makkai and Braithwaite (1994b) had measured inspectors' support for reintegrative shaming. However, theoretically regulatees are expected to react based on the extent to which they perceive to have been exposed to reintegrative shaming. Regulatees' perceptions are what Botchkovar and Tittle (2005) measured. Second, the latter tested the extent to which reintegrative shaming increases intentions to comply because it enhances feelings of shame and guilt, while Makkai and Braithwaite had assumed this. Third, Botchkovar and Tittle tested the extent to which gossiping—confirming social norms by expressing disapproval of deviance committed by others—resulted in increased intentions to comply, while Makkai and Braithwaite had assumed this as well.

Botchkovar and Tittle's test did not support the theory. Gossiping about transgressions committed by others did not increase respondents' own intentions to comply, while reintegrative shaming even decreased these intentions. Moreover, gossiping did not increase intentions to comply more when there was more interdependence, while reintegrative shaming decreased inclinations to comply even more when there was more interdependence. Finally, although feelings of guilt and shame increased intentions to comply, reintegrative shaming decreased feelings of shame instead of increasing them.

Possibly the societal context in which Botchkovar and Tittle (2005) undertook their study was not conducive to the theory. The transgressions respondents were asked to reflect upon might not have aroused strong feelings of guilt and shame shortly after the collapse of the former Soviet Union, because at that time Russia was badly integrated, and normlessness with respect to crime abounded. Yet they also refer to numerous other studies that did not support the policy idea of reintegrative shaming either (however, for a review of the literature supportive of reintegrative shaming theory, see Ahmed, Braithwaite, and Braithwaite 2001).[2] In particular, the common finding that reintegrative shaming undermines intentions to comply just as much as disintegrative shaming does is problematic for the theory. Botchkovar and Tittle's (2005) assumption that regulatees might no longer be receptive to reintegration after their behavior has been disapproved of has found some support in other research (Mascini and Van Wijk 2009, p. 40).

In short, research has neither unequivocally established that reintegrative shaming is a more effective way of showing disapproval for noncompliance than criminalizing corporate non-compliance is, nor has it shown that reintegrative shaming successfully mobilizes the need for social acceptance as a compliance motive. In other words, it is contested whether reintegrative shaming is a better strategy to express disapproval of noncompliance than criminalizing corporate non-compliance is.

III. The Enforcement Pyramid

While we have seen that reintegrative shaming presupposes a different compliance motive than does the criminalization of corporate non-compliance (social acceptance vs. rational calculation), the starting point of the enforcement pyramid is that rational calculation is not the only compliance motive for corporations that operate within a capitalist market. This starting point is based on the many studies showing that personal and social norms are at least as important compliance motives for entrepreneurs as is calculating the possible costs of penalties (Langevoort 2007; Goslinga and Denkers 2009; Piquero et al. 2011; Van Wingerde 2012). This is an important finding because other studies have shown that the effectiveness of a punitive enforcement style, like the criminalization of corporate non-compliance, depends on the compliance motives of regulatees. A punitive approach improves compliance when regulatees make decisions based on rational cost–benefit calculations, while it worsens compliance when they decide based on moral–emotional grounds (Makkai and Braithwaite 1994a; Simpson 2002).

According to the enforcement pyramid (figure 25.1), based on ample evidence that businesses' compliance motives vary, inspectors should encounter corporations with an open mind and should not doubt their willingness to comply a priori. They ought to start looking for strengths in the performance of regulatees and then seek to expand them. When corporations violate rules, inspectors should initially try to persuade regulatees to comply. Not until they encounter persistent opposition should they step up the rungs of the enforcement pyramid and start punishing or incapacitating the lawbreaker (Braithwaite 2007, p. 5). Moreover, enforcement agents should be patient, forgiving, and ready to deescalate at the first sign of goodwill (see arrows in figure 25.1). As long as regulatory inspectors make sure they will ultimately prevail whenever conflicts with regulatees escalate because they can revoke the business's license (see top of the enforcement pyramid in figure 25.1), a persuasive enforcement style can be applied in the majority of inspections (Braithwaite 2011).

Since Ayres and Braithwaite (1992) introduced the enforcement pyramid, its implementation has been studied extensively. These studies have shown that the implementation of the enforcement pyramid gives rise to a number of challenges and difficulties (for reviews, see Baldwin and Black 2008; Gunningham 2011; Heimer 2011; Mascini 2013). There are two fundamental problems connected to the implementation of the enforcement pyramid.

First, inspectors cannot always transmit unambiguously their intentions to regulatees because of communication problems. Frequently, there is not enough interaction between regulators and regulatees to transmit messages about how inspectors will react to regulatees' intentions and behavior. Sometimes inspection and enforcement activities are spread across different regulators with respect to similar activities or regulations. As a result, messages flowing between regulators and regulatees may be confused or subject to dispersion or interference (Baldwin and Black 2008, p. 63). Moreover, inspectors and regulatees often misinterpret each other's intentions. In particular, regulatees tend to perceive the inspector's behavior as more coercive than intended (Mascini and Van Wijk 2009).

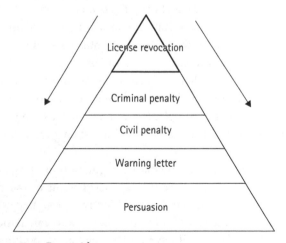

FIGURE 25.1 Enforcement Pyramid

By permission of Oxford University Press, USA: Responsive Regulation: Transcending the Deregulation Debate *by Ayres and Braithwaite (1992) "Enforcement Pyramid" p. 35; bold and arrows added.*

Second, often the preconditions necessary to enable inspectors to apply the most suitable enforcement style are absent. "Inspectors may lack the skills to read intentions, to distinguish an honest mistake from a calculated choice being represented as a simple mistake, and to discern how regulatees' attitudes are affected by regulators' actions" (Heimer 2011, p. 673). In addition, regulatory systems are usually not closely articulated to the core task of gradually stepping up the rungs of the enforcement pyramid whenever conflicts escalate, not least because the mix of tasks with which regulatory chores compete varies substantially between regulatory bodies or organizational levels (Heimer 2011, p. 691). Besides, inspectorates sometimes lack the juridical, public, business, or political support for escalation or deescalation (Baldwin and Black 2008, p. 64). "Furthermore, corporate behavior is often not driven by regulatory pressure but by the culture prevailing in the sector or by the far more pressing forces of competition" (Baldwin and Black 2008, p. 63).

In sum, unlike the criminalization of corporate non-compliance, the enforcement pyramid minimizes the perverse effects of a punitive inspection strategy and takes into account a range of compliance motives. However, communication problems between regulators and regulatees as well as institutional impediments pose difficult challenges to the implementation of the enforcement pyramid. Problems can result from ambiguous, infrequent, and interrupted contacts between regulators and regulates; from the lack of organizational or legal infrastructure; or because of political or economic pressure rendering it impossible to apply the enforcement style deemed most suitable.

IV. Risk-Based Regulation

A policy idea that has increasingly overshadowed the enforcement pyramid during recent years concerns risk-based regulation. Like the enforcement pyramid, the starting point of risk-based regulation is that regulatory inspectors ought to adjust their behavior to the specific context in which they operate. This implies inspectors should not automatically follow what the law dictates (as in case of criminalizing corporate non-compliance or reintegrative shaming). However, an important difference between policy ideas is that, according to the enforcement pyramid, regulatory inspectors should adjust their actions to the compliance motives they ascribe to regulatees, while risk-based regulation expects inspectors to preclude such subjective evaluations from their actions.

Baldwin and Black (2008) define risk-based regulation as "targeting of inspection and enforcement resources that is based on an assessment of the risks that a regulated person or firm poses to the regulator's objectives. The key components of the approach are evaluations of the risk of non-compliance and calculations regarding the impact that the non-compliance will have on the regulatory body's ability to achieve its objectives." "In its idealized form, risk-based regulation offers an evidence-based means of targeting the use of resources and of prioritizing attention to the highest risks in accordance with a transparent, systematic, and defensible framework" (Black and Baldwin 2010, p. 181). In practice, however, the implementation of risk-based regulation is riddled with challenges and difficulties, just like the previously discussed policy ideas are. Basically, there are four problems connected to the implementation of risk-based regulation.

First, an inherent danger of risk-based systems is "model myopia" (Black and Baldwin 2010, pp. 205–06). "Risk-based systems will tend to neglect lower levels of risk, which if numerous and broadly spread, may involve considerable cumulative dangers. Moreover, they tend to focus on known and familiar risks. They can fail to pick up new or developing risks and will tend to be backward looking and 'locked in' to an established analytic framework" (Baldwin and Black 2008, p. 66; see also Lloyd-Bostock and Hutter 2008, p. 76; and see Black and Baldwin 2012b for a deeper understanding and possible solutions of neglecting small risks). For example, Lloyd-Bostock (1992) showed that the risk of low-back injuries and repetitive strain injury had been neglected for years by British health and safety inspectors because these illnesses fell outside their usual risk categories. To prevent such model myopia, it is usually considered necessary to supplement risk-based regulation with random inspections. However, regulatory inspections often lack the means or the skills to do so, or random inspections do not break away from the normal risk-assessment framework (Black and Baldwin 2010, p. 206).

Second, risk-based regulation is often based on mock objectivity, which creates an illusion of control. The apparent objectivity and transparency of risk-based regulation are used as a justification for the way regulatory inspections allocate resources (Lloyd Bostock and Hutter 2008, p. 73). Indeed, central to risk-based regulation "is the promise that the challenges and complexities of regulation can be rationalized, systematized, ordered, managed, and controlled" (Black and Baldwin 2010, p. 203). The jargon of risk suggests that the likelihood of an adverse event occurring is based on probabilistic calculations. "However, regulators are often not dealing with risk but uncertainty" (Black and Baldwin 2010, p. 197). "There is often a frequent need to depart from the promise of a technical solution to regulatory issues and to incorporate qualitative judgments into analyses" (*Ibid.*). Moreover, risk categories can be so broad as to contain a huge diversity of cases. Consequently, it happens that cases are dealt with identically because they are put into the same category, while in fact they deserve a different approach because they are brought forth by different causes (Baldwin and Black 2008, p. 67; Black and Baldwin 2012a, p. 132). Not only might risk classifications suggest more objectivity than is justified, but also the same applies to the selection and prioritization of risks. These choices are inherently political. Moreover, precisely because political choices are debatable, inspectors tend to make them invisible and to bury them deep within the administrative process (Baldwin and Black 2008, p. 67; Black and Baldwin 2010, p. 204). This means the objectivity of risk-based systems is often fictitious, while the political choices underlying such systems are left out of the discussion as much as possible.

Third, risk-based systems give rise to considerable issues of accountability. The data needed by inspectors to estimate risks are often provided by the regulated companies. This dependence restrains regulatory inspectors from taking actions against these very same companies. After all, companies will be less inclined to supply data voluntarily when inspectors use those data against them (Black and Baldwin 2010, pp. 198–99). Moreover, companies or certification agencies may differ "in the models or 'codes' to evaluate risks," which means that "correlating the risk evaluation systems of the regulator with those of the firms may prove hugely demanding" (Black and Baldwin 2010, pp. 201, 203). Regulatory inspections might also be encumbered by the supposed transparency of risk classifications. For instance, for some time, Dutch and French food inspectors kept to themselves their suspicions that poisoned pork from Ireland had entered the European market, because they did not want to have to account for revealing their suspicions should they have been mistaken (Casey and Lawless 2011). Regulatory inspectors also hesitate to explicate which risks they have decided to tolerate because that makes them vulnerable in case precisely those risks manifest themselves (Baldwin and Black 2008, p. 66; Lloyd-Bostock and Hutter 2008, p. 77; Black and Baldwin 2010, p. 197).

In sum, the apparent objectivity and transparency of risk-based regulation could enable justification of the way regulatory inspections allocate resources. However, "risk information is neither generated nor used against a neutral background" (Lloyd-Bostock and Hutter 2008, p. 69). As far as the political character of risk-based regulation is not acknowledged, this policy idea will promise more than it can deliver. As far as this political character is acknowledged, it is less likely that risk-based systems will be legitimized automatically as an instrument to allocate the scarce resources of regulatory inspections.

V. RESPONSIVE REGULATION
AND REGULATORY GOVERNANCE

These regulatory inspection strategies have only been discussed in terms of what distinguishes them (i.e., compliance motives). However, they do have something in common as well: they all treat the state as the predominant regulatory body. The attention of these four policy ideas is primarily directed at the enforcement of legal rules by governmental agencies. It concerns, for example, the argument that regulatory bodies should apply criminal law more often, should adjust their actions to the willingness and capacities of companies to comply, and should allocate their scarce resources optimally. Besides, the state-centeredness of these policy ideas is not absolute. For example, in countries with a weak state, one proposal is to implement an enforcement pyramid that involves an increasing diversity of social actors in the regulatory process as companies persist more stubbornly in refusing to comply (Braithwaite 2006). Moreover, risk-based regulation is increasingly used as a strategy to decide whether regulatory inspection agencies should allocate their own scarce resources to regulate and inspect or to leave this up to regulatees themselves (Tombs and Whyte 2012; Verbruggen

2013). Nonetheless, while a polycentric view on regulation (Black 2008, see also Parker 2008) is exceptional for these policy ideas, it is the starting point of responsive regulation and regulatory governance.

Responsive regulation was introduced in 1992 as a third way between governmental regulation and self-regulation.[3] "It centers on regulatory delegation that is underwritten by escalating (and increasingly undelegated) forms of government intervention" (Ayres and Braithwaite 1992, p. 158). Allegedly, this way the advantages of competition are retained without the state losing the possibility to intervene when other parties fail to correct market failures. It advocates "a mixed institutional order, one where markets, community, state and associations each exercise countervailing power over the others and check the grave dangers when any one of these institutional orders dominates" (Ayres and Braithwaite 1992, p. 17). Since the introduction of responsive regulation, attention focused on the role of actors other than the state has dramatically increased in the literature on regulatory inspection. This trend is often addressed as the "governance turn." Regulatory governance is defined as "institutionalized modes of social coordination to produce and implement collectively binding rules or to provide collective goods" (Börzel and Risse 2010, p. 114).

Regulatory governance conceives of the different sectors—state, market, and civil society—as part of one comprehensive, interlocking system (Lobel 2012, p. 67). The premise of regulatory governance is that knowledge and commitment to corporate social responsibility are distributed among regulated companies, interest groups, and individual citizens (Vogel 2008). Regulatory governance aims to harness the knowledge and energy of these actors in the drafting, implementation, and enforcement of rules. "It tries to involve different actors in the regulation process by creating a fluid and flexible policy environment that fosters 'softer' processes, which will create an environment conducive to participation and dialogue" (Lobel 2012, p. 67). An important role of the state is to monitor actors that "undertake much of the work of governing . . . and at times they even regulate themselves" (Lobel 2012, p. 69). However, the conditions contributing to the effectiveness of involving market and civic parties in regulation are often absent. In a review, Saurwein (2011) enumerated these conditions for market parties. First, lack of experience with self-regulation systems decreases the chance that companies will successfully participate in them. By participating in self-regulation systems, companies can begin to see them as a necessary part of their identity or to experience that such systems can deliver financial benefits (Bernstein and Cashore 2007). Second, in case companies do not perceive a clear self-interest in preventing market failure, the chance that self-regulatory systems will work is slim (Gunningham 1995). For example, the aircraft industry has contributed to the improvement of the safety of air transport because in this sector consumers are potential victims of accidents, powerful elites fly more often than the average citizen, pilots are well organized, and the risk of claims is real. The maritime industry, on the other hand, basically has failed to improve unambiguously the safety of marine transport largely because these factors do not apply to this sector (Perrow 1984). Third, the larger the efforts companies have to make to meet the minimum standards of self-regulatory systems, the more likely it is that companies will withdraw from them. For example, an evaluation study following one of several disastrous fires in Bangladesh production factories revealed that Walmart had blocked an initiative to raise the minimum standards for fire safety in factories in Bangladesh because this would increase the costs of producing apparel (Greenhouse 2012). Fourth, the larger the size of the sector and the more heterogeneous it is, the more likely it is that self-regulation fails. After all, these factors make it harder for business associations to prevent opportunistic behavior by their members in the implementation of voluntary agreements (the free-rider problem) (Börzel and Risse 2010, p. 116). For example, small businesses in the chemical industry tried to free ride on the efforts of their larger competitors to implement "Responsible Care"—a self-regulatory system used in the chemical industry—because they were less convinced of the importance of self-regulation and had more difficulties in meeting its standards (Gunningham 1995). Fifth, the more active a role the government plays in self-regulation, the more effective it is (Short and Toffel 2010; Saurwein 2011). Governments can provide legal and technical support and commitment to self-regulatory systems (Hsueh and Prakash 2012). Conversely, the more self-regulation is treated as a substitute for governmental regulation, the less effective it is because this enables poorly performing firms to free ride (Havinga and Van Waarden 2013). Governments can counter free riding by threatening to switch to state regulation when self-regulation fails (Kesan 2000).

What are the conditions contributing to the effective involvement of civic parties in regulatory governance? First, civic parties must be powerful enough to exert influence on companies. Only in cases where interest groups or individual citizens pose a real threat to the reputation of companies do companies show a willingness to adjust their operations to the demands of civil auditors. This applies to the case of the international diamond trade, for example. The feel-good image of diamonds threatened to be undermined by the association of "blood" with diamonds, and this posed a severe threat to the whole industry. Second, civic parties must be able to assess and rank risks related to production processes. This is often particularly difficult in cases of what Ulrich Beck (1992) has called "Neue Risiken"—invisible, transnational, generation-transcending risks—identifiable only through scientific research. For instance, residents are more willing to take action against odor and noise pollution than against more harmful but less visible toxic pollutants (Thornton, Kagan, and Gunningham 2003). Furthermore, nongovernmental organizations can be selective in the choice of their targeted companies or goals. For example, in case of the sinking of the Brent Spar platform, Greenpeace crusaded against Shell but not the lesser-known co-owner of the platform, Exxon (Vogel 2005). Third, for civic parties to come into action, lawbreaking must be perceived as conflicting with social standards. This was not the case, for example, when the Dutch Financial Market Authority published the names of companies fined for financial offenses. This form of "naming" and "shaming" did not generate major media attention and did not result in consumer boycotts, and the transgressions were not perceived as meaningful and standard setting but as technical exceptions and as "splitting hairs" or "food for technicians" (Van Erp 2011a, 2013). That the offenses were not perceived as blameworthy shows that legal rules are not always legitimized and that interest groups or citizens will come into action only if legal rules are congru-ent with widely accepted social norms (see also Van Erp 2011b). In sum, what remains necessary is a government that has the power to collect information from and gain access to companies, that can facilitate objectifying risks, and that ensures that legal rules reflect widely accepted social norms.

We have seen that involving market and civil society in regulatory governance can be effective only in the shadow of the state (Gunningham 2009; Terpstra 2009). Indeed, initiatives of private self-regulation have been shown to collapse often the moment the credible threat of legal intervention by the state ceased to exist (Börzel and Risse 2010, p. 118). The importance attributed to the monitoring role of the state shows that the aim of regulatory governance is *not* to leave regulation entirely up to the market or civil society. It is intended as a third way—governance with government—that is half-way between unregulated markets (governance without government) and top-down government controls (governance by government) (Börzel and Risse 2010, p. 116; Lobel 2012, p. 3). Hence, governance itself involves a shift in the role of government, not the elimination of government itself (McGuire and Agranoff 2011, p. 278). However, even with an active monitoring role of government and the presence of preconditions con-ducive to regulatory governance, other challenges remain for this policy idea.

First, regulatory governance is connected to basic questions of legitimacy and accountability. The governance model enables parties to exert direct influence on the regulation process without the obligation to account politically for it (Lynn 2010). This entails the danger that powerful parties will influence the regulation process dispropor-tionately and that private interests will take precedence over public goals, which raises questions as to how legitimate such a regulation process is in terms of equality, freedom, and justice and how it can be accounted for (Black 2008; Wood and Shearing 2009).

Second, how can a stable balance in governance networks be reached wherein state authorities facilitate the contribution of market and civil society without losing con-trol? One challenge that governance takes on is "to promote legitimate, effective, and active participation in the work of regulation by the private regulated parties them-selves without devolving into deregulation" (Lobel 2012, p. 3). A second challenge is to avoid reverting to governmental control whenever cooperation between the parties does not work. The state retaining the ability to intervene when self-regulation fails can undermine the voluntariness of self-regulation, which is the key to its success. A related challenge is to prevent different actors who have developed a system of rules and moni-toring cooperatively and in joint consultation at the level of the governance network to revert to a rigid control system at the organizational level (Baer 2009). A third chal-lenge is to prevent the monitoring self-regulatory programs to bog down in a formal system of rules that is entirely decoupled from what actually happens on the shop floor (Parker 2002). In regulatory governance, the state has to ensure that regulatees write and enforce their own rules and see to it that noncompliance is reported to the rel-evant regulatory body (Ayres and Braithwaite 1992, p. 131–32). However, when such an approach is not combined with occasional on-the-spot inspections by the regula-tory body checking whether violations are indeed detected and acted upon by internal compliance systems, self-regulatory systems can easily boil down to window dressing (Gray 2006) or cosmetic compliance (Krawiec 2003).

In sum, creating effective regulatory governance networks is highly challenging. The conditions needed to involve the market and civil sector in regulation effectively are often absent. It is also a challenge to prevent powerful parties from influencing the regulation process disproportionately and private interests to take precedence over public goals. A further challenge is to create stable governance networks wherein the state facilitates the contribution of market and civil society without losing or imposing control.

VI. Conclusion

Compliance motives play a different role in policy ideas about regulatory inspection. According to the proponents of the criminalization of corporate non-compliance, rationally calculating companies have too many opportunities to ignore rules. Conversely, reintegrative shaming claims that the criminalization of corporate non-compliance is stigmatizing and just arouses anger and resistance. Instead, reintegrative shaming proposes to appeal to regulatees' need for social acceptance. The starting point of the enforcement pyramid is not to make any a priori assumptions about the compliance motives of regulatees but rather to adjust the enforcement style to regulatees' attitudes and behaviors as performed in practice. Risk-based regulation tends to ignore compliance motives altogether because its aim is to assess objectively the risks corporations pose to regulatory bodies to achieve their goals. Beside the different role that compliance motives play in these four policy ideas, these ideas have in common a state-centered view on regulatory inspection. This is what distinguishes them from the polycentric view on regulatory inspection characteristic of responsive regulation and regulatory governance.

Does this overview provide clues as to how to reach agreement on what policy ideas on regulatory inspection do or do not work? This is unlikely. The policy ideas are founded on different general perspectives. Proponents of the criminalization of corporate non-compliance use a conflict model in which a strong state is needed to curb the exploitive power of capital. Conversely, reintegrative shaming uses a harmony model assuming the existence of a sense of community that renders it possible to make an appeal to shared norms as well as to social actors' need to be included in a community. Furthermore, the enforcement pyramid and regulatory governance view regulatory inspection primarily as a *social* process, while risk-based regulation approaches view it predominantly as a *scientific* process. Moreover, on the one hand, state-centered policy ideas view regulatory inspection as part of a *representative* democracy process wherein regulatory bodies can be called to account by politicians. On the other hand, polycentric policy ideas consider regulatory inspection as part of a *deliberative* democracy process that assumes regulatory bodies can be called to account outside the official political arena as well.

These different perspectives underlying the various policy ideas are so general that, for every idea, examples can be found that prove them right or wrong: there are cases where companies flout rules for profit seeking, just as there are situations where they respond to appeals made to conform to social norms. Moreover, in some cases risks can be easily assessed scientifically, while in other situations uncertainty abounds. Furthermore, there are situations where the expertise and commitment needed to serve the public interest are concentrated in one enforcement body and situations where these assets are distributed among different actors. This means the comparative edge of the various policy ideas on regulatory inspection cannot be determined on the basis of empirical evidence only. Each of these policy ideas has its strengths and weaknesses and is founded on different perceptions. This means that political preferences will always contribute to the popularity of policy ideas on regulatory inspection.

NOTES

1. This essay is partly based on Mascini (2013) and Mascini and Van Erp (2011). The section "The Enforcement Pyramid" is a shortened and slightly altered version of Mascini (2013), while the sections "The Criminalization of Corporate Crime," "Reintegrative Shaming," and "Regulatory Governance" are translations, alterations, and updates from Mascini and Van Erp (2011).
2. Although Murphy and Harris's (2007) study basically is presented as a validation of the policy idea of reintegrative shaming, it actually shows the opposite. After all, the measurement shows reintegration is not a variant of shaming but its opposite. Apparently, reintegration and shaming are irreconcilable.
3. The enforcement pyramid is part of responsive regulation. However, in the literature, the enforcement pyramid is usually treated as an independent policy idea addressing the state as predominant regulatory body (see Mascini 2013).

REFERENCES

Abel, Richard L. 1985. "Risk as an Area of Struggle." *Michigan Law Review* 83: 772–812.

Ahmed, Eliza, Nathan Harris, John Braithwaite, and Valerie Braithwaite. 2001. *Shame Management through Reintegration*. Cambridge, UK: Cambridge University Press.

Ayres, Ian, and John Braithwaite. 1992. *Responsive Regulation: Transcending the Deregulation Debate*. New York: Oxford University Press.

Baer, Miriam Hechler. 2009. "Governing Corporate Compliance." *Boston College Law Review* 50: 51–71.

Baldwin, Robert, and Julia Black. 2008. "Really Responsive Regulation." *Modern Law Review* 71: 59–94.

Beck, Ulrich. 1992. *Risk Society: Towards a New Modernity*. London and New Delhi: Sage.

Bernstein, Steven, and Benjamin Cashore. 2007. "Can Non-State Global Governance Be Legitimate? An Analytical Framework." *Regulation and Governance* 1: 347–71.

Bittle, Steven. 2015. "Beyond Corporate Fundamentalism: A Marxian Class Analysis of Corporate Crime Law Reform." *Critical Sociology* 41: 133–51.

Black, Julia. 2008. "Constructing and Contesting Legitimacy and Accountability in Polycentric Regulatory Regimes." *Regulation and Governance* 2: 137–64.

Black, Julia, and Robert Baldwin. 2010. "Really Responsive Risk-based Regulation." *Law and Policy* 32: 181–213.

Black, Julia, and Robert Baldwin. 2012a. "When Risk-based Regulation Aims Low: A Strategic Framework." *Regulation and Governance* 6: 131–48.

Black, Julia, and Robert Baldwin. 2012b. "When Risk-based Regulation Aims Low: Approaches and Challenges." *Regulation and Governance* 6: 2–22.

Börzel, Tanja A., and Thomas Risse. 2010. "Governance without a State: Can It Work?" *Regulation and Governance* 4: 113–34.

Botchkovar, Ekaterina V., and Charles R. Tittle. 2005. "Crime, Shame, and Reintegration in Russia." *Theoretical Criminology* 9: 401–42.

Braithwaite, John. 2003. "What's Wrong with the Sociology of Punishment?" *Theoretical Criminology* 7: 5–28.

Braithwaite, John. 2006. "Responsive Regulation and Developing Economics." *World Development* 34: 884–98.

Braithwaite, John. 2011. "The Essence of Responsive Regulation." *University of British Columbia Law Review* 44: 474–520.

Braithwaite, Valerie. 2007. "Responsive Regulation and Taxation: Introduction." *Law and Policy* 29: 3–10.

Bunt, Henk van de, Judith van Erp, and Karin van Wingerde. 2007. "Hoe Stevig Is de Piramide van Braithwaite?" [How Solid Is the Pyramid of Braithwaite?] *Tijdschrift voor Criminologie* 49: 386–99.

Casey, Donald K., and James S. Lawless. 2011. "The Parable of the Poisoned Pork: Network Governance and the 2008 Irish Pork Dioxin Contamination." *Regulation and Governance* 5: 333–49.

Coglianese, Cary, and Robert Allan Kagan, eds. 2007. *Regulation and Regulatory Processes.* Aldershot, UK: Ashgate.

Erp, Judith van. 2011a. "Naming without Shaming: The Publication of Sanctions in the Dutch Financial Market." *Regulation and Governance* 5: 287–308.

Erp, Judith van. 2011b. "Naming and Shaming in Regulatory Enforcement." In *Explaining Compliance: Business Responses to Regulation*, pp. 322–42, edited by Christine Parker and Vibeke Nielsen. Cheltenham, UK: Edward Elgar.

Erp, Judith van. 2013. "Messy Business: Media Representations of Administrative Sanctions for Corporate Offenders." *Law and Policy* 35: 109–39.

Fineman, Stephen, and Andrew Sturdy. 1999. "The Emotions of Control: A Qualitative Exploration of Environmental Regulation." *Human Relations* 52: 631–63.

Goslinga, Sjoerd, and Adriaan Denkers. 2009. "Motieven voor Regelovertreding: Een Onderzoek onder Ondernemers" [Motives for Rule Violation: A Survey among Entrepreneurs]. *Gedrag en Organisatie* 22: 3–22.

Gray, Garry C. 2006. "The Regulation of Corporate Violations: Punishment, Compliance, and the Blurring of Responsibility." *British Journal of Criminology* 46: 875–92.

Greenhouse, Steven. 2012. "Documents Indicate Walmart Blocked Safety Push in Bangladesh." *The New York Times* (December 5). Available at http://www.nytimes.com/2012/12/06/world/asia/3-walmart-suppliers-made-goods-in-bangladeshi-factory-where-112-died-in-fire.html?_r=0

Gunningham, Neil. 1995. "Environment, Self-regulation, and the Chemical Industry: Assessing Responsible Care." *Law and Policy* 17: 57–109.

Gunningham, Neil. 2009. "The New Collaborative Environmental Governance: The Localization of Regulation." *Journal of Law and Society* 36: 145–66.

Gunningham, Neil. 2011. "Strategizing Compliance and Enforcement: Responsive Regulation and Beyond." In *Explaining Compliance: Business Responses to Regulation*, pp. 199–221, edited by Christine Parker and Vibeke Nielson. Cheltenham, UK: Edward Elgar.

Havinga, Tetty, and Frans van Waarden. 2013. *Veilig Voedsel: Toezicht Toevertrouwen?* [Safe Food: Entrust Enforcement?] Nijmegen, Utrecht, NL: WRR.

Hawkins, Keith. 1984. *Environment and Enforcement: Regulation and the Social Definition of Pollution.* Oxford, UK: Clarendon Press.

Heimer, Carol A. 2011. "Disarticulated Responsiveness: The Theory and Practice of Responsive Regulation in Multi-layered Systems." *University of British Columbia Law Review* 44: 663–93.

Hsueh, Lily, and Aseem Prakash. 2012. "Incentivizing Self-regulation: Federal vs. State-Level Voluntary Programs in US Climate Change Policies." *Regulation and Governance* 6: 445–73.

Kesan, Jay P. 2000. "Encouraging Firms to Police Themselves: Strategic Prescriptions to Promote Corporate Self-auditing." *University of Illinois Law Review* 2000: 155–84.

Krawiec, Kimberly D. 2003. "Cosmetic Compliance and the Failure of Negotiated Governance." *Washington University Law Quarterly* 81: 487–544.

Langevoort, Donald C. 2007. "The Social Construction of Sarbanes–Oxley." *Michigan Law Review* 105: 1817–56.

Lloyd-Bostock, Sally. 1992. "The Psychology of Routine Discretion: Accidence Screening by British Factory Inspectors." *Law and Policy* 14: 45–76.

Lloyd-Bostock, Sally, and Bridget M. Hunter. 2008. "Reforming Regulation of the Medical Profession: The Risks of Risk-based Approaches." *Health, Risk, and Society* 10: 69–83.

Lobel, Orly. 2012. "New Governance as Regulatory Governance." In *The Oxford Handbook of Governance*, pp. 65–82, edited by David Levy-Faur. Oxford, UK: Oxford University Press.

Lynn, Lawrence E., Jr. 2010. "Adaptation? Transformation? Both? Neither? The Many Faces of Governance." *Jerusalem Papers in Regulation and Governance* 20: 1–29.

Makkai, Toni, and John Braithwaite. 1994a. "The Dialectics of Corporate Deterrence." *Journal of Research in Crime and Delinquency* 31: 347–73.

Makkai, Toni, and John Braithwaite. 1994b. "Reintegrative Shaming and Compliance with Regulatory Standards." *Criminology* 32: 361–83.

Mascini, Peter. 2013. "Why Was the Enforcement Pyramid So Influential? And What Price Was Paid?" *Regulation and Governance* 7: 48–60.

Mascini, Peter, and Judith van Erp. 2011. "Waarom Zijn Sommige Vormen van Rechtshandhaving Effectiever dan Dndere?" [What Are Some Forms of Law Enforcement More Effective Than Others?]. In *Recht van onderop: antwoorden uit de rechtssociologie [Bottom Up Law: Answers for the Sociology of Law]*, pp. 109–26, edited by Marc Hertogh and Heleen Weyers. Nijmegen, NL: Ars Aequui Libri.

Mascini, Peter, and Eelco van Wijk. 2009. "Responsive Regulation at the Dutch Food and Commodity Authority: An Empirical Assessment of Assumptions Underlying the Theory." *Regulation and Governance* 3: 27–47.

McGuire, Michael, and Robert Agranoff. 2011. "The Limitations of Public Management Networks." *Public Administration* 89: 265–84.

Murphy, Kristina, and Nathan Harris. 2007. "Shaming, Shame, and Recidivism: A Test of Reintegrative Shaming Theory in the White-Collar Crime Context." *British Journal of Criminology* 47: 900–17.

Neale, Alan. 1997. "Organizing Environmental Self-regulation: Liberal Governmentality and the Pursuit of Ecological Modernization in Europe." *Environmental Politics* 6: 1–24.

Parker, Christine. 2002. *The Open Corporation: Effective Self-regulation and Democracy.* New York: Cambridge University Press.

Parker, Christine. 2008. "The Pluralization of Regulation." *Theoretical Inquiries in Law* 9: 348–69.

Pautz, Michelle C., and Sara R. Rinfret. 2012. *The Lilliputians of Environmental Regulation: The Perspective of State Regulators.* New York: Routledge.

Pearce, Frank, and Steve Tombs. 1990. "Ideology, Hegemony, and Empiricism." *British Journal of Criminology* 30: 423–43.

Pearce, Frank, and Steve Tombs. 1991. "Policing Corporate 'Skid Rows': A Reply to Keith Hawkins." *British Journal of Criminology* 31: 415–26.

Perrow, Charles. 1984. *Normal Accidents: Living with High-Risk Technologies.* New York: Basic Books.

Piquero, Alex R., Raymond Paternoster, Greg Pogarsky, and Thomas Loughran. 2011. "Elaborating the Individual Difference Component in Deterrence Theory." *Annual Review of Law and Social Science* 7: 335–60.

Saurwain, Florian. 2011. "Regulatory Choice for Alternative Modes of Regulation: How Context Matters." *Law and Policy* 33: 334–66.

Short, Jodi L. 2012. "The Paranoid Style in Regulatory Reform." *Hastings Law Journal* 63: 633–95.

Short, Jodi L., and Michael W. Toffel. 2010. "Making Self-Regulation More Than Merely Symbolic: The Critical Role of the Legal Environment." *Administrative Science Quarterly* 55: 361–96.

Shover, Neal. 2008. "Zelfregulering door Ondernemingen: Ontwikkeling, Beoordeling, en Bange Voorgevoelens" [Self-Regulation by Companies: Development, Assessment, and Foreboding]. *Tijdschrift voor Criminologie* 50: 169–81.

Simpson, Sally S. 2002. *Corporate Crime, Law, and Social Control.* Cambridge, UK: Cambridge University Press.

Simpson, Sally S. 2003. "White-Collar Crime: A Review of Recent Developments and Promising Directions for Future Research." *Annual Review of Sociology* 39: 309–31.

Terpstra, Jan. 2009. "Nodale Sturing van Veiligheid en Lokale Veiligheidsnetwerken: Over de Beperkingen van een Perspectief" [Nodal Governance of Security and Local Security Networks: About the Limitations of a Perspective]. *Justitiële Verkenningen* 35: 113–25.

Thornton, Dorothy, Robert A. Kagan, and Neil Gunningham. 2003. "Sources of Corporate Environmental Performance." *California Management Review* 46: 127–41.

Tombs, Steve, and David Whyte. 2010. "A Deadly Consensus: Worker Safety and Regulatory Degradation under New Labour." *British Journal of Criminology* 50: 46–65.

Tombs, Steve, and David Whyte. 2012. "Transcending the Deregulation Debate? Regulation, Risk, and the Enforcement of Health and Safety Law in the UK." *Regulation and Governance* 7: 61–79.

Verbruggen, Paul. 2013. "Gorillas in the Closet? Public and Private Actors in the Enforcement of Transnational Private Regulation." *Regulation and Governance* 7: 512–32.

Vogel, David. 2005. *The Market for Virtue: The Potential and Limits of Corporate Social Responsibility.* Washington, D.C.: The Brookings Institution.

Vogel, David. 2008. "The Private Regulation of Global Corporate Conduct." In *The Politics of Global Regulation*, pp.151–88, edited by Walter Mattli and Ngaire Woods. Princeton, NJ: Princeton University Press.

Wilthagen, Ton. 1993. *Het Overheidstoezicht op de Arbeidsomstandigheden: Een Onderzoek naar het Functioneren van de Arbeidsinspectie* [The Enforcement of Health and Safety Conditions: A Study of the Functioning of the Labor Inspectorate]. Groningen, NL: Wolters-Noordhoff.

Wingerde, Karin van. 2012. *De Afschrikking Voorbij: Een Empirishe Studie naar Afschrikking, Generale Preventie, en Regelnaleving in de Nederlandse Afvalbranche* [Beyond Deterrence: An Empirical Study of General Prevention, Deterrence, and Compliance in the Dutch Waste Industry]. Rotterdam, NL: Wolf Productions.

Wood, Jennifer, and Clifford Shearing. 2009. "De Nodale Politiefunctie" [The Nodal Police Function]. *Justitiële Verkenningen* 35: 11–28.

CHAPTER 26

....

THE CREDIBILITY
OF OVERSIGHT AND
AGGREGATE RATES OF
WHITE-COLLAR CRIME

....

WEI WANG AND HONGMING CHENG

THE general trend in our expanding and increasingly globalized market society is for regulation to grow, since harmful forces with economically and socially undesirable consequences can develop to threaten the society unless sufficient oversight is in place (Cheng 2004; Will, Handelman, and Brotherton 2012). The global economic and financial crisis that started in 2007 resulted from multiple causes, but fraud and regulatory failure have been cited as major factors (Friedrichs 2012). Despite an ongoing debate on the effectiveness of various regulatory approaches and the best model of regulation to deal with white-collar crime, criminologists generally agree that better oversight is needed to prevent and control the crimes of corporations and elites (Shover and Hochstetler 2006). The theoretical basis of this argument is that white-collar offenders are thought to be more calculating and more fearful of being caught, punished, and stigmatized than street criminals (Piquero, Exum, and Simpson 2005). The establishment of credible oversight in the form of government regulation, therefore, could restrain potential offenders from committing white-collar offenses and prevent existing offenders from continuing to offend (Shover and Hochstetler 2006).

Criminologists have examined various models of oversight and have established various theories to explain white-collar offenses and offenders, but limited efforts have been made to investigate the relationship between the credibility and power of oversight and aggregate rates of white-collar crime. This chapter will take an empirical approach to analyze the effect of the credibility of oversight on aggregate rates of white-collar crime. Its main conclusions are as follows:

- The establishment of credible oversight, as reflected by legislative reform and anti-fraud programs in this study, is generally an effective way to reduce the aggregate rate of white-collar crime in the long term.
- Credible oversight programs might increase public awareness and reporting of white-collar crime victimization, thus raising the apparent aggregate rate of such crime in the short run.
- More complete and methodologically sophisticated studies using more advanced measurements and data from different stages of legal proceedings can help further establish the relationship between the credibility of oversight and aggregate rates of white-collar crime.

Section I provides a brief review of the literature regarding definitions of white-collar crime and aggregate rates as well as theoretical perspectives about the concept and effects of credible oversight on controlling white-collar crimes. Section II describes two datasets and indicators of the credibility of oversight employed in this chapter. Section III discusses the results of empirical examples from Canada and assesses the proposed relationship between the credibility of oversight and aggregate rates of white-collar crime in Canada. Section IV concludes with academic and policy implications for reducing aggregate rates of white-collar crimes and proposes an agenda for future research.

I. Literature Review

A. Defining White-Collar Crime

Over seventy years have passed since Sutherland first distinguished white-collar from street crime, defining the former as a crime committed by a person of respectability and high social status in the course of his occupation (1940, p. 2). The definition of white-collar crime is still debated. While some scholars have attempted to clarify the ambiguities by using other terms such as corporate crime or organizational crime, others have incorporated those conflicts into broader definitions (e.g., Weisburd and Waring 2001; Langton and Piquero 2007; Bazley 2008). Some critics have proposed to use different terms to describe white-collar offenders and offenses.

Benson and Simpson (2009), for instance, argued that the concept of white-collar crime should not be limited to high-status individuals (also see Edelhertz 1970). They used the term "professionals" to refer to individuals who charge a fee for their specialized service. Professionals usually have specialized expertise in areas that ordinary people lack. When professionals are hired to do jobs that require specialized knowledge and/or experience, white-collar crime such as fraud is an ever-present possibility because it is difficult for nonprofessionals to ensure that the work was done properly for the price charged. Therefore, this definition not only includes the traditional under-standing of higher-status persons such as CEOs of Fortune 500 companies, lawyers, doctors, and business executives, but also covers individuals lower down the occupa-tional hierarchy, such as plumbers, mechanics, and electricians.

Shapiro (1990), moreover, defined white-collar crime as "violation and manipulation of the norms of trust" occurring in "agency relationships" (p. 350). She used "agency" to describe individuals or groups who act on behalf of others. She argued that modern agency relationships are highly unbalanced for three reasons: (1) the superior informa-tion held by the agents often cannot be assessed by principals; (2) the resources, power, property, assets, responsibility, and discretion controlled by agents can create wealth and distribute opportunity; and (3) conflicts can occur between principal interests and agents' self-interest. Because of the unbalanced relationships, agents who are employed based on trust can manipulate the trusted relationship to pursue illegitimate benefits for themselves.

These broad definitions help develop a possible system to evaluate aggregate statistics of white-collar crime. In the United States, the Federal Bureau of Investigation (FBI) defines white-collar crime as nonviolent offenses that rely on "guile or concealment" (Webster 1980, p. 276). Fraud is one of the most common types of white-collar crime, and it violates the norm of trust. Therefore, fraud, forgery/counterfeiting, embezzle-ment, and bribery have been measured in the official statistics regarding white-collar crime (Barnett 2002).[1] This, however, is far from a perfect measure of white-collar crime because it does not include offenses with victims who remain unaware that they have been victimized and it also does not include other types of white-collar offenses. Nevertheless, it is the best we can use at the present to assess the aggregate rate of white-collar crime. Therefore, to examine white-collar crime at a macro level, we use a broader definition of white-collar crime as violations of trust committed by individuals or groups. For the purpose of this essay, we will focus on fraud, including credit card fraud, check fraud, and other types of fraud.

B. Aggregate Analysis

Aggregate analysis emphasizes variations in crime rates across groups such as neighbor-hoods, cities, and countries (Osgood 2000). An aggregate crime rate can be defined as "the number of crime events (e.g., arrests, victimizations, crimes known to the police) divided by the population size, often reported as crimes per 100,000" (Osgood 2000, p. 21). Scholars have used this approach to analyze factors that are related to temporal and areal variation in crime, such as the effect of unemployment (Chiricos 1987), pov-erty and income inequality (Patterson 1991), changing age structure (Levitt 1999), and household crowding (Barkan 2000). Research, however, has been focused primarily on typical street crimes. Aggregate rates of white-collar crime have rarely been exam-ined in most general social surveys and scholarly studies. So far in the 21st century, no national uniform white-collar crime reporting system is in place in any country.

Part of the problem is the confusion over the definition of white-collar crime. As discussed in the previous section, due to the ambiguities and complexities involved in defining white-collar crime, it is difficult to analyze variations across groups as recorded by a whole range of regulatory agencies at the macro level using the concept of aggregate crime rate. Lack of an accurate way to measure white-collar crime is another reason for the difficulty. The typical methodologies used to obtain data on crime rates such as reports to police, victimization surveys, and self-reported questionnaires can only provide a partial picture of white-collar offenses. Victimization surveys are considered more precise than official statistical data to describe the nature of street crimes, but they are less effective in regard to white-collar offenses, as many people do not even realize they have been victimized by insider trading or price fixing. In a victimization survey conducted by the National White-Collar Crime Center in the United States (Huff, Desilets, and Kane 2010, p. 17), the largest number of victims reported minor fraud victimization such as credit card fraud, but no other type of white-collar crime was included in the study. Self-report surveys, in which respondents are asked to report their own offenses, could potentially reveal some illegal white-collar activities, but they are of little value for constructing a larger picture of white-collar crime. Importantly, no large-scale survey has been conducted asking people in white-collar positions to report on the criminal activities that they have committed (Coleman, 2005). Arguably, reports from law-enforcement agencies are the only available resource for examining aggregate rates of white-collar crime. Yet, the problems of official data, including limited recording of white-collar offenses, cannot be ignored.

C. Oversight and White-Collar Crime

Although many standard criminological theories have been applied to white-collar crime, the results have not been encouraging (e.g., Piquero and Piquero 2006; Langton and Piquero 2007; Benson and Simpson 2009). Criminologists have emphasized two aspects of causation when analyzing why individuals are involved in white-collar crime: motivation and opportunities (Coleman 2005). The first aspect explains why certain law-abiding persons without any records of juvenile delinquency start committing white-collar offenses in adulthood, while the second focuses on the circumstances that trigger the occurrence of such offenses. It is assumed that most white-collar offenders are psychologically normal or free from major psychiatric disorders (Benson, Madensen, and Eck 2009), and research has shown that they start older than their counterparts who commit street crimes (Piquero and Benson 2004). These offenders could be driven either by a desire to be successful (Coleman 2005) or by a fear of falling (Piquero 2012). They are considered to be rational in weighing costs and benefits (Shover and Cullen 2008) and to be skillful in using neutralizations to justify their behavior (Piquero, Tibbetts, and Blankenship 2005).

Opportunity theorists have argued that potential offenders might be highly skilled at committing crimes, but without proper opportunity, the possibility that such crimes could take place is quite low (Coleman 1987). Opportunities refer to certain conditions that make criminal activities available or attractive to a potential offender with little perceived risk of detection or penalty (Shover and Hochstetler 2006; Benson and Simpson 2009). Criminal opportunities are an important cause of criminal activities (Felson 2002). Studies on white-collar crimes further illustrate this argument. Benson and Simpson (2009), for instance, describe where opportunities exist and how they could affect fraud in healthcare. In the United States, most medical costs are paid by private insurance or government programs (which are not the actual persons who received service from the medical professionals). Claims filed with the insurance companies might not reflect the service or treatment that has been delivered. This gap between patients and insurance companies presents an opportunity for physicians to manipulate and file fake documents to receive payment for the nonexistent service they falsely claim to have provided. In other words, some medical professionals see the information asymmetry as a potential condition that makes fraud in healthcare possible. If the insurer could verify the information submitted in the file with patients and confirm that it reflects the precise situation occurring in the clinic, then the opportunity would be less attractive.

Criminal opportunities are the circumstances that indicate not only criminal rewards but also a low possibility of risks of detection or penalty (Coleman 1987). Shover and Hochstetler (2006) argued that lure becomes criminal opportunity only when there is an absence of credible oversight. With regard to white-collar crime, credible oversight means that potential offenders are aware that there is a not-insignificant probability that illegal behavior will be detected by regulatory agents, law-enforcement personnel, or others, such as consumers or employees. A widely accepted rationale for conducting oversight of white-collar crime in general is that oversight ensures that rules and regulations regarding white-collar crime are appropriately, effectively, and efficiently developed and implemented in order to prevent, detect, punish, and deter such crime. The concept of the credibility of oversight can be defined as the degree to which the oversight commitments are implemented. An oversight system is "credible" if it has followed its promised actions. From a more subjective perspective, credibility of oversight refers to perceptions and assumptions that the law and the operations of oversight agents dealing with a particular type of white-collar crime are trustworthy, responsible, desirable, appropriate, and most importantly effective. Therefore, the credibility of oversight must be fully understood in relation to public confidence, which requires that the public perceive that the law is effective and that the oversight agents have the ability and willingness to conduct extensive and systematic oversight consistently as has been promised.

Three types of oversight have been discussed in the academic literature in explanations of white-collar crime: private, state, and offshore. Private oversight refers to injured parties and nongovernmental organizations that "promulgate and enforce code of ethics and generally accepted practices" (Shover and Hochstetler 2006, p. 78). Professional associations, class-action lawsuits, and whistleblowers are examples of private oversight. However, the enforcement machinery is generally small and lenient.

Although the promise of private oversight (especially when it is used in conjunction with state oversight) is recognized by some leading criminologists (Braithwaite 1982; Simpson 2002), the effectiveness of private oversight alone is reduced in situations involving higher-status offenders sitting in vital positions in large companies because they have vast resources with which to resist this type of oversight (Shover and Hochstetler 2006).

Theoretically speaking, the most credible source of oversight comes from the state. Criminalization is a typical form of state oversight, which refers to the process that legislative bodies, courts, and administrative agencies use to categorize conduct as criminal offenses and to impose penalties on the offenders in order to restrain citizens and organizations in regard to certain types of behaviors and to thereby reduce the attractiveness of criminal opportunities (Shover and Hochstetler 2006). Although criminalization is a clear process of state oversight, in practice, the results could be more complicated because "the official response typically is weaker than promised, invariably challenged and softened by the difficulties of enforcement and prosecution" (Shover and Hochstetler 2006, p. 85; see also Cheng 2012b). Due to various political reasons and legal difficulties, the actions of white-collar offenders are less likely to be criminalized and prosecuted (Cheng 2008; Cheng and Ma 2009; Friedrichs 2010; Cheng 2012a). The penalties for white-collar crimes, moreover, are typically lenient since judges might empathize with white-collar offenders at times (Jesilow, Pontell, and Geis 1993; Croall 2001). Shover and Hochstetler (2006) proposed that unclear sentencing guidelines facilitate a lenient approach to white-collar offenders (p. 97). Economic and social regulation might also help reduce certain white-collar offenses. The monitoring process, however, is difficult to practice, and most regulatory agencies cannot effectively enforce laws regarding white-collar crime (Shover and Hochstetler 2006). For these reasons, oversight is less than it could be.

Transnational regulation refers to efforts conducted to control and regulate the transnational corporations in the global economic system. With increasing global oversight to criminalize certain conducts, corporations might relocate to other places. However, disunity that exists in each nation's legislation could challenge the power of national-level oversight and cause difficulties to control the crimes committed by the transnational corporations. Shover and Hochstetler (2006) argued that, although signatories to international trade agreements attempt to enforce their nationwide regulations on issues such as workers' rights, environmental protection, and product safety, lack of budget, inadequate expertise, and insufficient resources reduce the credibility of oversight, and this increases opportunities for white-collar crime moving from one country to another.

When examining white-collar offenses, it is obvious that both offenders' motivation and the available opportunity are important factors that work together to make crime occur. As Shover and Hochstetler (2006) emphasized, the absence of credible oversight would create more opportunities for potential offenders in the presence of lure. Scholars have provided numerous examples or case studies illustrating such a relationship between oversight and white-collar offenses (Gibbs et al. 2010; Levi 2010; van de Bunt 2010). Few studies, however, have examined how the credibility of oversight might affect the aggregate crime rate of white-collar crime. The current study attempts to address this gap by assessing the effects of the changes in legislation and oversight programs launched by the Canadian federal government on white-collar crime rates at a macro level.

Early theorists, such as Cloward and Ohlin (1960), argued that the most effective analysis unit to examine crime and delinquency is the community or neighborhood. When exploring white-collar crime, however, using such small areas as the unit of analysis would be difficult because most available data on aggregate crime rate are collected from national law-enforcement agencies, which provide information on a nation as a whole. Thus, the data used in the current study will be drawn from the official crime reports: Uniform Crime Reports (UCR) from Statistics Canada. The victimization reports from the Canada Anti-Fraud Center (CAFC 2011) will also be analyzed to complement the UCR data. We do not claim that the findings of this study can be generalized to other countries. However, since our focus is on the relationship between credible oversight and aggregate rates of white-collar crime in general, we hope that the theoretical argument we reach may have a more general applicability.

II. Data and Indicators

A. Data

Scholars have consistently argued that it is extremely difficult to estimate the prevalence of white-collar crime through official statistical data since most corporate crimes are not included. To provide some information on the larger picture, this chapter focuses on the aggregate rate of fraud. We understand that some may argue that fraud is not a good example of white-collar crime, as it does not require the perpetrators to have high occupational status or prestige. However, this measure is the best available from official statistics with which to assess aggregate rates of white-collar crime. The offenses of fraud reflect those prohibited in the Criminal Code.[2] It is arguable that the majority of the offenses included in this statistical data category are white-collar crimes, committed by middle-class individuals, as confirmed by the Chief Investigator of the Saskatoon Police Service in our interviews.

The first set of data used in the current study is drawn from the UCRs from Statistics Canada (the central office that provides statistics about the Canadian society). The surveys are conducted annually to measure rates and characteristics of the incidence of crime in Canada. It employs a cross-sectional design and collects data from all units of the target population. Police departments are the respondents, and more than 1,200 police detachments have responded to the survey (Statistics Canada 2012). Three separate categories are recorded as fraud: (1) check frauds, including false pretense, forgery, uttering, and fraud offenses involving checks; (2) credit/debit cards frauds, including fraudulent-type offenses involving use and/or theft of credit cards; and (3) other frauds, including all other frauds not scored as check or credit card fraud (Statistics Canada 2012).[3] For this study, we used data on the incidence of fraud from the UCR surveys between 1992 and 2011. The aggregate rates of fraud are presented per 100,000 population. The second set of data is drawn from the CAFC to complement the official data.

Due to the complexity and ambiguity of fraud, it is not surprising that there could be a certain number of unreported and undocumented offenses. This obviously weakens the reliability of official data. For street crime, it is argued that the victimization survey can enhance the analysis by way of consulting victims. However, white-collar offenses are not covered in the major victimization survey. Although both violent and nonviolent victimization experience has been investigated in the General Social Survey on Victimization, for instance, in the nonviolent category, respondents are only required to report victimization on breaking and entering, theft, motor theft, and vandalism (Perreault and Brennan 2009).

Fortunately, the intelligence unit of CAFC has made a tremendous effort to enter and analyze the complaints and reports from victims (or potential victims) and provide valuable information on white-collar offenses. The CAFC was initiated by members of the Ontario Provincial Police (OPP) and the Royal Canadian Mounted Police (RCMP) in Northern Ontario (Rosella 2010). The Criminal Intelligence Analysis Unit works with other law-enforcement agencies to detect and deter mass-marketing fraud. It provides annual reports on frauds targeting both Canadians and foreign victims. The victimization data are collected through phone calls and e-mails received by the CAFC. This chapter will analyze the reported fraud cases available from the CAFC between 2009 and 2011. Although the data are not a strictly aggregate rate of fraud, they are a good resource to assess white-collar crimes at the macro level as they offer a way to address the dark figures in the official data.

B. Indicators of Oversight Credibility

To our knowledge, the credibility of oversight is rarely measured and examined in a quantitative way. The ambiguity of its definition and lack of variation in the policies implemented in one particular country are the most important issues when determining the credibility of oversight. Since criminalization and regulation are key components of oversight, this chapter employs legislation changes and the development of antifraud programs implemented with the cooperation of federal agencies as indicators of the credibility of oversight. Again, this measurement is far from perfect, especially due to the lack of data regarding public perceptions of the credibility of oversight of white-collar crime, but it can provide a certain level of assessment on the relationship between a form of oversight and a particular form of white-collar crime—namely, fraud.

1. *Legislative Changes*

In Canada, white-collar crimes have traditionally been dealt with under the name of regulatory offenses, which are concerned with the enforcement of a federal or provincial regulatory scheme that addresses inherently legitimate yet potentially harmful activities, such as engaging in trade and commerce, advertising, and driving on the highways. Regulatory agencies merely impose penalties (usually financial) on those whose conduct falls below a standard of reasonable care. In the Criminal Code (Section 380), a general fraud is defined as an act of deceit, falsehood, or other fraudulent means. However, as this definition is rather broad, in legal practice other elements such as dishonesty and deprivation are often required in courts (*R. v. Théroux*, 1993). The punishment for fraud includes imprisonment, fine, probation, and other forms of sanction depending on the circumstances. Moreover, as it is not possible to sentence a corporation to imprisonment (Section 732), a fine can be imposed on a corporation convicted of fraud, although the amount of the fine varies depending on the economic harm to the public, the need of punishment, and deterrence to potential offenders. Due to these ambiguities, the government has made many efforts to amend the laws and regulations dealing with white-collar crime. The amendments in the recent decades were collected and analyzed as an indicator of the credibility of oversight.

In the past decade, several bills were passed that establish a more certain and harsher law against white-collar crime. "Service fraud," for example, was added to the list of fraud offenses in 1997. The federal government tabled Bill C-13, An Act to Amend the Criminal Code (Capital Markets Fraud and Evidence-Gathering), in February 2004. The bill received royal assent on March 29, 2004. It was created as a response to the corporate scandals that occurred in the United States, such as the Enron scandal. It created new offenses including fraud; market manipulation; and distributing false prospectuses, statements, or accounts, and it increased the maximum punishment of imprisonment for fraud from ten to fourteen years (Parliament of Canada 2004). Moreover, the amended Criminal Code prohibits insider trading and tipping inside information, with the maximum imprisonment of ten years for insider trading and five years for tipping inside information. The amendments also clarified certain aggravating circumstances that could be taken into the consideration of sentencing for market fraud offenses: (a) the amount exceeded $1 million; (b) the offense affected the stability of the Canadian economic or financial system or market; (c) large numbers of victims were involved; and (d) the elevated status or reputation of the offender was manipulated (Parliament of Canada 2004).

In March 2011, Bill C-21, An Act to Amend the Criminal Code (sentencing for fraud), also referred to as the Standing up for Victims of White-Collar Crime Act, received royal assent (Parliament of Canada 2011). The new law was created to address the concern that, although Section 380 states the maximum of imprisonment of fourteen years when the amount involved in fraud offenses exceeds $5,000 and two years' imprisonment for those under $5,000, minimum years of imprisonment were not clearly indicated (Parliament of Canada 2011). It also provided the aggravating circumstances that should be taken into consideration in courts,[4] and it added a discretionary order that prohibited the offender from offering professional service to others (Parliament of Canada 2011).[5] In addition, the new law states that courts might order offenders to make restitution to the victims and may consider the statement describing the harm made in the community where the offenses took place. Bill C-21 at least partially reflects the federal government's approach of "tough on crime" and attempts to provide more protection for victims from fraud offenses, even though such an approach is mainly adopted to target street criminals.

The Competition Act in Canada is a federal law that provides prohibition of criminal offenses under the criminal law as well as noncriminal provisions. Criminal offenses included in the act are price fixing, allocating sales, bid-rigging conspiracies, price discrimination, and misleading advertising; noncriminal activities include mergers, tied selling, and dealing misconduct. The act applies to all business in Canada. The Minister of Industry tabled Bill C-20 (An Act to Amend the Competition Act and to Make Consequential and Related Amendments to Other Acts) in November 1997. It clarified the ambiguities of the offense of misleading advertising and deceptive marketing practice and increased the maximum fine of a convicted offense from $25,000 to $200,000 (Parliament of Canada 1999). In addition, it created a new criminal offense of deceptive telemarketing practice and specified that a person would be fined or sentenced to imprisonment for a period not exceeding five years for a more serious conviction and be fined not exceeding $200,000 or be imprisoned for a term not exceeding one year if convicted for less serious offense (Parliament of Canada 1999).

2. *Antifraud Programs*

The reform of oversight programs of white-collar crime in Canada started in the early 1990s. The implementation of these programs can be another indicator of the credibility of oversight as they partially reflect the strategy of regulation. After the CAFC was established, the primary focus was on telemarketing, and "Project PhoneBusters" was created. A victim database has been created, and key perpetrators have been prosecuted. In 1997, another project, "SeniorBusters," was launched to increase the awareness of fraud among senior citizens and to protect them from victimization. In 2002, the Criminal Intelligence and Analytical Unit was developed. It provided research reports to law-enforcement agencies by analyzing the connections between victimization data and suspects. Since 2006, the CAFC has become a joint-force operation under OPP, RCMP, and the Competition Bureau Canada. In 2010, the CAFC expanded its programs to mass-marketing fraud and began to handle more types of fraud offenses, including telephone, postal mail, and Internet fraud.

Another notable antifraud program is the Fraud Prevention Forum. Chaired by the Competition Bureau Canada, it consists of various groups, government agencies, and law-enforcement organizations (Competition Bureau Canada 2011). Partner members have dramatically increased from 22 in 2004 to 125 in 2011. The aim of the forum is to fight fraud proactively and protect both individuals and businesses from victimization by mass-marketing fraud. Education programs play a major role in the forum. Fraud

Prevention Month has been organized by the forum since it was launched in 2004. The idea is to reduce fraud offenses by increasing public awareness so that people will be more alert when approached by potential perpetrators. It also encourages reporting cases to agencies, which could research the data, analyze the suspects, and share the information with law enforcement. It might accelerate the investigation process and increase the detection rate.

In addition, in 2004, the federal government launched the Anti-Spam Action Plan for Canada, which was overseen by a government/private sector Task Force on Spam and resulted in a report containing twenty-two recommendations on possible action by law enforcement regarding suspected spams (Task Force on Spam 2005). Since the 1990s, due to the government efforts to strengthen the regulatory environment, there has also been better diligence in implementing antifraud regimes within companies. From the survey conducted by PricewaterhouseCoopers LLP in 2009, most Canadian companies believe that an organization's ethical tone at the top and a strong internal control environment combine to provide the strongest deterrent to fraudulent activities. Canadian companies were almost twice as likely as their global counterparts to detect fraud through internal means, such as automated suspicious transaction reporting systems (PricewaterhouseCoopers 2009).

III. Analysis and Results

The amendments to the Criminal Code and the Competition Act can be treated as efforts to strengthen the credibility of oversight in regard to white-collar crime in Canada. The Canadian federal government attempted to send a message to the public and to potential offenders that white-collar crime has become one of the major concerns of the criminal justice system and of regulatory agencies and to restrain potential offenders from committing such as crimes by increasing the severity of punishment. Some scholars have suggested that it is possible to decrease the crime rate by increasing the certainty of sanctions (Wilson 1994; Shover and Hochstetler 2006), while others have argued that the bills are not effective (Bittle and Snider 2011). Our analysis is designed to investigate whether these changes in the law correlate with changes in indicators of fraud victimization.

Figure 26.1 presents the aggregate rates of fraud in Canada from 1992 to 2011. It shows that reported fraud decreased gradually during this period. The fraud rate was around 440 per 100,000 in 1992 and dropped twenty years later in 2011 to just over 250 per 100,000. It declined sharply in 1993 and trended downward until 2001. The rate increased slightly between 2001 and 2004, and this might have been due to the fact that several programs were launched to increase the awareness of fraud among citizens who might have reported more victimization cases to the police. Aggregate fraud rates have continued to decline since 2004 and were close to 250 per 100,000 in 2011. Although

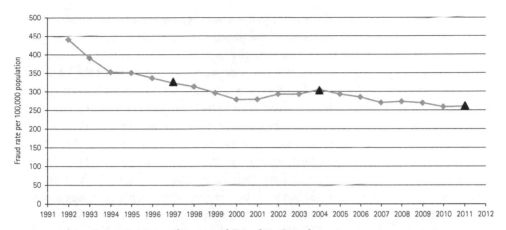

FIGURE 26.1 Aggregate Rate of Reported Fraud in Canada, 1992–2011

Notes: Fraud here includes check fraud, credit/debit card fraud, and other frauds as stipulated in the Criminal Code. The symbol of ▲ indicates the years when the Criminal Code was amended.

Source: Statistic Canada (2012).

there might be other factors that contributed to the decline, it is suggestive that the trend correlates with changes in legislation.

Figure 26.2 presents the results from the CAFC victimization survey. It indicates a similar pattern that the official data provide: the overall number of victims has been decreasing. For complaints, when using the 2009 data as a baseline, the total number increased 23 percent in 2010 and 13 percent in 2011. However, the total number of victims has been declining gradually since 2009. Indeed, these numbers were not strictly aggregate victim rates, but since the overall population of Canada has continued to

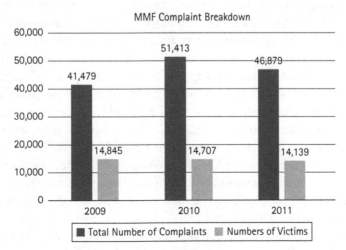

FIGURE 26.2 Numbers of Complaints and Victims of Mass-Marketing Fraud (MMF), 2009–2011

Source: Canadian Anti-Fraud Centre Criminal Intelligence Analytical Unit (2011).

increase in recent years, the downward pattern was clearly shown even without precisely dividing these actual numbers by the population. Although the changes in the victimization rate are quite small and it might be difficult to illustrate any statistical association with legislative changes, this figure arguably can supplement the UCR data.

Furthermore, the Global Economic Crime Survey by PricewaterhouseCoopers confirms this decline of fraud offenses. According to its surveys in 2003, 2007, 2009, and 2011, a decreasing percentage of Canadian respondents from businesses and the government said they were victims of some form of economic crime—a decrease of 14 percent from the survey in 2003, with slight fluctuations between some years. These findings not only provide some evidence that strategies implemented by both the Canadian government and companies work, but also they suggest that people are more aware of fraud offenses and have gained more knowledge to identify fraud and protect themselves from being victimized. The increased public awareness of white-collar crime victimization could increase reporting of white-collar crime cases in the short run yet reduce the aggregate rate of such crime in the long term.

IV. CONCLUSION

This chapter has analyzed the relationship between the credibility of oversight and aggregate rates of white-collar crime. Since several amendments of the Criminal Code of Canada have been passed in the recent decades and collaboration among different government agencies has been enhanced, aggregate rates of white-collar offenses have been decreasing in the short term after each legislative change. Although there likely are a variety of factors contributing to this decline (e.g., the changing nature of fraud and the increasing difficulty of cyberfraud), a possible contributing factor is the effect of the increases in the credibility of oversight, which makes commission of fraud more risky and costly (PricewaterhouseCoopers 2009). Those acts mentioned above appear to have reduced opportunities for white-collar offending or made them less attractive to potential offenders. Thus, they appear to have had a general deterrent effect on would-be offenders. The programs launched by law enforcement, government agencies, and companies also might have decreased the white-collar crime rate by reducing the number of suitable targets. As Canadians have become more aware of various types of fraud, it might have become harder for fraud offenders to deceive members of the general public. Therefore, legislation imposing more certain and harsher punishment on white-collar crime, coupled with efforts to increase awareness of white-collar offenses among the public, appears to be a feasible strategy to reduce the crime rate and prevent people from being victimized.

It is difficult to examine the relationship between credibility of oversight and aggregate rates of white-collar crime without controlling for other important factors, such as economic factors. The results presented in this chapter, thus, must be treated as preliminary and their limitations recognized. First, the definition of white-collar crime used here is quite broad. It is possible that some cases in the UCR data and the annual report from the CAFC are not really white-collar crimes. Second, only one broad type of white-collar offenses has been investigated. Corporate and high-status/occupational offenders might not be affected by the integrated model in the current study. For instance, Bittle and Snider (2011) argued that market fraud legislation is not very successful in handling corporate crimes, as few charges for market fraud have been made by the RCMP and fewer convictions have been secured six years since Bill C-13 has been implemented. It might not work for insider trading either, as individual victims are not specifically targeted by this type of offense.

Third, the credibility of the threat of harsher punishment is uncertain. Although it could indicate more risks and punishment, scholars have argued that the direct relationship between sanctions and criminal actions would be unobservable, and "the two must be linked through the intervening variable of subjective perceptions of the risks and rewards of committing an offense" (Decker, Wright, and Logie 1993, p. 135). Therefore, to have a better understanding of the effect of legislation on the aggregate crime rate of white-collar offenses, it is not sufficient to look at merely the amendments of legislation. The opinions of white-collar offenders are important indicators of whether new punishments have been perceived as an increased risk to committing criminal activities.

Last, the findings need to be supported by further studies using advanced measurements of white-collar crime and data from different resources, such as data on cases in adult criminal court and the type of sentences that white collar offenders have received. Information on the credibility of threats is also crucial to address the limitations in the current study. These data might provide information on the certainty and severity of the deterrence, which will help assess how the proposed strict legislation could reduce the crime rate and demonstrate a more solid understanding of the credibility of oversight on white-collar crime.

Furthermore, our analysis and argument do not suggest a universally applicable oversight model for other countries. Canada is a relatively small market with a small population. A certain and credible oversight system might be more visible to potential offenders in such a country. The emphasis on victim awareness could be more effective for Canadians since the population is only one tenth that of the United States. It would be much more challenging for the U.S. government to ensure that such a large number of the nation's people are provided with sufficient education on the knowledge and skills needed to protect themselves from being victims of fraud.

More empirical work is needed to comprehend the complex relationship between the credibility of oversight and aggregate rates of white-collar crimes. Due to limitations of space, here we can provide only the briefest outline of an agenda for this project. For instance, longitudinal studies would be a better approach to analyze the relationship between variation in the credibility of oversight and variation in aggregate crime rates of white-collar crime since criminal patterns often change slowly after new legislation has been implemented. Therefore, the effect of oversight needs time to be observed. Longitudinal research might overcome the delay and provide more precise data to assess the relationship. Other types of white-collar crime need to be considered in future studies as well. The mechanism of how oversight might have an impact on corporate crimes and white-collar offenders with high status remains unclear. Although it is difficult to obtain the proper data on such offenses for the investigation, it is incomplete if we focus only on fraud cases. White-collar crime scholars can and should make a range of useful contributions to the development of a quantitative criminology of white-collar crime, and such scholars can also learn much of great interest from this evolving white-collar criminology.

NOTES

1. Although there is a category of "all other offenses" in the reports that might also provide information on white-collar crime, this category is very limited in its measure and counts for white-collar crime (Barnett 2002).
2. Since Bill S-4 (An Act to Amend the Criminal Code [identity theft and related misconduct]) was passed in 2009, identity theft and identity fraud have been incorporated into the fraud category.
3. Specifically, according to the Canadian Criminal Code, other frauds include criminal breach of trust, false pretenses, forgery and uttering, false telegrams, counterfeiting revenue stamps, destroying or falsifying documents, frauds, fraud on creditors, fraud in relation to fares, mining frauds, falsification of books and documents, personation with intent, and trademark forgery and frauds.
4. The circumstances include the magnitude, complicity, and duration of the offense and impact of the victims.
5. The services include "seeking, obtaining, or continuing any employment or becoming or being a volunteer in any capacity that involves having authority over the real property, money, or valuable security of another person" (Parliament of Canada 2011).

REFERENCES

Barkan, Steven E. 2000. "Household Crowding and Aggregate Crime Rates." *Journal of Crime and Justice* 23: 47–64.

Barnett, Cynthia. 2002. *The Measurement of White-Collar Crime Using Uniform Crime Reporting (UCR) Data*. Washington, D.C.: Criminal Justice Information Services Division, Federal Bureau of Investigation, U.S. Department of Justice.

Bazley, Tom. 2008. *Investigating White-Collar Crime*. Upper Saddle River, NJ: Pearson.

Benson, Michael L., Tamara D. Madensen, and John E. Eck. 2009. "White-Collar Crime from an Opportunity Perspective." In *The Criminology of White-Collar Crime*, pp. 175–93, edited by Sally S. Simpson and David Weisburd. New York: Springer.

Benson, Michael L., and Sally S. Simpson. 2009. *White-Collar Crime: An Opportunity Perspective*. New York: Taylor and Francis.

Bittle, Steven, and Laureen Snider. 2011. "'Moral Panics Deflected: The Failed Legislative Response to Canada's Safety Crimes and Markets Fraud Legislation." *Crime, Law, and Social Change* 56: 373–87.

Braithwaite, John. 1982. "Enforced Self-regulation: A New Strategy for Corporate Crime Control." *Michigan Law Review* 80: 1466–507.

Bunt, Henk van de. 2010. "Walls of Secrecy and Silence." *Criminology and Public Policy* 9: 435–53.

Canadian Anti-Fraud Centre Criminal Intelligence Analytical Unit. 2011. *Annual Statistical Report 2011: Mass Marketing Fraud and ID Theft Activities.* Ottawa, CAN: Canadian Anti-Fraud Centre.

Cheng, Hongming. 2004. *Insider Trading in Canada and China: Globalized Market Economy and the Role of Law.* Fredericton, NB: CLSANA Publications.

Cheng, Hongming. 2008. "Insider Trading in China: The Case for the Chinese Securities Regulatory Commission." *Journal of Financial Crime* 15: 165–78.

Cheng, Hongming. 2012a. "Cheap Capitalism: A Sociological Study of Food Crime in China." *British Journal of Criminology* 52: 254–73.

Cheng, Hongming. 2012b. "Financial Fraud in China: A Structural Examination of Law and Law Enforcement." In *How They Got Away With It: White-Collar Crime and the Financial Meltdown*, pp. 296–314, edited by Susan Will, Stephen Handelman, and David C. Brotherton. New York: Columbia University Press.

Cheng, Hongming, and Ling Ma. 2009. "White-Collar Crime and the Criminal Justice System: Bank Fraud and Corruption in China." *Journal of Financial Crime* 16: 166–79.

Chiricos, Theodore G. 1987. "Rates of Crime and Unemployment: An Analysis of Aggregate Research Evidence." *Social Problems* 34: 187–212.

Cloward, Richard A., and Lloyd E. Ohlin. 1960. *Delinquency and Opportunity: A Theory of Delinquent Gangs.* New York: Free Press.

Coleman, James W. 1987. "Toward an Integrated Theory of White-Collar Crime." *American Journal of Sociology* 93: 406–39.

Coleman, James W. 2005. *The Criminal Elite*, 4th ed. New York: St. Martin's Press.

Competition Bureau Canada 2011. *Fraud Prevention Forum.* (November). Available at http://www.competitionbureau.gc.ca/eic/site/cb-bc.nsf/eng/03662.html#tab2

Croall, Hazel. 2001. *Understanding White-collar Crime.* Buckingham, UK: Open University Press.

Decker, Scott. H., Richard Wright, and Robert Logie. 1993. "Perceptual Deterrence among Active Residential Burglars: A Research Note." *Criminology* 31: 135–47.

Edelhertz, Herbert. 1970. *The Nature, Impact and Prosecution of White Collar Crime.* Washington, D.C.: U.S. Government Printing Office.

Felson, Marcus. 2002. *Crime and Everyday Life.* Thousand Oaks, CA: Sage Publications.

Friedrichs, David O. 2010. *Trusted Criminals: White Collar Crime in Contemporary Society*, 4th ed. Belmont: Wadsworth Cengage Learning.

Friedrichs, David O. 2012. "Wall Street: Crime Never Sleeps." In *How They Got Away With It: White-Collar Crime and the Financial Meltdown*, pp. 3–25, edited by Susan Will, Stephen Handelman, and David C. Brotherton. New York: Columbia University Press.

Gibbs, Carole, Edmund F. McGarrell, and Mark Axelrod. 2010. "Transnational White-Collar Crime and Risk: Lessons from the Global Trade in Electronic Waste." *Criminology and Public Policy* 9: 543–60.

Huff, Rodney, Christian Desilets, and John Kane. 2010. *The 2010 National Public Survey on White Collar Crime.* Fairmont, WV: National White Collar Crime Center.

Jesilow, Paul, Henry N. Pontell, and Gilbert Geis. 1993. *Prescription for Profit: How Doctors Defraud Medicaid.* Berkeley: University of California Press.

Langton, Lynn, and Nicole Leeper Piquero. 2007. "Can General Strain Theory Explain White-Collar Crime? A Preliminary Investigation of the Relationship between Strain and Select White-Collar Offenses." *Journal of Criminal Justice* 35: 1–15.

Levi, Michael. 2010. "Serious Tax Fraud and Noncompliance: A Review of Evidence on the Differential Impact of Criminal and Noncriminal Proceedings." *Criminology and Public Policy* 9: 493–513.

Levitt, Steven D. 1999. "The Limited Role of Changing Age Structure in Explaining Aggregate Crime Rates." *Criminology* 37: 581–98.

Osgood, Wayne D. 2000. "Poisson-Based Regression Analysis of Aggregate Crime Rates." *Journal of Quantitative Criminology* 16: 21–43.

Parliament of Canada. 1999. *Bill C-20: An Act to Amend the Competition Act and to Make Consequential and Related Amendments to Other Acts* by David Johansen (LS-309E).

Parliament of Canada. 2004. *Bill C-13: An Act to Amend the Criminal Code (Capital Markets Fraud and Evidence-Gathering)* by Robin MacKay and Margaret Smith (LS-468E).

Parliament of Canada. 2011. *Bill C-21: An Act to Amend the Criminal Code (Sentencing for Fraud)* by Cynthia Kirkby and Dominique Valiquet (40-3-21E).

Patterson, Britt E. 1991. "Poverty, Income Inequality, and Community Crime Rates." *Criminology* 29: 755–76.

Perreault, Samuel, and Shannon Brennan. 2009. *Criminal Victimization in Canada, 2009.* Statistics Canada, *Juristat* (Summer 2010).

Piquero, Nicole Leeper. 2012. "The Only Thing We Have to Fear Is Fear Itself: Investigating the Relationship between Fear of Falling and White-Collar Crime." *Crime and Delinquency* 58: 362–79.

Piquero, Nicole Leeper, and Michael L. Benson. 2004. "White-Collar Crime and Criminal Careers: Specifying a Trajectory of Punctuated Situational Offending." *Journal of Contemporary Criminal Justice* 20: 148–65.

Piquero, Nicole Leeper, M. Lyn Exum, and Sally S. Simpson. 2005. "Integrating Desire-for-Control and Rational Choice in a Corporate Crime Context." *Justice Quarterly* 22: 252–80.

Piquero, Nicole Leeper, and Alex R. Piquero. 2006. "Control Balance and Exploitative Corporate Crime." *Criminology* 44: 397–430.

Piquero, Nicole Leeper, Stephen G. Tibbetts, and Michael B. Blankeship. 2005. "Examining the Role of Differential Association and Techniques of Neutralization in Explaining Corporate Crime." *Deviant Behavior* 26: 159–88.

PricewaterhouseCoopers. 2003. *Global Economic Crime Survey 2009: Canada.* Toronto: PricewaterhouseCoopers LLP.

PricewaterhouseCoopers. 2007. *Global Economic Crime Survey 2009: Canada.* Toronto: PricewaterhouseCoopers LLP.

PricewaterhouseCoopers. 2009. *Global Economic Crime Survey 2009: Canada.* Toronto: PricewaterhouseCoopers LLP.

PricewaterhouseCoopers. 2011. *Global Economic Crime Survey 2009: Canada.* Toronto: PricewaterhouseCoopers LLP.

Rosella, Louie. 2010. "Anti-Fraud Center Launches Website." *Mississauga News* (November 10).

Shapiro, Susan P. 1990. "Collaring the Crime, not the Criminal: Reconsidering the Concept of White-Collar Crime." *American Sociological Review* 55: 346–65.

Shover, Neal, and Francis T. Cullen. 2008. "Studying and Teaching White-Collar Crime: Populist and Patrician Perspectives." *Journal of Criminal Justice Education* 19: 155–74.

Shover, Neal, and Andy Hochstetler. 2006. *Choosing White-Collar Crime*. New York: Cambridge University Press.

Simpson, Sally S. 2002. *Corporate Crime, Law, and Social Control*. New York: Cambridge University Press.

Statistics Canada. 2012. "Uniform Crime Reporting." Available at http://www23.statcan.gc.ca/imdb-bmdi/document/3302_D7_T1_V1-eng.pdf

Sutherland, Edwin H. 1940. "White-Collar Criminality." *American Sociological Review* 5: 1–12.

Task Force on Spam. 2005. *Stopping Spam: Creating a Stronger, Safer Internet*. Ottawa: Author.

Webster, William H. 1980. "An Examination of FBI Theory and Methodology Regarding White-Collar Crime Investigation and Prevention." *American Criminal Law Review* 17: 275–86.

Weisburd, David, and Elin Waring. 2001. *White-Collar Crime and Criminal Careers*. New York: Cambridge University Press.

Will, Susan, Stephen Handelman, and David C. Brotherton, eds. 2012. *How They Got Away with It: White-Collar Crime and the Financial Meltdown*. New York: Columbia University Press.

Wilson, James Q. 1994. "Penalties and Opportunities." In *A Reader on Punishment*, pp. 174–209, edited by Antony Duff and David Garland. Oxford, UK: Oxford University Press.

PART VIII

CRIMINAL SANCTIONS

CHAPTER 27

INVESTIGATING PROSECUTING WHITE COLLAR CRIMINALS

LUCIAN E. DERVAN AND ELLEN S. PODGOR

THIS chapter will discuss the fundamental elements of investigating and prosecuting white-collar criminals. Through an examination and analysis of the critical stages of such proceedings, this discussion will offer readers an overview of the unique aspects and difficult challenges found in this evolving field of law enforcement. Understanding the dynamics and nuances of white-collar investigations and prosecutions is vital because of the ever-increasing attention these types of crimes are receiving in the United States (Huff, Desilets, and Kane 2010).[1]

Though the investigation and prosecution of white-collar criminals has many similarities to proceedings against individuals charged with street crimes, there are significant differences throughout the process. First, and perhaps most noticeable, many white-collar cases have lengthy investigations. This is in part because white-collar cases are often document driven. Second, white-collar cases also include prosecutions against entities such as corporations or partnerships, which is less common in the non-white-collar setting. Third, although white-collar cases are found in both the state and federal system, the major fraud and corruption cases usually are handled in the federal criminal justice system. Note as well that a growing number of white-collar cases now occur in areas such as environmental and computer crimes. Fourth, white-collar cases do not always have prosecutions based upon statutes that are typically considered white-collar offenses, such as insider trading or antitrust. White-collar cases may use generic statutes or "short-cut" offenses because they allow for easier proof by prosecutors (Podgor 2011a). For example, a white-collar case can be brought using an obstruction of justice statute, as was seen in the *Arthur Andersen, LLP v. United States* (544 U.S. 696 [2005]) case, as opposed to the government bringing a charge alleging and requiring proof of te fraudulent conduct. Fifth, the number of indictments that are brought by al prosecutors far exceeds the number of cases that actually proceed to trial, 95 percent of the cases in the federal criminal justice system are resolved with lea agreements. As with non-white-collar cases, these prosecutions may include cooperators, or those receiving a lesser sentence in return for their assistance in other prosecutions.

This chapter reaches several conclusions regarding white-collar cases:

- White-collar investigations and prosecutions can involve various types of orga-nizational entities, such as private or public corporations, not-for-profit orga-nizations, and partnerships. While individuals are the most common targets of prosecution in the United States, organizational entities can also be prosecuted under the doctrine of respondeat superior. Because organizational entities and affiliated individuals, such as corporate employees, may sometimes have divergent interests and incentives during white-collar criminal investigations and prosecu-tions, complex ethical and strategic adversarial decision making is an important aspect of these cases.
- White-collar investigations involve complexities rarely present in other investiga-tions. First, they can involve both corporations and individuals. Second, there are various and distinct ways in which a white-collar investigation might begin. Third, both corporations and individuals involved in white-collar cases often conduct their own extensive investigations of the alleged misconduct in preparation for their defense. Finally, both corporations and individuals often present materials to the government before indictment in an effort to convince the government to decline the prosecution.
- Prosecutors have many choices in selecting criminal offenses for the prosecution of white-collar crime, but statutes and constitutional mandates provide limits, and internal guidelines offer guidance. "Shortcut" offenses—such as perjury, false statements, and obstruction of justice—often are used by prosecutors.
- The vast majority of cases are resolved by plea agreements. Sentencing in white-collar matters often requires a determination of the amount of loss suffered by the victims.

We begin in section I by discussing the investigation of white-collar criminals, with a focus on the prosecution of organizational entities, the origins of white-collar cases, the investigation of such cases by the corporations and individuals under suspicion, and the methods by which corporations and individuals make presentations seeking a declination of prosecution prior to indictment. Section II examines the prosecution of white-collar criminals, including the indictment, pretrial motions, discovery, nontrial resolutions, trial preparation, trials, and sentencing. Section III presents our conclu-sions and recommendations.

I. Investigating White-Collar Criminals

A. Prosecuting Individuals and Entities

Each year, numerous individuals stand accused of engaging in white-collar criminal activity (Bureau of Justice Statistics 2012, p. 2). Certain of these cases are so famous that the actors in these dramas have become household names—Charles Ponzi, Martha Stewart, Jack Abramoff, Jeffrey Skilling, Bernard Madoff. In the complex world of white-collar crime, however, cases often involve not just the investigation and prosecution of individuals, but also the targeting of various forms of organizational entities—such as private or public corporations, not-for-profit organizations, and partnerships—allegedly responsible for the actions of their employees or agents. As an example, according to the U.S. Government Accountability Office, there were 194 corporate criminal prosecutions by the federal government in 2009 (Government Accountability Office 2009, p. 16). One of the most famous examples of a corporate entity held responsible for the actions of its employees was Arthur Andersen, formerly one of America's "Big Five" accounting firms (U.S. Department of Justice 2002). In response to alleged destruction of documents related to the collapse of Enron in 2002, Andersen was indicted and convicted of obstruction of justice. The demise of Andersen illustrates both the power of corporate criminal liability and the complexities of its application. Although Andersen's conviction later was overturned unanimously by the U.S. Supreme Court, the reputational damage had been done, and the company quickly dissolved—along with 28,000 jobs (Greenhouse 2005).

The history of corporate criminal liability in the United States dates back to the 1909 U.S. Supreme Court case of *New York Central and Hudson River Railroad Co. v. United States* (212 U.S. 481 [1909]). In *New York Central*, the corporation argued that it could not be held criminally liable for the wrongful acts of its employees (at 492). In rejecting this argument and approving the application of corporate criminal liability, the U.S. Supreme Court noted that corporations should be held responsible for the actions of those entrusted with the authority to act on their behalf (*New York Central*, at 495–6). Today, corporations may be held criminally liable for an employee or agent's acts that are (1) within the scope of his or her duties and (2) intended—even if only in part—to benefit the corporation (Dervan 2011a). This standard permits a corporation to be held criminally liable even when the activity was conducted by low-level, rogue employees in direct contradiction of established policy and explicit direction from superiors (Bharara 2007).

One of the unique challenges in white-collar cases is the potential for conflict between organizations and individuals when both are under investigation (Green and Podgor 2012). This tension results, in part, from the low bar for establishing corporate criminal liability described above. When corporations can be charged so easily for the acts of even a single rogue employee, prosecutorial discretion often becomes the determining factor in whether a corporation will go unpunished or, perhaps, suffer a fate similar to Andersen's (Krug 2002; Green and Zacharias 2004).[2] As will be discussed more fully below, the exercise of this discretion is guided by several policies, including the U.S. Attorney's Manual (Podgor 2000, pp. 1516–18). Prosecutors hold broad discretion, however, and their choices regarding which individuals or entities will be prosecuted and for what criminal violations rarely are challenged (Podgor 2000, pp. 1517–18; Krug 2002, p. 643).[3] In such situations, therefore, the incentives for private corporations or other organizations to cooperate and assist the government in prosecuting employees and agents are significant and sometimes lead to complex ethical and legal considerations (Wray and Hur 2006, p. 1135; Green and Podgor 2012, p. 76).

B. The Government's Investigation

While the law allows both individuals and entities to be held criminally liable for white-collar offenses, the avenue by which each becomes aware of potential exposure often is different. For corporations, one vehicle through which potentially unlawful behavior is discovered is whistleblowing. Whistleblowing can occur in several forms (Dervan 2008). Almost all corporations have internal reporting mechanisms that encourage employees and agents to report issues of concern (Wellner 2005, p. 497). These mechanisms often include anonymous hotlines and designated compliance officers (Wellner 2005, p. 497). When a corporation is made aware of potential white-collar criminal liability through such internal reports, the entity is in an excellent position to investigate and correct the behavior before the government becomes involved (Dervan 2008, p. 671). However, in other situations—including when an internal whistleblower becomes dissatisfied with the organization's response—individuals with knowledge of potential unlawful behavior may report this conduct to parties outside the corporation. Such whistleblowing might include reporting the matter of concern to authorities—such as the Securities and Exchange Commission, Department of Justice, or Environmental Protection Agency—or to the plaintiff's attorneys, who might file a lawsuit regarding the matter, such as a retaliation lawsuit or a qui tam action.[4] During 2012, for instance, the Securities and Exchange Commission received more than 3,000 tips from potential whistleblowers (Henning 2012, p. 14). In one well-known whistleblower case, a former UBS banker was awarded $104 million in return for blowing the whistle on tax evasion by the bank (Fleischer 2012). When external whistleblowing occurs, it is possible that the corporation might not learn of its potential exposure until well after the government has been made aware of and begun investigating the matter.[5]

Although corporations sometimes learn of potential exposure through internal reporting prior to involvement by the government, individuals are more likely to be caught off guard by a government investigation of their behavior. While the individual might know he or she is engaging in conduct that could result in criminal liability, he or she might not be aware the government has learned of the conduct and is investigating it. There are various avenues through which the government might have learned of an individual's potentially unlawful behavior. These include an accomplice in the endeavor becoming a whistleblower, particularly if the accomplice is seeking a deal from the government in return for cooperation. Alternatively, the government might learn of the behavior through routine auditing or compliance reviews. Finally, the government might be conducting an unrelated investigation and could stumble upon the behavior inadvertently. In each of these scenarios, the individual target might be unaware of an investigation until the government makes its presence known.

When an entity or individual is unaware of a government investigation into potentially unlawful white-collar behavior, the first indication of such an inquiry might come from the government itself. This is because white-collar cases tend to be document intensive, and, therefore, the government sometimes must make its presence known to secure the materials necessary to understand the case. Typically, the government will use one of three approaches in collecting materials in a white-collar investigation.

First, the government might send the corporation or individual an informal request for production. Such requests typically seek documentary evidence the government needs to further examine and analyze the situation. Because such informal requests are nonbinding, they are commonly used in scenarios where the government believes the corporation or individual is willing to cooperate. Further, because such requests alert the receiving party to the government's investigation, they are used only in cases where the government is confident the recipient will not destroy evidence.

Second, the government might use the broad investigatory powers of a grand jury to gather evidence. Grand juries may "investigate merely on suspicion that the law is being violated, or even because it wants assurance that it is not" (*United States v. R. Enterprises, Inc.*, 498 U.S. 297 [1991]). One of the tools used to conduct such an investigation is the grand jury subpoena. Grand jury subpoenas are compulsory, and failure to provide the requested materials can result in civil or criminal contempt charges. As with informal requests to produce, grand jury subpoenas alert the recipient to the grand jury investigation, though the exact focus of the grand jury might be unclear. Once again, therefore, when the government fears the recipient will destroy documents, this investigatory tool might not be used.

Third, although still less common in white-collar than street-crime cases, the government might conduct a search to obtain evidence in the case (Henning 2010). Searches offer both advantages and disadvantages from the government's perspective. A search might be advantageous because it occurs without notice or an opportunity for the target to destroy evidence. Further, searches send a clear message to those involved and to the public regarding how seriously the government considers the matter. Searches afford collateral advantages, such as the ability to conduct on-the-spot interviews with employees when searching a business.

Alternatively, a search might be disadvantageous for the government because—unlike the broad investigatory powers of the grand jury—a search warrant can be obtained only upon a showing of probable cause. Further, in the context of a search governed by the Fourth Amendment of the U.S. Constitution, a failure to satisfy the probable cause requirement could result in suppression of any evidence collected. Another concern regarding searches is their public nature. While the issuance of informal requests to produce or grand jury subpoenas might go largely unnoticed, the execution of a search warrant, particularly against an entity, often will result in considerable media and public attention, thus making the existence of the government investigation obvious to all involved. Finally, while informal requests to produce and grand jury subpoenas can be specific and place the burden on the recipient to review files and collect the sought-after materials, the execution of a search warrant invariably results in the collection of volumes of irrelevant documents. As such, the administrative costs of executing a warrant are high compared with the other available avenues for evidence collection. Despite these disadvantages, the use of search warrants in white-collar cases is growing more prevalent (Henning 2010; Hortz and Sandick 2012).

It is important to note that in some cases, the government's investigation might only come to light after the arrest of the individuals involved. Although this is less common in white-collar cases than other areas of criminal law, this option for the government remains a possibility. For both corporations and individuals, it is always more desirable to learn of the government's investigation before an arrest is made in the matter. For an organization, being aware of the investigation early permits the launching of an internal investigation into the matter, the taking of corrective action, and an opportunity to attempt to persuade the government not to charge the company or its employees. For an individual, being aware of the investigation early permits the retention of counsel, the conducting of an investigation into the matter, and an opportunity to attempt to convince the government not to charge the individual or, perhaps, to enter into a cooperation agreement with the government (Mann 1985).

Finally, in today's enforcement environment, it is common for multiple governmental agencies and jurisdictions to enter an investigation once potential criminal conduct has been identified. In beginning to contemplate a response to a government inquiry as either an organization or an individual, therefore, the complexities of white-collar cases only grow larger as parallel investigations begin to compete for information and resolution.

C. The Entity's and Individual's Investigation

Upon discovering that the government is investigating potential criminal conduct, both organizations and individuals are wise to retain counsel (Creamer 2005). Although corporations often have their own in-house attorneys, it is advisable in such matters to retain outside counsel (Dervan 2008, p. 676). The retention of outside counsel will help ensure the independence and credibility of the representation, particularly when in-house counsel could have some involvement in the matter under investigation (Dervan 2008). For an individual, retaining counsel can be expensive—particularly in white-collar cases, which are often document intensive and complex.[6] When the matter under investigation relates to an individual's work for an entity, however, he or she may be entitled to indemnification and advancement. Indemnification means the corporation will reimburse the individual for the expenses incurred in defending the matter. Such indemnification obligations are controlled by statute, corporate bylaws, and employment contracts. Typically, indemnification only applies when the individual acted in good faith and in the best interest of the corporation and had no reasonable cause to believe his or her conduct was unlawful (Fla. Stat., title 36, chap. 607, sec. 0850 [2012]). While indemnification might mean an individual is refunded the significant legal costs associated with the successful resolution of a white-collar case, the expense of such cases often can bankrupt an individual prior to its conclusion. As such, individuals also should be aware of any advancement provisions that might be contained in applicable statutes, corporate bylaws, or employment agreements. Advancement provisions require or permit a corporation to advance an individual the funds necessary to cover legal expenses during the defense of such a case. In return for advancement of fees from the corporation, individuals often are required to sign undertakings promising to return the advanced funds should they later be found not to have been entitled to indemnification because they had not acted in good faith and in the best interest of the corporation or when there is reasonable cause to believe that the individual should have known that his or her conduct was unlawful.

Once an entity has retained counsel in a white-collar case, such counsel will often undertake an internal investigation to learn as much as possible about the matter (Dervan 2008).[7] An internal corporate investigation usually contains two distinct facets. First, employees and agents will be interviewed to learn about the events leading to the government inquiry. Importantly, prior to counsel interviewing employees, counsel must be sure to avoid any possible conflicts of interest (*Upjohn Co. v. United States*, 449 U.S. 383 [1981]). This is achieved by delivering an *Upjohn* warning to the employees before interviews begin.[8] An *Upjohn* warning typically includes the following statements:

- I represent the corporation and not any individual employees.
- The interview is covered by the attorney–client privilege, which belongs to, and is controlled by, the corporation, not the individual employee.
- The corporation may decide, in its sole discretion, whether to waive the privilege and disclose information from the interview to third parties, including the government.

Upjohn warnings serve several vital purposes during an investigation. First, they clarify to employees that the attorney conducting the investigation does not represent them, thus preventing the inadvertent creation of an attorney–client relationship that later might prevent disclosure of the information obtained during the session (Dervan 2008, p. 677). Second, these warnings protect the interview by cloaking the conversation with the corporation's attorney–client privilege. This allows the corporation to decide later at its discretion whether to protect the content of the interview or disclose the information as part of an effort to cooperate with the government (Dervan 2008, p. 677).

Along with interviewing employees, another important component of an internal investigation is the collection of documents (Dervan 2008, p. 677). This is achieved by distributing a document-search memorandum asking employees to provide counsel with materials relevant to the topic of the inquiry. Along with such document-search memoranda, however, counsel must ensure no purposeful or inadvertent document destruction occurs once the investigation is under way.[9] This is achieved by the simultaneous distribution of a document-preservation memorandum making clear employees' obligations to protect material relevant to the inquiry. Preservation of evidence is vital in white-collar cases because of the growing prevalence of obstruction of justice charges, even where the subject of the initial government investigation does not lead to charges or conviction (Emshwiller and Fields 2012). An example of this phenomenon was the prosecution of Martha Stewart. Although Stewart originally was investigated for engaging in insider trading, she was convicted only of obstructing justice and lying to federal agents (Ackman 2004).

Just as organizations conduct investigations after discovering the existence of potentially wrongful conduct or an active government investigation, individuals and their counsel similarly must prepare to defend the matter. For individuals and their counsel, however, the process of investigating the matter can be more difficult because they often lack access to all of the parties and documents. One mechanism by which to gain greater access to materials is a joint defense agreement. Joint defense agreements allow "counsel for clients facing a common litigation opponent [including the government] to exchange privileged communications and attorney work product in order to adequately prepare a defense without waiving either privilege" (*Haines v. Liggett Group, Inc.*, 975 F.2d 94 [3rd Cir. 1992]). Further, if a party withdraws from the agreement, the person remains bound not to reveal the privileged and confidential information obtained from the arrangement (*Haines*, at 94). Because white-collar cases tend to be complex and document intensive, joint defense agreements are an important mechanism by which individuals can pool resources and knowledge in an effort to prepare a defense (*Haines*, at 94).[10]

D. Presenting a Case to the Government Prior to Indictment

Once a corporation or individual has completed the investigation of the matter, counsel might seek the opportunity to present his or her case to the government and argue why prosecution is inappropriate. When an organization's counsel makes a presentation to the government, the exchange is guided by the Principles of Federal Prosecution of Business Organizations (U.S. Department of Justice 1997).[11] Section 28.300 of the

Principles provides nine factors for prosecutors to consider in deciding whether to charge an organization with a criminal offense:

1. The nature and seriousness of the offense, including the risk of harm to the public and applicable policies and priorities, if any, governing the prosecution of corporations for particular categories of crime (sec. 9.28.400);
2. The pervasiveness of wrongdoing within the corporation, including the complicity in, or condoning of, the wrongdoing by corporate management (sec. 9.28.500);
3. The corporation's history of similar misconduct, including prior criminal, civil, and regulatory enforcement actions against it (sec. 9.28.600);
4. The corporation's timely and voluntary disclosure of wrongdoing and its willingness to cooperate in the investigation of its agents (sec. 9.28.700);
5. The existence and effectiveness of the corporation's pre-existing compliance program (sec. 9.28.800);
6. The corporation's remedial actions, including any efforts to implement an effective corporate compliance program or to improve an existing one, to replace responsible management, to discipline or terminate wrongdoers, to pay restitution, and to cooperate with the relevant government agencies (sec. 9.29.900);
7. Collateral consequences, including whether there is disproportionate harm to shareholders, pension holders, employees, or others proven not personally culpable, as well as impact on the public arising from the prosecution (sec. 9.28.1000);
8. The adequacy of the prosecution of individuals responsible for the corporation's malfeasance; and
9. The adequacy of remedies such as civil or regulatory enforcement actions (sec. 9.28.1100).

Because corporate criminal liability is easily satisfied in many instances using the respondeat superior test, much of the case for an organization might rest on arguments based on the above factors. Importantly, however, even where a corporation has a strong argument that prosecution should not be initiated, the final determination rests with the prosecution. As the Principles themselves state, "[t]his memorandum provides only internal Department of Justice guidance. It is not intended to, does not, and may not be relied upon to create any rights, substantive or procedural, enforceable at law by any party in any matter civil or criminal. Nor are any limitations hereby placed on otherwise lawful litigative prerogatives of the Department of Justice" (U.S. Department of Justice 1997, sec. 9.28.1300).

As will be discussed in greater detail in section IIA, the government also has established Principles of Federal Prosecution upon which to rely in deciding whether to pursue criminal charges against individuals (U.S. Department of Justice 1997, section 27.220 et seq.). As with organizations, individuals often use these factors—along with arguments regarding innocence—in an attempt to persuade the government to decline prosecution. Counsel for an individual also might enter into a proffer agreement with the government (Tarlow 2005). These agreements permit an individual to meet with the government and to reveal his or her knowledge of the potential criminal conduct under investigation (Tarlow 2005, p. 53). Such proffers typically are conducted with an understanding that the government might offer immunity or a plea bargain if the individual's information is helpful in the prosecution of others. Such proffer agreements typically also contain an agreement from the government that the individual's statements during the meeting cannot later be used against him or her.

While presentations and proffers might be successful in bringing some cases to resolution, in other cases, the government might move forward with charging the corporation or individual. As seen below, when this occurs, the road ahead is complex.

II. Prosecuting White-Collar Criminals

A. Charging

As noted above, the grand jury serves as one of the major investigating tools of federal government prosecutors in white-collar cases. It is the grand jury that issues an "indictment," the legal writing that formally charges an individual with a crime. In some cases, the defendant will waive his or her constitutional grand jury rights, allowing the government to proceed with an "information." An information is the formal charging document that is signed by a prosecutor as opposed to the foreperson of a grand jury.[12] Absent the waiving of the indictment or the matter being under military jurisdiction, a defendant has a constitutional right to be charged by a grand jury with an indictment in cases where the term of imprisonment exceeds one year (U.S. Constitution, Fifth Amendment; Ex Parte *Wilson*, 114 U.S. 417 [1885]).

U.S. attorneys and their assistants prepare the charging document. They have enormous discretion in deciding who to charge, what crimes to charge, when to proceed with the charges, and the location where the charges will be brought (Podgor 2010b).[13] However, statutes, rules, and court precedents do place some restraints upon prosecutorial discretion. As described above, the U.S. Attorneys' Manual provides guidance to these attorneys, most importantly in its Principles of Federal Prosecution (U.S. Department of Justice, 1997, title 9, section 27.000).[14] Memoranda also have been prepared that elaborate on the preferences of specific attorneys general with regard to the charging process. Once again, however, the guidelines and memoranda are strictly internal to the U.S. Department of Justice and cannot be enforced by an individual charged with a crime (Podgor 2004).

The Principles of Federal Prosecution provide that a prosecution should be declined when there is "no substantial Federal interest" served by the prosecution, the individual "is subject to effective prosecution in another jurisdiction, or there exists an adequate non-criminal alternative to prosecution" (U.S. Department of Justice 1997, title

9, section 27.220).[15] In some instances, a defendant's activity may violate both state and federal criminal law. Under the Dual Sovereignty Rule, both jurisdictions may have the ability to charge the respective state or federal crime (*United States v. Lanza*, 260 U.S. 377 [1922]). However, the Petite Policy (U.S. Department of Justice 1997, title 9, section 2.031),[16] a policy emanating from the Supreme Court decision in *Petite v. United States* (361 U.S. 529 [1960]), guides federal prosecutors, absent special circumstances, from dual or successive federal proceedings when the conduct is or has been the source of a state prosecution. Often, when multiple agencies have jurisdiction to proceed against criminal activity, an internal agreement is reached as to who will go forward with the prosecution or who will go forward first with the criminal charge. These decisions could be a function of resources, expertise, location of the evidence and witnesses, and other factors that are beyond the statute. In the white-collar area, the state might be reluctant to proceed because of the intricate nature of the alleged activity or because the conduct involves state corruption and carries political ramifications for the state prosecutor. As noted in section I, prosecutors also are provided with guidance as to when to charge a corporation.

In some instances, prosecutors are instructed to secure approvals from beyond the individual U.S. Attorneys' Office to proceed with a criminal prosecution. For example, prior approval of the U.S. Department of Justice's Criminal Division is required to file a criminal indictment under the Racketeer Influenced and Corrupt Organization Act (RICO). Policies also provide that most charges being brought against attorneys should be vetted beforehand with the assistant attorney general of the Criminal Division.

There are more than 4,500 federal criminal statutes and an even greater number of regulatory offenses with criminal penalties, which often provide prosecutors with many options in their charging decisions (Baker 2008; Walsh and Joslyn 2010).[17] Because the U.S. Department of Justice does not group particular crimes into specific categories, such as white-collar offenses, it is difficult to list all the possible charges that would be considered white-collar crimes. Some crimes, such as securities fraud, are clearly white-collar crimes. Other criminal offenses, such as violations of RICO, could be either white-collar or street crimes. For example, mail and wire fraud are two common predicate acts used in the prosecution of RICO, and these two crimes are also often used with white-collar criminal activity. But RICO also includes many non-white-collar predicates, such as drug-related offenses. Recent white-collar prosecutions can be seen in areas such as corruption, which may use charges such as bribery (U.S. Code 18 [2006], sec. 201), or extortion under the Hobbs Act (U.S. Code 18 [2006], sec. 1951). Healthcare fraud, mortgage fraud, and financial institution fraud also have been among recent areas of focus in the U.S. Department of Justice.[18]

Prosecutors in white-collar cases also may use generic charges that are easier for the government to prove than it would be to prove the intricate underlying fraudulent criminal scheme. For example, statutes such as obstruction of justice (U.S. Code 18 [2006], sec. 1503), false statements (U.S. Code 18 [2006], sec. 1001), and perjury (U.S. Code 18 [2006], sec. 1623) allow the government to focus on conduct of the defendant that could involve the destruction of a document, a false statement to a federal agent, or a lie before the grand jury, as opposed to the entirety of a complex scheme.[19]

B. Bail and Pretrial Matters

Upon being charged, the individual or corporation usually will post bail. A controversial practice used by law enforcement in recent white-collar cases is to have the individual paraded in handcuffs publicly upon arrest (a "perp walk"). Other cases have the individual voluntarily surrendering with terms of house arrest, ankle bracelets, or other methods used to monitor the individual during the pretrial period.

An individual accused of a white-collar offense is afforded the same constitutional rights as those who commit street crimes, including the right to counsel. Although white-collar defendants are less likely to have public defenders, the need for appointed counsel is growing due to the high cost of defending a white-collar case. For example, the use of public defenders in cases involving allegations of mortgage fraud is not unusual.

As with all federal criminal matters, the defendant has an initial appearance, an arraignment, and the opportunity to file pretrial motions. Pretrial motions could include motions *in limine* that restrict the mention of specific prejudicial evidence during the trial.

Although all criminal cases could have orders providing for the prosecution and defense to receive discovery materials, white-collar cases sometimes can involve more elaborate processes. The materials accumulated by the grand jury and investigators in a white-collar matter can be voluminous. They may be housed in a separate location from the government agency, and they may or may not be accessible in a computer format. Discovery practices have become a significant problem in white-collar cases, with experts, such as computer specialists, being hired to organize the materials provided to the defendant by the government.

When multiple defendants are involved in a case, they might choose to split the costs of investigation and experts. To protect the confidentiality of the material, it is common to see the defendants enter into a joint defense agreement. As discussed above, this assists in keeping attorney–client privileged material and work-product material exclusive to the parties who entered into the joint defense agreement.

C. Pleas and Other Agreements

In the federal system, approximately 97 percent of the convictions are the result of a plea of guilt, while only approximately 3 percent of convictions are the result of a conviction at trial.[20] The government may provide benefits to defendants who cooperate and provide substantial assistance to the government. Thus, a defendant facing a severe penalty might not want to risk going to trial and choose instead to reach a plea agreement with the government that provides for a specific final outcome (Podgor 2010a; Dervan 2011b).

In regard to corporations, the government and the entity often will enter into a deferred or nonprosecution agreement.[21] In the case of a nonprosecution agreement, the government agrees not to proceed against the corporation in return for the payment of a fine and for the corporation's agreement to follow other specified terms. The same may be true for a deferred prosecution agreement, although in this case a charge typically is filed against the company and then held in abeyance for a set period of time specified in the agreement. These agreements often will require that the company institute or improve upon an existing compliance program that will detect and prevent future criminal activity. The agreements also could provide for a monitor who will provide oversight within the company to ensure future legal compliance. In recent years, deferred and nonprosecution agreements often have been conditioned upon the corporation cooperating with the government in providing evidence of individual wrongdoing within the entity. This information then is used by the government to bring prosecutions against corporate constituents, such as executives within the company.

D. Trial

Few corporations go to trial.[22] The fear held by some is that—like Arthur Andersen, the accounting firm that did proceed to trial—being charged and possibly convicted could cause devastating collateral consequences for the company. In the case of an accounting firm, it might mean bankruptcy if businesses will not hire the firm because of the pending indictment. There also can be collateral consequences for companies that do business with the government, such as defense contractors. A guilty verdict might cause a defense contractor to be debarred from doing business with the government. This can be true as well for healthcare providers, who might face exclusion from future government benefits as a result of a negative jury decision. Companies also need to factor in the collateral consequences of third-party civil actions, as shareholders or users of the company's product might sue based on the alleged or proven criminal activity.

Trials also can be problematic for individual white-collar defendants. Proceeding to trial in a white-collar case raises the challenge of how to present a complicated or sophisticated matter to a lay jury. This can be a problem for both the prosecution and defense. On one side, the prosecution needs to ensure that the jury understands how the evidence, which can be highly technical, meets the elements of the charged crime. On the other side, the defense—which does not need to prove anything—must nevertheless refute this same technical evidence and show that it does not support the prosecution's allegations. Both sides face the daunting task of trying to ensure that the lay jury agrees with their particular interpretation of complex technical evidence.

The trial will be a jury trial unless the defendant waives the right to trial by jury, the government consents to a nonjury trial, and the judge approves proceeding without a jury (Federal Rule of Criminal Procedure 23[a]). A trial where the judge is determining the facts, without a jury, is called a bench trial. Most cases that proceed to trial will have juries. The jury is composed of twelve people unless the parties agree otherwise or there is a court order for a jury of eleven as a result of a juror being excused after the jury has retired to deliberate (Federal Rule of Criminal Procedure 23[b]). The selection of the individuals for the trial is a process called voir dire. Each side has a set number of peremptory strikes (U.S. Code 19 [2006], sec. 1870; Federal Rule of Criminal Procedure 47), which attorneys may use without providing reason, and they also may ask the court to strike a juror for cause. Neither the prosecution nor the defense may strike jurors in a constitutionally impermissible manner, such as based upon race or gender (Podgor 2011b). In white-collar cases, a prospective juror's level of education and sophistication could be a reason for wanting or not wanting him or her to be on the jury.

The trial begins with the court giving preliminary instructions, instructions that tell the jury what the defendant has been charged with and the importance of keeping an open mind during the trial. This is followed by opening statements, wherein the parties provide a roadmap of the evidence that will be presented at trial. The government then calls its witnesses.

Depending on the charges filed in a white-collar case, some of the witnesses may need to be experts. If the government proceeds with "shortcut" offenses such as perjury, false statements, or obstruction of justice, the evidence presented by the government might be very simplistic. For example, in the prosecution of Martha Stewart mentioned above, the government contended that she lied to the Securities and Exchange Commission. Ms. Stewart was not charged with the more complicated statute of insider trading, so the evidence presented to the jurors was relatively easy for them to understand. The jurors were deciding the questions of whether she lied and whether she obstructed justice (Heminway 2007).

In cases involving schemes to defraud the government, the complicated nature of the scheme might necessitate an expert to explain the fraudulent activity. The defense also might want to use an expert to show that the transactions were proper and not criminal activity.

When the government is questioning a witness, it is called direct examination, and the prosecutor is limited to asking only open-ended questions of the witness. The defense may cross-examine the government witnesses if it chooses to do so and, unlike the prosecutor, is allowed to ask leading questions.

The court rules on evidentiary challenges presented by the parties, which can include precluding hearsay statements or including some of these statements when they are exceptions to the hearsay rule. For example, when there are multiple parties to the conduct and the government includes a charge of conspiracy, co-conspirators' out-of-court statements that are not under oath may be allowed as an exception to the hearsay rule (Federal Rule of Evidence 801).

The government is required to prove beyond a reasonable doubt each of the crimes presented in the indictment, which requires the government to show that the defendant committed a voluntary act with the appropriate *mens rea*, or guilty mind, specified in the statute. In some instances, white-collar offense may be strict liability crimes that do not require proof of *mens rea*. This is seen in some environmental and regulatory offenses, such as violations of the Rivers and Harbors Appropriations Act, commonly referred to as the Refuse Act (*United States v. White Fuel Corp.*, 498 F.2d 619 [1st Cir. 1974]). It also might be necessary to show that the act caused the resulting harm. Some statutes, moreover, will necessitate that the prosecution prove certain circumstances. For example, the false statement statute requires the government to prove that the statement was material—that is, whether the statement had "a natural tendency to influence, or [be] capable of influencing, the decision of the decision-making body to which it [was] addressed" (*United States v. Gaudin*, 515 U.S. 506, 509 [1995], quoting *Kungys v. United States*, 485 U.S. 759, 770 [1988]).

The crux of many white-collar cases is the *mens rea* of the accused (Mann 1985; Benson et al. 1988; Cullen et al. 2006). In some instances, the defendant might be arguing that he or she did not know that the conduct was criminal. Although knowledge of a specific statute is generally not required, some white-collar offenses require proof that the defendant acted willfully, which requires the prosecution to prove that the defendant knew his or her actions were criminal. For example, an accused who structures monetary transactions to avoid the filing of a required currency transaction report must have knowledge of the illegality of structuring, as the conduct is not "so obviously 'evil' or inherently 'bad' " (*Ratzlaf v. United States*, 510 U.S. 135, 146 [1994]).

At the conclusion of the government's case, the defense typically will make a motion for a judgment of acquittal (Federal Rule of Criminal Procedure 29). If the government has failed to provide sufficient evidence to sustain a conviction, the court will dismiss that count of the indictment. If the motion is not granted, the defense may make this motion again at the conclusion of the trial. The judge has the ability to reserve decision on an acquittal motion and may even grant it after the jury has been discharged.

Following the government's case, the defense may present evidence, but it has no obligation to do so. The government cannot comment on the defendant's failure to present any evidence (*Griffin v. California*, 380 U.S. 609 [1965]). After all the evidence has been presented, each side has the opportunity to present closing arguments. These statements allow each side to summarize the evidence presented.

At the conclusion of the trial, the court provides the jury with final instructions. These instructions will include the government's burden to prove the defendant guilty beyond a reasonable doubt, and that a not-guilty verdict should be entered if the government fails to meet its obligation. An instruction that tends to arise in white-collar matters is one concerning whether the accused acted with willful blindness. In the corporate setting, a CEO or president of the company could claim that he or she did not know of the illegal conduct occurring within the company. The government, in such cases, can request the court to read a final instruction allowing the jury to find that, if the defendant deliberately avoided learning the truth, the person could be found to have sufficient knowledge. The U.S. Supreme Court decision in *Global-Tech Appliances, Inc. et. al. v. SEB S.A.* (131 S. Ct. 2060, 2070 [2011]) held that, for willful blindness to be present, "(1) the defendant must subjectively believe that there is a high probability that the fact exists and (2) the defendant must take deliberate actions to avoid learning of that fact."

After the evidence, closing arguments, and jury instructions, the jurors deliberate until they return a verdict or the judge dismisses them. If the jury cannot reach a verdict on all or some of the counts, it is considered to be a hung jury. The prosecution may or may not decide to proceed with a second trial following a hung jury.

E. Sentencing

If the defendant is convicted, a presentence report is prepared by the probation department. Both the prosecution and defense also can decide to prepare sentencing memos to the court, advocating for the sentence each one believes fits the defendant and the crime.

The court issues a sentence that looks at the federal sentencing guidelines—which are now advisory for the court—in using statutory factors (U.S. Code 18 [2006], sec. 3553[a]). In a series of Supreme Court opinions, the U.S. Sentencing Guidelines moved from being mandatory guidelines to allowing judges some discretion in implementing them (*Apprendi v. New Jersey*, 530 U.S. 466 [2000]); *Blakely v. Washington*, 542 U.S. 296 [2004]); *United States v. Booker*, 543 U.S. 220 [2005]); *Gall v. United States*, 552 U.S. 38 [2007]); *Rita v. United States*, 551 U.S. 338 [2007]).[23] Both the government and the defense have the right to appeal a federal sentence.

White-collar sentences often rest on the amount of loss resulting from the criminal activity: higher losses often mean a longer possible sentence. Here again, both the prosecution and defense can use experts who can assess the loss that occurred.[24]

III. CONCLUSION

This chapter examined the prosecution and defense of white-collar crimes, noting where these activities differ compared to street crimes. It reflected on corporate criminality and the growth of internal corporate investigations, and it recognized key statutes used to prosecute these crimes—specifically, the use of "shortcut" offenses that carry easier burdens of proof for prosecutors in complex cases. Last, it provided an overview of the different stages of white-collar case processing, from investigation, through trial, and to the eventual sentencing.

The challenges that face the prosecution and defense involved in white-collar crime cases include the continual growth of federal statutes and the resulting administrative regulations and problems for corporations and corporate counsel. It will be important to watch how legislators react to conduct in the computer, environmental, and financial areas. The high cost to accused individuals associated with defending a white-collar case presents concerns for both criminal defendants and the judicial system. Finally, the rise of corporate internal investigations and the practices occurring in these investigations could cause corporate constituents to become less trustworthy of investigators and corporate counsel.

Notes

1. The 2010 National Public Survey on White-Collar Crime noted that, since its 2005 survey had been conducted, "white-collar crime has continued to be a topic 'of almost daily news'" (Huff, Desilets, and Kane 2010, p. 10). The report also noted that the Federal Trade Commission reported a 27 percent increase between 2007 and 2009 in fraud, identity theft, and other criminal complaints (Huff et al. 2010, p. 11).
2. As discussed more fully in section III, prosecutors exercise significant prosecutorial discretion in determining whether to charge a corporation. In the Principles of Federal Prosecution of Business Organizations, the government notes this significant power and states, "[i]n making a decision to charge a corporation, the prosecutor generally has wide latitude in determining when, whom, how, and even whether to prosecute for violations of federal criminal law" (McNulty 2008, p. 5).
3. According to Peter Krug (2002), "In the United States, prosecutors play the central role in the criminal justice systems of the federal and state governments. Their decisions determine the course of the criminal process, and in making those decisions, they act with broad, generally unregulated discretion. Indeed, the scope of *prosecutorial discretion* has steadily expanded in recent decades" (p. 643). For further discussion of prosecutorial discretion and concerns regarding the breadth of prosecutorial discretion, see Greene (1991).
4. A qui tam is a civil action brought by an individual against an entity on behalf of the government. Most commonly, these lawsuits allege the entity has stolen from the government through overbilling under the False Claims Act (U.S. Code 31 [2012], sec. 3729). Once filed, the government has the option to "intervene" and pursue the case to completion. Once the case is complete, the individual who brought the suit on behalf of the government receives a share of the damages recovered by the government.
5. In its 2012 "Report to the Nations on Occupational Fraud and Abuse," the Association of Certified Fraud Examiners reported that 43.3 percent of occupational frauds are detected by a "tip," 14.6 percent are detected by "management review," 14.4 percent are detected by "internal audit," 7.0 percent are detected by "accident," 4.8 percent are detected by "account reconciliation," 4.1 percent are detected by "document examination," 3.3 percent are detected by "external audit," 3.0 percent are detected by "notified by police," and the remaining 5.6 percent were detected by "surveillance/monitoring," "confession," "IT controls," or "other" (Association of Certified Fraud Examiners 2012).
6. As an example of the expense of white-collar cases, note that Jeffrey Skilling of Enron paid the law firm of O'Melveny and Myers LLP a retainer of $23 million, yet the law firm has stated that his defense cost much more than that amount (Johnson 2006).
7. It also should be noted that corporate internal investigations sometimes involve international components. In such situations, a myriad of additional complexities must be considered by counsel and the entity (Dervan 2012).
8. The need to provide the *Upjohn* warnings, also called "Corporate Miranda," emanate from the case of *Upjohn Co. v. United States* (449 U.S. 383 [1981]). In *Upjohn*, the Supreme

Court established that communications between employees and corporate counsel are protected by the attorney–client privilege.

9. It also must be noted that pursuant to U.S. Code 18 (2012), section 1519, an entity or individual may be criminally liable for the destruction of documents in "contemplation" of a government investigation. As such, neither a pending nor even foreseeable criminal investigation is required for obstruction of justice charges, as long as the destruction of evidence occurs in "contemplation" of a possible future investigation.

10. "In order to establish the existence of a joint defense privilege, the party asserting the privilege must show that (1) the communications were made in the course of a joint defense effort, (2) the statements were designed to further the effort and (3) the privilege has not been waived" (*Haines*, at 94, citing Matter of Bevill, Bresler, and Schulman Asset Management, 805 F.2d 126 [3rd Cir.1986]).

11. http://www.justice.gov/usao/eousa/foia_reading_room/usam/title9/28mcrm.htm#9-28.300

12. Approximately 70 percent of all defendants charged in criminal cases were initially indicted in 2010. Approximately 17 percent of cases were the result of a felony information (http://bjs.ojp.usdoj.gov/fjsrc/var.cfm?ttype=one_variable&agency=AOUSC&db_type=CrimCtCases&saf=IN).

13. U.S. Attorneys are appointed by the president and must be confirmed by the legislature, but the members of the office serve as civil servants in a nonpolitical capacity (Podgor 2010b).

14. http://www.justice.gov/usao/eousa/foia_reading_room/usam/title9/27mcrm.htm

15. http://www.justice.gov/usao/eousa/foia_reading_room/usam/title9/27mcrm.htm#9-27.220

16. http://www.justice.gov/usao/eousa/foia_reading_room/usam/title9/2mcrm.htm#9-2.031

17. As of 2010, there were "over 4,450 federal statutory crimes and an estimated tens of thousands more in federal regulations" (Walsh and Joslyn 2010, p. 4).

18. The U.S. Department of Justice has made preventing financial and healthcare fraud one of its priority goals. In fiscal year 2012, U.S. Department of Justice attorneys working on healthcare and financial fraud cases averaged 10.28 investigations (http://www.justice.gov/ag/annualreports/pr2012/par2012.pdf).

19. These can be seen as "shortcut" offenses and are used by prosecutors to simplify both the investigation of the case and the presentation for juries (Podgor 2011a).

20. According to the U.S. Sentencing Commission, in 2014, 97.1 percent of federal convictions were the result of a plea of guilt and 2.9 percent were the result of a conviction at trial. This percentage is relatively consistent with the previous four years (http://www.ussc.gov/sites/default/files/pdf/research-and-publications/annual-reports-and-sourcebooks/2014/FigureC.pdf).

21. According to the U.S. Government Accountability Office, the number of corporate criminal prosecutions between 2004 and 2009 decreased from 297 prosecutions to 194 prosecutions. Interestingly, however, the number of deferred and nonprosecution agreements increased from 4 to 17 (Government Accountability Office 2009, p. 16).

22. In 2014, 162 corporations were sentenced under Chapter Eight of the U.S. Sentencing Commission Guidelines Manual. Chapter Eight covers sentencing of organizations. One hundred forty-nine organizations pled guilty, twelve were convicted at trial, and one plead nolo contendere. (http://www.ussc.gov/sites/default/files/pdf/research-and-publications/annual-reports-and-sourcebooks/2014/Table53.pdf). Environmental crimes accounted

for 20.4 percent and fraud accounted for 25.9 percent of the cases (http://www.ussc.gov/sites/default/files/pdf/research-and-publications/annual-reports-and-sourcebooks/2014/Table51.pdf).

23. The cases require courts to use the guidelines but allow them to move beyond the numbers provided by the guidelines to ensure compliance with U.S. Code 18 (2012), section 3553(a). Section 3553(a) instructs a court to "impose a sentence sufficient, but not greater than necessary, to comply with" certain factors outlined in the statute. Among the factors are "the need for the sentence imposed to reflect the seriousness of the offense, to promote respect for the law, and to provide just punishment for the offense" and the need "to protect the public from further crimes of the defendant."

24. In 2014, 77.6 percent of offenders with a primary offense category of "Fraud" received imprisonment, while 22.4 percent received probation (http://www.ussc.gov/sites/default/files/pdf/research-and-publications/annual-reports-and-sourcebooks/2014/Table12.pdf).

REFERENCES

Ackman, Dan. 2004. "Martha Stewart Found Guilty." *Forbes* (March 5). Available at http://www.forbes.com/2004/03/05/cx_da_0305marthafinal.html

Association of Certified Fraud Examiners. 2012. *Report to the Nations on Occupational Fraud and Abuse*. Austin, TX: Author.

Baker, John S., Jr. 2008. "Revisiting the Explosive Growth of Federal Crimes." *Heritage Foundation Legal Memorandum* (No. 26). Available at http://www.heritage.org/research/reports/2008/06/revisiting-the-explosive-growth-of-federal-crimes

Benson, Michael L., and Francis T. Cullen. 1998. *Combating Corporate Crime: Local Prosecutors at Work*. Boston: Northeastern University Press.

Bharara, Preet. 2007. "Corporations Cry Uncle and Their Employees Cry Foul: Rethinking Prosecutorial Pressure on Corporate Defendants." *American Criminal Law Review* 44: 53–113.

Bureau of Justice Statistics. 2012. *Arrests in the United States, 1990–2010*. Washington, D.C.: U.S. Government Printing Office

Creamer, Robert A. 2005. "Criminal Law Concerns for Civil Lawyers." *Federal Lawyers* 52: 34–44.

Cullen, Francis T., Gray Cavendar, William J. Maakestad, and Michael L. Benson. 2006. *Corporate Crime under Attack: The Fight to Criminalize Business Violence*. Cincinnati, OH: Anderson Press.

Dervan, Lucian E. 2008. "Responding to Potential Employee Misconduct in the Age of the Whistleblower: Foreseeing and Avoiding Hidden Dangers." *Bloomberg Corporate Law Journal* 3: 670–79.

Dervan, Lucian E. 2011a. "Re-Evaluating Corporate Criminal Liability: The DOJ's Internal Moral Culpability Standard for Corporate Criminal Liability." *Stetson Law Review* 41: 7–20.

Dervan, Lucian E. 2011b. "Overcriminalization 2.0: The Symbiotic Relationship between Plea Bargaining and Overcriminalization." *Journal of Law, Economics, and Policy* 7: 645–55.

Dervan, Lucian E. 2012. "International White-Collar Crime and the Globalization of Internal Investigations." *Fordham Urban Law Journal* 39: 361–89.

Emshwiller, John R., and Gary Fields. 2012. "For Feds, 'Lying' Is a Handy Charge." *Wall Street Journal* (April 9). Available at http://online.wsj.com/article/SB10001424052702303299604577328102223038294.html

Fleischer, Victor. 2012. "A Strategy of Tattletales at the I.R.S." *The New York Times Dealbook Blog* (September 20). Available at http://dealbook.nytimes.com/2012/09/20/a-strategy-of-tattletales-at-the-i-r-s/

Government Accountability Office. 2009. "Corporate Crime: DOJ Has Taken Steps to Better Track Its Use of Deferred and Non-Prosecution Agreements, but Should Evaluate Effectiveness." *Report to Congressional Requesters* GAO-10-110.

Green, Bruce A., and Ellen S. Podgor. 2012. "Unregulated Internal Investigations: Achieving Fairness for Corporate Constituents." *Boston College Law Review* 54: 73–126.

Green, Bruce A., and Fred C. Zacharias. 2004. "Prosecutorial Neutrality." *Wisconsin Law Review* 2004: 837–904.

Greene, Dwight A. 1991. "Abusive Prosecutors: Gender, Race, and Class Discretion and the Prosecution of Drug-Addicted Mothers." *Buffalo Law Review* 39: 737–802.

Greenhouse, Linda. 2005. "Justices Unanimously Overturn Conviction of Arthur Andersen." *New York Times.* (May 31). Available at http://www.nytimes.com/2005/05/31/business/31wire-andersen.html

Heminway, Joan MacLeod. 2007. *Martha Stewart's Legal Troubles.* Durham, NC: Carolina Academic Press.

Henning, Peter J. 2010. "What a Search Warrant Means." *New York Times Dealbook Blog* (November 23). Available at http://dealbook.nytimes.com/2010/11/23/what-a-search-warrant-means/

Henning, Peter J. 2012. "Federal Regulators Stay on the Full-Court Press." *New York Times* (December 12), p. F14. Available at http://dealbook.nytimes.com/2012/12/11/federal-regulators-stay-on-the-full-court-press/

Hortz, Robert H., and Harry Sandick. 2012. "Search Warrants in White-Collar Crime Cases." *Review of Securities and Commodities Regulation* 45(12): 133–40.

Huff, Rodney, Christian Desilets, and John Kane. 2010. *The 2010 National Public Survey on White-Collar Crime.* Fairmont, WV: National White-Collar Crime Center.

Johnson, Carrie. 2006. "Enron Case a Grueling Trial for Its Lawyers." *The Washington Post* (May 29).

Krug, Peter. 2002. "Prosecutorial Discretion and its Limits." *American Journal of Comparative Law* 50: 643–64.

Mann, Kenneth. 1985. *Defending White-Collar Crime: A Portrait of Attorneys at Work.* New Haven, CT: Yale University Press.

McNulty, Paul J. 2008. *Principles of Federal Prosecution of Business Organizations.* Washington, D.C.: U.S. Department of Justice.

Podgor, Ellen S. 2000. "The Ethics and Professionalism of Prosecutors in Discretionary Decisions." *Fordham Law Review* 68: 1511–35.

Podgor, Ellen S. 2004. "Department of Justice Guidelines: Balancing 'Discretionary Justice.'" *Cornell Journal of Law and Public Policy* 13: 167–202.

Podgor, Ellen S. 2010a. "White-Collar Innocence: Irrelevant in the High Stakes Risk Game." *Chicago-Kent Law Review* 85: 77–88.

Podgor, Ellen S. 2010b. "The Tainted Federal Prosecutor in an Overcriminalized Justice System." *Washington and Lee Law Review* 67: 1569–85.

Podgor, Ellen S. 2011a. "100 Years of White-Collar Crime in 'Twitter.'" *Review of Litigation* 30: 535–58.

Podgor, Ellen S. 2011b. "The Role of the Prosecution and Defense Function Standards: S
or Progressive?" *Hastings Law Journal* 62: 1159–75.

Tarlow, Barry. 2005. "Rico Report: Queen for a Day–Proffer Your Life Away." *Champio*
19: 53–63.

U.S. Department of Justice. 1997. *United States Attorneys' Manual*. Washington, D.C.: Author.

U.S. Department of Justice. 2002. *Indictment of Arthur Andersen*. Washington, D.C.: Author.

Walsh, Brian W., and Tiffany M. Joslyn. 2010. *Without Intent: How Congress Is Eroding the Criminal Intent Requirement in Federal Law*. Washington, D.C.: The Heritage Foundation and National Association of Criminal Defense Lawyers. Available at http://s3.amazonaws.com/thf_media/2010/pdf/WithoutIntent_lo-res.pdf

Wellner, Philip A. 2005. "Effective Compliance Programs and Corporate Criminal Prosecutions." *Cardozo Law Review* 27: 497–528.

Wray, Chris A., and Robert K. Hur. 2006. "Corporate Criminal Prosecution in a Post-Enron World: The Thompson Memo in Theory and Practice." *American Criminal Law Review* 43: 1095–188.

CHAPTER 28

....

NCING RESPECTABLE
OFFENDERS

....

MICHAEL LEVI

THE notion of "the respectable offender" is very strongly associated with white-collar crime, dating from the loose Sutherland (1949) definition thereof. It raises particular issues of social fairness as well as of effectiveness: concern about the collateral damage of "just punishment" gives rise to some creative nonpenal sanctions for corporations in the shadow of the criminal law that may also be seen as social bias in formal "criminal justice" in favor of elites. This theme is seen, for example, in the evocative titles of texts such as *The Rich Get Richer and the Poor Get Prison* (Reiman and Leighton 2013), *Trusted Criminals* (Friedrichs 2010), *How They Got Away with It: White-Collar Criminals and the Financial Meltdown* (Will, Brotherton, and Handelman 2012), and *Too Big to Jail* (Garrett 2014). Note, however, that many poor people who commit relatively minor crimes can also be "respectable offenders," though they may not receive such sophisticated consideration.

Shapiro (1990) famously asked us to "collar" the crime, not the criminal, in order to concentrate on the abuse of fiduciary relationships that in her view was the core feature of white-collar crime. However, the opposite focus on "the respectable" is important in limiting the range of this chapter within that broader category of abuse. For example, the greater democratization of opportunities for some forms of financial crime has made outdated even the social status compromise title *Crimes of the Middle Classes* (Weisburd et al. 1991). Frauds today are actually committed by a broad range of social types, including "organized criminals," who are not "respectable offenders" within the rubric of this chapter.

The sentencing process comes at the end of a loosely coupled system of crime reporting, investigation, charge, and conviction (Levi 2013). The interplay between white-collar crime commission and the criminal process varies between countries and over time, but these influences are outside the scope of this chapter. The normal mode is that offending in the context of corporations is prosecuted only reactively, after a public event such as a corporate collapse and/or formal report, which may be influenced by media coverage. However, even in some elite cases, since the mid-1980s, American and to a far lesser extent British prosecutors have sometimes adapted the strategy used in organized-crime cases of rolling up white-collar offending networks via plea bargaining. This saw its apotheosis to date in the Michael Milken, Dennis Levine, Martin Siegel, and Ivan Boesky insider-trading web of the middle to late 1980s and in the Galleon insider-trading case in 2012. But this strategy applies only where (1) there are such networks of offenders, rather than individuals and small groups acting alone to defraud, and (2) the expected probability of conviction and expected sentences are high enough to incentivize betrayal rather than loyalty/self-interest in silence. It is assumed that respectable offenders will fear prison more than "organized criminals" would and therefore will need a lower threshold to inform against others.

This chapter will review the following:

- Levels of sentencing for white-collar crime (section II), which will note that if we exclude the more sensational cases that attract the most publicity, sentencing levels are relatively modest;
- Accounting for white-collar sentencing, including social bias in sentencing (section III), which will explore the paradoxes of leniency and severity in the attitudes of judiciary, showing that a combination of lack of public pressure, plea bargaining, and low to perceived future dangerousness are more salient than simple pro-business bias in accounting for sentencing; moreover, since many prosecuted frauds are against the interests of business, this must be taken into account when considering the bias question;
- Section IV examines the evidence on "what works" in sentencing "the respectable" and white-collar crimes—both individuals and corporations;
- Section V focuses on the sentencing of individual white-collar criminals and corporations—mainly in the United Kingdom and United States—while acknowledging that whether sentencing *should* take account of "fall from grace" is a question of broader remit than white-collar crime; and
- Section V also considers sanctions by professional bodies and by regulators, which to some extent are independent of the prosecution process but have some parallel characteristics to the dilemmas of criminal sentencing.

I. LEVELS OF SENTENCING
FOR WHITE-COLLAR CRIMES

Let us first examine some data on white-collar crime sentencing. Such crimes play a more prominent part in the U.S. federal system than might be expected. In 2012, fraud accounted for 10.5 percent of recorded offenses nationally, with "non-fraud white-collar" offenses (embezzlement, forgery/counterfeiting, bribery, money laundering, and tax) accounting for a further 3.5 percent (U.S. Sentencing Commission 2013). U.S. sentencing data show that nationally in 2011, imprisonment was imposed on 71 percent of those convicted of fraud (a further 7 percent received a split prison/community sentence); 38.5 percent of those convicted of embezzlement; 62 percent for bribery; 50 percent for tax evasion; and 74 percent for money laundering (which includes proceeds of drug trafficking as well as white-collar crimes). In 2011, the mean sentence for fraud was thirty months nationally, and the median sentence—less distorted by a small number of very long sentences—was eighteen months (twenty-four in the Southern District of New York, where the more sensational elite cases take place [U.S. Sentencing Commission 2012]). Other medians were eighteen months for tax, eighteen months for bribery, twenty-four months for money laundering, and twelve months for embezzlement. The sentencing guidelines intend to penalize offenders in relation to the financial harm caused. For fiscal year 2014 the median loss was $118,081. Almost 82 percent of fraud (§2B1.1) offenders had a loss amount of $1 million or less; almost ten percent of cases have a loss amount of $2.5 million or more; and less than one percent of cases are in the top four categories—64 cases in 2014 with losses above $50 million (Saris 2015).

Fines were imposed in almost 10 percent of white-collar crime cases in which an individual was sentenced and in three quarters of cases in which the offender was an organization. But the fact that the median fine for fraud was $100,000 suggests that most offenses were quite serious. The proportion of those convicted who are "respectable offenders" is unknown, but by U.S. and even British standards, these are not particularly severe sentencing levels: they are doubtless strongly influenced by the fact that around 94 percent of defendants plead guilty.

Hagan and Nagel (1982) noted differential patterns of sentencing regionally, which remains true today (though data are unavailable for cases prosecuted under New York law by the Manhattan district attorney, who has near-global jurisdiction because of the global dollar settlement banks headquartered there). Stadler, Benson, and Cullen (2012) noted that sentencing levels have risen substantially in this century, and though they do not seek to account for this rise, it may reflect awareness of the more systemic risks that arise from economic crime in an interconnected globalized world as well as greater public concern following the financial bubbles and then meltdown. We will return to explanatory accounts in later sections. Below is a selection of sentences in spectacular and mostly well-publicized (Levi 2006) U.S. white-collar crime cases in this century that shows what, by the standards of the rest of the world, are long sentences; where sentences are lower, this usually reflects plea and charge bargaining and/or substantial assistance to prosecutors:

- For a Ponzi scheme defrauding investors of around $17.3 billion, Bernie Madoff received a sentence of 150 years (and his brother received 10 years for assisting him).

- For a Ponzi scheme defrauding investors of around $7 billion, American Allen Stanford received 110 years (after a not-guilty plea) in 2012, and separately was stripped of his English knighthood.
- Russell Wasendorf Sr., ex-CEO of Peregrine, who defrauded clients of $215 million over twenty years, was given a fifty-year sentence.
- Minor Vargas Calvo, owner of Provident Capital Indemnity (PCI) Ltd., ran a criminal reinsurance company that fraudulently guaranteed almost half a billion dollars of life settlement investments worldwide, and was sentenced to sixty years.
- In the Galleon insider-dealing case, Raj Rajaratnam, CEO of Galleon, was sentenced to eleven years (plus $156 million in financial penalties) and Rajat Gupta, former director of McKinsey and of Goldman Sachs, was given a two-year sentence (plus a $5 million fine and one year of supervised release).
- Bernard J. Ebbers, the WorldCom Chief executive who masterminded an $11 billion accounting fraud, got twenty-five years.
- In Enron, Jeffrey Skilling initially received twenty-four years' imprisonment, reduced substantially in 2013 in a deal that led to his dropping his appeal and repaying $40 million in his seized assets to creditors (but not reinstating the more than 5,000 jobs and $1 billion in employee retirement funds lost when Enron collapsed).
- Andy Fastow got a reduced sentence of six years after pleading guilty and giving evidence against Skilling and Kenneth Lay (who died before serving his sentence).

A. Sentencing the Rogue Trader

One might have expected those causing huge losses for major financial institutions to be heavily sanctioned, since the offenses usually occurred over a lengthy period and the losers are elites. However, they appear to be treated as slippery-slope fraudsters who started out honest but whose losses escalated dramatically as they gambled to try to make up for earlier losses and conceal them, rather than as malevolent preplanned fraudsters who aimed from the outset to profit at the expense of their employers (see Levi 2008 for a developed typology) (table 28.1).

B. U.S. Sentencing Guidelines

There has been substantial literature on sentencing guidelines and adherence thereto, especially since the rules requiring conformity were relaxed after the *Booker* case in 2006 (see Richman [2013] and Bowman [2015] for thoughtful exegesis and critiques). Insider trading is an unusual crime, insofar as it is an abuse of confidence and trust, but—unlike manipulating the market to create a false price—it is not obvious what harm it causes to real individuals as contrasted with harm to the ideology of "the

Table 28.1. Sentencing Rogue Traders Around the World

Name of Offender and Corporate Victim	Loss to Corporation (US Dollars)	Sentence and Country
Toshihide Iguchi (Daiwa) 1995	1.1 billion	4 years (U.S.)
Nick Leeson (Barings) 1995	1.4 billion	6.5 years (England)
Yasuo Hamanaka (Sumitomo) 1996	2.6 billion	8 years (England)
John Rusnak (Allied Irish Bank) 2002	691 million	7.5 years (U.S.)
Luke Duffy and David Bullen (all National Australia Bank)	360 million	2.5 years (Australia)
Gianni Gray		16 months
Vince Ficarra		15 months
Jerome Kerviel (Société Générale) 2008	7.2 billion	5 years, 2 suspended (France)
Kweku Adoboli (UBS) 2012	2.3 billion	7 years (England)

market" in the abstract. There is substantial variation in how judges deal with it. At the low end is Judge Rakoff, who deals with many high-prestige cases. In 2010–13, he imposed an average sentence of twenty-one months on insider-trading defendants who did not cooperate with prosecutors—about 38 percent below the guidelines minimum. Judge Holwell's eleven-year sentence (plus $156.6 million in civil and criminal fines, forfeitures, and restitution) for the billionaire Raj Rajaratnam was 100 months below the minimum; he gave 30 months to Danielle Chiesi, Rajaratnam's co-conspirator in the Galleon case, which is 7 months under the guidelines range for her offense (Rothfeld 2010). Despite support from Bill Gates, Kofi Annan, and others for his substantial charitable work prior to coming under criminal investigation, former Goldman Sachs partner and McKinsey director Rajat Gupta was jailed for two years for leaking confidential information to Rajaratnam. Under Manhattan U.S. Attorney Preet Bharara, thirteen of the seventy-two persons charged with insider dealing cooperated with the government, all but one of whom got probation. Since 2010, the twenty-six insider-trading defendants who did not cooperate with prosecutors have received an average sentence of two years and ten months: this is a third under the average federal guidelines range (Rothfeld and Strumpf 2012) but significantly (to them) longer than what they would have received had they cooperated.

C. Organizational Cases

In addition to individuals, corporations and partnerships can be prosecuted for violating federal criminal law, and of the 187 cases for which the U.S. Sentencing Commission received complete sentencing information in fiscal year 2012, sentencing courts ordered restitution in 40 cases (21.4 percent), and imposed a fine in 144 cases (77.0 percent). The average restitution amount ordered was $447,440 (median $138,802), and the average fine imposed was $11,207,081 (median $200,000) (U.S. Sentencing Commission 2012). These data do not tell us anything about organizational size or prosperity or the social influence of those firms that were criminally sanctioned, nor about their prior records of law abidingness or career organizational criminality. Nor do they tell us about what proportion of daily profits or turnover this represented.

Deferred prosecution agreements are increasingly used in contexts where organizations such as KPMG and HSBC are what I would term "too big to be failed" (by the regulators). They are usually accompanied by burdensome and expensive requirements for monitoring and cultural/organizational reform that are intended as rehabilitative sanctions. Regulatory penalties can be very large (at least in absolute terms, if not as a proportion of turnover or profit) and can be accompanied by agreed texts setting out very extensive admissions of wrongdoing. In fiscal year 2012, the Securities and Exchange Commission (SEC) Division of Enforcement brought 734 enforcement actions—the second highest number of actions filed in a single year. Overall, in connection with the financial crisis, the SEC (2012) has imposed many professional and industry bars on individuals; returned more than $6 billion FY 2009–12 to harmed investors; obtained more than $11 billion in ordered disgorgements and penalties; and filed actions against 129 individuals and institutions stemming from the financial crisis, including more than 50 CEOs, CFOs, and other senior officers (though the firms from which they came do not all fit into the elite category). Mainly due to large LIBOR rate-fixing cases also being prosecuted, the U.K. Financial Services Authority levied fines of £312 million in the year ending 2012, three times higher than the next highest year (but well behind the $3.4 billion in fines and 1,084 cases opened by the SEC and the Commodity Futures Trading Commission, though more than the 1,541 disciplinary actions and fines totaling more than $68 million [£42.1 million] obtained by the U.S. Financial Industry Regulation Authority [*Financial Times* 2013a; FINRA, 2013]). In 2013, the U.K. Financial Conduct Authority (FSA renamed) imposed fines of £474 million; in 2014, this rose to £1.472 billion; and in the nine months to September 2015, its fines totaled £826 million.

In addition, in December 2013, the European Commission imposed fines of €1.7 billion for operating a rate-fixing cartel. The Euribor investigation 2005–08 settlement involved Barclays, Deutsche Bank, RBS, and Société Générale. In yen LIBOR, the banks involved were UBS, RBS, Deutsche Bank, Citigroup, and JP Morgan. These sharp increases in penalties all reflect the targeting of more prestigious firms, but also the fact that those firms had been allowed by management and by regulatory failures to commit egregious and in some cases endemic misconduct against the public. Altogether, it has been calculated that "conduct costs" for ten international banks in the period 2008–12 totaled £148.02 billion, including provisions against future costs (£100 bn. without) (McCormick 2013). Twenty of the world's biggest banks paid more than $235 billion in fines and compensation 2008–2015 for misconduct, ranging from fines for manipulation of currency and interest rate markets to compensation to customers who were wrongly sold mortgages in the United States or insurance products in Britain (*Reuters* 2015).

D. Some Historical Perspective

Reflecting on research from an earlier era, Clinard and Yeager (1980, p. 287) stated the following:

> In our study of 56 convicted executives of large corporations, 62.5 per cent received probation, 21.4 per cent had their sentences suspended, and 28.6 per cent were incarcerated. Almost all (96.4 per cent) also had a criminal fine imposed. Those convicted of price conspiracies and income tax violations frequently received the more severe sentences . . . . In view of the large salaries and benefits of most corporate executives, the fines imposed on officers . . . were not large. The maximum was $56,000, with an average fine of $18,250; the mean in financial cases was $22,700, and in manufacturing (one case) $2,000. The average fine for an officer in an antitrust conviction was $18,360.

Wheeler, Weisburd, and Bode (1982) noted that other factors being held constant, around half of those convicted for defrauding $10,000 to $100,000 and 68 percent of those defrauding over $2.5 million could expect to be imprisoned. For less respectable offenders committing serious crimes for gain, then and today, the proportion imprisoned might be expected to be nearer 100 percent.

1. *Sentencing in the United Kingdom*

In the United Kingdom, the Serious Fraud Office (SFO) deals with the top layer of serious frauds, starting at a minimum of $1.5 million losses but usually involving significantly more. However, most major fraud cases, including all tax cases, are handled by the Crown Prosecution Service, because the SFO only deals with about fifteen trials annually: in 2014-15, 18 people were convicted, and the year before, 11, but no aggregate sentencing is available. The time series is not long enough to be certain that this is an upward trend, and with small numbers the composition of cases makes a big difference. Thus in the first of LIBOR prosecutions, the principal organizer of the conspiracy to rig global prices was sentenced to 14 years' imprisonment, the highest sentence ever. In 2011–12, sentences averaged fifty-five months for each SFO-convicted fraudster, up from an average of thirty months in 2010–11 and thirty-two months in 2009–10. Levi (2010a) analyzed SFO cases up to 2005 in greater detail. Altogether, counting suspended prison sentences as zero (since none was activated), the 109 people convicted from 2000 to 2005 received an average of 31.7 months imprisonment. Out of the fifty-three *cases*, the average sentence of *the most severely sentenced* person per case was 37.7 months' imprisonment (median = 36 months). For frauds against business creditors, the average was 27.4 months; for investment frauds against business investors, 37.7 months; for investment frauds on individuals, 40.4 months; for market abuse, 12 months (though in one of the two cases, all four defendants received suspended prison sentences, showing how distorted averages can be); for procurement fraud/corruption, 19.9 months; and for frauds on government, 36.8 months (based on three cases). In about a third of cases, at least one defendant was disqualified from company director-ship, for an average of over seven years. This reflects not just legal powers but also a belief that this is an appropriate financial punishment (reducing future earnings) and will be as effective as incapacitation. The latter is an open question: it certainly would affect those who need to play an upfront role as a director, but the extent of "shadow directorships" among those subject to disqualification is unknown and very difficult to discover even in principle. The Sentencing Council (2013a) notes an upward trend in fraud sentencing in England and Wales and (2013b, 2014) recommends tougher sentences where vulnerable victims are defrauded or targeted.

The specialist business press in major economies (and increasingly elsewhere) report elite cases rigorously because these are issues that businesspeople need to know about, but the cases that receive publicity in the mainstream media are those that have a populist dimension of traumatized victims and/or celebrity corporate or individual defendants (Levi 2006). Particular attention to sentencing is given also when the sentences (including regulatory fines) are high or low outliers, though this is usually in terms of absolute figures rather than as a percentage of profit, turnover, or GDP. This can be culturally variable. At the other end of the sentencing spectrum from the United States is Iceland. Despite the devastating effects nationally and elsewhere of the economic collapse that followed the pricking of the financial services bubble, Jón Ásgeir Jóhannesson, former CEO of collapsed retail group Baugur, was sentenced for tax fraud to a year in jail, suspended for two years, and ordered to pay IKr62m ($488,882). His co-convicted were given shorter suspended sentences (*Financial Times* 2013b). In December 2012, the CEO of failed bank Glitnir was given a nine-month jail sentence, six months of which were suspended. (Suspended sentences are almost never activated against serious frauds, not least because of the length of time that it takes to investigate and try cases.) These light formal sanctions reflected cultural norms about their personal wrongfulness as well as general sentencing in Iceland.

Differential sentencing and perceptions of system fairness can generate tensions over extradition, such as from the United Kingdom to the United States. U.S. prosecutorial aggression toward Reddit cyber-guru and activist Aaron Swartz for alleged violations of intellectual property was seen by some as overreach in relation to morally ambiguous or even praiseworthy behavior, stimulating the hacker group Anonymous to bring down the U.S. Sentencing Commission website in early 2013 as a sort of vendetta following his suicide awaiting trial. Some forms of white-collar criminalization—though not Ponzi schemes—are morally contested by otherwise respectable or respected people.

2. *Fraud Sentencing in Continental Europe*

In many countries, mostly developing ones but also developed ones such as Russia and South Korea, out-of-favor politicians and businesspeople may be targeted by incoming regimes for corruption and fraud prosecutions to eliminate their political threat and, nowadays, to seek to confiscate their identified proceeds of crime worldwide. In others, such as France and Italy—and even, on occasions, Nigeria—independent investigative judges and police may go after those currently in power, subject to the important constraint that heads of state (and some other officeholders) normally are legally immune from prosecution. Thus, Chirac, former president of France, was not liable for prosecution when in power but was later prosecuted. At the age of 79 and stated to be suffering from dementia, he was given a suspended prison sentence for party finance corruption committed many years before when he was mayor of Paris (*New York Times* 2011). When they left office, French presidents Mitterrand and Sarkozy were also formally investigated for corruption committed to generate party finances—a common issue in many developed and developing societies. Kohl, former chancellor of Germany, agreed to pay a $150,000 fine to avoid prosecution for failure to declare $1 million in party finance donations and refusal to name the donors (*The Telegraph* 2001). Berlusconi, former Italian prime minister, was convicted of (1) perjury in 1990, though his conviction was set aside under a general amnesty; (2) illegal financing of a political party in 1997, though (as is the law in Italy) his conviction was set aside because the statute of limitations expired before he had exhausted all appeals; and (3) tax fraud in 2012, following which he was sentenced to four years' imprisonment, which was confirmed on appeal in 2013 but because of Italian rules about age and imprisonment, he was offered a choice and chose community service rather than house arrest, presumably to maintain an image of doing good works that would be carried by his media outlets.

Systematic research on European fraud sentencing practices is absent, and data are available only intermittently. In Sweden, where sentencing generally is not severe by U.K. standards, a former chief executive of Sweden's biggest insurance group, Skandia, was in May 2006 sentenced to two years in prison for agreeing to large bonuses for executives without board approval, a case that had aroused serious cultural concern in Sweden. Petersson, who was chief executive of the group from 1997 to 2003, had removed a ceiling on an executive-bonus program without authorization in 2000, which led to executives receiving an extra SKr156m (€21m) in payments, though there was no evidence that he benefited personally. In 2011, the average sentence for "serious fraud" was nineteen months; for tax fraud it was sixteen months; for crimes against creditors, thirteen months; for embezzlement, nine months; and for welfare fraud, eight months. This should be set against the average sentence for all crimes of nine months in the District Court (data supplied to the author by the Swedish government).

In her review of the way that Germany dealt with economic crimes, Huber (2003) noted that in the regular white-collar offenses contained in the Penal Code, 80 to 90 percent of sentences are fines; when a prison sentence is imposed at all, it is suspended in 90 percent of cases. Of the additional penalties contained in the Penal Code, only prohibition to work in one's profession (§§ 70 ff StGB) is of certain significance. Forfeiture and confiscation of assets and objects, however (§§ 73 ff StGB), are used more often (food and wine laws, copyright law). There can be large fines for breaches of competition law: examples are fines of $284 million against the producers of power cable who entered into a cartel. She noted that a characteristic of the specialist economic crime courts is the generally lower tariff than in the regular courts, especially following guilty pleas.

In May 2006, a Dutch court fined Cees van der Hoeven, Ahold's former chief executive, and A. Michiel Meurs, its former finance chief, €225,000 each after convicting them of fraud, but it rejected prosecutors' request to imprison them, giving them both nine-month sentences suspended for two years. Jan Andreae, former executive board member in charge of Ahold's European operations, was sentenced to four months in jail, suspended for two years, and was fined €120 million. Ahold had overstated its earnings by more than $1 billion from 1999 to 2002, mostly by inflating sales at its U.S. food service unit. In May 2012, multimillionaire oil trader and former South African sanctions buster John Deuss and his sister were each given a suspended prison sentence of six months and a fine of €375,000, and the bank they owned paid a fine of €1.2 million. They had been found guilty in a Dutch court of banking without a license and failing to report unusual transactions—in fact, many millions in proceeds of U.K. value-added tax frauds.

In the first of the Parmalat trials in Milan in 2005, eleven defendants pleaded guilty in "plea bargains." The longest sentence, two years and six months, was given to Fausto Tonna, a former CFO. Gian Paolo Zini, a lawyer who had set up some offshore companies used to hide billions of dollars in debt and losses, was given two years. In 2012, an Italian appeal court slightly trimmed to seventeen years and ten months a jail sentence for Calisto Tanzi for conduct that had led to the collapse of his global dairy products empire in 2003, an $18.5 billion accounting hole that wiped out the savings of more than 100,000 small investors who had bet on its investment-grade bonds. This was Europe's biggest corporate bankruptcy at the time. The prison sentence, which had been eighteen years in a previous verdict, is one of the harshest ever issued in Italy, where jail terms for white-collar crimes are rare (*Reuters* 2012). He was also stripped of national honors by the Italian President.

II. Accounting for White-Collar Sentencing

The comparability issue between white-collar and other offenses is particularly difficult because popular, media, and political constructions of harm prioritize offenses involving actual, threatened, or perceived threatened violence. Burglary and, especially, robbery contain those elements, whereas frauds very seldom do, especially when committed by "respectable offenders." Moreover, fraud offenders—particularly individual or corporate elites—typically have fewer previous convictions than is the norm for other offenses. In a system where prior convictions are important, this makes a big difference. There is no obvious metric for balancing very large sums obtained by fraud (or theft) against violence (though we implicitly do so in current practice and in the way we talk about the "fairness" of sentences). It is difficult to steal nonviolently very large amounts of money or property without an abuse of trust.

Do "the powerful" receive more lenient treatment than others? Buell (2014) argues that there is no evidence that they do, while Garrett (2014) suggests that most of the bias comes into the discretion not to prosecute. For the most part, they do not commit easily comparable "like for like" offenses; the exceptions are interpersonal violence and personal frauds against the government (such as tax vs. social security fraud). Van Slyke and Bales (2012) found that despite operating under sentencing guidelines designed to reduce disparities, white-collar offenders are afforded greater leniency, especially for those who embezzle or defraud the government, for higher-status offenders, and for white-collar offenders sentenced before the Enron scandal. However, it is not obvious how we adjudicate rationally between hypotheses that (1) there is an ideological and/ or social bias against imprisoning the powerful and (2) inequality of treatment is an *un*intended (and often unseen) product of wider criminal justice processes such as plea bargaining (Katz 1979) that are uneven in their application because better defense counsel and greater case complexity give more grounds for denying culpability. We also need to consider the conditions under which "respectable offenders" may become targets for status degradation, such as at times of general "moral panic" about corruption or white-collar crimes or "victor's justice" efforts to get rid of elite rivals or troublesome critics (in China, France, Russia and the United States as well as in the developing world). In other words, we need both to examine sentencing data themselves and to interpret how to make sense of them.

Note also that bias can occur (or be believed to occur) in allocation to categories of prison, parole decisions, and pardons. This is part of the sanctioning process, if not formally of the sentencing process. President Clinton was much criticized from many parts of the political spectrum for pardoning a number of people in jail for fraud and money laundering, plus especially Marc Rich and Pincus Green, who had been fugitives (in Switzerland) after their indictment in 1983 on charges of racketeering and of mail and wire fraud arising out of their oil business. Rich had been indicted for evading $48 million in taxes. Clinton felt obliged to try to defend his decision making and his reputation, not least against suggestions that donations by Rich's ex-wife to the Presidential Library and Democratic campaigns had facilitated the pardon (Clinton 2001).[1]

Wheeler, Weisburd, and Bode (1982, p. 644, emphasis added) observed the following:

> Repeatedly in the interviews, the judges came back to the nature of the criminal *act*. A more serious offense deserves a more serious sanction. . . . First, seriousness is measured by the dollar loss attributed to the offense. . . . A second consideration is the amount of complexity or sophistication shown in the commission of the offense. . . . Third, judges talk about the *spread* of illegality. . . . Fourth, judges report being attentive to the nature of the *victim*.

They found that *actor*-related variables were important too, and these tended to produce what they called a "paradox of leniency and severity" (p. 645; see further, Wheeler, Mann, and Sarat 1988). On the one hand, the high position of the offender makes the offense more grave; on the other hand, the offender's impeccable prior "community record" generates an overall picture of someone whose moral character is generally good.

From a statistical prediction viewpoint, the chances of being sent to prison rose dramatically and consistently with increased losses generated—from 27 percent of those defrauding less than $500 to 68 percent for those few who caused losses exceeding $2,500,000 (Wheeler, Mann, and Sarat 1988). It also rose with increased complexity/sophistication, geographic spread, role in the offense, and number of prior convictions. Judges seemed reluctant to imprison the young or the old, particularly the latter. Other factors being held constant, women are 30 percent less likely to be sent to prison than men. (Once imprisoned, however, they receive only slightly shorter sentences.) There were variations by type of offense. Tax offenders and securities and exchange violators stood a much stronger chance of being sent to jail (2/3) than bank embezzlers and those involved in bribery (1/3) and antitrust violators (1/4). The authors discovered that judges' insights into their sentencing decisions were sometimes mistaken, for example on the importance of direct loss to individuals and number of victims (Wheeler, Weisburd, and Bode 1982, p. 650).

Different criteria—particularly the importance of *actor*-related variables—come into play when deciding on the length of sentence, once the decision to incarcerate has been made. The social background and prior convictions of the defendant, the defendant's plea (to keep the caseload moving along), and the district in which sentencing occurs seem most important (Nagel and Hagan 1982). Mann, Wheeler, and Sarat (1980, p. 479) stated that general deterrence is most important to judges and that rehabilitation, incapacitation, and even retribution are unimportant (though this was at a time when there was less of a social movement against white-collar crime than there was in the aftermath of the financial crisis of 2008). One judge justified his view that prison sentences (even short ones) may be necessary to deter by reference to business reactions to the electrical equipment antitrust cases when he was in legal practice (p. 483). They concluded that both retribution and special deterrence are satisfied by the stigma and economic losses consequent upon conviction: by the time the offender has paid his legal bills, he has no money left because he has lost his job and has heavy routine financial commitments. Sometimes, a "deterrent" sentence will be passed for public consumption—an interesting mixing together of deterrence with denunciation—but despite their belief in the efficacy of deterrence, judges do not like to impose prison sentences unless they also feel that the offender *deserves* punishment. Moreover, judges consider that white-collar criminals have a special sensitivity to imprisonment (though Stadler, Benson, and Cullen [2012] have shown that this view is mistaken); that incarceration will harm innocent parties; that it may inhibit compensation; and that noncustodial "reparations" such as community service are possible (maybe because of less hostile social reaction). Perhaps, though there is no specific mention of it in their analysis or interviews, judges may consider that male and female businesspeople, unlike the male laboring and non-laboring poor, do not *need* the threat of severe sanctions to be generally law abiding.

Benson and Cullen (1998) similarly found that local prosecutors hold the same view as judges regarding the priority of general deterrence for corporate crimes.

Wheeler, Weisburd, and Bode (1982) suggested that *once they reach the sentencing stage*, high-status fraud offenders are more likely to be imprisoned than low-status fraudsters (though the former receive slightly shorter sentences than the latter). But Hagan and Parker (1985) and Benson and Walker (1988) found that at least as regards securities offenses, employers received more lenient treatment than managers, not because of bias but because employers were able to make their offenses more complex and difficult to prosecute and to portray them as more "technical" than "real" criminal offenses. The notion of "impeccability" referred to by Wheeler et al. (1982) is a form of unconscious social bias resulting from the greater identification of judges with the social world of the "respectable offender"—particularly professional persons like themselves—than that of the burglar or "organized criminal" as commonly construed.

However, let us reflect on what is meant by "impeccable" here. Social standing is not (or not only) a sign of superior moral worth but of superior *situation*. Indeed, there is even social status discrimination *within* the category of white-collar crime: Wheeler and Rothman (1982, p. 1422) noted that prior to sentence, those who committed their offenses through their organizations were four times as likely as other "white-collar criminals" to have a supporting letter in their file from someone in the community. In short, on the one hand, judges generally do regard the breach of trust by people in high positions as deeply reprehensible (except where it plausibly can be portrayed as inadvertent); on the other hand, they are normally faced with sentencing people for whom the offense is "out of character" (i.e., they have not been convicted previously) and who often have lost a good-paying job simply as a consequence of conviction or even for breach of organizational or professional rules. In some cases, not only may the accused lose much of their wealth but also—where a practicing license is mandatory—may be prevented by the fact of conviction or disciplinary sanctions alone from committing the offense again, at least directly in their own names (Benson 1984). This is a very rare situation for judges in substantial crimes for gain, since such offenders normally have a string of previous convictions or have been portrayed by the police and the media as a cunning "Mr. Big." Judges sometimes may see defendants from privileged backgrounds and/or living in privileged neighborhoods as being more affected by social degradation than they actually are, but errors can be made in either direction. One area where there are few parallels with most "ordinary" offenders is that professional sanctions can also create the possibility of what I term "incapacitation without custody" (Levi 2013). However, here too, it is important to make distinctions *within* fraud: it is much harder to cut off from crime opportunities those who defraud the government and banks as *external* actors than it is those people (like lawyers and bank directors) who need authorization as "fit and proper persons" to practice their professions; and though some payments to social security fraudsters can be cut off, other opportunities to defraud might be available to them. Paraphrasing the French writer Anatole France, street and household frauds (and other crimes), like the Ritz Hotel, are open to all.

III. Sentencing the Respectable Offender: What Works and When?

Social stereotyping may lead us to associate highly harmful offenses with highly dangerous offenders. In some frauds, the harm may be great but future probability of reoffending risks may be small (unless the offenders can commit crimes via nominees or, more colloquially, via "straw figures"). Another source of controversy lies in whether judges (and indeed "society" and "the media") have undervalued the seriousness of some or all types of fraud. Yet another question may arise from the social position of the perpetrator and whether that may also actually and/or *defensibly* have an impact on general social judgments of culpability and of harmfulness, as well as on judicial perceptions of the impact of conviction and sentence (or even media publicity and prosecution) on offenders. Normatively, sentencing theorists occupy a range of positions broadly between just deserts (perhaps modified by previous criminal records), deterrence, incapacitation, and restorative justice.[2] Restorative justice advocates may set aside other considerations and focus on the reduction of future offending by some sort of conciliation process; that, indeed, is the foundation of the regulatory approach to corporate crime (Sparrow 2012). However, by failing to appreciate that the regulatees may be what Sparrow (2008) referred to as "conscious opponents," regulators may misjudge the intentions of *some* white-collar criminals until they have done considerable further harm. In different terms, they need to be escalated up the "regulatory pyramid" of sanctions if their harms are to be stopped (see Ayres and Braithwaite 1992; Garrett 2014).

In relation to fraud and allied white-collar crimes such as money laundering by professional people, we know relatively little about what factors influence deterrence. Some important consequences for some high-status offenders arise from conviction or even bad publicity alone, irrespective of sentence level; for this subset of fraudsters, "the process is the punishment" (see Feeley 1979). Whether such consequences (or rather, since actual effects may not be known at the time of offending, *expected* consequences) *should* be taken into account in imposing sentences is a contested issue.

For specialist fraudsters, the "tipping point" for deterrence is whether, in their minds, the expected probability of conviction is high enough and sentences are long enough to outweigh the benefits from crime (however they represent their lawbreaking to themselves). For generalist "professional" or "organized" criminals—"nonrespectable offenders" in the context of this essay—the comparison is usually of conviction and of "jail time served" risks between fraud and any other types of crime (e.g., trafficking in drugs or people) that the offenders could plausibly commit. In addition, some fraudsters (and professionals providing money-laundering services to criminals) may be caught up on the fringes of "organized crime groups" without losing their "respectable offender" status.

In retributivism, there are two dimensions of sentencing—harm and culpability—around which various aggravating and mitigating factors are clustered. In practice, not always consciously, media anathematization (Levi 2006, 2009)—based around tropes of "evil offenders" or "serious harm to undeserving victims"—may have an impact on fraud sentences because of some need to express the denunciatory principle and to set a moral boundary, as Durkheim might have argued (von Hirsch 1993). General categories such as "elderly persons" are treated as especially vulnerable: in the case of fraud, one might argue that they have less working time to recoup their losses and therefore that the severity of harm might typically (though not invariably) be greater. (On the other hand, they have a shorter period to live and thus may have less time to suffer a lower standard of living.) How one translates broken dreams and damaged expectations (and the impacts of bribery, both domestic and transnational) into standardized criteria—especially monetary value—might be a matter of some dispute, but damage to mental and physical health has been measured by health economists in terms of QUALYS (Quality-adjusted life years) (Dubourg and Hamed 2005).

In England and Wales, following a Consultation, sentencing guidelines recommended a maximum sentence of ten years for frauds prosecuted under the Fraud Act 2006 and seven years for other cases, plus normally confiscation or compensation where appropriate (Sentencing Guidelines Council 2009), though these were reviewed and changed in 2014 (Sentencing Council 2014).

Much more attention has been paid to sanctions in the United States, where the Sentencing Commission (2003) was specifically tasked after the Enron scandal to review white-collar crime sentencing and where federal sentencing statistics generate more readily analyzable data. American sentencing levels (and imprisonment per capita population) are so much higher than anywhere in Europe that it is tempting to advocate using sentence *ratios* for fraud versus other crimes as indicators of (un)equal treatment rather than to look at fraud sentences in isolation as retribution or deterrence. On the other hand, at least for deterrent purposes if not for social justice and legitimacy, sentencing for business elites might better be considered in isolation from other offenses, since elites would seldom contemplate participating in mainstream crimes for gain. For those habitual offenders in a position to commit frauds of particular types, the *relative* consequences of conviction may stimulate a shift toward or away from particular offenses.

What is clear is that the general level of sentences has a powerful effect on the earlier decision stages, including plea negotiation and "proffers" and the trend toward "deferred prosecutions" used to elicit changes within institutions that, if prosecuted, might lose their licenses to do business (e.g., KPMG in the tax-shelter case). It is unlikely that senior staff and companies such as AIG, Arthur Andersen, Enron, HSBC, KPMG, UBS, and WorldCom would have cooperated with the prosecutors or settled cases had it not been for the prospect of lengthy prison sentences plus no sentencing discount unless they both confess first and implicate others. This is stimulated by the pressures placed on businesses that want to avoid indictment or to reduce financial penalties *not* to pay their staff's criminal defense costs, for fear of being viewed as "uncooperative" within the controversial Thompson guidelines, which hold that corporations do not receive credit for cooperation if they are not deemed by the prosecutors to be behaving appropriately (Martz 2006). (Because of such concerns, in 2012, News International unsuccessfully sought to cut off legal support for Andy Coulson, who had become the British prime minister's former head of communications and who later was convicted on charges related to phone hacking and the making of corrupt payments, while he was editor of the *News of the World*.) The "prisoners' dilemma" model has been incorporated into administrative penalties for cartel and allied offenses in Australia, Europe, the United Kingdom, and the United States. Equity apart, much of the deterrent and trial-success impact of these measures may depend on how plausible it is that fraudsters (of what "types" and in what contexts?) are part of some wider offender/rule-violator networks. Where white-collar defendants' prime motivation is to avoid a conviction that will have serious career consequences and/or public stigma, then the expected sentence levels on not-guilty pleas may be relatively unimportant unless they are very high. Plea negotiation might be expected to work best where there are rings of offenders or Enron-style hierarchies to unravel.

It is apparent that U.S. sentences in dramatic cases are typically far longer than would have occurred in the United Kingdom or *a fortiori* elsewhere in Europe. But it is important to appreciate that this is a relatively recent phenomenon transpiring since the turn of the 21st century. This punitiveness reflects the perceived need for deterrence for prevalent offenses as well as strong feelings of retribution toward people and companies that have caused serious harm, especially in a climate of austerity, but even preceding that in the dot.com bubble.

Ex hypothesi, whether regulatory sanctions (or formal monitoring) really deter fraudsters depends on what "sort of people" they are. Criminologists are broadly agreed that among the factors influencing involvement in crime are the following:

1. Personal values (though it is astonishing how readily ethical values can be reconciled with financial self-interest, via rationalizations);
2. Attachment to the social networks of respectability (which degree of attachment regulators and judges may misinterpret or be misled about); and
3. Expectations of being sanctioned—prosecuted, convicted, and punished, both in formal terms (exclusion from the profession or from contractor lists) and in informal terms (e.g., being snubbed by friends, losing business contacts through imputed disreputability).

Kerley and Copes (2004) described the effects on future employment of imprisonment for both white-collar and street criminals (see also Pinard [2010] and, for a pioneering early British study, Martin and Webster [1971]). Though it sometimes may be impossible to determine until after the fact whether shaming is going to be reintegrative or disintegrative, Braithwaite (1989) plausibly argued that reintegrative shaming is the key to successful crime control. But the effects of this depend on how much intending or more vaguely potential fraudsters care about such reactions (Levi and

Suddle 1989; Levi 2002, 2010b). If the stigmatized person remains useful to others in business or politics, then he or she will reemerge because of *realpolitik* unless effectively disqualified from the public sphere.

It is hard to disentangle the pure reputational effects from those connected with expected financial and legal losses (as well as the diversion of executives' time) from sanctions. What shaming might be expected to achieve remains obscure. Is it primarily social pressure to affect social prestige (in which case, this has to be affected and cared about)? Or is it some commercial incapacitation that operates through social mechanisms, like the importance the Chinese place on *guanxi* and its equivalence in other cultures?

Whatever the case, part of the effect of shaming depends on how much the particular business wants to continue operating. Few preplanned fraudsters will care, unless the publicity somehow incapacitates them—after all, they have already neutralized their crimes to their own ethical satisfaction and, though confrontation with the views of others may shake those neutralizations, they may regard the moral claims of "the respectable rackets" as unrealistic or hypocritical. Those who turn to fraud when their businesses are about to go bust may not care anyway, if they are focused narrowly on keeping going (though there are personality and cognitive dimensions here). The main people who care about shaming are (1) those whose social lives are embedded and are sufficiently distanced to appreciate the impact and (2) those who fear that they may be excluded economically from markets because others distrust them or fear that by associating with them, they themselves will attract unwelcome attention from regulators or police. The capacity to boost shame in contemporary societies is limited not just by the normally modest reactions of business and political elites, but also by the ability of the sociopathic to insulate themselves from the censurers.

IV. CONCLUSION

If offenders have both a low chance of conviction and a high chance of a "light" sentence for complex, multijurisdictional frauds obtaining sums of money that are vast compared with other types of crime for gain, then this reality is cause for reflection on the effectiveness, dissuasiveness, and proportionality of existing sentencing practices. The gap in probabilities of conviction and in sentencing between fraud and other types of crime for gain is important, both to those choosing between different forms of crime that they have the ability and capacity to commit and to justice between different sets of both offenders and victims. The systematic information is not yet there to make any clear evidence-based decisions as to the potential impact of sentencing upon different sorts of fraudsters. Nor, following the "corporate death" of Arthur Andersen, do we have any clear idea of whether the "deferred prosecutions" currently fashionable in the United States and now in place in the United Kingdom carry with them a credible threat that will produce either special or general deterrence. If conviction and formal censure alone were sufficient to put an end to the offending (as it is with many professionals who are thereby prevented from practicing officially), then the only reasons for tougher sentences would be retribution and a social demand for equality of suffering. We have seen how varied are the criminal careers of fraudsters and their stakes in respectability. The collateral damage from condign corporate punishment, especially though not exclusively in the financial sector, deters the authorities from establishing a consistently tough sanctioning regimen, even if they were minded to do so. Sending clear and consistent messages to the very different sorts of people who might plan frauds large and small, or who might stumble into disgrace, would be a major challenge even if one did not have to worry about systemic risk or the impacts on employment. These are elements in sentencing the respectable offender that are not present in the mainstream criminal justice system and that rightly tax those who aim for both effectiveness and social fairness in the sanctioning process.

NOTES

1. For a general discussion of pardons, see Linzer (2011).
2. For a good, accessible British review, see Ashworth and Roberts (2012).

REFERENCES

Ashworth, Andrew, and Julian Roberts. 2012. "Sentencing: Theory, Principle, and Practice." In *The Oxford Handbook of Criminology*, 5th ed., pp. 866–94, edited by Mike Maguire, Rob Morgan, and Robert Reiner. Oxford, UK: Oxford University Press.

Ayres, Ian, and John Braithwaite. 1992. *Responsive Regulation: Transcending the Deregulation Debate*. New York: Oxford University Press.

Benson, Michael L. 1984. "The Fall from Grace: Loss of Occupational Status as a Consequence of Conviction for a White-Collar Crime." *Criminology* 22: 573–93.

Benson, Michael L. and Francis T. Cullen. 1998. *Combating Corporate Crime: Local Prosecutors at Work*. Boston: Northeastern University Press.

Benson, Michael L., and Esteban Walker. 1988. "Sentencing the White-Collar Offender." *American Sociological Review* 53: 294–302.

Bowman III, Frank O. 2015. "Damp Squib: The Disappointing Denouement of the Sentencing Commission's Economic Crime Project (and What They Should Do Now)." 27 Federal Sentencing Reporter 270.

Braithwaite, John. 1989. *Crime, Shame, and Reintegration*. Cambridge, UK: Cambridge University Press.

Buell, Samuel W. 2014. "Is the White-Collar Offender Privileged?" *Duke Law Journal* 63: 101–67.

Clinard, Marshall B., and Peter C. Yeager. 1980. *Corporate Crime*. New York: The Free Press.

Clinton, William Jefferson. 2001. "My Reasons for the Pardons." *New York Times* (February 18). Available at http://www.nytimes.com/2001/02/18/opinion/my-reasons-for-the-pardons. html?n=Top%2fReference%2fTimes%20Topics%2fSubjects%2fA%2fAmnesties%20and%20 Pardons

Dubourg, Richard, and Joe Hamed. 2005. *The Economic and Social Costs of Crime against Individuals and Households 2003/04*. London: Home Office.

Feeley, Malcolm M. 1979. *The Process Is the Punishment: Handling Cases in a Lower Criminal Court*. New York: Russell Sage Foundation.

Financial Times. 2013a. "FSA metes out record £312m in fines." (January 13). Available at http://www.ft.com/cms/s/0/af9f6f42-54c6-11e2-a628-00144feab49a.html#ixzz2mpBleykm

Financial Times. 2013b. "Viking Raider" gets suspended jail term. (February 7). Available at http://www.ft.com/cms/s/0/5ecb00c4-715c-11e2-9056-00144feab49a.html#axzz2Xibf3dWS

FINRA. 2013. *FINRA 2012 Year in Review*. Washington, D.C.: Financial Industry Regulatory Authority.

Friedrichs, David O. 2010. *Trusted Criminals: White Collar Crime in Contemporary Society*, 4th ed. Upper Saddle River, NJ: Wadsworth.

Garrett, Brandon. 2014. *Too Big to Jail*. Cambridge: Belknap Press.

Hagan, John, and Ilene Nagel. 1982. "White-Collar Crime, White-Collar Time: The Sentencing of White-Collar Offenders in the Southern District of New York." *American Criminal Law Review* 20: 259–89.

Hagan, John, and Patricia Parker. 1985. "White-Collar Crime and Punishment: The Class Structure and Legal Sanctioning of Securities Violation." *American Sociological Review* 50: 302–16.

Huber, Barbara. 2003. "The Tribunal for Serious Fraud: The European Experience." *Journal of Financial Crime* 11: 28–37.

Katz, Jack. 1979. "Legality and Equality: Plea Bargaining in the Prosecution of White-Collar and Common Crimes." *Law and Society Review* 13: 431–59.

Kerley, Kent, and Heith Copes. 2004. "The Effects of Criminal Justice Contact on Employment Stability for White-Collar and Street-Level Offenders." *International Journal of Offender Therapy and Comparative Criminology* 48: 65–84.

Levi, Michael. 2002. "Suite Justice or Sweet Charity? Some Explorations of Shaming and Incapacitating Business Fraudsters." *Punishment and Society* 4: 147–63.

Levi, Michael. 2006. "The Media Construction of Financial White-Collar Crimes." *British Journal of Criminology* 46: 1037–57.

Levi, Michael. 2008. *The Phantom Capitalists*, 2nd ed. Andover, UK: Ashgate.

Levi, Michael. 2009. "Suite Revenge? The Shaping of Folk Devils and Moral Panics about White-Collar Crimes." *British Journal of Criminology* 49: 48–67.

Levi, Michael. 2010a. "Hitting the Suite Spot: Sentencing Frauds." *Journal of Financial Crime* 17: 116–32.

Levi, Michael. 2010b. "Serious Tax Fraud and Non-Compliance: A Review of Evidence on the Differential Impact of Criminal and Non-Criminal Proceedings." *Criminology and Public Policy* 9: 493–513.

Levi, Michael. [1987] 2013. *Regulating Fraud: White-Collar Crime and the Criminal Process*. London: Routledge.

Levi, Michael, and Shoaib M. Suddle. 1989. "White-Collar Crime, Shamelessness, and Disintegration: The Control of Tax Evasion in Pakistan." *Journal of Law and Society* 16: 489–505.

Linzer, Dafna. 2011. "The Shadow of Marc Rich." ProPublica (December 3). Available at http://www.propublica.org/article/the-shadow-of-marc-rich

Mann, Kenneth, Stanton Wheeler, and Austin Sarat. 1980. "Sentencing the White-Collar Offender." *American Criminal Law Review* 17: 479–500.

Martin, John P., and Douglas Webster. 1971. *The Social Consequences of Conviction*. London: Heinemann.

Martz, Stephanie. 2006. *Report from the Front Lines: The Thompson Memorandum and the KPMG Tax Shelter Case*. Washington, D.C.: National Association of Criminal Defense Lawyers. Available at http://www.nacdl.org/criminaldefense.aspx?id=9994

McCormick, Roger. 2013. "Bank Conduct Costs Results." Available at http://blogs.lse.ac.uk/conductcosts/bank-conduct-costs-results/

Nagel, Ilene, and John Hagan. 1982. "The Sentencing of White-Collar Criminals in Federal Courts: A Socio-legal Exploration of Disparity." *Michigan Law Review* 80: 1427–65.

New York Times. 2011. "Chirac Found Guilty in Political Funding Case." (December 15).

Pinard, Michael. 2010. "Reflections and Perspectives on Reentry and Collateral Consequences." *Journal of Criminal Law and Criminology* 100: 1213–24.

Reiman, Jeffrey, and Paul Leighton. 2012. *The Rich Get Richer and the Poor Get Prison: Ideology, Class, and Criminal Justice*. New York: Pearson.

Reuters. 2012. "Appeal Court Trims Jail Term for Parmalat Founder." (April 23).

Reuters. 2015. "Banking Misconduct Bill." (May 22).

Richman, Daniel. 2013. "Federal White Collar Sentencing in the United States: A Work in Progress." *Law and Contemporary Problems* 76: 53–73.

Rothfeld, Michael. 2010. "In Gupta Sentencing, a Judgment Call." *Wall Street Journal* (October 10).

Rothfeld, Michael, and Dan Strumpf. 2012. "Gupta Gets Two Years for Leaking Inside Tips." *Wall Street Journal* (October 25).

Saris, Patti. 2015. "The 2015 Economic Crime Amendments." Available at http://www.ussc.gov/sites/default/files/pdf/news/speeches-and-articles/speech_saris_20150414.pdf

Securities and Exchange Commission. 2012. *Fiscal Year 2012 Summary of Performance and Financial Information*. Available at www.sec.gov/about/secpar/secafr2012-summary.pdf

Sentencing Council. 2013a. *Fraud Offences Sentencing Data*. London: Sentencing Council.

Sentencing Council. 2013b. *Fraud, Bribery, and Money Laundering Offences Guideline Consultation*. London: Sentencing Council.

Sentencing Council. 2014. *Fraud, Bribery and Money Laundering Offences Definitive Guideline*. London: Sentencing Council.

Sentencing Guidelines Council. 2009. *Sentencing for Fraud—Statutory Offenses*. London: Sentencing Guidelines Council.

Shapiro, Susan. 1990. "Collaring the Crime, Not the Criminal: Reconsidering the Concept of White-Collar Crime." *American Sociological Review* 55: 346–65.

Sparrow, Malcolm K. 2008. *The Character of Harms: Operational Challenges in Control*. Cambridge, MA: Cambridge University Press.

Sparrow, Malcolm K. 2012. "Crime Reduction through a Regulatory Approach: Joining the Regulatory Fold." *Criminology and Public Policy* 11: 345–59.

Stadler, William A., Michael L. Benson, and Francis T. Cullen. 2012. "Revisiting the Special Sensitivity Hypothesis: The Prison Experience of White-Collar Inmates." *Justice Quarterly* 30(6): 1090–114.

Sutherland, Edwin H. 1949. *White Collar Crime*. New York: Dryden.

The Telegraph. 2001. "Kohl Escapes Prosecution." (February 9).

Van Slyke, Shanna, and William D. Bales. 2012. "A Contemporary Study of the Decision to Incarcerate White-Collar and Street Property Offenders." *Punishment and Society* 14: 217–46.

von Hirsch, Andrew. 1993. *Censure and Sanctions*. Oxford, UK: Oxford University Press.

U.S. Sentencing Commission. 2003. *Increased Penalties under the Sarbanes-Oxley Act of* 2002. Washington, D.C.: Author.

U.S. Sentencing Commission. 2012. *Statistical Information Packet, Fiscal Year* 2011, *Southern District of New York.* Washington, D.C.: Author.

U.S. Sentencing Commission. 2013. *2012 Annual Report.* Washington, D.C.: Author.

Weisburd, David, Stanton Wheeler, Elin Waring, and Nancy Bode. 1991. *Crimes of the Middle Classes: White-Collar Offenders in the Federal Courts.* New Haven, CT: Yale University Press.

Wheeler, Stanton, Kenneth Mann, and Austin Sarat. 1988. *Sitting in Judgment: The Sentencing of White-Collar Criminals.* New Haven, CT: Yale University Press.

Wheeler, Stanton, and Michael Rothman. 1982. "The Organization as Weapon in White-Collar Crime." *Michigan Law Review* 80: 1403–26.

Wheeler, Stanton, David Weisburd, and Nancy Bode. 1982. "Sentencing the White-Collar Offender: Rhetoric and Reality." *American Sociological Review* 47: 641–59.

Will, Susan, David Brotherton, and Stephen Handelman. 2012. *How They Got Away with It: White Collar Criminals and the Financial Meltdown.* New York: Columbia University Press.

CHAPTER 29

EFFECTS ON WHITE-COLLAR DEFENDANTS OF CRIMINAL JUSTICE ATTENTION AND SANCTIONS

BRIAN K. PAYNE

IN his classic book, *The Process is the Punishment*, Malcolm Feeley (1992) wrote "the fear of arrest and conviction does not loom as large in the eyes of many people brought into court as it does in eyes of middle-class researchers" (p. 200). He explained:

> I was . . . struck by the frequent lack of concern about the stigma of conviction and by the more practical and far more immediate concerns about what the sentence would be and how quickly they could get out of court. . . . There are several reasons for this. First, many arrestees already have criminal records, so that whatever stigma does attach to a conviction is already eroded, if not destroyed. Second, many arrestees, particularly young ones, are part of a subculture which spurns conventional values and for which arrest and conviction may even function as a celebratory ritual, reinforcing their own values and identity. . . . Third, lower-class people tend to be more *present*-oriented than middle-class people, and for obvious reasons. Many defendants are faced with an immediate concern for returning to work or their children, and these concerns often take precedence over the desire to avoid the *remote* consequences that a (or another) conviction might bring. (pp. 200–01)

Feeley goes on to point out that it is unlikely that, for reliable employees, loss of a job will follow a conviction. However, while blue-collar workers might be able to avoid the collateral consequences often thought to be associated with arrest and conviction, there are good reasons to think that the postconviction experiences of white-collar offenders are entirely different. For white-collar offenders, most assuredly, their conviction for a white-collar offense will result in the loss of the job in which they committed their offense. While Feeley, and others, have implied that the effects of being a white-collar defendant are different than they are for blue-collar defendants, very few researchers have focused specifically on the effects of criminal justice attention and sanctions on white-collar defendants.

In this chapter, attention is given to the effects of being investigated and prosecuted for white-collar misconduct, which is defined as criminal acts committed during the course of one's occupational routine by individuals of high status and respectability. It is important to note that the effects of criminal justice attention and sanctions on white-collar offenders are not necessarily worse than those effects experienced by conventional offenders, nor are the effects always different. As Schwartz and Skolnick (1962) commented more than four decades ago, "the social position of the defendant himself will serve to aggravate or alleviate the effects of any given sanction" (p. 134). However, in some situations, the effects, and the sources of the effects, likely vary between white-collar and conventional defendants. Addressing these effects promotes understanding about how white-collar defendants experience the criminal justice system.

It is also important to note that the effects of criminal justice attention and sanctions are intertwined with labeling theory and rational choice as perceived by the offender. The role of choice in conventional crimes is well established. From a rational choice perspective, offenders choose to commit crime after weighing the risks and benefits of the misconduct. For white-collar defendants, the role of choice applies in subtly different and more complicated ways, though they are as a group arguably more rational than conventional offenders (see Shover and Hochstetler 2006). In particular, one would expect that many white-collar offenders are initially surprised at the presence of criminal justice attention. The surprise exists for many reasons:

- Many white-collar defendants claim they did not do anything wrong, or at least they do not believe they did anything wrong. For these offenders, in their minds—or least in their narratives—they chose to engage in an appropriate behavior that others are defining as inappropriate.
- White-collar crime investigations and prosecutions are relatively rare and may not have a general deterrent effect. Some white-collar defendants chose to commit a crime because they thought they could get away with it. Hence, there is great surprise when criminal justice attention begins.
- Many white-collar defendants were, in their minds, committing the act for the good of their company and their behavior is seemingly defined as normal in their business. Upon realizing that others define their behavior as criminal, a series of negative effects will follow.

In the end, the effects are tied to interactions between the element of surprise and choice (or lack of acceptance about choice). If defendants (1) truly did nothing wrong or (2) believe they did nothing illegal, then the effects of criminal justice attention will potentially be much different than for those offenders who consciously admit and accept guilt, which demonstrates that they intentionally chose to commit the crime. From a labeling theory perspective, it is reasonable to suggest that the labels assigned to white-collar offenders might have different effects than those assigned to conventional offenders.

Using media reports, prior research on white-collar offenders, autobiographies by white-collar offenders, and biographies about white-collar offenders, a number of potential effects from criminal justice attention can be identified. In discussing these effects, narratives/quotes from white-collar professionals and their family members from news reports, studies, books, and even a few websites/blogs are included to highlight the themes. Section I addresses the psychological effects of criminal justice attention on white-collar defendants. Section II discusses the relationship effects. Section III explores the financial effects. Section IV considers the identity effects. Section V explores the effects white-collar offenders experience from criminal justice sanctions. Section VI addresses ways that some white-collar offenders have overcome the effects of criminal justice attention. The major conclusions of this essay are as follows:

- White-collar offenders experience an assortment of effects as a result of criminal justice attention and criminal justice sanctions.
- The sources of the effects are tied to different types of criminal justice practices and strategies.
- Many white-collar offenders can adjust to the negative consequences of criminal justice attention.
- For white-collar offenders, the process is as punitive, if not more punitive, than the sanction itself.
- Family members of white-collar defendants are often negatively affected.

I. Psychological and Emotional Effects

In this context, psychological/emotional effects refer to a range of psychological and emotional responses that white-collar defendants exhibit in response to criminal justice attention and sanctions. These effects include anxiety, shame, depression, and fear. For white-collar offenders, feelings of anxiety may persist throughout their contacts with the criminal justice system. Benson's (1985a) interviews with thirty white-collar offenders found that some offenders reported worrying about different aspects of their conviction.

In terms of shame, the weight of a criminal justice investigation alone carries a great deal of stigma for white-collar defendants, a conviction adds even more stigma, and a prison sentence still more. It seems obvious that this shame, while attributed to the defendant's actions, is the result of criminal justice attention and sanctions. If shame were the result of the behavior, white-collar offenders would more often experience shame prior to the criminal justice attention. More often than not, evidence of shame appears only after criminal justice attention or sanctioning.

Some white-collar defendants may also experience depression as a result of criminal justice experiences. Describing how one judge reacted after resigning in the wake of a bribery investigation, Joynt (1997) wrote the following:

> White took Jack home, and it did not take the attorney long to surmise that his friend was a wreck. He found pill bottles of anabolic steroids and the powerful anti-depressant Xanax and who knew what else. . . . Jack finally broke down and started talking about killing himself. (p. 8)

Perhaps attributed to depression, white-collar inmates have been identified by some researchers as being at risk for suicide (Fogal 1992). This degree of depression does not occur only among inmates but can surface earlier in the stressful criminal justice process for white-collar defendants. Not long after agreeing to testify before Congress about the Enron debacle, Clifford Baxter, a former Enron executive, committed suicide by shooting himself in the head in his car in an affluent suburb. His suicide note read:

> Carol,
>   I am so sorry for this. I feel I just can't go on. I have always tried to do the right thing but where there was once great pride now it's gone. I love you and the children so much. I just can't be any good to you or myself. The pain is overwhelming.
>   Please try to forgive me
>   Cliff. (Cruver 2002)

These effects can be attributed to the following factors, each of which is discussed below: (1) stress, (2) criminal justice bureaucratic practices, and (3) manifest criminal justice strategies.

A. Stress and Psychological Effects

Being accused of a crime, and being processed through the justice process, can be a very stressful process for white-collar defendants. Being investigated for committing a white-collar crime, prosecuted, and potentially convicted adds even more stress. Benson (1990) began one of the few articles on the emotional consequences of being labeled a white-collar offender with the following comments: "Few events produce stronger emotions than being publicly accused of a crime. Especially for the individual who has a stake in maintaining a legitimate persona, the prospect of being exposed as a criminal engenders 'deep emotions' (Denzin 1983): shame, humiliation, guilt, depression, and anger" (p. 515). These "deep emotions" arguably create levels of stress that defendants had rarely faced in their lives.

B. Criminal Justice Bureaucratic Practices and Psychological Effects

Criminal justice bureaucratic practices refer to the way that the criminal justice bureaucracy creates dynamics that lead to psychological and emotional consequences for white-collar defendants. The bureaucracy controls virtually every aspect of white-collar defendants' lives, and it moves very slowly. The element of time likely contributes to the emotional consequences of criminal justice attention for white-collar defendants. White-collar crime investigations frequently take a little longer to conduct than traditional investigations (Payne 2012). While the time element may make the investigation more difficult for law enforcement officials, having on ongoing investigation hanging over one's life, career, and livelihood can be a stressful situation. The longer the investigation lasts, the longer the offender must live in a state of uncertainty.

The criminal justice bureaucracy also produces negative emotional responses in white-collar defendants as part of the controlling nature of the criminal trial. Reports in the media and biographies of white-collar defendants show that depression, anxiety, and mental health problems persist through the trial, and white-collar crime trials can go on longer than traditional cases. In these situations, stress, anxiety, depression, and other emotional effects experienced by white-collar defendants have been connected to white collar defendants' (1) lack of exposure to trials, (2) lack of control when they are accustomed to being the ones in control, (3) potentially tremendous losses if they are found guilty, and (4) stigma and shame that comes from the daily public walks to the courthouse and subsequent media coverage (Payne 2012).

C. Manifest Criminal Justice Strategies and Psychological Effects

Manifest criminal justice strategies refer to actual practices of criminal justice professionals that are carried out to further the aims of the justice process. In some cases, the strategies may be intentionally designed to produce emotional reactions among white-collar defendants, while in other cases the actions may be carried out for a broader criminal justice purpose, with emotional consequences being a "side effect" of the criminal justice strategies. Interrogation practices and "perp walks" are examples of these strategies.

Interrogation practices are designed to produce strong emotional reactions among those being interrogated. The purpose of the interrogation is to elicit information that can be used to demonstrate the defendant's guilt. Interrogators will ask questions and communicate with defendants in such a way as to play on their emotions. It should not be surprising that white-collar defendants experience anxiety during law enforcement interrogations. Indeed, the nature of interrogations is such that they are structured to make defendants anxious.

"Perp walks," the very public arrests of white-collar defendants, represent another manifest criminal justice strategy that produces negative emotional effects for white-collar defendants. Arrests of white-collar defendants, or their trips to the courthouse, receive a great amount of media attention. Rudy Giuliani was one of the first officials to use perp walks for white-collar defendants when he ordered the arrests of three white-collar defendants from their Wall Street offices. The defendants were "handcuffed, and escorted from the building to a mob of press that had been previously alerted" (Mitchelson and Calloway 2006).

University of Toronto business professor Joseph d'Cruz described the perp walk as "justice as theatre" and said "this is very real punishment for them to be paraded before the public like this" (McFarland 2004, p. B7). According to Mitchelson and Calloway (2006), the perp walk is justified by prosecutors on four grounds. First, it is believed that the walk sends a clear "message that, regardless of ethnic background, wealth, or power, no one is above the law" (p. S1). Second, it is believed that the message will have a deterrent effect. Third, prosecutors suggest that it enlightens the public about the criminal justice process and "enhances transparency in the system." Finally, media attention may result in new witnesses contacting justice officials. The authors point out that defendants have challenged the perp walk in appeals and note that it was "described as a posture connoting guilt" in *Lauro v. Charles* 29F 3d202 212n7 (2d Cir. 200).

Currently, courts have ruled that perp walks staged by criminal justice professionals are unconstitutional (Hagglund 2012). This does not stop the media from covering the "perp walk" to the police station or courthouse, however; it simply stops criminal justice professionals from being the "producers" of the staged walk. Prosecutors and officials will use the media in other ways to paint a picture about the white-collar defendant. Benson (1990) noted that in some instances criminal justice officials share information with the media in a way that "shocks and degrades the white-collar offender" (p. 518). One white-collar offender told Benson the following:

> The prosecutors, they plant all kinds of things in newspapers. Some of those newspaper articles that came out were an abomination. They would seize on little key phrases and you could see how it was all planted by prosecutors. (p. 518)

Benson points out that the media depictions are not necessarily inaccurate, they are just "one-sided." Interviews with white-collar offenders by another researcher found that nine of the eleven subjects who had the media cover their case described the attention as "negative and biased" (Dhami 2007, p. 66).

II. Relationship Effects

White-collar defendants will also experience relationship effects with family members, friends, coworkers, and clients. These experiences are perhaps most salient and problematic for family members who are closest to the white-collar defendant. Family relations will be strained for numerous reasons: (1) family members might feel betrayed by the white-collar defendant, (2) the family will experience financial stress from the criminal justice attention, (3) the family will experience shame and stigma, and (4) the family will endure different types of legal ramifications.

In terms of legal ramifications, the defendant might be advised by his or her attorney not to share any information about the case with his or her spouse, even though spousal privilege exists. One attorney advises white-collar defendants:

> You should not even talk about the case with your spouse. If you and your spouse want to do so, however, this is difficult for your lawyer to prevent. Such communications should be permitted reluctantly, if at all, and only after your spouse is instructed not to speak to anyone else. . . . Remember that not all marriages survive a lengthy white-collar crime investigation. Male defendants often have a particularly hard time explaining to their wives how a portion of their ill-gotten loot went to refurbish a mistress' apartment. Remember also that a disgruntled spouse can waive the marital testimonial privilege and testify against her spouse with respect to matters falling outside of the marital communications privilege. (Wisenberg 2008)

The presence of criminal justice attention certainly must have some type of effect on the way spouses interact with one another. Indeed, white-collar defendants, many of whom come from stable families, will need to address their misdeeds with their loved ones. In *Daddy, Why Are You Going to Jail: A True Story of a Father's Descent into White-Collar Crime and His Amazing Restoration,* Stephen Lawson (1992) described his heart-wrenching memory of how he told his son about his impending departure to prison.

> "Daddy made a . . . mistake in business and broke the law. You know how Daddy has to punish you when you're naughty?"
> He nodded solemnly.
> "Well, it's the same thing when you're grown up—even when you're a daddy. I did some things wrong . . . very wrong . . . so I was sent to court where a judge told me I had to go to a place called a work camp, along with other daddies who have made mistakes. I'll have to stay there a long time."
> "No!" he cried, the tears gushing down his face now. "Don't go Daddy! Tell him I don't want you to go."
> . . . I pulled him close so that I wouldn't have to look into his eyes anymore. The sobs started. (p. 7)

Another white-collar offender told a researcher the following about familial relationship following his conviction:

> My own family disowned me and unfortunately I did not realize my father had died. I am responsible for a lot and not just breaking the law. My wife is supporting the relationship between my son and me . . . the devastation is colossal—I have caused

so much damage. I did not look at the overall picture. I did not realize my wife would get dragged in and that my family will disown me. I will walk out of prison on my own. (Gill 2005, p. 47)

From the spouse's perspective, the wife of a white-collar offender described her reaction to learning that her husband stole money to Slayton (2007):

In the morning, I rang him at his office, from my car to arrange to go to a parents-teacher meeting that night. His secretary said he wasn't at the office, he was at home, and so I called him there. He sounded odd. I asked, "What's the matter?" He wouldn't say. Finally he said: "I'm no longer at McCarthy's. I stole money. We've lost everything." I pulled over got out of the car and vomited. That evening we went to the parents-teacher meeting together and acted as if everything was okay. (p. 43)

In her memoir *The End of Normal*, Stephanie Mack (2011), daughter-in-law of Bernie Madoff, wrote the following about coping with the criminal justice and media attention that was thrust upon her husband Mark and her family: "My anxiety came from never knowing when the next bomb was going to drop. Mark, on the other hand, was convinced that each one would destroy him" (p. 141). Her husband eventually committed suicide, but not before his efforts to begin his own memoir, which included the following:

My own father has stolen my life from me. It's pain that is beyond description. The business that I spent twenty-three years building gone, I am unemployed, my livelihood destroyed, and my family will forever live with the shame of what my father has done. There are so many victims of my father's fraud, so many horrible stories. How do I explain to my children what I do not understand myself? (Mack 2011)

It is, of course, important to note that criminal justice attention and sanctions affect all families, not just white-collar families. However, as Mason (2007) pointed out, the stress experienced by white-collar families "may be more intense as compared to street offenders since working-class families are more likely to have some familiarity with crime and criminal sanctions" (p. 33).

III. Financial Effects

White-collar defendants also experience financial effects as a result of criminal justice attention and criminal justice sanctions. There are three ways that criminal justice experiences result in financial effects for white-collar defendants. First, many white-collar defendants lose their jobs, at least temporarily, as a result of criminal justice attention. Without a job, they lose lucrative salaries and could end up having to sell their home, to take money out of their retirement account, or to declare bankruptcy. Research shows that the financial losses likely vary across types of white-collar defendants. Benson's (1984) study of sentenced white-collar offenders concluded that "the most serious consequences of conviction undoubtedly fall on the licensed professional" (p. 588). The repercussions these professionals face from their professional associations or regulatory bodies could certainly affect the offender's career choice and subsequent income. Benson points out that "Lawyers, in particular, experience severe detrimental changes in their lifestyle" (p. 588).

Paying for high-priced defense attorneys is a second source of financial effects. White-collar defense work is a specialized area of the criminal law and attorneys are paid quite well for their services, especially in comparison to the salaries of criminal law attorneys for conventional offenders. It has been reported that former Goldman Sachs board member Rajat Gupta's defense cost $30 million and Jeff Skilling's cost $70 million (Lattman 2012). While these defendants may have been able to pass their costs along to their companies or insurance policies, the fact remains that many white-collar defendants will have to pay a high price for white-collar defense attorneys.

Financial effects are also experienced when white-collar defendants are fined for their misdeeds. These fines can be quite large, including restitution to pay back the victims and monetary penalties that go to the government. Interestingly, a Government Accountability Office (2005) investigation explored the recoupment of fines in five large white-collar crime cases and found that a relatively small percentage of the fines had been recovered. Among five cases, of the $568 million ordered for restitution, just 7 percent (roughly $40 million) had been collected. The fact that such a small amount of the fines is repaid at least tacitly suggests that the offenders were having problems (whether real or imagined) parting with their money. Or, it is also possible that—given the size of some of the fines levied in white-collar crime cases—the offender never had enough money in the first place to pay the fines. Indeed, larges fines may in some instances be awarded for symbolic reasons (similar to instances when conventional offenders are sentenced to more than 100 years in prison).

IV. Identity Effects

White-collar defendants will also experience identity effects in terms of how they see themselves, their loss of status, and how they present themselves. With regard to how the see themselves, many will grapple with the label of criminal or defendant. Consider the following exchange between a disgraced judge and a federal agent:

BRANNAN: I'm happy to leave it up to the jury about guilt, and I'm happy to leave it up to the judge for sentencing. I just try to do my job professionally and treat everyone with respect, even if they're a dope dealer or even if they are a white-collar criminal.

JACK: Is that what I am, a white-collar criminal?

BRANNAN: Mmm, it's more in what we would call public corruption.

JACK: Yeah, that's me. I'm a corrupt son of a bitch [laughs]. (Joynt 1997, p. 180)

For those who admit their crimes and accept responsibility, their identities change, at least temporarily, from respected employee to criminal.

Identity effects also include the status changes that occur as a result of criminal justice attention. In particular, white-collar defendants go from having power over those with lower statuses to being controlled by those with lower statuses (e.g., criminal justice officials). Consider interactions between police officers and white-collar defendants. Police officers are of a lower social status than many white-collar defendants, yet the legal power they wield gives them authority over white-collar defendants. Police officers typically have less education than white-collar defendants, but this lower education does not lessen their power. White-collar defendants have higher salaries than police officers, but this economic power does little to protect white-collar defendants beyond allowing them to hire high-powered attorneys (Payne 2012). A similar status relationship exists with other officials in the criminal justice process (Benson 1985a). In many ways, one of the effects of criminal justice attention is that white-collar defendants' identities change from being in control to being controlled.

Drawing attention to status differences between criminal justice officials and white-collar defendants, Jordan Belfort (2009), the "Wolf of Wall Street," wrote the following about his interactions with criminal justice official Joel Cohen (e.g., the "Bastard") while he was being interrogated for securities violations:

> At this particular moment, the Bastard was learning forward in his armchair with his bony elbows resting on the desktop. He was staring at me with narrowed eyes, licking his chops inwardly, no doubt. He wore a cheap gray suit, a cheap white dress shirt, a cheap red tie, and a sinister expression . . . He wasn't bad looking, though; he just looked unkempt as if he rolled out of bed and came straight to the office. But that was by design, I figured. Oh yes, the Bastard was trying to make a statement—that now that we were in *his* world, the price of your suit, the reputation of your dry cleaner, and the cash sense of your barber didn't matter a lick. It was the Bastard who had the power, and I was his prisoner—regardless of appearance. (p. 58)

After being convicted and upon his admission to prison, Belfort said that his first thought was "What's with all these mullets?" in reference to the hairstyle of the first two guards he encountered. Like other white-collar defendants, Belfort's identity changed from being the one with "power" to having others of a lower social status gain the power.

Also describing this adjustment, Herb Hoelter, a consultant with the National Center on Institutions and Alternatives, told a reporter the following about Conrad Black's impending prison sentence: "He is in for a tough time . . . one aspect is psychological. You were the CEO and now you're taking orders from a corrections officer who, but for prison, would be a dairy farmer. It's an extreme adjustment" (Bone 2007, p. 11).

With regard to how they present themselves, some white-collar defendants will engage in rituals with criminal justice officials and use denials to deflect guilt. It is well accepted, for example, that white-collar defendants are coached to present themselves in certain ways during the judicial process. As an illustration, consider the following remarks a reporter made about Rod Blagojevich's interactions with the judge at his sentencing hearing: "For sure, his body language, tone and demeanor as he sought mercy from Judge Zagel bore differences from what we've associated with the desperate-to-please politician-turned-celebrity" (Warren 2011, p. 29A).

Many criminologists who study white-collar crime have called attention to the way that white-collar defendants use different types of denials to resist the criminal identity. It has been suggested that many white-collar offenders have the "cultural capital" and the verbal skills to fend off criminal labels (Shover and Hunter, 2010). According to Stadler and Benson (2012), "there is considerable evidence that white-collar criminals are less accepting of the criminal label and stigmatization that typically accompany justice system processing." In effect, defendants use various denials in an effort to maintain their identity. Benson (1985b) used the phrase "denying the guilty mind" to refer to the process white-collar offenders use to avoid defining themselves as criminal. According to one research team, the use of denials "may be an outward manifestation of one's social and personal identity" (Klenowski, Copes, and Mullins 2011, p. 66).

V. Effects from Punishment

White-collar offenders will also experience effects from being sanctioned by the criminal justice system. These effects can be captured by considering the effects of incarceration and the effects of alternative sanctions.

A. Incarcerating White-Collar Defendants

With regard to incarceration, some white-collar offenders do, in fact, end up in prison and it has been suggested that over the past few decades their likelihood of incarceration has risen (Payne 2003). At the federal level, white-collar inmates are frequently sentenced to minimum-security prisons or work camps, which are euphemistically labeled "Club Fed" in reference to their supposedly plush surroundings.

Calling these institutions "clubs or club-like" is a misnomer and misleading, however. During their incarceration, white-collar inmates lose status, privacy, their identities, and their freedom (Payne 2003). Incarceration can be punitive for any type of offender. After all, "offenders have limited rights, they have no autonomy, they are away from their family members, there is nothing to do, and they have concern about their safety" (Payne 2012, p. 376). It has been reported that the federal government's Bureau of Prisons tightened regulations in minimum-security prison camps in response to allegations that white-collar inmates were enjoying their prison stay in club-like environments (Mullins 2007). Themes relevant to white-collar inmates include concerns about danger and the special sensitivity hypothesis.

1. *Danger and White-Collar Inmates*

Typically housed in lower-security prisons, the risk of violence against white-collar inmates is low. To be sure, some white-collar inmates experience harm in prison (Madoff was reportedly beat up in prison; see Payne 2012), and some are sent to prisons that are more violent. Still, for the most part, concerns tend to be exaggerated, but this is not surprising. Describing white-collar inmates' concerns about violence, one author writes, "But camp inmates also can't afford to relax. After all, most of their peers are gutsy streetwise men from hardscrabble backgrounds; these inmates may not be convicted of violent crimes, but that doesn't mean they don't have violent pasts" (Mullins 2007, p. 103).

Here is how two different white-collar inmates described their experiences with danger in their autobiographies:

- "Bizarre experiences and characters awaited me. . . . The second evening in my new home I walked in on a rape when I entered the showers. I exited quickly. I soon learned that no one got underneath his covers in bed without untucking both sides. That way you could escape an attack from either side without delay." (Lawson 1992, p. 148)
- "Prison is in many ways not as bad as one expects, and in some ways it is worse. It was different for me, as a white 58-year-old professional with no prior record . . . . If you follow the rules and hang out with the better people, you get along . . . . It was not, however, a day at the beach. I got punched out a couple of times, just deserts for my smart-ass lawyer's mouth directed at the wrong persons. I have a nice scar over my left eye and a permanent lump above my lip as badges of my prison experience." (Christensen 2005, p. viii)

Also summarizing the concerns about danger, Ron Cohen—a prison consultant who did time for mail fraud, theft, and money laundering—told a reporter, "and the biggest difference about being in jail is that being in jail is frightening. I don't mean physically frightening but emotionally, mentally, you are scared to a degree that on the outside, coming from the background that white-collar criminals come from, you will never have experienced before" (Doran 2002, p. 58).

Compared to conventional offenders, no research suggests that they have higher rates of violence while incarcerated. To some white-collar offenders, what appears to "hurt" the most is the boredom they experience while incarcerated. In fact, boredom appears to be one of the major challenges white-collar inmates confront. Boredom has been cited as among "the worst part of the white-collar inmate's incarceration experience" (Payne 2003, p. 105). According to one author, "boredom . . . can be a powerful enemy, especially for white-collar inmates who once held positions of tremendous power and responsibility" (Mullins 2007, p. 104).

2. *Special Sensitivity to Prison and White-Collar Inmates*

The special sensitivity hypothesis suggests that white-collar inmates experience incarceration as more punitive, or differently, than other offenders. Studies have called the hypothesis into questions. Interviews with thirteen white-collar inmates by Benson and Cullen (1988) revealed that the offenders had few problems adjusting to incarceration. The authors concluded, "Like ordinary offenders, they appeared to undergo a process of adjustment and reconciliation once the shock of confinement passed" (p. 209). In fact, according to Benson and Cullen, the negative consequences of anticipating the incarceration experience far outweigh the actual experiences and white-collar inmates are able to "reject the inmate culture" because of their positive perceptions of themselves, their differences from other inmates, their higher education level, and their ability to abide by prison rules.

A more recent examination of the special sensitivity hypothesis found that white-collar offenders experienced few problems adjusting to prison in some ways (Stadler, Benson, and Cullen 2012). Using a larger sample and conducting quantitative analyses, this latter study found that white-collar offenders were more likely to have friends in prison and less likely to experience general difficulties. Stadler and his co-authors concluded, "White-collar offenders appear to do fairly well in prison, or at least no worse than other types of offenders" (p. 18). Like Benson and Cullen's research, Stadler et al. suggested that the characteristics of white-collar offenders "may mitigate the negative effects of imprisonment" (p. 18). They pointed out that white-collar offenders tend to be older, and older inmates appeared to adjust better.

B. The Effects of Alternative Sanctions on White-Collar Offenders

Alternative sanctions also have an assortment of effects for white-collar offenders. Research on white-collar probationers show that the types of services and practices done with traditional probationers (e.g., monitoring and control) may not fit their needs (Mason 2007). A potential result is that offenders are forced to engage in routines that have little punitive, rehabilitative, or restorative value. By emphasizing monitoring and control over a group of offenders that needs very little monitoring or control, Mason suggested that the strategies "have negative consequences in that offenders lose respect for the legitimacy of the law and the criminal justice system and deny their own criminality" (Mason 2007, p. 28).

Some alternative sanctions, such as house arrest and community service, might be especially appropriate for some white-collar offenders (Payne 2012). These sanctions are experienced as punitive but have positive benefits in that they promote reintegration and, in the case of community service, help to meet community needs. Doctors have been ordered to provide free medical treatment, accountants have been ordered to perform public awareness campaigns, and other white-collar offenders have been ordered to help the homeless (Payne 2012). Unlike traditional probation strategies, the community service sanction involves the offender doing something that is controlling but ultimately beneficial for the offender and the community.

A degree of shame comes along with all types of alternative sanctions. This shame should not be seen as necessarily bad; in fact, strategies promoting reintegrative shaming may be especially appropriate for white-collar offenders, many of whom will feel embarrassment as a result of criminal justice attention (Benson 1990).

VI. Overcoming Effects of Criminal Justice Attention and Sanctions

The effects of the criminal justice process do not end when white-collar defendants depart from the justice process. Indeed, the justice system is designed to have lasting effects, particularly with the aim of deterring future misconduct. Describing his concerns about his life after incarceration, a lawyer who pled guilty to securities fraud after turning himself in wrote the following:

> What frightens me most is what awaits me upon my release. I am painfully aware that the end of my prison sentence will not mark the end of the consequences of my crime. I will be without a home or career to return to. I will confront decimated personal and business relationships. Then I'll face three years of supervised release, which will be followed by the lifelong label of convicted felon. That label carries with it limited employment and housing opportunities, and makes the prompt repayment of restitution nearly impossible. But I know that I must be held accountable, and I commit to spending the rest of my life trying to make the victims of my crime whole and doing all that I can to set things straight. This is no small undertaking, but I am absolutely dedicated to doing the very best that I can. (Tennies, n.d.)

One area that distinguishes white-collar offenders from traditional offenders is related to their employment opportunities. White-collar offenders, in comparison to traditional offenders, tend to have stronger work ethics that they can use to help them move on from the criminal conviction (see Benson 1985a), though obviously many will face obstacles in securing postconviction employment. As noted above, however, many white-collar offenders will have to seek new careers or purposes because they are often barred from their former careers. Businesses/livelihoods that some former white-collar offenders have sought include policy consulting, law-enforcement/security consulting, prison consulting, and speaking/writing careers.

Using their past experiences as a guide, some former convicted white-collar professionals have entered the policy consulting arena. Attorney Michael Sweig founded the Institute for People with Criminal Records after serving four years of probation for a trust-account violation. Sweig encountered numerous difficulties in his effort to find employment, which led him to the career path of lobbyist and public policy consultant. He told a reporter, "There are roadblocks everywhere . . . . But you must be the one who outs yourself. The worst thing you can do is try to hide it. Once you're rehabilitated, the issue should be what have you done since you got in trouble, not what did you do to get in trouble" (Trice 2010). To promote awareness about the issues facing those with criminal records, he created the institute, which advocates for those with a criminal record. On his website, Sweig (n.d.) wrote, "My own path as a felon and citizen has led me to conclude that education, prolonged and organized civic engagement, and aggressive use of the First Amendment is a key tool for people with criminal records to effect social change."

Past white-collar inmates have also served as law-enforcement/security consultants. Sam E. Antar, the former chief of Crazy Eddie Inc., admitted to his own share of misdeeds while providing the government information to help in its case against Crazy Eddie. He now works as a consultant informing law-enforcement agencies how to detect white-collar crime. He has been quoted saying, "the plain truth is that the accounting profession today, whether in the role of external auditor or individual auditor and accountant, does not have the sufficient education, training, skills, and experiences necessary to match wits with criminals of my former caliber" (Arvedlund 2012).

Barry Minkow, a former executive of a carpet-cleaning company who was sentenced to prison for security fraud in the late 1980s, "helped to found the Fraud Discovery Institute, a private online learning center that wants to help companies like banks and accounting firms detect . . . corporate fraud" (Dunn 2002, p. 2). In a twist, however, Minkow was recently sentenced back to prison for conspiracy involving his actions in spreading falsehoods about a builder in order to make the builder's stock prices fall (Reckard 2011).

Some former white-collar defendants have embarked upon careers that can be referred to as prison consulting: they consult and advise future white-collar inmates how to adjust to the prison experience. Jim Tayoun, who was a Philadelphia city council member before being sentenced to forty months for a corruption conviction, may have been one of the earliest white-collar inmates turned prison consultant. He developed a 900 number for white-collar offenders on their way to prison. At the time, calls cost between five and eight dollars, and callers were given a general introduction to prison (Timko 1995).

The white-collar inmate prison consulting business has grown significantly since then and is now a competitive consulting area. *New York Times* reporter Matt Richtel (2012) identified three dozen prison consulting groups with names such as "Executive Prison Coaching," "The Real Prison Consultant," and "The Prison Doctor." Richtel interviewed a former white-collar inmate who—in his early sixties—decided that after his prison sentence his best chance of earning a living would be as a prison consultant. The soon-to-be consultant—Michael Frantz—subsequently wrote a book titled *Jail Time: What You Need to Know . . . Before You Go to Federal Prison* (2009) and now runs Jail Time Consulting. According to the company's website, among other services, Jail Time Consulting provides information about the prison experience, how to increase the likelihood of being admitted to various programs, how to request furloughs, and what family members can expect.

Prison consultant Larry Levine runs Wall Street Prison Consultants. One of Levine's former clients offered the following support for Levine's services in an interview with a Forbes.com reporter: "Lawyers aren't worth a dime when it comes to this" (Feinberg 2009). Levine said he provided consulting services to forty clients in 2008 and made more than six figures in his business (Anton 2009). When clients ask if they can trust him, he responds, "You don't. . . . I can steal your money. But all you have to do is tell my probation officer. Think I'm going back to prison for a couple thousand dollars? That's your insurance policy" (Anton 2009). His website includes links to judicial ratings and inmate magazines. He offers consulting in the areas of medical care, surviving prison, accessing drug programs, determining custody levels, and related topics. One interesting irony that arises is that because inmates get time off for participating in certain drug abuse programs, Levine recommends future inmates show up drunk on the first day of prison because, as he was quoted by a reporter, "BOP is looking for reasons to put people in the [drug abuse] program" (Falkenberg 2008).

By all accounts, the white-collar prison consulting business is booming. There are at least four reasons why the business is doing so well. First, many of the businesses were developed and are run by former executives who have the business acumen to make the industry thrive. Second, because more white-collar offenders are being sentenced to prison, there are more possible clients. Third, many white-collar offenders who anticipate that prison awaits them after conviction have the resources to hire consultants to help alleviate their concerns. Fourth, the effects of criminal justice attention—depression, anxiety, fear of the unknown, and so on—are such that the prison consulting business fills a very real need for future white-collar inmates, and turning to those who have had similar experiences makes perfect sense. Describing his entrance into the career, white-collar prison consultant Ron Cohen said, "I had to draw on my experience, that's all I have . . . . I am banned from working in the securities industry. The only other thing I was good at was spending time in jail" (Doran 2002).

A handful of former white-collar inmates have developed writing/speaking careers. In terms of writing, at least a few former white-collar offenders have authored books about their experiences and some publish Internet blogs. Others focus on providing lectures and speeches about their experiences. Gary Zeune runs a speaker agency called The Pros and The Cons, which features former white-collar criminals who are "paid anywhere from $1,000 to $3,000 an appearance" (Stewart 2004, p. 15).

VII. CONCLUSION

White-collar defendants experience a range of effects from criminal justice attention and sanctions. These effects have been discussed separately, but it is important to recognize that they likely occur simultaneously for white-collar defendants throughout the justice process. Eventually, these effects will begin to play smaller roles in offenders' lives. Here is how one white-collar defendant described his experience with the criminal justice system:

> In 2008, I began serving an 18-month sentence following my conviction for violating securities laws. As I wrote in my first book *Lessons from Prison*, the real punishment wasn't imprisonment but the years preceding it, when authorities notified me with news that I was facing both civil and criminal charges. Fear, shame, and humiliation overwhelmed and owned me. Bouts of nausea and self-loathing came next, with clouds of depression hanging over me. Legal costs rose well into the six figures. Surrendering to serve time in federal prison, ironically, began the healing. While serving my term, I exercised extensively, recalibrated my values, and emerged with a commitment to share what I learned from the experience. (Paperny 2011)

Paperny's comments show the range of emotions experienced by white-collar offenders. As well, his recognition that it was the years before his imprisonment that was his "real punishment" reminds us once again of the title of Malcolm Feeley's classic book: *The Process Is the Punishment*. As noted in the introduction, Feeley speculated that those not accustomed to the justice process would experience it differently than those who are more accustomed to the process.

A number of questions should be addressed by future white-collar crime researchers. Do the effects of criminal justice attention on white-collar offenders vary across the criminal justice process? Do these effects vary by demographic characteristics of offenders, including gender, race, community type, age, and so on? Do different types of white-collar offenders experience different effects as a result of criminal justice attention and sanctions? Do these effects tend to have a deterrent effect or could they lead to future offending? These questions and many others should be addressed in future studies.

REFERENCES

Anton, Mike. 2009. "About to Do Time?" *Los Angeles Times* (February 27). Available at http://articles.latimes.com/2009/feb/27/local/me-prison-consultant27/2

Arvedlund, Erin E. 2012. "Crazy Eddie's Onetime CFO Offers Tips on Spotting Financial Fraud." *Philadelphia Inquirer* (May 23). Available at http://articles.philly.com/2012-05-23/business/31813311_1_eddie-antar-fraud-conference-white-collar-crime

Belfort, Jordan. 2009. *Catching the Wolf of Wall Street: More Incredible True Stories of Fortunes, Schemes, Parties, and Prisons*. New York: Bantam.

Benson, Michael K. 1984. "The Fall from Grace: Loss of Occupational Status as a Consequence of Conviction for a White-Collar Crime." *Criminology* 22: 573–93.

Benson, Michael L. 1985a. "Research Note: White-Collar Offenders under Community Supervision." *Justice Quarterly* 2: 429–38.

Benson, Michael L. 1985b. "Denying the Guilty Mind: Accounting for Involvement in a White-Collar Crime." *Criminology* 23: 583–607.

Benson, Michael L. 1990. "Emotions and Adjudication: Status Degradation among White-Collar Criminals." *Justice Quarterly* 7: 515–28.

Benson, Michael L., and Francis T. Cullen. 1988. "The Special Sensitivity of White-Collar Offenders to Prison: A Critique and Research Agenda." *Journal of Criminal Justice* 15: 207–15.

Bone, James. 2007. "Black's High Life Heading for a Fall." *The Times* (December 11), p. 4.

Cruver, Brian. 2002. *Anatomy of Greed: Telling the Unshredded Truth from Inside Enron*. New York: Basic Books.

Dhami, Mandeep. 2007. "White-Collar Prisoners' Perceptions of Audience Reaction." *Deviant Behavior* 28: 57–77.

Doran, James. 2002. "Voice of Experience for the Executive Facing Jail." *The Times* (December 7), p. 58.

Dunn, Julie. 2002. "Update/Barry Minkow: The Knowledge of the Perpetrator." *New York Times* (March 17). Available at http://www.nytimes.com/2002/03/17/business/update-barry-minkow-the-knowledge-of-the-perpetrator.html

Falkenberg, Kai. 2008. "Time Off For Good Behavior." *Forbes* (December 20). Available at http://www.forbes.com/2008/12/20/prison-crime-waksal-biz-beltway-cz_kf_1222prison.html

Feeley, Malcolm M. 1992. *The Process Is the Punishment: Handling Cases in a Lower Criminal Court*. New York: Russell Sage.

Feinberg, Lexi. 2009. "There's Something about Larry." *Forbes* (April 16). Available at http://www.forbes.com/2009/04/16/levine-madoff-prison-markets-faces-law.html

Fogal, Marcy. 1992. "Investigating Suicide." *Forum on Corrections Research* 4: 8–9.

Frantz, Michael. 2009. *Jail Time: What You Need to Know . . . Before You Go to Federal Prison*. Indianapolis, IN: Dog Ear Publishing.

Gill, Martin. 2005. *Learning from Fraudsters: Reinforcing the Message*. Leicester, UK: Protiviti.

Joynt, Jack. 1997. *Jack's Law: The Rise and Fall of Renegade Judge Jack Montgomery*. Birmingham, AL: Crane Hill.

Hagglund, Ryan. 2012. "Constitutional Protections against the Harms to Suspects in Custody Stemming from Perp Walks." *Mississippi Law Journal* 7: 1757–908.

Klenowski, Paul, Heith Copes, and Christopher Mullins. 2011. "Gender, Identity, and Accounts: How White-Collar Offenders Do Gender When Making Sense of Their Crimes." *Justice Quarterly* 28: 46–69.

Lattman, Peter. 2012. "Verdict Has Upside for Goldman." *International Herald Tribune* (June 20). Available at http://ihtbd.com/ihtuser/print/old%20THT/July-2012/20-07-2012/April-12/a2006x22xCQxxxxxx.pdf

Lawson, Stephen P. 1992. *Daddy, Why Are You Going to Jail? A True Descent into White-Collar Crime and His Amazing Restoration*. Wheaton, IL: Harold Shaw.

Mack, Stephanie Madoff. 2011. *The End of Normal: My Life as a Madoff*. New York: Penguin.

Mason, Karen A. 2007. "Punishment and Paperwork: White-Collar Offenders under Community Supervision." *American Journal of Criminal Justice* 31: 23–36.

McFarland, Janet. 2004. "When Executives Have to Walk the Walk." *Globe and Mail* (February 20), p. B7.

Mitchelson, William R. and Mark T. Calloway. 2006. "How to Avoid Letting a Perp Walk Turn into a Parade." *National Law Journal* 21: S1. Available at http://www.alston.com/files/Publication/e8d8c258-55cb-4ce4-8c23-327d6af83d54/Presentation/PublicationAttachment/3cab758a-5dee-45f5-a7f0-ba69ea42cab6/mitchelson%20calloway%20law%20com.pdf

Mullins, Luke. 2007. "Enter a Hellish Place." *The American* 98: 115.

Paperny, Justin. 2011. "White-Collar Crime Sentences Longer than Ones for Murder." *Forbes* (August 29). Available at http://www.forbes.com/sites/kellypope/2011/08/29/white-collar-crime-sentences-longer-than-ones-for-murder-by-guest-blogger-justin-paperny/

Payne, Brian K. 2003. *Incarcerating White-Collar Offenders: The Prison Experience and Beyond.* Springfield, IL: Charles Thomas.

Payne, Brian K. 2012. *White-Collar Crime: The Essentials.* Newbury Park, CA: Sage.

Reckard, E. Scott. 2011. "Barry Minkow Is Sentenced to Five Years in Prison." *Los Angeles Times* (July 22).

Richtel, Matt. 2012. "Making Crime Pay." *New York Times* (April 7). Available at http://www.nytimes.com/2012/04/08/fashion/prison-consulting-draws-new-crop-of-ex-cons.html?_r=0

Schwartz, Richard D., and Jerome H. Skolnick. 1962. "Two Studies of Legal Stigma." *Social Problems* 10: 132–42.

Shover, Neal, and Andrew Hochstetler. 2006. *Choosing White-Collar Crime.* Cambridge, UK: Cambridge University Press.

Shover, Neal, and Ben Hunter. 2010. "Blue-Collar, White-Collar: Crimes and Mistakes." In *Offenders on Offending: Learning about Crime from Criminals,* pp. 205–27, edited by Wim Bernasco. Cullompton, UK: Willan.

Slayton, Philip. 2007. *Lawyers Gone Bad: Money, Sex, and Madness in Canada's Legal Profession.* Toronto: Viking Canada.

Stadler, William A., and Michael L. Benson. 2012. "Revisiting the Guilty Mind: The Neutralization of White-Collar Crime." *Criminal Justice Review* 37: 494–511.

Stadler, William A., Michael L. Benson, and Francis T. Cullen. 2012. "Revisiting the Special Sensitivity Hypothesis: The Prison Experience of White-Collar Inmates." *Justice Quarterly* 30: 1090–114.

Stewart, Christopher. 2004. "White-Collar Convicts Hit the Lecture Circuit." *New York Times* (June 2), p. 15.

Sweig, Michael. n.d. "Michael Sweig, JD." Available at http://michaelsweig.wordpress.com/about/

Tennies, Steven. n.d. "Steven Tennies, JD." Available at http://michaelsweig.wordpress.com/steven-tennies/

Timko, Steve. 1995. "Fallen Angel." *USA Today* (April 26), p. 1A.

Trice, Dawn Turner. 2010. "From Practicing Law to Changing It: Former Attorney and Convicted Felon Works to Give Ex-offenders a Second Chance." *New Chicago Tribune* (August 1). Available at http://articles.chicagotribune.com/2010-08-01/news/ct-met-trice-0802-20100801_1_law-license-law-firm-ex-offenders

U.S. Government Accounting Office. 2005. *Criminal Debt.* Washington, D.C.: U.S. Government Printing Office.

Warren, James. 2011. "What Blagojevich's Sentence Says about Corruption and Greed." *New York Times* (December 9). Available at http://www.nytimes.com/2011/12/09/us/what-blagojevichs-sentence-says-about-corruption-and-greed.html

Wisenberg, Solomon. 2008. "White-Collar Crime: Crash Course." FindLaw for Legal Professionals. Available at http://corporate.findlaw.com/litigation-disputes/white-collar-crime-the-crash-course.html

···

CHAPTER 30

WHITE-COLLAR CRIME AND PERCEPTUAL DETERRENCE

···

RAY PATERNOSTER AND STEPHEN G. TIBBETTS

We don't see very far in the future, we are very focused on one idea at a time, one problem at a time, and all these are incompatible with rationality as economic theory assumes it.

Daniel Kahneman

Behind every great fortune is a crime.

Honoré de Balzac

WHEN most Americans are asked to think about crime, they think of burglaries, robberies, car theft, rape, murder, and other offenses that can victimize them and would require them to call the police. While these offenses, referred to often as "street crime," are serious events and cost the public billions of dollars and untold suffering, they do not represent the total crime picture. Millions of Americans every year are the victims of other kinds of crime, but these crimes are not caused by shady people lurking in the shadows, strung out on drugs, or armed with weapons. No, millions of Americans are victimized by people in suits, with college educations, who are armed with nothing more threatening than a pen and briefcase. These crimes are often referred to as "suite crimes" because they are hatched or occur in business suites, by businesspeople; they are crimes, like street crimes, that are intended to benefit the perpetrator. Suite crimes, or white-collar crimes, are crimes committed by bankers, business executives, accountants, lawyers, manufacturers, and other high-status, well-paid people. If most Americans had been unaware of the potential costs and damage that white-collar crime can unleash, they were no longer so naïve after the banking crisis and the near collapse of the U.S. and global economic system in 2008 brought on by corporate greed; chicanery; and criminal, civil, and regulatory violations. It is hard to depict precisely the damage that can be done by white-collar as opposed to street crime, but the American folksinger Woody Guthrie captured some of it in a song he wrote about the notorious Depression-era gangster "Pretty Boy" Floyd:

Yes, as through this world I've wandered
I've seen lots of funny men;
Some will rob you with a six-gun,
And some with a fountain pen.
And as through your life you travel,
Yes, as through your life you roam,
You won't never see an outlaw
Drive a family from their home.

In this song, Guthrie eloquently pointed out that there is a great deal of other crime committed by "respectable people" that is equally and arguably more damaging to people's spirits and lives than traditional street crime. Guthrie's words should ring particularly loudly today in view of the "robo-signing" of titles, illegal foreclosures, and other acts of dubious legality and morality perpetrated by some of this nation's banks during our current fiscal crisis.

In this chapter, we are going to examine the extent to which white-collar crime can be considered a "rational" crime that can be influenced by the threat of criminal, regulatory, or administrative sanctions. In section I, we present arguments as to why white-collar crime involves rational decision making and on what bases white-collar offenders are rational. We will also briefly examine the alternative that, like most criminal acts, white-collar crime is impulsive behavior that involves little foresight and contemplation. We find this latter view of white-collar crime unconvincing. In section II, we discuss some of the empirical studies that have investigated whether white-collar offenders behave in a rational way by seeing to what extent perceptions of sanctions, both formal or official and informal, affect their judgment and decision making. We find that white-collar offenders are not strongly affected by the threat of formal sanctions but are affected by the possibility of the financial and other benefits of offending, the possibility of social censure from others, and the extent to which criminal acts are morally condemned either personally or within the culture of the firm. We conclude with a discussion in section III of where we think white-collar crime research should go in the future. In the end, what we will have learned about white-collar crime is the following:

- The decision to commit white-collar crime is rational;
- Decisions to commit white-collar crime are affected by the perceived costs and benefits of the act, both to the firm and to the individual;
- Moral inhibitions that white-collar crime is wrong are among the most effective deterrents;
- The moral culture of the firm matters for white-collar crime;
- Informal censure and loss of one's own reputation or the reputation of the firm is more important in inhibiting white-collar crime than is the threat of formal sanctions; and
- The factors that affect white-collar crime are very similar to those that have been shown to affect street offenders.

I. Theoretical Speculations About White-Collar Crime

A. White-Collar Crime as Rational Choice

One of the most prominent theories in criminology today is rational choice theory, the essence of which is the assumption that would-be criminal offenders are at least minimally rational (Cherniak 1986) and, as such, they respond to the consequences of their actions. The latter point means simply that when making a decision as to whether or not to commit a criminal offense, a would-be offender takes into account the anticipated costs and benefits of the offense and tends to (probabilistically) make that decision that nets him or her more gains than losses in comparison with the anticipated gains and losses from noncriminal conduct. So, for example, if a person anticipates more gains than losses from selling fraudulent mortgage bundles in comparison with the expected utility of clearly informing prospective buyers of the financial risks, he or she will sell the fraudulent mortgages. This view of offender decision making does not have to assume that people collect all the available information before making a decision (after all, information collection is itself a cost), nor that they are astute Bayesians in updating and weighing the information before them, nor that they always make optimal decisions (optimal in the sense that they make the "best," highest net utility decision). The rational choice view is simply that people's actions are motivated by self-interest, that they have sufficient foresight to think about the consequences of their decisions and actions, that they are utility seekers (not necessarily maximizers) who weigh, however clumsily and ineptly, the costs and benefits of alternative courses of actions, and that they opt for the alternative that they *perceive* to have more rewards than costs.

Given these assumptions about the nature of human beings, criminal offenders or would-be criminal offenders included, the question we address in this chapter is whether and to what extent white-collar offenders behave in a rational manner. More simply, the question for us is whether white-collar offenders are affected by the perceived costs and benefits of their actions. We think of white-collar offenders in the way that Sutherland (1983, p. 7) did as "crime committed by a person of respectability and high social status in the course of his occupation." White-collar crime, then, is committed by *individuals* and for us is distinguished from corporate crime, which is crime committed by corporations at the aggregate level. So, while corporate-crime researchers can examine whether or not things like changes in the severity of regulatory law or sanctions imposed on corporations have any effect on compliance by the firm (see Block, Nold, and Sidak 1981; Simpson and Koper 1992; Smith and Vaughan 1986, for an example), here we will restrict our attention to individual-level decision makers.[1] Although we recognize that corporate decisions are frequently made by groups (e.g., a committee on compensation), we strongly affirm that the actors in these groups are guided by the anticipated costs and benefits of their group action and would, nevertheless, be explainable by rational choice considerations. While the group and corporate organizational context of the decision would certainly be important considerations, decisions to circumvent the law or regulatory rules would be affected by the anticipated utility of the decision, whether that decision is made as a result of the contemplation of an individual or a committee.

B. Looking at White-Collar Crime as Rational Decision Making

It may seem that white-collar crime would be particularly fertile, and perhaps too obvious, territory to examine a rational choice theory of criminal offending that puts a great deal of emphasis on sanction threats and the capacity of would-be offenders to consider them in their decision making. After all, white-collar workers could not have gotten their positions as accountants, managers, and executives, for example, without a more-than-average ability to act with rational deliberation. White-collar jobs generally require a college education, which in turns means that its incumbent has some capacity to defer gratification and persevere in a line of action over a long period of time. There is another reason why we might expect white-collar offenders to be particularly sensitive to sanction threats: it has been argued (Williams and Hawkins 1986) that formal sanctions (arrest, conviction, imprisonment) are most effective when they trigger informal costs like a loss of reputation or social censure, and Nagin and Paternoster (1994) found that formal sanctions have a stronger deterrent effect on those who have more investments in a prosocial life. Since white-collar offenders generally have made considerable investments in a prosocial life (including possessions, family, and social networks), we could reasonably presume that formal sanctions not only bring with them direct costs but put these conventional investments in jeopardy as indirect costs. Finally, white-collar offenders are likely on average older than regular criminal offenders ("street" offenders), whose crime peak is around late adolescence. Recent research has shown that the adolescent brain is not fully mature, particularly with respect to executive functioning and impulse control (Steinberg 2005; Casey, Jones, and Hare 2008). Older persons might, therefore, have a greater capacity for impulse control or stronger "willpower" (Ainslie 2001).

In spite of this, there is some debate within the criminological community as to the presumption that white-collar criminals can be thought of as rational decision makers who would be more sensitive than other types of criminal offenders to the costs and benefits of crime. The source for this view is Gottfredson and Hirschi (1990, p. 199), who have forcefully and eloquently argued that white-collar crimes share many of the same characteristics as other kinds of crime, the most important being that they require little skill and even less effort and forethought:

> One of the sources of difficulty for the white-collar-crime research tradition is that it fundamentally misconstrues the nature of crime. Starting with an image of crime as a complex, highly sophisticated, high-stake enterprise drive by large potential profits within the context of ambiguous moral codes, it is little wonder that the white-collar crime tradition came up with a white-collar offender distinct from ordinary offenders.

To Gottfredson and Hirschi, white-collar offenders are no different than other offenders in that they lack self-control, an important component of which is the capacity to contemplate and be affected by the short- and long-term consequences of their behavior (Hirschi 2004). Gottfredson and Hirschi's offender with low self-control, then, lacks foresight and, it is argued, thus cannot be moved rationally by sanctions or sanction threats. In part, it is easy to see why they would take this view of white-collar crime since the exemplar of it they chose was embezzlement, the vast majority of which we would agree involves little planning, modest forethought, and usually only negligible gain.[2] When most white-collar (or corporate) crime scholars think about what they want to explain, however, they think of a great many other offenses besides embezzlement, such as securities fraud, insider trading, price fixing, and antitrust violations—offenses that in general require more rational contemplation to execute successfully (Paternoster and Simpson 1996; Reed and Yeager 1996; Yeager and Reed 1998; Benson and Simpson 2009). We, therefore, disagree with the view that white-collar offenders either are not in general rational or cannot be deterred by sanction threats.

Our view (and one that would not be disputed by Gottfredson and Hirschi) is that the capacity to think rationally, to consider the short- and long-term consequences of one's actions, and therefore to exercise self-control, willpower, or impulse control lies along a continuum. We think that the human condition is to be able to think rationally and with foresight, and therefore that we all possess some element of rational thinking and deliberation, although some may possess more of it than others. The implication of this view is that all persons have the capacity to be deterred because they are thoughtful and able to accurately contemplate the subsequent costs and benefits of their actions. This means that some white-collar offenses—such as embezzlement, resetting car odometers, and pilfering from work supplies—are committed by persons with low self-control, but others—such as antitrust violations, violation of environmental regulations, and securities fraud—are committed by persons with higher self-control and enhanced rational capacity. Our prediction, therefore, would be that all criminal offenders can be deterred sometimes and to some degree because they all possess the power to reason and that, if we were to go looking for places where deterrence might be operative, it would be among white-collar offenses.[3] We move now to an examination of the existing literature as to whether white-collar offenders are deterred by the threat of sanctions, either formal or informal. We reiterate that our interest is in white-collar crime decision making, so we restrict our attention to studies at the individual level.

II. Empirical Studies of Perceived Sanction Threats and White-Collar Crime

A. General Studies of White-Collar Crime

When conducting a comprehensive review of the white-collar crime literature, one is immediately struck by the fact that, while there are literally scores of studies (both quantitative and ethnographic) relating perceptions of sanction threats to street crime and even more trivial kinds of antisocial acts, there is a dearth of literature in criminology with respect to white-collar offending,[4] and as a result "much less is known about white-collar decision making" (Shover and Hochstetler 2006, p. 112).[5] There have been, however, a few studies that have investigated white-collar crime from a deterrence/rational choice perspective.

Braithwaite and Makkai (1991) examined the effect of the threat of formal sanctions on nursing home managers' regulatory compliance. They found that of several measures of perceived sanction threats, only one (the probability of state detection) was related to compliance with nursing home regulations. In contrast with our expectation expressed above about the likely expectation of strong deterrent effects within the realm of white-collar crime, they concluded that there is a "stark failure of deterrence to explain compliance with regulatory law" (p. 29). In a second study with the same group of nursing home administrators, Makkai and Braithwaite (1994) reported that the probability of state detection was the only measure of sanction threat (of several) that had the expected deterrent effect on regulatory compliance. Even the risk of state detection did not uniformly inhibit rule breaking: a deterrent effect was observed only for those nursing home managers who were low on emotionality.

Simpson and Elis (1995) administered a factorial survey to first-year and second-year MBA students at three graduate schools and to a group of business executives attending an executive MBA program. The four offenses included in the hypothetical scenarios were price fixing, bribery, violation of environmental standards, and manipulation of sales data. They found that the respondents were less likely to report that they would commit the act if they had moral scruples about the misbehavior and if they believed that the firm's reputation would be damaged if they were to commit the act. Intentions to offend were higher when the scenario figure was ordered to commit the offense and if the firm was experiencing heavy competition from foreign companies. Consistent with deterrence/rational choice theory, the certainty that the individual would lose his or her job or have trouble finding a new job was inversely related to intentions to offend, as was the certainty of informal censure from friends, family, and business associates. In addition to a personal sense of morality, intentions to violate the law were reduced for those who thought the illegal act would tarnish the reputation of the firm.

In a follow-up study with the same data, Simpson and Piquero (2002) tested a theory of white-collar offending that combined organizational theory with a theory of stable individual differences in criminal propensity (self-control; Gottfredson and Hirschi 1990). They found that an individual trait of high propensity was unrelated to intentions to commit the four business crimes listed above, but intentions to offend were related to the perceived cost to the firm, the cultural climate within the firm, and a belief that the act would be a way to change an existing, disapproved law. The structural position of the manager within the firm (upper-level manager vs. middle- or lower-level manager) was not related to the reported intention to commit an illegal act. Several cost–benefit factors at the individual level also affected the likelihood of offending. Intentions to offend were significantly lower if there was a whistleblower hotline for employees to report misconduct, if an employee was recently fired for a similar act, if the person thought he or she might jeopardize any future job opportunity by the current illegal act, and if he or she had personal moral scruples against the act. Although Simpson and Piquero anchored their findings in organizational and individual trait theories of offending, it is clear that they are also harmonious with a rational choice perspective.

Although there had been several good studies of deterrence and white-collar crime, there was no formal articulation of a rational choice theory of white-collar crime that could provide guidance for research until Paternoster and Simpson (1996) outlined the principles of a rational choice theory of white-collar crime and an empirical test of that theory.[6] In brief, they constructed a subjective expected utility theory that is premised on two assumptions:[7] (1) decisions to offend are made on a balancing of both the costs and benefits of offending and (2) what is important are the decision maker's perceived or subjective expectations of reward and cost. According to this model, the rational individual will offend if $U(\text{Benefits}) > pU(\text{Costs})$, where $U(\cdot)$ represents a utility function for the benefits and costs, respectively, of the crime, and p is the perceived certainty of detection. The cost function would include the threat of formal and informal sanctions as perceived by the decision maker, and the benefits would include things like financial gain, promotions, and social approval.[8] With a sample of MBA students and business executives responding to four hypothetical scenarios (price fixing, bribery, manipulation of sales data, and environmental violations), they found that intentions to commit these white-collar offenses were influenced by the perceived costs and benefits. For example, intentions to offend were higher when committing the act was thought to bring with it career advancement and when it was intrinsically pleasurable, and intentions to offend were less likely when the possible formal and informal sanctions were likely. Net of these factors, the businesspeople in this study were less likely to offend when it was thought to violate their own moral code, and interestingly, Paternoster and Simpson also found that formal sanctions directed at the firm were effective in deterring criminal conduct only when it was perceived to directly affect the perceived costs for the individual. Indicative of the restraining power of morality, when moral inhibitions were high, sanction threats, either formal or informal, were unrelated to intentions to commit white-collar crimes. Finally, a corporate climate that was perceived to encourage or at least permit offending increased the reported intention to offend.

Subsequent to this, Simpson (2002) conducted a separate study of white-collar offending with a sample of middle- and upper-level executives employed by a Fortune 500 manufacturing company. Subjects responded to three hypothetical scenarios involving a criminal act: violation of environmental standards, bribery, and price fixing. Several interesting things came from this research. First, about half of the respondents said there was a non-zero chance that they would commit the offense described in the scenarios. The respondents perceived a higher risk of the certainty and severity of punishment (criminal, civil, and regulatory) for the company than for individual managers but believed that any sanctions imposed would be more costly for individuals rather than firms. Finally, individual respondents were sensitive to the costs and penalties for offending regarding their self-reported intentions to offend. For instance, if the respondents knew that a manager of the firm had been reprimanded or fired for his offending, they were substantially less likely to state that they would commit the offense. Notably, the presence of ethics training in the firm had no effect on intentions to offend. With respect to individual factors, offending was seen to be more likely if the individual stood to gain personally from the offense and less likely if the conduct was perceived to be against his or her personal moral code, if it would bring social censure, or if it would be seen to tarnish the reputation of the firm. The threat of formal sanctions, however, had absolutely no effect on these managers' intentions to commit crime. Moreover, most of the findings reported above were true both for the subset of managers who had weak moral constraints against offending and those who had strong inhibitions. This study, then, did not corroborate previous findings in the deterrence literature (both for white-collar and street crimes) that sanction threats are not salient when moral inhibitions are strong. However, recall that moral sentiments were independently related to intentions to offend. Nevertheless, the fact that the threat of formal sanctions was unrelated to intentions to offend cannot be good news for those pressing for greater enforcement of regulatory laws. Finally, a prominent finding in Simpson's study is that managers were particularly likely to offend when there was a direct benefit for them to do so, either in terms of a personal "sneaky thrill" (Katz 1988) of offending that has usually been associated with the pleasure of street crime or of the prospect of career advancement.

A relatively recent review of the rational choice perspective in explaining white-collar crime was presented by Shover and Hochstetler (2006). They placed much emphasis on the benefits of such crimes, which they refer to as the "lure," which cannot be argued against in terms of most corporate criminal decision making. After all, there is much to be gained, a relatively low risk of being caught, and even less likelihood of actually being punished—especially as an individual in the company. In the state of modern technology (such as the computer-based companies and the Internet), there are unlimited opportunities to commit fraudulent or other types of corporate malfeasance. Such ample opportunities are where the "lure" to commit such crimes becomes so overwhelming to so many individuals making decisions at the corporate level.

Shover and Hochstetler (2006) also explained that certain organizations, as well as individuals in such organizations, are more attracted to this lure via a predisposition toward such fast payoff, despite the potential costs. Specifically, certain organizations actually create a corporate climate in which such high-risk activity is fostered, encouraged, and even rewarded. In such a corporate environment, it is always likely that there will be a given supply of individuals—the tempted—who will probably take those risks, despite knowing the potential sanctions against them, or more likely the company they work for. The authors also state that there is a certain arrogance to most persons who make it to white-collar positions, knowing that there is a level of competition, and likely cheating, needed to be successful. Furthermore, there are many excuses or neutralization techniques (see discussion below) that alleviate any personal blame that the individuals making such unethical decisions may feel; after all, they see offending as being for the greater good, meaning the corporation they work for.

Shover and Hochstetler found that policies targeting individuals are not likely to be very effective, given individuals' typical dispositions toward a quick payout or career advancement. Private oversight likely will not work either, given the resources of the corporation versus any threat it may face. Rather, Shover and Hochstetler reasoned that the most efficient approach toward reducing such violations in the corporate world is to come from state oversight. Although such state oversight has many barriers—such as globalization, computer-based companies/finances, transnational corporations, and lack of certain and/or severe sanctions even when they are caught (see discussion of the recent research on the effects [or lack thereof] of the Sarbanes-Oxley Act below)—it is likely that this approach is the best chance we have of stemming the apparently exponential growth in misconduct among white-collar workers and corporations. One of the key findings reported by Shover and Hochstetler is that corporate climates often encourage employees to take certain risks, which frequently are unethical.

Related to such findings of the climate of corporate culture to affect decision making, Piquero, Tibbetts, and Blankenship (2005) found among a sample of 133 MBA students that perceived attitudes of agreement by coworkers and the board of directors were positively associated with decisions to further produce, market, and sell a drug that was about to be recalled by the U.S. Food and Drug Administration (FDA). This study presented the MBA students with a hypothetical scenario in which a drug was likely about to be recalled because a key federal government panel had "unanimously and without reservation" recommended that the FDA ban the sale of this drug due to a high likelihood of detrimental side effects, including death. The participants were presented with this situation, told to imagine that they were in the position in their corporation to make the overall decision of what to do, and then were given seven options (the dependent variable). These options ranged from the most ethical option of recalling the drug immediately and destroying all existing inventories to the least ethical option of continuing efforts to market the drug in other countries even after the

FDA ban takes place in the United States. Notably, as other previous vignette studies have shown (see Simpson 2002), the majority of respondents did *not* choose the most ethical option of recalling the drug immediately and destroying existing inventories. Rather, the median option was the third one: to stop all advertising and promotion of the drug but to continue distribution.

Other interesting findings reported by Piquero et al. (2005) include the fact that the participants' intentions to further produce, market, and distribute the drug were inversely related to perceptions of anticipated negative reactions of close friends and former business professors toward their decision. In other words, these MBA students chose their options of how to handle this controversial decision often in contrast to what they expected their close friends or former professors would think about their decision. Given the anticipated support of their coworkers and the board of directors, despite the anticipated negative reaction of their close friends and former business instructors, this study revealed the overwhelming influence of the corporate cultural climate in terms of individual decision making regarding unethical behavior. Although the findings of this study go against those of some previous studies—such as Simpson and Elis (1995), who found that some informal factors, such as social censure by friends, inhibit such unethical decision making—Piquero et al.'s findings do support the rather consistent finding that potential career advancement (see Paternoster and Simpson 1996) via the anticipated positive attitudes toward the decision to offend by boards of directors and coworkers facilitates a decision to commit a white-collar offense.

Piquero et al. (2005), whose sample included approximately 21 percent executive MBA students (i.e., experienced business managers), found that the more experienced executive MBA participants were actually more likely to use various neutralization techniques in making decisions of what to do about the dangerous drugs. Techniques of neutralization are psychological ways of avoiding guilt in making certain decisions (Sykes and Matza 1957). Although typically considered a more social learning type of concept, neutralization techniques have been applied to white-collar crime research in many recent studies. They can also be seen as a way to alleviate the moral constraints in making such corporate decisions, which have become a key element in rational choice/deterrence research regarding corporate offending (e.g., Simpson and Elis 1995; Simpson 2002). In fact, some techniques of neutralization—such as the metaphor of ledger (balancing good vs. bad of act), defense of necessity (if act is necessary, then no guilt felt), and fear of falling (scared of losing everything if act is not taken)—have been proposed specifically to address decision making in the corporate/business environment (Hollinger 1991; Minor 1981; Piquero 2011, respectively), and they can go a long way toward mediating or conditioning the formal deterrent effects—such as anticipated prison time or fines—in such corporate decisions.

In a follow-up to the Piquero et al. (2005) study, Vieraitis et al. (2012) examined gender differences in decisions regarding the marketing of this drug using the same methodology and data. Vieraitis et al.'s study revealed that female MBA students were far more likely to choose the most ethical option(s) in terms of what the corporation should do regarding the likely-soon-to-be-banned and potentially deadly drug.

Specifically, the modal and median score among females was the most ethical option of recalling it immediately and destroying all supplies of the drug. However, a notable proportion of female participants chose the more unethical options, even the most extreme option of continuing to market and distribute the drug overseas once it was actually banned by the FDA. Still, male participants were far more likely to choose the most unethical options, with twice as many males as females choosing the most extreme two options. Bivariate correlates revealed that the gender difference was significant, as it was in an estimated full regression model when controlling for other factors. Furthermore, females were found to be influenced more by techniques of neutralization—specifically denial of injury and denial of responsibility—than were males in their decision making.

Another recent study by Piquero (2011), which examined eighty-seven students in graduate-level business courses in a vignette study regarding price fixing, found that the perceived risk of sanctions (both formal and informal [via employer]) had an inverse influence on participants' intentions to commit such an act, as did participants' personal beliefs about the morality of the act. These findings are consistent with those found by previous studies (e.g., Simpson and Elis 1995; Paternoster and Simpson 1996; Simpson 2002). Also consistent with these prior studies, Piquero found that the perceived anticipated benefits from engaging in such price fixing were positively associated with higher intentions to commit the act. Furthermore, she found that the perceived fear of falling—or fear of losing what one has worked so hard to obtain—was inversely related to intentions to fix prices, given the context in the scenario. This study not only supported the findings of previous studies regarding formal and informal sanctions as well as benefits, but also supported the importance of a rather new concept in the rational choice perspective regarding white-collar offending, specifically the concept of fear of falling, which was introduced by Wheeler (1992) but was never fully incorporated into the rational choice perspective, at least in terms of white-collar crime.

As previously stated here as well as being advised by previous research, it is important to include both informal and internal factors into any theoretical model of offending, especially at the corporate or white-collar crime level. This was readily illustrated by a study by Smith, Simpson, and Chus-Yao (2007), who examined managers' decision making regarding a given act of misconduct. These researchers concluded that the threat of legal sanctions did not directly affect the likelihood of misconduct. Rather, the managers' evaluations of the ethics of the act were a primary factor, as was being associated with potential outcomes that had nothing to do with formal sanctions. However, the threat of formal sanctions did seem to operate indirectly, via influencing various ethical evaluations and anticipated outcomes. Another key finding of this study is that managers were significantly more willing to engage in questionable behavior when ordered to do so by their supervisors.

Perhaps one of the most thorough, and certainly the most recent, study of the effects of sanctions on white-collar decision making was done by Simpson et al. (2013). Their study used a vignette approach measuring how 237 business managers intended to act regarding two types of environmental offenses. Simpson et al. manipulated various contextual circumstances in the scenario across participants, making it a more experi-mental, factorial-based study. Specifically, the researchers altered the scenarios across respondents, such as "the industry is losing ground to foreign competitors" versus "the industry is economically healthy" versus "the industry is economically deteriorating," and these details were randomly assigned to the vignettes presented to the respon-dents. Other factors, such as locus of control, internal compliance structure/opera-tion, and managerial ethics, were also varied across the vignettes given to participants. Furthermore, the various risk factors examined were broken into separate components, such as individual-level factors (e.g., perceived career benefits), company-level factors (e.g., economic conditions), firm self-regulation factors (e.g., company participation in EPA emission reduction demands, internal compliance system), and perceived infor-mal sanction risk (e.g., loss of job, loss of respect by business associates, loss of future career prospects). Simpson et al. generally found that the most effective factors in such decision making were formal legal sanctions, as well as the likelihood and severity of informal sanctions, especially those by others in the company. Like other studies exam-ined in this chapter, the effect of anticipated benefits seemed to outweigh any potential sanctions, which emerges as a consistent finding among all studies examining white-collar crime decision making.

B. Research on Deterrent Effects of Sarbanes-Oxley Act

In response to public pressure regarding numerous acts of corporate misconduct in the area of financial statement fraud—such as the collapse of Enron, Tyco, and WorldCom—in July 2002 the Sarbanes-Oxley Act was enacted as federal law. Also known as SOX (or Sarbox), the purpose of the law was to establish enhanced stan-dards for public company boards and management and public accounting firms in the United States. One of the key elements of SOX is that top managers are required to cer-tify the accuracy of financial information (Ugrin and Odom 2010). Furthermore, the law raised the potential severity of penalties for corporations convicted of fraudulent financial activity. SOX also sought to increase the oversight role of companies' boards of directors and, importantly, to ensure the independence of outside auditors who are expected to objectively review the accuracy of financial statements of public companies (McEnroe 2006). One of the main goals of SOX was to ensure more serious penalties for offenders in order to deter such individuals and corporations, thereby reducing their attempts to commit such dishonest acts in their financial reporting practices, as well as other forms of malfeasance.

Although one main intention of SOX was specifically to increase the potential penal-ties for corporations that are caught "cooking the books," a key element in these poten-tial penalties reducing such corporate malfeasance from a rational choice/deterrence perspective is that the managers and other individuals in a given company must actu-ally perceive an increased risk of formal sanctions. More specifically, if a key manager or other decision maker in the company does not perceive an enhanced severity of sanctions and/or an increased risk of getting caught/convicted (likely both would be needed), the deterrent effects of SOX likely would be minimal in terms of reducing such corporate misconduct. A few recent studies have examined the level to which managers, auditors, and graduate business or accounting students perceive the impact of SOX. We will now review some of the key studies determining the influence that SOX had on individuals' perceptions in these key groups, who essentially are the decision makers (or likely future ones) for such public companies.

Relatively recent studies that sampled audit committee members (DeZoort, Hermanson, and Houston 2008; Cohen, Krishnamoorthy, and Wright 2010) concluded that they perceive that they have more power and independence since SOX was passed. However, the auditors generally still believe that top management is ultimately in control of decision making regarding the finances of the company, especially given that management still typically controls the decisions regarding which auditors to terminate or appoint (Cohen et al. 2010). Perhaps this is why research on the perceptions of financial executives show that most of them do not expect SOX to have much effect in reducing fraudulent earnings management practices, as shown by a survey of such executives by McEnroe (2006). Ultimately, if auditors do not feel they are primarily in control of decisions such as how to manage financial reporting practices, they can to some extent pass much of the blame on to the managers and executives and thereby not be deterred by the requirements stipulated by SOX.

A 2010 vignette study by Ugrin and Odom based on 130 master's-level accounting students and 43 corporate executives found that the threat of increased sanctions, particularly prison time, is likely to reduce fraudulent practices in financial statements, such as when potential incarceration time was increased from one to ten years (but the effect diminished when the potential length of the sentence was increased to twenty years). However, the efficacy of such formal sanctions in reducing financial statement fraud was bounded or mediated by a wide range of demographic and informal factors. Specifically, the perceived "social stigma" of potential jail sentences, such as the impact such an experience would have on their future employment or career opportunities, had more influence on their decision making than formal sanctions in scenarios involving whether or not to commit fraudulent reporting of finances for a company. This finding is consistent with prior research showing that it is often the informal factors, not the formal sanctions, that provide the most significant deterrent effects in such decisions. Furthermore, the amount of experience of participants in the corporate environment had a consistent effect on intentions to commit such fraud, with the more experienced students and executives being less deterred by such internal controls, or potential social stigma. This is rather alarming given the likelihood that it is these more experienced individuals who are the ones most likely to make such key decisions in terms of financial reporting fraud. Ultimately, Ugrin and Odom concluded, "the findings show that the incremental increase in potential jail time imposed by SOX creates little deterrence beyond the mechanisms that were in place pre-SOX" (p. 439).

III. CONCLUSIONS, IMPLICATIONS, AND RECOMMENDATIONS FOR FUTURE RESEARCH

In the final decades of the 20th century, as well as in the first decade or so of the 21st century, cultural and social learning theories of offending that had previously been the most supported explanations of crime were supplanted by the rebirth of a deterrence and rational choice theoretical framework. This shift led academic researchers to focus on decision-making models for explaining various street crimes, such as burglary, robbery, and drug dealing, and a large amount was learned using this approach, such as key insights regarding the decisions offenders make in selecting certain targets or processes in how they choose their offenses. However, as Shover and Cullen (2012) pointed out, there are still relatively few comparable studies into the decision making of white-collar criminals. The research that has been done, however, suggests that white-collar offenders are affected by very much the same factors as are street criminals. There appears to be consistent evidence that moral inhibitions and informal costs (like social censure and embarrassment) are much more effective in restraining rule breaking than formal sanction threats but that, when the former are weak, compliance can be created by the threat of formal legal sanctions. For both suite and street crime, therefore, would-be offenders are responsive to the anticipated costs and rewards of their behavior as well as to normative considerations.

Shover and Cullen (2012) cautioned that the typical strategies and methodologies used to study street criminals are more difficult to apply to white-collar offenders. Likewise, Shover and Hunter (2010) explained:

> Burglars and robbers do not take umbrage or argue when asked questions premised on their assumed criminality. Everything is different with white-collar criminals; questions exemplified by "tell me how you decided to do this crime" elicit denials of criminal intent and, therefore, of criminal decision making. Their refusal to acknowledge that they committed or were fairly convicted of crime means that white-collar criminals' decision making cannot be approached in the straightforward manner employed with muggers and burglars; circumspection is required. (p. 56)

This revelation based on empirical findings tends to support the use of vignette studies of business graduate students and executives, as has been done in many of the recent studies of white-collar decision making reviewed in this chapter. After all, these scenarios do not ask respondents about previous offenses they may have committed, but rather present a *hypothetical* scenario that does not explicitly state that the given act is a criminal offense. In such studies, there is far less of a chance that the participants will become defensive and deny any responsibility or guilt; as the authors recommend above, the vignette method is a way of circumventing such inherent feelings for such potential white-collar offenders. Thus, we conclude that the use of vignette studies is likely the best strategy toward gaining further understanding of the decision-making factors and processes that are most important in individuals' decisions to commit white-collar offenses.

However, vignette studies have their own limitations. First, vignettes do not address how people would actually behave in a given set of circumstances, or even how they have behaved in the past, but instead measure their behavioral *intention*. Although there is evidence to suggest a correlation between intentions and behavior (Pogarsky 2004), hypothetical scenarios are different from actual offending contexts and behavior. Another important limitation of hypothetical scenarios is that they request persons to respond while emotionally "cool," while many offending decisions are made in the presence of strong emotions or affect. Decisions made while "cool" may not be the same as those made while "hot" (Loewenstein 1996). For these reasons, we would also encourage the use of other methodologies such as extensive interviews with corporate offenders or corporate decision-making bodies, as has effectively been done with street offenders (Shover 1996; Wright and Decker 1997), in addition to quantitative work.

A final note. One of the criticisms of the rational choice framework is that it, and the theory of classical economics on which it is built, is silent with respect to the source of people's preferences and tastes that guide their decision making, such as the decision to commit corporate crime. This is illustrated in the rational choice theorists' notion that preferences are simply revealed by the choices one makes (Samuelson 1938) and that the springs of one's preferences are epiphenomenal—*degustibus non est disputandum* (in matters of taste there can be no dispute). Rational choice theorists in economics and criminology have, therefore, typically dealt with preferences as they have been given or revealed and have taken no interest in the possibility that human intentions or desires are the source of those preferences. Only the external conduct of *homo economicus* need be taken into account in understanding their preferences or goals of action (Becker 1968); consequently, there is no need to delve into the minds of people for their desires or preferences. An important avenue of future theoretical and then empirical work, therefore, entails dispensing with the assumption of revealed preferences and taking seriously the notion that beliefs and desires matter. One example may be the efforts in recent years by economists and criminologists to explicate the connection between people's identities and their preferences (Paternoster and Bushway 2009; Akerlof and Kranton 2010). One's personal identity—who one wants to be—may be an important factor in motivating behavior, both social and antisocial.

NOTES

1. We readily acknowledge that the distinction between white-collar and corporate crime we and others have adopted is somewhat arbitrary and ambiguous. We recognize that, despite what Mitt Romney says, corporations are "not people" in the sense that they do not "act" and so cannot be treated as judicial persons capable of committing criminal acts.

Some individuals act on behalf of corporations, but corporations can be subject to criminal, administrative, and civil sanctions, and as criminologists we can ascertain whether or not sanctions imposed on a given firm have a deterrent effect on its subsequent actions. We consider white-collar crime to occur when individuals commit illegal acts that stand to benefit either the business they work for (increased profits) or themselves (promotion, pay raises). In short, the distinction is the level of analysis rather than the nature of the criminality—white-collar crime is at the individual level and corporate crime is at the firm/company level.

2. Maybe what Gottfredson and Hirschi are characterizing is "workplace crime": criminal acts committed by employees against their companies. For example, *The New York Times* recently ran a story about a man who held a "low-level job" at a New York law firm and who over approximately a two-year period had stolen and resold more than $375,000 worth of copy-machine toner (Santora 2013). This is clearly an exception, with most of us stealing pens, paper, pencils, and envelopes from employers.

3. To say that deterrence processes are likely to be operative among white-collar offenders does not mean that we would expect to see strong evidence of deterrence among white-collar offenders. Deterrence may be lacking not because white-collar offenders are not rational and cannot easily be deterred but because white-collar crimes are enforced with very low certainty and severity of punishment, or the anticipated benefits simply outweigh any possibly anticipated costs of crime, or because sanction regimes are so complex that a failure to comply with rules is due to ignorance (Spence 2001).

4. Of course, there are ethnographies of white-collar and corporate offending: Vaughan (1997) and more recently McDonald and Robinson's (2010) description of the downfall of Lehman Brothers are but two examples. The point is that there are vastly more narrative accounts of robbers, burglars, and descriptions of the cognitive processing of shoplifters in the act than there are of white-collar and corporate offending.

5. There is probably more information about white-collar decision making in the business and economics literature than in criminology, and we will appeal to some of this literature in our review.

6. For excellent treatments of white-collar offenders as rational decision makers, see Shover and Hochstetler (2006) and Benson and Simpson (2009).

7. According to the seminal economic model of crime presented by Becker (1968), the rational individual will choose to offend if the expected cost of committing a crime (defined as the probability of detection, p, multiplied by the utility cost, C, of being punished) is less than the expected benefit (i.e., the probability of getting away with the crime, $1 - p$, multiplied by the utility benefit, B, of committing the crime). In other words, $E(C) = pC < E(B) = (1 - p)B$. Savage (1954) proposed Subjective Expected Utility (SEU) theory as an alternative descriptive model of choice. In SEU theory, individuals are allowed to have subjective beliefs regarding the probability of events, which allows for between-individual variation.

8. Paternoster and Simpson also include a moral component in the model as many rational choice scholars have done. While it is clear that one's moral evaluation of a given act affects one's decision making inhibiting offending, morality occupies an ambiguous place in the literature. Some consider morality a type of cost, a moral cost of offending, having a direct effect on decisions to offend that are independent of sanction threats, while it is also considered a moderating factor with instrumental considerations only salient when moral inhibitions (which act as an effective source of inhibition) are weak.

REFERENCES

Ainslie, George. 2001. *Breakdown of Will.* New York: Cambridge University Press.

Akerlof, George A., and Rachel E. Kranton. 2010. *Identity Economics.* Princeton, NJ: Princeton University Press.

Becker, Gary. 1968. "Crime and Punishment: An Economic Approach." *Journal of Political Economy* 76: 169–217.

Benson, Michael L., and Sally S. Simpson. 2009. *White-Collar Crime: An Opportunity Perspective.* New York: Routledge.

Block, Michael K., Frederick C. Nold, and Joseph G. Sidak. 1981. "The Deterrent Effects of Antitrust Enforcement." *Journal of Political Economy* 89: 429–44.

Braithwaite, John, and Toni Makkai. 1991. "Criminological Theories and Regulatory Compliance." *Criminology* 29: 191–220.

Casey, B. J., Rebecca M. Jones, and Todd A. Hare. 2008. "The Adolescent Brain." *Annals of the New York Academy of Sciences* 1124: 111–26.

Cherniak, Christopher. 1986. *Minimal Rationality.* Cambridge, MA: MIT Press.

Cohen, Jeffrey, Ganesh Krishnamoorthy, and Arnold M. Wright. 2010. "Corporate Governance in the Post Sarbanes-Oxley Era: Auditors' Experiences." *Contemporary Accounting Research* 27: 751–86.

DeZoort, F. Todd, Dana Hermanson, and Richard W. Houston. 2008. "Audit Committee Member Support for Proposed Audit Adjustments: Pre-SOX versus Post-SOX Judgments." *Auditing: A Journal of Practice and Theory* 27: 85–104.

Gottfredson, Michael R., and Travis Hirschi. 1990. *A General Theory of Crime.* Palo Alto, CA: Stanford University Press.

Hirschi, Travis. 2004. "Self-Control and Crime." In *Handbook of Self-regulation: Research, Theory, and Applications,* pp. 537–52, edited by Roy F. Baumeister and Kathleen D. Vohs. New York: Guilford Press.

Hollinger, Richard C. 1991. "Neutralizing in the Workplace: An Empirical Analysis of Property Theft and Production Deviance." *Deviant Behavior* 12: 169–202.

Katz, Jack. 1988. *Seductions of Crime: Moral and Sensual Attractions of Doing Evil.* New York: Basic Books.

Loewenstein, George. 1996. "Out of Control: Visceral Influences on Behavior." *Organizational Behavior and Human Decision Processes* 65: 272–92.

Makkai, Toni, and John Braithwaite. 1994. "The Dialectics of Corporate Deterrence." *Journal of Research in Crime and Delinquency* 31: 347–73.

McDonald, Lawrence G., and Patrick Robinson. 2010. *A Colossal Failure of Common Sense: The Inside Story of the Collapse of Lehman Brothers.* New York: Crown.

McEnroe, John E. 2006. "Perceptions of the Effect of Sarbanes-Oxley on Earnings Management Practices." *Research in Accounting Regulation* 19: 137–57.

Minor, W. William. 1981. "Techniques of Neutralization: A Reconceptualization and Empirical Examination." *Journal of Research in Crime and Delinquency* 18: 295–318.

Nagin, Daniel S., and Raymond Paternoster. 1994. "Personal Capital and Social Control: The Deterrence Implications of a Theory of Individual Differences in Criminal Offending." *Criminology* 32: 581–606.

Paternoster, Ray, and Shawn Bushway. 2009. "Desistance and the 'Feared Self:' Toward an Identity Theory of Criminal Desistance." *Journal of Criminal Law and Criminology* 99: 1109–56.

Paternoster, Raymond, and Sally S. Simpson. 1996. "Sanction Threats and Appeals to Morality: Testing a Rational Choice Model of Corporate Crime." *Law and Society Review* 30: 549–83.

Piquero, Nicole Leeper. 2011. "The Only Thing We Have to Fear Is Fear Itself: Investigating the Relationship between Fear of Failing and White-collar Crime." *Crime and Delinquency* 58: 362–79.

Piquero, Nicole Leeper, Stephen G. Tibbetts, and Michael Blankenship. 2005. "Examining the Role of Differential Association and Techniques of Neutralization in Explaining Corporate Crime." *Deviant Behavior* 26: 159–88.

Pogarsky, Greg. 2004. "Projected Offending and Contemporaneous Rule-Violation: Implications for Heterotypic Continuity." *Criminology* 42: 111–36.

Reed, Gary E., and Peter C. Yeager. 1996. "Organization Offending and Neoclassical Criminology: Challenging the Reach of a General Theory of Crime." *Criminology* 34: 357–82.

Samuelson, Paul A. 1938. "A Note on the Pure Theory of Consumers' Behavior." *Econometrica* 5: 61–71.

Santora, Marc. 2013. "For Thief in This Office, Paper Clips Wouldn't Do." *New York Times* (January 16). Available at http://www.nytimes.com/2013/01/16/nyregion/man-charged-in-theft-of-copy-toner-worth-over-376000.html

Savage, Leonard J. 1954. *The Foundations of Statistics*. New York: Dover.

Shover, Neal. 1996. *Great Pretenders: Pursuits and Careers of Persistent Thieves*. Boulder, CO: Westview Press.

Shover, Neal, and Francis T. Cullen. 2012. "White-Collar Crime: Interpretive Disagreement and Prospects for Change." In *Reflecting on White-Collar and Corporate Crime: Discerning Readings*, pp. 47–62, edited by David Shichor, Larry Gaines, and Andrea Schoepfer. Long Grove, IL: Waveland Press.

Shover, Neal, and Andy Hochstetler. 2006. *Choosing White-Collar Crime*. New York: Cambridge University Press.

Shover, Neal, and Ben W. Hunter. 2010. "Blue-Collar, White-Collar: Crimes and Mistakes." In *Offenders on Offending: Learning about Crime from Criminals*, pp. 205–27, edited by Wim Bernasco. Collompton, UK: Willan.

Simpson, Sally S. 2002. *Corporate Crime, Law, and Social Control*. New York: Cambridge University Press.

Simpson, Sally S., and Lori Elis. 1995. "Informal Sanction Threats and Corporate Crime: Additive versus Multiplicative Models." *Journal of Research in Crime and Delinquency* 32: 399–424.

Simpson, Sally S., Carole Gibbs, Melissa Rorie, Lee Ann Slocum, Mark Cohen, and Michael Vandenberg. 2013. "An Empirical Assessment of Corporate Environmental Crime Control Strategies." *Journal of Criminal Law and Criminology* 103: 231–78.

Simpson, Sally S., and Christopher S. Koper. 1992. "Deterring Corporate Crime." *Criminology* 30: 347–76.

Simpson, Sally S., and Nicole Leeper Piquero. 2002. "Low Self-Control, Organizational Theory, and Corporate Crime." *Law and Society Review* 36: 509–48.

Smith, N. Craig, Sally S. Simpson, and Huang Chun-Yao. 2007. "Why Managers Fail to Do the Right Thing: An Empirical Study of Unethical and Illegal Conduct." *Business Ethics Quarterly* 17: 633–67.

Smith, W. James, and Michael B. Vaughan. 1986 "Economic Welfare, Price, and Profit: The Deterrent Effect of Alternative Antitrust Regimes." *Economic Inquiry* 24: 615–29.

Spence, David B. 2001. "The Shadow of the Rational Polluter: Rethinking the Role of Rational Actor Models in Environmental Law." *California Law Review* 89: 917–98.

Steinberg, Larry. 2005. "Cognitive and Affective Development in Adolescence." *Trends in Cognitive Science* 9: 69–74.

Sutherland, Edwin. 1983. *White Collar Crime*. New York: Holt, Rinehart, and Winston.

Sykes, Gresham M., and David Matza. 1957. "Techniques of Neutralization: A Theory of Delinquency." *American Sociological Review* 22: 664–70.

Ugrin, Joseph C., and Marcus D. Odom. 2010. "Exploring Sarbanes-Oxley's Effect on Attitudes, Perceptions of Norms, and Intentions to Commit Financial Statement Fraud from a General Deterrence Perspective." *Journal of Accounting and Public Policy* 29: 439–58.

Vaughan, Diane. 1997. *The Challenger Launch Decision: Risky Technology, Culture, and Deviance at NASA*. Chicago: University of Chicago Press.

Vieraitis, Lynne M., Nicole Leeper Piquero, Alex R. Piquero, Stephen G. Tibbetts, and Michael Blankenship. 2012. "Do Women and Men Differ in Their Neutralizations of Corporate Crime?" *Criminal Justice Review* 37: 478–93.

Wheeler, Stanton. 1992. "The Problem of White-Collar Motivation." In *White-Collar Crime Reconsidered*, pp. 108–23, edited by Kip Schlegel and David Weisburd. Boston: Northeastern University Press.

Williams, Kirk R., and Richard Hawkins. 1986. "Perceptual Research on General Deterrence: A Critical Review." *Law and Society Review* 20: 545–72.

Wright, Richard T., and Scott Decker. 1997. *Armed Robbers in Action: Stick-up and Street Culture*. Boston: Northeastern University Press.

Yeager, Peter C., and Gary E. Reed. 1998. "Of Corporate Persons and Straw Men: A Reply to Herbert, Green, and Larragoite." *Criminology* 36: 885–97.

PART IX

PUBLIC POLICY

CHAPTER 31

THE PRACTICAL CHALLENGES OF RESPONDING TO CORPORATE CRIME

PETER CLEARY YEAGER

I hope we shall . . . crush in its birth the aristocracy
of our moneyed corporations, which dare already
to challenge our government to a trial of strength
and bid defiance to the laws of our country.[1]

WITH these words in his 1816 letter to George Logan, Thomas Jefferson expressed his condemnation of the role of corporate power in the young republic. The nation looked considerably different then, with a more decentralized politics and economy. Still, his comment prefigured some of the country's most enduring and important features: the close connections between state and economy, their intertwined fates, and the ambivalent relations between law and corporations, ranging over time and place from adversarial to cooperative, and at points even conspiratorial. The primary architect of the nation's Declaration of Independence from English colonialism worried that a new aristocracy now threatened the rights of citizens.

In the present moment, when the largest multinational corporations can be ranked in economic size alongside entire national economies,[2] and where—as in the United States—they have been granted such rights of citizenship as to expand their outsized influence on elections and public policy,[3] both their potential for great public harms and the difficulties of controlling them have grown substantially since Jefferson's time. This potential has recently been realized again in the American legal cases against major financial firms in connection with the 2008 financial crisis and its series of frauds associated with the mortgage lending industry. While some firms have been assessed civil penalties as high as nine figures, the government has not pursued criminal penalties against large companies and top executives. This reluctance, or inability, reflects a number of difficulties in regulating corporate misconduct, from its complexity (hence, difficult to prove in court) to the central role very large firms play in the nation's and world's financial stability and health (hence, a "too big to jail" problem) (Henning 2012; *New York Times* 2012). Whatever the sources of this pattern of selective (non)enforcement, its consequences range from reduced deterrence to wide public perceptions of compromised justice and the reduced legitimacy of law.

In this chapter I review some of the key challenges to the effective control of corporate crime, focusing on the U.S. case but with some comparative notes on other nations. However, I shall not discuss one major constraint on societies' abilities to regulate business misconduct. This is the problem of "the space between laws" (Michalowski and Kramer 1987), which refers to the fact that many nations, especially in the developing world, often permit as lawful activities of multinational corporations or their local subcontractors that would be illegal in the companies' home countries (e.g., the dumping of toxic industrial wastes, exposing manufacturing employees to unsafe work conditions).[4] This is a variant of the old problem that national corporations often played the individual American states off against each other, threatening to move factories to more legally permissive states if a state's laws weren't made more "reasonable," a problem that national legislation has reduced although not eliminated. The international variant raises many important issues in international law and relations and requires its own separate and lengthy treatment.

Instead, I concentrate on limitations on laws' effectiveness in a context in which arguably such rules should have their greatest effectiveness: a wealthy nation with an elaborate set of regulations and enforcement mechanisms and a history of popular eruptions against abuses of corporate power.

In the chapter, I draw the following conclusions:

- Constraints on the effective control of corporate harms are rooted in the structures and culture of the nation's political economy.
- These constraints are most clearly manifested in the complexities of offenses and of the relations between especially large corporations and enforcement agencies.
- Punishment for corporate offenses is uneven over targets (falling more heavily on smaller than on larger companies) and over time (being vulnerable to shifts in political administrations and ideologies).
- The consequences of such variability in enforcement are costs to both justice and deterrence.

In the next section, I discuss some important contextual issues to set the stage for consideration of some of the major challenges to effective control of corporate crime. In the following three sections, I take up, respectively, institutional, organizational, and legal limitations on the law's effective control of these offenses. These categories are not mutually exclusive, and the limitations in each are often synergistically related to those in the others. But I employ them as a convenient way to disentangle these interrelated phenomena in order to highlight something of their distinct natures. I end with a brief discussion of some implications of this analysis.

I. Initial Considerations

Conventionally, American society divorces practical from philosophical and theoretical considerations and much prefers solving problems than musing over their nature and sources. But the distinction is a false one, certainly as it relates to the matters at hand. The practical challenges of controlling corporate wrongdoing are rooted in cultural systems of belief, systems that include both professional and popular views about such issues as the relative roles of markets and governments in organizing social life. How these systems relate to problems in the social control of corporations can be seen in a number of ways in the American context.

One place to begin is at the beginning: with definitions of wrongs or crimes. Here I do not have in mind the seemingly endless academic debates about best definitions of white-collar crime. Those debates generally concern where to draw definitional boundaries around types of behaviors that have been officially deemed unlawful by statute or regulation. Instead, my interest is in when and how societies define corporate behaviors as illegal, selecting out some activities for legal prohibition from among various types of behaviors that cause social harms. These choices reflect changing public sentiments regarding, in effect, the morally correct balance between risks and rewards. At present it may be difficult or impossible for many Americans to imagine a time when toxic industrial pollution of air and water was largely a lawful business activity. But such a time existed only a few decades ago, prior to the flurry of environmental legislation in the 1970s that first criminalized many forms of pollution (Yeager 1991; forthcoming).[5]

The key point is that while public opinion was supportive of the new environmental laws, and segments demanded them of the Congress, the outlawing of corporate conduct has always been contested, certainly by companies and almost always on arguments about the risks to commerce and the economy of government intrusion into the prerogatives of businesses and the free operations of markets. Notably, this contest goes beyond the process of law creation and moves on to influence processes of law enforcement. Ideological views on the proper boundaries between the public sector of state and law and the private sector of markets, and relatedly on the very *nature* of corporate offenses, have long shaped and shadowed the decisions of law enforcers in the face of these offenses. I shall illustrate this dynamic in the sections to follow. For now I simply add three additional points.

First, enforcement decisions both reflect and reproduce particular *moral characterizations* of corporate violations of law. In contrast to violations of conventional criminal laws, such as robbery and burglary, these offenses are commonly—not to say always—treated as less blameworthy and at times even as morally ambivalent behaviors. This reduces law's deterrent effects not only by lowering punishments, but also by rendering the offending behaviors more normatively available to future corporate decisions.

Second, while these characterizations are related to such concrete matters as the complexity of some types of corporate offenses and the burden of proof in criminal cases, they are rooted in the American culture's distinctive bias favoring the perceived individualism and liberties of markets over the collectivism and controls of government. The criminologists Messner and Rosenfeld (2013) have argued persuasively that the United States is exceptional in the extent to which market norms of economic efficiency, productivity, and wealth creation have displaced or devalued nonmarket norms and values such as those emphasizing family and communal responsibilities. Because the market economy is in this way privileged over other institutions, and because corporate offenses are committed in the pursuit of competitive advantage and often resemble legal market conduct in form (2013, p. 98), corporate penalties tend to be relatively mild and to require justifications that the government need not supply in the case of conventional offenses. Even the form of the most common substantial penalties for corporate infractions, fines rather than incarceration, may be read as a sort of tariff on outlawed business activities rather than as a signal of their public condemnation.[6]

But, and this is the final point, culture does not act by itself. Its hierarchy of values is constantly reinforced by actors making arguments regarding the merits versus the blameworthiness of their conduct. Characteristically the arguments are not all equally weighted. In the context of suspected or alleged corporate misconduct, large companies especially have the reinforcing advantages of great resources and high status with which to negotiate the language of statutes, the nature of legal charges, and the outcomes of cases with their government opponents. As Marc Galanter demonstrated in his classic essay, "Why the 'Haves' Come Out Ahead" (1974), even where rules for making and enforcing laws are formally neutral and accessible to all parties—indeed, because of this very neutrality—they favor the input of more powerful, well-resourced organizations over other parties in legal cases. To his formulation I add here that such advantages not only generally confer better legal outcomes to large corporations than to their private-sector adversaries (as in civil suits), but also favor such companies over government bodies seeking to criminalize or to otherwise regulate harmful corporate conduct.

In his foundational analysis of the control of corporate misconduct, Christopher Stone made the important distinction between "absolutely disfavored conduct" and "qualifiedly disfavored conduct" (Stone 1975, pp. 30–31). The former is conduct that the society has determined is so evil that it wishes to eliminate it entirely, such as murder, regardless of other considerations (e.g., of any other value the perpetrator may have for society).[7] The latter is behavior that we wish to discourage with punishment, but not to the extent that we risk losing more than we gain, such as if we were to incarcerate the town's only doctor for illegally dispensing marijuana for pain control. If clear enough in the case of conventional offenses, for reasons I have suggested this distinction is considerably less so for corporate offenses and may have become even more blurred in recent decades, as suggested by the absence of criminal prosecutions of Wall Street banks implicated in the frauds associated with the worldwide financial collapse in 2008. Defining corporate behaviors as criminal (or simply illegal) and enforcing laws against violations are typically contested practices. As a result their perceived moral status commonly remains ambiguous rather than definitive, rendering these behaviors more available to corporate actors than deterred.

II. INSTITUTIONAL LIMITS

Because questions of the effective control of corporate wrongdoing involve two of society's key institutions, the economy and government, the limits on legal effectiveness are rooted in the nature of the relationships between them. As I have noted, in the American context the cultural privilege granted to markets over competing institutions requires government to meet a higher burden of proof, as it were, if it wishes to regulate corporate misconduct strictly. This cultural tilt toward the individualism and autonomy of markets is expressed in public opinion polls that reveal divided and inconsistent public views on government regulation of business, and perhaps most clearly in the consistent findings over the past thirty years that majorities believe big government is the biggest threat to the nation's future, while only a fifth to a third say big business is the largest threat (Yeager, forthcoming). It is also expressed in the degree to which traditional functions of government, including those in education, criminal justice, and the military, have been increasingly outsourced to private-sector businesses seeking profit opportunities in them (in the bargain creating new opportunities for corporate crime as well).

This cultural orientation reflects—and reinforces—the nation's institutional architecture. A key aspect of this design is that, compared to other capitalist democracies, the American state is separated from key profitmaking activities to an unusual degree. For example, among industrial nations, the United States has ranked at or near the bottom in percentage of government enterprise involved in such industries as manufacturing and mining, transportation, construction, and communications (Herman 1981, pp. 167–68). Thus government has been highly dependent on the financial health of markets to produce both the tax revenues and jobs necessary to political stability, and therefore is especially sensitive to signals from business as to the regulatory costs it will bear before adequate growth, or relocation of enterprises to more permissive legal environments, is threatened. The result, other things being equal, is less stringent regulation and enforcement for corporate misdeeds.

A second aspect of institutional architecture that limits effective control of corporate offenses is the complexity of government and law, as exhibited in the separation of powers. The division of government into executive, legislative, and judicial functions means that opponents of regulation need to prevail in only one branch of government, while supporters typically must see regulation successfully through all of them.[8] This is an especial challenge to law enforcement because of what Galanter (1974) referred to as the problem of the "penetration" of rules.[9] Forged in the publicly visible arenas of legislatures, often with dramatic assertions of the public interest and the importance of deterrent penalties, the impact of rules and enforcement stringency are often later diluted in the less visible levels of implementation and enforcement, for example by politically restricted enforcement budgets and quiet negotiations with powerful corporations (Alford and Friedland 1985; Yeager 1991; Stryker 2007).

Notably, this process of translating legislation into rules and enforcement practices commonly affects the moral force of law in ways that reduce the perceived offensiveness of corporate offenses in the eyes of offenders, thus rendering violations more likely to occur. For example, research on laws aimed at controlling companies' environmental harms has found that they lose much of their moral force as they move from the often passionate normative arguments for them in the legislature to the enforcement bureaucracies of government (Hawkins 1984; Shover, Clelland, and Lynxwiler 1986; Yeager 1991, 2007). In these agencies, laws are often translated into mundane, technical, and obscure procedures for enforcement, a prospect that is especially likely in areas of regulation that are inherently technical or that seek to control harms associated with such complex internal corporate matters as manufacturing and managerial processes, such as with environmental and securities regulation. Relatedly, this process of the "demoralization" of law amplifies the input of corporate offenders in the regulatory/enforcement dialogue because they control much of the knowledge on which government enforcers rely in making their determinations, while it simultaneously silences the voices of victims, who commonly lack the resources (knowledge, time, and wealth) to participate in such "obscured" enforcement negotiations. This imbalance in input is one of the reasons for the oft-noted bias in the use of cost–benefit analysis in regulatory matters: the costs of enforcement to violators are commonly more readily assessed than are its benefits to victims and to the wider society.

Another aspect of the institutional dynamics that limits law's effective control of corporate misconduct is variability in the rigor of enforcement. Driven by variegated and shifting political ideologies, this variability signals policy priorities but may also communicate the sort of inconsistency in law's purposes that undermines its moral force and deterrent effects. In the only large-scale study to produce comparative findings across types of corporate offenses, University of Wisconsin researchers found that the federal government more often used harsher criminal and civil sanctions for violations of financial laws (e.g., securities and tax laws) and antitrust laws than it did for other types of violations (Clinard et al. 1979). For such offenses as violations of environmental, labor and product quality and safety laws, the government more often used such lenient sanctions as warnings and orders to comply. This pattern of sanctions indicates the relative policy emphases in law, certainly at the time of that research. In particular, the pattern indicates that the government has more rigorously sought to prevent corporate offenses that threaten markets, such as antitrust assaults on competition and violations of trust in securities markets, than it has those offenses that don't directly undermine the needs of the economy.[10]

The Wisconsin research also found that large American corporations were less likely to commit antitrust and financial violations than they were the other types of offenses, suggesting the possibility of deterrent effects for harsher penalties. As a cross-sectional rather than a longitudinal study, the research could not test for deterrent effects so cannot prove them. A related explanation suggests that this pattern of violations may reflect differences in corporations' perceptions of the *legitimacy* of laws, violating more often those laws that seem less justified to them. Companies may "grant greater legitimacy to laws protecting markets than to those protecting values more remote from the core rules of competition that safeguard capitalist systems" (Yeager 2007, p. 30). The extent to which such patterns of corporate offenses and sanctions endure over time is a matter for future research, but such evidence as provided by journalistic and other reports of government policies and sanctions suggests that this pattern has remained fairly stable. For example, a major investigative report by *The New York Times* found that between 2004 and 2009 business facilities such as chemical factories and manufacturing plants had violated the nation's water pollution laws more than half a million times, that enforcement by state and federal agencies was routinely lax, and that as a result the nation's waters did not meet public health and other clean water goals nearly forty years after the passage of the major federal water pollution control legislation (Duhigg 2009; see also Yeager 1991).

Research also suggests the effect that political ideologies can have on the rigor of enforcement and thus also on the potential deterrence of corporate lawbreaking. In her study of antitrust offenses in the United States between 1927 and 1981, Sally Simpson (1986, 1987) found that companies were more likely to violate antitrust laws during Republican administrations in Washington as compared to Democratic ones, presumably because of the perception that Republicans oppose aggressive enforcement of laws regulating business. Similarly, Duhigg (2009) indicates that the high rates of water pollution offenses in the 2000s correlated with particularly lax enforcement of environmental laws during the Republican administration of President George W. Bush during 2001 to 2008. In another examination of this effect during that period, U.S. Environmental Protection Agency (EPA) professionals commented that enforcement had become politicized and thereby limited. For example, one water enforcement manager complained that "There is now always attention that we did not have in the past, to[:] 'What are the political ramifications [of our cases]?,'" while an anonymous EPA attorney said that, "[The Administration] is pro-energy and pro-industry. . . . Every time they can weaken the regulations they do so. They are trying to relax everything in sight" (Mintz 2004, p. 10941; footnote 59).

While those complaints refer explicitly to shifting ideological constraints on enforcement, Mintz's (2004, p. 10942) EPA and Department of Justice informants also pointed to insufficient budgets for enforcement that began during the second term of the Democratic Clinton administration. Notably this timing matched well the shift in control of Congress from Democratic to Republican majorities in the 1994 elections.

Because the Congress controls federal agencies' budgets, the Republican Party—which most consistently carries the neoliberal political ideology favoring market liberalization that was ushered firmly into American governance with the 1980 election of President Ronald Reagan—found itself in position to limit the enforcement of laws regulating corporate misconduct. Research has suggested that in general Republican administrations are more likely than Democratic ones to use their control of budgets and other means to restrict environmental regulation (Yeager 1991; Steinzor 2003; Mintz 2004; Yeager and Simpson 2009) and further that companies' investments in pollution control equipment is associated with the EPA's enforcement budget (Regens, Seldon, and Elliot 1997). But it is important to note that both major American political parties have shared in efforts to reduce regulation in ways that increased the risks and rates of corporate offenses. For example, both the Reagan and Clinton administrations saw to the deregulation of financial markets that contributed mightily to the waves of financial frauds from the 1980s to the 2008 economic crisis (see, e.g., Hagan 2010).

An important consequence of inconsistent regulation and enforcement over time is that the legitimacy of such laws is lost in the eyes of the regulated parties, a result that can help to increase rates of violation.

III. Organizational Limits

The organizational limits on effective enforcement of corporate offenses are largely embedded within the institutional constraints noted above. In general the enforcement agencies are limited structurally by the government's dual roles as facilitator of economic growth and as protector of the broader common good: regulation cannot be "too stringent" lest it be argued to threaten the health of the economy. And regulators are limited culturally by popular conceptions of crime and criminals. Criminal sanctions, arguably among the most deterrent of punishments for corporate offenders, are infrequently used in such cases, importantly (but not only) because the violators typically don't match the combination of clear intent and disreputable character that the culture attributes to "real" criminals (Yeager and Simpson 2009).

In this section I consider organizational constraints as they relate to the nature of offenses and to processes of enforcement. These are related phenomena, to be sure, but they each highlight different aspects of the social dynamics that limit the law's ability to punish and deter corporate offenses, especially those of large companies.

Corporate violations of law are often complex, either because they involve highly technical acts, because they are situated in complex organizational and interorganizational environments, or both. In the first case the law enforcers face difficulties in detecting and proving offenses that are sophisticated and that push the limits of legality in ways not anticipated by law. This was one of the features of the illegal conduct at the heart of the 2008 financial crisis. It was widely observed that even the senior executives of leading investment banks did not understand the complex financial products that they were buying and selling, such as credit default swaps and bonds built on suspect collections of home mortgages and sold as safe to trusting investors (Lewis 2010). Arguably this is one of the reasons that no bank executives were criminally prosecuted, along with lax regulation of these investments (see Morgenson and Story 2011; Henning 2012). The crimes of the convicted financier Bernard Madoff were much simpler—his massive fraud was a classic pyramid scheme—but for years they evaded detection by federal agents in part because they were hidden by sophisticated computer recordkeeping and programming ruses created in Madoff's firm (Henriques 2011).

In the second case—offenses that are situated in complex organizational environments—the social control of corporate offenses is limited not only by legal difficulties in attaching blame (i.e., proving criminal intent) but also by the problem of reaching the consciences of managers and executives. This is related to the familiar observation that people will often do things in crowds that they would not consider when acting alone, the moral hold of conscience having been diluted in the group context. But in contrast to the spontaneity of crowd deviancy, the corporate context of business often "disorganizes" moral perceptions in particular, patterned ways that are associated with the rational design of bureaucratized operations.

In his close analysis of this problem, Stone (1975) noted that formal legal controls carried more of the responsibility for protecting society from business crimes precisely because individual consciences could not be counted on to restrain behavior as they do for most people in the case of such conventional crimes as murder and burglary. Unfortunately, the organizational characteristics responsible for law's burden can also make it difficult for law to meet it. Authority relations, segmented responsibilities and (sub)cultures, and communication patterns in corporate hierarchies can work to reduce people's sense of accountability to law and even to their own moral views (see also Yeager 1995a; Simpson 2002, p. 53).

A characteristic dynamic involves organizational cultures in which discussion of ethical problems is implicitly discouraged (see also, Stone 1975: 53, 61–62). This occurs when top executives place high performance expectations on subordinates and the latter feel that they cannot communicate upward any difficulties they may experience in reaching corporate goals for fear that executives will find them incompetent. Notably, such communication blockages can occur not only in companies that exhibit unethical cultures given to law violations, but also in corporations with moral environments oriented more toward legal compliance. In either case, though, where it exists the dynamic reduces the inhibiting effect of law and punishment risks to the extent that no one may feel responsible for offenses: top executives can claim that they had no knowledge of the violations, while lower-level managers can argue that they had little choice but to break laws if they were to succeed or even survive in their jobs. In addition to this psychological or perceptual effect, the dynamic also poses obstacles to criminal law enforcement, denying proof of intent for executives while setting up lower-level actors as unfortunate scapegoats (cf., Laufer and Geis 2002). For both groups, then, the restraints of both law and conscience are diluted.[11]

There is another aspect of social complexity that restricts businesspeople's sensitivities to their consciences and law and thereby promotes illegality. This is perhaps best illustrated in the increasingly sophisticated financial industry that has come to dominate nations' economies via its mobilization of capital around the world. I have already suggested the difficulties posed to enforcement by increasingly complex financial investment products that render the offenses themselves complex. Here I have in mind another aspect of financial complexity: its tendency in the minds of offenders to render the notion of victims and victimization abstract to the vanishing point. Writing about the financial frauds of American corporations discovered in the early 2000s, but on a point that applies at least as well to the frauds associated with the economic crisis of 2008, I noted that

> [The victimization] was . . . abstract in the sense that corporate officials, dealing over long distances with intangible investment vehicles and absentee consumers rather than with local customers purchasing tangible products, could not easily perceive real victims and moral harm. These characteristics of the market facilitated the crimes by reducing the role of conscience in them. (Yeager 2007, p. 36)

In this sensibility, offenses take on the character of victimless crimes (cf., Geis 1995), thus neutralizing law's moral hold and leaving its potential effects only to those posed by the risk of substantial punishment. But as already noted, such punishments are infrequently imposed, especially for individuals in large and powerful corporate settings.

This dynamic also has implications for a nontraditional approach to corporate crime that is aimed precisely at reforming corporate cultures and managerial consciences. John Braithwaite (2002) has effectively argued for using restorative justice procedures to address corporate crimes instead of the traditional adversarial approaches of law. The approach calls for deliberative conferences between perpetrators and victims of corporate crimes in which the aim is to have the former come to appreciate and express true remorse for the harms they've caused and the latter to express authentic forgiveness. In theory, there are many advantages to this procedure, including the promotion of respect for law in a process that is cooperative rather than adversarial. But it could be challenged by difficulties in constructing effective representations of victims when they are as dispersed and abstract as are the countless institutional and individual victims of many complex corporate crimes (Yeager 2004).

The organization of enforcement efforts also shapes the effectiveness of law. At play here are factors that constrain justice's various purposes: deterrence, moral condemnation of wrongs, and equity. These factors range from dynamics of "turf protection" between agencies that share jurisdiction over offenses to the negotiating advantages especially large corporations have in their dealings with federal and state agencies. Collectively, they limit the use of the criminal sanction, the most deterrent and expressive of sanctions for corporate harms, and they often act to distribute sanctions disproportionately to less powerful offenders.

Enforcement agencies that share jurisdiction over cases engage in "turf battles" when, as is commonly the case, their annual budgets are determined importantly by how many cases they have successfully resolved. Because the federal regulatory agencies cannot themselves bring criminal prosecutions, being required to send cases of suspected corporate criminal activity to U.S. Justice Department prosecutors, they may instead keep such cases and work to resolve them using the more modest sanctions at their disposal (e.g., warnings and orders) that frame negotiations with offenders to come into compliance. These dynamics have been identified in past research for such agencies as the Federal Trade Commission and the EPA (Yeager 1991; Clinard and Yeager 2006).

Where this process occurs, it positions enforcement negotiations in the considerably less publicly visible and more technically oriented environs of agencies rather than in the more exposed and morally charged atmosphere of the criminal courts (but see limits on criminal cases in section IV). In doing so, it only enhances the advantages that powerful corporate organizations have at all stages of legal processes (cf., Mann 1985). These are the advantages of both wealth and knowledge of their businesses, resources that commonly outstrip those of the agencies when they are required to regulate technical aspects of business, and that can distort compliance in particular ways. In regulation by the EPA, for example, the need for the agency to negotiate the terms and conditions of compliance with companies both delayed compliance and reduced water pollution control (Yeager 1991); related processes and results have been found in environmental regulation in Europe (van de Bunt and Huisman 2007; Du Rées 2001). These negotiations also raise equity concerns when outcomes favor larger, more powerful firms over smaller companies because of the greater material and reputational resources larger companies bring to bear in discussions with government officials. In environmental regulation, for example, research has found that larger firms are less often cited for offenses—or are less seriously punished when cited—than smaller companies because they are better able to negotiate exceptions or persuade officials of their good-faith efforts to comply and/or their ability to appeal adverse legal decisions (Hawkins 1984; Shover et al. 1986; Yeager 1991; Firestone 2003).

Finally, governments' need to promote economic development may in various ways override their responsibilities for protecting the social welfare. This can be seen operating in connection with American federalism, in which national laws regulating corporations are sometimes delegated to the states for enforcement. For example, the federal EPA delegates much of the enforcement of environmental laws to the states, which may be more lenient than the federal government in enforcing them. A study of the federal hazardous waste law found that on average states issued fines for business offenses that were "less than half of what the federal government would impose in similar circumstances" (Atlas 2007, p. 972). Presumably having to do with states' concern to keep and attract businesses by being perceived as "reasonable" in their enforcement policies, this relative leniency can also reduce the deterrent effect of law. Research on the deterrent effects of the federal Clean Water Act in the chemical industry found evidence that federal fines were more deterrent than state fines (Glicksman and Earnhart 2007).

Interestingly, such patterns of delegation and reduced enforcement have also been found in China, where responsibilities for enforcing environmental laws and maintaining high levels of economic growth are handed to the same regional and local officials (Yeager and Simpson 2009).

IV. Legal Limits

When considering law's effects, deterrence is a good place to begin. For corporate offenses, deterrence is the primary function of punitive sanctions, the aim being to persuade corporations and their agents that law violations are not worth the risk of being caught and punished, especially by criminal law but also by large civil law fines. It has long been assumed that such punishments would be especially effective deterrents of corporate offenses because business decision makers rationally weigh the costs and benefits of their options before acting. Considerable research on organizations has since challenged the reach of the rationality assumption (e.g., Reed and Yeager 1996; Vaughan 1996; Simpson 2002). And even with the growth in recent years of nine- and occasionally ten-figure monetary penalties for major corporate offenses, the jury remains out as to just how much deterrence the law actually brings, especially for very large and wealthy companies.

As with research on corporate lawbreaking generally, the body of research on its deterrence by law is relatively sparse and the findings are equivocal overall (e.g., Simpson 2002; Ugrin and Odom 2010; Alexander and Cohen 2011). The deterrence from penalties for corporate offenses hinges on a number of circumstances, including the severity of penalties, the consistency with which they are imposed, the degree to which they change the incentives of individuals and groups inside firms to comply with laws (Stone 1975), the extent to which they impose collateral consequences of reputational damage that harm future business prospects (Fisse and Braithwaite 1983; Alexander and Cohen 2011), and so on. How much deterrence we get from what combination of sanctions for what sorts of offenses in what kinds of industries—this nexus remains to be much better deciphered by future research.

The need for such research is ever greater because the law proceeds to develop new sanctions and approaches to corporate misconduct. This is especially the case over the past quarter-century, with the creation of the federal sentencing guidelines for corporations in 1991, the Sarbanes-Oxley Act of 2002, and the Dodd-Frank Wall Street Reform and Consumer Protection Act of 2010. Collectively, these initiatives have increased penalties, established greater accountability of corporate executives for financial frauds, provided protections for whistleblowers inside companies, and given prosecutors new tools with which to seek reforms of internal corporate governance. Sarbanes-Oxley and Dodd-Frank were passed by the Congress in response to the waves of financial fraud that came to light both early and late in the first decade of the 21st century, and the resulting mix of sanctions may be especially promising for such offenses.

But implementation of these and other sanctions has raised a number of cautions regarding such matters as whether the severity, consistency, and publicity of corporate sanctions are adequate to deter companies and reform their cultures in more law-abiding directions. For example, between 2004 and 2007 federal prosecutors increased the use of deferred prosecution or nonprosecution agreements by over 300 percent in cases with fines of more than $1 million (Alexander and Cohen 2011, pp. 12–13). These are agreements not to pursue criminal charges against companies so long as they agree to pay the fines, reconfigure professional responsibilities, and establish internal compliance programs. From the government's viewpoint the agreements have the advantages of securing monetary penalties without costly litigation and the opportunity to insert monitors to impose governance reforms that may help to prevent future offenses. From the corporations' standpoint, the agreements avoid the stigma of criminal conviction, prevent broad public disclosure of the facts of bad corporate behavior, and offer the opportunity to present themselves as responsible corporate citizens, if rather newly minted ones. But these legal approaches—and similar agreements that mitigate penalties under the U.S. sentencing guidelines—also risk reduced deterrence. Critics argue that such negotiated approaches spare companies the stigma of criminal conviction and even the requirement to admit guilt, while imposing fines that do not deter large corporations (Laufer 2006; Lichtblau 2008).[12]

That even the biggest monetary penalties may not be sufficiently deterrent to large corporations is suggested by the federal government's settlement in 2011 with the pharmaceutical giant GlaxoSmithKline. For the illegal marketing of drugs the company agreed to pay $3 billion to settle criminal and civil investigations. The day the settlement was announced, the firm's stock rose 3 percent in value (Wilson 2011). Similarly, when the major Wall Street investment bank Goldman Sachs agreed in 2010 to pay $550 million to settle federal charges that it had misled investors regarding a subprime mortgage product, it amounted to only a fraction of its previous year's profit of $13.39 billion, and its stock price rose 5 percent after the settlement was announced (Chan and Story 2010). Such results suggest that the cases are not imposing sanctions that substantially affect profitability or that impose reputational penalties on large firms. On the latter point, there is some supportive research. In focus group research conducted after the financial frauds at major companies in the early 2000s, respondents said that they didn't generally make their own purchasing or investment decisions on the basis of companies' reputations for ethical behavior. Instead they commonly made these decisions in their own self-interest (i.e., on the basis of best price or best return on their investments) (Farkas et al. 2004).

Full-dress criminal trials—with their public disclosure of the facts of crimes and the stigma of conviction and condemnation by juries—may increase deterrent effects, especially for top corporate officials. But such cases are only infrequently brought against major companies and rarely against their top executives. As noted earlier, in contrast to the criminal cases brought for the savings and loan crimes of the 1980s and the financial fraud trials of Enron, Andersen, and a few other firms in the early 2000s, the U.S. Justice Department has not charged any major Wall Street banks or their executives with crimes for the pattern of fraud and other misconduct at the heart of the nation's (and world's) financial crisis of 2008. Lanny Breuer, assistant attorney general for the Department's criminal division, told a *Frontline* reporter that the potential cases raised problems in meeting the burden of proof for criminal cases, and that there was concern that bringing criminal cases would threaten the stability of large banks and by implication the economy, given the banks' central role in finance (Public Broadcasting System 2013).

The legal scholar Darryl Brown (2001) offers a related explanation for infrequent criminal cases against corporations. He argues that, ironically, the expansion of the concept of criminal responsibility to include the blameworthiness of the corporation as such—apart from individuals' own culpability—may spur prosecutors to proceed with civil rather than criminal cases against companies. This is because the idea that the organizational context is central to the motivation for crimes reduces the sense of blame and responsibility in such cases, relative to that attributed in conventional criminal cases. Thus, where enforcement officials have the choice between criminal and noncriminal (e.g., civil cases) means of proceeding against corporate crimes, they are likely to prefer the latter when they sense less blameworthiness, believe they can achieve the same preventative effects, and perceive a greater likelihood of success (less resistance from powerful companies) and lower risks of spillover costs to innocent third parties (customers, employees) than the stigma of criminal convictions might bring.

The other and related challenge to the deterrence of corporate offenses is inconsistency in enforcement. As noted earlier, enforcement waxes and wanes with changes in political leadership and ideology. It also varies with respect to the power of businesses: smaller firms and their employees more often receive harsher sanctions than large companies and their officials (Yeager 1991; Public Broadcasting System 2013). Such patterns raise basic questions of fairness and of whether the most serious harms are being punished proportionately. They also undermine the legitimacy of the law in the minds of business officials, increasing the likelihood of future offenses (Yeager 1995a; Gunningham, Thornton, and Kagan 2005; Yeager 2007).

V. Conclusion

Problems in protecting society from the harms done by corporations have been with us since the first corporate charters were issued. These problems today stem largely from the sources of the power of large companies: their organizational complexity and the political prowess that comes from their large financial resources and presumed centrality to economic health. In the face of such power, law often proceeds cautiously, its enforcers fearing losses in court to powerful adversaries, spillover costs, and the disapproval of political superiors whose allegiances might be biased by ideology and the material support of their corporate constituents. Among the consequences are reductions in law's legitimacy and deterrent impacts, and repeated waves of corporate offending, as history shows.

The factors in social power that insulate corporations from more effective law enforcement are also responsible for the growing risks that corporate corruption and irresponsibility pose to society, as illustrated in the role of fraud in the 2008 financial collapse. Whether law enforcement itself will be able to manage these risks more effectively, or whether it will be concluded that many of the world's dominant companies cannot adequately coexist with democratic societies and hence must themselves be restructured into smaller units, are questions that the future must resolve.

Notes

1. Quoted in Ford (1905).
2. For example, the world's largest corporation as ranked in 2012 (DeCarlo 2012), ExxonMobil, reported annual revenues of $453 billion that year (*Fortune.com* 2015), a sum greater than the gross domestic products (GDP) of most countries in 2012, including Austria, Israel, Finland, and Ireland, and 162 other countries among the 193 ranked by The World Bank (2015; see also Coll 2012). While national GDP and corporate revenues are not indicators of the same metric (Worstall 2011), their comparison nonetheless offers perspective on the great size and influence of especially the largest multinational companies.
3. The political influence of corporations was greatly expanded by the 2010 decision of the U.S. Supreme Court in *Citizens United v Federal Election Commission*, 558 U.S. 310 (2010). In the decision the Court overturned precedent and extended corporations' First Amendment rights to free speech to allow them to fund their own advertisements for or against candidates for political office.
4. For example, in late 2012, 112 workers were killed in a garment factory fire in Bangladesh. Through an opaque series of contracts and subcontracts the factory had been making garments for Walmart and Sears, among other companies. Both corporations denied responsibility for the factory's unsafe working conditions, saying that the factory was not authorized to make their clothing and that they were unaware that it was still doing so (Yardley 2012). Both companies fired the suppliers that had contracted with the factory to produce the goods, but in 2011 Walmart reportedly played a key role in "blocking an effort to have global retailers pay more for apparel to help Bangladesh factories improve their electrical and fire safety" (Greenhouse 2012).
5. For additional discussion of the points made in this section, see also Yeager (1995a, 1995b).
6. Cf., Garland (2001), who suggests that in the American cultural context criminal penalties for all forms of crime act as a sort of pricing mechanism for misconduct, a notion in keeping with the idea that economistic categories of interpretation dominate alternative perspectives on justice in the current era of neoliberalism.
7. For example, when my son's pediatric allergist, a world-renowned medical researcher and elite medical school faculty member, was convicted of murdering his wife, he was sentenced to life in prison without parole, notwithstanding his lack of any previous criminal record and his outstanding contributions to medicine.
8. See, for example, Yeager (1983, p. 979).

9. Galanter's analysis was focused on the penetration of court decisions, but his reasoning extends nicely to the context of legislation.
10. See also Cullen, Cavender, Maakestad, and Benson 2006: Ch. 7.
11. For an excellent case study of this dynamic see Vandivier (2002). For a somewhat different version of it, see Geis (1995). Our research in two companies on the ethical climates of corporations and their relations to organizational structures and processes is discussed in Kram, Yeager, and Reed (1989), Yeager (1995a), and Reed and Yeager (1996, pp. 370–75).
12. Experts also raise other concerns about such agreements, including whether prosecutors are the right persons to be imposing internal governance reforms on corporations (Barkow and Barkow 2011).

REFERENCES

Alexander, Cindy R., and Mark A. Cohen. 2011. "The Causes of Corporate Crime: An Economic Perspective." In *Prosecutors in the Boardroom: Using Criminal Law to Regulate Corporate Conduct*, pp. 11–37, edited by Anthony S. Barkow and Rachel E. Barkow. New York: New York University Press.

Alford, Robert R., and Roger Friedland. 1985. *Powers of Theory: Capitalism, the State, and Democracy*. New York: Cambridge University Press.

Atlas, Mark. 2007. "Enforcement Principles and Environmental Agencies: Principal–Agent Relationships in a Delegated Environmental Program." *Law and Society Review* 41: 939–80.

Barkow, Anthony S., and Rachel E. Barkow. 2011. *Prosecutors in the Boardroom: Using Criminal Law to Regulate Corporate Conduct*. New York: New York University Press.

Braithwaite, John. 2002. *Restorative Justice and Responsive Regulation*. New York: Oxford University Press.

Brown, Darryl K. 2001. "Street Crime, Corporate Crime, and the Contingency of Criminal Liability." *University of Pennsylvania Law Review* 149: 1295–360.

Bunt, Henk van de, and Wim Huisman. 2007. "Organizational Crime in the Netherlands." In *Crime and Justice in the Netherlands*, pp. 217–60, edited by Michael Tonry and Catrien Bijleveld. Vol. 35 of Crime and Justice: A Review of Research, edited by Michael Tonry. Chicago: University of Chicago Press.

Chan, Sewell, and Louise Story. 2010. "Goldman Pays $550 Million to Settle Fraud Case." *New York Times* (July 15). Available at http://www.nytimes.com/2010/07/16/business/16goldman.html

Clinard, Marshall B., and Peter Cleary Yeager. 2006. *Corporate Crime*. New Brunswick, NJ: Transaction Publishers.

Clinard, Marshall B., Peter Cleary Yeager, Jeanne Brisette, David Petrashek, and Elizabeth Harries. 1979. *Illegal Corporate Behavior*. Washington, D.C.: U.S. Government Printing Office.

Coll, Steve. 2012. *Private Empire: ExxonMobil and American Power*. New York: The Penguin Press.

Cullen, Francis T., Gray Cavender, William J. Maakestad, and Michael L. Benson. 2006. *Corporate Crime Under Attack: The Fight to Criminalize Business Violence*, 2nd ed. New York, NY: Routledge.

DeCarlo, Scott. 2012. "The World's Biggest Companies." *Forbes* (April 18). Available at http://www.forbes.com/sites/scottdecarlo/2012/04/18/the-worlds-biggest-companies/

Duhigg, Charles. 2009. "Clean Water Laws Are Neglected, at a Cost in Suffering." *New York Times* (September 13).

Du Rées, Helena. 2001. "Can Criminal Laws Protect the Environment?" *Journal of Scandinavian Studies in Criminology and Crime Prevention* 2: 109–26.

Farkas, Steve, Ann Duffett, Jean Johnson, and Beth Syat. 2004. *A Few Bad Apples? An Exploratory Look at What Typical Americans Think about Business Ethics Today.* New York: Public Agenda (www.publicagenda.com).

Firestone, Jeremy. 2003. "Enforcement of Pollution Laws and Regulations: An Analysis of Forum Choice." *Harvard Environmental Law Review* 27: 105–76.

Fisse, Brent, and John Braithwaite. 1983. *The Impact of Publicity on Corporate Offenders.* Albany: State University of New York Press.

Ford, Paul Leicester, ed. 1905. *The Works of Thomas Jefferson*, vol. 12 (Correspondence and Papers, 1816–1826). New York: G. P. Putnam's Sons.

Fortune.com. 2015. "Fortune 500 2012." Available at http://fortune.com/fortune500/2012/

Galanter, Marc. 1974. "Why the 'Haves' Come Out Ahead: Speculations on the Limits of Legal Change." *Law and Society Review* 9: 95–160.

Garland, David. 2001. *The Culture of Control: Crime and Social Order in Contemporary Society.* Chicago: University of Chicago Press.

Geis, Gilbert. 1995. "The Heavy Electrical Equipment Antitrust Cases of 1961." In *White-Collar Crime: Classic and Contemporary Views*, 3rd ed., pp. 151–65, edited by Gilbert Geis, Robert F. Meier, and Lawrence M. Salinger. New York: The Free Press.

Glicksman, Robert L., and Dietrich H. Earnhart. 2007. "The Comparative Effectiveness of Government Interventions on Environmental Performance in the Chemical Industry." *Stanford Environmental Law Journal* 26: 317–71.

Greenhouse, Steven. 2012. "Documents Indicate Walmart Blocked Safety Push in Bangladesh." *New York Times* (December 5). Available at http://www.nytimes.com/2012/12/06/world/asia/3-walmart-suppliers-made-goods-in-bangladeshi-factory-where-112-died-in-fire.html

Gunningham, Neil A., Dorothy Thornton, and Robert A. Kagan. 2005. "Motivating Management: Corporate Compliance in Environmental Protection." *Law and Policy* 27: 289–316.

Hagan, John. 2010. *Who Are the Criminals? The Politics of Crime Policy from the Age of Roosevelt to the Age of Reagan.* Princeton, NJ: Princeton University Press.

Hawkins, Keith. 1984. *Environment and Enforcement: Regulation and the Social Definition of Pollution.* New York: Oxford University Press.

Henning, Peter J. 2012. "Is That It for Financial Crisis Cases?" *New York Times* (August 13). Available at http://dealbook.nytimes.com/2012/08/13/is-that-it-for-financial-crisis-cases/

Henriques, Diana B. 2011. *The Wizard of Lies: Bernie Madoff and the Death of Trust.* New York: Times Books, Henry Holt and Company.

Herman, Edward S. 1981. *Corporate Control, Corporate Power.* New York: Cambridge University Press.

Kram, Kathy E., Peter Cleary Yeager, and Gary Reed. 1989. "Decisions and Dilemmas: The Ethical Dimension in the Corporate Context." In *Research in Corporate Social Performance and Policy*, vol. 11, pp. 21–54, edited by James E. Post. Greenwich, CT: JAI Press.

Laufer, William S. 2006. *Corporate Bodies and Guilty Minds: The Failure of Corporate Criminal Liability.* Chicago: University of Chicago Press.

Laufer, William S., and Gilbert Geis. 2002. "Corporate Crime and a New Brand of Cooperative Regulation." *Cahiers de Defense Sociale* 2002: 139–48.

Lewis, Michael. 2010. *The Big Short: Inside the Doomsday Machine*. New York: W. W. Norton and Company.

Lichtblau, Eric. 2008. "In Justice Shift, Corporate Deals Replace Trials." *New York Times* (April 9). Available at http://www.nytimes.com/2008/04/09/washington/09justice.html?pagewanted=all

Mann, Kenneth. 1985. *Defending White-Collar Crime: A Portrait of Attorneys at Work*. New Haven, CT: Yale University Press.

Messner, Steven F., and Richard Rosenfeld. 2013. *Crime and the American Dream*, 2nd ed. Belmont: Wadsworth.

Michalowski, Raymond J., and Ronald C. Kramer. 1987. "The Space between Laws: The Problem of Corporate Crime in a Transnational Context." *Social Problems* 34: 34–53.

Mintz, Joel A. 2004. "'Treading Water': A Preliminary Assessment of EPA Enforcement during the Bush II Administration." *Environmental Law Reporter* 34: 10933–53.

Morgenson, Gretchen, and Louise Story. 2011. "In Financial Crisis, No Prosecutions of Top Figures." *New York Times* (April 14). Available at http://www.nytimes.com/2011/04/14/business/14prosecute.html?pagewanted=all&_r=0

New York Times. 2012. "No Crime, No Punishment." (August 25). Available at https://www.google.com/#q=New+York+Times.+2012.+%E2%80%9CNo+Crime%2C+No+Punishment.%E2%80%9D+

Public Broadcasting System. 2013. "The Untouchables." *Frontline* (January 22). http://www.pbs.org/wgbh/pages/frontline/untouchables/

Reed, Gary E., and Peter Cleary Yeager. 1996. "Organizational Offending and Neoclassical Criminology: Challenging the Reach of a General Theory of Crime." *Criminology* 34: 357–82.

Regens, James L., Barry J. Seldon, and Euel Elliott. 1997. "Modeling Compliance to Environmental Regulation: Evidence from Manufacturing Industries." *Journal of Policy Making* 19: 683–96.

Shover, Neal, Donald A. Clelland, and John Lynxwiler. 1986. *Enforcement or Negotiation: Constructing a Regulatory Bureaucracy*. Albany: State University of New York Press.

Simpson, Sally S. 1986. "The Decomposition of Antitrust: Testing a Multilevel, Longitudinal Model of Profit Squeeze." *American Sociological Review* 51: 859–75.

Simpson, Sally S. 1987. "Cycles of Illegality: Antitrust Violations in Corporate America." *Social Forces* 65: 943–63.

Simpson, Sally S. 2002. *Corporate Crime, Law, and Social Control*. New York: Cambridge University Press.

Steinzor, Rena. 2003. *Testimony before the Subcommittee on Fisheries, Wildlife, and Water of the U.S. Senate Regarding Implementation of the Clean Water Act*. U.S. Senate. Available at www.epw.senate.gov/108th/Steinzor_091603.htm.

Stone, Christopher D. 1975. *Where the Law Ends: The Social Control of Corporate Behavior*. New York: Harper and Row.

Stryker, Robin. 2007. "Half Empty, Half Full, or Neither: Law, Inequality, and Social Change in Capitalist Democracies." *Annual Review of Law and Social Science* 3: 69–97.

Ugrin, Joseph C., and Marcus D. Odom. 2010. "Exploring Sarbanes-Oxley's Effect on Attitudes, Perceptions of Norms, and Intentions to Commit Financial Statement Fraud from a General Deterrence Perspective." *Journal of Accounting and Public Policy* 29: 439–58.

Vandivier, Kermit. 2002. "Why Should My Conscience Bother Me? Hiding Aircraft Brake Hazards." In *Corporate and Governmental Deviance: Problems of Organizational Behavior in Contemporary Society*, 6th ed., pp. 146–66, edited by M. David Ermann and Richard R. Lundman. New York: Oxford University Press.

Vaughan, Diane. 1996. *The Challenger Launch Decision: Risky Technology, Culture, and Deviance at NASA*. Chicago: University of Chicago Press.

The World Bank. 2015. "GDP (current US$)." Available at http://data.worldbank.org/indicator/NY.GDP.MKTP.CD?order=wbapi_data_value_2012+wbapi_data_value&sort=desc

Worstall, Tim. 2011. "GDP for a Country Is Not the Same Thing as Turnover for a Business." *Forbes* (June 28). Available at http://www.forbes.com/sites/timworstall/2011/06/28/gdp-for-a-country-is-not-the-same-thing-as-turnover-for-a-business/

Yardley, Jim. 2012. "Horrific Fire Revealed a Gap in Safety for Global Brands." *New York Times* (December 6). Available at http://www.nytimes.com/2012/12/07/world/asia/bangladesh-fire-exposes-safety-gap-in-supply-chain.html

Yeager, Peter Cleary. 1983. "The Limits of Law: On Chambliss and Seidman's *Law, Order, and Power*." *Law and Social Inquiry* 8: 974–84.

Yeager, Peter Cleary. 1991. *The Limits of Law: The Public Regulation of Private Pollution*. New York: Cambridge University Press.

Yeager, Peter Cleary. 1995a. "Management, Morality, and Law: Organizational Forms and Ethical Deliberations." In *Corporate Crime: Contemporary Debates*, pp. 147–67, edited by Frank Pearce and Laureen Snider. Toronto: University of Toronto Press.

Yeager, Peter Cleary. 1995b. "Law, Crime, and Inequality: The Regulatory State." In *Crime and Inequality*, pp. 247–76, edited by John Hagan and Ruth Peterson. Stanford: Stanford University Press.

Yeager, Peter Cleary. 2004. "Law versus Justice: From Adversarialism to Communitarianism." *Law and Social Inquiry* 29: 891–915.

Yeager, Peter Cleary. 2007. "Understanding Corporate Lawbreaking: From Profit Seeking to Law Finding." In *International Handbook of White-Collar and Corporate Crime*, pp. 25–49, edited by Henry N. Pontell and Gilbert Geis. New York: Springer.

Yeager, Peter Cleary. Forthcoming. *Corporate Crime and Punishment: A Sociology of Markets, Morality, and Malfeasance*. New York: Oxford University Press.

Yeager, Peter Cleary, and Sally S. Simpson. 2009. "Environmental Crime." In *The Oxford Handbook of Crime and Public Policy*, pp. 325–55, edited by Michael Tonry. New York: Oxford University Press.

CHAPTER 32

....

PUBLIC OPINION AND PUBLIC POLICY ON WHITE-COLLAR CRIME

....

SHANNA R. VAN SLYKE AND DONALD J. REBOVICH

THIS chapter discusses what ordinary people think about white-collar crime and the proper punishment for it, which was a topic of concern at the U.S. Sentencing Commission's Symposium on Economic Crime in September 2013. Like the commission's previous symposium on this topic in 2000, research evidence on public opinion about white-collar crime was solicited. The significance of the subject matter covered in this chapter therefore lies in its role in informing sentencing policy.

The purpose of the symposium was to discuss how the current sentencing guidelines for federal fraud offenders are too harsh. Most attendees were sentencing judges, many of whom explained how they respond to such "absurdly" harsh guidelines calculations by sentencing offenders far below what the guidelines recommend. Judge Preska, for example, shared her experience during the sentencing of Joe Collins of the now-defunct Refco Group Inc., which resulted in losses over $2.4 billion (Hurtado 2013). According to the guidelines, Collins deserved a lifetime prison sentence, yet he received a year and a day behind bars (Hurtado 2013). The judges seemed to share the sentiment that "long-firm fraud" (Levi 2008) is anomalous behavior and, therefore, not reflective of the person perpetrating it. Indeed, Preska explained her departure from the guidelines by saying, "There's no doubt that, but for this matter, Mr. Collins is a certifiable saint" (Hurtado 2013). Because they do not view these fraudsters as criminals, the judges refuse to sentence them to lengthy prison terms—despite the long sentences supposedly required by the guidelines.

The judges' sentiments are reminiscent of allegations from more than a century ago. For example, Sutherland (1949/1983) observed how "Legislators admire and respect businessmen and cannot conceive of them as criminals; businessmen do not conform to the popular stereotype of 'the criminal'" (p. 57). While the Sherman Antitrust Act

(1890) was being debated, a leading official in the Department of Justice explained why criminal prosecution is inappropriate for handling such offenses: "Most of the defendants in antitrust cases are not criminals in the usual sense. There is no inherent reason why antitrust enforcement requires branding them as such" (Wendell Berge 1940, cited in Sutherland [1949] 1983, p. 54).

Equally entrenched is the notion that public tolerance contributes to the underenforcement and punishment of white-collar crime:

> The immunity enjoyed by the perpetrator of new sins has brought into being a class for which we may coin the term criminaloid. By this, we designate such as prosper by flagitious practices which have not yet come under the effective ban of public opinion. Often, indeed, they are guilty in the eyes of the law; but since they are not culpable in the eyes of the public and in their own eyes, their spiritual attitude is not that of a criminal. The law-maker may make their misdeeds crimes, but, so long as morality stands stock-still in the old tracks, they escape both punishment and ignominy. (Ross 1907, pp. 47–48)

Writing at the turn of the 20th century, however, Ross did not have systematic empirical research upon which to base this statement. The purpose of the present analysis therefore is to review the available evidence on what the public thinks and wants about white-collar crime and its control. In doing so, we reach four main conclusions:

- Public opinion research is sufficiently rigorous to inform public policy debates;
- The public usually is less concerned with and punitive toward white-collar than street crime, although the magnitude and direction of this relationship differ according to the types of white-collar crimes about which people are surveyed;
- The public wants white-collar offenders to be punished more severely than is the norm when compared to actual sentences given to convicted white-collar offenders; and
- Public perceptions of white-collar crime punishment must be known to achieve the punishment goal of general deterrence.

Section I provides the definition of white-collar crime used in this essay and discusses limitations of the available research base on white-collar crime public opinion and of survey research more broadly. Section II summarizes the existing research on public perceptions of white-collar crime, while section III presents the current research about the public's punishment recommendations for white-collar offenders. Both literature review sections are limited to research using U.S. samples. Section IV concludes by suggesting directions for future research on public perceptions of and punitive attitudes toward white-collar criminals.

I. DEFINITIONAL AND METHODOLOGICAL CONSIDERATIONS

Disagreement over the definition of white-collar crime is noted in just about every white-collar crime research article and textbook. Similarly well recognized are challenges associated with designing valid survey research, which are discussed in social science research methods texts, political science public opinion literature, and scholarly work involving survey research designs.

A. Differing Definitions

Because the primary purpose of this chapter is to review the empirical literature on public opinion of white-collar crime, and due to its popularity in empirical research on white-collar crime, we will use the following offense-based definition of white-collar crime: "an illegal act or series of illegal acts committed by nonphysical means and by concealment or guile to obtain money or property, to avoid payment of money or property, or to obtain business or personal advantage" (Edelhertz 1970, p. 3). Using an offense-based definition not only casts a broader net in terms of selecting studies appropriate for inclusion but also allows for easier comparisons of punishments meted out to white-collar versus street offenders. (Refer to Chapter 2 by Geis and Chapter 3 by Pontell in this Handbook for more detailed treatments of these alternative definitions and their implications.) That said, when policymakers, practitioners, and the media discuss white-collar crime—as in the symposium mentioned at the outset of this essay—they usually are referring to upperworld offenders and thereby are invoking more of an offender-based definition.

B. Methodological Challenges

The limitations of public opinion research, however, must be taken into account. First, the average citizen is less informed than are the people involved in criminal justice processing about the sentencing considerations that are relevant to judges, which range from the facts of individual cases to the availability of prison space. The average citizen thus tends to rely on the media for information about criminal justice issues while the media, in turn, are influenced by society's elites (Lock 1999; Stimson 2004). Few dispute that the media provide misleading depictions of crime and criminals (e.g., Kappeler and Potter 2005). Regarding this concern, Page and Shapiro (1992, p. 34) cautioned, "Democracy has little meaning if public opinion is manipulated." A related matter centers on the notion that prejudice and discrimination—that is, antidemocratic motives—might drive public opinion (Barkan 2014). Research on public opinion of street crime and punishment serves as one example of this possibility; here, for instance, typification of offenders as African-American has been linked to more punitive punishment recommendations (Chiricos, Welch, and Gertz 2004).

Second, public opinion research long has been accused of measuring "nonattitudes" rather than for capturing peoples' genuine and adequately informed opinions about topics such as politics (Converse 1970; Page and Shapiro 1992; Manza and Uggen 2006). Asking the same question at different points in the survey, or asking the same question in a different context, for example, has elicited different responses from the same respondents. Indeed, the public has been described as apathetic if not ignorant about many things criminologists study, such as actual sentencing outcomes and resource allocations (Shaw et al. 1998). Beyond concerns about nonattitudes is the questionable relationship between attitudes expressed in public opinion surveys and actual behaviors. Although the results are mixed, research on voting behavior, for example, suggests a divergence between what people say they will do and how they actually behave (Chaiklin 2011).

The main purpose of this section has been to sensitize readers to possible limitations of the research about to be reviewed. But all social science research has limitations, and this section is titled "challenges" rather than "barriers" because improved methodological designs and careful interpretations can address the problems identified above:

> Taking everything into account, we believe that the available survey data are generally reliable and appropriate . . . We see survey research as a remarkably effective research tool, particularly in recent years when practitioners have been able to take advantage of long experience. Carefully worked out sampling schemes permit confident inferences about the opinions of millions of Americans, based on interviews with a few hundred of them. Modern instrument design and interviewing techniques, combining art and science, elicit meaningful responses. Aggregate results of the sort we are concerned with (percentages of respondents giving particular answers) tend to average out individual-level error and fluctuations. (Page and Shapiro 1992, p. 30)

II. Public Perceptions about White-Collar Crime

This section begins by summarizing the existing research on public perceptions and then moves into a closer look at a relatively recent series of national surveys. The most commonly measured aspect of public opinion on white-collar crime has been perceived seriousness; other aspects include perceptions of harmfulness, wrongfulness, frequency, risk of victimization, offender characteristics, offender risk of recidivism, and likelihood of apprehending and punishing offenders. The following subsections review this literature in terms of these different aspects.

A. Seriousness

Systematic research gauging public perceptions of white-collar crime using general population samples can be traced to Rossi et al.'s (1974) examination of the perceptions held by Baltimore residents regarding 140 Uniform Crime Report (UCR) crimes. After fatal crimes, the respondents perceived as the most serious, in descending order, the following offenses: drug selling; assault, rape, and incest; other crimes involving actual or threatened harm; non-white-collar economic crimes involving losses over $25; crimes against the police; prostitution and homosexuality; and then white-collar crimes. Only property crimes involving less than $25 and crimes against order (e.g., loitering and disturbing the peace) were rated as less serious than the white-collar crimes included. Schrager and Short (1980) extended Rossi et al.'s (1974) study by distinguishing between individual and organizational offenses and examining the role of physical versus economic harm in people's seriousness ratings. Seriousness perceptions did not differ by whether they were organizational and individual; instead, the respondents ranked as most serious those crimes that involved physical harm. Cullen, Link, and Polanzi (1982) compared their results with those reported a decade earlier by Rossi et al. (1974) to identify any shifts in public perceptions. They found that the white-collar offenses exhibited the greatest increase in seriousness scores. That said, the white-collar crimes were viewed as less serious than the other crime types included in the survey.

A different, more qualitative approach using a convenience sample identified factors influencing public perceptions of seriousness. After first ranking offenses in order of perceived seriousness, participants were asked why they ranked offenses the way they did and revealed that actual and potential harm were influential factors, as were amount lost and type of victim (i.e., individual vs. organizational victims yielded higher seriousness scores).

Consistent with the emerging pattern of greater seriousness perceptions for fatal (and potentially fatal) crimes, Meier and Short (1985) found that fatal "hazards" of all kinds (i.e., common crime, white-collar crime, and natural disasters) are perceived as more serious than nonfatal hazards. The white-collar crimes, on the other hand, were viewed as the least serious. Likewise, Warr (1989) found that the white-collar offenses were viewed as less serious than violent and most nonviolent economic crimes. The white-collar crime with the highest rate—polluting a river used for drinking water— was assigned a seriousness score lower than that assigned to robbing a person of $400 on the street. Also in line with the existing literature, Carlson and Wilson (1993) documented the following pattern of perceived seriousness (in descending order): crimes resulting in multiple fatalities, crimes resulting in a single fatality, public corruption, fraud, violent crimes, and then nonviolent economic crimes.

The National White Collar Crime Center and White Collar Crime Research Consortium (NWC3) has conducted three waves of national public opinion research regarding white-collar crime, and this series of public opinion surveys represents a break from the earlier research documenting greater seriousness perceptions of street than white-collar crime. The first of these studies (Rebovich and Kane 2000) employed the direct-comparison methods, asking the respondents which one of two offenses they feel is more serious. Of the four comparisons, the respondents more frequently reported white-collar crime to be more serious than street crime. Comparing seriousness perceptions regarding different forms of white-collar crime, Rebovich and Kane (2002) reported that offenses with organizational offenders as well as offenses involving high-status offenders are perceived as more serious. (For a reanalysis of this data reaching similar conclusions, see Piquero, Carmichael, and Piquero [2008]).

The second (Kane and Wall 2005) and third (Huff, Desilets, and Kane 2010) NWC3 surveys used a different method. Rather than directly comparing the perceived seriousness of two offenses at a time, the respondents were told that the case crime of car theft has a seriousness score of 4 and then were asked to assign seriousness scores to a variety of other street and white-collar crimes. Kane and Wall uncovered an unusually high level of seriousness perceptions for white-collar crimes. Table 32.1 summarizes the results of the second and third NWC3 surveys. Differences in the specific offenses included make it difficult to determine any shift in public perceptions of the seriousness of white-collar versus street crimes. The offenses included in both surveys, however, increased in perceived seriousness. Embezzlement, for example, went from place 7 to place 6, while insurance overcharge increased from place 8 to place 5. As with earlier research, Kane and Wall found that white-collar crimes committed by organizational and high-status offenders were perceived as being more serious than white-collar crimes committed by individual and low-status offenders.

Table 32.1 Rankings of Offense Seriousness (in Descending Order)

Kane and Wall (2005)	Huff, Desilets, and Kane (2010)
Carjacking/murder	Espionage
Toxic waste	False drug label
Omission of safety report	Identity theft
Insurance fraud—false claims	Market rigging
Assault	Insurance overcharge
Database hack	Embezzlement
Embezzlement	Assault
Insurance overcharge	Hacking
False earnings report	False charges
Robbery	Burglary
Auction fraud	Overbilling
Burglary	Counterfeit sales

Van Slyke (2009) surveyed Floridian adults in 2008 to determine perceptions and punishment preferences regarding various nonviolent economic offenders. She asked respondents for their seriousness perceptions regarding three categories of crimes: (1) elite white-collar crimes such as government bribery and corporate fraud, (2) consumer frauds such as false advertising, and (3) nonviolent economic street crimes such as burglary. These results indicate that elite white-collar crime was viewed as most serious (with 74 percent of respondents reporting it to be "extremely serious"), compared with 53 percent for consumer fraud and 48 percent for street crime.

B. Harmfulness and Morality

In his examination of public perceptions of the harmfulness of white-collar crimes, Warr (1989) reported that white-collar crimes generally are viewed as less harmful than street crimes. For instance, evading $500 in federal income taxes, illegally receiving monthly welfare checks, and a repair shop overcharging $60 on auto repairs are viewed as less harmful than stealing a handbag containing $15, breaking into a house and stealing a television, and stealing an unlocked car. The environmental crime of polluting a river used for drinking water, however, was ranked as more harmful than the majority of street crimes and all other white-collar crimes. This last finding is consistent with the larger body of literature finding that crimes resulting in actual or potential death/injury tend to be perceived in more serious terms than crimes than do not result in actual or potential death/injury.

An interesting variant in the research on public perceptions of white-collar crime is Retting and Pasamanick's (1959) study involving 500 undergraduate students who were asked to rank the "wrongness" of 50 "moral prohibitions." The researchers compared their survey results with those obtained in a 1929 survey to identify any shifts in severity of moral judgments over time. Paired with the substantial increase in the perceived wrongfulness of suicide and mercy killings are decreases in the severity of moral judgments for several white-collar crimes such as paying low wages, selling below cost for competitive reasons, and misrepresenting the value of goods. "These changes in moral attitudes on the part of college students indicate the increasing influence of the corporate system upon the educated in our society," Retting and Pasamanick explained (p. 325). "Those violations that involve collective irresponsibility and those violations on the part of business which tend to support the corporate system, the so-called 'sinning by syndicate' ... have become increasingly acceptable" (p. 324).

In addition to measuring perceptions of seriousness and harmfulness, Warr (1989) gauged public opinion on how morally wrong white-collar versus street crimes are perceived to be. Although the average wrongfulness score for white-collar crimes exceeds the average seriousness and harmfulness scores (5.107 vs. 5.338 and 6.847), the individual white-collar crimes typically were perceived as less morally wrong than most street crimes. Indeed, breaking into a house and stealing a television set was ranked as more immoral than all included white-collar crimes with the exception of environmental pollution.

C. Frequency and Risk of Victimization

Using audience panels, Graber (1980) assessed the public perceptions of the frequency of different crimes types. She found that 46 percent of the respondents believe that street crimes are more common than white-collar crimes. In contrast, only 16 percent of the respondents think that white-collar crimes are more common than street crimes (the remaining 39 percent indicated that white-collar and street crimes occur with equal frequency).

Meier and Short (1985) measured public perceptions of victimization risk for white-collar crime, street crime, natural hazards, and nuisances. In stark contrast to the results presented thus far, residents of eastern Washington following the Mount St. Helens eruption revealed these top five highest-risk hazards, in descending order of perceived likelihood of victimization: (1) vandalism, (2) being overcharged by physicians, (3) being sold products that prove to be worthless or badly defective, (4) being confronted by drunks in public places, and (5) illegal overcharging by manufacturers.

D. Offenders

Although this literature review has been restricted to research using U.S. samples, O'Connor's (1984) study conducted in Australia using nonprobability sampling methods fills a gap in our knowledge regarding how members of the public perceive the perpetrators of white-collar crimes. O'Connor asked community members and students for their opinions of swindlers and violent offenders and found pronounced differences. Violent offenders were perceived to be single, male, of low social status, in their twenties, minimally educated, and working in an unskilled occupation, whereas swindlers were described as professionals, male, in their thirties, married, and highly educated. The respondents also described the personality of violent offenders using negative words (e.g., dangerous, vicious, non-intelligent, immature, and inconsiderate) and the personality of swindlers using more positive terms (e.g., intelligent, good mannered, mature, and considerate of others). O'Connor's participants reported that substance abuse problems, a family history of vice and crime, increasing amounts of violence in the media, and gang membership explain participation in violent crime. To explain involvement in fraud, on the other hand, the respondents thought that such an offender was "seeking an easy life" (p. 266) or needed money because of gambling debts.

Van Slyke (2009) investigated whether social identification with white-collar offenders influenced punitive attitudes toward them. Specifically, participants were asked how many out of ten elite white-collar, consumer fraud, and nonviolent street offenders "[o]nce had the same opportunities in life as you, in terms of income, education, and/ or employment" (p. 52). A respondent who answered seven or higher to this question about, for example, elite white-collar offenders was classified as socially identifying with elite white-collar offenders. (Respondents who answered seven or higher to this question for consumer fraud offenders were classified as socially identifying with consumer fraud offenders, and respondents who answered seven or higher to this question for street offenders were classified as socially identifying with street offenders.) Van Slyke also measured respondents' racial identification with these three offender groups by asking how many out of ten offenders "are Non-Hispanic white."

Approximately 60 percent of the respondents expressed social identification with white-collar offenders in terms of social factors such as educational background, while 46 percent of the respondents identified socially with street offenders. Differences were more pronounced with regard to perceived racial similarity with these offender types: 56 percent of Caucasian respondents racially identify with elite white-collar offenders, whereas 40 percent of Caucasian respondents do so with consumer fraud offenders, and only 14 percent of Caucasian respondents believe most nonviolent street-level economic offenders are Caucasian too.

Bridging the literature on public perceptions with that of punitive attitudes are questions on the perceived likelihood of apprehension and punishment for white-collar versus street crimes. Two studies based on random, national samples of U.S. citizens have asked the same question: "Who is more likely to be apprehended—a robber or a fraudster?" (Rebovich and Kane 2002; Holtfreter et al. 2008). The majority of the respondents in both studies—75 percent (Rebovich and Kane 2002; for a similar analysis of the same data, see Schoepfer, Carmichael, and Piquero [2007]) and 63 percent (Holtfreter et al. 2008)—believe that the robber stands the greater chance of being apprehended. Not only do U.S. citizens generally agree that the robber is more likely to be caught, but there is an even greater consensus regarding perceptions of punishment severity: 82 percent of Rebovich and Kane's sample and 66 percent of Holtfreter et al.'s sample report that robbers are more likely to be punished severely than are fraudsters.

III. Punitive Attitudes toward White-Collar Criminals

This section reviews the existing empirical literature measuring punitive attitudes toward white-collar offenders. It begins with patterns and trends in this body of literature, continues with variables identified as correlates of punitive attitudes, and concludes with theoretical work on punitive attitudes toward white-collar offenders.

A. Trends and Patterns

Table 31.2 shows that many of the earliest studies compared public preferences to actual court dispositions (Newman 1957; Gibbons 1968–1969; Rossi, Simpson, and Miller 1985; Miller, Rossi, and Simpson 1986; Miller, Rossi, and Simpson 1991), whereas later studies often have asked whether respondents feel current sentences are adequate (Kane and Wall 2005; Holtfreter et al. 2008; Unnever, Benson, and Cullen 2008; Huff, Desilets, and Kane 2010; see also Cullen et al. 1983). In addition, corporate offenses in the past frequently included physically harmful (or violent) crimes such as product and worker safety violations (e.g., Newman 1957; Cullen et al. 1985b; Rossi, Simpson, and Miller 1985), while fraud by corporate executives has been included with some regularity in later surveys (e.g., Manza, Brooke, and Uggen 2004; Huff, Desilets, and Kane 2010). Unlike earlier studies, later studies also exhibit an interest in governmental crime-control resource allocations (e.g., Rebovich and Kane 2002; Holtfreter et al. 2008) and in felon disenfranchisement (e.g., Manza, Brooks, and Uggen 2004; Padgett et al. 2007).

Regardless of such methodological shifts, table 32.2 shows that the public has wanted harsher punishments for white-collar offenders since the 1950s (e.g., Newman 1957; Cullen et al. 1983; Unnever, Benson, and Cullen 2008). One of the most recent national studies, for example, reported that 90 percent of the respondents favor harsher punishments for corporate financial fraud than is believed to be the case (Unnever, Benson, and Cullen 2008). Gibbons (1968–1969) reached the similar conclusion of a more punitive public by comparing San Francisco residents' recommended sanctions with prison terms actually imposed in court. This research also has revealed that a minority of the respondents believe the government devotes adequate resources to white-collar crime control (Kane and Wall 2005; Huff, Desilets, and Kane 2010).

Looking closely at crime types reveals the growing popularity of offense-based definitions: credit fraud, unnecessary repairs, and other individual-level offenses appear frequently in the more recent surveys. Rossi and Berk (1997), for instance, found that respondents express more punitiveness toward counterfeiting and forgery offenders than toward antitrust and bribery offenders, while Cohen, Rust, and Steen (2002) similarly reported that people want to punish more severely lower-status offenses (e.g., credit fraud) as opposed to higher-status ones (e.g., Medicaid fraud). Van Slyke (2009), on the other hand, reported that Floridians exhibit more punitive attitudes toward high-status than low-status white-collar offenders.

B. Correlates and Causes

Perceptions of how serious the offense is often are positively related to harsh sanctioning preferences, but this relationship is not as strong as some might assume (Rossi, Simpson, and Miller 1985). This pattern in seriousness–punitiveness findings suggests

Table 32.2 Summary of Research Findings on Punitive Attitudes toward White–Collar Crime

Study	Sample	Measure(s) of White–Collar Crime*	Measure(s) of Punitiveness	Key Findings
Newman (1957)	178 Madison, Wisconsin, residents	Misbranding Distasteful but not physically harmful adulteration Physically harmful adulteration	Appropriate sentences Whether actual court dispositions were adequate	Most Rs want WC offenders punished more severely than in actual court dispositions.
Gibbons (1968–1969)	320 San Francisco residents	Antitrust Embezzlement False advertising Tax evasion	Appropriate sentences Whether actual court dispositions were adequate	Rs generally want the street offenders punished more severely than WC offenders. Rs want antitrust offenders punished more severely than actual court dispositions.
Thomas, Cage, and Foster (1976)	3,334 residents of a southeastern SMSA	Public official asking a bribe Tax evasion	Recommended length of prison sentence	Rs generally want the street crimes punished more severely than the WC offenders. Rs want bribery punished more severely than tax evasion.
Blumstein and Cohen (1980)	603 residents of a U.S. county	Employee safety Fraud on a bank loan application Medicaid fraud	Recommended length of prison sentence	Rs generally want street offenders punished more harshly than WC offenders. Rs want employee safety punished more severely than Medicaid fraud, and Medicaid fraud more severely than bank loan fraud.
Cullen et al. (1983)	240 Galesburg, Illinois, residents	NA; the term "white-collar crime" was used	Whether current sentences are adequate	Most Rs feel that WC offenders' punishments have been too lenient and should be more severe. Most Rs feel that we should punish WC offenders as severely as street thieves.
Cullen et al. (1985b)*	Same as Cullen et al., 2003	Knowingly manufacturing and selling contaminated food that results in a death Physician who receives false Medicaid payments from the government A public official accepting a bribe in return for favors Fixing prices of a product like gasoline	Punitiveness scale, 1–11	Excluding violent offenses, street crimes received more punitive punishment assessments. Of the WCCs, embezzlement received the highest punitive scores and nonviolent offenses committed against or by corporations received the lowest punitive scores.

Study	Sample	Offense/Scenario	Measures	Findings
Rossi, Simpson, and Miller (1985); Miller, Rossi, and Simpson (1986); and Miller, Rossi, and Simpson (1991)*	774 Boston residents, High school students, criminal justice college students, Job Corps members, and law students	Cheating on federal income tax return to avoid payment of . . . ; Embezzling money amounting to . . . ; As a public official, taking bribes amounting to . . . ; Knowingly selling contaminated food to a customer; Conspiring with several companies to fix illegally the retail prices of their products	Punitiveness scale, 1–125; Whether specified court dispositions were adequate	Corporate offenders received harsher sentencing recommendations than individual offenders; this finding persists despite amount of money involved.
Rossi and Berk (1997)*	1,500 U.S. citizens	Concealing evidence of a drug's dangerous side effects; Insider trading; Medicaid provider fraud; Conspiracy involving price fixing; Underreporting income; County commissioner accepting a bribe to award a contract		Violent street crimes, then violent WCCs received the most punitive judgments. Food and drug offenses were the highest-ranked white-collar offenses, followed by major fraud and then environmental offenses. Tax and forgery/counterfeiting offenses were rated more punitively than antitrust, bribery, minor fraud, and embezzlement.
Cohen, Rust, and Steen (2002)	1,130 U.S. citizens	Credit fraud; Medicaid fraud	Support for incarceration, home monitoring, fine, supervision, other, or no punishment	Rs generally were more punitive toward the street offenders than WC offenders. Rs were more punitive toward the credit fraud than Medicaid fraud offender.
Rebovich and Kane (2002); Schoepfer, Carmichael, and Piquero (2007); Piquero, Carmichael, and Piquero (2008)	1,169 U.S. citizens	Fraudster	Support for equal, harsher, or more lenient treatment than received by a robber; Resource allocations	The respondents are equally divided for both measures.
Manza, Brooke, and Uggen (2004); Manza and Uggen (2006)	1,000 U.S. citizens	Illegal trading of stocks	Support for restoring voting rights	Rs were more punitive toward the WC offender than violent offenders but not sex offenders.
Kane and Wall (2005)*	1,604 U.S. citizens	False stockbroker information; Business venture; Unnecessary repair (home, object); Monetary loss (Internet); Credit card fraud	Perceived adequacy of government resource allocation for white-collar crime control	About a third of the respondents believe the government devotes enough resources to combat white-collar crime.

(Continued)

Table 32.2 Continued

Study	Sample	Measure(s) of White–Collar Crime*	Measure(s) of Punitiveness	Key Findings
Padgett et al. (2007)	1,593 residents of Florida	Illegal trading of stocks	Opposition to restoring voting rights	Rs generally were more punitive toward the WC offender than violent and sex offenders.
Holtfreter et al. (2008)	402 U.S. citizens	Fraudster	Support for equal, harsher, or more lenient treatment than received by a robber Perceived adequacy of government resource allocation for white-collar crime control	Rs generally were more punitive to the street offender than the WC offender. About two thirds of the respondents want the government to devote equal or more resources to WCC control.
Unnever, Benson, and Cullen (2008)	1,512 U.S. citizens	Corporate executives who conceal their company's true financial condition	Support for stiffer penalties	Rs generally support harsher penalties for WCC.
Van Slyke (2009)	400 residents of Florida	Insider trading Medicaid fraud Welfare fraud Car sales fraud	Support for incarceration Length of incarceration Support for disenfranchisement Length of disenfranchisement	Rs generally support harsher penalties for high-than low-status WC offenders.
Huff, Desilets, and Kane (2010)	2,503 U.S. citizens	Credit card fraud Unnecessary repairs Monetary loss (Internet) False stockbroker information Mortgage fraud	Perceived adequacy of government resource allocation for white-collar crime control	Less than half of Rs believe the government devotes enough resources to WCC.

Notes: R = respondent. WC = white-collar. WCC = white-collar crime.

* Examples of white-collar crimes included in these surveys are provided where indicated to conserve space. In these cases, the offenses listed were chosen to reflect the diversity of offenses included in the survey.

at least two things: (1) one should not draw conclusions about punishment preferences based on research that asks only about seriousness and (2) other variables are needed to explain variation in punitive attitudes.

Certain offense, offender, and victim characteristics seem to inflame public punitiveness. Rossi and Berk's (1997) and Cohen, Rust, and Steen's (2002) national surveys, for example, found that people are most punitive toward violent street offenders, then white-collar offenders, followed by nonviolent offenders. Boston residents consistently assigned harsher sentences to corporate offenders than to individual offenders (Rossi, Simpson, and Miller 1985; Miller, Rossi, and Simpson 1986, 1991; but see Cullen et al. [1985b], who used a smaller sample of Galesburg, Illinois, residents), while Thomas, Cage, and Foster (1976) found that amount of money lost and premeditation lead to more punitive punishment recommendations.

An especially illuminating survey conducted in Galesburg, Illinois, focused on punitive attitudes and punishment recommendations for white-collar offenders (Cullen et al. 1983). More than 80 percent of the respondents agreed with the following two statements: "White-collar offenders have gotten off too easily for too many years; they deserve to be sent to jail for their crimes just like everyone else" and "We should punish white-collar offenders just as severely as we punish people who steal money on the street." Similarly, a slightly smaller percentage of the respondents disagreed that "Since white-collar offenders usually don't harm anyone, they shouldn't be punished as much as regular criminals." In an effort to understand the basis for these punishment preferences, the authors asked a series of questions about the consequences of white-collar crime relative to street crimes. For the sample respondents, they reported that:

- 90 percent agreed that "While white-collar crimes may cost Americans a lot of money, street crimes like assaults, murders, and muggings are worse because they are much more likely to injure or kill people."
- 84 percent agreed that "While white-collar crimes can hurt society, street crimes like robbery are worse because they make people afraid to walk the streets at night."
- 76 percent agreed that "The amount of money lost through white-collar crime is more than that lost as a result of street crimes such as robberies, burglaries, and thefts."
- 64 percent agreed that "People who commit street crimes are more dangerous than white-collar offenders."
- 55 percent agreed that "White-collar crimes do more to undermine the morality in our society than do street crimes."

Thus, Galesburg residents recognize the substantial losses and erosion of trust involved in white-collar crimes and want these crimes punished severely, but they consider street crimes to be "worse" and their perpetrators more dangerous.

Cullen and associates (1985a) hypothesized that beliefs about the causes of crime influence people's preference for punitive versus rehabilitative crime-control strategies.

Specifically, drawing from attribution theory, they predicted that a positivist view of crime causation (i.e., beliefs that crime is caused by external, social ills rather than internal, rational choice) would be associated with rehabilitation rather than punishment support. Although their subjects' attributional styles significantly predicted punitiveness toward street crime and support for rehabilitation-oriented strategies, the respondents' beliefs about the causes of white-collar crime were unrelated to their reported crime-control preferences for this type of crime.

While the public tends to be more punitive toward violent street criminals than white-collar criminals in terms of incarceration support, research on felon disenfranchisement presents a different picture. Padgett et al.'s (2007) survey of Florida residents, for instance, revealed that the respondents expressed more opposition to restoring voting rights for white-collar offenders (convicted of illegal trading of stocks) than for violent and sex offenders. Less drastic, Manza, Brooke, and Uggen's (2004; see also Manza and Uggen 2006) national survey found that people are less supportive of restoring voting rights for white-collar than for violent criminals, but that people were least supportive of restoring voting rights for sex offenders.

One of the most recent national studies investigated the extent to which race and politics predicted public support for stricter regulation of the stock market and harsher punishment of corporate financial fraud (Unnever, Benson, and Cullen 2008). Although the majority of the sample supported less regulation, more than 90 percent supported harsher punishments. Black respondents were more likely to support regulation and to support harsher punishments, while conservative political ideology was negatively associated with regulation support and was unassociated with punitiveness. The authors concluded, "It may be that individuals construct their opinions about which offenders are most deserving of punishment based on the degree to which the offender is similar to them" (p. 184).

What has emerged from the corpus of survey research on punitive attitudes toward white-collar criminals is a rather consistent pattern of the public expressing the desire for more punitive sanctioning of particularly corporate and government white-collar criminals. Drawing from the Cullen et al. (1983) study, ordinary people appear to attach more significance to physical harm and vulnerability than they do to economic losses and damage to society's moral fabric in formulating judgments of appropriate prison sentences. Yet the disenfranchisement research (e.g., Manza, Brooke, and Uggen 2004) suggests that abuse of trust and/or misuse of power could be powerful determinants of public support for civil liberties restrictions.

IV. Conclusion

The existing research indicates that the public generally is more punitive toward white-collar offenders than toward nonviolent street offenders. Sanctions recommended by the public are significantly longer than sentences reported by federal and state correctional agencies. The available literature, unfortunately, does not allow for straightforward distinctions in findings based on low-level versus upperworld white-collar crime, which limits to some degree the utility of this evidence in informing policy debates. That said, the public opinion research that has been conducted about white-collar crime appears to have at least three implications for public policy about crime and justice, which are discussed in the following subsection. The final subsection outlines potentially useful directions for future research.

A. Public Opinion and Public Policy

First and most fundamentally, democratic theory and consensus perspectives on the purpose of criminal law hold that crime control should reflect public wishes and prevailing social norms (Merton 1957; Hagan 1994; Dye 2008). The U.S. Supreme Court reinforced this ideal when it ruled that public opinion is a valid basis for a state's punishment practices (*Gregg v. Georgia*, 428 U.S. 153, 154, 1976). Enforcement of social norms, however, requires determining what public consensus is—and when it shifts.

Second, one of the goals of federal sentencing guidelines (and of punishment more generally) is deterrence. The guidelines were designed with an intention to deter potential offenders from breaking the law (Rossi and Berk 1997). Research on deterrence consistently shows that perceptions of punishment are a more powerful determinant of lawbreaking decisions than is objective reality (e.g., see Chapter 30 by Paternoster and Tibbetts in this Handbook). It makes little difference, in other words, whether a punishment is severe if potential offenders— members of the public—do not perceive a punishment as being severe. Here again, we find value in public opinion research. Findings that the public believes white-collar offenders should be punished more harshly than is currently believed to be the case—along with findings that the public believes street offenders are punished more harshly than white-collar offenders—suggest that current punishment practices for white-collar crime are not achieving the goal of deterrence.

Moreover, as Arlen (2013) explained during the first day of the Sentencing Commission's symposium described at the start of this chapter, and as others have documented before (e.g., Becker 1968; Nagin and Pogarsky 2006), the role of severity of punishment is less powerful in offender decision making than is the role of certainty. Findings that the public believes white-collar offenders have a smaller chance of being apprehended and punished—combined with qualitative interviews with convicted white-collar offenders that reveal a low perceived likelihood of apprehension (and of harsh punishment) (Copes and Vieraitis 2009)—likewise suggest that current law-enforcement practices in regard to white-collar crime most likely are failing to have much of a deterrent effect on potential offenders. However, more research is needed to ascertain this with certainty. Public opinion (and offender interview) research can inform policy in terms of whether would-be offenders consider existing punishment to be a realistic threat that outweighs the perceived benefits of white-collar criminal behavior.

Third, and related to the second point, is that the subjects of public opinion research are actual and potential white-collar crime victims and witnesses (not to mention jurors and agents of the criminal justice system). That the public perceives a low likelihood of apprehension and punishment for these offenders could partially explain the relatively low reporting rates for white-collar crime (Rebovich and Layne 2000). Victimization surveys tell us that we stand a much greater chance of being victimized by white-collar crimes than of street crimes, especially violent crimes (Titus, Heinzelmann, and Boyle 1995). Yet we are far less likely to report white-collar crimes than we are to report most street crimes (Kane and Wall 2005). When researchers ask victims why they do not report, a common response is that they feel nothing would be done about it and that it ultimately was not worth their time to go to the police (Walsh and Schram 1980). Public opinion research provides a gauge of citizens' perceived credibility of the threat of punishment, which can be used to understand patterns in people's responses to white-collar crime.

B. Directions for Research

The value of public opinion about white-collar crime and punishment laid out above indicates a need for carefully conducted research designed with the goal of informing penal policy. To maximize their policy potential, future research should involve the following features:

- A focus on specific offenses, which vary in terms of factors identified as influencing punitive attitudes and which include offenses committed by high-status people that are the primary concern of policymakers and the media and that have the most severe consequences;
- A focus on actual punishments, which range from traditional sanctions such as incarceration and fines to less traditional sanctions such as disenfranchisement and license revocation;
- Strong research designs including representative samples, probing, pretesting, and other methods that address common limitations of public opinion research identified in section I;
- Qualitative designs, which might clarify why respondents support certain penal policies;
- Hypothesis testing, which could help us understand the public's punitive attitudes; and
- Replicated designs, which produce the most credible evidence and which can be achieved by asking the same questions the same way.

By selecting relevant crimes and punishments and addressing major methodological criticisms of public opinion research, researchers can facilitate the use of empirical evidence in criminal justice discussions and decision making.

A policy-relevant and potentially helpful avenue for theoretical work revolves around the judges' notion of "anomalous" behavior, recounted in this chapter's introduction. Attribution theory and threat literature could guide this research. Attribution theory suggests that people accept situational explanations (e.g., pressure to provide for one's family) for white-collar criminal behavior, whereas dispositional explanations (e.g., bad, dangerous person) are preferred for street criminals. That Cullen et al. (1985a) found no support for attribution theory in relation to punitive attitudes toward white-collar offenders should not discourage future efforts in this direction. Such complex topics as attributional styles, for instance, doubtless should be measured using multi-item scales. Threat theory suggests another path for future research. The literature reviewed in section II suggests that white-collar crimes are perceived as less threatening than street crimes, while other research has linked threats to more emotional and punitive responses (Marcus et al. 1995). We can take lessons from the application of threat to punitive attitudes toward street crime, which is a more developed body of research than punitive attitudes toward white-collar crime. Whereas race as emerged as the dominant theme in the literature on threat and street crime, (high) social status and/or trust might emerge as central explanatory concepts for white-collar crime.

Noting that the primary impetus for the U.S. Sentencing Commission's latest symposium on white-collar crime was concern that a preoccupation with amount lost is resulting in inappropriately severe sanctions, future research could inform policy by examining factors that influence the public's punishment recommendations and perceptions of sanctioning severity. Researchers can frame this debate carefully by distinguishing between concepts and their empirical indicators for example, harm caused (a concept) and amount lost (an indicator). During a workshop at the symposium, judges listed the following as some of the most influential factors in their sentencing: harm to victims, thought processes that went into the crime, incorrigibility, reasons for the offense, and impact to the criminal justice system. These concepts are not easily quantifiable, nor are they mutually exclusive. Empirical indicators—such as money lost, number of victims, and duration of the crime—likely will prove necessary to translate these concepts into equitable punishments across cases.

Regardless whether they are rational and informed or not, ordinary people are the ones making decisions about whether or not to engage in crime. (They also are deciding whether or not to report the crime, and they serve on juries, to name a couple other roles filled by laypeople.) We argue that powerful reasons exist to conduct public opinion research and to use it to inform punishment policy. Whereas section I outlined several limitations to public opinion research, particularly as applied to crime matters, it also offered suggestions for controlling such methodological flaws. Sections II and III presented an unusually unequivocal conclusion for the social science: the U.S. public wants the government to take white-collar crime control more seriously, particularly in the form of punishing white-collar offenders more severely than street offenders. Section IV concluded by suggesting that carefully designed and replicated studies are needed to and can guide responsibly public policy on how to respond to white-collar crime.

References

Arlen, Jennifer. 2013. Presentation for the United States Sentencing Commission. Symposium on Economic Crime, September 18–19, New York.

Barkan, Steven E. 2014. *Criminology: A Sociological Understanding*, 6th ed. Upper Saddle River, NJ: Pearson Education.

Becker, Gary S. 1968. "Crime and Punishment: An Economic Approach." *Journal of Political Economy* 78: 169–217.

Blumstein, Alfred, and Jacqueline Cohen. 1980. "Sentencing of Convicted Offenders: An Analysis of the Public's View." *Law and Society Review* 14: 223–61.

Carlson, James M., and Tricia Williams. 1993. "Perspectives on the Seriousness of Crimes." *Social Science Research* 22: 190–207.

Chaiklin, Harris. 2011. "Attitudes, Behavior, and Social Practice." *Journal of Sociology and Social Welfare* 38: 31–39.

Chiricos, Ted, Kelly Welch, and Marc Gertz. 2004. "Racial Typification of Crime and Support for Punitive Measures." *Criminology* 42: 359–89.

Cohen, Mark A., Roland T. Rust, and Sara Steen. 2002. *Measuring Public Perceptions of Appropriate Prison Sentences* (Grant No. 1999-CE-VX-0001). National Institute of Justice, Office of Justice Programs, U.S. Department of Justice. Available at https://www.ncjrs.gov/pdffiles1/nij/grants/199364.pdf

Converse, Philip E. 1970. "Attitudes and Non-Attitudes: Continuation of a Dialogue." In *The Quantitative Analysis of Social Problems*, edited by Edward R. Tuft. Reading, MA: Addison-Wesley.

Copes, Heith, and Lynne M. Vieraitis. 2009. "Bounded Rationality of Identity Thieves: Using Offender-Based Research to Inform Policy." *Criminology and Public Policy* 8: 237–62.

Cullen, Francis T., Gregory A. Clark, John B. Cullen, and Richard A. Mathers. 1985a. "Attribution, Salience, and Attitudes toward Criminal Sanctioning." *Criminal Justice and Behavior* 12: 308–31.

Cullen, Francis T., Gregory A. Clark, Bruce G. Link, Richard A. Mathers, Jennifer Lee Niedospial, and Michael Sheahan. 1985b. "Dissecting White-Collar Crime: Offense Type and Punitiveness." *International Journal of Comparative and Applied Criminal Justice* 9: 15–28.

Cullen, Francis T., Gregory A. Clark, Richard A. Mathers, and John B. Cullen. 1983. "Public Support for Punishing White-Collar Crime: Blaming the Victim Revisited." *Journal of Criminal Justice* 11: 481–93.

Cullen, Francis T., Bruce G. Link, and Craig W. Polanzi. 1982. "The Seriousness of Crimes Revisited: Have Attitudes toward White-Collar Crime Changed?" *Criminology* 20: 83–102.

Dye, Thomas R. 2008. *Understanding Public Policy*. Upper Saddle River, NJ: Prentice Hall.

Edelhertz, Herbert. 1970. *The Nature, Impact, and Prosecution of White-Collar Crime*. Washington, D.C.: U.S. Government Printing Office.

Gibbons, Don C. 1968–1968. "Crime and Punishment: A Study in Social Attitudes. *Social Forces* 47: 391–97.

Graber, Doris. 1980. *Crime News and the Public*. New York: Praeger Publishers.

Hagan, John. 1994. *Crime and Disrepute*. Thousand Oaks, CA: Pine Forge Press.

Holtfreter, Kristy, Shanna Van Slyke, Jason Bratton, and Marc Gertz. 2008. "Public Perceptions of White-Collar Crime and Punishment." *Journal of Criminal Justice* 36: 50–60.

Huff, Rodney, Christian Desilets, and John Kane. 2010. *The 2010 National Public Survey on White Collar Crime*. Fairmont, WV: National White-Collar Crime Center.

Hurtado, Patricia. 2013. "Ex-Refco Lawyer Gets Year for Aiding $2.4 Billion Fraud." *Bloomberg* (July 15). Available at http://www.bloomberg.com/news/2013-07-15/ex-refco-lawyer-gets-year-for-aiding-2-4-billion-fraud.html

Kane, John, and April Wall. 2005. *The 2005 National Public Survey on White Collar Crime*. Fairmont, WV: National White-Collar Crime Center.

Kappeler, Victor E., and Gary W. Potter. 2005. *The Mythology of Crime and Criminal Justice*, 4th ed. Long Grove, IL: Waveland Press.

Levi, Michael. 2008. *The Phantom Capitalists: The Organization and Control of Long-firm Fraud*. Burlington, VT: Ashgate Publishing Company.

Lock, Shmuel. 1999. *Crime, Public Opinion, and Civil Liberties: The Tolerant Public*. Westport, CT: Praeger.

Manza, Jeff, Clem Brooks, and Christopher Uggen. 2004. "Public Attitudes toward Felon Disenfranchisement in the United States." *Public Opinion Quarterly* 68: 273–86.

Manza, Jeff, and Christopher Uggen. 2006. *Locked Out: Felon Disenfranchisement and American Democracy*. New York: Oxford University Press.

Marcus, George E., John L. Sullivan, Elizabeth Theiss-Morse, and Sandra L. Wood. 1995. *With Malice toward Some: How People Make Civil Liberties Judgments*. New York: Cambridge University Press.

Meier, Robert F., and James F. Short, Jr. 1985. "Crime as Hazard: Perceptions of Risk and Seriousness." *Criminology* 23: 389–99.

Merton, Robert K. 1957. *Social Theory and Social Structure*, revised and enlarged edition. New York: The Free Press.

Miller, Joann L., Peter H. Rossi, and Jon E. Simpson. 1986. "Perceptions of Justice: Race and Gender Differences in Judgments of Appropriate Prison Sentences." *Law and Society Review* 20: 313–34.

Miller, Joann, L., Peter H. Rossi, and Jon E. Simpson. 1991. "Felony Punishments: A Factorial Survey of Perceived Justice in Criminal Sanctioning." *Journal of Criminal Law and Criminology* 82: 396–422.

O'Connor, Michael E. 1984. "The Perception of Crime and Criminality: The Violent Criminal and Swindler as Social Types." *Deviant Behavior* 5: 255–74.

Nagin, Daniel S., and Greg Pogarsky. 2006. "Integrating Celerity, Impulsivity, and Extralegal Sanction Threats into a Model of General Deterrence: Theory and Evidence." *Criminology* 39: 865–92.

Newman, Donald J. 1957. "Public Attitudes toward a Form of White-Collar Crime." *Social Problems* 4: 228–32.

Padgett, Kathy, Ted Chiricos, Jason Bratton, and Marc Gertz. 2007. "Racial Threat and Opposition to the Re-Enfranchisement of Ex-Felons." Paper presented at the 59th Annual Meeting of the American Society of Criminology, November, Atlanta, GA.

Page, Benjamin I., and Robert Y. Shapiro. 1992. *The Rational Public: Fifty Years of Trends in Americans' Policy Preferences*. Chicago: University of Chicago Press.

Piquero, Nicole Leeper, Stephanie Carmichael, and Alex Piquero. 2008. "Research Note: Assessing the Perceived Seriousness of White-collar and Street Crimes." *Crime and Delinquency* 54: 291–312.

Rebovich, Donald J., and John Kane. 2002. "An Eye for an Eye in the Electronic Age: Gauging Public Attitudes toward White-Collar Crime and Punishment." *Journal of Economic Crime Management* 1: 1–19.

Rebovich, Donald J., and Jenny Layne. 2000. *The National Public Survey on White Collar Crime*. Morgantown, WV: National White Collar Crime Center.

Retting, Saloman, and Benjamin Pasamanick. 1959. "Changes in Moral Values over Three Decades, 1929–1958." *Social Problems* 6: 320–28.

Ross, Edward Alsworth. 1907. *Sin and Society: An Analysis of Latter-Day Iniquity*. Boston and New York: Houghton Mifflin Company.

Rossi, Peter H., and Richard A. Berk. 1997. *Just Punishments: Federal Guidelines and Public Views Compared*. Hawthorne, NY: Aldine De Gruyter.

Rossi, Peter H., Jon E. Simpson, and Joann L. Miller. 1985. "Beyond Crime Seriousness: Fitting the Punishment to the Crime." *Journal of Quantitative Criminology* 1: 59–90.

Rossi, Peter H., Emily Waite, Christine E. Bose, and Richard A. Berk. 1974. "The Seriousness of Crimes: Normative Structure and Individual Differences." *American Sociological Review* 39: 224–37.

Schoepfer, Andrea, Stephanie Carmichael, and Nicole Leeper Piquero. 2007. "Do Perceptions Vary between White-Collar and Street Crime?" *Journal of Criminal Justice* 35: 151–63.

Schrager, Laura Shill, and James F. Short, Jr. 1980. "How Serious a Crime? Perceptions of Organizational and Common Crimes." In *White-Collar Crime: Theory and Research*, edited by Gilbert Geis and Ezra Stotland. Beverly Hills: Sage.

Shaw, Greg, Robert Y. Shapiro, Shmuel Lock, and Lawrence R. Jacobs. 1998. "The Polls: Crime, the Police, and Civil Liberties." *Public Opinion Quarterly* 62: 405–26.

Stimson, James A. 2004. *Tides of Consent: How Public Opinion Shapes American Politics*. New York: Cambridge University Press.

Sutherland, Edwin. 1949 [1983]. *White Collar Crime: The Uncut Version*. New Haven, CT: Yale University Press.

Thomas, Charles W., Robin J. Cage, and Samuel C. Foster. 1976. "Public Opinion on Criminal Law and Legal Sanctions: An Examination of Two Conceptual Models." *Journal of Criminal Law and Criminology* 67: 110–16.

Titus, Richard M., Fred Heinzelmann, and John M. Boyle. 1995. "Victimization of Persons by Fraud." *Crime and Delinquency* 41: 54–72.

U.S. Sentencing Commission. 2013. *Application Rates for §2B.1: Fiscal Year 2012*. U.S. Sentencing Commission Symposium on Economic Crime, September 19–20, 2013, New York City.

Unnever, James D., Michael L. Benson, and Francis T. Cullen. 2008. "Public Support for Getting Tough on Corporate Crime: Racial and Political Divides." *Journal of Research in Crime and Delinquency* 45: 163–90.

Van Slyke, Shanna R. 2009. "Social Identification and Public Opinion on White-Collar Crime." Ph.D. Dissertation, Florida State University, College of Criminology and Criminal Justice.

Walsh, Marilyn E., and Donna D. Schram. 1980. "Victims of White-Collar Crime: Accuser or Accused?" In *White-Collar Crime: Theory and Research*, edited by Gilbert Geis and Ezra Stotland. Beverly Hills: Sage.

Warr, Mark. 1989. "What Is the Perceived Seriousness of Crimes?" *Criminology* 27: 795–821.

INDEX

Page numbers followed by *t* and *f* indicate a table or figure on the designated page
Page numbers followed by "n" and an additional number indicate a note on the designated page

CPSIA information can be obtained
at www.ICGtesting.com
Printed in the USA
LVHW060240110820
662888LV00007B/551

9 780190 947347